JOHN HENRY NEWMAN

John Henry Newman was born in 1801 and educated at Ealing School and Trinity College, Oxford. Elected a fellow of Oriel in 1822, he became vicar of the university church of St Mary's in 1828. In 1833 he began *Tracts for the Times*, but after his controversial *Tract 90*, which attempted to interpret the 39 Articles of the Church of England in Catholic sense, he retired in 1842 to monastic seclusion at Littlemore. Without completing his *Essay on the Development of Christian Doctrine*, he was received in 1845 into the Roman Catholic Church. Ordained a priest in 1847, he founded the Birmingham Oratory in 1848. In 1851 he was appointed first rector of the Catholic University of Ireland (resigning in 1858), and his Dublin lectures and articles were eventually published as *The Idea of a University*. His autobiography, *Apologia pro Vita Sua*, appeared in 1864 in response to public attack by Charles Kingsley. His poem on the afterlife, *The Dream of Gerontius*, was published in 1865 and later inspired Elgar's musical masterpiece. In 1870 he finally completed his philosophical justification of religious faith in *An Essay in Aid of a Grammar of Assent*. Created a cardinal in 1879, he died in 1890. He was declared 'Venerable' in 1991 and will be beatified by Pope Benedict XVI in September 2010.

Ian Ker teaches theology at Oxford University. He is the author and editor of more than twenty books on Newman. His *The Catholic Revival in English Literature 1845–1961* was published in 2003.

D1354912

JOHN HENRY NEWMAN 1873–4

Original sketch by Lady Coleridge.
Fineprint photography

John Henry Newman

A Biography

IAN KER

Oxford   New York

OXFORD UNIVERSITY PRESS

OXFORD
UNIVERSITY PRESS

Great Clarendon Street, Oxford, OX2 6DP,
United Kingdom

Oxford University Press is a department of the University of Oxford.
It furthers the University's objective of excellence in research, scholarship,
and education by publishing worldwide. Oxford is a registered trade mark of
Oxford University Press in the UK and in certain other countries

© Ian Ker 1988, 2009, 2019

The moral rights of the author have been asserted

First published 1988
Reissued in hardback with Afterword 2009
Reissued in paperback with Afterword 2010
Reissued in paperback with revised Afterword 2019

Impression: 8

Published in the United States of America by Oxford University Press
198 Madison Avenue, New York, NY 10016, United States of America

British Library Cataloguing in Publication Data
Data available

Library of Congress Control Number: 2019950764

ISBN 978-0-19-885680-1

Printed and bound by CPI Group (UK) Ltd,
Croydon, CR0 4YY

IN MEMORY OF
S.M.K.

PREFACE AND ACKNOWLEDGEMENTS

THE life of John Henry Newman presents unusual opportunities as well as problems for a biographer. Apart from the *Apologia* and the *Autobiographical Writings*, there are more than 20,000 letters extant, which, together with the diaries, will eventually fill thirty-one volumes. The corpus of published, including posthumous, works runs to well over forty volumes. The biographer of Newman who wishes to do justice to his thought and art as well as his life is faced by not so much a shortage as a surfeit of materials, with the result that he or she may well feel overwhelmed by the agonizing difficulty of selecting and distilling.

This biography has grown somewhat beyond its original conception, but it is still substantially shorter than the only other two published lives, both in two volumes, which can claim to be full-length studies: Wilfrid Ward's *The Life of John Henry Cardinal Newman* (1912) and Meriol Trevor's *Newman: The Pillar of the Cloud* and *Newman: Light in Winter* (1962). Ward's work has achieved an almost classic status, but it is less than definitive in at least three respects: first, Ward covers the entire Anglican half of the life in little more than a chapter; second, while he concentrates on Newman's theological stance as a Catholic, of which he gives a balanced and perceptive account, the picture he paints of Newman's personality is unbalanced and one-sided; third, since Ward wrote his biography, many hundreds of letters have come to light which were not available to him. Meriol Trevor's detailed and vivid life hardly purports to be a study of either the thinker or the writer.

My own purpose differs from that of my two predecessors. I have tried to write a book which is both a reasonably full personal life and also an intellectual and literary biography. So far as it is a study of the man, I hope it will finally dispel the myth of the hypersensitive, humourless, sad Newman. That he was unusually sensitive is beyond question; but sensitivity may be as much a virtue as insensitivity is a vice—even though it is as hard at times to distinguish it in practice from hyper-sensitivity, as it is difficult to differentiate in particular cases between courage and recklessness, tolerance and weakness, generosity and extravagance, kindness and indulgence ... Assuming that there is a significant distinction to be drawn and that it would be marvellous indeed if somebody as sensitive as Newman was never over-sensitive, I have tried to present the evidence fairly and squarely so that readers may make up their own minds. Again, it is true that the frustrations of the Catholic years brought much suffering, to which Newman was very sensitive; but it is fair to say, I think, that his humour and irony never failed him, even in the darkest of hours. The 'feminine' side of Newman's character has been much emphasized; without in any way denying it, I have endeavoured to stress also the other highly 'masculine' side of his temperament, which showed itself in an astonishing resilience and uncompromising toughness in the face of adversity, as well as in the kind of resourceful practicality one associates with the man of action rather than the thinker.

In so far as this book is a literary biography, it aims to break new ground in several ways: in shedding fresh light on Newman's rhetoric; in highlighting an exuberance of imagery and metaphor which at times invites comparison with Dickens; in evincing the fecundity of one of the most remarkable and prolific letter-writers in the English language; and in drawing attention to Newman's (neglected) genius as a satirical writer. As an intellectual biography, it is obviously largely concerned with the development and originality of Newman's religious thought, but due consideration is given to the full range of his intellectual interests, in particular his educational ideas. The mind of Newman, I argue, is characterized not by contradictions but by complementary strengths, so that he may be called, without inconsistency, both conservative and liberal, progressive and traditional, cautious and radical, dogmatic yet pragmatic, idealistic but realistic. I have drawn particular attention to that preoccupation with the 'real' and the 'unreal' which pervades his writings; an awareness of it is the key to a true understanding of Newman.

Both as an Anglican and as a Catholic, Newman has by any reckoning a central place in the religious history of the nineteenth century. As a critic of his own society and as one of its major prose writers, he is also to be counted among the great Victorian 'prophets' or 'sages'. I have tried to balance these important considerations against Newman's more universal significance as a Christian thinker who transcends his culture and his time, reminding one perhaps more of St Augustine than of any other comparable figure. The development of my own personal interest reflects these different perspectives. I first became fascinated by Newman while reading, as a student of English literature, his works alongside those of Matthew Arnold, Carlyle, and Ruskin; I became aware then of the extent to which his literary achievement is generally underestimated. Later, when studying theology, I came to appreciate the ways in which he anticipated so many of the central themes of the Ecumenical Council (Vatican II) which he predicted and which opened a new era in Christian history. And finally, my reading and rereading of his writings over the years has only deepened my conviction that John Henry Newman is to be numbered among the Doctors of the Church.

I have quoted generously from the letters, not only for the literary reason I have already implied, but also because my object has been to write the life of Newman rather than a book about him. 'It has ever been a hobby of mine (unless it be a truism, not a hobby) that a man's life lies in his letters', Newman once wrote.[1] Certainly, as he remarked in another context, there is no better way of discovering what a dead person's 'conversation' was like than through reading his or her correspondence.[2] I have endeavoured to quote judiciously and selectively, but without compromising my commitment to allowing the reader to hear, as far as possible, the actual sound of Newman's voice—and also to overhear him thinking aloud, particularly at certain critical junctures. Again, the subtlety of Newman's highly nuanced approach to complex issues constantly discourages any bland, reductive paraphrasing, in favour of the exact rendering of his own words which alone so often convey the fullness of his thought.

There is a vast literature on Newman, spanning several disciplines, which I hope I have taken proper account of; but I have referred only sparingly to specific secondary sources, when I have a definite debt or disagreement to record.

In writing this biography I have incurred a number of debts. I should like first to mention Professor John Dixon Hunt, once a colleague in the English department at the University of York, although he will have forgotten his kind invitation in 1970 which led eventually to my undertaking my first major work on Newman. I am grateful to my parents for providing me with a place in which to write during my summer holidays in the very early part of this work when I was engaged in full-time parish work. I must thank the Bishop of Portsmouth, the Rt. Revd Anthony Emery, for later appointing me to pastoral duties which gave me more leisure for scholarly work. Nearly all the actual writing of this book was done between 1982 and 1987, while I was Catholic Chaplain at the University of Southampton; a number of students (unwittingly) helped me by readily relieving me of various practical chores; but I should particularly like to thank Richard Grady for his help and support during the latter stages of this work.

I am grateful to the Very Reverend Gregory Winterton, Provost of the Birmingham Oratory, who arranged with the archivist, Mr G. Tracey, for photocopies of the still unpublished letters in the Newman

---

[1] *LD* xx. 443.　　[2] *HS* ii. 221.

archives to be sent to me, I must thank Park Place Pastoral Centre for enabling me to reproduce the drawing by Lady Coleridge. Most of my very rough manuscript was first deciphered, with admirable patience, and then typed into a fair typescript by Mrs Sandra Wilkins.

I express my thanks to the following, who, from their different points of view, read and commented on parts or all of the typescript: Hugh Black-Hawkins, Don Briel, Park Honan, Barry McCormick, Anthony Price, James Reidy, Jennifer Searle, Joanne Shattock, Georges Thiers, Gerard Tracey, and David Watson. I am particularly indebted to Professor Alan G. Hill for his careful, close criticism of the entire typescript.

When I began to study Newman some 20 years ago, Father Charles Stephen Dessain was still alive. Some of the happiest memories I have are of the many hours I spent talking Newman with him. It is a deep sadness to me that he did not live to read this life, which could hardly have been undertaken in the first place without his help and encouragement during the half-dozen years I enjoyed his friendship. The debt that this book owes to his monumental edition of *The Letters and Diaries of John Henry Newman*, which tragically he was unable to complete before he died suddenly and unexpectedly in 1976, is only too obvious. His death was a grievous personal loss to myself, as well as a devastating blow to Newman scholarship.

I.T.K.
Southampton
August 1987

PREFACE TO THE 1995 IMPRESSION

I am grateful to all those who have drawn my attention to errors and slips since the first publication of this book in 1988. Successive reprints have enabled me to make the necessary corrections, a few more of which are now incorporated in this new impression.

I.T.K.

CONTENTS

ABBREVIATIONS

THE abbreviations listed below for Newman's works are for the most part the ones used in Joseph Rickaby, SJ, *Index to the Works of John Henry Cardinal Newman* (London, 1914), supplemented by those in *The Letters and Diaries of John Henry Newman.*

References to Newman's works are usually to the uniform edition of 1868–81 (36 vols.), which was published by Longmans, Green, and Co. of London until the stock was destroyed in the Second World War. References to the volumes in the uniform edition are distinguished from those to other editions by not having a date or place of publication in brackets after the title. All references to *Apologia pro Vita Sua*, *The Idea of a University*, and *A Grammar of Assent* are to the Oxford critical editions.

Apo.	*Apologia pro Vita Sua*, ed. Martin J. Svaglic (Oxford, 1967)
Ari.	*The Arians of the Fourth Century*
Ath. i, ii	*Select Treatises of St. Athanasius*, 2 vols.
AW	*John Henry Newman: Autobiographical Writings*, ed. Henry Tristram (London and New York, 1956)
Call.	*Callista: A Tale of the Third Century*
Campaign	*My Campaign in Ireland, Part I*, ed. W. Neville (privately printed, 1896)
CS	*Catholic Sermons of Cardinal Newman*, ed. at the Birmingham Oratory (London, 1957)
Cons.	*On Consulting the Faithful in Matters of Doctrine*, ed. John Coulson (London, 1961)
DA	*Discussions and Arguments on Various Subjects*
Dev.	*An Essay on the Development of Christian Doctrine*
Diff. i, ii	*Certain Difficulties felt by Anglicans in Catholic Teaching*, 2 vols.
Ess. i, ii	*Essays Critical and Historical*, 2 vols.
GA	*An Essay in Aid of a Grammar of Assent*, ed. I. T. Ker (Oxford, 1985)
HS i, ii, iii	*Historical Sketches*, 3 vols.
Idea	*The Idea of a University*, ed. I. T. Ker (Oxford, 1976)
Jfc.	*Lectures on the Doctrine of Justification*
LD	*The Letters and Diaries of John Henry Newman*, ed. Charles Stephen Dessain *et al.*, vols. i–vi (Oxford, 1978–84), xi–xxii (London, 1961–72), xxiii–xxxi (Oxford, 1973–7)

LG	*Loss and Gain: The Story of a Convert*
MD	*Meditations and Devotions of the late Cardinal Newman* (London, 1893)
Mir.	*Two Essays on Biblical and on Ecclesiastical Miracles*
Mix.	*Discourses addressed to Mixed Congregations*
Moz. i, ii	*Letters and Correspondence of John Henry Newman during his Life in the English Church*, ed. Anne Mozley, 2 vols. (London, 1891)
NO	*Newman the Oratorian: His Unpublished Oratory Papers*, ed. Placid Murray, OSB (Dublin, 1969)
OS	*Sermons preached on Various Occasions*
PS i–viii	*Parochial and Plain Sermons*, 8 vols.
Phil.N. i, ii	*The Philosophical Notebook of John Henry Newman*, ed. Edward Sillem, 2 vols. (Louvain, 1969–70)
Prepos.	*Present Position of Catholics in England*
SD	*Sermons bearing on Subjects of the Day*
SE	*Stray Essays on Controversial Points* (privately printed, 1890)
SN	*Sermon Notes of John Henry Cardinal Newman, 1849–1878*, ed. Fathers of the Birmingham Oratory (London, 1913)
TP i	*The Theological Papers of John Henry Newman on Faith and Certainty*, ed. Hugo M. de Achaval, SJ, and J. Derek Holmes (Oxford, 1976)
TP ii	*The Theological Papers of John Henry Newman on Biblical Inspiration and on Infallibility*, ed. J. Derek Holmes (Oxford, 1979)
TT	*Tracts Theological and Ecclesiastical*
US	*Fifteen Sermons preached before the University of Oxford*
VM i, ii	*The Via Media*, 2 vols.
VV	*Verses on Various Occasions*
Ward i, ii	Wilfrid Ward, *The Life of John Henry Cardinal Newman*, 2 vols. (London, 1912)

I
Oxford

JOHN HENRY NEWMAN was born on Saturday, 21 February 1801 at 80 Old Broad Street in the City of London. His father, John Newman, was a banker, the son of a London grocer, originally from Cambridgeshire. His mother, Jemima Foudrinier, was the daughter of a papermaker, whose family were originally French Huguenot refugees. They had married in 1799 and John Henry was their first child. He was baptized on 9 April 1801.

In 1803 the Newmans moved to 17 Southampton Street (now Southampton Place), Bloomsbury. More than half a century later, John Henry recalled as one of his 'first memories . . . my admiring the borders of the paper in the drawing rooms'.[1] He could still remember every detail of the house. But there was another Georgian house, the memory of which was still more important, the family's country house at Ham, Grey Court House near Ham Common (it still stands). John Henry was only 6 years old when the house was given up, but he never forgot the morning of September 1807 when they left it for good. As a schoolboy he dreamed about it 'as if it was Paradise'.[2] His most vivid memory remained that of gazing 'at the windows of the room where I lay abed with candles in the windows in illumination for the victory at Trafalgar'.[3]

On 1 May 1808 Newman was sent to a private boarding-school at Ealing, run by a Dr Nicholas. Although it was not a public school, it enjoyed a considerable reputation and its pupils included some famous names such as Captain Marryat. Like any other boy at school, Newman looked forward to the holidays and his first known letter was written to his mother announcing the end of his first term: 'I am very glad to inform you that our Vacation commences on the 21st Inst when I hope to find you all well.'[4] As an old man, Newman told the story of how on his return to school at the beginning of the next term, he hung about in the hall after his father and mother had left, afraid to go into the room where the other boys were. The headmaster 'passed by and said, kindly enough, "Hadn't you better go into the big room?"—"No, no, I won't,

---

[1] *LD* xvi. 391. [2] Ibid. xxxi. 119. [3] Ibid. xx. 46. [4] Ibid. i. 4.

they'll bully me so, they'll do all sorts of things to me though I can't help crying." "Oh no, nonsense, they won't." At last, he said, "But they will! Only come into the room and see for yourself." Then he caught hold of Dr Nicholas' hand and dragged him into the room saying, "Come with me, sir, and then you can judge for yourself." In they went together, hand in hand, and no one said or did anything.'[5]

His subsequent letters were similarly terse announcements of the approach of holiday time, until December 1811, when at the age of nearly 11 he proclaimed the imminence of the Christmas holidays in a much more expansive letter, the exuberance and wit of which reveal the future writer:

Dear Aunt,

The joyful 21 again approaches when our books are closed according to delightful custom, and when I hope for the additional pleasure of seeing you all well and happy at home.

Already in imagination I pay my respects to the mince Pies, Turkies, and the other good things of Christmas.

In the mean time the Notches on my wooden Calendar diminish apace, but not so the duty and affection with which I am,

Dear Aunt, Your's ever John H. Newman.[6]

His first attempts to write (both prose and verse) date from 1812, when he was 11. He was 'of a studious turn', he later wrote in his autobiographical memoir, 'and his school-fellows have left on record that they never, or scarcely ever, saw him taking part in any game' (compulsory organized games had not yet been invented). But he excelled in his work, and the headmaster, 'to whom he became greatly attached, was accustomed to say, that no boy had run through the school, from the bottom to the top, so rapidly as John Newman'.[7] Fortunately, he succeeded, with the aid of his mother and Dr Nicholas, in avoiding being sent on to Winchester. He had a will of his own, and once, after failing to get his way with his mother, 'she reminded him, "You see, John, you did not get your own way." "No," was his answer, "but I tried very hard." '[8]

Saved from the ordeals of a public school, Newman continued to enjoy life at Ealing, acting in Latin plays, practising the violin, winning prizes for speeches, and editing periodicals, for which he wrote articles in the style of Addison. This happy period was brought to an abrupt end on 8 March 1816 when, as a result of the financial crisis at the end of the Napoleonic wars, his father's bank closed its doors. The depositors were all paid and there was no bankruptcy, but John Newman was left

[5] Cit. Meriol Trevor, *Newman: The Pillar of the Cloud* (London, 1962), 10–11.
[6] *LD* i. 9–10.   [7] *AW* 29.   [8] Moz. i. 16.

without a job and source of livelihood. Luckily, his partners in the bank were wealthy Windsor brewers who got him a job managing a brewery in Alton, Hampshire. The house in Southampton Street was let and the three girls in the family—Harriett, Jemima, and Mary—were sent to their grandmother's cottage at Norwood where the children had often enjoyed holidays. From being a prosperous banker, John Newman now found himself, at the age of nearly 50, managing a brewery, a trade about which he knew nothing. The decline in the family's fortunes was such that the Norwood cottage had to be given up in the autumn, when the girls joined their parents at Alton. Meanwhile John Henry, who had been summoned home to hear the traumatic news, remained at Ealing. He was to have left school at the end of the summer term, but because of the family crisis he stayed on through the summer holidays and the autumn term. The period from the beginning of August to 21 December, when term ended, he always regarded as the turning-point of his life.

He had been brought up as an ordinary member of the Church of England. His parents were in no way Evangelical, but belonged to what their son was later to call 'the national religion of England' or 'Bible Religion', which 'consists, not in rites or creeds, but mainly in having the Bible read in Church, in the family, and in private'.[9] He himself had been 'brought up from a child to take great delight in reading the Bible', particularly by his grandmother and aunt in whose house at Fulham he had stayed as a little boy (years later, on the eve of his leaving the Church of his baptism, he was to tell his Aunt Elizabeth, 'Whatever good there is in me, I owe, under grace, to the time I spent in that house, and to you and my dear Grandmother, its inhabitants').[10] At the same time he 'had no formed religious convictions'—that is, 'till I was fifteen'.[11]

Left at school by himself during the holidays ('my friends gone away'), he 'was terrified at the heavy hand of God which came down upon me'. It was not simply that his life had been turned upside down by his father's disaster; he was now afflicted by the first of the 'three great illnesses' of his life. Years later he referred to it as the 'first keen, terrible one, when I was a boy of 15, and it made me a Christian—with experiences before and after, awful, and known only to God'.[12] At the end of his life he confessed he found it 'difficult to realize or imagine the identity of the boy before and after August 1816'; as he looked back over seventy years, he could only see 'another person'.[13] When he recollected

[9] *GA* 43.

[10] To Miss E. Newman, 25 July 1844. The text of letters etc. not yet published in *LD* is in every case that of the original or draft or copy in the collection at the Birmingham Oratory.

[11] *Apo.* 15.   [12] *AW* 150, 268.   [13] *LD* xxxi. 31.

the crisis four or five years after the event, he discerned 'the wisdom and goodness of God' in the troubles that had come upon him, which allowed 'room' for particular 'influences' to be brought to bear—those of 'an excellent man, the Revd Walter Mayers . . . one of the classical masters, from whom he received deep religious impressions . . . Calvinistic in character, which were to him the beginning of a new life'.[14] Mayers himself had only been 'converted' two years previously, shortly after receiving Holy Orders.

A year before, at the age of 14, Newman had been rather enjoying reading objections to Christianity in writers like Thomas Paine. His general frame of mind was that he wanted 'to be virtuous, but not religious. There was something in the latter idea I did not like. Nor did I see the *meaning* of loving God.'[15] But now he 'fell under the influences of a definite Creed, and received into my intellect impressions of dogma, which, through God's mercy, have never been effaced or obscured'. It was not only 'the conversations and sermons' of Mayers ('who was the human means of this beginning of divine faith in me'), but, more important, there was 'the effect of the books which he put into my hands, all of the school of Calvin'. From one of them he learned the Calvinist doctrine of 'final perseverance', namely that 'the regenerate cannot fall away', a belief which 'gradually faded away' when he was 21, but which tended to influence him on the lines of certain 'childish imaginations', that is to say 'in isolating me from the objects which surrounded me, in confirming me in my mistrust of the reality of material phenomena, and making me rest in the thought of two and two only absolute and luminously self-evident beings, myself and my Creator'. The most important writer Mayers introduced him to was Thomas Scott, the famous Evangelical commentator on the Bible, 'who made a deeper impression on my mind than any other, and to whom (humanly speaking) I almost owe my soul'. Scott's autobiography *The Force of Truth* showed how he had 'followed truth wherever it led him, beginning with Unitarianism, and ending in a zealous faith in the Holy Trinity. It was he who first planted deep in my mind that fundamental truth of religion.' Significantly, Newman was also struck by 'the minutely practical character of his writings. They show him to be a true Englishman, and I deeply felt his influence; and for years I used almost as proverbs . . . "Holiness rather than peace", and "Growth the only evidence of life".'[16]

Profoundly influenced as he was by Evangelicalism, Newman had not been converted, as he soon became aware, 'in that special way which it laid down as imperative'. In 1821 he acknowledged in his journal that

---

[14] *AW* 150, 29.   [15] Ibid. 169.   [16] *Apo.* 17–19.

his own 'feelings' had been 'different from any account I have ever read'. A few years later he noted that his 'feelings' had not been '*violent*' in the prescribed Evangelical manner, 'but a returning to, a renewing of, principles, under the power of the Holy Spirit, which I had *already* felt, and in a measure acted on, when young'. He had not in fact had 'those special Evangelical experiences, which, like the grip of the hand or other prescribed signs of a secret society, are the sure token of a member'; for he had not undergone 'the evangelical process of conversion' with 'its stages of conviction of sin, terror, despair, news of the free and full salvation, joy and peace, and so on to final perseverance'. Not surprisingly, after his account of his conversion had been published in the *Apologia*, he received letters 'assuring him that he did not yet know what conversion meant, and that the all important change had still to be wrought in him, if he was to be saved'. But he did know about the 'reality of conversion', as 'cutting at the root of doubt, providing a chain between God and the soul'. He had attained to the certitude he was to analyse one day in the *Grammar of Assent*, which he anticipates by explaining, 'I know I am right. How do you know it? I know I know.'[17]

There were two other developments in those crucial months of 1816, both of enormous significance for the future. First,

I read Joseph Milner's Church History, and was nothing short of enamoured of the long extracts from St. Augustine, St. Ambrose, and the other Fathers which I found there. I read them as being the religion of the primitive Christians: but simultaneously with Milner I read Newton on the Prophecies, and in consequence became most firmly convinced that the Pope was the Antichrist predicted by Daniel, St. Paul, and St. John. My imagination was stained by the effects of this doctrine up to the year 1843; it had been obliterated from my reason and judgment at an earlier date . . .

These two very different works 'produced a deep impression' on him, 'each contrary to each, and planting in me the seeds of an intellectual inconsistency which disabled me for a long course of years'. The other 'deep imagination' which 'took possession' of him in the course of the autumn of 1816 was of a personal and spiritual nature, namely that it would be the 'will of God' that he should 'lead a single life', an 'anticipation' that was 'more or less connected' with the idea that his 'calling in life would require such a sacrifice as celibacy involved; as, for instance, missionary work among the heathen, to which I had a great drawing for some years. It also strengthened my feeling of separation from the visible world.'[18]

[17] *AW* 79–80, 150, 166, 172.   [18] *Apo.* 19–20.

2

On Saturday, 14 December 1816, Newman travelled to Oxford with his father and the Reverend John Mullens, a curate at St James's, Piccadilly, 'who had for some years taken an interest in the boy's education'. Even while the post-chaise was waiting at the door, John Newman had still not decided on whether to enter his son at Oxford or Cambridge. Mullens apparently persuaded him in favour of Oxford. When they reached Oxford, Mullens tried to obtain a place at his own old college of Exeter; since there was no vacancy there, he was advised to try Trinity, where Newman was offered a place as a commoner. On arriving back at Ealing, the young Newman was relieved to hear from Dr Nicholas—in response to 'his timid mention of a College of which he himself had never heard before'—' "Trinity? a most gentlemanlike College; I am much pleased to hear it." '[19]

Newman left Ealing School for good on 21 December. But he was not able to take up his place at Oxford till Sunday, 8 June 1817, when a set of rooms became vacant. He was only 16. He wrote his first letter home to his father three days later. As soon as his parents had left him, he had gone to buy a cap and gown. On returning 'HOME', he had 'hardly seated' himself when he 'heard a knock on the door, and, opening it, one of the commoners entered'. He had been sent by Thomas Short, who was to be Newman's tutor, 'to explain to me some of the customs of the College, and accompany me into the Hall at dinner'. Newman was delighted to learn that Short was not popular because he was considered too strict!

At dinner I was much entertained with the novelty of the thing. Fish, flesh and fowl, beautiful salmon, haunches of mutton, lamb etc and fine, very fine (to my taste) strong beer, served up on old pewter plates, and mis-shapen earthenware jars. Tell Mama there are gooseberry, rasberry, and apricot pies. And in all this the joint did not go round, but there was such a profusion that scarcely two ate of the same joint. Neither do they sit according to their ranks, but as they happen to come in.[20]

This marvellously vivid letter about his first impressions and his first dinner in hall again reveals the future writer. There is nothing of that 'unpleasant style' which Newman later complained of in his early writings and which he attributed to his composing with 'an eye to style', and also to his 'Evangelical tone', which 'contributed' to his 'bad taste'.[21]

It was already examination week and most of the undergraduates would be leaving the following week. There were no more lectures, but

[19] *AW* 30.   [20] *LD* i. 35.   [21] *AW* 149.

Newman hoped at least to find out what books he ought to be reading. His eyes had been giving him a lot of trouble that year, although for the past three months he had managed to study for about six hours a day. The first day or two at Trinity he could not see to read and felt depressed. 'Besides', he wrote home, 'I did not know any one, and, after being used to such a number about me, I felt very solitary.' He could hardly have chosen a worse time to arrive, as everyone else was preparing to leave: 'I am not noticed at all, except by being silently stared at.' He felt relieved, he added, to be left alone: he had been invited to meet some other students for a drink, but he was not 'entertained' by the company, 'with either their drinking or their conversation'. Their only object seemed to be to get drunk: 'I really think, if any one should ask me what qualifications were necessary for Trinity College, I should say there was only one,—Drink, drink, drink.' He could not help envying his younger brothers, Charles and Francis, now at home for the school holidays. Still, he only had to last out the three weeks needed for the residence qualification. Walter Mayers wrote encouragingly, exhorting him to stand by his religious principles and not to be deterred by 'the ridicule of the world'.[22]

On the nineteenth Newman wrote home to say that almost all the other students were either leaving or had left, including the 'Commoner' who had been detailed to look after him when he arrived. His name, he informed his mother, was 'Bowden', and he had gone down that morning. He was not to know that he and John William Bowden, also a freshman although exactly three years older, were to become the closest of friends, 'recognised in College as inseparables'.[23] During these 'solitary three weeks' his only real 'companion', he later recorded, was the 'snapdragon' on the wall separating Trinity from Balliol, which he could see from his window and which one day he would immortalize in the *Apologia*.[24] Short had also gone or was going away, so 'in his simplicity' he decided to ask the President of Trinity about his studies when he went to ask permission to leave for the vacation. The President told him in a kindly way that he must ask one of the tutors. He still had not discovered what he wanted to know up to the day before he left Oxford; but on the last Sunday, the twenty-ninth, as he was returning from a walk in the Parks,

he saw one of the Tutors in top-boots on horseback on his way into the country. Thinking it his last chance, he dashed into the road, and abruptly accosting him, asked him what books he should read during the Vacation. The person addressed answered him very kindly; explained that he was leaving Oxford for the Vacation, and referred him to one of his Colleagues still in College, who would give him the information he desired.[25]

[22] *LD* i. 36.   [23] *AW* 30.   [24] *LD* xxv. 106.   [25] *AW* 33.

The Oxford Newman was soon to love so much seemed to have little to recommend it. The climate only added to his discomforture: it was too windy and too hot. Whenever he went out he was conscious of being 'stared at; and the other day there was a party of people laughing at my dress'. There was hardly anybody now left in college. In hall he found himself at the head of the table and sometimes had almost finished his dinner before anybody else arrived:

The other day I had a nice dinner set before me of veal cutlets and peas, so much to myself that I could hear the noise I made in chewing through the empty hall; till at length one came in, and sat opposite to me, but I had not been introduced to him, and he could not speak to me. Consequently we preserved an amicable silence, and conversed with our teeth . . .

The best of the dinner now is that half a dozen servants wait behind me and watch me.[26]

On his last Sunday he wrote in his journal a Calvinistic critique of the sermon he had heard at the University Church of St Mary the Virgin. It is an early example of the logical powers he was to bring to bear so relentlessly in his controversial writings. But at this stage it is to his unstudied letters to his family, not to his more formal attempts at writing, that we must look for the first signs of literary greatness.

Oxford in October after the long vacation seemed, not surprisingly, much more attractive. His eyes were now better and he could read in the evenings. Bathing had always been a favourite recreation and he became a regular visitor to some baths near Holywell Church. Undergraduate social life still presented problems as Newman refused to join in the usual drinking binges. One evening early in November he was invited to what he thought would be a small party and asked to bring his violin. On arrival he was surprised to see a long table and 'to hear a smothered laugh . . . announcing "Mr Newman and his fiddle" '. Newman stood his ground, refusing both to play his violin and to fill his glass every time the bottle was passed to him. In spite of loud protests, he got up to go after an hour and three glasses. Some days later there was a similar ordeal when some undergraduates suddenly rushed into his room, asked 'in a laughing tone' how he was, ran and bolted the door saying they were hiding from someone, asked him to come and drink with them, and teasingly accused him of working too hard—'I said such conduct was not the conduct of gentlemen— and ordered them to leave the room.' One of them threatened to knock him down; but then came round the next day to apologize, saying that Newman 'had acted very well' and that 'he had seldom or never seen any one act more firmly'.[27]

On the last Sunday in November, he made his first Communion in the

[26] *LD* i. 40.   [27] *AW* 157.

college chapel. As an old man, he was reminded by a photograph of Trinity Chapel, which hung in his room, of his 'feelings' on the occasion, and how, because he was 'in mourning' for George IV's daughter, Princess Charlotte, who had recently died, he had on 'silk black gloves— and the glove would not come off when I had to receive the Bread, and I had to tear it off and spoil it in my flurry'.[28] He was not confirmed till the following summer.

He was now working nine or ten hours a day. He had surprised Mr Short by his proficiency in mathematics and had been moved up into the higher class. Very soon only he and Bowden were left in the group, having gone 'on too fast for the rest to keep up with them'.[29] A Latin declamation he had had to deliver in hall was praised by the Dean, and he found the classes in Classics 'childishly easy'. But he was painfully aware that there were several others who knew more Greek and Latin than he did: 'I now see', he told his father, 'the disadvantage of going so soon, and before I have the great addition of time of two or three years later.' Short, who had been second master at Rugby and was to lose the headmastership a few years later by only one vote to Thomas Arnold, symbolized the new reforming spirit at Oxford which had been inaugurated by a radical revision of the final examinations system in 1800. Newman wrote home delightedly to his mother:

If any one wishes to study much, I believe there can be no College that will encourage him more than Trinity. It wishes to rise in the University, and is rising fast. The scholarships were formerly open to members of the College alone; last year for the first time they were thrown open to the whole University . . . In discipline it has become the strictest of Colleges. There are lamentations in every corner of the increasing rigour; it is laughable, but it is delightful, to hear the groans of the oppressed.[30]

During the Lent term Short became still more impressed by his new youthful pupil. And when Newman's father came to collect him for the Easter vacation, 'he was quite overcome' with the tutor's 'warmth' about his son: 'He said Short went to meet him as an old friend, and holding out his hands said, "O, Mr Newman, what have you given us in your Son," or words to that effect.' On returning to London, Mr Newman decided to share the good news with Dr Nicholas at Ealing, where they had 'a very joyful' visit.[31] Not long after the beginning of the summer term Newman was called in by the two tutors of the college, who told him they wanted him to sit for a scholarship that term (rather than wait till next year, as he had intended). There were eleven candidates and the examination took place in the middle of May. On Monday, 18 May Newman won the scholarship, which was worth

[28] *Phil.N.* ii. 195, 197.   [29] *AW* 35.   [30] *LD* i. 47–8.   [31] Ibid. 50.

the princely sum of £60 a year. He had not told his parents he was a
candidate; he wanted to keep it a 'secret' to 'surprise' them.[32] His age
had been against him, and not even Bowden had thought he would be
successful. The fact that Short had wanted him to stand was a sign of
special favour, as he was supposed to have been responsible for
persuading the college to open the scholarship to all-comers, and so was
'naturally anxious for the success of his important measure'.[33] As so often
later in his life, Newman had 'felt the tortures of suspense' as he waited
for the result, not without some hope of success. Summoned by the
Dean to appear before the electors, he 'seemed' to himself 'to feel
no surprise'—although 'I am told I turned pale'. When, newly attired in
his scholar's gown, he met his unsuccessful rivals, he 'did not know what
to do' and 'held' his 'eyes down'.[34] He had prayed that he might not be
'too much set' on winning the scholarship, but there was no concealing
his delight.[35]

Trinity Monday was not only the day when elections to scholarships
and fellowships took place, it was also the gaudy day when there was 'a
grand drinking bout'. Newman himself left the scholars' party early to
avoid getting drunk and refused in future to attend. Such 'orgies' were
'the rule of the place; so much so, that it was a standing joke, in passing
Oriel College, which, as initiating a better way, was satirized as if
imposing on its Undergraduates tea instead of wine, to cry out to the
Porter, "Well, Porter, does the kettle boil?" ' Newman later commented
that his own 'disgust of drink' was 'no merit in him', since he 'had not a
grain in his composition of that temper of conviviality so natural to
young men'. He tried to keep his feelings to himself, too much so,
perhaps, he later thought, but every Trinity Monday his refusal to take
part was inevitably seen as a 'protest'. A year later on Trinity Sunday,
he wrote vehemently to Walter Mayers to express his disgust at the
imminent gaudy. What particularly outraged him was that on the
Sunday, which of course was the feast day of Trinity, the whole college
went to Holy Communion: 'O how the Angels must lament over a whole
Society throwing off the allegiance and service of their Maker, which
they have pledged the day before at His Table, and showing themselves
true sons of Belial.' He wished devoutly he could bring some influence to
bear—but 'I am intimate with very few'.[36] When he later re-read this
letter, he noted its fierceness and remarked that under 'his gentleness of
manner' lay 'very strong feelings', which, he admitted, 'as the sequel of
his life shows, had not always so much to justify them' as in the present
instance.[37]

Not long after arriving back for the new academic year in October

---

[32] *LD* i. 52.   [33] *AW* 35.   [34] *LD* i. 53.
[35] *AW* 157.   [36] *LD* i. 66.   [37] *AW* 38.

1818, he and Bowden together wrote a verse 'romance' called *St Bartholomew's Eve*, which was 'founded on the Massacre of St Bartholomew. The subject was the issue of the unfortunate union of a Protestant gentleman with a Catholic lady, ending in the tragical death of both, through the machinations of a cruel fanatical priest . . .'.[38] Newman was responsible for the theology of the poem, which was strongly anti-Catholic. The first canto was completed within a week and published at the beginning of November. It was not a success, as less than a third of the copies were sold. However, the second canto duly appeared in February. (Sixty years later Newman was asked to send a copy of his first published work to the Bodleian Library, which had omitted to acquire it when it first came out.) They had 'hurried the story to a conclusion' in order to bring out a periodical modelled on Addison's *Spectator* and called *The Undergraduate*. Several numbers appeared in February and it 'sold well, but, to his great disgust, Newman's name got out, and this was its death blow',[39] as he was too embarrassed and upset by the publicity to continue with it. Again, however, Newman's formal compositions evince his imagination and nascent powers as a writer much less than his more spontaneous writing, like, for example, this remarkably evocative entry in his journal one Sunday evening in March 1819:

Bells pealing. The pleasure of hearing them. It leads the mind to a longing after some thing I know not what. It does not bring past years to remembrance. It does not bring any thing. What does it do? We have a kind of longing after something dear to us and well known to us, very soothing. Such is my feeling at this minute, as I hear them.[40]

In the summer term, the Dean (who treated him 'with the familiar kindness of an older brother') took him to some lectures given by the Professor of Geology ('at that time a new and interesting Science').[41] The long vacation gave him another opportunity to read Gibbon, whom he had started studying the previous summer, but whose style impressed him even more this time. But he also had other, more romantic, literary tastes. Scott's *Ivanhoe*, which he read immediately it was published, made him exclaim: 'O what a poet! his words are not like a novelist . . . Author of Waverley, thou art a second Shakespeare.'[42] And Aeschylus' *Prometheus* struck him as 'a wonderful composition, the work of an author with gigantic conceptions, worth all the tragedies of the stiff, cold, artificial, dignified Sophecles'.[43] But the enthusiastic admiration he also expressed at the same time for the *Tales of the Hall* by Crabbe—'he seems to me one of the greatest poets of the present day'—reminds one of that

[38] Ibid. 42.   [39] Ibid 41.   [40] Ibid. 160–1.
[41] Ibid. 44.   [42] *LD* i. 72.   [43] Ibid. 82.

other side of Newman—his deeply-ingrained realism and respect for common sense.[44]

However, none of these various intellectual and literary activities was allowed to interfere with the heavy course of reading he and Bowden had undertaken. (The only time he took off completely from study was the long vacation of 1818 after winning the scholarship, and then he read Gibbon and Locke.) In the autumn term of 1819 they were working together for eleven or twelve hours a day in preparation for their final examinations, leaving themselves only an hour for a walk and an hour for dinner. In November, Newman became a member of Lincoln's Inn; rather than going into the Church, he was now thinking of the Bar as a career. He had prayed that winning the scholarship would be 'no snare', but he was now entertaining 'dreams of a secular ambition'; he was horrified later to note how 'cold and remiss and ungrateful' he had grown, 'so vain, so puffed up, so proud', after having been 'so lowly and resigned' before the scholarship examination and 'so thankful on succeeding'.[45]

There was a change of mood in 1820, as now he had the 'dread' of the approaching final examinations to 'awe' him 'into silence'. With the passing of months, he began to have a 'grave feeling, with something of sadness and even awe in it at the prospect before him'. Soberly he wrote to his mother that he had 'often remarked that undergraduate residence is a picture of a whole life, of youth, of manhood, and of old age; which could not be understood or felt without actual experience'.[46] Apart from a few weeks at home, he spent the whole of the long summer vacation working in Oxford by himself. For the third time in his life he was spending a solitary summer. Without even Bowden's company, 'he had Trinity College, its garden and library, all to himself; and in his solitude, pleasant as he found it, he became graver and graver'.[47] In August, he wrote to his brother Francis: 'The quiet and stillness of every thing around me tends to calm and lull those emotions, which the near prospect of my grand examination and a heart too solicitous about fame and too fearful of failure are continually striving to excite.' Once again it was his earnest prayer 'that I may not get any honours here, if they are to be the least cause of sin to me'. He was worried that he was too anxious for academic success, 'and that is coveting, for then we covet, when we desire a thing so earnestly as to be disappointed, if we fail in getting it'.[48] In confiding his spiritual anxieties to Walter Mayers, he revealed a typically tortuous kind of Evangelical introspection. He did not 'feel' his prayer as he ought, and in spite of 'all the earnestness I assume, how

[44] *LD* i. 83.   [45] *AW* 45, 158–9.
[46] *LD* i. 77; *AW* 45.   [47] *AW* 45–6.
[48] *LD* i. 81–3.

little does my heart go with my words'. He was afraid, too, of hypocrisy: 'I am buoyed up with the secret idea, that by thus leaving the event in the hands of God, when I pray, He may be induced, as a reward for so proper a spirit, to grant me my desire.'[49] But at the same time he pointed out to his spiritual mentor that he was in a difficult position because so much was expected of him by the college, which was now hoping to improve its undistinguished academic record and was consequently placing high hopes in him personally.

By September, he was working thirteen to fourteen hours a day. But at the beginning of October he sent a warning signal to Mayers not to be misled by his impressive industry. He had spent time on other things apart from study. More ominously, he complained: 'I have not been advised, or have been advised wrongly, what books to read.' He thought in fact that 'six months of very hard reading' had been 'thrown away'. His other reading had been so irregular 'and out of place that my mind is a labyrinth more than any thing else'. Moreover, the sense of his own 'ingratitude' after winning the scholarship 'lies heavy on my heart, and unnerves my arm in the day of battle'.[50] By the middle of October he thought 'a failure highly probable', and told his mother that he would have 'to throw all my Classics overboard to bring my Mathematics into port'.[51] He had not lost his nerve, though, he assured his father a fortnight before his examinations in November: 'Coolly reflecting I think I may attain a first class in mathematics and second class in classics.' The danger was that 'Those who have a double prize in view, have the chance of missing each through attention to both.'[52]

His examination began on 25 November and ended on 1 December. It was a disastrous week. He had by now lost all hope of a first, but he still hoped to get two seconds. As he later explained in his autobiographical memoir (written in the third person):

He had overread himself, and, being suddenly called up a day sooner than he expected, he lost his head, utterly broke down, and after vain attempts for several days had to retire, only making sure first of his B.A. degree. When the class list came out, his name did not appear at all on the Mathematical side of the Paper, and in Classics it was found in the lower division of the second class of honours, which at that time went by the contemptuous title of the 'Under-the-line', there being as yet no third and fourth classes.[53]

The fact was that he was still only 19, three years below the usual age. Dr Nicholas had opposed his going so soon to Oxford, but he had made such extraordinarily rapid progress at school that it was hard to see what

---

49 Ibid. 87.   50 Ibid. 89.

51 Ibid. 91.   52 Ibid. 93.

53 *AW* 47.

else he could have done. Lack of experience and maturity, he later realized, had meant that he had wasted a lot of time. Nor was he helped by being at a college whose tutors had never acted as university examiners under the new examination system and who were therefore at a disadvantage in preparing their students for honours degrees. Reform had so far only really touched a few colleges ('the very idea of study was new'), at least to the extent that it was only these colleges that provided effective teaching that was relevant to the final examinations. Newman could not blame Trinity for the fact (as he later saw it) that he 'had as little tutorial assistance or guidance as it is easy to conceive, and found myself left almost entirely to my own devices'.[54] For all its desire to share in the academic revival at Oxford, older, less specialized methods, which were not adapted to the new system, still prevailed in the college.

He assured his anxious mother that the only pain he felt was at having disappointed his parents and the college. But he found nothing but sympathy on all sides and admiration for the calm way in which he had suffered his reverse. At least he knew he had secured his degree. His father came to collect him and they returned to London, where Mr Newman was now trying to manage a brewery in Clerkenwell, having failed at Alton. There was still another shock in store when the class list appeared later in the month and showed that Newman had not even gained the second in classics which he had been expecting. His failure was indeed 'remarkable', he told Mayers, but he could hardly describe 'the peace of mind' he felt when the ordeal was over: 'Before there was darkness and dread—I saw the cataract, to which I was hurrying without the possibility of a rescue.' Nobody, not even Bowden, had taken his fears seriously. His great consolation now, his belief that failure was 'best' for him, was something he could not only believe but also feel, for 'God has given me to see and know it'. Anticipating his later celebrated distinction between 'real' and 'notional' knowledge, he pointed out, 'There is a great difference between believing a thing to be good, and feeling it.'[55]

He returned to Oxford in February 1821. Although his scholarship was for nine years, he had to vacate his college rooms at the end of the summer term. In October he moved into lodgings at a coffee-house (on the corner of Broad Street and Holywell), where Bowden had also lodged. It had been decided that his youngest brother Francis should live in the other spare set of rooms and study with him until entering a college himself. Meanwhile Short had found him a private pupil, a Trinity undergraduate, who was ready to pay £100 a year. He had not been back in Oxford long when his father, who had originally risen from comparatively humble origins to considerable affluence, was crushed by the final blow of bankruptcy. The house in Southampton Street, together with its contents, had to be sold, and the family moved to Kentish Town.

Newman wrote comfortingly to his mother that they ought to be thankful they were so happy and united a family and that the disaster would only bring them closer together. More practically, he offered to pay for Francis's education at Oxford—which he was able to do almost entirely, as it turned out, by taking private pupils. He was not slow to share with his family his reflections on the religious significance of the crisis, although aware that it might be 'called enthusiasm, but it is an enthusiasm which I wish never to lose'.[56] His mother had already accused him of 'verging upon enthusiasm' for wanting to go to Holy Communion once a fortnight during the summer, a frequency of devotion which was then highly unusual. Francis, who had also fallen under the influence of Mr Mayers, had refused at the end of the vacation to copy a letter for his father because it was a Sunday; he was, of course, backed up by his elder brother: 'A scene ensued more painful than any I have experienced.'[57] Newman could not but admire his poor long-suffering father's tolerance and readiness to make up the quarrel. He also humbly recorded part of the warning his father gave him in the Christmas vacation that his religious views would certainly change and that he should be less intense and avoid 'ultraism' of any sort. A lengthy letter he had had published the previous year in the *Christian Observer*, which had tried to show that mathematics offers an illuminating analogy for the apparent difficulties in Christianity (a parallel he was to develop fruitfully much later), was mercilessly criticized by his father for its tone—'more like the composition of an old man, than of a youth just entering life with energy and aspirations'.[58] Newman later noted that his father need not have worried, as the emotional side of Evangelicalism was alien to his nature.

The day before Newman returned to Oxford for the Easter term, his father told him he ought to make up his mind what he wanted to be; Newman already knew he wanted to go into the Church. His father's ambition in sending him to university had been that he would be called to the Bar, but he accepted that his eldest son would now be better off becoming a clergyman in view of his poor degree and his increasingly pronounced religious leanings. Newman had not been back long in Oxford before he began to receive offers of tutorships in private families, which he turned down. He had already in November 'conceived the audacious idea of standing for a fellowship at Oriel, at that time the

[56] Ibid. 116.   [57] *AW* 175–6.   [58] Ibid. 179–80.

object of ambition of all rising men in Oxford, and attainable only by those who had the highest academical pretensions'. He knew that his examination failure was no 'measure of his intellectual merits', and the dream he had sometimes entertained of becoming a fellow of one of the colleges began to take shape more definitely in his mind during the autumn of 1821.[59] He did not think that he had much chance of success the first time round, but it would be a useful trial attempt and he could not help thinking that one day he would be a fellow of Oriel, perhaps next year. His friends at Trinity were rather horrified at what seemed the certainty of another disastrous failure. It was quite true that most of his studies during that year had been irrelevant to the fellowship examination. Apart from dabbling in chemistry and attending lectures on mineralogy and geology, he had also turned his hand to musical composition, and had spent much of the summer studying the Bible and trying to draw up a systematic scriptural basis and shape for his Evangelical beliefs. What he should have been working at above all was Latin composition, which he had heard was the most important thing for winning an Oriel fellowship. Mr Short, however, was not against his standing, not because he thought he would be successful, but because he wanted Newman to show the Oriel examiners 'what was in him', and because Newman's failure in the schools had been an embarrassing setback to the start of the reforms at Trinity which Short had been responsible for initiating.[60] He had already tactfully intimated to Newman that he would like him to enter for one of the university prizes to vindicate the college for electing him to their first open scholarship. By a curious coincidence Oriel was even more self-conscious at this very time about its own academic reputation. Its traditional policy was to reward intellectual distinction and originality rather than mere academic ability, which meant that it used rather different criteria from the examiners in the schools. Thus, only very recently, in 1821, it had given a fellowship to a candidate with only a second-class degree in preference to someone with a first. The unsuccessful candidate had promptly written an (anonymous) article in the Whig *Edinburgh Review*, long hostile to Oxford and especially Oriel, attacking the impartiality of the examiners. There was good reason why the Oriel electors this year should be wary of taking any unnecessary risks.

On 21 February 1822 Newman came of age: it was an 'awful' moment. He was afraid that he was 'idolatrously' 'set on succeeding at Oriel'. He had certainly begun to feel the same kind of confidence as when he had stood for the Trinity scholarship—and whereas 'when I was going up for my Degree Examination, every day made my hopes

---

[59] *AW* 49.   [60] Ibid. 56.

fainter, so now they seem to swell and ripen, as the time approaches'.[61] But this surge of confidence did not last: the nearer the day came, the less confident, not surprisingly, he felt. The first examination began on Easter Saturday, 'and we were supplied with sandwiches, fruit, cake, jellies, and wine—a blazing fire and plenty of time'.[62] But it was 'stiff, oh how stiff! ... sitting 8 hours on hard benches' in Oriel hall. And 'possessed with the idea' that he 'had all but disgraced' himself, he 'crawled about in the most piteous condition on Easter Sunday'. He had a bad night, and halfway through the Monday felt so ill he had to hand in incomplete and unrevised work. He felt very nervous the next day, but his prayer for strength was 'wonderfully' answered'.[63] In fact, his papers had already so impressed the examiners that three of the Oriel fellows went to make enquiries about him at Trinity. Mr Short was 'so excited by this visit' that he sent for Newman on the pretext of asking him how he was getting on; Newman found Short 'at an early dinner in his rooms', whereupon Short 'made him sit down at table and partake of his lamb cutlets and fried parsley, a bodily refreshment' which, together with his old tutor's encouraging comments on his report of his answers, gave him enough reassurance to continue, as he had been thinking of withdrawing from the unequal contest. Thereafter he felt much better, and 'several times' was 'comforted' by the motto in the window of the hall, 'Pie repone te.'

On the morning of Friday, 12 April Newman was elected a fellow of Oriel. He later wrote a dramatic and funny account of how he heard the unbelievable news.

The Provost's Butler, to whom it fell by usage to take the news to the fortunate candidates, made his way to Mr Newman's lodgings in Broad Street, and found him playing the violin. This in itself disconcerted the messenger, who did not associate such an accomplishment with a candidateship for the Oriel Common Room; but his perplexity was increased, when, on his delivering what may be supposed to have been his usual form of speech on such occasions, that 'he had, he feared, disagreeable news to announce, viz. that Mr Newman was elected Fellow of Oriel, and that his immediate presence was required there,' the person addressed, thinking that such language savoured of impertinent familiarity, merely answered 'Very well' and went on fiddling. This led the man to ask whether perhaps he had not mistaken the rooms and gone to the wrong person, to which Mr Newman replied that was all right. But, as may be imagined, no sooner had the man left, than he flung down his instrument, and dashed down stairs with all speed to Oriel College. And he recollected after fifty years the eloquent faces and eager bows of the tradesmen and others whom he met on his way, who had heard the news, and well understood why he was crossing from St Mary's to the lane opposite at so extraordinary a pace.[64]

[61] Ibid. 183–4.　　　[62] *LD* i. 131.　　　[63] *AW* 185.　　　[64] Ibid. 61–2.

He was summoned to the tower above the Oriel gateway where the viva voce examinations had taken place, 'the scene of torture, to receive the congratulations of the assembled Fellows'—'I bore it till Keble took my hand, and then felt so abashed and unworthy the honour done me that I seemed desirous of quite sinking into the ground.' He dined in the Senior Common Room that evening and sat next to the great John Keble, whom he found 'more like an undergraduate than the first man in Oxford—so perfectly unassuming and unaffected in his manner'. His election caused a sensation throughout the university, but especially in Trinity: 'The Bells were set ringing from three different towers (I had to pay for it).' The Dean was 'in raptures', and Dr Ogle, who had privately tutored him and Bowden, 'declares that nothing has given him so great gratification since he came to his present situation, it being uncertain whether he means, since he took his first class, since he became MD, since he undertook the Tutorship of Trinity, or since he married Mrs Ogle'.[65] As for Newman himself, 'he ever felt this twelfth of April, 1822 to be the turning point of his life, and of all days most memorable.'[66]

3

It had required 'courage', the autobiographical memoir noted, on the part of Oriel to award one of their coveted fellowships to someone with such a poor degree. And if the fellows had had any misgivings, they would have been confirmed by the unimpressive figure the new fellow cut in the famous Oriel Common Room. His 'extreme shyness' meant that he 'shrank into himself, when his duty was to meet their advances'. In fact, it was his 'very admiration of his new associates' which 'made a sudden intimacy with them impossible to him'. There was also that 'vivid self consciousness' from which he always suffered through his life and which 'sometimes afflicted on him days of acute suffering from the recollection of solecisms, whether actual or imagined, which he recognized in his conduct in society'. Finally, there was no denying a 'real isolation of thought and spiritual solitariness, which was the result of his Calvinistic beliefs'.[67] Not feeling 'quite at home' but 'very much alone', he once met, on one of his solitary walks, the Provost, Dr Copleston, who 'turned round, and with the kind courteousness which sat so well on him' bowed to the young fellow and remarked that one was never less alone than when alone.[68] It was Copleston who was

---

[65] *LD* i. 131, 134, 139.   [66] *AW* 63.
[67] Ibid. 65–6, 168.   [68] *Apo.* 27.

later to single out Newman as the outstanding justification of the college's policy of discouraging the kind of technical expertise encouraged by more conventional examinations in favour of real intellectual distinction and originality. Little did they know, Copleston ruefully reflected, what this shy young man, so grateful for any kindness, would turn into.

Some of the leading fellows arranged for Richard Whately, who had only recently vacated a fellowship on marrying, to take the 'new bashful youth' in hand. Whately was the ideal person: 'a great talker, who endured very readily the silence of his company', he was 'free and easy in manners, rough indeed and dogmatic', but very kind to the young, who were 'happy to be knocked about in argument by such a man'. Newman was 'a good listener' with a 'special faculty of entering into ideas as soon as, or before, they were expressed'. It was not long before Whately was complimenting him on being 'the clearest-headed man he knew'. Newman was able to return the compliment when he emphasized in the *Apologia* that it was Whately who 'opened my mind, and taught me to think and to use my reason'. At this time Whately 'was full of the subject of Logic' and lent Newman 'the MS of his "Analytical Dialogues"', which Newman took copies of. Characteristically, as he enjoyed writing 'by the medium of other brains', Whately suggested that Newman should 'cast these dialogues into the shape of a synthetical Treatise', to form part of an article on logic by Whately, for the *Encyclopaedia Metropolitana*. By revising and rewriting the 'rude essays' which Newman produced, Whately was enabled to begin his famous *Elements of Logic*.[69]

In April 1823 E. B. Pusey was elected a fellow of Oriel. Newman was impressed by his religious seriousness, but regretted his lack of sympathy for Evangelicalism. Newman's memory of his appearance was not very flattering: 'His light curly head of hair was damp with the cold water which his headaches made necessary for comfort; he walked fast with a young manner of carrying himself, and stood rather bowed, looking up from under his eye-brows, his shoulders rounded . . .'.[70] In November, Newman and Pusey joined a small private class run by Charles Lloyd, the Regius Professor of Divinity at Christ Church, where Pusey had been an undergraduate. It was an experiment intended to supplement the usual public lectures with a view to improving the state of theology at Oxford. Whately and Lloyd belonged to rival colleges and 'in an intellectual and academical point of view' were 'diametrically opposite', representing respectively the Latitudinarian and the 'high-and-dry' schools of theology. But Lloyd's influence on Newman was

[69] *AW* 66–7; *Apo.* 23.   [70] *AW* 74.

complementary to that of Whately in overcoming his 'shyness and reserve'. As a teacher and man, Lloyd rather resembled Whately:

He was free and easy in his ways, and a bluff talker, with a rough lively good natured manner, and a pretended pomposity relieving itself in sudden bursts of laughter, and in indulgence in . . . *chaffing* at the expense of his auditors; and, as he moved up and down his room, large in person beyond his years, asking them questions, gathering their answers, and taking snuff, as he went along, he would sometimes stop before Mr Newman, on his speaking in his turn, fix his eyes on him as if to look him through, with a satirical expression of countenance, and then make a feint to box his ears or kick his shins, before he went on with his march to and fro.

Lloyd realized that his pupil 'held what are called evangelical views of doctrine, then greatly in disrepute in Oxford, and in consequence bestowed on him a notice, expressive of vexation and impatience on the one hand and of a liking for him personally and a good opinion of his abilities on the other'. But unlike Whately, Lloyd did not 'leave a mark' on Newman's mind: Lloyd was a 'scholar' not an 'original thinker', who stressed authoritative doctrine and tradition; whereas Whately's 'great satisfaction was to find a layman who had made a creed for himself', and he felt sympathetic to 'a heretic, for his heresy at least showed that he had exercised his mind upon its subject matter'. There was no doubting who was 'more Catholic in his tone of mind', but it was Whately who exerted the real 'intellectual influence' on Newman by teaching him how to think for himself, not the learned professor.[71] Not that Newman at this time despised exact scholarship: he likened theologians who lacked a close knowledge of the text of Scripture to 'insects who feed on the shell of a nut, instead of advancing to the kernel'.[72] However, it was Pusey, not Newman, who was the real disciple of Lloyd, who was soon to send him to Germany to continue his theological studies.

In May 1824 Newman decided to accept the curacy of St Clement's, a growing working-class parish with a population of about 2,000, situated on the other side of Magdalen Bridge. The Rector, the Reverend John Gutch, who was also Registrar of the University, was in his eighties and in poor health, but a new church was urgently needed to replace the present inadequate building, which could only hold about 200 people, and before an appeal could be launched a curate had to be found who would be 'a kind of guarantee to the subscribers that every exertion will be made, when the Church is built, to recover the parish from meeting houses, and on the other hand alehouses, into which they have been driven for want of convenient Sunday worship'.[73] A year before, Newman had been wondering how soon he should get ordained

---

[71] *AW* 69–71.   [72] *LD* i. 171.   [73] Ibid. 198–9.

and had been advised by Mayers that it was his duty to offer himself immediately so as to be able to aid the parochial clergy—although others had expressed doubts about the suitability of taking Orders while he was still teaching. At present he was tutoring as many private pupils as possible to support his brother Francis, and it seemed certain that he would soon be a college tutor, as the turnover of fellows was high (an Oriel fellowship was often sought simply for the honour and glory of it). Now he decided that it was 'necessary to get used to parochial duty early, and that a Fellow of a College after ten years residence in Oxford feels very awkward among poor and ignorant people'.[74] Pusey, who had recommended him for the curacy, advised him to accept the position, as did others in Oriel, as well as Walter Mayers. Accordingly, on 13 June he was ordained deacon in Christ Church Cathedral: 'It is over. I am thine, O Lord; I seem quite dizzy, and cannot altogether believe and understand it. At first, after the hands were laid on me, my heart shuddered within me; the words "for ever" are so terrible.'[75] Ten days later he preached his first sermon at Over Worton, near Banbury, where Mayers was curate. On Sunday, 4 July he took his first service at St Clement's and administered his first baptism. He began an intensive visitation of the parish, throwing himself into ordinary pastoral work as energetically and unsparingly as he had applied himself to academic study. After about ten days he calculated he had visited a third ('the most respectable third') of his parishioners. He found the people friendly and gratefully surprised to be visited by a clergyman. One problem Newman shared with the elderly rector was that people could not hear him in church; he had known beforehand that his voice would be a problem. But it became stronger, and the congregation rapidly increased from about 50 to more than the church could hold. He did not try to bring back 'regular' dissenters nor did he speak against their minister—there was 'too much irreligion in the place' to alienate 'so active an ally'. By the middle of August he had 'gone through the whole' parish 'from house to house'. He was much complimented on his preaching, although he later heard that people thought he was too severe. However, his own decided view was: 'Those who make comfort the great subject of their preaching seem to mistake the end of their ministry. *Holiness* is the great end. There must be a struggle and a trial here. Comfort is a cordial, but no one drinks cordials from morning to night.'[76] He told Pusey that the 'most pleasant part' of his duties was visiting the sick.[77]

It was during his time on the parish that he 'underwent a great change in his religious opinions'. To begin with, there was the 'atmosphere' of

[74] *LD* i. 175.   [75] *AW* 200.
[76] Ibid. 172.   [77] *LD* i. 184, 186, 191.

the Oriel Common Room, which was 'neither high Church nor low Church, but ... characterized by its spirit of moderation and comprehension'. Its leading lights, figures like Copleston, Whately, John Davison, Edward Hawkins, and Thomas Arnold, were objects of suspicion to 'the old unspiritual high-and-dry, then in possession of the high places of Oxford', who 'pronounced them unsafe'. Like other Evangelicals, Newman was 'grateful for that liberality of mind which was in such striking contrast with the dominant high-Church'. Because of his parochial duties he had to stay in Oxford in vacation time, as did Edward Hawkins, then Vicar of St Mary's, the University Church. In the long vacation, when all the other fellows were away, they were thrown into each other's company. Newman learned from Hawkins ('a man of most exact mind') intellectual rigour: 'He was the first who taught me to weigh my words, and to be cautious in my statements.' Theologically, Newman was deeply influenced by a university sermon which Hawkins had preached on tradition, to the effect that the Bible 'was never intended to teach doctrine, but only to prove it, and that, if we would learn doctrine, we must have recourse to the formularies of the Church'. But Hawkins influenced him more directly and personally by criticizing the first sermon he ever wrote, which 'divided the Christian world into two classes, the one all darkness, the other all light'. Newman maintained the usual Evangelical distinction between 'nominal' Christians, and 'real' Christians who had experienced true conversion. Hawkins argued that it was 'impossible for us in fact to draw such a line of demarcation', that people were 'not either saints or sinners' but somewhere in between, that there were differences of degree not of kind. To prove his point, Hawkins lent him J. B. Sumner's *Apostolical Preaching*, which showed how St Paul did not divide Christians into two categories, 'the converted and unconverted', but addressed them all as believers with the gift of the Holy Spirit, however much he might rebuke them for their actual behaviour. It was this book which 'was successful in the event beyond any thing else, in routing out' Newman's 'evangelical doctrines'. He had not, then, been in Orders long before he 'had taken the first step towards giving up the evangelical form of Christianity; however, for a long while certain shreds and tatters of that doctrine hung about his preaching, nor did he for a whole ten years altogether sever himself from those great religious societies and their meetings, which then as now were the rallying ground and the strength of the Evangelical body'.

The 'teaching of facts' also played an important part: he found from working in a parish that Evangelicalism did not 'work', that 'it was unreal', and 'not a key to the phenomena of human nature, as they occur in the world'. Although, he later readily recognized, Evangelical 'teaching had been a great blessing for England', for 'it had brought home to the hearts of thousands the cardinal and vital truths of Revelation, and ⟨...⟩ himself among others', still, 'much as he owed' to it, 'he never ha⟨...⟩ genuine evangelical'. True, Evangelicalism had 'converted' ⟨...⟩ spiritual life' (although his conversion had not followed th⟨...⟩ vangelical pattern), but 'considered as a system and in wh⟨...⟩ uliar to itself', it 'had from the first failed to find a response ⟨...⟩ wn religious experience, as afterwards in his parochi⟨...⟩ng to write sermons forced him to 'systematize and compl⟨...⟩eas, and he found that he had taken 'almost on trust' a num⟨...⟩octrines from Evangelical writers which did not seem to be suppo⟨...⟩y Scripture. In particular, he began to give up 'the doctrine of impu⟨...⟩ed righteousness' in favour of the traditional church doctrine of Baptismal regeneration, the rejection of which had come to be the hallmark of the true Evangelical but which Newman had never felt easy about dismissing: how otherwise, he had once asked Mayers, could unbaptized babies who died be saved?[79] Finally, there was an aspect of Newman's mind 'which seemed to intimate from the first that the ethical character of Evangelical Religion could not lastingly be imprinted upon it', and that was his 'great attraction' both to the Classics (whom, like the ancient Fathers, he valued 'as being in a certain sense inspired moralists and prophets of truths greater than they knew') and to the Fathers themselves. Had it not been for his love of the patristic writings, he would no doubt have embraced a 'cold Arminian doctrine' which was 'the characteristic aspect, both of the high and dry Anglicans of that day and of the Oriel divines'. But 'the permanent effect' of reading as a schoolboy Milner's *Church History* had been that 'the first centuries were his *beau idéal* of Christianity', and an 'imaginative devotion' to the Fathers 'saved him from the danger' of taking 'refuge in the flats' of the high-and-dry and Latitudinarian theologies on 'leaving the crags and precipices of Luther and Calvin'.[80]

On Saturday, 25 September, Newman took the night coach to London, after hearing that his father was seriously ill. He arrived on Sunday morning: 'He knew me, tried to put out his hand and said "God bless you." ' Mr Newman had told his wife that he would not live to see another summer; he was only 59 but his business failures had broken him. Now, however, he 'seemed in great peace of mind'. He died on the Wednesday. The next day he 'looked beautiful, such calmness, sweetness, composure, and majesty were in this countenance. Can a man be a materialist who sees a dead body? I had never seen one before.' Newman took the funeral service; he wondered whether he himself

---

[78] *AW* 73–4, 77–9; *Apo.* 21–2.   [79] *AW* 203–4.   [80] Ibid. 83.

would one day 'be followed to the grave by my children? my Mother said the other day she hoped to live to see me married, but *I* think I shall either die within a College walls, or a Missionary in a foreign land—no matter where, so that I die in Christ.'[81]

No sooner had Newman completed the subscription for the new church in the middle of October, than he decided to launch an appeal for a Sunday school. That Christmas the number of communicants was higher than ever before. Early in February the new Sunday school began; it had proved impossible to find a room anywhere, but money was soon raised to build a gallery to accommodate the children; for heating Pusey provided a stove.

In spite of all his enthusiasm and energy in the parish, Newman had not abandoned either the college or intellectual work. On 16 October 1824, he had been elected to the junior treasurership at Oriel, an appointment which brought a welcome increase to his income. In the spring he had been asked by Whately if he would like to write an article on Cicero for the *Encyclopaedia Metropolitana*, which he duly completed by the end of May. The editor, Edward Smedley, was delighted with the piece and hoped that Newman could be persuaded to contribute on other subjects. In his lengthy essay Newman said that he regarded the Roman orator as the most interesting and attractive figure of classical antiquity, self-revealed as he was in his letters. One day he was to say that the only writer who had really influenced his style was Cicero, whom he calls here 'the greatest master of composition that the world has seen'. Certainly something of his rhetorical influence on Newman is indicated clearly enough by this assessment of his orations: 'He accounts for everything so naturally, makes trivial circumstances tell so happily, so adroitly converts apparent objections into confirmations of his argument, connects independent facts with such ease and plausibility, that it becomes impossible to entertain a question on the truth of his statement.'[82] After Newman's death, his brother Francis maintained that Newman had learned his skills as a controversialist from Cicero, and that he could have been an 'eminent' barrister—as a writer he always had to have a 'thesis to attack or defend'.[83]

In February 1825 Whately arranged with Smedley that Newman should write a further two articles for the encyclopaedia, which would be connected and on theological subjects. Newman agreed to, not only because he was persuaded by Whately's advice that 'sermon writing *by itself* has a tendency to produce a loose rambling kind of composition, nay even of thought', but because he welcomed the opportunity of

[81] *AW* 202–3. [82] *HS* i. 297, 293.

[83] F. W. Newman, *Contributions Chiefly to the Early History of the late Cardinal Newman*, 2nd edn. (London, 1891), 44.

'influencing the religious tone' of such an important work of reference; moreover, writing on religious rather than secular topics was not incompatible with his desire 'to devote' his 'time to studies more connected with' his 'profession'.[84] The work would require a lot of reading, and he could not begin till June.

In the summer of 1823 he had had a long talk with his brother Charles, who was sceptical about the claims of Christianity, which he followed up with a letter at the end of the year, insisting in the usual Evangelical manner that religious truth cannot be attained without the right kind of moral seriousness and sincerity. In March 1825 he developed this apologetic approach by saying that he considered 'the rejection of Christianity to arise from a fault of the *heart*, not of the *intellect*', for a 'dislike of the *contents* of Scripture is at the bottom of unbelief': 'Hence the most powerful arguments for Christianity do not *convince*, only *silence*; for there is at the bottom that secret antipathy for the doctrines of Christianity, which is quite out of the reach of argument.' The idea of the crucial importance of 'antecedent probabilities' and 'first principles' is already clearly, if only implicitly, grasped: 'We survey moral and religious subjects through the glass of previous habits; and scarcely two persons use a glass of the same magnifying power. I venture confidently to say, that if the contents of a professed revelation on divine things are to be made the test of its genuineness, *no revelation could* be made us: for scarcely two persons can be got together, who will agree in their antecedent or self-originated ideas of God and his purposes towards man.' It is on its 'credentials' or 'claims', not its contents, that the Christian revelation, he insisted, must be judged.[85]

At the end of March Whately became Principal of Alban Hall and asked Newman to be his Vice-Principal, an invitation he accepted because he had 'all along thought it was more' his 'duty to engage in College offices than in parochial duty'.[86] There were only about a dozen undergraduates actually in residence, but Newman was to be 'Dean, Tutor, Bursar and all'. It would not mean much increase in his income, but it was 'a post of considerable authority and responsibility', he told his mother.[87] The hall, which was well-known for the poor quality of its undergraduates, was in urgent need of reform.

In May his father's mother died suddenly, his 'earliest benefactor'. In his journal he wrote, 'how she loved me!' He told his Aunt Elizabeth that she and his grandmother were chiefly responsible for 'having from my youth turned my thoughts towards religion'.[88] Unfortunately, his grandmother had not lived to see his ordination to the priesthood which

---

84 *LD* i. 210.   85 Ibid. 219, 225–6.
86 *AW* 205.   87 *LD* i. 222.
88 Ibid. 251.

took place exactly a week after her death on Sunday, 29 May. A year before, when he had been ordained deacon, Newman had thought that some of the other candidates might be 'without the Spirit of God', but now he considered that 'tho' there was difference of spirituality, yet all might be in some degree spiritual'—then he had assumed the onus of proof 'lay with those who asserted an individual to be a real Christian', but now he thought it lay with those who denied it.[89]

Yet another influence leading him away from Evangelicalism was brought to bear during the summer, when at the end of June he began reading Joseph Butler's classic *Analogy of Religion* (1736). It helped place 'his doctrinal views on a broad philosophical basis, with which an emotional religion could have little sympathy'.[90] Butler insisted on the similarities between the works of God as shown in nature and as revealed in revelation, arguing that the objections which can be made against Christianity are analogous to those which can be made against theism. In retrospect, it is obvious how deeply the idea of analogy influenced Newman both as an intellectual principle and as a mode of argument, strongly affecting him not only as a thinker but also as a writer. However, in the *Apologia* he merely points out the religious significance of 'the very idea of an analogy between the separate works of God', which 'leads to the conclusion that the system which is of less importance is economically or sacramentally connected with the more momentous system, and of this conclusion the theory, to which I was inclined as a boy, viz. the unreality of material phenomena, is an ultimate resolution'. In addition, Butler's doctrine that probability 'is the guide of life' was to have an important bearing on his writings on 'the logical cogency of Faith'.[91]

In July he began reading various writers on miracles, including Hume, as a preparation for one of the two promised articles, on which he made a start in August. And early in September he commenced writing the other article, on Apollonius of Tyana. Cheerfully, he assured his mother that 'parish, Hall, College, and Encyclopaedia go on together in perfect harmony'.[92] But in fact he was seriously overworking, and in January 1826 he began to suffer from chronic indigestion. Pusey was to have helped him at St Clement's, but he had been sent off by Lloyd to Germany to continue his theological studies. Nevertheless, in response to another invitation from Smedley to write an article on the Fathers of the second century, he offered to undertake a larger article which would cover the third century as well and which he would complete in two years. Smedley, however, wanted the shorter article within the year, which Newman felt did not give him enough time. He had suggested the

[89] *AW* 206.   [90] Ibid. 78.   [91] *Apo.* 23.   [92] *LD* i. 268.

larger project in 'the hope of gaining more time for the consideration of the important matter which the history of the early Church contains and of which I have at present but very slender knowledge'.[93]

4

On 20 January 1826 Newman accepted the invitation to become a tutor at Oriel after Easter. It would involve resigning the curacy at St Clement's, which he clearly felt was suffering from the amount of time he had to give to the problems of Alban Hall. (The parish clerk later remarked that the parochial work undertaken by Newman was on a scale unparalleled in Oxford at that time.) Whately was so anxious that he should stay and help him that he even offered to increase his salary to the amount he would receive as a tutor. Different as their minds were, their close association during 1825 had led to one important development in Newman's theological thinking, 'the idea of the Christian Church, as a divine appointment, and as a substantive body, independent of the State, and endowed with rights, prerogatives, and powers of its own'.[94]

On 21 March Newman moved into the rooms in college vacated by his predecessor—'those which of all others I have always wished to have'. Up till now he had lived in lodgings, except in vacations. He told his sister Harriett that he saw the tutorship as a spiritual undertaking and not 'merely as a secular office'; he was also aware of 'the danger of the love of literary pursuits'. But he warned her not to be too influenced by his religious views—he had already changed his opinions 'and I may change again'.[95] Pusey had recently accused him of becoming quite high church. On 31 March, R. I. Wilberforce, the second son of William Wilberforce the philanthropist, and R. H. Froude were elected fellows of Oriel. Newman was immediately impressed by Froude—'one of the acutest and clearest and deepest men', he told his mother.[96] It was a relief to be free of the parish and not to have to do several jobs at once, the effect of which he had felt as 'a *tearing* or *ripping open* of the coats of the brain and the vessels of the heart'.[97] But after only a few weeks of being a tutor, he was worried by the 'considerable profligacy' of the undergraduates, mostly 'men of family, in many cases, of fortune'. As at Trinity, he disapproved of the 'general reception of the Sacrament, which is expected'. He thought the tutors did not see enough of the students and

---

[93] Ibid. 276. [94] *AW* 69.
[95] *LD* i. 280. [96] Ibid. 282.
[97] Ibid. 309.

that there was not enough 'direct religious instruction'. Since he considered himself 'the minister of Christ', he might be forced to resign if he found he could not exercise a 'spiritual' influence over his pupils.[98] It was a sensitive point with him, as not only were his Evangelical mentors opposed to the conventional idea that ordination was a qualification for being a college tutor, but Hawkins himself regarded the office of tutor as hardly a natural fulfilment of the clerical vocation, however permissible it might be 'for a time or under circumstances'. Newman, on the contrary, held 'there were various modes of fulfilling' the vow of ordination, of which a college tutorship was one.[99]

Meanwhile, the article on Apollonius had been completed in March, and its sequel on the 'Miracles of Scripture' was also sent off to Smedley in April. Newman later regretted that in order to emphasize the special character of the miracles in the Bible he had depreciated the significance of later miracles in the history of the Church. He also confessed to using 'flippant language against the Fathers'. It was an example of 'a certain disdain for Antiquity' which had been 'growing' on him for 'several years'. At Easter the following year, for example, he was to preach a sermon in Oriel Chapel which implied that some clauses in the Athanasian (as opposed to the Nicene) Creed were 'unnecessarily scientific'. He was, he admitted in the *Apologia*, 'beginning to prefer intellectual excellence to moral' and 'drifting in the direction of the Liberalism of the day'. He was to be 'rudely awakened' from his 'dream at the end of 1827 by two great blows—illness and bereavement'.[100] From the point of view of Newman's intellectual development, the most interesting aspect of the article on miracles is the way in which some of the central concerns of the *Grammar of Assent* are already anticipated, not only the ideas of antecedent probability and the cumulation of probabilities (which were to be found in Whately's writings on logic) but also 'assent' and its relation to inference.[101]

He was hardly free of the encyclopaedia articles when he began talking of a new work which would perhaps (he gleefully warned his sisters) take him twenty years—'to trace the sources from which the corruptions of the Church, principally the Romish, have been derived'. It would involve reading all the Fathers—'200 volumes at least'.[102] During the long vacation he also began learning Hebrew and managed to get to the end of Genesis. Returning to Oxford for the new term, he felt as if he 'could have rooted up St Mary's spire and kicked down the Radcliffe'. The Dean of Oriel, J. E. Tyler, was to leave at Christmas, and it was not clear whether anybody could be found to take his place as

[98] *AW* 209.
[99] Ibid. 87.
[100] *Apo.* 25–6.
[101] See *GA*, pp. xxii–xxiii.
[102] *LD* i. 285.

tutor. 'We who remain are likely to have a great deal of work and responsibility laid upon us'—but, Newman remarked cheerfully, 'my spirits most happily rise at the prospect of danger, trial, or any call upon me for unusual exertion'.[103] Far from thinking of resigning as tutor, he intended to be 'very obstinate' with the undergraduates, 'though their curvettings and shyings are very teazing', 'for whenever they get a new coachman, they make an effort to get the reins slack'.[104] He had indeed 'come out of' his 'shell': becoming a tutor had given him a 'position', and his articles in the *Encyclopaedia Metropolitana* had been 'well received'. In July he had also preached his first university sermon. He was beginning 'to be known'. It was, he keenly remembered, 'like the feeling of spring weather after winter'.[105]

During the long summer vacation of 1827 Newman was once again hard at work, preparing for his first stint as an examiner for the BA degree. He stayed first at Brighton (where the family had moved) and then at Hampstead, where he took clerical duty for the Revd E. G. Marsh, a former fellow of Oriel. He was also tutoring privately two Oriel undergraduates, C. P. Golightly and Henry Wilberforce, the youngest son of William Wilberforce, who was to become one of his closest friends. He had made an immediate impression on Newman when he arrived as a freshman: 'He was small and timid, shrinking from notice, with a bright face and intelligent eyes. Partly from his name, partly from his appearance, I was at once drawn towards him . . .'[106] Newman caused 'quite a commotion' at Hampstead by quoting the Canons of 1603 against the Puritans in a sermon which provoked one of his congregation into observing that 'it was an exercise of charity (let alone any almsgiving) to listen patiently'. At the time, he later recalled, he was 'eagerly, but not very logically, High Church'. His mother and sisters had accompanied him from Brighton, but unfortunately they were 'obliged to leave' Mr Marsh's house because it was 'so full of bad vermin': when he wrote to the worthy clergyman about it, Marsh (who was 'a most meek, gentle, amiable man') replied simply that 'it was one of the trials of this life, and so must be borne'.[107]

Awaiting his return to Oxford in October was a set of the Fathers which Pusey had bought for him in Germany. 'I wish you could see them,' Newman wrote exultantly to his sister Harriett, 'they fit into my bookcases capitally.' To his mother he remarked: 'huge fellows they are, but very cheap—*one* folio costs a shilling!'[108]

This term he had no lectures to give; his fellow tutors had kindly given him the time off to get ready for examining in the Schools—which was not simply a matter of setting and marking papers, but of conducting a

[103] Ibid. 304. [104] Ibid. 305. [105] *Apo.* 27.
[106] *LD* ii. 21 n. 1. [107] Ibid. xxiii. 38. [108] Ibid. ii. 30.

largely viva voce examination which was open to the public. The ordeal
had been preying on his mind during the summer and he had read 'too
hard' for it: 'his mind had been too much on the stretch, and had
suffered from too intensely dwelling on the object'. Shortly before
coming back to Oxford he had suffered feverish symptoms, and the term
had only just begun when the long-expected crisis in his impecunious
aunt's financial affairs came to a head, which meant that he and Francis
would have to raise a large sum of money to pay off her debts. Finally,
when he was examining in November, feeling very nervous and tired, it
was announced that Copleston had been appointed Bishop of Llandaff
and that they would have to elect a new Provost. The excitement of the
news 'completed' his 'incapacity' and he was forced to leave the Schools,
his 'memory and mind gone'. He left Oxford on doctor's orders and
joined the family at Brighton. It was 'a curious coincidence' that this
nervous collapse should have taken place on the anniversary of his
previous failure seven years before.[109]

On 4 January 1828, Newman's youngest sister Mary was suddenly
taken ill during dinner. That night she suffered violent spasms, but
although she was in severe pain, she took 'great comfort' from being able
to recite to herself from memory verses she had learnt by heart from
Keble's *Christian Year*, which her brother had bought the previous
summer when the book was published and which he had lent to his
mother and sisters. She died next day later in the evening; she was barely
19. 'She was gifted with that singular sweetness and affectionateness of
temper', wrote Newman, 'that she lived in an ideal world of happiness,
the very sight of which made others happy.'[110] Indeed, for 'some time' he
had had a 'presentiment' that Mary would not live long: 'I was led to
this by her extreme loveliness of character, and by the circumstance of
my great affection for her. I thought I loved her too well, and hardly
ever dared to take my full swing of enjoyment in her dear society.' Now
he could only say, 'I cannot realize that I shall never see her again.'[111]
What upset him more than anything was that now they could only talk
of her 'in the third person', as though she were 'some inanimate object,
wood or stone'.[112] Later in the spring, as he rode in the countryside
round Oxford, the beauty of nature made him feel more 'intensely' than
ever before 'the transitory nature of this world'. But it was not 'possible
for words to put down those indefinite vague and withal subtle feelings
which quite pierce the soul and make it sick. Dear Mary seems embodied
in every tree and hid behind every hill. What a veil and curtain this
world of sense is! beautiful but still a veil . . .'[113]

[109] *AW* 212.   [110] *LD* ii. 49–50.
[111] *AW* 213.   [112] *LD* ii. 61.
[113] Ibid. 69.

There were two candidates for the Oriel provostship, Hawkins and Keble. Newman knew Hawkins much better ('he had taken me up'), while Keble had 'fought shy' of him ('in consequence of the marks which I bore upon me of the evangelical and liberal schools').[114] No less important was the consideration that Hawkins had the reputation of being a strict disciplinarian. At the end of January Hawkins was duly elected. Newman had defended his not voting for Keble by saying, 'You know we are not electing an Angel, but a Provost.'[115] He had been very pleasantly surprised by *The Christian Year*, which he found 'exquisite' and not at all 'heavy' as he had feared.[116] The 'two main intellectual truths' which its 'religious teaching' impressed upon him were the same as he had already learned from Butler, 'though recast in the creative mind of my new master': first, the sacramental idea that 'material phenomena are both the types and the instruments of real things unseen', and second, the view that 'it is not merely probability which makes us intellectually certain' in religious matters, 'but probability as it is put to account by faith and love'.[117]

On 12 March Hawkins resigned as Vicar of St Mary's, and Newman succeeded him two days later. Once again he was busy with parish work. But it did not stop him during the long vacation from starting to read the Fathers systematically, beginning with the early Apostolic Fathers, for 'as I moved out of the shadow of that liberalism which had hung over my course, my early devotion towards the Fathers returned'.[118]

At the end of September Newman began to write an essay which, as an example of late Romantic or early Victorian literary criticism, has received so much attention in recent times as would have surprised its author, for whom it was hardly more than an ephemeral article commissioned by a colleague for a new periodical. 'Poetry, with reference to Aristotle's Poetics' was completed in October and published the following January in the short-lived *London Review*, edited by Joseph Blanco White, a member of the Oriel Common Room, who was in Anglican Orders but had the novel distinction of being an ex-Catholic priest from Spain (though he was of Irish descent). Newman criticized Aristotle's emphasis on the importance of plot, arguing that Greek tragedy was in fact distinguished not for its action but for its characterization and poetry. He Platonized Aristotle's definition of poetry as 'a representation of the ideal', and insisted not only that a 'right moral state of heart is the . . . condition of a poetical mind', but that there was a 'connexion between want of the religious principle and want of poetical feeling'. He welcomed the corollary that 'Revealed

---

[114] Ibid. xxii. 209; *Apo.* 29.
[116] Ibid. ii. 20.
[118] Ibid. 35.

[115] *LD* xxx. 107.
[117] *Apo.* 29–30.

Religion should be especially poetical' and that 'a poetical view of things' was a Christian duty. The language of poetry, however, was dismissed as 'merely accessory to the poetical talent' and 'no essential part of poetry, though indispensable to its exhibition', so that 'attention to the language, for its own sake, evidences not the true poet, but the mere artist'.[119] Years later, in the *Idea of a University*, Newman was to avoid this crude dichotomy between content and form by producing a classic definition of style which directly contradicts what he had written as a young man: 'Thought and speech are inseparable from each other . . . style is a thinking out into language.'[120]

Early in 1829, Newman was able to boast to a friend of the reforms he and the other tutors had implemented at Oriel: 'We have gone through the year famously, packed off our lumber, parted with spoilt goods, washed and darned when we could, and imported several new articles of approved quality. Indeed the College is so altered that you would hardly know it again.' Two years earlier he had rejoiced at the departure of Tyler—'the evil which tuft and silk courting has been to the College, is best seen by the effect of its being withdrawn.' The 'tangible improvements' had been a reduction in the number of 'Gentlemen Commoners', the 'dismissal of the Incurables', the raising of qualifications for entry, the introduction of written work into the termly college examinations, and other measures designed to improve academic standards, as well as 'the revival of a Chapel Sermon at the Sacrament'. But

The most important and far reaching improvement has been commenced this term:—a radical alteration (*not apparent* on the published list) of the lecture system. The bad men are thrown into large classes—and thus time saved for the better sort who are put into very small lectures, and principally with their own Tutors quite familiarly and chattingly.

Newman added that the new Provost, while he had naturally not 'taken the initiative in these innovations', had nevertheless 'always approved, sometimes kept abreast with us', and at the termly 'collections' had 'slain the bad men manfully'.[121] The harmonious relationship was not to last.

At the beginning of February convocation passed a petition to Parliament against Catholic emancipation with an even larger majority than in the previous year. The fear of civil war in Ireland had led to a dramatic shift of policy on the part of the Tory government, in which Sir Robert Peel, who sat for the University, was a leading member.

[119] *Ess.* i. 9, 21–5.
[120] *Idea*, 232. See Geoffrey and Kathleen Tillotson, *Mid-Victorian Studies* (London, 1965), 256–7.
[121] *LD* ii. 8, 117–18.

Newman professed to indifference about the petition, regarding emancipation as a political rather than religious question, even if it was 'the *symptom* of a systematic hatred to our Church borne by Romanists, Sectarians, Liberals and Infidels'. But if he was not particularly in favour of the petition, he was very much in favour of not re-electing Peel, who had offered his resignation, as it would be humiliating for the University 'to have a Rat our member'.[122] He was more than happy that 'all the bigotry' that could be used against Peel should be used.[123] But his delight at the news that Peel's old college, Christ Church, had come out against him was short-lived: 'Unluckily our meddling Provost just then returned from London, where Oxford men, being chiefly liberal lawyers, were for Peel.' Hawkins began to canvass energetically for Peel, but most of the Oxford dons, although 'differing in their views on the Catholic question', agreed that Peel was 'unworthy to represent a religious, straightforward, unpolitical body, whose interests he had, in some form or other, more or less, betrayed'. Peel, who had been the leading Tory champion of the established Church and opponent of Catholic emancipation, was guilty of gross inconsistency. It would be 'an infamous thing, if Oxford were to be blown round by the breath of a minister' and used as a 'tool' by the government. Newman could not pretend that he was totally neutral on the question of emancipation—he was, he admitted, 'anti-catholic in *principle* . . . [I] consider the Church encompassed with inveterate foes, and only cannot make up my mind *where* the stand is to be made.'[124] As for the 'meddling' Provost of Oriel, far from consulting with his fellows, as was customary for the head of a college before taking an initiative on a public issue, he had 'contemptuously' called their opposition to Peel a 'cabal' and had 'suddenly got up an opposite party without speaking to any' of them.[125] Before he became Provost, Hawkins had the reputation of using 'the language of a Tribune of the people' in upholding the rights of fellows and tutors against usurpations by the head of the college. But after his election, 'he did not shrink from declaring that all was as it ought to be' and from 'assuming state and pomp' and 'separating himself from his own Fellows'.[126]

Peel's defeat at the election evoked an exuberant response from Newman:

We have achieved a glorious Victory. It is the first public event I have been concerned in, and I thank God from my heart both for my cause and its success. We have proved the independence of the Church and of Oxford.

---

[122] Ibid. 118–19.   [123] Ibid. 121.
[124] Ibid. 123.   [125] *AW* 98; *LD* ii. 124.
[126] *AW* 96–7.

A 'much nearer and holier interest than the pacification of Ireland' was resistance to the University being put 'under the feet' of the Duke of Wellington's government:

What is the reputation of the whole cabinet, great Captain and all, put together, compared with that of Oxford . . . Oxford has never turned with the turn of fortune. Mistaken we may have been, but never inconstant. We kept to the Stuarts in misfortune. Better be bigotted than time-serving . . .[127]

As so often later in his life, Newman justified the duty of resistance to a change, while at the same time allowing for the necessity of accepting it once it had happened. The religious aspect of the affair shows the influence of Keble and Froude who 'disliked the Duke's change of policy as dictated by liberalism'. Newman's emphasis on the value of asserting the Church's independence of the state reflects his growing friendship with Froude, who 'delighted in the notion of an hierarchical system, of sacerdotal power, and of full ecclesiastical liberty'.[128] Previously, Newman had voted with the minority in favour of Catholic emancipation, but then he had been under the influence of Whately's anti-erastianism and hostile to the high-and-dry party. Now he saw the granting of the Catholic claims as merely 'the first step in a long train of events' (such as, he correctly prophesied, the disestablishment of the Church of Ireland), but to be welcomed if it enabled them to 'fight the enemy on better ground and to more advantage'.[129] At any rate, it seemed inevitable.

The affair had set Newman thinking on the larger issues involved, both for religion and society.

We live in a novel era—one in which there is an advance towards universal education. Men have hitherto depended on others, and especially on the Clergy, for religious truth; now each man attempts to judge for himself. Now, without meaning of course that Christianity is in itself opposed to free inquiry, still I think it *in fact* at the present time opposed to the particular form which that liberty of thought has now assumed. Christianity is of faith, modesty, lowliness, subordination; but the spirit at work against it is one of latitudinarianism, indifferentism, republicanism, and schism, a spirit which tends to overthrow doctrine, as if the fruit of bigotry, and discipline as if the instrument of priestcraft.

There was general agreement that 'the stream of opinion is setting against the Church' and disestablishment seemed inevitable—a prospect that Newman contemplated 'with apprehension' because 'all revolutions are awful things', because 'the upper classes will be left almost religionless', because 'there will not be that security for sound doctrine without change which is given by an Act of Parliament', and for other reasons. Apart from the threat to the Church from freethinkers and Dissenters, there was another factor: 'the talent of the day is against the Church.' The 'church party', Newman candidly acknowledged, was 'poor in mental endowments' and depended 'on prejudice and bigotry'. That, however, did not prevent what they believed from being true, for 'great men alone can prove great ideas or grasp them', while moral truths are 'gained by patient study, by calm reflection, silently as the dew falls', and do not show well 'in the argument of an hour'.[130]

Not long after the election, Whately, who was 'considerably annoyed' at Newman's role in the affair, 'took a humorous revenge' by inviting him with 'a set of the least intellectual men in Oxford to dinner, and men most fond of port'. Whately saw 'more clearly' than he did that 'I was separating from his own friends for good and all'.[131] But Newman was not unconscious of how his views had 'enlarged and expanded', although not in the obvious sense those words might suggest. 'See what a bigot I am getting', he exclaimed to his sister Jemima. He was more than ever conscious of the importance of retaining his fellowship and remaining in Oxford, feeling 'more strongly than ever the necessity of there being men in the Church, like the R Catholic friars, free from all obstacles to their devoting themselves to its defence'.[132]

As the end of the summer term approached, he looked forward to returning to his patristic studies: 'I am so hungry for Irenaeus and Cyprian—I long for the Vacation.'[133] But college and parish duties kept him from reading the Fathers, and in the middle of August he told Froude that he would eventually have to resign his tutorship if he was ever to have time for scholarly work. He hoped to find somebody, preferably one of the fellows, to share the living of St Mary's with him, his plan being that his associate would look after the village of Littlemore, which would have its own church and become, practically speaking, a separate parish. It was not a scheme that was to find favour with the Provost. In the Christmas vacation he complained about the amount of his time the 'odious' junior treasurership took up, especially out of term.

His mother and sisters had come up from Brighton and rented a cottage at Horsepath, a village near Oxford, the previous summer; in October they had moved to Nuneham. In vacation time Newman used regularly to spend the night with them, walking out from Oxford to join them for dinner in the evening, and then back in the morning to breakfast in college. He had never been 'at home' so much since first coming up to Oxford. As he walked along 'the old road' from Oxford,

[130] Ibid. 129–31.   [131] *Apo.* 26.   [132] *LD* ii. 129, 133.   [133] Ibid. 150.

'King Charles and his Bishop seemed to rise before' him. He was, he wrote to Bowden, 'confirmed as a dull staid Tory unfit for these smart times'. But he felt 'amused rather than frightened at the prospect of coming events, though I suppose one ought to be serious and not speak lightly of what may be to masses of men productive of great evil'.[134] The threat of political interference in the Church raised questions about the urgent need for internal reforms. Newman was cautious about any attempt to change the liturgy: the 'influence' the Church of England 'chiefly' exerted 'in the hearts of her people' was 'by a reverential attachment to those prayers which they have heard from childhood and have been their solace often in their most trying seasons, and have shed a grace on the high solemnities of marriages and births.—Should we not dread disturbing this feeling?' As for objections to the damnatory clauses in the Athanasian Creed, 'if certain parts offend certain minds, is there not on the other hand an extreme danger of countenancing the false liberality of the age, which would fain have it believed that differences of *opinion* are of slight consequence?'[135] In March he started 'a Saints-day Service' in St Mary's, which he thought would be 'useful, both because it in some degree keeps up the memory of the Saints and so of old times' and also for a more pastoral reason, 'because it gives me an opportunity of knowing the more religious part of my Congregation'.[136] But once again he was distracted by college, or rather university, business—the 'insufferable nuisance' of appointment as Pro-Proctor (it was Oriel's turn this year to provide one of the two Proctors who were responsible for undergraduate discipline in the University).

Somewhat anomalously, he had been elected in March 1829 to the post of joint secretary of the Oxford branch of the Evangelical-orientated Church Missionary Society. For although, he later recalled, he had 'a growing disposition towards what is called the High Church', he was still 'on the whole Protestant in doctrine' and had long been very interested in missionary work. Before the year was out, however, he had lodged a formal protest about the doctrine of certain sermons preached in aid of the Society. He followed this up with a pamphlet, privately printed in January 1830, which was circulated among members of the university and intended 'at once to enlarge the circle of subscribers to the Society, and to direct and strengthen the influence of the University and thereby of the Anglican hierarchy, upon it'.[137] He was not re-elected secretary at the annual general meeting in March, after having already objected at a committee meeting to the Evangelical language in which the report had been drawn up. In June he withdrew from membership of the Bible Society on the ground that there was 'no *principle*, recognized

---

[134] *LD* ii. 188–9.   [135] Ibid. 191.   [136] Ibid. 201–2.   [137] *VM* ii. 3.

by the Society on which Churchmen could fall back and take their stand'.[138] He later explained to a friend that if it were 'recognized, e.g., that the Church were the divinely-sanctioned system, or that dissent was per se an evil, or that reading the Bible is not (ordinarily) sufficient for salvation, there would be something for Churchmen to cling to—whereas by coming *on common ground* with Dissenters, they seem to come on *middle* ground . . . and to allow that they ought to concede *as well* as Dissenters . . .'. 'I do believe', he solemnly pronounced, 'IT MAKES CHURCHMEN LIBERALS—it makes them undervalue the guilt of schism—it makes them feel a wish to conciliate Dissenters at the expence of truth. I think it is preparing the downfall of the Church.' But Newman's objection was to something much larger and less tangible, of which the Bible Society was only a symptom: 'The tendency of the age is towards *liberalism.*' Religion had to be 'enforced by authority of some kind', since '*moral* trust is not acceptable to man's heart'. It was the Church which was 'the *legitimate* enforcement of Christian truth. The liberals know this—and are in every possible manner trying to break it up.'[139]

Relations with the Provost had scarcely improved since the Peel affair. It was, Newman later admitted, 'a state of constant bickerings—of coldness, dryness, and donnishness on his part, and of provoking insubordination and petulance on mine. We differed in our views materially, and he, always mounting his high horse, irritated me and made me recoil from him.' They disagreed on 'the matter of testimonials for Orders, in which I naturally took the severer, he the laxer side', and on 'the custom of Gentlemen Commoners dining with the Fellows, which he maintained was one of the [praiseworthy customs] to which all were bound, but which I and others wished to dispense with'.[140]

When he had become a tutor in 1826, he had immediately 'commenced with an energy proverbial in the instance of "new brooms" '. Although he had not 'intentionally departed from the received ways of the College', there was no denying that 'there was something unusual and startling in his treatment of the undergraduate members of it who came under his jurisdiction'. He had begun 'by setting himself fiercely against the Gentlemen-Commoners, young men of birth, wealth or prospects, whom he considered (of course with real exceptions) to be the scandal and the ruin of the place'. He 'behaved towards them with a haughtiness which incurred their bitter resentment', and 'was much annoyed at the favour shown them in high quarters'. He particularly objected to the undergraduates 'being compelled, or even suffered as a matter of course to go terminally to communion, and shocked at the reception he met with from those to

[138] *LD* ii. 236.   [139] Ibid. 264–5.   [140] Ibid. 202–3.

whom he complained of so gross a profanation of a sacred rite'. The authorities preferred to turn a blind eye to any abuses of a hallowed custom, and not even Hawkins, the disciplinarian, supported him on this point.

With regard to his own pupils, Newman was anxious to stop the practice of hiring private tutors from among recent graduates: it meant expense for the undergraduate and lessened the influence of the official tutor. He regarded it as his own responsibility to find time outside the 'formal lecture routine' for the personal tutoring of the more serious students aiming at an honours degree.

With such youths he cultivated relations, not only of intimacy, but of friendship, and almost of equality, putting off, as much as might be, the martinet manner then in fashion with College Tutors, and seeking their society in outdoor exercise, on evenings, and in Vacation. And, when he became Vicar of St Mary's in 1828 the hold he had acquired over them led to their following him on to sacred ground, and receiving directly religious instruction from his sermons; but from the first, independently of St Mary's he had set before himself in his Tutorial work the aim of gaining souls to God.

The appointment of Froude and Wilberforce as tutors in 1828 meant that Newman was no longer alone in his views. As his new colleagues were both 'disciples' of Keble, they were 'in practical agreement' with Newman 'as to the nature of the office of College Tutor'. Because the fourth tutor, Joseph Dornford, 'was far from indisposed to the view' of the other three, 'there ensued in consequence a sudden, though at first unobserved, antagonism in the College administration between Provost and Tutors, the former keeping to that construction of a Tutor's duties . . . which may be called the disciplinarian, and the four Tutors adhering to the pastoral view of these duties'. The irony was that Newman, 'at the very moment of his friend Dr Hawkins's entering upon the Provostship, became conscious for the first time of his own congeniality of mind with Keble'. Froude's 'great argument in behalf of Keble, when the election of Provost was coming on,' had been 'that Keble, if Provost, would bring in with him quite a new world, that donnishness and humbug would be no more in the College, nor the pride of talent, nor an ignoble secular ambition. But such vague language did not touch Newman, who loved and admired Hawkins . . .' Moreover, an 'almost fastidious modesty and shrinking from the very shadow of pomposity, which was the characteristic of both Keble and Froude,' made them reluctant

to commit themselves in words to a theory of a Tutor's office, which nevertheless they religiously acted on. Newman on the contrary, when he had a clear view of a matter, was accustomed to formulate it, and was apt to be . . . considered irreverent and rude in the nakedness of his analysis, and unmeasured and even impatient in enforcing it. He held almost fiercely that secular education could be so conducted as to become a pastoral cure . . . He recollected that in the Laudian statutes for Oxford a Tutor was not a mere academical Policeman, or Constable, but a moral and religious guardian of the youth committed to him.

Newman made it very clear to the Provost that he was not interested in 'taking part in a heartless system of law and form, in which the good and promising were sacrificed to the worthless or uninteresting'. Hawkins for his part had 'no sympathy' for a principle which in his view meant 'sacrificing the many to the few, and governing, not by intelligible rules and their impartial application, but by a system . . . of mere personal influence and favoritism'. However, to begin with, 'all went on well, with the prospect of a future tinted with that rose-colour which prevails at the beginning of a new reign', and the Provost 'loyally and energetically backed up his Tutors in their measures for the enforcement of discipline and the purification of the College'. On the whole, then, there was a harmonious situation, with standards visibly rising, until the Peel affair at the beginning of 1829. Still, there was a 'grave, though latent, difference in principle . . . which was too likely at one time or another to issue in a serious collision between the one party and the other'.[141]

The re-election issue coincided with a change in the tutorial system in the Lent term of 1829. Up till then, the lecture list had been drawn up

without any regard to the existing relations between each Tutor and his own pupils, all the Tutors becoming Lecturers . . . to all the Undergraduates, whether their pupils or not, and taking this or that class by rotation, indiscriminately, whomsoever it was composed of. The principle now introduced was that each Tutor should in the first place be responsible and consult for his own pupils, should determine what subjects they ought to have lectures in, and should have the first choice as to taking those lectures themselves, and should in the second place consult for the pupils of others. Otherwise they considered the office of Tutor became that of a mere lecturer, and that teaching was not an act of personal intercourse, but an ungenial and donnish form.[142]

This new system was submitted by Newman, in collaboration with Froude and with the support of R. I. Wilberforce, to Dornford as Senior Tutor, who thought the plan worth trying, although he was afraid it would involve a lot of extra work for the tutors. The tutors considered that it lay within their power to make the alteration, at least as an experiment, and the Provost was not specifically told of the change,

---

[141] *AW* 89–92.   [142] Ibid. 99.

though he came to hear of it accidentally in the summer term after it had been introduced. But it was not until a college meeting on 2 November 1829 that Hawkins formally signified his disapproval of the change. Even then, matters did not come to a head until April 1830, when Newman was asked by the Provost to send him 'a short sketch' of the new system.[143] Newman's reply to Hawkins's complaint that the old system had worked perfectly well, was that this was only so when Oriel undergraduates had received extra private tuition (at their own request and expense) from the tutors: 'Nature . . . forces us into the private-tutor system—why not recognize it, control it, and make it economical?'[144] Hawkins's objection to this was that to place an undergraduate so exclusively under one personal tutor would put the Provost, who was responsible for assigning pupils to tutors, in a difficult and invidious position. The point cut little ice with Newman, for whom the tutorship was essentially 'of a Pastoral nature',[145] while 'the mere lecturing required' of him under the old system was 'incompatible with due attention to that more useful private instruction, which had imparted to the office of Tutor the importance of a clerical occupation'. So far as he was concerned, the university statutes entrusted undergraduates 'to the care of a particular Tutor'. If, however, this was not the case and they were actually 'committed to the Senior Tutor', as Hawkins had seemed to him to indicate, then he was more than ready to resign an appointment which he had misunderstood to be a university office.[146] He had never intended to introduce a '*new*' tutorial system, but considered he was only 'modifying' the existing practice which he had not understood to be 'immutably established in the College', particularly when he saw how in other colleges the tutors had 'an almost unlimited discretion'.[147] However, he was only prepared to relinquish the tutorship 'on the understanding, that in future . . . to all but to the Senior Tutor the name, not of *Tutor*, but of *Assistant Tutor*, shall be assigned in the University Calendar'.[148] Not surprisingly, Hawkins refused to make any such formal public distinction. And on 9 June, he warned Newman that if he refused to return to the previous system he would not be able to entrust any more pupils to him. On 15 June Newman accepted 'this gradual mode of removing me'.[149]

A compromise between the two positions would not, Newman later thought, have been impossible, but for 'an ever-widening theological antagonism between the two parties, and an impatience on the side of Newman, and an unsympathetic severity on the part of Dr Hawkins'. What particularly 'irritated' Newman was the Provost's 'imputing Newman's conduct to irritation, and refusing or not being able to see

[143] *LD* ii. 208.   [144] Ibid. 212.   [145] Ibid. 218.   [146] Ibid. 233–4.
[147] Ibid. 247.   [148] Ibid. 216.   [149] Ibid. 242.

that there was a grave principle in it earnestly held, and betraying a confident expectation that what was, he considered, mere temper in Newman, would soon pass away, and that he would eventually give in'.[150] The upshot of the whole affair, whereby Newman, Froude, and Wilberforce were to 'die off gradually with our existing pupils', was to Newman 'personally . . . a delightful arrangement': however bad he might think it for the college, 'it will materially lessen my labours, and at length reduce them within bearable limits'. More important, freedom from teaching duties meant that 'The Fathers arise up again full before me'.[151] The row over the Oriel tutorial system was not only of educational interest and significance for Newman's idea of his own vocation. It had much more momentous, albeit unforeseen, implications. 'Humanly speaking,' Newman later reflected, the Tractarian Movement 'never would have been, had he not been deprived of his Tutorship, or had Keble, not Hawkins, been Provost'.[152]

5

At the beginning of the long vacation of 1830, Newman rode on horseback down to Brighton to spend a fortnight with his family, who had returned there at the end of March. On the way back he complained that churches were not always open—'I conjecture they were some centuries ago. Though we have gained more, we certainly have lost something by old Luther.'[153] He also grumbled that not only were there 'no direction posts', but 'the mile stones are defaced, the labourers in the fields are deaf . . .'. When he did find passers-by to give him directions, he was supplied with the kind of maddeningly misleading information from which modern travellers still suffer: 'By going "straight on" they mean going "the right way". . . . I believe they habitually consider the road they know best to be the "right on" road.' As he rode along, 'the fascination of a country life' put to the test his conviction that he ought to remain a fellow of an Oxford college rather than move to a parish in due course as was then customary: 'It will indeed be a grievous temptation, should a living ever be offered me, when now even a curacy has inexpressible charms.' It was, however, 'the only great temptation' he feared—'for as to other fascinations which might be more dangerous still, I am pretty well out of the way of them'. Marriage, except for heads of colleges, then involved automatically relinquishing one's fellowship; but the religious call which he had felt since 1816 to a single life had (he later recalled) 'held its ground almost continuously ever since,—with

[150] *AW* 102–3.   [151] *LD* ii. 244–5.   [152] *AW* 96.   [153] *LD* ii. 250.

the break of a month now and a month then, up to 1829, and, after that date, without any break at all'. He had also set his face against an ecclesiastical career: the 'most useful men', he felt, were not the leaders of the Church but its teachers, whose memory endured not so much in their writings as in the 'school of pupils who trace their moral parentage to them'.[154]

In March 1831 Newman received an invitation from Hugh James Rose, the high churchman and Rector of Hadleigh in Suffolk—'the first to give warning . . . from the University Pulpit at Cambridge, of the perils to England which lay in the biblical and theological speculations of Germany'[155]—to contribute a history of Church Councils to a new library of theological works of which Rose was the co-editor. Newman had himself proposed a study of the Thirty-nine Articles, but the editors suggested that the history would be a useful introduction to such a work. Newman agreed to undertake the project. His formal teaching duties were to end in the summer.

However, he had other things on his mind apart from theological research. In March the new Whig government had begun passing the Reform Bill through parliament. Fundamental political changes threatened the position of the Established Church. A commission had already been set up to look into ecclesiastical abuses such as pluralism. 'The vital question was,' Newman later wrote, 'how were we to keep the Church from being liberalized?'[156] At the time he warned his friend Bowden gravely that the masses were 'for revolution'. There was a serious danger that people would be 'placed in the higher stations of the Church who are anything but real Churchmen'. He could not help suspecting that most people did not 'believe in Christianity in any true meaning of the word. No, they are liberals, and in saying this, I conceive I am saying almost as bad of them as can be said of any man.' He groaned over the 'incalculable mischief' the Duke of Wellington had perpetrated 'by his profligate mode' of passing Catholic emancipation: he had 'broken up the conservatives'. As for the effects on the Church of the 'vile' Whig ministry of Lord Grey, 'I would rather have the Church severed from its temporalities and scattered to the four winds than such a desecration of holy things. I dread above all things the pollution of such men as Lord Brougham affecting to lay a friendly hand upon it.' Even so, he added cautiously, he would 'preserve the present system' if possible.[157] And in spite of 'apathy . . . in some quarters' and 'imbecile alarm in others',[158] he took heart from 'the hidden moral strength of the Church in the midst of error. Depend upon it, we shall prove a tough

---

[154] *LD* ii. 254–5; *Apo.* 20.   [155] *Apo.* 45.   [156] Ibid. 39.
[157] *LD* ii. 317–18.   [158] *Apo.* 39.

mouthful, when the nation fastens upon us.' He wished, though, that 'our spiritual governors were more like men and less like cows'. There were too many churchmen whose only object was to be '*comfortable*', he remarked contemptuously—'Lovers of ease, with not even the self-mastery which a worldly ambition inspires'.[159]

In the long vacation of 1831 he began reading for the projected history, but soon interrupted his work early in July to take a holiday with Hurrell Froude in Devon, where Froude's high-church father was Archdeacon of Totnes and Rector of Dartington. The day after their arrival Froude went down with influenza; it was the beginning of the ill-health that was to end in his premature death. They had taken the night boat from Cowes in the Isle of Wight, and Froude had caught a cold from sleeping on the deck. Newman was fascinated by the Devonshire climate and countryside. The 'extreme deliciousness of the air and the fragrance of every thing' made him feel that he would 'dissolve into essence of roses, or be attenuated into an echo' if he lived there. He was amazed by the scenery, which drew from him one of his most sensuous descriptions:

What strikes me most is the strange richness of every thing. The rocks blush into every variety of colour—the trees and fields are emeralds, and the cottages are rubies. A beetle I picked up at Torquay was as green and gold as the stone it lay on, and a squirrel which ran up a tree here just now was not a pale reddish brown . . . but a bright brown red. Nay, my very hands and fingers look rosy, like Homer's Aurora, and I have been gazing on them with astonishment . . . The exuberance of the grass and the foliage is oppressive, as if one had not room to breathe, though this is a fancy—the depth of the valleys and the steepness of the slopes increase the illusion—and the Duke of Wellington would be in a fidget to get some commanding point to see the country from. The scents are extremely fine, so very delicate, yet so powerful, and the colours of the flowers as if they were all shot with white. The sweet peas especially have the complexion of a beautiful face—they trail up the wall, mixed with myrtles, as creepers[.] As to the sunset, the Dartmoor heights look purple, and the sky close upon a clear orange. When I turn back to think of Southampton Water and the Isle of Wight, they seem by contrast to be drawn in india-ink or pencil.[160]

Towards the end of August, he wrote to tell Rose that the Eastern Councils would need a volume to themselves and that he was now concerned with how to organize this first volume. He had decided it would be best to write 'a *connected* history of the Councils . . . not taking them as isolated, but introducing so much of Church History as will illustrate and account for them'. It was absurd to separate theology from history: 'What light would be thrown on the Nicene Confession *merely* by explaining it article by article? to understand it, it must be prefaced by a

---

[159] *LD* ii. 331–2.   [160] Ibid. 342–3.

sketch of the rise of the Arian heresy . . .' But there were obvious problems 'in combining history and doctrinal discussion', and he thought he would reserve detailed discussion of particular theological topics for notes in an appendix.[161] The Western Councils could be treated in another volume, with the exception of the Council of Trent, which would require a work on its own. In October he was well and truly 'set up in the Patristical line' when his pupils presented him with thirty-six volumes of the Fathers: 'They are so fine in their outsides as to put my former ones to shame—and the editions are the best.' The only problem was where to put them—they were 'too *deep*' for his bookshelves.[162]

At the end of September, Whately once again offered him the Vice-Principalship of Alban Hall. Whately had been appointed Archbishop of Dublin, and Newman's successor as Vice-Principal was accompanying him as his domestic chaplain. There was even talk of his succeeding Whately in the headship, but he had no ambition except 'to live and die a Fellow of Oriel'. He had 'no stomach' for a post involving responsibility—'I want a little peace; and expecting a persecution before I die, would gladly be cosy now.' Besides, he was taken up with his work on the Councils, on which he thought he could 'throw some lights', as he was not impressed by the ecclesiastical historians he was reading.[163] Nor did the possibility of a position under Whately in Dublin appeal to him. He was convinced it was his 'duty to remain' where he was. He felt he could contribute to 'the study of theology' which was 'very much neglected at Oxford'. And if the threat to the Church grew, 'Oxford will want hot headed men, and such I mean to be, and I am in my place'.[164]

An opportunity came in February 1832, when two candidates applied for the newly founded chair in Sanscrit. From the point of view of scholarship, the superior candidate was H. H. Wilson, but Newman was opposed to his appointment both on religious and also on more general educational grounds. Not only was he 'not a Clergyman or University man', but there was 'nothing to show that he is a classical scholar, or an Hebraist, or a divine, or a literary man in any sense, or that he has any formed religious opinions, or that he is a gentleman, or that he has the temper and judgment necessary for an academical man, or that his moral qualifications are such as to admit him into Oxford Society'. He was the 'best' Sanscrit scholar available, but 'since he is by education a Surgeon, he probably is not a generally well-read man'. Worse than lack of education and culture, however, was the danger that 'he may be a mere Liberal, and consider the Sanscrit-theology not far inferior to the Christian'.[165] The rival candidate, W. H. Mill, who was Principal of

[161] *LD* ii. 352–3.   [162] Ibid. 369.   [163] Ibid. 371.
[164] Ibid. 367.   [165] Ibid. iii. 15–16.

Bishop's College, Calcutta, had several disadvantages against him. He had been 'too warmly taken up' by the London clergy, which 'angered the resident members, who recollect besides the shuffling part they played at the time of Peel's election'. He was a Cambridge man, which 'is a worse thing for him than if he had been of neither University'. He also had the Evangelicals against him, because he had 'the reputation of having been a strict Churchman at Calcutta'. The 'liberals' were, 'of course', in favour of his rival.[166] In spite of Newman's efforts to rally opposition to Wilson, whose moral character was also in doubt, he was duly elected to the chair in March, albeit by a very narrow majority.

Meanwhile Newman was hard at work on his first book, which was turning out to be rather different from what he had originally envisaged. He did not see it as simply a work of research: it was 'on an extremely important subject', and in writing it he was 'resisting the innovations of the day, and attempting to defend the work of men indefinitely above me (the Primitive Fathers) which is now assailed'.[167] During June he made himself 'a hermit' in order to have the book ready for July, when it was due.[168] By the end of the month he was fainting from exhaustion, but a third of the manuscript was ready for the publisher at the beginning of July. He felt very dissatisfied with the result and wished there was 'time to rewrite it': the style, he admitted to Rose, was 'difficult', although he hoped it improved in the rest of the book, most of which had been 'written more than once or twice'.[169]

In the middle of July, he took a week's break to visit Samuel Rickards, a former fellow of Oriel, who had become a friend of the family, and who now had a living in Suffolk. On the way, Newman stopped off at Cambridge. He had come, he wrote to his mother, 'with no anticipations', but he was 'quite taken by surprise, and overcome with delight'. At first sight, he thought he would 'not be able to contain' himself—in spite of all his reservations about the university's political and religious 'present defects and past history', so very different from Cavalier and Tory high-church Oxford.

I do really think the place finer than Oxford, though I suppose it isn't, for every one says so. I like the narrow streets—they have a character—and they make the University buildings look larger by the contrast. I cannot believe that King's College is not far grander than any thing with us—the stone too is richer, and the foliage more thick and encompassing.

He had another third of the manuscript with him to give to Rose, and the remaining part was practically ready, but Rose was ill and not at home. He gave his mother a message for Froude about Rose: 'tell him, alas! he *is* married. This has quite troubled and grieved me,—still, if he

[166] Ibid. 27.   [167] Ibid. 43.   [168] Ibid. 55.   [169] Ibid. 65.

manages to give his whole soul to the Church, it matters not—though it seems impossible.'[170]

Apart from Newman's own personal sense of a vocation to the single life ('For years I have made up my *mind* to remain in single blessedness— but whether my *heart* be equally made up, time alone can tell'),[171] the ideal of celibacy was one of the religious views of Froude which had influenced him—'He [Froude] had a high severe idea of the intrinsic excellence of Virginity; and he considered the Blessed Virgin its great pattern.'[172] Far from being dogmatic, however, that clergymen should not marry, Newman thought that 'country parsons ought, as a general rule, to be married'. He was only anxious that 'there should be among the clergy enough unmarried, to give a character of strength to the whole—and that therefore, every one should ask himself whether he is called to the celibate'. Celibacy was 'a high state of life, to which the multitude of men cannot aspire', and although he could not claim that 'they who adopt it are necessarily better than others', still he felt it was the 'noblest' way of life. As for marriage, he was realistic rather than romantic: 'It is a fearful thing to tie yourself to one person for life.'[173] But celibacy was more than a personal idea; he felt it was of importance for the beleaguered Church: 'The Church wants *expeditos milites*—not a whole camp of women at its heels, forbye brats.'[174] The times demanded a totally dedicated clergy, and he was anxious to understand '*the mode* in which the Monastic orders rose, in order to see whether one could not in all simplicity and godly sincerity found such a society, if times get bad'.[175] Later, he agreed with Froude that 'the only way' of 'evangelizing' the new industrial cities was through 'monastic orders', for

great towns will never be evangelized merely by the parochial system. They are beyond the sphere of the parish priest, burdened as he is with the endearments and anxieties of a family, and the secular restraints and engagements of the Establishment. The unstable multitude cannot be influenced and ruled except by uncommon means, by the evident sight of disinterested and self-denying love, and elevated firmness. The show of domestic comfort, the decencies of furniture and apparel, the bright hearth and the comfortable table, (good and innocent as they are in their place,) are as ill-suited to the missionary of a town population as to an Apostle.'[176]

The book was finally completed on the last day of July. At last he could have a rest: 'I mean to be altogether idle, to keep no regularity of hours . . . It is true relaxation, when you undo the girths of time.' The opportunity of a prolonged holiday arose when Hurrell Froude invited

[170] *LD* iii. 66–7.   [171] Ibid. 34.   [172] *Apo.* 34.
[173] *LD* iii. 23, 70.   [174] Ibid. 43.   [175] Ibid. 107.
[176] Ibid. v. 17; *DA* 42.

him to join him and his father the Archdeacon on a trip to the Mediterranean which they were planning for the sake of Froude's health. The invitation 'quite unsettled' Newman. The thought of travelling in such company was 'very tempting', and he did not know when he would be so free again. He was also 'suspicious of becoming narrow-minded, and at least I wish to experience the feeling and the trial of expansiveness of views, if it were but to be able to *say* I had, and to know how to meet it in the case of others'. On the other hand, there were various objections: he was afraid of intruding on a family party, of being away from England for too long, and of having to spend too much money. Although he saw that a long holiday would be good for his health, he was also apprehensive of falling ill while abroad: he was aware of his own 'nervous' temperament ('I am so fidgety I cannot be still'), and there was the danger of another sudden collapse like the minor breakdowns he had already suffered.[177] Finally, he felt guilty at leaving his parish before a severe cholera epidemic had subsided: although he had a curate, his sense of his pastoral responsibilities had made him uneasy about even the short trip to Suffolk. In the end, the prospect of a vacation and the chance 'to enlarge one's ideas . . . and to have the name of a travelled man' proved too much.[178]

One consequence of the decision to go was that Newman could no longer be considered for the post of Dean. In the normal course of events, he would have been automatically elected as next in seniority to Dornford, who was leaving to take a country living. The Dean at Oriel was not only responsible for discipline, but was also Vice-Provost. The Provost's friends among the fellows wanted Newman to stand down to avoid a contested election and the embarrassment it would cause Hawkins if he were elected. Newman, however, saw no reason why he should be forced 'to retire from active work in the College', nor why he should aid and abet Hawkins in what he considered 'his usurpation on the rights of the Fellows'.[179] The most likely point of conflict was the compulsory service of Holy Communion: if he were ordered by the Provost to administer the sacrament against his conscience, he would not feel bound to obey. On the other hand, he recognized that the Provost had the right of veto to forbid any action on the part of the Dean. Although he objected to standing down, he dreaded being Dean and finding himself opposed by both undergraduates and Provost, and was determined not to take the post unless he could have his 'own way'.[180] The shortage of possible candidates put him in a strong position, but he was relieved when the Mediterranean trip settled the question.

Towards the end of October, Newman at last heard from Rose that

---

[177] *LD* iii. 88, 93–4.   [178] Ibid. 99.   [179] Ibid. 58.   [180] Ibid. 83.

his co-editor, Archdeacon Lyall, thought Newman's book unsuitable for the Theological Library, on the grounds that it was a history of the Arian heresy rather than of the Councils, and that it was too specialized for the general reader. Far from being a history of the principal Councils, it was not even a history of the Council of Nicaea, which, as Newman later admitted, 'occupied at most twenty pages', but on which he had 'set to work' only to 'launch' himself 'on an ocean with currents innumerable'.[181] Lyall also complained that some of Newman's views, particularly on tradition, seemed to be more Roman Catholic than Protestant. There was no question, however, about the distinction of the work, and the publisher Rivington readily agreed to publish it as a book in its own right.

6

The Arians of the Fourth Century may be primarily a historical work, but its author's own theological preoccupations are never far from the surface. Like contemporary religious liberalism, Arianism, unlike earlier heresies, was originally 'a sceptical rather than a dogmatic teaching', aiming 'to inquire into and reform the received creed, rather than to hazard one of its own', and as such enjoying all the advantages of 'the assailant' over 'the party assailed' in 'finding' rather than 'solving objections'.[182] In disputing the orthodox creed, the Arians, too, were guilty of misapplying human reason to the mysteries of revelation. Moreover, their objection to using 'words not found in Scripture, in confessions of faith' was of the very essence of the 'principle of liberalism'.[183] As for doctrinal 'comprehensiveness', Newman declares bluntly: 'If the Church would be vigorous and influential, it must be decided and plain-spoken in its doctrine . . . To attempt comprehensions of opinion . . . is to mistake arrangements of words, which have no existence except on paper, for . . . realities; and ingenious generalizations of discordant sentiments for that practical agreement which alone can lead to co-operation.' While it is only realistic to realize that 'there are no two opinions so contrary to each other, but some form of words may be found vague enough to comprehend them both', comprehensiveness is impractical because it is unreal: 'We may indeed artificially classify light and darkness under one term or formula; but nature has her own fixed courses . . . However plausible may be the veil thus thrown over heterogeneous doctrines, the flimsy artifice is discomposed so soon as the principles beneath it are called upon to move and act.' But comprehensiveness is, in fact, harmful to the Church, because of its

---

[181] *Apo.* 35.   [182] *Ari.* 26–7.   [183] Ibid. 361–2.

unreal substitution of 'words for things', in the form of 'statements so faintly precise and so decently ambiguous, as to embrace the greatest number of opinions possible, and to deprive religion, in consequence, of its austere and commanding aspect'.[184] Already, in his first book, Newman tends to define the true and the false in terms of the real and the unreal. As we watch his thought developing, we shall see that truth and reality become almost synonymous: to be true is to be real, and to be real is to be true.

The alternative to comprehensiveness is not necessarily dogmatism. We should notice how at the outset of his theological writing Newman maintains a careful and characteristic balance between opposing extremes. Far from dogmatic formularies being desirable for their own sake, he insists that 'freedom from symbols and articles is abstractedly the highest state of Christian communion, and the peculiar privilege of the primitive Church', for 'technicality and formalism are, in their degree, inevitable results of public confessions of faith', and 'when confessions do not exist, the mysteries of divine truth, instead of being exposed to the gaze of the profane and uninstructed, are kept hidden in the bosom of the Church, far more faithfully than is otherwise possible'. It were better for both liberals and Evangelicals if there were no formulated dogmas, for they 'are daily wrested by infidels to their ruin', while 'on the other hand, much of that mischievous fanaticism is avoided, which at present abounds from the vanity of men, who think that they can explain the sublime doctrines and exuberant promises of the Gospel, before they have yet learned to know themselves and to discern the holiness of God'. For these reasons, 'and again from tenderness both for the heathen and the neophyte, who were unequal to the reception of the strong meat of the full Gospel, the rulers of the Church were dilatory in applying a remedy, which nevertheless the circumstances of the times imperatively required. They were loath to confess, that the Church had grown too old to enjoy the free, unsuspicious teaching with which her childhood was blest . . .'[185] Throughout his life Newman was to keep the balance between insisting on the necessity of dogmatic formulations and yet allowing for their inherent limitations.

His awareness of the inadequacy of human language to express dogma came from his understanding of the early Church's principle of 'economy', the treatment of which is perhaps the most interesting aspect of the book.[186] He tells us in the *Apologia* how his study of the church of

---

[184] Ibid. 147–8, 274.   [185] Ibid. 36–7.

[186] For an excellent treatment of the importance of 'economy' and 'reserve' in Newman's thought and writings, see Robin C. Selby, *The Principle of Reserve in the Writings of John Henry Cardinal Newman* (Oxford, 1975).

Alexandria, where Athanasius, 'the champion of the truth', was Bishop, and where the 'battle of Arianism was first fought', introduced him to the 'broad philosophy' of Clement and Origen, which

carried me away . . . and I have drawn out some features of it in my volume, with the zeal and freshness, but with the partiality, of a neophyte. Some portions of their teaching, magnificent in themselves, came like music to my inward ear, as if the response to ideas, which, with little external to encourage them, I had cherished so long. These were based on the mystical or sacramental principle, and spoke of the various Economies or Dispensations of the Eternal. I understood these passages to mean that the exterior world, physical and historical, was but the manifestation to our senses of realities greater than itself. Nature was a parable: Scripture was an allegory: pagan literature, philosophy, and mythology, properly understood, were but a preparation for the Gospel. . . . There had been a directly divine dispensation granted to the Jews; but there had been in some sense a dispensation carried on in favour of the Gentiles . . . In the fulness of time both Judaism and Paganism had come to nought; the outward framework, which concealed yet suggested the Living Truth, had never been intended to last, and it was dissolving under the beams of the Sun of Justice which shone behind it and through it. The process of change had been slow; it had been done not rashly, but by rule and measure . . . first one disclosure and then another, till the whole evangelical doctrine was brought into full manifestation. And thus room was made for the anticipation of further and deeper disclosures, of truths still under the veil of the letter, and in their season to be revealed. The visible world still remains without its divine interpretation; Holy Church in her sacraments and her hierarchical appoint-ments, will remain, even to the end of the world, after all but a symbol of those heavenly facts which fill eternity. Her mysteries are but the expressions in human language of truths to which the human mind is unequal. It is evident how much there was in all this in correspondence with the thoughts which had attracted me when I was young, and with the doctrine which I have already associated with the Analogy and the Christian Year.[187]

The principle of economy meant that even that most fundamental of Christian dogmas, the doctrine of the Trinity, could be seen as only 'the shadow, projected for the contemplation of the intellect, of the Object of scripturally-informed piety: a representation, economical; necessarily imperfect, as being exhibited in a foreign medium, and therefore involving apparent inconsistencies or mysteries'. The 'systematic' dogma could be 'kept in the background in the infancy of Christianity, when faith and obedience were vigorous,' and only 'brought forward at a time when, reason being disproportionately developed, and aiming at sovereignty in the province of religion, its presence became necessary to expel an usurping idol from the house of God'. From the individual believer's point of view, to make explicit what was implicit was not

<hr />

[187] *Apo.* 36–7.

necessarily desirable: 'so reluctant is a well-constituted mind to reflect on its own motive principles, that the correct intellectual image, from its hardness of outline, may startle and offend those who have all along been acting upon it.' But having indicated how undesirable dogmatic formulations are, Newman immediately proceeds to show how necessary they are; for the fact that 'we cannot restrain the rovings of the intellect, or silence its clamorous demand for a formal statement concerning the Object of our worship', means paradoxically that the earlier insistence that 'intellectual representation should ever be subordinate to the cultivation of the religious affections' actually demands the 'intellectual expression of theological truth', not only because it 'excludes heresy', but because it 'directly assists the acts of religious worship and obedience'.[188]

The principle of economy had a practical application in the early Church's teaching of Christianity. The Alexandrian Church's 'economical method' or 'accommodation to the feelings and prejudices of the hearer, in leading him to the reception of a novel or unacceptable doctrine', rested on the idea that 'those who are strangers to the tone of thought and principles of the speaker, cannot at once be initiated into his system, . . . because they must begin with imperfect views; and therefore, if he is to teach them at all, he must put before them large propositions, which he has afterwards to modify, or make assertions, which are but parallel or analogous to the truth, rather than coincident with it'. Anticipating later criticism of the doctrine ('as intrinsically pernicious,—as if leading to lying and equivocation'),[189] Newman warns that it is important 'to be careful ever to maintain substantial truth in our use of the economical method'.[190] The warning is significant, for 'setting' truth 'out to advantage' can 'scarcely be disconnected from the *Disciplina Arcani*' of 'withholding the truth', in the sense that the early theologians 'write, not with the openness of Christian familiarity, but with the tenderness or the reserve with which we are accustomed to address those who do not sympathize with us, or whom we fear to mislead or to prejudice against the truth, by precipitate disclosures of its details'.[191] Newman takes the opportunity to point out that modern Evangelicals, who immediately appeal to the crucifixion of Christ to arouse the kind of emotion that is likely to lead to conversion, do the very opposite to the early Christian teachers whose 'uniform method' was 'to connect the Gospel with Natural Religion, and to mark out obedience to the moral law as the ordinary means of attaining to a Christian faith'.[192] To that sense of awe and the transcendent, which was to be so important a part of the Tractarian revival, the reticence of the 'secret tradition' was

[188] *Ari.* 145–6.   [189] *Apo.* 39.   [190] *Ari.* 71–2.

[191] Ibid. 65, 42.   [192] Ibid. 46–7.

also very important: 'Now, we allow ourselves publicly to canvass the most solemn truths in a careless or fiercely argumentative way; truths, which it is as useless as it is unseemly to discuss in public, as being attainable only by the sober and watchful, by slow degrees, with dependence on the Giver of wisdom, and with strict obedience to the light which has already been granted.'[193] Nor did the early Church use the Bible to teach the faith; it was the Church that taught what had to be believed, and it only appealed to 'Scripture in vindication of its own teaching'; heretics, on the other hand, like the Arians, relied on a 'private study of Holy Scripture' to elicit 'a systematic doctrine from the scattered notices of the truth which Scripture contains'.[194] The parallel with the contemporary situation was obvious.

Among the points which troubled the cautious Archdeacon Lyall was Newman's enthusiasm for the Alexandrian doctrine that all religion comes from God—'There never was a time when God had not spoken to man, and told him to a certain extent his duty.' It was true that 'the Church of God ever has had, and the rest of mankind never have had, authoritative documents of truth, and appointed channels of communication with Him . . . but all men have had more or less the guidance of Tradition, in addition to those internal notions of right and wrong which the Spirit has put into the heart of each individual.' Newman called this 'vague and uncertain family of religious truths, originally from God, but sojourning without the sanction of miracle, or a definite home, as pilgrims up and down the world, and discernible and separable from the corrupt legends with which they are mixed . . . the *Dispensation of Paganism*'. Arguing that this kind of economy is to be found in the Old Testament (in the figures, for example, of Job and Balaam), he claims that 'there is nothing unreasonable in the notion, that there may have been heathen poets and sages, or sibyls again, in a certain sense divinely illuminated, and organs through whom religious and moral truth was conveyed'. The practical conclusion is that the Christian apologist or missionary should 'after St. Paul's manner, seek some points in the existing superstitions as the basis of his own instructions, instead of indiscriminately condemning and discarding the whole assemblage of heathen opinions and practices', thus 'recovering and purifying, rather than reversing the essential principles of their belief'. What was then a radical approach, whether from a Catholic or Protestant point of view, stands in typically marked contrast to Newman's less than open attitude to 'deliberate heretics and apostates', towards whom such 'economy' is not to be shown. As always for Newman, superstition was far preferable to scepticism, for 'he who believes a little, but encompasses that little with the inventions of men, is undeniably in a better condition than he who blots out from his mind both the human inventions, and that portion of truth which was concealed in them'.[195]

A few years after the book's publication, Newman said that, apart from its contents, he had 'long thought it just the most imperfect work that was ever composed'. He did not change his mind, and years later declared that he found it 'a very imperfect work, from the circumstances of its composition'. It had been intended to be 'the beginning of a Manual on the Councils, and the gun went off in quite another direction, hitting no mark at all'. He had also had a deadline, so that the last few pages had been hurried. He came to feel it was 'inexact in thought and incorrect in language'; nevertheless, in spite of 'the many imperfections of the wording', not only did he hold to the 'substance' of what he had written, but he thought that 'with all its defects' it had 'good points in it, and in parts some originality'.[196]

[195] Ibid. 80–2, 84–5.   [196] *LD* xxiii. 46; xxviii. 172; xxx. 105, 240.

2

The Movement

TOWARDS the end of November 1832, Newman wrote to H. J. Rose to say that he and Froude were planning, on their return from their Mediterranean cruise, 'to systematize a poetry department' for the *British Magazine*, the review recently started by Rose 'to make a front against the coming danger'. Their 'object' would be 'to bring out certain truths and facts, moral, ecclesiastical, and religious, simply and forcibly, with greater freedom, and clearness than in the Christian Year'. They could not promise 'greater poetry' than Keble's best-selling collection. But they would undertake to produce for each number four short poems, 'each bringing out forcibly *one* idea'. The section, which would take up a couple of pages, could be called 'Lyra Apostolica'. To his pupil Frederic Rogers, who had taken a double first that year, Newman confided that they had 'hopes of making an effective quasi-political engine'—'Do not stirring times bring out poets? Do they not give opportunity for the rhetoric of poetry, and the persuasion?' Rose had been disappointed by Lyall's objections to the *Arians* and he had told Newman in confidence that he was afraid that the Theological Library would turn out to be as ineffective and useless as it was bland and inoffensive. Naturally, he was delighted with this new proposal. He had visited Oxford the previous summer term 'in order to beat up writers' for his magazine.[1]

On Sunday, 2 December Newman delivered the last university sermon he was to preach until 1839. The next day he left Oxford for Falmouth. From Whitchurch he wrote to his mother that he was beginning 'one of the few recreations, which I can hope, nay or desire, to have in this world'. But he did not want the forthcoming holiday to be 'any thing else than a preparation and strengthening-time for future toil—rather, I should rejoice to think that I was in this way steeling myself in soul and body for it'.[2] As he was waiting for the mail to Falmouth, he wrote the poem 'Angelic Guidance' which speaks of ' "the vision" which haunted me'; leaving Oxford 'for foreign countries and an unknown future', he 'naturally was led to think that some inward changes, as well as some larger course of action, were coming upon me'.[3]

---

[1] *LD* iii. 119–21; *Apo.* 45.   [2] *LD* iii. 123.   [3] *Apo.* 41.

At about one o'clock on Saturday, 8 December he set sail with the Froudes from Falmouth on board the packet *Hermes.* Three days later he penned the first of the many descriptive letters he was to send home. It was to his mother. They had crossed the Bay of Biscay and were now off Cape Finisterre, although they could not see it clearly because the moon had not yet risen. Early that morning they had caught sight of the Spanish mountains ('the first foreign land I ever saw'). The weather had suddenly brightened, 'and the sea, which had ever hitherto been very fine, now became of a rich indigo colour, and the wind freshening was tipped with the most striking white edges, which breaking in foam turned into momentary rainbows'. By evening it was obvious they were 'in a warmer latitude—The sea brightened to a glowing purple inclined to lilac—the sun set in a car of gold and was succeeded by a sky first pale orange, then gradually heightening to a dusky red—'. He also described, less sublimely, their preparations for departure from Falmouth:

It was most amusing to see the stores arrive. Fowls, Ducks, Turkeys, all alive and squatted down under legs of beef, hampers, and vegetables. One unfortunate Duck got away, and a chase ensued—I should have liked to have let him off, but the poor fool did not know how to use his fortune—and instead of making for the shore, kept quacking with absurd vehemence close to us—he was not caught for a considerable time, as he ducked and fluttered away, whenever the men got near him.

He had had time for a good deal of 'verse making' and had 'written a copy a day' since being on board.[4] He started transcribing specimens in his next letter to Harriett, which he began the next day.

On the thirteenth they came in view of the coast of Portugal—'in that indescribable peculiarity of foreign scenery which paintings attempt'. He did not know if the cause was the 'clearness of the air', but it was 'as different from England as possible'. It was 'like a vision', he wrote excitedly—'it is the first foreign soil I have come near.' It seemed incredible that 'scenes so unlike home should be so near home'; they were, after all, still in Europe.[5] On the evening of Saturday, 15 December they arrived at Gibraltar, but they had to stay on board all Sunday in quarantine because of the cholera epidemic. Fresh supplies of coal were brought on to the ship, 'the native coalmen loudly jabbering in that surprising way which distinguishes all races perhaps but the Saxon and German, about nothing at all'.[6] They were allowed on shore the next afternoon for a brief but 'wonderful' visit.

Newman was strangely disconcerted by the sights, as he explained uneasily to Harriett:

---

[4] *LD* iii. 129–31.   [5] Ibid. 138.   [6] Ibid. 144.

I no longer wonder at younger persons being carried away with travelling, and corrupted—for certainly the illusions of the world's magic can hardly be fancied while one remains at home. I never felt any pleasure or danger from the common routine of pleasures, which most persons desire and suffer from—balls, or pleasure parties, or sights—but I think it does require strength of mind to keep the thoughts [where] they should be while the varieties of strange sights, political moral and physical, are passed before the eyes.[7]

But the next day he wrote more confidently to his mother that, 'however interested' he had been in what he had seen, he did not think that he would 'ever for an instant' not have 'preferred . . . to find myself suddenly back again in the midst of those employments and pleasures which befall me in the course of ordinary duty'. He had 'good hope' that he would not be 'unsettled' by his 'present wanderings'. Resolutely he dismissed the temptation of 'all these strange sights' as 'but vanities, which bring no sensible good, and scarcely affect the imagination'. He had originally welcomed the prospect of travel as educationally beneficial, but now he simply saw it as a vacation, and 'the hope of benefitting my health, enlarging my powers of usefulness, and increasing my influence are really the main consideration which reconcile me to my present absence . . . Yet even these thoughts do not reconcile me to the length of time I shall be away—which is so vast, as quite to make me despond . . .' However, his protestation of indifference is partly belied by the reflection that immediately follows:

What has inspired me with all sort of strange reflections . . . is the thought that I am on the Mediterranean—for how much is implied in that one circumstance! Consider how the Mediterranean has been in one sense the seat of the most celebrated Empires and events, which have had their day upon its coasts— think of the variety of men, famous in every way in history to whom the sea has been known—Here the Romans engaged the Carthaginians—here the Phoenicians traded—here Jonah was in the storm—here St Paul was shipwrecked—here the great Athanasius voyaged to Rome and to Constantinople.

The thought of his hero prompted him to offer his mother some verses which began with the prayer for an Anglican Athanasius:

> When shall our northern Church her champion see,
>   Raised by high heaven's decree,
> To shield the ancient faith at his own harm?[8]

Reading the Fathers in Oxford, he had been unable to help comparing unfavourably the 'divided and threatened' Church of England with 'that fresh vigorous Power' of the first centuries. The heroism of the early Church had both 'exalted and abashed' him.

---

[7] *LD* iii. 146.   [8] Ibid. 155–6.

I felt affection for my own Church, but not tenderness; I felt dismay at her prospects, anger and scorn at her do-nothing perplexity. I thought that if Liberalism once got a footing within her, it was sure of the victory in the event. I saw that Reformation principles were powerless to rescue her. As to leaving her, the thought never crossed my imagination; still I ever kept before me that there was something greater than the Established Church, and that was the Church Catholic and Apostolic, set up from the beginning, of which she was but the local presence and organ.

He had already decided before leaving England that there was 'need of a second reformation'.[9]

They put into Algiers on 20 December. The city was stricken with the plague and they did not land. There was a French ship in port, but Newman 'would not even look at the tricolour'. The Bourbons had been dethroned in 1830, 'and I held that it was unchristian for nations to cast off their governors, and, much more, sovereigns who had the divine right of inheritance'. The sight of the republican flag reminded him unpleasantly of 'the success of the Liberal cause which fretted me inwardly'.[10] A gale blew up after they left port, and Newman was frequently violently seasick—

but the worst of seasickness is the sympathy which all things on board have with the illness, as if they were seasick too. First all the chairs, tables, much more the things on them are moving, moving, up and down, up and down—swing, swing—a tumbler turns over, knife and fork run down, wine is spilt—swing, swing. In this condition you go on talking and eating, as fast as you can, hiding your misery, which is provoking[ly] thrust upon you by every motion of the furniture which surrounds you. At length you are seized with sickness, up you get, swing, swing, you cannot move a step—you knock yourself against the table—run smack against the side of the cabin—you *cannot* make the door, the only point you want—you get into your berth at last, but the door will not shut—bang, bang, you slam your fingers. At last things go right with you and down you lie. You are much better, but now a new misery begins, the noise of the bulkheads (i.e. the wooden partitions thro' the vessel). This is not heard on deck—in the cabin it is considerable—but when you lie down, you are in a perfect millhouse. All sorts of noises tenfold increased by the gale; creaking, clattering, shivering, and dashing. And then your bed is seasick too—up and down—swinging without exaggeration as high and as fast (to your feelings) as a swing in a fair . . .[11]

He had not, in fact, had a proper night's sleep since he left England, apart from the time at Gibraltar; but he was nevertheless in excellent spirits.

They reached Malta on Christmas Eve, but again could not go ashore because of the cholera. The 'most wretched Christmas day I can

[9] *Apo.* 40.   [10] Ibid. 39, 42.   [11] *LD* iii. 159.

conceive it to be my lot to suffer' passed without any religious service, and as for the Christmas dinner in the evening it seemed 'so incongruous' that Newman determined, if he could do so 'with any decency, barely to taste of it'. He felt put to shame by a 'humble Romanist' whom he saw saying his prayers in the lazaretto facing the church across the water.[12] Leaving Malta, they set sail for Corfu. Now he was 'full of joy to overflowing—for I am in the Greek sea, the scene of old Homer's song and of the histories of Thucydides'.[13] Finding himself close to Ithaca, the home of Odysseus, he had difficulty expressing his feelings: 'They were not caused by any classical association, but by the thought that I now saw before me in real shape those places which had been the earliest vision of my childhood.' He 'thought of Ham and of all the various glimpses, which memory barely retains and which fly from me when I pursue them, of that earliest time of life when one seems almost to realize the remnant of a pre-existent state'.[14] The *Odyssey* was the first book (in Pope's translation) which he had 'ever learned from, as a child'.[15] When they reached Corfu, he was 'astonished' to realize how little the Greek authors like Homer and Thucydides had said about the magnificent scenery. In spite of all the excitement of travel, he insisted on the 'strange paradox' that

I do not think I should care, or rather I believe I should be very glad, to find myself suddenly transported to my rooms at Oriel, and with my oak sported be lying at full length on my sofa . . . and deliberately as I have set about my present wanderings, yet I heartily wish they were over, and only endure them; and had much rather *have* seen them than *see* them, tho' the while I am extremely astonished and almost enchanted at seeing them.[16]

While he was in Corfu he tried to find out about the Greek Orthodox Church. He heard the priests were ignorant but 'moral in their lives'. He suspected that 'outward ceremonies are the substitute for holiness, as among the Jews'; but in one country church he visited he found 'little objectionable . . . and much that was very good' in the devotional books he looked at.[17] While the strict fasts of the Orthodox impressed him—they seemed to him to be 'the distinguishing feature of the Greek communion as Masses etc is of the Latin'—nevertheless, he considered that 'they both answer the same purpose, and are a substitute apparently for moral obedience, and an opiate to the conscience.'[18]

They returned to Malta on 10 January 1833, but they were obliged to take up residence in the lazaretto because of the quarantine regulations ('the most absurd of all conceivable humbugs, but the British are obliged by other powers to keep it up').[19] Newman took the opportunity to

---

[12] *LD* iii. 162. [13] Ibid. 167. [14] Ibid. 172. [15] Ibid. 193.
[16] Ibid. 177–8. [17] Ibid. 181. [18] Ibid. 239. [19] Ibid. 189.

correct and transcribe the verses he had written for the planned 'Lyra Apostolica'. He enjoyed having some work to do, he told his mother: 'To any one like myself, who has been employing his mind actively for years, nothing is so wearisome as idleness, and so irksome as dissipation. I assure you I feel much more comfortable now than on that restless element which is the type of human life, and much less wearied in this prison than when seeing sights.'[20] Shut up in his Maltese prison, he felt at peace and certainly 'not cut out for a great politician, or as any instrument of change little or great in the Church, for it makes me wretched to be in motion'. Such a disclaimer was often to come to his lips in the course of his life, but the reality was as often the reverse as the admission which follows suggests: 'yet I suppose in these times we must all of us more or less expect to find our duty lie in agitation and tumult.' Indeed, his own trials on board ship, 'as I lay tossed in my luxurious berth in the steam-packet', had made him 'realize somewhat of the cross of that blessed Apostle who was in watchfulness and weariness so often'. St Paul's voyage to Rome had become real in all its arduous actuality for the first time. Similarly, actually seeing Greece had 'thrown a new light upon the whole of its history'; the country was so mountainous he could not conceive how communication had been possible—'how they ever could make war—how they ever extended the march of intellect'. He also now saw a value in the new realism which travel had given him: 'I think travelling a good thing for a secluded man, not so much as showing him the world, as in realizing to him the limited sphere of his own powers.' He could not think of 'one fact or impression about mankind' which he had gained as a result of his experiences, but he had 'deepened' his 'conviction of the intellectual weakness which attaches to a mere reading man—his inability to grasp and understand and appropriate things which befall him in life'.[21] A conviction of the unreality of deriving a religion from books was always to be an important element in Newman's thinking. Real life on a parish had seriously upset the Evangelicalism which he had gained from reading Evangelical authors. Now he was in a position to compare the primitive Church which he had read about in the Fathers with the actual 'unreformed' Churches of the East and West which traced their origins to that early undivided Church, and particularly, of course, with the Roman Church, which his reading as an Evangelical had convinced him was anti-Christian. An important part of this last conviction was to dissolve under the experience of seeing what sort of people real Roman Catholics actually were.

He wrote to tell Isaac Williams, his curate, who was looking after

[20] Ibid. 187.   [21] Ibid. 193-4.

St Mary's, that he had already written enough verses to fill up the proposed verse section in the *British Magazine*. But he was glad that he and Froude had decided not yet to begin the 'Lyra Apostolica'. He had found that Froude wanted to make it 'far more political' than he did, that is, more 'ecclesiastical'. He added that Froude took 'a very different practical view of the Church of Rome'; what he did not say was that his companion 'professed openly his admiration of the Church of Rome, and his hatred of the Reformers'.[22] He was determined not to 'submit' his verses to any sort of editorial 'board'—'I ever have felt strongly that one's power is diluted and usefulness diminished by *boards*—one checks another till something negative is produced—whereas a man does *more good tho'* with accidental evil by following out completely his own individual notion.' It was not long before a much more serious question would arise about boards and committees, again involving Rose, but affecting not a magazine but a movement. 'However this may be,' Newman concluded, 'at least it will never do for F. to be ever patronizing, and I opposing the Pope—so far I think I am resolved, not to join with F. in editing the work.' He had another criticism of Froude, that he did not have 'a sufficiently practical view of religious *teaching*— and that, from never having had a parish (I have often urged this upon him)'.[23] A striking example of Froude's difficulty in 'entering into the minds of others' was his failure to understand that Newman 'really' did hold 'the Roman Church to be Antichristian'. On the other hand, as Newman was to remark approvingly in the *Apologia*, Froude 'was an Englishman to the backbone in his severe adherence to the real and the concrete', and as a result he suffered from 'the contrariety between theory and fact', in the sense that, for instance, 'He was smitten with the love of the Theocratic Church; he went abroad and was shocked by the degeneracy which he thought he saw in the Catholics of Italy.'[24] Newman's own life-long concern to reconcile the ideal and the theoretical with the actual and the concrete, without sacrificing either, finds expression in that preoccupation with the 'real' which runs through his writings and colours all his thought.

The news that the Whigs controlled the first reformed parliament made Newman think that 'the Church's trial' would begin 'at once', which would be 'the best thing', as he had 'the greatest dread of any disturbance in *the State*', for then everybody would suffer—'but if the Church only suffers, then our own suffering, as Churchmen, is alone involved'. Jocularly, he warned Williams to prepare himself for being turned out of St Mary's by his 'vicar's turning Nonconformist'. He ended by asking him to choose out of the poems he had seen 'four *very*

---

[22] *LD* iii. 195; *Apo.* 34.   [23] *LD* iii. 196.   [24] *Apo.* 34-5.

easy, simple, popular ones' for the first number of the 'Lyra Apostolica', which he wanted to have ready for possible publication in June.[25]

A letter to his mother from Malta shows how ambivalent his feelings were becoming about the unreformed Churches of East and West. 'Every thing' in one Roman Catholic church he found 'admirable, if it did not go quite so far—it is a beautiful flower run to seed'. He insisted he had not changed his views, for, although he could not but admire what he saw, 'it is fearful to have before one's eyes the perversion of all the best, the holiest, the most exalted feelings of human nature'. One day he would develop a 'realistic' ecclesiology which would paradoxically characterize corruption as almost a note of the true Church. But for the moment he contented himself with remarking that it had to be admitted that many of the Protestant sects were far more heretical than either Rome or Constantinople. More interesting was the impact of experiencing the Orthodox Church for the first time: he wondered uneasily, 'what answer do Protestants make to the *fact* of the Greek Church invoking Saints, overhonouring the Virgin, and substituting ceremonies for a reasonable service, which they say are the *prophetic* marks of Antichrist?' The next day was Sunday, and the nostalgic thought of St Mary's and Littlemore steadied his feelings: 'We do not know how great our privileges are—all the quiet and calmness connected with our services etc is so beautiful in the memory and so soothing after the sight of that most excited religion which is around me—statues of Madonnas and Saints in the Streets, etc etc. A more poetical but not less jading stimulant than the pouring-forth in a Baptist Chapel.' Once again, he would one day provide a theological justification for the inevitable corruption of a popular religion. Now he admitted he was not only homesick but lonely; he had a bad cough and he was often left alone while the Froudes went out visiting: 'I wonder how long I should last without any friends about me.'[26]

They left Malta on 7 February bound for Sicily. This island 'filled' Newman 'with inexpressible rapture', and he felt 'drawn as by a loadstone'. The ruins of Egesta were 'the flower' of all that he had so far seen—'oh wonderful sight and full of the most strange pleasure, from the wonderful position of the town, its awful desolateness, the strange beauty of the scenery, rich even in winter, and its historical recollections, and, last not least, the misery of the population, the depth of squalidness and brutality, by which it is surrounded.'[27] The solitary ruined temple on the top of a hill, with the ruins of two towns on adjacent hills, had a 'piercing effect' on him—'Such was the genius of early Greek worship, grand in the midst of error; simple and unadorned in its architecture, it

[25] *LD* iii. 198–9.   [26] Ibid. 204–6, 209.   [27] Ibid. 213.

chose some elevated spot, and fixed its faith as a solitary witness on heights where it could not be hid.' Now there was only desolation, except for a 'miserable shepherd's hut with ragged dogs' and 'a savage looking bull prowling amid the ruins' on one of the neighbouring heights.[28] He hoped to return to Sicily in April on his way back to England: it was 'the most interesting (profane) country after Egypt', it 'had never been an unknown unrecorded place, and was the theme of every poet and every historian of antiquity, and . . . had remains in it more ancient and perfect than those of any country'.[29] They left Sicily on the thirteenth, and arrived in Naples the next day. Visits to Catholic churches led Newman to think the Latin Mass was 'less reverend than the Greek, being far more public—there is no skreen—the high altar is in sight'.[30] As a city, Naples did not particularly impress its English visitors: it was a '*watering place*' and, as such, was merely 'a place for *animal* gratification'.[31]

2

Rome, which they reached on 2 March, was very different—'a wonderful place', and the 'first city' to impress Newman.[32] Indeed, it was 'of all cities the first', and all the cities he had seen were 'but as dust, even dear Oxford inclusive, compared with its majesty and glory'. But his feelings were again very mixed. After all, Rome bore an 'awful' aspect as 'the great Enemy of God'; its 'immense . . . ruins, the thought of the purposes to which they were dedicated, the sight of the very arena where Ignatius suffered, the columns of heathen pride with the inscriptions still legible . . . brand it as the vile tool of God's wrath and again Satan's malice'. Certainly, from the religious point of view, 'pain and pleasure' were 'mixed': it was 'strange to be standing in the city of the apostles, and among the tombs of martyrs and saints'. With a glance at the situation at home, Newman thought he detected the 'timidity, indolence, and that secular spirit which creeps on established religion every where'.[33] He tried to explain his curious 'mixture of feelings, partly such as those with which one would approach a corpse, and partly those which would be excited by the sight of the spirit which had left it'; he had not seen much of the city, 'but the effect of every part is so vast and overpowering—there is such an air of greatness and repose cast over the whole, and . . . there are such traces of long sorrow and humiliation, suffering, punishment and decay . . .'.[34] His attitude to being abroad

---

[28] *LD* iii. 219–20, 245.   [29] Ibid. 216.   [30] Ibid. 214.   [31] Ibid. 226.
[32] Ibid. 227.   [33] Ibid. 232.   [34] Ibid. 233–4.

was at least as ambivalent: he intended to stay away as long as possible, and to see as much as he could,

> for I sincerely hope never to go abroad again. I never loved home so well as now I am away from it—and the exquisite sights, which foreign countries supply both to the imagination and the moral taste are most pleasurable in *memory*, but scarcely satisfactory as a present enjoyment. There is far too much of tumult in seeing the places one has read so much about all one's life, to make it desirable for it to continue.—I did not know before, the mind could be excited in so many various ways . . .[35]

His agitation arose out of the conflict between an exclusive and single-minded commitment to religion and an acute sensitivity and openness to the whole gamut of human experience.

Again and again in his letters to England, he spoke of his 'mingled feelings' about Rome, a conflict which induced a kind of emotional and intellectual paralysis in him:

> You are in the place of martyrdom and burial of Apostles and Saints—you have about you the buildings and sights they saw—and you are in the city to which England owes the blessing of the gospel—But then on the other hand the superstitions;—or rather, what is far worse, the solemn reception of them as an essential part of Christianity—but then again the extreme beauty and costliness of the Churches—and then on the contrary the knowledge that the most famous was built (in part) by the sale of indulgences—Really this is a cruel place.— There is more and more to be seen and thought of, daily—it is a mine of all sorts of excellences, but the very highest.

He also continued to analyse his feelings about foreign travel. He felt that he had 'learned thus much by travelling, to think all places about the same, which I had no notion of before—I never could believe that horses, dogs, men and houses were the same in other countries as at home—not that I exactly doubted it, but my imagination could not embrace the notion.' It is noteworthy how his later distinction between the 'notional' and 'real' was not just formulated for a specific philosophical purpose, but was already early on very much part of his ordinary language and thought. The wonder of sightseeing was strangely self-destructive: 'It is astonishing how little it seems to have been at places when one *has* been at them.' Walking around Corfu and Rome, 'and having the same thoughts, feelings, and bodily sensations as at home', made it hard to believe that one was actually in a foreign country. In a way, therefore, travel had an anti-romantic effect, for it 'in a measure destroyed the romance which I threw around every thing I had not myself witnessed . . .'. The romance that there was was necessarily short-lived: he did not, for example, want to see Egesta again

[35] Ibid. 238.

if possible, a place which had moved him more than any other except Ithaca, 'lest I should get familiar with it—as it is I have something for memory to dwell upon—the first impression of things is the poetical one.' He also maintained that he had 'experienced none of that largeness and expansion of mind' which he had been told he would 'get from travelling'.[36] But the claim was misleading: his religious vision had certainly been dramatically widened, and there is no question that his imagination, if not his mind, had been powerfully affected by witnessing at first hand the Church which his early Evangelical formation had convinced him was the Church of the Antichrist, a view which in a more modified and less extreme version he still held.

He could not at any rate 'boast', he told Thomas Mozley, one of his former pupils and now a fellow of Oriel, 'of any greater gift of philosophic coolness than before'. While at Naples he had read in the papers of the Irish Church Reform Bill, whereby ten sees of the established Church would be abolished, and a tax would be imposed on higher clerical incomes to pay for the upkeep of the churches, in place of the extremely unpopular church rates, which were levied on the largely Catholic population. He had commented then, 'well done, my blind Premier, confiscate and rob, till, like Samson, you pull down the political structure on your own head, tho' without his deliberate purpose and his good cause!' Now he confessed it had made him 'hate the Whigs . . . more bitterly than ever'. What, he wondered sarcastically, did the Provost and 'poor Whately' think of this latest development?[37] He had already sent word from on board ship that he would decline the Whitehall preachership, which he had conditionally accepted, if it was offered to him by Bishop Blomfield of London, who had supported the Reform Bill.

The situation, as he saw it, of the Italian Church gave him food for thought. It seemed to be 'in a miserable state': not only was its property confiscated, but 'it has lost its hold on the common people, and seems to go on merely from the force of habit. If a frost came one morning, it would fall off and perish (humanly speaking) as a withered leaf.' 'Infidelity' had 'spread considerably'; the Greek Orthodox Church appeared to be 'in a more hopeful state'. He admitted that the Roman clergy seemed to be 'more moral and decent than at Naples', and that Sunday in Rome was observed 'almost as it is in England'. His diagnosis of the decline led him to thoughts of the Church of England and his own personal position. He suspected that

all over Italy, and here pre-eminently, the Churches and fine buildings are the lure which makes the body so timid and poorspirited. It is not so much that

---

[36] *LD* iii. 240–2, 245.   [37] Ibid. 224, 242.

many of them would care to be pilgrims personally, as that they cannot bear to lose as a body such beautiful and rich structures.

Although he could hardly have guessed that one day the question of the temporal power of the papacy would bulk so large in his own life, he now recognized that if he were Pope himself he would 'feel very much the pain of parting with the Vatican Museum, St Peter's etc without any (strictly) selfish feeling coming into play'. True, there was an 'overabundance of formality . . . without *reverential* feeling, and such persons want no subtle temptation to make them temporizing and cowardly'. But the point was that the same choice was likely to face them in England: disestablishment might prove to be a painful necessity. He certainly did not relish the prospect of 'being ejected from St Mary's', but he hoped the clergy would acquit themselves 'like men—if some of the Bishops would but give the signal'. He was extremely anxious to know what the reaction at home was to 'the accursed Whig spoliation bill'. He could not himself be sorry 'to see things proceed so quickly to a crisis—since it is very annoying and disheartening to linger on in an ague, and to feel every one around you neither hot nor cold'. The time was coming when 'every one must choose his side'. But there was a practical objection which went to the heart of the matter and which Newman put his finger on with typical frankness and realism: they needed 'a little time to get . . . up' their 'own principles'. He told George Ryder, who had been one of his Oriel pupils, that he 'must get up the history of the Church changes at the time of the Reformation, and set others to do the same'. They were bound to make 'blunders' if they acted from only a 'partial view of a subject' without the 'comprehensive knowledge' and 'precedents for acting which history gives us'. He personally was determined 'not to move a step without some authority to back me'. Here was another surprising benefit of travel—'it takes one out of oneself, and reduces in one's eyes both the importance of one's own particular station and of one's own decisions in acting in it.'[38]

On 16 March Newman sent off two instalments of the 'Lyra Apostolica'. He wanted Rose to preface the section with an editorial note to the effect that the editor was not responsible for the views expressed; this would enable Newman and Froude 'to speak freely, which might be inexpedient in a known person such as yourself'. The motto they picked, Newman explained in the *Apologia*, indicated their feelings at the time: they had borrowed a copy of Homer from the Prussian minister and scholar, Baron Bunsen, and Froude 'chose the words in which Achilles, on returning to the battle, says, "You shall know the difference, now that I am back again." '[39]

[38] Ibid. 246–7, 249.   [39] *Apo.* 42.

The same day, Froude heard from Keble. Newman relayed the exciting news to his sister Jemima:

We are at present in good spirits about the prospect of the Church. We find Keble at length is roused, and (*if* once up) he will prove a second St Ambrose—others too are moving—so that wicked Spoliation Bill is already doing service, no thanks to it.[40]

They also learned from Keble about Thomas Arnold's plan for reforming the Church to avoid the disaster of disestablishment. It was, Newman remarked caustically, 'very comprehensive'.

If I understand it right, all sects (the Church inclusive) are to hold their meetings in the Parish Church—though not at the same hour of course. He excludes Quakers and Roman Catholics—yet even with this exclusion surely there will be too many sects in some places for one day? . . . If I might propose an amendment, I should say, pass an Act to oblige some persuasions to *change* the Sunday—if you have two Sundays in a week, it is plain you could easily accommodate any probable number of sects. . . . Nor would this interfere with the Jews' worship (which of course is to be in the Church)—they are too few to take up a whole day. Luckily the Mohammedan holiday is already on a Friday; so there will be no difficulty of arrangement in that quarter.[41]

This passage may be said to mark the beginning of Newman's career as a controversialist. It is the first striking example of his powers of irony and sarcasm, which were so much a part of his originality and strength as a writer, and which were to achieve their fullest expression in the marvellous exuberance of his early Catholic controversial writings—works which have been largely neglected by literary critics, but which ought to give him a prominent place among English satirical writers. There were two periods in his life when the controversialist was forced into silence, but without doubt it was the crisis of 1833 which first inspired and stimulated the genius that would eventually produce the *Tamworth Reading Room*, the satirical masterpiece of his Anglican period.[42]

The same letter also contains the typically tortuous reflection:

I cannot quite divest myself of the notion that Rome Christian is somehow under an especial shade as Rome Pagan certainly was—though I have seen nothing here to confirm it. Not that one can tolerate for an instant the wretched perversion of the truth which is sanctioned here, but I do not see my way enough to say that there is anything peculiar in the condition of Rome . . .[43]

---

[40] *LD* iii. 264.   [41] Ibid. 257–8.

[42] R. H. Hutton's astonishing view that Newman's 'keen and searching irony' did not really manifest itself until after he became a Roman Catholic (*Cardinal Newman*, 2nd edn. (London, 1891), 11) was followed by Wilfrid Ward's even more remarkable assertion, 'His powers of irony had never been displayed at all in his Oxford days' (*Last Lectures by Wilfrid Ward* (London, 1918), 109).

[43] *LD* iii. 258.

He could not disabuse himself of the deeply-ingrained conviction that Rome itself was 'one of the 4 beasts'.[44] With regard to the Book of Revelation, however, he actually wondered in a letter to Pusey whether it did not contain a prophecy of the Reformation, 'which, amid good, has been the source of all the infidelity, the second woe, which is now overspreading the earth'.[45] As to Roman Catholicism, on the other hand, he carefully assured Jemima that while there were 'great appearances . . . of piety in the Churches',

still as a system the corrupt religion (and it is very corrupt) must receive severe inflictions—and I fear I must look on Rome, as a city, still under a curse, which will one day break out in more dreadful judgments than heretofore—yet doubtless the Church will thereby be let loose from the thraldom.—Then as to Greece, the prospect is hopeful, considering its favorable leaning towards the English Church—and its corruptions seem in the retrospect light as air compared with those of Rome. It does not teach purgatory or the Mass, two chief practical delusions of Romanism. Its worst error (and I am far from undervaluing it) is the Saint worship, which is demoralizing in the same sense that Polytheism was—but this is not the Church's *act*, (tho' it in fact sanctions it) but the people's corruption of what is good—the honor due to Saints—whereas the doctrines of the Mass and Purgatory are not perversions but inventions.[46]

He had decided to make a return trip on his own to Sicily—'Think what Spring is! and in Sicily! it is the nearest approach to Paradise, of which sinful man is capable.' But although he was looking forward to it with keen anticipation, he was 'quite sure, it will be indefinitely more delightful in retrospect even than in actual performance'.[47] He had come to the general conclusion that 'the gratification of travelling' consisted 'chiefly in the retrospect—there is far too great hurry and excitement at the time to leave room for much actual enjoyment—but afterwards, the memory of every moment and of every little incident from without, awakes strange feelings of regret and almost tenderness'. Not only was it impossible to 'realize such things at the moment', but there was also the unreality of seeing sights without a proper perspective, for 'we cannot recollect all the associations with which the place is really connected in our minds'. The difficulty of deciding the merits of travelling had, not surprisingly, turned into a problem of reality: if sightseeing was inevitably unreal at the time, it could become real by recollection after the event. He compared the 'pure trouble' of travelling 'while it lasts' with the 'anxiety' he experienced when writing: it was something one wanted 'to have got through', and which 'has its enjoyment' in the end result.[48]

One interesting reason he had for going by himself to Sicily was that

---

44 Ibid. 249.   45 Ibid. 260.   46 Ibid. 265.
47 Ibid. 266.   48 Ibid. 253–5.

he thought it was no 'bad thing to be cast upon oneself as a discipline—
for no one can tell what may happen in time to come'.[49] But although it
would be a valuable 'privation' to be without companions, he could not
deny that he was 'drawn back by an irresistible love of Sicily, of which I
have seen just so much as to wish to see more'. Once again the special
attraction of the island was not just its ancient history, but its peculiar
symbolic value as a monument to paganism—'it is so beautiful and so
miserable that it is an emblem of its own past history, i.e. the history of
heathen countries, being a most noble record stone over the grave of
high hopes and aims, pride, sin, and disappointment.'[50] He had written
in the *Arians* about the truth to be found in pagan religion; now there
was an opportunity to have personal experience of that world which had
existed before Christianity and which was real to him only through the
medium of books.

He had hardly written any verse since leaving Malta: his 'Muse' had
'run dry' and he was 'now resting'.[51] How good a poet he was did not
matter all that much; the important thing was that he felt a greater
number of 'obvious ideas become impressive when put into a metrical
shape', many of which one would not 'dare to utter except metrically, for
thus the responsibility (as it were) is shoved off of oneself, and one speaks
[as if in play], though serious'. This was particularly true 'in time of
excitement'.[52] In so far, then, as verse was a kind of concealed way of
putting one's point across, it was a useful instrument for practitioners of
the principle of reserve.

On 25 March, the feast of the Annunciation, Newman went to High
Mass in the Church of Santa Maria Sopra Minerva. The Pope and his
'court' were present. Newman was scandalized by the 'unedifying
dumbshow', nor could he 'endure the Pope's foot being kissed,
considering how much is said in Scripture about the necessity of him that
is greatest being as the least, nor do I even tolerate him being carried in
on high'. But while he felt sure that Rome was 'a doomed city' as 'one of
the 4 monsters of Daniel's vision', and began 'to think that it was a sin, as
such, in the Church's uniting itself with that enemy of God, who from
the beginning sat on her 7 hills, with an enchantress's cup, as the
representative and instrument of the Evil Principle',

yet as I looked on, and saw all Christian acts performing the Holy Sacrament
offered up, and the blessing given, and recollected I was in church, I could only
say in very perplexity my own words, 'How shall I name thee, Light of the wide
west, or heinous error-seat?'—and felt the force of the parable of the tares—who
can separate the light from the darkness but the Creator Word who prophesied

[49] *LD* iii. 245.   [50] Ibid. 247–8.   [51] Ibid. 265.   [52] Ibid. 236.

their union? And so I am forced to leave the matter, not at all seeing my way out of it.—How shall I name thee?[53]

He was to ponder that question for a long time, but there is no doubt that the image of the 'Antichrist' had at least been dented. Recognizing both the revulsion and the attraction in him, he tried to distinguish between 'the Roman C. system' which he had 'ever detested' and 'the *Catholic* system' to which he was 'more attached than ever'. He was impressed by the clerical students he saw ('so innocent and bright, poor boys') and, while he feared that 'there are very grave and farspreading scandals among the Italian priesthood, and there is mummery in abundance', he nevertheless recognized that 'there is a deep substratum of true Christianity, and I think they may be as near truth (at the least) as that Mr B. whom I like less and less every day'.[54] Mr Burgess was the Anglican chaplain in Rome, whom Newman had earlier described with distaste as 'one of the most perfect watering place preachers I ever heard, most painfully so—pompous in manner and matter', with a 'doctrine mischievous semi-evangelical'.[55]

On Saturday, 6 April Newman's diary records that he and Froude called on Nicholas Wiseman, the Rector of the English College, and 'had long talk with him'. It was their second visit to him. In the *Apologia* Newman recalled that when they took their leave, Wiseman 'courteously expressed a wish that we might make a second visit to Rome; I said with great gravity, "We have a work to do in England." ' It seems his memory confused this conversation with something he did say nearly two months later in Sicily; whereas on this occasion the remark was rather less dramatic: as he remembered them a few years later, the words, 'though sincerely said . . . were not deeply pointedly? said, but in answer to the question how long we stayed there, I said that we had work at home'.[56] At any rate, their talk with Wiseman was not very encouraging: to their dismay, they discovered that there was no prospect of reunion without total acceptance of the Council of Trent. The shock of this discovery was worse for Froude, who now felt considerably less favourable to the Church of Rome, than for Newman:

As to my view of the Romanist system, it remains, I believe, unchanged. A union with Rome, while it is what it is, is impossible; it is a dream. As to the individual members of the cruel church, who can but love and feel for them? I am sure I have seen persons in Rome, who thus move me, though they cast out our name as evil. There is so much amiableness and gentleness, so much Oxonianism, (so to say) such an amusing and interesting demureness, and such simplicity of look and speech, that I feel for those indeed who are bound with an

---

[53] Ibid. 267–8. [54] Ibid. 273–4.
[55] Ibid. 227. [56] Ibid. 276; *Apo.* 43; *AW* 136.

iron chain, which cripples their energies, and (one would think,) makes their devotion languid. What a strange situation it is, to be with those who think one in a state of perdition, who speak calmly with one, while they have awful thoughts! what a mixture of grief and indignation, what a perplexity between frankness and reserve comes over one!

He was sorry to be leaving Rome—'it is a delightful place, so calm and quiet, so dignified and beautiful, that I know nothing like it but Oxford.' But he felt

drawn by an irresistible attraction to the fair levels and richly verdured heights of Sicily. What a country it is! a shadow of Eden, so as at once to enrapture and to make one melancholy. It will be a vision for my whole life; and, though I should not choose, I am not sorry to go alone, in order, as Wordsworth would say, to commune with high nature.[57]

Before he left the city, he came very close to adumbrating the theology of corruption which he would one day develop as part of his theology of the Church: he admitted in a letter to another don at Oriel that he did 'not like to talk of the lamentable mixture of truth with error which Romanism exhibits—the corruption of the highest and noblest views and principles, far higher than we Protestants have, with malignant poisons'. And while 'the pretension and fudge' of 'the Romish system' reminded him curiously of Evangelicalism, he was not thinking of the Evangelicals but of Roman Catholics when he remarked by way of conclusion, 'Dead flies cause the precious ointment to stink.' There were many stories of moral corruption among the clergy, although he had not himself come across any instances, but had been 'pleased' with the priests he had met, especially those from England and Ireland ('the only theatre left for the operation of the Romish system').[58]

3

On 9 April the Froudes left for Marseilles by sea, while Newman set off by land for Naples, which he reached the next day. He ate a solitary dinner at the hotel. He was now by himself for the first time in a foreign country. He wrote to Jemima that for a moment he half-repented his decision: 'I was going among strangers into a wild country, to live a wild life, to travel in solitudes and to sleep in dens of the earth; and all for what? for the gratification of an imagination . . . drawn by a strange love of Sicily to gaze upon its cities and mountains.' In leaving Rome, 'not as

[57] *LD* iii. 277.   [58] Ibid. 279–80.

a city, but as a scene of sacred history', he felt he had left behind 'a part' of his heart. Sadly he sighed to his sister,

Oh that Rome were not Rome; but I seem to see as clear as day that a union with her is *impossible*. She is the cruel Church—asking of us impossibilities, excommunicating us for disobedience, and now watching and exulting over our approaching overthrow.[59]

He had, however, now come to the conclusion that there was an important distinction between Rome as a place and Rome as a church: it did not follow from the fact that there was 'really a sort of Genius Loci which enthralls the Church which happens to be there' that that church itself was the 'new form of the old evil' of ancient Rome. Not unnaturally, he was perplexed: 'how a distinction is to be drawn between two powers, spiritual and devilish, which are so strongly united, is as much beyond our imagination, as it was beyond the power of the servants in the parable to pull up the tares from the wheat.' Indeed, the parable struck him as an astonishing prophecy of the scandals of the papacy—a point he would one day decide proved the opposite of what he now thought it proved. As he was to explain in the *Apologia*, his 'imagination' had been 'impressed' and his 'heart was touched also' by what he had seen of Roman Catholicism, but in spite of his 'tender feelings', his 'reason' had not been 'affected at all'—'My judgment was against her, when viewed as an institution, as truly as it ever had been.' The Roman Church seemed quite clearly to be a continuation of the old Rome—it even used the same language as 'its bond of union *as* an Empire'. Its 'policy' was still 'crafty, relentless, inflexible', it sacrificed 'the good of its members' to its own 'splendour and strength', as in enforcing celibacy on its clergy, and it upheld a 'polytheistic, degrading, idolatrous' religion. The obvious goodness, on the other hand, of so much of Catholicism merely proved that it was the 'slave' of the evil spirit which still ruled Rome. He was confident that the day would come 'when the captive will be set free'; in the meantime, it was all very distressing and puzzling.[60]

Newman was looking forward excitedly to seeing Sicily again.

Its history begins with the earliest times and lasts thro' both Greek and Roman annals, down to the eras of the Saracen invasions and Norman chivalry. In it I read the history of all that is great and romantic in human nature, and the man in all his strength and weakness, with high aims and manifold talents corrupted by sin and humbled by continual failure.

Apart from Rome, he had not been particularly interested in seeing Italy, 'but Greece has ever made my heart beat, and Sicily is Greece in a

---

[59] Ibid. 282, 284.   [60] Ibid. 288–9; *Apo.* 58–9.

way'. Its ancient Doric settlements seemed 'so wonderful', and the remains were better preserved than those of mainland Greece; there was 'something mysterious about them—their power is prior to the time of history'. Observing that 'the simplicity of their architecture seems to imply a corresponding simplicity in their religion', he wondered 'whether holy ones did not walk the rounds of these primitive temples, till the pride of science and literature extinguished the rays which had been providentially left among them'. Then there was the sheer beauty of the island, which was 'really a strange incentive' to revisit it, particularly at that time of year: 'Spring has been to me the most elevating and instructive time of the year—somehow it whispers of the good which is to come, when our bodies are to rise—and it throws the thoughts back upon Eden we have lost, and makes the heart contrite by the contrast between what is and what might be.' He hastened to add that he despised 'sentimentality' and was 'up in arms against the Shelleyism of the day, which resolves religion into feeling, and makes it possible for bad men to have holy thoughts. Doubtless no religious emotion is worth a straw, or rather it is pernicious, if it does not lead to *practice*.'

But rejection of a religion of feelings (whether the result of Romantic sensibility or Evangelical emotionalism) did not mean that psychological factors were irrelevant to action. And this, interestingly enough, was Newman's final justification for his return to Sicily alone, an adventure about which he not unnaturally had misgivings, particularly in view of his reservations about the value of travel in general:

Good thoughts are only good so far as they are taken as means to an exact *obedience* or at least this is the chief part of their goodness. Do not think me to be carried away with the mere poetical pleasure of an indulged imagination . . . In truth I find nothing is supporting in trouble and anxiety as bright seasons which remain in the memory and are recalled at pleasure. Why was St Paul caught into the third heaven but that he might have a vision to soothe him amid the dust of the world? and when it is put into our power to see scenes, which speak more of God than any thing which is not miraculous, surely we may innocently take them and use them with thankfulness. Thus I have reasoned with myself, and I think justly, when the time and expenses of my expedition seemed at first to shake me as devoted to a mere selfish gratification. But it is not so. Evil is before us. Clouds seem to gather round the Church. No one can tell what his lot will be. Certainly a Clergyman's office will be no pleasant one. Another holiday I shall never have.

The wild, primeval landscapes of Sicily might seem to have little to do with what Newman sarcastically called the Whigs' 'Piety towards the Church of Ireland', but they were to recreate and reinvigorate him for the battles that lay ahead. As for the particular conflict that was imminent, he had no doubt it was the established Church of Ireland which had been founded by St Patrick and 'continued by regular succession of clergy ever since', the 'Romish Priests being mere intruders, and a creation from Rome of these last centuries'. The Reform Bill had effectively separated Church and State, and so he was politically neutral, as between Whigs and Tories, but 'with a tendency, which may grow, towards agitating for a more effectual Church discipline, for the independence of Bishops of the Crown which has now become but a Creature of an Infidel Parliament, and for the restoration of the practice of excommunication'. There was an ironic afterthought: 'And surely the pious Whigs who are for the emancipation of negroes and receive in so edifying a spirit petitions for the better observance of the sabbath, cannot fail to aid the Church in purifying herself from worthless members.'[61]

While he was at Naples, he went up Vesuvius—'the most wonderful sight I have seen abroad'.[62] He also walked out to Virgil's tomb. He and the Froudes had been 'very hard on this poor place, which I begin to like if it were only out of remorse at having been violent against it'. He was, however, shocked by 'the very irreverent exhibitions of the Crucifix and of souls in purgatory which are stuck about', and he regarded 'the popular and exoteric religion as nearly pagan as you can fancy'. Not everything deserved censure: he told his mother that 'among the inconsistencies of these southerners' was 'the delicacy and abundance of their table and chamber linen, which is particularly white'. Not only were there always napkins and fresh tablecloths at meals, but at dinner 'two—the second smaller than the first and put anglewise on the table as a receptacle for the dishes and removed with them'. The hotel also provided 'two very large clean towels daily—and tho' they cannot make me use two, yet I cannot open a towel but it disappears and another is substituted'. On the other hand, the carpets were so 'intolerably dirty' that it was unwise to let one's towel touch them. As for the 'fashion of spitting', it was 'perfectly incredible to an Englishman—they are ever at it': he had seen a lady of fashion 'spit manfully', and even in the churches people spat while at prayer, including 'a priest at the altar in the most sacred part of the service'. He was still looking forward to Sicily—'yet how I wish it was over, tho' I shall enjoy it much at the time, for I wish to get home—and the memory of such sights is even more delightful than the seeing them.' One could then look back on one's experiences and enjoy the 'mental feelings', but without the 'bodily pain'.[63]

He wrote jocularly to his friend H. A. Woodgate, a fellow of St John's, 'Can there be a greater proof that I am become a liberal, a march-of-

[61] *LD* iii. 291–3.   [62] Ibid. 284.   [63] Ibid. 294–7, 308.

mind man, a man of the world . . . than my refusing to return home with
the Froudes and running down to Sicily instead?' He had 'already
overcome many prejudices'—although one had 'cost' him 'much to
surmount', namely, the local habit of serving the meat before the fish at
dinner. After hearing that, his friend would not be 'surprised' to learn
that 'I habitually desecrate the Sabbath by travelling and visiting; that
I visit the theatre, and am glad to accept invitations from the wealthy
English adulterers here, who are the attraction of the place'. He was now
'indeed quite polished' from his travels, as Woodgate had hoped he
would be—'and on my return shall be rational and dispassioned enough
to defend the Irish Church spoliation Bill, and to join hand and glove
with Dr Arnold in his views of Ecclesiastical Reform in England'. There
was 'one point indeed' in which he went further than the broad-minded
Arnold:

he is said to exclude the Jews, Roman Catholics, and Quakers from the
Churches—this seems to me illiberal. The only objection I can fancy is the want
of time in one day for these in addition to those already admitted to
participation in the Churches—I am aware the Quakers remain an indefinite
period at one sitting—and it would not do to keep the Sandemonians or the
Socinians waiting—there must be a punctuality, if all are to be accommodated.
Yet I think the difficulty might be met by forcing the Evangelicals to keep their
Sunday on the Saturday . . . The Jews could take Saturday too—and the
Roman Catholics would come in for Sunday in place of the Evangelicals. The
Mahometan Feast being Friday would not interfere.—Or on the whole, since it
is immaterial on what day the Christian festival is kept, the whole week might
be divided among the various denominations of Christians.—I have another
plan, which I hold to be altogether original and is the firstfruits of my late
conversion and runs Dr A hard. It is to allot the 24 Colleges and Halls of Oxford
among the various denominations—in this way you might meet the difficulty
about subscription . . . I would allow of exchanges or conversions . . .

Only a month had elapsed since his first real attempt at satire, but
already his irony had acquired a keen cutting-edge ('it would not do to
keep the Sandemonians or the Socinians waiting'). He ended the letter
with the first serious hint of an actual 'movement'. He begged Woodgate

to join the brotherhood of those who wish a return to the primitive state of the
Church, when it was not a mere instrument of civil government, which it
approaches to be now. I almost think the time is come to form clubs and
societies under the title of Apostolical—that we may have some approximation
towards a system of discipline. They should be somewhat on the plan of the
Temperance Societies, with the professed object of strengthening the Church,
and the promise to disband whenever the Church has recovered its power of
governing itself.[64]

[64] *LD* iii. 297–8, 300.

On 19 April the wind at last blew fair and Newman embarked on an English sailing-brig for Messina. He could have gone three days earlier on the steamer, but it was overcrowded and the weather was rough; nor did he want to arrive in Sicily with a hoard of tourists who would 'make inn room difficult to be got, and raise the price of every thing, besides creating a crowd in various objects of the traveller's search which spoils the beauty of them'.[65] He took with him as a servant a Neapolitan called Gennaro, who had been a sailor on board the *Victory* at the Battle of Trafalgar and had been in service with an English family for the past sixteen years.

They arrived two days later at Messina, and the next day set off by foot southwards. He 'felt amused and almost ashamed' to be 'the chief of a cavalcade' consisting of servant, muleteer, and mules. It seemed a somewhat 'princely' 'retinue', and the sight of his unclerical shadow, clad as he was in 'a straw hat and a flannel jacket', only added to his discomfiture.[66] The first day was not a great success: the luggage kept coming undone, the weather was threatening, the scenery not particularly inspiring, and he felt the lack of companionship. The next day, however, they reached Taormini—where the view from the ancient theatre was 'a nearer approach to seeing Eden, than anything' he 'had conceived possible'. The magnificent scenery had even a spiritual effect on him: 'I felt for the first time in my life with my eyes open that I must be better and more religious, if I lived there.' Words practically failed him as he attempted vainly to describe the astonishing sight: 'It realized all one had read of in books of the perfection of scenery—a deep valley— brawling streams—beautiful trees—but description is nothing—the sea was heard in the distance.' It was a 'superb view, the most wonderful I can ever hope to see'. They travelled on to the foot of Mt. Etna ('magnificent beyond description'),[67] but the snow still lay thick on it, so that he gave up the idea of attempting to climb it.

Not only was his leg strained and his feet covered in blisters from walking, but he was tired out after sleepless nights in mean, flea-infested inns. The 'so-called' inn at the foot of the mountain, where they spent the night before walking to Catania, 'was the most forlorn place I ever was in'. It was filthy, there was no glass in the one window, and the doors were broken with the 'boards gaping to the external air'. He was famished: Sicilian inns did not provide meals, and now he could not get his spirit-stove going to cook any of the provisions he had brought from Naples. Gennaro meanwhile had gone out to get himself something to eat.

I lay down on the so-called bed, and thought of the sick-room at Ealing, and my mind felt very dry, and I thought 'what if I should lose my reason?' and I was in

<hr />

[65] Ibid. 294.   [66] Ibid. 302.   [67] Ibid. 303–4.

dreadful irritation from the renewed attacks of the fleas and I was altogether out of sorts—and the bed was laid on a *board*, and the bed things looked dirty, and I fancied it would all come to pieces in the night—But my servant came in, and poached me some eggs, and threw down water under the bed to destroy my enemies and I laid down to sleep by 8 or 9 o'clock—and slept very sound for eight hours . . .[68]

Unfortunately, although Gennaro was very resourceful and a good cook, he was no help in finding their way about Sicily, of which he knew nothing, with the result that Newman had to rely on second-hand tips from others—'everyone was giving me advice to do things *they had not tried themselves*'![69]

They spent the night at Catania, where Newman cleaned up and rested, before taking the boat to Syracuse, where the sirocco, which had been threatening for several days, finally came down in heavy rain. Newman decided to return immediately the next day to Catania while the wind was still blowing in the right direction. However, they were blown off course and had to spend the night in a cove only a few miles from Syracuse. As before, the natives they met were polite and helpful, although obviously very poor, and Newman liked what he saw of them—'dirt, but simplicity and contentment'.[70]

On 1 May they set off inland from Catania in a north-westerly direction. Newman was already feeling under the weather with feverish symptoms, which was not very surprising after sleeping out of doors on a chilly night. After a night at Adernò they were back on the road again. The scenery was 'like the Garden of Eden most exquisitely beautiful'. By now he was in great pain, and as he walked he 'fell to tears thinking of dear Mary' while he 'looked at the beautiful prospect'.[71] They managed to reach Leonforte by evening, where unfortunately the best inn was already occupied by a Sicilian duke. Next morning Newman felt very ill but managed eventually to make his way to the better inn, which had now been vacated. As he lay in bed, he felt he was being punished for self-will (his last sermon before leaving Oxford had been on the sin of wilfulness) in leaving the Froudes and coming on his own; he remembered, too, that it was almost exactly three years ago that he had sent his ultimatum to Hawkins, and he wondered if the manner of this had not been too 'hasty and impatient' and whether he had not 'cherished resentment against the Provost'.[72] Still, nobody had actually advised him against coming to Sicily, and he 'kept saying' to himself 'I have not sinned against light.' Next day the feelings of self-reproach returned and he began to think his religious principles were hollow and

[68] *LD* iii. 305.   [69] Ibid. 313.   [70] Ibid. 310.
[71] *AW* 123.   [72] *LD* iv. 8.

shallow compared with Keble's. To stop his 'mind from thinking of itself' he 'kept counting the number of stars, flowers etc. in the pattern of the paper on the walls'. Some beggars started whining outside in the street, a 'low feeble monotonous cry' which seemed interminable. There was no doctor available nor any medicine, apart from some camomile tea his servant made. It was obvious to Gennaro that his employer was seriously ill with fever and that he might well die, so he hinted he might leave him the luggage. Newman gave him Froude's address in the event of his death, but emphatically discounted the possibility—'God has still work for me to do.'[73]

Refusing to accept that he was seriously ill, he insisted, in his somewhat delirious state, on setting out on the road again on 6 May. But they had hardly gone half a mile before he started to feel very hungry and then very thirsty. He 'began sucking some most delicious oranges which were on the way side' and 'kept thinking' what he would be able to tell his mother and sisters 'about the fineness of these oranges—not sweet or tart, but a fine aromatic bitter'.[74] He felt suffocated in his throat rather than actually thirsty; but it was some time before they came to a sort of hut or tent by the roadside where he could get water and rest. There was no floor, but he lay down on his blue travelling-cloak. Towards evening he had sufficiently recovered to be put on a mule, and there was an affectionate parting with the poor peasants who had kindly taken him in; he promised to remember them when he returned to England (at which the not especially soft-hearted Gennaro burst into tears).

He was then taken to the nearby town of Castro Giovanni, where the doctor attempted to bleed him. When no blood came at the first incision, Gennaro, who was a veteran of the Peninsula campaign, actually fainted away! Three incisions eventually produced blood, but not enough, and Newman was so weak that they were afraid to take any more. He corresponded in Latin with the doctor, who was hardly a match for the Oxford scholar and who 'pretended' Newman's Latin was 'nonsense', but it was in fact 'very good', his patient later triumphantly boasted, considering how ill he was! It seemed he had fallen victim to an epidemic of gastric or typhoid fever, from which numbers of people were dying, and which was often accompanied by cholera. He dreaded the long nights, when he dreamed deliriously that he was 'sitting on a staircase, wanting something'; but the heroic Gennaro exposed himself to infection by sleeping in the room with him. In the stifling heat he kept fainting, and there was 'nothing but vinegar to relieve' him, 'which the muleteer' (who also sat up with him) 'with his great bullet tips of fingers

---

[73] *AW* 125–7.   [74] Ibid. 128.

(so I recollect I called them, while he administered it with them) applied to my nose in the middle of the night'. Unfortunately, the doughty muleteer was dismissed after a dispute over wages. For some reason no attempt was made to reduce the heat and the doctor even refused to allow him to cool his burning head with cold water, but he 'managed to outwit' Gennaro by pretending to apply the prescribed vinegar to his temples with a cold cloth.[75]

There was a time when Newman's recovery was despaired of, and in fact the fever took a few days longer than usual to reach its crisis, which occurred on 13 May. Apart from a fair that took place outside his window, the most aggravating noise, ironically enough, was the church bell that rang for Mass every day: 'I used quite to writhe about, and put my head under the bed clothes—and asked Gennaro if it could not be stopped.' No doubt, he later reflected, his Sicilian attendants attributed his irritation to 'a heretic's misery under a holy bell'.[76] He had been visited by a local priest when he first arrived and had told Gennaro, 'when half light headed', that he wanted to 'dispute' with him.[77] After about a week he got up and took his first walk outside: 'As I sat in the chair, I could not command myself, but cried profusely, the sight of the sky was so piercing.'[78] He remembered vividly the return of his appetite—how he 'longed' for the tea Gennaro made for him and 'could not help crying out from delight'. He was totally dependent on the trusty Neapolitan, and 'could not bear him from the room five minutes', but was always calling out 'Gen-na-rooooo'!

At last, on Saturday, 25 May, they left Castro Giovanni. Newman was overwhelmed by the beauty of the countryside—'Spring in its greatest luxuriance'. He overcame his scruples about travelling on a Sunday, and on the Monday they reached Palermo. Either on that morning or the morning before, when he got up he 'sat some time by the bed side, crying bitterly and all I could say was, that I was sure God had some work for me to do in England'.[79] Needless to say, Gennaro had no idea what he was talking about. In the marvellously graphic account of his near fatal fever, which he began writing over a year later (and continued at intervals during 1834 and 1835, although not completing it till 1840), Newman said he thought that the Devil had seized the opportunity of his 'unlooked for' return to Sicily to destroy him before he could be 'a means of usefulness'.[80] Many years later he looked back on the episode as the third of the 'three great illnesses' in his life which had led to such decisive developments in his religious life.[81]

While he was staying in an English hotel in Palermo, he saw in an old newspaper that his favourite pupil, Frederic Rogers, had been elected to

[75] *AW* 130–1.   [76] Ibid. 132.   [77] Ibid. 135.   [78] Ibid. 133.
[79] Ibid. 136.   [80] Ibid. 121–2.   [81] Ibid. 268.

a fellowship at Oriel. He 'kissed the paper rapturously'.[82] To his sister Harriett he wrote excitedly, 'I could hardly dare trust my eyes, and have read it again and again.'[83] He sent off immediately his delighted congratulations to Rogers, to whom he gave an account of his adventures. He had returned to Sicily for two reasons: first, to see its antiquities, which he had failed to do, and second, to see the countryside, about which he could 'only say that I did not know before nature could be so beautiful'—it was indeed 'like the garden of Eden' and had surpassed all his expectations.[84]

Free from the cares of travelling, he found it easy once again to produce with facility verses for the 'Lyra Apostolica' ('anxiety', he had remarked, was 'the greatest enemy of poetry').[85] But all the time he was homesick and longing to return home. Day after day, for nearly three weeks, he waited for a sailing; his 'impatience' was 'calmed' by visits to churches, he recorded in the *Apologia*—although he 'knew nothing of the Presence of the Blessed Sacrament there', nor did he attend any services.[86] But the 'still retreats' which the cool churches offered from 'the city's sultry streets' inspired the ambivalent poem which begins:

> Oh that thy creed were sound!
> For thou dost soothe the heart, Thou Church of Rome,
> By thy unwearied watch and varied round
> Of service, in thy Saviour's holy home.[87]

At last, on 13 June, he was able to embark on an orange-boat bound for Marseilles. Gennaro, who had saved his life, had to be left behind to rejoin his family in Naples. Newman was convinced that no Englishman could have nursed him as Gennaro had done. He was also thoroughly honest, and none of Newman's belongings had gone missing.

On 16 June, while still at sea, Newman wrote 'The Pillar of the Cloud', better known by its opening words, 'Lead, Kindly Light'. It is not surprising that the poem has become one of the most famous hymns in the language, for its mood of thanksgiving and trust is easily applicable either to the individual believer's present predicament or to his or her more general pilgrimage of faith through life. But the words which are most characteristic of Newman come at the end of the first stanza:

> I do not ask to see
> The distant scene,—one step enough for me.[88]

It was a thought which was always to be at the heart of his spirituality, namely, that light is only given to us gradually bit by bit, but that we are

---

[82] Ibid. 134.   [83] *LD* iii. 305.   [84] Ibid. 315.   [85] Ibid. 307.
[86] *Apo.* 43.   [87] *VV* 153.   [88] Ibid. 156.

always given enough to see what we have to do next, and that when we have taken that step which has been lit up for us, we shall see the next, but only the next, step illuminated—while to attempt to see several steps ahead or the end of the path is not only futile but also self-defeating. We shall see how the eloquent idealism of the sermons is also balanced by a similar realism and relentless practicality about the humdrum means that realize high aspirations.

They were 'becalmed a whole week in the Straits of Bonifacio',[89] but eventually reached Marseilles on 27 June. The next day Newman set off for Lyons. Again he was held up, 'as tho' some unseen power, good or bad, was resisting my return'. For weeks now the tears had come into his eyes whenever he thought of home—but he was sure the 'severe lesson of patience' was God's will. The distance from Marseilles was only 200 miles, a journey of 48 hours, but on arrival he found his ankles so swollen that he was forced to rest a day in 'a miserably dirty inn'. The 'only anticipation' he now had 'of the future' was that 'thwarting awaits me at every step'.[90]

At last, on Monday, 8 July, he crossed the Channel from Dieppe and reached London the same night. He returned to Oxford the next evening. There he found his brother Francis at home, who had only himself arrived back a few hours before from Persia, where he had been involved in a somewhat bizarre Evangelical mission for the last three years, after resigning his fellowship at Balliol because of his nonconformist views. It was a strange coincidence.

The following Sunday, July 14th, Mr. Keble preached the Assize Sermon in the University Pulpit. It was published under the title of 'National Apostasy'. I have ever considered and kept the day, as the start of the religious movement of 1833.[91]

4

At the end of July, a meeting was held at H. J. Rose's rectory in Hadleigh, Suffolk to discuss the danger posed to the Church by the Irish Church Temporalities Bill, which was to become law on 14 August. The Oxford representatives were Froude and William Palmer of Worcester. There was a difference of opinion about whether or not the Church should remain established, and the meeting broke up without any agreement on what course of action to pursue.

Without the support of any of the bishops, and with the clergy 'dead', Newman felt that they had 'every thing against us but our cause'. Their

---

[89] *Apo.* 43.   [90] *LD* iii. 310–11.   [91] *Apo.* 43.

lack of theology meant they had no '*precedents* how to act'. He had no desire for disestablishment unless it became necessary—but he knew that the 'early Church threw itself on the *people*', and 'now that the Crown and aristocracy have deserted us, must we not do so too?'[92] He told Froude he thought Keble ought to be at their head, since he seemed now to be 'unchained', and 'a head we must have, and such a one as we know will go all lengths, when the time comes'. He also mentioned that he had begun writing a paper, which could be 'one of a series' for the *British Magazine*, 'called the "Church of the Fathers" . . . on the principle of popularity as an element of Church power, as exemplified in the history of St Ambrose'.[93] Froude reported with disappointment that Rose merely counselled caution and was 'hoping for a re-action'.[94] But the more pragmatic Newman warned, 'We *must* pull with Rose, and bide our time.' Rose might be only a 'conservative', but then who would not be one 'if things *could* return to their old state, provided something like discipline were enforced'?[95] It was important not to be 'prematurely violent', otherwise they would 'lose all' their 'influence when times are worse'; he 'heartily' wished 'things may keep quiet for a year or two, that we may ascertain our position, get up precedents, and know our duty'.

Already Newman was revealing himself as the master strategist. He urged on Keble the importance of making as much as possible 'of our situation in Oxford and the deference paid it through the Country'. They were the only party 'likely to be *active* in Oxford . . . so the field is before us'. He wanted them to 'agree on some plan' for 'writing letters to our friends, just as if we were *canvassing*'. They should certainly preach about the crisis to their congregations, otherwise they would be 'surprised at a call to follow us *from* the Establishment, should it come to that'.[96] He was already himself 'poking into the Fathers with a hope of rummaging forth passages of history which may prepare the *imaginations* of men for a changed state of things, and also be precedents for our conduct in difficult circumstances'.[97]

It was decided, with Keble's agreement, to form a 'society' at Oxford 'for the purpose of rousing the Clergy'. They needed to have names of clergy round the country to get up a petition to the Archbishop of Canterbury 'when the right moment comes', and to prepare the ground for the next parliament 'that we may not be taken by surprise'; the main point they would emphasize in canvassing support was the 'Apostolical Succession', but they would also defend the Prayer Book against any alterations and oppose 'heretical' appointments in the Church.[98] They hoped to form branches in other parts of the country and eventually to circulate books and tracts.

[92] *LD* iv. 14.   [93] Ibid. 18.   [94] Ibid. 20.   [95] Ibid. 17.
[96] Ibid. 21–2.   [97] Ibid. 24.   [98] Ibid. 28–9.

On 16 August Newman sent Rose four 'sketches of history from the Fathers' for publication in the *British Magazine*.[99] The first of these 'Letters on the Church of the Fathers' was on St Ambrose and came quickly to the point. The fact that hitherto the Church had 'depended' on the State 'is so natural and religious a position of things when viewed in the abstract, and in its actual working has been productive of such excellent fruits in the Church, such quietness, such sobriety, such external propriety of conduct, and such freedom from doctrinal excesses, that we must ever look back upon the period of ecclesiastical history so characterized with affectionate thoughts'. But mere conservatism should not prevent the question, 'what is intended by Providence to take the place of the time-honoured instrument, which He has broken (if it be yet broken), the regal and aristocratical power?' His own answer, which he knew would 'offend many', was, 'we must *look to the people*'. He conceded, 'Who at first sight does not dislike the thoughts of gentlemen and clergymen depending for their maintenance and their reputation on their flocks? of their strength, as a visible power, lying not in their birth, the patronage of the great, and the endowment of the Church (as hitherto), but in the homage of a multitude?' He had to confess that he had 'before now had a great repugnance to the notion' himself, but he had 'overcome it, and turned from the Government to the People', because he 'was forced to do so'. The suspicion of just the slightest hint of irony is confirmed by a later remark to the effect that 'St. Ambrose and his brethren' might 'have as reasonably disbelieved the possible existence of parsonages and pony carriages in the nineteenth century, as we the existence of martyrs and miracles in the primitive age'. At any rate, he is prepared to state bluntly here that 'what may become necessary in time to come, is a more religious state of things also'. The Bible prefers the poor to the rich, and in practice 'the Church, when purest and most powerful, *has* depended for its influence on its consideration with the many'.[100] Such was the primitive Church. It is not surprising that as a Roman Catholic Newman found so little difficulty with the idea of a disestablished and popular Catholicism. He had already seen that that was the shape of things to come at the start of the Oxford Movement.

As things were in the meantime, he told Bowden, 'the first thing' he would do if he were a bishop would be to 'excommunicate' the Prime Minister, Lord Grey, 'and a dozen more, whose names it is almost a shame and a pollution for a Christian to mention'.[101] He had already expressed the view that Whately, who had recently defended Lord Grey, had 'almost severed himself from Catholic Communion'; he 'really'

---

[99] *LD* iv. 30.   [100] *HS* i. 340–2, 364.   [101] *LD* iv. 32.

doubted 'whether one ought to hold intercourse with him', and thought that he would not be able 'to sit down to table with him'.[102] At least during the Arian heresy 'there was the possibility of true-minded men becoming Bishops, which is now almost out of the question'. If only, he groaned, 'we had one Athanasius, or Basil, we could bear with 20 Eusebiuses'. He wished the Archbishop of Canterbury 'had somewhat of the boldness of the old Catholic Prelates; no one can doubt he is a man of the highest principle, and would willingly die a Martyr; but, if he had but the little finger of Athanasius, he would do us all the good in the world'. (Archbishop Howley might have been a little surprised to learn that he was ready for martyrdom.) Newman admitted that the next ('stinging') 'Lyra Apostolica' in the *British Magazine* might seem 'somewhat violent'; but then, 'one gains nothing by sitting still. I am sure the Apostles did not sit still.' It was at least a good sign that they were accused of being 'enthusiasts'.

Although disestablishment would have serious economic consequences, he was not afraid of being 'thrown on the people'. However, he would not 'advocate a separation of Church and State, unless the Nation does more tyrannical things against us; but I do feel I should be glad if it were done and over, much as the Nation would lose by it—for I fear the Church is being corrupted by the union'. The fact was that although he was still a Tory 'theoretically and historically', he was beginning 'to be a Radical practically'. To him personally 'the most natural and becoming state of things' was 'for the aristocratical power to be the upholder of the Church'; and yet he could not 'deny the plain fact that in most ages the latter has been based on a popular power'.[103] In the present crisis, it might well be best if the Church were 'loose from the tyranny of the State', but it would be unwise 'to say so in print'. The principle of 'reserve' was implicitly invoked by Newman to justify caution on this point: 'I cannot help fearing that very plain speaking would be just now throwing pearls to swine. They must be roused a little, and then they will bear it.' Moreover, it was 'so very fearful a responsibility to remove our Candlestick from its present place, from which it gives light to the whole country', that he hoped 'the foes of the Church may have the burden of it instead of us'. Their main objective must be simply to preserve 'a pure doctrine to posterity' and 'to raise our witness in our generation as the Non-Jurors did'.[104]

On a personal note, Newman felt that his ordeal in Sicily, when he had 'certainly *roughed* it', was 'not a bad seasoning for the life of a pilgrim at home, if times become bad'. However, although all his hair had come out on his return home (which had meant having to wear a wig), he was

---

[102] Ibid. 26–7.   [103] Ibid. 33–6.   [104] Ibid. 40–1.

not only 'quite recovered' (except for weakness in his joints), but he was 'better now' than he had ever been all the seventeen years he had been in Oxford.[105]

The *Tracts for the Times* began to appear in September. They were Newman's idea, and he wrote the first one himself; it was on the doctrine of the Apostolic succession. Palmer wanted the Society's committee to authorize the Tracts, but Newman was strongly against 'putting forth Tracts *as a Society*', as that would mean 'entangling us in a timid cautious course'.[106] If 'a board' supervised their publication, 'you will have nothing but tame dull compositions, which will take no one'.[107] Palmer, who had links with 'the Establishment' and was the natural 'organ and representative' of 'the high-and-dry school', whose '*beau idéal* in ecclesiastical action was a board of safe, sound, sensible men', wanted 'a Committee, an Association, with rules and meetings'.[108] Newman, however, had never intended the original 'society' that had been formed at Oxford to be anything more than 'a mere name, which may give us a pretext for agitating'.[109] Now he told Palmer categorically that he was opposed to the idea of a formal, organized association, arguing that it would be inconsistent for them to form one without episcopal sanction, and that it was 'a dangerous thing to set up a large system at once', because it was likely to lead to 'ridicule and then disappointment', and also because 'a profession of something great excites jealousy and suspicion', whereas no one could 'complain of *individual* exertion'. But his real objection was that this was not the way to ensure the success of their cause. An association would involve compromise—but 'We feel our opinions are *true*; we are sure that, few tho' we be, we shall be able to propagate them by the force of the truth; we have no need, rather we cannot afford, to dilute them; which must be the consequence of joining those who do not go so far as we do.' He added that the problem with such societies was that 'the real movers are secret and irresponsible—and thus second rate men with low views get the upper hand.' 'Individuals', he declared, 'who are seen and heard, who act and suffer, are the instruments of Providence in all great successes.' Tracts issuing from a formal association would have to be 'weighed and carefully corrected', and they would 'become cold and formal and *im*personal'. A personal communication, on the other hand, might be more open to criticism, but at least 'coming from an individual mind, has a life about it, which is sure to make an impression'. Anyway, it would be difficult to set up an association without 'a very definite object', whereas at the moment their objections were 'very vague' because they were 'on the defensive', and not 'knowing *where* and *how* we shall be attacked'.

---

[105] *LD* iv. 43–5.   [106] Ibid. 52.   [107] Ibid. 55.
[108] *Apo.* 47.   [109] *LD* iv. 51.

Instead, Newman advocated individual personal contacts, including the circulation of tracts to friends up and down the country who could 'alter' them if they wanted, 'reprint them, and circulate them in turn'; this would in fact lead to 'certain centres' being formed, which would be in touch with each other and help spread the word. He was, however, in favour of the formal Address to the Archbishop, which Rose recommended; indeed, their various contacts through the country could start getting signatures, and this effort in itself would 'lay the rudiments of a number of Associations', which could in time develop into a formal Association with a bishop at its head—'whereas if we set up an Association at once, we commit ourselves'. He ended his letter by emphasizing again, 'I am for no committees, secretaries etc—but merely for certain individuals in every part of the country in correspondence with each other, instructing and encouraging each other, and acting with all their might on their respective circles.'[110] The principle that 'Living movements do not come of committees, nor are great ideas worked out through the post, even though it had been the penny post', was one which 'deeply penetrated' both Froude and him 'from the first'. When he was abroad, particularly when he was by himself, he tells us in the *Apologia*, 'the thought' came upon him that 'deliverance is wrought, not by the many but by the few, not by bodies but by persons'.[111] It was a heroic and romantic attitude that was alien to sober clergymen like Palmer and Rose. But the idea of the formal association was dropped, and Palmer turned his attention to trying to organize the Address.

Newman was now 'busy from morning till night' writing, printing, and distributing tracts.[112] He no longer had the help of Froude, who had left Oxford for Devonshire on his way to Barbados for the sake of his health. In addition to writing to clergy around the country, he began making personal visits. It did not matter whether they were high or low church, as his object was to rally opposition to 'the principles of liberalism'. He did not think later that 'much came of such attempts, nor were they quite in my way'. Towards the end of October he began a series of lengthy letters to the *Record* newspaper on the revival of church discipline. 'Acts', he later commented, of such an 'officious character' were uncharacteristic both of his own temperament and of the spirit and success of the Movement; but 'they were the fruit of that exuberant and joyous energy with which I had returned from abroad, and which I never had before or since'. His joy at being well again and home, and his delight at being at last in the thick of the battle about which he had dreamed for so long, gave him such an extraordinary vitality that friends in Oxford found it difficult to recognize the man they had known. He had 'a supreme confidence' in a 'momentous and inspiring' cause: 'we were upholding that primitive Christianity which was delivered for all time by the early teachers of the Church, and which was registered and attested in the Anglican formularies and by the Anglican divines.' What they were engaged in was 'a second Reformation' to restore that 'ancient religion' which 'had well nigh faded away out of the land'. There was no time to be lost: an image from his sea voyage summed up his feelings: 'I felt as on board a vessel, which first gets under weigh, and then the deck is cleared out, and luggage and live stock stowed away into their proper receptacles.' So confident was he about the 'Apostolical' position and so contemptuous of the Evangelical and high-and-dry alternatives to liberalism that his 'behaviour', he later recognized, 'had a mixture in it both of fierceness and of sport'. Afterwards he felt that 'perhaps those first vehement feelings which carried me on, were necessary for the beginning of the Movement.'[113]

He had not altogether, however, thrown caution to the winds, and sometime that autumn he drew up some instructions for friends on which 'to conduct their agitation', in which he warned against 'any intemperance of language' and advised caution where 'men are afraid of Apostolical ground'. But privately he exulted: 'We are in motion from the Isle of Wight to Durham and from Cornwall to Kent. Surely the Church will shortly be delivered from its captivity under wicked men, who are worse than Chushanrishathaim or the Philistines.'[114] In fact, his own vehemence of language, which arose from his 'absolute confidence' in their cause, was attracting attention. A passage in the *Arians*, for example, which was published at the beginning of November, led to the accusation that he wanted to bring back the Inquisition. It was, he admits humorously in the *Apologia*, 'a very fierce passage'—but 'it is only fair to myself to say that neither at this, nor any other time of my life, not even when I was fiercest, could I have even cut off a Puritan's ears, and I think the sight of a Spanish *auto-da-fé* would have been the death of me'. At the time, certainly, he was not only intense and vehement, but enjoyed himself at the expense of uncomprehending critics of the *Tracts*. He was 'amused' to hear that one of the bishops could not make up his mind whether or not he believed in the Apostolic Succession. He enjoyed teasing his bewildered opponents, and he 'used irony in conversation' which baffled 'matter-of-fact-men'.[115]

In the middle of November, Newman wrote to tell Froude that Palmer was pressing for the *Tracts* to be stopped. He wanted 'advice and encouragement'—he was afraid of being 'self willed'. He was well aware the *Tracts* were giving 'offence' and that '$\frac{1}{2}$ of all Oxford' were shaking

---

[113] *Apo.* 49–51, 44.   [114] *LD* iv. 79.   [115] *Apo.* 51–3.

'their heads'.[116] He told Keble that he had 'heard almost all of them abused, and again praised, by different readers'—he thought himself they were at present too 'vague and general, and too much in the way of hints'.[117] He now heard, too, through a third party, that Thomas Arnold was upset because he had heard that Newman had questioned in Rome whether he was a Christian. Newman responded that while he could not remember the words attributed to him, it was true that 'as far as' he understood Dr Arnold's 'ecclesiastical principles', he judged them to be 'unscriptural, unchristian, and open to ecclesiastical censure'. He was able, however, to assure the headmaster of Rugby that even where 'the essential Christian character' was lacking, 'there may yet be piety of an irregular and uncertain kind, which of course has its praise'.[118] As he was later to remark, he could certainly be 'very brusque and fierce' at this time—but then, 'Can one begin a movement in cold blood?'[119] Arnold's plan for Church reform had clearly revealed Newman's gift for satire; his complaint now elicited the first of the many superb snubs Newman was to administer in his long career as a controversialist.

To accompany the *Tracts*, Newman and his collaborators began publishing 'Records of the Church' or 'little stories of the Apostles, Fathers etc., to familiarize the imagination of the reader to an *Apostolical state* of the Church'. The 'Lyra Apostolica' had also been 'undertaken with a view of catching people when unguarded'.[120] In answer to a complaint from Samuel Rickards about the *Tracts*, Newman replied firmly that their authors were 'as men climbing a rock, who tear clothes and flesh, and slip now and then, and yet make progress . . . and are careless that bystanders criticize, so that their cause gains while they lose'. They were 'connected with no Association, answerable to no one except God and His Church, committing no one, bearing the blame, doing the work'. He did not mind if people said he went 'too far', provided he was able to 'push on the cause of truth some little way'. It was quite true that 'energy is ever incautious and exaggerated', but then 'it is energy' which 'gives edge to any undertaking'. It did not matter if people thought he was 'extreme' in his views, if only he could get them to advance 'a little way' in theirs. It was painful to be attacked by friends, but he did not mind now if 'the greater part of Oxford' was against him.[121] He also wrote to tell Rose that he was 'in all sorts of scrapes' over the *Tracts*—'abused in every quarter . . . and I doubt not with considerable reason'. But still no 'one person', he pointed out, 'can hit off the exact truth, much less exact propriety—yet individual exertions have a force about them, which perishes in the hands of a Committee—

---

[116] *LD* iv. 100–1. [117] Ibid. 113. [118] Ibid. 106.
[119] Ibid. 139. [120] Ibid. 109. [121] Ibid. 116–18.

so I must be forced to suffer criticism, in order to tend towards effecting certain ends—and take blows and wounds as in a battle.' He invited Rose to make what use of them he wanted and '*with whatever corrections you like*'. Above all, the writers of the *Tracts* wanted 'to avoid the pretence of authorship'. Newman himself was not the sole writer, but he was 'the chief' and also the editor. Like Froude, he told Rose, he was disappointed at the 'milk and water' Address that Palmer had drawn up—'however it effects three points—it teaches the Clergy to reflect and combine—it strengthens the Archbishop against his opponents;—and it brings out the Church as a body and power distinct from the State.' He had heard that some local associations were being started up, but he preferred the idea of having two or three 'energetic' men in each county, each of whom 'would be in correspondence with the rest elsewhere, and would be an organ of communication with his immediate neighbours'.[122]

In the middle of December Newman wrote to tell Froude the latest news. Everybody was signing the Address as a sign of support for the Archbishop, including some of those who had most vehemently opposed it originally. The *Record* had refused to publish his sixth letter, but had come out with an attack on the *Tracts*—'So these ganders have just managed to give us a most flaming advertisement.' Demand for the *Tracts* was growing, several had been reprinted, and new writers were coming forward, including one 'important' contributor 'who at present is nameless' (it was Pusey, who was now Regius Professor of Hebrew as well as a Canon of Christ Church). The 'furious' attacks on them were most encouraging—'men do not cry out till they are frightened.' He was, however, happy to tell Froude that he had managed to get 'thro' the Term without any kind of rumpus with the Provost', although he had just had 'a slight difference about shutting up Chapel' (he and Froude tried to keep the college chapel open during vacations 'on the ground that it was not a mere place for a roll call of undergraduates, but of worship for the Fellows').[123]

John Turrill, the London agent for the *Tracts*, who was also one of the publishers of the *British Magazine*, wanted to form the *Tracts* 'into a periodical', but Newman was 'against anything like a Tract Magazine': it was 'highly desirable each tract should be *separate*; we do not want regular troops, but sharpshooters'. On the other hand, 'to make the *issue* periodically, e.g. monthly, might be a good thing, as leading persons to look for them'. But he was anxious, he told Rose, not to interfere with the *British Magazine*, 'the first publication' to 'set up' the Church's 'Standard when others shrunk from doing so'.[124] He wished Rose was in

[122] *LD* iv. 120–1.   [123] Ibid. 141–2.   [124] Ibid. 143.

Oxford to adjudicate between himself and Palmer. Never had he appreciated so clearly the need for episcopal authority; if only the bishops would take the lead, then he would be delighted to be left in peace to pursue his own research and study. He had been ready to stop the *Tracts* at Palmer's insistence, and had only continued them because Rose had wanted him to and because not only Keble and Froude but many others very much preferred them to a formal association. They had also received 'powerful support' from Pusey and others. They might 'burst like bubbles', but he was convinced now they must 'go on' either 'to an end or to a development of truths which the world just now has forgotten'. He had made every effort to dissociate the *Tracts* from the Address; the draft he had sketched out for this had been 'milk and water', he had been so 'bullied' by Palmer, who had then 'diluted it still more'.[125] The Address, which received about 7,000 signatures, was eventually presented to the Archbishop on 6 February 1834. It was very bland and quite unlike Newman's original draft. Still, it was something to have actually addressed the Archbishop at all, and to have collected so many signatures.

The *Arians* had been reviewed very favourably in the January 1834 number of the *British Magazine*, but reservations were expressed about the treatment of the *Disciplina Arcani*, or 'the reserve of the Primitive Church in inculcating the more sacred doctrines of our faith'. Newman had never intended to imply that the *Disciplina* was a 'rule' rather than 'a feeling and a principle' in the early Church. It was not until the fourth century that 'the rule of secrecy was professed' as a systematic norm. Already he had grasped the essential idea of development: 'This is the case with the greater part of the theological and ecclesiastical system, which is implicitly contained in the writings and acts of the Apostles, but was developed at various times according to circumstances.' The fact that there was a '*rule* of secrecy' in the 4th century was 'evidence of the existence of the *principle* in the first'. At any rate, he was clear that the principle, which consisted 'rather in not insisting on, than concealing the truth', was part of the ethos of (Catholic) Christianity.[126]

Back in August 1833, he had mentioned to Froude 'a most audacious scheme in my mind about myself, which will not bear to be put on paper—the ink would turn red'.[127] The chair of moral philosophy was to fall vacant next year, and Newman thought that the election of the right man could help their cause. He later joked to Froude that he could not think of any one so well qualified as himself—'But if you think that you would do as well yourself. . . You shall be the man.'[128] The election was to be in the spring, and Newman thought he had 'a chance', but he had

[125] Ibid. 157–8.   [126] Ibid. 179–80.   [127] Ibid. 32.   [128] Ibid. 40.

'no especial wish' for the appointment. It would involve him in studies 'somewhat out of my present course'. On the other hand, 'it might be the means of giving me influence with the Undergraduates; and there is no situation which combines respectability with lightness of responsibility and labour so happily as the office of a Professor'.[129] As the day of the election approached, he thought he had 'a fair chance', if only because nobody else seemed to be standing. But he could not summon much enthusiasm for what was 'a sinecure of trouble'; he felt he had 'quite enough to do without mastering Hobbes and Epictetus'.[130] In the event, the electors did not choose him, but early in March elected R. D. Hampden, who had been appointed by Hawkins in 1832 to one of the vacant tutorial posts at Oriel.

5

March 1834 saw the publication of the first volume of Newman's *Parochial Sermons*. Just over a third of the pastoral sermons he wrote as an Anglican[131] were eventually published; and there is no doubt that they constitute one of the great classics of Christian spirituality. It is certainly almost as hard to conceive of the Oxford Movement without the *Parochial and Plain Sermons* as without the *Tracts for the Times*. However, far from the sermons being 'full of red-hot Tractarianism', they were deliberately 'humdrum' and 'plain', and being 'the same in Vacation as Term Time', were intended for his parishioners (unlike his lectures in church) rather than for members of the university—not that he was 'sorry' the latter came, but he 'would do any thing' he 'could to keep them from being excited'.[132]

At any rate, Newman's preaching in St Mary's became legendary and many descriptions were written of it, the most famous being Matthew Arnold's retrospective romantic evocation of 'the charm of that spiritual apparition, gliding in the dim afternoon light through the aisles of St. Mary's, rising into the pulpit, and then, in the most entrancing of voices, breaking the silence with words and thoughts which were a religious music,—subtle, sweet, mournful'. The characteristic most often noted was the 'sweetness' of the 'musical' voice, low and soft but also 'piercing' and 'thrilling'. This contrasted modulation was

---

[129] *LD* iv. 183.   [130] Ibid. 188.

[131] Back in Oct. 1831 he had 'devised the mode of writing Sermons which is my published mode' (*LD* ii. 366). Nearly all his earlier sermons were written in the Evangelical Charles 'Simeon's style, divisions 1, 2, 3, into different heads' (Moz. i. 249 n. 1). As for extempore preaching, he 'had from time to time diverse thoughts about turning evangelical so far—only I am afraid' (*LD* iii. 100).

[132] *LD* vi. 275; *Apo.* 411.

the most noticeable feature of a pulpit performance which on the one hand was the antithesis of normal oratory, but on the other hand had a mysterious power of its own. The only obvious oratorical device Newman used was the long pause, but even that appeared to be not for effect but the result of sheer intensity of thought. What was also so striking about the more eloquent passages was precisely that they gave the appearance of being the involuntary outbursts of a preacher unable to contain himself any longer, but whose sole conscious purpose was to convey the most practical and real of messages in as plain and simple a language as possible. The sermons were read, with hardly any change in the inflexion of the voice and without any gesture on the part of the preacher, whose eyes remained fixed on the text in front of him.[133]

The paradox of the power of Newman's style of preaching is reflected in the content of the sermons. Perhaps the most striking contrast concerns his treatment of the Holy Spirit. On the one hand, the doctrine of the 'indwelling' of the Holy Spirit, which was the most fundamental theological rediscovery that Newman had made from his study of Scripture and the Fathers,[134] is to be found prominently in the sermons. On the other hand, the sermons in a certain sense deliberately downgrade the role of the Spirit in the Christian life.[135] In answer to the inevitable criticism that came when the first volume was published, Newman distinguished the 'Spirit of Regeneration', which is the 'peculiar privilege' of Christians and which 'is the indwelling of the Holy Spirit in the soul as in a Temple—the spirit of adoption', from the 'sanctifying Spirit', which 'was given previously to Christianity', although 'more fully under it'. He explained the famous difference of emphasis on faith and works in St Paul and St James by arguing that the latter 'dwells more on sanctification' and the former 'on the regenerated state'. The reason why Newman preached in the way that he did was because he believed the Holy Spirit normally worked through ordinary human channels, such as conscience, reason, and feelings, and 'does not come immediately to change us'. It was in this sense that Newman could go so far as to say that 'salvation depends on ourselves'. And so in his preaching he had been 'led' to 'enlarge on our part of the work not on the Spirit's', convinced that what needed emphasis was '*the Law* not the Gospel in this age—we want rousing—we want the claims of duty and the details of obedience set before us strongly.' It was quite true that

[133] See R. D. Middleton, 'The Vicar of St. Mary's', in *John Henry Newman: Centenary Essays* (London, 1945), 127–38; David J. DeLaura, ' "O Unforgotten Voice": The Memory of Newman in the Nineteenth Century', in *Sources for Reinterpretation: The Use of Nineteenth-century Literary Documents. Essays in Honor of C. L. Cline* (Austin, 1975), 23–55.

[134] See Charles Stephen Dessain, *John Henry Newman* (London, 1966), 19–21.

[135] See C. S. Dessain, 'The Biblical Basis of Newman's Ecumenical Theology', in John Coulson and A. M. Allchin, eds., *The Rediscovery of Newman: An Oxford Symposium* (London, 1967), 101–2.

Christian works had to be done 'through the Spirit', but that did not alter the fact that they had to be done by ordinary human means. This was something 'this age forgets', which was why it was 'necessary to bring out the fact in all its details before the world'. Evangelicalism had led people to assume 'that a saving state is one, where the mind merely looks to Christ', with the result that actual moral behaviour could seem virtually irrelevant. The trouble with the 'Peculiars' or Evangelicals was that there was 'nothing definite or tangible' in their sermons, but they were always having to 'lug in' doctrines like the Holy Spirit and could 'never say a thing in a natural way'. Moreover, a sermon 'to be effective must be imperfect', because it ought 'to bring out' only 'one point'.[136]

Insistence on the indwelling of the Holy Spirit is, as we shall see, the key to Newman's solution to the classic problem of 'justification'. It is also at the heart of the new Tractarian emphasis on 'mystery' as opposed to the 'enthusiasm' of Evangelicals and the 'coldness' and 'dryness' of the liberal and high-and-dry Anglicans: 'Till we understand that the gifts of grace are unseen, supernatural, and mysterious, we have but a choice between explaining away the high and glowing expressions of Scripture, or giving them that rash, irreverent, and self-exalting interpretation, which is one of the chief errors of this time.' The alternative to the assumption that 'the gift of the Holy Ghost was almost peculiar to the Apostles' day, that now, at least, it does nothing more than make us decent and orderly members of society', did not have to be 'a sort of religious ecstasy . . . a high-wrought sensibility on sacred subjects . . . impassioned thoughts, a soft and languid tone of feeling, and an unnatural profession of all this in conversation'.[137] In order to describe the invisible presence of the Holy Spirit, Newman resorts to analogy— 'He pervades us . . . as light pervades a building, or as a sweet perfume the folds of some honourable robe; so that, in Scripture language, we are said to be in Him, and He in us.' The presence of the Spirit necessarily involves the presence of the other two Persons of the Trinity, and Newman is emphatic that invisible as this 'indwelling' is, there is nothing unreal about it—'we are assured of some real though mystical fellowship with the Father, Son, and Holy Spirit . . . so that . . . by a real presence in the soul . . . God is one with every believer, as in a consecrated Temple.'[138] But the life of a Christian is visible enough, and he 'who obeys God conscientiously, and lives holily, forces all about him to believe and tremble before the unseen power of Christ'.[139]

The sermons stress the mystery of Christianity, but, by contrast, there is nothing remotely mysterious about the demands which they prescribe as incumbent on the believer. The goal the preacher sets before his

---

[136] *LD* v. 14–16, 22, 38.   [137] *PS* iii. 267–8.
[138] Ibid. ii. 222, 35.   [139] Ibid. i. 292–3.

hearers is disturbingly simple ('Be you content with nothing short of perfection'), although one might think it was more idealistic than practical:

We dwell in the full light of the Gospel, and the full grace of the Sacraments. We ought to have the holiness of Apostles. There is no reason except our own wilful corruption, that we are not by this time walking in the steps of St. Paul or St. John, and following them as they followed Christ.[140]

But the ideal is trenchantly translated into a ruthlessly realistic spirituality, in which there is no room for merely uplifting platitudes and pious aspirations. This does not mean, however, that the ideal is not depicted with the eloquence of a great rhetorician:

Let us not be content with ourselves; let us not make our own hearts our home, or this world our home, or our friends our home; let us look out for a better country, that is, a heavenly . . .

Blessed are they who give the flower of their days, and their strength of soul and body to Him; blessed are they who in their youth turn to Him who gave His life for them, and would fain give it to them and implant it in them, that they may live for ever. Blessed are they who resolve—come good, come evil, come sunshine, come tempest, come honour, come dishonour—that He shall be their Lord and Master, their King and God! They will come to a perfect end, and to peace at the last.[141]

The paradox is that the ideal of holiness is as elevated and lofty as the means to attaining it are humble and mundane. For Newman, real spirituality is characterized by its utter unpretentiousness. He preached that 'the self-denial which is pleasing to Christ consists in little things . . . in the continual practice of small duties which are distasteful to us'. He warned his congregation not to be 'content with a warmth of faith carrying you over many obstacles', but to practise 'daily self-denial' in 'those little things in which obedience *is* a self-denial'.[142] There is the typically realistic reminder that

Nothing is more difficult than to be disciplined and regular in our religion. It is very easy to be religious by fits and starts, and to keep up our feelings by artificial stimulants; but regularity seems to trammel us, and we become impatient.[143]

Real holiness is attained by concrete acts of no particular significance in themselves, for we should remember 'how mysteriously little things are in this world connected with great; how single moments, improved or wasted, are the salvation or ruin of all-important interests'.[144] The hallmark of the truly spiritual person is that he or she 'is *consistent*' in a

---

[140] Ibid. i. 13, 82.   [141] Ibid. viii. 242–3.   [142] Ibid. i. 67, 69.
[143] Ibid. 252.   [144] Ibid. ii. 114.

'jealous carefulness about all things, little and great'.[145] One day as a Catholic he would say, 'I have ever made consistency the mark of a Saint', the greatest mortification being 'to do well the ordinary duties of the day'.[146] As an Anglican, he preached that real self-denial lies not in 'literally bearing Christ's Cross, and living on locusts and wild honey, but in such light abstinences as come in our way'.[147] In his spirituality, as in other things, there was not discontinuity but development after 1845; as the Superior of the Birmingham Oratory, he would one day warn his community:

Unless you prune off the luxuriances of plants, they grow bare, thin, and shabby at the roots. The higher your building is the broader must be its base—So it is with sanctity—Acts, words, devotions, which are suitable in saints, are absurd in other men.

The imagery may have become richer and subtler, but the teaching has not changed:

. . . if we would aim at perfection, we must perform well the duties of the day. I do not know any thing more difficult, more sobering, so strengthening than the constant aim to go through the ordinary day's work well.

And arguing that, 'if we wish to be perfect, we have nothing more to do than to perform the ordinary duties of the day well', Newman draws out the logic of his realism to its humorous conclusion, 'Go to bed in good time, and you are already perfect.'[148]

Far from assuming that Christians want to be holy, the sermons start from the eminently realistic assumption that the reason why people sin is that they want to. It is not just that it is unrealistic to expect sudden transformations, and that if there is to be change there has to be the will to change, but this willingness is itself something that only gradually develops: 'Is not holiness the result of many patient, repeated efforts after obedience, gradually working on us, and first modifying and then changing our hearts?'[149] Prayer itself has to be realistic: it is quite unreal to pray to be good when one does not in fact particularly want to be good, and when it is in fact this desire to be good for which one should be praying. A shrewdly practical psychology informs a highly idealistic spirituality. Thus, for example, voluntary acts of self-denial are recommended as a means to acquiring self-control in order to guard against unexpected temptations like anger, which 'are irresistible perhaps when they come upon you, but it is only at times that you are provoked, and then you are off your guard; so that the occasion is over, and you have failed, before you were well aware of its coming'.[150] False

---

[145] *PS* ii. 159.   [146] *LD* xi. 191; xiv. 153.   [147] *PS* iii. 211.
[148] *NO* 235, 359–60.   [149] *PS* i. 11.   [150] Ibid. 69.

illusions about self are mercilessly exposed. A man's real 'trial', for instance, lies in his 'weak point', and 'not in those things which are easy to him, but in that one thing, in those several things, whatever they are, in which to do his duty is against his nature'.[151] 'Any *one* deliberate habit of sin', Newman warns severely, 'incapacitates a man for receiving the gifts of the Gospel.'[152] A total commitment to Christ, he remarks, is 'rare', for most Christians retain 'a reserve' in their obedience, a 'corner' in their heart which they intend not to give up, if only because they feel they would not '*be*' themselves any longer, if they did 'not keep some portion' of what they 'have been hitherto', with the result that they take up only 'a pretence of religion instead of the substance'. People may 'profess in general terms to wish to be changed', but 'when it comes to the point, when particular instances of change are presented to us, we shrink from them, and are content to remain unchanged.'[153]

Newman may have abandoned Evangelicalism, but there can be little doubt that he had learned much from the kind of rigorous self-analysis to which the Evangelical habit of self-examination led and which was encouraged so strenuously by such standard spiritual books as William Wilberforce's *Practical View* and Hannah More's *Practical Piety*. In so far as this kind of introspection replaced a Christocentric spirituality, Newman rejected it, but it was certainly as important for the psychological penetration of his own sermons, as it was significant for the creative achievement of another former Evangelical, George Eliot, whose probing of intention and motive, and especially of self-delusion, was to raise the delineation of character in the novel to an altogether new level. Here, then, we find another apparent contradiction or paradox.

On the one hand, the sermons strongly advocate self-examination. We are told that without self-knowledge, it is impossible to understand Christianity properly, so that those who profess to believe but 'who neglect the duty of habitual self-examination are using words without meaning'.

For it is in proportion as we search our hearts and understand our own nature, that we understand what is meant by an Infinite Governor and Judge; in proportion as we comprehend the nature of disobedience and our actual sinfulness, that we feel what is the blessing of the removal of sin, redemption, pardon, sanctification, which otherwise are mere words.

This is 'real' belief as opposed to 'a mere assent, however sincere'.[154] Self-deception is seen as one of the great enemies of the Christian life: 'the more guilty we are, the less we know it; for the oftener we sin, the less

---

[151] *PS* i. 68.
[152] Ibid. 95.
[153] Ibid. iii. 238; iv. 5; v. 241, 244–5.
[154] Ibid. i. 41–3.

we are distressed at it.'[155] But there are much more subtle forms of self-deception which pervert what is otherwise right and true. For example, we may appreciate that 'Knowledge is nothing compared with doing; but the *knowing* that knowledge is nothing, we make to be *something*, we make it count, and thus we cheat ourselves'. Again, we may be 'proud' of our 'so-called humility': 'Many a man instead of *learning* humility in practice, confesses himself a poor sinner, and next *prides* himself upon the confession.' Or we may make confession of our faults 'a *substitute* for real repentance', which enables us 'to *put off* repentance'. The preacher's avowed aim is to lead his hearers 'to some true notion of the depths and deceitfulness of the heart, which we do not really know'.[156]

On the other hand, Newman is very alive to the danger of intro-spection degenerating into introversion. He advises, 'No harm can follow from contemplating our sins, so that we keep Christ before us, and attempt to overcome them.' But at the same time he warns against a situation where someone 'imprisons himself in his own thoughts, and rests on the workings of his own mind . . . instead of putting self aside, and living upon Him who speaks in the Gospels'.[157] The well-known sermon, 'Self-Contemplation', provides a sharp critique of this aspect of Evangelicalism: 'Instead of looking off to Jesus, and thinking little of ourselves, it is at present thought necessary . . . to examine the heart with a view of ascertaining whether it is in a spiritual state or no.' The 'inherent mischief' of the Evangelical theory of faith, Newman explains, lies 'in its necessarily involving a continual self-contemplation and reference to self':

He who aims at attaining sound doctrine or right practice, more or less looks out of himself; whereas, in labouring after a certain frame of mind, there is an habitual reflex action of the mind upon itself . . . for, as if it were not enough for a man to look up simply to Christ for salvation, it is declared to be necessary that he should be able to recognise this in himself. . . .

It was a strange contradiction that a theology which insisted on the absolute impossibility of any kind of self-justification should result in a complacent, not to say arrogant, self-sufficiency:

He who has learned to give names to his thoughts and deeds, to appraise them as if for the market, to attach to each its due measure of commendation or usefulness, will soon involuntarily corrupt his motives by pride or selfishness. A sort of self-approbation will insinuate itself into his mind: so subtle as not at once to be recognised by himself . . .[158]

---

[155] *PS* i. 51.
[157] Ibid. ii. 161–2.
[156] Ibid. 27–8, 35, 172.
[158] Ibid. 171.

That very self-deception which Evangelical self-scrutiny was supposed to eradicate ironically turns out itself to be the fruit of too much self-contemplation.

There is yet another paradox worth noting. Newman had come to the conclusion that the classic Evangelical distinction between so-called 'nominal' and 'real' Christians was itself an unreal distinction, but a preoccupation with the 'real' and the 'unreal' nevertheless runs through the sermons. Most Christians, he preaches, do not 'realize' what it is they profess to believe, but content themselves with 'an unreal faith', substituting 'a mere outward and nominal profession' for 'real' belief. An 'indolent use of words without apprehending them' is the natural concomitant of a merely 'passive faith'. He insists that all religion 'must be *real*'. To profess a religious belief as true, and yet not be able to 'feel, think, speak, act as if it were true', is to believe 'in an unreal way'. The reason why people do not 'act upon the truths they utter' is 'because they do not *realize* what they are so ready to proclaim'; it is only when people 'realize a truth' that 'it becomes an influential principle within them'. The reason, conversely, why holy people have 'such a remarkable simplicity' and can 'speak about themselves . . . in so unaffected a tone' is precisely because 'they do not feel' their goodness 'in that vivid way which we call realizing'—'They do not open their hearts to the knowledge, so that it becomes fruitful.' This is why, if the holy person speaks of an injury done to him, 'it will be in the same sort of strange, unreal, and (as I may say) forced and unnatural way in which pretenders to religion speak of religious joy and spiritual comfort, for he is as little at home with anger and revenge as hypocrites are with thoughts of heaven'.[159]

In one of the most penetrating sermons he ever preached, 'Unreal Words', Newman pointed out that when we subscribe to religious beliefs, we have to use words, and 'Words have a meaning, whether we mean that meaning or not', so that 'To make professions is to play with edged tools, unless we attend to what we are saying.' The expression of religious feelings, too, may be unreal, since someone may '*not* really believe' the doctrines of Christianity 'absolutely, because such absolute belief is the work of long time, and therefore his profession of feeling outruns the real inward existence of feeling, or he becomes unreal'. Unreality also affects religious, like other, knowledge: people who 'do not understand the difference between one point and another', who 'have no means of judging, no standard to measure by', are in consequence 'inconsistent' and 'unreal'. The conclusion is that 'unreality . . . is a sin; it is the sin of every one of us, in proportion as our hearts

---

[159] Ibid. i. 17, 54, 81; ii. 29, 179; v. 31; vi. 95, 263–4, 266.

are cold, or our tongues excessive.'[160] For God 'meant us to be simple, and we are unreal', with the result that 'the whole structure of society is . . . artificial'.[161]

A real religion reveals itself above all in actions as opposed to feelings and words. In 'Unreal Words' he remarked that 'Literature is almost in its essence unreal; for it is the exhibition of thought disjoined from practice.'[162] The point is developed in one of the most interesting of the sermons, 'The Danger of Accomplishments', which argues that the danger of a literary education is that 'it separates feeling and acting'. Newman complains that the effect of reading novels, for example, is that '*We* have nothing *to do*; we read, are affected, softened or roused, and that is all; we cool again,—nothing comes of it.' But

God has made us feel in order that we may *go on to act* in consequence of feeling; if then we allow our feelings to be excited without acting upon them, we do mischief to the moral system within us, just as we might spoil a watch, or other piece of mechanism, by playing with the wheels of it. We weaken its springs, and they cease to act truly.[163]

'It is easy', he remarks in another sermon, for religious people 'to make professions, easy to say fine things in speech or in writing, easy to astonish men with truths which they do not know, and sentiments which rise above human nature'. But in order to prove that faith is real, 'Let not your words run on; force every one of them into action as it goes . . .'.[164] It is not 'by giving utterance to religious sentiments' that we 'become religious', but 'rather the reverse', by 'obeying God in practice'.[165] To do 'one deed of obedience for Christ's sake' is better than any amount of religious eloquence, feeling, and imagination.[166] People who talk of love in general terms come in for some of Newman's sharpest sarcasm:

Such men have certain benevolent *feelings* towards the world,—feelings and nothing more;—nothing more than unstable feelings, the mere offspring of an indulged imagination, which exist only when their minds are wrought upon, and are sure to fail them in the hour of need. This is not to love men, it is but to talk about love.—The real love of man *must* depend on practice, and therefore, must begin by exercising itself on our friends around us, otherwise it will have no existence.[167]

He condemns 'mere feeling' as 'a sort of luxury of the imagination', which has no place in this world, which is intended to be 'a world of practice and labour', a place for 'obedience' not 'excellent words'.[168] Speaking, indeed, is positively discouraged, in terms strongly reminis-

[160] *PS* v. 33, 39, 36, 43.   [161] Ibid. viii. 265.   [162] Ibid. v. 42.
[163] Ibid. ii. 371.   [164] Ibid. i. 70.   [165] Ibid. 233.
[166] Ibid. 270.   [167] Ibid. ii. 55.   [168] Ibid. 367.

cent of Carlyle: 'Let us avoid talking, of whatever kind'—for 'That a thing is true, is no reason that it should be said, but that it should be done'. We shall, for example, be more moved by the thought of the Cross by 'bearing' it than by 'glowing accounts of it'. The call to silence may be terse, but it is not lacking in eloquence.

Think of the Cross when you rise and when you lie down, when you go out and when you come in, when you eat and when you walk and when you converse, when you buy and when you sell, when you labour and when you rest, consecrating and sealing all your doings with this one mental action, the thought of the Crucified. Do not talk of it to others; be silent, like the penitent woman, who showed her love in deep subdued acts.[169]

The realism of the sermons can be quite disconcerting, even shocking. It is true that, as always with Newman, one must guard against selective quotation emphasizing only one side of a question, but there is no doubt that he is remarkably unencouraging and unsanguine about the progress of Christianity in the world. The revival of religion in the nineteenth century did not impress him very much. He owned to being 'suspicious of any religion that is a people's religion, or an age's religion'. The 'token' of 'true religion' was rather 'The light shining in darkness', and, 'though doubtless there are seasons when a sudden enthusiasm arises in favour of the Truth . . . yet such a popularity of the Truth is *but* sudden, comes at once and goes at once, has no regular growth, no abiding stay'. It is, unfortunately, 'error alone which grows and is received heartily on a large scale'. Even though truth 'has that power in it, that it forces men to profess it in words', still, 'when they go on to act, instead of obeying *it*, they substitute some idol in the place of it'. In the face of any manifestation of religion, 'a cautious mind will feel anxious lest some counterfeit be, in fact, honoured instead of it'.[170] The fact of the matter is that people's 'real quarrel with religion . . . is not that it is strict, or engrossing, or imperative, not that it goes too far, but that it *is* religion'. As for the Church, 'she attempts much, she expects and promises little'.[171] The idea of a faithful remnant runs through the Bible, and 'when Christ came, the bulk of His own people rejected Him'.[172] Since then, redemption '*has* come to all the world, but the world is not changed thereby as a whole', for people have to be 'changed *one by one*'.[173] Christians should have 'no vain imaginings about the world's real conversion'. Indeed, Jesus spoke of the 'Gospel being preached, not chiefly as a means of converting, but as a witness against the world'.[174] A realist would have to ask whether the world is not 'as unbelieving now as when Christ came', and whether Christians, 'except a small remnant',

[169] Ibid. v. 45, 338–9.   [170] Ibid. i. 61–2.   [171] Ibid. iv. 14, 153.
[172] Ibid. v. 256.   [173] Ibid. i. 84.   [174] Ibid. ii. 389, 199.

would not, like the Jews, reject Christ if he came again.[175] In spite of all the good influences of Christianity, it has to be admitted that 'the great multitude of men have to all appearance remained, in a spiritual point of view, no better than before': the sad fact is that 'Human nature remains what it was, though it has been baptized'. The 'real triumph of the Gospel' has been to raise up a comparatively few 'specimens of faith and holiness, which without it are unknown and impossible'—'It has laboured for the elect, and it has succeeded with them.'[176] Most Christians, on the other hand, 'would go on almost as they do, neither much better nor much worse, if they believed Christianity to be a fable', for, although they 'wish to be religious' and 'feel a sort of respect for religious men', they 'do not get so far as to have any sort of love for religion'.[177] For the ordinary person, 'true religion' has a monotonous 'sameness' and 'plainness', for 'it is a weariness to the natural man to serve God humbly and in obscurity'.[178]

It was perhaps ironic that the sermons should insist with such a deeply pessimistic realism on the Gospel's inherent lack of appeal for fallen man, when the very same sermons were intended above all else to be '*real*' and to have 'reality in them', precisely by bringing out the Gospel in all its concrete actuality.[179] For the preacher's aim was to present the person of Christ not in an 'unreal way—as a mere idea or vision', but as 'Scripture has set Him before us in His actual sojourn on earth, in His gestures, words, and deeds'. Instead of using 'vague statements about His love, His willingness to receive the sinner, His imparting repentance and spiritual aid, and the like', the sermons present 'Christ as manifested in the Gospels, the Christ who exists therein, external to our own imaginings ... really a living being'.[180] It was this powerfully imaginative realization which helped make Newman's 4 o'clock Sunday sermons in St Mary's the most potent spiritual force of the Oxford Movement, as well as ensuring for them a permanent place among the classics of spirituality.

[175] *PS* vi. 80.   [176] Ibid. iv. 154–7.   [177] Ibid. 301; vii. 180.
[178] Ibid. iii. 30; vii. 22.   [179] *LD* v. 327.   [180] *PS* iii. 130–1.

3
The *Via Media*

ON 17 March 1834 Newman wrote to the *British Magazine* to protest against a new bill to admit Dissenters to the universities, by removing the obligation to subscribe to the Thirty-nine Articles, which was compulsory at Oxford on matriculating and at Cambridge on taking a degree. He strongly objected to the suggestion that Oxford should at least accept the Cambridge compromise of allowing non-Anglicans to reside as students but not to graduate: 'Have we not had experience enough of late years, that concession does not ensure contentment? Let all, who are inclined to retreat, ask themselves whether they contemplate any position in their rear, at which they propose to make a stand: rather, are they merely putting off the evil day, and purchasing a brief cessation of agitation?' The mere presence of Dissenters in a collegiate university was objectionable anyway: assuming that the tutorial system had a pastoral dimension, would it not be necessary for 'dissenting pupils' to have 'dissenting tutors'? It was true they might be 'improved' by being educated by tutors the ethos of whose religion was 'founded on reverence' rather than 'boldness and self-will', but 'will not the church pupils, nay the tutors themselves, be injured?' The Dissenters, Newman remarked, would certainly 'be improved in the way of gentlemanly feeling, modesty, and refinement', even if they were not 'made better Christians', but there would be a great danger of Anglicans lapsing 'into a mongrel faith, from the contact of laxer principles'. The fact that there seemed to be 'much greater laxity' at Cambridge was not surprising: 'The very subscribing the thirty-nine articles, which is exacted by us on entrance, is a check upon the words of unruly spirits, even if their imagination rove.' How, he demanded indignantly, could a college tutor be expected to 'look smilingly, and speak familiarly with those who have been baptized by strangers, and perhaps hold some deadly heresy'? Again, undergraduates were required to attend college chapel—but would it not be 'a tyranny of conscience to oblige men to attend upon forms which they disown'? If, however, chapel was not compulsory for some, how long would it be practical 'to insist upon attendance in the case of church pupils, when their companions do not attend'?[1]

[1] *LD* iv. 208–11.

Newman was also busy at this time composing a petition to the House of Commons against a new bill on marriage, which would require the Church to sanction marriages in Dissenting chapels. The great thing, he felt, was to make a public protest. But he was still against pressing for any change in the Church's position, except that '*in proportion* as changes are effected, so is it fair to agitate for corresponding changes in our state'.[2] However, he could not deny that 'every symptom of dissolution' was 'a ground for hope', and although he would do everything in his power 'to resist every change and degradation' to which the Church was 'subjected', still there was

a system *behind* the existing one, a system indeed which will take time and suffering to bring us to adopt, but still a firm foundation. Those who live by the breath of state patronage, who think the clergy must be gentlemen, and the Church must rest on the great, not the multitude, of course are desponding. Woe to the profane hands who rob us of privilege or possession, but they can do us no harm. In the mean time, should (by any strange accident) the course of events fall back into its old channel, *I* will not be a disturber of the Church . . .[3]

The 'Oxford Declaration against the Admission of Dissenters', insisting that education must be based on religion, came out on 24 April. Further declarations and petitions followed. Newman was delighted by the almost unanimously hostile response to the proposed bill—'the spirit of Oxford men is *up*', he exulted. In a letter to a newspaper, he remarked sarcastically that 'Practical men, men of enlarged views, should understand' that 'such inconvenient principles of action' as 'stupid prejudice, blind passion, epidemic fanaticism' have 'no *fears*'.[4] Privately, he was afraid of people 'getting *used* to the notion of having Dissenters, and so falling to sleep'. It was 'necessary to agitate . . . in order to prevent the skin growing over the sore'. A veritable 'system' of petitioning was needed to sustain the protest. On the subject of agitation, he told his sister Jemima that he could honestly say there was nothing in the *Tracts* he regretted, even though he doubted if he would 'have the *courage*' to do it all over again, 'for attacks make one timid'.[5] He wrote humorously to Froude that it was 'a strange mishap' that 'when the time of danger came, you should get out of the way and leave innocent me to trouble'. It was remarkable how he had got into a row with Arnold over a brief comment passed in front of friends, when he had always spoken so 'mildly' of him and Froude so 'bitterly'. Again, his *Tracts* 'were abused as Popish . . . especially for expressions about the Eucharist'—whereas it was Froude not he who was 'apt to be unguarded' in this respect. At the moment he was 'triumphing at our enemies being blunderers enough to attack the *Universities*, which are the

    [2] *LD* iv. 207.   [3] Ibid. 227.   [4] Ibid. 244–5.   [5] Ibid. 251, 253.

most organized, the most popularly constituted of our ecclesiastical institutions, and most intelligible to the nation'.[6]

On Monday, 30 June Newman began daily morning prayer in St Mary's. The service was enjoined in the Prayer Book, but the 'melancholy' fact was that this and other rubrics were ignored.[7] He had already in April started an evening service every Wednesday, which was followed by a lecture. To begin with, there was a congregation of about a hundred, mostly from the university, although the number fell off. For a year he had been anxious to have a celebration of Holy Communion once a week, but so far he had not been able to do anything about it; he hoped to make a start with Saints' days.

On 1 July Newman refused to marry a Miss Jubber, who lived in the parish, because she had not been baptized. The affair got into the papers. Newman would have preferred to consult the Bishop of Oxford, but there was no time, as he only heard about the wedding an hour and a half before the time fixed for the ceremony. It was a disagreeable surprise for him, because he already knew the family, as he and his curate, Isaac Williams, had been encouraging Mrs Jubber to have her children baptized (her husband was a Baptist). The couple were duly married in the bridegroom's parish. When reporting to the bishop, Newman referred to the rubric which forbade the burial of unbaptized persons, and appealed to the example of the primitive Church. There was no specific rubric on the point, presumably because, while the Prayer Book had had to take into account the case of babies who died before baptism, it had taken for granted that people getting married would be already baptized. He added that he was ready to obey the bishop in this and any other matter. A few days later he heard from the Archdeacon of Oxford that the bishop would have preferred him to take the wedding as there was no law against marrying an unbaptized person. In a statement to a local newspaper, Newman denied that he had told Mr Jubber he would not marry his daughter because she was an 'outcast', but admitted that he had said that he 'considered the unbaptized to be outcast from Christian privileges and blessings'.[8]

He advised his former pupil Thomas Mozley not to follow his example: 'one resistance is enough for an experiment.' He had the city, the clergy, the bishop, and the law against him. 'Abused beyond measure', he wrote to Froude, 'by high and low—threatened with a pelting, and a prosecution—having anonymous letters—discountenanced by high Church and low Church. It should be you.' The case had even got into *The Times*. He had certainly not looked for the confrontation, but he had never before, so far as he knew, married an

---

[6] Ibid. 270–1, 278.   [7] Ibid. 289.   [8] Ibid. 299, 279.

unbaptized person, and he did not want to start a precedent now. The law of the land would soon, no doubt, be changed, but as it stood at present the only way to get married legally was in the Established Church, and it would have been 'a most awkward thing' if Miss Jubber had been unable to find a clergyman willing to marry her. He did not know, in the meantime, what he would do if the bishop ordered him to marry somebody unbaptized; he had 'an excessive repugnance, almost amounting to a superstition, to doing such an act', but unless he resigned his living he would have to obey, although 'under a strong protest that it was not my free act'.[9] At least he had struck a blow in defence of two principles, 'that baptism is of importance, and that the Church is above Law', even if there were a lot of 'black faces'. The Church was 'asleep', he groaned to Henry Wilberforce: 'O that we had one Bishop for us!'[10]

Keble and Pusey had supported him in his stand. But he fully expected to be generally condemned: 'There is such a fear of offending the Dissenters, such a wretched unchurch-like conservative spirit among our own party, that the best view taken of such conduct as mine will be that "it was singularly deficient in judgment".' He received a sympathetic letter from Arthur Perceval, a leading high-church clergyman, who, however, also supported Palmer and the high-church party in expressing reservations about the *Tracts for the Times*. Newman replied that different people were bound to object to different things in them—'If we altered to please everyone, the effect would be spoiled.' The *Tracts* were intended to be 'the expressions of *individual* minds', and individuals, while

incidentally faulty in mode or language, are still peculiarly *effective*. No great work was done by a system—whereas systems rise out of individual exertions. Luther was an individual. The very faults of an individual excite attention—he loses, but his cause (if good, and he powerful minded) gains—this is the way of things, we promote truth by a self sacrifice.[11]

As for himself personally, he refused to accept that he was 'violent' or guilty of 'stern orthodoxy': rather, he boasted that if he had 'one merit', it was his 'extreme moderation'.[12]

John Bowden had already warned Newman that 'one day' he and the *Tracts* would be 'charged with rank Popery', and had suggested that a *Tract* should be specifically written to refute the accusation.[13] Newman was more than ready to admit that they contained doctrine which was not 'Protestant'. But then he disowned the word in its usual sense—'It is an uncomfortable perplexing word, intended to connect us, and actually connecting us, with the Protestants abroad.' In fact, they were a

---

9 *LD* iv. 300–1.   10 Ibid. 312.   11 Ibid. 307–8.
12 Ibid. 232.   13 Ibid. 304.

'Reformed' not a 'Protestant' Church: 'I "protest" as much against Calvin as against the Council of Trent.' It was, however, unfortunately true that 'the Puritanic spirit spread in England in Elizabeth and James's time, and did sad havoc, tainting even good and wise men'. As far as he could 'make out, the great and holy men of every age have not much differed from each other—Hooker and Taylor from St Bernard, St Bernard from St Chrysostom'. As for the Church of Rome, she had 'apostatized at Trent'.[14]

Back in March, Newman had begun work on an edition of St Dionysius of Alexandria for the University Press. It opened 'a wide field of reading', and he felt that 'to *have edited* respectably such a work, gives me a solid influence', as well as being 'abundantly useful if it bring me acquainted with the history of the early Church'.[15] In August, he told Bowden that he had 'managed nearly to break the neck of it—so I shall almost lay it by, and take it up from time to time, or keep it quietly in hand'. He had 'thought it was good to take something easy as a beginning'. The reason why he had turned to editing was that he had 'great fears of being superficial': it was a great 'temptation' when writing a book like the *Arians* 'to take facts and Fathers at *second hand*'. He wanted some day to correct the *Arians*. He was also anxious to try and learn some German: not only were they likely to be 'inundated with German divinity', but there were books in his own 'line' which he would like to be able to read. However, he was hardly at leisure for such projects. He had just begun studying the history of the Convocation of the Church of England, a subject he had for 'a long while plagued my friends on every side to undertake'. It was clearly a 'very important' question in the present crisis.

He had also followed up Bowden's 'hint' and had written two *Tracts* on the *Via Media*.[16] In the first he declared, 'The glory of the English Church is, that it has taken the VIA MEDIA . . . It lies *between* the (so called) Reformers and the Romanists.' The Prayer Book, he argued, was the 'depository' of the teaching of the Apostles, while the Thirty-nine Articles were 'polemical, and except as they embody the creeds, are mainly protests against certain definite errors'. He confidently assured his readers that 'no party will be more opposed to our doctrine, if it ever prospers and makes noise, than the Roman party'.[17] The second of the *Tracts* shows how even at this point Newman took the principle of doctrinal development for granted: the additional 'articles of faith', which 'are necessary to secure the Church's purity, according to the rise of successive heresies and errors,' were 'all hidden, as it were, in the Church's bosom from the first, and brought out into form according to

[14] Ibid. 314–15.   [15] Ibid. 274–5.
[16] Ibid. 320–1.   [17] *VM* ii. 28, 33–4.

the occasion'. He professed himself able to accept the Thirty-nine Articles, but he could not understand how Evangelicals could acquiesce in the Prayer Book, where there was 'not a word said of looking to Christ, resting on Him, and renovation of heart'.[18]

On 20 August Newman wrote to Rose to say that he was writing something on Convocation which might be suitable for the *British Magazine*.

> My simple object will be to *inform people* of the actual historical posture of our Church. I am not for the meeting of Convocation myself, though I can fancy the Church being actually driven to it, as the least of evils. Therefore I should by no means *advocate* it in any thing I put on paper. As far as I see, the danger from the Convocation would arise from its being (in a few years) too much, or rather an entirely, a Government instrument.

(Later, he thought that reviving Convocation would inevitably mean 'countenancing the notion, and furthering the success of alterations in doctrine professedly deduced in Protestant fashion from Scripture'.) He also warned Rose that his successful rival for the philosophy chair, R. D. Hampden, had

> just published a pamphlet which, I fear, destroys our glory. Hitherto Oxford was all on one side, as far as print goes, in this late dispute with the Commons and Co. I fear he calls all articles impositions of human authority, and advocates their removal as a test on matriculations . . .[19]

At the beginning of September he sent Rose the articles on Convocation. He mentioned that he had no regrets about the Jubber case: 'how could I more forcibly attest to every Dissenter who heard it that my notion was not a theory but a practical principle? men will not believe one is in earnest—they do not feel words—deeds startle them.'[20]

2

Newman's mother and sisters had been living permanently at Iffley, just outside Oxford, since October 1830. They had left Brighton because his mother wanted to be near her eldest son. Charles had left home when his father died, and John had managed to get him a job as a clerk in the Bank of England through Bowden, whose father was a director; but after five years he left and moved on to various jobs, becoming more and more strange and eccentric. Francis, who had been strongly influenced by the founder of the Plymouth Brethren, now complained of the family life-style at Iffley. His elder brother, who was helping to support his mother

---

[18] *VM* ii. 40, 44.   [19] *LD* iv. 323; v. 129.   [20] Ibid. iv. 327.

and sisters, retorted that the only ground for the charge of worldliness was 'my Mother's having a servant in livery'. They kept as few servants as possible, and, he remarked pointedly in reference to Frank's abortive mission to Persia, 'perhaps your own experience abroad will show you that to dispense with servants altogether and keep one's own house in order oneself is not the way to improve one's talents or to do most good'. It was 'invidious' to speak of 'high' and 'low' rather than 'right hand and left hand ranks, all being on a level'; employing domestic staff was 'a mutual engagement, for the good of all', since servants 'do what they are fitted to do, and which I, from want of training, cannot do'. The money he gave their mother and sisters was either given away in charity or was used to enable them to do good works at Littlemore, where they were helping him in the parish. They would do far less for 'God's glory' if they simply gave away all the money they did not strictly need to live on. They enabled Newman 'to spend a large sum upon the poor which I could not spend satisfactorily myself'. At any rate, he added tartly, 'I suppose my money goes further, than yours in journeying to Persia'.[21]

In the third week of September he left Oxford to stay with various friends. Between visits he stopped off at Alton, where painful memories were stirred, as he wrote to his mother:

As I got near the place, I many times wished I have not come, I found it so very trying. So many strong feelings, distinct from each other, were awakened. The very length of time since I was here was a serious thought, almost half my life; and I so different from what a boy, as I then was, could be;—not indeed in my having any strong stimulus of worldly hope then, which I have not now—for, strange though it may seem, never even as a boy had I any vision of success, fortune, or worldly comfort to bound my prospect of the future, but because, after fifteen years, I felt after all that I was hardly the same person as to all external relations, and as regards the particular tempering and colouring of my mind.

And then the number of painful events, and pleasant too, which have gone between my past and my present self. And further, the particular season at which we lived here, when I was just entered at Oxford, so that this place is, as it were, the record, as it was the scene, of my Undergraduate studies and opinions. The Oxford reminiscences of that time have been effaced by my constant residence there since, but here I am thrown back upon those years, which never can come again.

Chief among the 'many little incidents' he now remembered was the evening he returned home from Oxford after winning the Trinity scholarship to a delighted welcome from his father. As he remembered all his father's kindness and as Alton came into sight, he 'felt quite sick at heart'.

[21] Ibid. 329–30.

There was something so mysterious too in seeing old sights, half recollecting them, and doubting. It is like seeing the ghosts of friends . . . it seemed to me so very strange, that every thing was in its place after so long a time . . . it was as fearful as if I was standing on the grave of some one I knew, and saw him gradually recover life and rise again. Quite a lifetime seems to divide me from the time I was here. I wished myself away from the pain of it. And then the excitement caused a re-action, and I got quite insensible and callous—and then again got disgusted with myself, and thought I had made a great fool of myself in coming here at all, and wondered what I should do with myself, now that I was here.[22]

His mother replied that she was very relieved he had happy memories of his father; she herself never wanted to see Alton again because of its painful associations.

After leaving Alton Newman visited several friends. One, who had been a fellow of Oriel and now had a living in Sussex, lived in a splendid house and grounds. 'I confess', Newman wrote to Jemima,

I could not (I think) live in so beautiful a place—I should destroy the conservatory, and turn the inner drawing room into a chapel. *Natural* beauties I feel no grudge of—but artificial, whether exotic plants, foreign gems and marbles, rare viands, statues and paintings, seem as out of place as to be waited on by slaves.[23]

On his way to Tunbridge Wells, he passed through London, where he caught sight of Queen Victoria for the first and last time.

At Tunbridge Wells he had dinner with the Dean of Chester, but was disgusted to find that the Dean 'has no *views*, and in consequence is like a ship without rudder'. He wrote to Jemima that he himself, on the contrary, had been reading various books about the Church of Rome and as a result had 'more of a view'. He felt very confident that he had 'got hold somehow or other of an imposing view, call it right or wrong'. The theory of the *Via Media* needed developing, but it seemed very persuasive and very plausible.

To *become* a Romanist seems more and more impossible; to *unite* with Rome (*if* she would let us) not impossible—but *she* could not, without ceasing to be Rome. Somehow my own confidence in my views seems to grow. I am aware I have not yet fully developed them to myself yet; there are opinions as yet unknown to me which must be brought out and received, inconsistencies too (perhaps) to be set right—but on the whole I seem to have a grasp of a system very comprehensive—I could go a great way with Rome, and a great way with the peculiars, nay I should not despair of religious dissenters. I think our system will be very *taking*, from its novelty, its sublimity, and its argumentative basis. I see persons struck and puzzled at it.[24]

---

[22] *LD* iv. 331–2.   [23] Ibid. 333.   [24] Ibid. 337.

After his return to Oxford in October, Newman sent a long letter to the *British Magazine* on 'the principle of *centralization*'. He began by noting that 'it seems to have been a characteristic of the British constitution hitherto . . . to view the principle with jealousy, as hostile in its tendency to the liberty of the subject', whereas 'it is a growing peculiarity of the present age . . . to purchase a respite from present actual evils by the introduction of it into various departments of the body politic to which it was before a stranger'. It was now becoming the 'fashion to merge the nation in the government'. In the past, private enterprise had led the way: 'Waterloo Bridge was built, not by the government, but by individuals . . . our received English dictionary is the work of an individual, the French dictionary proceeding from the Institute . . . our East India empire was acquired by a mercantile company.' Recent reforms, on the other hand, like the Metropolitan Police, were 'all evidence of the growing popularity of the centralizing system'. The modern system was obviously much more efficient, but it was 'a strange inconsistency' to advocate 'a principle almost of tyranny, in the management of hitherto private matters, at the very time we were exulting in the triumph of a great Reform measure, which was to supersede the necessity of a government, and to make the House of Commons, and so the people, their own rulers'. But the inconsistency was more apparent than real: 'the destruction of local influences which centralization involves, and the disorganization of the parliament, *as* the seat and instrument of the administration,' both tended to increase the power of 'the executive, as the main-spring of all national power, and virtually identical with the government'.

It was true that the 'system of the church' was essentially 'of a centralizing character', with the bishop as the ruler of the diocese, but 'the genius of the English nation, jealous of centralizations, has actually broken up this ecclesiastical system, though of Divine origin'; for the parochial organization of the Church of England and the abolition of celibacy 'have long made the clergy *members of the state*,—a civil order, slightly bound one to another, compared with the local ties which make each . . . the religious member or chaplain of the parochial family'. But this 'parochial unit' was now being 'broken up', and 'when the magistrate is a paid professional man, subject to a distant board,—when the village constable is superseded by a police officer from a central board,—when the poor, and the young, and the sacred fabric itself are withdrawn from the superintendence or care of the clergyman,— especially when schoolmasters and school-books are submitted to the government of some foreign authority,' then clearly the 'parish minister, being solitary in his own place, will have to sustain the full and combined attack of all these various formidable systems which have sprung up around him'. The inevitable result would be that 'since he virtually belongs to nobody, the state will kindly undertake the office of centralizing for him, and will attempt to organize the clergy . . . into one manageable body, and will form the bishops, or certain of them, into a commission, in a bureau of public instruction'. Political and social changes meant that 'churchmen' must 'centralize by way of self-preservation' and 'rally round our ecclesiastical centres'. In order for the bishops to 'know' their clergy, it would probably be necessary either to divide dioceses or to provide suffragan bishops. On the heads of the bishops 'a fearful responsibility' would fall, as the 'successors of the apostles'.[25]

Privately, he admitted to Rose that he was well aware the clergy had little sense of episcopal authority, but he thought 'the first step *towards* raising it is to preach it up; not to acknowledge there is any difficulty except in men's ignorance of, and unwillingness to embrace Church principles'. He was 'much against putting new wine into old bottles; but is it not the first step towards obtaining new bottles to vaunt of our new wine? the demand creates a supply.'[26]

At the beginning of September, Newman had heard from Benjamin Harrison, a don at Christ Church and a contributor to the *Tracts*, about a French priest, the abbé Jean-Nicolas Jager, whom Harrison had met in Paris and who wanted to hold a debate about the theology of the *Tracts* in the *Univers* newspaper. Harrison contributed two letters, and then in October asked Newman to take over, who agreed, thinking that it would be useful experience, particularly in 'the Romanist mode of arguing'.[27] In a private letter to Jager, which he did not send, Newman admitted that most English divines were theologically unarmed and that their 'ignorance' of doctrinal differences was 'in proportion to' their 'long security'. He had decided, however, that 'if the controversy between the Churches was to be renewed, there must be a beginning; and that on our side that beginning must be attended with some mistakes in detail in the mode of conducting the argument; that the Romans once had no model for a ship of war but a chance vessel of the enemy's flung upon the beach, yet at last they became lords of sea as well as land'. And so he considered that he 'ought not to decline the challenge, believing as I do that truth is on my side'.[28] His first letter in reply to Jager was completed and translated into French before Christmas; the first part of his second letter was sent off at the end of July 1835, but the controversy came to an end and the second part was never published. The exchange was important, as it helped Newman to formulate his view of the *Via Media*, that would receive its classic

[25] *LD* iv. 339–42.   [26] Ibid. 344.   [27] Ibid. 347.   [28] Ibid. 350.

statement in the *Prophetical Office*, in which 'great portions' of his correspondence with Jager were 'incorporated'.[29]

Earlier in the summer, the bill to admit Dissenters to the universities had been thrown out by the House of Lords. But in November Newman was again in 'great anxiety', as the Heads of the colleges 'are proposing to remove the subscription to the Articles, and substitute a Declaration on the part of the youth matriculated'. He, Pusey, and others were prepared only to add an explanation of 'the meaning of subscription, if (as the objection is) it is obscure'. His inability to see only one side of any question made him feel much the same about the secularization of the University as he did about the disestablishment of the Church. He was

sure no harm (please God) can happen to Apostolical principles. If the University is liberalized, those who hold them will only be so much more thrown out into relief, detached from all those secular connections and influences with which it is their duty now to keep united—Nothing would tend more to the spreading of the Truth among those who could 'receive it,' than for it to be thrown out and embodied in a party. But so fearful is the misery to the Church generally, and so shocking the thought that Oxford should be the place desecrated, that one would strain every nerve to prevent it.[30]

Perhaps, he speculated mischievously to Froude, 'the apostolicals' might found a college themselves 'and introduce all sorts of abominations of the monastic kind'. If Froude's health, he joked, would not let him 'come home', then he 'ought to be a Bishop in India—there you might be a Catholic and no one would know the difference'. In fact, he was increasingly aware that his friend was unlikely if ever to recover sufficiently to go to India or anywhere else, and his sense of his approaching death was not inconsistent with the hopeful assurance, 'It is quite impossible that in some way or other you are not destined to be an instrument of God's purposes.' He told Froude that his own first volume of sermons, of which a thousand copies had been printed, had nearly sold out in less than a year, which was 'considered very good', although it had been attacked, not surprisingly, by Evangelicals. Rivington the publisher had just agreed to publish a second volume.

In the end, the proposal to relax the religious test at matriculation was withdrawn when the strength of the opposition to it became clear. Newman noted grimly that the Provost of Oriel and the Principal of St Mary's Hall, R. D. Hampden, were among the 'chief movers in the business'.[31] On 28 November he wrote to Hampden: 'The kindness which has led to your presenting me with your late pamphlet,

---

[29] *VM* i. xi. The original English drafts of Newman's letters have been published in *John Henry Newman and the Abbé Jager: A Controversy on Scripture and Tradition (1834–1836)*, ed. Louis Allen (London, 1975).

[30] *LD* iv. 355.   [31] Ibid. 364.

encourages me to hope that you will forgive me if I take the opportunity it affords me of expressing to you my very sincere and deep regret that it has been published.' A second edition of the original offending pamphlet, *Observations on Religious Dissent*, had appeared, *with particular reference to the use of religious tests in the university*. Its author wondered provocatively whether there was 'foundation for the common prejudice, which identifies systems of doctrine—or theological propositions methodically deduced and stated—with the simple religion of Jesus Christ, as received into the heart and influencing conduct'. Newman commented sharply that such a view tended 'altogether to make shipwreck of Christian faith'. He added solemnly: 'I also lament that by its appearance the first step has been taken towards interrupting that peace and mutual good understanding which has prevailed so long in this place, and which if once seriously disturbed will be succeeded by dissentions the more intractable because justified in the minds of those who resist innovation by a feeling of imperative duty.' Later, he noted that his letter 'was the beginning of hostilities in the University'.[32]

3

In January 1835 Newman went to London to seek medical advice about a symptom of his illness in Sicily which had reappeared and which was potentially serious if it was not treated in time. While there he stayed with Bowden, now married to Elizabeth Swinburne, the poet's aunt, and working as a Commissioner of Stamps. From there he wrote to Froude complaining of his 'solitariness, now you are away'. He felt none of his other friends could 'enter' in the same way into his 'mind', and he seemed 'to write things to no purpose as wanting your imprimatur'.[33] He and Froude, however, continued to view the Roman Church rather differently. While Newman admitted, 'I admire the lofty character, the beauty, the sweetness and tenderness of its services and discipline,' he also was convinced that 'there is that in Romanism which makes it a duty to keep aloof from it, there is a mixture of corruption, which, when seen, it is a duty to protest against'. 'The more', he declared, 'I examine into the R. C. system, the less sound it appears to me to be.' For example, unlike Froude, he could not accept the doctrine of Transubstantiation, which he interpreted as meaning that Christ's body and blood were literally present on the altar 'as they were on Calvary'.[34] Froude, on the other hand, did not shrink from following out the implications of the Tractarian theology of the Real Presence. It was Protestantism that he

[32] *LD* iv. 371.   [33] Ibid. v. 9.   [34] Ibid. iv. 367–8.

protested against—'Really I hate the Reformation and the Reformers more and more.' He refused to 'abuse the Roman Catholics as a Church for any thing except excommunicating us. If they would give up this I think they are indefinitely the purest Church of the two.' He hoped Newman had not been 'unnecessarily abusive' in his controversy with the abbé Jager. At the risk of offending Keble, he had to acknowledge that holiness among Anglicans did not include the 'austere beauty' of the Catholic ethos.[35]

Newman's second volume of *Parochial Sermons* was now in the press. He was aware that his preaching was criticized as 'cold and uninfluential'. But unlike those of the Evangelicals, his sermons were deliberately 'not adapted to *influence*', since it was the 'divinely ordered system' of sacraments—unfortunately 'but poorly developed among us'—which was meant to be 'full of persuasion'. These and 'the life of good men' were 'the great persuasives of the Gospel, as being visible witnesses and substitutes for Him who is Persuasion itself'. Anyway, preaching was not the way to convert people but the way to prepare them for conversion. Evangelical preachers might 'melt' their hearers, but it was only 'a blaze among the stubble'. It was one thing to arouse feelings, another to impress and persuade. As for his own sermons, he was quite ready to admit that on the whole they induced 'fear' and 'depression': they were 'meant to do so', for 'We need a continual Ash-wednesday'. In fact, he was rather dubious about the value of sermons in general, feeling that 'real profit' is 'the exception not the rule'. Of necessity they had to be formal and impersonal rhetorical addresses, and it was enough if they were 'merely unmeaning and harmless'. Unfortunately, Evangelical sermons were 'hurtful' in 'their rudeness, irreverence, and almost profaneness . . . of making a most sacred doctrine' like the Atonement 'a subject of vehement declamation, or instrument of exciting the feelings, or topic for vague, general, reiterated statements in technical language'. It was 'inexpressibly' distressing to hear 'our Lord's name and work used as a sort of charm or spell to convert men by, not in the selfabasement of prayer and praise, but in the midst of rhetorical flourishes or at best in an unreal mechanical manner'. Even in the religious 'prison' of the previous century, Bishop Butler's 'wonderfully gifted intellect caught the idea which had actually been the rule of the Primitive Church, of teaching the more Sacred Truths ordinarily by rites and ceremonies', which 'persuade' by their 'tenderness and mysteriousness', while they are 'prepared for' by a 'severity of preaching' that should 'enlighten the mind as to its real state' and 'dig round about the Truth'. It was far more 'reverential' that doctrines should be taught through sacraments rather

---

[35] Ibid. v. 12, 18–19.

than sermons. Unhappily, 'Popery' was the 'terror' used to frighten people from that 'continual revelation of the Incarnation', the 'Lord's Supper', rather 'like the unreal shapes which are represented as frightening champions of romance from the object of their search'. It was the loss of 'all the rich furniture of the Sanctuary' which had made 'the spiritual principle of Christianity, unable to live off the husks' of eighteenth-century religion, 'burst forth first into Methodism, then into the Evangelical School, which had the ardour and some of the depth of the Old Catholic Doctors, without their reverence, sanctity, and majesty'. He was convinced that 'the only way to arrest fanaticism, check profaneness, and take away the persuasiveness and influence of Popery, is to recur to this primitive Catholicism on which happily our Services are based.'[36]

He was not, however, simply hostile to the Evangelicals, but looked 'most hopefully towards numbers of them—They are a very heterogenous [*sic*] party, but contain some of the highest and noblest elements of the Christian character among them, which have been attracted to the existing system of seriousness and spirituality, defective as it was, since the time that the lowminded' Latitudinarians of the last century 'robbed the Church of all her more beautiful characteristics'. It was this 'want of deeper views' which had led to 'a large portion of the deepest and truest religious principle' being 'seduced' into a 'school' whose '*spirit*' tended to liberalism and Unitarianism.[37] Four years earlier, he had observed, 'The Children of evangelical parents, if they see the world, will generally turn liberals; on the same principles as the sons of Rome turn infidels.' The recipients of intensive Evangelical preaching became 'worn out, as a constitution which has undergone some dreadful disease, or more dreadful remedy. Give them education, they will turn *scoffers*, having already the evil heart of unbelief in them.' Bishop Butler was right when he said that, 'if we say things over without feeling them, we become worse not better. Children, who are taught, since they were weaned, to rely on the Christian atonement, and in whose ears have been dinned the motives of gratitude to it etc before their hearts are trained to understand them, are deadened to them by the time they are 21.' Emphasizing 'Christian motives' all the time, something the Apostles never did, 'leads ultimately to no men feeling them'.[38]

But nothing was 'so consoling as to see the indestructibility of good principles', which 'spring up' again and again, 'and in the least expected quarters'. Whatever the troubles besetting the Church, he was convinced that there was 'high and true principle . . . all through the Church . . . and this supported and consecrated by our great writers of

[36] *LD* v. 21, 32, 39–40, 44–7.   [37] Ibid. 21, 32.   [38] Ibid. ii. 308.

the seventeenth century; but from long quiet we were going to sleep'. Alexander Knox, for example, the Irish forerunner of the Tractarians, who had died in 1831, was 'a remarkable instance of a man searching for and striking out the truth by himself'. Coleridge, too, had 'his place in the growth and restoration . . . of Church principles', in spite of 'his defects of doctrine, which are not unlike Knox's'; and at present he was 'the oracle of young Cambridge men, and will prepare them (please God) for something higher'. Both Knox and Coleridge were 'laymen and that is remarkable. The very stones cry out.' (He had been particularly delighted when Bowden had contributed to the *Tracts*, because he was a layman.) In the previous century Dr Johnson had been 'another striking instance and in another line, taking the gloomy side of religion, as they have taken the mystical'. Again, Bishop Butler had been 'raised up to carry on the spiritual succession' just as the Non-jurors were 'disappearing'.[39]

What Newman thought the Church needed was not reform but restoration. In his pamphlet *The Restoration of Suffragan Bishops*, which came out in March, he wrote that the Church 'has from the first been thrown upon the world' and 'knows the world well in all its artifices and all its wants', and therefore 'It has a store of weapons for all times and circumstances . . . a vigorous principle of life, and an inherent self-renovating power'. It was not 'innovation' that was required, but the development of 'the latent powers of the Church'. One of these powers was the episcopacy, although there was 'a tendency in the age to dispense with' it and to treat the parochial clergy as 'mere instruments and adjuncts of the State'. But far from being 'the mere executive of a system', a bishop was 'the centre and emblem of Christian unity' and the guardian of 'soundness and unity of doctrine', as well as being intended to 'live among his people'. However, dioceses had grown too large, especially in the industrial areas, and a 'whirl of business' was 'always unfavourable to depth and accuracy of religious views'. Because human nature needed individual guides and leaders, 'Christianity has met our want in the Episcopal system'. If the practical conclusion was clear, the argument was fresh and not uninteresting:

Increase the number of our Bishops. Give the people objects on which their holier and more generous feelings may rest. After all, in spite of the utilitarianism of the age, we have hearts. We like to meet with those whom we may admire and make much of. We like to be thrown out of ourselves . . . Human nature is not republican.

It must have surprised the bishops of the Established Church to hear that 'the sight' of their persons was certain to bring out 'the purer and

[39] Ibid v. 26–7.

nobler feelings of our nature' and a 'flame of devoted and triumphant affection'. It is doubtful if they had ever seen themselves in such a light.[40] (Later, Newman remarked that he had only advocated the restoration of suffragan bishops 'as a transition state to a division of sees', and because it seemed a 'feasible' suggestion at the time—'The great thing is to put the wedge in.'[41])

Towards the end of April, the fellows of Oriel agreed that a chapel should be built at Littlemore and that the college would provide the land and a part of the cost. This welcome decision was followed a few days later by news, which, Newman told Henry Wilberforce, gave him 'most piercing pain' and made him feel 'sickish'—the 'authentication of the report that Keble is to be married'.[42] When Wilberforce himself had got married a year before, Newman had merely referred to 'his nonsense—preparing marriage settlements and doing all he can to make himself one of the children of this world'.[43] He was to observe more sadly a few years later that Wilberforce was the 'only' friend he had ever had who 'took that sort of affectionate interest in me . . . which a wife takes and none but she—and that interest, so be it, shall never be taken in me'.[44] Wilberforce's marriage had inevitably meant a lessening of friendship and was a reminder to Newman, if he needed one, to make his 'own mind' his 'wife, and anticipate and provide against that loss of friends which the fashion of the age makes inevitable'. He did not even 'dare . . . indulge affection without restraint' towards his sisters. He could hardly help feeling 'at times much the despondence of solitariness'—'God grant all this discipline will make me give my heart more to Him.'[45]

At the beginning of April, the college Heads had again produced a proposal to substitute a declaration of conformity to the Church of England in place of subscription to the Thirty-nine Articles. Newman immediately suspected that it was 'the first of a *series* of measures' and that only an '*overpowering* majority' against it in the University Convocation could 'save' them.[46] The 'innovating heads' had made it clear that 'unless they have a large majority against them, they mean to bring forward the question again'. Personally, Newman had little time for the Articles:

tho' I believe them to be entirely Scriptural, they are not such favourites of mine, that *if I consulted my own wishes*, I should make an effort to retain them. I think they accidentally countenance a vile Protestantism. I do not tell people this, lest I should encourage a scoffing at authority. I submit and obey.[47]

[40] *VM* ii. 54, 56, 63, 65–8, 70, 72–3.   [41] *LD* v. 379.   [42] Ibid. 64.
[43] Ibid. iv. 301.   [44] Ibid. v. 110 n. 1.   [45] Ibid. iv. 170.
[46] Ibid. v. 55.   [47] Ibid. 70–1.

That was the dilemma: subscription to the Articles was necessary to safeguard the Anglican integrity of the University, but how far were the Articles themselves Anglican in a sense the Tractarians could accept? On 20 May the college Heads' proposal was rejected at Convocation by an overwhelming majority. The previous day Hurrell Froude had arrived in Oxford to cast his last vote. On 4 June he left for Devonshire, never to return.

Towards the end of June, R. D. Hampden wrote a letter to Newman furiously complaining about a collection of pamphlets on the subscription question, of which he had heard that Newman was the editor, and particularly about those of the pamphlets which were attacks on him: 'I charge you with malignity, because you have no other ground of your assault on me but a fanatical persecuting spirit.' To Hampden's angry accusation of 'dissimulation', Newman replied with cool irony that he could not 'conceive that the fact of his being Editor has been "extorted" from him . . . considering Dr Hampden learned it without any difficulty immediately on his inquiring'.[48] He seemed to be acquiring a reputation for fanaticism, as he remarked with amusement to Froude: 'Some Head of a House, seeing me (!) pass, said . . . "I wonder how often he has flagellated himself this morning". Alas he does me too much honour.'[49]

In fact, the subject of mortification was worrying him. He admitted to Pusey that he had been unable to fast without suffering disquieting medical symptoms. He seemed to be just well enough to work, 'but hardly above the water's surface'. He could scarcely imagine 'a greater cross' than being unable to fast, but at least it reduced him to 'silence on the subject', which was 'a safeguard against spiritual pride'. However, he had not given up 'the attempt of observing the spirit of fasting in lesser matters' and still hoped that his health would recover enough for him to fast properly. Anyway, there were other penances available, such as adopting a strict rule of prayer and voluntarily enduring cold. There was indeed the whole subject of an 'Englishman's boast'—his '*comforts*. E.G. in Oxford you ring the bell, and have every thing done you wish in a moment. You ride in from the country, go in to the Common Room, wine and biscuits are brought you at once . . . we have no *wants*—we have everything our own way.' Perhaps the answer was deliberately not to 'employ a servant' on 'certain days'.[50]

A grant from the Church Building Society brought the money raised for the new church at Littlemore up to the contract sum of £630. Building began on 15 July, and Mrs Newman laid the first stone a few days later. Newman told his mother that when he was busy with parochial work such as preparing candidates for confirmation, he felt he

[48] Ibid. 83–4.   [49] Ibid. 90.   [50] Ibid. 91–2.

would 'like a parish with nothing but pastoral duties'. The great advantage 'of a large parish is that *one can do nothing else*', whereas nothing was 'so hampering to the mind as *two* occupations', as he had discovered when he was both a curate at St Clement's and a tutor at Oriel. St Mary's parish was not large enough to take up all his time, so he had to find himself other work, which, 'though necessary', was 'distracting'. He was at his best when he had only one thing to do, and he would gladly devote himself completely either to study or to pastoral work. There were, however, two problems about parish work: first, he complained, there was too much unavoidable 'secular business', and, second, he confessed, reading the Fathers had revealed 'how ignorant we are' in matters of pastoral practice.[51]

He was, in fact, preoccupied at the moment with pressing theological problems as he prepared his second letter to the abbé Jager. When he saw the French priest's reply to his first letter, he felt that the controversy was 'getting interesting', but that his opponent was 'so weak that so far it is no fun'; still, 'it is an object to make known our opinions'.[52] He told Froude now that he was 'fidgetted' with his letter and that it was 'a great bore', but at least 'it obliges me to get up the controversy—next it shows I am not a Papist'. His argument revolved around a critical distinction he wanted to make between, on the one hand, what he called '*prophetical*' tradition, that is, in the 'popular sense' of the word, 'the voice of the body of the Church, the received system in the Church, the spirit circulating through it and poured out through the channels of its doctors and writers', whose 'reception' was not 'necessary for Church Communion'—and, on the other hand, tradition, in a stricter sense, namely a 'strict Traditio from one hand to another, from definite person to definite person, official and exact, which I may call *Apostolical* or *Episcopal*', whose 'articles' such as the Apostles' Creed were 'necessary for Church Communion' and were 'fundamentals even if the Scripture said nothing about them'.[53]

On 30 July he had a visitor to dinner—John Maguire, a Roman Catholic priest on the staff of St Edmund's seminary at Ware, who had arrived with an introduction from Wiseman. 'It is quite painful', he wrote to Bowden, 'to see how they are hand and glove with O'Connell and Co.'[54] In March, Daniel O'Connell, who was responsible for the gaining of Catholic emancipation, had had a meeting with Whig and Radical politicians to co-ordinate a campaign against Peel's Tory government, at which it was agreed that O'Connell would suspend his agitation against the Union (of Great Britain and Ireland) and support the Whig opposition in parliament, while in return the Whigs, on being

---

[51] *LD* v. 111.   [52] Ibid. 25.   [53] Ibid. 100, 102–3.   [54] Ibid. 114.

returned to power, would commute the hated tithes that Irish Catholics had to pay to support the Protestant Church of Ireland, and introduce other reforms. Newman was particularly disgusted by the way English Catholics could support not only O'Connell (to whom he had 'an unspeakable aversion', on the ground that 'he associated himself with men of all religions and no religion against the Anglican Church, and advanced Catholicism by violence and intrigue'),[55] but also a Radical politician like Joseph Hume who was sympathetic to the Catholic cause. Doubtless, he wrote to Froude, Maguire 'does not see the difference between the dog and the hog—and we are but dogs in his eyes'. On the other hand, he had to admit, to his chagrin, that the objectionable priest exemplified 'one strong point of Romanism', that 'they have their system so well up', a strength 'which astonishes people so'. Maguire was an 'avant-courier' of Wiseman, who was coming himself shortly to look at manuscripts in Oxford libraries. Although he would rather like to know 'a Romanist to get into their system', he did not relish 'getting intimate' with Wiseman, since the 'Romanists seem so heartily to take up the cause of such vile persons as O'Connell, Hume etc.' He had seen in Maguire 'the very same spirit' he had seen in Wiseman in Rome, 'the spirit of the cruel Church'; the priest looked as if he would 'willingly annihilate the English Church', and no doubt 'we shall be honoured with the peculiar hatred of these people, if we are ever in a condition to show fight'.[56]

He told Froude that he was still working away at his projected edition of Dionysius; by the time he finished he should have collected enough material 'for a volume on the Incarnation to accompany the Arians'— although, without the exigencies of the edition, he would hardly have been able 'to rouse' himself 'to such subtle speculations', important as these were at a time when there was a serious danger of being 'swept away, Creeds, Church, and all'. He explained to his aunt Elizabeth that his research had 'far graver objects in view' than mere scholarship. They were facing 'a flood of scepticism' of which 'poor' Blanco White, whose recent 'defection' to Unitarianism had appalled Newman, was 'a most serious and impressive warning'. It was only too ominously clear that Unitarianism was the logical conclusion of the lack of interest in doctrine among Evangelicals, as revealed by the indifference to the Creeds shown in the recently published letters of Hannah More. What was 'most painful' was that the clergy were 'so utterly ignorant on the subject', thanks to their lack of any proper '*theological* education'.[57]

The more he himself studied the Fathers the more he saw that Scripture was used by them to prove the doctrines which they received

[55] *Apo.* 117.   [56] *LD* v. 119–20, 124, 132.   [57] Ibid. 51, 118, 120–1.

from the Church's Tradition, which was itself regarded as no more than the interpretation of Scripture; it was ironic to find how right Hawkins had been that 'Scripture proves, and the Church teaches'.[58] He was convinced of the inevitability of a major religious upheaval. 'Protestants' would have 'to be more consistent one way or other, to become rationalists or true Catholics' (in the Tractarian sense). It was 'intelligible though very offensive' to be a rationalist, but a 'piebald' kind of religion, which was nothing in particular, could not 'stand the sifting of controversy', and was only enforced by 'secular interests' of state.[59] It was hardly surprising that English Roman Catholics were beginning to proselytize with some success.

Although he had found Jager a mere 'chattering French Abbé, who says three words where one would do', still the controversy had proved another 'stimulus for reading'. He had discovered that it was unprofitable to try and read the Fathers 'without an object', or rather, 'without a previous knowledge of controversies which are built upon them'. Employing a couple of striking analogies, he explained what he meant:

Till then their writings are blank paper—controversy is like the heat administered to sympathetic ink. Thus I read Justin very careful[ly] in 1828—and made most copious notes—but I conceive most of my time was thrown away. I was like a sailor landed at Athens or Grand Cairo, who stares about—does not know what to admire, what to examine—makes random remarks, and forgets all about it when he has gone.[60]

4

In September, Newman went down to Dartington for a month's visit to Froude. When he left on the evening of 11 October, Froude's 'face lighted up and almost shone in the darkness, as if to say that in this world we were parting for ever'.[61] It was in fact the last time they would ever see each other. It was 'wonderful, almost mysterious', Newman thought, how he had 'just been kept afloat and nothing more' for the last four years—'Really I sometimes think, that he is merely kept alive by the prayers of his friends.' He had found Froude 'languishing' without his Oxford friends, and felt he had been of help 'in stimulating his spirits'.[62] On his return, he wrote to tell Froude that Keble had married the day before he left Devon, 'and told no one'. He had merely informed the college that he was resigning his fellowship, 'which silence the said

---

College puts down, I suspect, to a romantic delicacy and tenderness'; a keener observer, however, might see 'in it an opinion that marriage is a very second rate business'.[63]

While he was in Devon, Newman was busy compiling a third volume of selected sermons. He intended them 'to be milder and more affectionate' than those in the earlier volumes, for which he had deliberately chosen his 'severe' rather than his 'gentler' sermons to ensure that he was not taken up, or rather patronized, by the Evangelicals, who would readily 'have dropped what they did not like, and have incorporated the mangled fragments they chose to admit in their own hodge-podge'.[64]

He was also writing what was to become *Tract 73*, later to be republished under the title 'On the Introduction of Rationalistic Principles into Revealed Religion'. He defined rationalism as an 'abuse' of reason, 'that is, a use of it for purposes for which it never was intended, and is unfitted.'

To rationalize in matters of Revelation is to make our reason the standard and measure of the doctrines revealed; to stipulate that those doctrines should be such as to carry with them their own justification; to reject them, if they come in collision with our existing opinions or habits of thought, or are with difficulty harmonized with our existing stock of knowledge.

He was careful, however, not to exclude a legitimate use of reason in religious inquiry, and the passage is worth quoting at some length, if only because its sharply antithetical rhetoric is an early example of the kind of tension that is so marked a characteristic of Newman's developed style and thought.

As regards Revealed Truth, it is not Rationalism to set about to ascertain, by the use of reason, what things are ascertainable by reason, and what are not; nor, in the absence of an express Revelation, to inquire into the truths of Religion, as they come to us by nature; nor to determine what proofs are necessary for the acceptance of a Revelation, if it be given; nor to reject a Revelation on the plea of insufficient proof; nor, after recognizing it as divine, to investigate the meaning of its declarations, and to interpret its language. . . . This is not Rationalism; but it is Rationalism to accept the Revelation, and then to explain it away; to speak of it as the Word of God, and to treat it as the word of man; to refuse to let it speak for itself; to claim to be told the *why* and the *how* of God's dealings with us . . . and to assign to Him a motive and a scope of our own; to stumble at the partial knowledge of what He may give us of them; to put aside what is obscure, as if it had not been said at all; to accept one half of what has been told us, and not the other half; to assume that the contents of Revelation are also its proof; to frame some gratuitous hypothesis about them, and then to garble, gloss, and colour them, to trim, clip, pare away, and twist them, in order to bring them into conformity with the idea to which we have subjected them.

For Newman, the moral basis of rationalism is obvious enough: 'The Rationalist makes himself his own centre, not his Maker.' This 'narrow and egotistic temper of mind', he feared, was 'the spirit' that was pervasive in the modern world: 'Instead of looking out of ourselves, and trying to catch glimpses of God's workings, from any quarter,— throwing ourselves forward upon Him and waiting on Him, we sit at home bringing everything to ourselves, enthroning ourselves in our own views, and refusing to believe anything that does not force itself upon us as true.' The result was that 'the idea of Mystery' was 'discarded', and religion took on a subjective rather than objective character. The blame is laid squarely on Evangelical Christianity, which directs 'its attention to the heart itself, not to anything external to us, whether creeds, actions, or ritual', and which 'is really a specious form of trusting man rather than God,' and so 'in its nature Rationalistic.' In a postscript which he added in 1836, Newman explained the theology of Schleiermacher, which had just come to his attention, as the typical 'result of an attempt of the intellect to delineate, philosophise, and justify that religion (so called) of the heart and feelings, which has long prevailed'.

It is a measure of his genius that even in the middle of his furious struggle against anti-dogmatic liberalism, Newman avoids losing his balance and falling into the opposite kind of rationalism, an over-systematic approach to revelation. He is saved from this by a profound sense of the mystery of Christianity and by an idea of mystery completely distinct from any kind of mere vagueness. 'Considered as a Mystery,' revelation, he says, 'is a doctrine enunciated by inspiration, in human language, as the only possible medium of it, and suitably, according to the capacity of language; a doctrine *lying hid* in language, to be received in that language from the first by every mind, whatever be its separate power of understanding it . . .'. The necessity of verbal formulations, then, is taken for granted, but the inevitable inadequacy of language is also recognized, as well as the limitations of human thought. There is a brilliant exposition of how mystery is not only compatible with but is involved in the very idea of revelation:

No revelation can be complete and systematic, from the weakness of the human intellect; *so far as* it is not such, it is mysterious. . . . A Revelation is religious doctrine viewed on its illuminated side; a Mystery is the selfsame doctrine viewed on the side unilluminated. Thus Religious Truth is neither light nor darkness, but both together; it is like the dim view of a country seen in the twilight, with forms half extracted from the darkness, with broken lines, and isolated masses. Revelation . . . is not a revealed *system*, but consists of a number of detached and incomplete truths belonging to a vast system unrevealed, of doctrines and injunctions mysteriously connected together . . .[65]

In November, Newman wrote to his brother Frank to warn him that his religious views would lead him into unbelief. He demanded to know what rational or Scriptural ground there was for that 'wretched, nay (I may say) cursed', 'low arrogant cruel ultra-Protestant principle', according to which 'every one may gain the true doctrines of the gospel for himself from the Bible'. Until his brother could see that 'the unanimous witness of the whole Church' to the teaching of the Apostles was really 'as much the voice of God' as Scripture, there was 'no hope' for such 'a clearheaded man'. If one accepted the authority of Scripture, what 'antecedent probability' was there against also accepting the teaching of the Church? His prediction of Frank's religious development was as succinct as it was accurate: 'You will unravel the webb of selfsufficient inquiry.' He added that although he was obliged to refuse to meet Frank 'in a familiar way or to sit at table' with him, he had no objection at all to discussion with him in person or by letter.[66] He later noted that his justification for breaking off ordinary relations with his brother was that 'he was *originating* schism, when he returned from Persia—that he was a *teacher* and *organizer* of a *new* sect'.[67]

His New Year letter to Froude contained the news that the 'Heads of Houses' were 'much annoyed' at the success of his new theological society, which had held its first meetings in November, when Pusey and Newman read papers. Newman not only suspected that the Dissenters hated him 'with a perfect hatred', but he knew that there was 'a large party of people who abominate me'. He was a 'marked man', he was told. 'I am getting callous, I believe—all this would have made me quite sick at one time—but somehow I wag on sluggishly.'[68]

As a result of the Hampden affair, the apostasy of Blanco White, his brother's heterodoxy, and his own *Tract* on rationalism, Newman now saw subscription to the Articles in rather a different light. He was still 'no great friend of them—and should rejoice to be able to substitute the Creeds for them, were it not for the Romanists'. He thought 'it was to say the least a great mistake' that they had ever been drawn up. On the other hand, the 'advantage of subscription' lay in 'its witnessing to the principle that religion is to be approached with a submission of the understanding', which was very valuable, as students were wont 'to approach serious subjects, as judges—to study them, as mere sciences', reasoning rather than submitting, 'whereas the great lesson of the Gospel is faith'.[69]

---

[65] *Ess.* i. 31–4, 36, 95–6, 41–2.   [66] *LD* v. 166–7.   [67] Ibid. 315.
[68] Ibid. 190–1.   [69] Ibid. 196–7.

5

The death of Edward Burton, the Regius Professor of Divinity, in January 1836 was seen by Newman as a 'remarkable token', as though 'Providence were clearing' the middle ground 'and forcing men to choose their side'. Burton had 'represented and upheld more than any one else the middle party'. There was a real possibility that Hampden might be appointed to the vacant chair. It was obvious, Newman remarked scornfully to Pusey, that the 'mass of those called High Church' had 'no principles'.

Is it not very clear that the English Church subsists *in the State*, and has no internal consistency (in matter of fact, I do not say in theory) to keep it together? is bound into one by the imposition of articles and the inducement of State protection, not by . . . a common faith? If so, can we regret very much that a deceit should be detected? surely not, though we might think we had no right ourselves to disturb what we found established.

As for the Heads of Houses, the fact that they were manifestly unable to see that Hampden was unorthodox showed that he was 'not so far from representing their opinions'. Was it not better that they should 'speak out' what 'was latent in their opinions and feelings'? And was it 'not better to fight in light than in darkness?' What the Tractarians must do was to 'develop' their 'views into system', and if the Church was disestablished and had 'certain parties torn from it', although this would be 'most grievous . . . still the better sort will be brought into clearer and more complete Christianity and the Church will be purer'.[70]

There was some chance that Keble might be appointed to the chair; certainly, Newman thought, he was 'the only man among us who can take it without odium'. He told Froude that he could say 'with a clear conscience' that he had 'no desire for it'. He was 'too indolent' and too anxious to have his 'own way'. Besides, he would 'be entangled in routine business, which I abhor'. He would 'be obliged to economize and play the humbug in a way I should detest'. Apart from theological considerations, he had 'no love for the nuisance of house and furniture— adding up bills, settling accounts, hiring servants, and getting up the price of butcher's meat'. He did not covet the salary, even though he wished he were two or three hundred pounds a year richer.

All this does not apply to Keble who is already entangled in these delights— who moreover would not have the unpopularity, the fame of being a party man which I have, nor the care of Tracts and the engagements of agitation. I am more useful as I am; but Keble is a light too spiritual and subtle to be seen unless put on a candlestick.

[70] *LD* v. 214–15.

Anyway, he hoped and believed that his 'illname' would 'sound loud enough' in the 'ears' of Lord Melbourne, the Prime Minister, to prevent his promotion.[71]

He had some amusing news with which to regale Froude. The Provost had declared that St Paul's injunction against marriage was 'fulfilled *in College Tutors, who wished to marry, waiting for a living.* Ought not this to be perpetuated in some inscription, medal, or authorized comment?' He also reported that the Evangelicals were planning a massive church-building campaign in London: 'Let them fill the Churches with their people—our game is to convert these later.'[72] He thought that they ought to 'aim' particularly at the younger generation of Evangelicals, who would naturally 'feel a disposition (bad enough) to rise against the system they have been brought up in', but who could be prevented from 'taking up with liberalism' if 'the true one' was put before them.[73] In general, he thought the way to convert people to Tractarianism was 'by throwing oneself into their state of mind and presenting truth to them so far, and in such a way, as they can see and accept it'.[74] He discouraged any premature pressure ('every thing in its time'): 'Persons will not hear of things this year, who adopt them the next—and they bear *things* long before they bear *names*.'[75]

On 8 February it was announced that Hampden had been appointed to the professorship. Two days later, a meeting was held to organize a petition to the King against the appointment. Newman sat up all night working on a pamphlet, *Elucidations of Dr. Hampden's Theological Statements*, which came out anonymously on 13 February. He sent a copy to Hampden, who did not fail, in his indignation against the accusation that he had denied that the Trinity and Incarnation were revealed doctrines, to make a significant distinction: 'It is one thing to speak of truths themselves and another to speak of *modes of statement*, or the *phraseology* in which the truths are expressed.'[76] Newman was unimpressed. He sent an old Trinity friend, Simeon Lloyd Pope, a blistering indictment of Hampden. He was sure his friend's 'imagination' could not 'picture any thing a quarter so bad as he really is'. He was 'worse' than a Socinian or Unitarian:

There is no doctrine, however sacred, which he does not scoff at—and in his Moral Philosophy he adopts the lowest and most grovelling utilitarianism as the basis of Morals—he considers it a sacred duty to live to this world—and that religion by itself injuriously absorbs the mind. Whately, whatever his errors, is openhearted, generous, and careless of money—Blanco White is the same, though he has turned Socinian—Arnold is amiable and winning—but this

[71] Ibid. 219–20.   [72] Ibid. 221–2.   [73] Ibid. 59.
[74] Ibid. 226.   [75] Ibid. 285.   [76] Ibid. 235.

man, *judging by his writings*, is the most lucre loving, earthly minded, unlovely person one ever set eyes on.[77]

Newman was uncertain whether he wanted the petition to succeed or not. If Hampden was not appointed, then the Tractarian party would have 'gained a victory', and they would save themselves the 'extreme annoyance and mischief which must attend the appointment', as well as deterring anyone else from 'liberalistic propensities'. On the other hand, Hampden's appointment would mean that 'the Ministry will be at open war with the Church—the Archbishop will be roused, and a large number of waverers in this place will be thrown into our hands'. One cannot help suspecting that Newman inclined to the latter alternative. One of his chief motives in starting the theological society had been 'to restrain the vagaries' of Hampden 'and such as he'. It was 'lucky' it was already in existence and would now 'increase in consequence at once'. There was another rather attractive prospect: in the event of Hampden being appointed, 'we should be enabled to push a formal investigation into his opinions before the Vice Chancellor—and nothing would do us more good in these times than the precedent of a judicial investigation and sentence'.[78]

On 20 February Newman heard from Archdeacon Froude that Hurrell was dying. On his birthday the next day he told Jemima that on 'looking forward to the next 25 years of my life, and its probable occupations,' Froude's death was 'the greatest loss I could have. I shall be truly widowed . . .' God was teaching him 'to depend on Him only'.[79] News of his death came on 1 March. Newman wrote to Bowden that he could never 'have a greater loss':

for he was to me, and he was likely to be ever, in the same degree of continual familiarity which I enjoyed with yourself in our Undergraduate days; so much so that I was from time to time confusing him with you and only calling him by his right name and recollecting what belonged to him, what to you, by an act of memory. It would have been a great satisfaction to me, had you known him— you once saw him indeed, but it was when his health was gone, and when you could have no idea of him . . . I never on the whole fell in with so gifted a person—in variety and perfection of gifts I think he far exceeded even Keble— for myself, I cannot describe what I owe to him as regards the intellectual principles of religion . . .[80]

He told Keble that he 'earnestly' trusted that 'it will be granted to me, who have most claim on it, so to say, to receive his mantle—most claim, as having most need—and you, as his teacher, neither requiring it, nor naturally being heir to it—but I would fain be his heir'. He had 'for years' been expecting this 'irreparable loss'—'and realized it perhaps

[77] *LD* v. 251.   [78] Ibid. 237.   [79] Ibid. 240–1.   [80] Ibid. 249.

quite as much as I do now, which is, not at all'. When he had stayed with Froude in the autumn, he had simply wanted 'to drink out his thoughts', as it were, before it was too late.[81]

To Maria Giberne, a friend of the family, he wrote that he loved 'to think and muse upon one who had the most angelic mind of any person I ever fell in with—the most unearthly, the most gifted'. The devotion of Maria (to whom Frank twice proposed in vain) was at times to prove embarrassing to Newman. Having been a convert herself to Evangelicalism (her sister had married Walter Mayers), she had become an ardent supporter of the Movement. Newman now wrote to her delightedly:

The (so called) Evangelicals have thought to ride into the Church in this her hour of peril, to make certain reforms, to alter her liturgy in some matters, to fill her dignities with their own people . . . the wind was fair, and the sky bright, and they spread their sails and went on gaily, and they dreamed not of an enemy, and they thought high churchmen sluggards and drones, and that they alone were spiritual, and lo and behold they are suddenly encountered, Goliaths as they are . . . by one or two Davids, and they feel nervous to see these single shepherds aiming at them with their sling and stones, and they see the prey which was just in their hands suddenly snatched away, and they are called to controversy, and they find to their great indignation that these upstarts affect to be stricter than they, and call them carnal, and gallantly attack them, and so they cry out Murder and Fire and so forth.[82]

But the success of the Movement could not remove the pain Newman felt at Froude's death, which was especially painful 'because people will not consider it to be the pain, or show the consideration, which belongs to the loss of relatives'.[83]

A second instalment of 'Home Thoughts Abroad', which had begun appearing in January 1834, came out in March and April in the *British Magazine*. The previous September, Newman had told Froude that it would make clear his 'line' on 'the Popish question', at the same time warning that the 'great principle' was that 'one cannot go across country and make short cuts; you must go along the road.'[84] (He would one day recall in the *Apologia* that his friend 'was a bold rider, as on horseback, so also in his speculations', and not at all afraid to 'go a-head across country' regardless of the practical consequences.)[85] His object in writing the article, he now informed Rose, was 'to provide beforehand against prospective evils'. He was

persuaded that the half solutions which have hitherto really been enough, will not do in time to come. Men will probe deeper—and unless we manage to cut under their objections, they will take root and bear bad fruit. So I want to forestal [*sic*] objections and their answers. There seems that in the Church of

[81] Ibid. 253.   [82] Ibid. 263.   [83] Ibid. 268.   [84] Ibid. 140.
[85] *Apo.* 46.

Rome, as it is at present, which utterly precludes our return to her. Our Tracts at this very time in the Press are aiming to bring out this in a series. Again there is a possibility of a general crash—and then it is as well we should have some notion what our Church's capabilities are. Hitherto she has been supported by the State—but if it fails her, what is she to do? ... I wish to encourage Churchmen to look boldly at the possibility of the Church's being made to dwell in the affections of the people at large. At present it is too much a Church for the Aristocracy, and for the poor mainly *through* the Aristocracy; with few attractions for the middle classes.

He ended the letter with this diagnosis: 'The Roman Church stops the safety valve of the Excitement of Reason—we that of the Excitement of Feeling. In consequence Romanists turn Infidels, and Anglicans Westleyans.'[86]

The second part of 'Home Thoughts Abroad' was later republished by Newman in his collected works under the title 'How to Accomplish it'. The narrator meets an Anglican friend, who maintains that reunion with Rome is the way to revitalize the Church: but like those of so many people who now think 'it a duty to exercise the "sacred right of private judgment" ', his theories seem to the narrator (who, of course, largely represents the author) *'unreal*, as if he had raised his structure in the air, an independent, self-sustained pile of buildings . . . without historical basis or recognized position among things existing, without discoverable relations to the wants, wishes, and opinions of those who were the subject of his speculations'. What was needed was for the Church to teach 'those doctrines, which, to the eye of faith, give a reality and substance to religion'. Significantly, his interlocutor retorts that it is Anglo-Catholicism which is unreal—it is a

theory—a fine-drawn theory, which has never been owned by any body of churchmen, never witnessed in operation in any system. Laud's attempt was so unsuccessful as to prove he was working upon a mere theory. The actual English Church has never adopted it: in spite of the learning of her divines, she has ranked herself among the Protestants, and the doctrine of the Via Media has slept in libraries.

Unlike the Papist and the Protestant,

when a man takes up this Via Media, he is a mere doctrinarian—he is wasting his efforts in delineating an invisible phantom; and he will be judged, and fairly, to be trifling, and bookish, and unfit for the world. He will be set down in the number of those who, in some matter of business, start up to suggest their own little crotchet, and are for ever measuring mountains with a pocket ruler, or improving the planetary courses. The world moves forward in bold and intelligible parties; it has its roads to the east and north . . .

[86] *LD* v. 274–6.

The author would one day find himself in painful agreement with this view, although without abandoning the narrator's principle that, 'unless where conscience comes in, it is our duty to submit to what we are born under'. But the obligation—'We must not dare to move, except He bids us'—could be carried too far, and immobility as an end in itself could never be for Newman what, he came to suspect, it was for Keble at least.[87]

In December 1835, Nicholas Wiseman had given a series of public lectures in London on the Catholic Church; they attracted a good deal of attention and were twice repeated and then published in 1836. Newman heard that Wiseman had referred triumphantly to his own book on the Arians to prove that the Christian faith was taught in the early Church not by the Bible but by oral tradition. In April 1836 he noted with disgust that Wiseman had

begun what he calls the 'Dublin Review,' under the auspices of himself and O'Connell. Really, if one wished a plain practical direction as to one's behaviour towards Romanism, this surely would seem a sufficient one. As no one can suppose O'Connell is to *write* for the Review, it is plainly but his *name* which is put forward . . .[88]

But these developments were significant, particularly if Anglicanism as a 'system of doctrine' was 'in matter of fact not *complete*' and contained 'hiatuses', which needed to be 'filled up'. The best answer to Roman objections was to say, 'you have corrupted, we have only omitted'. The problems of the Church of England should be met 'by *submission*—let us thank God that matters are no worse—and let us contend against alteration as unsettling people and raising disputes'. Their attitude should be, '*we find ourselves where we are*—it is a religious duty, *not mere expedience*, to remain quiet.' It was at least 'setting an example of submission to Church authority which is most necessary at this day'.[89]

In response to Rose's fear that, 'by acknowledging our existing settlement to be in itself imperfect, we should be taking away the only *authority* which the mass of Churchmen have', Newman replied: 'Should we ultimately draw up a system of divinity from our Divines, surely we shall be free from the charge of unsettling,—and this, though *we should* grant that there were one or two points which in our private judgments might be added to those which they advocate.' It was essential to 'invest the Church with its treasures, and make communion with it a privilege as well as a duty; or schism will rise after schism, as the Westleyans arose when the nonjurors were disowned'. Indeed, he suggested to the cautious Rose, 'it strikes me, if we *are* reviving things, why not, while we are about it, raise them a peg or two higher, if the position gained be

---

[87] *DA* 1–2, 18–19, 32, 37.   [88] *LD* v. 290.   [89] Ibid. 291–2.

truer and securer?'[90] He told Rose confidentially that he could not say he 'loved' the Church of England.

> The Anglican Church, the old Church . . . the Church of the builders of our Cathedrals, the Church again of Andrews, Laud, Hammond, Ken, and Butler . . . the Church discriminated by imposition of hands, not a tyrant's jurisdiction, I love indeed, and the later not a whit less fervently than the earlier—On Ken or on Hammond, or on King Charles, I dwell far more affectionately than on any thing before them. But I do not like that adventitious encrusted system in which they found themselves. I do not like the Church of the Reformation . . . I love the Church too as embodying the good characteristics of the English [ethos]—I love it for its *human* traits so sanctified and assimilated into the substance of the Church Apostolical; but I cannot endure . . . the insults of the world which she has worn now three hundred years. In like manner I love our Church as a portion and a realizing of the Church Catholic among us—but this leads me to mourn over our separation from the Latins and Greeks . . . I cannot love the 'Church of England' commonly so designated—its very title is an offence . . .

The difference between the seventeenth century and their own day was that the Church was now being deserted by the State, which provided 'a *reason* for being bolder'. The fact was that the Church of England had 'never been one reality, except *as* an Establishment'. It was effectively a battleground between 'two opposite principles; Socinianism and Catholicism—Socinianism fighting for the most part by Puritanism its unconscious ally'. Its 'highest *praise*' was that it admitted 'a variety of opinions'. Even if 'there *was* a deliverance at the Reformation, I cannot be more than thankful for it, I cannot rejoice and exult, when it is coupled with doctrinal licentiousness'. And he could only 'deplore the hard heartedness and coarsemindedness of those . . . who gave up (practically) to the Church of Rome what *we might have kept*—so much that was high, elevating, majestic, affecting, captivating—so depriving us of our birthright that the Latins now claim it as if theirs solely'. Such 'primitive customs' as praying for the dead could still be recovered without the Roman 'corruptions' like purgatory. Personally, like Keble and Froude, he had once been 'bigotted' in favour of the Church of England—in his own case because of his 'failing' of 'looking up to those who happened to be just over me', so that 'for a while Whately and Hawkins beguiled me'. And so he could claim that he had begun, 'as all ought to begin, with reverence and enthusiasm towards the system I found myself in'. He ended this long, candid letter to Rose by admitting that he had 'one and but one point of conscience, or almost of conscience': the 'alterations in the Eucharistic Service seem to me *a sin*—not in us but in our forefathers. It is our *misfortune*—and I bear it resignedly, as I should the loss of a limb.' Indeed, ought they not to 'love the service more for its very misfortunes? as we should be more tender of a persecuted and mutilated brother'. In particular, the prayer of consecration in the Communion service lacked any prayer to the Holy Spirit, as well as any prayer for the dead, both 'defects in doctrine, looking at the matter by *Antiquity*'. He himself always secretly inserted his own silent commemoration of the dead—something he had hardly ever mentioned to anyone.[91] Praying for the dead, indeed, was 'so very natural, so soothing, that if there is no command against it, we have (it would seem) a call to do it'; and it was 'so great a gift, if so be to *be able* to benefit the dead', that he was 'sometimes . . . quite frightened at the thought how great a talent our Church is hiding in a napkin'.[92]

6

At the end of April, Jemima married Tom Mozley's elder brother John, who was a partner in the family publishing and printing business in Derby. Shortly after the wedding Mrs Newman collapsed, and after a brief illness she died on 17 May. Later Newman recalled how he had found himself getting into debt and had prayed that God would either enable him to go on helping his family or would 'remove the necessity': it was as if he had prayed for his mother's death, but it was remarkable how 'strangely' prayers were 'answered—so much so that to pray seems to be using an edged tool'.[93] 'If you knew', he now wrote to his aunt, 'how dreadfully she has suffered in mind, and how little her wanderings left her like herself, you would feel, as we do, that it really is a release.'[94] He told Jemima that he was distressed that his work had kept him from being more with his mother of late. But there was something else of a more serious nature which had come between them: 'I mean, of late years my Mother has much misunderstood my religious views, and considered she differed from me; and she thought I was surrounded by admirers and had everything my own way—and in consequence, I, who am conscious to myself I never thought any thing more precious than her sympathy and praise, had none of it. . . .' He continued:

Nearly in the last conversation I had with her, I saw she quite mistook something I said, and that she was hurt at it . . . All this brought me to see that I had taken a false step in wishing her to be at Oxford. I can never repent it for the good she has done to Littlemore, and for your most happy marriage; but I myself suffered by it . . . I know in my own heart how much I ever loved her,

91 Ibid. 301–5; vi. 263.   92 Ibid. v. 260.
93 Ibid. 322–3.   94 Ibid. 299.

and I know too how much she loved me—and often, when I had no means of showing it, I was quite overpowered from the feeling of her kindness.

There was the perennial problem of his shyness, as he explained:

I have some sort of dread and distress, which I cannot describe, of being the object of attention . . . I recollect about two years ago, after I had fainted away, my Mother most kindly stooping down to take up my feet and put them on the sofa. I started up—I could not endure it. I saw she was hurt, yet I did not know how to put things right. I felt it something quite shocking that any one, above all she, should so minister to me. Nay, when I seemed rude, it often rose from feelings very different from what appeared.[95]

He told Keble that he knew he was 'very cold and reserved to people; but I cannot ever realize to myself that any one loves me'.[96] (Years later, he remarked that he 'seemed sometimes . . . reserved, when the case really is, that, if I spoke I should say what was unreal and I should be next day sorry to have said'.[97])

Privately, Newman noted long afterwards that it was 'a great mistake in all of us, though a very natural one, to fancy that, if my Mother and sisters came nearer to me, they would see more of me. Their coming near me did not lessen the work of various kinds which engrossed my time; it did but involve them in a necessary disappointment, and made it seem as if I did not avail myself of opportunities of our meeting which they had done their part in securing.' When they had been in Brighton, he had paid lengthy visits to them and had been able to leave his work at Oxford behind him. Then there was the problem that 'they did not like some of my greatest friends'. Moreover, 'from the first they did not like the distinctive principles of the Oxford Movement; and, the more it developed, the wider did their difference from me in respect to it grow.' There was also the difficulty that they disagreed in their attitude to Frank and Charles. 'These differences, though they tried to hide them and to make the best of them, made me very sore. They had a full right to their own views; but I did not imitate them in bearing patiently what could not be helped.'

He assured his married sister that she should not worry about his being lonely, now that Harriett had also left to stay with relations.

I am not more lonely than I have been a long while. God intends me to be lonely. He has so framed my mind that I am in a great measure beyond the sympathies of other people, and thrown upon Himself . . .[98]

Newman had already understood that the essence of celibacy as a spiritual ideal as opposed to a pragmatic convenience, was not so much

---

[95] *LD* v. 313–14.   [96] Ibid. vi. 119.
[97] Ibid. xvii. 532.   [98] Ibid. v. 313–15.

that it provides freedom from the ties of marriage and family for a fuller commitment to the work of a religious profession, but rather that the very pain of the lack of intimate human love is meant to impel the celibate to find affective fulfilment in the exclusive love of God. As a poem he wrote in 1833 puts it, 'Thrice bless'd are they, who feel their loneliness'—for 'sick at heart, beyond the veil they fly,/Seeking His Presence, who alone can bless'.[99] Two decades later, after he had seen at first-hand how institutional celibacy in the Roman Catholic Church was all too often lived out in practice, he was to declare, 'To make a single life its own end, to adopt it simply and solely for its own sake, I do not know whether such a state of life is more melancholy or more unamiable, melancholy from its unrequited desolateness and unamiable from the pride and self-esteem on which it is based.' But

This is not the Virginity of the Gospel—it is not a state of independence or isolation, or dreary pride, or barren indolence, or crushed affections; man is made for sympathy, for the interchange of love, for self-denial for the sake of another dearer to him than himself. The Virginity of the Christian soul is a marriage with Christ.[100]

In 1836 he did not attempt to formulate the principle in a way that would have alarmed his uncomprehending sisters even more, but he did not mind puzzling them with the paradox that even when he did feel 'dejection', it was 'not unwelcome—I am speaking of dejection from solitude; I never feel so near heaven as then'. He had experienced solitude in the early years at Oriel, when in the midst of various worries he

on the whole had no friend near me—no one to whom I opened my mind fully or who could sympathize with me. I am but returning at worst to that state. Indeed, ever since that time I have learned to throw myself on myself. Therefore, please God, I trust I shall get on very well, and after all this life is very short, and it is a better thing to be pursuing what seems God's call, than to be looking after one's own comfort. I am learning more than hitherto to live in the presence of the dead—this is a gain which strange faces cannot take away.[101]

At the beginning of July he sent Bowden an amusing account of another little encounter he had had with Roman Catholics.

What has Dr. Wiseman done, but last night send me down two Papishers to entertain. This is somewhat cool—yet, as they are gentlemanlike men, nothing is left to me but to ask them to dinner. . . . Unluckily I can get no one . . . to meet them—so I shall seem to be holding a secret conclave with them. I unintentionally got them into a scrape this morning. At 8 o'clock they came to St. Mary's to see the Church, and not understanding me, got into the Chancel,

[99] *VV* 104.   [100] *NO* 277.   [101] *LD* v. 311–12.

took their seats, heard me read the Exhortation, and half the Confession when they took fright and absconded. I thought I had almost converted them. One is a Priest . . .'[102]

It was an early experience for Newman of Wiseman's notorious casualness, but he was not to know that; nor was he to know that the priest who had been foisted on him was none other than Wiseman's future coadjutor at Westminster, George Errington, whose famous quarrel with his patron was to have such far-reaching consequences both for Newman personally and for the Catholic Church in England.

On 17 July Newman wrote to ask Keble if he had any objection to the 'Lyra Apostolica' being published in book form, 'as far as your share in it goes'. He did not intend to give the names of the different writers, but 'to distinguish authors' alphabetically by the letters of the Greek alphabet. He also mentioned that he had 'thoughts of publishing some Lectures on Romanism'.[103] He had given the first of these lectures in the Adam de Brome chapel in St Mary's the day before his mother died, on Monday, 16 May, and the last on Monday, 11 July. He had so much work on his hands that he had no time even to visit his sisters. At the beginning of July he had begun going through Froude's papers. The church at Littlemore was soon to be opened. And then there were the October *Tracts* to be got ready, one of which would be concerned with 'giving authorities for Baptismal Regeneration'. In answer to the Roman Catholic demand to know what the Church of England believed, it was vital to '*systematize*' the writings of the Anglican divines of the seventeenth century (he had had the idea as early as 1826). He wanted to produce in the *Tracts* 'a Consensus Doctorum' or 'Catena Patrum', that is, a compendium of Anglican theology.[104] In August he and Pusey also began planning an English edition of the Fathers—'I am sure nothing will be like a good flood of divinity.'[105]

In September the church at Littlemore was finally consecrated by the Bishop of Oxford. Newman preached, and afterwards distributed buns to the children. He had deliberately 'secured a font large enough for immersion', and intended 'to urge the people to suffer their children to be immersed—or at least in the summer'.[106] The baptismal font was used for the first time on the day of the consecration. In spite of his strong views about celibacy, Newman was well aware that clergy wives were 'useful in a parish, and that in a way in which no *man* can rival them'.[107] He must have felt on that memorable day the absence of his own mother and sisters who had been so involved in Littlemore. He had already heard in August that Harriett was now engaged to Tom Mozley; he was

---

[102] *LD* v. 318–19.   [103] Ibid. 327–8.   [104] Ibid. 340.
[105] Ibid. 345.   [106] Ibid. 342.   [107] Ibid. 346.

'much pained', he told Jemima, 'the marriage' was 'so soon' after their mother's death.[108] However, he was present at the wedding, which took place at the end of September in Derby, where he stayed for a fortnight with Jemima. He told Bowden, not too seriously, that he could not 'approve' of his former pupil's 'offence against monastic rule', but still it was 'a great happiness to find him brought nearer to me'. He later remarked jocularly that he was wondering if Tom would ever get around to writing 'another letter' in his life—'every one when he marries is a lost man—a clean good for nothing.'[109]

Meanwhile, the future of the *Tracts* was in doubt, as Rivington (who had been 'very careless about them') had indicated to Newman that he wanted to give up publishing them, since they were not selling. Newman was not sorry, as he was tired of editing them. But he hoped they could continue in a new form, with Keble as editor. He thought they ought to come out less frequently, to be more substantial, and to be 'devoted . . . to the consideration of the Popish Controversy'.

I am deliberately certain that we must publish these Tracts against Popery for many reasons. First we shall have inquirers turning Papists, if we do not draw lines between ourselves and Popery. Next it will do us good, if we show we do differ from the Papists. Thirdly it is availing ourselves of a popular cry—this is what first got us on two years since (viz., when there was a cry against Dissent) and we shall miss our opportunity if we do not do the like now as regards Popery. Fourthly, it [will] be anticipating other parties by giving our own views of Romanism—and fifthly it is a very effectual though unsuspicious way of dealing a backhanded blow at ultra-protestantism.

To go on bringing out *Tracts* once a month was 'the way to make them mere trash'. Short *Tracts* were very useful at the beginning, but the need now was for 'treatises' rather than 'sketches'.[110] At present only 200 copies of the monthly *Tracts* were selling, of which Newman himself took 30. Publication was suspended when Rivington gave up publishing the *Tracts* in November. Keble declined to be editor. In January, Newman heard that the sales had improved and he decided to start a new series.

The plan for an English Library of the Fathers went ahead. Newman was surprised to hear from Pusey in October that the Archbishop of Canterbury had agreed to be its patron. There was no difficulty about finding translators—the problem was whom to choose. Towards the end of October his lectures on Romanism were accepted for publication by Rivington. He was confident they would 'indirectly'[111] answer Wiseman, whose lectures on the Catholic Church he reviewed in the October number of the *British Critic*. Shortly before the end of the month he took

---

[108] Ibid. 341.   [109] Ibid. 345; vi. 18.   [110] Ibid. 144, 136, 150.
[111] Ibid. v. 349.

his BD degree, which involved his reading out the Thirty-nine Articles to the Regius Professor of Divinity, Dr Hampden! At the end of November the *Lyra Apostolica* was published. He sent a complimentary copy to Maria Giberne, telling her that they seemed 'to be making way very remarkably here, in Apostolical views—so much so that our success quite frightens me, as being unnatural—may it be supernatural'. He was still slowly revising his lectures, parts of which he had rewritten 'an incredible number of times'.[112] He was very much in favour of her trying her hand at writing 'some Apostolic stories' for children and hoped she could collaborate with Jemima and her sister-in-law Anne Mozley.[113] What he thought was really needed was 'a library on all subjects for the middle classes and the Clergy'.[114]

In the new year of 1837 he wrote to Harriett to say that his book had 'gone to Press', but that he was 'very anxious' about it: 'I have taken immense pains with it, writing great portions of it from four to six times over.'[115] To Rose, he wrote more specifically:

I am publishing a sort of Via Media as far as it goes, and of course it makes me very anxious to be accurate. I do not think I deviate from our great writers in any point, certainly any point in which they agree—Doubtless, I shall make some mistakes after all—but not for want of pains—most of it has been re-written, not retranscribed, several times—good part from four to six times.[116]

He assured Jemima that it was 'no *advance* on any thing I have said—but a systematizing, consolidating, supplying premisses etc.' Excitement at his first sustained work of controversy stimulated the first really extended use of imagery to be found not only in the letters but also in his writings:

I say nothing, I believe, without the highest authority among our writers, yet it is so strong that every thing I have as yet said is milk and water to it—and this makes me anxious. It is all the difference between drifting snow and a hard snow ball. It seems to me like hitting the Peculiars [Evangelicals] etc. a most uncommon blow in the face. Pusey however compared it to a blow that takes the breath out of one. He says they will be so out of breath as not to be able to answer—and that before they recover, one or other of us must give them another. While I laugh, I am still anxious . . .[117]

In a letter to Frederic Rogers he noted that Pusey's graphic parallel was a 'curious' reminder of how Froude had compared his 1833 letter to Dr Arnold to 'a blow in the stomach', and how one of the bishops had compared the *Tracts* to 'shaking the fist in the face'.[118]

Newman asked the President of Magdalen, Martin Routh, the distinguished theological scholar and high churchman, who was

---

[112] *LD* v. 385. [113] Ibid. 387. [114] Ibid. vi. 32. [115] Ibid. 3.
[116] Ibid. 4–5. [117] Ibid. 6. [118] Ibid. 8.

sympathetic to the Movement, if he might dedicate the book to him, reiterating that he had 'tried, as far as may be, to follow the line of doctrine marked out by our great divines', particularly the Laudian John Bramhall who had written voluminously against both Rome and Protestantism.[119] Routh readily agreed, and the eventual dedication referred to him as one 'who has been reserved to report to a forgetful generation what was the theology of their fathers'.[120]

In December 1836 the Evangelical *Christian Observer* had violently attacked the *Tracts* by Pusey on Baptism[121] and sarcastically advised the Regius Professor of Hebrew to leave his Oxford chair and lecture instead at Maynooth or the Vatican. The paper challenged the Tractarians to say how they were able to accept the Articles and Homilies in the Prayer Book. Newman decided to take up the challenge and 'fervently' hoped he would be able to 'tease them usque ad necem, insaniam, or something else equally bad'.[122] In January and March he wrote twice, at length, to the magazine. In view of his later controversies as a Catholic, it is interesting to find him protesting that the vague, unsubstantiated abuse the Evangelicals showered on the Tractarians was 'not an English mode of proceeding': all that the Tractarians asked for was 'the right of an Englishman, a fair and uninterrupted hearing'. They were confident in their meekness: 'We know our place, and our fortunes; to give a witness and to be condemned, to be ill-used and to *succeed*.' As he was to say so often in his life, 'Such is the law which God has annexed to the promulgation of the Truth; its preachers suffer, but its cause prevails.' Again, as he was so often to do in controversy, he enjoyed trapping his opponents in their own inconsistencies: it was all very well, for example, to quote the Homilies against the Tractarians, but they could also easily be quoted against the Evangelical position; and moreover, to try and impose particular points of interpretation on them was ascribing an 'authority' to them which the Tractarians did not 'ascribe . . . in such matters even to the unanimous consent of all the Fathers'—'But *you* allow us no private judgment whatever; your private judgment is all particular and peculiar.' He ended by admitting, pointedly, that he had not discussed the 'most important' subject of Justification.[123]

He remarked to Pusey that nothing inspired him 'with greater hope for our own cause, or rather brings home to me the fact that we are on the whole right and they on the whole wrong than the circumstance that

[119] Ibid. 7.   [120] *VM* i. v.

[121] Pusey's first *Tract* (on fasting) was written at the end of 1833, but he had cautiously stipulated then 'that he might put his initials at the end of it, that he might separate himself from the movement party'—which was ironic, since 'the very reason why the movement was called "Puseyism" ' was 'because Pusey was the only writer whose name presented itself to the general public' (*LD* xxviii. 346).

[122] *LD* vi. 9.   [123] *VM* ii. 157, 170, 159, 184.

they have less humility than I think we have'.[124] He was struck, to take an extreme example, by the way his brother Frank complained that *he* was trying 'to make a sect': it seemed 'very uncharitable' to '*impute motives*' like that, when he himself did not attempt to 'judge' Frank in any way—'I only say that God tells me to avoid persons who make divisions—and he makes a division.'[125] At a recent London meeting of Evangelical clergy the Tractarians had been 'voted heretical, and open war declared', Newman informed Bowden excitedly: 'Earthen jars should not swing with iron ones, or the crockery will suffer.' At any rate, he had no doubt the Fathers were 'a match' for any number of Evangelicals.[126] When he sent the news to Maria Giberne, he again commented that he could not feel worried with 'all the Fathers round one'; as for the fury of the Evangelicals, he was amused 'beyond measure to see how angry these people are made by their very incapacity. They put me in mind of a naughty child put atop of the bookcase, very frightened, but very furious.'[127] The marvellously contemptuous image shows how Newman was developing his powers as a satirist under the pressure of controversy, and controversy in which he felt totally secure in his own position.

He was too busy to write anything for Anne Mozley's 'poetical collection', he told Jemima: he could not write poetry 'except in a season of idleness—When I have been doing nothing awhile, poems spring up as weeds in fallow fields.' However, he had found time to read Jane Austen's *Emma*, an experience that elicited one of his better-known literary judgements:

Every thing Miss A writes is clever, but I desiderate something. There is a want of *body* to the story. The action is frittered away in over-little things. There are some beautiful things in it. Emma herself is the most interesting to me of all her heroines. I feel kind to her whenever I think of her. But Miss A. has no romance, none at all. What vile creatures her parsons are! she has not a dream of the high Catholic [ethos]. That other woman, Fairfax, is a dolt—but I like Emma.

In the circumstances, his impatience with the world of Jane Austen was hardly less predictable than his dislike of Wesley, whose life by Southey he had also been reading: 'I do not like Westley—putting aside his exceeding self confidence, he seems to me to have a black self will, a bitterness of religious passion, which is very unamiable.'[128]

He was very pleasantly surprised to hear that the *Tract* he had published six months before ('at a dead time of year') on the Roman Breviary was already sold out. It had been a daring thing to write, but 'dear Froude wished it'. Its quite unexpected success was 'the most

[124] *LD* vi. 10.   [125] Ibid. 24.   [126] Ibid. 12.   [127] Ibid. 13.
[128] Ibid. 16.

promising event' in the history of the *Tracts*, which had 'suddenly begun to sell', so he heard from the publisher, who was going 'to double all editions in future'.[129] Given his intense preoccupation with the Movement and the *Tracts*, it was noted how, at the weekly Monday evening tea-parties which he started for Oriel undergraduates at the beginning of February, the conversation ranged freely round all sorts of subjects—*except* Tractarianism. It was noticed, too, how undergraduates seemed to feel much more at ease in his presence than in that of Professor Pusey.

7

On 11 March Newman's new book finally appeared, under the title *Lectures on the Prophetical Office of the Church viewed relatively to Romanism and Popular Protestantism*. He did not expect any 'mercy' from Protestants, who were sure to find mistakes in 'facts which touch people to the quick'. He was bound to be caught 'between the cross fires of Papists and Protestants'. What was 'amusing', though, was the way 'the unfortunate Peculiars are attacked on so many sides at once that they are quite out of breath with having to run about to defend their walls . . . No sooner do they recover their breath after one blow, but they receive another in their stomach.'[130]

The theology of the Church which Newman was painfully to develop during the next forty years begins and ends with the *Prophetical Office*, for the lengthy preface he wrote for the third edition of 1877 constitutes his last and greatest contribution to ecclesiology. He commences the 1837 work by pointing out that 'Roman Catholics having ever insisted upon' the Church 'and Protestants having neglected it, to speak of the Church at all, though it is mentioned in the Creed, is thought to savour of Rome'. Therefore, those 'who feel its importance, and yet are not Romanists, are bound to show why they are not Romanists, and how they differ from them', both 'in order to remove the prejudice with which an article of the Creed is at present encompassed; and on the other hand to prevent such persons as have right but vague ideas concerning it, from deviating into Romanism because no other system of doctrine is provided for them'. Leaving aside the 'directly political and ecclesiastical' aspects of the Church, his own object is to formulate 'a correct theory' of the 'Prophetical Office' of the Church, such as 'popular Protestantism' does not even attempt, while Rome provides 'an untrue one'. What, in fact, is demanded by the theory of the *Via Media* as

[129] Ibid. 18.   [130] Ibid. 34.

'the nearest approximation to that primitive truth which Ignatius and Polycarp enjoyed, and which the nineteenth century has virtually lost'?[131]

Unfortunately, the fact that the *Via Media* is only a 'theory' raises a serious objection at the outset:

A religious principle or idea, however true, before it is found in a substantive form, is but a theory; and since many theories are not more than theories, and do not admit of being carried into effect, it is exposed to the suspicion of being one of these, and of having no existence out of books.

However, that does not mean that an unrealized theory is necessarily unreal: 'The proof of reality in a doctrine is its holding together when actually attempted.' Christianity itself would have seemed 'at first a mere literature, or philosophy, or mysticism . . . till it was tried'. But although the doctrines of the *Via Media* purport to be the 'foundation' on which Christianity 'originally spread', still, since they 'related to extremes which did not then exist, and do exist now, they appear unreal, for a double reason, having no exact counterpart in early times, and being superseded now by actually existing systems'. The inescapable and damaging truth is that

Protestantism and Popery are real religions . . . but the *Via Media*, viewed as an integral system, has never had existence except on paper; it is known, not positively but negatively, in its differences from the rival creeds, not in its own properties; and can only be described as a third system, neither the one nor the other, but with something of each, cutting between them, and, as if with a critical fastidiousness, trifling with them both, and boasting to be nearer Antiquity than either.

There is no anxiety that the *Via Media* is not 'true', but the uneasy fear that it is not 'real' is palpably present in the sarcastic scepticism which Newman imagines in the minds of detached observers:

What is this but to fancy a road over mountains and rivers, which has never been cut? When we profess our *Via Media*, as the very truth of the Apostles, we seem to bystanders to be mere antiquarians or pedants, amusing ourselves with illusions or learned subtleties, and unable to grapple with things as they are.

However many learned theologians may have 'propounded' it, 'whatever its merits, still, when left to itself . . . it may not "work" '. Indeed, 'the very circumstance that it has been propounded for centuries by great names, and not yet reduced to practice as a system, is alleged as an additional presumption against its feasibility'. Candidly admitting the 'force' of the objections, Newman insists that 'it still remains to be tried whether what is called Anglo-Catholicism . . . is

[131] *VM* i. 5–7.

capable of being professed, acted on, and maintained on a larger sphere of action and through a sufficient period, or whether it be a mere modification or transition-state either of Romanism or of popular Protestantism'. Anglo-Catholics are 'certainly' required 'to exhibit' their 'principles in action', if only because it may plausibly be argued that

the Church of England, as established by law, and existing in fact, has never represented a doctrine at all or been the development of a principle, has never had an intellectual basis; that it has been but a name, or a department of the state, or a political party, in which religious opinion was an accident. . . . In consequence, it has been but the theatre of contending religionists, that is, of Papists and Latitudinarians, softened externally, or modified into inconsistency by their birth and education, or restrained by their interests and their religious engagements.

Newman draws comfort from the argument that, while the liberal and puritan parties 'have been shown to be but modifications' of Unitarianism and Calvinism, 'by their respective histories, whenever allowed to act freely', the Anglo-Catholic party, 'when it had the opportunity of running into Romanism, in fact did not coalesce with it'—a consideration that suggests 'some real differences in it from that system with which it is popularly confounded'.[132] But it can still be objected that the Anglican *Via Media* is not only a complex 'mean' but also has a certain 'indeterminateness', and because it has never been properly 'brought into operation', it is 'open to the suspicion of . . . being . . . a mere theory or fancy'.[133] Anglo-Catholics are 'accused . . . of drawing fine, and over-subtle distinctions; as if, like the Semi-arians of old, we are neither on the one side nor the other'.[134] However, although Anglo-Catholicism has never been 'practically reduced to system in its fulness, it does exist, in all its parts, in the writings of our divines, and in good measure is in actual operation, though with varying degrees of consistency and completeness in different places'. The task is clear:

We have a vast inheritance, but no inventory of our treasures. All is given us in profusion; it remains for us to catalogue, sort, distribute, select, harmonize, and complete. We have more than we know how to use; stores of learning, but little that is precise and serviceable . . .[135]

The Protestant insistence on 'the Bible as the only standard of appeal in doctrinal inquiries' inevitably leads to the conclusion that 'truth is but matter of opinion', for 'the Bible is not so written as to force its meaning upon the reader', nor does it 'carry with it its own interpretation'. Those who think that Christians must draw their faith from Scripture 'hold an unreal doctrine, and . . . to be consistent, they must . . . either cease to

[132] Ibid. 15–19.   [133] Ibid. 129.   [134] Ibid. 195.   [135] Ibid. 23–4.

think orthodoxy necessary, or allow it to be taught them'.[136] True, the Anglican, unlike the Roman Catholic, argues that the 'creed can be proved entirely . . . from the Bible'—but 'we take this ground only in controversy, not in teaching our own people or in our private studies'. None of the various denominations which claim to derive the Christian faith from the Bible alone actually 'embraces the whole Bible, none of them is able to interpret the whole, none of them has a key which will revolve through the entire compass of the words which lie within. Each has its favourite text, and neglects the rest.' As for Anglo-Catholics, 'we rely on Antiquity to strengthen such intimations of doctrine as are but faintly, though really, given in Scripture'—unlike Protestantism, which 'considers it a hardship to have anything clearly and distinctly told it in elucidation of Scripture doctrine, an infringement of its right of doubting, and mistaking, and labouring in vain'.[137]

Roman Catholics, on the other hand, appeal to Tradition as well as Scripture, maintaining that it was impossible to commit to writing all that the Apostles taught—'No one you fall in with on the highway, can tell you all his mind at once; much less could the Apostles . . . digest in one Epistle or Treatise a systematic view of the Revelation made to them.' The New Testament, they argue, is 'an incomplete document', without 'harmony or consistency in its parts' and without any 'code of commandments' and 'list of fundamentals'. Analogy and imagery are brilliantly employed to suggest the Catholic idea of Tradition:

It is latent, but it lives. It is silent, like the rapids of a river, before the rocks intercept it. It is the Church's unconscious habit of opinion and sentiment; which she reflects upon, masters, and expresses, according to the emergency. We see then the mistake of asking for a complete collection of the Roman Traditions; as well might we ask for a complete catalogue of a man's tastes and thoughts on a given subject. Tradition in its fulness is necessarily unwritten . . . and it cannot be circumscribed any more than a man's countenance and manner can be conveyed to strangers in any set of propositions.

Newman agrees that it is certainly the case that 'we receive through Tradition both the Bible itself, and the doctrine that it is divinely inspired', as do most Protestants, who 'believe in the divinity of Scripture precisely on the ground on which the Roman Catholics take their stand in behalf of their own system of doctrine, viz. because they have been taught it'.[138] The fact is that Christians 'derive their faith' not from Scripture but from Tradition.[139] And it is not the concept of Tradition that Anglo-Catholics object to, but the fact that Rome 'substitutes the authority of the Church for that of Antiquity', merely

---

[136] *VM* i. 26–7, 245, 150.   [137] Ibid. 28–9, 159, 239.   [138] Ibid. 31–4, 281.
[139] Ibid. 244.

keeping the Fathers 'around her to ask their advice when it happens to agree with her own', but otherwise superseding them 'because they are hard of hearing, are slow to answer, are circuitous in their motions, and go their own way to work'. True Tradition is attested to by 'Catholicity, Antiquity, and consent of Fathers', and how far this test is met 'must be decided by the same principles which guide us in the conduct of life . . . which lead us to accept Revelation at all, for which we have but probability to show at most'.[140] Certainly, while 'Private Judgment' may interpret Scripture to a considerable extent as it pleases, it cannot 'so deal with Antiquity'—for 'History is a record of facts', and the Fathers 'are far too ample to allow' selective interpretation.[141]

The key distinction that Newman now tries to make between two different kinds of Tradition is the most significant part of the book, attempting as it does to preserve the centrality of Tradition without damage to the uniqueness of Scripture. He divides Tradition into 'Episcopal Tradition', which is derived from the Apostles, and 'Prophetical Tradition', which consists of the interpretation of the Revelation, a 'body of Truth, pervading the Church like an atmosphere', and 'existing primarily in the bosom of the Church itself, and recorded in such measure as Providence has determined in the writings of eminent men'. It is this latter kind of Tradition which Newman claims may be 'corrupted in its details', so that the doctrines which develop out of it 'are entitled to very different degrees of credit'. The decrees of the Council of Trent may reasonably claim to be 'Apostolic', and yet 'they are the ruins and perversions of Primitive Tradition'.[142]

This view of 'Prophetical Tradition' is in keeping with 'the Tradition of the Fathers', which 'witnesses' not only 'to its own inferiority to Scripture,' but also to the fact that 'Scripture is the record' and 'the sole record of saving truth'.[143] And this 'fundamental faith' or 'the doctrine of the Apostles' was what the 'Ancient Church' taught before 'it broke up into portions, and for Catholic agreement substituted peculiar and local opinions'—although it 'still remains to us, and to all Christians all over the world'.[144] Given that 'the Church Catholic' must be 'indefectible in faith, we have but to inquire what that common faith is, which she now holds everywhere as the original deposit', and we shall find it is those 'fundamental or essential doctrines . . . which are contained in the Creed'—which 'has become almost sacred from being the chief remains left us of apostolical truth; as the likeness of a friend, however incomplete in itself, is cherished as the best memorial of him, when he has been taken from us'.[145] As for the 'Catholic Church' of the early centuries, she was now only the 'Church Catholic' because of the loss of 'Unity . . . the

[140] Ibid. 49, 51, 56, 71, 107.   [141] Ibid. 38.   [142] Ibid. 250–2.
[143] Ibid. 286.   [144] Ibid. 189, 203, 209.   [145] Ibid. 217, 232.

sacramental channel through which . . . purity of doctrine' is 'secured to the Church', and because, consequently, 'the separate branches of the Church do disagree with each other in the details of faith'.[146]

The book ends with the consoling reflection that

the whole course of Christianity from the first . . . is but one series of troubles and disorders. Every century is like every other, and to those who live in it seems worse than all times before it. The Church is ever ailing. . . . Religion seems ever expiring, schisms dominant, the light of Truth dim, its adherents scattered. The cause of Christ is ever in its last agony . . .

It was a comforting thought that would often come to Newman's mind long after he had come to believe that the 'Catholic Church' of the Fathers had not in fact been broken into pieces. But the difference is that the author of the *Via Media* can offer no confident prospect of ultimate victory, only the assurance that in the end God will save his people 'in the intervals of sunshine between storm and storm . . . snatching them from the surge of evil, even when the waters rage most furiously'.[147]

8

Whatever Newman's unease about the *Via Media* position, the success of the Movement gave every reason for confidence. He was even afraid that 'Apostolicity' was 'growing . . . too fast' in Oxford. There was no doubting the Evangelical 'froth and fury' at 'the spread of Apostolical opinions'.[148] He also heard that his new book was selling 'very well'. He thought it would probably 'conciliate' some and 'frighten' others.[149] The eventual favourable response only showed 'how deep the absurd notion was in men's minds that I was a Papist; and now they are agreeably surprised'. He told Jemima 'frankly' that the Anglican ethos differed 'in some important points' from 'Popery', but that 'on the whole' it was 'far more like it than like Protestantism'.[150] He hoped that perhaps, 'under cover of this surprise and the relentings attending it', he would be 'able to discharge some darts against common Protestantism without molestation'. In Oxford everyone was commenting on how 'mild a book' it was.[151] He wondered 'how long the powder of the Popery cry will last—they must sooner or later come to the shot of argument'. His growing confidence was reflected in the increasingly bold and exuberant imagery of his letters: 'new ideas *will* startle people—it is like a souse in the water—there must be the contact with the cold. . . . The age is so very sluggish that it will not hear unless you bawl—you must first tread

---

[146] *VM* i. 199, 201–2.   [147] Ibid. 354–5.   [148] *LD* vi. 42–3.

[149] Ibid. 50–1.   [150] Ibid. 61.   [151] Ibid. 64.

on its toes, and then apologize.'¹⁵² Not only the 'great clamour' but also the 'grotesque reports' about the Tractarians were a 'proof' of the success of the Movement: 'The Coachman of the Coach which passes Littlemore at three when the bell is ringing seems regularly to give the passengers an account of us about as veracious I suppose, as those of Oxford guides generally are;' he could 'see the said Coachman touch his companion and turn to the passengers behind him when I meet them'.¹⁵³

After Easter he began a weekly early Communion service at 7 o'clock on Sundays. Meanwhile he had been using the Roman Breviary now for over a year, having chosen, at Rogers's suggestion, Froude's personal copy from among his books as a memento of his friend (he had first selected Butler's *Analogy*, but somebody else had already asked for it). He found that saying all the offices took up three or four hours a day—'a time which may be easily redeemed from the world. I like them uncommonly. They are very unexciting, grave, and simple.' As opposed to Greek 'devotions', which were 'pathetic and animated', the Latin ones were 'majestic and austere'. He was convinced that the Psalms, of which the Breviary very largely consists, 'should be the basis of all devotion'. A 'peculiarity' of the Breviary was its salutary emphasis on prayer in the morning, as opposed to night time, which was 'like putting off religion to a deathbed'; it was in 'curious contrast' to 'peculiarism' (Evangelicalism), which concentrated on 'exciting' evening services. 'Another characteristic' of the Breviary offices was 'the shortness of the prayers they contain'; lengthy prayers were 'peculiar', Froude had maintained, 'and came in at the Reformation'. The Psalms were more meditative and restful than '*continual addresses*' to God. The precise, methodical nature of the Breviary, like the Rosary, helped one to concentrate and seemed right in principle, although it might 'be abused into formalism'. More actual Scripture was read by Anglicans, but there again the short passages of the Breviary held one's attention better.¹⁵⁴

Just as the *Prophetical Office* had originated in Newman's correspondence with the abbé Jager, so his controversy with the *Christian Observer* (his second letter was published in the April and May numbers) had given him the idea of writing 'what will be almost a book on Justification'.¹⁵⁵ The first of the *Lectures on Justification* was delivered in the Adam de Brome chapel at St Mary's on 13 April, and the last on 1 June.

Meanwhile, Hurrell Froude's papers had been given to Newman and Keble to publish at their discretion. After consulting with various friends, it became clear that 'all parties' were in favour of 'immediate publication'. Only Newman had 'fears' of what he saw as 'a leap', but he

¹⁵² Ibid. 74.   ¹⁵³ Ibid. 149.   ¹⁵⁴ Ibid. 46-8.   ¹⁵⁵ Ibid. 53.

had nothing 'definite' against it and agreed to go ahead while he had the time.[156] He thought it would be best to bring out only one volume to begin with, rather than two or three volumes together, which would be 'a formidable purchase'. It would contain Froude's 'Private Thoughts', which were 'so very interesting and instructive' that he was 'sanguine about their selling', particularly among 'University men'. Since they were 'more touching as far as they are private', they would 'prepare the way for others—would interest men's sympathies and excite their respect, before their political prejudices' were upset by the more political papers on Church and State. He was so 'deeply impressed with their *attractive* character' that he proposed to send them to the printer straightaway, if Keble approved. Spiritual journals were much in vogue among Evangelicals, but these 'Private Thoughts' would 'show people what is the real use of such memoranda . . . not to ascertain our spiritual state in God's sight', but for 'improving ourselves, discovering our faults'. They also showed '*how* a person may indulge *metaphysical* speculations to the utmost extent and yet be *practical*', which 'might be a good lesson to various Cambridge men and others'. Furthermore, they presented 'a remarkable instance of the temptation to rationalism . . . subdued'. The paradoxical view that theological creativity is actually encouraged rather than discouraged by constraint and discipline would one day be eloquently applied by Newman on a much larger scale to the problem of freedom and authority in the Roman Catholic Church.

We see his mind only breaking out into more original and beautiful discoveries, from that very repression which seemed at first likely to be the utter prohibition of his powers. He used playfully to say 'His highest ambition was to be humdrum', and by sacrificing the *prospect* of originality he has become in the event more original. His profound Church views, as brought out in the Becket Papers, have sometimes seemed to me as a sort of gracious reward for his denying himself that vulgar originality which is rationalistic.

Newman proposed that a selection of letters should follow the 'Thoughts'—

to show his mind, his unaffectedness, playfulness, brilliancy. . . . His letters approach to conversation, to show his delicate mode of implying, not expressing, sacred thoughts; his utter hatred of pretence and humbug. I have much to say on the danger which (I think) at present besets the Apostolical movement of getting *peculiar* in externals, i.e. formal, manneristic etc. Now, Froude disdained all *show* of religion.[157]

He wrote to Keble that he had hesitated about publishing the letters as too personal. But they contained the 'first hints of principles which had been taken up by himself and others and for which he ought to have the credit'. Besides, 'We have often said the movement ... must be *enthusiastic*—now here is a character fitted above all others to kindle enthusiasm—should we not show what he was in himself?' He was 'really sanguine any how that the book will be a somewhat romantic one—and therefore do not like to lose the chance of this addition. Considering the state of the University, everything that can be effected against lowminded Hampdenism will be a gain.'[158] But when Rogers wrote to say that he and others were concerned about some of the more provocative passages in the letters, Newman replied that his friends now understood why he had had a 'dread of publishing' in the first place.[159]

On 25 August he received a parcel from William Froude containing his dead brother's private journal. It gave details of his fastings and temptations. Apart from the letters to Keble, they were the most interesting papers Newman had seen and 'quite made my head whirl, and have put things quite in a new light'.[160] He wrote to Keble begging him to consider the obvious religious objection that would be made: the Tractarians denied they were crypto-Papists, but it would be said that Froude's private journal showed 'a young man deeply oppressed by the feelings of his imperfections . . . coming to God for forgiveness, yet not a hint in his most intimate thoughts that he recollected he had a Saviour'. Since Christ's name was not even mentioned, it would be alleged that he had 'no real *apprehension*' of being saved, and it was no 'wonder that in his later papers he actually expresses his leaning to Popery, nay his bitter hatred of our Reformers'. Surely some 'explanation' was 'required. I think it was his profound awe and remorse. Is mine too Roman?'[161] Keble asked him to make the proposed explanation.

In October, Newman went down to Hursley to consult with Keble about the Froude papers which were now being printed. He told Bowden that he thought they would prove to be 'a fresh instrument of influence' for the Movement. He was convinced they portrayed 'a saint', whose ethos was 'as different from what is now set up as perfection as the East from the West'—'All persons of unhacknied feelings and youthful minds must be taken by them—others will think them romantic, scrupulous, over refined.'[162] Rivington had been so struck by reading the first few pages of the journal that he had decided to increase the edition from 750 to 1,000 copies. It had been decided to publish two volumes together; a third, and possibly a fourth, would follow later and would contain the papers on St Thomas à Becket. From Hursley, where he stayed a week, Newman mentioned in a letter to Jemima that he had been reading with delight Manzoni's novel *I promessi sposi*, which he had

[158] Ibid. 96–7.   [159] Ibid. 100.   [160] Ibid. 120.
[161] Ibid. 118–19.   [162] Ibid. 145.

found 'most inspiring' and which had 'quite transported' him 'in parts'; although it did not have 'the vigour or richness of Walter Scott', it showed 'a depth of religious feeling' not to be found in Scott.[163]

October also saw the publication in the *British Critic* of an interesting review article on de Lamennais, who, with Lacordaire and Montalembert, was one of the leading opponents of the Erastianizing Gallican church in France. Opposition to state control of the local church led Lamennais to the 'Ultramontane' view that Rome is the 'resting-point and centre of Catholicism', in so far as it is 'a court of final appeal between the Church and the local civil government'—'Hence it is the interest of the civil government, if it would subject its own Church to itself, to break it off from its centre of power . . . in other words, to *establish* it.' But ironically, hostility to 'the temporal establishment of religion' involved criticism of the Pope himself as 'a temporal prince'. We can see the seed of Newman's own later attitude to the temporal and spiritual powers of the papacy in his pointed remark that Lamennais found the 'See of St. Peter . . . removed from the rock on which it was originally built, and based upon the low and marshy ground which lies beside it'. At present Newman can only himself admit to a deeply ambivalent view of the papacy, which 'may be a human and rebellious work, and yet, in the divine counsels, a centre of unity may have been intended for the Church in process of time'—rather as, by analogy, he suggests, 'In the Mosaic law we find an anticipation of a time when the government of Israel should be kingly, yet the actual adoption of that form of polity was, under the circumstances, a sin in the people.' And he is reduced to speaking somewhat incoherently of 'the Papal power as an evil, yet not a pure evil, as in itself human, yet, relatively to the world, divine'. Where Newman can happily agree with Lamennais is in the historical fact that 'the Latin Church rose to power, not by the favour of princes, but of people'. Although the Church was not 'developed upon its original idea' of 'appealing to the people', nevertheless, 'what we do see from the first . . . is, religion throwing itself upon the people'. This essential truth provokes Newman into a gleefully sarcastic reflection on the establishment of the Church of England:

Doubtless, in the long run, the gridiron of St. Laurence would be found a more effectual guarantee of Church property than a coronation oath or an act of parliament. A broiling here and there, once or twice a century, would, on the whole, have ensured to the Church the unmolested enjoyment of her property throughout her dominions down to this day.

Corruptions there may have been in the papacy, but 'It was not the breath of princes or the smiles of a court which fostered the stern and lofty spirit of Hildebrand and Innocent. It was the neglect of self, the renunciation of worldly pomp and ease, the appeal to the people.' However, the radical conclusion reached by Lamennais that the Pope should not only renounce his 'temporalities' but 'place himself at the head of the democratic movement throughout Europe' (for 'Liberty is the cry of the day') finds no echo in the more cautious Anglican Newman, for whom 'rebellion is a sin' and 'innovation' to be suspected 'on principle'.[164]

By December the first volume of the *Remains* had been printed, and as the date for publication drew nearer, Newman again became 'very anxious' that, while they 'would arrest and bring forward very many', they would also 'much scandalize and . . . throw back some persons by their uncompromising Anti-protestantism'; they were certainly calculated 'to make people disloyal towards the Establishment', but not, he hoped 'to make them Romanists', on whom after all Froude was 'very severe'.[165] Before Christmas he sent to the publishers the first of his *Lectures on Justification*. He had been getting them ready for publication since the summer. The fact that the theological problem of justification had first been raised at the Reformation explained the absence of the 'peculiar' Evangelical 'ethos' in the early Church.[166] He had had to rewrite the original lectures. He was 'quite' frightened at the prospect of the appearance not only of the *Remains* but also of the *Lectures*, in which he was 'so afraid' of making 'some floors'—'and I know not whom to ask'.[167] However, the book was still 'in a very unfinished state, so I have to work like a horse', he told Harriett.

I am very anxious about the *unity* of the composition. One always exaggerates what is in hand—or I should say for certain that nothing I have done has given me such anxious thought and so much time and labour. I have written it over, and recast parts, so often that I cannot count them. Now as I print, I am rewriting it in fact . . . and I cannot help hoping, that, if all that is to come is like them, my trouble will be repaid—but, since an Author always has an affection for his worst productions, perhaps this is a bad sign.[168]

He wrote to Bowden that he was in a state of anxiety about both publications. The *Remains* would surely 'open upon' him 'a flood of criticism, and from all quarters': he had no regrets about the general 'picture of a mind' which they depicted, but he was very conscious that there would be considerable disagreement about individual passages which had been included—'It is just a case where no two persons have the same judgment about particulars'—but so long as the main point was 'gained . . . the details must be left to take their chance'. As to his

[164] *Ess.* i. 147–54, 157, 159.   [165] *LD* vi. 177.   [166] Ibid. 98.
[167] Ibid. 182.   [168] Ibid. 186.

own work on justification, he was 'a good deal fussed': it was 'the first voyage' he had 'yet made' on his own, 'with sun, stars, compass and a sounding line, but with very insufficient charts'. He was 'so afraid, not of saying things wrong so much, as queer and crotchety—and of misunderstanding other writers for really the Lutherans etc. as divines are so shallow and inconsequent, that I can hardly believe my own impressions about them'.[169]

There are many detailed descriptions in Newman's letters of the endless trouble he took to revise and rewrite his books, and the letter he wrote to Jemima at the end of January 1838 contains the first and perhaps the most vivid of the graphic accounts of the agony of writing, a pain which the writer in him could not help giving expression to.

I write—I write again—I write a third time, in the course of six months—then I take the third—I literally fill the paper with corrections so that another person could not read it—I then write it out fair for the printer—I put it by—I take it up—I begin to correct again—it will not do—alterations multiply—pages are re-written—little lines sneak in and crawl about—the whole page is disfigured—I write again. I cannot count how many times this process goes on.—I can but compare the whole business to a very homely undertaking . . . washing a sponge of the sea gravel and sea smell. Well—as many fresh *waters* have I taken to my book.[170]

Still, he was 'very diffident' how it would 'turn out' in the end, and was afraid it would be 'hard and laboured to read'.[171]

On 15 March, after completing the book, he told Henry Wilberforce that he had spent more time on it than on either of his two previous books, although it was 'a subject which ought to have taken less as having been in my thoughts, of course years and years before a scientific treatment of either Church Authority or the Arian Question could be, and continually before me as being the matter of Sermons, and yet I had nothing produceable scientifically'. He did not think he had changed his view since delivering the lectures, apart from 'very minor matters' of expression. 'What has taken me so much time is first the adjustment of the ideas into a system, next their adjustment in the Lectures, and thirdly and not the least the avoiding of all technicalities and all but the simplest and broadest reasonings'. He was even now uncertain how it would 'take as a whole—that there are good bits, I am aware'.[172] His 'great difficulty' had been how 'to avoid *being* difficult' on a subject which was 'so entangled and mystified by irrelevant and refined questions'.[173] *Lectures on Justification* was finally published on 30 March 1838.

[169] *LD* vi. 188–9. [170] Ibid. 193. [171] Ibid. 199.
[172] Ibid. 212–13. [173] Ibid. 222.

9

Newman begins by saying that the lectures were originally intended to show that 'certain essential Christian truths, such as Baptismal Regeneration and the Apostolical Ministry', are not in fact 'incompatible with the doctrine of justifying faith'.[174] It is another attempt to steer a *Via Media* between Protestantism and Romanism, between the 'erroneous' idea of justification by 'faith only' and the 'defective' theory of 'justification by obedience'. These two 'rigid' and 'extreme' views are both partially right, for the idea that 'we are absolutely saved by obedience, that is, by *what we are*, has introduced the proper merit of good works; that we are absolutely saved by faith, or by *what Christ is*, the notion that good works are not conditions of our salvation'.[175]

Lutheran theology assumes that 'justifying faith' will always be 'lively' and 'lead to good works'; but it is quite possible to believe fully that one has been saved by Christ 'without any fruit following': 'Trusting faith is not necessarily living faith.' The explanation that the 'life of faith' must be 'love' is rejected by Luther on the ground that this would be 'to deny the innate life and power of faith as such, and to associate another principle with it as a joint instrument in justification'.[176] Instead, it is claimed that justifying faith is defined 'not by what *it is*, but by what it *does*', for it is 'trust *in Christ*, and it differs from all other kinds of faith in That towards which it reaches forward and on which it rests'. Such a faith hardly 'admits of a definition', but derives 'its character' and 'its form' from the 'Object of the faith . . . which makes the faith what it is'. Newman criticizes the evasiveness of the explanation: 'They seem to allow that faith *is* in itself something more than trust, though men may be unable to say what it is more.'[177] It is claimed that faith '*sees* the purchased redemption, and therefore must be able to *take* and *apply* it': in other words, 'it *apprehends* Christ; a suitable, or rather convenient term as vaguely including both ideas, of accepting the message and receiving the gift, without making the distinction between them'.[178] To the Roman and Anglican objection that 'the thought of Christ may be possessed by those who have not Christ, and therefore that it is in no sense the form or characteristic principle of justifying faith; rather that love . . . is the true form, the discriminating mark and moulding principle under which belief is converted into Faith and made justifying', Luther's answer is that such a doctrine 'makes our thoughts centre on ourselves . . . fixes our faith on that love with which it is supposed to be instinct, instead of its mounting up worthless, rude, and

---

[174] *Jfc.*, p. v.   [175] Ibid. 2.   [176] Ibid. 8–9.   [177] Ibid. 11–13.
[178] Ibid. 19.

unformed, to receive subsistence, fashion, and acceptableness in Christ'.[179] It was his 'wish to extirpate all notions of human merit' and 'to give peace and satisfaction to the troubled conscience' that accounts for his vehement insistence on a doctrine which arose 'from his opposition to the Roman doctrine concerning good works'.[180] Faith also in his view 'is the instrument by which' Christ's 'Righteousness becomes ours', for 'He is our Righteousness, in the sense of His obedience being the substitute for ours in the sight of God's justice', with the result that 'every believer has at once a perfect righteousness, yet not his own', which 'precludes all boasting' because 'it is not his own' and 'all anxiety' because 'it is perfect': 'The conscience is unladen, without becoming puffed up.'[181] The 'doctrine of faith as the instrument, and Christ's righteousness as the form, of justification' is supposed 'to secure us against self-contemplation' and all forms of self-reliance, as well as destroying 'the state of doubt about our justification which must ever attend the belief that it depends on our graces and works'.[182] The fact that faith makes Christ's fulfilment of the moral law ours as well 'places us above the Law'. It is true that Christians will obey the moral law and be 'fruitful in good works', but only 'naturally' as a result of faith, and not out of a sense of duty or conscience.[183]

Newman now turns 'to consider the opposite scheme of doctrine, which is not unsound or dangerous in itself, but in a certain degree incomplete,—truth, but not the whole truth', in so far as it must not be 'detached and isolated', as 'in the Roman schools', from 'other truths'. This is the traditional view that 'justification consists in love, or sanctity, or obedience', and that to be justified is not just to be counted righteous but actually to be made righteous—'not a change merely in God's dealings towards us, like the pale and wan sunshine of a winter's day, but . . . the possession of Himself'.[184] Like the Arians, Protestants 'entrench themselves in a few favourite texts', but unlike the 'one or two texts only, detached from their context' of Lutheranism, the whole of Scripture testifies to this 'actual inherent righteousness' which is 'not a shadow but a substance, not a name but a power, not an imputation but an inward work'.[185] As usual for Newman, there is one decisive consideration: 'it is what the rival doctrine is not, a real doctrine, and contains an intelligible, tangible, practical view which one can take and use.'[186] By contrast, the Protestant 'idea of faith' is damned as 'a mere theory', from which it follows that 'their whole theology is shadowy and unreal'. The theme of reality is developed with superbly telling imagery:

---

[179] *Jfc.* 21.　　　　　[180] Ibid. 23.　　　　　[181] Ibid. 24.
[182] Ibid. 26.　　　　　[183] Ibid. 27–8.　　　　　[184] Ibid. 30–1, 34.
[185] Ibid. 36–7, 61.　　　[186] Ibid. 56.

The one view then differs from the other as the likeness of a man differs from the original. The picture resembles him; but it is not he. It is not a reality, it is all surface. It has no depth, no substance; touch it, and you will find it is not what it pretends to be . . . I wish to deal with things, not with words. I do not look to be put off with a name or a shadow. I would treat of faith as it is actually found in the soul; and I say it is as little an isolated grace, as a man is a picture. It has a depth, a breadth, and a thickness; it has an inward life which is something over and above itself; it has a heart, and blood, and pulses, and nerves, though not upon the surface. . . . Love and fear and obedience are not really posterior to justifying faith for even a moment of time, unless bones or muscles are formed after the countenance and complexion. It is as unmeaning to speak of living faith, as being independent of newness of mind, as of solidity as divisible from body, or tallness from stature, or colour from the landscape. As well might it be said that an arm or a foot can exist out of the body, and that man is born with only certain portions, head or heart, and that the rest accrues afterwards, as that faith comes first and gives birth to other graces.

In short, just as 'the presence of the soul changes the nature of the dust of the earth, and makes it flesh and blood . . . so love is the modelling and harmonizing principle on which justifying faith depends, and in which it exists and acts'.[187]

According to Newman, the word 'justifying' means literally ' "counting righteous", but includes *under* its meaning "making righteous" '.[188] By 'calling righteous what is not righteous till He calls it so', God not only declares we are justified, but 'He *justifies* us'.[189] After all, it would be 'a strange paradox to say that a thing is not because He says it is'.[190] Rather, it is characteristic of God's word in Scripture that it 'effects what it announces'.[191] Justification, then, means both God's '*justifying*' and man's '*being justified*', just as 'work' means 'both the doing and the thing done'; and while Protestants generally use it in the first active sense, and Roman theologians employ it in the second passive sense, in the standard Anglican writers there is no attempt to separate 'the seal and the impression, justification and renewal'.[192]

In the last analysis of what 'our state of justification . . . consists in', Newman dismisses both the archetypal Protestant and Roman answers as superficial and unsatisfactory. If 'the inward principle of acceptance' is held to be faith, then 'the question rises, what gives to faith its acceptableness?' And the answer must be that the reason why faith rather than unbelief is 'acceptable' is because the former has 'a something in it' which the latter does not, namely, 'God's grace'. And so we are driven to the conclusion that 'the having that grace or that presence, and not faith, which is its result, must be the real token, the

---

[187] Ibid. 263–6.   [188] Ibid. 65.   [189] Ibid. 72–3.   [190] Ibid. 78.
                           [191] Ibid. 81.   [192] Ibid. 96, 99, 174.

real state of a justified man'. Conversely, 'if we say that justification consists in a supernatural quality imparted to the soul by God's grace, as Roman writers say, then in like manner, the question arises' whether 'this renovating principle' does not necessarily involve 'grace itself, as an immediate divine power or presence'. But if so, 'then surely the possession of that grace is really our justification, and not renewal, or the principle of renewal'. It can thus be shown, 'by tracing farther back the lines of thought on which these apparently discordant views are placed', how they in fact 'converge' in 'an inward divine presence or grace, of which both faith and spiritual renovation are fruits'. Having, incisively and penetratingly, cut through the apparently impenetrable thicket of a controversy deeply rooted in a late medieval scholastic theology of grace which had lost touch with Scriptural and patristic sources, Newman can now put forward a solution to the age-old problem which transcends both the rival positions and whose brilliant originality lies simply in the rediscovery of the central New Testament doctrine of the 'indwelling' of the Holy Spirit: 'the presence of the Holy Ghost shed abroad in our hearts, the Author both of faith and of renewal, this is really that which makes us righteous, and . . . our righteousness is the possession of that presence.' Justification, then, 'is wrought by the power of the Spirit, or rather by His presence within us', while 'faith and renewal are both present also, but as fruits of it'.[193] The 'connection' between 'justification and renewal' is that they are 'both included in that one great gift of God, the indwelling of Christ [through the Holy Spirit] in the Christian soul', which constitutes 'our justification and sanctification, as its necessary results'—'And the one cannot be separated from the other except in idea, unless the sun's rays can be separated from the sun, or the power of purifying from fire or water.'[194] Faith, on the other hand, as the 'correlative' to God's grace, is first the 'condition' and then the 'instrument' of justification; while 'love is the modelling and harmonizing principle on which justifying faith depends, and in which it exists and acts'.[195]

It would be impossible to leave these lectures without paying special attention to the most powerful and striking final lecture, 'On Preaching the Gospel', where Newman maintains that Protestantism—'having fallen, after the usual manner of self-appointed champions and reformers, into the evil which it professed to remedy'—is itself guilty of the very charge of *legalism* which it wrongly makes against 'Catholic Truth'. It charges that just as 'Judaism interposed the Mosaic Law between the soul and Christ . . . so the Christian Church, Ancient and Catholic, also obscures the right and true worship of Him . . . by

[193] *Jfc.* 136–8.   [194] Ibid. 154.   [195] Ibid. 243, 303, 266.

insisting on Creeds, on Rites, and on Works'.[196] In so far, Newman agrees, as Roman theology, for instance, 'makes itself co-extensive with the Gospel Dispensation' and 'keeps pace with what is infinite and eternal, and exhausts the Abyss of grace, such a system is certainly open to the objection'.[197] But doctrinal statements, which are negative rather than positive, are necessary and useful as 'landmarks' and summaries of belief, 'intended to forbid speculations, which are sure to spring up in the human mind, and to anticipate its attempts at systematic views by showing the ultimate abyss at which all rightly conducted inquiries arrive, not to tell us anything definite and real, which we did not know before, or which is beyond the faith of the most unlearned'.[198] And just as bigotry is 'making the statement itself our end', so supersitition 'is the substitution of human for divine means of approaching God', but 'a rite is not properly superstitious, unless it is such self-worship'.[199]

By refusing 'what has been actually given', Protestantism was 'sure to adopt what had not been given'. Thus Protestants 'congratulate themselves on their emancipation from forms and their enlightened worship, when they are but in the straight course to a worse captivity, and are exchanging dependence on the creature for dependence on self'. Ironically, 'they substitute faith for Christ', and 'so regard it, that instead of being the way to Him, it is in the way'. Pithily, he presses home the point: 'they make it a something to rest in . . . they alter the meaning of the word, as the Jews altered the meaning of the word Law . . . they have brought into the Gospel, the narrow, minute, technical, nay, I will say carnal and hollow system of the Pharisees.' With contemporary Evangelicals in mind, he explains:

a system of doctrine has risen up during the last three centuries, in which faith or spiritual-mindedness is contemplated and rested on as the end of religion instead of Christ. . . . And in this way religion is made to consist in contemplating ourselves instead of Christ; not simply in looking to Christ, but in ascertaining that we look to Christ, not in His Divinity and Atonement, but in our conversion and our faith in those truths.

Instead of preaching Christ, the 'fashion of the day' is 'to preach conversion', to tell people 'to be sure they look at Christ, instead of simply holding up Christ to them', and 'to tell them to have faith, rather than to supply its Object'—with the result that 'faith and . . . spiritual-mindedness are dwelt on as *ends*, and obstruct the view of Christ'. It would be as if one were to 'affect people by *telling* them to weep or laugh'. Rather than feeling 'spontaneously, as the consequence of the objects presented to them', people 'will feel this and that, because they are told

---

[196] Ibid. 313–14.   [197] Ibid. 319.   [198] Ibid. 316.
[199] Ibid. 317–18.

to feel it'. This explains 'the absence of . . . composure, unobtrusiveness, healthy and unstudied feeling, variety and ease of language, among those who are thus converted, even when that conversion is sincere'.[200] There follows a splendidly sarcastic denunciation of the slavery of self-preoccupation:

Poor miserable captives, to whom such doctrine is preached as the Gospel! What! is *this* the liberty wherewith Christ has made us free, and wherein we stand, the home of our own thoughts, the prison of our own sensations, the province of self. . . . This is nothing but a specious idolatry . . .[201]

Referring to Luther's condemnation of 'the conscience-stricken Catholics of his day', Newman remarks tersely and satirically, 'surely it is better not to have Christ and to mourn, than to let Him go and to think it gain.'[202] Protestants picture faith 'as a sort of passive quality which sits amid the ruins of human nature, and keeps up what may be called a silent protest, or indulges a pensive meditation over its misery'; whereas

True faith is what may be called colourless, like air or water; it is but the medium through which the soul sees Christ; and the soul as little really rests upon it and contemplates it, as the eye can see the air. When, then, men are bent on holding it (as it were) in their hands, curiously inspecting, analyzing . . . they are obliged to colour and thicken it, so that it may be seen and touched. That is, they substitute for it something or other . . . which they may hang over, and doat upon. They rather aim at experiences . . . within them, than at Him that is without them.

Such 'being the difference', Newman concludes, 'between true faith and self-contemplation, no wonder that where the thought of self obscures the thought of God, prayer and praise languish, and only preaching flourishes'.[203] Yet another brilliant aphorism sums up the argument: 'To look at Christ is to be justified by faith; to think of being justified by faith is to look from Christ and to fall from grace.' The reader is left with the great paradox:

[Luther] found Christians in bondage to their works and observances; he released them by his doctrine of faith; and he left them in bondage to their feelings. . . . For outward signs of grace he substituted inward; for reverence towards the Church contemplation of self. And . . . whereas he preached against reliance on self, he introduced it in a more subtle shape; whereas he professed to make the written word all in all, he sacrificed it in its length and breadth to the doctrine which he had wrested from a few texts.

The moral with which Newman draws to a close the lecture is that this is 'what comes of fighting God's battles in our own way'; for just as the Pharisees, who 'were more careful of their Law than God who gave it',

---

[200] *Jfc.* 323–8.   [201] Ibid. 330.   [202] Ibid. 332–3.   [203] Ibid. 336–7.

and Judas, who 'was concerned at the waste of the ointment, which might have been given to the poor', were 'bad men' who 'professed to be more zealous ... than the servants of God', so 'in a parallel way Protestants would be more spiritual'.[204]

It was an arresting irony with which to conclude his final, most sustained repudiation of what he scathingly called earlier

this modern, this private, this arbitrary, this unscriptural system, which promising liberty conspires against it; which abolishes Christian Sacraments to introduce barren and dead ordinances; and for the real participation of the Son, and justification through the Spirit, would, at the very marriage feast, feed us on shells and husks, who hunger and thirst after righteousness! It is a new gospel, unless three hundred years stand for eighteen hundred; and if men are bent on seducing us from the ancient faith, let them provide a more specious error, a more alluring sophism, a more angelic tempter, than this. It is surely too bold an attempt to take from our hearts the power, the fulness, the mysterious presence of Christ's most holy death and resurrection, and to soothe us for our loss with the name of having it.[205]

From a literary point of view, the *Lectures on Justification*, and especially the last one, contain for the first time the full range of Newman's developing powers as a writer—in the increased richness of imagery, in a new brilliance of aphorism and skill in controversy, in a sharpened sarcasm and satirical wit, and in the assured poise of the eloquent rhetorician. As a theological work, the *Lectures*, although hardly eirenic in intention or tone, can now be seen to be a pioneering classic of 'ecumenical' theology; they are also, by the same token, an outstanding early example of Newman's many anticipations of much later developments in Roman Catholic theology.

[204] Ibid. 339–41.   [205] Ibid. 57.

4
Doubts

T H E first two volumes of Froude's *Remains* were published in the last week of February 1838. Newman waited, 'prepared but not comfortable in expectation of the first report of the explosion . . . having applied the match'.[1] However, he hoped the publication of the papers would be like 'the frost' which 'by its rigor hardens' the 'roots' of plants: he did 'not wish the Truth to spread too fast', and a 'check' would be 'providential'; he was confident that 'bold hearts' would 'stand the gust, but the reeds are bending, and the shallow' trees 'may be uprooted'.[2] At the beginning of April he noted: 'We are getting into considerable hot water in some places about the Remains—but it was to be expected—if we can but turn it into steam, and direct it aright, it may accelerate our motion towards desirable objects.'[3] The variegated images in a way reflected his own alternating feelings, but 'more and more' he saw the book as 'a call on the Church to repentance, (not to change)'.[4]

Back in May 1837 Newman had mentioned to Henry Wilberforce an idea he had of starting up a series of small volumes of prose and verse, which he hoped to 'get Ladies to write for'; they would be 'for the edification of young persons of the fair sex'. To counteract Evangelical and Roman Catholic fiction, 'we do want tales on our side very much— to take people's imagination'.[5] However, he had to give up the idea of beginning such a library himself after he agreed in January 1838 to take over the editorship of the *British Critic* from J. S. Boone. Two years before he had helped save the review from closing, when it was running at a loss, by promising unpaid contributions from himself and other members of the Movement, who had long wanted a specifically Tractarian review of their own; but, as he told Froude at the time, 'Perhaps this would be better than starting a fresh journal, not only as easier and less expence, but with a more Economical regard to the hearer'.[6] However, an article on Hampden in the July 1837 number caused great offence, and Newman also found out that Boone was allowing articles by a Methodist. It was especially galling that Wiseman's *Dublin Review*, amongst others, referred to the *British Critic* as

---

[1] *LD* vi. 210. [2] Ibid. 213. [3] Ibid. 224.
[4] Ibid. 228. [5] Ibid. 66, 72, 238. [6] Ibid. v. 201.

the organ of the Tractarians. Newman's fellow-Tractarian contributors had now 'struck', and a further offending article made him decide to 'strike' himself.[7] When Boone resigned, Newman made it clear that Tractarian support would only be forthcoming if the right editor was appointed, who would personally ensure the Catholic character of the journal. Typically, he dismissed the idea of a committee or board to run the review: 'All great things are done by concentration and individuality. We have been ruined by coalitions—if we are saved, it must be by God's single instrument, though defective . . .'.[8] One name he thought of was that of Henry Edward Manning—'an exceedingly sound man—a clever man'—the rising young Rector of Lavington, who had written earlier in 1837 to express his enthusiastic support for the work of Newman and Pusey. Newman knew that Manning had 'some time his own', for his wife Caroline had died from consumption in July after they had been married less than four years.[9] After Manning had declined, it was decided that S. R. Maitland, a friend of Rose and a contributor to the *British Magazine*, would edit one issue of the review 'on trial'. Newman liked him, but he was uneasy about his association with Rose (who seemed to Newman never to have '*a view*' but to be 'deficient in the power of taking an accurate and firm view of any subject which was clouded by political interests and the influences of friends and superiors'). They would have 'to break him in'; he was, Newman remarked with amusement, 'in a state half pleasurable half nervous—alternately soothed and startled, as a little boy being ducked in the sea, or a horse brought up to a post he shies at'.[10] If he refused to publish their 'strong articles', they would have to 'retire'.[11] In fact, it was Maitland who withdrew after one issue, and in January 1838 Newman was asked to take on the editorship himself. He felt 'sick at the thought', but 'there was no one else', and he 'did not like so important a work to get into hands' he 'could not trust'. He would 'come into play in July'. Maitland was the librarian at Lambeth Palace, and he had taken fright at a forthcoming review article by Pusey, which would put him in an embarrassing situation with the Archbishop. It was 'no wonder', Newman thought, he did not want to be editor—'he was setting out on a voyage of adventure with a rum crew and thought twice before he cut cable.'[12] At the end of March, after finishing the *Lectures on Justification*, Newman began 'clearing decks' for his new job.[13]

But he had other projects too on hand. A month later he arranged to rent in the summer a house opposite Pusey's in St Aldate's. The plan was to use it for young scholars who would help with the Library of the

---

[7] Ibid. vi. 147.   [8] Ibid. 170.   [9] Ibid. 175.
[10] Ibid. 186–7; iv. 230.   [11] Ibid. vi. 189.   [12] Ibid. 191–2, 194–5.
[13] Ibid. 221.

Fathers. Another of the Mozley brothers, James, a graduate of Oriel, was to be in charge; but there was no prospect of immediately filling the house, as it was highly unlikely that anyone hoping for a college fellowship would risk his chances by being seen to be so closely involved with Newman and Pusey. This idea of a 'monastery' or 'house of young Apostolicals' had first been mooted at the end of 1837.[14]

Then on 8 May Newman began another series of lectures in the Adam de Brome chapel at St Mary's, returning again to the crucial question of the relation of the Bible to Christianity. Of the twelve 'Lectures on the Scripture Proof of the Doctrines of the Church', the last of which was given on 7 August, eight were published as *Tract 85*. Newman begins by arguing that it is inconsistent for Bible Protestants to deny a Church doctrine like the Apostolic Succession 'because it is not clearly taught in Scripture', while accepting 'the divinity of the Holy Ghost, which is nowhere literally stated in Scripture'. The 'kill-or-cure remedy' for such 'inconsistency' lies either in 'adding to their creed, or . . . giving it up altogether'. It was a similar 'fearful' alternative with which one day he would confront Anglo-Catholics themselves.[15] Now he insists that it is facile to suppose that doctrines are either in or not in Scripture: 'Indeed . . . the more arguments there are for a certain doctrine found in Scripture, the more objections will be found against it.'[16] Moreover,

The arguments which are used to prove that the Church system is not in Scripture, may as cogently be used to prove that no system is in Scripture. If silence in Scripture, or apparent contrariety, is an argument against the Church system, it is an argument against system altogether. No system is on the surface of Scripture; none, but has at times to account for the silence or the apparent opposition of Scripture as to particular portions of it.

The conclusion is relentlessly pressed home: '*either* Christianity contains no definite message, creed, revelation, system . . . nothing which can be made the subject of belief at all; *or*, secondly, though there really is a true creed or system in Scripture, still it is not on the surface of Scripture, but is found latent and implicit within it.' The only third possibility is that, 'though there is a true creed or system revealed, it is not revealed in Scripture, but must be learned collaterally from other sources'.[17] The second possibility is the Anglican, while the first and third positions are the Latitudinarian and Roman Catholic points of view.

It is hard to take liberal Protestantism seriously: 'Why should God speak, unless He meant to say something? Why should he say it, unless He meant us to hear?' If there has been a Revelation, then 'there must be some essential doctrine proposed by it to our faith'; and therefore it is

---

[14] *LD* vi. 174.   [15] *DA* 112–13.   [16] Ibid. 125.   [17] Ibid. 126–7.

difficult 'to be a consistent Latitudinarian', because even he will hold on to 'his own favourite doctrine, whatever it is'.[18] It is against 'the common sense of mankind' to have 'a religion without doctrines': 'Religion cannot but be dogmatic; it ever has been.'[19] Not only do the New Testament writers themselves acknowledge that they 'did not in Scripture say out all they had to say', but they actually refer to a 'system' of doctrine and worship which has existed from the earliest times and which would have survived even if Scripture had been lost.[20] To suppose that all beliefs are equally true in the eyes of God, provided they are sincerely held, is simply 'unreal' and a 'mere dream of religion'. On the contrary, says Newman, invoking the pragmatic principle to which he was so often to appeal, 'We must take things as we find them, as God has given them', however inconvenient or unsatisfactory we may find them.[21]

Given, then, that the 'structure of Scripture' is so 'irregular' and unmethodical, we either have to say that it contains no definite 'message' (in which case we must say that there is 'no message at all given' or that 'it is given elsewhere'), or else 'that it is but indirectly and covertly recorded there, that is, under the surface'. Using a vivid, and not uncomical, image, Newman depicts Protestants, who like to ask where 'Church doctrines' are to be found in the Bible, as having themselves, in order to justify their own special so-called Biblical doctrines, 'to wind their way through obstacles, in and out, avoiding some things and catching at others, like men making their way in a wood, or over broken ground'.[22] Although the Bible is inspired, the actual 'history' and 'mode of its composition', he points out, are like those of other books. In fact, it is 'not one book' but 'a great number of writings, of various persons, living at different times, put together into one, and assuming its existing form as if casually and by accident'. To deduce 'the true system of religion' from such an unsystematic 'collection' would be like trying 'to make out the history of Rome from the extant letters of some of its great politicians, and from the fragments of ancient annals, histories, laws, inscriptions, and medals'. The New Testament writers 'did not sit down with a design to commit to paper all they had to say' about the Gospel, but they wrote with more limited, specific purposes in mind. Newman sees a corroborative analogy in the 'confused' and apparently fortuitous evolution and history of the world, which is none the less 'overruled' by God. It is no wonder that the 'doctrines of faith' are in Scripture 'only in an implicit shape', for, he ventures to suggest, 'humanly judging, they would not be there but for divine interposition'; and it should be no more surprise to 'find revealed doctrines scattered about high and low in Scripture, in places expected

[18] Ibid. 130–1.   [19] Ibid. 134.   [20] Ibid. 136–7.
[21] Ibid. 140–1.   [22] Ibid. 142–3.

and unexpected' than not to find the natural environment 'laid out in order'.[23] In fact, he goes on to argue, 'the Bible is written throughout with this absence of method', so that there is 'an order in the very disorder'.[24] Even its narrative of facts is 'unsystematic and unstudied' without any 'completeness or consistency'.[25]

There is also the consideration that 'two attributes' characterize the Bible 'throughout', which 'have a sort of necessary connexion, and set off each other—simplicity and depth'. This helps, too, to explain why Scripture is not luminous: 'Simplicity leads a writer to say things without display; and depth obliges him to use inadequate words.'[26] And this prompts Newman to contrast the 'fashion of this day', which 'is ever to speak about all religious things at once, and never to introduce one, but to introduce all, and never to maintain reserve about any'.[27] But the early Church always regarded the Bible as 'a book with very recondite meanings' and characterized by the same kind of 'secrecy' and 'concealment' which it practised itself.[28] A series of examples shows how simplistic it is to suppose that the meaning of Scripture is patently obvious, even on the most central of doctrines like the divinity of Christ. It is again inconsistent to accept without question the canon of Scripture, which cannot itself be proved from Scripture and which did not exist before the fourth century, and yet not to accept Church doctrines clearly attested to before that date and implicit in Scripture. Provocative Biblical analogies are employed to arouse a shocking realization of the inherent inconsistencies involved: 'The doctrines of the Church are not hidden so deep in the New Testament, as the Gospel doctrines are hidden in the old; but they are hidden; and . . . were men but consistent, who oppose the Church doctrines as being unscriptural, they would vindicate the Jews for rejecting the Gospel.'[29]

Tract 85 (which Newman later republished in his collected works under the title 'Holy Scripture in its Relation to the Catholic Creed') not only contains some of his most brilliant Biblical criticism, particularly in respect of the literary form of Scripture, but also is notable for its effective use of analogies to show up inconsistencies—a technique which he would one day perfect in the satirical masterpieces of his Catholic period.

2

On 19 June Newman began a pamphlet in answer to a sermon which Godfrey Faussett, the Lady Margaret Professor of Divinity, had preached on 20 May against the Tractarians. On 22 June, after sitting

[23] *DA* 146–51.   [24] Ibid. 153.   [25] Ibid. 170.   [26] Ibid. 173–4.
[27] Ibid. 181.   [28] Ibid. 194–5.   [29] Ibid. 246.

up all night, he completed the pamphlet, which was chiefly concerned with defending what Froude had written on the Eucharist. Faussett had deliberately withheld publication of his sermon, hoping that its appearance in time for Commemoration Day at the end of June would ensure it maximum publicity, but without leaving any opportunity for a reply. He had already preached against Hampden: 'He is like an old piece of ordnance,' Newman snorted, 'which can do nothing but fire—or like an old macaw with one speech . . . He can do nothing but fire, fire.'[30] He protested in the pamphlet, in the same terms he would one day use as a Roman Catholic about the intolerance of the Ultramontanes, against the Professor's presumption that members of the Church of England were Protestants: it was 'narrowing our terms of communion' when 'we must bear differences of opinion, however "offensive" '.[31] He had the 'satisfaction' of finding that his own pamphlet sold 750 copies as against 500 copies of Faussett's sermon.[32] 'Just at this time, June 1838,' he later noted, 'was the zenith of the Tract movement.' The 'beginning of a change of fortune' soon came.[33]

On 14 August the Bishop of Oxford delivered a *charge* which Newman had heard would be favourable to the *Tracts*. In the event, Dr Bagot, while commending their high doctrine of the Church and their attempts to restore the discipline of the Church, voiced disquiet about the effect on 'Disciples' of 'a peculiar temperament' and expressed fear about the dangers of further dividing the Church of England and encouraging 'practices which heretofore have ended in superstition'.[34] Newman wrote to Keble that he was 'disappointed' and thought it 'rather hard that he should publicly attack things in the Tracts without speaking to me about them privately and hearing what had to be said for them'. As he was so often to say later in his life with regard to Church authority, 'it seems hard that those who work and who *therefore*, as men, *must* mistake, should not have those mistakes put to the score of their workings, and be thanked for that work which others do not.' He thought at first that he would write and ask if the bishop wanted the *Tracts* to be stopped: but if so, he could not promise he would write nothing else in defence of the 'Faith' when it was 'in jeopardy'—although he would like nothing better personally than 'to retire into myself and to set about reading without writing'. If, on the other hand, he wrote to ask what specifically was objected to, he could be put in the position of having to retract statements or views he could not in conscience disavow. Then there was the danger of forcing the bishop 'to say more and command more than he intended, *in order* to give his words a definite and consistent meaning'.

[30] *LD* vi. 254.   [31] *VM* ii. 216–17.   [32] *LD* vi. 270.
[33] Ibid. 248.   [34] Ibid. 285–6.

And so, while it was 'disheartening to be snubbed', he had decided not to treat the matter seriously but 'to take it as one of those rebukes one reads of in history, which are like a smack in the face and nothing more'. The bishop had 'several times' shown favour to individual members of the Movement, and no doubt now he had been '*forced* to say something, conniving at us all the while', so that it would be 'unkind and unwise to make him commit himself to a meaning'.[35]

On second thoughts, however, the prospect of putting himself in opposition to the authority of his bishop filled Newman with unease. He decided to write informally to the Archdeacon to try and ascertain what exactly Dr Bagot objected to. 'I say with great sorrow', he wrote, 'that it is quite impossible for me to continue the Tracts with this indefinite censure upon them from my own Bishop.' It was not 'any undue sensitiveness' which made him say this, but 'A Bishop's lightest word ex cathedrâ is heavy. His judgment on a book cannot be light. It is a rare occurrence.' If the Archdeacon could let him know which *Tracts* were disapproved of, he would 'at once withdraw them without a word'. He ended the letter by acknowledging 'some pain . . . now expressed for the first and last time, that the first notice I should have of his dissatisfaction with any part of my writings, should be on so solemn and public an occasion'.[36] He told Bowden that while he knew that what the bishop had said 'was very slight indeed', still, 'a Bishop's lightest word ex Cathedra is heavy'. It was not 'usual' for a bishop to refer to a book in a *charge*, 'and, since he has not said *what* the exceptionable things are, he has thrown a general suspicion all over the volumes'. It would involve 'a considerable loss of money' if they had to stop the *Tracts*, but at least it would show people 'we are sincere and not ambitious'.[37] He did not doubt the bishop had only intended a 'mild' warning, which would act as 'merely a *check*', but Dr Bagot did not apparently appreciate that the 'Apostolical' principles and teachings of the *Tracts* meant that 'I cannot be party to any thing which he censures ex cathedrâ ever so slightly'.[38]

The Archdeacon replied that he could not answer Newman's question, but that he did not think the bishop wanted the *Tracts* to be withdrawn; he advised Newman to get in touch with the bishop himself. After being shown Newman's letter to the Archdeacon, the bishop wrote to say that he was astonished by his reaction: much he had approved, nothing had been censured, and he had 'only lamented things which from ambiguity of expression might . . . by others be misunderstood or misrepresented'; he had expected disapproval from opponents of the *Tracts* because of his support for them, but he had not dreamed that his

---

[35] *LD* vi. 286–7. [36] Ibid. 290. [37] Ibid. 291–2. [38] Ibid. 295.

remarks would cause offence on the other side.[39] He asked Newman to look again at his *charge* when it was printed—when he took the precaution himself of adding a footnote to deny that he had intended to censure the *Tracts*. Newman replied that he felt 'a more lively pleasure in knowing that I am submitting myself to your Lordship's expressed judgment . . . than I could have even in the widest circulation of the volumes in question'. He told Pusey, however, that although the bishop had been very kind, he still thought that the bishop had not taken into account their view of 'the power of a Bishop's word', nor that 'we are so bound by professions (to say nothing else) to obey it'.[40] It was unlikely he had any definite objections to anything in the *Tracts*, but he had simply wanted to placate 'the popular cry with a vague disapprobation, just as men revile Popery in order to say strong Catholic things'. Probably, too, he was annoyed about the *Remains*. At any rate he had failed to see that 'a Bishop's word is an act' and that he, Newman, was strictly 'under his jurisdiction', so that 'his word would not act as a damper merely but as a command'. A bishop, he insisted, 'cannot *criticize* ex-cathedrâ those under him'.[41] However, as Keble pointed out, the bishop was hardly accustomed to such deference to his views among the clergy and was obviously astonished by Newman's reaction.

Newman explained his feelings more fully to Pusey. He had

for several years been working against all sorts of opposition, and with hardly a friendly voice. Consider how few persons have said a word in favor of me. Do you think the thought never comes across me, that I am putting myself out of my place? what warrant have I for putting myself so forward against the world? am I bishop or professor, or in any station which gives me right to speak?

His only 'comfort' had been that the bishop had never actually 'spoken against' him, but he had never been a '*friend*' or 'supported' him. He could 'truly say' that he 'would do any thing to serve him'. Indeed, he confided, in words that would certainly have startled the worthy Dr Bagot, 'Sometimes as I have stood by as he put on his robes, I felt as if it would be such a relief if I could have fallen at his feet and kissed them . . .'. The fact was that the bishop had not even replied to his letter over the 'unpleasant Jubber business' when 'I needed a great deal to cheer me'. It looked as if the *Tracts* would have to cease.

It is very well for people at a distance, looking *at* me, to say (as they will) I am betraying a cause and unsettling people. My good fellows, *you* make me the head *of a party*—that is *your external* view—but I know what I am, I am a clergyman under the Bishop of Oxford and any thing more is accidental.

Shortly after, he wrote to Keble, 'No one has encouraged me but you—

[39] Ibid 296.   [40] Ibid. 298.   [41] Ibid. 301, 305.

Pusey was so cast down when he heard it, that he himself needed comfort.'[42] He told Bowden that he would wait until he saw the *charge* in print, but he was certain that in '*consistency*' lay their 'strength (as to every thing, or person, political, religious, philosophical)'—'If we show we are not afraid of carrying out our principles in whatever direction, humanly speaking, nothing can hurt us—And it seems the most likely way to receive a blessing.'[43] In the end, the note which the bishop added to the *charge* persuaded him that he could 'proceed with the *Tracts* without inconsistency', as he told Dr Bagot.[44]

Meanwhile, Newman was busy trying to edit the *British Critic*. He suggested to Keble that an article might usefully be written to show 'that nothing but Apostolicity is poetical—that religious poets are forced to go *out of* their religion, (e.g. into domestic matters etc) for poetry when their religion is Peculiarity etc.'[45] He was very keen that Keble should write a review of Manzoni's *I Promessi sposi*: they knew so little about the actual workings of Roman Catholicism, 'but still the contrast with our own way of going on is so striking that a person may know much negatively'. He also mentioned in the same letter, written in the middle of October, that there was a plan for 'building a "Church of the Reformers", in order to force your humble servant either to subscribe to it *or* not'.[46] The idea apparently was to erect 'a sort of Cranmer and Latimer testimonial', although it had not been decided whether it should be 'a Church or a Cross or a monument'.[47]

At the beginning of November Newman heard that some supporters of the Movement were dismayed about a projected English translation of the Roman Breviary, on which two of his former Oriel pupils, S. F. Wood and Robert Williams, had been working during the past year, and to which he himself had contributed translations of hymns. Keble thought that the publication of the *Remains* had caused alarm in certain Tractarian quarters and that the project should be suspended temporarily, although he did not see how the whole of it could ever be published, as parts concerning the Saints and the Virgin Mary would have to be omitted. Newman himself had already suggested that a corrected version should be published, although it was not clear by what '*standard*'.[48] He felt very depressed, he confided to Bowden:

I am so bothered and attacked on all sides by friends and foes. . . . It is just like walking on treacherous ice—one cannot say a thing but one offends some one or other. I don't mean foe, for that one could bear, but friend. You cannot conceive what unpleasant tendencies to split are developing themselves on all sides. . .[49]

[42] *LD* vi. 307–9. [43] Ibid. 314. [44] Ibid. 334. [45] Ibid. 322.
[46] Ibid. 329. [47] Ibid. 331. [48] Ibid. 338. [49] Ibid. 344.

Towards the end of the month he wrote to tell Keble that Wood and Williams had decided, at some cost, to abandon their project. As for other criticisms, he wanted to put himself 'entirely' in Keble's hands—'I will do whatever you suggest. I really do hope I have no wish but that of peace with all parties, and of satisfying you.' He wished some people

would seriously ask themselves *what* they desire of me. Is it to stop writing? I will stop any thing you advise. Is it to show what I write to others before publishing? it is my rule. . . . Is it to stop my weekly parties or any thing else? I will gladly do so. Now this being understood, may I not fairly ask for some little confidence in me as to what, under these voluntary restrictions, I do? People really should put themselves into my place, and consider how the appearance of suspicion, jealousy, and discontent is likely to affect one, who is most conscious that every thing he does is imperfect, and therefore soon begins so to suspect every thing that he does as to have no heart and little power remaining to do any thing at all. Any one can fancy the effect which the presence of ill-disposed spectators would have on some artist or operator engaged in a delicate experiment? Is such conduct kind towards me? is it feeling? If I ought to stop, I am ready to stop; but do not in the same breath, chide me, for instance, for thinking of stopping the Tracts, and then be severe on the Tracts which appear. . . . This I feel, that if I am met with loud remonstrances before gentle hints are tried, and suspicions before proof, I shall very soon be silenced, whether persons wish it or no.

In his reply to this *cri de cœur* from his friend, Keble admitted that his brother Thomas, whose criticisms had hurt Newman, failed to 'understand the keenness of your feelings—(for you know, my dear N. you are a very sensitive person—)'. Newman's response was that Thomas Keble understood the country clergy, but that he himself was writing not for them but for the younger generation, especially those at Oxford, for whom he did not consider he was 'going too fast'.

One cannot stop still. Shrewd minds anticipate views, anticipate objections, oblige one to say yes or no—oblige one to defend oneself, oblige one to anticipate *their objections* . . . who must be anticipated and treated, lest *they* do harm. It is better surely to refute objections than to let others be the prey of them. In fact, in a place of this kind, if one *is* to speak (which is another matter) one must be prepared to pursue things, and admit or deny inferences.

But it was perfectly true it could well be asked, '*ought* one to say, though one *may* be making way here, if it is at the expence of the country clergy?' After all, he had '*no call*' and no 'station': 'When then a man like your brother *does* object, he has my own latent feelings on his side—and he goes just the way, whether he wishes it or no, to reduce me to silence.' But, 'though silent', he had no intention of 'doing nothing'. He wondered whether he would 'not be doing better by reading and preparing *for future* writing on the Fathers, than by offhand works; and with this view giving up the Tracts, the B.C. and preaching at St Mary's'. To read the Fathers would give him 'most peace of *conscience*', as well as being preferable to writing tracts and pamphlets which he only did 'under the stimulus of external things which I witness'. He had a 'constant feeling' when writing 'that I do not realize things, but am merely drawing out intellectual conclusions', which was 'very uncomfortable'. But, if he did withdraw from the fray, he warned rather ominously, 'many things would occur, which one should wish otherwise and which would pain me—and I should be blamed by those who now, without knowing it, are certainly going the way to bring it about'.[50] It was a foretaste of his later discomfort as a Roman Catholic, painfully caught as he was between the older Tractarians, who urged caution and moderation, and the younger, more adventurous, inquiring adherents of the Movement.

Sensitive he might be, but this did not exclude an exuberant robustness in responding to attacks, such as the one that appeared in a newspaper at the end of November:

There is a great fat lie, a lie to the back bone, and in all its component parts, and in its soul and body, inside and out, in all sides of it, and in its very origin, in the Record. . . . It has no element of truth in it—it is born of a lie—its father and mother are lies and all its ancestry—and to complete it, it is about me.[51]

The gloating fascination with which Newman pursues the metaphor is typical of the kind of gleefully grotesque imagery he was to develop so effectively later in his satirical writings.

3

At the beginning of January 1839 Newman wrote to Bowden, 'What a great thing it is that our Bishop is for us!' He had heard that Dr Bagot was 'extremely pleased' with his letters—'and has done every thing to counteract any effect such as I feared'. He had to admit that he had not been 'fully reconciled' till he realized 'the poor Bishop had got into trouble'; he had now begun 'to feel very grateful to him'. A 'most grotesque' news item about him in the current *Christian Observer* made him feel that 'one step alone is wanted—to say' that he was the very Pope himself 'in disguise'![52] However, he could honestly say that he did not 'care about the attacks of strangers; it is only when friends fall upon me, that I am touched'. The newspapers, anyway, would not be making 'this great noise unless we were making way'. He did not know what their

---

[50] *LD* vi. 347–8, 350, 353–4.   [51] Ibid. 352.
[52] To J. W. Bowden, 3 Jan. 1839.

'length of tether' was to be—'no one can know—it is a fearful and interesting thought—but at present it is lengthening out.'[53]

The publication of Froude's *Remains* seems to have provoked the idea, which was first mooted in the autumn of 1838, of erecting by subscription some kind of a monument to Cranmer, Ridley, and Latimer, who had been burned at the stake in Broad Street, as a kind of test of the loyalty of Newman and Pusey, in particular, to the Church of England. From the outset Newman had no intention of subscribing:

. . . I have no sort of confidence in, Cranmer etc, and I will not commit myself to them. Practically speaking, to subscribe is to make them the representatives of the English Church—This is the reason they are brought forward; in order to be watchwords against the Romanists . . . it is to acknowledge them theologically. This, I am sure, will be the practical effect of it. I will not tie, what may prove a millstone, round my neck . . . now when through happy fortune I am emancipated, when I walk in the light of day and the free air, and no longer need invent all sort of fictions and artifices to make out Cranmer or others Catholic . . . it would be sheer absurdity to bury myself again in the world of shadows, and give myself in the eyes of our adversaries, Romanists and Dissenters, that appearance of unfairness and disingenuousness which they have ever imparted to the English controversialist. No—I can say, do your worst on Cranmer, you do not touch the English Church.—I am perfectly aware indeed that what I gain *controversially*, I lose *at home*. I alienate and disgust brother Churchmen, while I strengthen myself against opponents . . . [But] I say that Cranmer will not stand *examination*—that they are worst friends to him who put him up to be criticized—that they are best friends who keep silence . . . Men are for him now—they will be less and less so. The more he is talked of, the less he will be borne. It is an unpopular thing to seem to take part against him now—but men will come over to us . . . and therefore, though unpopular at the moment, it is long sighted policy . . . to keep free of him. The controversial gain then is permanent, the unpopularity at home transitory . . .[54]

Now he merely noted that the bishops were 'en masse . . . joining the testimonial'. He could think of 'worse things'; perhaps 'good' might even come out of it.[55]

'Poor Rose' had died shortly before Christmas in Florence—'or happy, that he is taken off just as the battle begins!' It was wrong, Newman told Rogers, to be over-anxious over the progress of the Movement:

. . . Apostolicity is nothing till it is tried, and less than nothing if it cannot bear a puff. I do not know how I should feel were I in the world; but here I cannot realize things enough either to hope or fear. It sometimes comes on me as an alarming thing, almost a sin, that I doubt whether I should grieve though all that has been done melted away like an ice palace. I do not mean, of course, I

[53] To Mrs J. Mozley, 9 Jan. 1839.   [54] *LD* vi. 364.
[55] To F. Rogers, 14 Jan. 1839.

should not grieve in the case of individuals I knew, or should not be annoyed about opponents, whom I knew, triumphing—but I speak of the whole as a *work*. I wish I lived as much in the unseen world as I think I do not live in this. The fear is, lest one lives in a world between the two, a selfish heart.

Meanwhile, the good news was that the *Tracts* 'are selling faster than they can print them': the fourth volume had sold out after only six months, and a second edition was now coming out. As a safeguard, Newman had had the idea of 'printing extracts from our works against Popery—and they will appear stitched into some of the February magazines': after all, 'if our beauties are strung together in the Newspapers on the side of Romanism, there is reason why elegant Extracts should be made against it'; and anyway, people 'need the same thing being said a hundred times over in order to hear it'.[56] He had heard that the clergy of the Church of Ireland were 'rising en masse to call on the English Bishops to hold a Council and condemn us'. But this was nothing to the popular rumours that were circulating:

the Master of University [College] [has] been assured by a lady at Cheltenham that we offered sacrifices every morning. He explained it by morning prayers. No, she said, it was not that—she knew for certain we killed *something*, she did not know what—

Was it 'little children?' Newman wondered, 'or each other? or frogs and spiders? or what?' However, he could not feel anxious about their 'prospects . . . when souls have once tasted of immortal truth'.[57] Nor was he worried about misrepresentations in the press: as he was so often to do in the course of his life, he consoled himself with the reflection that 'time will set a great many matters right, and time only'. At any rate, there must surely be 'a reaction' and 'the gradual growth of better views'.[58]

At the end of January a meeting was held at which it was decided to build a church as a memorial to the Protestant martyrs. Newman expected most senior members of the university to subscribe, but with reluctance. The idea that it was 'a shocking thing' if he, Pusey, and Keble were 'left alone in the whole Church' in not subscribing struck him as 'most curious'. People assumed they were 'a party' and could not understand how they could be so 'unmindful' of their 'interests'; but he had 'never felt, never acted as having a party—so such an argument is but an insult'. So far as he was concerned, 'nothing on earth' would make him put his name to the subscription. 'One thing' was 'clear', namely, that 'the scheme' was 'an egregious failure' with regard to 'its first purpose' of 'showing the feeling of Oxford'.

[56] To F. Rogers, 22 Jan. 1839.
[57] To F. Rogers, 22 Jan. 1839; to H. Wilberforce, 22 Jan. 1839.
[58] To A. Belamy, 25 Jan. 1839.

It seemed, however, now, as if they were 'in the thick of the fight', with the heads of colleges 'annoyed' and the bishops 'frightened'. Newman did not in any way regret the publication of the *Remains*, although it appeared that 'the Tracts are in certain high quarters taken up as perfection *now*, and the Remains made the scapegoat', while the '*tone* of the Tracts is now *perfect*—but the Remains all that is unpleasant'. Five years ago, he remembered sardonically, it was 'the tone of the Tracts' which 'was thought most insulting; and the whole conduct of them most injudicious'.[59] He had heard that people had been startled by *Tract 85*, but he also knew that others had found it helpful: what pleased one person displeased another, and he was learning to ignore criticism, 'so much so that in due time I suppose *no one* will have any influence over me in questions connected with *expedience*'.[60]

The January number of the *British Critic* included an article by Newman on St Ignatius, which contained some not altogether dissimilar autobiographical reflections on patristic studies. The reason why there were such contrary reactions to reading the Fathers was that people 'do not know what to look for, or are possessed with one or more ideas which they in vain seek to find in them. Their notion of the matter of divinity is so different from what prevailed in primitive times, that the surface of their minds does not come into contact with what they read . . .' To analyse the Fathers in accordance with modern categories and criteria was futile, especially when the 'ancient Church cannot speak for herself'. Newman's approach to the Fathers reminds one of his attitude to religious belief in general: 'if a man begins by summoning them before him, instead of betaking himself to them,—by seeking to make them evidence for modern dogmas, instead of throwing his mind upon their text, and drawing from them their own doctrines,—he will to a certainty miss their sense.' To come to the Fathers with preconceived modern ideas was like trying 'to criticise Gothic architecture by the proportions of Italian, or to attempt the mysterious strains of Beethoven on the flute or guitar'. Apart from divesting oneself of 'modern ideas and prejudices', one had to take 'the trouble of a personal inspection' rather than rely on 'antecedent reasoning', in order to discover the 'Catholic' sense of the Fathers; otherwise, one merely illustrated 'how the age of railroads' was bound to 'behave towards the age of martyrs'.[61]

At the beginning of February, Newman told Maria Giberne that he felt 'sanguine' about the present 'clamour' against them: 'Clamour makes our principles known—and then tires, and leaves us to prove them.' They were in the process of publishing some more volumes of the

[59] To H. Wilberforce, 1 Feb. 1839.   [60] To J. F. Christie, 5 Feb. 1839.
[61] *Ess.* i. 227–9, 232–3.

Remains, but he admitted he was a 'little' worried about the bishop—'I wish to do what he would wish—yet it is so very difficult to get at his wishes, without committing him.' He mentioned that C. P. Golightly, who had been at Oriel and on friendly terms with Newman (who indeed had invited him to be his curate at Littlemore on the completion of the church there) was now 'making himself a Scaramouch here. He has got up a project of a Testimonial to Cranmer—but has stuck half way in the important matter of *funds*. . . . This precious project was mainly devised against me and others—they will pay dear for their frolick.' He asked her to 'send . . . at once any GOOD absurd lies about us which are current in your parts—a whole budget, if they would do to be printed'.[62]

His exuberance was soon checked by a letter from S. F. Wood—'one of the heaviest I ever had in my life'. It contained the completely unexpected news that Bowden's lungs were giving serious cause for concern. He had simply 'taken it for granted that a long course of usefulness was reserved' for his friend: 'I think this news has brought home to me, more than any thing else, how in the midst of life we are in death. It is as if one were standing in a fight, and any one might be shot down.'[63] On the birthday they shared he wrote to his oldest Oxford friend: 'It is a day which among its other thoughts must ever bring before me the image of one of the kindest, most generous, and most sweet-minded persons I ever have been allowed to know.'[64]

By March the promoters of the Martyrs' Memorial had still not raised even a quarter of the sum they had hoped for. Perhaps they would have to be 'contented with busts in the Bodleian'. They wanted to build a church and had 'a grand scheme of pulling down and rebuilding St Mary Magdalen', just round the corner from Broad Street. 'Would it not be a remarkable and quite ominous satire on . . . Cranmer, if they are obliged to pull down a church?' Pulling it down would, in any case, cost them at least the sum they had already raised. 'I long to see them all,' Newman remarked gleefully, 'as a point of honor, doubling, trebling, and quadrupling their subscriptions.' He would love to see 'old Faussett' and others 'pulling out their £100s to build a thing which no one cares for, where no one wants it—and just completing it by the time that all sensible people . . . have given up Cranmer as a bad job'.[65] It seemed to him 'a very curious proof of the hollowness of the apparent system of Protestantism' that even a projected memorial to its great martyrs could not 'touch' people's 'hearts'.[66] It was in fact nothing but a 'ramshackle tumbledown . . . concern . . . begun in spite against myself and others'.[67] And the only result of the activities of 'goose Golightly and

[62] To Miss M. Giberne, 6 Feb. 1839. [63] To S. F. Wood, 8 Feb. 1839.
[64] To J. W. Bowden, 21 Feb. 1839. [65] To H. A. Woodgate, 3 Mar. 1839.
[66] To Mrs J. Mozley, 4 Mar. 1839. [67] To S. L. Pope, 21 Apr. 1839.

Co' had been to start 'an inquiry upon Cranmer, whom it is the truest charity to say nothing about'.[68]

He had decided not to continue his annual lectures in the Adam de Brome chapel in the summer term. He had intended them to be 'a continuation of Tract 85', and the 'question of the Pope's being Antichrist would have come in'.[69] He wanted instead to rewrite his *History of the Arians* for a second edition and to try and finish his edition of St Dionysius, with which he could conveniently combine other editorial work on the Library of the Fathers.

Newman was still busy editing the *British Critic*, the sales of which, rather to his surprise, had slightly risen under his editorship. The 'one thing' he aimed at ('which other publications fail in') was 'avoiding frothy, empty articles, from which you rise up and have gained nothing'. The *British Critic* might be 'dull or lively, obscure or striking, but, if I can help it, it shall not be unreal'.[70] There was certainly nothing dull or obscure or unreal about the important article he wrote in the April number, which was called 'The State of Religious Parties' (later republished as 'Prospects of the Anglican Church').

He records in the *Apologia* how 'In the spring of 1839 my position in the Anglican Church was at its height. I had supreme confidence in my controversial *status*, and I had a great and still growing success, in recommending it to others.' But, as he recalled the April article, he realized that it contained 'the last words which I ever spoke as an Anglican'. Although he 'little knew it at the time', it could in retrospect 'be read as my parting address and valediction, made to my friends'.[71]

Apart from the more obvious causes of the Movement, in the article Newman singles out 'a growing tendency towards the character of mind and feeling of which Catholic doctrines are the just expression' and which 'manifested itself long before men entered into the truth intellectually'. The first of the Romantic influences he mentions is that of Walter Scott:

During the first quarter of this century a great poet was raised up in the North, who, whatever were his defects, has contributed by his works, in prose and verse, to prepare men for some closer and more practical approximation to Catholic truth. . . . stimulating their mental thirst, feeding their hopes, setting before them visions, which, when once seen, are not easily forgotten, and silently indoctrinating them with nobler ideas . . .

And while history in prose and verse was thus made the instrument of Church feelings and opinions, a philosophical basis for the same was under formation in England by a very original thinker, who, while he indulged a liberty of speculation which no Christian can tolerate, and advocated conclusions which

---

[68] To Mrs J. Mozley, 23 Apr. 1839.   [69] Ibid.
[70] To Mrs J. Mozley, 20 June 1839.   [71] *Apo*. 91–2.

were often heathen rather than Christian, yet after all instilled a higher philosophy into inquiring minds, than they had hitherto been accustomed to accept. . . . It has indeed been only since the death of Coleridge that these results of his writings have fully shown themselves . . . Two living poets [Southey and Wordsworth] may be added, one of whom in the department of fantastic fiction, the other in that of philosophical meditation, have addressed themselves to the same high principles and feelings, and carried forward their readers in the same direction.

These wishes, however, are to be noticed far more as indications of what was secretly going on in the minds of men, than as causes of it. The reaction in the Church . . . was long ago anticipated . . .

People who complain about 'the impetuosity of the current' of the Movement, should rather criticize the previous century which 'dammed up our majestic river till it has become a flood'. Anyway, it is 'not a movement' but 'a spirit'. And it is the result of 'the spiritual awakening of spiritual wants', for people 'feel in themselves a moral need, which certain doctrines supply' and 'they embrace the doctrines because they need them'. These 'yearnings' are very different from 'merely enthusiastic' feelings which 'often argue impatience and want of discipline'. On the other hand, Newman admits that among the Tractarians there is 'much that is enthusiastic, extravagant, or excessive':

Truth and falsehood do not meet each other here by harsh lines; there are ten thousand varieties of intermixture between them. There will ever be a number of persons professing the opinions of a movement party, who talk loudly and strangely, do odd or fierce things, display themselves unnecessarily, and disgust other people; there will be ever those who are too young to be wise, too generous to be cautious, too warm to be sober, or too intellectual to be humble . . . Such persons will be very apt to attach themselves to particular persons, to use particular names, to say things merely because others say them, and to act in a party-spirited way . . .

But, argues Newman, 'dust and din . . . attends every great moral movement', and the 'truer doctrines are, the more liable they are to be perverted'.

Of the other two main parties in the Church of England, Newman sees 'Liberalism' as 'too cold a principle to prevail with the multitude', whereas Evangelicalism ('the largest, most compact, most prominent party in our Church at this moment') lacks any 'internal principle of union, permanence, and consistency', in the absence of which, 'a principle of life is wanting, and all is outward show'. Because it 'is made up of the fragments of religion which the course of events has brought together', it 'contains within it the seeds of ruin, which time only is required to develop'. Its very inconsistency ensures that Evangelical Protestantism is *unreal*:

It does not stand on entrenched ground, or make any pretence to a position; it does but occupy . . . the space between contesting powers, Catholic truth and Rationalism; neither of these owning it, or making account of it, or courting it; on the contrary, both feeling it to be a hindrance in the way of their engaging with each other, and impatiently waiting to be rid of it. Then, indeed, will be the stern encounter, when two real and living principles, simple, entire, and consistent, one in the Church, the other out of it, at length rush upon each other, contending not for names and words, or half views, but for elementary notions and distinctive moral characters.

As Newman's survey of the religious scene reaches its conclusion, the central issue becomes one of consistency versus inconsistency, reality versus unreality. The idea of 'comprehensiveness' is dissected with brutal sarcasm:

In the present day mistiness is the mother of wisdom. A man who can set down half a dozen general propositions, which escape from destroying one another only by being diluted into truisms, who can hold the balance between opposites so skilfully as to do without fulcrum or beam, who never enunciates a truth without guarding himself from being supposed to exclude the contradictory, who holds that Scripture is the only authority, yet that the Church is to be deferred to, that faith only justifies, yet that it does not justify without works, that grace does not depend on sacraments, yet is not given without them, that bishops are a divine ordinance, yet those who have them not are in the same religious condition as those who have,—this is your safe man and the hope of the Church; this is what the Church is said to want, not party men, but sensible, temperate, sober, well-judging persons, to guide it through the channel of No-meaning, between the Scylla and Charybdis of Aye and No.

Grotesque physical imagery, not unreminiscent of Dickens, is employed to convey the frustration of those who cannot continue in this kind of unreal religion:

They will not keep standing in that very attitude, which you please to call sound Church-of-Englandism or orthodox Protestantism. It tires them, it is so very awkward; and for the life of them they cannot continue in it long together, where there is neither article nor canon to lean against; they cannot go on for ever standing on one leg, or sitting without a chair, or walking with their legs tied, or grazing, like Tityrus's stags, on the air.

People who read and think are bound eventually to adopt some view or other which is consistent, and therefore real:

Premises imply conclusions; germs lead to developments; principles have issues; doctrines lead to action. . . . They may take one view or another of the English or the Primitive Church; but, whatever else it be, on the long run, it will be a consistent view. It may be Rationalism, or Erastianism, or Popery, or Catholicity; but it will be real. It will not be a merely transitional view; it will not be Lutheranism, or Presbyterianism . . . Effects will sooner or later be seen to presuppose causes; correlatives to imply each other; contradictions to exclude each other . . . The most intense horror of Popery cannot undo facts or legitimatize fallacies.

Given that Protestantism is unreal, Roman Catholicism and unbelief are not the only alternatives, but

our true wisdom now is to look for some Via Media which will preserve us from what threatens . . . The spirit of Luther is dead; but Hildebrand and Loyola are still alive. Is it sensible, sober, judicious, to be so very angry with those writers of the day, who point to the fact, that our divines of the seventeenth century have occupied a ground which is the true and intelligible mean beween extremes? . . . The current of the age cannot be stopped, but it may be directed; and it is better that it should find its way into the Anglican port, than that it should be propelled into Popery, or drifted upon unbelief.

The 'real alternative' to Rome is Anglo-Catholicism, which 'is a road leading off the beaten highway of Popery', from which 'it branches off at last, though for some time it seems one with it'. Roman Catholics may see Anglicanism as a bogus counterfeit of real Catholicism, but they 'recognize in us their real and most formidable opponents'.[72] But how real was the theory of the *Via Media*? At the end of the *Prophetical Office* he had even wondered if 'what has been said is but a dream, the wanton exercise, rather than the practical conclusion of the intellect'.[73] In the *Apologia*, Newman notes that he was 'still, in some way or other, feeling about for an available *Via Media*'. Nevertheless, he little dreamed that 'while I was thus speaking of the future of the Movement, I was in truth winding up my accounts with it'. For he 'was soon to receive a shock which was to cast out of my imagination all middle courses and compromises for ever'.[74]

4

'The Long Vacation of 1839 began early', the *Apologia* records with an almost ominous terseness.[75] Newman had spent a solitary summer in the fateful year 1816. Now once again he was alone. He wrote to Isaac Williams: 'I am solus in College and am likely to be—a comfort I have not had for several Long Vacations—'. He wanted now to return

---

[72] *Ess.* i. 268–9, 272, 274–5, 277, 281, 294–5, 297, 302–3, 306–7.
[73] *VM* i. 331.   [74] *Apo.* 99–100.   [75] Ibid. 108.

to my *own* line of reading—the early controversies of the Church, which I have suspended since 1835; not suspended of my own wish, but it was pressing that subjects should be treated more connected with what was going on in the Church. I have done enough now in that way, at least for the present—and, as I have never engaged in those subjects from any pleasure of mine, so now that I may, I return with great pleasure to my own subject—and shall not quit it in a hurry;—though one can promise oneself nothing in such a shifting state of things.[76]

And so he turned again to study the theological problems of the fifth century, 'preparatory (I trust) to my finishing my edition of Dionysius of Alexandria—and editing (for the Library of the Fathers) Theodoret, Leo, and Cyril'.[77] He was also hoping to rewrite *The Arians of the Fourth Century*. Meanwhile, the new volumes of the *Remains* were nearly out. There was also a plan (which again would fit in with his own reading) to begin publishing a translation with notes of Claude Fleury's monumental church history, commencing (where his own book had left off) with the Council of Constantinople in 381.

As he studied the Monophysite controversy, he was struck by two 'very remarkable' features of the Council of Chalcedon—'the great power of the Pope (as great as he claims now almost), and the marvellous interference of the civil power, as great almost as in our kings'.[78] The first aspect could usefully be employed against Anglican Erastians, and the second against Roman Catholics. Meanwhile, he remained 'solus in College—always excepting the mice, which' (he wrote to Robert Wilberforce) 'are at this moment making a sociable rustling among my papers and behind the arras'.[79] He had no thought of the Church of Rome, about which he had written nothing controversial or polemical for the past two years. But during the course of his reading, 'for the first time a doubt came upon me of the tenableness of Anglicanism'. He recalled in the *Apologia* the day at the end of July when he mentioned 'to a friend, whom I had accidentally met, how remarkable the history [of the Monophysites] was'. By the end of August he was 'seriously alarmed'. What had so startled him?

My stronghold was Antiquity; now here, in the middle of the fifth century, I found, as it seemed to me, Christendom of the sixteenth and the nineteenth centuries reflected. I saw my face in that mirror, and I was a Monophysite. The Church of the *Via Media* was in the position of the Oriental communion, Rome was, where she now is; and the Protestants were the Eutychians.

To an imagination acutely sensitive to analogies, the sight of Pope Leo upholding the Catholic faith, while the heretics divided into an extreme

---

[76] To I. Williams, 1, 18 July 1839.   [77] To J. W. Bowden, 11 July 1839.
[78] To F. Rogers, 12 July 1839.   [79] To R. I. Wilberforce, 12 July 1839.

and a moderate party, was disturbing. Looking back twenty-five years later at the experience, Newman could not help smiling at his own analogy:

Of all passages of history, since history has been, who would have thought of going to the sayings and doings of old Eutyches, that *delirius senex*, as (I think) Petavius calls him, and to the enormities of the unprincipled Dioscorus, in order to be converted to Rome![80]

At the beginning of August, he had written to H. A. Woodgate that the Tractarians had succeeded in drawing attention to the importance 'of going to antiquity'; the question now was, '*what* do the Fathers say?' Pusey's Library of the Fathers was the natural consequence of the *Tracts*, and he was confident that the translations of the writings of the Fathers would show how 'consistent' and 'edifying' they were: 'It was well enough for theologians to go on arguing, refuting and oversetting each other in the dark—I mean by extracts—and appeals to what their audience had not read—but this is an age of light.'[81] But what if the shedding of light on the age of the Fathers cast an unexpected shadow on the Anglo-Catholic position?

As that fateful summer wore on, Newman refrained from revealing his new anxiety in his correspondence. But something of his disquiet is reflected in a rather despairing comment he made at the end of August to Isaac Williams that he could 'never . . . be sorry when a friend refuses a Bishoprick in the Establishment'—for 'How can a person enter upon the office of defender of the Church without almost a promise on entering it, that he will not defend it?'[82] He even toyed with the idea of leaving Oxford—'my imagination has for some time roved after being a sort of brother of charity in London—but I fear it is more imagination than heart.' He certainly had no intention of abandoning the celibate state, to which he was 'virtually bound': people might not believe him, but 'I do not mean to marry at 60'.[83]

Back in June he had noted with satisfaction that Tractarian 'principles' were still 'on the growth' at Oxford—but 'when they will stop, at what point, and at what extent, is quite hidden of course'.[84] Now, naturally, he had his own personal reasons for fearing the eventual outcome of the Movement. Without divulging his own secret doubts, he admitted to Henry Manning that he was 'very anxious' about the possibility of defections to Rome, 'from the consciousness that our Church has not the provisions and methods by which Catholic feelings are to be detained, secured, sobered, and trained heavenwards. Our

[80] *Apo.* 108.
[81] To H. A. Woodgate, 11 Aug. 1839.   [82] To I. Williams, 28 Aug. 1839.
[83] To T. Mozley, 30 Aug. 1839; to H. Wilberforce, 30 Aug. 1839.
[84] To Mrs J. Mozley, 20 June 1839.

blanket is too small for our bed.' He was only too 'conscious that we are raising longings and tastes which we are not allowed to supply—and till our Bishops and others give scope to the development of Catholicism externally and visibly, we *do* tend to make impatient minds seek it where it has ever been, in Rome'. He thought that 'whenever the time comes that secessions to Rome take place, for which we must not be unprepared,' they

must boldly say to that Protestant section of our Church—'*You* are the cause of this. You must *concede*—you must conciliate—you must meet the age. You must make the Church more efficient—more suitable to the needs of the heart, more equal to the external pressures. Give us more services—more vestments and decorations in worship—give us monasteries ... Till then, you will have continual defections to Rome.'

Given the present state of the Church, Newman admits: 'I think nothing but *patience* and *dutifulness* can keep us in the Church of England—and remaining in it is a test whether we have these graces.' Manning's friend, who is thinking of becoming a Roman Catholic, must be reminded of 'the duty of remaining in the calling in which God has found her' and of her obligations to 'the poor Church, through which she has her baptism, by stopping in it':

Does she not care for the souls all around her steeped and stifled in Protestantism? How will she best care for them, by indulging her own feelings in the Communion of Rome, or in denying herself and staying in sackcloth and ashes to do them good? Will she persuade more of her brethren by leaving them or by continuing with them? Is she unmarried? is there any chance of making her a 'Mother Superior'?

If she actually has doubts about the 'Catholicity' of the Church of England, then she must be confronted not only with the objections to Rome but also 'with the additional reflection that she is *taking a step*, and therefore should have some abundant evidence on the side of that step'—for it 'is either a clear imperative duty or it is a sin'. Again,

can she deny that the hand of God is with our Church, even granting *for argument's sake* Rome has some things which we have not. Is it dead? has it the signs of death? has it more than the signs of disease? has it not lasted through very troublous times? has it not from time to time marvellously revived when it seemed to be losing all faith and holiness? is it to be *given up* ...[85]

On 8 September Newman told Jemima that he had written a 'flippant' article for the *British Critic* on the 'American Church'.[86] It was published in the October number. Newman confessed in it that he was

[85] To H. E. Manning, 1 Sept. 1839.   [86] To Mrs J. Mozley, 8 Sept. 1839.

delighted at the progress of the daughter church—'It gives us some taste of Catholic feelings, and some enjoyment of Christian sympathy.' After all, the Church of England herself was in 'captivity', albeit 'a most honourable captivity', in the sense that 'power, wealth, authority, rank, consideration, have been showered upon her, to make her as happy as the day is long'. Satire is not spared to describe the Establishment:

She has been among strangers; statesmen, lawyers, and soldiers frisked and prowled around: creatures wild or tame have held a parliament over her, but still she has wanted some one to converse with, to repose on, to consult, to love. The State indeed . . . has thought it unreasonable in her, that she could not find in a lion and a unicorn a sufficient object for her affections. It has set her to keep order in the land, to restrain enthusiasm, and to rival and so discountenance 'Popery'. . . .

Much more important, however, is the fact that 'the daughter is the evidence of the mother's origin; that which lives is the true Church; that which is fruitful lives; the English Church, the desolate one, has children'. This proves that the Church of England has 'life' and 'a living principle', and is not one of those 'unreal' systems in the world. American Episcopalians have shown they are different from the surrounding Protestant sects, which remind Newman of the early heretical bodies 'to which the presence of the true Church gave rise, as the sun breeds reptiles'. They alone have 'a creative principle in them'— 'Baptists might form and reform, resolve and change like a calidoscope; Shakers, Dunkers, Swedenborgians, Mormonites, might flit around them, but they . . . were ever . . . breaking forth into the Apostolic polity and the Catholic faith.' Not that the American Church is not also, like the English Church, wont 'to call it moderation and judgment to sit down deliberately between two stools, or to leap into the ditch, and ultraism to clear it'. (Of one particular Anglican divine, Newman was to say, 'he leads persons a certain way and then breaks down, depositing them and their luggage in the road, about half way between Geneva and Oxford. People cannot remain long in so exposed a state, but get on as they can in omnibuses.'[87])

However, the particular danger which threatens to make the American Church 'inconsistent and unreal' is 'the influence of a refined and covert Socinianism', for which a 'trading country' is the natural '*habitat*', for 'there is a moral condition of mind to which this dismal creed *is* alluring'. Newman offers an interesting socio-religious analysis:

Not to the poor, the forlorn, the dejected, the afflicted, can the Unitarian doctrine be alluring, but to those who are rich and have need of nothing . . .

---

[87] To W. F. Hook, 3 Jan. 1840.

Those who have nothing of this world to rely upon need a firm hold of the next, they need a deep religion . . .

Such is the benefit of poverty; as to wealth, its providential corrective is the relative duties which it involves, as in the case of a landlord; but these do not fall on the trader. He has rank without tangible responsibilities; he has made himself what he is, and becomes self-dependent . . . If he thinks of religion at all, he will not like from being a great man to become a little one; he bargains for some or other compensation to his self-importance, some little power of judging or managing, some small permission to have his own way. Commerce is free as air; it knows no distinctions; mutual intercourse is its medium of operation. Exclusiveness, separations, rules of life, observance of days, nice scruples of conscience, are odious to it.

It is not that the commercial middle classes do not want a religion, but they want an undogmatic, unhierarchical religion:

A religion which neither irritates their reason nor interferes with their comfort, will be all in all in such a society. Severity whether of creed or precept, high mysteries, corrective practices, subjection of whatever kind, whether to a doctrine or to a priest, will be offensive to them. They need nothing to fill the heart, to feed upon, or to live in; they despise enthusiasm, they abhor fanaticism, they persecute bigotry. They want only so much religion as will satisfy their natural perception of the propriety of being religious. Reason teaches them that utter disregard of their Maker is unbecoming, and they determine to be religious, not from love and fear, but from good sense.

The danger is that decorous, moderate, reasonable Anglicanism may encourage 'a sleek gentlemanlike religion' to 'grow up within the sacred pale, with well-warmed chapels, softly cushioned pews, and eloquent preachers'. But 'pews, carpets, cushions, and fine speaking are not developments of the Apostolical Succession'.[88]

To his closest friends Newman did not attempt to disguise his growing unease about the Anglican Church. In a letter of 15 September to Frederic Rogers he asked, '*Can* the R.C.'s have any tender feeling towards Anglicanism? Who among us ever showed them any kindness? Are we not the pets of a State which has made it a felony to celebrate Mass even . . . in private . . . '? And he confided his deep attraction to the religious life:

You see, if things were to come to the worst, I should turn Brother of Charity in London—an object which, *quite* independently of any such perplexities, is growing on me, and, peradventure, will some day be accomplished, if other things do not impede me. That Capuchin in the 'Promessi Sposi' has stuck in my heart like a dart. I have never got over him. Only I think it would be, in sober seriousness, far too great an honour for such as me to have such a post, being little worthy or fit for it.[89]

---

[88] *Ess.* i. 311–13, 327, 333–6, 347–50.   [89] To F. Rogers, 15 Sept. 1839.

A week later, he wrote again to Rogers, 'Since I wrote to you, I have had the first real hit from Romanism which has happened to me.' Robert Williams had drawn his attention to an article by Wiseman in the August *Dublin Review* on the 'Anglican Claim'.

I must confess it has given me a stomach-ache. You see the whole history of the Monophysites has been a sort of alterative. And now comes this dose at the end of it. It does certainly come upon one that we are not at the bottom of things.

They had 'sprung a leak', and 'the worst of it' was that 'sharp fellows' like W. G. Ward of Balliol, one of the leaders of the younger Tractarians, 'will not let me go to sleep upon it'. He had 'not said so much to any one'. He 'seriously' thought it was 'a most uncomfortable article on every account'. He ended:

It is no laughing matter. I will not blink the question, so be it; but you don't suppose I am a madcap to take up notions suddenly—only there is an uncomfortable vista opened which was closed before. I am writing upon my first feelings.[90]

In the *Apologia*, Newman explained what had happened. On first reading the article, which was on the Donatist controversy, but with special reference to Anglicanism, he 'did not see much in it'. After all, the Donatists had caused a schism within the African Church and it was 'not the case of one Church against another, as of Rome against the Oriental Monophysites'.

But my friend . . . pointed out the palmary words of St. Augustine, which were contained in one of the extracts made in the Review, and which had escaped my observation. 'Securus judicat orbis terrarum.' He repeated these words again and again, and, when he was gone, they kept ringing in my ears. 'Securus judicat orbis terrarum'; they were words which went beyond the occasion of the Donatists: they applied to that of the Monophysites. . . . They decided ecclesiastical questions on a simpler rule than that of Antiquity; nay, St. Augustine was one of the prime oracles of Antiquity; here then Antiquity was deciding against itself. What a light was hereby thrown upon every controversy in the Church! not that, for the moment, the multitude may not falter in their judgment,—not that, in the Arian hurricane, Sees more than can be numbered did not bend before its fury, and fall off from St. Athanasius,—not that the crowd of Oriental Bishops did not need to be sustained during the contest by the voice and the eye of St. Leo; but that the deliberate judgment, in which the whole Church at length rests and acquiesces, is an infallible prescription and a final sentence against such portions of it as protest and secede.

The passage, one of the most dramatic and powerful in all Newman's

90 To F. Rogers, 22 Sept. 1839.

writings and worthy of that fateful moment, concludes on a note of conversion—or rather, deconversion:

Who can account for the impressions which are made on him? For a mere sentence, the words of St. Augustine, struck me with a power which I never had felt from any words before. To take a familiar intance, they were like the 'Turn again Whittington' of the chime; or, to take a more serious one, they were like the 'Tolle, lege,—Tolle, lege', of the child, which converted St. Augustine himself. 'Securus judicat orbis terrarum!' By those great words of the ancient Father, interpreting and summing up the long and varied course of ecclesiastical history, the theory of the *Via Media* was absolutely pulverized.[91]

After another week had passed following his second letter to Rogers, Newman wrote more circumspectly to S. F. Wood to say that he thought that Wiseman's article needed to be considered and answered. He was afraid, though, that it might lead 'this or that person to anticipate a truth to which others are advancing also—and his anticipating it throws others back'—whereas they ought to be 'keeping together, *though* moving on the same road'. If there was 'something' in Wiseman's argument, then it would eventually be accepted. He felt 'very diffident' about his 'own judgment', particularly with regard to 'doctrines beyond what one's Church admits'. But he felt confident that if there was anything in the article, 'Keble will eventually see it—and am glad, as well as bound, to wait to see what he says. It is more likely that he should be right than my own judgment.'[92] Anyway, he realized that however good Wiseman's arguments might be, there were also arguments on the other side.

A few days later he wrote again to Rogers to say that he thought St Augustine would agree that grace could be 'given even in a schismatical Church'. A Church, he argued,

which has broken away from the centre of unity is not at liberty at once to return, yet is not nothing. May she not put herself into a state of penance? Are not her children best fulfilling their duty to her—not by leaving her, but by promoting her return, and not thinking they have a *right* to rush into such higher state as communion with the centre of unity might give them. If the Church Catholic, indeed, has actually commanded their return to her at once, that is another matter; but this she cannot have done without pronouncing their present Church good-for-nothing, which I do not suppose Rome has done of us.[93]

Also at the beginning of October, he visited Henry Wilberforce in his parish at Bransgore in Hampshire. Years later Wilberforce recalled the 'astounding confidence' his friend made to him:

---

[91] *Apo.* 110–11.
[92] To S. F. Wood, 29 Sept. 1839.   [93] To F. Rogers, 3 Oct. 1839.

He added that he felt confident that when he returned to his rooms [in Oriel], and was able fully and calmly to consider the whole matter, he should see his way completely out of the difficulty. But he said, 'I cannot conceal from myself that, for the first time since I began the study of theology, a vista has been opened before me, to the end of which I do not see.' He was walking in the New Forest, and he borrowed the form of his expression from the surrounding scenery. His companion, upon whom such a fear came like a thunderstroke, expressed his hope that Mr. Newman might die rather than take such a step. He replied, with deep earnestness, that he had thought, if ever the time should come when he was in serious danger, of asking his friends to pray that, if it was not indeed the will of God, he might be taken away before he did it.[94]

In the *Apologia* Newman tells us that his excitement did die away: 'After a while, I got calm, and at length the vivid impression upon my imagination faded away.' But it remained true that he 'had seen the shadow of a hand upon the wall'.

It was clear that I had a good deal to learn on the question of the Churches, and that perhaps some new light was coming upon me. He who has seen a ghost, cannot be as if he had never seen it. The heavens had opened and closed again. The thought for the moment had been, 'The Church of Rome will be found right after all'; and then it had vanished. My old convictions remained as before.

The 'three original points of belief' he fell back on were 'the principle of dogma, the sacramental system, and anti-Romanism'. Since 'the first two were better secured in Rome', his 'main argument for the Anglican claims lay in the positive and special charges, which I could bring against Rome', for now he 'had no positive Anglican theory'. But this 'pure Protestantism', or anti-Popery, 'was really a practical principle', since he had 'so fully imbibed' it at the age of 15 that 'it still had great hold on me' like 'a stain upon my imagination'—although his 'reason' was no longer 'convinced' that Rome was the Antichrist. At any rate, he now 'determined to be guided, not by my imagination, but by my reason'.[95]

5

The October number of the *British Critic* carried a review article by Newman on the Protestant idea of 'Antichrist'. He admitted that there was 'a strong temptation' to 'call the Pope Antichrist' because of 'the ease with which it disposes of the plausible and apparently cogent proofs with which Rome fights her battles'. It was the Protestant counterpart to 'the dogma of the Pope's infallibility in the Roman system'. But one

[94] Cit. Moz. ii. 287.   [95] *Apo.* 111–13, 115.

would have to be 'almost an Angel' to unchurch 'the greater part of Christendom', and to hold that 'the great multitude of Christian bishops are children of the devil' was no light matter. Only a saint would attempt to 'establish the paradox' that St Charles Borromeo 'sucked the breast of Babylon, and that Pascal died in her arms'. Certainly the 'private life' of Thomas Newton, whose *Observations upon the Prophecies of Daniel and the Apocalypse* was 'the main source' for the English Protestant tradition of Antichrist, hardly inspired confidence. True, there was no doubt as to his 'kindness of heart and amiableness',

but a man so idolatrous of comfort, so liquorish of preferment, whose most fervent aspiration apparently was that he might ride in a carriage and sleep on down, whose keenest sorrow that he could not get a second appointment without relinquishing the first, who cast a regretful look back upon his dinner while he was at supper, and anticipated his morning chocolate in his evening muffins, who will say that this is the man, not merely to unchurch, but to smite, to ban, to wither the whole of Christendom for many centuries, and the greater part of it even in his own day. . .

This superb sneer is followed closely by the sarcastic admission, 'Who would not rather be found even with Whitfield and Wesley, than with ecclesiastics whose life is literary ease at the best, whose highest flights attain but to Downing Street or the levee?' And once again the satire of *Present Position of Catholics* is foreshadowed in this assault on the inherent inconsistency of anti-Popery—'how men, thinking that the Pope is the Beast of the Apocalypse, can endure the sight of any of his servants . . . or can sit with them in the same Council or Parliament, or can do business with them, buy and sell, trade and traffic, or can gaze upon and admire the architecture of churches built by Antichrist, or make much of his pictures,—or how they can read any book of his servants . . . all this is to us inexplicable.' The fact is, Newman claims, that 'Antichrist' is 'almost foretold to be the *title* which His representatives and servants should bear', the 'imputation' of which 'may almost be called one of the Notes of the Church'. And far from Rome having any monopoly to such 'titles' of reproach, 'Anglo-Catholics inherit them from the Roman family', and must be allowed to 'share them with Rome'—for it is the very mark of heretics like Protestants to call 'the Church by foul and frightful names'.[96]

Apart from his own personal situation, Newman was now beginning for the first time to be seriously worried about the future of the Movement. The 'practical difficulty' was that they were 'raising feelings and aspirations' for which, till the Church of England was 'reformed', only Rome could provide the '*objects*'. His uneasy reflection was that it

---

[96] *Ess.* ii. 131–2, 134, 138–9, 140, 148–9, 151–2.

was 'comparatively easy to get up a Catholic movement', but 'not easy to see what barriers are to be found to its onward progress'.[97] While he had been away, J. B. Morris of Exeter, 'a most simple minded conscientious fellow—but as little possessed of tact or common sense as he is great in other departments', had been looking after St Mary's for him. He wrote to Bowden (who was now much better) that he had 'cautioned him against extravagances' in his preaching, 'as he had given some specimens in that line once before'.

What does he do on St Michael's day but preach a Sermon, not simply on Angels, but on his one subject for which he has a monomania, of fasting, nay and say it was a good thing, whereas Angels feasted on festivals, to make the brute creation fast on fast days. . . . May he . . . have a fasting horse the next time he goes steeple chasing. Well this was not all. You may conceive how the Heads of Houses . . . fretted under this—but next Sunday he gave them a more extended exhibition . . . He preached to them . . . the Roman doctrine of the Mass, and, not content with that, added in energetic terms that every one was an unbeliever, carnal, and so forth, who did not hold it.

The Vice-Chancellor had said not a word to Newman, but he and his family had stopped coming to St Mary's. He had also complained to the Bishop of Oxford. It seemed the 'authorities' were becoming 'very much frightened about the spread of Apostolicity'; and although they could not 'stop matters now', there was a real danger 'of persons going too far'.[98] He did not know what effect the new volumes of the *Remains* would have, but some people would be unpleasantly surprised to discover that the Library of the Fathers contained rather more doctrines than they expected to find. Evangelicals, who had 'just nibbled', would no doubt 'be off at once', while others would 'go further the other way'. The undeniable fact was that 'from the first the Fathers do teach doctrines and a temper of mind which we commonly identify with Romanism'. He fully expected individuals to join the Church of Rome, but what he was more afraid of was 'a schism *in* the Church', with the high and the low parties 'gathering up into clear, distinct, tangible, forces—and colliding'. If the 'Apostolical party' was 'cast out, and without Bishops', what would they do?[99] He contemplated with equanimity the possibility of having to resign both his living and his fellowship.

In November he heard that a report was circulating that his curate J. R. Bloxam, who had paid a visit in the summer to Alton Towers, the home of the Roman Catholic Earl of Shewsbury, had not only attended Mass but had bowed at the elevation of the Host. Newman himself had been dismayed to hear from Bloxam that he had been in the chapel—

---

[97] To H. A. Woodgate, 20 Oct. 1839.   [98] To J. W. Bowden, 4 Nov. 1839.
[99] To Mrs J. Mozley, 17 Nov. 1839.

although he himself would not have hesitated to go into a church abroad to pray. Now he promptly wrote to the Bishop of Oxford explaining that Bloxam had simply been present in the gallery of the chapel while saying his own prayers from the Prayer Book. But it was still highly indiscreet, and he apologized to the bishop, assuring him he was doing everything in his power to restrain the younger Tractarians. Privately, he had been expecting an incident like this: they had 'raised desires, of which our Church does not supply the objects', and the younger generation of Tractarians did not have 'the patience, or humility, or discretion to keep from seeking those objects where they are supplied'. He had always thought that 'nothing but a quasi miracle' would carry them 'through the trial with no proselytes whatever to Rome'.[100] Now he was much more pessimistic:

I think the tide is turning and we shall be left on the beach—there seems a more consistent firing at us from high quarters . . . persons are more and more breaking from us—and the younger men are getting fiercer the other way. I should not be surprised to see conversions to Romanism some where or other. I think the women will be going, unless nunneries are soon held out to them *in* our Church. In a word the Church is getting into the attitude of a split.[101]

Meanwhile, Newman had been writing an article for the January *British Critic*, called 'Catholicity of the English Church'. It was an attempt to begin 'to stop up the leak in our boat' which Wiseman's article had made.[102] Newman begins by pointing out that the 'strong point' in the Anglican position 'is the argument from the past', namely, 'that Rome has added to the Creed', while 'that of the Romanists is the argument from the present', namely, that Anglicans 'are estranged from the great body of Christians over the world'. The Anglican difficulty, then, is that on the one hand the 'mark or note' of the Church is that it is 'one kingdom or polity in all lands', and that on the other hand 'there *is* a body mainly answering to this description, the communion of Rome, lineally descended from the ancient Church'. The Roman position has two advantages: first, 'want of Catholicity' is 'far more level to the apprehension of men in general than . . . want of primitiveness in doctrine'; second, 'it is no difficulty that the great body should have added to the faith, when we grant their assumption that they have the power', that is, the power 'of developing the faith'. Newman also admits that the traditional 'Anglican view' that the 'separate portions' of the Church 'need not be united together, for their essential complete-ness, except by the tie of descent from one original' ('Apostolical

---

[100] To W. Dodsworth, 19 Nov. 1839. [101] To T. Mozley, 12 Dec. 1839.
[102] To J. W. Bowden, 5 Jan. 1840.

Succession')—for the individual Churches are like 'branches of an extended family, or colonies of a mother country'—was not apparently held by St Augustine. But, he pleads, 'Christians now are in a different position'. The Jewish Temple was demolished, but Israel remained 'a holy people'; so, too, the early unity of the Church was 'a divine witness', but its loss was not 'fatal' to the Church. As for St Augustine's 'striking and beautiful principle against the Donatists, "securus judicat orbis terrarum"', it was hardly 'intended as a theological verity equally sacred as an article in the Creed'. Again, Roman Catholics claim the Church is still the Church although it has developed into a Papal 'monarchy', so why should the Church not still be the Church when it has 'dissolved' into 'fragments'? Or again, the Roman Church, which claims its 'Catholicity' is 'an essential mark of the Church', hardly exists in England, let alone in Russia—and is not 'reality' also a 'Note of the Church'? Another essential 'Note' is '*life*', which certainly belongs to the Church of England, as is shown by all the vicissitudes she has survived and by her wonderful revival in recent times when 'temporal defences have been removed'.

Newman concludes that if only the Church of England had the 'one Note' of 'sanctity', her claim to be a branch of the Church would be irresistible; he is 'almost content to say to Romanists, Account us not yet as a branch of the Catholic Church, though we be a branch, till we are like a branch . . .'. However, the Church of Rome is also gravely lacking in this Note:

When we go into foreign countries, we see superstitions in the Roman Church which shock us; when we read history, we find its spirit of intrigue so rife, so widely spread, that 'jesuitism' has become a by-word; when we look round us at home, we see it associated everywhere with the low democracy, pandering to the spirit of rebellion . . . We see it attempting to gain converts among us, by unreal representations of its doctrines . . . We see its agents smiling and nodding and ducking to attract attention, as gipsies make up to truant boys, holding out tales for the nursery, and pretty pictures, and gold gingerbread, and physic concealed in jam, and sugar-plums for good children.

The quite exceptional satirical dig at the Roman Church is explained by the apologetic sentence that follows: 'Who can but feel shame when the religion of Ximenes, Borromeo, and Pascal is so overlaid?' In other words, for once Roman Catholicism appears inconsistent and therefore unreal and therefore ridiculous. But the article ends with an ominous warning to his own Church:

We Englishmen like manliness, openness, consistency, truth. Rome will never gain on us till she learns these virtues . . . but if she does reform . . . then it will be our Church's duty at once to join in communion with the Continental

Churches, whatever politicians at home may say to it, and whatever steps the civil power may take in consequence.[103]

The new volumes of the *Remains* were selling 'excellently', and the preface by Keble had been well received. 'Old Faussett', Newman reported mischievously to Bowden, 'started half off his seat when he heard of new volumes, as if he should say "Why I annihilated Mr F's writings last year—what is meant by the absurdity of continuing them?" ' Newman himself was planning to put together in book form his *British Magazine* 'Letters on the Church of the Fathers'. But he was 'very anxious' about their publication—'I have not put my name to any *strong* thing yet—and this is regularly strong meat. I suppose I must expect a clamour unless persons are tired of clamouring.' They were 'so dreadfully monastic, that I have some tremours what will happen to me'. Meanwhile his time was taken up with rewriting a 'great part' of them.[104]

They had been intended to show how different both the Established Church and Bible Protestantism were from the religion of the first centuries. Thus St Antony, for example, would seem a clear case of 'an enthusiast', and 'had he lived a Protestant in this Protestant day, he would have been exposed to a serious temptation of becoming a fanatic', for 'minds with ardent feelings, keen imaginations, and undisciplined tempers' are unable to reconcile themselves to that 'special resignation to worldly comforts . . . we see around us', but instead abandon 'the Protestant Establishment' which 'provides no occupation for them, does not understand how to turn them to account, lets them run to waste, tempts them to dissent, loses them, is weakened by the loss, and then denounces them'. Antony's 'enthusiasm', however, did not take a 'vulgar, bustling, imbecile, unstable, undutiful' form, but was 'calm and composed, manly intrepid, magnanimous'. Monasticism, indeed, in the early Church provided an outlet for the kind of religious aspirations which in England found expression in Methodism, because 'the Established Church . . . will admit nothing but what it considers "rational" and "sensible" in religion'. The Protestant, of course, prides himself on the fact that Protestantism never could 'be corrupted, to use his word, into monasticism', but if it is true that 'his system never could become superstitious' in this way, then 'it is not primitive', for clearly the 'religious temper' of the primitive Church did lead to monasticism. The lack of the monastic element in the English Church prompts Newman into making a remarkable observation on the rights of women in a male-dominated world:

[103] *Ess.* ii. 6, 9, 11–12, 18, 33, 39–40, 44, 50, 53, 56, 69–72.
[104] To J. W. Bowden, 5 Jan. 1840; to Mrs J. Mozley, 14 Jan. 1840; to H. A. Woodgate, 17 Jan. 1840.

I know not any more distressing development of the cruel temper of Protestantism than the determined, bitter, and scoffing spirit in which it has set itself against institutions which give dignity and independence to the position of women in society. As matters stand, marriage is almost the only shelter which a defenceless portion of the community has against the rude world . . .

Newman appeals to the reader to take 'a large view' of the faith of the early Christians, and asks, 'Is there any family likeness in it to Protestantism?'

When we ask, 'Where was your Church before Luther?' Protestants answer, 'Where were you this morning before you washed your face?' But, if Protestants can clean themselves into the likeness of Cyprian or Irenaeus, they must scrub very hard . . .

He concedes, 'It is natural and becoming in all of us to make a brave struggle for life; but I do not think it will avail the Protestant who attempts it in the medium of ecclesiastical history. He will find himself in an element in which he cannot breathe.' In more than one marvellously sarcastic passage, the satire again strikingly anticipates *Present Position of Catholics*:

'We [Protestants] uphold the pure unmutilated Scripture; the Bible, and the Bible only, is the religion of Protestants; the Bible and our own sense of the Bible. We claim a sort of parliamentary privilege to interpret laws in our own way, and not to suffer an appeal to any court beyond ourselves. We know, and we view it with consternation, that all Antiquity runs counter to our interpretation; and therefore, alas, the Church was corrupt from *very* early times indeed. But mind, we hold all this in a truly Catholic spirit, not in bigotry. We allow in others the right of private judgment, and confess that we, as others, are fallible men. We confess facts are against us; we do but claim the liberty of theorizing in spite of them. Far be it from us to say that we are certainly right; we only say that the whole early Church was certainly wrong. We do not impose our belief on any one; we only say that those who take the contrary side are Papists, firebrands, persecutors, madmen, zealots, bigots, and an insult to the nineteenth century.'

The fact is, Newman scornfully concludes, 'the model Protestant of this day' would not 'have a chance of finding himself at home' in the early Church—

With his religious societies for the Church, with his committees, boards, and platforms instead of Bishops, his . . . newspapers instead of Councils, his concerts for prayer instead of anathemas on heresy and schism, his spoutings at public meetings for exorcisms, his fourths of October for festivals of the Martyrs, his glorious memories for commemorations of the dead, his niggard vestry allowances for gold and silver vessels, his gas and stoves for wax and oil, his denunciations of self-righteousness for fasting and celibacy, and his exercise of private judgment for submission to authority . . .'[105]

On 8 January Newman received a visit from George Spencer, the youngest son of Earl Spencer, who had been converted to Roman Catholicism several years before and was now a priest teaching at the seminary at Oscott. Newman had been invited to meet him at dinner the previous evening but had refused on the ground that Spencer, who had been in Anglican Orders, was an apostate—and 'that if R.C.'s and A.C.'s meet together, it should be in sackcloth, rather than at a pleasant party'. They talked together for an hour. Afterwards Newman wrote to Bowden:

I wish these R.C. priests had not so smooth a manner, it puts me out. He was very mild, very gentlemanlike, not a controvertialist [*sic*], and came to insist only on one point, that we would take steps to get Anglo-catholics to pray for the R.C's. He said he was sure that if we felt the desirableness of unity, and if we prayed for each other, where there was a will there would be a way . . . He said that he had been instrumental in beginning the practice in France, that it had spread all over that country, and was now being taken up in Germany— Thursday being the day fixed on. It is certainly, a most dreadful thing that we should be separated from them—but your account of the Southern Churches, makes one almost feel as if a formal union would do no good. If we could make strong terms with them so as to *act upon* them, that would be the thing.

Newman wondered if the priest's 'sadly smooth' manner was the result of the Roman clergy's 'habit of internal discipline, the necessity of confession, etc.'[106] (Later he was to note, 'Demureness is the Roman manner, as pompousness is the Church of England's.')[107] But he was taken with the idea of a fixed day for mutual ecumenical prayer. Too many people reviled Roman Catholics, instead of praying for them.

If they practise duplicity, they need our prayers the more. I do not think we should be outdone by them and whatever be the motives of certain scheming leaders and agents, I never will believe that the multitude among them who pray for us wish us any thing but good. They pray that we may be changed— and we should pray that they should.[108]

He wished there were more Roman Catholics like Spencer, who had even gone out to Littlemore 'and put some money in the box'—which would no doubt 'one day be magnified into my letting him say Mass at Littlemore'.[109]

Later, he decided to write to Spencer to explain why he had not been

[105] *HS* ii. 98–9, 164–5; i. 402–3, 417, 420–1, 442.
[106] To J. W. Bowden, 5 Jan. 1840; to F. Rogers, 8 Jan. 1840.
[107] To F. Rogers, 10 Jan. 1841.   [108] To H. E. Manning, 16 Jan. 1840.
[109] To Mrs T. Mozley, 29 Jan. 1840.

more friendly on the occasion of his visit to Oxford: 'you invite us to a union of hearts, at the same time you are doing all you can, not to restore, not to reform, not to re-unite, but to destroy our Church. . . . You are leagued with our enemies.' In spite of the fact that of all religious bodies in England the Anglican Church was the closest to the Roman Catholic Church, the latter was hand-in-glove with her foes—'this is what impresses us irresistibly with the notion that you are a political, not a religious party; that in order to gain an end on which you have set your hearts, an open stage for yourselves in England, you ally yourselves with those who hold nothing against those who hold something.' This was why he personally could not 'meet familiarly any leading persons of the Roman communion, and least of all when they come on a religious errand. Break off . . . your alliance with Mr O Connell in Ireland and the liberal party in England, or come not to us with overtures for mutual prayer and religious sympathy.' He also resented the lack of even a 'trace of an acknowledgement of the English Church' as a Church and of his own orders as a priest. He did not want to enter into an argument or controversy with Spencer, but simply to explain his own 'feelings'.[110]

Meanwhile, he was more than pleased with the response to his article against Wiseman. 'Things are progressing steadily,' he assured Bowden—

but breakers ahead! the danger of a lapse into Romanism I think gets greater daily. I expect to hear of victims. Again, I fear I see more clearly that we are working up to a schism *in* our Church, i.e., a split between Peculiars and Apostolicals . . . If a Convocation were now to meet, I think there would be a schism.

According to the Evangelical *Record* newspaper, the Tractarians were 'far worse than the unspiritual High Church of last century, as, sinning more against light i.e., there was no Record then'.[111] The paper's 'stern extravagance' amused him—'it is the bitterness of a person who feels he can do nothing *but* be bitter.'[112] He was also delighted by a story a friend had heard in London that 'I carried my austerity to such an extent that I would not let my wife wear anything but sad coloured ribbons in her bonnet'![113]

When he wrote again to Bowden on 21 February, his thirty-ninth birthday ('how old I am getting'),[114] he seemed to have more or less got over the Wiseman article, remarking in a matter-of-fact way, 'it made me for a while very uncomfortable in my own mind'. But he admitted that 'the great speciousness of his argument' was 'one of the things'

[110] To G. Spencer, 9 Feb. 1840.
[111] To J. W. Bowden, 17 Jan. 1840.
[112] To H. A. Woodgate, 17 Jan. 1840.
[113] To J. W. Bowden, 17 Jan. 1840.
[114] To H. Wilberforce, 27 Feb. 1840.

which had made him 'despond so much'. The 'misery' of the lack of a Catholic ethos in the Church remained ('one dare not hardly *move*'), and it tended to make him 'despondent and sluggish—as if nothing *could* be done'. Pusey was anxious to start up nunneries—'I feel sure that such institutions are the only means of saving some of our best members turning Roman Catholics, and yet I despair of such societies being *made* externally. They must be the expansion of an inward principle.'[115]

He wrote at greater length to Jemima about his mood of despondency, which extended beyond Tractarian problems to the larger religious crisis of the time, of which he was so acutely aware in the midst of all his preoccupations with the progress of the Movement. He had 'long' been expecting 'a great attack upon the Bible', and 'at the present moment indications of what is coming gather'. Carlyle, 'a man of first rate ability, I suppose, and quite fascinating as a writer', whose book on the French Revolution was 'quite taking', held the view 'that Christianity has good *in* it, or is good *as far as it goes*—which when applied to Scripture is of course a picking and choosing of its contents'. (He had earlier called the *French Revolution* 'a queer, tiresome, obscure, profound, and original work', while its author had 'not very *clear* principles and views. . . . but they are very deep.') Apart from the growing attacks by liberal Biblical critics on the historicity and inspiration of the Scriptures, there were the 'political Economists, who *cannot* accept . . . the Scripture rules about almsgiving, renunciation of wealth, self-denial, etc etc., and then your Geologists, giving up part of the O.T.' It was not just that 'these and many more spirits seem uniting and forming into something shocking', but he was beginning 'to have serious apprehensions lest any religious body is strong enough to withstand the league of evil, but the Roman Church'. Not only had it '*tried* strength' after all it had endured over the centuries, but 'it is stronger than ever'.

We on the other hand have never been tried and come out of trial without practical concessions. I cannot see that we *can* receive the assault of the foe. We are divided among ourselves . . . So that it seems to me as if there were coming on a great encounter between infidelity and Rome, and that we should be smashed between them. Certainly the way that good principles have shot up is wonderful—but I am not clear that they are not tending to Rome—not from any necessity in the principles themselves, but from the much greater proximity between Rome and us than between infidelity and us . . .[116]

[115] To J. W. Bowden, 21 Feb. 1840.
[116] To Mrs J. Mozley, 23 Apr. 1839; 25 Feb. 1840.

6

Newman decided to go out and stay at Littlemore in March, partly because Bloxam, who had resigned his curacy and gone home to his father, who was seriously ill, was no longer there. But he was also worried about the state of the Littlemore school; not only was the teacher lazy, but he was afraid that she drank. He arrived 'a little after nine' on Monday morning, 9 March. The unfortunate schoolmistress, Mrs Whitman, was still 'sweeping out the school room'; only a few children had arrived and 'hardly any girls'. Newman himself took the prayers, which should have begun at 9, and then called the roll, which did not take place normally till 10, but this morning was over by 20 to 10; only just over half the children (nearly a hundred) who should have been present were there. The boys were ill-behaved, the Vicar noted disapprovingly, and 'most of the girls dirty' with uncombed hair (one little girl of about 5 was actually '*in ringlets*'—the schoolmistress's daughter).[117] But although he could 'see the girls' hair wants combing', he could not 'go further' in his 'analysis of the general air of slatternness which prevails', he solemnly informed Henry Wilberforce.[118] To his sister Jemima he boasted: 'I have been reforming, or at least lecturing against, uncombed hair and dirty faces and hands; but I find I am not deep in the philosophy of school-girl tidiness.'[119]

After a week he wrote to Bloxam to thank him for all he had done at Littlemore. As for himself, he was 'so drawn' to the place that it would 'be an effort to go back to St Mary's'—

Every thing is so cold at St Mary's—I have felt it for years. I know no one. I have no sympathy. I have many critics and carpers—If it were not for those poor undergraduates, who are after all *not* my charge, and the Sunday Communions, I should be sorely tempted to pitch my tent here.

He wondered if he might not be able to buy some more ground at Littlemore and build 'a house' on it. At any rate he was seriously thinking of dividing his time in future between Oxford and Littlemore. He had not only been inveighing against uncombed hair and unwashed hands and faces, but, more agreeably, he had been teaching the children to sing—'their voices are so thrilling as to make one sick with love.'[120]

He wrote more openly to Pusey that the 'idea' had 'revived' in his mind, which they had already discussed, of his 'building a monastic house . . . and coming up to live in it myself'. The 'feeling' had been

---

[117] Memorandum: 'State of the School at Littlemore', 9 Mar. 1840.
[118] To H. Wilberforce, 10 Mar. 1840.   [119] To Mrs J. Mozley, 12 Mar. 1840.
[120] To J. R. Bloxam, 15 Mar. 1840.

'growing' on him that his 'duty as well as pleasure' directed him to be more at Littlemore.

It has long been a distress that I know so little of my Parishioners in Oxford, but tradespeople it is next to impossible to know, considering how they have hitherto been educated—at least impossible to me. It has pained me much to be preaching and doing little more than preach—knowing and guiding only a few, say about half a dozen . . . preaching more for persons who are *not* under my charge, members of the University.

He had no intention of severing his connections with Oxford. He could still take the Sunday afternoon service at St Mary's. Nor did he think that he would be 'neglecting the duty of residence at Oriel' by staying there, as the college had after all appointed him, by virtue of his being a fellow (if he resigned his fellowship he would also have to resign the living), to be Vicar of the parish which included Littlemore. Indeed, he even wondered whether his projected community might not take in theological students and come to be recognized as 'a Hall dependent in a way on the College, as St Mary's Hall was'. What had reminded him of his original idea of a religious house at Littlemore was the thought that he could only live there if he had his library with him, and this would involve a building to house it (at present he was staying in lodgings). He did not think 'such a scheme' could be started at Oxford or London or any 'other great towns'. But he would like to 'begin with a complete type or specimen, which may *preach* to others', and if such a community could be 'set up at Littlemore, it would set the example both in great towns and for female societies'. It might also 'serve as a place to *train up* men for great towns'. It 'should be an open place, where friends might come for a time if they needed a retreat, or if they wished to *see* what it was like'. Finally, 'a plan like this' would settle him permanently at Oxford—'I should conceive myself as much fixed as you are by your Canonry, whereas at present I am continually perplexing myself whether I am not called elsewhere, or may not be.'[121] The problem was not so much whether the money could be raised as whether the ground could be bought. To Pusey's response that he hoped Newman would at least spend the greater part of term-time in Oxford, he replied that being in two places at once would cause 'irregularity', nor would it be 'compatible with having others here besides myself'—but he could at least begin by building 'two rooms—one for me, one for my books, so that the building could afterwards be increased'. However, he did not yet own the ground, nor did he think it would be an 'easy matter to persuade the owner, a strange old man living at Dorchester, to sell it. The whole plan necessarily is a work of time.'[122] Later, when other

---

[121] To E. B. Pusey, 17 Mar. 1840. [122] To E. B. Pusey, 20 Mar. 1840.

friends also objected to the idea of his not residing in college, he began to wonder if the college would let him keep the living if he resigned his fellowship. In the meantime, he thought he would spend vacations at Littlemore, but without deserting St Mary's on Sundays.

He continued practising the schoolchildren in their singing, accompanying them himself on the violin. He told Bloxam proudly at the end of March that in the preceding week he had already taught them three new tunes, and that he was even hoping to introduce them to Gregorian chant! He was also thinking of having a practice in church on Sunday evenings, to keep them out of idleness and mischief. He held catechism classes on Sunday afternoons, which he claimed to Jemima were holding their attention. He had even won a victory in the field of female hygiene:

I have effected a great reform (for the time) in the girls' hands and faces—lectured with unblushing effrontery on the necessity of their *keeping their work clean*, and set them to knit stockings with all their might. Also, I am going to give them some neat white pinafores for Church use, and am going to contrive to make them make them.[123]

But other schoolgirl problems were less easy to solve, and in April he had to write to Bloxam for enlightenment about 'a strange request' passed on to him by Mr Whitman, the schoolmaster, 'from "some young ladies" to be allowed to have a ball in the schoolroom next week. It does not look well—but they say you have hitherto allowed it.'[124] He had not done so much ordinary parochial work since he left St Clement's, and he looked forward to building on the foundations he had laid. He was, in fact, enjoying himself, as he admitted to his Aunt Elizabeth: 'I came up here as a sort of penance during Lent; but though without friends or books, I have as yet had nothing but pleasure. So that it seems a shame to spend Lent so happily.'[125] At least he had 'infused a little animation for the time', and perhaps the new diocesan school inspectors would prevent a 'relapse' on his return to Oxford. One reform in the curriculum had occurred to him: why did all the singing have to be religious?—'A taste for music would be a great resource to the poor.'[126] He felt so happy at Easter, before leaving Littlemore, that he 'quite' dreaded 'some reverse'.[127]

While he was out at Littlemore, he finally completed the extraordinary account of his illness in Sicily in 1833, which he had begun writing in 1834. The last part, which is dated 25 March 1840, concludes with a reflection on the ideal and the pain of celibacy:

The thought keeps pressing on me, while I write this, what am I writing it for?

[123] To Mrs. J. Mozley, 1 Apr. 1840.   [124] To J. R. Bloxam, 14 Apr. 1840.
[125] To Miss E. Newman, 1 Apr. 1840.   [126] To Mrs S. Rickards, 14 Apr. 1840.
[127] To Mrs J. Mozley, 18 Apr. 1840.

For myself, I may look at it once or twice in my whole life, and what sympathy is there in *my* looking at it? Whom have I, whom can I have, who would take interest in it? I was going to say, I only have found one who ever took that sort of affectionate interest in me as to be pleased with such details—and that is H. Wilberforce and what shall I ever see of him? This is the sort of interest which a wife takes and none but she—it is a woman's interest—and that interest, so be it, shall never be taken in me. Never, so be it, will I be other than God has found me. All my habits for years, my tendencies, are towards celibacy. I could not take that interest in this world which marriage requires. I am too disgusted with this world—And, above all, call it what one will, I have a repugnance to a clergyman's marrying. I do not say it is not lawful—I cannot deny the right—but, whether a prejudice or not, it shocks me. And therefore I willingly give up the possession of that sympathy, which I feel is not, cannot be, granted to me. Yet, not the less do I feel the need of it. Who will care to be told such details as I have put down above? Shall I ever have in my old age spiritual children who will take an interest such as a wife does?

But he had not yet ended his account. There was still the story of his parting with Gennaro at Palermo. His faithful Neapolitan servant had hinted he would like as a parting-present

an old blue cloke of mine which I had since 1823; a little thing for him to set his services at—at the same time a great thing for me to give for I have an affection for it. It had nursed me all through my illness; had even been put on my bed, put on me when I rose to have my bed made. . . . I had nearly lost it at Corfu—it was stolen by a soldier but recovered. I have it still. I have brought it up here to Littlemore, and on some cold nights I have had it on my bed. I have so few things to sympathize with me, that I take to clokes.[128]

Towards the end of May he and Bloxam managed to buy nine or ten acres near the church at Littlemore. He immediately began to make plans for the proposed monastic building: he wanted 'a cell to contain three rooms', sitting-room, bedroom, and bathroom. He even wondered if he could get rid of fireplaces by using 'pipes of hot water'.[129] He joked to Woodgate, 'when parsons are turned out of their livings, and rail roads have superseded turnpikes, and you and yours are mounted on horses with one or two poneys for luggage, I will give you bread and beer at the House of the Blessed Mary of Littlemore.'[130] And he wrote to Maria Giberne, 'We . . . aspire . . . to build a magnificent Abbey upon it, which is to rival Glastonbury or Osney.' But in September he warned her not to be taken in by his 'fine words'—he only had in mind 'a hovel such as St Martin lived in or St Basil'.[131]

Meanwhile, Newman's 'monastic' *Church of the Fathers* ('strong meat

---

[128] *AW* 137–8.   [129] To T. Mozley, 20 May, 10 June 1840.
[130] To H. A. Woodgate, 11 June 1840.
[131] To Miss M. R. Giberne, 15 July, 16 Sept. 1840.

perhaps—but it is very sweet meat too'),[132] which had appeared early in March, was drawing the predictable criticism—but he had ample 'experience of the *indignation* and *horror* which has been the process through which men have been persuaded and converted', and of the protests 'against points which can now be quietly assumed as first principles'. In the end he was confident it would find acceptance, if not approval: 'The newest Tract or Volume has always been *the* indiscreet one, and our last point but one has been that at which we ought to have stopped.'[133] But he remained very concerned about disunity within the Church of England, and he had already in March suggested to Pusey weekly prayers for internal unity instead of prayers for union with Rome. Pusey and others warmly welcomed the idea, and it was agreed that Friday should be the day on which people would be asked to pray for unity in the Church of England. It would, he hoped, help 'to allay the violence of party spirit'.[134]

Robert Williams, who had been responsible the previous summer for drawing Newman's attention to the fateful passage in the Wiseman article, was now himself seriously thinking of going over to Rome. Newman wrote to warn him that only 'the clearest and most constraining view' that it was his 'absolute duty' to become a Roman Catholic could 'justify' acting on his 'private judgment' and 'against the advice of all you look up to'. If the Church of England was indeed 'in error', at least it was not his 'responsibility' that he had been 'born in a state of error' since he had not 'chosen it', whereas he might be 'choosing and changing into error' by joining the Roman Church. There were 'so many ways', he concluded, 'of misleading onself in such a question', that it was 'much safer' to 'remain' where he was. It was the first of many such letters that Newman was to write. In a later letter to Williams, he admitted that he too felt 'difficulties', but was 'convinced' according to his own 'best light' that he ought to remain where he was.[135] At the end of July he advised another waverer against being 'perplexed and deceived by argument', and claimed that God 'usually gives overpowering evidence' when he 'asks of us *singly* to follow Him'. If a number of people felt the same, that would be 'an external *note*' to follow, but going over by oneself was simply going by 'private judgment'. He was even ready to concede that 'our state is inferior in point of privilege to Rome', but this was the state they found themselves in, and the 'simple question' was, '*What* is God's will concerning me'—not ' "What is best?" "What is most Catholic?" but "What is *my* duty?" ' But far from leaving his enquirer entirely to his own conscience and thoughts, he added this significant rider:

[132] To H Wilberforce, 27 Feb. 1840.
[134] To R. I. Wilberforce, 25 May 1840.

[133] To H. Moore, 21 May 1840.
[135] To R. Williams, 11, 19 July 1840.

A great experiment is going on, whether Anglocatholicism *has* a root, a foundation, a consistency, as well as Roman Catholicism, or whether . . . it be 'a sham.' I hold it to be quite impossible, unless it be *real*, that it can maintain its ground—it must fall to pieces—This is a day in which mere theories will not pass current. If *it* be a mere theory, it will not *work*. . . . Nothing is allowed to remain undeveloped—but inferences are drawn, or must be refuted—questions are asked and must be satisfactorily answered—the internal consistence of the whole is being severely tested. I securely leave it to this issue—I will not defend it if it will not stand it.

As always for Newman, *reality* was the ultimate test: was Anglo-Catholicism consistent, would it stand up to *facts*—or was it a mere *theory*? One real fact that could not be denied was that 'it really is being taken up with the utmost seriousness' by people 'who have embraced Apostolical doctrines . . . in a deeply religious, practical, earnest and . . . spiritual way'. They included some of the most 'holy' members of the Church of England—was it 'likely that God would leave these men in error?' And, he concluded, even if 'Rome be true', these would be 'her Messengers guiding you to her'.[136]

Back in April he had heard that his brother Frank was no longer 'heading a congregation, or making a schism, which Scripture seemed to me to make a cause for withdrawing from him'. He therefore wrote to say that there was no longer any 'reason for separating from his society'.[137] He also took the opportunity to apologize for 'much infirmity' in his behaviour towards Frank, and especially his lack of 'meekness' in 1821 and 1822. He knew, however, that 'free unrestrained intercourse' between them was 'impossible and that to attempt it would be a great mistake', although he hoped they could keep in touch with one another.[138] His own private view of Frank was that he had a 'great defect of imagination' which would always militate against his coming to a 'Catholic' point of view.[139] In October he reminded Frank, who had by now broken with the Plymouth Brethren, that he had always known that he would 'arrive' at his 'present opinions' if he adhered to 'principles' which 'lead to scepticism on all points whatever'.

I think your reasonings are irresistible, granting certain latent principles which you all along assume. And since I anticipate that these will be generally assumed by the coming age, as they are in great measure already, I am prepared for almost a downfall of Christianity for a time.

Frank's 'conclusions' were only 'the legitimate issue of Protestant principles, when followed out'. What gave his brother hope, however, was that

---

[136] To W. C. A. Maclaurin, 26 July 1840.   [137] To F. W. Newman, 11, 16 Apr. 1840.
[138] To Mrs J. Mozley, 10 Apr. 1840.   [139] To Mrs J. Mozley, 28 Apr. 1840.

Latitudinarianism is an unnatural state; the mind cannot long rest in it; and especially if the fact of a revelation be granted, it is most extravagant and revolting to our reason to suppose that after all its message is not ascertainable and that the divine interposition reveals nothing. The more scepticism abounds, the more is a way made for the revival of a strong ecclesiastical authority; Christianity arose in the beginning, when the popular religions had lost their hold upon the mind. So strongly do I feel this, that, averse as the English people are to Romanism, I conceive that did their choice lie in the mere alternative they would embrace even Romanism rather than acquiesce in absolute uncertainty.[140]

Towards the end of October Newman wrote to ask Keble's advice about whether he should act on 'a feeling' which had been 'growing' on him over the past year that he 'ought to give up St Mary's'. He neither knew his parishioners nor was he 'conscious of influencing them' or of having any 'insight into their spiritual state'.

In my excuse I am accustomed to say to myself, that I am not adapted to get on with them, while others are. On the other hand, I am conscious that by means of my position at St Mary's I do exert a considerable influence on the University, whether on Undergraduates or Graduates. It seems then, on the whole, that I am using St Mary's, to the neglect of its direct duties, for objects not belonging to it; I am converting a parochial charge into a sort of University office.

Although he could honestly say that he had 'begun scarcely any plan but for the sake of my parish', still 'every one has turned, independently of me, into the direction of the University'. The extra Saints' days and weekday services, as well as the lectures in the Adam de Brome chapel, had all been started for his parishioners—'but they have not come to them'. As a result he had stopped the lectures, although, while they lasted, he had 'naturally' had in mind 'those who did come, instead of those who did not'. It was no doubt true that the weekly Communion services had been intended for members of the university (he had been encouraged by how well attended they were, especially by graduates). Meanwhile, 'the authorities of the University, the appointed guardians of those who form great part of the attendants on my Sermons, have shown a dislike to my preaching'—which, he was bound to admit, was

not calculated to defend that system of religion which has been received for 300 years, and of which the Heads of Houses are the legitimate maintainers in this place. They exclude me, as far as may be, from the University Pulpit; and though I never have preached strong doctrine in it, they do so rightly so far as this, that they understand that my sermons are calculated to undermine things established. I cannot disguise from myself that they are. No one will deny that most of my Sermons are on moral subjects, not doctrinal; still I am leading my

[140] To F. W. Newman, 22 Oct. 1840.

hearers, to the Primitive Church if you will, but not to the Church of England. Now ought one to be disgusting the minds of young men with the received religion, in the exercise of a sacred office, yet without a commission, and against the wish of their guides and governors?

He also had to admit that whether he liked it or not, he was influencing his hearers towards Rome; not only was she 'the only representative of the Primitive Church besides ourselves', but 'as they are loosened from the one they will go to the other', particularly as 'many doctrines which I hold have far greater, or their only scope, in the Roman system'. He felt sure that if heresy entered high places in the Church of England and if English Roman Catholics broke their present political links, 'strong temptations will be placed in the way of individuals, already imbued with a tone of thought congenial to Rome, to join her communion'. It was said that he was exercising a useful influence on the future clergy of the Church—but what if he was really leading them to Rome? 'The *arguments* which I have published against Romanism seem to myself as cogent as ever; but men go by their sympathies, not by argument; and if I feel the force of this influence myself who bow to the argument, why may not others still more who never have in the same degree admitted the argument?' He could say no more against Rome: not only had he 'shot' his 'last arrow' in his article on the 'Catholicity of the English Church', but 'I am troubled by doubts, whether, as it is, I have not in what I have published spoken too strongly against Rome; though I think I did it in a kind of faith, being determined to put myself into the English system, and say *all that* our Divines said whether I had fully weighed it or not'. It was 'painful', too, that his very attacks on Rome had had 'the effect of setting to sleep men's suspicions about me', just when he was beginning 'to have suspicions about myself'. He had mentioned his problem to Rogers a year ago, who had advised him to give up St Mary's if he continued to feel the same.

Keble dismissed his scruples about the parishioners and college heads, and warned that resigning St Mary's was liable to cause scandal and would lead people either to look towards Rome, or, alternatively, to assume that Newman repented of the Tractarian cause altogether; whereas by staying he could exercise a restraining influence. Newman accepted the advice, and replied more cheerfully:

I do not think that we have yet made fair trial how much the English Church will bear. I know it is a hazardous experiment, like proving Cannon. Yet we must not take it for granted the metal will burst in the operation. It has borne at various times, not to say at this time, a great infusion of Catholic Truth without damage. As to the result, viz whether this process will not approximate the whole English Church, as a body, to Rome, that is nothing to us. For what we know, it may be the providential means of uniting the whole Church in one, without fresh schismatising, or use of private judgment.

As for his arousing sympathy towards Rome, the same could be said of the high-church Anglican divines of the seventeenth century. Anyway, 'the great evil of the day' was rationalism, and he felt entitled to consider his 'post at St Mary's as a place of protest against *it*'. He was 'more certain' that the Protestant ethos he opposed 'leads to infidelity than that which I recommend leads to Rome'. This was the 'spirit' with which they had to do 'battle'—'May we not leave to another age its own evil,—to settle the question of Romanism?'[141] It was hopeful, if wishful, thinking.

He told Rogers that he had only wanted '*leave*' from Keble to stay at St Mary's—'there are so many reasons making it a duty to remain, so soon as one comes to the conclusion that it is not a duty to go.' It was inevitable that the Movement would 'create a sympathy towards Rome so far as our system does not realise what is realised in Rome'. As for his own doubts, he confided, he felt 'more comfortable', though he found it hard to say exactly why.

My only solicitude has been to have an answer in *controversy* why an *individual* is not bound to leave the English Church. That we are suffering dreadfully (so are the Romanists), and that we are wrong in our separation, I do not doubt. It is quite consistent to say that I think Rome the *centre* of unity, and yet not to say that she is infallible, when she is by herself. . . . I do not fear at all any number of persons as likely to go to Rome, if I am secure about myself. If I can trust myself, I can trust others. We have so many things on our side, that a good conscience is all that one wants.[142]

He felt confident enough to joke to Tom Mozley, 'Apostolicity may be like the eau medicinale—kill us at last into Papists, but at present it does and will do wonders.'[143]

Certainly Newman was well aware of the possibility of future developments in Tractarianism as a religious system. He had been keenly alive for some time to the need for monastic establishments in the Church of England. But he also felt that they were 'not ripe for it yet': for a religious community, 'tight discipline would be necessary'. Nevertheless, he was sure that it was 'a very good thing for people to be thinking about'. Again, on the question of auricular confession he felt that there was 'rather a call for agitating and urging the subject, than proceeding to practice'; and again, people would have first to 'count the cost'. He had no doubt that they would all be 'in a much better state, were it practised', but he saw 'very good obstacles to reviving it'. In his view, 'it

---

[141] To J. Keble, 26 Oct., 6 Nov. 1840.   [142] To F. Rogers, 25 Nov. 1840.
[143] To T. Mozley, 15 Dec. 1840.

should be *sacramental*—performed in Church and face to face'.[144] He had, in fact, heard his first confession back in March 1838, early one Sunday morning in St Mary's, when he had sat at the altar-rails while his penitent knelt before him. Fasting before receiving Holy Communion he thought 'better' but not 'necessary'; however, although it might involve 'too great an effort', it certainly was 'very desirable to place some sort of selfdenials round the participation of the Holy Sacrament lest we should grow familiar with so awful a mystery'.[145]

In general, Newman still felt confident about the progress of the Movement, as a letter of January 1841 shows. Just as in later years when the prospect seemed gloomy, he put his faith in the ultimately invincible power of truth.

The one thing I feared and deprecated years ago, when we began the Tracts for the Times, was utter neglect of us on the part of the Church. I was not afraid of being misrepresented, censured or illtreated—and certainly hitherto it has done no harm. Every attack hitherto has turned to good, or at least is dying a natural death. But *Controversy* does but delay the sure victory of truth by making people angry. When they find out they are wrong of *themselves*, a generous feeling rises in their minds towards the persons and things they have abused and resisted. Much of this reaction has already taken place. Controversy too is a waste of time—one has other things to do. Truth can fight its own battle. It has a reality in it, which shivers to pieces swords of earth. As far as we are not on the side of truth, *we* shall shiver to bits, and I am willing it should be so. The only cause of the prevalence of fallacies for the last 300 years has been the strong arm of the civil power countenancing them. This can hardly continue now. I see too that in the rising generation the most influential and stirring men in Church and State have in them a root of Catholic principles.[146]

The depreciation of controversy—'I declare I think it is as rare a thing, candour in controversy, as to be a Saint'[147]—was rather curious considering Newman was himself about to publish a brilliant controversial work. But then that, like the review article he published in the January 1841 number of the *British Critic* of Henry Hart Milman's *History of Christianity*, was concerned not with the question of the Catholicity of the Church of England, but with the more fundamental and more serious problem of religious belief.

7

Milman had already caused a stir in 1829 with his *History of the Jews*. Newman's initial opinion, that it was 'very dangerous' and apparently

---

[144] To Miss M. R. Giberne, 23 Nov., 22 Dec. 1840.
[145] To Miss M. Holmes, 31 Dec. 1840. [146] To R. Belaney, 25 Jan. 1841.
[147] To F. Rogers, 10 Jan. 1841.

'rationalistic', he later modified, explaining that 'the great evil' of the book lay 'not in the *matter of the* history, but in the profane *spirit* in which it is written'—while adding the remarkable admission, 'In *most* of his positions I agree with him but abhor the irreverent scoffing Gibbon-like tone of the composition.' It was a very early example of the carefully balanced approach to the problems for religious belief that were raised by progress in scholarly and scientific research which Newman was to develop over the years, in sharp contradistinction to the polarized reactions of so many of his contemporaries. He was not slow, however, to offer a moral diagnosis of Milman's motives in writing the book, which he considered to be 'the fruit of a supercilious liberalistic spirit, which liked to be . . . philosophical and above the world, and to appear so—to show that a Clergyman could take an enlarged view of things, and yet be a firm believer'. He saw then that the effect of 'the flattery of liberals and the severe censure of others' would only be to force Milman into a more extreme position.[148] When Milman's new book appeared in 1840, he was wary of a concerted Tractarian attack on it 'bad' as it no doubt was: he saw no point in getting involved 'prematurely' in a very large problem which the Church would sooner or later have to face—let the Evangelicals 'try their heads' instead ('it will do them good to find we are good for something').

The controversy is not yet begun. I am in no hurry to begin it. When it begins, it may last out our days. . . . Feeling all this, I am not *anxious* to assail poor Milman, than whom there may be to come more powerful and deeper men.

It seemed, indeed, that 'a great battle is coming on of which Milman's new book is a sort of earnest'.[149] In the first book, he felt Milman had been 'treading on the brink of danger, and now and then letting precious things fall over, without knowing where exactly he was'.[150] Now, on reviewing its sequel, he considered Milman 'indefinitely *unreal*, and that he does not know where he is'.[151]

The review starts from the premiss that not only Christianity, 'but all God's dealings with His creatures, have two aspects, one external, one internal'. This 'is the one great rule on which the Divine Dispensations with mankind have been and are conducted, that the visible world is the instrument, yet the veil, of the world invisible'. Since, then, 'All that is seen,—the world, the Bible, the Church, the civil polity, and man himself,—are types, and . . . representatives and organs of an unseen world, truer and higher than themselves', it is not surprising that, when God 'would make a Revelation, He does not begin anew, but uses the

[148] *LD* ii. 160, 299, 309.
[149] To E. B. Pusey, 29 Mar. 1840; to H. Wilberforce, 25 July 1840; to J. Keble, 6 Nov. 1840.
[150] *LD* ii. 309.   [151] To Mrs J. Mozley, 8 Jan. 1841.

existing system'. And so, like Judaism, Christianity, 'though not of this world, yet is in the world, and has a visible, material, social shape'. It is therefore possible to 'write its history, and make it look as like those which were before or contemporary with it, as a man is like a monkey'. This, Newman argues, is what Milman 'has been doing. He has been viewing the history of the Church on the side of the world.' But by simply 'viewing Christianity as an external political fact', he 'has gone very far indeed towards viewing it as nothing more'. As for Milman's 'professing to keep to fact, and yet insinuating a theory', Newman is so unimpressed as to produce the provocative paradox: 'As liberals are the bitterest persecutors, so denouncers of controversy are sure to proceed upon the most startling, irritating, blistering methods which the practice of their age furnishes.' Now the undoubted fact that 'great portion of what is generally received as Christian truth, is in its rudiments or in its separate parts to be found in heathen philosophies and religions' does not necessarily lead to Milman's theory that therefore these things are not Christian. Rather,

we prefer to say, and we think that Scripture bears us out in saying, that from the beginning the Moral Governor of the world has scattered the seeds of truth far and wide over its extent; that these have variously taken root, and grown up as in the wilderness, wild plants indeed but living; and hence that, as the inferior animals have tokens of an immaterial principle in them, yet have not souls, so the philosophies and religions of men have their life in certain true ideas, though they are not directly divine. What man is amid the brute creation, such is the Church among the schools of the world; and as Adam gave names to the animals about him, so has the Church from the first looked round upon the earth, noting and visiting the doctrines she found there . . . claiming to herself what they said rightly, correcting their errors, supplying their defects, completing their beginnings, expanding their surmises, and thus gradually by means of them enlarging the range and refining the sense of her own teaching.

It was an eloquent development of the point Newman had already forcefully made in the *Arians* that all religions have elements of truth in them. But it was also, he well realized, a very different theory from that which assumed that 'Revelation was a single, entire, solitary act . . . introducing a certain message', and Christianity 'some one tenet or certain principles given at one time in their fulness'. For on this view, revealed religion was 'various, complex, progressive, and supplemental of itself'. As opposed to people like Milman who 'are ever hunting for a fabulous primitive simplicity; we repose in Catholic fulness'. Newman concludes that, if we follow out the implications of Milman's approach, 'Christianity will melt away in our hands like snow'.[152]

---

[152] *Ess.* ii. 190, 192–4, 196, 213–14, 231–3, 242.

Before leaving the review, it is worth noticing how at the beginning Newman had commented, 'It is notorious that the English Church is destitute of an Ecclesiastical History; Gibbon is almost our sole authority for subjects as near the heart of a Christian as any can well be.' In another review, published three months later, of Bowden's life of Hildebrand, he added that it was 'difficult justly to estimate the injury done to our whole view of Gospel truth by our ignorance of ecclesiastical history. Every department of theology acts upon the rest, and if one is neglected the others suffer.' He was to make the same point on a much larger scale in the *Idea of a University*, but now he was concerned to emphasize not only the importance of history—'the present is a text, and the past its interpretation'—but also the impossibility of a totally unbiased judgement: 'We always judge of what meets us by what we know already. There is no such thing in nature as a naked text without note or comment.'[153] Again, a knowledge of historical facts was essential if people were not to indulge in mere theorizing.

On 19 January, at the opening of a new library and reading-room at Tamworth, Sir Robert Peel delivered a speech which attracted a lot of publicity because of its markedly utilitarian tone. John Walter, the son of the proprietor of *The Times*, who had come under Newman's influence at Oxford, persuaded his father, who had till now been opposed to the Tractarians, to ask Newman to write a reply. The older John Walter called on Newman at Oriel and 'pressed' him 'several times' to write before he 'consented'.[154] The resulting seven letters appeared in *The Times* during February under the name of 'Catholicus'.

Apart from their political and social interest and the ways in which they anticipate the *Idea of a University*, the letters constitute the one sustained work of satire that Newman wrote as an Anglican. He begins by remarking that Sir Robert Peel's speech could just as well have been delivered in 1827 or 1828 at the founding of secular University College, London by the former Lord Chancellor, Lord Brougham, one of the leading promoters of the Reform Bill.

It is, indeed, most melancholy to see so sober and experienced a man practising the antics of one of the wildest performers of this wild age . . .
    Yet let him be assured that the task of rivalling such a man is hopeless, as well as unprofitable. No one can equal the great sophist. Lord Brougham is inimitable in his own line.

Although unable to conceal altogether his 'personal religious feeling', Peel, when faced with the question whether a society consisting of 'persons of different religions' is 'a positive standing evil, to be endured at best as unavoidable, or a topic of exultation', replies (according to

---

[153] *Ess.* ii. 186, 250, 252.   [154] *LD* xiv. 52.

Newman), 'Of exultation . . . the greater differences the better, the more the merrier.'[155]

In establishing a library where all discussions or lectures on denominational or political lines will be excluded, Sir Robert treats religious distinctions exactly as if they were mere local party differences—'such, I suppose, as about a municipal election, or a hole-and-corner meeting, or a parish job, or a bill in Parliament for a railway'. However,

Christianity is faith, faith implies a doctrine; a doctrine propositions; propositions yes or no, yes or no differences. Differences, then, are the natural attendants on Christianity, and you cannot have Christianity, and not have differences.

Sir Robert 'advocates concessions', but 'he must be plainly told to make presents of things that belong to him, nor seek to be generous with other people's substance. There are entails in more matters than parks and old places.' It is not that Sir Robert 'considers all differences of opinion as equal in importance; no, they are only equally in the way'. It is a 'remarkable example of self-sacrifice' to become 'the disciple of his political foe, accepting from Lord Brougham his new principle of combination, rejecting Faith for the fulcrum of Society, and proceeding to rest it upon Knowledge'. Whereas faith was 'once the soul of social union', now it is 'but the spirit of division'. So far as Sir Robert is concerned,

We must abandon Religion, if we aspire to be statesmen. Once, indeed, it was a living power, kindling hearts, leavening them with one idea, moulding them on one model, developing them into one polity. Ere now it has been the life of morality: it has given birth to heroes; it has wielded empire. But another age has come in, and Faith is effete; let us submit to what we cannot change; let us not hang over our dead, but bury it out of sight. Seek we out some young and vigorous principle, rich in sap, and fierce in life, to give form to elements which are fast resolving into their inorganic chaos; and where shall we find such a principle but in Knowledge?[156]

English literature owes a debt to Sir Robert Peel's educational project, for the idea of knowledge as a substitute for religion strikes Newman as so grotesquely absurd that it inspires the first really extended display of his powers of irony. He wonders how a knowledge of science will produce moral effects—'Can the process be analyzed and drawn out, or does it act like a dose or a charm which comes into general use empirically?' It would appear that 'To know is one thing, to do is another'—an objection, of course, which Bentham would answer by

---

[155] *DA* 255, 259–60. [156] Ibid. 283–6.

saying 'that the knowledge which carries virtue along with it, is the knowledge how to take care of number one', for 'Useful Knowledge is that which tends to make us more useful to ourselves;—a most definite and intelligible account of the matter, and needing no explanation'. But the Utilitarian philosopher 'had not a spark of poetry in him; on the contrary, there is much of high aspiration, generous sentiment, and impassioned feeling in the tone of Lord Brougham and Sir Robert'. It is true, Newman concedes, that 'Sir Robert does *obiter* talk of improved modes of draining, and the chemical properties of manure, yet he must not be supposed to come short of the lofty enthusiasm of Lord Brougham, who expressly panegyrizes certain ancient philosophers who gave up riches, retired into solitude, or embraced a life of travel, smit with a sacred curiosity about physical or mathematical truth'. What, then, is the connection supposed to be between knowledge and morals?

When a husband is gloomy, or an old woman peevish and fretful, those who are about them do all they can to keep dangerous topics and causes of offence out of the way, and think themselves lucky, if, by such skilful management, they get through the day without an outbreak. When a child cries, the nurserymaid dances it about, or points to the pretty black horses out of window, or shows how ashamed poll-parrot or poor puss must be of its tantrums. Such is the sort of prescription which Sir Robert Peel offers to the good people of Tamworth. He makes no pretence of subduing the giant nature, in which we were born, of smiting the loins of the domestic enemies of our peace, of overthrowing passion and fortifying reason; he does but offer to bribe the foe for the nonce with gifts which will avail for that purpose just so long as they *will* avail, and no longer.

And so Lord Brougham's 'notions of rigour and elevation, when analyzed, will be found to resolve themselves into a mere preternatural excitement under the influence of some stimulating object, or the peace which is attained by there being nothing to quarrel with'. It is the modern heresy that 'our true excellence comes not from within, but from without; not wrought out through personal struggles and sufferings, but following upon a passive exposure to influences over which we have no control'. It is 'the theory that diversion is the instrument of improvement, and excitement the condition of right action; and whereas diversions cease to be diversions if they are constant, and excitements by their very nature have a crisis and run through a course, they will tend to make morality ever in request, and will set the great teachers of morals upon the incessant search after stimulants and sedatives, by which unruly nature may . . . be kept in order'. Lord Brougham

frankly offers us a philosophy of expedients: he shows us how to live by medicine. Digestive pills half an hour before dinner, and a posset at bedtime at the best; and at the worst, dram-drinking and opium,—the very remedy against broken hearts, or remorse of conscience, which is in request among the many, in gin-palaces *not* intellectual.

But 'who was ever consoled in real trouble by the small beer of literature or science?' Or when, Newman asks sarcastically, 'was a choleric temperament ever brought under by a scientific King Canute planting his professor's chair before the rising waves?' Anyway, it is not very realistic to imagine that the 'pleasures' of 'intellectual pursuit and conquest' will not be 'outbid in the market by gratifications much closer at hand, and on a level with the meanest capacity'. The colloquial tone of voice only adds to the sense of the outrageously incongruous: 'Such is this new art of living, offered to the labouring classes,—we will say, for instance, in a severe winter, snow on the ground, glass falling, bread rising, coal at 20d. the cwt., and no work.' The most sarcastic of satirists never managed to write anything better than this:

that the mind is changed by a discovery, or saved by a diversion, and can thus be amused into immortality,—that grief, anger, cowardice, self-conceit, pride, or passion, can be subdued by an examination of shells or grasses, or inhaling of gases, or chipping of rocks, or calculating the longitude, is the veriest of pretences which sophist or mountebank ever professed to a gaping auditory. If virtue be a mastery over the mind, if its end be action, if its perfection be inward order, harmony, and peace, we must seek it in graver and holier places than in Libraries and Reading-rooms.[157]

As a great proponent of realism himself, Newman has a certain reluctant respect for that 'stern realist' Jeremy Bentham (whose 'system has nothing ideal about it'), even though 'he limits his realism to things which he can see, hear, taste, touch, and handle'. But nothing could be more unreal than to imagine that knowledge ever 'healed a wounded heart' or 'changed a sinful one'. The imagery used is disconcertingly tactile, culminating in an image of physical confinement to satirize the theorizing of Brougham and Peel (the figure of imprisonment would be put to similar effect in the later satirical writings):

Christianity raises men from earth, for it comes from heaven; but human morality creeps, struts, or frets upon the earth's level, without wings to rise. The Knowledge School does not contemplate raising man above himself; it merely aims at disposing of his existing powers and tastes, as is most convenient, or is practicable under circumstances. It finds him, like the victims of the French Tyrant, doubled up in a cage in which he can neither lie, stand, sit, nor kneel, and its highest desire is to find an attitude in which his unrest may be least.[158]

Anticipating his later idea of a university, Newman is careful, on the one hand, to deny that he has any 'fanatical wish to deny to any

---

[157] *DA* 261–8.   [158] Ibid. 269–70, 272.

whatever subject of thought or method of reason a place altogether, if it chooses to claim it, in the cultivation of the mind' (the essential principle being 'to sacrifice none—to combine, and therefore to adjust, all'), while, on the other hand, to insist that

Christianity, and nothing short of it, must be made the element and principle of all education. Where it has been laid as the first stone, and acknowledged as the governing spirit, it will take up into itself, assimilate, and give a character to literature and science. Where Revealed Truth has given the aim and direction to Knowledge, Knowledge of all kinds will minister to Revealed Truth.

The distinction would be elaborated later, but here Newman's concern is to emphasize that any 'attempt to effect a moral improvement' by means of knowledge is to 'misplace what in its place is a divine gift'.[159]

Lord Brougham, who 'understands that something more is necessary for man's happiness than self-love' and that 'man has affections and aspirations which Bentham does not take account of', dismisses Christianity as 'dogmatism': 'Human nature wants recasting, but Lord Brougham is all for tinkering it.'[160] Sir Robert Peel, on the other hand, is sure that the study of science will lead to religious faith. But, Newman warns ironically, 'The way is long, and there are not a few half-way houses and traveller's rests along it . . .'. Anyway, 'common sense and practical experience' show that if people 'give their leisure and curiosity to this world, they will have none left for the next'. He wonders, incidentally, why the Tamworth Reading-room only admits '*virtuous* women' as members—

A very emphatic silence is maintained about women not virtuous. What does this mean? Does it mean to exclude them, while bad *men* are admitted? Is this accident, or design, sinister and insidious, against a portion of the community? What has virtue to do with a Reading-room? It is to *make* its members virtuous . . .

How inconsistent that 'bigotry should have left the mark of its hoof' on so liberal a philosophy!'[161]

To the objection that 'it is but a dream to suppose that Christianity should regain the organic power in human society which once it possessed', Newman replies:

I cannot help that; I never said it could. I am not a politician; I am proposing no measures, but exposing a fallacy, and resisting a pretence. Let Benthamism reign, if men have no aspirations; but do not tell them to be romantic, and then solace them with glory; do not attempt by philosophy what once was done by religion. The ascendancy of Faith may be impracticable, but the reign of

---

[159] *DA* 274–5.   [160] Ibid. 277, 281–2.   [161] Ibid. 279–82.

Knowledge is incomprehensible. The problem for statesmen of this age is how to educate the masses, and literature and science cannot give the answer.

Science can only give us 'facts': we have to 'give them a meaning, and to draw our own conclusions from them'. Newman's critique of Peel's sanguine belief that science leads to Christianity is not only a striking anticipation of the argument of the *Grammar of Assent*, but shows Newman at the height of his literary powers. He would certainly write as well again, but hardly with greater force than in these passages where the aphoristic, the colloquial, and the ironic come together in a dazzling display of imagery.

First comes Knowledge, then a view, then reasoning, and then belief. This is why Science has so little of a religious tendency; deductions have no power of persuasion. The heart is commonly reached, not through the reason, but through the imagination, by means of direct impressions, by the testimony of facts and events, by history, by description. Persons influence us, voices melt us, looks subdue us, deeds inflame us. Many a man will live and die upon a dogma: no man will be a martyr for a conclusion. A conclusion is but an opinion . . . To say that a thing *must* be, is to admit that it *may not* be. No one, I say, will die for his own calculations; he dies for realities. This is why a literary religion is so little to be depended upon; it looks well in fair weather, but its doctrines are opinions, and, when called to suffer for them, it slips them between its folios, or burns them at its hearth . . .
  I have no confidence, then, in philosophers who . . . sit at home, and reach forward to distances which astonish us; but they hit without grasping, and are sometimes as confident about shadows as about realities. They have worked out by a calculation the lie of the country which they never saw, and mapped it by means of a gazeteer; and like blind men, though they can put a stranger on his way, they cannot walk straight themselves, and do not feel it quite their business to walk at all.
  Logic makes but a sorry rhetoric with the multitude; first shoot round corners, and you may not despair of converting by a syllogism. . . . After all, man is *not* a reasoning animal; he is a seeing, feeling, contemplating, acting animal.

Newman now introduces the crucial concept of 'first principles':

Life is not long enough for a religion of inferences; we shall never have done beginning, if we determine to begin with proof. . . . We shall never get at our first principles. Resolve to believe nothing, and you must prove your proofs and analyze your elements, sinking further and further . . . till you come to the broad bosom of scepticism. . . . Life is for action. If we insist on proofs for everything, we shall never come to action: to act you must assume, that assumption is faith.

It is all very well, he concludes, 'to analyze our modes of thought; but let this come second', for, 'if we commence with scientific knowledge and argumentative proof, or lay any great stress upon it as the basis of personal Christianity, or attempt to make man moral and religious by Libraries and Museums, let us in consistency take chemists for our cooks, and mineralogists for our masons'. It is not simply realism that is at stake, but the very nature of revealed religion:

Why we are so constituted that Faith, not Knowledge or Argument, is our principle of action, is a question with which I have nothing to do; but I think it is a fact, and if it be such, we must resign ourselves to it as best we may, unless we take refuge in the intolerable paradox, that the mass of men are created for nothing, and are meant to leave life as they entered it. So well has this practically been understood in all ages of the world, that no Religion has yet been a Religion of physics or philosophy. It has ever been synonymous with Revelation. It never has been a deduction from what we know: it has ever been an assertion of what we are to believe. It has never lived in a conclusion; it has ever been a message, or a history, or a vision.[162]

As for science, however wonderful nature may be, 'wonder is not religion, or we should be worshipping our railroads'. Moreover, the 'essence of Religion is the idea of a Moral Governor and a particular Providence'—not 'the animating principle' of the universe, which is 'co-extensive with matter' and which 'is not the Almighty God'. In a way reminiscent of his criticism of the tendency to internalize and so lessen the external reality of the object of faith, Newman dismisses this kind of pantheism as ultimately 'the worship of self', for 'our admiration terminates in man'. It is also *qua* religion as absurd as it is practically useless: 'Meditate indeed on the wonders of Nature on a death-bed! Rather stay your hunger with corn grown in Jupiter, and warm yourself by the Moon.'

Just as in the *Idea of a University*, Newman has no doubt that science is 'worthy of a place in a liberal education'; still, that does not alter the fact 'that knowledge does but occupy, does not form the mind; that apprehension of the unseen is the only known principle capable of subduing moral evil, educating the multitude, and organizing society; and that, whereas man is born for action, action flows not from inferences, but from impressions,—not from reasonings, but from Faith'. How 'melancholy', Newman concludes by exclaiming, that Sir Robert Peel should have 'so little of romantic aspiration, and of firm resolve, and stern dutifulness to the Unseen', that he thought 'to be safe was his first merit, and to kindle enthusiasm his most disgraceful blunder'![163]

[162] *DA* 292–6.   [163] Ibid. 301–5.

5
Crisis

❧

In February 1841 Newman reached the age of 40. He felt it as a watershed: 'I never had such dreary dismal thoughts as on finding myself 40. 21 was bad enough.'[1] Later in the year he sighed to his aunt, 'I am getting such an age, I hardly know how to bear the thought of myself.' And he mused: 'What a great difference there is in the length of lives! When a person is young, 60 and 80 seem much the same—but what a strange thing it is that a person has as much as 20 years more than another.'[2] The previous new year he had been quite startled by the date: 'who would have thought that 1840 would *ever* come! it used to look like a fabulous date; like some of the idle prophecies of the end of the world, as in this year or that.'[3]

Word soon spread that Newman was the author of the letters by 'Catholicus', which he was now correcting and revising for publication as a book under the title *The Tamworth Reading Room*. On 22 February he wrote delightedly to Henry Wilberforce that they had upset the preconceptions of those who 'thought Puseyism a thing of copes and lighted tapers. Geese, they never read a word, till the fist is shaken in their face.' He also mentioned that A. W. N. Pugin, the Gothic architect who had become a Roman Catholic in 1834, had been in Oxford. Newman admitted he could not 'help liking him, though he is an immense talker'.[4] The 'rough tongue-free unselfgoverned' Pugin, as Newman described him to Tom Mozley, had given a 'dreadful account of the politicism of the RCs.', but had also given an assurance that 'a better spirit is beginning among them, and that Dr Wiseman has set his face firmly against political priests'. Pugin had paid an earlier visit to Oxford in November when he had spoken 'strongly against the R.C. body' and said 'that if 200 of the ablest and best of our men were to go over, they would be received coldly'. Although Newman had heard then that Wiseman, who had left the English College in Rome to become Coadjutor to the Vicar Apostolic of the Midland district and President of Oscott College, had 'begun a *Conservative* line on taking possession of his post' and was 'silencing political priests', he had concluded from

[1] To Mrs J. Mozley, 24 Feb. 1841. [2] To Miss E. Newman, 27 June 1841.
[3] To Mrs J. Mozley, 14 Jan. 1840. [4] To H. Wilberforce, 22 Feb. 1841.

Pugin's discouraging report that 'our way certainly is to form alliances with *foreigners*; the jealousies (natural) with R.C.'s at home preclude anything good'. He now passed on the gratifying news to Mozley that not only was the *British Critic* 'extensively' read by Roman Catholics and 'really doing them good', but also Pugin thought that it was 'the most Catholic publication going'.[5] It had already been decided in the previous autumn that Mozley should succeed Newman as editor in the summer.

Overtures from such converts as Pugin and his friend Ambrose Lisle Phillipps made Newman wonder 'why', when their 'sympathies' were 'so much the same', they should be 'separated'—

except that there is a strong body in both Churches whose antipathies are more powerful still, and because this body has the governing authorities on its side. I cannot wonder that *our* authorities should feel as they do, considering what the Church of Rome practically is—nor can I wonder that the Church of Rome should feel as it does considering what we are and have been, at least the majority of us.

This long letter to Bloxam, setting out Newman's feelings, continues rather less even-handedly as he attempts to justify the continuing separation from Rome:

This I feel most strongly and cannot conceal it, viz. that, while Rome is what she is, union is impossible—that we too must change I do not deny.

Rome must change first of all in her spirit. I must see more sanctity in her than I do at present. Alas! I see no marks of sanctity—or if any, they are chiefly confined to converts from us. . . . I do verily think that, with all our sins, there is more sanctity in the Church of England and Ireland, than in the Roman Catholic bodies in the same countries.

His principal objection remained the same:

What Hildebrand did by faith and holiness, they do by political intrigue. Their great object is to pull down the English Church. They join with those who are *further* from them in creed to oppose those who are *nearer* to them. They have to do with such a man as O Connell. Never can I think such ways the footsteps of Christ. If they want to convert England, let them go barefooted into our manufacturing towns, let them preach to the people, like St Francis Xavier, let them be pelted and trampled on—and I will own that they can do what we cannot; I will confess that they are our betters far . . . This is to be Catholics . . . Let them use the proper arms of the Church, and they will prove they are the Church by using them.

Although 'difficulties would not be at an end', he nevertheless felt that 'sanctity being secured, everything would ultimately follow'. In the meantime he saw no reason why

[5] To T. Mozley, 22 Feb. 1841; to F. Rogers, 25 Nov. 1840.

it would be other than a sin for any of us to *leave* our Church. We must make our Church move. If indeed, so far from moving, she rushed (which God forbid and which it is profane even to suppose) into open heresy instead, and the Church of Rome on the other hand had cleansed herself of her present faults, in such a state of things I can conceive its being a duty to leave our own Church and join the Roman. I do not feel it a duty on any other hypothesis.

For the time being, their 'duty' seemed

rather to lie in trying to be one with each other in heart, and doing what we can to improve our own bodies respectively. No one can say that much has not been done on the part of many of our members to improve the state of the English Communion—let Roman Catholics do as much. . . . they have much to do before they will have done as much as some of us have done. I long to see them begin the work of Christian charity. I wish I could see a movement on the part of their *clergy*. I earnestly wait for the time when men of learning and ability will come forward, not to advocate any recognition of our Church,—I am not asking for that,—but to speak and act kindly towards a body which has done much to repress many heresies . . . and is nearer them than any other Christian communion. I would call upon them to break their connections with those who agree with them in no one principle; to give up the uncatholic proceedings which disgrace their worship so commonly, (such as music meetings in Chapels—); to be preachers of sanctity and to raise a feeling of the necessity of a moral reformation. Their success rests with themselves. The English never will be favorably inclined to a plotting intriguing party—but faith and holiness are irresistible.[6]

In its essentials, Newman's view of the situation never changed, although he came ultimately to believe that there was more hope of the Roman Catholic Church becoming more 'Christian' than of the Church of England becoming more 'Catholic'.

Later, in March, he told Bloxam, who was in correspondence with Phillipps, that the latter greatly exaggerated the 'importance and influence' of the leaders of the Movement, some of whom were 'not even in authority, nor are likely to be. To ask us to propose terms of negociation, is to invite us to forget our place and to take on us the duties of our rulers.' Given Newman's sense of episcopal authority, he considered 'it would be wrong in me to hold intercourse with any one who comes hither on such an understanding'. He reiterated his own important ecumenical principle:

Faith is but the expression of love. If they and we were animated by one spirit, we *should* unite in one Church. The belief of the heart would lead to the confession of the lips. Reverse the process, and you but sew a new piece into an old garment.

And he concluded by hoping that enlightened Roman Catholics might

[6] To J. R. Bloxam, 23 Feb. 1841.

'incur as much odium, in their own communion, for what they knew to be truth, as Dr Pusey has done and incurred among ourselves for what they allow to be the same truth'.[7] But he had to admit to Tom Mozley that Phillipps, who had been defending the Anglican Church and particularly the Tractarians in the *Tablet,* had been 'so attacked by his own party as to be a sort of Confessor'. People like him and Pugin should be 'encouraged on every account', not least because 'it would be *politic* to get up a split in the R.C. body'. It was amazing, too, how *The Times* had changed its attitude to the Movement. On the other hand, people had warned him that the new *Tract* he had brought out would get him 'into a scrape', although he was not unduly worried, nor did he regret writing it.

It has been sent off by enemies to various Bishops, and is selling very fast here. *I* think people are *sick* of the subject, and will in weariness let us rest. They have cried wolf till they have no voice. The Tract was necessary to keep our young friends etc from stumbling at the Articles and going to Rome.[8]

2

Tract 90 had appeared on 27 February. It was, as usual, anonymous, but there was little doubt who its author was. Newman had long thought of writing about the Thirty-nine Articles. In the *Apologia* he says that he could not 'conjecture' whether, 'as time went on', he would 'have been forced, by the necessities of the original theory of the Movement, to put on paper the speculations which I had about them'. What actually forced the issue was 'the restlessness . . . of those who neither liked the *Via Media,* nor my strong judgment against Rome'. The bishop had asked him 'to keep these men straight', but the problem of 'subscription to the Articles' was 'thrown in our teeth'. After his shock in the summer of 1839, he realized that not only had he to say what 'Notes of the Church' could be said to belong positively to the Anglican Church (which he did in the article of January 1840), but 'the great stumbling-block' of the Articles had to be surmounted, as here, it was 'urged', 'was a positive Note *against* Anglicanism'.

Anglicanism claimed to hold, that the Church of England was nothing else than a continuation in this country . . . of that one Church of which in old times Athanasius and Augustine were members. But, if so, the doctrine must be the same; the doctrine of the Old Church must live and speak in Anglican formularies, in the 39 Articles. Did it? Yes, it did . . . it did in substance, in a true sense. Man had done his worst to disfigure, to mutilate, the old Catholic Truth;

[7] To J. R. Bloxam, 2 Mar. 1841.   [8] To T. Mozley, 7 Mar. 1841.

but there it was, in spite of them, in the Articles still. It was there,—but this must be shown. It was a matter of life and death to us to show it.

He had gone out to Littlemore in March 1840 with this intention, but 'other things interfered to prevent' his 'accomplishing' the work then. By the time he did undertake the investigation, he had become 'reconciled to the prospect of it, and had no apprehensions as to the experiment'; but to begin with, although he genuinely thought it could be done, he had no doubt that 'it would be a trial of the Anglican Church, which it had never undergone before,—not that the Catholic sense of the Articles had not been held or at least suffered by their framers and promulgators', or taught by later Anglican theologians, 'but that it had never been publicly recognized, while the interpretation of the day was Protestant and exclusive'.[9]

Tract 90 begins with an unequivocal disavowal of any wish to join with the liberals in securing the relaxation of the obligation to subscribe to the Articles. Newman makes only too clear his deep distrust of religious change, however seemingly desirable:

Religious changes, to be beneficial, should be the act of the whole body; they are worth little if they are the mere act of a majority. No good can come of any change which is not heartfelt, a development of feelings springing up freely and calmly within the bosom of the whole body itself. Moreover, a change in theological teaching involves either the commission or the confession of sin . . . Even supposing . . . that any changes in contemplation, whatever they were, were good in themselves, they would cease to be good to a Church, in which they were the fruits not of the quiet conviction of all, but of the agitation, or tyranny, or intrigue of a few; nurtured not in mutual love, but in strife and envying; perfected not in humiliation and grief, but in pride, elation, and triumph.

Rejecting any 'untrue desire of unity', Newman insists that it is only by 'returning to each other in heart, and coming together to God to do for us what we cannot do for ourselves', that any 'change can be for the better'.

Till we, her children, are stirred up to this religious course, let the Church, our Mother, sit still; let her children be content to be in bondage; let us work in chains; let us submit to our imperfections as a punishment; let us go on teaching with the stammering lips of ambiguous formularies, and inconsistent precedents, and principles but partially developed.

Breaking off his passionate plea for a completely spiritual, as opposed to 'political', approach to the Church's disunity, he turns to the purpose in hand—'which is merely to show that, while our Prayer Book is

---

[9] *Apo.* 78, 122–3.

acknowledged on all hands to be of Catholic origin, our Articles also, the offspring of an uncatholic age, are, through God's good providence, to say the least, not uncatholic, and may be subscribed by those who aim at being catholic in heart and doctrine'.[10] The detailed and lengthy examination of the individual Articles that follows was, Newman explains in the *Apologia*, intended to prove that 'the Articles do not oppose Catholic teaching; they but partially oppose Roman dogma; they for the most part oppose the dominant errors of Rome'.[11] He also hoped to reduce the real differences between the two communions as far as possible, on the assumption that 'each creed was obscured and misrepresented by a dominant circumambient "Popery" and "Protestantism" '. The conclusion reached is that 'it is a *duty* which we owe both to the Catholic Church and to our own, to take our reformed confessions in the most Catholic sense they will admit; we have no duties towards their framers.' Moreover, 'the Articles are evidently framed on the principle of leaving open large questions, on which the controversy hinges'. Again, 'the variety of doctrinal views contained in the Homilies . . . views which cannot be brought under Protestantism itself . . . is an additional proof, considering the connexion of the Articles with the Homilies, that the Articles are not framed on the principle of excluding those who prefer the theology of the early ages to that of the Reformation'. Finally, it is clear that 'their framers constructed them in such a way as best to comprehend those who did not go so far in Protestantism as themselves'. Thus, Newman concludes triumphantly, 'What was an economy in the Reformers, is a protection to us. What would have been a perplexity to us then, is a perplexity to Protestants now.'[12]

On 8 March a letter from four senior college tutors was sent to the editor of *Tracts for the Times* protesting that *Tract 90* opened the door to the teaching of Roman Catholicism in the University. Newman now realized that he could be in 'a serious mess'. He had not even thought the *Tract* 'likely to excite attention'.[13] He had shown it to Keble before its publication, who had made no objection. There was one consolation: the learned William Palmer of Worcester, who had distanced himself early on from the Movement, now congratulated Newman on having written the most valuable of the *Tracts*. At any rate, he told Pusey, he could not be sorry he had written it: either a 'legitimate interpretation' of the Articles must be allowed, or there would be 'quasi secessions, if not real ones, from the Church'.[14] People were 'so angry' that they were capable of anything, he reported to Bowden.[15] The Heads of Houses

[10] *VM* ii. 269–72.   [11] *Apo*. 79.   [12] *VM* ii. 344–6, 348.
[13] To Mrs T. Mozley, 9 Mar. 1841.   [14] To E. B. Pusey, 10 Mar. 1841.
[15] To J. W. Bowden, 11 Mar. 1841.

especially were furious and were planning some action, he heard. He explained to Henry Wilberforce that the reason why he was 'in a regular scrape' was all because of Golightly, who had 'stirred up the world, who else would have slept'. At least people now knew what he thought, which was one 'comfort'.[16] He only hoped Pusey would not become involved. He told Harriett that he was afraid he was 'clean dished': 'The Heads of Houses are at this very moment concocting a manifesto against me. Do not think I fear for my cause. We have too great a run of luck.'[17] But he had had to write *Tract 90*, 'to keep people either from Rome or schism or an uncomfortable conscience'. It was also 'necessary for my own peace so much as this, that I felt people *did not know* me, and were trusting me when otherwise they would not'. It was true he had never expected it to make 'a noise', but thought it would 'come in quietly'.[18] He had not, however, bargained for Golightly fanning the flames. Still, he thought it would 'turn to good', although he was 'sorry' that his 'friends should suffer through me'.[19] He decided to write immediately 'a *short* explanation'—not that he thought 'any thing I could say would satisfy them'—which he suggested to Hawkins the Heads might like to see before they made any public statement.[20] But they did not wait: on 15 March the Vice-Chancellor, Heads of Houses, and Proctors decided on a public censure of *Tract 90*, which appeared early next morning, only a few hours before Newman's own 'explanation' was published. The same day Newman wrote to Bowden:

The Heads ... have just done a violent act—they have said that my interpretation of the articles is an evasion. Do not think that this will pain me; you see no doctrine is censured, and my shoulders shall manage to bear the charge.

If you know all, or when you know all, you will see that I have asserted a great principle, and I ought to suffer for it . . .[21]

He had hoped the Heads would not come to a decision till his pamphlet was out, but he had tried to prepare himself for 'the worst'.[22] And now he was 'not at all *troubled*', he assured Harriett and Jemima: 'No one ever did a great thing without suffering.'[23] To the Vice-Chancellor he sent a formal note (which he had printed) acknowledging that he was the author of *Tract 90*: 'I hope it will not surprise you if I say, that my opinion remains unchanged of the truth and honesty of the principle maintained in the Tract, and of the necessity of putting it forth.'[24]

[16] To H. Wilberforce, 11 Mar. 1841.   [17] To Mrs T. Mozley, 12 Mar. 1841.
[18] To A. P. Perceval, 12 Mar. 1841.   [19] To J. W. Bowden, 13 Mar. 1841.
[20] To E. B. Pusey, 12 Mar. 1941; to E. Hawkins, 14 Mar. 1841.
[21] To J. W. Bowden, 15 Mar. 1841.   [22] To Mrs J. Mozley, 15 Mar. 1841.
[23] To Mrs J. Mozley, 16 Mar. 1841; to Mrs T. Mozley, 16 Mar. 1841.
[24] To P. Wynter, 16 Mar. 1841.

In his 'explanation', which took the form of *A Letter addressed to the Rev. R. W. Jelf* (whom Newman chose as an impartial observer, according to the practice of the time), he did not flinch, much as he now disliked speaking against the Roman Church, from affirming publicly once again his view that to all appearances

the present authoritative teaching of the Church of Rome . . . goes very far indeed to substitute another Gospel for the true one. Instead of setting before the soul the Holy Trinity, and heaven and hell; it does seem to me, as a popular system, to preach the Blessed Virgin and the Saints, and Purgatory. If there ever was a system which required reformation, it is that of Rome at this day, or in other words . . . Romanism or Popery.

He also maintained, however, that his own Church had 'in it a traditionary system, as well as the Roman, beyond and beside the letter of its formularies, and to be ruled by a spirit far inferior to its own nature'. As for *Tract 90*, the 'only peculiarity of the view' he had put forward of the Articles was that, 'whereas it is usual at this day to make the particular *belief of their writers* their true interpretation, I would make the *belief of the Catholic* Church such'. He ended by explaining that the *Tract* had been written for the benefit of a particular kind of person:

. . . there is at this moment a great progress of the religious mind of our Church to something deeper and truer than satisfied the last century. . . . The poets and philosophers of the age have borne witness to it for many years. . . . The age is moving towards something, and most unhappily the one religious communion among us which has of late years been practically in possession of this something, is the Church of Rome. She alone, amid all the errors and evils of her practical system, has given free scope to the feelings of awe, mystery, tenderness, reverence, devotedness, and other feelings which may be especially called Catholic. The question then is, whether we shall give them up to the Roman Church or claim them for ourselves, as we well may, by reverting to that older system, which has of late years indeed been superseded . . . But if we do give them up, then we must give up the men who cherish them. We must consent either to give up the men, or to admit their principles.[25]

On 18 March Newman heard from the Bishop of Oxford, who wrote a kind but distressed letter, asking that there should be no more discussion of the Articles in the *Tracts*. Newman immediately replied that he had no 'intention that there should be'. Two days later he wrote again to the bishop to say that he was 'altogether unsuspicious' that the *Tract* 'would make any disturbance'. He tried to explain his own personal difficulty:

When persons interrogate me, I am obliged in many cases to give an opinion, or I seem to be underhand. Keeping silence looks like artifice. And I do not like persons to consult or to respect me, from thinking differently of my opinions

[25] *VM* ii. 368–9, 378, 385–7.

from what I know them to be. . . . Hitherto I have been successful in keeping people together—but that a collision must at some time ensue between members of the Church of opposite opinions I have long been aware.[26]

To W. F. Hook, the high-church Vicar of Leeds, he wrote that he had said practically all he could say in his *Letter to Jelf* and that he sincerely hoped the bishops would not press him to elaborate further. He was afraid, too, he told Pusey, that Thomas Arnold was preparing an attack, in order 'to *drag out* things from me which I do not wish to say, and which the Bishops would not wish'. The difficulty was that if he replied only in generalities, this would suggest the worst to the bishops. He prayed that the Bishop of Oxford would not ask him 'to commit myself on points on which I cannot'.[27]

He might have created a 'sensation', but he had not lost his sense of humour: 'have they caricatured me yet?' he asked Jemima.[28] Now that things were out in the open, he felt a sense of relief: he told Rogers, 'I now am in my right place, which I have long wished to be in, which I did not know how to attain, and which has been brought about without my intention, I hope I may say providentially.' He did not know what would be the outcome for himself personally, but he did not 'fear for the *cause*'.[29] His 'explanation' seemed to have rather nonplussed his critics, and he hoped 'the storm' would now 'blow over'. He expected two or three bishops to come out with statements—'but on the whole, I do trust, quiet is the order of the day.'[30] He was quite sure that 'Golightly was the *sole* concoctor of the whole matter'.[31]

The next day, however, 23 March, the Bishop of Oxford, after consulting with the Archbishop of Canterbury, asked Pusey to come and see him. At their meeting on the following day, Dr Bagot asked that the *Tracts* should cease, and that not only should *Tract 90* not be reprinted, but that Newman should let it be known publicly that he was suppressing the *Tract* at the request of his bishop. To begin with, Newman was ready to comply; but on second thoughts, he told Pusey, he had decided that to do so would mean 'surrendering *interests* with which I am providentially charged at this moment, and which I have no right to surrender'. He had 'offered the Bishop to withdraw the Tract', but he had not offered 'to concur, by any act of mine, in his *virtual censure* of it, which is involved in its being suppressed at his bidding'. He was also

pained to see that authorities in London have increased their demands according to my submissiveness. When they thought me obstinate, they spoke only of not writing more in the Tracts about the Articles. When they find me

---

[26] To R. Bagot, 18, 20 Mar. 1841.
[27] To E. B. Pusey, 20 Mar. 1841.
[28] To Mrs J. Mozley, 21 Mar. 1841.
[29] To F. Rogers, 21 Mar. 1841.
[30] To A. P. Perceval, 22 Mar. 1841.
[31] To H. Wilberforce, 22 Mar. 1841.

obedient, they add the stopping of the Tracts and the suppression of No 90.

And they use me against myself. They cannot deliver charges of a sudden, but they use me to convey to the world a prompt and popular condemnation of my own principles.

What too is to be our warrant, that, in addition to this, the Bishops . . . will not charge against the Tract though suppressed? And what is to stop pamphlets against it? . . .

I feel this so strongly, that I have almost come to the resolution, if the Bishop publicly intimates that I must suppress it, or speaks strongly in his charge against it, to suppress it indeed, but to resign my living also. I could not in conscience act otherwise.[32]

He felt very strongly that he could not stay at St Mary's if the bishop, as well as the Heads of Houses, was against him—'I cannot be a demagogue, or a quasi schismatiser.'[33] It was true the bishop personally was 'all kindness'—but 'not so the authorities in London': he had even heard that there had been 'talk of the Bishops condemning the Tract as a body'.[34]

It was a dangerous situation: to Maria Giberne he wrote, 'If as you say a destiny hangs over us, a single false step may ruin all.'[35] He had heard that 'the general feeling' among both undergraduates and graduates was that he had been 'unceremoniously used': indeed, in three colleges, Oriel, Balliol, and Trinity, the notice of censure of *Tract 90* had been '(most improperly) torn down'.[36] But it was certainly humiliating to be 'posted up by the marshall on the buttery-hatch of every College of my University, after the manner of discommoned pastry-cooks'.[37]

On further thoughts, he told Pusey that suppressing the *Tract* would only strengthen people's '*first* impressions', whereas he felt sure that people would come to 'alter their opinion very much'—indeed, they had already done so to some extent. Besides, there were already enough 'gross misrepresentations . . . put forth and believed' about his works which were 'in circulation'—'how much more will this be, when a tract is not forthcoming to speak for itself?'[38]

In the end the bishop agreed that *Tract 90* should not be suppressed, but he insisted that Newman should immediately write him a letter for publication, recording the bishop's view that the *Tract* was 'objectionable' and that the *Tracts* should be 'discontinued'. This Newman did on 29 March. One particularly contentious matter was the question of 'the Invocation of Saints', on which he admitted he had not come to 'any

[32] To E. B. Pusey, 24 Mar. 1841.   [33] To J. Keble, 25 Mar. 1841.
[34] To W. F. Hook, 25 Mar. 1841.   [35] To Miss M. R. Giberne, 25 Mar. 1841.
[36] To Mrs T. Mozley, 25 Mar. 1841.   [37] *Apo.* 88.
[38] To E. B. Pusey, 26 Mar. 1841.

definite conclusion at all' (from the 'feeling' that to 'say *how far* a person may go, is almost to tempt him to go up to the boundary-line'); but he wanted now 'to state as plainly as I can, lest my brethren should mistake me, my great apprehension concerning the use even of . . . modified invocations. Every feeling which interferes with God's sovereignty in our hearts, is of an idolatrous nature.' He had always spoken against and still spoke against the 'system' he called 'Romanism or Popery', while on the other hand he considered the Church of England 'to be the Catholic Church in this country'. His own 'obedience' was shown in his 'habitual submission to things as they are' and in his avoidance of 'any indulgence of private tastes and opinions, which left to myself perhaps I should have allowed'. Thus his sermons had been 'far more practical than doctrinal; and this, from a dislike of introducing a character and tone of preaching very different from that which is generally to be found among us'. Again, he had 'altered nothing' which he had 'found established' at St Mary's, and

when I have increased the number of the Services, and had to determine points connected with the manner of performing them for myself, if there was no danger of offending others, then indeed I have followed my own judgment, but not otherwise. I have left many things, which I did not like, and which most other persons would have altered.

All along indeed he had refused 'to take part in any measures which aim at changes' in the Church. He had also opposed conversations with other Churches:

Our business is with ourselves—to make ourselves more holy . . . Let the Church of Rome do the same, and it will come nearer to us, and will cease to be what we one and all mean, when we speak of Rome. To be anxious for a composition of differences, is to begin at the end. . . . political reconciliations are but outward and hollow, and fallacious.

Generally, he had 'tried to feel that the great business of one and all of us is, to endeavour to raise the moral tone of the Church'.

It is sanctity of heart and conduct which commends us to God. If we be holy, all will go well with us. . . . sanctity is the great Note of the Church. . . . I will unite with all persons as brethren, who have this Note, without any distinction of party.

And finally, he disclaimed all personal ambition:

I have never taken pleasure in seeming to be able to move a party, and whatever influence I have had has been found not sought after. I have acted because others did not act, and have sacrificed a quiet which I prized.[39]

---

[39] *VM* ii. 397, 410, 412, 417–19, 421–2, 424.

The letter was published on 31 March. Newman wrote to tell Jemima that the 'affair' of *Tract 90* was now 'settled': he had complied with the 'terms' of the bishop and was 'quite satisfied with the bargain I have got, if this is all, as I suppose it will be'.[40] Considering 'what was threatened', he told Tom Mozley, he had 'reason well to be satisfied'; and he could not complain about the bishop, who had 'been most kind and tender'.[41] He confided to Bowden, 'I *trust* I am now out of the wood.'[42] At any rate, his letter seemed to have satisfied his critics in Oxford. Even though he had agreed to stop the *Tracts*, there was no question that 'a *great step*' had been taken.[43] In his letter to Dr Bagot, he had 'managed to wedge in a good many bits of Catholicism, which *now* come out with the Bishop's sanction'. It was important, he urged Keble,

to let the matter drop at present. We have got the *principle* of our interpretation admitted in that it has not been condemned—Do not let us provoke opposition—Numbers will be taking advantage silently and quietly of the admission for their own benefit. It will soon be *assumed* as a matter of course.

He had heard, too, that the bishops were 'sorely bent on keeping the peace'. Meanwhile, they were 'all in very good spirits . . . and jubilant'.[44] It really seemed 'things' were 'mending'—not that he had ever 'had a misgiving for a minute'.[45] He felt he had really got his 'full penny worth out of the business' and was 'well content to sustain the weight' of the public censure by the Heads of Houses, so long as he could get his '*principle* allowed, which it now seems to be'.[46] As for the bishop, he wrote on 2 April to say that he was more than satisfied by Newman's letter. But 'kind' as his own bishop was, he felt very strongly that 'the more men yield' the more 'severe' the 'moving powers of the Church' would be, and 'the more men threaten' the more the authorities would 'give way'—'We are hit, because we are dutiful.'[47] On the other hand, discretion was the better part of valour, and he told Keble he was sure that 'the *one* thing' the bishops were afraid of was 'a *disturbance*', which was why he was convinced they could not be happy about the condemnation of *Tract 90*:

We may do any thing if we keep from *disturbance*. The more then we can yield, the better policy. We can gain any thing by giving way.[48]

The end of the *Tracts*, he promised Ambrose Phillipps, could not, 'humanly speaking, stop the spread of opinions which they have inculcated. . . . I trust that the fire is kindled, and will make progress,

[40] To Mrs J. Mozley, 30 Mar. 1841.
[41] To T. Mozley, 30 Mar. 1841.
[42] To J. W. Bowden, 1 Apr. 1841.
[43] To Miss M. R. Giberne, 1 Apr. 1841.
[44] To J. Keble, 1 Apr. 1841.
[45] To T. Mozley, 1 Apr. 1841.
[46] To H. A. Woodgate, 1 Apr. 1841.
[47] To Mrs J. Mozley, 5 Apr. 1841.
[48] To J. Keble, 10 Apr. 1841.

even though the original torch is extinguished. But ... it is *not* extinguished. The Tracts are not *suppressed*.' It was true that a particular *Tract* had been called 'objectionable' by the Bishop of Oxford, but 'no reason' had been 'stated', nor had any 'doctrine or principle ... been conceded by us, or condemned by Authority'. Disobedience to the bishop, however, was out of the question:

Our Bishop is our Pope. It is our theory that each Diocese is an integral Church, intercommunion being a duty, (and the breach of it a sin) but not essential, to Catholicity. To have resisted my Bishop would have been to place myself in an utterly false position ... the strength of any party lies in its being true to its theory, consistency is the life of a movement.

He added that 'it is a profound gospel principle that victory comes by yielding. We rise by falling.' But there was yielding and there was yielding—'I have no intention whatever of yielding any one point which I hold on conviction—And that the authorities of the Church know full well.'[49] In answer to an anxious letter from Richard Westmacott, the sculptor, who had been a contemporary of his at Ealing School, he assured him that the '*very view*' taken of the Articles in *Tract 90* was the one 'all our chief divines have ever taken; only it has never been systematically put out'.[50]

At Easter Newman received a letter from a young Irish Roman Catholic priest, called Charles Russell, who was a professor at Maynooth and co-editor with Wiseman of the *Dublin Review*, and who had followed the Oxford Movement with keen interest, protesting against various misunderstandings of Roman Catholic doctrines, particularly the treatment of Transubstantiation in *Tract 90*. Newman hastened to assure him that he knew the Roman Church was not committed to a carnal view of the Real Presence such as was condemned in the Articles. But he could not refrain from exclaiming:

O that you would reform your worship, that you would disown the extreme honors paid to St Mary and other Saints, your traditionary view of Indulgences, and the veneration paid in foreign countries to Images! ... It would do your highest and most religious interests as much benefit in our eyes, as it would tend to rid your religious system of those peculiarities which distinguish it from primitive Christianity.[51]

To Russell's co-religionist, Ambrose Phillipps, he wrote again, warning him against 'entertaining sanguine hopes in which you may be disappointed':

[49] To A. L. Phillipps, 8 Apr. 1841.   [50] To R. Westmacott, 8 Apr. 1841.
[51] To C. W. Russell, 13 Apr. 1841.

You over rate our exertions, our influence, our tendencies. We are but a few, and we are what we are. Many times before now in the course of the last 300 years has a hope of concord arisen among Christians, but as yet it has ever come to nothing. When was a great schism ever healed? Why would ours cease, if that between the East and West has continued so long? And if a growth in sanctity be the necessary condition of it in both parties, what stipulation can be more costly, more hopeless?[52]

At the end of April he wrote again to Russell to say that he had

every reason to be made sanguine by the disturbance which has followed Tract 90, which I never have been before. When I began the Tracts 7 or 8 years since, I did so in a sort of despair—and felt surprised to find persons influenced by them. I had intended them mainly as a protest. I have never courted, or anticipated success—yet success came. I may be as mistaken now when I have become more sanguine—yet in matter of fact not only myself, but others too, have had their spirits raised by what has happened. My only anxiety is lest your branch of the Church should not meet us by those reforms which surely are *necessary*—It never could be, that so large a portion of Christendom should have split off from the communion of Rome, and kept up a protest for 300 years for nothing. I think I never shall believe that so much piety and earnestness would be found among Protestants, if there were not some very grave errors on the side of Rome.

It is interesting to see how Newman now justifies the continuing separation from Rome on the ground that it would be 'unreal' to ignore the significance of the 'protest' of Protestants:

To suppose the contrary is most unreal, and violates all one's notions of moral probabilities. All aberrations are founded on, and have their life in, some truth or other—and Protestantism, so widely spread and so long enduring, must have in it, and must be witness for, a great truth or much truth.[53]

He wrote again at the beginning of May to Russell, arguing that the 'principle and temper of obedience' and 'horror of the principle of private judgment' were too imbued in them 'to allow of our separating ourselves from our ecclesiastical superiors because in many points we may sympathise with others'. The only 'conceivable causes of our leaving the Church in which we were baptized' would be their expulsion from the Church of England on its declaring 'heresy to be truth'. He concluded:

That my *sympathies* have grown towards the religion of Rome I do not deny; that my *reasons* for *shunning* her communion have lessened or altered, it will be difficult perhaps to prove. And I wish to go by reason not by feeling.[54]

[52] To A. L. Phillipps, 16 Apr. 1841.   [53] To C. W. Russell, 26 Apr. 1841.
[54] To C. W. Russell, 5 May 1841.

Early in June Faussett began 'firing away' against *Tract 90* 'and glorying that the University is at length beginning to persecute', after W. G. Ward had been stripped of his lectureship in Mathematics at Balliol for a pamphlet he had written. Newman guessed that 'the line' of the bishops would be to bring pressure to bear through the university. But he continued to insist that he was still 'for letting the whole controversy *sleep*'. As for Professor Faussett, he was 'a fat dog who comes out to bark' occasionally, and '*whose work* we are doing'.[55] However, he was worried about the provocative tone of the *British Critic*. He had himself tried hard, without success, 'to make it *literary* and scientific'. But if it was going to be a 'theological' review, he warned Pusey, it would 'to a certainty take a (so called) ultra tone, if clever men are to write for it'. At any rate he promised to do all he could 'to turn it into the literary channel' and, if possible, to 'put a stop to all attacks on the Reformers'. Unfortunately, the two leaders of the younger generation of Tractarians, Ward and Frederick Oakeley (himself a former fellow of Balliol and now at the Margaret Street Chapel, the centre for Tractarian worship in London), were obsessed with the subject. But he would do what he could to restrain them. Newman himself was 'in no hurry' to see the reformers 'exposed', as he was 'sure that it is only a question of time *when* they would be seen in their true colours'. And he felt Oakeley and Ward were too impatient about 'running' them 'down . . . for the sake of doing so'. As always, he advocated leaving the issue to '*time*'—'Truth *will* work.' Unlike Pusey—'I do fear that his historical view of the Reformation is his great bulwark against Rome'—he felt nothing but 'dislike' of the Reformation—'Whence all this schism and heresy, humanly speaking, but for it?' And it would never have 'succeeded', he thought, but for the 'disingenuous' way in which the Reformers had misrepresented Roman Catholic doctrine ('when they would attack some tenet or practice of Rome, they attacked something which RC's could and do condemn as much as their opponents do').[56]

3

The July number of the *British Critic* carried an article by Newman on 'Private Judgment'. He begins by stating that 'serious religious changes have a *primâ facie* case against them . . . and their agents may be called upon to suffer, in order to prove their earnestness, and to pay the penalty of the trouble they are causing.' The principle that it is change itself

---

[55] To T. Mozley, 3, 12 June 1841.
[56] To E. B. Pusey, 30 July, 13 Aug. 1841; to R. W. Church, 12 Sept. 1841.

which requires justification could hardly be stated with a more conservative rigour:

> . . . considering, in a word, that change is really the characteristic of error, and unalterableness the attribute of truth, of holiness, of Almighty God Himself, we consider that when Private Judgment moves in the direction of innovation, it may well be regarded at first with suspicion and treated with severity. Nay, we confess even a satisfaction, when a penalty is attached to the expression of new doctrines, or to a change of communion. We repeat it, if any men have strong feelings, they should pay for them; if they think it a duty to unsettle things established, they should show their earnestness by being willing to suffer. . . . Such disadvantages do no harm to that cause in the event, but they bring home to a man's mind his own responsibility; they are a memento to him of a great moral law, and warn him that his private judgment, if not a duty, is a sin.

Newman then goes on to argue that the unfavourable response to changes of religion, which are generally attributed to personal feelings and motives rather than rational conviction, proves that 'this great people is not such a conscientious supporter of the sacred right of Private Judgment as a good Protestant would desire'. He seizes gleefully on the inconsistency in a marvellously satirical sally:

> Is it not sheer wantonness and cruelty in Baptist, Independent, Irvingite, Wesleyan, Establishment-man, Jumper, and Mormonite, to delight in trampling on and crushing these manifestations of their own pure and precious charter, instead of dutifully and reverently exalting, at Bethel, or at Dan, each instance of it, as it occurs, to the gaze of its professing votaries? If a staunch Protestant's daughter turns Roman, and betakes herself to a convent, why does he not exult in the occurrence? Why does he not give a public breakfast, or hold a meeting, or erect a memorial, or write a pamphlet in honour of her, and of the great undying principle she has so gloriously vindicated? Why is he in this base, disloyal style muttering about priests, and Jesuits, and the horrors of nunneries, in solution of the phenomenon, when he has the fair and ample form of Private Judgment rising before his eyes, and pleading with him . . . All this would lead us to suspect that the doctrine of private judgment, in its simplicity, purity, and integrity,—private judgment, all private judgment, and nothing but private judgment,—is held by very few persons indeed; and that the great mass of the population are either stark unbelievers in it, or deplorably dark about it; and that even the minority who are in a manner faithful to it, have glossed and corrupted the true sense of it by a miserably faulty reading, and hold, not the right of private judgment, but the private right of judgment; in other words, their own private right, and no one else's. . . . It is undeniable, then, if the popular feeling is to be our guide, that, high and mighty as the principle of private judgment is in religious inquiries, as we most fully grant it is, still it bears some similarity to Saul's armour which David rejected, or to edged tools which have a bad trick of chopping at our fingers, when we are but simply and innocently meaning them to make a dash forward at truth.

In a more serious vein, Newman claims that the Scriptures justify the exercise of private judgement in ascertaining 'not what has God revealed, but whom has He commissioned?' In other words, they 'sanction, not an inquiry about Gospel doctrine, but about the Gospel teacher'. When, therefore, 'an appeal *is* made to private judgment, this is done in order to settle who the teacher is and what are his notes or tokens, rather than to substantiate this or that religious opinion or practice'. Since St Paul tells us that the Church is our teacher, the 'simple question . . . for Private Judgment to exercise itself upon is, what and where is the Church?' All this should hardly surprise us—

Religion is for practice, and that immediate. Now it is much easier to form a correct and rapid judgment of persons than of books or of doctrines. Every one, even a child, has an impression about new faces; few persons have any real view about new propositions. . . . The multitude have neither the time, the patience, nor the clearness and exactness of thought, for processes of investigation and deduction. Reason is slow and abstract, cold and speculative; but man is a being of feeling and action . . .

He then turns on those who do not exercise their private judgement 'in looking out for a teacher at all':

They must not act like the dog in the fable . . . who would neither use the manger himself, nor relinquish it to others: let them not grudge to others a manifest Scriptural privilege which they disown themselves. Is an ordinance of Scripture to be fulfilled nowhere, because it is not fulfilled in them?

On the awkward problem of choosing between teachers, he points out that 'even in the Apostles' age very grave outward differences seem to have existed between Christian teachers'—'Is not this, at least in great measure, the state of the Churches of England and Rome?' True, the Church of England 'has certain imperfections', but then the Church of Rome has 'certain corruptions'. As for the damaging fact of the separation of the Anglican Church 'from the rest of Christendom', he admits that Anglicans tend not to treat Christians abroad as 'brethren' but 'in an arrogant John Bull way' as foreigners rather than Christians. But again he falls back on the defence that if 'the English glories in what looks so very like schism', still 'the Roman Church practises what looks so very like idolatry'. Given that 'Few men have time to scrutinize accurately', but 'all men may have general impressions, and the general impressions of conscientious men are true ones', then the 'quasi-idolatry' of the Roman Church is as much a 'Note' to dissuade 'a man of Catholic feelings from her communion, as the taint of a Protestant or schismatical spirit in our communion may tempt him to depart from us'. This, concludes Newman, 'is the Via Media which we would maintain'. There was only one 'cloud' he could foresee which would 'darken and bewilder our course': if the Church of England made itself formally schismatic or professed itself to be Protestant, while superstition were disowned by the Church of Rome—'then doubtless, for a season, Catholic minds among us would be unable to see their way'.[57]

But it was a somewhat half-hearted *Via Media*. In August he advised Mary Holmes, a governess and convert to Tractarianism, whose spiritual director he had effectively become after she had introduced herself by letter, that for 'all great changes, a season of thought and preparation is a necessary introduction, if we would know what God's will is'. He had already warned her earlier, even more severely, that 'so great a matter as a change of religion ought not to be thought of without years . . . of prayer and preparation.' It was also wrong, 'generally speaking, for *individuals* to leave one religion for another—it is so much like an exercise of private judgment.' Now he could only offer this encouragement:

Grievous as are the defects of the English system, painful as is the position of Catholicly minded persons in it, still these persons do *remain* in it. They have waited, they do not recognise that clear voice of God directing them to change, which they desiderate. They do not find that England is out of the Covenant; or they cannot overcome their repugnance to much that is Roman.

The possibility of leaving the Church of England is openly allowed for: 'If persons patiently wait some time, they may see the English Church get better or worse and in either case will be more able to discern God's will concerning them.' Anyway, it was 'better to go with a number than by oneself, if one must go'. And yet it could not be denied that Roman Catholic 'worship' of the Virgin Mary, albeit not formally defined but still sanctioned in official 'devotional forms', was so obviously unprimitive as to be manifestly 'a new doctrine and observance' rather than a development. And so, considering how much Scripture warned against idolatry, it did seem that 'their difficulty is to say the least as great as ours'. Meanwhile, was not the extraordinary 'burst of hidden life' in the Anglican Church 'the greatest note of the Catholicity of our Church'?

Only let us be patient. Let us wait and see. If this counsel and work be of men it will come to naught. Should Catholic influences die away among us, I grant that the Church of England will seem to have had a trial and to have failed under it.[58]

Naturally he did not give away so much when he wrote again in September to Ambrose Phillipps on the subject of unity. 'Suspicion and distrust are the main existing causes of the separation between us.' But

[57] *Ess.* ii. 337–41, 350–1, 353, 356, 360, 363, 365, 367–8, 370, 374.
[58] To Miss M. Holmes, 8 Apr., 8 Aug., 6 Sept. 1841.

'*we cannot remove the obstacles*—it is with you to do so. You do not fear us— we fear you. Till we cease to fear you, we cannot love you.' Roman Catholics must abandon their 'alliance with the liberal party', he insisted, adding the memorable indictment, 'The spirit of lawlessness came in at the Reformation—and Liberalism is its offspring.' There were also doctrinal problems such as the worship of Mary and Transubstantiation, neither of which were 'primitive'. Let Roman Catholics work for unity by helping to make the Church of England more Catholic; then, if she 'were prepared for a union, she might make her terms' with Rome—although there must be no 'grudging bargaining'.[59]

4

During the summer of 1841 Newman was busy translating St Athanasius for the Library of the Fathers. He found it 'very anxious work', but still it was certainly 'a great refuge after other things'.[60] As he explains in the *Apologia*, he had deliberately decided 'to put aside all controversy'. But 'between July and November, I received three blows which broke me'.

I had got but a little way in my work, when my trouble returned on me. The ghost had come a second time. In the Arian History I found the very same phenomenon, in a far bolder shape, which I had found in the Monophysite. I had not observed it in 1832. Wonderful that this should come upon me! I had not sought it out; I was reading and writing in my own line of study, far from the controversies of the day . . . but I saw clearly, that in the history of Arianism, the pure Arians were the Protestants, the semi-Arians were the Anglicans, and that Rome now was what it was then. The truth lay, not with the *Via Media*, but with what was called 'the extreme party.'[61]

He did not talk about this new blow in letters to friends. Writing from Littlemore, he apologized flippantly to H. A. Woodgate that he could not come and visit him:

You forget that I am an incipient Monk, in my noviciate at the least. I am preparing a Monastery at Littlemore and shall shortly retire from the world— so that if the great prospects are destined for me you speak of, I shall be the first Bishop from the Cloister for the last three hundred years—and while I am about it, think . . . that I will not come out of it except for the Papacy.[62]

---

[59] To A. L. Phillipps, 12 Sept. 1841.
[60] To Mrs J. Mozley, 1 Sept. 1841; to J. Keble, 4 Sept. 1841.
[61] *Apo.* 130.
[62] To H. A. Woodgate, 22 Sept. 1841.

The joke was too close to the bone to suggest that anything was seriously amiss.

He certainly gave nothing away to Wiseman, when he wrote to him at the beginning of October to thank him for the gift of his 'Letter on Catholic Unity'. It was 'very satisfactory' that a Roman Catholic could admit that there was 'corruption and scandal' in his Church: 'I really do not know why so great a Communion should not feel itself at liberty to confess many things of itself.' The fact was 'that the more candid the Apologists of the Church of Rome are, the more they will weight with Englishmen, and gain their favour'. He could hardly have known how often such sentiments would come to his lips in later years when he was in a very different position. He emphasized to Wiseman that 'the answers made by Roman disputants' often seemed to people to be 'shuffles'. Roman Catholic writers ought to 'enter into and study our impressions. They are worth attending to.' An authoritative statement on the efforts made by the Roman Catholic authorities 'to repress what we consider the extravagances of your members' with regard to devotions to Mary and the Saints 'would have great effect in conciliating our minds towards the Church of Rome'. Yet again, he refused 'directly' to advocate reunion; rather, he intended 'to remain quite silent and quiet'. For eight years the Tractarians had been trying to make Anglicans 'more Catholic':

We have brought opinions some way towards the question of union. It is our turn to rest. When you have done with your own members or with public opinion as much as we have done, then there will be a call upon us. At present there is none in *justice*.

Anyway, the great thing was to go gradually:

Enough has been written on Church subjects by us to last a long while—it has not yet spread among our members, it has not done its work. I trust it will in time—but we must have patience. On the other hand nothing would be so likely to throw inquirers back as others going very much ahead of them. To consider the terms of re-union, the concessions and explanations to be made on either side, would be the way to produce a re-action.

Nevertheless,

If a true seed has been sown by the books which have proceeded from this place, it will in time bear fruit. If it has life, if it is worthy any thing, it will do its own work.

In the meantime, it was

A duty and a matter of expedience in us to remain quiet—and to occupy ourselves in attempts to teach and improve our own body. If we can make our members more apprehensive of . . . high theological truths . . . and more holy in their lives and aspirations, it will be a gain so great that I do not know why I should desire any thing beyond it, though of course more would and must follow. And on the other hand if influential persons among yourselves raised and purified your own tone, reformed abuses, and conciliated us in word and deed, the happiest results would follow. Such conduct on both sides must tend eventually to unity, *in God's time*, though, it may be, not in our day.[63]

The second of the 'three blows which broke' Newman had in fact already begun to fall upon him. The bishops' *charges* against *Tract 90* had started coming out, including one on 23 September from Keble's bishop. It was, Newman recalled, 'a formal, determinate movement'— 'This was the real "understanding"; that, on which I had acted on the first appearance of Tract 90, had come to nought.' He had been given to understand that possibly two or three bishops might allude to the *Tract* in their *charges*. But he was not prepared for the more or less hostile *charges* which bishop after bishop issued in the course of the next three years: 'I recognized it as a condemnation; it was the only one that was in their power.'[64] At the time he tried to put a brave face on it. He told Maria Giberne that it might be 'necessary in some shape or other to re-assert Tract 90—else it will seem after these Bishops' charges, as if it were silenced—which it has not been, nor do I intend it should be'. He had wanted 'to keep quiet', but he could not if the bishops spoke out: 'If the view were silenced, I could not remain in the Church, nor could many others—and therefore since it is *not* silenced, I shall take care to show that it is not.'[65] To his lawyer friend James Hope, he put forward the argument that bishops' *charges* had 'no direct authority except in their own dioceses', and that anyway a bishop's 'word is to be obeyed, not as doctrine, but as part of discipline—only in Synod do they prescribe doctrine'. On the other hand, he had 'candidly to own that the . . . charges are very serious matters—as virtually silencing portions of the truth in particular dioceses, and as showing that it is not impossible that our Church *may* lapse into heresy'. He had to admit that 'a great and anxious *experiment* is going on, whether our Church be or be not Catholic—the issue may not be in our day. But I must be plain in saying that, if it does issue in Protestantism, I shall think it my duty, if alive, to leave it.' Of course he trusted that would not be the outcome, but 'the way to hinder it, is to be prepared for it'. Indeed, he had begun to think that 'the only way to keep in the English Church is steadily to contemplate and act upon the possibility of leaving it'. Still, 'on the whole', he hoped for 'better things—the Clergy were at their worst some years since—and now the Bishops are at their worst'. But whatever

---

[63] To N. Wiseman, 4 Oct. 1841.   [64] *Apo.* 130.
[65] To Miss M. R. Giberne, 17 Oct. 1841.

happened, he was 'sure that to leave the English Church, unless something very flagrant happened, must be the work of *years*'.[66]

As for the third of the 'blows', which 'finally shattered' his 'faith in the Anglican Church', he had already given a warning of the threat to install a bishop in Jerusalem in his July article in the *British Critic*. The King of Prussia wanted 'to introduce Episcopacy into the new Evangelical Religion, which was intended in that country to embrace both the Lutheran and Calvinistic bodies'. Newman's old friend in Rome, Baron Bunsen, had been sent as Prussian minister to London in 1841, and began to make arrangements with the Archbishop of Canterbury for the bishopric, which was to alternate between England and Prussia. From the Prussian point of view, Jerusalem 'was considered a safe place for the experiment', since 'it was too far from Prussia to awaken the susceptibilities of any party at home'. From the English point of view, there were obvious political advantages, as 'it gave Protestantism a *status* in the East', and so 'formed a political instrument for England, parallel to that which Russia had in the Greek Church, and France in the Latin'.[67] Religiously, the plan was welcomed by the Evangelicals as a reverse for the Tractarians, and by liberals like Thomas Arnold as a step towards a comprehensive Protestant church. A day after writing to Wiseman, Newman hastened to warn Keble of the Act before Parliament that was to establish the odious bishopric:

It really does seem to me as if the Bishops were doing their best to uncatholicize us—and whether they will succeed before a rescue comes, who can say? The Bishop of Jerusalem is to be consecrated forthwith—perhaps in a few days—Mr Bunsen is at the bottom of the whole business, who, I think I am right in saying, considers the Nicene Council the first step in the corruption of the Church.[68]

He wrote less gravely, but with no less disgust, to his more familiar friends. He asked Bowden if he had 'heard of this fearful business'—

It seems we are *in the way* to fraternize with Protestants of all sorts, Monophysites, half converted Jews and even Druses. If any such event should take place, I shall not be able to keep a single man from Rome. They will be all trooping off, sooner or later.[69]

It was a 'hideous business'—'Dr Wiseman may sit still—our Bishop[s] will do his work.'[70] To Henry Wilberforce he wrote in greater detail:

The Bishops, keeping it snug till it is done and over, are, at Bunsen's suggestion, sending out a Bishop to Jerusalem, where is *no* Anglican at present, and but few

[66] To J. R. Hope, 17 Oct. 1841.   [67] *Apo*. 131–3.
[68] To J. Keble, 5 Oct. 1841.   [69] To J. W. Bowden, 10 Oct. 1841.
[70] To W. Dodsworth, 10 Oct. 1841.

Jews (i.e. anglicanized—*4*, a man told me who's just returned from the Holy Land) He is to go out to head the Protestants of every class—and the power of the British government will soon make him the head of a very large and flourishing communion. The Druses (all but infidels) have applied for an English Bishop. He is Mr Alexander, a *Jew*, because the Jews wish for a Bishop of the Circumcision . . .'[71]

He told S. F. Wood that to say that the plan was 'to collect a communion out of Protestants, Jews, Druses and Monophysites, conforming under the influence of our war-steamers, to counterbalance the Russian influence through Greeks, and the French through Latins,' was to put it 'concisely, but I assure you not epigrammatically or with exaggeration'.[72] For those who had doubts about the Catholic nature of the Church of England, 'every act . . . such as this of coalescing with heretics *weakens* the proof, and in some cases it may fulfil the proverb of being the last straw that breaks the horse's back'. To Keble he wrote, 'Really . . . considering Jerusalem is the spot, there is something almost awful in this.'[73] He himself had no intention of doing anything 'publicly', although he would be ready to sign 'a Protest—but I think it would be out of place in me to agitate, having been in a way silenced'.[74] He did, however, write an unsigned letter to *The Times*, which was not published, in which he agreed with bitter sarcasm that the Church was not 'worth' much 'if she is to be nice and mealy-mouthed when a piece of work is to be done for her good lord the State. Surely, surely, in *such* a case, some formula can be found for proving heresy to be orthodoxy and schism to be charity.' As for bringing Episcopacy to the Prussians, 'Surely it is an evil great enough to find Bishops heretics, without going on to make heretics Bishops.' He concluded, 'Is all this the way to keep certain of our members from Rome? or is it on the whole desirable that they should go, and a good riddance?'[75]

Dark as the prospect was, Newman continued to counsel patience. At the beginning of November he warned Miss Holmes that even if Rome was the true Church, 'yet those who join it against God's will, that is, impatiently, may be as really cut off from God's blessings as those who remained patiently according to God's will in a Church which was cut off from Rome'.[76] It was an interesting point which he put in a slightly different form to Henry Wilberforce: he agreed that it was possible that

the English Church is not part of the Church Catholic, but only visited with overflowings of grace—and that God may *call* some persons on to higher things. They must *obey* the calling; but that proves nothing against those who do not receive it. I have no call at present to go to the Church of Rome; but I am not

[71] To H. Wilberforce, 10 Oct. 1841.
[72] To S. F. Wood, 10 Oct. 1841.
[73] To J. Keble, 24 Oct. 1841.
[74] To J. W. Bowden, 12 Oct. 1841.
[75] To the Editor of *The Times*, 1 Nov. 1841.
[76] To Miss M. Holmes, 7 Nov. 1841.

confident I may not have some day. But it seems to me that there is something most unnatural and revolting in going over *suddenly*—unless indeed a miracle is granted.

However, it seemed to him obvious that the bishops were

sowing the seeds of future secessions. They speak all against us or are silent. We have no thanks for what is well done. For 8 years not a word of *direct* praise has been granted . . . A jealous suspicion has been the only feeling. All sorts of irregularity have been committed on the other side impuné. All sorts of liberties are taken with the Services. All sorts of heresies are promulgated.[77]

Bunsen he infinitely distrusted. He would not be surprised if he did not have 'ambitious views of reforming our Church'. He darkly suspected that there was 'a great scheme afloat to unite us in a Protestant league', a kind of 'union of Protestants, the Church of England being at its head'. He had reluctantly come to the decision that he must make a public protest—even if it did 'make people think me a bitter fanatic—I have nothing to lose.' The Church authorities 'will believe nothing but *acts*. Representations have been made to them without end. . . . Why may I not be troublesome as well as another?—especially when thereby I seem to ease my conscience.' It would be going against his own principles to 'excite and unsettle people', but 'unless a protest is made, others will determine that our Church is given up and uncatholicized'.[78] He sent his protest, dated 11 November, to both the Archbishop of Canterbury and the Bishop of Oxford. Afterwards he saw the 'great misfortune' of the Jerusalem bishopric as 'one of the greatest of mercies. It brought me on to the beginning of the end.'[79]

5

Incredible as it may seem, all during this time since the last week in September Newman had been working ten to twelve hours every day at his translation of St Athanasius. Meanwhile, there was yet another crisis looming, the choice of Keble's successor as Professor of Poetry. Although Isaac Williams was the obvious candidate, the election had taken on a controversial religious aspect because of Williams's prominence as a leading Tractarian. 'It is *most important* to make a demonstration,' Newman wrote to Henry Wilberforce. 'Every fact which makes us seem strong keeps men from Rome, every thing which implies we are weak and few, draws men on.' They had 'a fair chance of success . . . but any

[77] To H. Wilberforce, 8 Nov. 1841.
[78] To J. R. Hope, 11 Nov. 1841; to J. W. Bowden, 13 Nov. 1841; to J. Keble, 13 Nov. 1841.
[79] *Apo.* 136.

how to record a large number of votes is a great point'.[80] In the present situation,

Unless some stir is made, to a dead certainty we shall have men going over to Rome. Contrary pressure is the only chance we have of not being carried off our legs by the pressure of the Protestants upon us. If our friends have no *hope*, they will leave us.

If the Tractarians did not achieve at least 'a large minority' in the election, it would surely 'hasten the catastrophe of men going to Rome'.[81] Newman had been against Williams standing in the circumstances, but he could not 'say that he ought lightly to give up now'. What he was afraid of was a humiliating defeat: success would hardly be worth 'the *risk* of great interests', but to retire now would seem '*equivalent* with defeat'.[82] It was being said in Oxford that, 'if Williams is beaten, Convocation is to go on to other stringent measures against us'. 'Nothing', Newman warned James Hope, would more 'delight the heads, in their own dominions supreme, as they are, than to drive certain people out of the Church'.[83] It was because of his 'great dread of Convocation' that he had been opposed to Williams's candidature 'throughout'—'but considering *I* am the cause of the opposition by Number 90, it would have been ungenerous to press my objection.' He was also afraid that some of the Tractarians 'would not be sorry' if Williams was defeated.

They feel the misery of the present state of the Church, with only half the robes of the Church Catholic upon her—they look out for signs of God's providence one way or the other—and, since they despair of the Church actually righting, they look with some sort of relief, as the second best event, for signs of her retrograding and withdrawing her notes. And though the mere defeat of a person in a University Election is a little thing enough, yet if there is a movement of the Church as a whole in all its ranks to disown Catholic truth . . . the fact of a series of disavowals on the part of a University is an important fact as part of a series or collection. And it cannot be denied, I suppose, that a series of such facts might happen amounting to a moral evidence that our Church was quite severed and distinct from the Church of the first ages.

If the accumulating weight of probabilities against the Church of England proved to be unbearable, then people 'would say, since the Church must be somewhere and is not in England, it must be in the Communion of Rome—and on the strength of the inference they would submit *in faith* to what they did not like in the Roman system'. But the Roman Church anyway had its obvious attractions to such people, especially when they found '*sympathy* there and *none* at home'. It was true

[80] To H. Wilberforce, 24 Oct. 1841.   [81] To T. Mozley, 29 Oct. 1841.
[82] To J. Keble, 6 Nov. 1841.   [83] To J. R. Hope, 19 Nov. 1841.

that those 'most in danger here and elsewhere' had promised to 'do nothing' which Newman would not 'approve' of, but it was hard to prevent their meeting and talking with Roman Catholics, particularly when these were found to be 'in private amiable and devout men'. He still believed that the 'Catholic' ideas which the Movement had spread could 'strengthen the Church against Rome', but it could not be denied that they

are a powerful weapon—they have not come into the world for nothing—They must tell either for us or against us—If we will not use them, others will. If a physician promises to cure a patient, it is on condition of his taking his medicine, not if he chucks it out of the window.[84]

He was aware that his 'Protest' was strongly worded, but he had no choice when there was a threat 'to prove all I hold a mere theory and illusion, a paper theology that facts contradict'. Despairingly, he told James Hope that he could not 'see that any thing else was left' for him to do—although doubtless his 'days of *controversy* on such subjects' were now 'past'. He even thought of inserting his 'Protest', when it was published, into every new book or new edition he brought out—'If people are driving me quite against all my feelings out of the English Church, they shall know they are doing so.' He ended by remarking sarcastically that he thought people believed he had 'some secret understanding with the Pope'.[85] He told Tom Mozley that he thought 'silence would do every thing for us', but then, since everything they said in the *British Critic* would be 'misinterpreted', perhaps the best thing would be to close it down. He wondered how long he could go on 'putting out sparks, which might blow up into secessions', when 'the notes of the Church are crumbling away day after day'.[86] But he was insistent that there was a 'general' outcry against the *British Critic*, which was certainly 'advancing things to a crisis'; for by constantly stirring up controversy it was encouraging waverers among the Tractarians 'to look towards Rome', either because of 'enemies telling them to go' or by 'well meaning friends imploring them not to go'. This kind of suspicion was very dangerous, because it made people feel self-conscious, as well as familiarizing them with the idea that others were fully expecting them to leave the Church; it also created an atmosphere that was hardly conducive to their wanting to stay. He wished Tom would give up the editorship, as in the present circumstances anything that appeared in the *British Critic* was bound to be seized upon as objectionable. And just as he was to complain later of the liberal Catholic writers in the *Rambler*, so now he bemoaned the evident 'animus' with which the extreme

---

[84] To Mrs J. Mozley, 21 Nov. 1841.　　　[85] To J. R Hope, 24 Nov. 1841.
[86] To T. Mozley, 13 Dec. 1841.

younger Tractarians like Oakeley and Ward could not help writing 'even on common subjects'.[87]

It was true there was no knowing what the bishops might do next: they might 'bring out some tests which will have the effect of precipitating us, and leaving the Church clean Protestant'. If so, the Tractarians would have to 'look out for cheap lodgings'—but where, Newman wondered half-humorously, would he be able to 'stow' all his books?[88] Perhaps he would be 'driven' into the Littlemore 'refuge for the destitute'; if so, he promised he would do his 'utmost to catch all dangerous persons and clap them into confinement there'.[89] But he resented being pressed as to what he would do under hypothetical circumstances: there were 'things which I neither contemplate, nor wish to contemplate—but when I am asked about them ten times, at length I begin to contemplate them'. As always, he insisted on doing 'simply *what we think right* day by day', rather than attempting 'to trace by anticipation the course of divine providence'. With regard to the English Church, this did not mean 'being afraid to look difficulties in the face'. The result of trying to 'whitewash' events like the Jerusalem bishopric was that 'our Church has through centuries ever been sinking lower and lower'.[90] He wrote to Maria Giberne that he would never be unwilling 'to call heresy heresy, and am never going to retreat before heresy, until like mephytic gas it is suffocating outright'. But he still thought that their 'strength' lay in 'quiet':

People will find it most difficult to oust us, if we sit down, fold our arms, hunch up our shoulders, and turn sulky. They will think us dangerous—and if they attempt to lift us, will find us so dismally heavy, as to make the work hopeless—we the while looking at them with grave faces.

He hoped that they had now reached 'the lowest point'.[91] However, he confided to another friend that he had lost all confidence in the bishops, whose recent actions had produced an 'irremediable evil':

Confidence is shaken—and when once a *doubt* of our Catholicity gets into the mind, it is like a seed—it lies for years to appearance dead—but, alas, it has its hour of germinating or is ever threatening.[92]

It was an ominous image with which to close a fateful year.

1841 did not end without Newman attempting to place his diminished faith in the Church of England on some kind of theological basis. For the last two years he had fallen back on the note of sanctity to prove that the Church of England, as having the Apostolic succession

[87] To T. Mozley, 19 Dec. 1841.
[88] To J. R. Hope, 23 Dec. 1841.
[89] To R. W. Church, 24 Dec. 1841.
[90] To R. W. Church, 25 Dec. 1841.
[91] To Miss M. R. Giberne, 27 Dec. 1841.
[92] To W. Dodsworth, 27 Dec. 1841.

and creed, was part of the Catholic Church. Now, he says in the *Apologia*, 'I sunk my theory to a lower level'. During December he preached four sermons at St Mary's, the first he had ever delivered on 'the exciting topics of the day'. He had already in the *Prophetical Office* used the 'analogy' or 'parallel' of Judaism in defence of the Anglican claim to be a branch of the Catholic Church.[93] Now, using the same analogy, he tries to show something much less.

The point of these Sermons is, that, in spite of the rigid character of the Jewish law, the formal and literal face of its precepts, and the manifest schism, and worse than schism, of the Ten Tribes, yet in fact they were still recognized as a people by the Divine Mercy; that the great prophets Elias and Eliseus were sent to them; and not only so, but were sent to preach to them and reclaim them, without any intimation that they must be reconciled to the line of David and the Aaronic priesthood, or go up to Jerusalem to worship. They were not in the Church, yet they had the means of grace and the hope of acceptance with their Maker. The application of all this to the Anglican Church was immediate . . .[94]

The justification for the Church of England was now of a personal and spiritual nature. As he had reassured Mary Holmes at the beginning of December, 'the Presence of Christ is still with us'.[95] Indeed he was very afraid of 'turning' his 'back . . . on a Divine Presence' and leaving 'what is given' for 'another system, though that system might be in itself better', in which he might not 'ever find it again'. It seemed suspiciously like a theology of feelings: 'I trust I have been favored with a much more definite view of the (promised) inward evidence of the Presence of Christ with us in the Sacraments, now that the outward notes of it are being removed. And I am content to be with Moses in the desert—or with Elijah excommunicated from the Temple.'[96] Not surprisingly, the 'moderate' Tractarians were astonished by the replacement of the old objective *Via Media* with this kind of 'methodistic self-contemplation' (as Newman stigmatizes it in the *Apologia*).[97] However, he felt strongly at the time that 'all moderate Churchmen' were 'on their trial'—'They are not worth much, all such, as are offended at our *words* yet can digest the *acts* of others, acts which commit the Church, which our words could not do.'[98]

At the beginning of 1842, Newman told Charles Crawley, the new high-church squire of Littlemore, that he thought his 'days of battle' were 'over'—'It must be something very unforeseen that makes me controvert any more.'[99] In the meantime he could at least remain in the Church of England, still convinced that it was 'quite as improbable that

[93] *VM* i. 198.
[94] *Apo.* 142–3.
[95] To Miss M. Holmes, 6 Dec. 1841.
[96] To S. F. Wood, 13 Dec. 1841; 17 Jan. 1842.
[97] *Apo.* 145.
[98] To W. Dodsworth, 2 Jan. 1842.
[99] To C. Crawley, 2 Jan. 1842.

Rome should purify herself as that England should fall away'.[100] He consoled himself with the Scriptural reflection that they had had their 'seven years of plenty' and 'now come those of the lean kine'.[101] But he was 'almost in despair' of holding the more advanced Tractarians in the Church:

The only possible way is a monastery. Men want an outlet for their devotional and penitential feelings—and if we do not grant it, to a dead certainty they will go where they can find it. This is the beginning and the end of the matter. Yet the clamour is so great, and will be so much greater, that, if I persist, I expect . . . that I shall be stopped. Not that I have any intention of doing more at present than laying the foundation of what may be.[102]

He told Jemima that the one thing he resented in newspaper reports about himself was the allusions to his 'going to Littlemore, which is so personal a thing, that it is a great rudeness'. He explained that they had leased some cottages which had been converted out of a granary, and had then had some adjacent stables turned into rooms to take his books ('which now are actually covering the greater part of my floor in Oriel'). He hoped to use the cottages to 'take in persons, either as pupils or as friends'. (The land he had bought in 1840 for a monastic house had been planted with trees but not built on, and was later sold.) He ended his letter by expressing his confidence that the Tractarians would win through: 'What I dread is, the Church taking some desperate steps . . . and changing the Church's character. Things would be hopeless then.'[103]

On 12 January he wrote to Isaac Williams to say that he was absolutely opposed to his retiring from the election for the poetry professorship under pressure from the Bishop of Oxford, who had been persuaded by Gladstone (fearful of a major defeat for the Tractarians) to intervene. Such an act of 'submission' to the bishop, however commendable in itself, would be 'pregnant with evil to the *integrity* of the Church'. It would be yet another sign that the Church was not 'Catholic'. Anyway, his college would be unlikely to 'acknowledge the Bishop's jurisdiction'.[104] Such proved to be the case: the President of Trinity became 'excited beyond measure—kept discharging notes at the fellows every half hour, and his very head kept shaking', as he declared 'he would rather go to the *stake*' than give in to the bishop—'thus we were near having another Protestant Martyr'.[105] Perhaps the Archbishop of Canterbury himself might intervene, in order to avoid the embarrassment of a large vote for the Tractarians. But why should

[100] To W. Dodsworth, 2 Jan. 1842.
[102] To J. R. Hope, 3 Jan. 1842.
[104] To I. Williams, 12 Jan. 1842.
[101] To S. Rickards, 2 Jan. 1842.
[103] To Mrs J. Mozley, 9 Jan. 1842.
[105] To Miss M. R. Giberne, 28 Feb. 1842.

Williams have to withdraw because his opponent would not? What had they done to deserve this latest rebuff, Newman asked indignantly.

Last March I submitted, and was told that *therefore* nothing would be done from authority. What has happened since? I have been silent—has any thing happened but *clamour*? is it not then the *clamour* which calls up the Archbishop?[106]

In the event, there was an informal comparison of votes which showed a majority of 3 to 2 against Williams, whereupon he withdrew. Newman was more than pleased at the support he had received and thought Williams could have won or nearly won, had the election been a little later and a proper vote taken. At any rate, this was surely too 'large a minority' for the authorities to think of trying to coerce.[107]

Meanwhile, it was precisely 'the *clamour* against Popery' which more than anything else was calculated to turn the minds of undergraduates towards Rome.[108] Before the Heads of Houses condemned *Tract 90* and the bishops issued *charges* against it, there had been no talk or threat of conversions to Rome. The former, Newman pointed out,

have proclaimed all over the world that their University is Popish. Well then, the country replies, you must put the evil down. But we can't. Then the Church must. It seems then as if some strong acts were inevitable. People up and down the country, clergymen, squires, and the like, *demand* that the University should not be a place where Popery is imbibed; and while vast numbers of the higher and middle classes feel this grievance, popular addresses are commencing to the Archbishop to the same effect. All parties are desirous of doing something.

Indeed, Newman agreed, '*something* must be done'—which was why, he told Jemima, he thought the *British Critic* 'should be as mute as a fish'. He could 'boast' that all his own friends were 'in a very tranquil state', but there were threatening noises from the undergraduates—'and were any of *them* to conform to the Church of Rome it would raise the popular commotion to boiling point and would all be imputed to me'.[109]

6

At the end of January Newman let another friend into his secret. He told Robert Wilberforce that he was 'much put to it' when asked about his state of mind, 'not thinking it right to speak out, yet feeling the difficulty and pain of shuffling'. After describing what had happened in the summer of 1839, he went on:

---

[106] To Mrs J. Mozley, 19 Jan. 1842.
[108] To E. B. Pusey, 24 Jan. 1842.
[107] To R. Palmer, 21 Jan. 1842.
[109] To Mrs J. Mozley, 25 Jan. 1842.

Since then whatever line of early history I look into, I see as in a glass reflected our own Church in the heretical party, and the Roman church in the Catholic. This is an appalling fact—which, do what I will, I cannot shake off.

One special test of the heretical party is absence of *stay* or *consistence*, ever crumbling ever shifting, ever new forming—ever self consumed by internal strife. Our present state . . . is a most miserable and continual fulfilment of this Note of error . . .

Another is a constant effort to make alliance with other heresies and schisms, though differing itself from them. . . . Now, I confess, miserable as this Prussian business is to my mind in itself, it is rendered still more startling and unsettling by its apparent fulfilment in this Note of error. . . .

Nor is it the mere *coincidence* between the state of things now and formerly which harasses me, but it seems something *prophetic*—it scares me.

This had led me anxiously to look out for *grounds* of remaining where Providence has placed me . . .

After referring to the case of St Meletius as 'the most remarkable historical evidence'—whose gentle qualities, he had already averred in 'The Catholicity of the Anglican Church', 'seem to have been notes of his churchmanship, which outweighed his separation from Rome and Alexandria, and prove that saints may be matured in a state which Romanists of this day would fain call schism'—[110] he continued:

It has also forced me back upon the *internal or personal Notes* of the Church; and with thankfulness I say that I have received great comfort there. But, alas, in seeking to draw out this comfort for the benefit of others, who (without knowing my state) have been similarly distressed, eager inquisitive sensitive minds have taken the alarm, and (though I acted with the greatest anxiety and tried to do what I could to avoid the suspicion) they are beginning to guess that I have not an implicit faith in the validity of the *external* Notes of our Church.

My present purpose is from sheer despondency lest I should be doing harm, to give over, at least for the present, preaching at St Mary's. Nothing I can say, though I preach Sermons 17 years old, but is made to have a meaning—much more when I write fresh ones. And I think it may be of use in itself, in the present excited stated of Oxford and the country. My going to be at Littlemore, which has long been in contemplation and progress, will be an excuse, to save appearances.

One obvious consequence is to be mentioned besides—a growing dread lest in speaking against the Church of Rome I may be speaking against the Holy Ghost. This is quite consistent with a full conviction of the degraded state of that Church whether here or elsewhere.

He knew 'what pain' his letter would give Robert, but he had wanted to be 'open'. Only two other people knew about his feelings—and then only 'generally': Robert was 'the first person to whom' he had 'drawn it out'. Of course, he felt 'very differently' at 'different times', and what he

[110] *Ess.* ii. 65.

had said in his published letters to R. W. Jelf and the Bishop of Oxford was 'said quite sincerely', for his 'fears' had 'slept for very many months', and had 'only lately been re-animated by our dreadful divisions, the Bishops' charges, and this Prussian affair'. On the other hand, he had to admit to the 'painful thought' whether, contrary to what he had said in his letter to the Bishop, 'if Rome be the true Church, the divinely appointed method of raising her from her present degradation be not to *join her*. Whether either she or we *can* correct our mutual errors while separated from each other.' Perhaps it was '*unity*' which would bring holiness to both Churches rather than the other way round.[111] He certainly felt that 'the want of unity has injured both them and us'[112]—a thought which would often recur to him later as a Roman Catholic.

In the *Apologia* Newman recounts how, 'While my old and true friends were thus in trouble about me, I suppose they felt not only anxiety but pain, to see that I was gradually surrendering myself to the influence of others . . . younger men, and of a cast of mind in no small degree uncongenial to my own'. This 'new school of thought', which 'was sweeping the original party of the Movement aside, and was taking its place', had 'rapidly formed and increased, in and out of Oxford' just at the very time that Newman's doubts had started in the summer of 1839. They 'knew nothing about the *Via Media*, but had heard much about Rome'. And Newman admits that

though I neither was so fond (with a few exceptions) of the persons, nor of the methods of thought, which belonged to this new school, as of the old set . . . yet I had an intense sympathy in their object and in the direction in which their path lay, in spite of my old friends, in spite of my old life-long prejudices. In spite of my ingrained fears of Rome, and the decision of my reason and conscience against her usages, in spite of my affection for Oxford and Oriel, yet I had a secret longing love of Rome the Mother of English Christianity, and I had a true devotion to the Blessed Virgin . . . And it was the consciousness of this bias in myself . . . which made me preach so earnestly against the danger of being swayed in religious inquiry by our sympathy rather than by our reason.[113]

In reply to a distressed letter from Robert Wilberforce, Newman retorted that he had brought 'the pain' on himself by asking about his state of mind. Robert was free to tell his wife, but 'dreadful mischief would ensue' if so 'serious a secret' got out. Anyway, Newman assured him, not only had he no intention of leaving the Church in which he believed Christ was 'present', but the only 'reason for so awful and dreadful a step' would be 'the quiet growth of a feeling through many years'. He could 'sincerely say' that 'no one' had 'exerted himself more.

[111] To R. I. Wilberforce, 26 Jan. 1842. [112] To J. Keble, 29 Dec. 1844.
[113] *Apo.* 150–2.

... to make a case for the English Church and theory, from the Fathers': having 'honestly' undertaken the attempt and 'spared no pains', he could 'perhaps' say that he had '*succeeded*'. At any rate, 'I really think I have examined and replied to more objections than most people. I don't think argument will help me.'[114] He confided to Robert's brother, Henry, that he 'sometimes thought' that if he was 'seriously prompted to join the Church of Rome', he would 'beg' his 'friends' prayers' that he 'might die rather than do it, if it were wrong'.[115]

On 6 February he wrote to tell Jemima that he was moving to Littlemore: 'my books are all in motion—part gone—the rest in a day or two. It makes me very downcast—it is such a nuisance taking *steps* . . .'. A few days later he wrote again to reassure his anxious sister:

For some years, as is natural, I have felt that I am out of place at Oxford, as customs are. Every one almost is my junior. And then added to this is the hostility of the Heads, who are now . . . taking measures to get the men from St Mary's.

He had more or less decided for the time being to stop preaching at St Mary's ('a cause of *irritation*') to forestall such moves. Eighteen months ago he had wanted to retire from St Mary's altogether, while retaining Littlemore. The reason why he felt so old at Oxford, of course, was because he had not married and left college for a living like most fellows. Now he thought he would be ready to lose his fellowship on condition he could keep Littlemore. 'Perhaps', he drily remarked, 'the Provost might listen to so great a bribe.'[116]

Not long before, Newman and the Provost had spent a rather embarrassing evening together at the annual college Gaudy on 2 February. It was announced that Dr Arnold was coming, and Newman realized that, as the senior fellow, taking the place of the Dean, C. P. Eden, who was ill, he would have to sit next to Hawkins and Arnold both at dinner on high table and afterwards in the Senior Common Room. At first he felt like not going, but then thought that would be 'cowardly'. Arnold had apparently forgotten he had met him before, but on being introduced by the Provost, Newman, as he later recounted to Jemima, 'was sly enough to say very gently and clearly, that I had before then had the pleasure of knowing Dr Arnold, for I had disputed with him in the Divinity School for his B.D. degree, when he was appointed to Rugby'. At this 'Arnold seemed a little awkward'. When they sat down to dinner, Newman 'thought of all the matters possible which it was safe to talk on'. He afterwards remembered that 'the productions of North Africa was a fruitful subject'. After dinner,

---

[114] To R. I. Wilberforce, 1 Feb. 1842. [115] To H. Wilberforce, 12 Feb. 1842.
[116] To Mrs J. Mozley, 6, 15 Feb. 1842.

they retired to the Common Room, where 'the contrast was very marked between Arnold and the Provost—the Provost so dry and unbending and seeming to shrink from whatever I said, and Arnold who was natural and easy'. Arnold died in June, and Newman never saw him again. Newman had 'always separated' him 'from the people he was with, always respected, often defended' him—though accidentally Arnold had got the idea that 'I was a firebrand, and particularly hostile to him. There is no doubt he was surprised and thrown out on finding that I did not seem to be what he had fancied.' As for Newman, he 'was secretly amused from the idea that he certainly would be taken aback by coming across me' in person. At any rate, he could congratulate himself on being 'most absolutely cool, or rather calm and unconcerned, all through the meeting from beginning to end'. It was really no 'affectation' that he seemed on such occasions 'to put on a very simple, innocent, and modest manner. I sometimes laugh at myself, and at the absurdities which result from it, but really I cannot help it, and I do really believe it to be genuine.'[117]

It was not only the Heads of Houses who were displeased with Newman. He remarked to his lawyer friend Edward Bellasis, who had been converted to Tractarianism by Newman's writings, that he was grateful for his support because 'hardly any thing is said to me or comes to me, even from friends, of a sympathetic character'. This only made him 'more grateful' to those who did show sympathy. Still, years of opposition had hardened him. In the meantime, it was best 'to do nothing', in view of the 'irritation against us even among our friends, which in time will be succeeded by *resignation*'. In the end, there must surely be 'a re-action' in their favour, which they should 'quietly' wait for.[118]

On 21 February he reached the age of 41. He wrote to his Aunt Elizabeth, 'Really I marvel more and more at my age, and cannot get reconciled to it. I mean I do not *feel* so old as I am; and it dismays one that life is going with so little to show for it.' He told her they were 'fitting up a very pretty little parsonage' at Littlemore, which they had leased for seven years. They were spending a lot of money on it, but hoped it would look nice by the summer. He was busy arranging all his books, which he was going to insure for £1500 or £2000: 'They are a very fine collection, and I am afraid to say what they are worth. . . . My rooms at Oriel look so queer without them.'[119] To Bowden he joked, 'I hope I shall not get to idolize my Library.'[120] He reported that the 'Bishops seem to have decided on doing nothing—and Golightly has happily so little tact,

[117] To Mrs J. Mozley, 31 Oct. 1844.　　[118] To E. Bellasis, 16 Feb. 1842.
[119] To Miss E. Newman, 21 Feb. 1842.　　[120] To J. W. Bowden, 28 Feb. 1842.

as to have disgusted his own friends by his ultra statements'. The first part of his edition of Athanasius was coming out. He and Pusey had decided that the advantages outweighed the disadvantages of publishing straight away without waiting till the second part was ready.

At the end of March Newman was able to report to Maria Giberne that he had no news—and that was good news. He mentioned they were 'trying to set up a half College half monastery at Littlemore', but there were no 'inmates' yet.[121] A fortnight later a letter arrived from the Bishop of Oxford asking him to deny a newspaper report that he was erecting a monastery at Littlemore. He replied that he felt it was 'hard' that he should have to provide an 'explanation' to satisfy 'the restlessness of the public mind'. For a year now he had been 'the subject of incessant misrepresentation', although he had complied with the bishop's commands and had ceased from all controversial activities. He had been concerned solely with scholarly research (his translations of St Athanasius) and ordinary pastoral parochial work, and that was what he intended to do in the future. However, for many years he had wanted to lead 'a life of greater religious regularity', although it was 'very unpleasant' to mention the fact as it seemed 'arrogant' and committed him to 'a profession which may come to nothing'. He thought it was 'very cruel' that 'very sacred matters between me and my conscience are made a public talk'. It was a private concern of his own, although it would be comforting to find that 'God had put it into the hearts of others to pursue their personal edification in the same way, and unnatural not to wish to have the benefit of their presence and encouragement'. He added that, in his view, 'such religious resolutions are most necessary for keeping a certain class of minds firm in their allegiance to our Church'. Apart from the conversion of the stable into a library, no alterations had been made in the buildings he had leased, although he had had a 'shed' erected to connect the doors of the cottages which opened on the back (a 'cloister' had been mentioned in the newspaper report), 'so that an inmate can now pass from one to another without exposure to the weather'. He had a resident curate, David Lewis, looking after St Mary's. There were at least as many parishioners living at Littlemore, which had been 'very much neglected'. Anyway, it seemed better, under the circumstances, that he should stay away from Oxford for the time being. His curate at Littlemore, W. J. Copeland, might move into one of the cottages, and he hoped to get a young unmarried man as the new schoolmaster who would live in one of the other cottages. The rest of the six two-roomed cottages might be used by helpers, or students studying for Holy Orders, or friends staying. All would be

[121] To Miss M. R. Giberne, 30 Mar. 1842.

involved 'in study and in joint devotion'.[122] The bishop replied that he deplored the calumnies and that Littlemore would benefit from the Vicar residing there.

On 25 April Newman wrote to tell Henry Wilberforce about the move. They were only 'a small household', but had held their first 'Breviary Service' that morning. He did not know what would come of the undertaking—'yet a good Providence has so wonderfully guided me on step by step, without my seeing the path before me, that I cannot but think that something will come of it.' He wished that he 'was a hundredth part as sure' that he 'was in God's favor' as he was sure that God was 'using' him 'as an instrument'.[123]

A month later the Bishop of Oxford delivered his own *charge* on *Tract 90*. Newman reported to Keble that on the whole it was 'very favourable' to the Movement, although *Tract 90*'s interpretation of the Articles was criticized for not being 'the obvious' one. But while Dr Bagot had declared he was 'against all interpretations which made the Articles mean every thing or nothing', he had also said that he did not see why the Tractarians should not enjoy the same liberty of interpretation as the Evangelicals. His real 'censure' was reserved for 'the *disciples* of the movement', but he warned that 'if people attempted to dam up the movement, there would be a great inundation, and a fearful schism'.[124] It seemed 'plain which way' the bishop leaned, and he was even expected to pay a friendly private visit to Littlemore. They were 'doing *capitally*', Newman told Jemima in June, after an attempt by the Heads of Houses to have the statutes against Hampden repealed had failed in Convocation by the same proportion of 3 to 2 as in the contest for the poetry professorship. It seemed to Newman like a 'reward' for having allowed themselves to be 'bullied' then. He had refused himself to take any initiative in organizing opposition to the Hebdomadal Board's proposal, which was obviously intended to be an anti-Tractarian move in support of the liberals. He apologized to Jemima that he could not stay with her in Derby—but now 'I am a family man and cannot leave home'.[125]

There was another reason. He was 'plagued' with his 'Essay on Miracles which I cannot finish or write'. Towards the end of July he complained to Pusey that it had 'become very much longer' than he 'wished'. It was 'now nearly done'—but he had 'thought' he 'ought to give some instances', otherwise he would 'leave people in a vague dreamy state of mind, as to what' he 'meant', and that had 'taken time'.[126] The essay, which he 'thought never would come to an end', was

[122] To R. Bagot, 14 Apr. 1842.   [123] To H. Wilberforce, 25 Apr. 1842.
[124] To J. Keble, 24 May 1842.   [125] To Mrs J. Mozley, 12 June 1842.
[126] To E. B. Pusey, 23 June, 12 July 1842.

more or less finished at the end of the month.[127] It was 'not much of a thing', but it had 'taken a good deal of time'.[128] The part which had taken the 'most time' was the last part on historical examples, but he was 'sure' it was the part which would 'excite most interest' and 'have the best chance of selling the book'.[129] The essay was a preface to the forthcoming annotated translation of Fleury's *Ecclesiastical History*; it was to be published separately in 1843 as *An Essay on the Miracles Recorded in the Ecclesiastical History of the Early Ages*, and was later incorporated, together with Newman's earlier essay for the *Encyclopaedia Metropolitana*, in *Two Essays on Biblical and on Ecclesiastical Miracles*, under the title 'The Miracles of Early Ecclesiastical History, compared with those of Scripture, as regards their Nature, Credibility, and Evidence'. Using the 'argument from Analogy', Newman claims that 'there exists in matter of fact that very connection and intermixture between ecclesiastical and Scripture miracles', which is suggested by 'the richness and variety of physical nature'.[130] At one point in the historical part of the essay, Newman suddenly remarks, with obvious reference to his own predicament:

belief, in any true sense of the word, requires a certain familiarity or intimacy of the mind with the thing believed. Till it is in some way brought home to us and made our own, we cannot properly say we believe it, even when our reason receives it.[131]

When Maria Giberne wrote in August and asked for news of him, he replied:

really I have nothing to tell. I wish to have no goings on—that is, I wish to have no prospects or plans . . . Of course I wish things very different from what they are—of course too I see things changing—and I cannot but see that my own principles, by which I defend our Church, go far beyond the use to which I put them. But I speak honestly when I say that there is no *definite idea* of things which I have set up as right and perfect, and no *positive end* at which I am aiming. Rather I am aiming at no end at all. I defended the state of things as it is, for *its own* sake—and now that defence has proved not acceptable to the ruling part of the Church I am willing to do nothing. . . . Had I my will, I really think I should write nothing more—for what I do, is misinterpreted, not only by enemies, which I can bear, but by friends.

He was able to report that the cottages at Littlemore were 'full'—but 'men come and go; I have hardly one constant inmate, and in winter perhaps I may be left alone'.[132] He could not complain about people suspecting that he had 'misgivings' about the Anglican Church, but

---

[127] To Mrs J. Mozley, 31 July 1842. [128] To W. H. Anderdon, 1 Aug. 1842.
[129] To J. H. Parker, 2 Aug. 1842. [130] *Mir.* 147, 161.
[131] Ibid. 259. [132] To Miss M. R. Giberne, 12 Aug. 1842.

what really 'hurt' him, he told Pusey, was that people could think him 'capable of *holding an office* in the Church, and yet countenancing and living familiarly with those who were seceding from it'. That would indeed be 'treachery', and surely the fact that he held a living was proof that he was still 'in the *service* of the English Church'.[133] Hostile rumour had it that he was 'actually in the service of the enemy' and was 'rearing at Littlemore a nest of Papists'; whereas the truth was that he was offering Littlemore as 'a place of retirement' for young Anglo-Catholics who were in difficulties like himself and whom he was doing his best to dissuade from going over to Rome.[134] At present, he had 'two regular inmates' living with him, who were reading for Holy Orders, as well as his curate Copeland and 'a number of visitors from time to time'.

By the end of August he had been there 'going on for 19 weeks', he told his Aunt Elizabeth, 'and the time has glided on so calmly and happily that it seems incredible it should be so long'. He might be under strain, but he could still enjoy a good joke, and he regaled his aunt with the practical joke they thought of playing on one visitor, who, they had suspected, would use the place as a hotel in order to visit Oxford:

> but still we do not find it in our hearts to let him off so easily, and have thought of various plans to inflict Littlemore upon him. One idea is to lock the street doors, a simple expedient, unless he gets out of the windows which a thinner man could do. But the most approved idea is to make him sleep on the straw mattress, and, as there are no servants on the premises, when he is once shut in for the night, he must make the best of it.

However, in the event, there was no need for any practical tricks, for as their visitor walked out from Oxford, he

> was (unintentionally on the part of his Oxford companion) so mystified and terrified about this place, which I suppose he thought before to be some sort of rural villa, that, when he at length reached us, he was as grave and solemn as an old cat, and we could make nothing of him. I thought marriage had spoiled him. He looked thin too, and yellow, and was full of fidget. The shock his nerves had experienced went further still—for he was sick all night, and had not a wink of sleep. Next Morning he went to Oxford, and contrived to breathe more freely—and in no long time took up his abode in Christ Church—and soon became as lively and chirping as usual, and his face lost all its gibbous effect and swelled into a gleaming glistening full moon.—So you see we had our fun, without practising any tricks upon him. His *imagination* did it for us.[135]

At the beginning of September Newman sent his old Trinity friend, Simeon Lloyd Pope, a rather more serious letter on the state and prospects of the Church of England. It was not all pessimistic.

[133] To E. B. Pusey, 24 Aug. 1842.   [134] *Apo*. 162.
[135] To Miss E. Newman, 29 Aug. 1842.

The laity say, *Whom* are we to believe? ... How can that be practically a church, how can it *teach*, which speaks half a dozen things in the same breath? Of course things cannot stand here. . . . My great hope and belief is, that the so-called Evangelical party is a failing and declining one; so that we may hope that the clamour will be less and less every year. And the very circumstance that there is reason for so thinking is what makes the clamour louder at present. These good people feel and know that they are losing ground, and therefore they cry out so much the louder. They cry while they can.

The rising generation are almost to a man of another way of thinking. Even at Cambridge, where the want of mental discipline is so great that one cannot augur any thing very superfine in time to come, a very much truer view of religious matters is appearing . . . The great point seems to be to stave off any serious collision between the parties for (say) 20 years—by that time the old Protestant generation will be extinct—and one may trust there will be more of unity. But if not, if either zealots force matters on to a collision, or the old party does not disappear in time, our church must inevitably go to pieces. For this reason I am very much against the meeting of Convocation for despatch of business—fearing it would bring on a crisis. The Protestant party would do all in their power to eject their opponents from the church.

The disunity of the Church was indeed 'a great triumph to the Roman Catholics', who, he was full of hope, would 'turn over a new leaf'. He knew it was impossible to eradicate superstition from a popular church, but he wished the Roman Church would take 'a truer, more manly, more sensible, more Christian line, removing scandals, and unlearning bigotry, and ceasing their vile connexion with liberals and democrats'. In the meantime it was 'lucky' for Anglicans that the Roman Catholics were in such a 'deplorably low ethical state', as otherwise 'they would be most formidable opponents'.[136]

A few days later he wrote to Keble about plans for a memorial to Dr Arnold (who had died that year). He saw no reason why he should not subscribe, provided 'the *object* of the memorial' was 'confined to Arnold's merits in his School'. After all, they could 'do things *now*, which we could not do ten years ago, because now we are so well known that no one can mistake our meaning'. In 1832 he and Froude had kept away 'from the meeting in Oxford about the Walter Scott Testimonial, because it was taken up by Liberals—but then our opinions were unknown; and to have joined it would have seemed adopting Liberal notions'. Anyway, there was 'nothing inconsistent or hypocritical' in his taking part—'because I am conscious I have always done justice to his great merits at Rugby, nay have always defended him in many other respects, as considering him widely different from Whately, Hawkins, and many other persons with whom he is associated, as more real and

---

[136] To S. L. Pope, 4 Sept. 1842.

earnest than his friends, as having done a work, when they are merely talkers'. It would therefore be 'painful' for him not to subscribe. Apropos of Scott, he remarked that he had just been reading Lockhart's life, which had 'brought more tears' into his eyes than any other book he had ever read, while at the same time leaving 'an impression . . . like a bad dream'. He could not 'get the bitter taste' out of his mouth—'it is so like vanity of vanities—except that I really do trust that he had *done a work*; and may be an instrument in the hands of Providence for the revival of Catholicity.' But he ended his letter by commenting characteristically that there would be no religious progress 'till the doctrine of post-baptismal sin is recognized'. Moderate high churchmen like W. F. Hook collaborated with the Cambridge Camden Society 'in making a fair outside, while within are dead men's bones. We shall do nothing till we have a severer religion.'[137] His own position on any kind of provocative ritualism was summed up in his usual epithet of condemnation—it was 'unreal'.[138]

. . . I have myself a very great repugnance to reviving obsolete usages on private authority without very strong reason for doing so. And, great indeed as is the good which the Campden has done and is doing . . . I confess they seem to me to carry too much sail. There are after all things of greater consequence than ceremonies; and though the very business of the Society is with externals, and therefore it is not to be blamed for being silent upon theology and ethics, yet I cannot but fear that some of its promoters have given too little time to the foundation, before they began to build. . . . they are not always so serious and reverent as the sacredness of their subject requires them to be.[139]

However, his dislike of ritualistic innovations did not extend to a procession with singing on the anniversary of the dedication of the church at Littlemore, although it provoked a raucous demonstration, he reported not without some satisfaction to Maria Giberne:

There was a vulgar riotous stranger there, making a noise, all through the service, crying popish etc. If I had heard him, I should have had him turned out for brawling—he was a little man—and we had some stout fellows among us. Then he would have said 'What persecution already! I thought the wily Puseyites would have kept the cloven foot out of sight a little longer.'[140]

He told Jemima he could not but feel uneasy in general at 'the spread of Catholic opinions'—for 'spread as they may, they have no solid bottom—at least Anglicanism is not a bottom. But I suppose, if one feels certain things to be right and true, it is want of faith not to preach them merely because one cannot systematize.' When she saw him, his sister

[137] To J. Keble, 12 Sept. 1842.
[139] To R. Belaney, 7 Sept. 1842.
[138] To T. Lloyd Coghlan, 18 July 1841.
[140] To Miss M. R. Giberne, 25 Sept. 1842.

would find him 'vastly aged in this year and a half'. He had begun to think of himself as 'an old man'.[141]

In view of the *charge* by the Bishop of Oxford, in which he had complained about the *British Critic*, Newman again advised Tom Mozley to get rid of Oakeley and Ward—'they *cannot* write, without bringing in their notions'. If Tom agreed, he was ready to take the 'responsibility' for it.[142] When Tom demurred, Newman suggested that perhaps the best thing would be to give up the editorship, 'which is cutting the knot, and the best for your comfort'. The only trouble was that 'this is just what the Conservative Apostolicals want', as it would appear to have the effect of 'reducing ourselves to silence . . . and giving up an important engine to other hands'. Although he would be 'sorry' if Tom decided to, it was 'probably' what he would do in his situation, trusting that the Movement would 'make its way by some means or other'. Alternatively, Tom could obey the bishop, 'by changing the tone of the Review and keeping out those articles and views which you know to be the offenders'. But then the 'disgust' would no doubt be transferred to himself and Tom; so they might as well 'have something to show for it', and not only did he agree with the views of Oakeley and Ward, but at least they were 'doing a *work*, by breaking down prejudices', and it had to be borne in mind that 'all reformers create disgust'. If he himself did not 'write like them', it was only because he could not 'say what they say without unreality'. The only other course open to Tom ('a very bold one') was to disobey the bishop on the ground that this was not a case in which he had authority.[143]

Newman admitted to Pusey that, unlike him, he had never himself been '*pained*' at what Oakeley and Ward wrote—adding rather ambiguously:

I think my sympathies *are* entirely with them; but really I cannot determine whether my opinions are. I do not know the limits of my own opinions. If Ward says this or that is a development from what I have said, I cannot say yes or no— It is plausible; it *may* be true—I cannot assert it is not true; but I cannot with that keen perception, which some people have, appropriate it. It is a nuisance to me to be *forced* beyond what I can fairly go.[144]

He continued to warn Tom Mozley against the 'Romanism' of the *British Critic*, which he prophesied would eventually alienate the whole Church, and strongly advised him to avoid all compromising 'doctrinal articles'. When Tom replied that he proposed to ignore the bishop's *charge*, Newman typically rebuked him for not acting on any '*theory*' or 'principle'. From the point of view of public opinion, he insisted,

---

[141] To Mrs J. Mozley, 17 Sept. 1842.   [142] To T. Mozley, 17 Sept. 1842.
[143] To T. Mozley, 26 Sept. 1842.   [144] To E. B. Pusey, 16 Oct. 1842.

'Consistency is better than truth . . . Take what theory you please, but act upon it.'[145] Certainly, the episcopal pronouncement should not be treated lightly.

In November Newman was once again in correspondence with Charles Russell, who had sent him a volume of St Alfonso Liguori's sermons. He wished the Roman Church was 'more known among us by such writings'. She would not win 'the heart of England' by 'learned discussions, or acute arguments, or reports of miracles', let alone by political activity, so much as 'in her true functions of exhorting, teaching, and guiding'. But before he could answer Russell's question whether the sermons were 'not calculated to remove my apprehensions that another gospel is substituted for the true one in your practical instructions', he would need to know how far they were only a selection. If he proved to be wrong, he promised that his 'public' admission would 'only be a question of time'. He warned Russell that the 'unwearied efforts' by Roman Catholic leaders to make individual conversions among Anglicans would merely hinder the 'incipient movement of our *Church* towards yours'. In December he thanked Russell for his assurance that the sermons were not unrepresentative, but regretted that the silent omission of some passages about the Virgin Mary in one of the sermons was 'very likely to be discovered, and then great offence is given'.[146] Later he recalled that this 'at least showed that such passages as are found in the works of Italian Authors were not acceptable to every part of the Catholic world'. He also recorded in the *Apologia* that Russell 'had, perhaps, more to do with my conversion than any one else. . . . he was always gentle, mild, unobtrusive, uncontroversial. He let me alone.'[147]

Newman did not tell Russell that he had already written out a retraction of the more extreme anti-Roman statements to be found in his writings of the 1830s, which he hoped could be slipped unobtrusively into an Oxford newspaper. He showed it to R. W. Church, an Oriel friend, warning that it would 'scare' him—'but I hardly think my conscience will let me off'.[148] It was only 'a little demonstration', but it might get him 'into trouble'.[149] After listing the passages (together with Hurrell Froude's scathing criticisms) in an (unsigned) announcement rather than letter to the Editor of the *Conservative Journal*, Newman explained that he had only been following Anglican divines in what he had said, although he had to admit that 'such language is to be ascribed, in no small measure, to an impetuous temper, a hope of approving myself to persons I respect, and a wish to repel the charge of Romanism'. He added that he was making the 'retractation' for 'personal reasons'

[145] To T. Mozley, 18, 30 Oct. 1842.   [146] To C. W. Russell, 22 Nov., 10 Dec. 1842.
[147] *Apo.* 176.   [148] To R. W. Church, 29 Nov. 1842.
[149] To T. Mozley, 26 Dec. 1842.

and 'without consulting others'. He concluded ambivalently that he was 'as fully convinced as ever' that Anglicanism was still 'the strongest' or rather 'the only possible antagonist' of Roman Catholicism—'If Rome is to be withstood, it can be done in no other way.'[150]

Of the 'daily restraints' which Newman had come to find so 'painful' in the exercise of his Anglican ministry, none was more galling than the absence of sacramental confession, particularly at a time like Christmas.[151] In answer to an enquiry from Keble about his pastoral practice, he replied with surprising vehemence:

As to reminding my People about Confession, it is the most dreary and dismal thought which I have about my Parish that I dare do so little, or rather nothing. I have long thought it would hinder me ever taking another cure. Confession is the life of the Parochial charge—without it all is hollow—and yet I do not see my way to say that I should not do more harm than good by more than the most distant mention of it.[152]

The mere fact that there was no practice of confession in the Church of England seemed to him to be in itself a sufficient reason for not holding an Anglican 'pastoral cure'—'I cannot understand how a clergyman can be answerable for souls, if souls are not submitted to him.'[153] If the priesthood without the confessional seemed unreal, there was a distinctly unreal feel about the development of the aesthetic side of Anglo-Catholicism. Its proponents he found

deficient in *inside* . . . I think we are in great danger of becoming . . . *theatrical* in our Religion. All true attention to rites must be founded of course on deep inward convictions, and this makes me dread the fine arts when disjoined from what is practical and personal. All about the country people are taking up architecture. I rejoice at it, *if* they take the severer side of Religion as well as the imaginative and beautiful—but no good can come of all sunshine and no shade.[154]

Newman was just as severe about anything that seemed unreal in the view others had of himself. He wrote sternly to Miss Holmes about her blatant adulation:

. . . I am *not* venerable, and nothing can make me so. I am what I am. I am very much like other people, and I do not think it necessary to abstain from the feelings and thoughts . . . which other people have. I cannot speak words of wisdom; to some it comes naturally. Do not suffer any illusive notion about me to spring up in your mind. No one ever treats me with deference and respect who knows me—and from my heart I trust and pray that no one ever may. I never have been in office or station; people have never bowed to me—and I

[150] To the Editor of the *Conservative Journal*, 12 Dec. 1842.
[151] To W. H. Anderdon, 1 Aug. 1842. [152] To J. Keble, 20 Dec. 1842.
[153] To Mrs J. Mozley, 15 Sept. 1843. [154] To J. F. Russell, 29 Dec. 1842.

could not endure it. I tell you frankly, my infirmity I believe is, always to be rude to persons who are deferential in manner to me.

In fact, Miss Holmes had already been forced to be more realistic about her spiritual director through meeting him in the flesh for the first time—'you are not the first person who have been disappointed in me. Romantic people always will be. I am . . . a very ordinary person.'[155] Another lady, he joked to Harriett, 'was almost disgusted to find me so young. She said she thought my hair was grey—so you see I must like Pythagoras shut myself up in a cave and never be seen by any one.'[156] In view of the intense publicity that his retreat at Littlemore had attracted, the joke was, perhaps, not without a serious note.

[155] To Miss M. Holmes, 27 Dec., 20 Nov. 1842.
[156] To Mrs T. Mozley, 16 Nov. 1842.

6

Development

BEFORE the end of 1842 Newman began to turn his thoughts to the problem of the development of doctrine, to which he was to devote the last of the university sermons he was now preparing for publication. He thought it would be his 'best book'—if it were not that authors were usually wrong about their own writings, 'and if I boast I certainly shall be out'.[1] He was prepared for the sermons being 'thought sad dull affairs—but having got through a subject I wish to get rid of it'.[2]

In January 1843 he was 'much plagued' with the final university sermon, which he was due to deliver on 2 February, but 'which won't write'.[3] However, it was completed before the end of the month—'I am clear about its being long—I am not clear about any thing else.'[4] He warned Jemima that 'some' of the sermons were 'very hard':

but I have now for 12 years been working out a theory, and whether it is true or not, it has this recommendation, that it is consistent—and this is the only encouragement I have to publish, considering its unpopularity and my own ignorance of metaphysical writers. I have kept to the same views and arguments for 12 years, and am obliged to watch myself lest in new sermons I stumble on what I have already said—therefore I think I may fairly publish. They are not theological or ecclesiastical, though they bear immediately upon the most intimate and practical religious questions. The first are much better written I fear than the last . . .[5]

As the feast of the Purification, on which he was to deliver the last sermon on development, drew near, he advised Pusey, 'If any one values his Luncheon . . . he must not go to hear me at St Mary's, for my sermon is of portentous length.'[6] In fact, it 'lasted an hour and a half', he reported to Jemima! 'People went about saying there was a good deal of mischief in it, and that it must be answered; but I am under no apprehensions.'[7] When all the sermons were collected together in one volume, he thought it would be 'the best, not the most perfect, book' he had published—'I mean there is more to develop in it, though it is

[1] To T. Mozley, 26 Dec. 1842.   [2] To J. W. Bowden, 29 Dec. 1842.
[3] To T. Mozley, 13 Jan. 1843.   [4] To R. W. Church, 21 Jan. 1843.
[5] To Mrs J. Mozley, 23 Jan. 1843.   [6] To E. B. Pusey, 30 Jan. 1843.
[7] To Mrs J. Mozley, 21 Feb. 1843.

*im*perfect.'[8] It was true the sermons did not exactly form a '*whole*', but they would 'have more in them than any thing I have published'.[9] People would 'wonder' why he wanted to 'drag some of them from obscurity—but I could not draw the line—some of them are partly on the subject which is the main subject of the volume, though not wholly, and if *they* were to be admitted, it did not seem worth while omitting only one or two.'[10] The book came out in February.

2

The first of the *Sermons, chiefly on the Theory of Religious Belief, preached before the University of Oxford* had been delivered on 2 July 1826. For such an early sermon it is striking for the way in which it warns against 'answering every . . . objection to the words of Scripture, which has been urged . . . from successive discoveries in science', not only for fear of losing a sense of proportion and exaggerating the problem, but also because 'succeeding discoveries' may solve the difficulty. As Newman was so often to insist as a Catholic, 'To feel jealous and appear timid, on witnessing the enlargement of scientific knowledge, is almost to acknowledge that there may be some contrariety between it and Revelation.'[11] In fact, as Newman makes clear in a subsequent sermon of 1831, 'Scripture communications . . . are intended for religious purposes' and not 'to the determination of physical questions', just as so-called 'Reason' is not the 'judge of those truths which are subjected to another part of our nature, the moral sense'.[12] However, the most important of the *Oxford University Sermons*, which rehearse central themes of both the *Grammar of Assent* and the *Development of Christian Doctrine*, were the last six preached between 1839 and 1843. There had been an interval of some six years since the sermon Newman delivered in December 1832 on the eve of his departure for the Mediterranean. Still, the earlier series of sermons are by no means without interest, and contain points which would receive further amplification later, such as the comment that 'it is as absurd to argue men, as to torture them, into believing', or the insistence that 'Conscience is the essential principle and sanction of Religion in the mind', or the paradox that 'They who are not superstitious without the Gospel, will not be religious with it', or the warning that 'The influence of the world, viewed as the enemy of our souls, consists in its hold upon our imagination.'[13]

---

[8] To J. R. Hope, 3 Feb. 1843.
[9] To H. Wilberforce, 3 Feb. 1843; to J. W. Bowden, 10 Feb. 1843.
[10] To J. W. Bowden, 10 Feb. 1843.
[11] *US* 4.   [12] Ibid. 59.   [13] Ibid. 63, 18, 118, 149.

The relation of faith to reason is the principal theme of the *Oxford University Sermons*. Although it is not treated systematically, there is a gradual development which becomes 'more precise, as well as more accurate', as Newman noted in his 1872 preface, where he provides a useful summary of the salient points, which is especially helpful in view of the confusion over the senses in which the term 'reason' is used.[14] Nevertheless, a sustained discussion of the relationship does not really begin until the tenth sermon, 'Faith and Reason, Contrasted as Habits of Mind', preached in 1839, and concludes with the penultimate sermon, preached in 1841.

In the tenth sermon, Newman starts by rejecting the current idea that 'Faith is but a moral quality, dependent upon Reason,—that Reason judges both of the evidence on which Scripture is to be received, and of the meaning of Scripture; and then Faith follows or not, according to the state of the heart; that we make up our minds by Reason without Faith, and then we proceed to adore and to obey by Faith apart from Reason; that, though Faith rests on testimony, not on reasonings, yet that testimony, in its turn, depends on Reason for the proof of its pretensions, so that Reason is an indispensable preliminary'. Just as a judge 'does not make men honest, but acquits and vindicates them', so 'Reason need not be the origin of Faith, as Faith exists in the very persons believing, though it does test and verify it.' There is a difference between 'a critical' and 'a creative power'. We give reasons for our actions by analysing our motives, but the reasons are not the same as the motives. Certainly, Scripture sees 'Faith . . . as an instrument of knowledge and action, unknown to the world before . . . independent of what is commonly understood by Reason'. If it were 'merely . . . a believing upon evidence, or a sort of conclusion upon a process of reasoning', then it would hardly be 'a novel principle of action', as the Bible regards it. Conscience is not 'against Reason', but it does not 'depend . . . upon some previous processes of Reason'. Nor can it be denied that 'a child or uneducated person may . . . savingly act on Faith, without being able to produce reasons why he so acts'. Faith is 'mainly swayed by antecedent considerations', whereas reason demands 'direct and definite proof'. After all, 'Faith is a principle of action, and action does not allow time for minute and finished investigations.' Such investigations, indeed, 'have a tendency to blunt the practical energy of the mind', although they may 'improve its scientific exactness'. Religious faith, like all beliefs, 'is influenced . . . less by evidence, more by previously-entertained principles, views, and wishes', that is, by 'antecedent probabilities'. It is when these 'prepossessions' are right, that 'we are

---

[14] Ibid., p. x.

right in believing', even if 'upon slender evidence'. Faith, then, is a 'moral principle' in the sense that it is 'created in the mind, not so much by facts, as by probabilities', which vary according to one's 'moral temperament'—'A good and a bad man will think very different things probable.' This is why 'a man *is* responsible for his faith, because he is responsible for his likings and dislikings, his hopes and his opinions, on all of which his faith depends'. It is those 'feelings' which 'come only of supernatural grace' that 'make us think evidence sufficient, which falls short of a proof in itself'. And so it is that 'religious minds embrace the Gospel mainly on the great antecedent probability of a Revelation, and the suitableness of the Gospel to their needs.' On the other hand, not only are 'Evidences . . . thrown away' on 'men of irreligious minds', but too much emphasis on them leads people 'to think that Faith is mainly the result of argument' and that 'religious Truth is a legitimate matter of disputation' without any 'preparation of heart': for 'the ways towards Truth are considered high roads open to all men, however disposed, at all times', given that 'Truth is to be approached without homage'. But he rejects the

wild notion that actually no proof at all is implied in the maintenance, or may be exacted for the profession of Christianity. I would only maintain that that proof need not be the subject of analysis, or take a methodical form, or be complete and symmetrical, in the believing mind; and that probability is its life. I do but say that it is antecedent probability that gives meaning to those arguments from facts which are commonly called the Evidences of Revelation; that, whereas mere probability proves nothing, mere facts persuade no one; that probability is to fact, as the soul to the body; that mere presumptions may have no force, but that mere facts have no warmth. A mutilated and defective evidence suffices for persuasion where the heart is alive; but dead evidences, however perfect, can but create a dead faith.

Newman concludes this brilliant sermon with a well-known passage in which he claims merely to have defined 'the sense in which the words Faith and Reason are used by Christian and Catholic writers':

Half the controversies in the world are verbal ones; and could they be brought to a plain issue, they would be brought to a prompt termination. Parties engaged in them would then perceive, either that in substance they agreed together, or that their difference was one of first principles. . . . We need not dispute, we need not prove,—we need but define. . . . Controversy, at least in this age, does not lie between the hosts of heaven, Michael and his Angels on the one side, and the powers of evil on the other; but it is a sort of night battle, where each fights for himself, and friend and foe stand together. When men understand each other's meaning, they see, for the most part, that controversy is either superfluous or hopeless.[15]

[15] *US* 177, 179, 182–4, 187–8, 190–3, 197–201.

In the next sermon, 'The Nature of Faith in Relation to Reason' (preached a week later on 13 January 1839), Newman defines faith as 'the reasoning of a religious mind, or of what Scripture calls a right or renewed heart, which acts upon presumptions rather than evidence; which speculates and ventures on the future when it cannot make sure of it'. The world regards faith as 'bad' reason 'because it rests on presumption more, and on evidence less'. Certainly an act of faith is 'an exercise of Reason', in so far as it is 'an acceptance of things as real, which the senses do not convey, upon certain previous grounds'. As such, it 'is not the only exercise of Reason, which, when critically examined, would be called unreasonable, and yet is not so'. The 'pursuit of truth' is not solely 'a syllogistic process', and 'the experience of life contains abundant evidence that in practical matters, when their minds are really roused, men commonly are not bad reasoners', if only because 'the principles which they profess guide them unerringly to their legitimate issues'. People 'may argue badly, but they reason well; that is, their professed grounds are no sufficient measures of their real ones', which 'they do not, or cannot produce, or if they could, yet could not prove to be true, on latent or antecedent grounds which they take for granted'. However 'full' and 'precise' the 'grounds' and 'however systematic our method, however clear and tangible our evidence, yet when our argument is traced down to its simple elements, there must ever be something assumed ultimately which is incapable of proof'. Faith, then, is no different from other kinds of intellectual activity where 'we must assume something to prove anything, and can gain nothing without a venture'. Indeed, the more important the knowledge is, the more subtle is 'the evidence on which it is received'—'We are so constituted, that if we insist upon being as sure as is conceivable, in every step of our course, we must be content to creep along the ground, and can never soar.' And just as 'Reason, with its great conclusions, is confessedly a higher instrument than Sense with its secure premisses, so Faith rises above Reason, in its subject-matter, more than it falls below it in the obscurity of its process'. Like 'the most remarkable victories of genius', the act of faith involves 'grounds of inference' which 'cannot be exhibited', so that the 'act of mind' of an uneducated believer 'may be analogous to the exercise of sagacity in a great statesman or general, supernatural grace doing for the uncultivated reason what genius does for them'.[16]

In 'Love the Safeguard of Faith against Superstition', preached in May 1839, Newman explains that the 'antecedent probabilities' on which faith depends are 'grounds which do not reach so far as to touch

---

[16] Ibid. 203–4, 207, 209, 211–13, 215, 218.

precisely the desired conclusion, though they tend towards it, and may come very near it'. An 'active', 'personal and living' faith is created by 'anticipations and presumptions', which 'are the creation of the mind itself,' and is an acceptance of an 'external religion' which 'elicits into shape, and supplies the spontaneous desires and presentiments of their minds'. The 'evidence' for Christianity 'tells a certain way, yet might be more', and a person will believe or not believe 'according to . . . the state of his heart'. Moreover, 'the antecedent judgment, with which a man approaches the subject of religion, not only acts as a bearing this way or that,—as causing him to go out to meet the evidence in a greater or less degree, and nothing more,—but, further, it practically colours the evidence.' This is exactly how 'judgments are commonly formed concerning facts alleged or reported in political and social matters, and for the same reason, because it cannot be helped'. Unbelief itself 'criticizes the evidence of Religion, only because it does not like it, and really goes upon presumptions and prejudices as much as Faith does, only presumptions of an opposite nature'. Newman allows that 'some safeguard of Faith is needed, some corrective principle which will secure it from running (as it were) to seed, and becoming superstition or fanaticism.' What, accordingly, 'gives . . . birth' to faith is also what 'disciplines it'—namely, 'a right state of heart'. In a word, 'We *believe*, because we *love*.' And so it is the 'divinely-enlightened mind' which 'sees in Christ the very Object whom it desires to love and worship,—the Object correlative of its own affections'. Newman sums up the intellectual and moral elements in faith:

Right faith is the faith of a right mind. Faith is an intellectual act; right Faith is an intellectual act, done in a certain moral disposition. Faith is an act of Reason, viz. a reasoning upon presumptions; right Faith is a reasoning upon holy, devout, and enlightened presumptions. Faith ventures and hazards; right Faith ventures and hazards deliberately, seriously, soberly, piously, and humbly, counting the cost and delighting in the sacrifice.

Although faith 'is itself an intellectual act', still 'it takes its character from the moral state of the agent' and 'is perfected, not by intellectual cultivation, but by obedience'.[17]

To reject the preoccupation of the 'age of reason' with 'evidences' did not mean for Newman that the only alternative was a 'romantic' religion of feelings and imagination. As we have seen, his own understanding of 'reason' led him not to contrast it with faith but to define faith in terms of a wider concept of reasoning. In the next sermon, 'Implicit and Explicit Reason', preached in 1840, he is careful to insist on the importance of the explicitly rational element.

[17] *US* 224–8, 230, 232–4, 236, 239, 249–50.

Nothing would be more theoretical and unreal than to suppose that true Faith cannot exist except when moulded upon a Creed, and based upon Evidence; yet nothing would indicate a more shallow philosophy than to say that it ought carefully to be disjoined from dogmatic and argumentative statements. To assert the latter is to discard the science of theology from the service of Religion; to assert the former, is to maintain that every child, every peasant, must be a theologian. Faith cannot exist without grounds or without an object; but it does not follow that all who have faith should recognize, and be able to state what they believe, and why.

It is clear from Scripture that faith is sometimes 'attended by a conscious exercise of Reason', but sometimes is 'independent not of objects or grounds (for that is impossible,) but of perceptible, recognized, producible objects and grounds'. The difference between 'the more simple faculties and operations of the mind, and that process of analyzing and describing them, which takes place upon reflection', is the difference between implicit and explicit reasoning. No one surely has ever written more evocatively of the extraordinary power of the human mind:

The mind ranges to and fro, and spreads out, and advances forward with a quickness which has become a proverb, and a subtlety and versatility which baffle investigation. It passes on from point to point, gaining one by some indication; another on a probability; then availing itself of an association; then falling back on some received law; next seizing on testimony; then committing itself to some popular impression, or some inward instinct, or some obscure memory; and thus it makes progress not unlike a clamberer on a steep cliff, who, by quick eye, prompt hand, and firm foot, ascends how he knows not himself, by personal endowments and by practice, rather than by rule, leaving no track behind him, and unable to teach another. It is not too much to say that the stepping by which great geniuses scale the mountains of truth is as unsafe and precarious to men in general, as the ascent of a skilful mountaineer up a literal crag. It is a way which they alone can take; and its justification lies in their success. And such mainly is the way in which all men, gifted or not gifted, commonly reason,—not by rule, but by an inward faculty.

For reasoning is 'not an art', Newman insists, but 'a living spontaneous energy within us', which the mind may later 'analyze' in its 'various processes'. No one can help reasoning, 'but all men do not reflect upon their own reasonings, much less reflect truly and accurately, so as to do justice to their own meaning'.

In other words, all men have a reason, but not all men can give a reason. We may denote, then, these two exercises of mind as reasoning and arguing, or as conscious and unconscious reasoning, or as Implicit Reason and Explicit Reasoning.

Anticipating the *Grammar of Assent*, Newman points out that different subjects call for different kinds of reasoning—'Some men's reason becomes genius in particular subjects, and is less than ordinary in others.' Somebody may be very good at analysing someone else's reasoning, and yet be 'as little creative of the reasoning itself which he analyzes, as a critic need possess the gift of writing poems'. The corollary is that faith, 'though in all cases a reasonable process, is not necessarily founded on investigation, argument, or proof; these processes being but the explicit form which the reasoning takes in the case of particular minds'. But he warns that 'No analysis is subtle and delicate enough to represent adequately the state of mind under which we believe, or the subjects of belief, as they are presented to our thoughts.' It is natural, therefore, that the advocates of Christianity should put forward 'as reasons for belief' those 'secondary points' which 'best admit of being exhibited in argument'—in other words, the so-called 'evidences'—rather than 'our more recondite feelings' which are usually 'the real reasons' for faith; for it is these latter 'momentous reasons' which are not susceptible of analysis and demonstration. Even the 'evidences' generally convince only 'upon a number of very minute circumstances together, which the mind is quite unable to count up and methodize in an argumentative form'. He ends on a warning note: the 'argumentative forms' which analyse or test reasoning are 'critical, not creative', and therefore are 'useful in raising objections, and in ministering to scepticism'. As he put it earlier in the sermon, there is a danger of 'weakening the springs of action by inquiring into them'.[18]

If there is one work of Newman which may truly be called 'seminal', it is surely the *Oxford University Sermons*, where he first explores some of his most brilliantly original ideas. The last two sermons, in fact, contain respectively the genesis of the *Idea of a University* and of the *Development of Christian Doctrine*. 'Wisdom, as Contrasted with Faith and with Bigotry' (1841) begins by distinguishing between faith as 'an exercise of the Reason, so spontaneous, unconscious, and unargumentative, as to seem at first sight even to be a moral act, and Wisdom being that orderly and mature development of thought, which in earthly language goes by the name of science and philosophy'. This leads to a more general consideration of the 'philosophical' mind. We are told that 'knowledge itself, though a condition of the mind's enlargement, yet, whatever be its range, is not that very thing which enlarges it', but that 'this enlargement consists in the comparison of the subjects of knowledge one with another'. Such a theory of the mind has educational implications:

It is not the mere addition to our knowledge which is the enlargement, but the

[18] *US* 253–60, 262, 266–7, 271–2, 274, 276.

change of place, the movement onwards, of that moral centre, to which what we know and what we have been acquiring, the whole mass of our knowledge, as it were, gravitates. And therefore a philosophical cast of thought, or a comprehensive mind, or wisdom in conduct or policy, implies a connected view of the old with the new; an insight into the bearing and influence of each part upon every other; without which there is no whole, and could be no centre. It is the knowledge, not only of things, but of their mutual relations. It is organized, and therefore living knowledge.

Newman is emphatic that 'knowledge without system is not Philosophy', whereas 'Philosophy is Reason exercised upon Knowledge', for 'Reason is the power of proceeding to new ideas by means of given ones.'

It is the power of referring every thing to its true place in the universal system ... It makes every thing lead to every thing else; it communicates the image of the whole body to every separate member, till the whole becomes in imagination like a spirit, every where pervading and penetrating its component parts, and giving them their one definite meaning.

There is no question of the truly 'philosophical' mind being 'possessed by some one object' or, on the other hand, lacking a 'firm grasp of principles' or a 'view':

... Philosophy cannot be partial, cannot be exclusive, cannot be impetuous, cannot be surprised, cannot fear, cannot lose its balance, cannot be at a loss, cannot but be patient, collected, and majestically calm, because it discerns the whole in each part, the end in each beginning, the worth of each interruption, the measure of each delay, because it always knows where it is, and how its path lies from one point to another.

The difference between 'genius' and 'philosophy' suggests an analogous distinction between 'faith' and 'wisdom' (the religious equivalent of 'philosophy'):

There are men who, when in difficulties, by the force of genius, originate at the moment vast ideas or dazzling projects; who, under the impulse of excitement, are able to cast a light, almost as if from inspiration, on a subject or course of action which comes before them; who have a sudden presence of mind equal to any emergency, rising with the occasion, and an undaunted heroic bearing, and an energy and keenness, which is but sharpened by opposition. Faith is a gift analogous to this thus far, that it acts promptly and boldly on the occasion, on slender evidence, as if guessing and reaching forward to the truth, amid darkness or confusion; but such is not the Wisdom of the perfect. Wisdom is the clear, calm, accurate vision, and comprehension of the whole course, and whole work of God ...

Because 'elementary principles' are 'necessary to the human mind', some kind of 'dogmatism and system' is inevitable—'it forms the stamina of thought, which, when it is removed, languishes, and droops.'

'Principle' is 'the life' of 'Wisdom, Bigotry, and Faith'—but 'Wisdom is the application of adequate principles to the state of things as we find them, Bigotry is the application of inadequate or narrow principles, while Faith is the maintenance of principles, without caring to apply or adjust them.' It is easy to confuse faith with bigotry, for 'what is Faith but a reaching forth after truth amid darkness, upon the warrant of certain antecedent notions', that is to say, 'a presumption about matters of fact, upon principle rather than on knowledge; and what is Bigotry also but this?' Moreover, although its 'grounds' are 'conditional', it issues in 'the absolute acceptance of a certain message or doctrine as divine'. But faith, though 'a presumption of facts under defective knowledge', is 'altogether a practical principle' and 'is exercised under a sense of personal responsibility'. Bigots, on the other hand, 'far from confessing ignorance and maintaining Truth mainly as a duty, profess . . . to understand the subjects which they take up and the principles which they apply to them'. The difference between bigotry and the wisdom 'it lays claim to' is highlighted when there are advances in new knowledge, Newman claims, using the kind of 'imperial' image so characteristic of the *Idea of a University*:

True philosophy admits of being carried out to any extent; it is its very test, that no knowledge can be submitted to it with which it is not commensurate, and which it cannot annex to its territory. But the theory of the narrow or bigoted has already run out within short limits, and a vast and anxious region lies beyond, unoccupied and in rebellion.[19]

The last and most brilliant of the sermons is 'The Theory of Developments in Religious Doctrine', preached on 2 February 1843. Taking as his text 'Mary kept all these things, and pondered them in her heart', Newman points to the Virgin Mary as 'our pattern of Faith, both in the reception and in the study of Divine Truth. She does not think it enough to accept, she dwells upon it . . . not enough to assent, she developes it.' In the course of the history of Christianity, 'a large fabric of divinity' has been 'reared, irregular in its structure, and diverse in its style, as beseemed the slow growth of centuries . . . but still, on the whole, the development of an idea, and like itself, and unlike any thing else'. The study of the formulation of particular dogmas is full of 'deep interest', for it shows 'how the great idea takes hold of a thousand minds by its living force . . . so that the doctrine may rather be said to use the minds of Christians, than to be used by them'.

Wonderful it is to see with what effort, hesitation, suspense, interruption,—with how many swayings to the right and to the left—with how many reverses, yet with what certainty of advance, with what precision in its march, and with

[19] *US* 279, 287, 289–93, 296–300, 305, 309.

what ultimate completeness, it has been evolved ... Wonderful, to see how heresy has but thrown that idea into fresh forms, and drawn out from it further developments, with an exuberance which exceeded all questioning, and a harmony which baffled all criticism ...

And this world of thought is the expansion of a few words, uttered, as if casually, by the fishermen of Galilee. ... Reason has not only submitted, it has ministered to Faith; it has illustrated its documents; it has raised illiterate peasants into philosophers and divines; it has elicited a meaning from their words which their immediate hearers little suspected. ... Its half sentences, its overflowings of language, admit of development; they have a life in them which shows itself in progress; a truth, which has the token of consistency; a reality, which is fruitful in resources; a depth, which extends into mystery: for they are representations of what is actual, and has a definite location and necessary bearings and a meaning in the great system of things, and a harmony in what it is, and a compatibility in what it involves. ... Here, too, is the badge of heresy; its dogmas are unfruitful; it has no theology; so far forth as it is heresy, it has none. Deduct its remnant of Catholic theology, and what remains? Polemics, explanations, protests. It turns to Biblical Criticism, or to the Evidences of Religion, for want of a province. Its *formulae* end in themselves, without development, because they are words; they are barren, because they are dead. If they had life, they would increase and multiply ... It develops into dissolution; but it creates nothing, it leads to no system, its resultant dogma is but the denial of all dogmas ...

(A few pages later, he remarks with smooth sarcasm that 'heretics in general, however opposed in tenets, are found to have an inexplicable sympathy for each other, and never wake up from their ordinary torpor, but to exchange courtesies and mediate coalitions.')

Newman now turns to consider the actual process of development:

Theological dogmas are propositions expressive of the judgments which the mind forms, or the impressions which it receives, of Revealed Truth. Revelation sets before it certain supernatural facts and actions, beings and principles; these make a certain impression or image upon it; and this impression spontaneously, or even necessarily, becomes the subject of reflection on the part of the mind itself ...

He is careful once again to insist that, 'naturally as the inward idea of divine truth ... passes into explicit form by the activity of our reflective powers, still such an actual delineation is not essential to its genuineness and perfection', so that a 'peasant may have such a true impression, yet be unable to give any intelligible account of it'. Indeed, the 'impression made upon the mind need not even be recognized' by the person 'possessing it'. Such 'unperceived impressions' are commonplace in life: thus people may not even be 'conscious' of 'an idea' of which they are actually 'possessed'. Nor is the 'absence, or partial absence, or incompleteness of dogmatic statements' any 'proof of the absence of impressions or implicit judgments, in the mind of the Church. Even centuries might pass without the formal expression of a truth, which had been all along the secret life of millions of faithful souls.' In the case of developments relating to the 'Objects of Faith', like the Trinity or the Incarnation where 'what was at first an impression on the Imagination' becomes 'a system or creed in the Reason', the 'developments . . . are mere portions of the original impression, and modes of representing it'. Such impressions 'are obviously individual and complete above other theological ideas, *because* they are the impression of Objects', and 'all our attempts to delineate' our impressions 'go to bring out one idea, not two or three or four . . . but an individual idea in its separate aspects'. On the other hand, 'Ideas and their developments are commonly not identical, the development being but the carrying out of the idea into its consequences', so that, for example, penance may be seen as a development of baptism, and 'yet still is a distinct doctrine'.

As we have seen, Newman's rejection of dogmatic liberalism does not lead him into the trap of fundamentalism. Dogmatic statements are 'necessary only because the human mind cannot reflect . . . except piecemeal' upon 'the one idea which they are designed to express', but they are only expressions of 'aspects' of the 'idea' and 'can never really be confused with the idea itself, which all such propositions taken together can but reach, and cannot exceed', and indeed to which they 'are never equivalent'—for 'dogmas are, after all, but symbols of a Divine fact, which, far from being compassed by those very propositions, would not be exhausted, nor fathomed, by a thousand.' Newman now goes on to give a classic statement of the relation of dogma to personal faith, which once again offers an alternative to the formalism of 'orthodoxy' on the one hand and the feelings of emotional Evangelicalism on the other:

That idea is not enlarged, if propositions are added, nor impaired if they are withdrawn: if they are added, this is with a view of conveying that one integral view, not of amplifying it. That view does not depend on such propositions: it does not consist in them; they are but specimens and indications of it. And they may be multiplied without limit. They are necessary, but not needful to it, being but portions or aspects of that previous impression which has at length come under the cognizance of Reason and the terminology of science. . . . [These] propositions imply each other, as being parts of one whole; so that to deny one is to deny all, and to invalidate one is to deface and destroy the view itself. One thing alone has to be impressed on us by Scripture, the Catholic idea, and in it they all are included. To object, then, to the number of propositions, upon which an anathema is placed, is altogether to mistake their use; for their multiplication is not intended to enforce many things, but to express one . . .

The error of 'doctrinal innovators', he adds, is 'to go away with this or that proposition of the Creed, instead of embracing that one idea which all of them together are meant to convey; it being almost a definition of heresy, that it fastens on some one statement as if the whole truth'— which 'is a proof that it does not really hold even that very statement for the sake of which it rejects the others'. Heresy, then, is something fundamentally *unreal*, whereas 'Realizing is the very life of true developments; it is peculiar to the Church, and the justification of her definitions.' As for the objection that dogmas cannot 'convey . . . knowledge of the Divine Nature itself', Newman is more than ready to admit that they 'convey no true idea of Almighty God, but only an earthly one, gained from earthly figures, provided it be allowed, on the other hand, that the senses do not convey to us any true idea of matter, but only an idea commensurate with sensible impressions'. For 'earthly figures and images' can only give us 'an approximation to the truth'. For that matter, the very 'diversities of language' in the world are a hindrance to 'communicating ideas', given the infinite complexity of ideas. Understanding between individuals is often difficult because of the lack of 'a common measure or economy to mediate between them'.[20]

The sermon would soon be developed into the full-length book on the development of doctrine that is one of the great classics of theology.

3

Newman's 'Retractation of Anti-Catholic Statements'[21] had finally appeared anonymously on 28 January 1843 in the *Conservative Journal*, not unobtrusively, as he had hoped, but under the eye-catching title 'Oxford and Rome' and with the editorial comment that the identity of the author would be obvious to readers. The timing was especially unfortunate as it coincided with the furore which followed the well-publicized conversion to Rome of a clergyman in the Lincoln diocese, called Bernard Smith. Newman had intended his conscientious attempt 'to eat a few dirty words of mine' to appear in December at 'a time of peace . . . when all was quiet', but the 'operation' had been 'delayed' against his wishes.[22] He asked Pusey to forgive him for what he would no doubt regard as a 'rash' act, 'but my conscience would not stand out'. He pointed out that Pusey himself had 'before now' remarked that Newman had said 'far severer things against Rome' than he had ever said; the time had come 'to unsay them'.[23] He explained at greater

---

[20] Ibid. 312–13, 316–18, 320–1, 323, 326, 329–32, 336–7, 339–42.
[21] See *VM* ii. 427–33, where (as in *Apo.*) the date of publication is wrongly given as Feb.
[22] To J. R. Hope, 25 Jan. 1843.　　　[23] To E. B. Pusey, 30 Jan. 1843.

length to James Hope that he had had two reasons for publishing the statement (not that he wanted it '*said* that I directly inserted it—I don't wish it talked about'): first, there was his 'long continued feeling of the great inconsistency I was in of letting things stand in print against me which I did not hold and which I could not but be contradicting by my actions every day of my life'; second, and more compelling, was the feeling that he

was taking people in—that they thought me what I was not, and were trusting me when they should not—and this has been at times a very painful feeling indeed. I don't want to be trusted . . . people *won't* believe I go so far as I do—they will cling to their hopes. . . . I am not aware that I have any great motive for this paper beyond this, setting myself right, and wishing to be seen in my proper colours, and not unwilling to do such penance for wrong words as lies in the necessary criticism which such a retractation will involve on the part of friends and enemies . . .[24]

He expressed the fervent wish to Tom Mozley that his statement, now that it was 'afloat', would just 'swim away and be forgotten'. He intended, so far as possible, 'to keep a dead silence' himself, although it was painful 'to be puzzling people' and also 'very annoying to know that any doing of mine is public talk'.[25] If people wanted to 'criticize' the way he had made the announcement, 'let them'—he no longer had a 'character to lose'. He begged Pusey to reply, if asked, that he 'knew nothing about it. Please say I am obstinate and dangerous and impracticable.'[26]

When he talked about having 'a guilty conscience', he meant, he confided to Henry Wilberforce,

to express my deep feeling that people do not know me, and that I am a Roman in my heart when they think me an Anglican. I am sure I have no wish to take people in, yet, having out grown former faith by present convictions, I have managed effectually to do so . . . I can truly say that the idea of people's trusting me when I am not trustworthy has long made me very uncomfortable. Yet what can I do? how is it possible to give persons a right impression of what I would say when every word is sure to be misunderstood, every admission to be exaggerated, every avowal to be considered but a hint of what is unsaid, when there is the certainty of unsettling people, and when it is far easier to say what I have not confidence in, than what I have.

If there was anything that would give him 'confidence' in the Church of England, it was the presence of 'such good' people in it—but then there was the danger of the argument becoming circular—'they continuing good Anglicans, because they think that I am'. Finally, he was

---

[24] To J. R. Hope, 3 Feb. 1843.   [25] To T. Mozley, 3 Feb. 1843.
[26] To E. B. Pusey, 3 Feb. 1843.

despondent because he would like 'to be out of hot water, and something or other is always sousing me again in it. It is so very difficult to steer between being hypocritical, and revolutionary.'[27] If only, he groaned to Pusey, people would 'not have confidence in me—because I have not confidence in myself'. One of his 'greatest troubles' was that 'younger persons trust me, who should not'.[28] Indeed, friends reproached him for using words in his writings which were strictly true in the sense in which he used them, but which had a much more anti-Roman effect on his readers.

On his birthday he wrote to Jemima to reassure her that his retraction appeared to have caused remarkably little excitement at Oxford. Not only that, but the redoubtable President of Magdalen, Martin Routh, had asked him for the fifth time, in spite of earlier vociferous objections, to examine for a scholarship in theology; it was a nuisance as he wanted to stay 'quietly' at Littlemore—'but it is so good a joke that I can scarcely wish it otherwise.'[29] He had another joke with which to regale Tom Mozley—how the eccentric J. B. Morris 'once at a breakfast table after long silence turned round to a nice and pretty young lady who was next to him and said with his peculiar smile that he thought it not worse to burn a man for heresy than to hang him for sheepstealing'![30]

It was a relief to laugh now that he had unburdened himself of his confessional statement, particularly when it seemed to have caused so little hostile reaction. But meanwhile he was continuing to lead a far from light-hearted life at Littlemore, which he described in a letter to Maria Giberne:

We have one joint-meal . . . during the day, at 5 PM, which four days in the week consists of meat, generally cold. We break fast . . . not before noon . . . but separately and standing. We keep silence till 2 or 3 PM according as it is winter or summer, and resume it at 8 or 9. We begin services at 6 AM—in Advent we begin at 3.

When they were 'out of cloister', for example in Oxford, they were 'free from all rules'. Friends who came to stay for a few days also kept the rule, with the exception sometimes of the long fast in the morning. The cottages were 'full' and they needed 'more room', so he was going to 'cut off' his own bedroom and another in order to 'get two more cells'. The new squire, Mr Crawley, and his wife were 'a great acquisition', being 'thoroughly Catholic people'. He mentioned that he intended 'to master' the 'very instructive' *Spiritual Exercises* of St Ignatius Loyola. (Some weeks later he was to note that 'finding the holiness of the Roman Saints *since* our separation', particularly of the Jesuits, had 'very much' 'affected' his 'feelings' and seemed to be an answer to his complaint that the Roman Church lacked the note of sanctity.[31]) He was writing, he reminded Maria, on the anniversary of Hurrell Froude's death: 'What would have been his thoughts, what his views, had he lived to this day?'[32] The day was Shrove Tuesday and, although he did not say so, he was about to begin the most severe of his Lenten fasts at Littlemore.

Quiet as things might be in Oxford, Newman was not free of controversy. Newspaper reports had appeared alleging that Bernard Smith had been encouraged to retain his living after going over to Rome, which Newman took to be an allusion to himself. For the benefit of the Bishop of Lincoln he reiterated the categorical denial of the story which he had sent to the papers, but he added emphatically and pointedly that he could 'see nothing wrong' in 'a person holding Roman Catholic opinions' and at the same time 'continuing in communion with us, provided he holds no preferment or office, abstains from the management of ecclesiastical affairs, and is bound by no subscription or oath to our doctrines'.[33]

In March he heard that his *University Sermons* were already going into a second edition. It was 'unaccountable', considering both that all his other sermons had taken a year to exhaust the first edition and also that many of these sermons were on 'very abstruse subjects'—it was impossible to believe that they had been 'bought for their contents'. Meanwhile, the library at Littlemore was beginning to overflow, and all the rooms in the cottages had been 'full for months'; they would have to divide all the 'sets of rooms into two to admit more inmates'.[34] Because they lacked in the Church of England the customary forms and safeguards of 'religious' life, Newman felt it was 'allowable or necessary to pick and choose our associates, and to make personal attachment the principle of admission', although it seemed to be agreed that the practice of 'sacramental confession' should be a condition of belonging to the community.[35] They used the offices in the Roman Breviary for their services, but they omitted the invocations to the saints (as incompatible with the Articles) and kept to the Anglican calendar, only adding those saints who were mentioned in the Homilies. What he particularly liked about Roman devotional works was 'their great and business-like practicalness': they met definite spiritual needs. The only problem was that

RCs cannot write English. Our literature is essentially Protestant—All our great writers are such—all the strength, richness, and elegance of the language is devoted to the maintenance of Protestantism. RCs are driven to foreign

[31] Memorandum, 17 Mar.–12 Apr. 1843. [32] To Miss M. Giberne, 28 Feb. 1843.
[33] To Bishop of Lincoln, 7 Mar. 1843. [34] To S. Rickards, 7 Mar. 1843.
[35] To W. Dodsworth, 18 Mar. 1844.

writers—they write their own language, in consequence, like foreigners—It is not English—It is Latin or French.

As for Anglicans, they would not have 'devotional writers' till they had 'ascetical livers'. For real spiritual writing could only come from spiritual people—'It cannot be done by the stroke of a pen.' In a similar way, he warned Mary Holmes, the question of converting to Rome was much more than a mere intellectual exercise:

You must be patient, you must wait for the *eye* of the soul to be formed in you. Religious truth is reached, not by reasoning, but by an inward perception. Any one can reason; only disciplined, educated, formed minds can perceive.[36]

In the middle of March Newman contacted Keble again about the possibility of retiring from St Mary's. His 'difficulty' had not 'diminished' since he wrote two and half years ago. He was 'so bewildered' that he felt he did 'not know right from wrong' and had 'no confidence of being real in any thing I think or say'. His position had been made even more invidious by the almost 'unanimous condemnation' by the bishops of *Tract 90*. How could he continue at St Mary's 'with any sense of propriety'? He wondered at himself for not having resigned long ago. He could not even feel secure in the knowledge that he was 'in the right': after all, his interpretation of the Thirty-nine Articles had 'never been drawn out, to say the least, before', and the undeniable fact was that he was 'not advocating . . . not promoting, the Anglican system of doctrine, but one very much more resembling . . . the doctrine of the Roman Church. I have nothing to *fall back upon*.' There was another factor to be considered: against the objection that by resigning he would be 'recklessly tossing away influence' was the fact that he was increasingly busy 'directing . . . the consciences of persons'—so much so that he guessed he would have a great deal more 'pastoral' work to do if he left St Mary's. The main argument against doing so was that it would 'seem to imply a great dissatisfaction with the Church of England'.[37] Perhaps some arrangement could now be made whereby he could keep Littlemore. Still, it was hardly likely that his resignation would cause any surprise.

At the end of April came news of the death of S. F. Wood, who had been ill for some time. He had lost 'a very dear friend', Newman wrote to Jemima, adding confidentially, 'I think, he considered the Church of Rome the true Church,—but thought God had placed him where he was.' He ought to be grateful to God for sending him 'new friends' in place of 'old' ones, although they did make him 'feel so very antique'.[38] It

---

[36] To Miss M. Holmes, 8 Mar. 1843.   [37] To J. Keble, 14 Mar. 1843.
[38] To Mrs J. Mozley, 30 Apr. 1843.

was Wood who had first suggested to Newman the idea of taking the cottages at Littlemore. He was a genuinely spiritual man at a time when 'to try to cultivate personal holiness, is all that is left us'.[39]

At the beginning of May Keble wrote to say that he would not be against Newman's retiring from St Mary's provided he could continue to exercise his ministry at Littlemore. On the same day, C. P. Eden, Newman's prospective successor at St Mary's, made it clear that he would not let him take weekday prayers at Littlemore in the event of his resigning as Vicar. He decided now to tell Keble 'something which has at last been forced upon my full consciousness'.

There is something about myself, which is no longer a secret to me—and if not to me, surely it ought not to be so to someone else; and I think that other person should be you whose advice I have always wished to follow.

He felt extremely diffident about trying to decide properly his real state of mind—particularly when

Some thoughts are like hideous dreams, and we wake from them, and think they will never return; and though they do return, we cannot be sure still that they are more than vague fancies; and till one is so sure they are not, as to be afraid of concealing within what is at variance with one's professions, one does not like, or rather it is wrong, to mention them to another.

He had put down what he had to say on a separate sheet of paper, which he knew would cause Keble 'most dreadful suffering'.

After telling of the traumatic summer of 1839, he confessed that his 'feeling' about Rome, 'though fading and reviving, has been on the whole becoming stronger and deeper'. Now that he had come to the point, he did not spare his friend:

as far as I can realize my own convictions, I consider the Roman Catholic Communion the Church of the Apostles, and that what grace is among us . . . is extraordinary, and from the overflowings of His Dispensation.

I am very far *more* sure that England is in schism, than that the Roman additions to the Primitive Creed may not be developments, arising out of a keen and vivid realizing of the Divine Depositum of faith.

All this is so shocking to say, that I do not know whether to wish that I am exaggerating to you my feelings or not.

You will now understand what gives edge to the Bishops' charges, without any undue sensitiveness on my part. They distress me in two ways; 1. as being in some sense protests and witnesses to my conscience against my secret unfaithfulness to the English Church; and 2. next, as being average samples of her teaching and tokens how very far she is from even aspiring to Catholicity.

Rogers, who perhaps knew his mind better than any of his friends, had

---

[39] To Miss M. Giberne, 11 May 1843.

refused for the past two years to advise him 'one way or the other', and had only very recently explained why: 'that it would be treachery in him to the English Church, to assist one who is conducting a movement, tending to carry over her members to Rome'. Rogers had touched a sore point, for 'being unfaithful to a trust is my great subject of dread'.[40]

Keble replied that he was afraid that if Newman retired altogether from active ministry, the danger of his going over to Rome would be greatly increased. He did not know enough to comment on the historical evidence from the early Church which had so impressed Newman, but he did think that Newman was being too impatient about the Church of England, especially its bishops, from whom one could not at present expect much, and also perhaps reacting excessively against his earlier attacks on Rome. Certainly Newman's secession from the Church of England would be the gravest possible set-back to all the progress the Movement had made. But he begged him not to be too influenced by anything he said.

Newman replied that he did not feel he was being impulsive, although it was true 'I have now laid down my arms rather suddenly', thanks to the recent rebuffs from Rogers and Eden. By staying at St Mary's he was 'exposing' himself 'to a constant risk of detection', considering all 'the eyes, friendly and hostile,' which were upon him; 'A detection would be far more calamitous, than a quiet withdrawal while things were so tranquil.' He had done his best to dissuade people from going over to Rome, but his 'arguments', however 'efficacious' with those for whom they were intended, were such as 'to infuse suspicions of me in the minds of lookers-on'. The fact was that he was 'an offence and stumbling block' by remaining at St Mary's. People were 'keen sighted enough to make out' what he thought 'on certain points', and then they inferred that having 'such opinions' was 'compatible with holding situations of trust in the Church'. Was it not the case that his 'present position' was 'a cruelty' to these people, 'as well as a treachery towards the Church'? Last summer he had thought of 'publishing the Lives of the Saints', thinking 'it would be useful, as employing the minds of persons who were in danger of running wild, and bringing them from doctrine to history, from speculation to fact; again, as giving them an interest in the English soil and English church, and keeping them from seeking sympathy in Rome as she is; and further, as tending to promote the spread of right views'. Unfortunately, he had begun to realize that if the project went ahead, it would be 'a practical carrying out' of *Tract 90*, 'from the character of the usages and opinions of Ante-reformation times'. However, plans had so far advanced that 'it would create much surprise

---

[40] To J. Keble, 4 May 1843.

and talk, were it now suddenly given over'. Yet how was it 'compatible with my holding St Mary's, being what I am'? On the other hand, he wondered, with his usual readiness to look at every possible argument and aspect of a problem, would not his commitment as editor of such a series be 'in itself a sort of guarantee, in addition to the Editorship of the Library of the Fathers and my Fellowship, of my remaining quiet, though I did not retain St Mary's for that purpose'?[41]

He could at least make use of his own misery to help those who were looking to him for guidance. 'I have no doubt you often feel forlorn—', he wrote to Mary Holmes, 'but recollect that is the fate, not only of yourself, but of all . . . who wish to live a life to God and religion—they are pilgrims on earth, and have no business here—and seem in the way to other people.'[42] It is noticeable how he did not speak in some special (unreal) way when he gave spiritual counsel, but in his usual colloquial and even ironic tone of voice. However, he groaned to Henry Wilberforce, there was nobody who needed 'guidance and comfort' more than he himself, who was in no position to offer advice to others. The irony was that he could have 'a clear path' if only he could 'trust' himself, so 'flourishing' was the Movement, with new adherents 'coming over' and new 'openings' and 'lines of influence' offering themselves.[43] Unfortunately, he could no longer even give an 'opinion' on 'Church matters', but felt 'like a person whose fingers are numbed'.[44]

At the beginning of June, however, 'the first formal University act' was taken against the Tractarian party.[45] It was announced that Pusey had been suspended from preaching for two years on account of a (quite restrained) sermon on the Eucharist he had preached in May in Christ Church Cathedral, which had been denounced as heretical by Faussett to the Vice-Chancellor. Newman thought there should be 'some demonstration' in defence of Pusey—'if one thing after another is done against the holders of Catholic doctrines, without protest from any quarter, the imagination of certain persons will be gradually affected with the notion that the Church of England does not hold them, and is not their place.'[46] If there was widespread support for Pusey, then the authorities could well come to regret what seemed a very injudicious act—for not only was there no 'Puseyite' so generally 'revered' as Pusey, but the unfair way in which he had been condemned had alienated moderate opinion.[47] But, on the other hand, the University statutes gave the authorities a power unheard of elsewhere except in the army, and it looked as if there was a concerted and determined effort 'to put down

[41] To J. Keble, 18 May 1843.
[43] To H. Wilberforce, 16 May 1843.
[45] To Mrs J. Mozley, 24 May 1843.
[47] To Miss M. Holmes, 4 June 1843.

[42] To Miss M. Holmes, 14 May 1843.
[44] To C. Anderson, 21 Jan. 1843.
[46] To W. Dodsworth, 4 June 1843.

Catholicism at any risk', even that of driving people out of the Church.[48] Never had Oxford been in such turmoil since the beginning of the Movement. Newman was afraid of the effect on Pusey, who seemed to him to live 'in a sanguine imagination about the state of things', and whose deeply 'conservative' instincts were not conducive to adapting to a position of 'opposition' as opposed to 'authority'.[49] But his anxiety did not prevent him from entertaining his Aunt Elizabeth with the marvellous story of 'the Devonshire Farmer' who

had heard Dr Pusey very much abused, and had believed and joined in the abuse. At last he was undeceived, and being a generous fellow, and not knowing how else to relieve the painful feeling of remorse which came upon him, being just then about to send up a bull to Derby to stand for the prize, he gave it the name of Dr Pusey—and as such I believe it has been entered in the books, perhaps in the report, of the British Agricultural and Farming Society. . . . You see how Puseyism is spreading. It has reached our very cattle. Here is the first Puseyite bull. Our domestic animals will be the next victims. Homer talks of the plague falling first on mules and dogs, then on man. This has observed a reverse order; except that I think Heads of Houses will catch it last. We shall have Puseyite lapdogs and kittens—butcher's meat and grocery will come next—till at last we shall be unable to pay a morning call, or put our candle out at night without Puseyism.[50]

At the end of July Newman, in reply to an enquiry from William Froude's wife Catherine, wrote that he wished he could write her

a real open letter, saying just what I think—but I feel it so difficult to bring out what I would say, that when I attempt it, I become unreal. One difficulty is the analysing and knowing one's feelings—but another is to be able to exhibit them on occasion. I do not carry them in my hand, and, much as I wish it, I cannot put you in possession of them on the mere asking.

There was no question that he was 'approximating towards Rome' or that 'those who are very much about me see this, little as I wish it'. He had decided to resign St Mary's, feeling he was 'no longer able to fulfil such a *trust*, as a pastoral charge in our Church implies'. He was 'dissatisfied' with the Church of England and its authorities were 'dissatisfied' with him: 'I do not see what good can come of continuing a relation, which each party wishes brought to an end.' By continuing to hesitate about taking the step, he might get into 'serious difficulties' if his situation changed. But at the moment he did not 'see beyond' retiring from St Mary's and continuing to live at Littlemore as he was already doing. He promised he would 'do nothing sudden, or without people in general being prepared for it'. Providence might 'leave' him 'just' where

[48] To A. St John, 20 June 1843.   [49] To W. Dodsworth, 28 June 1843.
[50] To Miss E. Newman, 28 July 1843.

he was—or 'lead' him on 'further': 'His guidance is commonly slow.' In the meantime, it was important to live in the present rather than the future. It was 'a very cool letter' he was sending her, but then she had asked him 'a very cool question—and as you are about the only person who have so asked, you are the only person who has been so answered'.[51]

Towards the end of August he approached Keble about the possibility of his publishing the sermons he had preached at the end of 1841 as part of a volume to be called, perhaps, 'Sermons on Subjects of the Day'. These sermons had had the desired effect of 'quieting some persons who felt unsettled as to Rome'. He himself had 'felt the argument' of the four sermons in question when he had written them—

I feel it now (tho' not so strongly, I suppose.)—I think it is mainly (whether correctly analyzed in them and drawn out, or not) what reconciles me to our position. But I don't feel confident, judging of myself by former changes, that I shall think it a good argument 5 years hence. Now, is it fair, I think it is, to put forward the argument under such circumstances? I think it *is* fair to stop people in a headlong movement, (if that is possible)—to give them time to think—to give the English cause the advantage of this argument—and to see what comes of it, as to myself, so to others.

He thought, then, that he could with honesty publish them now as fairly representing his position, even if he could not be sure he would not change his mind. As for the objection that his argument involved a use of private judgement on Scripture, which was not authorized by any authority, he could only say that they were in an unprecedented situation. If it seemed to be 'holding water' and really convincing people, then this 'ought to have a great effect upon me'. Their publication now 'would be a sort of guarantee that my resigning St Mary's (to which I am more and more strongly drawn) did not involve an ulterior step—for no one could suppose that I should be publishing today, and leaving the Church tomorrow'. A few days later he wrote to say that he had just heard that one of the Littlemore 'inmates', William Lockhart, was about to go over to Rome: 'Would *this* be a good excuse for giving up St Mary's?'[52] He was very shaken by the news, because he had only taken Lockhart in on the understanding that he would wait for three years before making any move. Since Lockhart had been teaching in the school up to the time he left, it would cause 'a great scandal'. He warned Jemima of the step which he was about to take and which he had postponed deliberately till October 'for safety'. He was very sorry that it would upset her and others, but he too was very upset at the prospect of losing Littlemore. He was comforted by the conviction that 'Every thing that one does honestly, sincerely, with

[51] To Mrs W. Froude, 28 July 1843.   [52] To J. Keble, 20, 25 Aug.; 6, 29 Sept. 1843.

prayer, with advice, must turn to good.'[53] He was more open with her brother-in-law James Mozley, to whom he wrote in confidence, 'I am not a good son enough of the Church of England, to feel I can in conscience hold preferment under her. I love the Church of Rome too well.' He asked him to burn the letter, 'there's a good fellow, for you sometimes let letters lie on your mantle piece'.[54] Against Keble's suggestion that he should wait till things quietened down again, he argued that his resignation would cause a sensation whenever it took place, that the more he delayed it the more difficult it would become, and that the Lockhart scandal at least provided a *'reason'* for resigning—indeed, 'I do not know how I can hold up my head again while I have St Mary's'.[55]

Lockhart's announcement was followed rapidly by the much more disturbing news that Tom Mozley himself was on the point of going over. Newman hastened over to Cholderton to try and dissuade him. Travelling suggested a strikingly vivid metaphor to him when he told James Hope of the latest developments: 'the movement is going so fast, that some of the wheels are catching fire.'[56] Tom, who was now more than ready to give up the *British Critic*, refused to give any undertakings. In Newman's view he was much too inclined to be self-willed 'and not to mind others'.[57] In the end Tom did not leave the Church of England, but Harriett, who had become more and more alienated from her brother's religious views, blamed him for her husband's attack of 'Roman fever' and effectively broke off relations.

Newman complained to Keble that his attempts to keep others from Rome were only doing himself 'harm—for I feel that the collision which drives them from Rome drives me . . . in the other direction': it was impossible to 'speak in a sufficiently real way about it' and his words could only be 'cold upon paper', but he was very much afraid that his talk with Tom had done him 'a good deal of harm, that is, has increased my conviction of the false position we are in, if that is harm'.[58] There was no question but he would have to give up St Mary's. He had originally wanted to wait till October, by which time all the bishops' triennial *charges* since *Tract 90* would be out; but it was obvious by September that there were to be no exceptions to the chorus of condemnation, the only differences being in the degree of censure. Anyway, the Lockhart affair in itself was sufficient reason for resigning.

On 7 September he sent his letter of resignation to Bishop Bagot. He pointed out that nobody should be surprised at his going now, 'when so many Bishops have said such things of me, and no one has taken my part

---

[53] To Mrs J. Mozley, 28, 31 Aug. 1843.
[54] To J. B. Mozley, 1 Sept. 1843.
[55] To J. Keble, 1 Sept. 1843.
[56] To J. Hope, 5 Sept. 1843.
[57] To T. Mozley, 7 Oct. 1843.
[58] To J. Keble, 5 Sept. 1843.

in respect to that interpretation of the articles under which alone I can subscribe them'. He had done his best to serve the Church of England: 'I am not relaxing my zeal, till it has been disowned by her rulers; I have not retired from her service till I have lost or forfeited her confidence.'[59]

On 25 September he preached on the anniversary of the consecration of the church at Littlemore. 'The Parting of Friends' was the last sermon he preached as an Anglican, and appropriately enough he took as his text the same verse of the Psalms which he had taken for the first sermon he ever wrote: 'Man goeth forth to his work and to his labour until the evening.' After movingly recalling some of the great farewells and partings of Scripture, the preacher concludes with his own deeply emotional leave-taking:

And, O my brethren, O kind and affectionate hearts, O loving friends, should you know any one whose lot it has been, by writing or by word of mouth, in some degree to help you thus to act; if he has ever told you what you knew about yourselves, or what you did not know; has read to you your wants or feelings, and comforted you by the very reading; has made you feel that there was a higher life than this daily one, and a brighter world than that you see; or encouraged you, or sobered you, or opened a way to the inquiring, or soothed the perplexed; if what he has said or done has ever made you take interest in him, and feel well inclined towards him; remember such a one in time to come, though you hear him not, and pray for him, that in all things he may know God's will, and at all times he may be ready to fulfil it.[60]

When Manning remonstrated with Newman for resigning out of pique, he was warned that he was engaging in 'a dangerous correspondence'. And Newman proceeded to tell him about the fateful summer of 1839. Events since then had not caused his present state of mind, but they had acted as 'keen stimulants and weighty confirmations of a conviction' which his 'theological reading', undertaken '*in the course of duty*' (he had not noticed this fact till now), had 'forced' on him. He knew he was innocent of the charge of 'impatience'. But he had to point out that an intervention like that of Manning had the opposite effect of that intended:

It makes me realize my views to myself, it makes me see their consistency, it assures me of my own deliberateness—it suggests to me the traces of a Providential Hand. It takes away the pain of disclosures, it relieves me of a heavy secret.

He had told his secret to only a few people, either because they asked or because they guessed, but he realized that many suspected it, and he was

---

[59] To Bishop of Oxford, 7 Sept. 1843.   [60] *SD* 409.

'quite haunted by the one dreadful whisper repeated from so many quarters, and causing the keenest distress to friends'.[61]

4

At the beginning of April he had mentioned to Bowden a plan he had of editing a series of lives of the 'Saints of the British Isles'. He intended 'the work to be historical and devotional, but not controversial'; miracles he thought could be 'treated as matters of fact, credible according to their evidence'.[62] At the beginning of November he told James Hope that Pusey's fear that the projected 'Lives of the Saints would cause a sensation' had thrown him into 'great perplexity'. He had only 'entered into the scheme, after the delay of months, for the sake of others', and now he was afraid that 'stopping it may in various ways tend to precipitate certain persons (readers, if you will) towards Rome'. It was all very well to reply, 'Give facts without comment', but nothing was 'so dry as mere facts', and in order to sell the work had to be 'ethical—but to be ethical, is merely to colour a narrative with one's own mind, or to give a *tone* to it'. Now since church history was made up of 'three elements—miracles, monkery, popery', it was impossible to view it sympathetically without betraying 'a feeling in favour of miracles, or monkery, or popery, one or all'. Nor was it possible to present facts with total detachment—'Opinion comes in at every step of the history.' Having heard Pusey's objection, he was very doubtful whether to go ahead with publication; but what he did know was that the lives could not be published without causing 'offence'. He had thought at first very seriously of abandoning the project. On the other hand, he had a responsibility towards those who had already started writing and who stood to lose financially if nothing came of their work; besides, he knew from his own younger days 'how very annoying such a disappointment is'. However, work was so far advanced on the series that it was 'most unlikely' it would stop if he withdrew; others would take over who would 'go further'. Anyway, given that he had 'no misgivings' himself, perhaps now after nearly three years he had no right to be silent any longer, when he had 'the means of making a protest'. Was he 'never to move'? Was it to be said that the Church of England 'cannot . . . bear the Lives of her Saints'? If the lives had 'a strong Roman effect', this was inevitable, because 'the times were Roman'.[63] It was the same with publishing the Breviary, he warned Pusey: 'however corrected', it could

---

[61] To H. E. Manning, 25, 31 Oct. 1843. [62] To J. W. Bowden, 3 Apr. 1843.
[63] To J. Hope, 2, 6, 26 Nov. 1843.

not but 'prepare minds for the Church of Rome'—'I do not think our system will bear it. It is like sewing a new piece of cloth on an old garment.' When Pusey wondered if it might not lead the Church of England rather than its individual members towards Rome, Newman responded that it would be 'like attempting to bend a stick—if it does not bend, it will break'.[64]

Pusey had raised his objection to the 'Lives of the Saints' after seeing by chance in Newman's room some proofs of the first *Life*, that of St Stephen Harding by J. D. Dalgairns, a member of the Littlemore community. However, he did not want Newman to go by his opinion alone. So Newman consulted Hope and also Gladstone, who both expressed strong misgivings. He immediately decided to abandon the project, although it was disheartening to find that the Church of England 'cannot hear the lives of her Saints'. (As he later remarked, it was events like this which forced upon the 'imagination' the conclusion of the reason or intellect that the Church of England lacked Catholicity: 'Propositions become facts.') Such *Lives* as had already been written would be published as individual works, but not as parts of a uniform series bearing his name as editor. He had taken the decision, he told Hope, to avoid 'administering a continual blister to the kind feelings' of sympathizers like Gladstone. He was also reluctant to expose himself by giving the bishops a sitting target to 'aim at'.[65] He still hoped that enough *Lives* would come out individually as eventually to make up a series.

In December he wrote again to Mrs William Froude, expressing his sorrow for 'unsettling' her by his abandonment of the *Via Media*: it was only natural that she should begin 'to be sceptical about all arguments, and to question whether truth can be found, or is any where'. But he could at least plead that it had been plain throughout the *Prophetical Office* that he was very afraid 'lest the view should prove a mere paper view, a fine theory, which would not work, which would not move. I felt strongly the objection that it has never been carried into effect, and in the opening sentences of the last Lecture I speak in the language of despondency.' One conclusion to be drawn was 'that it is a duty to be very slow in taking up and acting upon any new belief'. It was true that his earlier view 'was biassed (properly so) by a deference to the system in which one found oneself', whereas his present view was 'unwillingly forced upon the mind'—but there was still very good reason 'for dreading lest one should be the sport of mere argumentative demonstrations'. Only time could tell whether a view would 'hold', but then there was the 'consolation, that, if time has shown the untenableness of one, it

---

[64] To E. B. Pusey, 2, 18 Dec. 1843.   [65] To J. Hope, 11, 16 Dec. 1843; 14 Mar. 1844.

will do the like service to another, if it be untenable'. Fortunately, his own developing philosophy of religious belief provided a theory to fit the situation:

Time alone can turn a view into a conviction—It is most unsatisfactory to be acting on a syllogism, or a solitary, naked, external, logical process. But surely it is possible in process of time to have a proposition so wrought into the mind, both ethically and by numberless fine conspiring and ever-recurring consider-ations as to become part of our mind, to be inseparable from us, and to command our obedience.

With an obvious allusion to his own possible move to Rome, he added: 'And then the greater the sacrifice, the more cogent the testimony shall we have to its authority, for to overcome impediments is a token of power.' There was finally the consideration that only time could 'show whether what forces itself upon us, influences others also': if others 'were not moved' by the same arguments ('and their impassibleness could not be referred to definite causes'), this would be 'a very strong' reason for not going on one's own 'private judgment'. He was upset that he had been so little able in the time available to explain his position at his last meeting with William—'Every thing I said seemed to be shot out like bullets, round and hard and sudden—Arguments ought to grow out of the mind'; but this was hardly possible when friends only saw each other rarely.[66]

Towards the end of January 1844 he wrote to Keble to report on his current state of mind, at the risk of 'saying what is unreal'. He had 'a steadily growing conviction about the English Church', not from any 'effort' of his own but from his study of the early Church. He still wanted to 'resist' it, as well as feeling it his 'duty' to do so. He was 'sure, *if* it be right to go forward,' that he would be 'forced on in spite of' himself, but he had reservations on the question of 'dutifulness'—'Was it undutiful-ness to the Mosaic Law, to be led on to the Gospel?' What he wanted was, 'not to go by my own judgment, but by something external, like the pillar of the cloud in the desert'—such as the 'united movement of *many*'. Or again, if the publication of the four sermons 'were permanently to stop people, this would have a great influence on me'. He would then 'think there was something *real* in the view', whereas he was afraid they were 'only ingenious', in other words, unreal. But what he did know from the letters he received was that 'a movement is going on in cases which are little suspected and in minds which are struggling against it'. Sometimes, he added, he had 'uncomfortable feelings' about dying a member of the Church of England, and if his time were 'cut short' he would have to make a decision on 'what seemed most probable'.[67] In

[66] To Mrs W. Froude, 9 Dec. 1843.   [67] To J. Keble, 23 Jan. 1844.

February he told Pusey bluntly that he was not in a state of 'perplexity or anxiety', but rather that ever since the summer of 1839,

I have had a conviction, weaker or stronger, but on the whole constantly growing, and at present very strong, that we are not part of the Catholic Church. I am too much accustomed to this idea to feel pain at it. I could only feel pain, if I found it led me to action. At present I do not feel any such call. Such feelings are not hastily to be called convictions, though this seems to me to be such. Did I ever arrive at a full persuasion that it was such, then I should be anxious and much perplexed.[68]

He admitted to Bowden that with his 'opinions, to the full of which I dare not confess,' he felt 'like a guilty person': people kindly sympathized with him over his disappointments and trials—but 'I have nothing to bear but the anxiety which I feel for my friends' anxiety for me and perplexity'.[69] The deepening of his conviction about Rome involved a change or rather development in his own doctrinal views. He tells us in the *Apologia* that it was perhaps 'some way into 1844' before he could be said 'fully to have got over' his objection to invocations of the Saints.[70] In March he admitted to Keble, 'for myself I have no difficulty in the Breviary in toto, though you are the first person to whom I say so.'[71]

Once again he was in correspondence with Mrs Froude, contending that changes of view were inevitable, if truth and falsehood really were 'objective realities'. He saw no need to apologize for having 'defended the system' in which he had been brought up:

For is it not one's duty, instead of beginning with criticism, to throw oneself generously into that form of religion which is providentially put before one? Is it right, is it not wrong, to begin with private judgment? May we not on the other hand look for a blessing *through* obedience even to an erroneous system, and a guidance by means of it out of it? Were those who were strict and conscientious in their Judaism, or those who were lukewarm and sceptical, more likely to be led into Christianity, when Christ came? Yet in proportion to their previous zeal, would be their appearance of inconsistency. Certainly I have always contended that obedience even to an erring conscience was the way to gain light—and that it mattered not where a man began, so that he began on what came to hand and in faith . . .

He stressed that his fateful study of the Monophysite controversy and the Council of Chalcedon in the summer of 1839 had come about 'in the course of my *regular* reading'. What he found had astonished him. Up till then he had read the history of the early Church 'with the eyes of our Divines, and taken what they said on faith', but now he had '*a key*, which

---

[68] To E. B. Pusey, 19 Feb. 1844.   [69] To J. W. Bowden, 21 Feb. 1844.

[70] *Apo.* 178.   [71] To J. Keble, 2 Mar. 1844.

interpreted large passages of history which had been locked up from me'. Everywhere he found 'one and the same picture, prophetic of our present state, the Church in communion with Rome decreeing, and heretics resisting'. With regard particularly to the Arians, he could not understand how he could have been 'so blind before! except that I looked at things bit by bit, instead of putting them together'.

There were two parties, a Via Media, and an extreme, both heretical—but the Via Media contained pious men . . . there were the kings of the earth taking up the heresy against the Church—there was precisely the same appeal to Scripture, which now obtains, and that grounded on a literal interpretation of its text, to which St Athanasius always opposed the 'ecclesiastical sense'—there was the same complaint of introducing novel and unscriptural terms into the Creed of the Church. . .

Shaken as he was, he immediately proceeded—on principle—to try and find arguments in defence of

the form of doctrine and the religious system in which we find ourselves. I think such resistance pleasing to God. If it is His will to lead us from them, if the doubt comes from Him, He will repeat the suggestion. . . . Fancies, excitements, feelings go and never return—truth comes again and is importunate. The system in which we have been placed is God's voice to us, till He supersede it . . .

The long letters to Mrs Froude continued, with Newman obviously relieved to have a sympathetic confidante to whom he could pour out the thoughts that had troubled him for so long. He had great difficulties, he explained, with the Anglican theory that the Church was 'one' because it was 'a *succession*' as opposed to 'one *kingdom*, one body politic'. This meant that every bishop was quite independent, and only joined to other bishops so far as 'the civil power or his own choice happens to unite him'. But it seemed very 'unreal' to try and pretend that, since there could only be one bishop and one Church in any given place, therefore the Anglican Church was the true Church in England because its 'succession' was in 'possession', when everybody knew that the real division between the two Churches concerned not succession but doctrine. The fact that Anglicans did not feel they were in communion with the Roman Church when they were in Roman Catholic countries showed that the theory could not be 'acted upon—it is a mere set of words—facts confuse it'. He also told Mrs Froude that he did 'not mind it being said, as an historical fact . . . that you have reason to know that I was very much unsettled on the subject of Rome in the year 1839'. He did not want her to say anything about his '*present* state of mind' nor how she got her 'information'; but he felt it was 'unfair that people who think well of me should not be made acquainted with this *fact*, considering so much has come of it. I know it will shock them, but it is better than a greater shock afterwards, and it is very unpleasant to be trusted when I do not deserve it.'[72]

When he wrote to Henry Wilberforce with the same request, he admitted that friends might think that 1839 was so long ago now, that he must have 'got over' his doubts. He had never wanted to be 'the head of a party', so he was not concerned if people gave him up once they knew; if they still wanted to 'follow' him, 'let them do it with their eyes open'. Recently, for the first time, he admitted, he had sometimes had 'fears of the lawfulness of my remaining where I am, of the responsibility of knowing without acting'.[73] He warned Jemima not to be surprised if he resigned his fellowship; but he insisted that he was very happy living quietly in his retreat at Littlemore, even though he was upset by the 'pain' of his friends—'and I do not know how I shall bear it—but He gives us strength according to our day'.[74]

In June he wrote again at agonizing length to Keble about his 'state of mind'. If he was in 'a spirit of delusion', then what was his 'fault'? Certainly his 'convictions' all continued to 'grow in one direction'. As he looked back over his life, it seemed to him very clear that God had never deserted him since his conversion when he was 15, particularly when he had nearly died in Sicily, but had 'led' him on step by step until he had reached his present situation. Ever since the summer of 1839 he had 'attempted to lead a stricter life', spending every Lent as far as he possibly could at Littlemore. He felt he could 'certainly' say 'that in many respects my heart and conduct have improved in the course of this five years, and that, in respects in which I have prayed for improvement. Then the question comes upon me, why should Providence have granted my prayers in these respects, and not when I have prayed for light and guidance?'

And then, as far as I see, all inducements and temptations are for remaining quiet, and against moving. The loss of friends what a great evil is this! the loss of position, of name, of esteem—such a stultification of myself—such a triumph to others. It is no proud thing to unsay what I had said, to pull down what I have attempted to build up. And again, what quite pierces me, the disturbance of mind which a change on my part would cause to so many . . . the temptation to which many would be exposed of scepticism, indifference, and even infidelity.

On the other hand, he dreaded the thought of being the 'cause' of others dying out of the Church of Rome, 'who have had a *call* to join it'. How much longer was he to wait?—'I have fought against these feelings in myself and others long enough.' He was very afraid that 'a sort of latitudinarianism and liberalism *may* be the end of those . . . whom I am

---

[72] To Mrs W. Froude, 4, 5, 9 Apr.; 19, 28 May 1844.
[73] To H. Wilberforce, 8 June; 17 July 1844.   [74] To Mrs J. Mozley, 3 June 1844.

keeping from Rome.' Sometimes, indeed, he felt 'uncomfortable' about himself—'a sceptical, unrealizing temper is far from unnatural to me—and I may be suffered to relapse into it as a judgment.' He ended as he began: 'Am I in a delusion, given over to believe a lie?' Was there 'any subtle feeling or temptation' which he could not 'detect' but which was influencing him? If so, would not God show him what it was? 'Has he led me thus far to destroy me in the wilderness?'[75]

The next day he wrote Mrs Froude another long letter, this time on the development of doctrine—in which, he explained, he had always believed, although he had limited it to the Apostolic, or at least to the primitive, Church. However, the idea he had formulated in his *Lectures on the Prophetical Office* of a 'Prophetical Tradition' existing within the Church had allowed for the possibility of development 'at any time'. Then, in the last of his *University Sermons*, he had gone even further, by saying that 'developments are not only *explanations* of the sense of the Creed, but further doctrines involved in and arising from its articles.' It was an 'argument or theory' which he had been trying to put into words for years, at least since 1836. It was true that it did not 'go the whole length of theory which is necessary for the Roman system', but still he had 'no difficulties about receiving the system in matter of fact'. He was 'far more certain' that they were in schism than that Roman Catholic developments in doctrine were '*not* true ones'. Granted they were 'not found drawn out in the early Church', still there was 'sufficient trace of them in it, to recommend and prove them, *on the hypothesis* of the Church having a divine guidance, though not sufficient to prove them by itself'. Moreover, there 'was more evidence in Antiquity' for some Roman doctrines than there was for certain doctrines which Anglicans also held—for instance, 'for the necessity of Unity than for that of the Apostolic Succession—for the supremacy of the See of Rome than for the Presence in the Eucharist—for the practice of the Invocation than for certain books in the present Canon of Scripture'.[76]

5

In July Newman began to go over regularly to Roehampton to give Holy Communion to Bowden, whose health had broken down again and who was now very seriously ill. On one of these overnight visits, while waiting for a coach, he decided to have 'a peep' at his grandmother's house in Fulham which he had not seen for nearly forty years. Part of the front of the house had been turned into a chemist's

[75] To J. Keble, 8 June 1844.　　[76] To Mrs W. Froude, 9 June; 15 July 1844.

shop. The 'good chemist', he recounted to his aunt, did not unfortunately take his 'hints', so he did not see anything except the hall and staircase through the open door. However, he was able to describe the 'lie of the house', which the chemist confirmed. The sight of the house powerfully reminded Newman of the very first religious influence on him. It also had the usual effect of evoking in him an overpowering sense of the mystery of the passing of time.

How strange it is, I wish I could describe it, to stand in a house which was so much to me, as that house was, and it so different, and I so different! Whatever good there is in me, I owe, under grace, to the time I spent in that house, and to you and my dear Grandmother, its inhabitants. I do not forget her Bible and the prints in it. Alas, my dear Aunt, I am but a sorry bargain, and perhaps if you knew all about me, you would hardly think me now worth claiming; still I cannot help it—I am what I am—and I have grown into what I am from that time at Fulham.

What a strange change forty years makes. How little did the little child whom you used to fondle, think of what *he* thinks now! He had no thoughts. . . . I know not now of course what is before me, before my end comes—still more strange may be the contrast—but it is very touching and subduing as it is.

It was a veiled warning to his beloved aunt, of course. Sadly, he ended by remarking that 'really' he loved peace, although he seemed 'destined' for a life of conflict. 'Only think', however, he added on a gayer note in a postscript to the letter, he had just had his picture taken for Henry Wilberforce by the famous portrait-painter George Richmond! At the end of the year he assured her that whatever the uncertain future held, at least 'The past is our own. What you have done for me is irrevocable—it is mine—and I can delight in it.'[77] On the other hand, his nostalgic fascination for places associated with his past life contained not so much pleasure as pain, as he tried to explain to Jemima:

There is something quite mysterious to me which I cannot communicate in early scenes—not pleasurable, I can't tell why. When the Bowdens in 1836 took me to Ham, my pain was most piercing. I had no pleasure—yet I am so drawn to them. I cannot understand it.[78]

Returning to Oxford now was also like revisiting a scene of the past. He told Jemima that Bowden's impending death was not only perhaps intended by God to 'prepare' him 'for separations on a larger scale and still more painful', but strangely it seemed already to 'cut' him 'off from Oxford':

I do fancy I am getting changed. I go into Oxford, and find myself out of place. Every thing seems to say to me, this is not your home. The College seems strange to me, and even the College servants seem to look as if I were getting strange to

[77] To Miss E. Newman, 25 July; 9 Dec. 1844.   [78] To Mrs J. Mozley, 23 Jan. 1845.

them. I cannot tell myself whether it is a fancy or not, but to myself I seem changing. I am so much more easily touched than I used to be . . .[79]

Hearing that Pusey was very depressed, Newman urged him to accept that it was 'a hundred times more certain' that all that had come out of Pusey's part in the Movement was 'good than that joining the Church of Rome is evil'. Moreover, the 'certain good' ought to be 'a comment and more true interpreter of what seems to you evil'. Anyway, it was God's 'work' and one had to believe that He would 'perfect and complete it in a way suitable to His original design'. Besides, he asked pointedly, 'can a true Church lose her children and those her better ones?' It would be strange indeed 'if her better sort of children, after years of patient waiting, and steady personal improvement, and against their feelings, wishes, and interests, leave a true Church'. At the end of August he decided he must try and confront Pusey with the certainty of his leaving the Church of England. In his own case he liked 'to know and prepare for the worst of things—it distresses me not to look things full in the face, and in my case it is on the whole a saving of pain.' He knew that Pusey preferred to 'shut' his 'eyes' to 'painful' facts—but 'it does seem better to me to have all out once and for all . . . than to keep hacking and hacking bit by bit'. After all, 'great part of our pain is from suspense, anxiety, suspicion, anticipation—surely if I could but make you feel the worst, it must be a relief to you.' He thought, however, that Pusey greatly overrated his importance, as well as the consternation his leaving would cause—'I believe a great number of persons are prepared for it—more and more are coming to expect it daily.' Indeed, it was much easier for others who were not 'close to the act' to realize it—'I cannot realize it myself. . . You cannot realize it.' But what he did know was that he was 'about' as sure that the Anglican Church was 'not part of the Church' as of anything else that he believed; in fact, he was sure that 'the struggle' against this conviction was 'doing injury to his faith in general, and . . . spreading a film of scepticism over his mind', so much so that he was 'frightened, and cannot tell what it may end in, if he dares to turn a deaf ear to a voice which has so long spoken to him'. He was even scared, when travelling, that he might be killed before he could do what he knew he had to do. He had long waited, and was ready to go on waiting for some 'decisive proof' that he was not deluding himself, but if 'brought down to the brink of life', he supposed that 'he would feel he must act, as is on the whole safest, under circumstances'.[80] He sincerely hoped that this last letter would finally 'break the neck of all incredulity' in Pusey 'once for all'.[81]

[79] To Mrs J. Mozley, 13 Aug. 1844.   [80] To E. B. Pusey, 18, 23, 28 Aug. 1844.
[81] To H. Wilberforce, 29 Aug. 1844.

Although it seemed to Newman that he was often 'talking in an unreal way' because he could not 'master and bring out' his 'real feelings at a moment', it was becoming more and more urgent that he should reveal his state of mind to his friends. In September he explained to Edward Badeley, a lawyer friend and Tractarian:

Convictions are things which cannot be transferred—one would not wish they could be. As well could persons change hands, as opinions, which are worth any thing. I never then like talking to another on matters of doctrine or principle; what right has one to do so? he is he, and I am I. It seems an impertinence.

Merciless as he was towards any kind of outward inconsistency, Newman was always keenly sensitive to the essentially personal nature of belief, if only because he thought all beliefs rested on 'first principles' which lay outside the range of logical argument and belonged to the inner life of the individual, where conscience not logic reigns supreme. However, without attempting to argue, he wanted to try and share his feelings. For several years, he told Badeley, he had been acting 'like persons who pinch themselves to be sure that they are not asleep and dreaming'. He had done everything he could to dispel what might be a 'delusion', but he could not 'shake it off'. Others might try and explain it away (like the friends of 'a patient in a consumption' who 'show that not one of his symptoms but may be referred to some cause short of the fatal malady'); but then for those who had grown up in 'this dying or dead system in which we have lived all our days', it was inconceivable to accept 'what the real state of the case is':

We cannot be persuaded to open our eyes. Every ominous fact admits of an explanation, and in it we take refuge. . . . There is no bier and funeral of a Church. The fact then escapes unwilling minds; yet it may be as certain to others, as the prospective termination of a fatal malady is to the physician.

He could not say that he had yet achieved this 'certainty' about the Church of England, but he was 'approximating to it', and indeed was now 'certain of reaching it some time or other'.[82]

On 11 September he went over to Clifton to see Bowden, who had moved there with his family from Roehampton. He had not seen him for a month and was shocked by his appearance. He stayed overnight and hoped to visit him again in a week's time, although he could ill afford the time, for he was so preoccupied with the second part of his edition of St Athanasius which was now in the press. If it became necessary, he would stay on at Clifton—'I cannot lose him twice.'[83] Three days later Newman wrote to Keble that he did not think he had ever felt such 'pain

---

[82] To E. Badeley, 23 Aug.; 9 Sept. 1844. [83] To Mrs J. Mozley, 14 Sept. 1844.

before'. Although he had long given up all hope of his friend's recovery, he had 'not realized his loss till now, if now'. He was his 'oldest friend' and was his 'link' with Oxford—'I have ever known Oxford in him. In losing him I seem to lose Oxford.' For the last few years he had 'shrunk from him feeling that I had opinions that I dared not tell him, and that I must be constrained or almost hypocritical if I was with him'.[84] Before he could finish the letter, news came of Bowden's death. He had not felt 'such distress' since the death of his sister Mary.[85] The Bowdens had returned to London so that John Bowden could die at the family house in Grosvenor Place, which Newman had so often visited. From there he wrote to Jemima, 'What long and many recollections this house has to me; so many, so far back, they make me feel like an old man . . .'.[86] He also wrote to Ambrose St John, a former curate of Henry Wilberforce, who had come to live at Littlemore in the summer of 1843 as a result of doubts about the Church of England: 'I am full of wrong and miserable feelings, which it is useless to detail—so grudging and sullen when I should be thankful.'[87] The house, with its all too familiar rooms and furnishings, had not changed, and evoked many memories of happy past times; but now his 'oldest friend' lay dead in one of the rooms, and he himself 'with so little of faith or hope, as dead as a stone and detesting myself'.[88] In the *Apologia*, he records a note he made at the time: 'I sobbed bitterly over his coffin, to think that he left me still dark as to what the way of truth was, and what I ought to do in order to please God and fulfil His will.'[89]

Newman's own doctor had become seriously worried about his health and had 'been firing a gun over my head with such noise and fury that I am going to see him in London. He threatens to make me as idle as the day is long, to go the whole hog in eating, and to sleep like a top.'[90] After examining him early in October, Dr Babington pronounced him to be better than he expected. Newman caught the early morning train back to Oxford from Paddington Station; it was still dark, he reported to Mrs Bowden: 'Three persons were in the parallel carriage, and they began talking at the pitch of their voice in the dark, forgetting that walls had ears.' One of them reported to his travelling companions that 'the soundest divine in the Church' had told him,

'Depend on it, Newman, Newman (very loud) is a jesuit, a jesuit.' Somehow I could not help interfering . . . So I put my head through the cross window which separates the carriages and said (in the dark) 'Gentleman, please don't speak so loud, for persons are here whom you would not like to speak before.'

[84] To J. Keble, 14 Sept. 1844.
[85] To H. A. Woodgate, 14 Sept. 1844.
[86] To Mrs J. Mozley, 16 Sept. 1844.
[87] To A. St John, 16 Sept. 1844.
[88] To J. Keble, 17 Sept. 1844.
[89] *Apo.* 204.
[90] To A. St John, 3 Oct. 1844.

On which there was a deep silence—but in a while the conversation was resumed in a lower pitch.

On arriving back in Oxford in time for an important meeting of Convocation, he met a former resident who asked him if it was true he did not go to church at Littlemore: 'I was obliged to assure him I thought it irreligious not to go to Church, and that I did go.'[91]

At the end of October he set down on paper an account of his religious position for Henry Wilberforce to make whatever use of he thought fit; he did not want personally to make the 'confession' public, but he felt very strongly that he had a responsibility towards people who had been influenced by his writings. After once again recounting the events of the summer of 1839, he went on to say that he could not resist the conclusion that it was 'irrational to believe so much' as Anglo-Catholics did without believing 'more'. It was hard to 'do justice' to his 'reasonings':

They are not present—the impression remains, but the process of argument is like a scaffolding taken down when the building is completed. I could not recollect all the items which went to make up my convictions, nor can I represent it to another with that force which it came to my mind. Corroborations too are generally coincidences resulting from distinct courses of thought or from the bodies of fact which require a certain frame of mind to appreciate . . .

He had long wondered on what ground Anglicans only accepted the first Councils: why was Trent 'not a true council also'? If it was because the first Councils were 'scriptural', then they were not really receiving these Councils *as* Councils. With regard to individual doctrines, he could not 'see why prayers for the dead are primitive, and not the Pope's Supremacy'. He thus found himself in the position that he 'must either believe all or none'.[92]

A report appeared in the papers that Newman was leaving the Church of England. He immediately wrote to friends to assure them that it was 'entirely without foundation'. Perhaps some 'Protestant foe or Popish friend' was responsible, hoping 'to precipitate matters'. At least, he wrote to Maria Giberne, it was now clear that 'every one is prepared for such an event, next that every one expects it of me'. But still he did not seem to have any 'call' to make the move, which he was practically certain he would eventually have to make—although 'the expression of opinion and the latent and habitual feeling about me which are on every side and among all parties, has great force', as he had 'a great dread of going merely by my own feelings, lest they should mislead me'. One had to act only according to 'one's sense of duty . . . but external facts

---

[91] To Mrs J. W. Bowden, 8 Oct. 1844.   [92] To H. Wilberforce, 30 Oct. 1844.

support one in doing so'. He had 'little doubt' where he would be 'this time two years', even though his 'imagination' could not 'embrace the idea'.[93]

To Mrs Froude, he wrote:

The pain I suffer from the thought of the distress I am causing cannot be described—and of the loss of kind opinion on the part of those I desire to be well with. The unsettling so many peaceable, innocent minds is a most overpowering thought, and . . . my heart literally aches . . . I am conscious of no motive but that of obeying an urgent imperative call of duty—alas what am I not sacrificing! and if after all it is but for a dream?

There was other pain too:

. . . what with this long continued inward secret trial, and the unwearied violence of the attacks upon me, most cruel, though they mean it not so, at a time when I most need peace, I am just now in straits. Dying people are commonly left in quiet. If I *am*, as people think, unsettled, what great thoughtlessness to be watching every look and gesture and reporting it at the market place![94]

He told Manning he was 'going through what must be gone through', although he hoped that 'every day of pain is so much from the necessary draught which must be exhausted'. It was 'like drinking a cup out'— and 'the more of it the sooner over'. He had only one real reason for joining the Roman Church, and that was his belief that the Church of England was in schism.

I have no visions whatever of hope, no schemes of action, in any other sphere, more suited to me. I have no existing sympathies with Roman Catholics. I hardly ever, even abroad, was at one of their services—I know none of them. I do not like what I hear of them.

And then how much I am giving up in so many ways—and to me sacrifices irreparable, not only from my age, when people hate changing, but from my especial love of old associations and the pleasures of memory.

Nor am I conscious of any feeling, enthusiastic or heroic, of pleasure in the sacrifice—I have nothing to support me here.

What keeps me yet, is what has kept me long—a fear that I am under a delusion—but the conviction remains firm under all circumstances, in all frames of mind.

And this most serious feeling is growing on me . . . that the reasons, for which I believe *as much* as our system teaches, *must* lead me to believe more—and not to believe more, is to fall back into scepticism.[95]

But, he told Henry Wilberforce, he still felt he had to 'try' himself 'further'—even though he was 'not conscious of having omitted any

[93] To Miss M. Giberne, 7 Nov. 1844.   [94] To Mrs W. Froude, 12 Nov. 1844.
[95] To H. E. Manning, 16 Nov. 1844; to Mrs J. Mozley, 30 Nov. 1844.

thing by way of breaking the spell, if it is a spell'.[96] Indeed, he admitted to Keble, 'I doubt whether I *can* have clearer convictions than I have without a miracle, if then.' The fact was that he was far more convinced about Rome than he had ever been about the Catholic doctrines which he had learned as a young fellow of Oriel and which he would never have professed if he had gone on in the same 'shilly shally way' as now. As for his sense of the intellectual inconsistency of Anglicanism, that by itself would not be enough 'to make me tear myself from my friends, from their good opinion, from my reputation for consistency, from my habitual associations, from all that is naturally dear to me'.[97] Of all the attacks he had to endure, the one really hurtful one was the accusation that he was dishonest and a liar. But the 'atrocious lies' which 'circulated' about him made him wonder about the 'popular', 'plausible' feeling against Roman Catholicism, particularly when it had always been 'a note of the Church' to be 'under odium and in disgrace'. Certainly, by becoming a Roman Catholic himself, he knew, he told Jemima, that he would be 'giving up every thing' and 'throwing' himself 'away'. Nevertheless he would not hesitate to go over to Rome 'tomorrow—it is the fear that there is some secret fault which is the cause of my belief, which keeps me where I am, waiting'. He had no 'confidence whatever' that he was 'acting from faith or love', although he could not 'detect bad motives'.[98] While he could say what did '*not* influence' him, he could not 'analyze' his mind—'I feel myself very unreal'.[99]

6

W. G. Ward's notorious *Ideal of a Christian Church, considered in Comparison with Existing Practice* had been published in the summer in answer to a pamphlet by William Palmer of Worcester, which was severely critical of Ward's Romanizing articles in the *British Critic*. Ward maintained not only that the Roman Church alone could claim to be the 'ideal' Church, but also that he was entitled to hold and teach all the doctrines of Rome while remaining a member of the Church of England and retaining his fellowship at Balliol. Newman dismissed this paradoxical view as a mere 'theory'.[100] But then why should the Church of England refuse to accommodate 'Wardism' when it was tolerant of heresies like Unitarianism? He noted with amusement that the Master of Balliol was 'ill of his emotion, or what the Italians, I believe, call arrabiato'.[101] Naturally the

[96] To H. Wilberforce, 16 Nov. 1844.
[98] To Mrs J. Mozley, 24, 30 Nov.; 2 Dec. 1844.
[100] To J. W. Bowden, 17 June 1844.

[97] To J. Keble, 21 Nov. 1844.
[99] To J. Keble, 21 Nov. 1844.
[101] To J. Keble, 3 July 1844.

high-church allies of Tractarianism, like W. F. Hook, who had been led to believe that Anglo-Catholicism did not lead to Rome, felt 'deceived' and angry to 'find the ground cut under them'—although Newman could not feel much sympathy for Palmer, who seemed to him 'like a walking folio, or a theological nine pounder'.[102] He assured Keble that he had had no part in the book's publication, and had already told Ward that he did not approve of his articles in the *British Critic*. He certainly 'could not entertain' Ward's 'main theory . . . that a man may hold all that the Church of Rome holds yet remain under subscription to our formularies, or . . . that a Church could have the Sacraments without the doctrines of the gospel, or could impart grace yet not possess authority'.[103]

In December the Hebdomadal Board announced that it would ask Convocation to condemn Ward's book, to deprive the author of his degrees, and to add to the compulsory subscription to the Thirty-nine Articles a declaration that the subscriber accepted them in the sense in which they were originally drawn up and which the University now received and imposed. The Heads of Houses had been infuriated by the attempt in October to challenge in Convocation the nomination of the Warden of Wadham, who was well known for his special hostility to the Movement, as the next Vice-Chancellor according to the usual custom of succession; but the overwhelming defeat of the Tractarian party then had emboldened them to take full advantage of Ward's extraordinary book to launch a new attack on the 'Puseyites'. Newman had been very much against this challenge to the Heads of Houses. Opposed as he was to their autocratic powers, he did not feel it was his 'line to be in the position of a democrat or a demagogue'.[104] Not only did he predict that the Tractarians would be roundly beaten, but he disapproved of this 'first aggressive act' on their part, especially on a matter that was not even strictly religious.[105] Now he was appalled by the proposed additional 'test' for subscription: since the Statutes empowered the Vice-Chancellor to require any member of the University at any time to prove his orthodoxy by subscribing to the Articles, it would be a new 'Inquisition', or rather, 'the reign of Go-lightlyism'.[106] As for Ward, he could see no justification for Convocation 'degrading' an individual who, unlike Pusey, represented no one but himself and Oakeley.

In the event, the attempt to impose the 'test' aroused such bitter opposition, and not only from the Tractarians, that it was withdrawn. Instead, determined to exploit to the full the feeling against Ward, the Heads voted in February 1845 to submit to Convocation a formal

---

[102] To Mrs J. W. Bowden, 7 Dec. 1844.
[104] To Mrs J. W. Bowden, 15 Oct. 1844.
[106] To Mrs J. W. Bowden, 27 Dec. 1844.

[103] To J. Keble, 16 Dec. 1844.
[105] To M. Johnson, 3 Oct. 1844.

censure of *Tract 90*. Newman was completely unconcerned: he was to all intents and purposes 'a dead man—and Hebdomadal Boards can do me neither good nor harm'.[107] He even confessed to Pusey, he would 'be glad, selfishly speaking,' if the censure was passed—'Long indeed have I been looking for external circumstances to determine my course—and I do not wish this daylight to be withdrawn.'[108] The move was so 'unexpected' that he felt sure 'something must be intended to come of it'.[109] It gave him 'nothing but relief and ease', although he was afraid 'it must pain others'.[110] He had rather hoped in December that the measures against Ward would prove to be the kind of 'external' 'direction' he was looking for, and certainly it did seem 'as if external events were taking matters into their own hands'.[111] At any rate, he assured Manning, he had as much interest in what transpired as in 'the merest occurrence I might read of in a newspaper, and not even the curiosity which unconcerned spectators might feel about it'. He had 'ills which Heads of Houses can neither augment nor cure. Real inward pain makes one insensible to such shadows.'[112] However, the threatened censure had arouse 'sympathy' for him, and this was 'a satisfaction' in that it covered his 'retreat—preparing people for it as a thing not unnatural under my circumstances', as well as 'creating a kindly feeling and a compassion which may blunt the edge of resentment', but also 'a pain' because it only increased the 'distress' he felt in disappointing and troubling his friends.[113]

On 13 February Convocation met. The condemnation of Ward's book was easily carried, but there was a much narrower majority for stripping the author of his degrees. When the Vice-Chancellor put the censure of *Tract 90* to the vote, the two Proctors, one of whom was Newman's friend, R. W. Church, immediately vetoed the proposal, as they had earlier warned they would. Newman had anticipated the veto, but expected the censure would come up for vote again when the present Proctors' term expired—'for John Bull is a determined man'.[114]

In March Newman began to warn people that he could not promise that he would still be in the Church of England after Christmas. He could not afford to wait much longer, he told Jemima, who was very alarmed and upset by the news.

Pass a very few years, and I am an old man. What means of judging can I have more than I have? What maturity of mind am I to expect? If I am right to move at all, surely it is high time not to delay about it longer. Let me give my strength

[107] To J. B. Mozley, 5 Feb. 1845.   [108] To E. B. Pusey, 6 Feb. 1845.
[109] To Mrs J. W. Bowden, 7 Feb. 1845.   [110] To I. Williams, 7 Feb. 1845.
[111] To Mrs W. Froude, 8 Dec. 1844; to J. Keble, 16 Dec. 1844.
[112] To H. E. Manning, 9 Feb. 1845.   [113] To Mrs J. Mozley, 10 Feb. 1845.
[114] To I. Williams, 7 Feb. 1845.

to the work, not my weakness—years in which I can profit His cause who calls me, not the dregs of life. Is it not like a deathbed repentance to put off what one feels one ought to do?

. . . At my time of life men love ease—I love ease myself. I am giving up a maintenance, involving no duties, and adequate to all my wants; what in the world am I doing this for, (I ask *myself* this) except that I think I am called to do so? I am making a large income by my Sermons, I am, *to say the very least*, risking this; the chance is that my Sermons will have no further sale at all. I have a good name with many; I am deliberately sacrificing it. I have a bad name with more—I am fulfilling all their worst wishes and giving them their most coveted triumph—I am distressing all I love, unsettling all I have instructed or aided—I am going to those whom I do not know and of whom I expect very little—I am making myself an outcast, and that at my age. Oh, what can it be but a stern necessity which causes this?

Ever since he had had his first 'doubts', he had begun 'to live more strictly—and really from that time to this, I have done more towards my inward improvement, as far as I can judge, than in any time of my life'. Was it really possible that he was under some terrible delusion when he himself had prayed so hard for light and so many were praying for him? Ought he to go on living in a Church where he 'could not bear to die'? If he were suddenly to be on the point of death, he thought he would immediately send for a Catholic priest. Indeed, travelling made him nervous, in case of a serious accident.

Have I lived so many years, have I made such high profession, have I preached to others so peremptorily, to be myself now in fear of death? What is the difference between me and a poor profligate? We both feel we have a work to do which is undone.

He had wanted to wait for seven years till the summer of 1846, but recently his 'resolution to move' had grown 'so much stronger' that he could not promise he would wait beyond Christmas. He expected to resign his fellowship in October or November at the latest. He comforted himself with the thought that the Jews regarded St Paul as 'the prince of apostates', and that he was literally obeying the injunction of the Gospels in 'quitting friends and relations and houses and goods, for Christ's sake'.[115] As for hurting others, he admitted to Pusey that the pain had become 'more bearable', the more sure he became that he must go and the more he consequently hoped that others would go too.[116] None the less, his 'mind and heart' were simply 'tired out' from continuous 'dull aching pain'.[117] Still, he was 'getting more callous about consequences, from feeling that there are dangers on all sides, on

---

[115] To Mrs J. Mozley, 15 Mar. 1845.   [116] To E. B. Pusey, 14 Mar. 1845.
[117] To R. W. Church, 3 Apr. 1845.

any course of conduct, so my mind is like the nautical needle in a box cased all round with iron'.[118]

But he did not yet have quite enough certainty to act, as he explained to Maria Giberne: 'it is so difficult to know whether it is a call of *reason* or of *conscience*. I cannot make out if I am impelled by what seems to me *clear*, or by a sense of *duty*.'[119] He was planning to publish a book after giving up his fellowship, which would give his reasons for becoming a Roman Catholic and which might help others in the same position as himself. He would then see how he felt. In fact, as he explains in the *Apologia*, he had decided at the end of 1844 to write 'an Essay on Doctrinal Development; and then, if at the end of it, my convictions in favour of the Roman Church were not weaker, of taking the necessary steps for admission into her fold'.[120]

In April he was reading Blanco White's recently published autobiography, and he was again haunted by the fear that, just as Blanco White (and Arnold, for that matter) had in his view obvious weaknesses which accounted for their religious views, so too he might have secret faults, unknown to himself, which were responsible for his present convictions. He was horrified by the life which showed how Blanco White, having abandoned belief in the divinity of Christ, had ended as a pantheist. He had been hailed as a ' *"Confessor"*—confessor to what? not to any opinion, any belief whatever—but to the *Search* after truth; ever wandering about and changing, and therefore great. Is this the *end* of Life?' But what the book did eloquently demonstrate was that 'to be consistent one must believe more or less than we are accustomed to believe'. Blanco White's praise of himself personally was hardly of 'this old dry chip who am worthless' but of a past Newman, and ('like light showing the previous darkness') it brought home to him how unpopular and out of favour he had become. He realized, he sighed to Henry Wilberforce, 'My spring, my summer, are over.' His 'prime of life' was 'past' and he was 'nothing'. What did 'often' seem 'mysterious' to him was how he had 'all along been so wonderfully kept out of' the kind of work he seemed especially suited to, namely, the 'tuition or the oversight of young men'. He admitted that he got 'intellectually (not morally) fidgetted at the mystery' and could not help thinking what his 'influence would have been in any thing like station, when it has been what it is among people who never saw me'. But now that it was all over, he did not believe there was any frustrated 'ambition' in him: after all, he was 'so desperately fond' of his 'own ease, like an old batchelor, that having *duties*, being in office . . . is in idea insupportable to me'. As for the future,

---

[118] To Mrs W. Froude, 20 Apr. 1845. [119] To Miss M. R. Giberne, 30 Mar. 1845.
[120] *Apo.* 205.

he dreaded having 'to act on great matters so much in the dark—yet I, who have preached so much on the duty of following in the night whenever God may call, am the last person who have a right to complain.'[121]

In spite of having reached virtual certainty that the Church of England was in schism, Newman continued to believe that she had the Apostolic Succession and valid sacraments. He therefore advised Maria Giberne, who was in the same situation as himself, that she could continue to attend Holy Communion. He confided to her that he was very busy writing a book, although he did not want this to be known and he did not tell her what it was about. He was more informative to Mrs Froude about the work he had been turning over in his mind since March of the previous year and had started writing at the beginning of the year. But he had

lost, if that is the word when it could not be helped, or rather consumed several months this Spring, in working upon it in ways which will not turn to any direct account. I have had to remodel my plan, and what it will be at last I cannot yet foretell. All I know is that body and mind are getting wearied together, and the book not yet written through for the first time.

He did reveal to her that it would be 'a sort of obscure philosophical work . . . with little to interest and much to disappoint'. He was not letting it be known that he was writing a book, otherwise 'people will be expecting something which they will not have'. He was dismayed by the recent 'confident reports' that he was leaving the Church of England— 'for if the whole world believes I am going, I suppose I ought for the appearance of the thing to resign my Fellowship at once; whereas I do not wish to do so before October, because that is the time I have fixed.' At least people generally seemed to be recovering from the 'shock' of his impending move. He wrote again a few days later on 10 June, complaining of exhaustion. He had still not recovered from a series of virus infections during the previous winter, brought on by all the trials of 1844, including the death of his best friend and the pain of having to tell people his secret. He was also tired after finally completing the second part of his edition of St Athanasius, and would have liked to have had a complete rest from intellectual work. And now his new book, he groaned, had 'cost' him, he thought, more 'hard thought and anxiety' than anything else he had attempted. He had found that he 'had vastly more materials' than he 'knew how to employ'.

The difficulty was to bring them into shape, as well as to work out in my mind the principle on which they were to run. I spent two months in reading and

[121] To H. Wilberforce, 27 Apr. 1845.

writing which came to nothing, at least for my present purpose. I really have no hope at all it will be finished before the Autumn—if then. I have not written a sentence, I suppose, which will stand or hardly so. Perhaps one gets over-sensitive even about style, as one gets on in life. . . . Our time is so divided here, that I have not above 6 or 7 hours a day at it, and it is so exhausting, I doubt whether I could give more. I am now writing it for the first time, and have done three chapters, out of 4 or 5. Besides re-writing, every part has to be worked out and defined as in moulding a statue. I get on, as a person walks with a lame ankle, who does get on and gets to his journey's end—but not comfortably. Now, after all this, you will expect the work to be something out of the way—alack, that is the worst of it—it is much cry and little wool.[122]

They were modest words to describe the book that is the theological counterpart of the *Origin of Species*, which it pre-dates by over a decade.

As the summer wore on, Newman began to regret that he had said he would not move before Christmas, as the 'suspense' was becoming 'almost intolerable' to everybody. Pusey had at last accepted the inevitable, but, with his usual reluctance 'to look at trouble in the face', was now 'trying to smooth it over—as if it involved no great separation necessarily'.[123] Pusey had been asked to try and persuade Newman to go abroad to join the Roman Church. Newman indignantly rejected the idea, which was presumably intended to hide the fact that he was leaving the English Church because he thought she was in schism. When he pointed out that such a misrepresentation of his motives would only lead to disappointment later, he 'found the plan was that I should leave England for life. I could hardly help saying how cool.' He was writing to J. D. Dalgairns, and mentioned that when he and Ambrose St John had visited W. G. Ward and his bride (whom he had married shortly after his condemnation in Convocation) in their new home in Littlemore, St John had 'reminded me on our catching them at a good piece of mutton, that it was the Vigil of St John Baptist. What a shame.' Everybody in Oxford seemed to know about his situation, and he found it 'very uncomfortable to meet acquaintances, tradesmen', and so on.[124]

He was growing 'more and more sure' what he must do, and, although his distress at upsetting others had 'been like a sword through me', he was 'getting better now, and almost think the crisis over'.[125] In July he wrote calmly as well as confidently to Richard Westmacott: 'I do not see any medium between disowning Christianity, and taking the Church of Rome.' He could not 'believe only just as much as our Reformers out of their own heads have chosen we should believe—I must believe less or more. If Christianity is one and the same at all times,

---

[122] To Mrs W. Froude, 1, 10 June 1845.
[123] To Mrs J. W. Bowden, 25 June; 31 Aug. 1845.
[124] To J. D. Dalgairns, 29 June 1845.   [125] To E. Coleridge, 3 July 1845.

then I must believe, not what the Reformers have carved out of it, but what the Catholic Church holds.'[126] Why, he demanded, should he 'believe just what the English Church allows me to believe and nothing more'?[127] The hint of sarcasm signals a new self-confidence and suggests that at last he had attained to that full certitude which is 'to know that one knows'.[128]

In August he warned Jemima that the publication of his book would be 'the signal of my going—and people must take it as such'. But still it was not finished and he was unable to 'arrange the last and most important chapter', which he had written 'several times in vain'. Never before had he written and rewritten anything so many times. He wondered if John Mozley would be willing to print the book in Derby, 'where it could be printed with less chance of the subject getting known'.[129] In the end the book did not go to press till late in September, but he wanted it to be kept a secret till he had resigned his fellowship, when he would advertise it. On 3 October he sent his resignation to the Provost of Oriel: 'I shall be obliged to you if you will remove my name from the books of the College and the University.'[130] To friends he wrote warningly, 'anything may happen to me now any day.'[131] Two members of the Littlemore community, Dalgairns and St John, had been received into the Roman Catholic Church within the last few days, and Father Dominic Barberi, the Italian Passionist, who had received Dalgairns, was to visit Littlemore. Newman thought he would ask to be received by him, but he was not absolutely 'sure', he was so busy with the publication of his new work.[132]

The 'Advertisement' to the book is dated 6 October, with a 'Postscript' which informs the reader that

Since the above was written, the Author has joined the Catholic Church. It was his intention and wish to have carried his Volume through the Press before deciding finally on this step. But when he had got some way in the printing, he recognized in himself a conviction of the truth of the conclusion to which the discussion leads, so clear as to supersede further deliberation.

According to the 'Advertisement', the book is not 'a finished composition',[133] and in the *Apologia* Newman explains why: 'Before I got to the end, I resolved to be received, and the book remains in the state in which it was then, unfinished.'[134]

[126] To R. Westmacott, 11 July 1845.   [127] To C. Crawley, 14 July 1845.
[128] *Apo.* 195.   [129] To Mrs J. Mozley, 17 Aug. 1845.
[130] To E. Hawkins, 3 Oct. 1845.
[131] To Mrs J. W. Bowden; to E. B. Pusey, 3 Oct. 1845.
[132] To R. Stanton, 4 Oct. 1845.   [133] *Dev.*, pp. x–xi.   [134] *Apo.* 211.

7

'Christianity has been long enough in the world to justify us in dealing with it as a fact in the world's history.'[135] So begins the *Essay on the Development of Christian Doctrine*, which, its author tells us,

is directed towards a solution of the difficulty . . . of our using in controversy the testimony of our most natural informant concerning the doctrine and worship of Christianity, viz. the history of eighteen hundred years. The view on which it is written has at all times, perhaps, been implicitly adopted by theologians . . . This may be called the Theory of Development of Doctrine . . .

Newman admits that 'It is undoubtedly an hypothesis to account for a difficulty'—but then so too are the 'explanations' of science.[136] The 'difficulty' is that Christianity has apparently undergone so many changes and variations over the centuries that the question arises whether there has been any 'real continuity of doctrine' since the time of the Apostles.[137] This has led to Protestants 'dispensing with historical Christianity altogether, and . . . forming a Christianity from the Bible alone'—which is understandable, given that 'the Christianity of history' is certainly 'not Protestantism'.[138] Anglicans, on the other hand, have traditionally appealed to the famous dictum of Vincent of Lerins that 'Christianity is what has been held always, everywhere, and by all', a rule which

is irresistible against Protestantism, and in one sense indeed it is irresistible against Rome also, but in the same sense it is irresistible against England. It strikes at Rome through England. It admits of being interpreted in one of two ways: if it be narrowed for the purpose of disproving the catholicity of the Creed of Pope Pius, it becomes also an objection to the Athanasian; and if it be relaxed to admit the doctrines retained by the English Church, it no longer excludes certain doctrines of Rome which that Church denies. It cannot at once condemn St. Thomas and St. Bernard, and defend St. Athanasius and St. Gregory Nazianzen.[139]

Newman's idea of development cannot be understood without first understanding his concept of an 'idea' and its 'aspects'.

The idea which represents an object or supposed object is commensurate with the sum total of its possible aspects, however they may vary in the separate consciousness of individuals; and in proportion to the variety of aspects under which it presents itself to various minds is its force and depth, and the argument for its reality. Ordinarily an idea is not brought home to the intellect as objective except through this variety; like bodily substances, which are not

---

[135] *Dev.* 3.   [136] Ibid. 29–30.   [137] Ibid. 5.
[138] Ibid. 7.   [139] Ibid. 11–12.

apprehended except under the clothing of their properties and results, and which admit of being walked round, and surveyed on opposite sides, and in different perspectives, and in contrary light, in evidence of their reality. And, as views of a material object may be taken from points so remote or so opposed, that they seem at first sight incompatible, and especially as their shadows will be disproportionate, or even monstrous, and yet all these anomalies will disappear and all these contrarieties be adjusted, on ascertaining the point of vision or the surface of projection in each case; so also all the aspects of an idea are capable of coalition, and of a resolution into the object to which it belongs; and the *prima facie* dissimilitude of its aspects becomes, when explained, an argument for its substantiveness and integrity, and their multiplicity for its originality and power.

He warns that there is 'no one aspect deep enough to exhaust the contents of a real idea, no one term or proposition which will serve to define it'. Thus no 'one aspect of Revelation must . . . be allowed to exclude or to obscure another; and Christianity is dogmatical, devotional, practical all at once; it is esoteric and exoteric; it is indulgent and strict; it is light and dark; it is love, and it is fear'.

Ideas such as mathematical ones are 'real' enough, but can 'hardly properly be called living':

When an idea, whether real or not, is of a nature to arrest and possess the mind, it may be said to have life, that is, to live in the mind which is its recipient. . . . then it is not merely received passively in this or that form into many minds, but it becomes an active principle within them, leading them to an ever-new contemplation of itself, to an application of it in various directions, and a propagation of it on every side.

A living idea grows gradually into a 'body of thought,' which 'will after all be little more than the proper representative of one idea, being in substance what that idea meant from the first, its complete image as seen in a combination of diversified aspects, with the suggestions and corrections of many minds, and the illustration of many experiences'. It is the 'process . . . by which the aspects of an idea are brought into consistency and form' which Newman calls 'its development, being the germination and maturation of some truth or apparent truth on a large mental field'. But again he warns, 'this process will not be a development, unless the assemblage of aspects, which constitute its ultimate shape, really belongs to the idea from which they start.' Far from being passive,

A development will have this characteristic, that, its action being in the busy scene of human life, it cannot progress at all without cutting across, and thereby destroying or modifying and incorporating with itself existing modes of thinking and operating. The development then of an idea is not like an investigation worked out on paper, in which each successive advance is a pure evolution from a foregoing, but it is carried on through and by means of communities of men and their leaders and guides; and it employs their minds as its instruments, and depends upon them, while it uses them.

As usual, Newman portrays the intellectual life in terms of conflict and conquest—'It is the warfare of ideas under their various aspects striving for the mastery, each of them enterprising, engrossing, imperious, more or less incompatible with the rest . . .'. The context, too, is not unimportant: 'an idea not only modifies, but is modified, or at least influenced, by the state of things in which it is carried out, and is dependent in various ways on the circumstances which surround it.' There may be 'the risk of corruption from intercourse with the world around', but 'such a risk must be encountered if a great idea is duly to be understood, and much more if it is to be fully exhibited. It is elicited and expanded by trial, and battles into perfection and supremacy.' In other words, an idea is brought out rather than obscured by development, as Newman argues in a classic passage, which concludes with one of the most frequently quoted sentences from his writings:

It is indeed sometimes said that the stream is clearest near the spring. Whatever use may fairly be made of this image, it does not apply to the history of a philosophy or belief, which on the contrary is more equable, and purer, and stronger, when its bed has become deep, and broad, and full. It necessarily rises out of an existing state of things, and for a time savours of the soil. Its vital element needs disengaging from what is foreign and temporary . . . It remains perhaps for a time quiescent; it tries, as it were, its limbs, and proves the ground under it, and feels its way. From time to time it makes essays which fail, and are in consequence abandoned. It seems in suspense which way to go; it wavers, and at length strikes out in one definite direction. In time it enters upon strange territory; points of controversy alter their bearing; parties rise and fall around it; dangers and hopes appear in new relations; and old principles reappear under new forms. It changes with them in order to remain the same. In a higher world it is otherwise, but here below to live is to change, and to be perfect is to have changed often.[140]

Far from being unexpected, there is an 'antecedent probability' in favour of developments in doctrine. After all, 'If Christianity is a fact, and impresses an idea of itself on our minds and is a subject-matter of exercises of the reason, that idea will in course of time expand into a multitude of ideas, and aspects of ideas, connected and harmonious with one another, and in themselves determinate and immutable, as is the objective fact itself which is thus represented.' The more an idea claims to be 'living, the more various will be its aspects', for 'whole objects do not create in the intellect whole ideas, but are . . . thrown . . . into

---

[140] *Dev.* 34–6, 38–40.

a number of statements, strengthening, interpreting, correcting each other, and with more or less exactness approximating, as they accumulate, to a perfect image'. It is not possible to 'teach except by aspects or views, which are not identical with the thing itself which we are teaching'. Since Christianity in particular is not a local but a universal religion, 'it cannot but vary in its relations and dealings towards the world around it, that is, it will develope,' for 'Principles require a very various application according as persons and circumstances vary, and must be thrown into new shapes according to the form of society which they are to influence.' New problems and questions arise which 'must be answered, and, unless we suppose a new revelation, answered by means of the revelation which we have, that is, by development'. Scripture, for instance, does not solve the difficulties which are raised about its own authority and interpretation, but 'in matter of fact the decision has been left to time, to the slow process of thought, to the influence of mind upon mind, the issues of controversy, and the growth of opinion'. And the fact that 'Scripture needs completion' suggests that the 'defect or inchoateness in its doctrines' constitutes 'an antecedent probability in favour of a development of them'. In the Bible itself we find a 'prophetic Revelation' in the form of 'a process of development', in which

the earlier prophecies are pregnant texts out of which the succeeding announcements grow; they are types. It is not that first one truth is told, then another; but the whole truth or large portions of it are told at once, yet only in rudiments, or in miniature, and they are expanded and finished in their parts, as the course of revelation proceeds.

The truth is that 'the whole Bible, not its prophetical portions only, is written on the principle of development. As the Revelation proceeds, it is ever new, yet ever old.' Moreover, the sayings of Christ and the Apostles

are of a typical structure . . . predictions as well as injunctions of doctrine. If then the prophetic sentences have had that development which has really been given them, first by succeeding revelations, and then by the event, it is probable antecedently that those doctrinal, political, ritual, and ethical sentences, which have the same structure, should admit the same expansion.

It is not surprising that after the Ascension it is impossible 'to fix an historical point at which the growth of doctrine ceased, and the rule of faith was once for all settled', or to find 'one doctrine . . . which starts complete at first, and gains nothing afterwards from the investigations of faith and the attacks of heresy'.[141]

---

[141] Ibid. 55–6, 58, 60, 62, 64–6, 68.

If there is an antecedent probability for developments, then 'this is a strong antecedent argument in favour of a provision in the Dispensation for putting a seal of authority upon those developments'. After all, Christianity 'is a revelation which comes to us as a revelation, as a whole, objectively, and with a profession of infallibility', for, 'unlike other revelations . . . except the Jewish, of which it is a continuation, [it] is an objective religion, or a revelation with credentials'.

We are told that God has spoken. Where? In a Book? We have tried it and it disappoints; it disappoints us, that most holy and blessed gift, not from fault of its own, but because it is used for a purpose for which it was not given. . . . The Church undertakes that office; she does what none else can do, and this is the secret of her power.

Again, 'a revelation is not given, if there be no authority to decide what it is that is given.' And so, in order to distinguish true from false developments, a 'supreme authority' is necessary—without an 'infallible chair' the only unity possible is 'a comprehension of opinions' such as the 'hollow uniformity' of the Church of England. Nor is 'the notion of development under infallible authority' an implausible 'hypothesis . . . to account for the rise of Christianity and the formation of its theology'.[142]

The various developments of doctrine that took place in the East and West are 'suggestive, or correlative, or confirmatory, or illustrative of each other'; whereas 'the heretical doctrines were confessedly barren and short-lived, and could not stand their ground against Catholicism'. After the Great Schism the Orthodox did not 'present more than a negative opposition' to Rome, while after Trent there were 'no rival developments' and 'no antagonist system'. It would have to be generally accepted that, 'of all existing systems, the present communion of Rome is the nearest approximation in fact to the Church of the Fathers, possible though some may think it, to be nearer still to that Church on paper'. There follows one of the most rhetorically daring passages in Newman's writings, as eloquent and evocative as it is pointed and specific:

Did St. Athanasius or St. Ambrose come suddenly to life, it cannot be doubted what communion he would take to be his own. All surely will agree that these Fathers, with whatever opinions of their own, whatever protests, if we will, would find themselves more at home with such men as St. Bernard or St. Ignatius Loyola, or with the lonely priest in his lodging, or the holy sisterhood of mercy, or the unlettered crowd before the altar, than with the teachers or with the members of any other creed. And may we not add, that were those same Saints, who once sojourned, one in exile, one on embassy, at Treves, to come more northward still, and to travel until they reached another fair city, seated among groves, green meadows, and calm streams, the holy brothers would turn from many a high aisle and solemn cloister which they found there, and ask the way to some small chapel where mass was said in the populous alley or forlorn suburb? And, on the other hand, can any one who has but heard his name, and cursorily read his history, doubt for one instant how, in turn, the people of England . . . would deal with Athanasius—Athanasius, who spent his long years in fighting against sovereigns for a theological term?'[143]

The general point that there has existed since Apostolic times a continuous, developing body of doctrine called Catholicism becomes vividly real for Newman through the concretely personal argument that it is 'the nearest . . . to say the least, to the religious sentiment, and what is called *ethos*, of the early Church, nay, to that of the Apostles and Prophets . . . [who were] saintly and heroic men . . . more like a Dominican preacher, or a Jesuit missionary, or a Carmelite friar, more like St. Toribio, or St. Vincent Ferrer, or St. Francis Xavier, or St. Alphonso Liguori, than to any individuals, or to any classes of men, that can be found in other communions'.[144]

Although it is undeniable that modern Catholicism is 'the historical continuation' of early Christianity, it may still be objected that the 'expansion' which has taken place consists not of developments but of corruptions. It is therefore 'necessary . . . to assign certain characteristics of faithful developments . . . as a test to discriminate between them and corruptions'. But it is important first to understand what the word 'corruption' means 'when used literally of material substances'. It cannot, for example, be used of 'a stone', which 'may be crushed to powder, but . . . cannot be corrupted'. On the other hand, it can be applied to the human body, when it signifies 'the breaking up of life, preparatory to its termination'. On the basis of this 'analogy', Newman proposes seven 'Tests' or 'Notes'[145]

of varying cogency, independence and applicability, to discriminate healthy developments of an idea from its state of corruption and decay, as follows:— There is no corruption if it retains one and the same type, the same principles, the same organization; if its beginnings anticipate its subsequent phases, and its later phenomena protect and subserve its earlier; if it has a power of assimilation and revival, and a vigorous action from first to last.[146]

The first characteristic or mark, that of 'unity of type',

must not be pressed to the extent of denying all variation, nay, considerable alteration of proportion and relation, as time goes on, in the parts or aspects of

---

[143] Ibid. 93, 95, 97–8.   [144] Ibid. 100.
[145] This is the more cautious, less definite word he uses in the revised 1878 edition, although the word 'test' is still to be found there.
[146] *Dev.* 169–71.

an idea. Great changes in outward appearance and internal harmony occur in the instance of the animal creation itself. The fledged bird differs much from its rudimental form in the egg. The butterfly is the development, but not in any sense the image, of the grub.

The 'variations' in 'political and religious developments' are more 'subtle still and mysterious'. Thus the 'same man may run through various philosophies or beliefs, which are in themselves irreconcilable, without inconsistency, since in him they may be nothing more than accidental instruments or expressions of what he is inwardly from first to last'. Similarly, 'real perversions and corruptions are often not so unlike externally to the doctrine from which they come, as are changes which are consistent with it and true developments.' A familiar 'cause of corruption in religion is the refusal to follow the course of doctrine as it moves on, and an obstinacy in the notions of the past'.[147]

In the *Lectures on Justification*, Newman had made an important and subtle distinction in recognizing justification by faith as an abstract *principle* but not as a practical *rule*. So here, in explaining his second 'Note', he distinguishes doctrines from the 'principle which they embody' and according to which they develop:

Principles are abstract and general, doctrines relate to facts; doctrines develope, and principles at first sight do not; doctrines grow and are enlarged, principles are permanent; doctrines are intellectual, and principles are more immediately ethical and practical. Systems live in principles and represent doctrines. Personal responsibility is a principle, the Being of God is a doctrine; from that doctrine all theology has come in due course, whereas that principle is not clearer under the Gospel than in paradise, and depends, not on belief in an Almighty Governor, but on conscience.

However, 'the difference between the two sometimes merely exists in our mode of viewing them; and what is a doctrine in one philosophy is a principle in another'. For example, personal responsibility 'may be made a doctrinal basis, and develope into Arminianism or Pelagianism'. Or there may be doubt as to 'whether infallibility is a principle or a doctrine of the Church of Rome, and dogmatism a principle or doctrine of Christianity'. The same doctrine will develop differently according to different principles. Principles may be 'exemplified' rather than actually develop, as in the case of the Protestant sects, which are 'applications and results' rather than 'developments of the principle of Private Judgment'. In order to be 'faithful', a development

must retain both the doctrine and the principle with which it started. Doctrine without its correspondent principle remains barren, if not lifeless, of which the Greek Church seems an instance; or it forms those hollow professions which are

[147] *Dev.* 173–7.

familiarly called 'shams,' as a zeal for an established Church and its creed on merely conservative or temporal motives. . . .

Pagans may have, heretics cannot have, the same principles as Catholics . . . Principle is a better test of heresy than doctrine. Heretics are true to their principles, but change to and fro, backwards and forwards, in opinion; for very opposite doctrines may be exemplifications of the same principle. . . . Thus Calvinists become Unitarians from the principle of private judgment. The doctrines of heresy are accidents and soon run to an end; its principles are everlasting.[148]

For his third 'Note', Newman argues that because 'doctrines and views which relate to man are not placed in a void, but in the crowded world', they 'make way for themselves by interpenetration, and develope by absorption'.

Facts and opinions, which have hitherto been regarded in other relations and grouped round other centres, henceforth are gradually attracted to a new influence and subjected to a new sovereign. . . . A new element of order and composition has come among them; and its life is proved by this capacity of expansion, without disarrangement or dissolution. An eclectic, conservative, assimilating, healing, moulding process, a unitive power, is of the essence, and a third test, of a faithful development.[149]

Fourthly, although development is not 'a logical operation' in the sense that it is 'a conscious reasoning from premises to conclusion', and 'the spontaneous process which goes on within the mind itself is higher and choicer than that which is logical', still the 'rules' of logic 'must not be transgressed', and the 'logical character which the whole wears becomes a test that the process has been a true development, not a perversion or corruption'. 'Logical Sequence', then, includes 'any progress of the mind from one judgment to another, as, for instance, by way of moral fitness, which may not admit of analysis into premiss and conclusion'.[150]

Fifthly,

since developments are in great measure only aspects of the idea from which they proceed, and all of them are natural consequences of it, it is often a matter of accident in what order they are carried out in individual minds; and it is in no wise strange that here and there definite specimens of advanced teaching should very early occur, which in the historical course are not found till a late day. The fact, then, of such early or recurring intimations of tendencies which afterwards are fully realized, is a sort of evidence that those later and more systematic fulfilments are only in accordance with the original idea.[151]

Sixthly, a true development is 'one which is conservative of the course

---

[148] Ibid. 178–81.   [149] Ibid. 186.   [150] Ibid. 189–91, 383.
[151] Ibid. 195–6.

of antecedent developments being really those antecedents and something besides them: it is an addition which illustrates, not obscures, corroborates, not corrects, the body of thought from which it proceeds'. Thus, for example, 'a gradual conversion from a false to a true religion, plainly, has much of the character of a continuous process, or a development, in the mind itself', inasmuch as 'such a change consists in addition and increase chiefly, not in destruction'.[152]

The seventh and final 'Note' is that of 'chronic vigour':

Since the corruption of an idea, as far as the appearance goes, is a sort of accident or affection of its development, being the end of a course, and a transition-state leading to a crisis, it is . . . a brief and rapid process. While ideas live in men's minds, they are ever enlarging into further development: they will not be stationary in their corruption any more than before it; and dissolution is that further state to which corruption tends. Corruption cannot, therefore, be of long standing; and thus *duration* is another test of a faithful development.

A heresy is always short-lived, because 'it is an intermediate state between life and death'—although 'an heretical principle will continue in life many years, first running one way, then another', if it does not die but 'is resolved into some new, perhaps opposite, course of error, which lays no claim to be connected with it'. Although 'decay' is a 'form of corruption' which is 'slow', it is 'a state in which there is no violent or vigorous action at all, whether of a conservative or a destructive character, the hostile influence being powerful enough to enfeeble the functions of life, but not to quicken its own process'. And so, 'while a corruption is distinguishable from decay by its energetic action, it is distinguished from a development by its *transitory character*'.[153]

The rest of the *Essay* is concerned with applying the seven 'Notes' to the actual historical development of Christian doctrine. By far the largest space is devoted to the first, not surprisingly: for of course, it was the recognition of the essential identity of contemporary Catholicism and early Christianity which was the cause of Newman's own conversion. There are several rhetorical passages where Newman delineates, vividly and tersely, the various general features of the continuing Church, of which the first serves as an introduction to the lengthy chapter on the first of the 'Notes'.

There is a religious communion claiming a divine commission, and holding all other religious bodies around it heretical or infidel; it is a well-organized, well-disciplined body; it is a sort of secret society, binding together its members by influences and by engagements which it is difficult for strangers to ascertain. It is spread over the known world; it may be weak or insignificant locally, but it is strong on the whole from its continuity; it may be smaller than all other

[152] *Dev.* 200.   [153] Ibid. 203–5.

religious bodies together, but is larger than each separately. It is a natural enemy to governments external to itself; it is intolerant and engrossing, and tends to a new modelling of society; it breaks laws, it divides families. It is a gross superstition; it is charged with the foulest crimes; it is despised by the intellect of the day; it is frightful to the imagination of the many. And there is but one communion such.[154]

The conclusion to this chapter offers the most explicit and dramatic identification:

If then there is now a form of Christianity such, that it extends throughout the world, though with varying measures of prominence or prosperity in separate places;—that it lies under the power of sovereigns and magistrates, in various ways alien to its faith;—that flourishing nations and great empires, professing or tolerating the Christian name, lie over against it as antagonists;—that schools of philosophy and learning are supporting theories, and following out conclusions, hostile to it, and establishing an exegetical system subversive of its Scriptures;—that it has lost whole Churches by schism, and is now opposed by powerful communions once part of itself; that it has been altogether or almost driven from some countries;—that in others its line of teachers is overlaid, its flocks oppressed, its Churches occupied, its property held by what may be called a duplicate succession; that in others its members are degenerate and corrupt, and are surpassed in conscientiousness and in virtue, as in gifts of intellect, by the very heretics whom it condemns; that heresies are rife and bishops negligent within its own pale;—and that amid its disorders and fears there is but one Voice for whose decisions the peoples wait with trust, one Name and one See to which they look with hope, and that name Peter, and that see Rome;—such a religion is not unlike the Christianity of the fifth and sixth Centuries.[155]

In connection with this first 'Note', Newman insists (as he was so often to do as a Roman Catholic in controversy with Anglicans) that the 'universality which the Fathers ascribe to the Catholic Church' did not lie 'in its Apostolical descent, or again in its Episcopacy,' but rather in the fact that it was 'one Kingdom': for

who will in seriousness maintain that relationship, or that sameness of structure, makes two bodies one? England and Prussia are both of them monarchies; are they therefore one kingdom? England and the United States are from one stock; can they therefore be called one state? England and Ireland are peopled by different races; yet are they not one kingdom still? If unity lies in the Apostolical succession, an act of schism is from the nature of the case impossible; for as no one can reverse his parentage, so no Church can undo the fact that its clergy have come by lineal descent from the Apostles.

Just as 'a kingdom admits of the possibility of rebels, so does such a Church involve sectaries and schismatics, but not independent portions'.[156] The unspoken implication is that the separate Churches of Rome and England cannot both be parts of one Church, any more than two countries with different governments can constitute one kingdom.

One of the most important of the principles which arise out of the discussion of the second 'Note' and which characterize Christianity and the development of its doctrines, that of dogmatism ('a religion's profession of its own reality as contrasted with other systems'),[157] is described in a famous passage calculated to provoke many readers:

That there is a truth then; that there is one truth; that religious error is in itself of an immoral nature; that its maintainers, unless involuntarily such, are guilty in maintaining it; that it is to be dreaded; that the search for truth is not the gratification of curiosity; that its attainment has nothing of the excitement of a discovery; that the mind is below truth, not above it, and is bound, not to descant upon it, but to venerate it; that truth and falsehood are set before us for the trial of our hearts . . . this is the dogmatical principle . . .

Contrasted with this is the principle of liberalism—

That truth and falsehood in religion are but matter of opinion; that one doctrine is as good as another; that the Governor of the world does not intend that we should gain the truth; that there is no truth; that we are not more acceptable to God by believing this than by believing that; that no one is answerable for his opinions; that they are a matter of necessity or accident; that it is enough if we sincerely hold what we profess; that our merit lies in seeking, not in possessing; that it is a duty to follow what seems to us true, without a fear lest it should not be true; that it may be a gain to succeed, and can be no harm to fail; that we may take up and lay down opinions at pleasure; that belief belongs to the mere intellect, not to the heart also; that we may safely trust to ourselves in matters of Faith, and need no other guide . . .[158]

In discussing the third 'Note', the power of assimilation, Newman characterizes the contribution of heresies to the development of doctrine with an arresting image. For just as 'the statements of the early Fathers are but tokens of the multiplicity of openings which the mind of the Church was making into the treasure-house of Truth; real openings, but incomplete or irregular', so

the doctrines even of the heretical bodies are indices and anticipations of the mind of the Church. As the first step in settling a question of doctrine is to raise and debate it, so heresies in every age may be taken as the measure of the existing state of thought in the Church, and of the movement of her theology; they determine in what way the current is setting, and the rate at which it flows.[159]

With regard to the sixth 'Note' or 'Test' of conservation of the past,

---

[156] *Dev.* 265–6. [157] Ibid. 439. [158] Ibid. 357–8. [159] Ibid. 362.

Newman argues that ironically it is generally heretics who profess to be 'but serving and protecting Christianity by their innovations; and it is their charge against what by this time we may surely call the Catholic Church, that her successive definitions of doctrine have but overlaid and obscured it'.[160] But this claim is falsified by history. Thus, for example, 'it is not those religious communions which are characterized by devotion towards the Blessed Virgin that have ceased to adore her Eternal Son', but rather it is 'their accusers' who 'have ceased to worship Him altogether'.[161]

With regard to the seventh 'Note', the 'chronic vigour' of the Catholic Church is shown in 'the development of dogmatic theology' as it has been 'wrought out and carried through under the fiercest controversies, and amid the most fearful perils'—

but these disorders were no interruption to the sustained and steady march of the sacred science from implicit belief to formal statement. The series of ecclesiastical decisions . . . alternate between the one and the other side of the theological dogma especially in question, as if fashioning it into shape by opposite strokes.[162]

This last point would one day take on heightened significance for Newman in the aftermath of the Vatican Council. And as for the vicissitudes of the Church, on which again he would so often have occasion to reflect as a Catholic, 'her wonderful revivals, while the world was triumphing over her, is a further evidence of the absence of corruption in the system of doctrine and worship into which she has developed'.

She pauses in her course, and almost suspends her functions; she rises again, and she is herself once more; all things are in their place and ready for action. Doctrine is where it was, and usage, and precedence, and principle, and policy; there may be changes, but they are consolidations or adaptations; all is unequivocal and determinate, with an identity which there is no disputing.[163]

At the beginning of the chapter on the sixth 'Note', Newman had remarked: 'this Essay has so far exceeded its proposed limits, that both reader and writer may well be weary, and may content themselves with a brief consideration of the portions of the subject which remain.'[164] He now ends on a personal note of appeal to the reader:

And now, dear Reader, time is short, eternity is long. Put not from you what you have here found; regard it not as mere matter of present controversy; set not out resolved to refute it, and looking about for the best way of doing so;' seduce not yourself with the imagination that it comes of disappointment, or

---

[160] Ibid. 419.   [161] Ibid. 426.   [162] Ibid. 439.   [163] Ibid. 444.
[164] Ibid. 419.

disgust, or restlessness, or wounded feeling, or undue sensibility, or other weakness. Wrap not yourself round in the associations of years past, nor determine that to be truth which you wish to be so, nor make an idol of cherished anticipations. Time is short, eternity is long.[165]

It was his public farewell to the Church of England.

A couple of decades later Newman was to write again on doctrinal development (the occasion was the controversy over papal infallibility). The resulting paper (of 1868) contains such a concrete and succinct statement of his theory as to make it a very useful supplement to the *Essay*. In particular, Newman makes it quite clear that he does not envisage the original revelation as having been given partly in wordless experiences or feelings such as could hardly be capable of being developed into new dogmatic propositions (as has been claimed):[166]

the Apostles had the *fullness* of revealed knowledge, a fullness which they could as little realize to themselves, as the human mind, as such, can have all its thoughts present before it at once. They are elicited according to the occasion. A man of genius cannot go about with his genius in his hand: in an Apostle's mind great part of his knowledge is from the nature of the case latent or implicit . . .

Indeed, the 'idea' which the Church has received is cognitive enough to be called a 'Divine philosophy'—

not a number of formulas . . . but a system of thought . . . in such sense that a mind that was possessed of it, that is, the Church's mind, could definitely and unequivocally say whether this part of it, as traditionally expressed, meant this or that, and whether this or that was agreeable to, or inconsistent with it in whole or in part. I wish to hold that there is nothing which the Church has defined or shall define but what an Apostle, if asked, would have been fully able to answer and would have answered, as the Church has answered, the one answering by inspiration, the other from its gift of infallibility . . .

As an analogy, Newman cites the situation of someone who has complete knowledge of Aristotle's philosophy, and yet who cannot have 'before his mind' every thought and saying of Aristotle, any more than Aristotle himself could have had 'a host of thoughts present' to his mind 'at once'.

The philosophy, as a system, is stored in the *memory* . . . and is brought out according to the occasion. A learned Aristotelian is one who can answer any whatever philosophical questions in the way that Aristotle would have answered them. If they are questions which could not occur in Aristotle's age,

[165] *Dev.* 445.

[166] See Owen Chadwick, *From Bossuet to Newman: The Idea of Doctrinal Development* (Cambridge, 1957), 157–60, 195. For this and other criticisms that Newman's theory involves 'new revelation' rather than development, see Ian T. Ker, 'Newman's Theory—Development or Continuing Revelation?', *Newman and Gladstone Centennial Essays*, ed. James D. Bastable (Dublin, 1978), 145–59.

he still answers them . . . In one respect he knows more than Aristotle; because, in new emergencies after the time of Aristotle, he *can* and *does* answer what Aristotle would have answered, but for the want of the opportunity did not. There is another point of view in which he seems to have the advantage of Aristotle, though it is no real superiority, viz that, from the necessities of the interval between Aristotle and himself, there has been the growth of . . . a scientific vocabulary, which makes the philosophy easier to remember, easier to communicate and to defend . . .

So, for example, St Paul could hardly have understood what was meant by the 'Immaculate Conception', but 'if he had been asked, whether or not our Lady had the grace of the Spirit anticipating all sin whatever, including Adam's imputed sin, I think he would have answered in the affirmative'. The 'living idea', then, of Christianity, or what Newman as a Roman Catholic calls 'the deposit of faith',

is in such sense committed to the Church or to the Pope, that when the Pope sits in St. Peter's chair, or when a Council of Fathers and doctors is collected round him, it is capable of being presented to their minds with that fullness and exactness . . . with which it habitually, not occasionally, resided in the minds of the Apostles;—a vision of it, not logical, and therefore consistent with errors of reasoning and of fact in the enunciation, after the manner of an intuition or an instinct.[167]

[167] *TP* ii. 156–9.

7

From Oxford to Rome

ON 7 October 1845 Newman wrote to tell Henry Wilberforce of his decision to ask Father Dominic Barberi to receive him into the Roman Catholic Church. Father Dominic had been invited to stay a night at Littlemore by Dalgairns, whom he had received into the Church a few days before.

He does not know of my intentions, but I shall ask of him admission into the one true Fold of the Redeemer . . . I could have wished to delay till my book was actually out, but having all along gone so simply and entirely by my own reason, I was not sorry . . . to submit myself to what seemed an external call. Also I suppose the departure of others has had something to do with it . . .[1]

Close friends had asked Newman not to upset them by making the break later during the Advent or Christmas season. Again, to his disappointment, so far only 128 out of 400 pages of the *Essay on the Development of Christian Doctrine* had been set up in type, so slow were the printers. And already four of his companions at Littlemore had left to become Roman Catholics. It was true that there was little in common between Newman, the famous Oriel don, and Barberi, the son of an Italian peasant; but

Father Dominic has had his thoughts turned to England from a youth, in a distinct and remarkable way. For thirty years he has expected to be sent to England, and about three years since was sent without any act of his own by his superiors. He has had little or nothing to do with conversions, but goes on missions and retreats among his own people.[2]

Unlike other of his co-religionists, too, he was not pressing for conversions but was 'most singularly kind in his thoughts of religious persons in our communion'.[3] It seemed not just the right time but the providential time for Newman to make the final break.

On 8 October, Newman's diary records, 'Father Dominic came at night. I began my Confession to him.'[4] On the next day he completed his confession and was received into the Catholic Church with two others of the Littlemore community, Frederick Bowles and Richard Stanton.

---

[1] *LD* xi. 3.   [2] Ibid.   [3] Ibid. 5.   [4] Ibid. 4.

Very early on the morning of his reception, Newman wrote an answer to a letter from Jemima remonstrating with him for his intention to remain at Littlemore. On the one hand, he does not hesitate to compare his new position with that of the first Apostles who remained in Jerusalem to preach to the Jews. There is an uncompromising assertion of the claims of the Roman Catholic Church. On the other hand, he is no less quick to point out, 'All this is quite consistent with believing, as I firmly do, that individuals in the English Church are invisibly knit into that True Body of which they are not outwardly members—and consistent too with thinking it highly injudicious, indiscreet, wanton, to interfere with them in particular cases . . .' He enclosed a note for his Aunt Elizabeth, 'written with a trembling hand and great intensity of feeling'—God 'alone knows how much you are in my heart, or how it pierces my heart so to distress you'. A few days later he wrote again to Jemima to assure her that nothing she had said about his 'loss of influence' had 'any tendency to hurt' him:

I never have thought about any influence I had had—I never have mastered what it was—it is simply no effort whatever to give it up. The pain indeed, which I knew I was giving individuals, has affected me much—but as to influence, the whole world is one great vanity, and I trust I am not set on any thing in it . . .

Nor had he any

distinct views about remaining at Littlemore; but to *move* would be to *decide* one way. *While* I am undecided, I *remain*. So far from being a sacrifice to go, as you suppose, it is a great trial to remain—to remain in the midst of known faces, perplexed, and whose perplexity I cannot possibly relieve—to remain in a place where I have myself built up a system against myself, to remain where there are no outward tokens or means of Catholic communion. It is said that the one support to persons in my case has been the daily Mass—now mass is only twice a week at St Clement's, and at the distance of 2 or 3 miles. Nor is it a slight trial . . . to go to what to outward appearance is a meeting house.

Anyway, where was he to go?—'am I to take a house for my books in the first town I come to?' Moreover, 'so many providential circumstances' had brought him to Littlemore that 'I fear to move'.[5]

At the end of October Newman went to Oscott College, near Birmingham, to be confirmed and to see Nicholas Wiseman, who had been appointed President in 1840 and also Coadjutor to the Vicar Apostolic of the Midland district, in which Oxford was situated. It was eventually decided that Wiseman should not censor the proofs of the *Development of Christian Doctrine*, not only because it simply 'professed to be the course of reasoning' which had led to his conversion,[6] but also

---

[5] Ibid. 14, 16–17.   [6] Ibid. 23.

because any ecclesiastical revision would spoil the influence the book
might have. Wiseman offered the Oxford converts the use of the old
Oscott College (later renamed Maryvale by Newman). It could be
'Littlemore continued', 'a place of refuge', to which 'any one' could
'come who would have come to me at Littlemore'. Ultimately, Wiseman
envisaged a body of priests engaged in apostolic work of an intellectual
rather than parochial nature. Newman appreciated that the offer would
at least enable them 'to keep together'. He also saw that to remain at
Littlemore would be to offend members of both Churches, nor was there
any point unless they were 'simply to be literary laymen': 'It seems the
right thing, as well as necessary, in the first place to submit ourselves *to
the existing system*, and to work ourselves out *through* it.' London or Oxford
as 'a centre' would be preferable to Birmingham, but at least old Oscott
could be a beginning, perhaps of a new religious 'congregation' as
Father Dominic had suggested. It was 'dismally ugly', but it had a
chapel and enough rooms for twenty or thirty people.[7]

At this point it was still 'not clear' to Newman whether he had a 'duty
to be a priest'. Indeed, he later recalled, 'For a while after my reception,
I proposed to betake myself to some secular calling.'[8] However, before
the end of November his ordination as a Catholic priest was taken for
granted.

Meanwhile, the publication of the *Essay on the Development of Christian
Doctrine* (it was soon sold out and a second edition was published in 1846)
brought Newman a number of enquiries and objections, the beginning
of more than forty years' voluminous correspondence with critics and
potential converts to the Church. It was essential, he urged, 'to begin
with antecedent probabilities and general presumptions, and to take
large and broad views of the subject, instead of entangling ourselves with
particular questions'. He complained of one critic that: 'When we have
lost our way, we mount up to some eminence to look about us, but he
plunges into the nearest thicket to find out his bearings.'[9] Equally, the
opposite danger of over-simplification should also be avoided, for
'Catholicism is a deep matter—you cannot take it up in a teacup.' As for
Newman's own reasons for becoming a Catholic, 'You cannot buy them
for a crown piece'—in fact, 'you cannot get them, except at the cost of
some portion of the trouble I have been at myself.'[10] He noted ruefully
that the Evangelical hostility which he had suffered as an Anglican was
now replaced by exactly the same kind of misrepresentation from his old
high-Anglican allies.

Leaving Littlemore, unlike leaving Oxford or St Mary's, was very

---

[7] *LD* xi. 29–30, 48.
[9] *LD* xi. 69.
[8] Ibid. xxxi. 20*; *Apo.* 212.
[10] Ibid. 110.

painful for Newman. And as he cleared out his letters and papers, he felt an overwhelming sense of desolation:

So many dead, so many separated. My mother gone; my sisters nothing to me, or rather foreign to me; of my greatest friends Froude, Wood, Bowden taken away, all of whom would now be, or be coming, on my side. Other dear friends who *are* preserved in life *not* moving with me; Pusey strongly bent on an opposite course, Williams protesting against my conduct as rationalistic, and dying— Rogers and J. Mozley viewing it with utter repugnance. Of my friends of a dozen years ago whom have I now? and what did I know of my present friends a dozen years ago? why, they were at School, or they were freshmen looking up to me, if they knew my name, as some immense and unapproachable don; and now they know nothing, can know nothing of my earlier life; things which to me are as yesterday are to them as dreams of the past; they do not know the names, the state of things, the occurrences, they have not the associations, which are part of my own world, in which I live.[11]

Newman would be the last to leave Littlemore as he had been the first to arrive. 'A happy time indeed I have had here, happy to look back on, though suspense and waiting are dreary in themselves;—happy, because it is the only place perhaps I ever lived in, which I can look back on, without an evil conscience.' His few years at Littlemore meant far more to him than all his years at Oxford.

Doubtless if my life here for these last years were placed in the light of God's countenance, it would be like a room when a sunbeam comes into it, full of hidden unknown impurities—but still I look back to it as a very soothing happy period. I came into this house by myself, and for nights was the sole person here, except Almighty God Himself, my Judge . . . And now, so be it, I shall go out of it by myself, having found rest.

Still he was very 'loath to leave'; would he ever 'have quiet again'? Despite having been 'in such doubt and suspense', it had been the 'happiest time' in his life, 'because so quiet'.[12]

While he was 'burning and packing . . . reading and folding—passing from a metaphysical MS to a lump of resin or an ink-glass',[13] he was shocked to read a virulent attack on Anglo-Catholics in a pamphlet by F. W. Faber, a former fellow of University College and a promising young poet who had attracted Wordsworth's attention. Faber had come over to Rome a few weeks after Newman and founded in Birmingham a community called 'Brothers of the Will of God', which included a number of youths from his former Anglican parish. Nothing was more calculated than such invective to dissuade people like Pusey and Keble from becoming Roman Catholics. On the other hand, Newman had no hesitation in criticizing to Pusey the lack of charity shown towards

---

[11] Ibid. 102.   [12] Ibid. 113, 125–6.   [13] Ibid. 117.

converts, who had made considerable 'sacrifices' to join the Church of Rome, only to find themselves accused of moral 'deterioration'.[14]

On the afternoon of 22 February 1846 Newman left Littlemore—'I quite tore myself away—and could not help kissing my bed, and mantelpiece, and other parts of the house.'[15] He spent a final night in Oxford at the home of a friend, Manuel Johnson, the Radcliffe Observer, who was Bowden's first cousin. Late that night Pusey came to say goodbye. It was another twenty-two years before Newman was to see Littlemore again, and another thirty-two years before he was to visit Oxford again.

Old Oscott, or Maryvale as it was now called, could hardly rival Littlemore in Newman's affections, but it did have one inestimable advantage which deeply impressed its new occupant from the outset: the reservation of the Sacrament in the chapel, which made Christ 'really' present. 'I am writing next door to the Chapel', he told Henry Wilberforce; '—It is such an incomprehensible blessing to have Christ in bodily presence in one's house, within one's walls, as swallows up all other privileges and destroys, or should destroy, every pain. To know that He is close by—to be able again and again through the day to go in to Him . . .'[16] Before he left the Church of England, not only had Newman been less than enthusiastic about English Roman Catholicism, but his determined resolve to keep his distance meant that he was remarkably ignorant in many ways about the Church to which he now belonged, and particularly with regard to the central feature of Catholic devotional life which so moved him now:

We went over not realizing those privileges which we have found *by* going. I never allowed my mind to dwell on what I might gain of blessedness—but certainly, if I had thought much upon it, I could not have fancied the extreme, ineffable comfort of being in the same house with Him who cured the sick and taught His disciples . . . When I have been in Churches abroad, I have religiously abstained from acts of worship, though it was a most soothing comfort to go into them—nor did I know what was going on; I neither understood nor tried to understand the Mass service—and I did not know, or did not observe, the tabernacle Lamp—but now after tasting of the awful delight of worshipping God in His Temple, how unspeakably cold is the idea of a Temple without that Divine Presence! One is tempted to say what is the meaning, what is the use of it?[17]

The tabernacle with the Blessed Sacrament was not simply a source of spiritual comfort, but it was what above all helped to produce 'the deep impression of religion as an objective fact'[18] which so impressed Newman as a convert. He admired 'every where the signs of an awful and real

[14] *LD* xi. 124.   [15] Ibid. 132.   [16] Ibid. 129.   [17] Ibid. 131.
[18] Ibid. 65.

system'.¹⁹ Far from being 'a vague generality' or 'an idea', Catholicism was indeed 'a working religion'.²⁰ Had he not as an Anglican 'kept aloof from Catholics from a sense of duty' but 'known them and their religion from personal acquaintance', he would have been 'exposed to a set of influences in their favour, from which in matter of fact' he 'was debarred'.²¹ He told Mrs Bowden that he now possessed a 'confidence' he had made the right decision which he had not enjoyed at the moment of conversion: 'The moment before acting may be . . . peculiarly dreary—the mind may be confused—no reason for acting may be forthcoming in our mind . . . I could do nothing but shut myself up in my room and lie down on my bed.'²²

But there was another painful side to his new Catholic life. 'How dreary', he remembered, was 'my first year at Maryvale . . . when I was the gaze of so many eyes at Oscott, as if some wild incomprehensible beast, caught by the hunter, and a spectacle for Dr. Wiseman to exhibit to strangers, as himself being the hunter who captured it!' There was also 'the strangeness of ways, habits, religious observances, to which, however, I was urged on to conform without any delicacy towards my feelings'. Younger men like Dalgairns, who had been disciples of Newman, now felt 'on a level' with him and did not hesitate to 'lecture' him. The one-time Vicar of St Mary's, Oxford now 'had to stand at Dr. Wiseman's door waiting for Confession amid the Oscott boys'.²³ But there was a funny side to it, too. He found that his new co-religionists had 'the most absurd notions' about his asceticism—'they fancy I never eat, and I have just lost a good dinner in consequence . . .'.²⁴

2

It was decided in April that Newman should go in the summer to Rome to the College of Propaganda (the seminary for students from mission countries). He had told Wiseman he wanted 'a regular education' and also to 'be strictly under obedience and discipline for a time'. The college was known to be 'one of the strictest schools' in Rome, where he would be 'under the discipline of all but a school boy'. Indeed, he would be 'like a child going to a new school'. His 'difficulty' about being reordained ('I could not say that Anglican orders were invalid') had been removed by the assurance that, although ordination would not be explicitly conditional, the 'condition' would be 'implied . . . in the Church's *intention*'.²⁵

¹⁹ Ibid. 102.   ²⁰ Ibid. xii. 336.   ²¹ Ibid. xi. 146.   ²² Ibid. 141.
²³ *AW* 255.   ²⁴ *LD* xi. 43.   ²⁵ Ibid. 151–2, 283.

The community at Maryvale began in May 'to read divinity and make syllogisms'. They had to read by themselves, as they had no one to teach them. 'Only fancy', exclaimed Newman, 'my return to school at my age.' He began to wonder if Maryvale might become 'the *school* of Theology for the whole of England'. However, they would not want 'to be mere divines, but something more active. A mere theological school is not monastic enough.' Later in the summer he toyed with the idea of 'an institution having the express object of propagating the faith . . . and opposing heresy'. But the impossibility of finding a priest to teach theology to the community meant that they would probably all have to go abroad to study 'by relays'—'The use of instruction is first for discipline—secondly for the name of it.' One (convert) priest they had tried to get had been at the College of Propaganda himself, and he gave Newman a forbidding description of seminary life there, which he passed on to the Maryvale community ('you will all laugh at his information'). Rules regulated every minute in the day; 'no private confabs.' were allowed or visits to other students' rooms; all letters were opened; no one was allowed to have any personal money, or even clothes of their own ('It is a great object to use up the old clothes'). The last prohibition made Newman comment with mock alarm, 'Why, one might catch the plague, for depend on it, there are Egyptians and Turks there.' The only concession apparently was as much free snuff as one wanted, 'and I should be allowed to take a snuffbox'.[26]

The June number of the *Dublin Review* carried a review by Newman of Keble's new collection of poems, *Lyra Innocentium*, which had been published in May. Keble's *Christian Year*, he said, had made the Church of England 'poetical':

Poetry is the refuge of those who have not the Catholic Church . . . for the Church herself is the most sacred and august of poets. Poetry, as Mr. Keble lays it down in his University Lectures on the subject, is a method of relieving the overburdened mind; it is a channel through which emotion finds expression, and that a safe, regulated expression. Now what is the Catholic Church, viewed in her human aspect, but a discipline of the affections and passions? . . . She is the poet of her children; full of music to soothe the sad and control the wayward,—wonderful in story for the imagination of the romantic; rich in symbol and imagery, so that gentle and delicate feelings, which will not bear words, may in silence intimate their presence or commune with themselves. Her very being is poetry . . .

But while the 'Catholic Church speaks for itself, the Anglican needs external assistance', and Keble's poetry 'made the Anglican Church seem what Catholicism was and is'.[27]

[26] *LD* xi. 165, 195–6, 211, 200–1.   [27] *Ess.* ii. 442–5.

Newman commented to Mrs Bowden that he could find 'no coherence' in Keble's 'doctrine—I do not find *why* he holds so much of the Roman doctrine, yet not more,—unless he asserts the right of believing what he pleases.' Nor could he find any 'consistency' in Pusey: 'He says one thing to one person, another to another. He has never been yet from year's end to year's end one and the same . . . *whom* does *he* follow? himself.'[28] Mrs Bowden was herself trying to make up her mind whether or not to become a Catholic (she was received in July), but Newman refused to enter into complicated historical and theological questions with her—'I am not capable of stunning you with arguments, or stifling you with folios, or subduing you by an urgent tone or a confident manner.' Instead, he urged, 'You can have general impressions, and take general views, but you cannot go into details.'[29]

Although it was his own personal decision to go to Rome, it was still 'a very great trial' at his 'time of life' and with his 'stationary habits'.[30] On 7 September he and Ambrose St John set off from Brighton for France, where they were given a great welcome and treated as distinguished guests by the French Church. The feather beds and elaborate fare failed to agree with him, but he liked the French clergy and tried to imitate their incessant formal bows—'I can hardly keep my countenance, as I put my elbows to my hips and make a segment of a circle, the lower vertibrae being the centre and my head the circumference.'[31]

They reached Milan on 20 September. Newman was delighted with the church attached to the priests' house where they stayed. He feared he liked its 'style of architecture more than some of our . . . friends would approve', for he had to admit that he preferred the 'brightness, grace, and simplicity of the classical style' to Gothic architecture.

It has such a sweet, smiling, open countenance—and the Altar is so gracious and winning—standing out for all to see . . . Perhaps I do but follow the way of elderly persons, who have seen enough that is sad to like to be able to dispense with officious intentional sadness—and as the young prefer autumn and the old spring, the young tragedy and the old comedy, so in the ceremonial of religion, younger men have my leave to prefer gothic, if they will [but] tolerate me in my weakness which requires the Italian.

However much his 'reason' might 'go with Gothic',

my heart has ever gone with Grecian. I loved Trinity Chapel at Oxford more than any other building. There is in the Italian style such a simplicity, purity, elegance, beauty, brightness, which I suppose the word 'classical' implies, that it seems to befit the notion of an Angel or Saint . . .

But the style of architecture also meant that the Blessed Sacrament,

---

[28] *LD* xi. 171–2.   [29] Ibid. 187.   [30] Ibid. 238.   [31] Ibid. 246.

reserved on the high altar, was the focal point of the church: 'Nothing moves there but the distant glimmering Lamp which betokens the Presence of our Undying Life, hidden but ever working . . . .'. Again and again in these early days of his life as a Catholic, Newman alluded to this 'Real Presence':

It is really most wonderful to see the Divine Presence looking out almost into the open streets from the various Churches. . . . I never knew what worship was, as an objective fact, till I entered the Catholic Church . . .[32]

This was 'a real religion—not a mere opinion such, that you have no confidence that your next door neighbour holds it too, but an external objective substantive creed and worship'.[33] They constantly visited the Duomo (an 'overpowering place'):

. . . a Catholic Cathedral is a sort of world, every one going about his own business, but that business a religious one; groups of worshippers, and solitary ones—kneeling, standing—some at shrines, some at altars—hearing Mass and communicating—currents of worshippers intercepting and passing by each other—altar after altar lit up for worship, like stars in the firmament—or the bell giving notice of what is going on in parts you do not see—and all the while the canons in the choir going through matins and lauds, and at the end of it the incense rolling up from the high altar, and all this in one of the most wonderful buildings in the world and every day—lastly, all of this without any show or effort, but what everyone is used to—every one at his own work, and leaving every one else to his.[34]

Newman was captivated by Milan, 'a most wonderful place—to me more striking than Rome'. True, he had not been a Catholic when he had been in Rome—'but then Milan presents more associations with the history, which is familiar to me, than Rome. Here were St Ambrose, St Augustine, St Monica, St Athanasius . . .'. He was reading the life of St Charles Borromeo, the great Counter-Reformation Archbishop of Milan, who 'was raised up to resist that dreadful storm under which poor England fell—and as he in his day saved his country from Protestantism and its collateral evils, so are we now attempting to do something to resist the same foes of the Church in England . . . So I trust, and my mind has been full of him, so that I have even dreamed of him—and we go most days and kneel at his shrine . . .'. He thought Milan was 'the most interesting place' he had ever been to. He had a special personal interest because it was the see of St Ambrose—'whom I have heard and read of more than other Saints from a boy. It is 30 years this very month . . . since God made me religious, and St Ambrose in Milner's history was one of the first objects of my veneration.' Here, too,

[32] *LD* xi. 249–50, 252–3.　　　[33] Ibid. xii. 168.　　　[34] Ibid. xi. 253.

Augustine had been converted, and here Athanasius had come in his exile—'I never have been in a city, which moved me more—not even Rome . . .'.

And then too, it is not a mere imagination, as it might be in a ruined city, or in a desolate place where Saints once dwelt—but here are a score of Churches which are open to the passer by . . . and the Blessed Sacrament ready for the worshipper even before he enters. There is nothing which has brought home to me so much the Unity of the Church, as the presence of its Divine Founder and Life wherever I go—All places are, as it were, one . . .[35]

However wonderful the religion, Italian life on the more mundane level could be alarming. As on his previous visit, Newman was appalled by the 'vile practice of spitting [which] is a serious drawback on our enjoyment':

They spit everywhere—they spit on the kneeling boards—they encourage it, and as if for amusement go on every ten seconds. . . . They spit over the floors of their rooms—their floors are filthy principally with dust—if you drop your coat or stocking in undressing, it is far worse than if you dropped them in the street. . . . I could have fancied they liked spit . . . except that I saw a neighbour in the caffee spit by mistake on his coat, and I had great satisfaction in seeing the pains he was at to get rid of it.[36]

There was as much interest in Italy as in France in the famous convert, although the philosopher Rosmini, when he passed through Milan, excused himself from a meeting on the rather flimsy ground of language difficulties. Newman did not profess to understand the great Italian reformer's philosophy, but he could not help being suspicious of it. Rosmini's views were indeed controversial, but there Newman had something in common with him, for his own *Essay on the Development of Christian Doctrine* had recently been attacked in America by the convert Orestes Brownson as 'essentially anticatholic and Protestant'.[37] The problem of his own future vocation (and that of the Maryvale community) continued to preoccupy him, but he felt no attraction to Rosmini's newly founded order, which was active in England as well as northern Italy. He was also unimpressed by what he heard and saw of the great orders like the Jesuits and Dominicans (even the allegedly observant Dominicans of Florence turned out to be 'manufacturers of scented water', with 'very choice wines in their cellar'), and he began to feel that Wiseman had been right to advise them to become Oratorians, as 'external secularism with a gentle inward bond of asceticism' seemed to meet the contemporary situation.[38]

[35] Ibid. 249–54.   [36] Ibid. 259.   [37] Ibid. 228 n. 1.
[38] Ibid. 263.

3

On 28 October, after five weeks in Milan, the two travellers reached Rome. First impressions were not very encouraging. The dirt and fleas of the hotel ('a palace of filth') were such that they did not even venture to unpack their clothes. And the cumbersome formal dress they were obliged to wear as 'gentlemen' rather than ordinary seminarians (including 'a large heavy cocked hat'),[39] in anticipation of a sudden summons to attend on the Pope, plunged Newman into such miserable agony that he felt like joining a religious order immediately. After the Duomo at Milan, St Peter's, at this time standing outside the city and usually empty, was very disappointing. Nor did Newman 'like the people of Rome—One is struck at once with their horrible cruelty to animals—also with their dishonesty, lying and stealing apparently without any conscience—and thirdly with their extreme dirt'. On the other hand, he observed '*every where* a simple certainty in believing which to a Protestant or Anglican is quite astonishing'. Unfortunately, it was 'not that *living* faith which leads to correctness or sanctity of character', but rather 'they show in a wonderful way how it is possible to disjoin religion and morality'.[40] Still, the Roman parochial clergy struck Newman as 'exemplary' (unlike the 'lazy bad priests' of the surrounding Campagna).[41]

After about a fortnight Newman and St John entered the College of Propaganda, where specially decorated rooms had been prepared for the distinguished new students, who were treated as though they were 'princes'.[42] The end of a corridor had been cut off with a glazed partition to create a private apartment, where all the furniture was new, with expensive fittings. To add to their embarrassment, tea was provided for them every night. However, they refused to be exempted from the discipline of seminary life, which was their reason for coming in the first place; the only concession they took advantage of was the freedom to go out when they wanted. The Jesuit Rector, Padre Bresciani, was extremely solicitous, 'anticipating all one's thoughts and wishes'. Newman was highly impressed by the 'self denying life' of the Jesuit staff, who had 'no enjoyment of life' and nothing to look forward to but only the consolation of 'the thought of the next world'.[43]

Intellectually, Newman's chief concern was the theological reaction in Rome to the *Essay on Development*. Two leading Jesuit theologians, who knew of the American attack, felt that Newman had gone too far in his application of the principle of development. But they knew little of the

---

[39] *LD* xi. 267, 273.   [40] Ibid. xii. 24.   [41] Ibid. 26.
[42] Ibid. 272.   [43] Ibid. 24.

book apart from the fact that American Unitarians, much to the alarm of American Catholics, were making play of the admission that the Trinitarian teaching of Nicaea was not always in accord with the Antenicene Fathers. Later, Newman discovered that the book was 'accused of denying moral certainty' and holding that 'we cannot get beyond probability in religious questions',[44] although he had in fact used the word 'probable' in opposition not to 'certain' but to 'demonstrative'.

In general, Newman was shocked by the poor state of both philosophy and theology. There was no study of Aristotle, nor of St Thomas Aquinas. A few searching questions from his distinguished student completely confused the startled lecturer at Propaganda. The Roman theologians, Newman realized with dismay, simply had no 'view'.[45]

What impressed Newman about the college was not the education provided but the number of different nationalities represented; there were thirty-two languages spoken, which gave the community Mass a Pentecost flavour. There was a heroic aspect, too. Some of the students were marked out for martyrdom in their own countries. Others were to die prematurely in Rome of fever. Of eight students from New York, only one or two returned—the rest died in Rome. 'The native tribes wished to send some youths here—they proposed to send 12 that they might have six back'.[46] Apart from endless colds, Newman's only suffering was nostalgia for old friends in England ('no one here can sympathize with me duly'). It was 'a kind of dream' to find himself in the College of Propaganda, 'so quiet, so safe, so happy—as if I had always been here—as if there had been no violent rupture or vicissitude in my course of life—nay more quiet and happy than before'. He did not know what people in Rome would make of him, considering his shyness and how little Italian he spoke: 'speaking languages is not my gift, I am not glib, and never was even in English—and I am bashful when I ought to be bold.'[47]

After Mass at half past 6 or 7 (the Roman clocks varied widely, thus offering 'an outlet and exemplification of the Protestant principle of private judgment which is forbidden in religion'), there was a continental breakfast. There were two hour-long lectures in the morning ('at which N. goes to sleep and nods', noted Ambrose St John as a parenthesis in the account Newman was writing for the community at Maryvale), which one was required to attend, 'lecture after lecture,—to drawl through a few tedious pages . . . quite necessary for boys, not for grown men'.[48] In the afternoon they visited the city, the streets of which were so clogged up with dung (on a scale Newman had never seen before), after weeks of more or less continuous rain, that one was forced

44 Ibid. xi. 289.   45 Ibid. 280.   46 Ibid. 292.
47 Ibid. 284, 294.   48 Ibid. 298; xii. 48.

either to try and hold up one's cassock and mantella at the same time or else don the hated cocked hat with dress coat. At 3 there was another lecture. This did not leave much time for reading, but there were plenty of free days, and lectures could be skipped, especially on Saturdays, when the students were examined on the preceding week's lectures. (In the end they gave up going to lectures and read by themselves.) However, there were other distractions—visits from ecclesiastics, and English lessons for an aspiring young Italian missionary.[49] As for the formal 'recreations', Newman found himself as tongue-tied as he had been in the early days in the Oriel Common Room. After tea made in a tea-machine by Ambrose St John, there was time for more reading, followed by Rosary in the chapel, supper, and then bed.

Towards the end of November Newman and St John were summoned to see the Pope, Pius IX, who was very cordial and friendly, even though Newman had knocked his head against the Pope's knee as he bent to kiss the papal foot! What seemed to the Pope rather more clumsy was the sermon Newman was pressed to preach extempore at the funeral of a young Catholic niece of the Countess of Shrewsbury. The sermon noticeably lacked the fluency customary in Rome, while it offended English Protestants by its tone (one gentleman expressed the view that its deliverer should be thrown into the Tiber). The Pope was not amused when he heard about it.

4

On the day after Christmas Newman and St John visited the Roman Oratory. With its library and sets of rooms, it reminded Newman of an Oxford college. As a community of secular priests living under a rule but not under vows, the Oratory of St Philip Neri offered a middle way between a religious order and the diocesan priesthood. Oratorians were allowed to keep their own property, and Newman admitted it would 'try' his 'faith very much' to take a vow of poverty. Another objection to joining a religious order was his 'own previous history'. Apart from the difficulty of taking on 'new habits' at his age, he had perhaps 'begun a work' at Oxford which he was 'to finish', whereas by becoming a member of an order he would be 'beginning life again' by 'becoming a sort of instrument of others'.[50] Wiseman's original suggestion that they should become Oratorians began to seem very attractive.

---

[49] Julius Cesare Mola (1823–?), who went on the Ceylon mission, but left the Church in 1865 after the publication of the Ultramontane *Syllabus of Errors*. Ironically, he was able to put the knowledge of English which he had acquired from Newman to practical use when in the late 1880s he took charge of an Anglican mission to Italians in London (see *LD* xi. 347).

[50] *LD* xi. 306.

The Oratory offered opportunities for learning and scholarship, as well as for active pastoral work. Oratories were always situated in towns, and there was ample scope for apostolic and evangelistic work among the de-Christianized population of a manufacturing town like Birmingham. Without attempting to run a school or theological college, an Oratory could also support educational and theological work. The obvious place for such an Oratory was London, but a start could be made in Birmingham without giving up Maryvale. The Oratory idea was flexible enough to admit of a variety of possibilities. As for its founder, the sixteenth-century Philip Neri reminded Newman vividly of Keble with his mixture of 'extreme hatred of humbug, playfulness, nay oddity, tender love for others, and severity'.[51]

The former plan of a theological college or seminary at Maryvale faded away. It did not provide the religious framework that Newman wanted, and there were practical difficulties. But there was also the peculiar problem of Newman's position as a theologian. The leading dogmatic theologian in Rome, Carlo Passaglia, disapproved of the *Essay on Development*. There was enough suspicion of the converts in England without opposition from Rome as well. Newman had thought of writing a preface to the projected French translation of the *Essay*, in order to rebut the charge that he was substituting probability for certainty. But in the event he began to fear any further publicity for the book—'I don't like to begin my career in the Catholic Church with a condemnation or retraction.'[52] One suggested line of defence was to publish a French translation of some of the *Oxford University Sermons*, for which Newman wrote a preface in Latin[53] to explain that they clarified the *Essay on Development*, particularly the aspect of antecedent probability. But then he began to be afraid that the *Sermons* might themselves fall under ecclesiastical censure. It seemed 'hard, since nations now converse by printing not in the schools, that an English Catholic cannot investigate truth with one of France or Rome, without having the Inquisition upon him'. Having re-read the *Sermons*, he thought that on the whole they were 'the best things' he had written—'and I cannot believe that they are not Catholic, and will not be useful'. There were times when he 'vividly' felt that he had 'not yet been done justice to', but there was even less chance of his writings being appreciated at Rome where there seemed to be 'an iron form' and where 'people are at no trouble to deepen their views'.[54]

---

[51] Ibid. xii. 25.

[52] Ibid. 36.

[53] Published in Henry Tristram, ed., 'Cardinal Newman's Theses de Fide and his Proposed Introduction to the French Translation of the University Sermons', *Gregorianum*, 18 (1937), 248–60.

[54] *LD* xii. 29, 32.

In the end he decided to send to the other leading theologian in Rome, Giovanni Perrone, a list of formal propositions summarizing his views on faith and reason.[55] He also sent him a paper on his theory of development.[56] Finally, as an extra precaution, in the spring of 1847 he published 'in Latin some dissertations which have in substance appeared in my translation of St. Athanasius'.[57] They underwent the full rigours of ecclesiastical censorship and were intended to show that the *Essay* rested on an accurate and deep knowledge of the Fathers.

Meanwhile, the Oratory plan had met with general approval in Rome. True, Newman foresaw that friends in England might prefer a more distinguished sphere for him. But he had no doubt that what he wanted was active priestly work, with time for reading and writing. However, he could not help the depressed feeling that his 'time' was 'past' and that all he could now do was to be the 'bond of union' for the English Oratory.[58]

He began to plan the new foundation. Assuming that Oratories would be founded in other towns apart from Birmingham, he suggested to Wiseman that Maryvale could become 'a sort of mother house', combining novitiate, retreat, and holiday house. An experimental foundation (without a public church) could be made first in the centre of Birmingham. On a lighter note, Newman felt they needed 'companions who have a good deal of fun in them', for if 'we have not spirit, it will be like bottled beer with the cork out'.[59] So far as the membership of the new Oratory was concerned, the attitude at Rome was not one of suspicion at converts collaborating (as English Catholics complained), but the fact of their having lived together at Littlemore was a recommendation and could serve as part of the novitiate. Newman also discovered that the English Oratory was expected to meet an important need by providing a more educated type of pastoral priest for the Church in England. He wondered if he would return home with the same revitalized energy with which he had returned in 1833. Later, he lamented, 'How I wish I had in me the energy which I had when I began the Tracts for the Times! Now I am . . . so stiff so wooden.'[60] However, some of the old exuberance was certainly coming back as various projects and ideas caught his imagination. A surprise offer from the Pope of the defunct but magnificent Malta Oratory as a Mediterranean novitiate was extremely tempting (although in the end the idea never came to anything).

[55] Published in Tristram, op. cit., 226–41.

[56] See T. Lynch, ed., 'The Newman–Perrone Paper on Development', *Gregorianum*, 16 (1935), 402–47.

[57] *LD* xii. 60. See *TT* 1–91.

[58] *LD* xii. 45.   [59] Ibid. xii. 51, 54–5.   [60] Ibid. xiii. 16.

5

At the end of June, when he left the College of Propaganda, Newman sent a memorandum to the Rector on the general discontent among English-speaking students. He complained of the ban on visits outside and the reading of books. Mature students had no one to talk to in their own language and there were no opportunities for philosophical and theological discussion. In spite of the flood of Protestant books on the perils of 'Jesuitism', Newman found the Jesuits disappointingly lacking in craft and subtlety. Clever academically as many of them were, they lacked originality and the intelligence needed for new initiatives; hard-working and self-sacrificing, they struck him as 'plodding, methodical, unromantic'. He realized that they were unthinking *conservatives*, astonishingly reminiscent of Anglicans like the Kebles at the time of the Reform Bill. He concluded—and the words were to ring through the rest of his life as a Catholic: 'There is a deep suspicion of *change*, with a perfect incapacity to create any thing *positive* for the wants of the times.'[61]

Unlike the Jesuits, who were the equivalent of Spartans, the Oratorians resembled the Athenians in their comparative freedom: unlike soldiers in a phalanx, but like legionaries, they had to fight by themselves, and yet with others, as responsible individuals. So, at any rate, Newman liked to imagine the Oratorian vocation. The papal 'Brief' established the Oratory at Birmingham, but Newman was certain that sooner or later they would be brought nearer to London, if only because Wiseman was moving there. He hoped that old Catholics might join them to leaven the convert lump, even wondering if Charles Newsham, the President of Ushaw, might agree to be Superior.

When Newman left the College of Propaganda, a month after his ordination to the priesthood on 30 May 1847, he went to begin his Oratorian novitiate at Santa Croce with other members of the Maryvale community, who by now had come out to Rome to join him and St John. 'How dreary,' Newman later recalled, was this novitiate under Father Rossi of the Roman Oratory ('room-sweeping, slop-emptying, dinner-serving, bed making, shoe blacking')[62] after the 'happy months' at Propaganda.[63] However, it did not last long, and at the end of November Father Rossi left, the official papal Brief arrived, and Newman said his goodbyes. He was now an Oratorian priest and Superior of the English Oratory. Returning via Germany and Munich, where they went to tea with the church historian Döllinger, he and St John arrived in London on Christmas Eve.

On Christmas Day they lunched with Wiseman. The news he gave them was to have far-reaching consequences. Faber had offered—with Wiseman's approval—to join the Oratory together with his 'Brothers of the Will of God' or 'Wilfridians', Faber's convert community now at Cotton Hall, St Wilfrid's, Staffordshire. Before Newman had left Littlemore, he had already been politely discouraging about Faber's suggestion that the two communities might join up—'I cannot help thinking you should be a distinct centre of operation and collect people about you.'[64] Apart from Faber's own colourful personality, there was the objection that neither his collection of lay brothers nor his devotionalism seemed to fit the Oratory of St Philip Neri. It was all too 'poetical'.[65] However, Newman's own community favoured the merger, even though Newman himself was worried that they did not know enough about Faber's followers. No doubt he remembered the warning of his Jesuit confessor in Rome that everything depended upon their 'own internal union'.[66]

6

On New Year's Day 1848 Newman celebrated Mass at Maryvale for the first time. Eight days later occurs the first reference to his first novel, *Loss and Gain: The Story of a Convert*, of which there is no previous mention in the extant letters or even in the diaries. It was not until the sixth edition of 1874 that Newman actually put his name on the title-page, and in the 'advertisement' he explained that the book was an answer to a 'tale, directed against the Oxford converts to the Catholic Faith', which 'was sent from England to the author of this Volume in the summer of 1847, when he was resident at Santa Croce in Rome'.[67] This was *From Oxford to Rome: And how it fared with Some who lately made the Journey* (1847) by Elizabeth Harris, a convert who had left the Church. There was another reason for writing the novel: Newman wanted to help the publisher James Burns, who had recently become a Catholic and who stood to lose business as a result. In the event, the novel sold very well. It was published in 1848, with an advertisement dated 21 February.

Newman was careful to insist that *Loss and Gain* was not intended to be an apologetic work but 'a description of . . . the course of thought and state of mind'[68] of a particular convert to Catholicism. Obviously, the book contains certain specific arguments for Catholicism, but Newman's purpose goes deeper than that. He himself pointed out that the book contained hardly any theological argument—'*Doctrine* is hardly

---

[64] *LD* xi. 105. [65] Ibid. xii. 137, 140. [66] Ibid. 53.
[67] *LG*, p. ix. [68] Ibid., p. vii.

touched upon.'[69] What he is really concerned with is the kind of underlying 'first principles' that underpin explicit assent to Catholic doctrine.

At the outset, the hero, Charles Reding, is contrasted with his college friend Sheffield who is better informed and better read, but more superficial. The difference is expressed by Newman in his favourite distinction between 'view' and 'viewiness'. To have a view is to have an understanding and a perspective; to be 'viewy' is to be over-anxious to have a 'view', to be dissatisfied 'intellectually with things as they are . . . critical, impatient to reduce things to system', argumentative.[70] When it comes to religious conviction, Reding knows that to gain a true view is a gradual process of growth, 'not a conclusion from premises': 'all the paper-arguments in the world are unequal to giving one a view in a moment.'[71]

There are obvious similarities between the author and his hero. Perhaps the most important of all is the same sensitiveness to the *real*. Running through the novel is a strong, often comic, sense of reality and unreality. Whatever its alleged superstitions, Roman Catholicism is real. Conversely, whatever high Anglicans may believe or say, the Church of England is a 'Protestant reality' but 'a Catholic sham'. Whatever changes may be made in externals and ritual, 'the living body abjures Catholicism, flings off the name and the thing'.[72]

As the debate progresses, increasingly the issue becomes one of reality versus unreality. And because two contradictions cannot 'both be real',[73] there must be truth and falsehood in religion. Thus, the principle of reality supports a dogmatic rather than a liberal theology. For example, Mr Vincent, a tutor, 'was for ever mistaking shams for truths, and converting pompous nothings into oracles' in his pursuit of the *Via Media*, denouncing all parties and 'holding all opinions', however contradictory.[74] He warns the hero against 'pushing things *too far*, and wishing to form a *system*'.[75] On the contrary, religious truth is divided among the different insights of the different denominations—none 'is entirely right or entirely wrong'.[76] The unreality of Mr Vincent's munificent comprehensiveness is marvellously captured by Newman's rendering of his final eulogy of the Church of England:

'Our Church,' he said, 'admitted of great liberty of thought within her pale. Even our greatest divines differed from each other in many respects; nay, Bishop Taylor differed from himself. It was a great principle in the English Church. Her true children agree to differ. In truth, there is that robust, masculine, noble independence in the English mind, which refuses to be tied down to artificial shapes, but is like, I will say, some great and beautiful

[69] *LD* xii. 194.   [70] *LG* 19–20.   [71] Ibid. 294.   [72] Ibid. 52.
[73] Ibid. 34.   [74] Ibid. 74.   [75] Ibid. 81.   [76] Ibid. 82.

production of nature—a tree, which is rich in foliage and fantastic in limb, no sickly denizen of the hothouse, or helpless dependent of the garden wall, but in careless magnificence sheds its fruits upon the free earth, for the bird of the air and the beast of the field, and all sorts of cattle, to eat thereof and rejoice'.[77]

Then there is Lord Newlights, who is equally unreal because he has 'no fixed, definite religious principle'—'You don't know where to find him.'[78]

Charles's religious quest is abruptly interrupted by his father's death, which for a time makes the pursuit of truth itself seem unreal. Theological questions suddenly appear 'shams' compared with the 'great realities' of the old-fashioned undoctrinal parsonage which was his home.[79] However, the change is only temporary, and as Charles gradually becomes more and more 'Catholic', it seems to him as if he 'is coming out of shadows into realities'.[80] The change is symbolized by the difference between one of his Oxford friends, Willis, a convert to Roman Catholicism who actually enters a real monastery, and another friend, the Anglo-Catholic Bateman, with an industrial parish with 10,000 parishioners, who is toying with 'plans for the introduction of the surplice and gilt candlesticks among his people'.[81]

The intended contrast between two representatives of a real and an unreal religion is caricatured by a later comic scene when Charles, by now close to reception into the Church, comes across in a religious bookshop at Bath another Anglo-Catholic friend from Oxford, White, who had once idealized clerical celibacy, but is now a clergyman engaged to be married. The absurd dialogue between White and his pretty bride accounts for the Puseyite charge that Newman had sunk lower even than Dickens. (Newman himself claimed, 'I have laughed at nothing . . . which I did not laugh at when a Protestant.'[82]) Again, it is the unreality rather than the comfortable worldliness of the Anglican clergy which disgusts Charles and his author. Louisa cannot remember the name of a book she wanted. Can it be 'The Catholic Parsonage'? or 'Modified Celibacy'? No, it is 'Abbeys and Abbots'—' "I want to get some hints for improving the rectory windows when we get home; and our church wants, you know, a porch for the poor people." '[83]

In the advertisement to the novel, Newman had been careful to deny that any of the characters was properly representative of Tractarianism, and in a later letter he stressed that his satire was directed against the same 'unreality and inconsistency' which he had laughed at as an Anglican, in other words at the *abuse* of Tractarian views.[84] This does not affect his serious criticisms of the inconsistency and unreality of the

[77] *LG* 84–5.　　[78] Ibid. 121.　　[79] Ibid. 157.　　[80] Ibid. 255.
[81] Ibid. 338.　　[82] *LD* xv. 399.　　[83] *LG* 351.　　[84] *LD* xv. 399; xiv. 360.

Via Media position, but it does mean that the comic element in the novel should be seen in perspective. Thus there can be no question about the seriousness of Tractarian insistence on fasting, or its preoccupation with the Church's calendar—in spite of Mr Vincent's order to the astonished college servant to check if it was a fasting day: ' "The Vigil of St. Peter, you mean, Watkins; I thought so. Then let us have a plain beefsteak and a saddle of mutton; no Portugal onions, Watkins, or currant-jelly; and some simple pudding, Charlotte pudding, Watkins—that will do." '[85]

Imagery is often used to devastating effect. Thus to the Very Revd Dr Brownside, 'Revelation . . . instead of being the abyss of God's counsels, with its dim outlines and broad shadows, was a flat, sunny plain, laid out with straight macadamised roads.'[86] There is no problem about 'religious dogmas', which are neither true nor false, but merely relative and more or less appropriate modes of expressing eternal truths. On the other hand, imagery can be used as humorously but no less positively in support of Catholicism. To the objection that converts must use their 'private judgment', Newman agrees, but adds:

they use it in order ultimately to supersede it; as a man out of doors uses a lamp in a dark night, and puts it out when he gets home. What would be thought of his bringing it into his drawing room? . . . if he came in with a great-coat on his back, a hat on his head, an umbrella under his arm, and a large stable-lantern in his hand?[87]

And when Charles has his decisive meeting on the train with a Catholic priest, he is told, ' "A man's moral life is concentrated in each moment of his life; it lives in the tip of his fingers, and the spring of his insteps." '[88] In a sense, the whole novel is intended to illustrate the truth of this.

As the hero moves to the point of conversion, he is assured by Willis that the Mass ' "is not a mere form of words,—it is a great action, the greatest action that can be on earth" '.[89] And when Charles attends a Catholic church for the first time, it is not the beauty of the ritual that impresses him so much as the objective reality of the worship, made possible especially by 'the Great Presence, which makes a Catholic Church different from every other place in the world'.[90] It is not so much the quality of the devotion that is important, it is the sense that the worship is real because there is a real object for the worship—unlike the Church of England, where Charles finds to his dismay that it is not even clear why only the clergyman may 'read prayers'.[91] To use a striking analogy from one of the letters, the presence of the Blessed Sacrament, the communion of saints, the sacraments and sacramentals all ensure that 'the Atonement of Christ is not a thing at a distance, or like the sun

---

[85] *LG* 80. [86] Ibid. 68. [87] Ibid. 203. [88] Ibid. 379.
[89] Ibid. 328. [90] Ibid. 427. [91] Ibid. 28.

standing over against us and separated off from us, but that we are surrounded by an *atmosphere* and are in a medium, through which his warmth and light flow in upon us on every side'. It is this concrete reality that makes Catholicism even a *'different religion'* from Anglicanism.[92]

Closely connected to reality and unreality are consistency and inconsistency. Trying to graft Catholic observances and ritual on to the liturgy of the Church of England is not only unreal but impossible to reconcile with Anglican formularies. Anglican comprehensiveness is self-contradictory, because two opposing points of view cannot both be right. As in his correspondence with high Anglicans, Newman argues that it is inconsistent to reject the Roman Catholic insistence on the papacy, and yet at the same time to insist against Nonconformists on the necessity of the episcopacy. Or again, what right has one to object to devotion to the Virgin Mary interfering with worship to God, when that is exactly the kind of charge that is brought against Anglicans themselves for believing, for example, in Baptismal regeneration when that seems to undermine faith in Christ's atonement? Why, in short, should one believe in parts of Catholicism and not the whole of it? Moreover, it seems inconsistent to regard as essential faith in certain basic doctrines while at the same time commending in general an open mind in religious belief. As for the Thirty-nine Articles, Charles concludes that they are inconsistent with other parts of the Prayer Book, and also with themselves. And finally, is it not the supreme inconsistency to refuse members of the Church of England the right to become Roman Catholics, when they have all along been urged to use their own private judgement in matters of religion?

Loss and Gain, without being an autobiography or in any full sense an apologetic for Catholicism, contains a number of interesting autobiographical elements as well as familiar arguments for conversion to the Catholic Church. But it remains essentially a sketch, often very funny, but not as serious or as well constructed as the novel that was to follow, which contains a more profound analysis and dramatization of the essential nature of religious faith. It does, however, foreshadow Newman's two brilliant satirical polemics, which were soon to absorb his creative powers.

[92] *LD* xii. 224.

8

Controversy and Satire

AFTER only three weeks back at Maryvale, Newman began preaching a
series of eight popular parochial sermons at St. Chad's, Birmingham.
The manuscript of the first sermon is lost, but the rest have survived and
have been published posthumously.[1] After he had read out the second
one he gave up the Anglican practice of reading sermons. The young
Edward White Benson, the future Archbishop of Canterbury, went to
hear one of the sermons. His reaction, an extraordinary mixture of
admiration and revulsion, suggests the kind of deeply divided feelings
Newman inspired in contemporaries whose extreme antipathy to
Catholicism was only matched by their fascinated reverence for
Newman himself.

He is a wonderful man truly, and spoke with a sort of Angelic eloquence . . .
Sweet, flowing, unlaboured language in short, very short, and very pithy and
touching sentences . . . he was very much emaciated, and when he began his
voice was very feeble, and he spoke with great difficulty, nay sometimes he
gasped for breath; but his voice was very sweet . . . it was awful—the terrible
lines deeply ploughed all over his face, and the craft that sat upon his retreating
forehead and sunken eyes.[2]

As for the facial lines that struck Benson so forcibly, Newman himself
was painfully aware that 'those sad long years of anxiety have stamped
themselves on my face—and now that they are at an end, yet I cannot
change what has become a physical effect'.[3]

On 1 February the English Congregation of the Oratory was formally
set up by Newman, when he admitted nine members—five priests, one
novice, and three lay brothers. On the 14th the St Wilfrid's community
was also admitted. Immediately a problem arose—a foretaste of things
to come. There was an obligation to Lord Shrewsbury to keep the
mission at St Wilfrid's going, into which the community had already
invested £7,000. But the Pope's Brief specified Maryvale, nor did the
community there feel like moving yet again. It had been difficult to

[1] In CS.
[2] A. C. Benson, *The Life of Edward White Benson, sometime Archbishop of Canterbury* (London, 1899),
i. 62.
[3] *LD* xii. 223.

retain Maryvale—and only as linked to a future house in Birmingham—since Oratories were supposed to be in cities; it would be out of the question, apart from the expense, to have an Oratory at St Wilfrid's. The obvious solution was for Lord Shrewsbury to find another religious community for St Wilfrid's, and for the Wilfridians to give up the place without losing their money. But Newman refused to accede to Faber's insistent demand that an immediate decision should be taken either (preferably) to give up Maryvale, or, failing that, St Wilfrid's. Time and patience were needed to reach a compromise that was as fair as possible to all three parties. Faber's unconditional 'surrender' of himself and his community to the Oratory appeared after all to be not so unconditional.

An important element in the eventual rift between Faber and himself is revealed in Newman's warnings against gratuitously introducing into sermons miraculous legends likely to offend and inappropriate allusions to the Blessed Virgin Mary. 'We must avoid every thing extreme'[4] was Newman's advice to Faber's community. Later Newman even had to warn against an exaggerated enthusiasm for St Philip himself, as if he were 'the instrumental Saint of modern times' and as if everybody ought to become Oratorians.[5] It was important to recognize the 'necessity of being men, of pruning luxuriances, lest we get thin and shabby about the roots'.[6]

To begin with, though, Newman loyally supported Faber through the controversies in which he became embroiled. As an enthusiastic Oratorian, Faber, of course, preferred the classical architecture of the Italian Renaissance to Gothic. His insistence that the elevation and benediction of the Blessed Sacrament should be clearly visible to everybody in the church led to a comical row with Pugin, when he visited St Wilfrid's. Faber, apparently, retorted to Pugin in a quarrel over rood screens, 'Why, Pugin, you might as well treat the Blessed Sacrament as Henry VIII's people did, as do what you do at a benediction . . .'.[7] The dispute was continued by Ambrose Phillipps, who complained to Newman about Faber's 'violent and excessive' ideas and methods. However, as Newman patiently pointed out, the excess and violence were not all on one side: Pugin's Gothic fanaticism was well known. As for Phillipps, it seemed that he had '*cursed*' the Oratory: 'Now if this was the case, did it become a person who had used strong language of this kind to treasure up and divulge the strong language of another?'[8]

The extravagance and inconsistency of Phillipps's quaintly spelt 'Gothick' reply must have reminded Newman of Faber's own letters, which alternated between querulous demands and abject protestations

---

[4] *LD* xii. 197. [5] Ibid. xiv. 30. [6] Ibid. 144.
[7] Ibid. xii. 212 n. 2. [8] Ibid. 212.

of love and obedience. ('Save me', Newman once wrote in exasperation, 'from such affection and devotion, and give me a little more tenderness for others, and a little less self will.'[9]) After denying the alleged curse, Phillipps went on to claim that he was only 'a simple Catholick' who was 'not conscious . . . of being overbearing or intolerant to the opponents of *Gothick ideas*'. On the other hand,

I have a strong conviction that Gothick is Christian architecture, and Italian or Grecian Pagan, in their respective origin and destination, but I have no desire to *quarrel* with those who would build their Churches on the model of a Pagan Temple . . . But really I cannot plead guilty to a charge of intolerance even on ritual questions—In my own chapels I would certainly insist on Church principles being carried out, but if other people have other views on these questions I have no idea of quarrelling with them on that account. On the occasion before alluded to at St Wilfrid's I did not quarrel with Fr. Faber, because he had no skreen, but he shocked me by his awful expression in denouncing the skreen . . .[10]

Newman admitted that Faber had actually accused Phillipps of uttering the following denunciation rather than curse: 'Father Faber, God for your pride destroyed and brought to nought your first effort: He will curse and destroy *your order*, and it will perish if you go on thus.' But was 'it not somewhat *exclusive* to call Grecian or Italian *Pagan*, as you do?' And moreover, 'If it is *Pagan*, it is *Popish* too, for I suppose the Pope has given quite as much sanction to it as he has to Gregorian music, which by the bye seems to be Pagan in the same sense that Italian architecture is.' Indeed, so far as Pugin was concerned, 'half Christendom' was '*pagan*', including St Peter's itself. Unfortunately, Pugin had 'the great fault of a man of genius': he was a 'bigot'. He was 'notoriously engaged in a revival', for there was no 'continuous' Gothic tradition. But the Church's liturgy, which was always changing 'according to the times', required a 'living architecture', whereas Gothic was 'now like an old dress, which fitted a man well twenty years back but must be altered to fit him now'. Personally, Newman remarked, he had never sympathized as an Anglican with 'parties, or extreme opinions, of any kind', including the antiquarianism of the Camden Society, which struck him as 'unreal'.[11]

2

In the Lent of 1848 Newman was asked by Wiseman, along with Faber and other members of the Oratory, to preach a series of sermons in London. This kind of preaching, like the unfortunate sermon in Rome,

[9] Ibid. xiii. 41.   [10] Ibid. xii. 216 n. 1.   [11] Ibid. 216. 220–2.

was not Newman's style: 'I can preach to people I know, but any thing like a display is quite out of my line.'[12] It turned out, as Newman anticipated, to be a 'blunder' and a 'failure', about which he was to feel 'a raw sensitiveness' long after.[13] However, one positive result was the offer of a piece of ground in Bayswater with money for building an Oratory and church—the 'only drawback is that it is *not London*'.[14] The scheme finally foundered because the real inducement for going so far out of London as Bayswater was that there was sufficient land for building a large enough house for an Oratory community, whereas the condition of the offer was that a church had to be built first without any assurance that there would later be enough money for a proper Oratory. But still London remained the goal: after all, the Papal Brief specified the educated upper classes as the principal aim of the Oratory's apostolate, and these were to be found in the capital, not in Birmingham.

Meanwhile, the incipient Oratory was having its own internal difficulties. Because of his shyness, Newman was experiencing problems in communicating with some of the younger members, and, as he wrote to Ambrose St John, he sometimes felt tempted to wish that he had been an individual convert without any of the responsibility that came from his connection with the Littlemore community—but then, he reminded himself, he would never have known St John. There were also all sorts of teething problems inevitable in any new community.

Moreover, Pugin was not the only fanatic among the converts. Newman's followers contained more than one enthusiast. One priest, Henry Formby, who was for a short time a member of the Oratory, considered that Plain Chant was 'predestinated', and was anxious to burst into print on the subject. But Newman was ruthless about such 'literary vanity': 'I own I am hard hearted towards the mere literary [ethos], for there is nothing I despise and detest more.'[15] The trouble was that the community consisted of a number of gifted individuals who were not bound by formal religious vows. Much, therefore, depended on Newman's own personal position and influence.

Unfortunately, there was already another centre of authority in the Oratory. At the end of September 1848 it was decided that Maryvale should be given up and the community should move to St Wilfrid's. It was hoped to start an Oratory in the city of Birmingham itself in the New Year. This was not against the Brief, which merely allowed Maryvale as a temporary site for an eventual Birmingham foundation. At the end of October Newman himself moved to St Wilfrid's. There Faber had already objected to the traditional Oratorian custom of silent

---

[12] *LD* xii. 198.　　[13] *AW* 256.　　[14] *LD* xii. 215.　　[15] Ibid. 311.

meditation in common. This was partly because he alleged it interfered with the work of the mission (i.e. parish). Newman soon found that his Oratory in practice had to give way to Faber's mission. Nevertheless, there was no doubting Newman's support for Faber when the first major crisis came.

In 1847 Faber had begun a series of translations of continental lives of the saints. They soon fell under criticism from some 'old Catholics' for their extravagant accounts of miracles and their revelations about ecclesiastical scandals. When Faber joined the Oratory, a decision about whether the Oratory should itself take over the series was postponed for a year by a hesitant Newman. But in September 1848 a Catholic magazine published a violent attack on Faber for promoting idolatry because of a passage on addressing prayers to an image. Faber, with his usual provocative exuberance, was ready for a fight. But Newman warned him: 'I cannot see that we have any call, whether as Oratorians or as converts, to begin our course by preaching to the old Catholics— and good part of your argument is this—first, that we must anyhow get into trouble, next that these Lives will tend to supernaturalize the Nunneries.'[16]

W. B. Ullathorne, who had succeeded Wiseman as Vicar Apostolic, after the latter had moved to London, and who was to become the first Bishop of Birmingham two years later, not only refused to give his official sanction to the continuation of the series when asked to do so by Newman, who was now ready to give the Oratory's backing to it, but advised it should be stopped. Years later, in his *Letter to Pusey*, Newman admitted the wisdom of Ullathorne's reservations about such publications in Protestant England and implied that perhaps he had been influenced against his better judgement by his younger fellow converts. Certainly, at the time, he could sound sometimes quite like Faber: 'I think a blow has been struck . . . at the timid unreal views, which have so prevailed for years past among Catholics . . .'.[17] And he was quick to spring to Faber's defence, expressing impatience at Ullathorne's warnings about the 'jealousy' of the clergy—are 'we . . . on every occasion to give way to this indefinite terror'?[18] In the circular announcing suspension of the lives, Faber was able to quote his superior's written assurance that 'no one can assail your name without striking at mine'.[19] As for Ullathorne's reminder of the Oxford principle of 'reserve in the communication of religious knowledge', Newman replied that he himself had not been converted by 'half measures and uncertain statements' or by evasions of Catholic scandals.[20] Ullathorne refused to budge, insisting that the lives should be rewritten—on the

---

[16] Ibid. 285.   [17] Ibid. xiii. 8–9.   [18] Ibid. xii. 304.
[19] Ibid. 316.   [20] Ibid. 319.

restrained lines of the Oxford lives of the saints. In fact, Newman himself privately wished that the particular life that had been objected to had never been published. However, he stood firm when Ullathorne complained about the 'sensitiveness' displayed in the circular, and announced his intention of publishing Ullathorne's admission that the personal attack on Faber had been unwarranted. In the end the magazine concerned printed a public apology for the hostile review and the lives were resumed under the auspices of the Oratory at the beginning of 1849. The episode ended not with Newman enjoying the fruits of victory over his bishop but with his firmly maintaining to Wiseman that while Ullathorne had every right to 'lecture' him (*'any one may lecture me'*), unfortunately Ullathorne had judged him *'without knowing me'* and 'on a *theory'*.[21]

3

Towards the end of January 1849 Newman left St Wilfrid's for Birmingham—'for a gloomy gin distillery of which we have taken a lease, fitting up a large room for a Chapel'.[22] The new Oratory in Alcester Street was formally opened on the Feast of the Purification, the second of February; it was on the eve of the same feast at first vespers a year ago that the Oratory as a religious institute had been set up in England. Newman preached a sermon called 'The Salvation of the Hearer the Motive of the Preacher', which became the opening sermon in the collection *Discourses Addressed to Mixed Congregations*.

The volume was the first work Newman published under his own name as a Roman Catholic priest. The sermons are in obvious ways conventionally 'Catholic'. Indeed, in answer to the criticism that they were too severe, Newman pointed out that one of the strictest is modelled on a sermon of the Italian saint, Alfonso Liguori (in fact, he thought they were no more stern than his *Parochial and Plain Sermons*). They are concerned to a considerable extent with the unending battle between the Church and the World, the Flesh, and the Devil. Natural man without grace can do nothing. The inevitable tendency to commit 'mortal' sin is so overwhelming that it is hard for anybody to be saved. The only salvation is to be found in the Catholic Church—'because she brings a universal remedy for a universal disease', which is sin.[23] Newman acknowledged that they were 'more rhetorical than my former Sermons'.[24] Certainly the rhetoric is often more Italianate than Newmanian:

---

[21] *LD* xii. 363–4.   [22] Ibid. 382.   [23] *Mix.* 246.   [24] *LD* xiii. 335.

If the world has its fascinations, so surely has the Altar of the living God; if its pomps and vanities dazzle, so much more should the vision of Angels ascending and descending on the heavenly ladder; if sights of earth intoxicate, and its music is a spell upon the soul, behold Mary pleads with us, over against them, with her chaste eyes, and offers the Eternal Child for our caress, while sounds of cherubim are heard all round singing from out the fulness of the Divine Glory.[25]

However, Newman's characteristic genius is not altogether absent. The argument from analogy is deployed effectively and at length in 'Mysteries of Nature and of Grace' to show that the difficulties of belief in God are parallel to those of believing in the Catholic Church. Imagery is used, often humorously, to make a point. Thus Catholic converts are believed by the world to be constantly repressing doubts, so that 'after the likeness of a vessel which has met with some accident at sea, we are ever baling out the water which rushes in upon us, and have hard work to keep afloat . . .'.[26] There is another very startling sea image in Newman's evocation of the modern city with its 'population of human beings, so vast that each is solitary, so various that each is independent, which, like the ocean, yields before and closes over every attempt made to influence and impress it . . .'.[27] Again, 'they who stumble at the Catholic mysteries may be dashed back upon the adamantine rocks which base the throne of the Everlasting, and may wrestle with the stern conclusions of reason, since they refuse the bright conclusions of faith.'[28] The elaborateness of this imagery of cliffs, and rocks, and sea is unusual but in keeping with the ornate character of the volume. The Established Church is contemptuously dismissed in terms of a lifeless monster: 'National religions . . . lie huge and lifeless, and cumber the ground for centuries, and distract the attention or confuse the judgment of the learned.'[29] Finally, the sermons are not without a satirical element: 'The world professes to supply all that we need, as if we were sent into it for the sake of being sent here, and for nothing beyond the sending', so that 'It is a great favour to have an introduction to this august world'.[30] As for so-called Bible Christians, 'I can fancy a man magisterially expounding St. Paul's Epistle to the Galatians or to the Ephesians, who would be better content with the writer's absence than his sudden re-appearance among us . . .'.[31]

4

Newman had not left St Wilfrid's completely behind him. He soon heard from Faber that members of the community there were

[25] *Mix.* 70. [26] Ibid. 222. [27] Ibid. 238. [28] Ibid. 269.
[29] Ibid. 282. [30] Ibid. 105. [31] Ibid. 200.

grumbling about Newman's reserve and shyness towards them in contrast to his 'particular friendship' with the allegedly unpopular Ambrose St John. Newman quickly countered the latter charge by referring to friendships in the Gospels themselves. To one novice who had felt hurt, Newman wrote movingly:

It is strange to write to you a note about nothing; but such is my fate just now and for some time, that, since I have nothing to say to you, I must either be silent or unseasonable.

Many is the time I have stood over the fire at breakfast or looked at you at Recreation, hunting for something to talk about.[32]

More seriously, Newman learned from Faber that there was talk at St Wilfrid's questioning the assumption that the two communities would eventually be united in Birmingham. Newman began to wonder if the answer might not be to separate into two communities, one in Birmingham and one in London, which would eventually become a separate Oratory.

Meanwhile the Alcester Street Oratory, which also (rather against Newman's inclinations) had a mission or parish attached, was flourishing. The policeman 'in waiting'[33] (the arrival of a Catholic mission could mean trouble) calculated that there was a congregation of 600 on Sunday evenings, when it was crammed and people had to be turned away. A hundred children soon began crowding in for catechism classes, but there seemed little possibility of a school: city children in those days over the age of about 7 went to work till 8 p.m. In fact, the work of the Oratory was concentrated into two hours between 7 and 9 p.m. when there was 'a *rush* of all sorts'.[34] Two evenings a week there were lectures. Converts were beginning to flow in, in spite of the tremendous prejudice against Catholics. Newman confessed that he was almost loth to convert working-class girls who would as a result have great difficulties going 'into service' and getting married. The house itself, which formed three sides of a quadrangle, had sixteen bedrooms, three sitting-rooms, a private community chapel, and a library. Once again Newman dragged his folios of the Fathers into place, hurting his wrist as he did so. He hoped that at last he was 'where I may live and die, having been for 10 years without what promised to be a home'.[35] He could not help remarking, with a certain sadness, to Mrs Bowden on what a very different world it was from the Oriel of the old days, about which he had no one now to talk with. It was different, if only because Newman had now so little to live on (although the sale of his books was holding up better than he had feared) that at the end of 1849 he

[32] *LD* xiii. 32.   [33] Ibid. 26.   [34] Ibid. 44.   [35] Ibid. 108.

confessed that for the last year he had not even been able to afford new shoes or stockings, let alone give to charity.

The Alcester Street congregation hardly corresponded to the 'doctior et honestior ordo',[36] or educated upper class, which the Pope had specified in his Brief as the proper object of the Oratory's apostolate. But Newman refused to agree with Faber that their situation in Birmingham was purely the accidental result of Wiseman having been there, and that the whole Oratory should move to London. In his formal proposal to the Roman authorities of an English Oratory, Newman had particularly mentioned Birmingham and other provincial towns as 'the main holds of political power at this day among us'. And so '*if there* be a class in Birmingham of sharp intellects, who are the recipients of political power, and who can be made Catholics, I think we are fulfilling the Brief'.[37] This did not mean, though, that for the literal fulfilment of the 'doctior et honestior ordo' directive, London was not more suitable and certainly more congenial to the St Wilfrid's community of Faber. It was also true that at the moment they were too large for an Oratory, which was meant to be a small, intimate community, like a family—ideally, Newman thought, not more than twelve members altogether. This was another reason for splitting up. That there must be a separation one day, perhaps in ten years, Newman accepted, but he would have much preferred to let it gradually happen 'as fruit ripens on the tree and falls', whereas he was being forced 'to take a knife and cut it off'.[38] The separation into two independent bodies required much more time and consideration.

So far as Newman was concerned, London, not Birmingham, would have been the place he would have chosen for himself. On the other hand, Birmingham had possession, and, more important, in spite of its obvious attractions, London would not provide him with the time for study and writing that Birmingham would. And if he had to choose between an active apostolate and a more intellectual life, he would choose the latter. So, because London would be more appropriate for the former, Birmingham would now be his choice. London would mean public engagements, not all of them very congenial, whereas his present life in Birmingham 'is just the life I have ever coveted, time for study, yet missionary work of the most intimate kind'.[39] This of course did not remove the fact that Birmingham was outwardly the most unlikely place for him to be—not so far geographically from Oxford, but thousands of miles away intellectually and in every other respect. But then it had once been asked, 'Can any good come out of Nazareth?' As for his personal influence, it was his writings which had converted people. Still, he was

---

[36] Ibid. xii. 239, n. 1.   [37] Ibid. xiii. 50.   [38] Ibid. 62.   [39] Ibid. 95.

seriously considering spending three months a year at the projected London house. Not that his apostolate in Birmingham was wholly pastoral and unintellectual. In June 1849 he 'gave a flash Lecture on Poetry—to the Birmingham Catholic Reading Society Association'; it 'was a splendid concern', although 'really I quite laughed when I was delivering it', as 'I said absurd things which I knew they would applaud'.[40]

In spite of all the tensions, Newman was able to laugh at the contrast between Faber's repeated demand that he use his authority as Father Superior more vigorously and the actual wilfulness shown by members of the community: 'And you lecture me and say "My dear F.S. do take us at our word—you can make minced meat of us—you can turn us into Bolognas or Germans—don't be consulting for us—speak, speak out what *you* think—and all difficulty is at an end." '[41]

In fact, Newman could use his authority when necessary. Father Richard Stanton, who seemed to have set himself up as the 'Keeper of the Rule', had to be warned against forgetting 'equity' 'in zeal for the law'.[42] But Newman could be ruthlessly blunt in a much more personal way. (He was aware of this: 'I am quite conscious *always* of not liking to tell people how keenly I feel things, both from tenderness to them, and again from a consciousness that, when I once begin, I am apt to let out and blow them out of the water.'[43]) Father Bernard Dalgairns, who was to be the source of so much discord between the two Oratories, was told, quite simply, that he had 'a great fault'—'contempt of others'. A long and blistering catalogue of his offences followed, including a marvellously vivid indictment of the misbehaviour of certain youths Dalgairns had taken up and allowed the freedom of the house to: '. . . I found them strumming on the Piano, they ate the sugar and the jam and stole the candles; you laughed when it was complained of . . . They flung about the ink in the guest room, broke the chairs, squandered coal and gas, broke into the closet, took out the Crucifix and put it back head downwards.'[44] But Newman ended the letter by blaming his own lack of self-confidence and self-possession for his failure as Superior to gain more of the confidence of his subjects. Or again, Father William Penny was told very plainly that he used the Oratory 'as a lodging house, for which you paid so much per week grudgingly . . . In vain have I remonstrated with you again and again; my words were as bullets upon wet sand. You have been simply passive and impassive; have listened, consented, and gone on as before.'[45]

[40] The newspaper report of the lecture is rpt. in Fernande Tardivel, *La Personnalité littéraire de Newman* (Paris, 1937), 387–92.

[41] *LD* xiii. 100.   [42] Ibid. 110.   [43] Ibid. xiv. 143.   [44] Ibid. xiii. 130.
[45] Ibid. 200.

As the separation of the two communities became final, Newman still hoped that at least a community spirit could be maintained, perhaps by keeping St Wilfrid's as a kind of common novitiate where future Oratorians could study together for the priesthood and where a school too might be opened from which vocations might come. Already the poor state of Catholic schools in England had suggested to Newman the possibility of starting a school. Perhaps indeed St Wilfrid's might be a sort of 'Eton of the Oratory—a place where Fathers would turn with warm associations of boyhood or at least youth'. And then with a whimsical humour that Faber seemed to bring out in him, he speculated on the memorials that might be gathered there—'a gin bottle or cayenne phial of the Venerabile Serve di Dio, il Padre Wilfredo Faber, an old red biretta of his Eminence C. Robert Coffin, and a double tooth and the knuckle bone of St Aloysius of Birmingham'.[46]

Faber had by now arrived in London with his Oratorians, who paraded the streets in their habits. Newman wondered, half-afraid, what the effect might be of one novice spreading out 'his cloke like a peacock's tail in the sight of Sir R. Inglis', the staunchly Protestant Member of Parliament for Oxford University. Under the humour one senses Newman's unease at an exuberance and extravagance very far from Tractarian reserve. The Catholic periodical the *Tablet* might advertise the new London Oratory 'to the universe as its destined saviour', but what with their flaunting of habits, irreverent slang, and disrespect for the ecclesiastical authorities, the Oratorians might soon arouse 'fear, odium, jealousy' on all sides.[47] In parting from the Birmingham community the Londoners were leaving the mother Oratory and its privileges, but in return they were gaining all the advantages of a metropolis over a mere provincial manufacturing town. Given, too, that the Londoners were individually the wealthiest members, it was clear that 'the balance was more in favor of the London House than it ought to be'.[48] The London Oratory was opened on 31 May, and Newman preached in the evening at Benediction, 'Prospects of the Catholic Missioner'.[49] In spite of his extreme dislike of such formal 'occasional sermons',[50] Newman felt when it was over that he had been himself.

St Wilfrid's remained a problem. Newman suggested that both communities should provide a priest to maintain the mission there as they had promised. The objections raised to this suggestion by the Londoners brought out how independent they had become of their founder. Faber's letter is characteristic. After protesting that he 'would prefer doing anything to thwarting any deliberate plan of yours',

[46] Ibid. 143.   [47] Ibid. 145.   [48] Ibid. 166.
[49] *Mix.* 238–59.   [50] *LD* xiii. 167.

especially since Newman was the founder enjoying the Pope's original mandate, he went on to remark with a kind of studied insolence: 'It sometimes crosses me to think that you take a more French view, others of us a more Italian view, of the work of the Congregation; I don't like to say this, because of the associations one has with the French Oratory; but it has passed thro my mind at times—Well—I think your proposal a great bore for this particular house . . .'.[51] To appreciate the full flavour of this one needs to know that the French Oratory, which was an organized society with seminaries and colleges, had developed heretical Jansenist and Gallican tendencies before its temporary demise at the French Revolution. Newman pointed out in reply that the Italian Oratory could boast at least as many learned men as the French. Dalgairns also wrote to Newman to complain, but his letter was couched in more extreme, even violent, terms:

. . . a Philippine is meant to be rooted in one spot, to be glued to one confessional, to spout out of one pulpit . . . has not F. Superior a different idea altogether of St Philip's institute from mine? Does not his view approach the French Oratory . . . Since I have been a priest my intellect is gone; gradually what was once a pleasure has become a pain. I loath literature; I am not even easy if I dip into a modern historical book. It troubles my mind, and I am forced to mention it in confession. Saints' lives on the contrary fill me with peace. In a word my intellect has disappeared.[52]

The letter ends with the familiar protestations of loyalty and obedience, but the implication that intellectualism is un-Oratorian and leads to spiritual pride is strangely reminiscent of Ambrose Lisle Phillipps's mixture of affected humility and arrogant dogmatism. The real objection was not to lending a priest but to Newman's idea of the educational possibilities of St Wilfrid's. This was Newman's heresy—to suggest running any sort of school, even if it was only for the Oratory itself. As for the pastoral duties of the confessional, Newman drily pointed out that 'if *every* Father were so glued, you would not get breakfast or dinner, nor indeed a confessional to be glued to'.[53] It was all very well for Dalgairns to despise culture, but he had had the advantage of Oxford. The fact was that traditionally an Oratory consisted of well-educated priests and had more facets to it than simply the confessional. It had, for example, traditionally included church history as a speciality. Certainly the future members of the English Oratory would have to receive a theological education somewhere. The clause in St Philip's Rule forbidding the running of colleges (which in fact referred to educational institutions external to and independent of the Oratory)

[51] *LD* xiii. 176 n. 2.   [52] Ibid. 177 n. 1.   [53] Ibid. 177.

had been modified by Newman when he had adapted the Rule for England with papal approval.

It was becoming more and more obvious that not only was Newman's overall authority no longer acknowledged, but his view of the Oratory was specifically rejected. There were to be two Oratories separate in identity and theory. Whatever Newman stood for was simply to be dismissed as 'French'. As for Faber, he pleaded that mere intellectual dissent from Newman's view of the educational role of the Oratory was not to be regarded as actual disobedience. But the fact remained that the London Oratory had said it was unwilling to provide a priest for St Wilfrid's. To Dalgairns Newman sent a carefully worded letter congratulating him on his tacit admission that the Oratory did have an 'intellectual' side (on which he again pointedly insists) and concluding with the devastatingly innocent: 'How could I doubt that you would kindly receive any conclusion I came to about St. Wilfrid's, or any provision I was contemplating for the future wants of the novices of the Oratory?' 'But why spoil', Newman wondered, 'an acquiescence so like yourself, with large views, and those beside the point, and moreover unfounded, and expressed in allusions of which you cannot yourself approve, about your and my respective "ideas" of the Oratory?'[54] The tone of the letter is as unremittingly courteous and polite, as the note of authority is insistent and the logic merciless. It is an ironic snub by a superb controversialist.

The humour of the letters foreshadows the exuberant satirical writings that were soon to follow. Of an Irish priest called Dr Whitty, who was procrastinating about joining the Oratory, he wrote, 'his notion is that he is sent to the poor, that is to the Irish poor, that is to those who are in gross sin, that is to those who have in them the materials of saints, that is not to those who are going on to perfection, that is not to the many for he is not strong enough, that is to London, that is to Lord this or Lady that.'[55] To Faber, who complained about the dirt and smell of the Irish poor turning away 'respectable' people, he gave practical advice on how to prevent 'the lean kind eating the fat'.[56] But he admitted that his own experiences of smells and bugs in the confessional were beginning to drive him to the un-Catholic notion that 'cleanliness is next to Godliness.'[57] In another letter to Faber he described how a convert priest who hesitated to join the Oratory because of his suspicions of Newman's orthodoxy, in conversation about theology 'took the same demure way which an old maid would with a Magdalene or a puritan with a Papist'.[58] Amused as well as embarrassed by a lady who called him a saint, Newman remarked:

[54] Ibid. 190–1.   [55] Ibid. 212.   [56] Ibid. 211.   [57] Ibid. 254.
[58] Ibid. 337.

I may have a high view of many things, but it is the consequence of education and of a peculiar cast of intellect—but this is very different from *being* what I admire. I have no tendency to be a saint—it is a sad thing to say. Saints are not literary men, they do not love the classics, they do not write Tales. I may be well enough in my way, but it is not the 'high line.' People ought to feel this, most people do. But those who are at a distance have fee-fa-fum notions about one. It is enough for me to black the saints' shoes—if St Philip uses blacking, in heaven.[59]

The work of the Oratory in Birmingham 'amid our labyrinth of lanes and beneath our firmament of smoke'[60] continued. During a serious outbreak of cholera at Bilston in Staffordshire, Newman and St John were asked to go and help the priests, but the epidemic was practically over; it was estimated that two-thirds of the population would become Catholics, but 'alas, could not be received for want of instructors and confessors . . . the sight of the sick in the hospitals was terrible—and brought before one most awful thoughts.'[61] One besetting problem was how to set up a confraternity of young men—who did not exist—on the traditional Oratorian model of St Philip's 'little Oratory'.

As for St Wilfrid's, it had at last been reluctantly agreed that Birmingham and London should each provide one priest, not only to maintain the mission there, but to establish a college for youths over the age of 16; it was a temporary expedient, as either the college would fail or, if it succeeded, it could be made independent of both Oratories. It would not be a direct help to the Oratory either for its members or for vocations, but at least it was a way of trying to make St Wilfrid's pay for itself.

Newman had been asked by the London Oratorians to give a series of Lenten lectures in 1850. He was very uncertain what to lecture on, but belatedly he was given a subject by the so-called Gorham case, on which on 9 March 1850 the judicial committee of the Privy Council in effect ruled that Baptismal regeneration was not an essential doctrine of the Church of England. Apart from the sacramental aspect, this interference by the State in the Church eventually led to a wave of converts to Rome, including Henry Wilberforce, Hope, and Manning. Newman thought the crisis could be turned to good account, and on 9 May he delivered at the London Oratory the first of his *Lectures on Certain Difficulties felt by Anglicans in submitting to the Catholic Church*. These continued twice a week on Thursdays and Fridays, with three breaks,

---

[59] *LD* xiii. 419. Years later he remarked to a nun, 'I always feel like a hypocrite who can be detected by holy eyes, just as an accomplished thief . . . is at once recognized by a police officer. But at a distance I look like a great man, without any hang dog look which I can't throw off, do what I will, when I am in places where brass will not go for gold' (*LD* xx. 427).

[60] *LD* xiii. 445.

[61] Ibid. 378.

until 5 July. Newman could not remember ever before writing so 'intellectually against the grain'.[62]

5

The lectures are specifically intended not to prove Catholicism, but to remove difficulties in the way of Anglo-Catholics. Newman admits that they are necessarily incomplete as not touching on a whole range of disputed questions. More than half of them, which form the first part of the work, are concerned exclusively with the relation between the Established Church and what Newman calls 'the movement of 1833'.

Although the argument is more detailed and explicit than in *Loss and Gain*, it is directed and underpinned by much the same general principles. The contrast, in particular, between reality and unreality is central. Indeed, it is the first consideration that Newman presses on the high Anglicans:

We must not indulge our imagination, we must not dream: we must look at things as they are . . . we must not indulge our imagination in the view we take of the National Establishment. If, indeed, we dress it up in an ideal form, as if it were something real . . . as if it were in deed and not only in name a Church, then indeed we may feel interest in it, and reverence towards it, and affection for it, as men have fallen in love with pictures, or knights in romance do battle for high dames whom they have never seen. Thus it is that students of the Fathers, antiquaries, and poets, begin by assuming that the body to which they belong is that of which they read in times past, and then proceed to decorate it with that majesty and beauty of which history tells, or which their genius creates.[63]

This, of course, was how Newman himself, as 'a student of the Fathers', had once tried to picture the Church of England.

But at length, either the force of circumstances or some unexpected accident dissipates it; and, as in fairy tales, the magic castle vanishes when the spell is broken, and nothing is seen but the wild heath, the barren rock, and the forlorn sheep-walk, so is it with us as regards the Church of England, when we look in amazement on that we thought so unearthly and find so commonplace or worthless.[64]

It is true that Newman says that on such occasions we find 'we have not been guided by reason',[65] but this does not mean that imagination or idealism, or even 'romance', is rejected. Far from it. If there were no place for such, Newman himself would never have become a Catholic:

Even when I was a boy, my thoughts were turned to the early Church, and

---

[62] Ibid. 470. [63] *Diff.* i. 4–5. [64] Ibid. 6. [65] Ibid.

especially to the early Fathers, by the perusal of the Calvinist [Joseph] Milner's Church History, and I have never lost, I never have suffered a suspension of the impression, deep and most pleasurable, which his sketches of St. Ambrose and St. Augustine left on my mind. From that time the vision of the Fathers was always, to my imagination, I may say, a paradise of delight . . .[66]

Newman certainly allows a very special place for imagination, but the object of the imaginative vision must be a real one, and it is reason that helps to determine and locate this reality. He argues that it is not the picture of the early Church that is a fantasy, but it is the imaginative effort to identify this picture with the Church of England that is fantastic; for the picture is in fact a picture of the Roman Catholic Church. In the end, for Newman himself it was 'the living picture' which the study of 'history presents to us'[67] that opened his eyes to the identity of the Church of the Fathers with the Roman Catholic Church.

This was possible only through the ability to 'see' the historical analogy. Newman describes (as he was to do in greater detail in the *Apologia*) how in 1839 his study of the Monophysite controversy and the Council of Chalcedon 'implanted' a doubt in his mind as to 'the fundamental principle of Anglicanism . . . which never was eradicated': 'I thought I saw . . . a clear interpretation of the present state of Christendom.' This 'new view of things' was deepened by Wiseman's article on the Donatists. Again, in 1841 the renewed study of the Arian controversy and the Council of Nicaea brought before Newman's eyes 'the same phenomenon'.[68] What Newman 'saw' were 'a series of prototypes'[69] of the Anglican *Via Media*:

what the See of Rome was then such is it now . . . what Arius, Nestorius, or Eutyches were then, such are Luther and Calvin now; what the Eusebians or Monophysites then, such the Anglican hierarchy now; what the Byzantine Court then, such is now the Government of England . . . That ancient history is not dead, it lives . . . we see ourselves in it, as in a glass, and if the *Via Media* was heretical then, it is heretical now.[70]

Newman concluded, 'there was an awful similitude, more awful, because so silent and unimpassioned, between the dead records of the past and the feverish chronicle of the present.'[71]

It is not possible to prove an analogy like this, which has to be 'seen', and Newman admits that 'I do not know how to convey this to others in one or two paragraphs.'[72] As for the analogy between the development of doctrine in the primitive Church and that in the modern Roman Catholic Church, 'the force of this, to me ineffably cogent argument, I cannot hope to convey to another'.[73] Although reason is involved,

[66] *Diff.* i. 370–1.   [67] Ibid. 379.   [68] Ibid. 373.   [69] Ibid. 374.
[70] Ibid. 379.   [71] Ibid. 387–8.   [72] Ibid. 379.   [73] Ibid. 396.

so is imagination, and this alone makes it something not publicly demonstrable.

As usual in Newman, the argument from analogy plays a continuous and crucial role in his critique of Anglo-Catholicism. For it is through the recognition of analogies that identities are discovered and realities revealed. Thus, Newman allows that 'The Fathers have catholicised the Protestant Church at home', but only 'pretty much as the Bible has evangelised the Mahometan or Hindoo religions abroad'.[74] And indeed, 'as the Turks would feel serious resentment at hearing the Gospel in the mouths of their Muftis and Mollahs, so was, and is, the English nation provoked, not persuaded, by Catholic preaching in the Establishment.'[75] Or again, if Anglo-Catholics want to argue from the 'sensible effects of supernatural grace' that they are part of the Catholic Church, then what, Newman unkindly asks, is to be said of Methodists who display 'more remarkable phenomena in their history, symptomatic of the presence of grace among them, than you can show in yours'?[76] The fact is, Newman points out, holiness is to be found among all kinds of Protestants whose theological views may be very far from Catholic. Then the charge that the Roman Catholic Church does not in fact enjoy any more real unity than the Church of England, as shown for example by the widespread Jansenist heresy, lasting nearly 200 years, is a charge as easily levelled at the early Church infected from within by the heresy of the Monophysites which lasted for between 400 and 500 years. As for the mere presence of rival Christian bodies, these do not detract from the claims of the Catholic Church. For 'this phenomenon is but one instance of a great and broad fact . . . that truth is opposed not only by direct contradictions which are unequivocal, but also by such pretences as are of a character to deceive men at first sight'.[77] The false prophets in the Old Testament illustrate this. And so, from the beginning, 'the Church was but one Communion among many which bore the name of Christian, some of them more learned, and others affecting a greater strictness than herself. . . Hence the famous advice of the Fathers, that if one of the faithful went to a strange city, he should not ask for the "Church" . . . but for the Catholic Church.'[78] Unlike the modern Orthodox churches, some of the early heretical bodies actually rivalled the Catholic Church in their universality. Corruptions of the truth, declares Newman, are as much to be expected as rejections. And if Roman Catholics are to be called to account for their divergences from the patristic Church, are not Anglicans to give account 'for their own serious departure in so many respects from the primitive doctrine and ritual'?[79]

---

[74] *Diff.* i. 9–10. [75] Ibid. 68. [76] Ibid. 88. [77] Ibid. 337.
[78] Ibid. 342. [79] Ibid. 365.

Reality, then, is attained by a balanced combination of imagination and reason. Imagination, without 'the judgment of reason', is over-whelmed, for example, by the sight of 'so many nations and races, which have kept the name of Christian, yet given up Catholicism',[80] or for that matter by the 'number, power, and nobleness'[81] of the Orthodox. It is possible to dream about what the Established Church might have been, but history shows that it never had in reality been Catholic.

Ranged on the side of reality against unreality are common sense and consistency. Thus Newman declares it makes no sense to insist on certain dead formularies as proving the Catholic character of the Church of England, when they are but 'the shrivelled blossom about the formed fruit'.[82] Common sense is not deceived by the 'zeal and ingenuity'[83] of Anglo-Catholic arguments, for it knows that the Church of England is really a Protestant state church and not a 'branch' of the Catholic Church. It is an 'intellectual absurdity'

that such as you, my brethren, should consider Christianity given from heaven once for all, should protest against private judgment, should profess to transmit what you have received, and yet from diligent study of the Fathers, from your thorough knowledge of St. Basil and St. Chrysostom, from living, as you say, in the atmosphere of Antiquity, that you should come forth into open day with your new edition of the Catholic faith, different from that held in any existing body of Christians anywhere . . . and then, withal, should be as positive about its truth in every part, as if the voice of mankind were with you instead of being against you.[84]

It is at least as absurd as arrogant to profess to 'have a mission to teach the National Church, which is to teach the British empire, which is to teach the world'.[85] And it is not common sense to claim that 'the latest fashion of opinion which the world has seen' is in fact 'the oldest'. Nor is it consistent to provide a defence for the Church 'which she has no dream of appropriating', to 'innovate on her professions of doctrine' and then 'bid us love her for your innovations', to 'cling to her for what she denounces', and 'almost anathematise us for taking a step which you would please her best by taking also'.[86]

Newman claims to appeal 'rather to common sense and truths before our eyes than to theology and history'.[87] It is by concentrating too much on the latter that Anglo-Catholics find a difficulty in reconciling the patristic Church with the modern Roman Catholic Church, a problem which 'the world at large' does not experience.[88] Traditional Anglic-anism, on the other hand, which sees itself as the *Via Media* between

---

[80] *Diff.* i. 330.   [81] Ibid. 344.   [82] Ibid. 19.   [83] Ibid. 49.
[84] Ibid. 154, 157.   [85] Ibid. 158.   [86] Ibid. 161.   [87] Ibid. 366.
[88] Ibid. 364.

Catholicism and Protestantism, prides itself precisely on appealing to 'the good sense of mankind', refusing 'to run into extremes' on the ground that 'the human mind is naturally prone to excess'. This comprehensive, liberal religion, not Anglo-Catholicism, is true Anglicanism—'it is this, or it is nothing; deny this, and it forthwith dissolves into Catholicism or Protestantism.'[89] Here, if anywhere, Newman concludes, is an Anglican reality.

Again, Erastianism 'is the doctrine of common sense',[90] if there is to be no authoritative, visible church. But unfortunately the Anglo-Catholic is in a less happy position than the hated Erastian, for 'it is worse still to become a Sectarian', that is, to be one's 'own Doctor and . . . Pope'.[91] And this is what the Anglo-Catholic has to be without church authority and without even the definite creed of a united sect. Newman enjoys showing how Anglo-Catholicism, which began in reaction to Erastianism and sets itself up against Protestantism, is in fact quintessentially Erastian. The theory may be that the Catholic Church has been divided into 'branches', but the practice is that 'it is the normal condition of a Branch Church to be a National Church; it tends to nationality as its perfect idea.' And 'a National Church ever will be and must be what you have found your own to be,—an Erastian body', so that 'Erastianism, the fruitful mother of all heresies, will be your first and your last'.[92] The reason is that 'as a branch cannot live of itself, therefore, as soon as it is lopped off from the Body of Christ, it is straightway grafted of sheer necessity upon the civil constitution, if it is to preserve life of any kind.'[93] Branches cannot live apart from the tree to which they belong: the 'branch' theory, therefore, ingenious as it is, is wholly unreal.

The unsurprising conclusion is that it is the Catholic Church alone which possesses reality. Unlike other 'visible' churches, it is not a 'sham', for it is not merely intended 'for the protection of private judgment'.[94] Instead, as the embodiment of Christianity, it is 'an external fact' with 'a bodily occupation of the world', 'one continuous fact or thing, the same from first to last'.[95] That it is the 'heir and representative' of the early Church is obvious and 'a fact attested by mankind'.[96] Common sense recognizes its reality, and this reality is confirmed by its own consistency.

Newman's attempt to persuade his former fellow co-religionists of the falsity of their position does not of course rest only on the broad issue of reality and unreality. The rhetoric of the lectures is carefully modulated to allow a range of different tones, sometimes sharply contrasted. On the personal, autobiographical level, for example, he appeals to the sympathy of his audience. He has no reason 'to be harsh' against the Anglican Church when he has 'only pleasant associations of those many

[89] Ibid. 374.   [90] Ibid. 203.   [91] Ibid. 197.   [92] Ibid. 171–2.
[93] Ibid. 186.   [94] Ibid. 212.   [95] Ibid. 368.   [96] Ibid. 369.

years when I was within her pale', and when he is 'come to a time
of life, when men desire to be quiet and at peace'.[97] He appreciates
the Established Church as one of the remaining 'bulwarks' of the 'dogmatic principle', and recognizes the contribution made by Anglican
theologians.[98] 'Can I wipe out from my memory, or wish to wipe out,
those happy Sunday mornings, light or dark, year after year, when
I celebrated your Communion-rite, in my own church of St.
Mary's . . .?'[99] What makes him speak out 'is my intimate sense that the
Catholic Church is the one ark of salvation, and my love for your
souls'.[100] And whose writings can he more fairly refute than his own,
'without misrepresenting him or hurting his feelings'?'[101] As for his own
conversion, he can state from experience that it was the Fathers, the very
fount of Tractarian theology, who far from proving an obstacle had in
fact been the ultimate cause of his submission to Rome. And so it is
Newman's own eloquent testimony to the story of his conversion that
forms the climax of the book. It is not an account of how he fell in love
with the papacy or the medieval Church; it is rather the history of an
Oxford patristic student whose first 'vision of the Fathers'[102] as a boy
remained with him until the scales fell from his eyes and he realized that
with all his ingenious and learned controversies on behalf of Anglicanism against the Roman Church he 'was but forging arguments for
Arius or Eutyches, and turning devil's advocate against the much-
enduring Athanasius and the majestic Leo . . . whose image was
continually before my eyes, and whose musical words were ever in my
ears and on my tongue!'[103]

Newman certainly has some hard things to say about the high-church
party. He is even 'obliged in candour to allow' that if he 'wished to find
what was striking, extraordinary, suggestive of Catholic heroism' he
would go rather to the early Methodists—why, 'even old Bunyan . . . is
. . . more Apostolical than you'.[104] He is critical of their disunity, their
superiority, their arrogance, their complacency, their compromises with
the Establishment, their lack of principle, their superficiality. And yet,
when all is said and done, the 'brethren' to whom Newman is speaking
are indeed his brothers, for but five years before he was one of them, 'a
body of persons whom I have loved, revered, and sympathised with'.[105]
In spite of his criticisms, he has 'ever been trustful in that true Catholic
spirit which has lived in the movement of which you are partakers . . .
steady in my confidence in that supernatural influence among you,
which made me what I am,—which, in its good time, shall make you
what you shall be'.[106] Newman ends as he began in commiseration for

---

[97] *Diff*. i. 3.   [98] Ibid. 2.   [99] Ibid. 81–2.   [100] Ibid. 4.
[101] Ibid. 141.   [102] Ibid. 371.   [103] Ibid. 388.   [104] Ibid. 89, 91.
[105] Ibid. 17–18.   [106] Ibid. 398.

Anglo-Catholics held 'in bondage' by the Established Church, whereas in fact they are 'born to be Catholics'.[107] He refuses to allow that they have been 'deformed' by 'secret doubts', 'self-will', 'disregard of authority', 'an unmanly, disingenuous bearing', 'the spirit of party',[108] although he is aware that there are 'close around you men who look like you, but are not',[109] men too concerned with externals and pretensions (such as he mocked himself in *Loss and Gain*).

His one object is that Anglo-Catholics too should 'be lodged safely in the true home of your souls and the valley of peace'.[110] They look up to their own 'Mother' church and find her 'silent, ambiguous, unsympathetic, sullen, and even hostile', 'with ritual mutilated, sacraments defective, precedents inconsistent, articles equivocal, canons obsolete, courts Protestant, and synods suspended; scouted by the laity, scorned by men of the world, hated and blackened'.[111] Unwanted by their own church, their true home awaits them elsewhere, where 'you will almost see invisible mysteries, and will touch the threshold of eternity'.[112] The Catholic Church, which 'is the one ark of salvation', is waiting to receive Anglo-Catholics 'who have thrown themselves' from the 'wreck' of the Established Church upon 'the waves, or are clinging to its rigging, or are sitting in heaviness and despair upon its side'.[113] A little later, 'the power of a nation's will' becomes the 'giant ocean' which 'has suddenly swelled and heaved, and majestically yet masterfully snaps the cables of the smaller craft which lie upon its bosom, and strands them upon the beach', so that the great high Anglican divines, 'names mighty in their generation, are broken and wrecked'.[114] Anglo-Catholic theology itself is 'most uncongenial and heterogeneous, floating upon it, a foreign substance, like oil upon the water'.[115] Anglo-Catholic theologians had appealed to the authority of the Fathers:

there they found a haven of rest; thence they looked out upon the troubled surge of human opinion and upon the crazy vessels which were labouring, without chart or compass, upon it. Judge then of their dismay, when, according to the Arabian tale, on their striking their anchors into the supposed soil, lighting their fires on it, and fixing in it the poles of their tents, suddenly their island began to move, to heave, to splash, to frisk to and fro, to dive, and at last to swim away, spouting out inhospitable jets of water upon the credulous mariners who had made it their home.[116]

What had been felt as a profound shock of tragic dimensions can now be depicted in comic imagery which is also deployed against other targets.

Unlike their high Anglican counterparts, the Evangelical clergy

[107] Ibid. 5, 398.   [108] Ibid. 17.   [109] Ibid. 397.   [110] Ibid. 360.
[111] Ibid. 16.   [112] Ibid. 361.   [113] Ibid. 4.   [114] Ibid. 25.
[115] Ibid. 35.   [116] Ibid. 150.

'glide forward rapidly and proudly down the stream' of the age which is so congenial to them.[117] Whereas the spiritual power of the Catholic Church is real though imperceptible—in the same way that the air which 'gives way, and . . . returns again . . . exerts a gentle but constant pressure on every side'[118]—the faith of Protestants is 'a sickly child', brought out 'of doors only on fine days'; and Protestants lose their 'vision of the Unseen' 'if they turn about their head, or change their posture ever so little', so 'they keep the exhibition of their faith for high days and great occasions, when it comes forth with sufficient pomp and gravity of language, and ceremonial of manner'.[119] The Established Church is pictured as a 'huge creature' which, in spite of the Movement, 'has steadily gone on its own way, eating, drinking, sleeping, and working, fulfilling its nature', and which, oblivious of the defections to Rome, 'showed no consciousness of its loss, but shook itself, and went about its work as of old time'.[120]

The marvellous comic imagery is meant to laugh Anglo-Catholics out of their unreal fantasies and pretensions. They had invested their bishops with unfamiliar Apostolic powers, and these same bishops had then

fearlessly handselled their Apostolic weapons upon the Apostolical party . . . It was a solemn war-dance, which they executed round victims, who by their very principles were bound hand and foot, and could only eye with disgust and perplexity this most unaccountable movement, on the part of their 'holy Fathers, the representatives of the Apostles, and the Angels of the Churches.'[121]

The very first *Tract* wished

nothing better for the Bishops of the Establishment than martyrdom . . . It was easy to foresee what response the Establishment would make to its officious defenders, as soon as it could recover from its surprise; but experience was necessary to teach this to men who knew more of St. Athanasius than of the Privy Council or the Court of Arches.[122]

In place of a teaching authority, the Anglo-Catholic theologian has to put forward his 'own private researches into St. Chrysostom and St. Augustine', which his followers are required to accept unreservedly as 'the teaching of the old Fathers, and of your Mother the Church of England'.[123] Newman employs imagery uncannily reminiscent of Dickens to express the discomfort of the Anglo-Catholic's life in the Church of England, where

there is no lying, or standing, or sitting, or kneeling, or stooping there, in any possible attitude . . . when you would rest your head, your legs are forced out

[117] *Diff.* i. 15.   [118] Ibid. 178.   [119] Ibid. 289–90.   [120] Ibid. 10, 12.
[121] Ibid. 152.   [122] Ibid. 106.   [123] Ibid. 162.

between the Articles, and when you would relieve your back, your head strikes against the Prayer Book; when, place yourselves as you will, on the right side or the left and try to keep as still as you can, your flesh is ever being punctured and probed by the stings of Bishops, laity, and nine-tenths of the Clergy buzzing about you . . .[124]

A totally unoriginal image can be used to devastating effect, as when with the gentlest irony Newman recommends the Anglo-Catholic to

have nothing to do with a 'Branch Church.' You have had enough experience of branch churches already, and you know very well what they are. Depend upon it, such as is one, such is another. They may differ in accidents certainly; but, after all, a branch is a branch, and no branch is a tree. Depend upon it, my brethren, it is not worth while leaving one branch for another.[125]

In national churches, doctrine is not determined by Bible or tradition 'but by its tendency to minister to the peace and repose of the community, to the convenience and comfort of Downing Street, Lambeth, and Exeter Hall'.[126] A national church reflects the will of the nation, which reflects the will of the world: 'Provided it could gain one little islet in the ocean, one foot upon the coast, if it could cheapen tea by sixpence a pound, or make its flag respected among the Esquimaux or Otaheitans, at the cost of a hundred lives and a hundred souls, it would think it a very good bargain.'[127] The Catholic Church, on the other hand, says Newman, in a brilliant and notorious passage (which he was later to defend in the *Apologia*),

holds that it were better for sun and moon to drop from heaven, for the earth to fail, and for all the many millions who are upon it to die of starvation in extremest agony, so far as temporal affliction goes, than that one soul, I will not say, should be lost, but should commit one single venial sin, should tell one wilful untruth, though it harmed no one, or steal one poor farthing without excuse . . . she would rather save the soul of one single wild bandit of Calabria, or whining beggar of Palermo, than draw a hundred lines of railroad through the length and breadth of Italy . . .[128]

6

In the end the plan for St Wilfrid's petered out. When it came to the point, the London Oratorians pleaded lack of resources to help staff the place. It was a blow to Newman because he had been anxious that St Wilfrid's should be what he had intended Maryvale to be, a community house common to both Oratories. His argument was that

---

[124] Ibid. 167. [125] Ibid. 169. [126] Ibid. 193.
[127] Ibid. 235. [128] Ibid. 240.

Oratories, because they had no overall government, either had to be totally independent on the Italian model, or else bound together by common bonds and ˜sympathies. It was this kind of union which Newman saw as necessary in England, where physical separation was not possible, especially if he was to continue to be superior of both houses, but which London rejected in favour of complete separation. The two Oratories were formally separated in October, when Faber was elected the first Superior of the London Oratory.

The formal erection of the London Oratory coincided with the establishment of a new Roman Catholic hierarchy in England on 29 September and the elevation of Wiseman to the cardinalate. Newman felt very uneasy about the excitement it was bound to create in Protestant England. Worse was to follow with Wiseman's triumphalist pastoral letter 'from out the Flaminian Gate', which was read out by the clergy on Sunday, 20 October and violently condemned in the press. The Roman Catholic Church had long existed privately and silently in England, but now it was entering on to the public and political stage without the proper legal, theological, and practical resources. Perhaps, Newman hoped, it might force a new maturity on the Catholic community. The campaign against the so-called 'Papal Aggression' began to mount, with leading articles and letters in the newspapers, protest meetings, and satirical cartoons in *Punch*. Many of these were personal attacks on Newman himself, who did not however lose his sense of humour. He enjoyed describing how the clergyman brother of one of the convert Oratorians 'was followed by the rabble the other day in London, having on a long cloke which they took for an Oratorian. He faced round, pulled aside the cloke, and showed his trousers—When they saw him all sound below, they gave him a cheer and left him.'[129]

In spite of his reservations about the restoration of the hierarchy, Newman was soon hard at work on a sermon to mark the installation of Ullathorne as first Bishop of Birmingham, 'Christ upon the Waters'.[130] Formally religious though the occasion was, the sermon contains all the elements of Newman's satirical genius, not least the kind of imagery typical of this period of his writings. Thus, for English Protestants, who 'shrink from the great road of travel which God has appointed' and 'run . . . their own private conveyance . . . on their own track',[131] there is no 'calumny too gross' and 'no imputation on us so monstrous which they will not drink up greedily like water', and because there is 'a demand for such fabrications', there is 'a consequent supply' of slanders against Catholics, who 'are fair game for all comers', and who can only expect 'to be treated as shadows of the past, names a thousand miles away,

---

[129] *LD* xiv. 117–18.   [130] *OS* 121–62.   [131] Ibid. 147–8.

abstractions, commonplaces, historical figures, or dramatic properties, waste ground on which any load of abuse may be shot, the convenient conductors of a distempered political atmosphere . . .'.[132]

The gulf between what Newman sees as the Catholic values of the Gospel and those of Protestant England, because of rather than in spite of which England has become the most powerful nation in the world, finds expression in his claim that when, after the Reformation, Englishmen rejected the external reality of the Church, they 'fell back, with closed affections, and haughty reserve, and dreariness within, upon their worldly integrity, honour, energy, prudence, and perseverance; they made the most of the natural man, and they "received their reward" '.[133] This spiritual philistinism is matched by a theological philistinism. The vaunted 'private judgment' of the Englishman turns out to be little more than the 'passive impression' which he receives through his 'intellectual servants', the periodicals and newspapers, that are employed to tell him 'what to think and what to say', the sole criterion being that this 'cheap knowledge' should be 'ready to hand, as he has his table-cloth laid for his breakfast'. In matters of religion the Englishman 'is bent on action, but as to opinion he takes what comes, only he bargains not to be teased or troubled about it', so that he 'is satisfied to walk about, dressed just as he is' and very much 'resents the idea of interference', for 'it is an insult to be told that God has spoken and superseded investigation', especially since 'he thinks the Englishman knows more about God's dealings with men, than any one else'.[134] Where Dickens caricatured the materialism and snobbery of the great Victorian middle class, and where Arnold sneered at its cultural superficiality, Newman satirized its religious and spiritual provincialism and shallowness. But like Arnold and Dickens, Newman's harshness is only possible and tolerable by virtue of the very pride he takes in his Englishness. And he is careful here to praise those qualities which, 'despite the loss of heavenly gifts', the English excel in—'the love of justice, manly bearing, and tenderness of heart'.[135] As in *Present Position of Catholics*, which this sermon strikingly anticipates, the criticism is so effective precisely because it comes from within the family.

Newman hoped the tone of the sermon was not too '*violent*—but my experience tells me that the more you show a bold face to the world, so cowardly is it, the more you gain. It does not appreciate concession.'[136] He thought that the Prime Minister, Lord John Russell, should be 'brought to account for calling the religion of one third of the British Empire a superstition and a mummery'.[137] Hostile crowds gathered outside the Oratory in Alcester Street, and the police had to be called.

[132] *OS* 156–7. [133] Ibid. 132. [134] Ibid. 148–51. [135] Ibid. 161.
[136] *LD* xiv. 121. [137] Ibid. 125.

But in spite of the fury of 'the British Lion', Newman knew that 'his keepers' were too 'sharp-sighted' to think of trying to put Catholic priests into prison.[138] His own sermon had aroused wrath in high places on the ground that he had blasphemously likened Ullathorne to Christ. What Newman had really said was that the contemporary revival of Catholicism was like the resurrection of Christ. And even if he had—which he had not—applied words about Christ to a bishop, it was no more, to use another analogy, than what the Church of England did in the service for King Charles the Martyr. As for the misrepresentation, Newman was too used to public attacks to mind; in the end, truth would prevail.

As he was to do much later over the proceedings of the Vatican Council, he took the line that 'what our [ecclesiastical] rulers have done is right, *because* it is done.' The workings of Providence, however mysterious, had to be acknowledged. And, however uncongenial 'external manifestation' and 'rows' might be, 'humbug' was just as hateful: at least it was now clear that the 'British Lion' had not 'become a lamb', and that England was as anti-Catholic as ever.[139] Nor was it just a national aversion to the doctrines of Catholicism, it was an almost superstitious dread and fear of all things Catholic. In Birmingham itself, the rumour was spreading that Newman was married and had shut up his wife in a convent! An MP in the House of Commons also made the lurid allegation that 'At this moment, in the parish of Edgebaston, within the borough of Birmingham, there was a large convent of some kind or other being erected, and the whole of the *underground* was fitted up with *cells*; *and what were those cells for?* (hear, hear).' Newman replied suavely in the *Morning Chronicle*:

The underground cells . . . have been devised in order to economize space for offices commonly attached to a large house. I think they are five in number, but cannot be certain. They run under the kitchen and its neighbourhood. One is to be a larder, another is to be a coal-hole; beer, perhaps wine, may occupy a third. As to the rest . . . we have had ideas of baking and brewing; but I cannot pledge myself . . . that such will be their ultimate destination.

Larger subterraneans commonly run under gentlemens' [*sic*] houses in London; but I have never, in thought or word, connected them with practices of cruelty . . . and never asked their owners what use they made of them.[140]

Newman was not particularly worried about the Ecclesiastical Titles Bill, which might turn out to be very useful: 'We are not ripe ourselves for a Hierarchy. Now they have one, they can't fill up the sees, positively can't.' There was another side to the question, too. New bishops did not touch the real English Catholic problem—lack of education: 'We want

---

[138] *LD* xiv. 130.   [139] Ibid. 154.   [140] Ibid. 283.

seminaries far more than sees.'[141] Before this, Newman had complained about the tendency of Catholics to lay out money on '*showy* works', as exemplified by their naïve enthusiasm for neo-Gothic churches.[142] More important were proper schools: 'How few Catholics can compose! for instance, Dr. Ullathorne's style!'[143] It was the same lack of education which led to the appalling taste of Catholics (in the matter of sermons, for example). The current persecution of Catholics could profitably be exploited by making it an excuse for 'getting up a great organization, going round the towns giving lectures, or making speeches, . . . starting a paper, a review etc.' There ought to be lay speakers and public meetings in the big towns. Young Catholics should band together as the Tractarians had. At this point one senses a feeling on Newman's part that here was the potential beginning of a new Tractarian movement, the occasion being again the persecution of the Church, but this time the object being to make England truly Catholic. Now the condemnation of tracts and the suspension of university preachers might be matched by the fining, imprisonment, even transportation of recalcitrant bishops. But, as in the past, Newman sadly sensed that the bishops would not rise to the occasion—had they bothered or did they intend to consult any of the laity on the best course of action? Again, was there any '*unanimous* plan of action, and a *view*' among the bishops?[144] His own Bishop Ullathorne, Newman could not help acknowledging, 'has a terror of laymen, and I am sure they may be made in this day the strength of the Church'.[145] However, for all his new-found energy and excitement, he was careful, unlike some converts, to advise against direct attacks on the Church of England, which at present was the only 'bulwark against Infidelity', the Catholic Church being too weak to take its place as the guardian of revealed Christianity in the country at large. As for his own satire in his recent novel and lectures, 'such ridicule only disparages it in the eyes of Puseyites who *ought* to leave it, not in those of Erastians and Establishmentarians, who constitute its strength.'[146]

The no-Popery agitation began to subside. Against its own liberal principles, Lord John Russell's Whig government was forced to carry through Parliament the Ecclesiastical Titles Bill, for which they were responsible through encouraging popular anti-Catholic feeling. Newman wrote triumphantly:

. . . Lord John has struck his foot against a rock and has fallen. A sunken rock, for they did not believe so insignificant a thing as British Catholicism would harm them—but it has shivered them . . . they have gone down in a smooth sea and under a smiling heaven. They are in again, to their own disgrace; like slaves, obliged to finish their own set work, and drink their own brewing.[147]

[141] Ibid. 213.   [142] Ibid. xii. 366.   [143] Ibid. xiii. 6.   [144] Ibid. xiv. 214.
[145] Ibid. 252.   [146] Ibid. 173.   [147] Ibid. 232.

Meanwhile, the new Birmingham Oratory house was rising in Edgbaston, then just outside the city. The plans had been laid in the summer of 1850, when an appeal for the church was launched. Newman wanted a 'Roman style' for the church, with 'a smack of moorish and gothic—. . . the beauty of Greece with something of the wildness of other styles—yet without the extravagance of the moor and the gloom of the Goth'.[148] He certainly admired the strength of the house, on which 1,700,000 bricks were used, but not the taste of the architect.

At the end of June 1851 Newman began 'a set of Public Lectures at the Corn Exchange'.[149] Delivered weekly, except for the first Monday in August, and concluding on 1 September, they were each published separately a week after delivery and collected together as *Lectures on Catholicism in England*, but they were published in book form as *Lectures on the Present Position of Catholics in England: Addressed to the Brothers of the Oratory*. The 'Brothers of the Oratory' constituted the 'Little Oratory', the confraternity of laymen traditionally attached to an Oratory, which Newman considered as 'more important than any thing else'.[150] It was ostensibly for the benefit of this body that he now launched his 'attack upon John Bull', which he 'ever considered' to be his 'best written book'.[151]

7

Newman begins the first lecture by announcing that his intention is to investigate the reasons for the universal prejudice against Catholics ('how it is we are cried out against by the very stones, and bricks, and tiles, and chimney-pots'), a prejudice which 'is not only a trial to flesh and blood, but a discomfort to the reason and imagination'.[152] His aim is to show that the actual prejudice is founded not on reason but on illusory imagination. Scandalous stories circulated against Catholics may be proved to have no basis in fact, and yet an 'impression' has been 'created or deepened . . . that a monk commits murder or adultery as readily as he eats his dinner'.[153] Imagination, of course, is open to various impressions. It is because 'Catholicism appeals to the imagination, as a great fact, wherever she comes', that Protestantism has to impress upon the popular imagination that the Church is 'Anti-Christ'.[154] Such

---

[148] *LD* xiv. 290. In fact, because of the donations towards the expenses of the 1852 Achilli trial, there were no further appeals, and there was never more than a temporary church in Newman's lifetime; but after his death, the present church, on the lines of the Roman church, San Martino ai Monti, was built as a memorial.

[149] Ibid. 298.   [150] Ibid. 274.   [151] Ibid. xxvi. 115.   [152] *Prepos.* 2.
[153] Ibid. 95.   [154] Ibid. 224.

impressions 'do not depend afterwards upon the facts or reason-ings by which they were produced, any more than a blow, when once given, has any continued connection with the stone or the stick which gave it'.[155] The anti-Catholic prejudice remains as a 'stain on the mind'.[156]

In his effort to show that the English imagination has been fatally poisoned at the wells, Newman deploys some of the most startling and vivid imagery to be found in his writings. He enjoys turning the images that have stained the Protestant imagination against Protestantism itself. Thus it is not a Catholic country but Protestant England which, 'as far as religion is concerned, really must be called one large convent, or rather workhouse; the old pictures hang on the walls; the world-wide Church is chalked up on every side as a wivern or a griffin; no pure gleam of light finds its way in or from without; the thick atmosphere refracts and distorts such straggling rays as gain admittance'.[157] The fact is, Newman argues, the 'anti-Catholic Tradition' is the most effective weapon the Established Church has, and so its special duty is 'to preserve it from rust and decay, to keep it bright and keen, and ready for action on any emergency or peril'.[158] The Church of England's mission lies in 'cataloguing and classing the texts which are to batter us, and the objections which are to explode among us, and the insinuations and the slanders which are to mow us down'.[159] The 'Establishment is the Keeper in ordinary of those national types and blocks from which Popery is ever to be printed off'.[160]

Some facts are useful for nurturing the tradition, and so it is not surprising that 'preachers and declaimers' have 'now a weary while been longing, and panting, and praying for some good fat scandal, one, only just one . . . to batten upon and revel in'!'[161] The Prejudiced Protestant is the child of the tradition, 'and, like a man who has been for a long while in one position, he is cramped and disabled, and has a difficulty and pain . . . in stretching his limbs, straightening them, and moving them freely'.[162] In his view the Catholic Church in England 'ought to be content with vegetating, as a sickly plant, in some back-yard or garret window';[163] for his part, he 'is intensely conscious that he is in a very eligible situation, and his opponent in the gutter; and he lectures down upon him, as if out of a drawing-room window'.[164] Meanwhile,

the meetings and preachings which are ever going on against us on all sides, though they may have no argumentative force whatever, are still immense factories for the creation of prejudice,—an article, by means of these exertions, more carefully elaborated, and more lasting in its texture, than any specimens

[155] Ibid. 231.   [156] Ibid. 233.   [157] Ibid. 44.   [158] Ibid. 74.
[159] Ibid. 75.   [160] Ibid.   [161] Ibid. 139.   [162] Ibid. 178.
[163] Ibid. 195.   [164] Ibid. 200.

of hardware, or other material productions, which are the boast of a town such as this is.

Sometimes the imagery has a savage, Swiftian flavour, at other times, as here, the effect is grotesque in the Dickens manner. Or again, the imagery may be characteristically Newmanian in its sharply concrete psychological detail:

If, for instance, a person cannot open a door, or get a key into a lock, which he has done a hundred times before, you know how apt he is to shake, and to rattle, and to force it, as if some great insult was offered him by its resistance: you know how surprised a wasp, or other large insect is, that he cannot get through a window-pane; such is the feeling of the Prejudiced Man when we urge our objections—not softened by them at all, but exasperated the more . . .[165]

Faced with the inescapable fact that people are converted to Catholicism,

the Prejudiced Man has a last resource, he simply forgets that Protestants they ever were . . . they merge in the great fog, in which to his eyes everything Catholic is enveloped: they are dwellers in the land of romance and fable; and, if he dimly contemplates them plunging and floundering amid the gloom, it is as griffins, wiverns, salamanders, the spawn of Popery, such as are said to sport in the depths of the sea, or to range amid the central sands of Africa.[166]

Catholic attempts to be conciliatory are doomed, for 'our advances are met as would be those of some hideous baboon, or sloth, or rattlesnake, or toad, which strove to make itself agreeable.'[167] As for Catholic beliefs, they are as likely to 'gain admittance into his imagination, as for a lighted candle to remain burning, when dipped into a vessel of water'.[168] Catholic doctrines 'stand in Reformation Tracts, torn up by the roots or planted head-downwards', not 'as they are found in our own garden'.[169] And they are too 'great to be comfortably accommodated in a Protestant nutshell'.[170] For just as Protestantism has its Scripture 'texts', so it has 'its chips, shavings, brick-bats, potsherds, and other odds and ends of the Heavenly City, which form the authenticated and ticketed specimens of what the Catholic Religion is in its great national Museum'.[171] Protestants prefer to 'keep at a convenient distance from us, take the angles, calculate the sines and cosines, and work out an algebraic process, when common sense would bid them ask us a few questions'.[172] It is because 'Catholics are to be surveyed from without, not inspected from within', that 'texts and formulas are to prevail over broad and luminous facts' and 'one grain of Protestant logic is to weigh

---

[165] *Prepos.* 240. [166] Ibid. 245. [167] Ibid. 265. [168] Ibid. 303.
[169] Ibid. 331. [170] Ibid. 332. [171] Ibid. 342. [172] Ibid. 350.

more than cartloads of Catholic testimony'.[173] As for personal acquaintance, 'Did the figures come down from some old piece of tapestry, or were a lion rampant from an inn door suddenly to walk the streets, a Protestant would not be more surprised than at the notion that we have nerves, that we have hearts, that we have sensibilities.'[174] 'They will' even 'do all in their power not to see you; the nearer you come, they will close their eyelids all the tighter; they will be very angry and frightened, and give the alarm as if you were going to murder them.'[175]

The fact is that if 'Catholicism were taken from the market', then 'scandal' would be without 'its staple food and its cheap luxuries', while prejudice 'could not fast for a day', 'would be in torment inexpressible, and call it Popish persecution, to be kept on this sort of meagre for a Lent, and would shake down Queen and Parliament with the violence of its convulsions, rather than it should never suck a Catholic's sweet bones and drink his blood any more'.[176] Indeed, 'Prejudice is ever craving for food, victuals are in constant request for its consumption every day; and accordingly they are served up in unceasing succession, Titus Oates, Maria Monk, and Jeffreys, being the purveyors, and platform and pulpit speakers being the cooks.'[177]

As Newman warms to his theme, the humour becomes more and more fantastically grotesque, in the Dickensian vein. Protestantism, declares Newman, 'is the current coin of the realm', so that 'there is an incessant, unwearied circulation of Protestantism all over the country, for 365 days in the year from morning till night'.[178] But converts present an unfamiliar phenomenon to the Protestant Tradition, whose champions Newman advises to 'be sure to shoot your game sitting; keep yourselves under cover', and from there, 'Open your wide mouth, and collect your rumbling epithets, and round your pretentious sentences, and discharge your concentrated malignity.'[179]

Nowhere else in his writings is Newman more exuberantly funny. Bully and monster as the Protestant Tradition may be, it is also depicted as absurd and ridiculous. For example, Newman's own cellars at the Oratory have fallen under its suspicion. But the reason for the cellars is that the unevenness of the ground dictates some such construction under the building—and 'there is a prejudice among Catholics in favour of horizontal floors.'[180] No doubt, Newman muses, if the 'nascent fable' had not 'been lost by bad nursing', but had 'been cherished awhile in those underground receptacles where first it drew breath', it might have lingered in the Protestant consciousness, and one day 'a mob might have swarmed about our innocent dwelling, to rescue certain legs of mutton

[173] Ibid. 358–9.   [174] Ibid. 355.   [175] Ibid. 372.   [176] Ibid. 341.
[177] Ibid. 371.   [178] Ibid. 366.   [179] Ibid. 376.   [180] Ibid. 119.

and pats of butter from imprisonment, and to hold an inquest over a dozen packing-cases, some old hampers, a knife-board, and a range of empty blacking bottles'.[181] Instead, Newman has exposed the slander—although 'it is a matter of surprise' that 'we dare to speak a word in our defence, and that we are not content with the liberty of breathing, eating, moving about, and dying in a Protestant soil'.[182] As for a Catholic priest, 'there is peril in his frown, there is greater peril in his smile . . . whether he eats or sleeps, in every mouthful and every nod he ever has in view one and one only object, the aggrandisement of the unwearied, relentless foe of freedom and progress, the Catholic Church.'[183] Prejudice, after all, 'is superior to facts, and lives in a world of its own'.[184]

Apart from imagery, the lectures contain lines of argument familiar from *Difficulties of Anglicans*. Most important is the argument from analogy. The first lecture culminates in the comic account of an imaginary indictment of the British Constitution by a Russian count, who has never actually seen or visited England or studied its history and literature, 'but who has dipped into Blackstone and several English writers, and has picked up facts at third or fourth hand, and has got together a crude farrago of ideas, words, and instances, a little truth, a deal of falsehood, a deal of misrepresentation, a deal of nonsense, and a deal of invention'.[185] The resulting picture is an absurd caricature—like the picture of Catholicism which the Protestant Tradition has impressed on the English imagination. The next lecture begins by pointing out how it is

familiar to an Englishman to wonder at and to pity the recluse and the devotee who surround themselves with a high enclosure, and shut out what is on the other side of it; but was there ever such an instance of self-sufficient, dense, and ridiculous bigotry, as that which rises up and walls in the minds of our fellow-countrymen from all knowledge of one of the most remarkable phenomena which the history of the world has seen?[186]

[In an] inquisitive age, when the Alps are crested, and seas fathomed, and mines ransacked, and sands sifted, and rocks cracked into specimens, and beasts caught and catalogued, as little is known by Englishmen of the religious sentiments, the religious usages, the religious motives, the religious ideas of two hundred millions of Christians poured to and fro, among them and around them, as if, I will not say, they were Tartars or Patagonians, but as if they inhabited the moon.[187]

And so the English Protestant who despises the enclosed monk or nun is shown to be as 'enclosed' himself, while in spite of his boasted knowledge

---

[181] *Prepos.* 124–5.   [182] Ibid. 199.   [183] Ibid. 248–9.   [184] Ibid. 261.
[185] Ibid. 26.   [186] Ibid. 43.   [187] Ibid. 44.

of the world he is wholly ignorant of Catholics, about whom he has so much to say.

Charges made against Catholics can just as easily be levelled at Protestants. Is it not better to venerate a crucifix than a statue of King William? The Catholic system of dispensations may be criticized, but what Protestant would not justify himself in breaking an unlawful oath? As for persecution, Protestants are just as culpable as Catholics. It is in fact the very similarity of the accusations made against Catholics that links them to the early Christians, who were persecuted on parallel grounds. Their pagan persecutors also judged and condemned them on their own and not on Christian principles; similarly, Protestants judge Catholics on their own preconceived grounds. But if, for example, Protestants really believed in the most stupendous of all miracles, the Incarnation, they would not find Catholic miracles so hard to believe. Again, relics and miracles in the lives of the saints may not all be authentic or true, but then neither are all the familiar stories of English history. Just as Protestants pick out key 'texts' from the Bible from which they construct a 'Scriptural Religion', so they pick up scraps from Catholic theology and call it 'Popery'; of real live Catholics they know no more than they know about the early Christians whose Gospels they presume to know better than they did; they would not welcome St Paul if he came back to explain some of his 'texts'; nor do they welcome Catholic explanations. For example, the 'omnipotence' of the Virgin Mary is no more to be taken literally than the 'Omnipotence of Parliament'. Just as the notice 'Ring the Bell' presupposes 'if you have business within', so indulgences presuppose but do not convey absolution, whatever their written form may suggest to the uninitiated. Protestants understand that the Old Testament has to be understood in the light of a particular context; why cannot they appreciate that Catholic forms and words also have to be placed in their context?

Analogies reveal inconsistencies: in comparing and seeing similarities between facts and situations it is impossible not to note lack of consistency in attitudes to comparable phenomena. As in the *Difficulties of Anglicans*, Newman makes much play of the inconsistencies of the other side. He especially enjoys stressing that anti-Catholicism rests on '*tradition* immemorial, unauthenticated *tradition*'—whereas it is precisely the Catholic insistence on tradition that Protestants object to.[188] Again, Protestants like to emphasize the value of freedom of thought, 'but towards us they do not dream of practising it'.[189] The original Reformers had used their 'private judgment' against the Church—but 'There was enough of private judgment in the world, they thought, when they had

---

[188] Ibid. 45.   [189] Ibid.

done with it themselves. So they forcibly shut-to the door which they had opened, and imposed on the populations they had reformed an artificial tradition of their own, instead of the liberty of inquiry and disputation.'[190] The Protestant Tradition totally rejects the very notion of infallibility, but in practice regards as infallible its own objections to Catholicism. Protestants disapprove of images in Catholic churches, and yet they are quite happy to burn the Pope in effigy—but 'How is it childish to honour an image, if it is not childish to dishonour it?'[191] Toleration is the special boast of Protestants—but at this very moment they are busy persecuting Catholics in England! It is true that the Catholic Church does not recognize the absolute right to religious freedom in the same sense that Protestants do—but are Protestants to 'bring their own inconsistency as the excuse for their crime' of atrocities at least as bloody as any perpetuated by Catholics?[192] Certainly the Protestant readiness to persecute Catholics is inconsistent with the view that Catholicism 'is so irrational that it will fall to pieces of itself'.[193] And considering the Protestant emphasis on freedom of thought, they of all people 'ought to abstain from bigotry'.[194] They certainly should not abuse fellow Protestants for using this liberty to become Catholics.

Inconsistency, for Newman is the hallmark of unreality. The true reason for anti-Catholicism is that 'Protestantism is at best but a fine piece of wax-work, which does not look dead, only because it is not confronted by that Church which really breathes and lives'.[195] And so Catholicism is abolished 'by Act of Parliament', and 'not by sight or hearing, but by the national will'.[196] Again, the reason why Protestants 'ever persecute, in spite of their professions', is because 'this doctrine of private judgment . . . is extreme and unreal, and necessarily leads to excesses in the opposite direction'.[197] So is the whole Protestant attitude to the Bible—to think 'most unnaturally, that the accidental and occasional writings of an Apostle convey to them of necessity his whole mind': in secular matters they would not dream of relying solely on letters 'to arrive at the real state of a case'.[198] It is just as unreal to imagine that Catholicism can be understood from a few texts without personal contact with its living reality.

The rhetoric of the lectures is more subtle than has perhaps been suggested. As in *Anglican Difficulties*, there is a personal appeal. Part of Newman's indignation lies in his pride that he is an Englishman. More than that, he and his fellow converts were in fact 'nourished . . . in the bosom of the great schools and universities of Protestant England'.[199] He himself has written against Catholicism as a Protestant controversialist.

---

[190] *Prepos.* 55.   [191] Ibid. 180.   [192] Ibid. 219.   [193] Ibid. 275.
[194] Ibid. 292.   [195] Ibid. 9.   [196] Ibid. 11.   [197] Ibid. 221.
[198] Ibid. 318–19.   [199] Ibid. 123.

But the English Tradition is more than the Protestant Tradition. It is true that there is a parochialism and a provincialism which militate against anything that is 'foreign' or calculated to disturb English complacency. Thus from one point of view the lectures represent an assault on a central aspect of Victorian philistinism. The following passage, for example, is pure Newman, but it is a remarkable anticipation of Dickens's delineation of Mr Podsnap in *Our Mutual Friend* (1865):

They themselves are the pattern-men; their height, their dress, their manners, their food, their language, are all founded in the nature of things; and everything else is good or bad, just in that very degree in which it partakes, or does not partake, of them. All men ought to get up at half-past eight, breakfast between nine and ten, read the newspapers, lunch, take a ride or drive, dine. Here is the great principle of the day—dine; no one is a man who does not dine; yes, dine, and at the right hour; and it must *be* a dinner, with a certain time after dinner, and then, in due time, to bed. Tea and toast, port wine, roast beef; mincepies at Christmas, lamb at Easter, goose at Michaelmas, these are their great principles. They suspect any one who does otherwise. Figs and maccaroni for the day's fare, or Burgundy and grapes for breakfast!—they are aghast at the atrocity of the notion.

More serious is it when English people, without the benefit of education and travel, though 'with right intentions, but yet, I think, narrow views, wish to introduce the British Constitution and British ideas into every nation and tribe upon earth'.[200] It is this same insular self-complacency which makes it possible for anyone to be 'thought qualified to attack or to instruct a Catholic in matters of his religion; a country gentleman, a navy captain, a half-pay officer, with time on his hands, never having seen a Catholic, or a Catholic ceremonial, or a Catholic treatise, in his life, is competent, by means of one or two periodicals and tracts, and a set of Protestant extracts against Popery, to teach the Pope in his own religion, and refute a Council'. Matthew Arnold, no Catholic, saw the point: it was not just religious prejudice but a serious cultural deprivation that the most powerful nation in the world could not treat with respect a religion 'which has occupied the lives and elicited the genius of some of the greatest masters of thought whom the world has known'.[201] (At one point Newman actually quotes an article to this effect from the secular *Westminster Review*.)

But, for all that, Newman is glad to be an Englishman. For example, 'personal attachment', a quality conspicuous in his own character, is one of the distinguishing characteristics of the English. Indeed, he remarks prophetically that the Pope himself would doubtless be 'received with

---

[200] Ibid. 295–7.   [201] Ibid. 330.

cheers, and run after by admiring crowds, if he visited this country, independent of the shadow of Peter which attends him, winning favour and attracting hearts, when he showed himself in real flesh and blood, by the majesty of his presence and the prestige of his name'! The concrete, not the abstract, appeals to the Englishman, and he would never have been attracted by 'the unnatural speculations of Calvin' or 'the dreamy and sensual doctrines of Luther'.[202] Again, it is strange that a people renowned for their 'love of justice and fair dealing'[203] should be so unfair and unjust to a section of their fellow countrymen. Paradoxically, since honesty is one of the great English virtues, it is by 'wholesale, retail, systematic, unscrupulous lying . . . that the many rivulets are made to flow for the feeding the great Protestant Tradition'.[204] Even ridicule and satire, which are 'good natured' and a 'healthy' 'safety valve' in 'a free country' like England ('our boast among the nations'), are used for blasphemous and insulting attacks on Catholicism itself.[205] It is all so un-English, Newman exclaims: 'where is the generosity of the Briton, of which from one's youth up one has been so proud? where is his love of fair play, and his compassion for the weak, and his indignation at the oppressor, when we are concerned?' What has come over the 'most sensible people on the earth, the most sensitive of moral inconsistency, the most ambitious of propriety and good taste', who cannot even display 'simple reasonableness and common sense' towards Catholics?[206]

8

The fifth of the lectures, which was delivered on 28 July, contained a denunciation[207] of Giacinto Achilli, an ex-Dominican priest, who had become a Protestant after being sentenced to imprisonment by the Roman Inquisition for sexual immorality, including assault. He was brought to England by the Evangelical Alliance in 1850 and toured the country, denouncing before enthusiastic audiences the corruptions of Rome, and claiming he had been punished for heresy. In June 1850 Wiseman had written an article in the *Dublin Review* exposing in detail Achilli's real offences, which was reproduced as a pamphlet. Newman had taken informal legal opinion on whether he could safely use the material in Wiseman's indictment. He was advised that he could do so without much risk because no action had been taken out against

---

[202] *Prepos.* 61–2.
[203] Ibid. 394.   [204] Ibid. 126.   [205] Ibid. 203.   [206] Ibid. 235–6.
[207] Omitted in the second edition, it is reproduced in *LD* xiv. 501–3.

Wiseman for libel ('at so exciting a time, and when he was such a mark'),[208] and because the proof for Wiseman's allegations would not be hard to produce. However, Newman's lectures were making 'the extreme party so very angry'[209] that he began to wonder if the rumour that Achilli had decided to sue might not turn out to be true. In the frenziedly anti-Catholic climate of the time, Achilli was likely to receive a lot of support if he challenged Newman. Newman, for his part, was clear in his own mind that his position in Birmingham, where he was a public figure but where he was unknown as a person, meant that he had to reply to personal attacks. A clergyman, for example, who announced that the whole of Newman's public life had been 'one unmitigated lie' was publicly lacerated:

He has professed to quote two passages from me, in support of his charge. He does so in the received Protestant fashion on such occasions; for he has *cut off the beginning* of the first sentence of the former of the two; and he has *cut out the middle* of the latter.'[210]

There was an important difference between the two attacks on Achilli: Wiseman's name had not actually appeared, but Newman's had. And the repetition of the charges might goad Achilli into counter-attack. In August came definite news that Achilli intended to take legal proceedings. And so in September Nicholas Darnell and Joseph Gordon from the Birmingham Oratory set off for Italy to gather documents and evidence. This mission was the more imperative because it seemed that Wiseman's documentary evidence, on which Newman had relied, had been mislaid. On 4 November Achilli denied on oath all the charges made against him. This affidavit enabled him to institute criminal proceedings rather than a civil action against Newman's publishers, which forced Newman to acknowledge personal responsibility for the alleged libel. Newman's lawyers drew up a counter-affidavit for Newman to swear, to the effect that if he were given time he would be able to produce sufficient evidence for the truth of his charges against Achilli. At this early stage, clear proof of only one of Newman's allegations would have been enough to stop the case. Unfortunately, not only had Wiseman apparently mislaid his papers, but he had been dilatory about obtaining alternative documents from Italy and he had failed to ensure that the two Birmingham Oratorians were given the evidence they needed.

As it was, Newman knew that he had English public opinion against him. At the first court hearing the Lord Chief Justice, Lord Campbell, showed the usual anti-Catholic prejudice, while Newman's own

---

[208] *LD* xiv. 339.   [209] Ibid. 335.   [210] Ibid. 331.

counsel, Sir Alexander Cockburn, the Attorney-General, did not hide his strong disapproval of the passage in question. On the other hand, Newman knew he had the whole Catholic body behind him, even if he had had great difficulty in getting Catholics, from Wiseman down, to take seriously the threat of Achilli's prosecution. The blow fell on 20 November when the court refused to give Newman an extension of time to collect evidence and committed him to stand trial on a criminal charge. There had been so much delay that he had no primary documents or witnesses even to promise, let alone produce. Because of the difficulty of securing justice at this time of 'Papal aggression', his lawyers advised him not to fight the case, in the hope of avoiding both punishment and legal expenses; otherwise there was the danger of a year's imprisonment. Newman felt that to do this would be to 'betray a great Catholic interest'.[211] However, after various consultations he agreed to the suggestion of a compromise, that he should declare that his accusations against Achilli were based on the evidence cited in Wiseman's article (not on personal knowledge) and should agree to withdraw the offending passage.

Nothing came of the suggested compromise. Wiseman had discovered his documents, but it was too late. Vital evidence had arrived from Rome, again only when it was too late, thanks to the procrastination of the egregious Mgr. George Talbot, the convert Papal Chamberlain to Pius IX. Cockburn's confident assumption that there would be no trial till after Easter had been disproved. Catholics, who had refused to take the danger seriously, were confounded. As for Newman, the whole affair seemed like some strange nightmare: 'If the devil raised a physical whirlwind, rolled me up in sand, whirled me round, and then transported me some thousands of miles, it would not be more strange, though it would be more imposing a visitation.'[212] Local urchins had already begun gleefully to cry out 'Six months in quod!' As so often in Newman's life, it was the suspense that really tried him. However, the documents from Rome had at last arrived and a committee had been set up to collect money for the legal expenses. Newman's old friend Maria Giberne (who had also become a Catholic in 1845) was to bring back the key women witnesses from Italy.[213] Newman consoled himself that if he

---

[211] *LD* xiv. 431.

[212] Ibid. 442.

[213] She assembled them in Paris in the new year, where they had to wait till they were needed. On the problem of keeping them amused, Newman advised: 'We think you don't allow Gippina's husband cigars enough—let him have an unlimited supply. Let him have any thing else he takes to—perhaps he would get tired if he rode in legno every day—but is there nothing else? is there no equestrial exhibition? no harmless play? no giant or dwarf? no panorama, cosmorama, diorama, dissolving views, steam incubation of chickens, or *menagerie* (the jardin des plants!) which he would like to see. Surely beasts are just the thing for him. I wonder he has no taste for a review. I should not *ask* him, but I should *take* him to the jardin des plants, as if I wished to see them myself' (*LD* xv. 24).

could not unmask Achilli, at least he would win a moral victory, and by suffering for the truth would ultimately help the Catholic cause. He was soon indefatigably engaged in preparing his defence and organizing the collection of evidence and witnesses, throwing himself with his usual zest into all the practical details, so that his letters at this time have all the flavour of a military campaign.

9
The Idea of a University

APART from the Achilli affair (and the preparations for the new Oratory at Edgbaston), Newman had another preoccupation. On 15 April 1851 Archbishop Paul Cullen of Armagh had written to ask him if he could advise on the appointment of staff for the new Catholic University of Ireland, and also if he 'could spare time to give us a few lectures on education'.[1] Newman's initial response was cautiously non-committal, although he took the opportunity to hint that suitable candidates might be found among the English married clerical converts (he had been disturbed since he became a Catholic about the Church's failure to make use of them).

The origins of the new university dated from the spring of 1845, when Sir Robert Peel successfully moved, as part of his conciliatory policy towards the Irish, his bill to establish a secular and non-denominational 'Queen's University of Ireland', which would provide an alternative to Anglican Trinity College, Dublin, where partial religious tests were still in force. However, this scheme of so-called 'mixed education' only met with the approval of a minority of the Irish bishops, and Rome in turn forbade the Irish Church to take any part in such a university, instead urging the establishment of a Catholic university on the model of the Belgian Louvain. This led to the appointment of a Catholic University Committee in 1850, of which Cullen had become the recognized head.

In spite of his apparent reticence at first, Newman's imagination was soon fired by the idea: 'It will be the Catholic University of the English tongue for the whole world.'[2] In July Cullen called twice at Birmingham to discuss the project with him. On the second visit he proposed that Newman himself should become the first Rector. Newman responded that he thought it would be sufficient if he became simply the Prefect of Studies; this could be more of a temporary post, and would not interfere so much with his responsibilities to the Birmingham Oratory. But shortly afterwards he indicated to Cullen that his fellow Oratorians felt he should not take a subordinate position in the new university: 'What I should desire is, to do as much work for the University as possible with *as*

[1] *LD* xiv. 257 n. 2.   [2] Ibid. 262.

little absence as possible from this place. This problem being satisfied, I do not care what you are pleased to make me.'[3] For the time being, however, he merely became a member of a subcommittee of three charged with making preliminary plans.

On 16 September Newman wrote to tell Cullen that he would 'most readily' give the lectures Cullen had asked for—'but I consider I ought to know better than I do the state of public opinion and knowledge in Ireland on the subject of education, and your own ideas what Lectures ought to be about, in order to be useful'.[4] Cullen replied, 'What we want in Ireland is to persuade the people that education should be religious.' Newman promised cautiously that he would do what he could, but 'I ought to know some thing of the state of feeling of my audience before I actually do any thing'.[5]

At the beginning of October Newman made his first visit to Ireland, where the report of the subcommittee was completed and presented to Cullen. If he had had any illusions about the extent of the task in front of him, he had lost them: 'The quantity of work I shall have is enormous, and grows on me. The very patronage I shall have, will be a business. All things are parts of a whole and must be done on an idea . . '.[6] Writing to Ambrose St John, he mentioned the possibility of a Dublin Oratory to justify his presence there. On 12 November the University Committee accepted the report and appointed Newman 'President of the Catholic University of Ireland'. It was agreed that at first no professors should be appointed to chairs, but that the Rector at this experimental stage should have complete control (under the bishops). As Newman remarked humorously, 'I mean to be Chancellor, Rector, Provost, Professor, Tutor all at once, and no one else any thing'![7] Another three whole years were to elapse before the University could begin. Cullen favoured some delay, especially in view of the distinct lack of support from Archbishop Murray of Dublin, who had been in favour of accepting the Queen's Colleges. As for Newman himself, he still had the Achilli affair hanging over his head, as well as the lectures to prepare. But whatever his unfamiliarity with Ireland and his reservations about prolonged absences from the Birmingham Oratory, there is no doubt that his heart was fully in the project—and for a number of reasons:

It is a most daring attempt but first it is a religious one, next it has the Pope's blessing on it. Curious it will be if Oxford is imported into Ireland, not in its members only, but in its principles, methods, ways, and arguments. The battle there will be what it was in Oxford 20 years ago. Curious too that there I shall be opposed to the Whigs, having Lord Clarendon instead of Lord Melbourne—that Whately will be there in propriâ personâ—and that while I found my tools

[3] Ibid. 316.   [4] Ibid. 357–8.   [5] Ibid. 364–5 and n. 2.
[6] Ibid. 377.   [7] Ibid. 394.

breaking under me in Oxford, for Protestantism is not susceptible of so high a temper, I am renewing the struggle in Dublin, with the Catholic Church to support me. It is very wonderful—Keble, Pusey, Maurice, Sewell, etc who have been able to do so little against Liberalism in Oxford, will be renewing the fight, alas, not in their persons, in Ireland.[8]

2

Newman now began to sketch out his lectures, although uncertain of 'the lie of the ground in Dublin'.[9] He decided to prepare the first three or four and then be guided by the reaction to them. He hinted to Cullen that he might not be able to cover all the subjects originally specified in his somewhat extensive brief, but he warned that he would 'almost confine' himself to the general theme, 'the great subject of the connection of religion with literature and science'.[10] At the end of February 1852 came news that Archbishop Murray of Dublin, one of the chief opponents of the new university, had died. He was immediately succeeded by Cullen. It now looked as if a real beginning could be made.

On 16 February Newman had moved into the new Oratory out in Edgbaston ('we are to fight the workmen out by our presence').[11] However, the whole community did not leave the Alcester Street house until two months later. From there he wrote to Dublin that he would be ready to give his first three lectures on three consecutive days in the first week of May; since they would be on the same subject, they could suitably be delivered together. In the end five, not three, lectures were delivered on successive weeks; no definite number seems ever to have been agreed or promised. Newman wrote rather nervously to Dalgairns's convert brother-in-law, Robert Ornsby, in Dublin: 'Will you get me a desk made of plain wood, a plan of which I enclose, by when I come? the *height*, and the *angle* at which the book part is placed upon the stem, are the two most important points about it. And there should be *lead* in the foot to prevent it overturning.'[12] He was worried about the reception his lectures were likely to receive, although they had given him 'more trouble than ever any one could by a stretch of fancy conceive. I have written almost reams of paper;—finished, set aside—then taken them up again, and plucked them . . . The truth is, I have the utmost difficulty of writing to people I do not know. . . .' He had decided to begin with Oxford, because it was important to show the sceptical part of his audience that he was not arguing simply 'on the assumption of

---

[8] *LD* xiv. 389–90.   [9] Ibid. 429.   [10] Ibid. xv. 28.
[11] Ibid. 37.   [12] Ibid. 65.

Catholicism, but in the way of reasoning, and as men of all religions may do'.[13] However, Newman's own antecedents were not, he judged, irrelevant to the task of persuading educated Catholics to support the new venture. Even so, he remained cautious about saying too much about Oxford for fear of antagonizing the Irish nationalist party. He admitted that the advertised subjects of his first lectures would seem '*dry*—but (in confidence) they were suggested by high authority, and I think may please those whom I wish most to please, if I begin with them'. Having dealt with the theological aspect, he proposed to 'go on to give a normal idea of a University'.[14] Having judged it to be diplomatically more prudent to stay in lodgings than with any particular person, English or Irish, he asked Ornsby to procure 'a low iron bed with a single hard mattress (and no curtains)'.[15]

The first lecture was given on Monday, 10 May in the Exhibition Room at the Rotunda, where public meetings in Dublin normally took place. The next day Newman wrote with great relief to Ambrose St John that it seemed to have been 'a hit'. Apart from being rather dark the room was ideal, as it held only about 400 people and there had been no problem at all about being heard—'It was just the room I have ever coveted, and never had.' There had been few seats left, and Newman was told that 'all the intellect, almost, of Dublin was there'. Leading members of the clergy and laity who had supported the Queen's Colleges as opposed to a Catholic university seemed to have been placated, if not won over. Ladies, too, had been present, 'and I *fancied* a slight sensation in the room, when I said, not Ladies and Gentlemen, but Gentlemen'.[16]

The next lecture was to be a week later, but unfortunately the same room was no longer available. Newman discovered that the publication of the first lecture in the English Catholic periodical the *Tablet* had caused unfavourable comment, so he gave the Irish publisher James Duffy the right to publish the lectures after delivery. Newman was puzzled by this kind of Irish grumbling, 'like the going off of ginger beer; the minute after I am an object of veneration'.[17] But he was also

amused at the great cleverness of the Irish, which far surpasses any thing I ever saw elsewhere. The very ticket takers in the room followed my arguments, and gave an analysis of the Discourse afterwards. The printer makes most judicious remarks and alterations in the proof—always clever and well meant, though generally wrong. As to the poor servant girl here, she is supernaturally sharp-sighted and subnaturally dirty; but her eyes seem every where, she anticipates every want, and how she discovers some things I really find a deep mystery. She closed up both windows in my bedroom with the shutters the first night—when

[13] Ibid. 66–7.   [14] Ibid. 71.   [15] Ibid. 79.

[16] Ibid. 83–4.   [17] Ibid. 86.

I went to bed I opened the right, *after* putting out my candle; the first thing in the morning, I opened the left also. How she found it out I cannot conceive—but next night and ever since the left was closed up, and the right open. She has taken to sort my papers and put away books, and fill my drawers—but here she is beyond her province, and I have been obliged to snub her just now. As I generally seem very cross or very stupid, sometimes both, she puts me down doubtless as a specimen of an English Priest.[18]

The second lecture gave him great trouble. As he sat in his lodgings at 22 Lower Dorset Street on the afternoon before the lecture, he wrote to Ambrose St John that he had not felt such confusion of mind since his illness in Sicily and his examination for the Oriel fellowship:

I have *just* discovered *how* I ought to have written my lectures—what would have been the true rhetoric—and how I have plunged into a maze of metaphysics, from which I may be unable to heave myself. When this broke on me, I half thought of lecturing ex tempore quite a different lecture—but I am not equal to it.[19]

However, the lecture in the Concert Room at the Rotunda passed off without incident (apart from background music from a brass band), as did the third lecture on the Monday following, after which Newman left for England. It was only a brief break, necessitated by his presence in Birmingham for the feast of St Philip Neri, the founder of the Oratory, on 26 May. He had to be back in Dublin for the fourth lecture on the last Monday of May. The lectures, he wrote, 'try me more than any thing I ever did—I mean, the thinking them out'. They were 'seriously hurting' his health.[20] The fourth lecture went off well and the room was full. In spite of all his anxiety, he began to feel the lectures were 'telling'.[21] He had now secured more permanent lodgings in Harcourt Street. Unfortunately, the housekeeper had taken it upon herself to arrange not only his clothes but his papers, including ones for the lectures, which she had laid out 'most neatly according to their *size*': 'She then came in to make an apology, but was so much amused at her own mischief, as to show she had no deep sense of its enormity.'[22] The fifth and final lecture was delivered on Monday, 7 June, after which Newman again left for England. The lectures had gone off far better than he ever expected, but they 'have oppressed me more than any thing else of the kind in my life'.[23] Newman had now 'intermitted the course, merely because I could not proceed to my satisfaction'. He hoped to 'be strengthened to begin again'.[24] The original three lectures had been expanded into five and delivered publicly as a fulfilment of his original brief from Archbishop Cullen. He could now go on to give 'a normal idea of a University' in his

---

[18] *LD* xv. 88.   [19] Ibid. 90.   [20] Ibid. 92.   [21] Ibid. 94.
[22] Ibid. 95.   [23] Ibid. 98–9.   [24] Ibid. 100.

own time on paper. It was the sixth lecture, 'Philosophical Knowledge its own End' (Discourse V in *The Idea of a University*), which was giving him serious trouble. While he was preparing it for the printers in July, he gave it to Joseph Gordon to read, who objected that Newman had excluded 'any notion of a religious end as the object of a Catholic University Education'.[25] The objection was predictable and was likely to come from other quarters, not least from Ireland. In order to meet it, Newman wrote a four-page introduction, which he had printed, saying that he was concerned not with 'the *indirect effects* of University Education', which 'are *religious*', but with 'the *direct end* of a University', which 'is Knowledge'. When Dalgairns criticized it as unnecessary, since the author was concerned with general principles and not a Catholic university specifically, Newman substituted a considerably abridged version consisting of a couple of paragraphs, which was printed on a separate page immediately before the lecture when it was first published on 18 August. (Neither introduction was retained when the lectures were collected into a volume.)

The Achilli trial began on 21 and ended on 24 June 1852, when the jury gave their verdict that Newman had failed to prove his charges. Newman himself was not too depressed: he had lost legally but he had won morally. It was Achilli's word on oath that had put him on trial, and now it was the same word on oath that had prevailed in the eyes of a prejudiced jury against numerous testimonies. He had known all along that he would be found guilty if he could not prove *all* his charges against Achilli, which of course was impossible. *The Times* in a leading article strongly criticized the Judge's conduct of the trial and commented that Roman Catholics could no longer have faith in British justice. As so often, Newman was relieved that at least the suspense was over—'It is nearly the only thing that ever tries me.'[26] The manifest injustice of the verdict had ensured that there were no anti-Catholic demonstrations against the Oratory in Birmingham. Certainly, here was an opportunity to practise what Newman had so often preached, that one must suffer for the truth. Sentence was postponed till November.

On 13 July Newman delivered his famous sermon 'The Second Spring' at the first synod of the new hierarchy at Oscott. In an age which worshipped progress—'The past is out of date; the past is dead'—a miracle had apparently occurred: 'The past has returned, the dead lives.'[27] The Catholics of England had survived, but, like the early persecuted Christians, 'in corners, and alleys, and cellars, and the housetops, or in the recesses of the country; cut off from the populous world around them, and dimly seen, as if through a mist or in twilight, as

---

[25] Ibid. 129 n. 2.   [26] Ibid. 116.   [27] *OS* 168–9.

ghosts flitting to and fro, by the high Protestants, the lords of the earth'.[28] The sermon celebrates their revival to life with an exuberant, even (to modern ears) embarrassing triumphalism—but Newman warns, prophetically, though from experience, that this spring of the Church may 'turn out to be an English spring, an uncertain, anxious time of hope and fear, of joy and suffering,—of bright promise and budding hopes, yet withal, of keen blasts, and cold showers, and sudden storms'.[29] It was an emotional occasion, and most of the bishops and clergy were in tears, including Wiseman.

At the end of July Newman went over to Ireland again for a fortnight, one week of which he spent quietly at Tervoe in the country home of his convert friend William Monsell, the MP for Limerick. There he worked on the seventh and eighth lectures. By the last week in September the ninth lecture, 'an anxious one', was 'half in the Press'.[30] On 22 October the lectures were 'all but finished', 'the most painful of all' his books to write.[31] Completed by the end of November, including appendix and preface, they were collected in one volume, *Discourses on the Scope and Nature of University Education: Addressed to the Catholics of Dublin*, dated 1852 on the title-page but not in fact published until 2 February 1853. Newman considered what was to become the first half of his classic *The Idea of a University* one of 'my two most perfect works, artistically', though the one which put him to the 'greatest' trouble, whereas the other work, *Present Position of Catholics in England*, had been the easiest of his books to write.[32] This judgement on the *Discourses* is not necessarily contradicted by his remark in the advertisement to the 1859 abridged edition that it had given him 'less satisfaction when written than any of his Volumes': the dissatisfaction was intellectual, not literary, and expressed his frustration at dealing adequately with his subject in the lectures—as he wrote at the time, 'I am out on the ocean with them, out of sight of land, with nothing but the stars . . .'.[33]

3

The *Discourses*[34] are the first of Newman's Roman Catholic works to evince that new ambivalence which was to achieve its classic expression in the last part of the *Apologia*. Although his ostensible target is Utilitarian criticism of liberal education within a confessional religious framework, there is another less obvious and diametrically opposite

---

[28] *OS* 172–3.   [29] Ibid. 179–80.   [30] *LD* xv. 168.
[31] Ibid. 183.   [32] Ibid. 226.   [33] Ibid. 133.
[34] The following discussion is an adapted and condensed version of part of the introduction to my critical edition of *The Idea of a University* (Oxford, 1976).

point of view under more or less covert attack—the narrow dogmatism of a defensive clerical Catholicism. Certainly, Newman's own public stance has sharply changed. In place of polemic and satire against Anglo-Catholicism, Newman now resumes his old Tractarian position on university education.

The opening Discourse reveals Newman's predicament, as well as his skill in meeting it. He had to satisfy Dr Cullen's insistence on a strictly Catholic university, but he also had to cope with nationalist fears that the university would not be properly Irish; then there was Dr Murray's view that the university was impractical, which also had to be taken into account. Somehow Newman had to satisfy all three parties. The first Discourses were intended to follow in general the lines laid down by Cullen, but without giving offence to those who were prepared to acquiesce in non-denominational education as an inevitable necessity. And so he begins by speaking of his lifelong interest in liberal education and his close connection with English Protestant Oxford, both to demonstrate his neutrality as an outsider in Irish affairs, and also to appeal to the potentially anti-clerical lay element in his audience. Turning to the burning question of 'mixed' education, he invokes the history of the Catholic Church to show that the controversy does not involve 'immutable truth', but merely 'practice and expedience'.[35] And then, to avoid coming down on either side himself in the dispute, he reminds his listeners that in this case the Pope 'has spoken, and has a claim on us to trust him'—even if he 'has enjoined that which seems to us so unpromising'.[36] Finally, with masterly tact, Newman concludes by adducing as a special reason for such a claim that it was the Bishop of Rome who once gave both England and Ireland the 'faith' and the 'civilization' that united them in that 'memorable time':[37] 'and now surely he is giving us a like mission, and we shall become one again, while we zealously and lovingly fulfil it'.[38]

This careful balance between differing perspectives and points of view is typical of the *Discourses*, and is the key to understanding them. The failure to do so has resulted in various charges of inconsistency and incoherence.[39] There is indeed a central thesis in Newman's argument which is unambiguous and unequivocal, but it is deliberately modified by various qualifications and reservations.

At the very outset Newman may startle some readers by asking abruptly whether the Pope, who has recommended the establishment of the Catholic University, can be said to have 'any obligation or duty at all towards secular knowledge as such? . . . does he not contemplate such

---

[35] *Idea* 24.   [36] Ibid. 28.   [37] Ibid. 29–31.
[38] Ibid. 32.   [39] See ibid., pp. xlvi ff.

achievements of the intellect, as far as he contemplates them, solely and simply in their relation to the interests of Revealed Truth?' To which Newman's immediate answer is that certainly, 'if he encourages and patronizes art and science, it is for the sake of Religion.' If the suspicious reader is not disarmed, he will certainly be taken by surprise at the turn the argument now takes: 'He rejoices in the widest and most philosophical systems of intellectual education, from an intimate conviction that Truth is his real ally, as it is his profession; and that Knowledge and Reason are sure ministers to Faith.'[40] The Church 'fears no knowledge',[41] for 'all branches of knowledge are connected together, because the subject-matter of knowledge is intimately united in itself, as being the acts and the work of the Creator'.[42] It is, then, ultimately a religious conviction that supports Newman's supremely confident vision of the wholeness of intellectual knowledge and truth. Underlying his belief in man's 'imperial intellect'[43] is his belief in God. What may seem to some an intolerable paradox is at the heart of Newman's theme, and it is important not to confuse our own disinclination to believe with any ambiguity or evasion on Newman's part.

Religion and knowledge are not opposed to each other—and not because they are irrelevant to each other, but because they are indivisibly connected, or rather because religion forms part of the subject-matter of knowledge. This is Newman's claim, and it is crucial to his case. It may be provocative, but it is not illogical (given the premiss) for him to state: 'If the Catholic Faith is true, a University cannot exist externally to the Catholic pale, for it cannot teach Universal Knowledge if it does not teach Catholic theology.'[44]

What gives the *Discourses* their special character is not an unresolved and unresolvable conflict between knowledge and religion, which Newman would deny could ever really occur ('truth cannot be contrary to truth'),[45] but the tension between the genuinely unconditional insistence on the absolute value of knowledge in itself and the equally firm conviction that knowledge is emphatically not the highest good. Thus, while on the one hand Newman will have no party with those who wish to justify education solely on moral or religious grounds, on the other hand, without any self-contradiction, he insists that it is better to have a simple religious faith than an educated intellect without religious belief. There is no question of any necessary incompatibility for Newman, but he recognizes the fact that religion and education, faith and reason, are not always found together: 'Right Reason, that is, Reason rightly exercised, leads the mind to the Catholic Faith, and

[40] *Idea* 6.   [41] Ibid. 198.   [42] Ibid. 94.
[43] Ibid. 371.   [44] Ibid. 184.   [45] Ibid. 372.

plants it there, and teaches it in all its religious speculations to act under its guidance. But Reason, considered as a real agent in the world, and as an operative principle in man's nature . . . is far from taking so straight and satisfactory a direction.'[46] If, then, there has to be a choice between this kind of reason and simple faith, Newman leaves us in no doubt as to his own preference. Whatever one may think of this priority, the fact is that Newman contrives to keep both considerations in sharp equipoise throughout the *Discourses*.

The point can be illustrated first by some simple examples. For instance, the various eulogies of man's 'imperial intellect'[47] receive their counterpoint, as it were, in the eloquent expositions of the omnipotence and omniscience of God and the authority of the Catholic Church and the papacy. Or there is the contrast in the final Discourse between the admission that a *Christian* literature is an impossibility, because it 'is a contradiction in terms to attempt a sinless Literature of sinful man', and the insistence that nevertheless the study of literature must not be omitted from education, because education is 'for this world' and 'it is not the way to learn to swim in troubled waters, never to have gone into them'.[48] Conversely, the rapt evocation of the wonder of music in the fourth Discourse is promptly followed by a warning against its temptation 'rather to use Religion than to minister to it'.[49]

In short, a sustained eulogy of a liberal education is systematically qualified by reminders of its limitations. Thus the definition of a 'liberal' pursuit does not attempt to pretend that 'in point of worth and importance' there need be even any comparison with an 'illiberal' study: 'even what is supernatural need not be liberal, nor need a hero be a gentleman, for the plain reason that one idea is not another idea.'[50] Newman is keenly aware of the danger of exaggerating the importance both of the university and of a liberal education. It is, he insists, 'as real a mistake to burden' liberal knowledge 'with virtue or religion as with the mechanical arts':

Its direct business is not to steel the soul against temptation or to console it in affliction, any more than to set the loom in motion, or to direct the steam carriage . . . it as little mends our hearts as it improves our temporal circumstances . . . Quarry the granite rock with razors, or moor the vessel with a thread of silk; then you may hope with such keen and delicate instruments as human knowledge and human reason to contend against those giants, the passion and the pride of man.[51]

Again, the 'perfection of the Intellect, which is the result of Education', may have 'almost the beauty and harmony of heavenly contemplation,

---

[46] Ibid. 157.   [47] Ibid. 371.   [48] Ibid. 195, 197.
[49] Ibid. 80.   [50] Ibid. 101.   [51] Ibid. 110–11.

so intimate is it with the eternal order of things and the music of the spheres'—but, Newman emphasizes, it is not to be confused with the 'vast ideas or dazzling projects' of genius.[52] In practice, too, 'a so-called University, which dispensed with residence and tutorial superintendence, and gave its degrees to any person who passed an examination in a wide range of subjects', may even be *'morally* the better' than 'a University which had no professors or examinations at all, but merely brought a number of young men together for three or four years'—but 'if I must determine which of the two courses was the more successful in training, moulding, enlarging the mind . . . I have no hesitation in giving the preference to that University which did nothing': such a university, with 'a heathen code of ethics', at least 'can boast of a succession of heroes and statesmen, of literary men and philosophers, of men conspicuous for great natural virtues, for habits of business, for knowledge of life, for practical judgment, for cultivated tastes, for accomplishments, who have made England what it is,—able to subdue the earth, able to domineer over Catholics.'[53]

An element of suspense hangs more or less continuously over the *Discourses* as evaluations are constantly modified by the author's changing point of view. Thus the Discourse from which we have just quoted ends with a description of 'the poor boy' in Crabbe's poem who managed 'to fashion for himself a philosophy' from his humble country experiences—'how much more genuine an education', Newman exclaims, than that of those university students 'who are forced to load their minds with a score of subjects against an examination'![54]

But the most remarkable and dramatic shift of perspective in the *Discourses* is to be found in its most famous part—the celebrated portrait of the 'gentleman' in the eighth Discourse. It is here that Newman concludes his exposition of intellectual culture with an eloquent depiction of its 'momentous' moral influences 'all upon the type of Christianity . . . so much so, that a character more noble to look at, more beautiful, more winning, in the various relations of life and in personal duties, is hardly conceivable'. However, 'the work is as certainly not supernatural as it is certainly noble and beautiful', for there is a 'radical difference' between this 'mental refinement' and 'genuine religion'.[55] And Newman proceeds to show how 'the tendency of the intellectual culture' is to become 'a false philosophy' and a 'spurious religion'.[56] He takes as an example the Emperor Julian, 'in whom every Catholic sees the shadow of the future Antichrist', but who 'was all but the pattern-man of philosophical virtue'.[57] Indeed, it is from the very 'shallowness of philosophical Religion . . . that its disciples seem able to fulfil certain

---

[52] *Idea* 124.   [53] Ibid. 129–30.   [54] Ibid. 132–3.
[55] Ibid. 164.   [56] Ibid. 165.   [57] Ibid. 167.

precepts of Christianity more readily and exactly than Christians themselves', so that 'the school of the world seems to send out living copies' of 'St. Paul's exemplar of the Christian in his external relations . . . with greater success than the Church'.[58] Modesty is substituted for humility, and 'pride, under such training, instead of running to waste in the education of the mind, is turned to account'. A passage of marvellous irony follows, in which Newman admiringly extols the great and real social fruits of this new quality 'called self-respect', only to conclude with devastating effect: 'It breathes upon the face of the community, and the hollow sepulchre is forthwith beautiful to look upon.' Still, however, we are not allowed to forget that secular education can accomplish objects which seem to defeat religion, and we are reminded that it is a refined self-respect which 'is now quietly but energetically opposing itself to the unchristian practice of duelling . . . and certainly it seems likely to effect what Religion has aimed at abolishing in vain'.[59]

The famous passage which follows, beginning with the well-known words, 'Hence it is that it is almost a definition of a gentleman to say he is one who never inflicts pain',[60] is so eloquent and presents such an attractive picture that many people have supposed that this is in fact Newman's ideal. And indeed they are right in the sense that it is the ideal end of a liberal education, which

makes not the Christian, not the Catholic, but the gentleman. It is well to be a gentleman, it is well to have a cultivated intellect, a delicate taste, a candid, equitable, dispassionate mind, a noble and courteous bearing in the conduct of life;—these are the connatural qualities of a large knowledge; they are the objects of a University; I am advocating, I shall illustrate and insist upon them; but still, I repeat, they are no guarantee for sanctity or even for conscientiousness, they may attach to the man of the world, to the profligate, to the heartless . . .[61]

Implicit in much of the criticism of the *Discourses* is a disregard of Newman's initial premiss that theology is a part of knowledge. But the whole argument rests on this principle, which Newman admits is not universally accepted. This is not seen as special pleading for theology, for it is possible in principle to conceive of a university where 'the moral and mental sciences' are also excluded because of 'the extreme sensitiveness of large classes of the community, clergy and laymen, on the subjects of necessity, responsibility, the standard of morals, and the nature of virtue'.[62] The analogy is suggested with the gentle irony characteristic of the *Discourses*. 'What relieves . . . their regret', observes Newman, 'is the reflection, that domestic feelings and polished manners are best

---

[58] Ibid. 174.   [59] Ibid. 177–8.   [60] Ibid. 179.

[61] Ibid. 110.   [62] Ibid. 59.

cultivated in the family circle and in good society, in the observance of the sacred ties which unite father, mother, and child, in the correlative claims and duties of citizenship, in the exercise of disinterested loyalty and enlightened patriotism.'[63] In such a university it will be as simple to deny that 'intelligence and volition' are 'real powers'[64] as to refuse to accept the God of monotheism. Newman's case, then, rests on the premiss that theology is a genuine branch and religion a genuine part of the subject-matter of knowledge. Otherwise the eighth Discourse may well appear to contradict what has preceded, with liberal culture and religion appearing as irreconcilable enemies.

Now what Newman in fact is discussing in the most famous of the *Discourses* is not so much the relation between intellectual culture and religion, as that between the *religion of* intellectual culture and religion itself. The distinction is crucial. At the beginning of the Discourse Newman is careful to say that 'the Religion of Civilization' is not incompatible with 'the profession of Catholicism', and that he is concerned 'to compare and contrast, not the doctrinal, but the moral and social teaching of Philosophy on the one hand, and Catholicism on the other'. The conflict is over 'Catholicism chiefly as a system of pastoral instruction and moral duty' and its bearing on those 'subjects to which the cultivated intellect will practically be turned'.[65] Newman's point is simply that the 'educated mind' or 'cultivated intellect' has a tendency to substitute a 'self-reproach' which 'is directed and limited to our mere sense of what is fitting and becoming' for conscience, 'which ought to lead to God': this 'is the danger which awaits a civilized age'.[66] But at the same time he is very insistent that in practice intellectual culture has also in moral matters 'a special claim upon our consideration and gratitude'.[67] We should not be misled by the dramatic vividness with which Newman depicts the effects of religionless culture into imagining a conflict that is not there.

Theoretical as the *Discourses* are, we are not allowed to forget that universities are not self-sufficient, totally independent entities. Even the particular branches of knowledge which they teach arise out of the discoveries and creations of genius, the work of scientists and artists who are as likely as not to be outside the university. It is obvious that what a particular university teaches is determined by what is available and what is recognized as knowledge at a particular period of a particular society. What is necessarily true for Newman, also, is that a university has some kind of ethos and directing philosophy—although it may only be the kind of fragmented and disintegrated vision of knowledge

---

[63] *Idea* 60.   [64] Ibid. 61.   [65] Ibid. 158–9.
[66] Ibid. 165.   [67] Ibid. 162.

depicted in the original fifth Discourse (which was omitted from *The Idea of a University* chiefly, it seems, because of its largely theological character, which was deemed to be out of keeping with a work of educational theory).[68] It is not possible to have a university which is not founded on some particular form of the general idea that a university teaches universal knowledge. In this sense a university can never be 'uncommitted'. At the very least decisions have to be made about what subjects constitute worthwhile academic study. And so Newman's insistence on the jurisdiction of the Church over a Catholic university, which after all is the creation of a Catholic community, may be regarded as hardly more than a specific application of the general principle that a university is inevitably limited and defined by its concept of what constitutes knowledge and truth. The emphasis on the control of the Church in the ninth Discourse need not, therefore, imply any sinister opposition between the liberal cultural ideal and religion; it is, rather, a sharply explicit reminder that a university must teach all the knowledge it professes to teach—in accordance with its idea of what constitutes knowledge—unequivocally and without compromise.

A university, then, where ethics, for example, is not recognized as a branch of knowledge is certain to be a different kind of university from one where it is; just as a university which teaches Catholic theology is a radically different kind of university from one which does not teach any theology at all. Ultimately, a university must have its own particular identity—whether voluntarily or involuntarily, consciously or unconsciously. And this will determine the nature of its 'conception of what is meant by Philosophy . . . and of a philosophical habit of mind'. There need not be any essential difference over Newman's basic definition— 'the comprehension of the bearings of one science on another, and the use of each to each, and the location and limitation and adjustment and due appreciation of them all, one with another'.[69] But clearly the 'philosophical habit of mind' is bound to vary with the kind of subjects that are taught and how they are taught. A Christian, a secular humanist, and a Marxist will not be of one mind as regards the conclusions of 'that Architectonic Science or Philosophy, whatever it be, which is itself the arbiter of all truth, and which disposes of the claims and arranges the places of all the departments of knowledge'.[70] Marxist theory demands a university committed to a specific dialectic, while Anglo-Saxon empiricism may refuse to recognize as 'knowledge' any system of 'metaphysics'. Nor is the 'utilitarian' university that is mocked in the suppressed fifth Discourse any less 'dogmatically' conceived, in

---

[68] See ibid., p. xxxvii. It is rpt. ibid. 419–34.   [69] Ibid. 57.   [70] Ibid. 87.

principle, than a Catholic university—for it denies no less emphatically what the latter asserts.

It is important to be clear what Newman means by this 'special Philosophy', this 'Liberal or Philosophical Knowledge' which he calls 'the end of University Education' and which he defines as 'a comprehensive view of truth in all its branches, of the relations of science to science, of their mutual bearings, and their respective values'.[71] Essentially, he means nothing more than what he defines as 'real cultivation of mind' in the Preface: 'the intellect . . . properly trained and formed to have a connected view or grasp of things'.[72] Although it is true that the more sciences we know the more comprehensive will our actual knowledge be, Newman's philosophical ideal is not at all quantitative. 'Science and Philosophy', he says, 'in their elementary idea, are nothing else but this habit of *viewing* . . . the objects which sense conveys to the mind, of throwing them into system, and uniting and stamping them with one form.'[73] The 'Architectonic Science or Philosophy' is the same, though on an altogether larger scale. But to aspire to a cultivated intellect and the philosophical habit is not to attempt to pursue every subject. Newman is quite explicit on this point when he advocates enlarging 'the range of studies which a University professes, even for the sake of the students':

> . . . though they cannot pursue every subject which is open to them, they will be the gainers by living among those and under those who represent the whole circle. This I conceive to be the advantage of a seat of universal learning, considered as a place of education. An assemblage of learned men, zealous for their own sciences, and rivals of each other, are brought, by familiar intercourse and for the sake of intellectual peace, to adjust together the claims and relations of their respective subjects of investigation. They learn to respect, to consult, to aid each other. Thus is created a pure and clear atmosphere of thought, which the student also breathes, though in his own case he only pursues a few sciences out of the multitude. He profits by an intellectual tradition . . . which guides him in his choice of subjects, and duly interprets for him those which he chooses. He apprehends the great outlines of knowledge, the principles on which it rests, the scale of its parts, its lights and its shades, its great points and its little . . . Hence it is that his education is called 'Liberal'. A habit of mind is formed which lasts through life . . . or what . . . I have ventured to call a philosophical habit.[74]

That 'form of Universal Knowledge' which is the 'perfection' of 'the individual intellect' is not knowing all branches of knowledge, but simply 'is the power of viewing many things at once as one whole, of referring them severally to their true place in the universal system, of understanding their respective values, and determining their mutual

[71] *Idea* 96–7.   [72] Ibid. 10–11.   [73] Ibid. 75.   [74] Ibid. 95–6.

dependence'.[75] It is where this understanding of order and wholeness is lacking or rejected that individual disciplines will inevitably encroach on the territories of other disciplines and their proponents will make normative judgements under the cloak of their special discipline, which may in fact arise from their professional preoccupations but which certainly fall outside their area of competence. Newman cites economics as an example: 'Of course if there is a science of wealth, it must give rules for gaining and disposing of wealth', but 'it cannot itself declare that it is a subordinate science, that its end is not the ultimate end of all things, and that its conclusions are only hypothetical, depending on its premisses, and liable to be overruled by a higher teaching.'[76] This simple logical truth, so often neglected in practice, is one of the central insights of the *Discourses*. Not only must a university inevitably reflect and embody certain values in its organization and structure, but individual branches of study are bound to give rise to normative questions which cannot be settled exclusively within the terms of reference of the particular intellectual discipline. When, therefore, Newman explicitly denies that he is opposed to professional or vocational studies in a university, he does make this significant reservation:

I do but say that there will be this distinction as regards a Professor of Law, or of Medicine, or of Geology, or of Political Economy, in a University and out of it, that out of a University he is in danger of being absorbed and narrowed by his pursuit, and of giving Lectures which are the Lectures of nothing more than a lawyer, physician, geologist, or political economist; whereas in a University he will just know where he and his science stand, he has come to it, as it were, from a height, he has taken a survey of all knowledge, he is kept from extravagance by the very rivalry of other studies, he has gained from them a special illumination and largeness of mind and freedom and self-possession, and he treats his own in consequence with a philosophy and a resource, which belongs not to the study itself, but to his liberal education.[77]

The charge that Newman excluded professional studies from his idea of a university is part of the general criticism that he contradicts his own initial definition of a university as a place for teaching all branches of knowledge. The assumption is that because the end of the university is liberal knowledge, therefore only the so-called liberal arts are to be taught. Apart from Newman's own practice in Dublin which manifestly belies the accusation, the fact that the liberal arts formed for Newman the centre and nucleus of university studies did not mean that other subjects were excluded. Nor were they seen as essentially external to the idea of a liberal education. Thus, to take Newman's own example, the study of theology ceases to be a liberal study only when it 'becomes an art or a business making use of Theology' for the specific practical purposes of the catechism and pulpit.[78] The illustration could not be more apt, for Newman can hardly be suspected of undervaluing religion. But his point is that when theology is studied in a seminary or catechetical college in this kind of way, it is not a theological education that the students are receiving but a theological training. For the primary object is not that they should learn to think about theology, but that they should learn to apply certain given theological information and skills to meet certain concrete demands and situations. And so, while it is true that Newman did not include either theology or applied science among the central disciplines of a university, this did not preclude either from providing a liberal education if 'cultivated as a contemplation' or 'exercised' as 'simple knowledge' within the university context of the whole circle of knowledge.[79] Although Newman did regard an education in the traditional liberal arts as the best, in the sense of the most 'liberal', education, this did not prevent him from acknowledging pure science as one 'main constituent portion of the subject-matter of Liberal Education', the other being literature.[80]

It is also claimed that Newman places a disproportionate emphasis on theology, which is again inconsistent with his definition of a university. Now it is quite true that the *Discourses* make it clear that the different branches of knowledge 'differ in importance', and that theology is the most important of all, for 'it comes from heaven . . . its truths were given once for all at the first . . . they are more certain on account of the Giver than those of mathematics'.[81] Indeed, to leave out theology from the circle of knowledge is to throw it into 'a far worse confusion' even than by omitting 'man's agency' from the 'circle of universal science', in view of the 'important influence' which theology 'does and must exercise over a great variety of sciences, completing and correcting them'.[82] And in the original fifth Discourse it is stated categorically that although 'Theology is one branch of knowledge, and Secular Sciences are other branches', nevertheless 'Theology is the highest indeed, and widest.'[83]

It should, however, be noted that far from ever speaking of a 'hierarchy' of branches of knowledge, Newman's favoured image is the 'circle', which is intended to imply interdependence not equality, since certain key branches of knowledge like ethics and theology, whose importance is commensurate with the precariousness of their status, impinge upon (not rule over) a number of other branches of knowledge. And so there is no reason why one science should not be the principal science, in the sense of being first among equals rather than sovereign over the others.

[78] *Idea* 101.
[79] Ibid.
[80] Ibid. 193.
[81] Ibid. 54, 57–8.
[82] Ibid. 63, 92.
[83] Ibid. 427–8.

4

The preoccupation with theology in the *Discourses* should be put into perspective by a comparison with 'Christianity and Letters', the 1854 inaugural lecture which opens the collection of *Lectures and Essays on University Subjects* (1859), later published as the second part of *The Idea of a University* under the title 'University Subjects Discussed in Occasional Lectures and Essays'. The lecture begins with the emphatic statement that the subjects of the 'School of Philosophy and Letters' form the central studies of a university, 'in spite of the special historical connexion of University Institutions with the Sciences of Theology, Law, and Medicine'. Newman points out that 'the Classics . . . or . . . the Arts, have ever, on the whole, been the instruments of education' which Western civilization has adopted.[84] This system of liberal education became known as the seven liberal arts in the Middle Ages. By 'Classics', Newman does not mean a narrowly linguistic or even literary course of studies. Not only do the Classics include ancient history and philosophy, but also 'the subjects of thought and the studies to which they give rise'.[85] Newman's words allow for even further developments than the seven liberal arts. 'I take things', he says, 'as I find them on the surface of history, and am but classing phenomena.' It is true that he finds something providential in the fact that 'the world was to have certain intellectual teachers, and no others', and he remarks on how 'Even to this day Shakespeare and Milton are not studied in our course of education'.[86] But there is no reason to suppose that Newman, who was responsible for setting up one of the first university chairs of English Literature, would not have admitted modern arts courses as legitimate heirs of the old liberal tradition based on the Classics, although he would have had justifiable regrets.[87]

In the medieval period the liberal arts were able to withstand the challenge of the new sciences of Scholastic theology, law, and medicine, because they were 'acknowledged, as before, to be the best instruments of mental cultivation, and the best guarantees for intellectual progress'. This for Newman is the crucial test: 'how best to strengthen, refine, and enrich the intellectual powers'. And what seems to him self-evident is that 'the perusal of the poets, historians, and philosophers of Greece and Rome will accomplish this purpose, as long experience has shown'. The liberal arts are again threatened by modern applied sciences (which, however, are no more to be excluded from a university than is theology

---

[84] Ibid. 211, 216.   [85] Ibid. 216.   [86] Ibid. 213, 219.

[87] He held the advanced view that it was necessary 'to lay a great stress on English Literature', for it is 'next best to Latin and Greek' (*LD* xvi. 426).

or law or medicine), and the same question arises as before: will these sciences be able to educate the mind as the humanities do? Newman contents himself with observing merely that it 'is proved to us as yet by no experience whatever'. The champion of the place of theology in a university curriculum regards neither theologians nor scientists as being central to its chief business:

. . . the question is not what department of study contains the more wonderful facts, or promises the more brilliant discoveries, and which is in the higher and which in an inferior rank; but simply which out of all provides the most robust and invigorating discipline for the unformed mind. And I conceive it is as little disrespectful to Lord Bacon to prefer the Classics in this point of view to the sciences which have grown out of his philosophy as it would be disrespectful to St. Thomas in the middle ages to have hindered the study of the Summa from doing prejudice to the Faculty of Arts.[88]

There can be no question that for Newman theology is far more important as a branch of knowledge than literature, but this does not prevent him from holding that literature is more important as a study for a liberal education. The fact is that Newman has exactly the same reservations about applied science as he has about theology. It was not after all empty rhetoric to write of Bacon in the *Discourses*:

Almost day by day have we fresh and fresh shoots, and buds, and blossoms, which are to ripen into fruit, on that magical tree of knowledge which he planted, and to which none of us perhaps, except the very poor, but owes, if not his present life, at least his daily food, his health, and general well-being. He was the divinely provided minister of temporal benefits to all of us . . .[89]

If there had to be a choice between bodily and spiritual health on the one hand and intellectual culture on the other, there is no doubt that Newman would have chosen hospitals and seminaries in preference to universities.

By bringing the *Discourses* and *Lectures and Essays* together into one volume under a common title, Newman was not merely assembling a miscellaneous collection of papers on university education. The second part was intended to be seen as the practical application of the theoretical first part. Thus the second Lecture on 'Literature' shows Newman in the chair of the 'Science of Sciences', defining and evaluating a particular branch of knowledge: the educated mind considers literature and appreciates the importance of its place in the circle of knowledge, a judgement not open to the literary student as such. The pre-eminent position assigned to literature ('the personal use or exercise of language') is justified by the overriding importance of language, 'a gift as great as any that can be named'.[90]

---

[88] *Idea* 221-2.   [89] Ibid. 108.   [90] Ibid. 231, 245.

The most impressive example of Newman professing the 'Science of Sciences' is to be found in 'Christianity and Scientific Investigation', where he presents his final ideal of the university as 'an empire . . . in the sphere of philosophy and research',

the high protecting power of all knowledge and science, of fact and principle, of inquiry and discovery, of experiment and speculation; it maps out the territory of the intellect, and sees that the boundaries of each province are religiously respected, and that there is neither encroachment nor surrender on any side. It acts as umpire between truth and truth, and, taking into account the nature and importance of each, assigns to all their due order of precedence.

The 'philosophy of an imperial intellect . . . is based, not so much on simplification as on discrimination'.[91]

When it comes to discriminating between the spheres of religion and science, Newman once again has to keep different points of view in careful balance. Thus, on the one hand, he insists that the scientist 'should be free, independent, unshackled in his movements'; on the other hand, he warns the scientist against rashly intruding into the territory of religion—after, he hastens to add, the manner of 'religious men, who, from a nervous impatience lest Scripture should for one moment seem inconsistent with the results of some speculation of the hour, are ever proposing geological or ethnological comments upon it, which they have to alter or obliterate before the ink is well dry, from changes in the progressive science, which they have so officiously brought to its aid'.[92] As for errors, they are sometimes 'the way to truth, and the only way', as the 'inseparable accidents' of important new systems of thought. Not, he is quick to warn, that 'great care' must not be 'taken to avoid scandal, or shocking the popular mind, or unsettling the weak; the association between truth and error being so strong in particular minds that it is impossible to weed them of the error without rooting up the wheat with it'.[93] Still, there must be freedom for scientific research, whose progress may not be altogether smooth or straight-forward—but then 'No one can go straight up a mountain; no sailing vessel makes for its port without tacking.'[94]

Newman's treatment of the relation between religion and science is not only an illustration of the kind of 'discrimination' that belongs to the 'imperial intellect', but constitutes his own significant and valuable contribution to the solution of what was becoming one of the most critical problems for religious belief in the nineteenth century. In 'Christianity and Physical Science' he yet again employs the key image of the circle:

---

[91] Ibid. 370–1. [92] Ibid. 379–80. [93] Ibid. 382, 384, 381.
[94] Ibid. 382.

These two great circles of knowledge . . . intersect; first, as far as supernatural knowledge includes truths and facts of the natural world, and secondly, as far as truths and facts of the natural world are on the other hand data for inferences about the supernatural. Still . . . the two worlds and the two kinds of knowledge respectively are separated off from each other; and . . . therefore, as being separate, they cannot on the whole contradict each other.[95]

Not only are theology and science completely different ways of looking at the world, but they employ diametrically opposite methods, theology being deductive and science inductive. The two separate kinds of knowledge are 'like the distinct subjects represented by the lines of the same drawing . . . accordingly as they are read on their concave or convex side'.[96] No science can actually be hostile to theology, but it is 'Private Judgment that infects every science which it touches with a hostility to Theology'.[97]

After the eloquent generalities of the *Discourses*, the *Lectures and Essays* provide a striking contrast in their relentless practicality. Thus we find that the 'imperial intellect' is formed not by lofty generalities but by 'accuracy of thought', which cannot be learned 'by any manual or treatise' but only by 'a really good education' which is founded on the principle 'really know what you say you know' and which eschews 'general education' in favour of 'clearness of head, accuracy, scholarlike precision'.[98] The ability to write is essential: 'Till a man begins to put down his thoughts about a subject on paper he will not ascertain what he knows and what he does not know; and still less will he be able to express what he does know.'[99] Again, 'formation of mind' results not from 'that barren mockery of knowledge which comes of attending on great Lecturers, or of mere acquaintance with reviews, magazines, newspapers', but from 'that catechetical instruction, which consists in a sort of conversation between your lecturer and you', and from having 'really studied and mastered' a subject.[100] The end of a liberal education may be idealistic, but (as in Newman's spirituality) the means to attaining it are strictly practical as well as practicable.

The *Idea* may be seen as the triumphant culmination of Newman's most intensely creative period as a writer. After 1858, Newman wrote virtually nothing until the *Apologia*, by which time he had begun to develop his own Catholic ecclesiology. And what is so striking is the resemblance between his idea of the Church and his earlier idea of the university, a similarity which suggests if not influence at least a common source in a unified vision.

---

[95] *Idea* 347–8.   [96] Ibid. 324.   [97] Ibid. 92.
[98] Ibid. 273, 275, 285.   [99] Ibid. 341.   [100] Ibid. 394, 402–4.

10

The Catholic University of Ireland

In spite of the success of the *Discourses* which Newman had delivered in the presence of Cullen, a cloud had already appeared on the horizon, the harbinger of many troubles to come. On 4 July 1852 Newman had written to Cullen to ask that a Vice-Rector should not at present be appointed. He explained that he regarded this office as so important that he ought to have absolute control over the appointment. Whoever was appointed must not only have the requisite abilities and enjoy Newman's complete confidence, but he must 'see things from the same point of view as I do'. But because Newman was not in the position at the moment of knowing enough people to choose from (he had already in 1851 unsuccessfully asked Manning to take on the post), it would be inexpedient to make an appointment at present—it might be 'ruining every thing'.[1] To this letter Newman never received any answer. The silence was ominous, and it turned out to be the first of many episcopal snubs by Cullen. In the memorandum he wrote in the early 1870s about the Catholic University, Newman noted that the problem over a Vice-Rector was his first as well as his last difficulty, and proved to be his chief problem with Cullen.

Not that there was any doubt about his reception in Ireland. He was 'killed with kindness', and he was amazed at the universal warmth with which he was received. All the excitement, however, was physically exhausting, and he longed for some quiet and solitude. He felt stimulated, on the other hand, intellectually, and sensed that his mind had never been 'more vigorous'.[2] As usual, he felt much better after his week's solitude at Tervoe, free from the strain of meeting people. He had not had a holiday for two years.

On 22 November Newman appeared again in court. To the dismay of the presiding judge and the prosecution, Newman's leading counsel, Sir Alexander Cockburn, demanded a new trial on three grounds, only one of which was ruled admissible, namely, that the verdict had been against the weight of evidence. Newman had opposed the idea because of the cost and the trouble involved; he was quite resigned to the prospect of

---

[1] *LD* xv. 117–18.   [2] Ibid. 140.

prison, which was the penalty for criminal libel. But when all his lawyers were unanimously in favour of pressing for another trial, he gave in at the very last moment in court. One of the lawyers, a non-Catholic, had actually refused to accept any fee and said he would collect money from Protestants to defray the expenses. On reflection, Newman saw the advantage of the application, for even if it was rejected, at least his counsel would have the opportunity of showing up the injustice of the judge and jury. If, on the other hand, it were granted, it could only be on the ground that the verdict was inconsistent with the evidence. Achilli had everything to lose by the application, while Newman had everything to gain—even the expense would be tolerable now that he knew what witnesses to produce. The court would decide in January after hearing the prosecution's reply.

On 16 December Newman left for six weeks' holiday at Abbotsford on the banks of the Tweed in Scotland, the house built by Sir Walter Scott, where James Hope, who had married Scott's granddaughter, now lived. He was desperately in need of a real rest; he had never had 'such a year' as 1852.[3] He felt so much at home at Abbotsford that he began to feel rather uneasy: 'I am in danger of arguing too much, or of laughing too much—and, though I ought not *personally* to care that persons should go away with a lower and truer notion of me, the thought of giving scandal comes before me, and annoys me.'[4] (The previous year he had taken a very strict line, saying to Faber that he doubted whether priests should 'live in a family at all'—'I certainly mean to *try* never to sleep a night under a gentleman's roof.'[5]) The house itself he did not find very impressive: it was dark, the rooms small, and the passages so narrow that 'I could shake hands with the nursery maids in the rooms opposite me, without leaving my own room—and sometimes of a morning or evening in going down stairs, seeing nothing, I hear a step approaching, and am obliged to stand still where I am, for fear of consequences, and then a little light figure shoots past me on the right or left . . . Once there was an awful moral stoppage, neither daring to move.'[6] Back in Birmingham, there was trouble over a lay brother who had misbehaved. Newman sent a letter stating categorically that he would have to be asked to leave— but adding that the brother's defence must be heard and then sent on to him. As so often in his life, Newman's forthrightness was misunderstood. The lay brother was summarily dismissed before his defence could be heard and judged by his Superior. Newman was not only appalled at the way the affair had been mishandled, but deeply upset that important decisions had been taken without proper consultation with him: 'Does it not come to this, that I am unnecessary to you?' There is also the note of

---

[3] *LD* xv. 227.　　　[4] Ibid. 247.　　　[5] Ibid. xiv. 392.　　　[6] Ibid. xv. 247.

personal sensitivity in his letter to Ambrose St John: 'I thought of taking a *year* ticket for the Rail, when I went to Ireland, so that, any night I pleased, I might come home, if needed—but what is the good of it?'[7] St John, the acting Superior, had shown too his lack of control in an excited situation, and it was a foretaste of things to come in the future when Newman was away in Ireland. As for the lay brother, Newman insisted that it was not his improper behaviour that he could not tolerate—he could have forgiven even an act of fornication—but his general 'unfaithfulness—he has committed the unpardonable sin'.[8]

On 31 January 1853 Newman again appeared in court. A new trial had been refused on the ground that the jury had correctly found that not all Newman's allegations had been legally proved. After a lengthy lecture from one of the judges, Sir John Taylor Coleridge, a Tractarian and a friend of Keble, 'of which the theme was "deterioration of converts" ',[9] Newman was fined a mere £100, with the alternative of imprisonment. This anticlimax was greeted with laughter, 'and we walked off in triumph amid the hurrahs of 200 paddies'.[10] Newman's request to address the court was rejected, but Coleridge wrote in his diary that he felt 'overpowered' by the 'strange mysterious cloudy face' and the 'sweet musical, almost unearthly voice' of the defendant.[11] Newman himself merely commented that after twenty years of scorn and slander, 'mere habit, as in the case of the skinned eels, would keep me from being annoyed'.[12] As Newman had known from the beginning, the verdict must go against him because it would be impossible to prove legally everything he had alleged against Achilli. The judges could have taken the opportunity explicitly to correct the manifestly prejudiced finding of the jury that except for one charge all the rest against Achilli were unproved. However, the lightness of the sentence was itself an implicit admission that the jury had been misguided. Newman contemplated publishing a letter or pamphlet on his feelings about the trial, but it was judged inadvisable by his legal adviser.

The trials and tribulations of 1852 seemed to continue unabated into the new year. On 13 February Joseph Gordon died. Newman was shattered: 'He was the *life* of our Oratory.'[13] Gordon not only had powers of leadership (unfortunately, he had been seriously ill during the crisis over the lay brother), but he was extremely devoted and loyal to Newman. His death left a serious gap and was 'the greatest blow' the Oratory had had. Newman recorded his sense of desolation with a chilling image from the past. In 1826, 'after a most glorious Summer, there was a week of pouring rain, and then it was fine again and the sky

---

[7] Ibid. 254. [8] Ibid. 241. [9] Ibid. 280. [10] Ibid. 278.
[11] Ibid. 284 n. 2. [12] Ibid. 285. [13] Ibid. 295.

as radiant for weeks as before. But the season was changed—the ground had been thoroughly chilled, and never recovered itself. Autumn had unequivocally set in, and the week of wet divided the two seasons as by a river. And so I think I have now passed into my Autumn . . .'.[14]

2

Certainly, Newman's honeymoon period as a Catholic was fast coming to an end, if it had not already ended. There were desolations undreamed of still to come. In the meantime he was alarmed by the report that Wiseman had sent his name to Rome for one of the new dioceses—'The very thought of it makes me ill.'[15] Such responsibility was not his line, nor did he relish the exercise of power. He was eminently suited, on the other hand, for the Irish University; but still there was no news of any definite development. In spite of the irritating suspense, he was sufficiently confident to say, 'I *expect* to have every thing my own way.'[16] He wrote to Cullen in March pressing that the University should begin in the autumn without further delay. At the moment things were still in the hands of the University Committee, of which Newman was not even a member and of whose powers of initiative he was sceptical. As in the Oxford Movement, so now, he was convinced that individuals not committees shaped the course of events. The undertaking was difficult enough: normally the rise of universities was a gradual process, but in the case of this university,

private men were to dispense with time and circumstance, and to create it in a day, not only without, but against the civil Government, and in a population, Catholic indeed, but indifferent to the undertaking[,] under a Catholic hierarchy, divided as to its expediency, before a Catholic public viewing all things in a mere political aspect, and for the sake of a Catholic gentry both suspicious and hopeless of Episcopal enterprises.[17]

It was not that Newman wanted to do things all by himself, although he was anxious to avoid committing himself to any particular faction or party in the Irish Church. What he needed were advisers chosen by himself whom he could trust. With this end in view, he proposed the setting up of a small subcommittee. As on the subject of the Vice-Rectorship, Cullen's refusal to co-operate remained a bone of contention till the end. Three months after he had received Newman's letter asking that a Vice-Rector should not be appointed at present, Cullen wrote (not in reply, since he ignored the letter) that he had found an

---

[14] *LD* xv. 309.   [15] Ibid. 311.   [16] Ibid. 309.   [17] *AW* 285–6.

excellent candidate for the post, a priest called Dr Taylor. After Newman had demurred and suggested instead that Taylor should be made the Dean, Cullen eventually arranged for him to be made Secretary to the University. Newman drily noted that he was not so much his secretary as Cullen's, 'to save the trouble of writing to me'.[18]

There were differences of opinion about where the University should be situated. More seriously, there were differences about how to commence it. The dilemma was,

If we followed the course of history and nature, we should commence on a small scale and gradually get into shape and expand; but this was only to sow the seed, whereas we were required to raise a crop, to vaunt it in the faces of the friends of the Queen's Colleges, and to send specimens of our produce to Rome, to be handed round the circle of the Cardinal Prefect of Propaganda. On the other hand, we might begin with a complete staff of officials and a handsome material structure, trusting or hazarding its being filled with students; and then it might turn out in the event that we were in the condition of a carriage, with state coachmen and lacquies, but without horses to draw us on.[19]

Ironically, Newman was in the minority with Cullen in favouring an informal, provisional beginning; but whereas Cullen was for delay for the sake of delay in the classic Roman fashion because it was more 'prudent' to wait to see how things turned out, Newman was at least for beginning, not for dawdling. It was particularly important that he should be publicly installed as Rector without further delay. In the meantime, not only was he left in suspense, but it was impossible to commit himself to any other work. Delay was also annoying because he only intended to give a limited number of years to the University. Again, unless he was on the spot, appointments and decisions would be made without his knowledge—as had already been done.

Twice in January and February 1853, Newman wrote to press Cullen for definite instructions, but received no reply. Cullen had his difficulties—he was a stranger to Ireland and was viewed with suspicion by the other bishops, especially Archbishop MacHale of Tuam, a vehement Irish Nationalist, who believed, not without reason, that Cullen wanted sole control over the University. But instead of confiding in or consulting with Newman, he did what he had learnt to do at Rome, 'to act, not to speak—to be peremptory in act, but to keep his counsel; not to commit himself on paper; to treat me, not as an equal, but as one of his subjects'.[20] These words were the fruit of a great deal more experience of the Roman side of the Church than Newman had in 1853. When he did finally hear from Dublin, it was a letter not from Cullen but from 'his secretary', Dr Taylor, to say that the Archbishop proposed

---

[18] Ibid. 295.   [19] Ibid. 286.   [20] Ibid. 298.

that each of the Irish bishops should make Newman his Vicar-General with special responsibility for the University. However, the news that Newman might be made a bishop seems to have given Cullen even more cause for delay. A further urgent letter in March pleading that the University Committee should take the necessary action for the University to begin in the autumn was again ignored. It was not until October that the Committee finally met, and Newman was summoned to Ireland at his earliest convenience. But this was not quite the same as official and public recognition from all the bishops of Ireland. Years later, Newman thought he had made a mistake in not ensuring that Archbishop MacHale in particular was ready to give full approval and support, but then MacHale had after all been a member of the University Committee and had personally supported Newman's appointment (although he had not been present at the Committee's latest meeting). No specific date was given for Newman's arrival, but at the beginning of November he went over for a night to Dublin to look at the 'University House' that had just been acquired (without Newman's prior knowledge) in St Stephen's Green, in the centre of the city, a location the disadvantages of which easily in his view outweighed the advantages. He warned that there was no possibility of his beginning in Ireland till the new year. He now had two other time-consuming projects on his hands. One was the new church for the Oratory in Edgbaston, which had been supposed to be opened on All Saints' Day, 1 November, although in fact there was a delay of three weeks. As at the old Oratory, there was to be a parish or 'mission' attached to the church, and that had to be organized.

3

The other project was a course of six lectures which Newman gave at the recently founded Catholic Institute in Liverpool in October and November. The institute was dedicated to St Philip Neri, and Newman had been asked in March to speak at its opening, but had refused on the ground of ill-health. He was ready, though, to give the lectures as a contribution to Catholic adult education, a cause close to his heart. He had been working on them since July, and after their delivery he prepared them for publication under the title *Lectures on the History of the Turks in its Relation to Christianity*.[21] He referred to them disparagingly as 'trash'.[22] They were published, however, in January 1854 in a volume some 300 pages long.

[21] They were republished in *HS* i, under the title *Lectures on the History of the Turks, in their Relation to Europe*.   [22] *LD* xv. 477.

The background to the lectures was the hostility between Russia and Turkey, which had led to the outbreak of war in October and was soon to lead to the outbreak of the Crimean War involving England and France in March 1854. Newman was firmly opposed to his country's policy, believing that England and France ought to support Russia, which, as a Christian power, was attempting to deliver Eastern Europe from the domination of Muslim Turkey, which, 'since the year 1048', he insisted, has been 'the great Antichrist among the races of men'.[23] The strict monotheism of Muhammadanism is recognized by Newman, but he criticizes its 'consecration of the principle of nationalism' (in which it resembles the Eastern Orthodox Church)[24] as well as its 'sternness, its coldness, its doctrine of fatalism', which 'wrought both a gloom and also an improvement in the barbarian, not very unlike the effect which some forms of Protestantism produce among ourselves'.[25] As a popular lecturer addressing a Catholic audience, Newman enjoys drawing another provocative analogy when he contrasts Rome, which exchanged Emperor for Pope, with Constantinople, which passed from Orthodoxy to Islam. The long separation from the West of the Orthodox Church Newman simply dismisses as eight centuries of 'religious deadness and insensibility'.[26] The papacy itself, as in the *Discourses*, is idealized as an earthly power invested with supernatural authority, which in the person of Pope St Pius V almost miraculously reversed the Turkish advance into Europe at the Battle of Lepanto. And yet at one point Newman refers unambiguously to the way in which during the Arian heresy it was the laity rather than the papacy that 'transmitted so faithfully, generation after generation, the once delivered apostolic faith'.[27] It was for developing this very point that Newman himself a few years later was to fall into disfavour with the Holy See.

The most interesting of these rather uninteresting lectures is the seventh, 'Barbarism and Civilization', where Newman distinguishes between '*barbarous* states', which 'live in a common *imagination*, and are destroyed *from without*', and 'civilized states', which 'live in some common object of *sense*, and are destroyed from *within*'.[28] A barbarous state will exist, for example, on the basis of a belief in the divine right of kings, while the life of a civilized state lies in common shared secular interests. Because barbarous states are governed by instinct they do not develop, whereas civilized states are governed by intellect, so that 'their distinguishing badge is progress'.[29] However, the strength of civilized states is also their weakness, because, while barbarous states have 'the strength of conservatism', in civilized states the 'cultivation of reason

---

[23] *HS* i. 105.   [24] Ibid. 203.   [25] Ibid. 72.   [26] Ibid. 192.
[27] Ibid. 209.   [28] Ibid. 162.   [29] Ibid. 167.

and the spread of knowledge for a time develop and at length dissipate the elements of political greatness', in the sense that 'where thought is encouraged, too many will think, and will think too much', with the result that the 'sentiment of sacredness in institutions fades away' and 'at length the common bond of unity in the state consists . . . simply in the unanimous wish of each member of it to secure his own interests.'[30] Barbarian states do not decay, but 'simply cease to be', for they have 'the life of a stone, and, unless pounded and pulverized', are 'indestructible'.[31] Newman does not miss the opportunity to make his favourite point that 'civilization is not necessarily Christianity', since it is possible to substitute 'natural religion for faith, and a refined expediency or propriety for true morality'.[32] But against this should be balanced the later comment that because Christianity 'admits the principle of progress on all matters of knowledge and conduct' where Revelation is not directly involved, Christianity, even if only negatively, remains 'the religion of civilization'.[33]

4

November 1853 was a busy month for Newman. On 9 November, immediately after the last of his Liverpool lectures and the hasty visit to Dublin, he preached a sermon, 'Order, the Witness and Instrument of Unity',[34] at the first Birmingham Diocesan Synod. The sermon, which is unremarkable, argues that the combination of order and unity, which is essential to the nature of the Church, is also characteristic of the Triune God and of human society.

Towards the end of December 1853 Newman again wrote to Cullen. His appointment was now two years old, but he had still received no public episcopal recognition. Again there was no reply, but it was intimated to Dr Taylor that the lack of support from the bishops was the chief obstacle. Newman was also worried that the failure might be seen to indicate a lack of awareness of the difference between a college and a university. He wrote a second letter pointing out that unless he received the necessary mandate without further delay there would be no hope of beginning the University in the autumn of 1854. At last Cullen replied, personally promising that this would now be given. Newman had seriously contemplated resigning, but he had been urged by his friend Hope-Scott (as he was now called) and others not to abandon the University, which would then, in their view, be doomed to failure. Even

[30] *HS* i. 173–4. [31] Ibid. 220. [32] Ibid. 165.
[33] Ibid. 202. [34] *OS* 183–98.

now Cullen's promise of a 'document'[35] fell short of Newman's plea for 'but an inch of Irish ground, or the point of a needle', since 'unless they let me come in, I can do nothing.'[36]

Early in the new year, Newman received much more encouraging news, this time from Rome, where Wiseman had intervened with the Pope, who had agreed to issue a formal Brief as the best way of starting up the university. Cullen seemed to welcome the idea with enthusiasm. To Newman's suggestion that he himself should go to Rome (he was afraid Wiseman might interfere too much), Cullen replied that it would be better not, if only because the publication of the Brief would most probably 'be accompanied by some mark of distinction to yourself as its Rector', and therefore it would be 'more appropriate that you should not be on the spot at the time'.[37] This was the first hint to Newman of Wiseman's plan that he should be made a titular bishop to give him extra authority. This was confirmed shortly after by a letter from Wiseman in which he said that both the Pope and Cullen favoured the idea, and that he himself looked forward to consecrating Newman personally. In fact, the day after Wiseman had written to Newman, Cullen wrote to Wiseman to say that it would be better to wait a little before Newman was made a bishop. Newman himself, who thought the idea really would solve the whole problem, was never told about Cullen's reservation. From Wiseman's tone and words it appeared that a decision had been made. News of the proposed bishopric soon spread, and friends even sent appropriate gifts. His own bishop treated Newman as if he had already been raised to the episcopal rank. But behind the scenes Cullen had prevented the promotion by officially asking Rome to postpone it on the ground that the time was not ripe and that the appointment could arouse opposition. He repeated the objection twice in 1855. Looking back later Newman could not help marvelling that nothing was ever said officially to him again on the subject by Wiseman or anyone else; but at the same time he was thankful, as the bishopric could have prevented his ever resigning and returning to England. In the meantime, however, he was amused to think that what with the Oratory and the University and now the titular bishopric of 'Ptolemais, Megalopolis, or Rhinocorura', he would have 'a field of action on which pretty nearly the sun will never set'.[38]

Wiseman's letter crossed with one from Newman warning that it was important that the papal Brief should not be too definite or explicit, as 'we must be at first in a *provisional* state'. What were needed were two things—'an external *manifestation* and the beginning of an inward and real *formation*'. The latter meant getting together a small teaching staff

[35] *AW* 312.   [36] *LD* xvi. 5.   [37] Ibid. 21 n. 1.   [38] Ibid. 41.

who could work together closely and intimately, the former, finding some popular lecturers who might only be temporary appointments. There was as much danger of doing too much as too little, and constitutions and statutes were no substitutes for personal dedication and initiative.

On 7 February 1854 Newman set off again for Dublin, this time at last to start up the University. His first object was a tour of Ireland to visit the bishops and to make enquiries about the state of the colleges and schools, as well as to advertise the University to potential students and teachers. (He was even toying with the idea of a similar tour of the United States.) Unfortunately, the country was experiencing its worst winter since 1814, and it was snowing hard as Newman set off for Kilkenny with a bad cold. The cabman at Kilkenny station, instead of taking him to the Catholic bishop, took him to the Protestant bishop's residence. Fortunately, the Protestant bishop, an old foe of Newman and Tractarianism, was away in London, and nobody answered the door, otherwise the bishop would have had the surprise of receiving Newman's card. Perhaps, the Catholic bishop suggested, the trouble lay with the plaid which Newman had mistakenly bought in Dublin and which marked him out as a Protestant parson, in spite of his Roman collar. At Carlow a large number of priests had been invited to meet Newman at dinner, but after dinner Newman, as he described to his community back in Birmingham,

went to sleep—and was awakened from a refreshing repose by his next neighbour on the right shouting in his ear, 'Gentlemen, Dr N is about to explain to you the plan he proposes for establishing the new University,' an announcement, which the said Dr N. does aver most solemnly took him utterly by surprise, and he cannot think what he could have said in his sleep which could have been understood to mean something so altogether foreign to his intentions and his habits.[39]

His stay at Waterford included a visit to a convent school; he described how he found assembled there seventy young ladies:

all dressed in blue, with medals on, some blue, some green, some red; and how he found he had to make them a speech, and how he puzzled and fussed himself what on earth he should say impromptu to a parcel of school girls—and how in his distress he *did* make what he considered his best speech—and how, when it was ended, the Mother Schoolmistress did not know he had made it, or even begun it, and still asked for his speech. And how he would not, because he could not make a second speech; and how, to make it up, he asked for a holiday for the girls, and how the Mother Schoolmistress flatly refused him, by reason (as he verily believes) because she would not recognise and accept his speech, and

[39] *LD* xvi. 52.

wanted another, and thought she had dressed up her girls for nothing—and how he nevertheless drank her rasberry's vinegar, which much resembles a nun's anger, being a sweet acid . . .[40]

Newman's cold had got much worse, he could not sleep on the feather-beds, and he could not eat the undercooked mutton. Faced with the prospect of his next destination, Tuam, the see of Archbishop MacHale, the 'lion of the West', Newman's heart sank, and he decided to cut short his tour and return to Dublin. He had succeeded in visiting six bishops.

5

Three weeks after his return, on 20 March 1854, the expected Brief was issued. Although the Pope explicitly ordered the Irish bishops to meet in synod and make arrangements for the new University, Newman noted with dismay that the language of the Brief sometimes suggested something less than a university, while the strict emphasis on the religious aspect of the curriculum and teaching also suggested something different from the idea of a university which he had set out in the *Discourses*. There were other inauspicious signs. Newman's consultations had been more extensive than conversations with the bishops. And the reactions had been less than favourable. His first meeting in Dublin had been with the Jesuit provincial, who informed him in no uncertain terms that it would be impossible to find enough potential students in Ireland: the 'middle class was too poor', while 'the gentleman class wished a degree for their sons, and sent them to Trinity College: and the upper class, who were few, sent their sons to English Universities.'[41] Nor would there be enough part-time students available for the evening classes which Newman had planned on the lines of those at King's College, London. Fr. Curtis's damning advice was that the whole idea of the university ought to be given up as hopeless. The President of Maynooth, the national seminary, was distinctly unenthusiastic, and so was Newman's old friend, Dr Russell. Some of the bishops, privately, were still sceptical. The educated laity were especially opposed to the project. An exclusively Catholic university was seen as impractical, undesirable, and unnecessary in a mixed Catholic–Protestant community. It was regarded as a negative ecclesiastical reaction to the Queen's Colleges, and there was the strong suspicion that it was to be an excessively clerical undertaking, with little lay involvement. Finally, there was the antagonism of the Irish nationalist party to be reckoned with, hostile as

[40] Ibid. 53.   [41] *AW* 323.

it was both to Cullen and to English involvement. Irish Catholics were, Newman noted sadly, as 'divided as dissenters in England'.[42] Looking back in 1873, Newman recognized that in view of all the opposition from different quarters, the attempt to found a Catholic university in Ireland was apparently 'to attempt an impossibility'.[43] At the time he certainly appreciated that his 'work was that of raising the dead'—even more so than the Oxford Movement had been[44]—but then that had succeeded beyond all expectations.

However, in 1833 Newman had been in a very different situation as a fellow of Oriel, whereas his position in Ireland was still very uncertain. The Pope's Brief had said nothing about the proposed bishopric, and at an interview with Cullen at the end of April Newman received the first evasive hint that the expected elevation was not after all to take place, when the Archbishop pointed out some complimentary words about Newman in the Brief, 'and said in an awkward and hurried manner, "You see how the Pope speaks of you—*here* is the 'distinction'." '[45] Cullen made no reply to Newman's subsequent request that the May synod of bishops should appoint him Vicar-General to the whole hierarchy in order to ensure full episcopal support in the future. Newman did not waver from his conviction that while 'the University must start in a provisional state, without any constitution', still in the early stages 'the whole power must be vested in one person, that is, the Rector'.[46] The foundations of the University had to be laid by Newman without interference, particularly in the matter of appointments. In the long run Newman intended the University to be governed not by the Rector alone, but by the Rector together with the professors, who would be mostly laymen.

In retrospect, Newman thought that the principal cause of the friction between himself and Cullen was his 'desire . . . to make the laity a substantive power in the University'.[47] First of all, he felt that the management of the finances ought to be in the hands of the lay people for whom the University was intended, but this was against all Irish clerical tradition, according to which the laity were 'treated like good little boys—were told to shut their eyes and open their mouths'.[48] Much worse than his abortive desire to have a lay finance committee was Newman's attitude to the 'young Ireland' or nationalist party, some of whose leading members were appointed to chairs in spite of Cullen's strong opposition. Newman wanted all but the theology chairs to be filled with the ablest laymen available (whatever their politics) rather than by inferior priests. Another initiative of Newman, to draw up a 'list of

---

[42] *LD* xvi. 54.   [43] *AW* 326.   [44] *LD* xvi. 68.   [45] *AW* 318.

[46] *LD* xvi. 129.   [47] *AW* 327.   [48] Ibid. 328.

honorary members of the University, principally laymen from Ireland or elsewhere',[49] was also viewed with suspicion by Cullen.

On 18 May 1854 the bishops at last met in synod to approve the University's statutes and recognize Newman formally as Rector. Not long afterwards, he met Archbishop MacHale, who 'shook his hand with so violent a cordiality, when I kissed his ring, as to punish my nose'![50] On 4 June he was finally installed as Rector by Cullen. Although always insistent that the real growth of the University had necessarily to be gradual and slow—and although always preferring by inclination 'to begin on a small scale and without pretence'[51]—Newman realized from the beginning that it was nevertheless important to 'make a *show*'.[52] For example, it was essential that the professors should be distinguished and well known. This was the thinking which lay behind his interest in establishing as soon as possible, for instance, a medical school, which in the end turned out to be the most successful institution in the University.

6

The *Catholic University Gazette* began now as the official organ of the University. It was a weekly publication, edited until the end of the year by Newman, with news about the University, and articles, many of them written by Newman himself. As well as some of the *Lectures and Essays on University Subjects*, Newman published in the *Gazette* during 1854 a number of 'illustrations of the idea of a University', which were collected into one volume in 1856 called *Office and Work of Universities*, and later republished as part of the third volume of *Historical Sketches* under the new title of *Rise and Progress of Universities*.[53]

Although primarily historical, these papers are not purely academic in interest. They have a topical interest, and sometimes provide fruitful and illuminating footnotes to the *Idea of a University*. Newman takes the opportunity to reaffirm once more his confidence in the ultimate success of the University as an English-speaking venture, owing its inspiration to the Pope, and destined to unite once again the English and Irish in a common Catholic undertaking. Again he emphasizes that the 'great instrument, or rather organ' of a university is 'the personal presence of a teacher', although he himself has

experienced a state of things, in which teachers were cut off from the taught as by an insurmountable barrier; when neither part entered into the thoughts of

---

[49] *AW* 326. [50] *LD* xvi. 172. [51] Ibid. xiv. 416.
[52] Ibid. xvi. 155. [53] *HS* iii., p. vii.

the other; when each lived by and in itself; when the tutor was supposed to fulfil his duty, if he trotted on like a squirrel in his cage, if at a certain hour he was in a certain room . . . and the pupil did his duty too, if he was careful to meet his tutor . . . at the same certain hour . . . I have known places where a stiff manner, a pompous voice, coldness and condescension, were the teachers' attributes . . .

His conclusion is that 'the personal influence of the teacher is able in some sort to dispense with an academical system', but an 'academical system without the personal influence of teachers upon pupils, is an arctic winter; it will create an ice-bound, petrified, cast-iron University'.[54]

On the question of teaching in a university, Newman is anxious to maintain both the professorial system, which 'fulfils the strict idea of a University', and the college tutorial principle, which is necessary for the '*integrity* of a University'.[55] The college provides community life and personal supervision. Whereas in England the college system is strong and the university is weak, it is the opposite on the Continent. In England at the Reformation 'the civil power could as little bear a University as it bore a Church'.[56] And so the individual colleges of Oxford and Cambridge displaced the universities, without whose jurisdiction they fell into isolation and decay. A university, however, 'seated and living in Colleges, would be a perfect institution'.[57] This, in fact, is what Newman attempted to create in Dublin. While he carefully preserved the Oxford college principle, he also modelled the University's constitution on that of the Catholic University of Louvain, ensuring that its effective government lay in the hands of the Rector and professors rather than the Heads of colleges (as at Oxford).

The reiteration of the assurance that an undertaking commanded by the Pope cannot fail (a confidence which was to be considerably modified as the years went by) is not the only eulogy of the papacy. Arguably the most interesting part of *Rise and Progress of Universities* is the ninth chapter on Pope St Gregory the Great, not one of the better-known parts of Newman's writings, but remarkable in retrospect. In view of the many allusions elsewhere to 'liberalism', it is interesting to read here Newman's definition of 'conservatism'. The Popes, he says, 'have been, and are, of course Conservatives in the right sense of the word; that is, they cannot bear anarchy, they think revolution an evil, they pray for the peace of the world . . . and they effectively support the cause of order and good government'.

But a Conservative, in the political sense of the word, commonly signifies something else, which the Pope never is, and cannot be. It means a man who is at the top of the tree, and knows it, and means never to come down, whatever it

[54] *HS* iii. 14, 74–5.   [55] Ibid. 182.   [56] Ibid. 230.   [57] Ibid. 229.

may cost him to keep his place there . . . It means a man who defends religion, not for religion's sake, but for the sake of its accidents and externals; and in this sense Conservative a Pope can never be . . .

However, Newman continues, 'there is a more subtle form of Conservatism, by which ecclesiastical persons are much more likely to be tempted and overcome, and to which also the Popes are shown in history to be superior'. How far this last point may be true is debatable, but what Newman proceeds to say is nevertheless of the highest significance for the Church's understanding not so much of doctrinal development as of changes in discipline, policy, and worship, which may be far more radical and far-reaching in their consequences than new formulations of dogma.

To prefer the establishment of religion to its purity, is Conservatism, though in a plausible garb. It was once of no uncommon occurrence for saintly Bishops, in the time of famine or war, to break up the Church plate and sell it, in order to relieve the hungry or to redeem the captives . . . Now this proceeding was not unfrequently urged against them in their day as some great offence; but the Church has always justified them . . . This fault is an over-attachment to the ecclesiastical establishment, as such . . . to traditional lines of policy, precedent, and discipline,—to rules and customs of long standing. But a great Pontiff must be detached from everything save the deposit of faith . . . He may use, he may uphold, he may and will be very slow to part with, a hundred things which have grown up, or taken shelter, or are stored, under the shadow of the Church; but, at bottom, and after all, he will be simply detached . . .

Far from being conservative in the bad sense, Newman concludes that although the 'Popes have been old men', they 'have never been slow to venture out upon a new line, when it was necessary'.

And, thus independent of times and places, the Popes have never found any difficulty, when the proper moment came, of following out a new and daring line of policy . . . of leaving the old world to shift for itself and to disappear from the scene . . .[58]

And when Newman gives as an example the bold initiatives of the previous Pope Gregory XVI, 'a man of eighty, of humble origin, the most Conservative of Popes, as he was considered',[59] the modern reader can hardly help but think of Pope John XXIII, the aged peasant Pope, who was elected as a 'caretaker', but who, against all expectations, called the Second Vatican Council, which has been called 'Newman's Council', and which so dramatically changed the Catholic Church's course from that Ultramontanism which had apparently received its irreversible sanction from the First Vatican Council's definition of papal infallibility.

[58] Ibid. 131–4.   [59] Ibid. 134.

7

The main problem in finding teachers for the University was whether to appoint Irishmen who were more suitable, or Englishmen who were sometimes better qualified and also known personally to the Rector. Newman's policy was to appoint Irishmen whenever possible, but not to hesitate to appoint Englishmen when academic priorities justified it. To exclude English teachers would be self-defeating, as part of Newman's job was to try and persuade the Irish class that would normally send their sons away for an English education to send them instead to the new Catholic University. The deans in charge of the halls—or rather hostels, as they were only to hold twenty students—would be Irish priests. Newman was very insistent on the importance of a residential university, and wanted there to be resident tutors, young unmarried graduates, who would provide the kind of close personal tuition that he had advocated so vehemently at Oriel and who, with the Rector, 'would be the nucleus of a tradition or genius loci'.[60] The tutor would represent 'that union of intellectual and moral influence, the separation of which is the evil of the age'. He would not be involved in college discipline, nor would he have 'any academical authority'. The halls were to be small for disciplinary reasons, as 'Personal influence requires personal acquaintance.'[61]

The University was officially opened on 3 November 1854, with about twenty students actually in residence, and another forty expected. On 9 November Newman delivered the inaugural lecture, 'On the place held by the Faculty of Arts in the University Course'. It was immediately published in the *Catholic University Gazette*, and was reprinted as 'Christianity and Letters' in *Lectures and Essays on University Subjects* in 1859.

Newman had intended to have a University church or chapel as soon as things were under way. At the beginning of December he wrote to Cullen proposing to build one at his own expense. He did not want to use University funds as that would mean a committee. Nor did he want to commit the University to a permanent church. There was also still the thought in his mind that one day there might be a Dublin Oratory which would need a church. Apart from anything else, it would help advertise the University.

8

In January 1854 Britain and France had commenced hostilities, which would soon lead to the Crimean War, against Russia on the side of

---

[60] *LD* xv. 85.   [61] *Campaign*, 39, 120.

Turkey. Newman was against the war—'a simple piece of Johnbullism'.[62] He wondered, indeed, if public opinion would tolerate the war for long. Modern newspaper reports made the carnage and destruction horrifyingly present and real to people at home, who were more sensitive to pain and suffering than in the past and less tolerant of the loss of human life and limb. It was now possible to be spectators through the eyes of the war correspondents, like 'Children on a rainy day who spend hours . . . in tracing the wayward course of each particular drop of rain, as it strikes against the window pane, and runs down to the frame at the bottom in its own way'.[63] It seemed anyway more than futile in the long run to take the side of a declining non-European nation against a growing European power, just because one was afraid of the latter. And it was doubly hypocritical both to condemn the Russians and to pretend that Turkish power could be re-established. A constructive, positive policy was needed in the face of growing Russian strength and the Turkish decline. The first of a series of letters by Newman on the war, *Who's to Blame?*, was published on 3 March in the *Catholic Standard*, which Henry Wilberforce was now editing. Newman employed the pseudonym 'Catholicus', which he had used years earlier in the *Tamworth Reading Room* letters. The letters were later reprinted in *Discussions and Arguments on Various Subjects* (1872). Their title was characteristically and deliberately low-key and unpretentious: 'From a child a description of Ulysses's eloquence in the Iliad seized my imagination and touched my heart. When he began, he looked like a fool. This is the only way in which I have done anything.'[64] In this particular case Newman was uneasy about his authorship becoming known, as he was writing on a non-religious, political topic. As Newman's first sustained attempt at political theory, the letters are a good deal more interesting than the earlier lectures on the Turks. As a further contribution to his cultural and social criticism, they are well worth comparing with *Present Position of Catholics*.

A comparison with his satirical masterpiece is inevitable when one reads at the beginning of the first letter the author's 'decided view that Catholicism is safer and more free under a constitutional *regime*, such as our own, than under any other':

I have no liking for the tyranny whether of autocrat or mob; no taste for being whirled off to Siberia, or tarred and feathered in the far West, by the enemies of my religion. May I live and die under the mild sway of a polity which certainly represses and dilutes the blind fanaticism of a certain portion of my countrymen,—a fanaticism which, except for it, would sweep us off these broad lands, and lodge us, with little delay or compunction, in the German Sea![65]

---

[62] *LD* xvi. 340.   [63] Ibid. 334.   [64] Ibid. 429.   [65] *DA* 307.

A cynic might point out that the fury over Papal Aggression had now died down, and that Newman's Irish experiences had given him a strong taste of religious absolutism. But the truth is that Newman is concerned here not with the undoubted 'bigotry of our middle class', but with British 'Constitutional Government', and his analysis of its nature follows from his avowed object to demonstrate that it 'shows to extreme advantage in a state of peace, but not so in a state of war'.[66] No longer concerned with bigotry, the imagery has none of the extravagant quality of *Present Position of Catholics*, but is light-heartedly good-humoured: 'I am not denying that, with great exertion, we are able to hoist up our complex Constitution, to ease it into position, and fire it off with uncommon effect; but to do so is a most inconvenient, expensive, tedious process; it takes much time, much money, many men, and many lives.'[67] This is what has had to be done, since 'the British Lion . . . was bent on puffing the Muscovite into space with the mere breath of his growl'.[68] More serious, however, than the cost and danger of the war is the threat it presents to 'that remarkable polity, which the world never saw before, or elsewhere, and which it is so pleasant to live under'.[69] As for English Catholics, Newman tartly remarks, their enthusiasm for rescuing Turkey from Orthodox Russia might be lessened by the consideration that 'after planting Protestant Liberalism there instead', they might find 'on looking homeward that despotism or democracy had mounted in these islands on the ruins of the aristocracy'.[70]

To explain the peculiar nature of the British constitution and state, which makes them suited to peace rather than war, to home rather than foreign affairs, Newman embarks on a digression into general political theory. His main point is that a constitution 'is the embodiment of special ideas' which are the 'first principles', that is, the 'creative and conservative influences of Society'.[71] The state 'has two main elements, power and liberty,—for without power there is no protection, and without liberty there is nothing to protect. The seat of power is the Government; the seat of liberty is the Constitution.'[72] That 'set of traditions' in which a constitution consists may, depending on the country, be more or less 'scientifically developed', or 'distinctly recognized', or 'skilfully and fully adapted to their end'.[73] Newman distinguishes four chief constitutional principles—'co-ordination', 'sub-ordination', 'delegation', and 'participation'—of which the last is especially relevant to his case, because it implies self-government by a people. In every political system the question is, 'what is the most advisable compromise' between power and liberty—'what point is the

---

[66] *D.A* 308.   [67] Ibid.   [68] Ibid. 309.   [69] Ibid. 310.
[70] Ibid.   [71] Ibid. 315–16.   [72] Ibid. 317–18.   [73] Ibid. 320.

maximum of at once protection and independence'. Newman's answer in general is that those 'political institutions are the best which subtract as little as possible from a people's natural independence as the price of their protection'.[74] But, at the same time, the fact is that 'a despotic government is the best for war, and a popular government the best for peace.'[75]

Newman draws a clear distinction between a nation and a state. Thus the British 'are free, considered as a State; they are strong, considered as a Nation'.[76] This enables him to make a patriotic comparison with the Athenians, who, 'as unlike us, as beauty is unlike utility', nevertheless as 'a People . . . could do what democracy itself could not do', having 'the self-reliance, the spirit, and the unflagging industry of the individual Englishman'.[77] Both Athenian and Englishman are characterized by 'that inward spring of restless independence, which makes a State weak, and a Nation great'.[78] What the strong state does through government action, the strong nation does through 'private energy'.[79]

The argument is developed with a positive evaluation of the qualities of the individual Englishman, who may be 'rough, surly, a bully and a bigot', but 'if ever there was a generous, good, tender heart, it beats within his breast'. He is also endowed with a 'shrewd sense, and a sobriety of judgment, and a practical logic, which passion does not cloud'.[80] All this makes for good 'private enterprise', unlike those nations which 'require a despot to nurse, and feed, and dress them, to give them pocket money, and take them out for airings'.[81] The eulogy of Victorian energy is generous but humorous: 'He is on the top of the Andes, or in a diving-bell in the Pacific, or taking notes at Timbuctoo, or grubbing at the Pyramids, or scouring over the Pampas, or acting as prime minister to the king of Dahomey, or smoking the pipe of friendship with the Red Indians, or hutting at the Pole.'[82]

Unfortunately, 'rare energy, self-possession, and imperturbability'[83] do not provide the strong government necessary in time of war. The English nation has 'erected itself into a personality, under the style and title of John Bull', who 'wishes to form his own judgment in all matters, and to have everything proved to him', at the same time disliking 'the thought of generously placing his interests in the hands of others', but preferring to place his rulers 'in the fetters of Constitutional red tape'. The other side of the picture, then, is that England 'is the paradise of little men, and the purgatory of great ones'.[84] It is 'a capable people' which creates an 'incapable Executive'.[85] The nation's great aim is that 'the Government should not do too much, and next, that itself should

[74] Ibid. 325.	[75] Ibid. 326.	[76] Ibid. 326.	[77] Ibid. 327–8.
[78] Ibid. 330.	[79] Ibid. 331.	[80] Ibid. 334.	[81] Ibid. 336.
[82] Ibid. 338.	[83] Ibid. 339.	[84] Ibid. 342–3.	[85] Ibid. 345–6.

have a real share in the Government'.[86] As a result, 'power is committed, not to the highest capacity, but to the largest possible constituency'.[87] This affects the judiciary, which has to interpret the law in the light of public opinion. The recent Gorham case, in which the judicial committee of the Privy Council refused to adjudicate on the truth of the doctrine or the meaning of the Prayer Book, on the ground that a 'neutral reading ... was more congenial with the existing and traditional sentiments of the English people', shows that 'neither does English law seek justice, nor English religion seek truth'.[88]

Newman scarcely conceals his ambivalence about England, which on the one hand 'has not the climate ... the faith ... the grace and sweetness, the festive cheerfulness, the social radiance' of some countries, but on the other hand 'is, in a political and national point of view, the best country to live in in the world'.[89] The price to be paid, however, for its freedom is that institutions like the Army and the Church, which are 'the instruments of moral and material force' and therefore 'real powers', lose their independence. (As in *Rise and Progress of Universities*, Newman also notes the English substitution of colleges for universities, 'that the intellect may not be too strong for us'.[90]) As with the parson, precautions are taken to 'tie ... up' the soldier, 'to pare his claws' and 'to keep him low'.[91] This hardly helps in time of war, but is one of the necessary evils of the British constitutional system.

That individualism, then, which Newman condemns in religion as 'private judgment', he now commends (with reservations) as 'private enterprise' in politics. Insistence on the authority of the Church has been replaced by a rejection of state control. There has been a sharp shift of perspective from the view of *Present Position of Catholics*. But there is no real inconsistency. As he explained when advocating the private enterprise of the Catholic University, 'We confess to having a great jealousy of authority, prescription, prerogative, protection, so far as they are not based upon ecclesiastical principle and enjoined by a sacred sanction'; and so in secular matters 'it is but an acquiescence in the custom of our country and the traditions of the day to adopt private judgment and free trade for our watchwords, and to denounce monopolies'.[92] Nevertheless, the emphasis here on the necessary balance between 'power and liberty' in the political system may be said to prefigure the later concern with authority and freedom in the Church.

---

[86] *DA* 347.   [87] Ibid. 348.   [88] Ibid. 350.   [89] Ibid. 353.
[90] Ibid. 357.   [91] Ibid.   [92] *LD* xviii. 567–8.

I I
Oratory and University

ARCHBISHOP CULLEN was away in Rome for nearly a year from the autumn of 1854 to July 1855. The purpose of his stay there was not only to take part in the solemn definition of the dogma of the Immaculate Conception, but also to defend his pro-government policy against Irish nationalists like Archbishop MacHale. While he was in Rome he wrote to Newman to warn him to keep the University free of Young Irelandism. Newman's response was limited to an assurance that he intended to exclude politics, but it fell short of a promise not to appoint Young Irelanders to the staff. As a result, his further letters were left unanswered, and he had no more contact with Cullen till the latter's return to Dublin, when he took the opportunity to press on the Archbishop the urgent need not only for an effective committee to look after the finances (otherwise it was 'like putting one's hands into a bag') but also for lay involvement in the affairs of the University. If not, the educated upper class in Ireland would continue to stand aloof. Cullen did not reply immediately, but instead wrote to Rome complaining about Newman's lack of practicality and stressing that he did not wish him to be made a bishop until the University was properly established. When he did reply it was only to say that he heard complaints about the discipline and the expenditure of money, implying, however, at the same time that it was impossible for him to give Newman an answer as he was back in Birmingham for the long summer vacation and was not available for consultation. Afterwards Newman realized that his only partial residence in Dublin was a constant irritation for Cullen, who blamed this factor for whatever went wrong in the University. Perhaps Cullen had assumed that Newman would either leave the Birmingham Oratory (for 'the superior attractions of the Rectorship') or else transplant it to Dublin.[1]

By the time Newman did return to Dublin, in October in time for the new term, he had just heard of an alarming new development in the relations between the two Oratories. He was very preoccupied and upset by the news given to him on the eve of his departure, by Dalgairns, that

[1] *AW* 327.

the London Oratory had applied in August to Rome for a relaxation of the clause in the Oratorian Rule adapted by Newman in 1847 which forbade the spiritual direction of nuns, a work the London Oratory was increasingly being asked to undertake. Dalgairns added that the Roman Congregation of Propaganda had consulted Wiseman and also Ullathorne, who was keen that Dalgairns should continue to act as a confessor and director to nuns, an apostolate which the Birmingham house had decided the previous month should be discontinued in spite of Dalgairns's own inclination. Newman had in fact been told in September that the London Oratory had 'just applied for instructions, as to whether we ought to continue' looking after convents.[2] The information was contained in a letter from Stanton, in answer to a request from Newman for details of activities for an annual report on the two Oratories. As a description of an official application to the Roman authorities to be dispensed from part of the English Oratory's Rule it was somewhat disingenuous (as was the London house's reference, in its formal application, to the official *Instituta Congregationis Anglicae Oratorii* as merely 'the Edition printed for our use by the press of Propaganda'[3]). On the other hand, perhaps Newman should have realized that something more was conveyed by the words 'applied for instructions' than merely an approach to the Roman and other Italian Oratories inquiring about their practice. No doubt because he could not conceive that the daughter house would ever appeal to Rome against his Rule, without first consulting or at least informing him, Newman failed to read between the lines of Stanton's casual remark, or, apparently, to suspect anything out of the ordinary.

The provision about nuns was 'only one part', Newman maintained, 'of a great principle of the Oratory, by which the Fathers are confined to one spot, and which forbids unless in the way of exception, distant jurisdictions or outlying labours'.[4] Newman's own distant jurisdiction and outlying labour in Dublin were presumably covered by the exception 'without grave necessity' in the clause in the Rule which, ironically, immediately followed the one about nuns' confessions, and which excluded educational work associated with seminaries, colleges, or universities.[5] But he insisted in a letter of complaint to Wiseman that an Oratory 'is a home institution, bringing work into its homestead, and not seeking it at a distance'.[6]

More important, however, was the principle that 'to suspend or alter the Rule of the Oratory in so vital a point, is in some measure to change its vocation, to remove a protection which its subjects have hitherto enjoyed, and to endanger their perseverance'.[7] The London Oratorians

---

[2] *LD* xvii. 9 n. 1.   [3] Ibid. 8 n. 2.   [4] Ibid. 9.
[5] Ibid. 9 n. 2.   [6] Ibid. 13.   [7] Ibid. 10.

had only intended to ask for a dispensation which would apply to themselves, but the Roman authorities simply assumed that the request had been made with Newman's concurrence. This explains why Ullathorne was consulted, and why, when the dispensation, which was merely permissive, was issued in late November, it seemed to be intended for both Oratories, although it was only actually sent to London.

The application was bitterly resented at Birmingham, because it seemed to imply that the London Oratory, relying on its position in the capital, could force on the mother house and the founder in Birmingham its own understanding of what an Oratory was supposed to be. This was the underlying cause of the row that ensued. Newman favoured the suggestion of John Stanislas Flanagan (an Irishman who had joined the Birmingham Oratory in 1848) that two Oratorians from Birmingham should be sent to Rome to present their case. He also told Flanagan now—what he had never told anyone before except Ambrose St John— 'that I utterly cannot trust Fr Faber',[8] whose 'ambition' he was 'getting in truth, more and more to see'.[9] He suspected that Faber was influenced by the assumption that Newman's position in Dublin had virtually cut him off from the Birmingham Oratory.

2

Apart from strongly urging resistance to Faber, Flanagan was busy looking over the proofs of Newman's new novel *Callista: A Tale of the Third Century.* As a competent theologian, he was asked by Newman to check doctrinal points in the book, which he had begun in the early spring of 1848 (as 'a sort of romance' about St Cyprian),[10] put aside, and then resumed at the end of July 1855. He had started writing it immediately after successfully completing *Loss and Gain,* 'but could not get on with it, though I strove hard. So it remained, one or two chapters alone written'.[11] Then, in January 1854, Newman was told that Wiseman had suggested that he should write a sequel to Wiseman's novel *Fabiola or the Church of the Catacombs* (which had been written for the 'Popular Catholic Library'), to illustrate the next period of the Church's history. Newman responded that it was 'a beautiful plan—but what time and strength shall *I* have for writing, while life lasts, if I have this University on my hands?'[12] However, during the long vacation of 1855 he 'suddenly resumed the thread of his tale' and completed it.[13]

[8] Ibid. 27.	[9] Ibid. 29.	[10] Ibid. xiv. 343.
[11] Ibid. xxii. 61.	[12] Ibid. xvi. 7.	[13] *Call.*, pp. vii–viii.

In the original advertisement to the first anonymous edition (1856), Newman described the novel as 'an attempt to imagine and express, from a Catholic point of view, the feelings and mutual relations of Christians and heathens at the period to which it belongs'.[14] He admitted that it was a less ambitious work than the one Wiseman had suggested. What Newman does not mention, and what gives the book so much of its interest, is the largely unexpressed analogy between the situation of those early Christians and that of English Catholics in nineteenth-century Protestant England.

In both cases an esoteric faith found itself in involuntary collision with the established religion of an imperial power. Unlike a variety of other faiths to be found within the Roman empire, this one was distinguished by the 'irrational and disgusting obstinacy' with which it refused to conform in matters of conscience to what 'the tradition of ages had sanctioned'.[15] Newman makes the analogy explicit, however, when he remarks that the Christians of the age he is writing about had enjoyed freedom from persecution for so long that they practised their religion as freely in private 'as now in England, where we do not scruple to raise crucifixes within our churches and houses, though we shrink from doing so within sight of the hundred cabs and omnibuses which rattle past them'.[16]

As the story develops, numerous points of intended comparison strike the reader. Jucundus, the guardian and uncle of Agellius and Juba, like any good Victorian father, is 'warmly attached to the reigning' religion, 'both as being the law of the land and the vital principle of the state';[17] while the idea of religious 'truth' means nothing to him.[18] For Jucundus, Christianity is 'idiotic cant and impudent fee-fa-fum', and its typical priest a 'sour hypocrite', quite unlike the pagan priests, men of the world, 'who enjoyed this life'.[19] Insignificant as the Christians might be in importance or numbers, still it 'could not be denied that the bigoted and ignorant majority, not only of the common people, but of the better classes, was steeped in a bitter prejudice, and an intense, though latent, hatred of Christianity'.[20]

The actual conversion of the Greek heroine Callista is bound to remind the reader of Newman's own gradual conversion, as he passed agonizingly from Anglicanism to Catholicism.

She was neither a Christian, nor was she not. She was in the midway region of inquiry, which as surely takes time to pass over, except there be some almost miraculous interference, as it takes time to walk from place to place . . . To see that heathenism is false,—to see that Christianity is true,—are two acts, and involve two processes.

---

[14] *Call.*, p. vii. [15] Ibid. 24. [16] Ibid. 26. [17] Ibid. 21.
[18] Ibid. 249. [19] Ibid. 21, 61. [20] Ibid. 75.

Apart from the intellectual difficulties, there is the emotional fear of a new and strange religious community ('what did she know of Christians?'),[21] which Newman himself had once painfully experienced. Agellius, whose faith was to be revitalized by Callista and Caecilius (St Cyprian), shares another side of his creator—the need for sympathy:

He needed the sympathy of his kind; hearts which might beat with his heart; friends with whom he might share his joys and griefs; advisers whom he might consult; minds like his own, who would understand him—minds unlike his own, who would succour and respond to him. A very great trial certainly this, in which the soul is flung back upon itself . . .[22]

Like Newman when he began to doubt the *Via Media*, Agellius suffered too from intellectual and spiritual isolation, cut off as he was from the fellowship of the Church: 'He wanted to know whether his guesses, his perplexities, his trials of mind, were peculiar to himself, or how far they were shared by others, and what they were worth.'[23]

The most interesting part of the book is the analysis of the process of conversion as it takes place in Callista. The starting-point is the need for some external reality to give actuality to one's own personal identity: ' "Here am I a living, breathing woman, with an overflowing heart, with keen affections, with a yearning after some object which may possess me. I cannot exist without something to rest upon." '[24] When Callista protests against the idea of hell, Caecilius points out that if there is a life after death, then Callista ' "will still be the same being, but deprived of those outward stays and reliefs and solaces, which, such as they are, you now enjoy. You will be yourself, shut up in yourself." '[25] As Juba discovers, the terrifying truth may be that ' "You cannot escape from yourself!" '[26] Caecilius explains the corollary:

'Assuming, then, first, that the soul always needs external objects to rest upon; next, that it has no prospect of any such when it leaves this visible scene; and thirdly, that the hunger and thirst, the gnawing of the heart, where it occurs, is as keen and piercing as a flame; it will follow there is nothing irrational in the notion of an eternal Tartarus.'

The burden of Caecilius's argument is that there are 'needs, desires, aims, aspirations, all of which demand an Object, and imply, by their very existence, that such an Object does exist also'—and that 'nothing here does satisfy them', except for that 'message which professes to come from that Object'.[27] The more Callista thinks about Christianity, 'the more it seemed . . . to have an external reality and substance'.[28] Her

[21] Ibid. 317.   [22] Ibid. 27.   [23] Ibid. 93.   [24] Ibid. 131–2.
[25] Ibid. 219.   [26] Ibid. 265.   [27] Ibid. 220.   [28] Ibid. 292.

intellect 'could not frame' the Object, but it could 'approve and acknowledge, when set before it, what it could not originate'.[29]

Antecedent probability is not the only characteristic Newman doctrine that is dramatized in Callista. Her conversion is not a sudden event, but a development: 'while she was continually differing from herself, in that she was changing, yet it was not a change which involved contrariety, but one which expanded itself in (as it were) concentric circles, and only fulfilled, as time went on, the promise of its beginning.'[30] Nor is she simply converted by either 'logic' or 'reason' or 'feeling'; but, on the lines of the discussion of faith in the *Oxford University Sermons*, 'the more she thought over what she heard of Christianity, the more she was drawn to it, and the more it approved itself to her whole soul, and the more it seemed to respond to all her needs and aspirations, and the more intimate was her presentiment that it was true.'[31]

In both the *Oxford University Sermons* and the *Essay on the Development of Christian Doctrine*, Newman had touched on the fact of conscience as an argument for the existence of God, but the point is now fully personalized for the first time here, when Callista declares that the dictate of conscience is not ' "a mere law of my nature . . . it is the echo of a person speaking to me . . . An echo implies a voice; a voice a speaker. That speaker I love and I fear." '[32]

Years later, Newman referred to the philosophical and theological significance of the novel, when he commented, 'I don't think Catholics have ever done justice to the book; they read it as a mere story book—and I think Protestants are more likely to gain something from it.'[33]

3

On 8 November 1855 Newman wrote to Faber to protest against the London application. He also demanded that the London house petition Rome 'to recognise . . . that fundamental principle of the Oratory of St Philip, whereby its Houses are entirely independent of each other, and what one does is not the act of the other'.[34] He asked for a reply 'almost by return of post that your Congregation intends doing it', and for the petition to be given to him as the founder of the English Oratory to transmit to Rome. The 'deputies' (or governing council) of the Birmingham house were quite confident that London would agree. The next day Newman wrote a long letter from Dublin to his community explaining the situation. He added that he was well aware 'that *I* am despised, and that *you* as a body and as individuals are despised, by

[29] *Call.* 326.　　　　[30] Ibid. 291.　　　　[31] Ibid. 292.
[32] Ibid. 314–15.　　　[33] *LD* xxvi. 130.　　　[34] Ibid. xvii. 39.

persons whom we do not despise. I cannot conceal from myself that we
are considered as slow, and humdrum, and twaddling, and unready,
and incapable, and idle, and unfruitful, and unspiritual . . .'. Perhaps,
however, 'all that the complaint means is that we do not puff and
advertise [our work] to the four quarters of the earth'. In Birmingham
'we are not seen', and 'those, to whom we minister, are persons of low
state, of whom the world thinks little'. It was a fulfilment of St Philip's
maxim, 'amare nesciri', and Newman welcomed the opportunity of 'our
being overlooked, passed by, and not known to be true children of our
Father, till men come close to us', especially as 'I know well, that, as to
myself, all through life, when I have been despised most, I have
succeeded most'.[35]

Early in September Dalgairns, who was arguing in favour of the
Birmingham Oratory undertaking the spiritual direction of nuns, had
complained to Newman that they were 'stagnating for want of objects to
fix themselves upon' and that 'We have no right to be living as
comfortably as we do unless we are wearing ourselves out with work for
Christ.'[36] In response, Newman proposed that Dalgairns should develop
the Oratorian mission at neighbouring working-class Smethwick,
enlisting those of the Fathers who 'were ill for want of work—or any
others who were not ill'. The 'project languished on for months',
Newman later recalled, 'and then as I had foreseen, almost silently
died'.[37] In his letter to Birmingham, obviously alluding to Dalgairns's
obsession with the confessional, Newman cautioned that 'a great
variety of occupations and studies' were possible in an Oratory, and
that the 'error' was to suppose that 'one particular mode of life' is
'*essential*'. Nor was it right for London 'to hold up itself as a *pattern*
Oratory'.[38] With the exception of Dalgairns, this long letter was well
received at Birmingham.

The London Oratory replied immediately, regretting any misunderstanding that might have arisen over their application, which had been
not 'for a dispensation from the Rule', but 'for an interpretation of it,
and a direction in our own particular case'.[39] However, they could not
clarify the matter with Rome until they had had an answer from
Propaganda, when it would become plain if, as seemed unlikely, there
had been any confusion. Newman's response to this was that
Propaganda had already been in correspondence with the Bishop of
Birmingham, who had recommended the suspension of the part of the
Rule relating to nuns, 'without our knowing any thing about what was
going on'. On the ground that an 'injury' had been done, Newman now
made it 'a demand' that London should petition Rome as he had

[35] Ibid. 48–9. [36] Ibid. 33 n. 3. [37] Ibid. 34 and n. 1.
[38] Ibid. 50. [39] Ibid. 51.

asked.[40] Newman still thought that Faber would want to avoid a quarrel with him—although the Birmingham deputies were now less than sanguine. Meanwhile, he wrote again to Wiseman, having 'lost a precious month' by the Cardinal's failure to reply to his earlier, strongly worded letter, addressed to 'one of the gentlest, kindest hearts in the world', and 'on a matter affecting almost the existence of the Oratory in England'.[41] Wiseman immediately wrote back, offering to write to Rome to rectify any misunderstanding in whatever way Newman wanted. He had sent Faber Newman's first letter, and he now sent the second one, remarking, 'let us exert ourselves to the utmost to heal and soothe this noble wounded spirit.' Faber, who claimed his nerves were completely shattered, replied excitedly that they were ready to sacrifice anything, 'except the rights of our Congregation', but that 'the Padre' was 'bent, as it seems, to cast us from him altogether', although they were 'completely *his in heart*', and 'nothing shall wring from us one complaining word'.[42] On the same day that Wiseman wrote to Newman, the London Oratory formally rejected Newman's demand on the grounds that it would be disrespectful to anticipate Propaganda's answer and to assume it had misunderstood the application; nor was there any need to remind Rome of something so fundamental as the autonomy of individual Oratories; and if indeed a rescript was sent to Birmingham as well, then it was for Birmingham not London to take up the matter.

So serious was Newman's fear that the whole affair was an attempt by London to obtain an ascendancy over Birmingham that he even began to speculate what their position would be if London did gain 'an actual sovereignty' over them.[43] More practically, he was coming to the reluctant conclusion that he would have to go to Rome—'On the broad face of the matter they have a plausible case, unless we had reason to suspect more than is on the surface.' 'How odd it is,' he mused, 'all thro' life this is the sort of way I have been treated.'[44] Faber, however, had only 'acted according to his nature'.[45]

Instead of writing to Wiseman, Newman came over from Dublin to see him personally. It was agreed that Wiseman should forward a letter from Newman to the Cardinal Prefect of Propaganda, which he did with a covering note asking that any dispensation should be limited to London and should be only temporary, but without giving explicit support to Newman's request that no change or suspension of the English Oratorian Rule should be sanctioned without his first being consulted. However, neither letter nor note arrived in time to stop the Rescript, in which Faber was referred to as 'Provost of the Oratorians of

---

[40] *LD* xvii. 60.   [41] Ibid. 65.   [42] Ibid. 67 n. 3.
[43] Ibid. 68.   [44] Ibid. 71.   [45] Ibid. 72.

England', and which granted the application temporarily and under certain circumstances. Cardinal Fransoni told Wiseman that Propaganda had taken it for granted that Faber had not written without Newman's approval. When Faber heard from Wiseman what had happened, a stiff note of protest against Newman's alleged attempt to interfere in the affairs of another Oratory ('practically an attempt to exercise an act of *generalate* over us')[46] and against Wiseman's collaboration was drawn up, but not sent.

Newman took the night boat back to Ireland. He had a revealing dream on the passage over of a parson getting into his berth, 'and threatening my face with his feet; and my resolving to convert him; and choosing as my instrument a glass jar of large preserved gooseberries; and failing, because he found them undeniably full of large maggots!'[47] A few days later he was advised not to deliver his lecture on 'Christianity and Scientific Investigation', as it was felt to be too dangerous in the prevailing theological climate, although he was to publish it four years later. He felt that 'perhaps I never was so worked as I am just now.'[48] And he could not remember when he last had found time even to take a walk. He was engaged in Dublin on 'what is the work of a life', more suitable for 'some one twenty years younger, and who can feel it is his *work*'. But in addition, he had all the Oratory worries on his mind. 'No one can be two things at once—all through life my trouble has been just that—that not one, but two or three distinct duties are upon me—So it is now.'[49]

On 10 December he wrote again to Wiseman to consult him about the two proposals he intended to make to Propaganda to safeguard the autonomy of the separate English Oratories. The first was simple enough, that no directive to one Oratory should affect another. The problem was that this provision did not remove the possibility of Rome issuing an interpretation of the Rule of the English Oratory to one community, which would inevitably affect indirectly another community. He proposed secondly, therefore, that no Oratory should be allowed to make an application for an interpretation without first informing other houses, which would then have the opportunity of making known their views to Rome. Wiseman immediately sent the letter on to Faber for his comments, who complained bitterly that Newman seemed intent not only on no reconciliation, but on trying to introduce a 'generalate' over the English Oratory. The double irony was that Newman himself, who had earlier been accused of leaning towards French Oratorianism, now suspected he 'saw a tendency in the direction of the French Oratory, *which many persons wish to be developed, of uniting the*

[46] Ibid. 74.   [47] Ibid. 76.   [48] Ibid. 80.   [49] Ibid. 82.

Houses of the English Oratory'.[50] Certainly, on the face of it, Newman's second proposal was quite innocuous, but then the London Oratory might argue that, as the founder of the English Oratory and the author of its Rule, Newman would always be in a special position to veto any independent development on its own part. Whatever Faber's private ambitions may have been, the whole previous history of relations between the two communities shows clearly enough a desire not only to be independent of Newman but to cultivate a very different style. In some ways it was a natural, perhaps inevitable, reaction of younger men impatient of Newman's authority. It is expressed in some notes left by Dalgairns, who after a retreat in Paris decided after all not to leave the Birmingham Oratory, and informed Newman that the thought of leaving was 'a temptation of the devil brought on by pride': however, in spite of all his professed admiration and love for Newman, he confided to his retreat director that Newman did not have that 'zeal for the salvation of souls' characteristic of St Philip, but instead was more interested in education and literature.[51] The trouble, from Newman's point of view, was that the Brompton Oratory had a natural advantage over the mother house because of its central position in London, where Wiseman, who had been the original patron of the new English Oratory, was now the local bishop and was for obvious reasons anxious not to alienate the Oratorian house in his own diocese. Unfortunately, too, Wiseman was the only person who could have effected a reconciliation. But in the end the seeds of discord between the two Oratories lay too deep in the personalities of the two Superiors. Newman had never felt at home with Faber's dramatic personality, however amused he may have been at times by it. With all his gifts, it would have been hard for Faber not to feel, however unconsciously, some jealousy and sense of inferiority, which almost inevitably led to his advocating an idea of the Oratory very different from Newman's. Probably the fatal spark that lit the fire was not Newman's 'sensitiveness', but that uncompromising firmness, even peremptoriness, in matters of what he saw as principle; it was a trait of which he was well aware, but which was bound to bring out the worst side of Faber. Had Newman written to Faber in the first place an emotional, self-pitying letter such as Faber would have written, the response would no doubt have been much more accommodating. Again, with a more carefully diplomatic letter, Newman might well have outmanoeuvred Faber. But both responses would have been out of character. Newman, not without good reason, thought that an important principle was involved and that Faber had disloyally gone behind his back to subvert the Birmingham position. In such

---

[50] *LD* xvii. 98.   [51] Ibid. 87.

circumstances, he confronted Faber straightforwardly and uncompromisingly. On the face of it, of course, as he himself acknowledged, Birmingham might appear to have overreacted, but the justification, if there was one, lay in past conflicts and difficulties which suggested that more was involved than met the eye. Wiseman may have spoken of Newman's 'wounded spirit' in order to persuade Faber to be more conciliatory, but it is quite misleading as a description of Newman's attitude at this time, which shows a coolly determined and deliberate resolve to frustrate any attempt by Faber to undermine the autonomy of his Oratory. Faber's own angry reaction does not suggest that he thought Newman was suffering from hurt feelings. Whatever Wiseman may have liked to believe, both the Superiors of the two Oratories knew perfectly well what the real issue was and what was at stake.

4

On returning to Birmingham for the Christmas vacation, Newman found a letter from Propaganda, to say that the Rescript was too limited in its force to cause him any disquiet. Satisfactory as this was, Newman still felt that a personal visit to Rome was important to make clear 'the real state of the difficulty about the Oratory, which will be greater, I am sure, as time goes on'.[52] He wanted in particular to put to Propaganda the two proposals he had made to Wiseman. On 27 December he and Ambrose St John crossed to Calais via London. The London Oratory heard the next day, and promptly sent a circular letter to the Italian Oratories accusing Newman of trying to impose a kind of 'generalate' on the Oratory. They also wrote 'a report' to Propaganda containing the same accusation, as well as their version of the quarrel.

On his way to Rome Newman visited several northern Italian Oratories. He wanted to consult them on various points and problems that had arisen. He found that it was generally agreed that an application to Rome from one Oratory for a particular dispensation from the Rule could not impose any obligation on another Oratory, and that the direction of nuns was possible, but not usual. Newman did not know about the London Oratory's circular letter, but the replies from the Provosts of the Oratories Newman had visited assured Faber that Newman's only object seemed to be to safeguard the individual autonomy of the English Oratories, and that his only concern was that Rome in its dealings with one Oratory would not bind or compromise another.

[52] Ibid. 103.

On 12 January 1856 Newman arrived in Rome and moved into lodgings which his faithful friend Maria Giberne had found at 47 Piazza di Spagna. The Roman Oratory had obviously renewed itself since 1847 when he and his companions had had to make their novitiate at Santa Croce. However, it 'was quite plain' to Newman that both the new Provost, Fr. Concha, and the Secretary of Propaganda, Mgr. Barnabò, had been prejudiced by what they had heard from the London Oratory, 'and that both looked on our House as unwilling to throw ourselves into the age, and to work to purpose'.[53] Both Concha and Barnabò made no bones about the fact that they thought Newman was fussing unnecessarily.

On 25 January Newman and St John had an audience with Pius IX, who had on his desk the London Oratory's 'report' to Propaganda accusing Newman of trying to make himself 'general' of the English Oratories. St John, whose Italian was better than Newman's, understood the Pope to say hurriedly at the beginning that he had heard Newman had come to make himself head of the English Congregation of the Oratory. However, the audience went off well, and St John was able to give their version of the affair, which the Pope seemed to accept. The Pope even remarked that he did not want them to occupy themselves with nuns. To avoid seeming merely negative, Newman asked for his approval of other apostolic works which he proposed the Birmingham Oratory should undertake, including 'the formation of a female [little] Oratory'.[54] The result of the audience was that Barnabò was far more gracious, but to Newman's great surprise, on his finally producing his petition 'that nothing done by the Holy See by one Oratory might affect another', Barnabò said that he would present it to the Pope 'if I wished, but he advised *not*, because the grant of it would *diminish* my power, inasmuch as I was *Deputato Apostolico* for setting up the Oratory in any part of England'.[55] (Of course, once an Oratory was founded, Newman had no more power over it.) Newman was happy now to withdraw the proposal that had provided the basis for the accusation that he wanted a generalate. 'Every thing is turning out well—and I can never feel any thing but thankfulness and satisfaction that I have come here.'[56]

Barnabò's information, however, was as puzzling as it was welcome. It agreed with what Mgr. Palma had said, the official at Propaganda who had originally arranged for Newman to adapt the Oratorian Rule for England, and who had befriended Newman—the only friend, Newman used to say, he ever had at Rome. (Unfortunately, Palma met with an untimely death in 1848.) But it disagreed with what he had been told at the various Oratories and by the canon lawyer he had consulted

---

[53] *LD* xvii. 131.   [54] Ibid. 137.   [55] Ibid. 138.   [56] Ibid. 139.

at Rome. The only explanation he could think of was that Propaganda had extraordinary powers in a missionary country like England. The reason why the news was so welcome was that he had been anxious to discover '*who* had power to found Oratories'.[57] There had been two earlier plans for more than one Oratory in London, and he had even envisaged several for a capital city which was really a number of towns or boroughs joined together. He now fully appreciated that if there was only one Oratory in London, then the head of the London Oratory would inevitably be a kind of rival to the head of the mother house in Birmingham, especially if there were only two Oratories in England. At Rome, in fact, Newman and St John had found that England simply meant London. Accordingly, at their farewell audience with the Pope, who 'was very free and pleasant, and made us laugh', Pius IX granted Newman's request that the Birmingham Oratory 'might be called the Chiesa Nuova [i.e. Rome Oratory] of England'.[58] The next day, 4 February, the two English Oratorians set out for home.

On his return to Dublin Newman received two personal letters from Brompton, one from Stanton and the other from Antony Hutchison. Both claimed that Newman had been harsh and unfair. His original demand, formally addressed to 'Father Faber', had caused great offence. As a result, London's reply had come formally through their secretary, Stanton. Although both letters professed admiration and affection for Newman, neither gave any indication that any special deference was due to the founder, although Hutchison allowed that their failure to inform Newman in the first place might be open to criticism. Both implied that they thought that he was in fact angry with them for other reasons. Newman replied in a friendly tone, but was adamant that he refused to discuss the matter any further, except formally through official channels.

The whole affair led Newman to think more deeply about the idea of the Oratory, and he began to put down on paper some thoughts on the nature of the Oratorian vocation. At the beginning of March these remarks were written up and sent to the community in Birmingham (which later in the year decreed that they should be printed).

Newman begins by insisting that because an Oratory is not strictly a 'religious' community bound by the three vows, this does not imply any sort of inferiority, as there are various roads to perfection and the saints themselves differ enormously in their spirituality. Thus the Oratory is not even dedicated exclusively to 'religious' work—'learned studies and literary pursuits and the fine arts . . . have had a distinct place there from the first.'[59] This humanistic emphasis extends to the actual community

---

[57] Ibid. 150 n. 1.   [58] Ibid. 147.   [59] *NO* 323.

life, which should be 'founded on human affection' as well as on Christian charity, in other words, 'the sort of mixed or twofold love which St Paul, for instance, felt for his converts, whom he loved not simply as the regenerate sons of God, but as having certain associations with his own history'.[60] As he had explained in an early 'chapter address', the 'religious' is bound by vows, but the Oratorian by 'personal attachment',[61] by 'an influence stronger, wider, surer, than the most cunningly organized association'.[62] The Oratory is to be a 'home'[63] for members of a family who know one another. The Oratorian relies on 'personal influence', and is formed by his general education and culture rather than by any specific religious exercises. Indeed, the nearest secular equivalent to an Oratory that Newman can think of is an Oxbridge college. Oratorians are traditionally drawn from the educated classes and are therefore 'gentlemen'. As had already been recognized in *The Idea of a University*, 'refinement is worthless without saintliness', but at the same time it does not follow that 'it is needless and useless with it', for it 'may set off and recommend an interior holiness, just as the gift of eloquence sets off logical argument'. And although 'true refinement of thought, word, and manners is the natural *result* of Christian holiness, and the necessary result when it is carried out into its full and ultimate effect', it by no means always happens in practice even in the saints. And so 'inferior principles' and 'secular instruments' may help to provide 'that refinement which ought to follow, and often does follow even in the humblest and least educated, from Christian faith and love'. Among the institutions, then, of the Church, Newman claims for the Oratory a special humanizing role in fostering 'this external polish and refinement, which is so valueless in itself morally, yet so useful as a sort of rhetoric in conduct'.[64] For the virtues of culture and education 'are Christian *in* a Christian—When a Christian mind takes them up into itself they cease to be secular, they are sanctified by their possessor, and become the instruments of spiritual good.'[65] Oratorians should not be content to be 'mere University men', but at the same time they should 'not throw away those advantages . . . but perfect them' by letting 'grace perfect nature'.[66] Like his idea of a university, Newman's idea of the Oratory is based on an ideal of an authentic Christian humanism, in which mere religiosity is as out of place as mere secularism.

The attempt to integrate secular culture and religion was to bring him much hostility and misunderstanding in the years ahead. As for his deeply felt sense of the Oratory as a home and its members as a family, this had already caused him pain and suffering. Back in February 1854 he had been told that his request for reports on the observance of the

---

[60] *NO* 302.   [61] Ibid. 169.   [62] Ibid. 171.   [63] Ibid. 192.
[64] Ibid. 189–91.   [65] Ibid. 214.   [66] Ibid. 221.

Rule (in the light of a list of points he had drawn up) was resented by some of the community. He had not intended by this anything 'inquisitorial' (he had been misunderstood to mean that he wanted private reports by the members of the community on each other), but he was anxious the Rule should be kept better. He also wanted to keep in as close a contact as possible with the community, which after all had urged him to accept the Dublin rectorship, even though this necessitated his being an absent superior, thus preventing, for example, his presence at the fortnightly 'chapter of faults', where breaches of the Oratorian Rule were publicly acknowledged (as was the custom then in religious communities and orders). It was merely the record of these public admissions that he had asked for. One of the community, Nicholas Darnell, had even spoken of making a 'protest' at a meeting of the deputies. It was not simply that no attempt had been made to find out first what in fact Newman had meant by his instruction, but it seemed (to Newman at least) as if he were no longer recognized as Superior, because he was no longer resident. In order to keep in constant touch, he had gone out of his way to write frequently, pay brief visits whenever possible, and send chapter addresses to the whole community. But instead of communicating directly with him, the community had apparently talked about him behind his back. Deeply hurt, he wondered if his chapter addresses were also resented:

will you cut me off from speaking to you, as well as from hearing of you? Will you thus, I may say, in my old age, throw me on the world without a home? No one knows but myself the desolateness I sustain in leaving Birmingham, and being thrown among strangers . . .

Since they had been written 'in a simple confidence in the *sympathy* of the *whole* community for me', he gave up sending them—reluctantly, because he had 'got up the steam', and a number of subjects had occurred to him. Later, when asked to continue them, he felt he could not 'get up the steam . . . and where are the coals and the fire to get it up withal?'[67] The whole painful episode seemed to him to strike at the concept of a loving, trusting community. Certainly his own most sensitive feelings about friendship and loyalty had been deeply hurt.

Inevitably, the absence of the Superior had caused problems, or rather aggravated the problem endemic to an Oratory, that of authority, especially where there was 'an enormous tendency' in its members 'to act each for himself, as if [he] were in a lodging house, and to be impatient of control'.[68] As Newman complained to St John, 'if people loved me, they would show their love by attending a little more to my wishes'; till there was 'practical consideration' for his wishes, he

[67] Ibid. 294; *LD* xvi. 58, 176.   [68] *LD* xvi. 150.

could not 'have confidence' in the absent community.[69] In a letter to one
of the lay brothers about his vocation, he commented caustically on the
way he had been looked after on a week's visit to Birmingham, as if he
had not 'a certain right to have a room of my own, and think it quite as
strange that you should pull my room about, as you would, did I do the
same to yours'.[70] On the other hand, he told Edward Caswall, the acting
Superior, not to interfere with the lay brothers who came under the
Father Minister, adding severely:

> I am somewhat pained, my dear Edward, to hear you speak of us as
> 'Gentlemen—' We are not Gentlemen in contradistinction to the Brothers—
> they are Gentlemen too, by which I mean, not only a Catholic, but a polished
> refined Catholic. The Brothers are our equals . . . The Father is above the
> Brothers sacerdotally—but in the Oratory they are equal.[71]

5

In March 1856 Newman was alarmed to hear reports of the possibility of
English Catholics going to Oxford, where religious tests had been
abolished two years earlier. It was not simply that he regarded it as 'a
place very dangerous to a young man's faith', where he 'might be
preserved from defection' but also 'might be indelibly stamped with
indifferentism', although he might 'be saved from this, if there were a
Catholic *Hall* or *College* there'. But, he pointed out, 'the Holy See
decided that Dublin was to be the place for Catholic education of the
upper classes in these Islands, and, under this decision, I acquiesced in
the wish of the Irish Bishops to have me here'. Personally, 'of course I
would far rather do good to English Catholics in Oxford than in
Dublin'. Not only would he himself be unsettled 'if there is a College for
Catholics in Oxford, or anything approaching to it', but the students at
the Catholic University, English and Irish, 'would wish to go there and
this University would have to seek not only Rectors and Professors, but
students altogether'. There was always the fear that students would use
the Catholic University as merely a stepping-stone to Oxford—'but, if it
is known here that a Catholic youth actually is in Oxford with the leave
of a Catholic Bishop, the consequences may be serious'.[72] An unwelcome
analogy struck him as he wrote in protest to Ullathorne: '*We shall merely
have created the taste*, and shall have done for Catholic education in favor of
Protestantism just what Puseyism has done for Protestants in favor of the
Catholic Church.'[73] In the event, his fears were not realized.

[69] *LD* xvi. 127–8.   [70] Ibid. 154.   [71] Ibid. 267.
[72] Ibid. xvii. 178–9.   [73] Ibid. 183.

The thought of a University church had, not surprisingly, been in the mind of the former Vicar of St Mary's from the beginning. It would advertise the University, it would symbolize 'the great principle of the University, the indissoluble union of philosophy with religion', and it would provide a suitable place for university ceremonies.[74] In June of the previous year, after a scheme for using a local parish church had fallen through, he had bought some ground beside the University House in St Stephen's Green. He had asked John Hungerford Pollen, the convert Professor of Fine Arts, to draw up plans for a church in the style of the early Roman basilicas. After some last-minute objections from Cullen, the new University Church was opened on Ascension Day, 1 May 1856. Newman had used money left over from the Achilli trial fund to pay for it.

There was another reason why a University church had been a priority in his mind. From the beginning he had hoped to found another Oratory in Dublin. And it was with Cullen's support that he had brought up the possibility when he saw Barnabò in Rome. As envisaged by Newman, the Oratory would not actually be a part of the University, but would act as a kind of university chaplaincy. He already had two priests in mind who might join him in the foundation.

On the Sunday after the opening of the church, he delivered the first of the eight university sermons he was to preach in the course of the next year. Unlike his *Oxford University Sermons*, they are more pastoral than academic. Unlike his Catholic parish sermons, they were written before delivery, although one of them was a rewritten version of one of his Anglican parochial sermons, and another borrowed a few pages from one of his *Sermons bearing on Subjects of the Day*. The first, 'Intellect, the Instrument of Religious Training', is the most important, concerned as it is to oppose those 'who would set knowledge against itself, and would make truth contradict truth, and would persuade the world that, to be religious, you must be ignorant, and to be intellectual, you must be unbelieving'.[75] As a pastor of students, Newman admits disarmingly that 'from the disorder and confusion into which the human mind has fallen, too often good men are not attractive, and bad men are; too often cleverness, or wit, or taste, or richness of fancy, or keenness of intellect, or depth, or knowledge, or pleasantness and agreeableness, is on the side of error and not on the side of virtue.'[76] What was once joined together by God has been put asunder. There is no question of a compromise between the two. And in a well-known passage, the Rector sets out his purpose in presiding over a Catholic university:

It will not satisfy me, what satisfies so many, to have two independent systems,

---

[74] *Campaign* 290.   [75] *OS* 5.   [76] Ibid. 8.

intellectual and religious, going at once side by side, by a sort of division of labour, and only accidentally brought together. It will not satisfy me, if religion is here, and science there, and young men converse with science all day, and lodge with religion in the evening. It is not touching the evil . . . if young men eat and drink and sleep in one place, and think in another: I want the same roof to contain both the intellectual and moral discipline. Devotion is not a sort of finish given to the sciences; nor is science a sort of feather in the cap, if I may so express myself, an ornament and set-off to devotion. I want the intellectual layman to be religious, and the devout ecclesiastic to be intellectual.[77]

Newman admits in a later sermon of 1857 that there are many great saints undistinguished for learning. But on the other hand, there are other saints 'in whom the supernatural combines with nature, instead of superseding it,—invigorating it, elevating it, ennobling it; and who are not the less men, because they are saints'.[78] His favourite early Father, St Athanasius, is characterized by this kind of Christian humanism, as is St Paul. St Philip Neri, too, who 'lived in an age . . . when literature and art were receiving their fullest development', was anxious 'not to destroy or supersede . . . but . . . to sanctify poetry, and history, and painting, and music'.[79] Very different, he emphasizes, is 'the religion of the natural man', even when 'embellished . . . with the refinements of a cultivated intellect'; for when 'virtue is something external' and 'has little to do with conscience and the Lord of conscience', the devotees of such a religion 'pace round and round in the small circle of their own thoughts and of their own judgments', with 'self' as 'their supreme teacher'. Instead of allowing conscience to lead them 'into the fulness of religious knowledge', they 'succeed in pleasing themselves' by fulfilling the 'contracted, defective range of duties' which they allow conscience to put before them.[80]

A few days after the opening of the University Church, Faber finally broke his long silence, due, he said, to illness. Newman again insisted that he would not discuss their differences except through the London Oratory's secretary, because 'Great confusion arises from going to and fro, beginning formally, continuing informally, and thus dissipating responsibility.'[81] The most revealing of Faber's complaints was that he knew that Newman did not trust him. Newman refused to be drawn. His reply was cool but courteous, firm but uncontentious. So was his reply to another emotional letter from Faber, pleading for a reconciliation and again asking what London could do to repair the breach.

At last, on 22 May, the London house wrote formally to apologize, not for the original application to Rome, but for having (unintentionally) offended their founder. Newman was now prepared to state explicitly

[77] *OS* 13.   [78] Ibid. 92.   [79] Ibid. 118–19.
[80] Ibid. 20–3, 25.   [81] *LD* xvii. 236.

his objections to the application. By appealing to Rome for an interpretation of the Rule (which was uncalled for, since individual Oratories were empowered to interpret the Rule for themselves), and by not giving Birmingham the opportunity also to submit its opinion, the London house was in effect tampering with the Rule, which was the basis of their common vocation. Birmingham had not been forewarned, let alone consulted. The essential principle at stake was the autonomy and independence of two neighbouring Oratories. This, Newman concluded, was the 'substance' of his complaint—although he had also been hurt by the formal tone of their rejection of his protest.[82]

Privately, Faber wrote back to plead that Newman had in fact been informed about the original application through Dalgairns; to which Newman replied that he had indeed learned of it from Dalgairns, but by accident and when it was too late. In their official reply the London Oratory claimed that the tone of their letter which had given such offence had been influenced by the highly formal tone of Newman's original letter. As for the main point of Newman's present letter, they argued that they had regarded their application to Propaganda as an unimportant practical query on the legitimacy of an apostolate which Wiseman had asked them to undertake. On both points they admitted it was not impossible that they had 'fallen into an error of judgment'. In the light of Newman's view of the matter, which they alleged was 'new' to them, they promised in the future not to appear 'unmindful of the obligations we owe you, and your relation to us, as the Founder of our House'. The Birmingham deputies thought the letter was 'written in the same diplomatic and evasive spirit as the former ones'.[83] There was nothing about reparation for the past or remedy for similar problems in the future. 'They seem simply to decline to do any thing', commented Newman.[84] A day after this letter was written, on 7 June, Wiseman himself wrote to Newman insisting that he be allowed to dedicate a 'panegyric' he had delivered on St Philip jointly to Faber and Newman. The Cardinal's purpose was clear enough. But Newman in his turn insisted that if 'I am not to stand by myself in the Dedication, you will be kind enough to include the Birmingham Fathers in it'.[85] Wiseman, however, published the dedication as it stood, in which Faber and Newman are closely associated, 'the one planting' intellectual seeds, 'the other watering' and gathering 'sweet flowers of devotion'. It was galling enough to have his name coupled with Faber's after all that had happened, without the implication that Faber's devotionalism was complementary to or associated with Newman's intellectual work. Later in the year Newman indeed heard that not only were Faber's devotional books disapproved of in Rome, but it was a source of surprise that he, Newman, presumably approved of them both as the founder of the English Oratory and (according to Wiseman) as Faber's close collaborator. He then had the satisfaction of informing, with studied ambiguity, the Rector of the Scots College in Rome that while he had 'a great admiration of Fr Faber's genius', he had never seen 'a line of any of [his] publications before they were given to the world'.[86] After Wiseman had ignored Newman's condition, he then 'proceeded, through Fr Faber, freely to show my private letter to various persons, without my leave or knowledge, and to comment on it through Fr Faber behind my back in most disrespectful terms'. So Newman wrote three years later when he sent to several friends a letter explaining the rumour that he had refused to allow Wiseman to make the joint dedication. He pointed out that the letter to the Cardinal was a private one, which he for his part had kept secret, that it had been written 'not under the influence of any personal feeling, but on motives of grave duty and with a definite object', and that he did not regret having done so.[87]

So far as Faber was concerned, Newman proceeded to do two things. First, he invited him to preach at the University. Personally unwelcome as this would be, at least it would put 'an end to all the reports, which he urges on me, of my causing *scandal*, by separating from him'.[88] Second, he sent Wiseman a letter containing five proposals Faber had put forward just before the foundation of the London house, which would have curtailed that house's independence and would have certainly ensured that nothing like the application to Rome (such a petition was expressly excluded) could have been made without Newman's permission, but in place of which Newman had put forward three less restricting propositions, which were only valid for three years. Although the three years were up, Newman still felt that Faber's original guarantees were morally binding, at least in the sense that Newman had taken them in good faith as representing the intentions of London. A copy of this 'melancholy memorial of the past'[89] was sent by Newman to Faber, who promptly wrote to Wiseman complaining that they had already twice written to Newman to apologize in vain, and that the initial checks on their early independence were no longer in force.

To his community in Birmingham Newman wrote a long letter giving his account of the breach with the London Oratory. He begins by stating that 'the whole question between us turns' on his 'relation to that community, peculiar to myself', no longer their superior but still their founder. As for the particular issue, an attempt had virtually been made by means of Propaganda to force Birmingham 'into a line of missionary

---

[86] *LD* xvii. 456.   [87] Ibid. xix. 101.   [88] Ibid. xvii. 265.   [89] Ibid. 259.

work which it held to be unoratorian'. As for his original letter to Faber which had given so much offence, he 'had written to them in the least formal way' in which an Oratory could be addressed. In reply, London had shown neither courtesy nor charity, let alone sympathy, but had advised Newman to have recourse to Propaganda if in the event their application proved to apply to Birmingham as well. When Newman went to Italy he found that London had attempted to prejudice the Oratories there and also the Curia against him, although he himself had been careful not to attack the daughter house. Newman concludes by pointing the moral that because Oratories have no common Superior, 'they are best friends at a distance':

Each must fall back upon its own centre, throw itself upon its own friends, and surround itself with its own association and traditions. This has struck us from the first in the Oratories abroad; we then suspected, now we painfully feel, the reason of it . . . St Philip is not the Saint of far spreading associations; but of isolated bodies, working severally in their own sphere.[90]

To accept and to formalize the separation seemed to Newman to be preferable to trying to extract from London any guarantee for the future. Accordingly, he drew up a decree that stated that other Oratories were in the same position as other religious communities, and forbade communication with other Oratorians about internal community matters. Then on 2 July the Birmingham Oratory formally sent the London Oratory a letter expressing their unanimity with Newman (Dalgairns fortunately was out of the country) and enclosing a copy of his letter to them. Brompton sent back a protest rejecting Newman's account and reiterating that they had already apologized for any trouble they had unintentionally caused.

Newman did not altogether correctly judge the mood at London. He remembered how, back in 1847, Faber had resented his setting up the Oratory 'as if I were encroaching on his province' (at the time Faber had complained that he had already had the same idea, but had been discouraged by Wiseman). Faber, he thought, saw no point in trying to heal relations, because he was convinced that the quarrel lay much deeper in Newman's distrust of his ambitions; and he was right in the sense that Newman thought he had originally 'joined the Oratory, seized some of our more valuable subjects, went off, and now simply sets up for himself'.[91] As for the other London Oratorians, Newman on the whole supposed they had not appreciated the full import of the application to Rome and had therefore been shocked by his strong reaction. In actual fact, the idea of making the application in the first place apparently came from Stanton, who thought Faber was inclined

90 Ibid. 270.   91 Ibid. 314.

to be too generous to Newman. Certainly on his deathbed in 1863 Faber assured Newman that he had been in a minority of one in wanting him consulted about the application. Although Newman at this point tended to blame Faber for the whole affair, he could not help feeling that 'it annoys him intensely to be out of joint with me'. His own view was that Faber had simply casually, as it were, 'come into my house, asked for a certificate from me [,] looked round the room, put some silver spoons and mantel piece ornaments into his pocket, and wished me good morning'—but without any particular deliberation or malice.[92] However, Stanislas Flanagan's view that the application was quite deliberate and was designed to prove the London Oratorians' independence as soon as their three years were up was confirmed by Newman's last talk with Faber, who told him that he 'wanted me consulted, and only gave in, when they said that, though I proved to be against the particular application which they proposed to make to Rome, still they would make it'.[93]

Faber, of course, was right in implying that the real causes of the rupture lay deeper. From the beginning there had been tension between Faber's 'Wilfridians' and Newman's 'Oratorians'. Nor was it only a question of resentment of Newman's authority: his idea of the Oratory and St Philip as representing an ideal of Catholic humanism was very different from the devotional and more exclusively spiritual Oratorianism of Faber and Dalgairns. What was bound to exacerbate the difference was that the London house had a natural geographical advantage and superiority over the Birmingham house. There were also two other practical factors—Newman's appointment in Dublin and Dalgairns's presence in the Birmingham house. It seemed very clear to Newman that 'efforts were making to take advantage of my temporary absence, to remodel my Oratory after the pattern of the London, and to merge my own Oratorian character in my position at the University'. Not only had Dalgairns been told privately about the London application, but Bishop Ullathorne had also been consulted by Rome and had lent his support 'both to please' Dalgairns 'who was his director, and to use him as director of convents through his diocese'—although he had not informed Newman, 'his excuse being that Propaganda bound him to secrecy'. A dispensation from Rome, would, then, be dangerous 'as giving the Bishop an entrance into our Congregation, as scattering our members, as forcing us into a particular line of study (that of Direction) for which we had no calling, and as securing for the Father in question an undue pre-eminence in our body'.[94]

The final correspondence between the two Oratories was not quite

---

[92] *LD* xvii. 318–19. [93] Ibid. 559. [94] Ibid. xix. 444.

the conclusion of the affair. During the summer, Stanton and Hutchison were in Rome seeking a separate foundation Brief for the London Oratory. They were delighted with Barnabò's nickname for Newman, 'il Babbo' ('the Daddy'), which now in their letters replaced the old 'il Padre'. They were less happy to learn that the Pope had insisted that Newman should be consulted. When he replied, Newman reminded Barnabò, who was now a Cardinal and Prefect of Propaganda, that he had suggested a separate Brief himself when he was in Rome, but had been told it was unnecessary. His only reservation now concerned the future foundation of other Oratories in the metropolis. The London Oratorians, who were particularly nervous about this, were anxious that the possibility should be expressly excluded in the Brief. However, the Brief which was issued only stipulated, on the advice of Bishop Grant of Southwark, that no other Oratory could be erected within a 10-mile radius.

In August Dalgairns finally decided to leave Birmingham and rejoin the London Oratory. He told Faber he wished he could 'have submitted my rationale to the old gentleman [Newman]', but that he could not be other than himself. He consoled himself by trusting that 'Mama [the Virgin Mary] will get me some grace'. The immediate cause of Dalgairns's departure was the occasion of a community vote formally adopting Newman's 'Remarks on the Oratorian Vocation', when he told Newman privately that they did not concur with 'his view of the Oratory, which agreed with that of the London House' and 'was the *historical* view'. Dalgairns wrote an account of his interview with Newman to Faber, describing how he asked Newman if he thought that he, Dalgairns, had 'the Spirit of the Birmingham house'. After telling Dalgairns that he had a perfect right to hold his view of the Oratory, Newman asked him to wait while he considered.

I cannot tell you how kind he was. Do you remember an expression in Callista about 'eyes blue as the sapphires of the Eternal City.' His eyes looked then just like a Saint's and he spoke and acted like one, so disinterestedly, so gently. He said how much he loved me; he then said that he felt quite sure he had no resentful feeling against the London house; and lastly he said that since I asked him the question he could not but answer that I had not the spirit of the Birmingham house.[95]

Newman himself was relieved. Dalgairns's departure removed 'a source of weakness' in the community, as well as 'removing what might ever be a cause of irritation against me and us in the minds of the Brompton Fathers'.[96] He confessed to the community that he thought that if he had more of 'the art of government'—or rather, 'the art of management'—he might have coped better with Dalgairns. But the fact was that they had spoiled him in trying to make him feel at home, while 'in all that relates to an Oratorian life, he despises and has ever despised us'. Dalgairns's restlessness had led to his being 'used', however unconsciously, 'by the London Oratory to new-make us after the pattern of the London Oratory'.[97] Later, however, Newman came to think less tolerantly of Dalgairns, who, he felt, had caused the quarrel with London by 'thinking he might do what he pleased in my absence'.[98]

Newman had been responsible in the first place for Dalgairns returning to Birmingham in 1853, when he had asked to be taken back 'as being much bullied by Fr Faber and hardly treated by the London Fathers'. After his final meeting with Faber in 1863, Newman reflected that his 'application', or rather 'demand', for Dalgairns, which 'was imprudent extremely', probably 'set up the Londoners' back, and, in spite of granting my desire, they never forgave it'.[99] At the time Newman had been very upset because he thought Faber had given encouragement to a potential novice at Birmingham to break his commitment there and join London. So he took the opportunity to press Faber to allow Dalgairns to return, pleading the 'destitution' of the Birmingham house since Joseph Gordon's death, and his excessive generosity in giving up 'too many, on whom I had a claim, in the division of the Houses'.[100] Faber had reacted very angrily, but put no obstacle in the way of Dalgairns going. Newman seems to have been almost embarrassed at having got his way so easily, and even told Faber he felt ashamed at the way he had demanded to have Dalgairns back. His obvious uneasiness about the whole affair was reflected in his almost effusive praise at the time of the noble generosity of Faber and the London house.

As for the Londoners now, they were delighted to receive back their 'Prodigal Son', who was able to give them a report on the Birmingham house. Faber sent Stanton his own characteristically vivid version of the account:

He describes their feeling against us as something awful . . . from time to time the Padre transmitted from Dublin bitter papers, which Ambrose was ordered to read . . . One of these papers lashed them to perfect phrenzy . . . He says Ambrose's bitterness is chiefly, as we might expect, from personal feeling about the Padre; but that Stanislas' is a fixed view about the Institute. He is entirely in the Padre's confidence and he told Bernard candidly that the Padre avoided study of precedents because *he did not wish the Institute as St Philip left it*, but his intention was to change it for the nineteenth century, and for England; and we

⁹⁷ *NO* 352, 354, 357.   ⁹⁸ *AW* 329.   ⁹⁹ *LD* xvii. 560.
¹⁰⁰ Ibid. xv. 434.

stand in the way . . . I am sure . . . if we keep simply to our Saint and do his work and follow his rule, we shall be all right and triumph in the end.[101]

The letter is not only an amusing example of Faber's gift for comic dramatization, but is interesting because of the implied contrast between Newman's view of the necessity for adaptation and change if the Oratory was to remain true to St Philip's original inspiration, and Faber's idea that a real Oratory was one that imitated as exactly as possible the sixteenth-century Philip Neri and his Oratory. In a way the argument was the same as that with Pusey and Pugin: did loyalty to the past mean development or revival? Did fidelity to the tradition imply growth or imitation? It was one of Newman's deepest convictions that to cling to the literal letter of the past was to lose its essential spirit, and therefore to betray it.

6

On 26 June 1856 Newman appeared before the Irish bishops' Synod in Dublin. Archbishop MacHale 'kept a dead silence, and asked no question whatever', although the Rector 'wished the lion to attack me, I was so cool and so prepared'. Most of the bishops seemed favourable, and he 'thanked them most pointedly and earnestly for their great kindness to me, ever since I came to Ireland, which I quite feel'.[102] In the printed letter which they had before them, he had mentioned some immediate objectives, which included forming links between the University and secondary schools, preparing students for the new competitive examinations 'in the engineering and artillery departments, in the civil service, and in the India appointments', and especially the establishment of a medical faculty.[103] Reference was also made to the need to encourage the physical sciences in general (although not to the plan of an observatory, on which Newman had been keen in 1854, when he had tried in vain to find a suitable Observer with the help of Manuel Johnson, who, he suggested half-seriously, should 'fling off that shabby Protestantism of yours, and come here yourself').[104] Again, as he had done in 1854, Newman advocated a department of ancient Irish studies. He admitted that there would not immediately be enough students to justify the staff of professors, which was an investment for the future. For their part, the bishops unanimously approved not only the provisional rules and regulations, but also Newman's appointments and prospective expenditure for a period of three years. This meant that his rectorship

[101] Ibid. xvii. 361–2.   [102] Ibid. 298–9.   [103] Ibid. 281.
[104] Ibid. xvi. 123.

would not terminate before 1859, although his official papal leave of absence from the Oratory expired in 1857, when he had hoped to return for good. But at least he now had 'a definite and intelligible term put to my duties here'.[105] The statutes however, did not bind him to any particular period of residence in Dublin, and he looked forward to spending more time in Birmingham. As for the proposal of a finance committee of three laymen (with a clerical secretary), this predictably fell on deaf episcopal ears.

The provisional statutes included a section on discipline in which Newman quoted from his first Report for 1854–5, where he had laid down the

> guiding principle, what I believe to be the truth, that the young for the most part cannot be driven, but, on the other hand, are open to persuasion, and to the influence of kindness and personal attachment; and that, in consequence, they are to be kept straight by indirect contrivances rather than by authoritative enactments and naked prohibitions.

It must have sounded strange to bishops used to strict seminary discipline to hear that 'We could not do worse than to continue the discpline of school and college into the University, and to let the great world, which is to follow upon it, be the first stage on which the young are set at liberty to follow their own bent.' As for the notion that one of 'the characteristics of that discipline which is peculiar of a University' is 'a certain tenderness, or even laxity of rule',[106] Archbishop Cullen had already complained to Rome about the 'unsuitable' state of affairs in which 'young men are allowed to go out at all hours, to smoke etc., and there has not been any fixed time for study'.[107] Such freedom would have been as out of place in a seminary as lay control of the finances.

Newman's great problem was to attract students in sufficient number and of reasonable calibre. There were only ninety-four so far enrolled in courses. The Catholic aristocracy and gentry preferred the established universities, even when they were not actually hostile to the new University. The middle class could not afford a university education, and such secondary schools as there were did not inspire confidence. This was why it was so important that the University should help to raise the standard of Irish secondary education. The response from Ireland as a whole had been negligible. Many of the bishops and priests, Newman guessed, were at heart deeply suspicious of the whole idea of the University, if only because they thought it 'a mistake and a misfortune that they have any of the upper or middle classes among them . . . and in fact . . . they think that then only Ireland will become again the Isle of Saints, when it has a population of peasants ruled over by a patriotic

[105] *LD* xvii. 310.   [106] *Campaign* 36–8, 115–17.   [107] *LD* xvi. 551 n. 4.

priesthood patriarchally'.[108] It was all very well and good to try and attract students from the less well-off section of society with scholarships, but where was the '*inducement* sufficient to induce' them to '*accept* an almost gratuitous education', since the 'love of learning does not seem a sufficient inducement in this day, if it is not coupled with the prospect of a livelihood'?[109]

Dublin itself offered the best prospects—if only because it was felt in the schools in the country that the metropolis was not the right place for a residential university (like Cullen, Newman had wanted the University to be just outside the city, but he was forestalled by the premature purchase of the University House). The University's brightest hope was the medical school, which promised to be the best in the city. It was not simply a question of producing qualified doctors, but of 'securing the moral and liberal education of the Medical Profession, a profession which can, of all others, be an aid and support to the parish priests in the country at large'.[110] In the last lecture he would deliver in Dublin, on 4 November 1858, the day of his final departure, Newman (once again professing the 'Science of Sciences') was to warn the medical students that 'bodily health is not the only end of man, and the medical science is not the highest science of which he is the subject', since 'man has a moral and a religious nature, as well as a physical'. With the aid of one of his most arresting images, he pointed out that moral and religious truths are as superior to the knowledge derived from the senses as they are vulnerable before the 'hard, palpable, material facts' of physical nature:

... the phenomena, which are the basis of morals and Religion ... are the dictates either of Conscience or of Faith. They are faint shadows and tracings, certain indeed, but delicate, fragile, and almost evanescent, which the mind recognizes at one time, not at another,—discerns when it is calm, loses when it is in agitation. The reflection of sky and mountains in the lake is a proof that sky and mountains are around it, but the twilight, or the mist, or the sudden storm hurries away the beautiful image, which leaves behind it no memorial of what it was ...[111]

Apart from the university environment itself, the 'liberal' side of the medical students' education would in fact merely consist in the two-year preliminary course compulsory for all students from the age of 16 to 18. Newman wanted to provide scholarships for this initial course which would be open to prospective students of medicine, engineering, and agriculture—rather than lay out a similar sum of money on a house intended for the sons of the gentry, who might never come. This preliminary course of liberal studies involved compulsory Latin, but the

---

[108] Ibid. xvii. 385.   [109] Ibid. 369.   [110] Ibid. xvii. 281.
[111] *Idea* 412–13.

options from which the other two subjects had to be taken included mathematics and science. In effect, it was the equivalent of an English school sixth-form course not easily available in Ireland because of the lack of secondary education. Where, of course, it was available, then it was not necessary to repeat it at the University. Specialized study for a degree, whether in the arts or sciences or professional studies, began, as in England, at the age of 18, although it was expected that the majority of students who came at 16 would in fact leave at the end of the two-year course.

In the summer of 1856 Newman felt sufficiently encouraged to say, 'I have broken the neck of my work at Dublin; by which I mean, that I have launched the boat, and progress is a matter of wind and tide and time.' The passage between England and Ireland would 'be less formidable' in a few months with the introduction of larger ships, and he wanted now to spend more time with his community in Birmingham. He felt he had

not been so well, as I am, perhaps for forty years, since, that is, I was a boy—but these autumn days, with their bright noons and chill evenings, remind me that my prime of health, though it comes late like September, and promises fair, is close upon sudden twilight hastening down and melancholy hours. Years are precious, because they are rare, like jewels . . .

He was so 'strangely without crosses . . . as to make me fear'. The old friends he had lost by becoming a Catholic had been replaced by new friends. Some of his old friends had become Catholics and others, like William Froude's wife, were about to come over. As for his beloved Oratory, it was now 'most singularly of one mind and spirit, and of one heart', although Dalgairns's departure meant even more work for the depleted community. His only cross was his work in Dublin, and he looked forward to giving that up soon.[112]

At the end of August he was obliged to ask Cullen for a loan of £2,000 from the University funds, as the cost of the University Church, which was to have been £3,500, came to £5,600. The Archbishop agreed, provided two of the other archbishops gave their consent. This was forthcoming, but when Newman's lawyers applied for the loan they were told that the security of the church was not sufficient, but that the Archbishop would be writing to the Rector. Newman then wrote to Cullen to point out that he was 'doing the University a great service in wanting the money at all',[113] as the church was for the University. Not only had he taken on himself the trouble of building the church, but he had also provided the original outlay. An immediate decision was needed. A fortnight passed and still no word came. Newman then

[112] *LD* xvii. 378.   [113] Ibid. 390.

offered as security £2,300 worth of property in the church for a loan of £850 'to release me from my immediate embarassments'.[114] This time Cullen did reply, though not to Newman himself but to his lawyers, again intimating that the security offered was inadequate, but suggesting that if Newman could return to Dublin in time for a meeting of the bishops the matter could be arranged. Newman, who was occupied with business in Birmingham, borrowed the £2,000 from the Oratory.

His six years as Rector would be up next autumn in 1857, when he was determined to resign. The Birmingham Oratory was too weak to do without him. He felt he was too old himself for the job. The University needed now a different kind of Rector:

A Rector ought to be a more showy, bustling man than I am, in order to impress the world that we are great people. This is one of our great wants. I feel it vividly—but it is difficult to find the man who is this with other qualifications too . . . I ought to dine out every day, and of course I don't dine out at all. I ought to mix in literary society and talk about new gasses and the price of labour—whereas I can't recollect what I once knew, much less get up a whole lot of new subjects—I ought to behave condescendingly to others, whereas they are condescending to me—And I ought above all to be 20 years younger, and take it up as the work of my life. But since my qualifications are not those, all I can do is to attempt to get together a number of clever men, and set them to do what is not in my own line.[115]

A young Irish Rector 'with *real* views in opposition to theories'[116] was what was needed, but unfortunately it was more likely, Newman reflected sadly, that 'both Rectorship and Vice Rectorship will fall into the hands of men, who have little other idea of a University than a place for imposing fines . . . on those who are slow at lecture and for sending out students into the Town two and two'.[117] His departure would, no doubt, be welcomed by Cullen and MacHale, even though resented by the professors. Years later, in 1872, Newman noted acidly that it was 'not Ireland that was unkind to me'—for the 'same thing would have happened in England or France. It was the clergy, moved as they are in automaton fashion from the camarilla at Rome.'[118] By this time he had also discovered to his cost that 'these Bishops are so accustomed to be absolute that they usurp the rights of others, and rough ride over their wishes and their plans quite innocently, without meaning it, and astonished, not at finding out the fact, but at its being impossible to them.'[119] If he was now really 'driven into a corner, from the urgency of those who wish me to stay', he would 'insist on quasi nonresidence'.[120]

---

[114] Ibid. 405. [115] Ibid. xvi. 535. [116] Ibid. xvii. 221.
[117] Ibid. 259. [118] Ibid. 415 n. 2. [119] *AW* 293.
[120] *LD* xvii. 415.

Whatever the frustrations, his real attachment and devotion to the University could not be doubted. And he was deeply gratified when he later heard that one of the Irish professors at a University dinner had called him 'one of the greatest and most enduring benefactors of Ireland'. As an Englishman he had to admit that 'Englishmen have deep reasons for shame when they think how they have treated Ireland.'[121]

Newman was uncomfortably aware that the shadow of the London Oratory still hung over the Birmingham house. He had discovered that Robert Tillotson, an American whom he had received into the Church at Alcester Street and who had subsequently joined the community, was in correspondence with Dalgairns, who had been his novice-master. He warned Tillotson that Faber 'cannot keep from meddling with us, and I am sure that correspondence or communication with any of his subjects will tend to our *ruin*'—'Some one says that priests should treat women as souls in purgatory—whom we pray for and hope to meet in heaven. I say the same of the Fathers at Brompton.'[122] He also asked John Hungerford Pollen not to speak of his Dublin affairs—'least of all to Fr Faber or any of the Oratorians at Brompton—who like to pump out from all comers all they can about me, and to retail it'.[123] He was delighted, though, with Pollen's church, especially with the beautiful apse, 'and, to my taste, the church is the most beautiful one in the three Kingdoms'.[124]

In a letter to Henry Wilberforce, he had referred in passing to 'secret enemies' in England, but without naming Faber and Wiseman.[125] In his reply, Wilberforce deprecated a 'sensitiveness, which is the penalty of great ability'.[126] Newman asked him,

did you *ever*, since you knew me, hear me speak of 'my enemies' before? I don't think I ever did in my life.

Is then what you surmise of a connexion between my sensitiveness and my thus speaking, an inference in reason, or a theory?[127]

He scolded Ambrose St John for lacking 'moral courage' when he advised him not to risk Cullen's complaining to Rome and also to thank Wiseman for the odious dedication which had just been published. Far from grovelling, if he said anything he would 'fire off':

I go to Rome to be snubbed. I come to Dublin to be repelled by Dr McHale and worn away by Dr Cullen. The Cardinal taunts me with his Dedications, and Fr Faber insults me with his letters . . . What enormous irritation Job must have felt, when his friends came and prosed to him . . .

This flash of the old pugnacious humour reassured St John, who retracted his advice ('you always gain when you show your monkey').[128]

---

[121] *LD* xvii. 470.   [122] Ibid. 431–2.   [123] Ibid. 433.   [124] Ibid. 440.

[125] Ibid. 419.   [126] Ibid. 426.   [127] Ibid. 423.   [128] Ibid. 426–7.

A letter from Mrs Bowden, whose younger son Charles (Newman's godson) had recently joined his older brother John at the London Oratory, convinced Newman that 'the tack is to sooth and butter me'. It was quite unlike the tone of any of her previous letters. He had heard from Pollen how Wiseman was 'full of admiration, interest and sympathy' for him. Wilberforce, he predicted, would soon begin 'to butter my sensitiveness in his paper'. 'None of them can rise above the idea that I am *personally* wounded!' Concern for the Birmingham Oratory was hardly 'considered a sufficient *object*' to account for his 'conduct'.[129] He agreed with William Monsell, who had returned from a visit to Rome, that he had 'no one to represent' him there, with the result 'Out of sight, out of mind'. But he complained that though Monsell had emphasized the importance of the University, he had said nothing of the Birmingham Oratory. Wiseman 'placed us at Birmingham by his sole act, and then *left* us. He has simply shelved us. *Me* they wish to use—me they wish to detach in every way from my own Fathers.' Newman was useful in Dublin at the University; the less he was associated with Birmingham the better for the London Oratory and its supporters. The Birmingham Oratory, to which he had 'given' himself 'deliberately', was 'simply ignored' in Dublin, London, and Rome, and what made him most 'sore' was the way people like Wilberforce praised him, but made no reference at all to his Oratory. Monsell replied that he did not undervalue the Birmingham Oratory (indeed, he especially appreciated its 'masculine character') but he valued the Catholic University more.[130] Newman himself wondered if there was any privilege for which he could petition the Holy See, for his Oratory as the mother house. He now suspected that Barnabò had 'wished to throw dust in my eyes' in dissuading him from his original petition in Rome by assuring him that he was already 'Deputato Apostolico' for the Oratory in England. The fact was 'there is no such word in Canon Law', and so he 'might as well have declared I was the Pope's Grand Visier'.[131]

Meanwhile, Newman was feeling the effects of overwork in Dublin. He wrote in despair at the beginning of November:

My chattels stand about my room in the same confusion as on the night I came, near three weeks ago, from my inability to find leisure for removing them to their places. My letters are a daily burden, and, did I not answer them by return of post, they would soon get my head under water and drown me. Every hour or half hour of the day I have people calling on me. I have to entertain strangers at dinner, I have to attend inaugural Lectures . . . I have to stop Professors resigning, and Houses revolting. I have to keep accounts and find money, when I have none . . . I have to Lecture on Latin Composition, and examine for

[129] Ibid. 447.   [130] Ibid. 502–3.   [131] Ibid. 506.

Exhibitions. In ten days I rush to Birmingham for their sheer want of me—and then have to throw myself into quite a fresh world. And I have the continual pain of our Fathers sighing if I am not there, and priests and professors looking blank if I am not here.[132]

He was also very busy preparing his University sermons for publication in *Sermons Preached on Various Occasions* (1857). In one of them, he ventured on his first veiled public criticism in print of the authorities of the Church, when he denied that 'when we use great words of the Church' this necessarily involves any interest in 'the praise of earthly superiors' or that 'we are living on the breath, and basking in the smile, of man'.[133] Later, he specifically referred to this 'implied' criticism when he wrote in his journal that 'while I have Him who lives in the Church, the separate members of the Church, my Superiors, though they may claim my obedience, have no claim on my admiration, and offer nothing for my inward trust.'[134] The University Church, which could hold 1,200 people, was crowded on both the successive Sundays in November on which Newman preached. It was noted that the congregation by no means consisted entirely of educated people. Even working-class Irish men and women appreciated the famous Englishman in their midst.

Newman could not help thinking of the future when he hoped he would no longer be Rector. His own choice as his successor would have been David Moriarty, the newly appointed Bishop of Kerry. Moriarty had stayed at Alcester Street in 1849 and had become a trusted friend and ally in Ireland. Newman saw distinct advantages in such an appointment, although it would have seemed presumptuous to think of it if he had not heard that Moriarty's name was being mentioned at Rome. The relationship between the University and the hierarchy was critical, and the Rector needed qualities which the present incumbent did not have:

For myself, even were I Bishop and Irishman, I have not the talent of ruling. I never had—I never ruled—I never have been in a position of authority before—I can begin things—and I never aspired to do more.

Now it was time to retire, 'because I have done my work, and cannot do the work which lies before me'.[135] He had 'got together a number of very clever men, and *they pull well together*—but *of course* they want a strong hand over them; they want an Irishman too; and to deal with the Hierarchy a Bishop is wanted'. In addition, 'they ought to get a man 15 years younger than I am; one *who can form plans* for the future', since Newman himself was 'too old to promise myself a future—*my* government can never be more than provisional'.[136] Another Rector

[132] *LD* xvii. 444–5.   [133] *OS* 56–7.   [134] *AW* 251–2.
[135] *LD* xvii. 460–1.   [136] Ibid. 492.

might be able to 'manage' the priests on the staff (especially the '*intolerable*' Father Forde, Cullen's nominee to the chair of Canon Law), who formed a distinct group in opposition to the lay professors.[137] For his part, Moriarty predicted that Newman's resignation would seriously damage the University. He also pointed out that Ireland had no university tradition, and that his own personal experience lay in seminaries; nor did he relish the thought of working in Dublin, with its authoritarian Archbishop. If the worst came to the worst, it might even be best if Newman remained as a non-resident Rector.

The relationship between clergy and laity was something that was beginning to occupy Newman's attention more and more. The 'fearful' 'breach' between the two threatened the University in particular. Most of the money for it was collected by the priests from the Irish poor. Apart from a few converts, the Irish gentry and aristocracy did less for the University than their English counterparts. If it was to be a proper lay institution, then the laity, and not least the English laity (after all, the Rector was English), must take the initiative in raising money for it. However, Newman himself, in spite of all the difficulties, felt detached:

> . . . I know myself, if no one else knows, what little interest I take in the success or failure of schemes in which I am engaged. If I needed it, the failure of Puseyism, and the advance of years, have been sufficient to secure one against over earnestness in working, and the zest of business. I am working very hard, but I take as little (natural or human) interest in it as I do in the cotton plantations of India. I have never doubted a moment of our success—I am *quite satisfied* with our progress. To look back two years, and see the *substantial* improvement of things, is wonderful . . .

In criticizing the English and Irish gentry, he was merely making the objective point that '*you cannot have a University, till the gentlemen take it up*'. The 'narrowness and party-spirit' of Archbishop Cullen was certainly damaging, but the only 'personal annoyance' was 'his *rule* of acting—not once, or twice, but his rule and principle—to let me ask a question in June, to call about it again and again, to let me write to him about it in July, to let me write to his intimate friend to get an answer for me in August, to give up the chance of one in September, and in January accidentally to find he all along has been telling others that he *has* decided it in the way I asked him *not* to decide in, though even now in February he has not, directly or indirectly, answered me'.[138]

Newman was right: the University was progressing. In the autumn term of 1856 Thomas Arnold was appointed Professor of English Literature. He had recently become a Roman Catholic, in spite of his wife's violent opposition; but he had had to leave Tasmania, where he

---

[137] Ibid. 499.   [138] Ibid. 513–14.

was Inspector of Schools, because of anti-Catholic feeling. Although he had been at Oxford in Newman's time and had heard him preach once or twice, he had not been under his influence. It was 'strange' and 'marvellous' to Newman that a son of Dr Arnold should not only have entered the Church (after a period of agnosticism), but should now be joining his staff in Dublin.[139] It was 'one of the most wonderful instances of conversion', considering his father's implacable opposition to the Oxford Movement.[140]

The Rector's aim was 'to make as many *self supporting* Institutions' as he could, 'so that, even though the Bishops and people of Ireland flagged in their zeal, the Institution would go on, at least in its constituent parts'.[141] An archaeological institute, an observatory, and other scientific establishments were planned. His own University House was full and was at last paying for itself. The University Church, the professors, and the Medical School were more or less self-sufficient.

7

In March 1857 Newman prepared letters to the bishops announcing his impending resignation from the beginning of the next academic year, when his original leave of absence would be up. He did not necessarily anticipate leaving the University altogether: perhaps he might revert to the original post he had wanted, that of Prefect of Studies. He was also thinking of trying to found a special house for English students, as well as 'a literary and scientific journal' for 'depositing professorial *work*, and to advertise the University'.[142] If he was to maintain some residence in Dublin, he would want some work to do. The letters were dispatched on 3 April, the day he returned to Birmingham for Easter. The principal reason he gave for his retirement was 'the fatigue of journeying between Birmingham and Dublin', but in fact 'it was a real great difficulty, and it went to the root of the question how I could continue Rector', since Cullen wanted permanent residence.[143] The other reasons given were the need for a more active Rector, and his responsibilities to the Oratory. Cullen himself did not apparently reply to the formal but polite letter he received—nor did MacHale to the somewhat terser one sent to him. Other bishops responded warmly, deeply regretting Newman's decision and fearing for the future of the University. But he was adamant that he had made his contribution in starting up the University; a younger, full-time Rector was now needed. Members of staff remonstrated in vain; his

---

[139] *LD* xvii. 416–17.   [140] Ibid. 545.   [141] Ibid. 548.
[142] Ibid. 543.   [143] Ibid. xviii. 9.

principal loyalty must be to his Oratory in Birmingham. Finally, in May, when he was back in Dublin, the Archbishop called, 'so nervous and distressed, as to melt me internally, though I was very stiff or very much moved, both at once perhaps, during the short interview'. He wanted Newman to stay at least another three years, to make six from the opening of the University. He was reminded 'how I had urged him to begin sooner, for I had lost my first years in waiting'; besides, he had been warned a year ago of the impending resignation. To the point that Rome would have no objection to dispensing him from non-residence at Birmingham, Newman rejoined that the Oratory would not tolerate it. But he left open the door to Cullen's final suggestion that some arrangement might be possible whereby the Rector could spend more time in Birmingham, with a permanent, resident Vice-Rector in Dublin. The conversation 'took place with pauses of silence on my part and his— and when I spoke, I spoke with great momentum'. The Archbishop ended by saying that he thought the bishops would shortly agree to buy Newman's church for the University.[144] The resignation was the talking-point of Dublin, and Cullen was obviously under great pressure, but his new position of strength only made Newman 'wish more than ever to get away, before I am found out—for I am an ass in a lion's skin'.[145] However, he did not 'object, for a year or two, to be a non-resident Rector, with a real acting Vice-Rector—but it will be a very large pill for the Irish clergy to swallow—and I doubt the capacity of their throat'.[146] His one object was still 'to do some service to Catholic Education'.[147] As for the Vice-Rector, he saw no reason why he had to be a cleric. The important thing was that he should be effective and on the spot. A Dr Leahy had been appointed Vice-Rector in 1854, but in 1855 he was made Vicar-General of Cashel, although he did not formally resign until the spring of 1857, when he became Archbishop. Newman later drily noted that the fact that his one and only Vice-Rector, with whom he always got on extremely well, was 'hardly there at all', did not appear to cause Cullen any displeasure.[148]

As the months passed, Newman began to suspect that the Birmingham Oratory was more than simply ignored and despised. A number of things happened to make him feel that 'we are whispered against'. There was a kind of studied ignorance as to whether they had a church or a parish or any novices. He noticed that Mrs Bowden, with her connections at the London Oratory, had stopped writing to him on his birthday. They should 'expect', he concluded, 'any quantity of contempt from the influences which are at work against us': the important thing was to 'make ourselves in every way *strong in*

---

[144] Ibid. 34–5. [145] Ibid. 41. [146] Ibid. 58.
[147] Ibid. 45. [148] Ibid. xvi. 551 n. 1.

Birmingham', for 'while we have *local* opinion, we may defy public, and
while we are strong at home, we may defy the world'. If they stood firm,
they would find many 'elsewhere falling back upon us'.[149] He
remembered how Faber had originally predicted that he would leave
Birmingham for London; no doubt he now dismissed him as 'thrown
away'. It was certainly true that they were unlikely to attract the
recruits their 'antecedents' ought to draw.

All the world goes to London—to know people up and down the world, is to
know people in London. That is Fr Faber's position—and he is, as they say,
master of the situation. I knew it, when I let him go there—I refused it myself,
because it is not my line. I never have liked publicity, and could not do justice to
it. I should have been in a most false position. Providence did not mean it—but
it follows that my whole Oxford connexion, and whatever comes through it,
and again all the interest I might have excited by my former works, goes to
London, not to Bm, and so to Fr Faber. All he has not himself, and wished to
have, is my *name*. As long as he can make his Oratory looked on as mine, he has
all from me he wishes . . . I never should be surprised if they put up my portrait
in a conspicuous place at Brompton—the guest room—and thus would have a
double advantage, would show gratitude and forbearance, and would use my
name.

This very frank and revealing letter to Ambrose St John continues with
a realistic estimate of his present reputation:

To the rising generation itself, to the sons of those who knew or read me 15 or
20 years ago, I am a character of history—they know nothing of me; they have
heard my name, and nothing more—they have no associations with it . . . I
made influence at Oxford by my Parochial Sermons—they are not only
Protestant but simply unknown, unheard of by the young generation.
Fr Faber's books are to it, just what those sermons were to the foregoing, and do
the same work of creating influence.

As a place for an Oratory, Birmingham was less suitable than
Manchester or Liverpool. None of their difficulties, Newman ended
cheerfully, arose from their own fault; they should not be discouraged.
For new members for the community, they must look to conversions in
their own non-Catholic neighbourhood among the affluent Protestant
middle class of Birmingham. The problem was how to make conversions
when the Oratory had already more than enough ordinary work to
do.[150]

On 6 August 1857 the Fathers of the Birmingham Oratory refused a
formal request from the three Irish Archbishops, contained in a letter of
20 July, to allow Newman to continue to reside in Dublin as Rector 'for
some time longer'.[151] In a letter composed by Newman, they pointed out

[149] *LD* xviii. 76.   [150] Ibid. 92–5.   [151] Ibid. 112–13.

that 'since he has been our Superior, your University has had the use of him far more than ourselves; it has had two thirds of his whole time.' They also mentioned the unsettlement caused by the Superior's absence. But they left the door open to compromise when they concluded by saying, 'everything we *can* do, we will gladly offer; but we can consent to a non-resident Superior, even less than you perhaps can contemplate a non-resident Rector.'[152] Included, too, in the letter was a reference to his doctor's fear that Newman had heart trouble, with the consequent need to avoid anxiety as far as possible. Not only was the present community overworked, so depleted were their numbers, but Newman was afraid that no new novices would come in the absence of the Superior. He was disappointed that the idea of a 'middle plan' involving residence for a limited number of weeks had not been followed up. It would have been feasible for a couple of years, provided a suitable Vice-Rector could be found. When this was put to the Archbishops, they agreed to try the plan as an experiment for one academic year. Newman suspected that Cullen, who had always wanted him to be permanently in residence, did not like the proposed compromise, but would be glad if he left, provided a suitable successor could be found. Once again there was a problem over the Vice-Rector. The Archbishops proposed the objectionable Father Forde, but asked the Rector to suggest some other Irish priests if this was not acceptable. Newman would have preferred to choose from the present University staff, who were mostly laymen; but since this was not open to him, he put forward the names of four Irish priests, including his friend Dr Russell of Maynooth. Once again a decision was deferred, though the Rector was given leave to appoint a Pro-Vice-Rector, on condition he was a priest—a restriction, Newman drily noted, which effectively limited his choice to the one suitable cleric available on the staff, Fr. O'Reilly, the Professor of Dogmatic Theology, since it was too late to try and find anyone outside the University. O'Reilly refused the post, and Newman refused to accept Forde or the other priest in residence. The result was that when Newman left Dublin on 19 November 1857, after being present for the opening of the new academic year on 3 November, not only was there still no Vice-Rector to represent him, but there was not even a Pro-Vice-Rector to act as head of the University in the absence of the Rector.

Newman himself, who was now only an acting non-resident Rector, wondered whether, if more English interest and support were forthcoming, there might be a possibility of actually moving the arts faculty (in which only a minority of the professors were Irish) and setting it up as a college in England, although it would still be an integral part of the

---

[152] Ibid. 114–15.

University. However, there seemed as little chance of arousing any enthusiasm in England for the University, as of finding students in Ireland. English Catholics did not want to go to Ireland for a university education. As for the potential Irish students that were available, even if they were offered an almost free education, they still needed an object in coming. In the arts faculty the number of students had remained static at about fifty. Nor did the poor numbers at the Queen's Colleges suggest the situation was likely to improve. The failure to increase the student numbers was hardly Cullen's fault, whatever his enemies might say. The only hope seemed to be to try and gradually attract students from Dublin itself. However, there was no doubt about the success of the medical faculty, and the forthcoming University journal would boost the science faculty. The unpalatable fact was that the arts faculty, the one closest to the Rector's own heart, was the least promising and successful of all the faculties. After the compulsory preliminary course of two years, only two or three Irish students had stayed on to do an arts honours degree. What made it worse was that the faculty cost twice as much as the other faculties, and the staff were predominantly English. It was embarrassing for the Rector to feel that 'for what does good to two or three Irish only, I am making a sort of job in favor of the English of Irish money'. He was aware of the complaint that 'the Irish people will have no return for their contributions, unless the Faculty of Arts be given up to the purposes of a grammar and commercial school'.[153] If only England would subscribe '£1000 a year, it might at any time ship off the Philosophy and Letters Faculty to England . . . leaving it an integral part of the Dublin University still'.[154] Perhaps (although he did not say so) Newman would then be able to maintain a link with the University as well as develop Catholic higher education in England—and perhaps even find a new important role for the Birmingham Oratory.

Not very surprisingly, a crisis soon broke in the absence of the Rector. It involved a matter of discipline which was in fact the responsibility of the Vice-Rector. But since there was no Vice-Rector, Newman was asked by the University Council to discipline the two students involved. Apart from the fact it was not really his business, he also felt strongly that 'the essence of good punishment is, its being *immediate*'.[155] He began to think that perhaps it would be 'better to resign now, while people like me—than to outlive my popularity, and leave unpleasant associations behind me'. 'On the spot' he knew what people were thinking and feeling, but away in Birmingham he was 'walking in the dark' and could easily cause offence without even knowing it.[156] It was true that he never had experienced the confidence of his episcopal superiors (who 'never

---

[153] *LD* xviii. 572.   [154] Ibid. 187.   [155] Ibid. 206.   [156] Ibid. 211.

have asked my advice—it has always been a bargaining, and they getting all they can'). But now that he was 300 miles away, it seemed inevitable that there would be 'continual little collisions' without that 'continual action and re-action between all members of the University and myself, which has hindered any thing of the kind'; hitherto there had been the 'most perfect harmony', but this could hardly last if he was 'to act in the dark in another place'.[157] Besides, he had always 'acted, not by formal authority and rule, but by influence, and this power cannot be well exerted when absent'.[158] Unless a trustworthy Vice-Rector was appointed, he could not continue as Rector. Not that that was at all likely, since 'Dr Cullen's idea of a Vice Rector from the first was, not as an official who would represent me but one who would represent the Archbishop against me, as a regulator of my movements.'[159] For he was viewed 'rather as the Archbishops' representative and as their security and safeguard against me, than as my own helper and backer up'.[160] In fact, the Vice-Rector, not the Rector, was, according to the statutes, in charge not only of discipline but of the routine administration of the University.

However, the situation was not all gloom, there were brighter aspects. Surprisingly perhaps, in view of all the problems, the annual contribution collected in Irish churches seemed to be still holding up. The quality of the professors boded well for the future. And on 1 January 1858 the first number of the new University journal, called the *Atlantis*, was published, which Newman hoped would 'act as considerable advertisement and puff'.[161] It was to appear twice a year and to contain research in the arts and sciences, but not (specifically) theology proper (though there were three professors of theology, Newman had deliberately refused to set up a faculty on his own authority, but had handed over responsibility for this to the Irish hierarchy). Newman had been insistent that the professors should not be 'overburdened with lectures', so that they would have time for writing and research.[162] (The fact that in the *Discourses* he had maintained that universities were primarily teaching rather than research institutions did not mean that research was in any way excluded.) Perhaps the *Atlantis* might be one way in which he could keep up a connection with the University, even if he had to give up the rectorship completely.

In September 1857 he had completed an article for the opening number on 'The Mission of St. Benedict'. The essay begins with a division of the history of Catholic education into three periods, the ancient, the medieval, and the modern, each of which Newman sees as typified by one of three religious orders, the Benedictines, the

---

[157] Ibid. 214.   [158] Ibid. 217.   [159] Ibid. 221 n. 3.

[160] *AW* 294.   [161] *LD* xviii. 218.   [162] *Campaign* 110.

Dominicans, and the Jesuits. To St Benedict is assigned as 'his discriminating badge, the element of Poetry; to St. Dominic, the Scientific element; and to St. Ignatius, the Practical'.[163] Newman calls the
monastic life 'the most poetical of religious disciplines' because it was 'a
return to that primitive age of the world', to 'the simple life' in which
poetry is predominant rather than reason or science. Without
attempting here to define poetry, he contrasts it with reason or science in
the sense that it 'delights in the indefinite and various as contrasted with
unity, and in the simple as contrasted with system', for it 'demands, as its
primary condition, that we should not put ourselves above the objects in
which it resides, but at their feet; that we should feel them to be above
and beyond us, that we should look up to them, and that, instead of
fancying that we can comprehend them, we should take for granted that
we are surrounded and comprehended by them ourselves'.[164] In its
'flight from the world,'[165] monasticism sought for 'such a rest of intellect
and of passion as . . . is full of the elements of the poetical'.[166] Nor did
monasticism spread on a plan or system, but 'with a silent mysterious
operation . . . and through the romantic adventures of individuals'.[167]
But Newman is careful to emphasize that though the monks preferred
the country to the town, they 'were not dreamy sentimentalists, to fall in
love with melancholy winds and purling rills, and waterfalls and
nodding groves; but their poetry was the poetry of hard work'.[168] The
purpose of St Benedict was neither poetical nor romantic, but the
history of Benedictinism is highly 'romantic'.[169] Because (like Oratorians) the early monks did not engage in theological controversy or
speculation, that did not prevent them from quietly studying the
Scriptures and the Fathers. In a second article, 'The Benedictine
Centuries',[170] which appeared in the January number of 1859, Newman
used a bold topical analogy for the growth of primitive monasticism,
which he called 'a sort of recognized emigration from the old world', in
which 'thousands took their departure year after year' in quest of 'the
true *eldorado* or gold country'.[171] As for the scholarship of Benedictine
monasteries, it reminds him of an older Oxford which 'thought little of
science or philosophy by the side of the authors of Greece and Rome'.[172]
He does not say so, but their conservative theology ('a loving study and
exposition of Holy Scripture, according to the teaching of the Fathers')
may also recall the Oxford of the Tractarians. Keenly aware of the
limitations of a static theology, Newman, for all his natural sympathy for
it, does not hesitate to point out that unlike patristic and scholastic

---

[163] *HS* ii. 366.   [164] Ibid. 386–7.   [165] Ibid. 375.   [166] Ibid. 386.
[167] Ibid. 388.   [168] Ibid. 398.   [169] Ibid. 400.
[170] Republished in *Historical Sketches* under the title 'The Benedictine Schools'.
[171] *HS* ii. 436.   [172] Ibid. 466.

theology, monastic theology involved no 'creative action of the intellect'; whereas the Fathers themselves were 'authors of powerful, original minds, and engaged in the production of original works'. Merely to conserve is not necessarily to preserve true doctrine when new problems arise: 'There is no greater mistake, surely, than to suppose that a revealed truth precludes originality in the treatment of it.' Indeed, the 'reassertion of what is old with a luminousness of explanation which is new, is a gift inferior only to that of revelation itself'.[173] A further article which he had planned on the Dominicans was unfortunately never written. After a criticism of what he had said about the Benedictines, he was afraid to write more about the religious orders without a great deal more research. Later he remarked rather sadly, 'It has been my misfortune through life, never to have been able to devote myself to one subject in consequence of the urgent calls upon me of the passing hour, so that I have ever been beginning and never ending.' It weighed upon him that his life had been 'cut up so that I have followed out nothing, and have got just a smattering of many things, and am an authority in none'.[174]

In the spring of 1858 he began work on a highly technical article on St Cyril of Alexandria's christology, which was published in the July number for 1858.[175] It was only fitting that the Rector should contribute some of his great patristic learning to the University's research journal. Newman was a bit worried about 'the ticklish part'[176] at the beginning, which acknowledged that revealed doctrines, which 'are from the nature of the case above our intellectual reach', required for their formal definition a new technical terminology 'not definitely supplied by Scripture or by tradition, nor for centuries by ecclesiastical authority'. It was therefore inevitable, he boldly stated, that in the early Church there was in fact 'variety in the use, and confusion in the apprehension' of these 'new words, or words used in new senses'.[177] In spite of his slight unease at the possible reaction, the article was approved by Fr. O'Reilly.

On 15 April 1858, evening lectures for part-time students at the University resumed. Ninety 'young men of the Middle Class' attended. Newman had had the idea before the University opened, on the lines of the experimental courses that had begun at King's College, London in 1848. And evening classes had been organized when the University opened in 1854. But they had been discontinued because of the poor attendance. This was the result not only of the bad weather, but of the failure to retain the attention of young men who had 'been all day in the

---

[173] Ibid. 475–6.   [174] *LD* xxviii. 130; xix. 508.
[175] 'St. Cyril's Formula . . . ', *TT* 329–82.
[176] *LD* xviii. 357.   [177] *TT* 335.

shops'. Sceptical as he was of the students' 'power of attention', and unwilling to turn his professors into 'mere popular Lecturers', the Rector none the less agreed that the demand for a resumption of the lectures should be met if possible. He had to admit that it was 'a great thing to *employ* the time of young men of an evening', and that it was 'better they should be awake or asleep in a lecture room, than in many other places which they might otherwise frequent'. Apart from that, in theory, 'a system of such Lectures is highly desirable.'[178] Later in the year, Newman was to address these sleepy, inattentive students in one of the last lectures he gave in Dublin. But not before he had expressed scepticism about the future of their evening classes without some kind of an examination leading to a diploma. In general he saw that the 'Examination system is the key to the whole University Course',[179] since the examinations inevitably dictate the way subjects are taught and studied.

During January, February, and March 1858 Newman wrote six leading articles for Henry Wilberforce's *Weekly Register* on 'The Catholic University'. Cullen apparently had complained that the University was not being advertised enough in the press, so Newman first wrote three provocative letters under a pseudonym to the paper, maintaining that the University was really an Irish institution which had got nothing to do with English Catholics, who had their own colleges where they could obtain external degrees from London University. He argued that the failure of English Catholics to support the University proved his point. The idea was to stir up some controversy, and Newman got Robert Ornsby, one of the two Classics professors, to write in defence of the University; but the response was poor, and Newman noted with disgust that not 'a word came in advocacy of the University from any English College or centre'.[180] It was becoming more and more clear to him that whatever its prospects, the University was likely to remain essentially Irish, and had no real claims on him. And yet when he had first accepted the rectorship, he had assumed the University was intended for all English-speaking Catholics, not just the Irish; this, after all, was how the original University Committee had first advertised it to English Catholics in 1851, and how the Rector himself always referred to it in his reports to the Irish bishops. The articles drew attention to the achievements and strengths of the University, singling out for special attention the religious importance of a Catholic medical faculty and the academic significance of the *Atlantis*. And Newman was careful to justify the appointment of so many professors when there were so few students,

[178] *LD* xviii. 263.   [179] Ibid. 445.   [180] *AW* 330.

on the grounds that it was the professors who would have to attract the students by creating the demand through their own abilities.

As for the Rector himself, Ornsby wrote feelingly to him: 'Your unsparing exertions—in the whole idea and scheme and each point of it, worked out step by step, with nothing to blame yourself for—statutes—lectures—essays—sermons—the church and all its cost and troubles, with the provoking treatment you have sustained, and all this merely the visible points of a whole world of business and vexation; I can only wonder you have not broken down under it long before.'[181]

Still no Vice-Rector had been appointed, and until that was done Newman adamantly refused to go to Dublin. He was determined not to have to bear the responsibilities of the Vice-Rector as well. In fact, the Archbishops had been looking for a Vice-Rector, but they did not consult Newman. ('They had given me up, or at least Dr Cullen had'.[182]) Since the beginning of February he had refused to accept any salary. There was one advantage in this stalemate: Newman thought his absence had 'done considerable good, by putting the Professors on their mettle—and making them advertise themselves'. But there was no question that morale was low: 'The state of the young men is suffering considerably—and this is our real evil, though we try to remedy it.' There was, however, a move on the part of Cullen (without telling the Rector) to secure a charter for the University from the government. Ironically, in view of the battles and controversies ahead, Newman himself wondered if this concession might be obtained by Catholics 'giving up the right to a position in the English Universities' and 'the power, with other religious communions, of setting up Halls there'.[183] There was no doubt that Rome was very hostile to Catholics attending non-Catholic universities, and the bishops would follow whatever directives were issued. As for educated English Catholics who would be in favour of Catholic halls or colleges at Oxford, Newman could 'not sympathise with them from my great dislike of mixed education'. He felt confident that, with a charter, the Catholic University ought to become 'as attractive to Catholic youths, as Trinity [Dublin] can be, or even Oxford'.[184] Not that recognized degrees, although obviously desirable, were absolutely essential; entry to the army, for example, and the Indian Civil Service was by open examination. More important than degrees, which not many students would in fact take, was recognition by the state. If a charter could not be obtained, Newman advocated an affiliated connection with the degree-conferring Queen's University, as opposed to the totally integrated status of one of the constituent Queen's

[181] *LD* xviii. 222 n. 2.   [182] Ibid. 359 n. 1.   [183] Ibid. 343.
[184] Ibid. 501.

Colleges; 'but the two are so closely associated together in the minds of the people of Ireland' that he never 'got one single person to second me'.[185] On the model of Louvain, he thought the University should award its own theological degrees, while other degrees would be obtained from the Queen's University. This would be greatly preferable to affiliation with the secular London University, which would certainly refuse the Catholic University the right to have its own examiners in sensitive subjects like history and philosophy.

Not only was Newman confident that the July number of the *Atlantis* would be 'a prodigy',[186] but he began to think about the possibility of starting up a university press. There were also plans afoot for the establishment of a faculty of law and the erection of museums. If a charter could be secured, although it would not bring any 'immediate *direct* benefit', at least it seemed to Newman's tactical mind that 'to succeed is of great importance from the fact that it *will* be success'.[187] In July he wrote a letter on behalf of the University staff to Disraeli, who was then Chancellor of the Exchequer and Leader of the House of Commons, petitioning for a charter. When Cullen heard of this and wrote at last to tell Newman of his own attempt to sound out the government on a charter, he spoke, Newman noted wrily, as if the Rector had never resigned, but had merely absented himself because he had been 'troubled and annoyed'.[188] Cullen was suffering from chronic insomnia, which seriously affected his health. At the end of August he wrote complaining to Cardinal Barnabò about Newman's extravagance in nominating so many professors with so few students, and about the discipline at the Rector's University House, where the students went dancing and riding in a manner suitable to Oxford but not to a country where the University was being supported by the pennies of the poor. With a non-resident Rector, he concluded, and with MacHale's bitter opposition, it was hard to see how the University could be kept going. Then, in October, Archbishop Leahy, whose own residence as Vice-Rector had been somewhat intermittent, wrote to ask Newman to spend much longer in Dublin during the forthcoming academic year than he had in the last, but without alluding to the limited nine weeks' residence which the Archbishops had accepted in 1857 as an experiment for a year. This letter possibly crossed with one from Newman written the day before and containing the pointed request that since for the last year 'I have been holding the Rectorship only provisionally until a successor is appointed', he would be very grateful 'if they proceeded to the appointment of a new Rector'.[189] Leahy replied that the bishops would

[185] *LD* xviii. 77.   [186] Ibid. 386.   [187] Ibid. 397.   [188] Ibid. 420.
[189] Ibid. 473.

probably not be meeting again that year, and asked Newman to consider the possibility of helping the University through the crisis by spending 'some time' in Dublin during the next year or two. With exasperation, Newman noted, 'I was quite ready to do so,—so was the Oratory,—if the Archbishops would grant my conditions, which were not unreasonable.' 'If they wished me to stop,' he wondered, '*why* did they not grant them?'[190] The fact was that Cullen was not prepared to allow only partial residence. Leahy again wrote to tell Newman that in his view the solution to the whole problem lay in the removal of the Birmingham Oratory, or a part of it, to Dublin, since 'The Oratory in Birmingham . . . dwindles . . . to a small thing in comparison with the Catholic University, for which . . . it is my belief that Providence was preparing you long years before your secession from the Church of England.'[191] Tempting as the suggestion might have been in different, happier circumstances, Newman knew now that his only course was to resign the rectorship. His memories were very pleasant, apart from his treatment by Cullen and MacHale; it was a 'mortification . . . to separate myself from persons I love so much and from a work to which all my human feelings so much incline me'. This was in reply to John O'Hagan, a Young Irelander and the Professor of Political Economy, who wrote that 'so far as regards the Irish Professors in the University (I speak of those whom I know as laymen) . . . We have always felt that you only wanted power and freedom of action to make the institution march.'[192] As for the 'silent, impenetrable'[193] Cullen, it was now clear to Newman that he was 'perfectly impracticable,'[194] and that further dealings with him would be useless: 'He has treated me from the first like a scrub . . . he never has done any thing but take my letters, crumple them up, put them in the fire, and write me no answer.'[195] It was not that the Rector was singled out for special treatment: Cullen's 'great fault' in Newman's eyes was that 'he makes no one his friend, because he will confide in no body, and be considerate to no body'.[196] It was a wonder really he did not 'cook his own dinners,' he was so distrustful of everyone.[197]

On 26 October 1858 Newman set off for Dublin for the last time. On 2 November he gave a lecture to the evening classes, called 'Discipline of Mind', in which he again reiterated the need for an educated Catholic laity, but warned against 'the mere diversion of the mind' as opposed to 'its real education'.[198] On the third and the fourth he delivered consecutively 'Literature', a lecture for the Faculty of Philosophy and Letters, and 'Christianity and Medical Science', the lecture given to

---

[190] Ibid. 474.   [191] Ibid. 478.   [192] Ibid. 483.
[193] Ibid. 491.   [194] Ibid. 490.   [195] Ibid. 487.
[196] Ibid. xvii. 220.   [197] Ibid. xix. 379.   [198] *Idea* 393.

medical students. All three were later published among the lectures and essays which form the second part of the *Idea of a University*. On the evening of the fourth he left for Birmingham. He was never to see Ireland again. Later, he calculated that he had 'crossed the St. George's Channel 56 times in the service of the University'.[199] On the twelfth he sent to the Archbishops his formal resignation of the rectorship. It was seven years to the day since his appointment.

In retrospect, Newman thought that he ought never to have accepted the rectorship in the first place without the full confidence of all the Irish Archbishops (even though MacHale had originally voted for his appointment), without the formal participation of the English bishops, without lay control of the finances, and without a mutual agreement on the length of his annual residence in Dublin and the term of his rectorship. These conditions would not of course have been met, but if they had been, perhaps his relations with Cullen would not have been so fraught with difficulties and tensions, nor would his responsibilities to the Oratory have complicated matters as they did. Had the Archbishops been united, too, perhaps there would not have been that desperate 'reign of impenetrable silence'.[200] Anyway, there was consolation to be found in the consideration that sooner or later he would have wanted to resign because of the strain; what was needed was a younger, more vigorous, Irish Rector. Moreover, the more Irish the University, the more likely, suspected Newman, it was to get a charter.

When years later he reflected on his connection with the Catholic University, he concluded that if the Pope 'had known more of the state of things in Ireland', he would never have decreed the University, even though he could not have officially recognized the Queen's Colleges. His earlier belief that history on the whole showed that 'a gift of sagacity' characterized the acts and policies of the papacy, had been 'considerably weakened as far as the present Pope is concerned'.[201] He certainly no longer believed that the Pope 'is divinely guided in all he does'.[202] As for Ireland, he had been 'a poor innocent' and had 'relied on the word of the Pope, but from the event I am led to think it not rash to say that I knew as much about Ireland as he did'.[203] However, he had to admit that even without the Pope's 'express wish', he would have wanted to take part in establishing the University, since he had 'from the very first month of my Catholic existence, when I knew nothing of course of Catholics, wished for a Catholic University'.[204]

[199] *AW* 333.
[200] *LD* xviii. 517.
[201] *AW* 320.
[202] *LD* xii. 214.
[203] *AW* 320.
[204] *LD* xxvi. 58.

12

The Idea of the Laity

DURING the year that Newman continued as Rector but was no longer in residence, he was still heavily involved in the affairs of the University. But, in spite of the burden of correspondence with Dublin, fresh developments in England were increasingly occupying his attention. The English Catholic community had been revitalized and enormously strengthened, intellectually by the wave of conversions from the Oxford Movement and numerically by the influx of Irish immigrants. The restoration of the hierarchy had given it a new status, and the resulting Papal Aggression agitation had unified Catholics and closed the ranks in the face of a common foe. But the phenomenal growth of a tiny, despised sect into a major religious body brought with it new strains and tensions. The clash with the London Oratory turned out to be the prelude for Newman of a much larger conflict, in which similar principles were at stake, although the issue was no longer the nature of the Oratory, but the nature of the Church itself; the problem became not how to be an Oratorian, but how to be a Catholic in the nineteenth century. Back in 1856 Newman had guessed that it suited Faber and Wiseman that he should be out of the way in Dublin. It was not very long before his disappearance from the scene would be welcome to other people as well, for other and more important reasons.

Newman certainly did not see himself as a theologian in any technical sense of the word. If he had an intellectual mission, apart from education, it lay in the field of apologetics—not in narrow polemic against Anglo-Catholics over the claims of Rome, but in a philosophical justification of 'the Church and its position in the world in the 19th century as confronted with, and as against the penetrating knowledge, learning and ability of the scientific men and philosophers of the day'. These words conclude a short paper of notes dated 12 March 1857, which he called 'the beginning of a large work'.[1] In January 1857 he had told J. M. Capes (originally an opponent of the Tractarians, who had been converted to Rome in 1845 and subsequently founded the *Rambler* in 1848) that he was 'opposed to laymen writing Theology, on the same principle that I am against amateur doctors and still more

---

[1] See *Ward* i. 423–5. See also *LD* xvii. 534 n. 1.

lawyers', not because they were laymen, but because they were self-taught. He himself had not written on dogmatic theology proper since he became a Catholic, 'because I gave up private judgment when I became one'.[2] The subject had arisen because of an article on original sin, of which Newman disapproved as being unorthodox, by Richard Simpson, the literary critic and Shakespearian scholar, who had become a Catholic in 1846. But the reason for Newman's writing was not to attack Simpson, but to commiserate with Capes, who had written complaining about an (anonymous) assault by Wiseman in the *Dublin Review* on the *Rambler* for causing dissension by advocating an improvement of educational standards among Catholics. Thus from the beginning of the *Rambler* controversy Newman was caught in the middle ground between the two opposing sides, between the 'liberal' and the Ultramontane parties. The vital dogmatic principle was to be carefully safeguarded, but without recourse to anti-intellectualism.

Also in January 1857, plans began to be considered for the foundation of a new Catholic school. One obvious difficulty was the likely hostility of already existing schools, which would have the support of the bishops, who, without proper autonomous seminaries, still depended on them for the support of their seminarians. Newman thought they should begin with younger boys and see how things developed. The idea of the Birmingham Oratory running a school appealed to Newman: it would give him an outlet for his interest in education. More was involved than simply setting up another Catholic school: there was the need for a new kind of school to cater for the needs of converts who wanted a typical English public school education for their sons, which would also be Catholic, but without the narrowness of English Catholic schools. As Sir John Simeon, the close friend and neighbour of Tennyson, who had become a Catholic in 1851, remarked in a letter, what was required was 'Eton, minus its wickedness, and plus the inculcation of the Catholic faith'; and Newman was the person who was ideally suited for the task because, unlike some other converts (especially Oratorians), who seemed determined 'to denationalize the English Catholic, and to set up as a model for his imitation, some foreign type', Newman had not rejected his English past on becoming a Catholic.[3]

Newman saw a connection between the letters he had received from Capes and Simeon, independent as the two complaints were. On 7 May 1857 he wrote from Dublin to St John:

It seems to me that a time of great reaction and of great trial is before us . . . it seems to me that really I may be *wanted* in England, and that there may be a providential reason . . . for me to return. I have too little perhaps made myself

---

[2] *LD* xvii. 504.   [3] Ibid. xviii. 17 n. 1.

felt—and, while some like Fr Faber are going ahead without fear, others are in consequence . . . backing and making confusion.

The Bishops are necessarily engaged in the great and momentous ecclesiastical routine . . . meanwhile, the party of the aristocracy and the party of talent are left to themselves without leaders and without guides.

It makes me wish I were to live twenty years in full possession of my mind—for breakers are ahead.[4]

Amongst other possibilities, he was thinking of turning his attention again to the question of religious faith. W. G. Ward, who had become a Catholic shortly before Newman in 1845, and who had been teaching first philosophy and then theology at St Edmund's College, Ware, had recently urged him to return to the subject as soon as he was relieved of his duties in Dublin. An interest in the philosophical nature of faith was what united the two converts, whose views on the Church were to diverge more and more as time went on. Unlike other of his opponents, Newman always found Ward disarmingly candid and frank. Ward had made no bones about his disapproval of the emphasis Newman had placed on the secular liberal arts as opposed to theology in his idea of the university. For his part, Newman had made no secret about his objection to a layman teaching theology in a seminary. By coincidence, both men were in fact about to resign their positions; both were to make their influence felt in the years ahead by means of their writings.

In July 1857 Newman found himself again in correspondence with Ambrose Lisle Phillipps; this time, the subject was not architecture but ecumenism. Earlier in the year, Phillipps had contributed letters to the newly founded Anglo-Catholic *Union* newspaper advocating the corporate reunion of the Church of England with Rome. Newman had been critical of the implication that the Church of England enjoyed as an ecclesiastical body a 'religious existence'; he thought that it was as odd to pray for the Established Church as such as to pray for the 'Fishmongers Company as such', in contradistinction to individual Anglicans or fishmongers.[5] However, even if he could not recognize the Church of England as a church, he told Phillipps that he appreciated that it was in the long-term interests of Catholicism that high Anglicans 'should not join us, but should remain to leaven the mass'—although as individuals he had not the 'heart' to try and persuade 'them to preach to others, if they themselves thereby become castaways'. Nor was he 'one of those who wish the Church Establishment of England overthrown'.[6] As for corporate reunion, he was only against discussions if 'persons, who ought to be Catholics, should allow themselves to *bargain* and make *terms*'.[7] But he was also afraid that the apparently friendly noises from

<hr>

[4] Ibid. 30.   [5] Ibid. 12.   [6] Ibid. 70–1.   [7] Ibid. 78.

Rome might turn out to be deceptive: 'they know so little of the English character, and have so little tact, (as much as I should have in dealing with the Sepoys,) that they may give great offence, as soon as ever they emerge out of the vague terms of courtesy and kindness which Christian charity will elicit from them at the outset.'[8] Unlike other converts, including Henry Wilberforce, who was attacking the *Union* in his *Weekly Register*, Newman was anxious not to discourage any promising movement among Anglo-Catholics; a certain 'economy' was necessary in dealing with them: 'they cling to points which never can be granted, but to tell them so' might 'throw them back'.[9] As for Anglican Orders, he had never 'been able to prove them not valid by any clear logical process, and I was surprised, when I got to Rome in 1846, to find various persons there in the belief that they were valid, and none, I think, clear that they were not'. On the other hand, there were 'many strong *indirect* proofs against their validity', as well as 'many reasons for *wishing* them invalid'. After all, it was not uncommon for consecrated bread left over from the Communion service to be scattered to the birds, and the wine poured back into the bottle to be drunk perhaps 'at a vestry merry meeting'. Was it possible that God could have permitted such sacrilege for 300 years if the Church of England possessed true priestly orders?[10] Tractarians argued that the doctrine of the Real Presence implied a priesthood; but by analogy, one could argue that the Real Presence implied a rite to protect it, whereas the absence of any such ritual in the Anglican service implied that Christ was not in fact sacramentally present in the Catholic sense in the Anglican eucharist. Phillipps pointed out that Catholic apostate clergy had also been guilty of sacrilege, but thanked Newman warmly for his sympathy, which contrasted with the hostility shown by other converts. On 8 September the 'Association for the Promotion of the Unity of Christendom' was founded in London at Phillipps's instigation. Catholics were not forbidden to join, although Wiseman was wary of anything that might discourage individual conversions.

At the end of August Newman received a letter from Wiseman informing him that the bishops at the Synod of Westminster in July 1855 had entrusted him with the task of preparing a new English translation of the Bible. He was to choose his own collaborators, who would presumably be Oratorians. It was noticeable not only that he had not been consulted in the first place, but that over two years had since elapsed. Newman suspected that the original intention had been to give the work to the London Oratory, but to use his 'name and general superintendence'. At the time of the bishops' meeting he was already in

---

[8] *LD* xviii. 91.   [9] Ibid. 100.   [10] Ibid. 104.

Ireland, fully committed to his work there. Although his own bishop had mentioned it to him at the time, Wiseman had chosen to say nothing official, presumably because of the quarrel with the London Oratory which had begun just when the bishops' resolutions were being sent to Rome for approval. Newman could only assume that Wiseman had 'waited to the last minute, hoping things would come straight'.[11] Newman's own feeling was: 'there is no work I should less have liked committed to me. I had cut out my own work for myself—for which I consider myself adapted—and here comes an undertaking, which I cannot decline, to occupy the few years of mental vigour which may remain to me.'[12] The 'two works' he had '*wished* to undertake, in what remains of life, were an argument for Theism and a review of the mythical theory of the Gospel History'.[13] On the other hand, it was extremely important for the Birmingham Oratory to find its 'place, *as an Oratory*, in the English Church', which was 'a reason for doing the New Version ourselves, if we possibly can'. It was also a reason for starting a school. They had to be seen to 'do *things which secular Priests cannot do*'. Otherwise, what was the point of a number of priests living together in one house? It was essential to 'exhibit a visible, tangible, serviceableness, in that red brick house which stands upon a triangular island close to the Plough and Harrow [hotel]'.[14] Newman would not always be there to defend his Oratory, which did not have the protection of a regular religious order, and until it was 'something more than a flourishing mission', they stood 'a chance in time to come of being swept away', because, although 'the parochial work which we have actually done and are doing is *very* important', still they had to show a 'visible utility more than the average'. The Oratory was 'a most versatile, elastic, institution, and can take any sort of work'; all that mattered was to have 'a real work'. There was no problem about finding a sphere for action in London, but in Birmingham there were very few educated Catholics for an Oratorian apostolate, while the dearth of well-to-do Catholics meant that the church collection scarcely covered the expenses of the sacristy, let alone supported the mission. Unless they could make conversions among the wealthy Protestants in the neighbourhood, which did not seem very likely, the only alternative seemed to be some kind of educational work, if they were to be more than simply a parish. It was good that followers of St Philip should be despised, but 'there is a certain point of contempt', Newman ruefully noted, 'which leads from being ignored to being annihiliated.'[15]

Accordingly, he proposed to Wiseman that a 'scriptorium' should be

---

[11] Ibid. 191.   [12] Ibid. 134.   [13] Ibid. 326.
[14] Ibid. 159.   [15] Ibid. 165–6.

set up in the Birmingham Oratory, where he and three other members of the house, together with two other non-Oratorian scholars, would work on the translation. None of the London Oratorians were included, although Faber had been on a tentative list of helpers he had drawn up in 1855. A week after his letter to Wiseman, a review appeared in the *Weekly Register* by Faber full of praise of a recent translation of a devotional work by St John and of the work of the Birmingham Oratory, praise which Newman resented as impertinent and patronizing. But he thought he saw the motive for it: 'He is the fox, complimenting you [St John] on your beauty, and hoping to get hold of the cheese, which is myself.'[16] Wiseman, he guessed, had told Faber to 'sooth' and 'coax' Birmingham, when he saw that Newman intended to exclude the London Oratory from the work.[17]

In January 1858 Newman went to see Ullathorne about the projected Oratory school; he was relieved to find that not only did the bishop not object, but he actually welcomed the prospect of a separation of Catholic schools from seminaries. Newman thought that up to fifty boys could be accommodated on the top floor of the Oratory house (which would be self-contained); a new building could be built alongside, in front of the temporary church, which would contain the school rooms. The Oratory would provide a headmaster and the necessary spiritual services, but not the teaching staff. Among the laymen who were involved in the plan was the young baronet Sir John Acton, who had been educated at Oscott and then at Munich as a private pupil of Döllinger, who had deeply influenced him both as a historian and as a liberal Catholic. Acton told Newman that the London Oratory regarded the proposal as against the Oratorian Rule; he also wrote to Döllinger to express his astonishment at the contemptuous hostility towards Newman of many of the converts. All the laymen interested in the school wanted it to be under the control of Newman, but some were less enthusiastic about its connection with the Oratory. Newman himself stipulated that the Birmingham Oratory would commit itself for not more than twenty years, and that strictly speaking the school would not be the responsibility of the community as a whole, but only of Newman and the prospective headmaster, Nicholas Darnell (who had been one of Faber's original 'Wilfridians', after resigning an Oxford fellowship to become a Catholic). Thus the school would be no more un-Oratorian than any other of the projects associated with the Oratory and looked after by individual Oratorians; in fact it would be less so, since their original Brief had directed them to the educated class.

Newman learned that Ullathorne was now uneasy about the school,

[16] *LD* xviii. 175.   [17] Ibid. 175, 191.

partly perhaps because Wiseman (influenced by Faber) was against it, and partly because he was afraid the discipline would be too lax. Newman admitted, 'I have it as little in me to be a good schoolmaster ... as to be a good rider or successful chess player. But this does not hinder my feeling the *need* of strict discipline for boys—for many a man approves what he cannot practise.' No doubt Ullathorne had heard 'stories about our goings on in Dublin, which, though not so exact and well managed as I should like them to be, are not what some good people represent them'. The fact that Newman did not think the discipline of a university should be like that of a school did not mean that he therefore thought a school should resemble a university in this respect. Anyway, the Vice-Rector, not the Rector, was supposed to have been in charge of discipline at Dublin. As for Ullathorne's suspicion that converts in general thought the discipline in Catholic schools too strict, Newman commented: 'The only point of *principle* on which we should differ from the Colleges, is that we should aim at doing every thing above board— and abjure espionage, listening at doors etc.' The great thing was to encourage openness and trust.[18] On 21 April the Birmingham Oratory formally decreed that Darnell should undertake the school as Newman's representative, but without any teaching commitment on the part of the rest of the community. Newman felt 'great and dark suspense' about the success of the venture, considering 'the great blows we have, whenever we attempt any thing'.[19] As always for him, the real trial was 'being in *suspense*', the 'misery is the beginning *in* twilight';[20] nor was this the same as the inevitable uncertainty of 'having to begin without seeing endings'.[21]

During 1858 he had become seriously anxious and worried about the Oratory. In January he had been to see a specialist in London about apparent heart palpitations; to his relief, the complaint was diagnosed as the effect of the indigestion he had long suffered from. On his return to Birmingham, he found Flanagan seriously ill in bed with bronchitis. He was the hardest worker in the community, ready to turn his hand to anything. Then, towards the end of February, Henry Bittleston (who had joined the community in 1850, after being received into the Church by Newman in 1849) fell seriously ill with pleurisy. Both went abroad to recuperate. Newman took on their confessional duties in the church, which gave him the opportunity of observing that out of a congregation of more than 600 there seemed to be a disproportionate number of women. He also replaced Flanagan as novice-master, having the previous year given his opinion that novices should be given as much freedom and personal responsibility as possible. A dozen novices could

---

[18] Ibid. 314–15.   [19] Ibid. 341.   [20] Ibid. 352.   [21] Ibid. 361.

not make up for the loss of Flanagan; and while an Oratory should not normally 'want novices except like so many drops now and then falling upon it',[22] there was still an urgent need for new members. At one point in the summer holidays, Newman found himself virtually alone in the house, and felt ashamed when visitors came who witnessed the depleted state of the community. He was embarrassed by his new, unfamiliar, pastoral duties, afraid that he might confuse penitents, and worried that a baptism he had to perform was not valid ('The water was exhausted out of the abominable shell before I made the three crosses—and I made a hash of it').[23] There seemed no end to the troubles that befell the Oratory, but he wrote encouragingly to Flanagan:

. . . from the first it has been my fortune to be ever failing, yet after all not to fail. From the first I have had bad strokes of fortune—yet on the whole I have made way. Hardly had I begun life, when misfortunes happened to my family—then I failed in the Schools; then I was put out of office at College; then came Number 90—and later the Achilli matter. You talk of 'brilliant success' as not our portion—it is not, because you are all joined to me. When I was a boy, I was taken beyond any thing in Homer, with Ulysses seeming 'like a fool or an idiot,' when he began to speak—and yet somehow doing more than others, as St Paul with his weakness and foolishness.[24]

Newman was also trying to encourage himself. He felt he had the right, if not to despond, at least to complain of St Philip Neri that he could not be 'detached' so long as he had Philip's Oratory on his hands: '*He* has implicated me in the world, in a way in which I never was before, or at least never since my sisters married and my mother died. For his sake I have given up my liberty, and have . . . done, almost as much as if I had married.' Anyway, it was a relief, and not 'an unlawful one', to vent his feelings, like Job, to a few friends.[25] He felt that 'never in my life till this last year have I felt it any thing of a difficulty even for a moment to feel resignation.'[26]

At the end of July he received an invitation from Sir John Acton to meet Döllinger at Aldenham, Acton's country seat in Shropshire. Newman declined, on the ground that he never stayed away from home—apart from his solitary visit to Abbotsford, where he had gone on the orders of Wiseman for reasons of health. However, he saw both Acton and Döllinger when they passed through Birmingham at the end of September. As it turned out, he was very relieved he had not attended the meeting at Aldenham, news of which soon spread. Wiseman (who wanted to know if Newman had attended it) was informed by Talbot in Rome that the object of the meeting was to attack the hierarchy. The

---

[22] *LD* xviii. 338.   [23] Ibid. 378.   [24] Ibid. 271.
[25] Ibid. 376–7.   [26] Ibid. 436.

meeting was attended by Capes, who had told Newman in August that he had begun to doubt Catholicism. When his doubts became publicly known, the wildest rumours spread about the Aldenham meeting, the participants in which (mostly converts) were supposed either to be about to leave the Church or to be intent on subverting it through the medium of the *Rambler*. Newman had decided, with 'full deliberation', not to attend: 'People are strange to say, so watching me, that I find I must be most cautious, for every thing I do is known.'[27] He was well aware that certain people were 'looking at every thing I do in the way of theology', so that he was in constant danger of being 'whispered about at Rome', where he knew he had no friends (apart from the Pope).[28] He was grateful for a review in the December number of the *Rambler* in which Richard Simpson alluded to this self-imposed silence by remarking that the 'oblivion to which Dr. Newman has been assigned in the communion which he has left has found too faithful an echo among ourselves'.[29] Newman was worried that the whispering campaign against him might damage the prospects of the school; but he had no intention of speaking out in defence of himself—truth would prevail, and self-vindication was undesirable in principle. He smiled at the caution of his convert lawyer friends, Bellasis and Hope-Scott, who deleted parts of the school prospectus he had drawn up as imprudent: 'Alas, it has been my fault through life to have spoken out . . . I do really believe it arises from an impatience of not being above-board.'[30] And he wondered why, after all the trouble he had had with the University, he was now involving himself in yet another undertaking likely only to bring him 'anxiety and mortification'.[31]

However, he was more cautious and circumspect about the other project to which he had reluctantly committed himself. At the beginning of December, in reply to a request from the American hierarchy to co-operate with Archbishop Kenrick of Baltimore in preparing a joint translation of the Bible for use in all English-speaking countries, he said that he was happy to co-operate in any way, provided the English bishops were agreeable; he did not want to compete with Kenrick, who had already translated the New and part of the Old Testament from the Vulgate. Wiseman had already been informed of the proposal, but, instead of replying, he merely forwarded the letter to Ullathorne to show Newman. The English bishops, who never responded to the American invitation, also never arranged with Newman the conditions and duration of the copyright which they had agreed should belong to him to cover the heavy expenses of the work. It was becoming clear that Wiseman wanted to throw all the responsibility on Newman, who had already agreed to handle the negotiations with the publishers. And so Newman decided to do nothing till he heard something more from the bishops about the American difficulty. It was a wise decision, as he never heard anything more from the bishops about the matter. Such preliminary plans and preparations as he had made had been a waste of time.

It certainly seemed that Wiseman had washed his hands of Newman personally, of whom he was supposed to have said that he had '*shelved*' himself. Newman had heard from two sources that Faber had in his possession the 1856 letter he had sent Wiseman objecting to the joint dedication to himself and Faber. Faber apparently talked openly about the letter and how the Cardinal had spoken of Newman's 'impudence' and 'insolence' in rejecting his attempt to 'make up matters'. The Duke of Norfolk, among others, had been shown letters of Newman to Faber, who told Sir John Acton that the Duke had commented on reading them, 'Shall we then never have a Saint?' The Duke had promised a donation to the school, but he now withdrew his support. Faber was also supposed to have said that all Newman's enterprises as a Catholic had failed. Newman noted the various reports at the end of December in a memorandum which he called 'Defamatory Talk in London'.[32] It was possible that Faber's hostility might frustrate the foundation of the school.

2

The quarrel between Faber and Newman was to some extent only part of a larger split in the Catholic Church, that was to widen finally into a chasm with the agitation for the definition of papal infallibility. On 30 December Acton, who had become the chief proprietor of the *Rambler*, came to see Newman about a letter that Simpson, who had replaced Capes as editor, had received from Wiseman, complaining about an article in the December issue by Döllinger. Wiseman referred to the possibility of its being denounced to Rome, a course of action which Faber and Dalgairns, whom he had consulted, had strongly recommended. Newman himself had already written to tell Acton that he was 'exceedingly interested' by the article, which attributed 'The Paternity of Jansenism' to St Augustine.[33] Now he correctly guessed that Faber was behind Wiseman's threat. Acton described to Simpson his three-hour talk with 'the venerable Noggs'—

[32] *LD* xviii. 549–50.   [33] Ibid. 525.

who came out at last with his real sentiments to an extent which startled me, with respect both to things and persons . . . I did not think he could ever cast aside his diplomacy . . . so entirely, and was quite surprised at the intense interest he betrayed in the Rambler. He was quite miserable when I told him the news and moaned for a long time, rocking himself backwards and forward over the fire, like an old woman with the toothache.[34]

The next day, Newman wrote to say that he did not see how Rome could condemn taking a 'historical view of the person of heretics, while condemning their writings'. However, he could not help thinking that 'the Rambler was in a false position', in so far as untrained laymen were writing about theology in a secular magazine, and attacking authority into the bargain. In conversation with Acton, he had admitted the misuse of authority, but now he warned that the 'position of the Holy See must be considered, especially in a missionary country', where it 'has to act, to act promptly and forcibly, and is forced to use such instruments as come to hand', to 'adopt courses which are immediately effective, and measure services by what is showy, telling, and successful'. In an imperfect world, even famous saints had been badly treated by Rome. Although it was true that the Holy See had sometimes supported laymen even against their own bishops, this was always because they were acting in defence of Rome itself. By becoming embroiled in theological controversy, the *Rambler* united its opponents; but if it abstained, they would soon fall out among themselves, and the dictum 'All converts are dangerous', which was being applied to Simpson, would soon 'find its fulfilment in other converts'. Newman ended this perceptive and subtle letter by advising the *Rambler* to avoid controversy and to conciliate ordinary Catholic opinion, which naturally sided with authority:

Then it will be able to plant a good blow at a fitting time with great effect—it may come down keen and sharp . . . and without committing itself to definite statements of its own, it may support authority by attacking views which authority will be the first to be jealous of, if the Rambler is not the first to attack them—Power, to be powerful, and strength, to be strong, must be exerted only now and then—It then would be strong and effective, and affect public opinion without offending piety or good sense.[35]

Acton agreed about the need to avoid theology, but doubted if it would be possible to discuss history or politics without also giving offence to those whose bigotry naturally opposed itself to all free inquiry.

As the new year of 1859 began, Newman looked back on the thirteen years he had been a Catholic, during which time he had 'been in many true senses a servant', but for which he had received 'so little thanks from any one', although there 'never was a time, when apparently I am more likely than now to be visited with those suspicions and jealousies which in one shape or other have been my portion through life'. Still, he was aware of 'much secret brooding discontent' among others 'whose zeal and honesty have not been acknowledged'. Moreover, he could not wish himself to be without so light a cross. Nor ought he to forget 'the wonderful act of substantial sympathy shown me by the Catholic body in the Achilli matter, which showed in time of need that I was not forgotten, and balanced all absence of those other acknowledgements to which I have been referring'. Meanwhile, he told his correspondent J. H. Pollen that a 'firm unruffled faith in the Catholic Church' should not preclude giving 'strong expression to our common conviction of the miserable deficiencies which exist'.[36]

He was glad to hear from Acton that Simpson agreed that the *Rambler* should avoid theology: 'I have a great opinion of his powers, and a great respect for his character, and a great personal liking for him . . .'.[37] But he added 'how much' he 'liked' Acton's article in the January issue on the kind of individual liberty which the Catholic doctrine of conscience demanded, a freedom which was better observed in Protestant England than in some Catholic countries.[38] This was a daring comparison to make, when it is remembered that before the Second Vatican Council religious liberty was not even explicitly or officially recognized by the Catholic Church as either desirable or permissible in practice in countries where Catholicism was the official religion, on the ground that error (regardless of the people in error) had no rights. However, Newman was alarmed by another 'very startling' article by a leading government inspector of Catholic schools, implicitly criticizing the bishops for their sectarian refusal to co-operate with a Royal Commission into the state of primary education: Catholic schools received substantial support from the state, and they should not resent an inquiry, even if it involved investigation into the way religion was taught. Violently attacked by the *Tablet* for encouraging disobedience to the bishops, the writer replied that no episcopal decision had been made public, there had been no involvement of the laity, nor were faith and morals involved; the bishops could not object to the loyal expression of views which were irrefutable.

Towards the end of January, Newman wrote to warn Acton that he had heard definitely that the *Rambler* was to be 'denounced at Rome on several grounds' apart from the article by Döllinger.[39] He even wondered if an attempt would be made to link his name with it. In the event, he was asked by Ullathorne to mediate and to secure Simpson's resignation as editor of the *Rambler* on behalf of Wiseman and the other

---

[36] *LD* xix. 10–11.   [37] Ibid. 13.   [38] Ibid. 17.   [39] Ibid. 28.

bishops concerned. Newman told Simpson he was 'exceedingly' pained at 'the very idea of the Rambler, which has done so much for us, and which is so influential, being censured from authority'.[40] To Ullathorne he wrote that Simpson felt aggrieved that he had to make up his mind so quickly and without knowing 'the definite charges, which lie against him, as he might in equity demand'.[41] But he was able to assure the bishops that Simpson was ready to abide by Newman's decision, namely, that he should resign as editor on the understanding that the article on the schools question would not be condemned in the bishops' pastorals. Simpson remained, however, one of the three proprietors of the magazine. He wanted Newman to take over as editor. Although Newman only agreed for the moment to look over the proofs of the next issue, his fateful association with the *Rambler* ('the *name*' of which 'from the first I have never liked')[42] had begun. He suggested that there should be a special section for letters, where controversial material could be deposited more safely. He was well aware that, apart from its tone, which was sometimes felt as offensive, the *Rambler* in fact appealed to a great many Catholics; this was why the bishops were so afraid of it. He tried to comfort Simpson by pointing out that he too had suffered at the hands of Wiseman; however, to 'fret, and to be troubled, does not pay— it is like scratching a wound, instead of letting it heal'.[43] He agreed with Simpson about the bishops' scant regard for the rights of the laity. He was very anxious that the *Rambler* should continue, and it was becoming clear that to enable it to do so he would have to become editor. Wiseman had made it clear that Acton was as unacceptable as Simpson; the only person acceptable to both parties was Newman, who stipulated that he could only contemplate doing the job till the end of the year. It was even in the interests of the bishops that the *Rambler* should continue as a 'safety valve',[44] if nothing else; they were nervously aware of the growing opposition to Wiseman and his policies. For Newman, it was a matter of conscience that he should do anything possible to keep in print a periodical whose '*principles*' he was as anxious to further as he was to moderate its offensive '*tone*'.[45]

On 21 March Newman reluctantly agreed to take on the editorship. It seemed to him the greatest 'mortification' of his life, 'like a bad dream, and oppresses me at times inconceivably'.[46] He drew up a notice for the next issue in May, scrupulously refraining from referring to any change of editorial policy, but also carefully reaffirming the 'animating principle' of the *Rambler*, namely, 'the refinement, enlargement, and elevation of the intellect in the educated classes'. The intention

[40] Ibid. 42–3. [41] Ibid. 45. [42] Ibid. 228. [43] Ibid. 52.
[44] Ibid. 69. [45] Ibid. 76. [46] Ibid. 96.

remained the same—'to combine devotion to the Church with discrimination and candour in the treatment of her opponents; to reconcile freedom of thought with implicit faith; to discountenance what is untenable and unreal, without forgetting the tenderness due to the weak and the reverence rightly claimed for what is sacred; and to encourage a manly investigation of subjects of public interest under a deep sense of the prerogatives of ecclesiastical authority'.[47] He had, in fact, every intention of changing what had given offence, but without apologizing for or criticizing the previous management; their aims were his aims, even if their methods were different. The essential principles had not changed, but to anyone reading between the lines a new caution as well as a new emphasis was obvious. When the new advertisement was published, a warning was inserted that neither theological nor devotional works could be reviewed, since for different reasons they were both unsuitable for discussion in a magazine. Newman knew, of course, that he was caught 'between two fires'.[48] But if he was once again in an impossible position, it was '*because*, as in so many cases in my life, I have done (what I never can repent) what seemed to me at the moment my duty, without looking at consequences'.[49] He had told Acton at the end of 1858 that he did not want to become involved in writing for a periodical, as he felt 'used up—at least for such purposes', too old 'to write with freshness and energy', and 'things seem to have gone past me, and I don't know whom I am likely to influence'. Besides, he was 'very tired' and wanted a rest before he returned to his 'old studies, and to do something, if life is given me, more solid than I have done hitherto'.[50] He refused to write for Henry Wilberforce's paper, for the same reason that it would take him 'from those more arduous subjects, on which I wish to engage myself; and, as Almighty God speaks to the heart when it is in retirement, so does He to the intellect when it is still and at rest'.[51]

Early in April he decided at last to break his silence about Faber and Wiseman. Back in the summer of 1856 he had told his community not to talk outside the house about the rupture with London; news of it would inevitably spread from one person to another until 'the whole affair is thrown upon the judgment of society'. He himself always deliberately refrained from defending himself, since 'dirt does not stick'. It was better anyway that he should be thought 'tyrannical' than that Faber should appear to be 'double-dealing'. To justify oneself was to put oneself in the wrong: besides, 'to plead a cause, and leave it to the decision of a third person, when *nothing can come of it*, is most distasteful to me.'[52] But now he had come to the conclusion that the Oratory was being 'harmed by the tittle tattle in question'. He therefore wrote a very deliberately worded

---

[47] *LD* xix. 88–9.   [48] Ibid. 90.   [49] Ibid. 75.
[50] Ibid. xviii. 547.   [51] Ibid. xix. 24.   [52] Ibid. xvii. 317.

letter, copies of which were shown or sent to various people, including Ullathorne. In it he explained that his refusal to allow Wiseman to make a joint dedication to himself and Faber had been made 'not under the influence of any personal feeling, but on motives of grave duty and with a definite object'. He had not mentioned this letter outside his community; he had not been the cause of any scandal. But Wiseman, through Faber, had made his letter public and commented on it behind his back in the 'most disrespectful terms'. This was only one of several instances in which Faber's Oratory had used their position in London to damage him by making allegations about him which were as false or misleading as they were uncharitable.[53] He told Miss Mary Holmes, whose spiritual director he had been till her conversion to Catholicism in 1844 (after which she became a regular and trusted correspondent), that Wiseman had 'ten thousand good points—but, as an individual, you cannot *trust* him; not from any moral fault, but from his character'. He had used exactly the same words to Henry Wilberforce a couple of years earlier, when he remarked that it was the Achilli affair which had first shown him how unreliable Wiseman was. Now he spoke frankly of Faber:

I never have been so intimate with Fr Faber from any *personal* tie, as to make it strange that I have no personal trust in him now. He was never one of my intimate friends—not at Littlemore—not at Rome. On my return from Rome the Cardinal made him and his people Oratorians. I took them as a duty, and made them my friends. In process of time they swarmed. In the interval I found that there was that in Fr Faber, with all his good qualities and talents, which made it impossible to trust him. I did not even tell my own people here of this.

He was not in the least ashamed about his letter to Wiseman refusing the joint dedication—'there is nothing violent in it.'[54]

3

On 1 May the new school opened its doors to seven boys, all sons of converts, including the nephew of Scott Nasmyth Stokes, the school inspector whose article had had such far-reaching results. It was, in fact, the *Rambler*, not the Oratory School, which made the month of May 1859 a memorable one in Newman's life. On 13 May he received a letter from John Gillow, a professor of theology at Ushaw College, the leading seminary in England, enclosing a pamphlet against Döllinger's article on Jansenism, and protesting against a passage in the May *Rambler*

[53] Ibid. xix. 100–1.   [54] Ibid. 112–13.

about the bishops' recent pastorals on the Royal Commission on education. Newman acknowledged that the passage which Gillow described as 'objectionable' was written by himself. In the passage objected to, Newman, while apologizing for any offence the *Rambler* had inadvertently caused the hierarchy, stated boldly and uncompromisingly his view that the bishops must

really desire to know the opinion of the laity on subjects in which the laity are especially concerned. If even in the preparation of a dogmatic definition the faithful are consulted, as lately in the instance of the Immaculate Conception, it is at least as natural to anticipate such an act of kind feeling and sympathy in great practical questions . . .

And he concluded with a general warning against 'the misery of any division between the rulers of the Church and the educated laity', coupled with a strong plea to the bishops: 'Let them pardon, then, the accidental hastiness of manner or want of ceremony of the rude Jack-tars of their vessel, as far as it occurred, in consideration of the zeal and energy with which they haul-to the ropes and man the yards.'[55]

   Newman immediately wrote back to Gillow, tersely enquiring what the grounds of the objection were. He also informed Ullathorne of the complaint, explaining that in the reference to the definition of the Immaculate Conception, to which Gillow had taken especial exception, he had only been pointing out that 'the Christian people at large were consulted on the *fact* of the *tradition* of the Immaculate Conception in every part of the Catholic world'.[56] He was not very surprised by Gillow's attack: 'Of course the Rambler will get me into trouble, as nearly every thing I do does.'[57] What he did not know was that it was to elicit from him his first original theological work as a Catholic, which marked the beginning of a theology of the Church that was to develop slowly but surely during the next two decades. Gillow wrote to explain that Newman's words seemed to mean that the infallibility of the Church lay with the laity rather than the hierarchy. Newman replied that Gillow had misunderstood the world 'consult':

To the unlearned reader the idea conveyed by 'consulting' is not necessarily that of asking an opinion. For instance, we speak of consulting a barometer about the weather. The barometer does not give us its opinion, but ascertains for us a fact . . . I had not a dream of understanding the word . . . in the sense of *asking an opinion.*[58]

Gillow accepted the explanation without demur: it had never even occurred to him as a theologian to use the word 'consult' in such an untheological sense.

---

[55] *LD* xix. 129–30.   [56] Ibid. 131.   [57] Ibid. 133.   [58] Ibid. 135.

Ullathorne called on Newman on 22 May. He regretted that there seemed to be 'remains of the old spirit' in the *Rambler*: 'It was irritating. Our laity were a *peaceable* set, the Church was *peace*. They had a deep faith—they did not like to hear that any one doubted.' Newman pointed out that he knew from experience that the laity in Ireland, for example, was 'docile' but 'unsettled'. In the course of their talk, the bishop 'said something like, "Who are the laity?" I answered that the Church would look foolish without them ...'. Newman added that he saw his connection with the *Rambler* as 'substantially the same work' as his mission in Dublin.[59] However, it was much less attractive, and even more impossible—

but I suppose it would be allowable in a fire, old as one was, or dignified, to throw off one's coat, tuck up one's shirt sleeves, and work at the pump. And then, if a fireman came and said, 'My good old boy, you are doing your best, but don't you see you are doing nothing but drowning all your friends in your ill directed attempts,' I should with the best heart in the world say, I take your hint, and leave the management of the fire and its extinction to others.[60]

At this interview Ullathorne advised him to give up the editorship after the July number. Newman agreed without hesitation: 'I never have resisted, nor can resist, the voice of a lawful Superior, speaking in his own province.' He had offered to submit any theological articles to censorship, but the bishop pointed out that 'theological difficulties cropped up in half sentences'; however, to submit the whole *Rambler* to 'the slow machinery of a theological revision' would be quite impractical.[61] Newman later reflected that it was

rather strange the Bishop let me off my engagement so easily, or rather pressed a release on me, when I had gained his side of the bargain, and had not paid my own. Though I had rescued Simpson etc. from the Pastorals, I was allowed, or rather urged, to give him back the Magazine. Perhaps it was that the Cardinal etc. were seized with a panic, lest they had got out of the frying pan into the fire.[62]

Still, the original object of removing Simpson as editor had been secured, as Newman was succeeded by Acton. But Newman did not allude to 'retirement' in the July number, any more than he had referred in the May issue to his 'undertaking' the editorship—'I have refused all along to recognise any change of Editors.'[63] The July number in fact was 'nearly entirely written' by him; he had discovered that he '*must do every thing*', and he had been wrong to think that he could be editor 'without its interfering too much with my time'.[64] On the other hand, he told

---

[59] Ibid. 140–1.   [60] Ibid. 144.   [61] Ibid. 149–50.
[62] Ibid. 151.   [63] Ibid. 163.   [64] Ibid. 178–9.

Wilberforce that, although he was accustomed to being 'plucked' from his Anglican days,

> I assure you it has made me feel that my occupation was gone, when the Bishop put his extinguisher on the Rambler. I never meant to have kept it for long— but it is one thing to set a thing off, another to be made throw it away.

Still, he could now look forward to lying 'fallow' for the rest of the year, as he had originally intended doing for the whole of 1859 after resigning from the University and before becoming involved with the *Rambler*. He thought that he might then turn to re-editing some of his Anglican theological works; there were also all his papers to sort out for his literary executors:

> It is some time since I have wished to set my house in order. To look over my papers, burn, arrange and the like. To have done this, will be an amazing comfort to me, for at present everything is in confusion, and I feel like a person who has been long out in the dust and rain, and whose hat, coat and shoes show it. There are many things I want to do for the sake of my *Congregation*; as to *personal* matters my prospect is curious, as most others must feel who are of my age. According as a man dies at 60, 70, or 80 his heirs are different, and his papers come into different hands . . . I have not a notion who it is to be who will read any direction I give . . . This makes it very difficult to determine what to keep and what to destroy. Things most interesting and dear to myself may be worthless in the eyes of those to whom my papers fall. Fancy my properties coming into possession of Dr Ullathorne, whom I mention with all respect—or of others whom, from want of respect for them I don't mention![65]

Before, however, relinquishing the editorship, he was determined to deal more fully with the place of the laity in the Church. The famous article 'On Consulting the Faithful in Matters of Doctrine' was completed in time for the July number. He begins by defending his use of the word 'consult', which he says in ordinary English 'includes the idea of inquiring into a matter of *fact*, as well as asking a judgment'. Thus, for example, a 'physician consults the pulse of his patient; but not in the same sense in which his patient consults *him*'. It is in the former sense that the Church 'consults' or 'regards' the faith of the laity before defining a doctrine. The *Rambler* was written for lay people, not for scholastic theologians, to whom the word 'consult' would naturally signify its Latin sense of 'consult *with*'. But if the laity's 'advice, their opinion, their judgment on the question of definition is not asked', nevertheless, 'the matter of fact, viz. their belief, *is* sought for, as a testimony to that apostolical tradition, on which alone any doctrine whatsoever can be defined'.[66] Newman not only refuses to offer any apology for his use of the word, but implicitly rebukes his critics by remarking, 'if we do not

---

[65] *LD* xix. 181–2.					[66] *Cons.* 54–5.

use the vernacular, I do not see how the bulk of the Catholic people are to be catechised or taught at all.'[67] Because the 'perfect accuracy' of a theological lecture in Latin was lacking, 'a want of this exactness' did not necessarily indicate 'self-will and undutifulness'.[68] On the other hand, as usual, Newman balances his criticism of scholastic orthodoxy by rejecting the suggestion that he is

comparing such precision (far from it) with that true religious zeal which leads theologians to keep the sacred Ark of the Covenant in every letter of its dogma, as a tremendous deposit for which they are responsible. In this curious sceptical world, such sensitiveness is the only human means by which the treasure of faith can be kept inviolate. There is a woe in Scripture against the unfaithful shepherd. We do not blame the watch-dog because he sometimes flies at the wrong person. I conceive the force, the peremptoriness, the sternness, with which the Holy See comes down upon the vagrant or the robber, trespassing upon the enclosure of revealed truth, is the only sufficient antagonist to the power and subtlety of the world, to imperial comprehensiveness, monarchical selfishness, nationalism, the liberalism of philosophy, the encroachments and usurpation of science.[69]

Having defended his use of the word 'consult',[70] he now turns to consider the question, why consult the laity? The answer is plain, he says: 'because the body of the faithful is one of the witnesses to the fact of the tradition of revealed doctrine, and because their *consensus* through Christendom is the voice of the Infallible Church'. There are 'channels of tradition', through which 'the tradition of the Apostles, committed to the whole Church . . . manifests itself variously at various times', none of which 'may be treated with disrespect', even though the hierarchy has sole responsibility for 'discerning, discriminating, defining, promulgating, and enforcing any portion of that tradition'.[71] He himself, he explains, is 'accustomed to lay great stress on the *consensus fidelium*' in order to compensate for the lack of testimony from bishops and theologians in favour of defined points of doctrine. At the time of the definition of the Immaculate Conception, Bishop Ullathorne had referred to the faith of the laity as a 'reflection' of the teaching of the Church, and Newman comments with dry irony: 'Reflection; that is, the people are a *mirror*, in which the Bishops see themselves. Well, I suppose a person may *consult* his glass, and in that way may know things about himself which he can learn in no other way.'[72]

---

[67] Ibid. 56.   [68] Ibid. 62.   [69] Ibid. 61.

[70] It did not satisfy Ullathorne, who pointed out that 'to take advise [*sic*], that is, to seek guidance from another's judgment, is both the Latin sense, the technical theological sense, and the literal and primary English sense of the word' (*LD* xix. 146 n. 1). However, it is not clear what other word Newman could have used to convey his meaning.

[71] *Cons.* 63.   [72] Ibid. 72.

He now proceeds to his celebrated historical example drawn from that period of the early Church's history which he had studied so deeply and intensely as an Anglican. In spite of the fact that the fourth century was the age of great doctors and saints, who were also bishops, like Athanasius, Ambrose, Chrysostom, and Augustine, 'nevertheless in that very day the divine tradition committed to the infallible Church was proclaimed and maintained far more by the faithful than by the Episcopate'. During the Arian heresy, 'in that time of immense confusion the divine dogma of our Lord's divinity was proclaimed, enforced, maintained, and (humanly speaking) preserved, far more by the "Ecclesia docta" than by the "Ecclesia docens" . . . the body of the episcopate was unfaithful to its commission, while the body of the laity was faithful to its baptism.'[73] The importance of the illustration is shown by the fact that it occurred so early in the history of the Church and involved the very identity of Christ. Newman boldly concludes by saying that 'there was a temporary suspense of the functions' of the teaching Church, the unpalatable truth being that the 'body of Bishops failed in their confession of the faith'.[74] The danger of the present time, when the hierarchy was so faithful and orthodox, was that the role of the laity would be neglected—but 'each constituent portion of the Church has its proper functions, and no portion can safely be neglected'. The article ends with an almost defiant challenge, in the well-known words:

I think certainly that the *Ecclesia docens* is more happy when she has . . . enthusiastic partisans about her . . . than when she cuts off the faithful from the study of her divine doctrines . . . and requires from them a *fides implicita* in her word, which in the educated classes will terminate in indifference, and in the poorer in superstition.[75]

Newman avoided discussing in the article whether or not a periodical like the *Rambler* should include theology at all; but he told Acton that if the *Rambler* continued to be as theological as in the past, it would not survive almost certain episcopal condemnation. He advised, more or less as he had done before, that the occasional quasi-theological article, far from being objectionable, 'would come now and then with great effect'. His own article had been exceptional, and had arisen out of a controversy he had inherited. Like the *Edinburgh Review* and *Quarterly Review*, the *Rambler* should stick to secular subjects. He agreed with Acton that Simpson should be advised to turn his attention away from religious subjects (to Mill's *On Liberty*, for example, which had just been published). But even to have him involved in any editorial capacity was dangerous—he would be sure to 'compromise the work', if only by 'some ironical praise to the Cardinal—or even fling at the Holy See'. As for the

---

[73] *Cons.* 75–6.   [74] Ibid. 77.   [75] Ibid. 106.

latter, Simpson failed to distinguish between 'the proceedings of the Holy See' and 'people round about it':

There will necessarily always be round about the Pope second rate people, who are not subjects of that supernatural guidance which is his prerogative. For myself, certainly I have found myself in a different atmosphere, when I have left the Curia for the Pope himself.[76]

In general, he was concerned to insist

that large subjects and delicate subjects want a lengthy and careful treatment *in order to do justice to them*. They cannot be knocked off in a few sentences. There are explanations which *ought* to be given, definitions which are of primary importance in the discussion, relations and bearings on other truths which have to be settled—and if all this is not done, great scandal is caused.[77]

The difficulty was that Simpson appeared to be incapable of writing on any subject without introducing theology. On the other hand, by excluding theology, Acton would be more likely to achieve the real object of the *Rambler*, which was to raise the intellectual level among English Catholics:

The great point is to open men's minds—to educate them—and to make them logical. It does not matter what the subject matter is, which you use for this purpose. If you make them think in politics, you will make them think in religion.[78]

One sees what Newman meant by saying that there was a continuity for him between his Dublin and his *Rambler* work.

4

In the May number of the *Rambler*, Newman had published the first part of a series called 'The Ancient Saints'. It had upset some Catholics with its frank remarks, for which he was criticized in the *Tablet*, on the biographies of saints.

I take but a secondary interest in books which chop up a Saint into chapters of faith, hope, charity, and the cardinal virtues . . . They do not manifest a Saint, they mince him into spiritual lessons.[79]

Now he hesitated to continue the series, 'because it makes enemies, and thus does more harm than at the moment it can do good'.[80] However, another instalment appeared in the November issue, and two more in

---

[76] *LD* xix. 167.   [77] Ibid. 185.   [78] Ibid. 190.
[79] *HS* ii. 229.   [80] *LD* xix. 166.

1860; they were later republished in *Historical Sketches* under the title
'St Chrysostom'.

Newman begins by confessing 'to a delight in reading the lives . . . of
the Saints of the first ages, such as I receive from none besides them; and
for this reason, because we know so much more about them than about
most of the Saints who come after them'. He is 'touched by what I read
about, not by what I myself create', for 'mere imagination does not lead'
him 'to devotion'.[81] What he wants 'to trace and study is the real, hidden
but human, life' of the saints.[82] In their correspondence, particularly,
the early saints have left behind what 'more than any other approaches
to conversation'.[83] Again (like Newman himself), instead of 'writing
formal doctrinal treatises, they write controversy' and 'mix up their own
persons . . . with the didactic or polemical works which engaged them',
writing 'for the occasion, and seldom on a carefully-digested plan'.[84] The
true life of a saint is 'a narrative which impresses the reader with the idea
of moral unity, identity, growth, continuity, personality . . . the
presence of one active principle of thought, one individual character . . .
an inward life'.[85] And if 'history is to mirror the actual course of time, it
must also be a course itself'. Truth, too, Newman remarks pointedly,
should be observed: 'facts are omitted in great histories, or glosses are
put upon memorable acts, because they are thought not edifying,
whereas of all scandals such omissions, such glosses, are the greatest.'[86]
As for St John Chrysostom, he attracts Newman like St Paul because of
his humanity—'his intimate sympathy and compassionateness for the
whole world, not only in its strength, but in its weakness; in the lively
regard with which he views every thing that comes before him, taken in
the concrete'.[87]

Another piece, 'The Mission of the Isles of the North', was published
in the May and July issues, and republished in *Historical Sketches* as 'The
Northmen and Normans in England and Ireland'. It opens with a
tribute to the Irish, including a contrast which reminds one of Matthew
Arnold's comparison of the French and English peasantry—'an
innocence in the young face, and a piety and patience in the aged voice,
which strikingly and sadly contrast with the habits of [England's] rural
population'.[88] When in Ireland, an Englishman comes 'as the representative of persons, and actions, and catastrophies, which it is not pleasant
to any one to think about', as 'one of a strong, unscrupulous, tyrannous
race'.[89] But the writer consoles himself with the thought that it is
'Protestantism which has been the tyrannical oppressor of the Irish', and
their 'serious evils did not begin till the English monarchy was false to

---

[81] *HS* ii. 217.   [82] Ibid. 219.   [83] Ibid. 221.
[84] Ibid. 223.   [85] Ibid. 227.   [86] Ibid. 231.
[87] Ibid. 285.   [88] Ibid. iii. 257–8.   [89] Ibid. 258.

the Pope as well as to Ireland'.[90] The point that Newman, with an eye still on the University in Dublin, wants to make is that although in so many ways dissimilar and alienated, still in obvious ways England and Ireland have always been closely connected with each other, so much so that they 'have seemed to the Pope as one, and as one he has treated them'.[91] The paper remains 'but a fragment', noted Newman, 'in consequence of the author's suddenly retiring from the Editorship of the *Rambler* Magazine'.[92] In fact, however, he was still trying to finish the article in September, although he had become afraid of 'treading on the toes of my Irish friends without knowing it', as well as feeling that he had not read enough on the subject to do justice to it.[93]

Finally, he published several (anonymous) letters in the May, July, and September numbers. In one he raised the sensitive issue as to whether 'temporal prosperity' is a Note of the Church. The standard Catholic response to Protestant strictures on the 'contemptible' state of a country like Italy was to deny it. But Newman admits that he 'cannot see the flaw' in the Protestant argument that religion should be 'the foster-parent, if not the natural mother, of industry, thriftiness, order, honesty, and equitable dealing'. Unfortunately, 'religion must not be merely existing or vegetating in a country', as in Italy, 'but be in a really *vigorous* state, if it is to develop itself in *temporal prosperity*'. He also blames the intellectual and spiritual decadence of the upper classes for the poor government of Italy, a criticism from which the Papal States are not exempted. Good government, however, he insists, is not the result of any particular constitution, as John Bull may like to imagine, but means 'good laws vigorously and impartially enforced'.[94] Typically, he modified his stricture in another letter, in which he pointed out that humiliation and poverty must always be Notes of the Church, as they were characteristics of Christ. In addition, 'intellect, and even moral virtues, will frequently be found dissociated from the Church' because she 'calls especially the poor, the sinful, and the ignorant: not that she calls them *peculiarly*, but because her *including them* repels the rich, the self-righteous, and the intellectual'.[95] In another letter, to which Ullathorne specifically objected, he argued that where 'education is widely promoted, and thought in consequence is active and incessant, it is a great thing to have a safety-valve, lest in particular minds there should be a formidable generation of steam and an explosion'.[96] It was dangerous to try and stop Catholics asking questions, for example about the literal meaning of the Bible, and about what was of faith and what was not.

On 14 July several visitors from the synod which was being held at

---

[90] Ibid. 262.   [91] Ibid. 264.   [92] Ibid. 312.   [93] Ibid. 208–9.
[94] *LD* xix.   [95] Ibid. 540.   [96] Ibid. 530.

Oscott visited the Oratory. They included Manning, who had been sent to remonstrate with Newman about 'On Consulting the Faithful in Matters of Doctrine'. It was Bishop Brown of Newport, a Benedictine from Downside and an old Catholic, who had raised the subject with Wiseman, Ullathorne, and Manning, all of whom agreed that Newman had expressed himself most unfortunately. Newman assured Manning that he had never intended to say that the Church itself had fallen into error during the Arian heresy. At the end of August he received another letter from Gillow saying that the article appeared to contradict the doctrine of the infallibility of the Church. He replied briefly: Gillow had taken the word 'suspense' to mean 'failure', but 'I think it has a meaning far lighter even than "suspension" '; Gillow understood the 'body of the Bishops' to mean the 'Ecclesia docens', but 'I think it merely means the actual mass at the particular time spoken of'. He protested strongly against the gravely offensive implication that he was guilty of heresy. He also made a private note to the effect that he had not meant that 'the (dispersed) body of Bishops were not sound in faith', nor that 'they deliberately gave witness to or taught heresy', but that 'there was a temporary confusion, arising from the number who got puzzled or were deceived or were timid or were heretics such, that, as a cloud obscures the heavens, so the testimony of all was for a time suspended, as being bishop against bishop'—not that there were not 'gleams of confession in the midst of this confusion', just as there 'may be gleams of sun during a cloudy day'.[97] At the beginning of October, Bishop Brown wrote to Rome to complain about the article. He explained that he had asked Manning to write to Newman after no correction or explanation had appeared in the September *Rambler*, but that Newman had still not published anything to offset the heretical impression of the offending article. He had also been in touch not only with Wiseman and Ullathorne but also with Gillow, who had not been satisfied by Newman's reply and who complained that the article had widened the gulf between the old Catholics and the converts, who seemed to be forming a party within the Church. Brown thought that Rome should intervene.

Not only, however, were there two rather different kinds of converts, but not all old Catholics were opposed to converts. On 11 November Newman preached 'The Tree Beside the Waters' at the funeral of Henry Weedall, the President of Oscott, 'whom there is no one I more revere or love in the whole Catholic body'.[98] Weedall was 'one of the old school,—of that old school of Catholics which has characteristics so great and so special'.[99] He is quietly and movingly eulogized under the

---

[97] *LD* xix. 206–7.   [98] Ibid. xviii. 340.   [99] *OS* 260.

image of a tree which 'grows up gradually, silently, without observation; and in proportion as it rises aloft, so do its roots, with still less observation, strike deep into the earth'.[100] He exemplifies Newman's idea of sanctity as consisting in the careful observance of 'routine duties',[101] which constitute a man's 'work *in* his day . . . not the work of any other day, but of his own day', inevitably incomplete, but 'necessary in order to the work of that next day which is *not* his, as a stepping-stone on which we, who come next, are to raise our own work'.[102] An old Catholic like Weedall, Newman suggests, combined complete loyalty to Rome with an unashamed attachment to English traditions.

While at Oscott, Newman heard about Brown's delation of him to Rome, and he wrote him a letter of protest, which he did not send. Ironically, he was himself again busy trying to moderate the *Rambler*'s tone, much as he agreed with the substance of what it had to say on such matters as the distinction between religious indifference and religious tolerance, and the need to improve the educational standards of Catholic schools. Brown had written a second letter to Propaganda at the end of October; he was told that Cardinal Barnabò had been informed, and was not surprised by the new delation, since Newman had been delated already a few years previously (by the London Oratory). Rome now wanted a copy of the offending article and commended Brown's pastoral zeal.

On 13 January 1860 Ullathorne asked to see Newman, who was in bed with a bad cold; St John went instead. When Newman heard that it was about the delation, he immediately got out of bed, though it was late in the evening, and went to see Ullathorne, who had just returned from Rome. (The matter was serious enough, but there was something to laugh at in the bishop's mysterious hint to St John that Newman might return a bishop himself from Rome if he would only go there and explain himself!) It appeared that Barnabò had shown Brown's letters to Ullathorne and told him the Pope was worried about the offending passages. Ullathorne had agreed to take the matter up with Newman. But he had also seen Wiseman, who was in Rome too, and taken up with him the matter of Newman's letter about the joint dedication, which Wiseman had shown to others and about which Newman had written the letter of which Ullathorne had received a copy. He had also referred to the various 'annoyances' to which Newman had been subjected: 'At last the Cardinal burst into tears, and said—"Tell Newman I will do any thing I can for him." '[103] The result was that Newman now agreed to write and tell Wiseman that he was ready to comply with any demands

---

[100] Ibid. 245. [101] Ibid. 246. [102] Ibid. 262. [103] *LD* xix. 276–7.

made by Rome. In view of Newman's own lack of confidence in Wiseman's reliability, it was an unfortunate suggestion.

Newman admitted to himself that he felt 'a considerable temptation to despise and to be angry with various persons who are engaging in this matter—as very shallow, as not knowing the English language—as not looking at the drift and context of what I wrote, but as taking my isolated words to comment on'. As so often before in his life, he saw himself as the 'scapegoat'—just as it was he, not Wiseman, who had been taken to court over Achilli, so now it was he, not Döllinger, who was in danger of a Roman condemnation. As he looked back on his life, he seemed like Sisyphus, 'rolling my load up the hill for ten years and never cresting it, but falling back': the failure in the Schools in 1820, the retirement from the Oriel tutorship in 1830, the condemnation of *Tract 90* in 1841, the Achilli trial of 1851 (when he had actually predicted, 'in another ten years, I shall be had up before Rome'). Clearly, it was 'the manifest disposition of Providence'. He wondered if the most straightforward course of action was not simply to ask why he was being attacked for an article which did not bear his name and which had appeared in a magazine of which he was not publicly known as the editor. He knew now enough of the workings of the Roman Curia to realize that it would not be

good policy to be too eager to put myself simply in to their hands, though it would be extremely wrong policy to seem to shuffle. They think me very irritable—this to an Italian, I suppose, means that I am apt to go in to a rabbia, and take to my bed. In consequence they are afraid to touch me as some unknown animal . . . the more I take on myself, the less will be done to me, and the more I give way, the more I shall be expected to do. At present Cardinal Barnabò is afraid and gives good words; he would use the violent or rude language which he can use, as soon as he knew that it was safe.[104]

On 19 January he wrote to Wiseman in Rome to say that he would like to know what dogmatic propositions of the Church the article was supposed to have infringed, as he was ready not only to accept these propositions in their entirety, but to show that the article was, in its English text (as opposed to a translation), completely consistent with them. He remarked pointedly,

I marvel, but I do not complain, that, after many years of patient and self denying labour in the cause of Catholicity, the one appropriate acknowledgement in my old age should be considered to consist in taking advantage against me of what is at worst a slip of the pen in an anonymous un-theological paper. But I suppose it is a law of the world, that those who toil much and say little, are little thought of.[105]

---

[104] *LD* xix. 280, 282–3.   [105] Ibid. 289–90.

His request for information was forwarded to the Congregation of Propaganda, which sent Wiseman a list of the passages in the article which were objected to. This list was never sent on to Newman. Instead, he received a letter from Manning three months later to say that Wiseman would settle the matter on his return to England. Wiseman was in poor health and preoccupied: together with Manning, who had become the Provost of the Westminster Chapter, he was busy in Rome working towards the removal of his coadjutor, Archbishop Errington. Barnabò simply assumed that Newman was disobedient when no explanation was forthcoming. As for Newman, he thought the matter was closed when he heard nothing further. His intention had all along been 'studiously' to avoid the dangerous subject of theology, but he had 'put' his 'foot into it' against his 'wish and expectation' by merely 'stating historical facts' which he assumed 'no one would deny'.[106]

[106] Ibid. 420.

13
The Years of Silence

❧

On 15 December 1859 Newman started a new private journal. The first entry, which laments his loss of 'sensible devotion and inward life',[1] picks up again the theme of the last notes he had written in his old journal during his pre-ordination retreat in Rome in April 1847. There, too, he had noted sadly how much of the vigour and vitality of youth seemed to have vanished. At the time the uncongenial strangeness of certain peripheral Catholic devotions did not help, nor much of the ceremonial and ritual, which left him feeling embarrassed and uncomfortable. But the disconcerting, almost alarming, fact then was how little enthusiasm he felt at the prospect of becoming an Oratorian priest. His mood of despondency could not all be blamed on the recent trauma of his conversion. Nor was it simply the inevitable waning of the spiritual exuberance and freshness of a younger man. He could not help, therefore, feeling that his depression was the numbing effect of years of conflict in the Church of England, coupled with the loss of his two closest friends. The old fervour was definitely gone, and he had sensed in himself a 'reaction' even against the austere life he had led at Littlemore.[2] Indeed, he had felt quite strongly tempted by the thought of a life of leisure among his books and friends.

Now, more than twelve years later, he had very similar feelings as he contemplated his Catholic life. He recognized, though, as he had noted more than once in his sermons, that the devotion of youth might be more natural than supernatural; whereas 'Old men are in soul as stiff, as lean, as bloodless as their bodies, except so far as grace penetrates and softens them',[3] for 'age is a frost upon them, chilling devotion and binding and hardening the heart'.[4] As a young man he had prayed earnestly to give up all worldly ambitions to serve God, but he suspected now that his prayers had been 'immediately prompted . . . by natural rashness, generosity, cheerfulness, sanguine temperament, and unselfishness', rather than by pure love of God. Would such prayers now come so readily to him? 'O my God,' he wrote with painful insistence, 'not as a matter of sentiment, not as a matter of literary exhibition, do I put this down':

---

[1] *AW* 249.   [2] Ibid. 241.   [3] Ibid. 249.   [4] *LD* xx. 43.

O rid me of this frightful *cowardice*, for this is at the bottom of all my ills. When I was young, I was bold, because I was ignorant—now I have lost my boldness, because I have . . . advanced in experience. I am able to count the cost, better than I did, of being brave for Thy sake, and therefore I shrink from sacrifices. Here is a second reason, over and above the deadness of my soul, why I have so little faith or love in me.

A few weeks later, in January, he took up the journal again, noting how in his last entry he had 'had something to say, but I lost my thread . . . and now I will recover it, if I can'. As he looked back on the failures and setbacks of his life as a Catholic, he did not exactly blame the jealousy or malice of others; the root cause lay in himself: he had not pushed himself enough, gossiped and flattered and intrigued in the right places—he was a 'nobody', with 'no friend at Rome'. The hostility he had attracted resulted from his unwelcome attempts to raise the intellectual level of Catholics. On the other hand, he could not help contrasting the indifference of his co-religionists with a certain 'drawing towards me on the part of Protestants'. His Catholic writings were more appreciated by non-Catholics, and there was a new interest in some of his neglected Anglican works. People who had ignored him for years had begun to make overtures. He felt a 'temptation of looking out for, if not courting, Protestant praise'. It was very tempting, he admitted, 'to desire more of that sympathy, feeling lonely, and fretting under, not so much the coldness towards me, (though that in part), as the ignorance, narrowness of mind, and selfconceit' of his fellow Catholics, whose faith and virtue he nevertheless recognized. Once again he renewed his prayer to 'be set aside in this world'. His two principal anxieties he put in God's hands: the precarious future of the Oratory and his frustration at not knowing what long-term work he should undertake in the time left to him. His years as a Catholic seemed wasted: 'What I wrote as a Protestant has had far greater power, force, meaning, success, than my Catholic works—and this troubles me a great deal . . .'.[5]

2

The disappointments and sufferings of the last decade had certainly taken their toll. Far from being the hoped-for year of rest, 1859 had proved to be one of the most critical and trying years of Newman's life.

All through last year I fell off in flesh, and suppose I shall at least never recover it, if I don't go on. My fingers are so thin that I can't get accustomed to the sight

[5] *AW* 249–53.

of them. My skin is getting to gleam like parchment, and I have had difficulty of lying at night from the prominency of my bones.

Still, the strange thing was that his 'general health' had never been 'better', in spite of 'a deal of anxiety and sorrow'.[6] However, like Tennyson's Tithonus (the poem had just been published), he felt he was 'fading out from the world, and having nothing to do with its interests or its affairs'; not only had he 'fallen off in flesh', but he had 'shrunk up during the past year' and was 'like a grey grasshopper or the evaporating mist of the morning'.[7] To an old friend he wrote that he could 'almost say that a pleasant event has not happened to me for more years than I can count', with one trial succeeding another like 'the clouds . . . returning after the rain'.[8] Now he had no time to rest, because he was so busy with Oratory work. Apart from Ambrose St John, there was no one left capable even of preaching. Flanagan and Bittleston had still not recovered. Robert Tillotson, who had been allowed leave for a few months to visit his aged father in America, had decided to leave the Oratory at the end of 1859 and join the new American Paulist order. Newman was deeply upset, but he never sent the letter he wrote which contained the sentence, 'Never since we have been a Congregation have we had so great, so unexpected, so undeserved a blow.'[9]

The daily business of the community—'the trifles of the day'—had at least the advantage that 'those trifles are wholes, and have their value, such as it is—whereas one does but waste time, if one makes preparations for a future which is never to be one's own'. Again Newman meditated, 'What a strange accident of human life it is that the age for death is so various!' Compared with the life-span of some people, others enjoyed 'a second life'. But what was the good of making plans, 'of laying out work for many years, when . . . we may be cut off when we have only placed the foundations?'[10]

At the end of May 1860 he received a call from Ullathorne's secretary, E. E. Estcourt, a convert Anglican clergyman, who proposed that he should be on a committee to build a new Catholic church in Oxford, for which land had become available; Newman's name would draw subscriptions from converts, and the church would be a kind of memorial to his role in the Oxford Movement. Estcourt also talked of the possibility of converting an old workhouse that had come onto the market into a college for Catholics. Newman's reactions were very mixed. Before replying definitely to Estcourt, he drew up a memorandum and also drafted a letter, which he showed to several friends. Considering the Church's official opposition to 'mixed' education, he

---

[6] *LD* xix. 310.   [7] Ibid. 311.   [8] Ibid. 313.
[9] Ibid. 235.   [10] Ibid. 331.

'thought it cool, that, whereas the English hierarchy had in no way supported me at Dublin, they should now turn round, and . . . ask me without any explanation to assist them at Oxford, to the reversal of all that I had done or written'. Another consideration struck him. Suppose one day 'it seemed desirable for me to show myself at Oxford, or commence any thing there in the shape of a College, this hostile act might be thrown in my teeth'; there was, after all, no need for a new Catholic church, unless the intention was to make converts among members of the University. Otherwise, with the lapse of time, he could expect the ill-feeling against him at Oxford to fade away. Far from wanting to enter into a 'war', Newman felt that

Oxford deserves least, of any part of the Anglican territory, to be interfered with. That there are also false traditions there, I know well; I know too that there is . . . scepticism and infidelity; but till things are very much changed there, in weakening Oxford, we are weakening our friends . . . Catholics did not make us Catholics; Oxford made us Catholics. At present Oxford surely does more good than harm. There has been a rage for shooting sparrows of late years under the notion that they are the farmer's enemies. Now, it is discovered that they do more good by destroying insects than harm by picking up the seed.

This remarkable draft letter, the boldest parts of which were deleted in the copy actually sent, continued even more boldly:

The Establishment has ever been a break water against Unitarianism, fanaticism, and infidelity. It has ever loved us better than Puritans or Independents have loved us. And it receives all that abuse and odium of dogmatism, or at least a good deal of it, which otherwise would be directed against us. I should have the greatest repugnance to introducing controversy into those quiet circles and sober schools of thought, which are the strength of the Church of England. It is another thing altogether to introduce controversy to individual minds which are already unsettled, or have a drawing towards Catholicism. Altogether another thing in a place like Birmingham, where nearly everyone is a nothingarian, an infidel, a sceptic or an inquirer. . . . In Oxford you would unsettle many, and gain a few, if you did your most.

A Catholic church 'would attract just those who were likely to be unstable, and who perhaps in a year or two would lapse back into Protestantism', and would 'create great bitterness of feeling and indignation against Catholics'. When Newman himself had become a Catholic, he had immediately left the vicinity of Oxford. He had 'never acted in direct hostility to the Church of England', although in *Difficulties of Anglicans* he had encouraged Anglo-Catholics to draw certain 'conclusions', and in *Present Position of Catholics* he had written against Anglicans in so far as they were representatives of the 'National Protestantism'.

In all that I have written, I have spoken of Oxford and the Oxford system with affection and admiration. I have put its system forward, as an instance of that union of dogmatic teaching and liberal education which command my assent.[11]

Later in the summer he again became involved with the *Rambler*. A student for the priesthood called H. N. Oxenham, a convert, wrote an unsigned letter to the magazine attacking the narrowness of the seminary system and invoking Newman's name. The attack was comprehensive and penetrating, and certainly reflected Newman's own views on Catholic education in general. The letter appeared in the July number; an unsigned reply by Newman was published in the September issue. Newman agreed that certainly 'free discussion should be allowed us on all matters which the Church has not ruled', and he lamented 'that bigotry and jealousy which would enthrone the decisions of individuals, or of parties, or of schools, as if divine truths, unassailable and irreversible'. He also acknowledged that 'the secular education of Catholics in the middle and upper classes should be the best of its kind, and such as to enable them to take their place in society by the side of Protestants'. His complaint, however, was that 'a purely clerical subject' had been discussed 'in a lay magazine'; if it was 'a mistake in ecclesiastics . . . to lecture laymen on secular subjects', the same applied even more to lay discussion of the education of the clergy.[12] The letter was anonymous, partly in order to avoid hurting 'persons whom I don't wish to hurt'.[13] In fact, these very persons (so W. G. Ward indignantly informed him) refused to believe that Newman, whom they regarded as the authority for their views, could be the author of the letter. But not only (Newman reassured Ward) did he think it 'most extravagantly novel' for laymen to advance their opinions on clerical education, but he also added, characteristically, that 'devotion and self rule are worth all the intellectual cultivation in the world', and moreover that 'in the case of most men, literature and science and the habits they create, so far from ensuring those highest gifts, indispose the mind towards their acquisition'.[14] As a matter of fact, he did not see why 'the clergy considered as a *class* . . . should be literary men'.[15] It was absurd that the clergy as a whole, who had their own professional calling, should receive the same kind of liberal education that only a small minority of the laity enjoyed.

In November Newman began a correspondence about Christian civilization with T. W. Allies, an Oxford convert who had become a Catholic in 1850, and whom he had appointed to a lectureship in history at the Catholic University. His approach was predictably

[11] *LD* xix. 350–3. [12] Ibid. 554–5. [13] Ibid. 397.
[14] Ibid. 417. [15] Ibid. 455.

unconventional. He agreed that 'it is the tendency of Christianity to impress itself on the face of society', but then it is also 'the tendency of devotion to increase Church lands and property', which may lead to corruption and secularization. The fact is 'the world is one of our three deadly enemies. Did it cease to be so in the Middle Age?' Far from it. Papal Rome was 'spoken of, not only as the world, but even as Babylon'. True, Christianity was able to impress 'its image on the social framework', but it 'never has been able to do so on literature and science'. Admittedly, 'ages of barbarism', which 'are more susceptible of religious impressions than other ages', may 'call for, need, the visible rule of Religion'; but the fact is that a 'mediaeval system now would but foster the worst hypocrisy,—not because this age is worse than that, but because imagination acts more powerfully upon barbarians, and reason on traders, *savants*, and newspaper readers'.[16] Was there any 'proof that the Church saves *more* souls when established, than when persecuted, or than when tolerated?'[17] Certainly, the establishment of religion inevitably tends to lead to hypocritical profession as well as to state interference. Where there is establishment, it should be only when '*Catholicism comes first and establishment comes second*', and when 'establishment is the spontaneous act of the people' and not of the Church; in such cases 'it is the will of the masses', but 'it is not necessary for Catholicism'. Nor is it necessarily preferable: 'Is God glorified more by many saved or by great saints?'[18]

Before the end of the year Newman was again unpleasantly reminded of the London Oratory, which was again, not for the first time, criticizing Birmingham for allegedly breaking the Oratorian Rule in starting a school. He told Hope-Scott in confidence that he had 'a profound and intense *distrust*' of Faber, in spite of 'a thousand attractive points', because of 'a restless spirit of intrigue which nothing can quench':[19]

A little reverence on his part towards me, a little gratitude, would be worth all the 'affection and admiration' of which you speak. But it is not in his nature. With many shining, many winning qualities, he has no heart.[20]

However, he 'gladly' took 'the reproach' for the rupture between them on himself, as Faber was 'doing so much good in his important position'.[21]

His own Oratory continued to give him anxiety, and he was burdened with even more work since Father Frederick Bowles (an old companion from Littlemore days), who was depressive by temperament and had been gradually withdrawing from community life, suddenly left in

---

[16] Ibid. 421–3.   [17] Ibid. 432.   [18] Ibid. 473.
[19] Ibid. 427.   [20] Ibid. 446.   [21] Ibid. 428.

August. This meant that Newman was now also in charge of the music in church, which was being enlarged and decorated under his personal supervision. As in Dublin, he felt that it was very important that there should be a proper church for the school. Inevitably, the school was growing in importance. After the Dublin and *Rambler* failures, here at least was a work that 'falls under those objects, to which I have especially given my time and thought'. And even if there were 'other works, more directly suitable to St. Philip's Oratory, as such', this one did fit their special brief from the Pope.[22]

The storm over *Essays and Reviews* (published in the autumn of 1860), the famous collection of radical essays by seven well-known Anglican liberals, elicited from Newman a typically complex response, which was distinct from both the predictable orthodox and progressive reactions. He told the new Rector of Lincoln College, Oxford, Mark Pattison, who had come under his influence at Oriel, but who had long since given up Tractarianism, that he had no objection to theological speculation, provided it was published in learned journals and not broadcast abroad unsettling ordinary people's faith. This would not have been so much of an objection in the eighteenth century, but 'now every one is alive to religious subjects': the 'growth of scepticism' was 'appalling', and 'Christianity is tending to go out in whole classes'. The fatal process of compromise had begun in the last century, when Bishop Butler ('to whom I owe so much') in practice seemed to reduce faith to 'a mere *practical certainty*'. All along, 'Anglican defenders of Christianity' had been 'fighting and retreating'; this latest crisis would surely lead to further erosions of belief.[23] But Newman had another, more subtle, view of the significance of the book.

The religion of England is 'the Bible, the whole Bible, and nothing but the Bible'—the consequence is that to strike a blow at its inspiration, veracity or canonicity, is directly to aim at whatever there is of Christianity in the country. It is frightful to think where England would be, as regards Revelation, if it once got to disbelieve or to doubt the authority of Scripture. This is what makes the Volume so grave a matter—and the responsibility of those who have had to do with it so great.

This was 'one illustration' of why he could not 'defend Christianity on the Anglican basis'. True, a Catholic had to believe in the inspiration of the Bible, but then 'the Church has defined very little upon the subject ... and we should have a sufficient ground of faith and teacher of doctrine, though ... the whole Bible were miraculously to vanish out of the world'. Not only does a Catholic believe 'in the word of God thro' His Church', but, he added significantly, 'there is nothing which binds

---

[22] *LD* xix. 464.   [23] Ibid. 480.

the Catholic to belief in various portions of Genesis etc as popularly interpreted'.[24] To the obvious objection that the Bible was not in fact the religion of the Church of England, he replied, 'But the [historical] Church of England's religion is not the religion of England.'[25] English popular religion was bound up with the Bible, and also depended, 'humanly speaking', he added, 'on the observance of the Calvinistic Sabbath'. He did not himself wish to become involved in the controversy, although he was well aware of the religious situation at Oxford, and 'it was one of my severest trials in leaving it, that I was undoing my own work, and leaving the field open, or rather infallibly surrendering it to those who would break down and crumble to powder all religion whatever'. He wondered if the contributors to *Essays and Reviews* saw 'the termination, or rather the abyss, to which these speculations lead', and whether they realized that, 'before attempting to sift facts, they ought to make sure that they have a firm hold of true and eternal principles. To unsettle the minds of a generation, when you give them no landmarks and no causeway across the morass is to undertake a great responsibility.' But if the whole question of the literal meaning and truth of the Bible was not 'one of life and death' to a Catholic (whereas 'the beginning of the end of Protestantism' lay in 'the breaking of that bubble of "Bible-Christianity" which has been its life'),[26] nevertheless, '*we* shall have a controversy of our own, viz with Atheism':

My own belief is, that, if there be a God, Catholicism is true; but this is the elementary, august, and sovereign truth, the denial of which is in progress. May He Himself give grace to those who shall be alive in that terrible day, to fight His battle well. All the forms of Protestantism . . . are but toys of children in the great battle between the Holy Catholic Roman Church and Antichrist.[27]

This grim prophecy Newman was to go on repeating for the rest of his life. Increasingly, he saw the justification of religious belief as the critical problem facing the Catholic Church. In 1858, free of the University, he had expressed a wish 'to go back to my old studies, and to do something, if life is given me, more solid than I have done hitherto'.[28] He felt then, as he looked back on his life, 'how little I have done', and 'all I have done is unfinished'.[29] Now he lamented 'how for years and years, indeed, I have wished to write on Faith and Reason—but the good time for it has never come, and now I am too old; too weary, too weak, and too busy'. There was also the danger that if he attempted anything, he would 'at once be attacked in my rear by some narrow-minded disputant of our own Creed'. It was necessary to be patient—'time alone will overcome it.'[30] The need to write something substantial on the philosophy of religion, to

[24] Ibid. 482–3. [25] Ibid. 485. [26] Ibid. xx. 465. [27] Ibid. xix. 487–8.
[28] Ibid. xviii. 547. [29] Ibid. 248, 218. [30] Ibid. xix. 500.

complete what he had only adumbrated with such brilliant originality in the *Oxford University Sermons*, continued to nag him, until finally the *Grammar of Assent* was conceived. On and off almost throughout the 1850s and 1860s, he constantly returned to the question of the certainty of faith, recording his thoughts and conclusions in letters, notes, and papers. Although he had refused to enter the controversy over *Essays and Reviews*, he did begin to think seriously about the problem of Biblical inspiration; again, his reflections during the years 1861–3 are contained not only in letters, but in several papers which ultimately bore fruit in two published articles of 1884.

In June 1861 the crisis over the Pope's temporal power, which was seriously in jeopardy because of Garibaldi's successful assault on the Papal States, threatened to drag Newman into a dangerous controversy. It was assumed by most Catholics that the Pope's spiritual authority would be seriously weakened if he ceased to be a temporal sovereign. From the beginning, Newman's view was that not only would the Pope's 'real power' not be touched, but that 'when matters are finally settled, he will be stronger and firmer than he has been for a long while'— 'Nothing is more wonderful in the past history of the Holy See than the transformation of its circumstances, and its power of beginning, as it were, a new life in them.'[31] The peril posed by Garibaldi was at least an 'evil that speaks' rather than 'evil that rankles and plots', and therefore 'less dangerous' because 'it has a safety valve'.[32] There was another consideration that weighed with Newman. As in Ireland, he was aware that there was a

distance . . . between the clergy and gentry in Italy—and that is at the root of all the mischief there. As far as I can make out, not instruction, but repression is the rule. I don't mean that they do not know their catechism, but their intellect is left to grow wild; in consequence it rebels; and is not met with counter and stronger intellect, but by authority.

If the Pope lost his temporal power, perhaps this would indicate that it was impossible 'to remedy the above dead lock without a revolution'.[33] In fact, history showed that Popes could be spiritually independent when dependent on or even subject to external political power; there was no reason why this should not be just as true if Rome became a neutral city.

But Newman refused to speak out in public in spite of an appeal from Acton. The *Rambler* had come out in support of the British government, which was opposed to the Temporal Power, for which it had been sharply attacked. Faber and Manning had both come out strongly in support of the Pope's claims. Newman certainly thought it was 'very

[31] *LD* xix. 300, 308–9.   [32] Ibid. 401–2.   [33] Ibid. 450.

hard we may not say what we think on a point of ecclesiastical expediency',[34] but he saw no reason why he personally should say anything publicly. The mere fact that he had not spoken on the other side was eloquent enough: 'You may be sure that there are people watching me very narrowly, and who would rejoice if I brought out in any tangible form what they believe I hold in my heart.' He had to consider, too, the welfare of the Oratory, which could be destroyed 'by a stroke of the pen' at Rome. Loyalty to the Pope, who had stood by him against Propaganda in the crisis over the Rule, also dictated that he should remain silent.[35] He warned Acton that Simpson, through his provocative style in the *Rambler*, was 'doing high interests a disservice': for example, it would be much better to 'say, like a man, that the Pope is surrounded by a clique who mislead him, than insinuate it from the history of a past age'.[36] However, he advised Acton not to be bullied by Rome into withdrawing support from the Liberal government, which favoured Italian nationalism: 'How *wonderful*', he exclaimed, that Cardinal Antonelli, the Papal Secretary of State, should connect the failure of Catholic Members of Parliament to support the Temporal Power with the editorial policy of the *Rambler*! He immediately also wrote bluntly to Manning (who had seen Acton on Wiseman's behalf to inform him of an impending censure by Rome), to say that he would not remain a member of Wiseman's recently established 'Academia of the Catholic Religion', if the Cardinal used his impending inaugural address to insist that Catholics were bound to support the Temporal Power. But he told Acton flatly that he did not see how, with Simpson's involvement, the *Rambler* could continue: it was true that it was no business of Cardinal Antonelli's, who was not 'a legitimate authority', but 'Propaganda and the Cardinal Archbishop are', and

It seems to me that a man who opposes legitimate authority is in a false position . . . If they do not allow the Rambler to speak against the temporal power, they seem to me tyrannical—but they have the right to disallow it—and a Magazine, with a censure upon it from authority, continues at an enormous disadvantage.

It does not seem to me courage, to run counter to constituted superiors—*they* bear the responsibility and to them we must leave it . . .

If I felt with you it was doing a real work, which otherwise would not be done,—of course I should not find a determination of the difficulty so easy . . .[37]

To Acton's response that the Church authorities had no jurisdiction over the *Rambler*, since theology had been deliberately excluded, Newman replied that, far from this being the case, in fact it 'certainly does seem to me ever nibbling at theological questions'. Apart from the

[34] Ibid. 506.   [35] Ibid. 509.   [36] Ibid. 506.   [37] Ibid. 523.

offending article on the education of priests, a canonized Pope had been treated by Simpson 'very much as if, in showing a Church, the Sacristan were to take an axe and knock off a piece of an Altar—and then, when called to account, were to say that the Altar was about to be removed, as it was in the way, and he was only by his act beginning the intended reforms'. It was quite true that the magazine's views on 'homeopathy, or the broad gauge', or on literature were none of the bishops' business. The trouble was that Simpson could not keep away from theology, and would 'always be clever, amusing, brilliant, and *suggestive*'.

He will always be flicking his whip at Bishops, cutting them in tender places, throwing stones at sacred Congregations, and, as he rides along the high road, discharging pea shooters at Cardinals who happen by bad luck to look out of window.

Nor did he think non-Catholics would 'say that an independent organ of opinion is silenced, but one that loved to assail, and to go out of its way to assail what was authoritative and venerable'.[38]

3

Towards the end of July 1861, suffering from insomnia and strain, Newman left Birmingham for a three-week holiday. He was accompanied by William Neville, whom he had received into the Church in 1851 and who had joined the Oratory the same year, but was not ordained till ten years later because of his indecisiveness (he was eventually to become Newman's secretary and literary executor). Newman had been advised by a London specialist to rest for several months. He had now passed his sixtieth birthday, but the signs were not auspicious for a serene old age. He could hardly have guessed that nearly three decades of life were still left to him, as he travelled from London 'going about seeing once again, and taking leave for good, of the places I knew as a child'. He went to Ham, where he gazed 'at the windows of our house . . . where I lay . . . looking at the candles stuck in them in celebration of the victory of Trafalgar'. He felt he knew more about the house than any other he had been in since, and 'could pass an examination in it. It has ever been in my dreams.' Strangely enough, he thought he had not seen the house since September 1807. His memory was curiously at fault. He had in fact ridden over in 1813 with his father and brother from Norwood (then 'the wild beautiful haunt of gypsies'), where the family had a cottage, which he could not now find ('the whole face of the country is changed').[39] On

<hr />

[38] *LD* xx. 3–5.   [39] Ibid. 23.

that earlier visit the gardener had offered them three apricots, and when his father had allowed him to choose, 'I took the largest, a thing which still distresses me, whenever I think of it.' He had again visited the house in 1836 with Bowden and his wife, as he had recalled as recently as 1853:

It was then, I believe, a school—and the fine trees, which were upon the lawn, were cut down . . . A large magnolia, flowering (in June I think) went up the House, and the mower's scythe, cutting the lawn, used to sound so sweetly as I lay in a crib . . .

When later as a schoolboy he 'dreamed of heaven, the scene was Ham'.[40]

He also visited Brighton, where the family had gone after selling the house at Ham and where his sister Mary was buried. He had not been there for nearly thirty years, years that seemed full of failures ('and continual disappointment wears away the mind'), beginning with his dismissal from the Oriel tutorship in 1830.[41] One place he went to had no nostalgic or poignant memories; he had only been to Cambridge once before, for a few hours in 1832:

Then, I recollect, my allegiance to Oxford was shaken by the extreme beauty of the place. I had forgotten this—but a second sight has revived the impression. Certainly it is exquisitely beautiful.[42]

It was impossible to escape from his past and his reputation. The only other resident in the hotel's coffee-room, an Evangelical lay theologian, recognized Newman from hearing him preach thirty years before in St Mary's, Oxford.

This was no annoyance to us; but what did annoy us was, that, when we were in King's College Chapel to hear the chanting and see the place, a little man at once fastened his eyes on us, whom William instantly jaloused as having been at the Oratory. William, who acts as a sort of Guardian Angel or Homeric god, instantly enveloped me in darkness, rustling with his wings, and flapping about with a vigor which for the time was very successful. But, alas, all through the day, wherever we were, this little man haunted us. He seemed to take no meals, to say no prayers, or elsewhere to know our times for these exercises with a preternatural exactness. William was ever saying, whether we were here or there, in garden or in cloister—'Don't look that way—turn this way—there's the little man again.' His anxiety led him to make matters worse, for he boldly approximated him to be sure of the individual, but with too little caution, for the little man caught his hand and asked him how he was. However, his generalship kept me out of harm's way, and we dined peaceably at six. There was then no further danger—we lounged out at seven, and were tempted, by the merest accident to turn aside into PeterHouse. We were not two seconds in the Court, when William cried out, 'There's the little man—don't look.' But it would not do—he pounced upon his prey . . .[43]

[40] Ibid. xv. 396-7.   [41] Ibid. xx. 23.   [42] Ibid. 17.   [43] Ibid. 17-18.

In Brighton, Newman picked up the *Quarterly Review* and found an attack on the alleged disingenuousness of *Tract 90* by Bishop Samuel Wilberforce in the course of a critical article on *Essays and Reviews*. Nor did a reply by A. P. Stanley in the *Edinburgh Review* miss the opportunity to condemn Newman's *Elucidations* of Hampden as calumnious and disgraceful. 'These are little and ridiculous things taken separately, but they form an atmosphere of *flies*—one can't enjoy a walk without this fidget on the nerves of the mind.' 'They are nothing', he admitted, 'in the eye of reason, but they weary.' He was not aware of having made any personal attacks on anyone except Achilli. He was only conscious of thirty years of disappointment—'every thing seems to crumble under my hands, as if one were making ropes of sand.' Like St Paul, he could not be indifferent to those 'wounds which one bears speechlessly, the dreadful secrets which are severed from the sympathy of others, the destruction of confidences, the sense of hollowness all around one, the expectation of calamity or scandal'; nor, even if he were much more advanced 'in that higher life which lasts and grows in spite of the ills of mortality', could he avoid 'that mental burden which consists in the perception of evil with the consciousness one cannot avert it'. He had seldom replied, except where the interests of others or a cause were at stake, to all the 'gross misrepresentations' of thirty years, 'since I have been a sort of target for a shot, when any one wished to try his hand, and had nothing better to do'. The worst thing, as 'in a naval engagement, while the vessels near, and the men are standing quite still, the knees of the bravest shake', was to be 'simply passive in suffering':

When we act as well as suffer, the effort alleviates the pain; in that case men are wounded without knowing it; but it is otherwise when you are hit, without hitting. It would have been better with me humanly and naturally, had I given as good as I took.[44]

His own long-suffering self-restraint had not stopped the attacks, nor could he now respond with the old, carefree glee that had once come so naturally to him in happier days: 'people throw things out from time to time *to bring us out*—just as you make a noise, or put in a stick or throw in some food to make a beast in a cage show itself. They want to trot me out.'[45]

So deep was his depression that he could only describe it in physical terms. He felt there was something the matter with 'the *physical* texture' of his 'soul'. Even if it was not quite literally true, still he could not remember having received any 'piece of (personal) good news for thirty years and more'. He even wondered whether he had ever had 'any success' apart from his scholarship at Trinity and fellowship at Oriel;

[44] *LD* xx. 29–31.   [45] Ibid. xiii. 5.

and 'I think I never have been praised for any thing I did, except once, for my Lectures on Catholicism in England by the Bishop and Catholics of Birmingham.' Recently, his experience had been that whenever he 'attempted to do any thing for God, I find after a little while that my arms or my legs have a string round them—and perhaps I sprain myself in the effort to move them in spite of it'.[46] At least his imagination did not desert him, as he varied the imagery in his descriptions of his semi-breakdown—'I have been in constant hot water, of one sort or degree or another, for full thirty years—and it has at length boiled me': the worry was 'sucking life' out of him.[47]

After returning from his holiday, Newman spent most of the rest of the summer at the small country house which the Oratorians had built at Rednal just under the Lickey hills, about 8 miles from the Oratory. The land had been bought in 1854, mostly out of money from the Achilli fund, partly as a burial-ground for the community, and partly as a quiet place of retreat. From there, at the end of August, he wrote a letter to Nicholas Darnell, after a sleepless night. He was very worried about lack of discipline, poor academic standards, and the general religious tone in the school. With the beginning of the new school year approaching, it was important to make some reforms. To this letter Darnell made no answer either by letter or in conversation. There the matter rested for the time being. But it was an additional anxiety to bear; perhaps the school would turn out to be yet another abortive work. Not only was there legitimate criticism of the school, but there were also false rumours circulating, which could easily be denied, 'but lies are long-lived, and die hard'.[48]

The second week of October he spent at Ventnor in the Isle of Wight. He had not been back there since 1825. He was reminded of how much the face of England was changing. Then there had been only one bathing-machine and no accommodation; now it was a sizeable resort. He was again delighted with the spot: 'The undercliff is the most beautiful sea place I know in England.' And once the English coast and railway were left behind, 'the journey is a succession of beautiful pictures, which throws one back to the time when steam was not,—and people travelled for the sake of travelling.'[49] At the end of November he went for a month's visit to the London home of Henry Bowden, the younger brother of J. W. Bowden, who had been married by Newman in 1838 and who had become a Catholic with his wife and family in 1852. From there he wrote with sardonic amusement to Ambrose St John the latest news of the London Oratory:

Fr Faber, having been in his own belief given over, and in immediate prospect

---

[46] Ibid. xx. 34.   [47] Ibid. 35–6.   [48] Ibid. 23.   [49] Ibid. 56–7.

of death, suddenly got up, shaved himself, and announces his intention of coming to town next Monday. John Bowden gave us a sort of hagiographical account of it, said that the doctor pronounced that there had been an organic or structural change suddenly effected, and gave the Brompton judgment that it was a grazia.

Fr Faber has dictated a letter to me to beg pardon for any wilfulnesses of his in his—noviceship! and any disedification he gave any of our Fathers when he was a novice.[50]

Much less amusing was the not unexpected news of a crisis at the school. At the beginning of December, the matron, Mrs Wootten, offered to resign after Darnell issued new rules which curtailed her authority and restricted the boys' free access to her. Newman was horrified to hear of the row. If Darnell resigned, it 'would ruin us with the world', but if Mrs Wootten did, it would 'ruin us with mothers, and rob us of the *only* real advantage that we have over other schools.'[51] As with the University, it was the *personal* side of the school that Newman was so anxious to emphasize: he wanted not only 'to combine the advantages of a large school with those of private tuition',[52] but especially to 'lay stress on, more than other schools . . . the quality of our matrons'.[53] He wanted small boys, who were away from home, to have the kind of maternal care and sympathy that was not usually available in boarding-schools. The closure of the school, he wrote to St John, would 'shipwreck us'; it would also, he added significantly, 'act on the mind' of Stanislas Flanagan 'to show that the Oratory cannot succeed in any thing and is going to the dogs'.[54] Newman had 'feared what was coming for a year past', and it was one of the causes of his illness.[55] He could hardly arbitrate when he thought Mrs Wootten, who was the convert widow of the Tractarian doctor in Oxford, and one of his most loyal supporters, entirely in the right. Indeed, the burden of Darnell's complaint was that Mrs Wootten was a member of his staff and should not be able to communicate directly with Newman. Newman had tried to make peace by urging that the headmaster and the matron had different spheres of responsibility, although in any cases of collision Mrs Wootten was bound to give way to Darnell. Darnell responded by accusing Mrs Wootten of gross insubordination, and suggesting sarcastically that it would be best if she were appointed headmistress. Newman's reply was characteristically blunt: Darnell appeared not to admit 'the right of appeal on the part of subordinates in the school to me as President—and this I cannot for an instant allow'. He also sharply reminded Darnell that 'you must never forget that without my name the School would not be, and that many, to say the least, of the

[50] *LD* xx. 75.   [51] Ibid. 76.   [52] Ibid. xix. 398.
[53] Ibid. xx. 68.   [54] Ibid. 76.   [55] Ibid. 81.

parents, make me responsible for their children.'[56] However, he told the community that Darnell and Mrs Wootten, who had previously been close friends, were 'the two pillars of my undertaking',[57] and proposed as a compromise that the school should divide in two, with Darnell as the headmaster of the senior school and Mrs Wootten as the matron of the junior school.

Two days after Christmas Darnell rejected the compromise plan, and made public his resignation as headmaster; either he went or Mrs Wootten went. He also announced that the other masters were ready to resign if he resigned. If the Oratory School was to be a proper English public school, then no matron could presume to such independence. But Newman told the community at a meeting 'that the mode of conducting the great schools of Eton, Winchester, etc, necessarily end in subordinating religion to secular interests and principles; and that this consequence would ensue in ours, but for the presence of Matrons of a high class, and of spiritual directors'.[58] This was another complaint against Darnell, that he had not allowed free scope to the priests who were the confessors in the school. There was an irony in Newman's warning against the danger of the school sacrificing its moral and spiritual character to other priorities; he himself, after all, had been accused of something similar with regard to his idea of the Oratory. As usual, he occupied the middle ground, this time between conventional Catholic educators and those like Darnell who wanted the Oratory School to be as like an English public school as possible; his ideal was rather a new type of school which would combine Catholicism with the best elements of Protestant education.

He remained surprisingly resilient under the new disaster, 'the heaviest blow' they had suffered as an Oratory.[59] But whereas before he had stood by in helpless inaction, now as usual the possibility of action galvanized him into an extraordinary burst of activity for an elderly man in poor health. It was always suspense and uncertainty that undermined his morale, not work with a purpose. If Darnell thought that by resigning along with the other masters he would force Newman to get rid of Mrs Wootten, he had seriously miscalculated. While before Newman had hesitated and agonized, now he had no doubt what to do. Not only had Darnell forced the issue by refusing any compromise, but by making public his resignation he had been responsible for any scandal. The vital question was whether new staff could be found during the Christmas holidays before the next term began. Darnell let it be known that he was leaving the Oratory and that Flanagan was leaving with him (he had discovered that Flanagan, who was still not fully

---

[56] Ibid. 82.   [57] Ibid. 86.   [58] Ibid. 91.   [59] Ibid. 96.

recovered, was thinking of leaving, though for quite different reasons). He was in contact, too, with parents of boys, in the hope that he could continue the school elsewhere. Early in January he moved out of the Oratory. Meanwhile, Newman's determined efforts had met with success: new masters were appointed, and two of the staff who had resigned apologized and were reinstated. He even managed to persuade Thomas Arnold to leave Dublin and come as first master for a term. He had no regrets about the course of action he had taken. The issue was not really Mrs Wootten, but whether the school was independent of or under the jurisdiction of the Oratory. He was not unaware of the possible danger of Mrs Wootten becoming too dominant a force, but it 'would have been unjust, ungrateful, cowardly, disloyal to the Oratory, and utterly disgraceful' to have agreed to 'the immediate dismissal of an helpless lady, who had no kind of warning of what was coming, and who had in many ways sacrificed herself for us'.[60] If anything, he felt he had been too indulgent to Darnell. The real damage was not to the school, but to the community—'the severance of such long and intimate ties— and the enormous scandal': 'We have already had blows enough to knock the life out of us, but this . . . is worse than all before it.'[61] Darnell had been a member of the Oratory since its foundation in 1848, when he had joined with Faber's Wilfridians.

H. N. Oxenham, who had been refused ordination by Wiseman because of his letters on seminary education, and who had subsequently become a master at the school, informed Newman that his support for Darnell arose not from any desire to subvert Newman's ultimate authority over the school, but from his agreement with Darnell that Mrs Wootten's position prevented the school from being a proper public school. He received a short, sharp reply from Newman disclaiming any interest in his motives: 'We here are only concerned with your act; and, as to that, I have no difficulty in accepting your assurance that it was deliberate and that you are not sorry for it.'[62] Newman certainly had no intention of even contemplating Darnell's reinstatement. Darnell had not only betrayed the trust reposed in him, but had broken his religious obedience to the Oratory; he had also tried to force the unjust dismissal of Mrs Wootten without notice. Newman's problem had been that he had followed his usual practice of giving 'a generous liberty to those I put in trust with any work—and, having put power out of my hands, there was no way of getting it back'. He thought he saw the 'immediate cause' of Darnell's precipitous action:

He had committed himself to an Order, prohibitory of her just power over the boys, (e.g. in sending for them to the doctor, giving them medicine etc etc) *which would not work.* He professed openly, that he *could* not withdraw it, without prejudice to his own dignity (This in my mind was an absurdity)—and so his only way out of this cul de sac was her instantaneous departure . . .

The real reason, however, for the growing alienation between Darnell and Mrs Wootten, who had been such close friends, was, Newman discovered, that she had known about and vigorously opposed a plan Darnell and the other masters had resolved on, without telling Newman, to move the school away from Edgbaston (a location that Newman himself recognized was unsuitable in the long term). The gossip among local Protestants, Newman noted with mischievous amusement, was that Darnell had run off with Miss French ('I whisper, she is 50'), the assistant matron, a great friend and supporter of his who had also resigned: 'I am malicious enough to wish this to get to her ears.'[63] More seriously, he recognized that while 'No trial has been keener', still 'none has been shorter'—'And it is the long wearing trial, with suspense . . . which is the greatest.'[64]

But the result was even more work for a seriously depleted community, since, although William Neville had been ordained at last the previous year, Flanagan's resignation from the Oratory was only a matter of time (he finally left in August). Ambrose St John had agreed to take over as headmaster, and Newman himself became quite heavily involved in teaching and administration. There was no doubting the success of the school, which by the end of the third year had grown from a dozen to seventy boys. But Newman felt the pressure: the sheer *'endlessness* of the task to me (at my age) is a serious trial'.[65] He almost forgot it was his birthday in February—'*Have* old people birthdays? somehow they die out of my memory, and the death day, could it be known by anticipation, ought to stand instead of them.'[66] Although his sense of humour did not fail, a new mordant note is perceptible. To J. L. Patterson, a London convert priest, closely involved with Wiseman and Manning, who wondered with apparent innocence why he no longer published anything, he sent a message that there were several reasons, including: 'Because Hannibal's elephants never could learn the goose step', and 'Because Garibaldi's chaplains in ordinary never do write'.[67] The latter was a sardonic reference to the rumour, which Newman knew had reached Rome, that on St Philip's day in 1860 he had preached a sermon in favour of Garibaldi (actually, he had asked for prayers for the Oratory in Sicily, a country which was being 'overrun by an able general'). Finally, he was too busy 'teaching little boys'.[68] To Mark Pattison he wrote: 'I wish I could get some rest—I wish I could

---

[63] Ibid. 138–42.   [64] Ibid. 144.   [65] Ibid. 153.
[66] Ibid. 156.   [67] Ibid. 178.   [68] Ibid. xix. 359 n. 2.

look into my books; I wish I could think out half a dozen questions, which I seem to myself to be able to answer, but have no leisure to set about.'[69]

One result of the school affair was a further alienation from Acton, who had strongly supported Darnell and who now thought that not only was Newman opposed to the idea of a public school, but that he had changed his views on education since his Dublin lectures and now favoured a more narrowly Catholic education. As usual, Newman found that he was equally suspected by the opposite party of continuing to hold dangerously secular ideas about education. Half-amused, half-exasperated, he complained to W. G. Ward, 'I have to endure, in spite of your real affection for me, a never-dying misgiving on your part that I am in some substantial matter at variance with you—while I for my part sincerely think that on *no* subject is there any substantial difference between us . . .'.[70] In view of the deep gulf that was to open between the two men during the next few years on the most contentious of theological issues, perhaps Ward's instincts were sounder than Newman guessed.

4

News of Newman's discomfiture in the Church inevitably began to filter outside. Ever since he had become a Catholic it had been rumoured that he was about to 'return from the Mother of Saints to the City of Confusion'.[71] Now there were well-publicized cases of former Anglican clergymen returning to the Church of England. Extraordinary rumours spread. One extreme Protestant correspondent in a Lincolnshire paper announced that the famous 'clerical pervert' was now a sceptic living in Paris! Newman immediately wrote to the editor to demand:

In an age of light, where in the world has the unfortunate man been living? Of what select circle is he the oracle? What bad luck has seduced him into print? What has ailed him to take up a position so false, that the Law might come down upon him, and every Englishman must cry shame upon him?[72]

Depressed and disillusioned and weary as he was, his brilliance as a controversialist had lost none of its cutting-edge; if anything, it had been tempered by successive trials. After hearing from a friendly source that it was also said that he discouraged others from becoming Catholics, he characteristically confirmed what was true in the damaging allegation, namely, that he had indeed warned '*many* Protestants that they would be disappointed in the Catholic body, if they knew it experimentally', as

[69] *LD* xx. 195.   [70] Ibid. 191.   [71] Ibid. xix. 111.
[72] Ibid. xx. 208–9.

they 'not unfrequently view us in an imaginative way'. A blistering catalogue of the actual, practical deficiencies of contemporary Catholicism follows. Far from being 'a powerful organization', the undeniable fact was that they 'often acted in a second best way in a worldly aspect'; far from being 'crafty . . . with deep, subtle, powerful intellects', Catholics were generally lacking in education; far from having 'an inexhaustible supply of money, and a consummate prudence, and a great economical exactness in its use . . . we commonly live from hand to mouth'; far from having excellent spiritual direction, 'first rate direction is rare'; and as for theology, 'since the revolutions of the end of last century, theological schools are sparse'. Catholics had the faith, but that meant, unwelcome as the fact might be to many Catholics, they possessed not 'natural excellence, but supernatural'. Educated Protestants who thought of becoming Catholics ought to know the real state of affairs, as otherwise there was a danger they might 'suffer a reaction of mind'.[73]

At the end of June, Newman took the opportunity of a categorical announcement in the *Globe*, the Whig newspaper, to deny no less categorically that he had left or was about to leave the Oratory as a step to rejoining the Church of England. The paper was too important to ignore, and its wide circulation gave him the full publicity he wanted to quash the rumours. After denying that he had any intention of leaving the Oratory, or that he had ever 'had one moment's wavering of trust in the Catholic Church', or anything but 'an unclouded faith in her creed in all its articles; a supreme satisfaction in her worship, discipline, and teaching; and an eager longing and a hope against hope that the many dear friends whom I have left in Protestantism may be partakers of my happiness', he went on to add that to deny he had any intention of leaving the Church 'would be superfluous, except that Protestants are always on the look-out for some loophole or evasion in a Catholic's statement of fact':

Therefore, in order to give them full satisfaction, if I can, I do hereby profess *ex animo*, with an absolute internal assent and consent, that Protestantism is the dreariest of possible religions; that the thought of the Anglican service makes me shiver, and the thought of the Thirty-nine Articles makes me shudder. Return to the Church of England! no; 'the net is broken, and we are delivered.' I should be a consummate fool (to use a mild term) if in my old age I left 'the land flowing with milk and honey' for the city of confusion and the house of bondage.[74]

The letter naturally provoked a flurry of anger and resentment. But Newman refused to apologize or retract what he had said. His purpose

---

[73] Ibid. 209–10.   [74] Ibid. 215–16.

had been to put an end to the rumours once and for all, by stating his feelings unambiguously in words which no one could doubt were his own words. He had meant what he said when he said that Protestantism was the dreariest of religions—in the sense that there was no religion '*less* adapted to popularity', going 'as near to the wind, as a religion can', if religion 'must have something by which to *take* people'. Who could say, for example, that the Protestant Sabbath was calculated to have popular appeal? The worship of the Book of Common Prayer was not popular religion (apart from the additions and embellishments of Tractarianism). But having said that, it was characteristic that he should proceed to emphasize, on the other hand, that the Church of England was still

indefinitely superior to *no* religion, to irreligion, and to various other English forms of religion. I account it to be a breakwater against infidelity, and do not wish it destroyed. Catholics in England could not take its place at this time . . . it is a necessity *in the present state of things*.[75]

Later Newman was asked to explain how he could consistently say that the thought of the Anglican service made him 'shiver', when in his Anglicans sermons he had spoken eloquently of daily worship and weekly communion in the Church of England. His answer was that the latter was an accurate reflection of the devotion he had felt at the time, though even then he had found the actual liturgy 'clumsy and dreary'. He could now look back with great nostalgia to St Mary's and Littlemore and 'still feel nevertheless an extreme distaste and dislike' of Anglican services. As an Anglican, it was his duty to make 'the best of things', although he had sometimes 'covertly' expressed his feelings in print even then. As a Catholic moreover, he had written glowingly of his religious devotions and feelings in the Church of England. So far as he was concerned, 'God's mercy did for me, what the system which I was in did not.' The Sunday service, 'not as I and others had attempted to mend it, but as we found it, and as I for years and years bore the burden of it in St Mary's', was indeed 'intensely dreary':

two or three Catholic services mutilated and thrown together, without any respect to due arrangement, or dependence of part; psalms, lessons, prayers, huddled up together, and read over and over again week after week . . . preached aloud in high reading desks . . . and the clerk and charity children responding and singing instead of the congregation.

As for the daily service he had introduced, it became 'a *growing* burden', and 'its intense dreariness forced itself on me more and more . . . as an unhealthy climate grows into the body', because although it was supposed to be common prayer, 'there was hardly any one at it', and so it had to be read 'in a forlorn empty Church'.[76] Finally, the joy of Sunday communion was quite compatible with having little love for the actual service.

Charles Crawley, the high-church squire at Littlemore, at the time wrote reproachfully to express his astonishment that Newman could have written such a public letter after having recently written to him privately in a friendly manner. Newman replied that he was sorry to have hurt his Anglican friends, but they had themselves broken off relations with him when he became a Catholic. As for the vehemence of his letter, it was not his fault, but the fault of the Protestants who circulated the rumours that he was leaving the Church. Silence only encouraged them. They had begun immediately after his conversion. Even Catholics had begun to believe them. Their appearance in the newspapers had given him the long-awaited opportunity for a public denial. He could not allow it to be said after he was dead that he had died a Protestant.

Tastes, sentiments, affections, are deeper, more permanent, more trustworthy, than conclusions in logic. Convictions change: habits of mind endure. Had I mildly and courteously said that my reason was antagonistic to Protestantism ... I should not have obliterated the general anticipation and instinctive suspicion that I should return to it. It would have been said that my words were dictated, nay written by someone else . . .[77]

Perhaps the rumours would at last cease now that he had made clear his 'dislikings, aversion, and moral alienation to Protestantism'.[78]

Crawley was not the only Anglican Newman was in touch with. In the autumn of 1861 Isaac Williams had written, to Newman's great joy, proposing a meeting. At the very time of the row over the letter in the *Globe*, Newman was in affectionate correspondence with another of his old curates, W. J. Copeland, begging him to pay a visit. 'You must not disappoint me,' he wrote with almost boyish delight, 'I have a hundred questions to ask you, and a hundred things to show you.'[79] He wrote again in July pressing him to come, and was overjoyed when a date was fixed—'Do *let us have a long* confab.'[80]

Former Catholic associates and collaborators afforded less consolation. At the beginning of August Newman wrote sadly and tersely to Darnell, who had sent him a furious letter about Mrs Wootten's claim to some furniture she had given him:

What I have done to deserve the letter, which has just now come to me from you, I cannot imagine.
I think you will be sorry for it some day.[81]

[76] Ibid. 339–41.	[77] Ibid. 236.	[78] Ibid. 242.
[79] Ibid. 213.	[80] Ibid. 225.	[81] Ibid. 250.

A French priest who had recently resigned as a master at the school turned out to have been a thief—'Moustaches, coloured neckties etc have been found in his room.'[82] Newman had opposed his original appointment by Darnell, but had reinstated him as a master after he had dissociated himself from the other staff who left with Darnell.

Newman was trying to be more on his guard in the world of ecclesiastical politics. He warned Ambrose St John not to let out too much to Wiseman's aide, J. L. Patterson—but to be 'suave, bland, and reticent'. Bishop Ullathorne had just preached at the Oratory at one service 'two sermons, agglutinated—an hour and half about'.[83] He and the other English bishops had recently won a victory over Wiseman in forcing the Pope to agree that their votes at episcopal meetings were not merely consultative; but they had been dismissed with a rebuke by Pius IX. Rome was firmly behind Wiseman and his policies. His closest collaborator, Manning, also came to Birmingham, 'very kind as always . . . primed to console' Newman about the troubles at the school (which was criticized by more than one of the bishops for being too secular and lax in discipline). Newman refused to help with the *Dublin Review*, which Manning was reorganizing as the Ultramontane answer to the *Rambler*. Innocently, Newman told him in confidence that while in his letter to the *Globe* he had called the Church 'the land of Canaan', in fact 'looking at it in a temporal earthly point of view, it was just the contrary. I had found very little but desert and desolateness ever since I had been in it . . . all my human affections were with those whom I had left.' Years later he noted that this 'was one of the last times that Manning wormed things out of me'; Ullathorne had warned him that he 'never went any where but to fish out something'. Indeed, Newman came to feel, 'he is quite violent sometimes in his effort to gain secrets. He does not fish, but extorts by force . . . He is ever prying about . . .'.[84]

Meanwhile Newman was wearing himself out with school business. St John had had a severe attack of asthma, to which he was prone, at the beginning of the summer holidays. It was serious news, as the school depended on him—'We hang on a thread.'[85] Newman was left to do the accounts by himself. An unhappy slip in his arithmetic one night brought back the old nervous symptoms and a bout of insomnia (accompanied by his 'usual dream' of having to 'preach before the University of Oxford' without 'a notion what I was to preach about, and then a misgiving coming on me that it was a communicatio in sacris').[86] Almost never before in his life had he felt so much the need for a holiday. In the middle of August came Flanagan's long-expected resignation; he blamed the school for having changed the character of the Oratory. For

[82] *LD* xx. 251.   [83] Ibid.   [84] Ibid. xx. 253–4; xxiv. 33–4.

[85] Ibid. xx. 239.   [86] Ibid. 255.

Newman it was not only yet another defection, but 'the most tragical event, which has befallen the Oratory, since it has been set up'.[87] Apart from himself, there were now only six members in the community, together with a novice, who left the next year.

5

At the end of September Newman went down to the Kent coast for a much-needed break. On the train to London he was recognized by Benjamin Jowett of Balliol, who came and sat down next to him. He decided to go to Deal, where he found lodgings at 43 Walmer Road. He wrote to J. R. Bloxam, his old curate, who had always kept in friendly contact, that he wanted to avoid well-known resorts like Brighton where his name was likely to attract publicity:

I can't tell how long I shall be here. Perhaps I shall suddenly abscond . . . This is not the most ornate place in the world—but the Deal boatman and the pipe-loving sailor are more welcome objects to me in the landscape, than fine gentlemen, watering-place cockneys, crinolines, porkpie hats, and little dogs with blue ribbons on.[88]

He remembered 'the soft charm which the chalk gives to the landscape', but he was pleasantly surprised by the autumnal fields and heather, 'rich yellow or salmon coloured'.[89] The 'esplanade' was no more than 'a long strip of pebbly green, uneven and slanting the wrong way, and strewed with oyster shells and broken bottles', but it was preferable to 'the smooth majestic esplanade' of a fashionable resort, where his name was likely to get into the local paper in the 'list of arrivals'. The one drawback was the prohibitive cost of a sea-bathing machine—half-a-crown (not much less than the cost of a dinner in a hotel). He guessed his landlord was a waiter—'at least he has all the appearance, being an upright melancholy young man in sad attire'.[90] He thought it 'a very good sign' that his wife was 'neat, clean, and pretty looking; for women lose this when they have the duties of a family, and have no one to please but their families'. Her cooking was less appealing: he had asked her to get in some mutton chops,

and I reckoned accordingly on my Sunday's meal, when they were to come into play. Alas, to my dismay, when the cover was lifted off, I saw nothing but a piece of meat the size of a fritter, and when I attempted to cut it, it was nearly all bone. She said I had ordered '*a chop*' . . .[91]

---

[87] Ibid. 261. [88] Ibid. 277. [89] Ibid. 276.
[90] Ibid. 279. [91] Ibid. 283.

He was enjoying reading Trollope's recent novel *The Bertrams*, although he was disturbed by 'a touch of scepticism which I have never seen in him before',[92] and was very disappointed by the last volume ('few people can end').[93] He was also enjoying being able to wear his 'worst things—a very great lounge. I am almost a guy . . . I don't wear gloves, and I carry three novel volumes under my arm without a scruple.'[94] The seclusion was perfect: it was only a pity that there was no sandy beach and no cliffs. A more serious drawback was the fact that there was no hotel where he could get a decent dinner. Nor was his weekly bill at the lodgings cheap, in spite of the poor food; it only confirmed all his experience that 'First rate places are not dearer than second rate', which 'do not know how to charge, and therefore charge at random'.[95]

Secluded as he was, he could not avoid correspondence. He heard from St John that Edward Bellasis had met the Bishop of Shrewsbury on the train, who had launched an attack on the religious instruction given at the school. It was indeed 'astonishing', Newman mused, 'how near the wind people allow themselves to go in the matter of false witness— and persons, who from their position and weight of metal, are able to do so much against small craft'. Perhaps in the end the 'continual cannonadings' would 'work their purpose'. 'I suppose,' he remarked, with weary sarcasm, 'Bishops are above the 10 commandments.'[96] The suggestion (readily advanced by the bishop) that it was not surprising the religious instruction was unsatisfactory, since it was given by converts, was calculated to deter old Catholics especially from sending their sons to the school—and old Catholics, Newman thought, 'hold together like a bunch of currants; one go, all go'.[97] The convert teachers suspected by the bishop included Newman himself, who was involved in giving catechetical talks to the boys—which St John thought were so good that they should be published. Still, Newman recognized that the standards at the school needed to be raised, although this would take time.

On 16 October he left Deal for Ramsgate, where he stayed a fortnight at the Royal Hotel. He read Dickens's *Bleak House* and was struck by how much a passage about Deal resembled his own description of it. While he was there at Ramsgate, a copy of Bishop Ullathorne's letter to the Birmingham clergy, censuring both the *Rambler* and its successor the *Home and Foreign Review*, was forwarded to him. He wrote immediately to Ullathorne accepting the condemnation, but with the significant reservation, 'of the doctrines which you find in those publications'.[98] He also agreed that the doctrines in question should be repudiated and the offending passages withdrawn. The bishop thanked him, and promised

---

[92] *LD* xx. 281. [93] Ibid. 284. [94] Ibid. 285. [95] Ibid. 293.
[96] Ibid. 313–14. [97] Ibid. 282. [98] Ibid. 324.

that he would make sure the contents of the letter were made known to the Roman authorities to dispel any lingering suspicions of Newman; a copy of the letter was also sent to Wiseman, who showed it to Manning.

Earlier in the summer Newman had advised Acton against the idea of Simpson making any sort of public apology for his more extreme statements in the *Rambler*; such a gesture, far from conciliating, would only be exploited by his enemies. The first number of the new *Home and Foreign Review* had been published in July. There was an unwitting allusion to a report in a French paper that Wiseman had advocated excommunicating leading opponents of the Temporal Power. For Wiseman it was the last straw, stung as he was by Simpson's continual jibes. Already in May he had successfully arranged for Propaganda to send the bishops an order to issue official condemnations of the *Rambler*. Now he responded with a bitter public attack on the orthodoxy of the *Home and Foreign Review* and its predecessor. Newman thought that Wiseman had overreacted and that Acton should not contemplate closing down the review: 'Such a course would be a smothering of feelings and opinions which exist, which are allowable in a Catholic, which it is healthy to out with, dangerous or injurious to bottle up.' The *Home and Foreign* had to be shown to be unorthodox, not just out of line with a particular party in the Church. The actual reply to Wiseman in the October issue struck him, however, as disappointingly casual and evasive. But he was even more displeased by a review article by Simpson which digressed into a theological discussion of the beginning of Genesis; it was 'a speculation edged with an insinuation, or an insinuation hoisted on a speculation'. And he had 'a lifelong disgust at speculations, as opposed to carefully argued theories or doctrines'.[99] He certainly had no intention of becoming involved himself in writing for the *Home and Foreign*. Indeed, Ullathorne's letter of censure almost seemed to him to give 'the coup de grace'[100] to his ever writing anything again: whatever he wrote, he would be sure to become involved in controversy. Unlike Wiseman's letter, Ullathorne's was at least specific and was apparently mostly directed at Simpson's articles. Disinclined as he was to defend Simpson, Newman found the bishop's argument too obscure to decide how far he was fair to Simpson. He was, however, slightly worried by Ullathorne's remark that the *Rambler* and *Home and Foreign Review* were wont to hint they were secretly supported by an unnamed authority of great weight. The reference would be taken to be to himself. Did the bishop really trust him? He knew he had doubts about the school. Perhaps Flanagan's strange, unaccountable departure would be attributed to a want of confidence in Newman's orthodoxy. Perhaps the

---

[99] Ibid. 295.   [100] Ibid. 319.

crimes of Rougemont, the former French master, would also be used against the Oratory. He confided to St John his nightmarish premonition that even worse might be in store. After all, he had predicted, with alarming prescience, at the time of the Achilli trial,

that, as, when I was 20 I was cut off from the rising talent of the University by my failure in the Schools, as, when 30, I was cut off from distinction in the governing body by being deprived of my Tutorship, as, when 40, I was virtually cast out of the Church of England, by the affair of Number 90, as when 50 I was cast out of what may be called society by the disgrace of the Achilli sentence, so, when I should arrive at 60 years, I should be cast out of the good books of Catholics, and especially of ecclesiastical authorities.

If, then, he lived to be 70, 'Am I to lose all of you and to be left desolate? or is our house to be burned to the ground? or am I to be smitten with some afflicting disorder?'[101]

Whatever the lack of cogency in Ullathorne's letter, Newman was adamant that his response to it had been right. It was irrelevant that Simpson had not been proved to be guilty of the heterodoxy of which he was accused. The fact was that authority had spoken, and what was the point of subscribing to the principle of episcopal authority if one disallowed the exercise of it? In words he would have used as an Anglican, he insisted, 'What a Bishop says is law to those over whom he has jurisdiction.' As for the right of appeal, Ullathorne's judgement was patently upheld by the Metropolitan (Wiseman) and by Propaganda at Rome. Still, a careful distinction had to be made between 'an internal consent on such subtle and delicate questions' (which was not required), and the duty to acquiesce, as a matter of discipline rather than doctrine, in the condemnation.[102] The authoritative nature of Ullathorne's letter was beyond dispute; how far it was correct or true was another question altogether. In fact, Newman suspected he had misrepresented Simpson's views (on original sin, specifically), 'but no good ever came of disobedience, and I submit as a duty'.[103]

There was another reservation that had to be made. He did not wish his acceptance of Ullathorne's condemnation to be seen to imply any sort of recantation on his part. The delighted W. G. Ward had to be warned that disapproval of the *Home and Foreign* did not mean approval of the *Dublin Review*, with which 'under no circumstances should I connect my name': 'If I ever wrote on the subjects in question, I should say neither what Simpson has said, nor what you have said; but any how the true judgment about me lies, not with clubs or with coteries, but in my own acts . . .'.[104] For Newman, as for other moderate Catholics, it was a tragedy that a review which had the right ideas and principles

[101] *LD* xx. 328–9.   [102] Ibid. 331.   [103] Ibid. 376.   [104] Ibid. 337.

should unnecessarily alienate general Catholic opinion because of its style and tone. The failure of the *Home and Foreign* would have the disastrous consequence that the *Dublin Review* would have the field to itself. Because the *Home and Foreign* was really more or less a continuation of the *Rambler*, Newman's connection with the latter tended to be used by the editors to suggest an involvement with its successor. However, to dissociate himself publicly from Acton and Simpson would be very awkward, as that might imply support for Ward. To explain his real position would involve more than 'a little explanation; and if I attempted one, I might be making a dozen fresh holes while I darned one'.[105]

On Boxing Day he received a visit from Bishop Ullathorne, who came to talk about the pamphlet Simpson had just issued in reply to his letter to the clergy and about his own projected reply to it. Afraid that the bishop had misunderstood his position, Newman wrote formally a few days later. He showed a draft of his letter to Ward, who complained that he misled people by not speaking out clearly and directly, and advised him to draw out unambiguously for the bishop's benefit the distinction between 'external submission' and 'internal assent'. Newman, however, saw no need to offend the bishop unnecessarily. He pointed out that he had given his 'obedience' or 'submission' to Ullathorne's letter, although he could not express a judgement himself on its contents, as he had not read the particular writings in question. But he warned that 'a certain sympathy' with Simpson's 'intentions has been at the root of my pain at his performances'. Strongly disapprove as he did of Simpson's style and tone, he could not deny that his real complaint was that he had 'dealt so unworthily with questions, which are real and great, and which demand, not only free discussion, but a grave and comprehensive treatment'. It was precisely because Simpson's 'dissatisfaction with the present mode of handling subjects of controversy was my own' that he had decided immediately to 'subject what was so near my heart and intellect to the judgment of the Church'. However, his submission had been freely given as soon as Ullathorne (unlike the Cardinal) had spoken out 'like a Bishop, clearly, distinctly'. And just as when he became a Catholic he had been ready to burn his *Essay on the Development of Christian Doctrine*, so now, had he 'been writing on those subjects which most deeply interest and distress me at this time', he would have been 'equally ready to suppress my own convictions at the bidding of the Church'.[106] In its careful balance and subtle distinctions, this pointed but respectful letter is certainly a masterly piece of tactful candour. In his first draft, Newman had spoken less politely of 'the shallowness of the

[105] Ibid. 353.   [106] Ibid. 378–9.

polemic with which we ordinarily meet the intellectual difficulties of the day' (a charge Ward had to admit was perfectly true). What was good enough for the old Catholic gentry of Ullathorne's generation was not necessarily going to satisfy 'active minds and the generation to come': 'I earnestly pray, that the ecclesiastical policy, which in one shape or other has been pursued toward the Anglo-Saxon race during the last 300 years, may be in the long run as successful as it has been absolute and peremptory.'[107] These daring words, which contain an unmistakable allusion to Simpson's outspoken views on the folly of excommunicating Queen Elizabeth and the long-standing refusal to allow English Catholics to take oaths of allegiance denying the Pope's power to depose the sovereign, were, not surprisingly, not in the letter actually sent.

Ullathorne replied that he perfectly understood Newman's position, and that the cautious tone of his original response had not been lost on him. Unlike Ward, he had not misunderstood. Newman sent Ward a copy of Ullathorne's letter and took the opportunity to reject the suggestion that he was still practising '*economical half speakings*', a practice he had been forced to advocate as an Anglican, but which 'I have given up since I was a Catholic'.[108] Ullathorne's reply refuted Ward's charge that Newman 'never spoke out . . . always hinted things', and that this was what made him unpopular among Catholics.[109] Although Newman thought that Ullathorne had been unfair to Simpson, he also had to admit that what had offended the bishop was likely to 'scandalize and mislead ordinary Catholics'. And they were the people who read the *Rambler*, which was not an academic journal but a periodical, so it was not surprising that the Church should show 'a vigour' in dealing with it which corresponded to 'that which the new description of literature exhibits'. As a quasi-missionary country, England came under Propaganda, which in turn came more directly under the Pope than any other department of the Roman Curia; any episcopal pronouncement inspired by Propaganda, therefore, carried special weight. Rome was wont 'to meet rude actions by a rude retort', and, since the Pope was 'not a philosopher, but a ruler', Simpson really could not complain.[110] What he saw as the 'real grievance' drew from Newman one of his first important observations on the relationship in the Church between the teaching authority and the freedom of theologians:

The wisdom of the Church has provided many courts for theological questions, one higher than another, and with an appeal from the lower to the higher. I suppose, in the middle ages, which had a manliness and boldness of which there is now so great a lack, a question was first debated in a University; then in one University against another; or by one order of friars against another; then

[107] *LD* xx. 376–7.   [108] Ibid. 385.   [109] Ibid. 388.   [110] Ibid. 390–1.

perhaps it came before a theological faculty; then it went to the metropolitan; and so by various stages and after many examinations and judgments, it came before the Holy See. But now what do the Bishops do? All courts are superseded, because the English-speaking Catholic population all over the world is under Propaganda, an arbitrary, military power. Propaganda is our only court of appeal; but to it the Bishops go, and secure it and commit it, before they move one step in the matter which calls for interference . . . And who *is* Propaganda? one sharp man of business, who works day and night, and dispatches his work quick off, to the East and the West, a high dignitary . . . but after all little more than a clerk . . . with two or three clerks under him.

Faced with what he could only view as an abnormal situation, he still counselled patience: 'All this will be overruled.' Characteristically, he warned that to resist would only be 'to complicate matters, and to delay the necessary reforms'. He was quite ready to speak his mind to his bishop, but only if he were asked to (which was unlikely). In the end, the 'logic of facts will be the best and most thorough teacher'. Meanwhile, it was a sobering thought that 'in England, as things are, upon theological questions the Pope and the individual Catholic meet each other face to face, without media for collision, without the safeguard of springs or cushions, with a jar; and the quasi-military power of Propaganda has the jurisdiction and the control of the intellect'.[111] When he himself had been ordered to resign the editorship of the *Rambler*, it had been, he joked, 'the same shock to my nerves that a pat from a lion would be': when 'great powers' are 'brought into exercise', then 'one seems to feel one's breath taken away'.[112]

Nevertheless, Simpson's recent pamphlet had given Newman real grounds for hope that the *Home and Foreign Review* would, after all, be able to survive. For Simpson had taken on himself personal responsibility for most of the offending articles in the *Rambler*, and had disclaimed any editorial responsibility for the *Home and Foreign*. Apart from the one offending article on Genesis, the *Home and Foreign* had only fallen under censure because of its close connection with the *Rambler*. It now had the opportunity to wipe the slate clean and make a new start, hopefully without Simpson's help. Unfortunately, it soon began to look as if Acton intended to play down the Catholic character of the review and to publish Protestant contributions even on subjects with a religious bearing: the result, Newman sadly predicted, would be 'neither fish, fowl, nor good red herring'.[113] He had discovered this uncomfortable fact himself when he had tried to make a Catholic revision of his own *Oxford University Sermons*. But he did not despair, and before long he felt more encouraged by the prospects of the review.

---

[111] Ibid. 391–2. [112] Ibid. xxi. 23. [113] Ibid. xx. 403.

6

Apart from the wider issues, Newman was weighed down with work and worry. 'One gets', he wrote, 'into a dull passive state, such as one may fancy to be the frame of mind of a wearied and jaded cab-horse.'[114] His lethargy sank to a new trough on 21 January 1863, when he could not even bring himself to take a shower on getting up in the morning:

for what is the good, I said, of prolonging strength, when I do nothing? And yet every way seems blocked up to me by which I could be of use. There are plenty of things I could attempt, which I am *not* fit for—but a veto seems to come whenever I try at any thing I feel I could do. And how to get through the thick underwood, and over the ravines, I see not. So year goes on after year; and no man hires me.[115]

For solace he turned once again to his private journal, where he could pour out his sorrows without the risk of seeming to complain. He had intended to make regular entries, but this was only the third time he had written in it in over three years. For the last year or two, he noted, he had been trying to preserve his health: he had taken holidays and, in the attempt to ward off the colds to which he was so vulnerable, he had not only papered and carpeted his room, but also installed double windows and a shower. But now, he wondered listlessly, to what purpose? 'O how forlorn and dreary has been my course since I have been a Catholic! here has been the contrast—as a Protestant, I felt my religion dreary, but not my life—but, as a Catholic, my life dreary, not my religion.' Till his retirement to Littlemore after *Tract 90*, 'I had my mouth half open, and commonly a smile on my face', but ever since then 'my mouth has been closed and contracted, and the muscles are so set now, that I cannot but look grave and forbidding'. Indeed, he was 'so conscious' of his 'stern look' that he hardly liked even 'to see people'.

It began when I set my face towards Rome; and, since I made the great sacrifice, to which God called me, He has rewarded me in ten thousand ways, O how many! but he has marked my course with almost unintermittent mortification.

He had had few successes in life apart from his scholarship at Trinity and his fellowship at Oriel, but 'since I have been a Catholic, I seem to myself to have had nothing but failure, personally'.[116] It was not all his various trials he complained of, but the fact that they had '(to all appearance) succeeded in destroying my influence and usefulness'. Converts, with ingratitude, had treated him much worse than the old Catholics. It was true that the Oratory, the Catholic University, and the Oratory School

[114] *LD* xx. 381.   [115] Ibid. 398.   [116] *AW* 254–5.

were all foundations associated with his name, but he himself personally had not been able to do any of the things which he felt specially qualified to do. He knew that at Rome the only thing that counted was converts, especially important converts, such as Faber and Manning made in London. Ever since the Oxford conversions, Rome had had 'visions of the whole of England coming over to the Church' and saw 'the conversion of persons of rank' as the obvious means to this end ('Such an idea is perhaps even conveyed in our Brief, which sends us to the upper classes'). His own way had been 'altogether different': when he became a Catholic, it seemed to him that 'one, who had taken a prominent part against the Church', should not take 'a prominent part against Anglicanism, but that my place was retirement, which indeed was my nature too'. But the real problem was that he did not in fact see conversions as 'the first thing, but the edification of Catholics'. Indeed, in his view, the Church had to be 'prepared for converts, as well as converts prepared for the Church'. This attitude was hardly likely to appeal to the Roman authorities, who did not understand the English situation; as for English Catholics, they were bound to resent the suggestion that they were ignorant and ill informed. But 'from first to last, education, in this large sense of the word, has been my line'. It had caused offence in two other ways. Rome did not appreciate the implication that there was 'room for improvement' in Catholic apologetic. In England, the Oratory School was resented as interfering with existing establishments, which explained the attacks on it. It was not surprising, then, that since

these have been the two objects of the Rambler,—to raise the status of Catholics, first by education, secondly by a philosophical basis of argument,— and the Rambler has attempted it injudiciously, intemperately, and erroneously, at least at times, I come in for the odium of all the Rambler's faults . . .

Finally, there was the all-important question of the Temporal Power, on which Newman was known to be 'lukewarm': Wiseman had once said he had put himself 'on the shelf'—'But the position I occupy at the moment is, in his mind, a less harmless one.'[117]

Anyway, it was not the Temporal Power, or even education, that was at present occupying his time. He was again immersed in the school accounts; they had not been kept properly by Darnell—which was partly why the Oratory was losing money on the school. Without Flanagan, and with St John in poor health and fully occupied as headmaster, not only all the responsibility, but many of the routine chores of the community fell on his shoulders. The few priests left in the community had their energies absorbed by the school, the Oratory

[117] Ibid. 257–60.

parish, the mission they had opened at Smethwick, and the workhouse (where they had even succeeded in setting up a Catholic chapel). There were no lay brothers, and Newman had on his hands much of the work connected with the church sacristy and choir, the library, and the community housekeeping. These routine jobs and his correspondence filled the day. But his health was good, and he hardly could believe he was now 62:

I am an old man; my hair white, my eyes sunk in, and my hand so shrivelled, that I am sometimes quite startled to see it;—but, when I shut my eyes and merely think, I can't believe I am more than 25 years old, and smile to think how differently strangers must think of me from my own internal feelings.[118]

Before the end of March, Newman heard of the possibility of a private venture to establish a Catholic college at Oxford. His cautious response was that while the Oratory School was not at present preparing boys for either Oxford or Cambridge, it was not an impossibility, if parents asked for it (but so far, few had). And of course, if Catholics were to go to either university, it was better they should go to their own college, provided the bishops gave permission—which was not certain, as Rome might well forbid it in line with its strict policy in favour of Catholic education. It was clear that English Catholics must have proper access to university education, but what the best solution was he did not profess to say.

Meanwhile, the news from the Catholic University in Dublin was not very reassuring. There had been a demonstration against the government by the students. Newman commented acidly, 'While there were other students, besides Irish, in the University, the national feeling was kept *diluted*, but now it is the genuine high proof whisky and no mistake.'[119] If the students were not very Catholic, it was only to be expected from Cullen's idea of religious education—'Denunciation neither effects subjection in thought nor in conduct.' It was like the harsh treatment meted out to the *Rambler*—'You cannot make men believe by force and repression'; rather, 'you train the reason to defend the truth'. And the 'cut and dried answers out of a dogmatic treatise are no weapons with which the Catholic Reason can hope to vanquish the infidels of the day'.

Newman again reverts in his correspondence to the crucial question of intellectual freedom in the Church, this time employing the kind of physical imagery which he had once used satirically to describe the discomfort of Anglo-Catholics in an essentially Protestant church. 'Why was it that the Medieval Schools were so vigorous? because they were allowed free and fair play—because the disputants were not made to feel the bit in their mouths at every other word they spoke, but could move

[118] *LD* xx. 409.   [119] Ibid. 425.

their limbs freely and expatiate at will.' Not that the importance of authority is in any way rejected by Newman, but rather it is, he hints, in the creative interplay between the magisterium and private judgment that truth is attained: 'when they went wrong, a stronger and truer intellect set them down—and, as time went on, if the dispute got perilous, and a controversialist obstinate, then at length Rome interfered—at length, not at first—Truth is wrought out by many minds, working together freely.' Indeed, it is in these exploratory letters that we see a vigorously independent and original mind, yet imbued with a profound sense of authority and tradition, in the actual process of forming a balanced theory of the teaching office of the Church. And his analysis is not confined only to 'missionary' English-speaking countries, which suffered from the special disadvantage of immediate dependence on Propaganda, but is applied to the whole Catholic Church affected by the rise of Ultramontanism: 'As far as I can make out, this [kind of freedom] has ever been the rule of the Church till now, when the first French Revolution having destroyed the Schools of Europe, a sort of centralization has been established at headquarters—and the individual thinker in France, England, or Germany is brought into immediate collision with the most sacred authorities of the Divine Polity.'[120]

On a more practical plane, increased familiarity with the life and practice of the Church had not caused Newman to withdraw his first impressions as a convert of the faith of ordinary Catholics, but he had had to modify them as he became more realistic about actual practice. He had never advocated the 'ecclesiastical prohibition to doubt and inquire' as a means of preserving belief, but he was now very conscious that Catholics could and did lose their faith:

A Catholic is kept from scepticism . . . by admiration, trust, and love. While he admires, trusts, and loves our Lord and His Church, these feelings prohibit him from doubt; they guard and protect his faith; the real prohibition is from within. But suppose these feelings go . . .[121]

There was the rub, and it was one to which he was increasingly to advert as society drifted into deeper disbelief and the Catholic Church diverged into more and more isolated obscurantism.

Feeling increasingly cut off from the world and other Catholics (by whom he was regarded, he noticed, 'as *dead*, in a sort of historical way'),[122] he continued to think aloud in his letters on the theme which was soon to achieve classic expression in the *Apologia*. Not that he had any thought of writing for an audience, for although he felt 'as full of thought and life as ever', he was conscious that 'a certain invisible chain

---

[120] Ibid. 425–6. [121] Ibid. 430. [122] Ibid. 394.

impedes me, or bar stops me, when I attempt to do any thing'. He was happy to be out of controversy, but for the fact that 'I feel to myself I could do much in it.' It was not that he himself was not loyal to the Holy See—indeed, he was personally devoted to the Pope—

But Propaganda is a quasi-military power, extraordinary, for missionary countries, rough and ready. It does not understand an intellectual movement. It likes quick results—scalps from beaten foes by the hundred. Our Bishop once on his return from Rome, said pointedly to me what I am sure came as a quasi message from Propaganda, that at Rome 'they liked good news.'

This was his mistake—'I had not preached sermons, make speeches, fussed about, and reported all my proceedings to Propaganda. I had been working away very hard in Ireland at the University, and saying nothing about it.' Then as editor of the *Rambler*, he would have been in a position 'to ventilate a hundred questions',[123] but he had not been given the 'elbow room' necessary. Unlike earlier times (he reiterates with a new, vivid image),

Now, if I, as a private priest, put any thing into print, *Propaganda* answers me at once. How can I fight with such a chain on my arm? It is like the Persians driven on to fight *under the lash*. There was true private judgment in the primitive and medieval schools—there are no schools now, no private judgment . . . That is, no exercise of the intellect. No, the system goes on by the tradition of the intellect of former times.

However, he refused to despair:

This is a way of things which, in God's own time, will work its own cure, of necessity; nor need we fret under a state of things, much as we may feel it, which is incomparably less painful than the state of the Church before Hildebrand, and again in the fifteenth century.

As for himself personally, if he had suffered at the hands of the Roman authorities, so had his patron St Philip. The one prospect he had to fear was a summons to Rome to defend himself, which meant 'to sever an old man from his Home, to subject him to intercourse with persons whose languages are strange to him . . . to bring him to a climate, which is unhealthy to him—to food, and to floors, which are almost starvation on one hand, and involve restless days and nights on the other . . . to oblige him to dance attendance on Propaganda week after week and month after month—it means his death.'[124] It was indeed a far cry from his sanguine belief, after the visit to Italy in 1856, that they could 'be sure, that, if we are really doing work, Rome will never be hard on us, even if we are informal, imprudent, or arbitrary'![125]

---

[123] *LD* xxi. 23. [124] Ibid. xx. 445–8. [125] Ibid. xvii. 151.

7

During the summer, the question of Catholics attending English universities began increasingly to occupy Newman's attention. He was quite clear in his own mind that 'mixed' or 'unmixed' education was only a matter of 'expedience'. However, not only had Rome a very definite and insistent policy in favour of exclusively Catholic education, but he himself had 'personally a great dislike to mixed education'—and indeed, he added:

I love Oxford too well to wish its dogmatism destroyed, tho' it be a Protestant dogmatism. I had rather it was dogmatic on an error, than not dogmatic at all. At present I had rather it excluded us, from dogmatism, than admitted us, from liberalism. Dogmatism is not so common in these days, that we can dispense with any one of its witnesses. Oxford has been a breakwater against latitudinarianism; I don't wish to have part in letting the ocean in. It is another thing altogether what one ought to do when the breakwater is gone.[126]

The paradox was typical. But so too was the opposite conclusion, acknowledging the practical rather than advocating the ideal: Catholics were bound to want to go to Oxford, and therefore it was better not to oppose a Catholic college or hall there. Nevertheless, he personally could not bring himself to support the idea; apart from anything else, it would be inconsistent with his position on mixed education, it would be tacitly admitting that the Catholic University had failed, and it would involve opposition to Rome. His predicament was that the Catholic University was not in fact meeting the needs of English Catholics and that some provision had to be made for them. Perhaps the time might be coming when a Catholic presence at Oxford would turn out to be a welcome ally for Anglicans in the fight to defend religion there. Privately, he was embarrassed by the consideration that he had himself once written to Propaganda opposing English Catholics going to Oxford and Cambridge in order to protect the interests of the Catholic University; he had also urged the granting of a charter for the University as an alternative to the English universities opening their doors to Catholics. The irony was that it was the only time Propaganda had ever supported him! At any rate, if there was to be a Catholic hall at Oxford, he was strongly of the opinion that it should be a decent size and in a respectable building, even if a start had to be made with small lodging-houses. There was also some talk of the possibility of starting a Catholic university in England, and Newman wondered if a suitable mansion might be acquired cheaply in a provincial town away from the

---

[126] Ibid. xx. 455–6.

big cities and centres. An alternative would be a hall affiliated to
Oxford—perhaps, he suggested, at Oscott, where it could replace the
school there and support the seminary, which could then be separated;
unlikely as the plan was to be accepted, it had obvious advantages for
the Oratory School. The more he thought about it, the more he inclined
towards a college rather than a Catholic university, which would be
expensive and risky, if only because it was unlikely to attract Catholic
students. The English bishops did not seem to be opposed to the idea,
provided it did not create a precedent for mixed education. But he
thought that unless the interested laity put pressure on the hierarchy,
'the strong *will* of Manning'[127] would prevail. Either plan, however,
seemed better than Catholics going to Anglican colleges at Oxford—
although, unfortunately, Catholics might not be very interested in their
sons going to Oxford at all, unless they could go to one of the established,
traditional colleges.

In July of the previous year Faber had mentioned in a letter that there
was the danger of his suffering a stroke as a result of strain; so, Newman
commented unsympathetically to Ambrose St John, 'he now has some
portions of the anxieties, which I, which we, have had so many years. It
was good fun sailing on the stream, speaking against the Brummagem
Oratory, and criticizing me as slow ... But now anxious times are
coming on *him*.'[128] In the summer of 1863, reports continued to arrive in
Birmingham of Faber's imminent death. Newman was inclined to take
them with a pinch of salt: 'How many times has Fr Faber been
a-dying?'[129] But this time it was true. Faber was indeed dying. To
Wiseman, who in July wrote urging him to visit Faber before he died,
Newman replied with icy formality:

I thank your Eminence for the feeling which dictated your Eminence's letter.
I am perfectly aware of the hopeless state in which Fr Faber lies.
Your Eminence will be glad to know that Fr Faber has already been
informed by me, not only of my wish to see him, but of the precise time when I
hope to have that sad satisfaction[.][130]

Newman was leaving Birmingham for London anyway, for his first
continental holiday since his trip with Hurrell Froude, thirty years
before. On the way he stopped to see Faber. At Ostend he wrote up an
account of this last meeting. On medical advice he had only stayed a
quarter of an hour. Faber did most of the talking, 'for he seemed to wish
to disburden his mind'. To Newman, he gave the appearance of 'arguing
with himself that he had not been unkind to me'. He protested his love
and admiration for Newman, as well as his gratitude for his influence
and support. He claimed that he had been in a minority of one in

[127] *LD* xx. 518.   [128] Ibid. 248.   [129] Ibid. 468.   [130] Ibid. 494.

wanting Newman consulted before they applied to Rome for the dispensation from the Oratorian Rule, and had only given in when the rest of the community made it clear that they would still make the application even if Newman was against it. 'My own view about Faber, poor fellow,' commented Newman, 'is not much changed.'[131] There was no doubt that Faber had been disloyal, and he knew it: he had certainly talked against Newman behind his back. At least the mystery of the application was now cleared up: Flanagan had been right in saying that it was a deliberate act to show the Brompton house's independence. What the Londoners had not calculated on was Propaganda's unfortunate decision to consult Ullathorne rather than Newman, presumably on the assumption that the latter was aware of the application. Faber finally died on 26 September, and Newman attended the funeral.

Basking in the August sunshine on the pier at Ostend, Newman looked out over a

vast hard dry expanse of sand—lots of children making castles on it. Bathing machines without end, and bathing all day—a continual landing, more or less dexterous, of the clumsy machines, drawn by clumsier horses scarcely in harness, from the pier into the level sea-line of deep ploughed-up sand—hosts of donkey boys stretched at full length, with their donkeys not knowing what to think of it—an awning over head, and a restorateur at our backs—where we had a good dinner at 4 francs, and a military band.

As the sun set, the Belgian King, Leopold I, Queen Victoria's uncle, suddenly walked past.

We were quite by ourselves, and received a most gracious bow . . . I was surprised at his young appearance. The last time I saw him was at the Coronation of George the iv, July 1821! What a time he has been before the world! since 1816, nearly 50 years—a man who has born arms against the first Napoleon . . . Of course he is some years older than I am, but still to persons of my age he is a sort of compendium of the whole political history of their times.[132]

On his return to Birmingham, Newman found another reminder of the past: a letter was awaiting him from John Keble, the first for seventeen years. The tone was characteristically affectionate and gentle. Keble apologized for not having written for so long: he had heard that the silence of old friends had pained Newman—although in fact he himself had been the last to write (Newman could not now remember why he had never replied)—and he felt 'it was the duty of us all to diminish rather than aggravate' the 'sore burthen' he was 'bearing' for the sake of 'conscience'. Newman replied immediately:

[131] Ibid. xvii. 559–60.   [132] Ibid. xx. 499.

Never have I doubted for one moment your affection for me—never have I been hurt at your silence. I interpreted it easily—it was not the silence of men, nor the forgetfulness of men, who can recollect about me and talk about me enough, when there is something to be said to my disparagement. You are always with me a thought of reverence and love—and there is nothing I love better than you, and Isaac [Williams], and Copeland and many others I could name, except Him whom I ought to love best of all and supremely. May He Himself, who is the over abundant compensation for all losses, give me His own Presence—and then I shall want nothing and desiderate nothing—but none *but* He, *can* make up for the losses of those old familiar faces which haunt me continually.[133]

He also found on his return—and the contrast was eloquent—that the first number of the *Dublin Review*, edited by W. G. Ward, which had come out in July, contained an article by Manning referring to the Catholic schools of England, but pointedly omitting any reference to the Oratory School. The article advocated a Catholic university, and referred to Newman's Dublin lectures to oppose the plan of a Catholic college at Oxford. But, Newman protested, 'what I have said is, that Catholic youths should not go to Protestant *Tutors* and *Lecturers*—and in the plan of a *College*, they would not'. His own difficulty was the dilemma that Catholics in Oxford would either be 'few, and then despised, or many and then feared and hated'.[134]

Nothing, however, could spoil his delight at renewing contact with old Anglican friends. The previous Christmas he had written to Copeland to thank him for the gift of a turkey (which was to become an annual present)[135] and to express the hope of another meeting soon. Copeland was thinking of writing a history of the Oxford Movement, and Newman was enthusiastic about the idea. He wanted him to come and see his own letters of the period, which he was busy trying to sort out; besides, 'There are so many things I could talk to you about.' He ended with the moving assurance, 'You could not be kinder to me than you are in telling me that persons whom I love have not forgotten me.'[136] A few weeks later, he wrote affectionately, 'I want you to live many years, and never, never again to be so cruel to me as you were for near 17 long years.' No one, he continued, knew 'how great an affliction' it had been to be 'simply treated . . . as *dead*'.[137] And now, at the end of August, he received a visit from Frederic Rogers, whom he had not seen for twenty years, and who burst into tears when he saw him, he was so changed. 'We talked exceedingly freely on all subjects—my *own*

---

[133] *LD* xx. 503.   [134] Ibid. 512.

[135] This Christmas he was to write in thanks to his dear 'heretical' friend: 'What a turkey! it is as large as a baby—we shall make a good Catholic of it by means of a hot fire, before it comes to table' (*LD* xx. 564).

[136] Ibid. 372.   [137] Ibid. 399–400.

difficulty is to keep from speaking *too* freely . . . It was a sad pleasure to me to find how very closely we agreed on a number of matters . . . It was almost like two clocks keeping time.' Rogers was upset to see him 'almost alone in a large house with none of his old friends about him, overworked, and that in a way which is not his own . . . thrown away by the communion to which he has devoted himself'. He told his wife how they had joked about Ward and his eccentricities, 'and it was a pleasure to get a good hearty laugh out of him in the old fashion'.

He set me criticising his beginnings towards a church, and, though there is much I did not like, I happily hit more than once on a thing to admire warmly, which made him stop and look at me hard in his old amused way and ask, 'Now, do you really mean what you say?' 'Certainly'. 'Because, my dear Rogers, that is my own.'

As for Newman, he was relieved to find that Rogers, although no nearer to Catholicism, 'had not gone back'.[138] (It had been one of his great dreads on becoming a Catholic that friends whom he had influenced towards a high view of the church, 'instead of going on with myself, would relapse into indifference or doubt'.[139])

There were some former Tractarians who, far from entertaining doubts, were confidently adopting the most extreme positions. To a potential convert who had expressed amazed dismay at a recent book of sermons by Manning, Newman wrote without reserve:

It seems to me like madness for English Catholics to bind up the Infallible Church and the See of St. Peter with every act of every person who in the course of 1800 years has held eminent authority in it. Why do we not bind up the Church with what St. Peter himself did at Antioch as referred to in Galatians ii? or say that there was nothing human in the contention between St. Paul and St. Barnabas? That an Italian should wish to force a score of irrelevant beliefs upon Englishmen I can understand, because he does not know us; but how Englishmen, who wish the conversion of England, can indissolubly connect it with Dogma, that a Pope cannot err as a private doctor or in particular points of conduct, is to my mind incomprehensible . . . or to consider it practically a point of faith to hold the necessity of the Pope's temporal power. Where are we, if individuals or parties, according to their own feelings or views, can inflict on us additions to the Catholic Faith as once delivered? Why, even our Lady's Assumption is not de fide.[140]

---

[138] Ibid. 513.

[139] Ibid. 495; He also recalled how, at the time, 'the sort of earthquake . . . I was causing in men's minds threw me into a bodily indisposition which I never had before or since. Many men had with great difficulty screwed themselves up into Anglicanism, and now they were told by me, that the operation was nothing worth, and they must begin again. This was, they felt, too much of a good thing' (*LD* xx. 551).

[140] Ibid. 537–8.

Scriptural analogies, which Newman had used so often against
Evangelicals and Liberals in the Church of England, and then as a
Roman Catholic against Anglo-Catholics, are now effectively used
against the Ultramontane position. The Italian element in the Church
was already too prominent, without the added reinforcement of English
converts. While in the early days he had been tolerant (though with
misgivings) of Faber's Italianate devotionalism, now he took an
uncompromising line against Manning's doctrinal exaggerations. Even
more frankly, he had already told another potential convert to

take into consideration the serious loss (humanly speaking) Catholicism has
sustained by the loss of the Teutonic element, which is the consequence of the
Reformation. As an Englishman, I do not like a Romaic religion—and I have
much to say, not (God forbid) against the Roman Catholic, but against the
Romaic Catholic Church. I have no great sympathy with Italian religion, as
such—but I do not account myself the worse Catholic for this.[141]

So many Catholics were 'narrowminded' and had no more understanding of Protestants than Protestants had of Catholics. Typically, though,
when asked about the worship of images, Newman's answer contains an
element of surprise, which cuts across both conventional points of view:

In England Catholics pray *before* images, not *to* them. I wonder whether as
many as a dozen pray *to* them, but *they* will be the best Catholics, not ordinary
ones. The truth is, that sort of affectionate fervour which leads one to confuse an
object with its representative, is skin-deep in the South and argues nothing for a
worshipper's faith, hope and charity, whereas in a Northern race like ours, with
whom ardent devotional feeling is not common, it may be the mark of great
spirituality . . . Do we not love the pictures which we may have of friends
departed? Will not a husband wear in his bosom and kiss the miniature of his
wife?[142]

Against the Ultramontane view of Manning as to what one had to
accept to be a Catholic, Newman set out in impressively succinct, but
comprehensive, terms, the theory of authority and freedom in the
Church which he was soon to elaborate in his first major theological
writings as a Catholic:

To submit to the Church means this, first that you will receive as de fide
whatever she proposes de fide; that you will submit to the decisions of Schola
Theologorum, when unanimous in matters of faith and morals, as being so sure
that it is forbidden to contradict them—that you obey the commands of the
Church in act and deed, though as a matter of policy prudence etc. you may
think that other commands would be better. You are not called on to believe de
fide any thing but what has been promulgated as such—You are not called on
to exercise an internal belief of any doctrine which Sacred Congregations,

[141] *LD* xx. 471.   [142] Ibid. 543–4.

Local Synods, or particular Bishops, or the Pope as a private Doctor, may enunciate. You are not called upon ever to believe or act against the moral law, at the command of any superior.[143]

Just as he had defended the right of theologians to express their views before authoritative pronouncements were made, so too, 'all parts of the Catholic world should say their say on those matters in which they have a right to have an opinion from their local interests, experience etc', before decisions were made by Rome affecting the local church, whose members 'know more than Monsignores at Rome'.[144]

It is interesting to compare this view of freedom and restraint in the Church with Newman's carefully nuanced attitude to slavery in the world. He told T. W. Allies (still busy on his history of Christian civilization) that he regarded slavery as a form of despotism, but not necessarily as intrinsically evil: after all, a father is despot over his young children, and slavery was not condemned in the New Testament. But, like despotism, slavery was certainly in practice evil and to be resisted in whatever way was practical. He could not help thinking that the military profession was 'a greater instrument of sin than slavery', because it led to both slavery and despotism, but was not in itself sinful. If, then, the effects of an army did not make it evil as an institution, it was not clear why 'a wicked origin should make slavery per se evil'. 'True, to enslave is a horrible sin, yet comparative good may come out of sin in this sinful world'; thus, for example, 'American slavery admits the introduction of more antagonistic good, than African despotism'. He claimed, with characteristic paradox, 'I had rather have been a slave in the Holy Land, than a courtier of Xerxes or a soldier of Zingis Khan.'[145] Still, slavery 'came of sin and tended to sin', so that, but for St Paul, he would have been tempted to say that it was 'a sinful institution in itself'. A contemporary note is struck by Newman's astonishment that people could be shocked by slavery, but not by war, which involves 'more immorality';[146] but if war may be a necessary evil, so, arguably, might slavery be, under certain circumstances in the past.

Christmas 1863 brought news of the death of Thackeray, who had attended Newman's lectures on *Difficulties of Anglicans* in 1850. Newman had been looking forward to reading his new (unfinished) novel—'and now the drama of his life is closed, and he himself is the greatest instance of the text, of which he was so full, Vanitas vanitatum, omnia vanitas.' 'What a world this is', he lamented to Mary Holmes (who had tried to interest the novelist in Catholicism),

—how wretched they are, who take it for their portion. Poor Thackeray—it seems but the other day since we became Catholics—now all his renown has

---

[143] Ibid. 545.   [144] Ibid. 568.   [145] Ibid. 555.   [146] Ibid. 558.

been since that—he has made his name, has been made much of, has been fêted, and has gone out, all since 1846 or 1847, all since I went to Propaganda and came back a Philippine[.]'[147]

Little did Newman guess that his own new hour of fame was at hand. To be ignored and unnoticed seemed to be the best he could hope for. For another, much more potentially dangerous, opponent had taken the place of Faber—namely, Manning. As for Faber, Newman remarked to Miss Holmes, with studied detachment, he 'was a person of great natural gifts, and of high aspirations, and of an impulsive affectionateness. His great fault was that he was not the same man two days running—you never could be sure of him.'[148]

[147] Ibid. 566.   [148] Ibid. 560.

14
Apologia

ON 30 December 1863 Newman received in the post a copy of the January number of *Macmillan's Magazine*. It was sent (anonymously) by William Pope, a Catholic priest in Yorkshire and a former Anglican clergyman who had been converted by Newman's writings; curiously enough, he was a nephew of Whately and related to Newman's undergraduate friend Simeon Lloyd Pope. The issue contained an enthusiastic review (signed 'C.K.') of J. A. Froude's anti-Catholic *History of England*, in which various passages had been marked in pencil, including the following:

Truth, for its own sake, had never been a virtue with the Roman clergy. Father Newman informs us that it need not, and on the whole ought not to be; that cunning is the weapon which Heaven has given to the saints wherewith to withstand the brute male force of the wicked world which marries and is given in marriage. Whether his notion be doctrinally correct or not, it is at least historically so.

Newman immediately wrote to the publishers, quoting the passage. His letter was not the complaint of an aggrieved Roman priest, but the protest of an affronted English gentleman to other English gentlemen:

There is no reference at the foot of the page to any words of mine, much less any quotation from my writings, in justification of this statement.

I should not dream of expostulating with the writer of such a passage, nor with the editor who could insert it without appending evidence in proof of its allegations. Nor do I want any reparation from either of them. I neither complain of them for their act, nor should I thank them if they reversed it. Nor do I even write to you with any desire of troubling you to send me an answer. I do but wish to draw the attention of yourselves, as gentlemen, to a grave and gratuitous slander, with which I feel confident you will be sorry to find associated a name so eminent as yours.[1]

On 7 January 1864 Newman received a letter from Charles Kingsley defending his words as justified by many passages in Newman's writings, but particularly by his Anglican sermon 'Wisdom and Innocence', published in *Sermons bearing on Subjects of the Day* (in consequence of which

[1] *LD* xx. 571–2.

'I finally shook off the strong influence which your writings exerted on me').[2] Kingsley was not only a successful novelist, but a clergyman (who had reacted strongly against the Oxford Movement) and, since 1860, Regius Professor of Modern History at Cambridge. He offered to retract what he had said if Newman could show that he had done him an injustice. Newman coldly and stiffly acknowledged his letter, commenting that he 'was amazed' to learn that Kingsley was the author of the review article.[3] The initials at the end had meant nothing to him ('I live out of the world'), nor had he noticed Kingsley's name in the table of contents. He explained to Alexander Macmillan, the head of the publishing firm, that he had assumed the author was some 'young scribe, who is making a cheap reputation by smart hits at safe objects'. Macmillan had written courteously to say that he had never dreamed Newman or any other Roman Catholic would object to what he thought was the accepted Catholic strategy towards 'heretics', namely, the wisdom of the serpent. 'Most wonderful phenomenon!' exclaimed Newman, that an 'educated man, breathing English air, and walking in the light of the nineteenth century,' should think that 'such is the standard of morality acknowledged, acquiesced in', by Catholics. There follows one of the most superbly indignant passages in the whole of Newman's controversial writings, including a brilliant analogy that recalls the satire of *Present Position of Catholics* at its most devastating.

I, on my side, have long thought, even before I was a Catholic, that the Protestant system, as such, leads to a lax observance of the rule of purity; Protestants think that the Catholic system, as such, leads to a lax observance of the rule of truth. I am very sorry that they should think so, but I cannot help it; I lament their mistake, but I bear it as I may. If Mr. Kingsley had said no more than this, I should not have felt it necessary to criticize such an ordinary remark. But, as I should be committing a crime, heaping dirt upon my soul, and storing up for myself remorse and confusion of face at a future day, if I applied my abstract belief of the latent sensuality of Protestantism, on *à priori* reasoning, to individuals, to living persons, to authors and men of name, and said (not to make disrespectful allusion to the living) that Bishop Van Mildert, or the Rev. Dr. Spry, or Dean Milner, or the Rev. Charles Simeon 'informs us that chastity for its own sake need not be, and on the whole ought not to be, a virtue with the Anglican clergy,' and then, when challenged for the proof, said, '*Vide* Van Mildert's Bampton Lectures and Simeon's Skeleton Sermons *passim;*' and, as I should only make the matter still worse, if I pointed to flagrant instances of paradoxical divines or of bad clergymen among Protestants ... so, in like manner, for a writer, when he is criticizing definite historical facts of the sixteenth century, which stand or fall on their own merits, to go out of his way to have a fling at an unpopular name, living but 'down,' and boldly to say ... of *me*, 'Father Newman *informs* us that Truth for its own sake *need not be, and on the*

---

[2] *LD* xxi. 10.   [3] Ibid. 11.

whole ought not to be, a virtue with the Roman clergy,' and to be thus brilliant and antithetical (save the mark!) in the very cause of Truth, is a proceeding of so special a character as to lead me to exclaim, after the pattern of the celebrated saying, 'O Truth, how many lies are told in thy name!'

Newman could hardly not have sensed the irony of his reference to a writer using a historical review to introduce a contentious and unfair attack on a living person; what he did not know was that Kingsley's side-swipe was to prove far more counter-productive and self-defeating than any of Simpson's insinuations in the *Rambler* against Wiseman. He ended the letter to Macmillan by repeating that he was not looking for an apology or explanation; but he warned, with the cynicism of a veteran, that if the editor and writer

propose merely to smooth the matter over by publishing to the world that I have 'complained,' or that 'they yield to my letters, expostulations, representations, explanations,' or that 'they are quite ready to be convinced of their mistake, if I will convince them,' or that 'they have profound respect for me, but really they are not the only persons who have gathered from my writings what they have said of me,' or that 'they are unfeignedly surprised that I should visit in their case what I have passed over in the case of others,' or that 'they have ever had a true sense of my good points, but cannot be expected to be blind to my faults,' if this be the sum total of what they are to say . . . then . . . they had better let it all alone, as far as I am concerned, for a half-measure settles nothing.[4]

In his reply to Newman's acknowledgement of his letter, Kingsley justified Newman's sarcastic prophecy by expressing his willingness to accept that the 'tone' (even more than the 'language') of Newman's letters 'makes me feel,—to my very deep pleasure—that my opinion of the meaning of your words was a mistaken one'. He enclosed the famous 'apology' he proposed to have published in *Macmillan's Magazine*:

Dr. Newman has, by letter, expressed in the strongest terms, his denial of the meaning which I have put upon his words.

No man knows the use of words better than Dr Newman. No man, therefore, has a better right to define what he does, or does not, mean by them.

It only remains, therefore, for me to express my hearty regret at having so seriously mistaken him; and my hearty pleasure at finding him on the side of Truth, in this, or any other matter.[5]

After consulting Edward Badeley, the convert lawyer friend who had helped him in the Achilli affair, Newman wrote to Kingsley expressing his strong objection to the professed 'apology', not only because it implied that he had been confronted with definite passages from his writings, but because it would not in fact be taken to be a retraction at

---

[4] Ibid. 12–15.   [5] Ibid. 18–19.

all. Wittily, he set out Kingsley's letter with his own paraphrase juxtaposed:

I have set before Dr. Newman, as he challenged me to do, extracts from his writings, and he has affixed to them what he conceives to be their legitimate sense, to the denial of that in which I understood them.

He has done this with the skill of a great master of verbal fence, who knows, as well as any man living, how to insinuate a doctrine without committing himself to it.

However, while I heartily regret that I have so seriously mistaken the sense which he assures me his words were meant to bear, I cannot but feel a hearty pleasure also, at having brought him, for once in a way, to confess that after all truth is a Christian virtue.[6]

In reply, Kingsley agreed to omit the second sentence and the second half of the last sentence from his 'apology', and pointed out that he had specifically referred to the sermon on 'Wisdom and Innocence' as the basis for his allegations. However, he did not withdraw the first sentence Newman had taken exception to. Again Newman consulted Badeley, who again advised that the reparation was unsatisfactory: Kingsley had not only failed to quote any particular passages in the sermon, but had left the impression that his interpretation of it was the fair and natural one. The truncated apology appeared in the February number of *Macmillan's Magazine*. Already, Newman had decided to print the correspondence in the form of a pamphlet; it was to be published by Longman ('I wish it very largely advertised').[7] As a conclusion he wrote three pages of 'Reflections', which he submitted to Badeley; he was afraid they were 'too strong', but he also thought that if he was going to write any comment, it ought to be written 'con amore'; and when he did try and write something else, he found it 'as flat as ditch water'.[8] Fortunately, Badeley wrote fully approving the 'Reflections', which he called not 'ditch water', but 'champagne'.[9] He was right: the marvellously comic dialogue takes one back to 1851 when Newman's satirical genius was at its most exuberant.

Mr. Kingsley begins then by exclaiming,—'O the chicanery, the wholesale fraud, the vile hypocrisy, the conscience-killing tyranny of Rome! We have not far to seek for an evidence of it. There's Father Newman to wit: one living specimen is worth a hundred dead ones. He, a Priest writing of Priests, tells us that lying is never any harm.'

I interpose: 'You are taking a most extraordinary liberty with my name. If I have said this, tell me when and where.'

Mr. Kingsley replies: 'You said it, Reverend Sir, in a Sermon which you preached, when a Protestant, as Vicar of St. Mary's, and published in 1844;

[6] *LD* xxi. 20–1.   [7] Ibid. 32.   [8] Ibid. 37, 39.   [9] Ibid. 44.

and I could read you a very salutary lecture on the effects which that Sermon had at the time on my own opinion of you.'

I make answer: 'Oh . . . *Not*, it seems, as a Priest speaking of Priests;—but let us have the passage.'

Mr. Kingsley relaxes: 'Do you know, I like your *tone*. From your *tone* I rejoice, greatly rejoice, to be able to believe that you did not mean what you said.'

I rejoin: '*Mean* it! I maintain I never *said* it, whether as a Protestant or as a Catholic.'

Mr. Kingsley replies: 'I waive that point.'

I object: 'Is it possible! What? waive the main question! I either said it or I didn't. You have made a monstrous charge against me; direct, distinct, public. You are bound to prove it as directly, as distinctly, as publicly;—or to own you can't.'

'Well,' says Mr. Kingsley, 'if you are quite sure you did not say it, I'll take your word for it; I really will.'

My *word*! I am dumb. Somehow I thought that it was my *word* that happened to be on trial. The *word* of a Professor of lying, that he does not lie!

But Mr. Kingsley re-assures me: 'We are both gentlemen,' he says: 'I have done as much as one English gentleman can expect from another.'

I begin to see: he thought me a gentleman at the very time that he said I taught lying on system. After all, it is not I, but it is Mr. Kingsley who did not mean what he said.'[10]

The pamphlet, which began with a long extract from Kingsley's review, appeared on 12 February. Newman explained to Alexander Macmillan that he felt it would have been cowardly to have done nothing, especially when Kingsley had made no real attempt to apologize. He told Thomas Harper, a convert Jesuit, that the fact that people like Kingsley kept on referring to him showed that he was 'still feared': the abuse and slander which had rained down on him for thirty years he was ready to accept 'as the price I pay for the victory, or at least the great extension, of those principles which are so near my heart;—and, I think, while I live, I shall go on paying it, because I trust that, even after my life, those principles will extend.'[11]

2

In spite of all the excitement of the controversy, his life continued in its familiar pattern. Still overworked, he was busy as usual with the school accounts and correspondence with parents: he was also taking some of Thomas Arnold's classes, since he had gone sick, and preparing an expurgated edition of Terence's *Phormio*. He was enjoying the teaching,

---

[10] *Apo.* 352.   [11] *LD* xxi. 53–4.

'and, if I could believe it to be God's will, would turn away my thoughts
from ever writing any thing, and should see, in the superintendence of
these boys, the nearest return to my Oxford life'.[12] He was now 63: 'old
age has come on me like the falling snow, so gently that I cannot realize
it.' He felt better than he had for years, although he was growing thinner
and thinner. He told his sister Jemima how for the last two years he had
taken up again his morning cold shower ('not later than six o'clock'),
which helped him enormously through the winter, especially in keeping
away colds (the fact he could stand it was a proof in itself of how strong
he was). But while as a young man he had never used a great coat, now
'I could not carry more clothes without becoming a beast of burden'.[13]
In fact, he found the damp and raw Birmingham climate very trying compared with the South; 'much snow again melting—a long
illnatured, sullen, stern and weeping winter', a bleak, laconic entry in
his diary for March records.[14] As for the prospect of death, it was what
gave meaning to life: 'We seem to live and die as the leaves; but there is
One who notes the fragrance of every one of them, and, when their hour
comes, places them between the pages of His great Book.'[15]

At the beginning of February he had heard from William Monsell,
who was in Rome, that there was a concerted move to have the French
lay Catholic leader Montalembert condemned for advocating religious
freedom (against which Ward had recently published a pamphlet). He
was very concerned at this 'fearfully important'[16] news. The standard
Catholic view at this time was that since Catholicism was the true
religion, both the Church and the State had the right to persecute
heresy. But even if this was defensible (and Newman was prepared to
accept it was), it did not alter the practical fact that 'persecution does
not answer . . . the feelings of the age are as strongly against it as they
were once for it. The age is such, that we must go by reason, not by
force.'[17] Indeed, he wondered if the opposite was not true: for 'the
presence of Protestantism, where it is tolerated, stirs up Catholics and
keeps them from sinking . . . into tyranny, superstition, and
immorality'.[18] Admitting that religion could be established by the state
if (and only if) this was the will of the people, even so, he argued,

I am not at all sure that it would not be better for the Catholic religion every
where, if it had no very different status from that which it has in England. There
is so much corruption, so much deadness, so much hypocrisy, so much
infidelity, when a dogmatic faith is imposed on a nation by law, that I like
freedom better. I think Italy will be more religious, that is, there will be more
true religion in it, when the Church has to fight for its supremacy, than when

[12] *LD* xxi. 51.   [13] Ibid. 57.   [14] Ibid. 73.   [15] Ibid. 51.
[16] Ibid. 41.   [17] Ibid. xx. 477.   [18] Ibid. xxi. 43.

that supremacy depends on the provisions of courts, and police, and territorial claims.

Such thoughts were of course extremely radical for a Catholic to express at this time—

but we see every where a new state of things coming in, and it is pleasant to believe one has reasons not to fear it, but to be hopeful about it, as regards the prospects of religion. It is pleasant not to be obliged to resist a movement, which is so characteristic of the age; and with these feelings one may concur with Protestants in no small measure . . .[19]

Having spent so much of his life fighting against the spirit of the age, it certainly was a surprising development for Newman to be able to welcome this particular instance of 'progress'. Comforting as this consideration was, it did not alter the fact that it would be impossible for him to write anything without making it obvious that he agreed with liberal Catholics like Döllinger and Montalembert, and this would mean a head-on collision with the Roman authorities, who now, unprecedentedly, 'acted on the individual thinker without buffers'.[20] But he advised Monsell that even if Rome, most unadvisedly, did condemn Montalembert, the condemnation would be of the theory of religious freedom, and would not prevent a Catholic politician from advocating toleration as the most practical policy in particular circumstances.

3

Towards the end of February Newman began one of his most interesting correspondences. Richard Holt Hutton, the literary editor of the *Spectator*, had written a review of Newman's pamphlet, a two-part article called 'Father Newman's Sarcasm'. Hutton was the son of a Unitarian minister and had been a student at University College, London. He had intended to enter the Unitarian ministry, but had been drawn towards the Church of England. He had heard Newman's lectures on *Difficulties of Anglicans* and had been influenced by his other writings. His review called Newman 'not only one of the greatest of English writers, but, perhaps, the very greatest master of . . . sarcasm in the English language'. Sarcastically, he commented himself that one of Kingsley's books, ' "Loose Thoughts for Loose Thinkers," represents too closely the character of his rough but manly intellect, so that a more opportune Protestant ram for Father Newman's sacrificial knife could scarcely

[19] Ibid. xx. 477.   [20] Ibid. xxi. 49.

have been found'.[21] Although he never became a Catholic, Hutton was not only the first serious critic of Newman's distinctive literary genius, but his insight into Newman's mind enabled him to write one of the first and best studies of Newman after his death. Certainly, this first published essay was a turning-point. Newman wrote at once to express his warm gratitude for the unusual generosity of the review; it was not what he was accustomed to read.

He was beginning to be aware that the clash with Kingsley might develop into an affair of much larger significance than he could have guessed when he first saw the passage in *Macmillan's Magazine*. It was more than possible that Kingsley would reply to his pamphlet with a compilation of every passage from his works that could support the charge.

This would lead me to a survey of my whole course, which I should not be sorry for, tho' I dread the wear and tear of it. The chance that such a task is sooner or later in store for me, is what makes me wish to get about me as many letters and memoranda as I can. I have never defended myself . . .[22]

He told Badeley that he had 'prepared' himself 'from the first' for this eventuality, and indeed had 'always looked forward to the possibility' of 'an opening to defend myself as to various passages in my life and writings'. He had arranged his letters and papers up to 1836, but it was those for the vital period 1841–5 which he would most need for the vindication of his submission to Rome. In the quickening tempo of his letters we sense at last the return of the old creative impulse; at last that essential 'external stimulus' without which, as he told Hutton, he had 'scarcely written any' of his books had come again. But he knew that the 'pain' of writing would be 'a mental child-bearing'.[23]

The controversy with Kingsley also provided an opportunity for Wiseman's opponents in the Westminster diocesan chapter to demonstrate their public support for Newman by organizing an address of thanks for his defence of the Church, which was signed by more than half the clergy of the diocese. Manning was not one of the signatories. Newman suspected correctly that the address was really intended as a demonstration against Manning, who the Westminster clergy were very afraid was to be made coadjutor to Wiseman, with automatic right of succession (Archbishop Errington having been removed for his opposition to the Cardinal). He also noted that it was on the whole the old Catholics rather than the converts among the clergy who were the first to put their signatures to the address. Hardly had Newman written to thank the organizers, when he received a letter from Acton to say that he had decided to end the *Home and Foreign Review*. The 'Munich Brief' of

Pius IX had just been published, rejecting the freedom claimed for Catholic thinkers at a recent conference for theologians at Munich. An official censure of the *Home and Foreign* would cause a scandal and be fatal to the review, which upheld principles diametrically opposed to those contained in the Pope's strictures. Newman replied that he was very sad at the news, as he had hoped the review, which he thought had made excellent progress, would be read by non-Catholics as well as eventually win the bishops' confidence. He was particularly alarmed by the way in which the Brief might be applied in a country like England by 'the military regime of Propaganda'. He tried to console Acton:

But good may come out of this disappointment. There is life, and increasing life in the English Catholic body; and, if there is life, there must be re-action. It seems impossible that active and sensible men can remain still under the dull tyranny of Manning and Ward.[24]

In his own private analysis and summary of the papal document he noted particularly what the Pope had to say about scientific research. His reaction was characteristically ambivalent; in theory he could only deplore the language used, but in practice perhaps it was paradoxically opportune:

I thought it was commonly said that Galileo's fault was that he meddled with *theology*, and that, if he had confined himself to *scientific conclusions* he would have been let alone; but surely the language of the Brief . . . is as if even men of science must keep theological conclusions before them in treating of science . . . I certainly could not write a word upon the special controversies and difficulties of the day with a view to defend religion from freethinking physicists without allowing them freedom of logic in their own science; so that . . . it is simply a providential intimation to every religious man, that, at this moment, we are simply to be silent while scientific investigation proceeds—and say not a word on questions of interpretation of Scripture . . . when perplexed persons ask us—and I am not sure that it will not prove to be the best course.[25]

Early in the morning of Passion Sunday, 13 March, Newman wrote down a final profession of faith 'in prospect of death'.[26] He had been so extraordinarily depressed for so long that he suddenly became afraid that he really must be about to die, although there appeared to be nothing actually wrong with his mental and physical health. He could not know that he had reached his lowest point; and he certainly could not have dreamed how dramatic and rapid the reversal would be.

On 20 March Kingsley's pamphlet '*What, then, does Dr. Newman mean?*' appeared. Again Newman wrote gratefully to thank Hutton for his review in the *Spectator*, which scornfully dismissed Kingsley for

[24] Ibid. 84.   [25] *Ward* i. 642.   [26] *MD* 437.

merely compounding his original offence by hurling angry aspersions and insinuations against the craft and subtlety of Newman and Catholics in general. Newman now knew what he had to do. On 31 March, a few days after Easter, he wrote confidentially to Copeland:

I am writing my answer to Kingsley's pamphlet . . . The whole strength of what he says, *as directed rhetorically* to the popular mind, lies in the antecedent prejudice that *I was a Papist while I was an Anglican* . . . The only way in which I can destroy this, is to give my history, and the history of my mind, from 1822 or earlier, down to 1845. I wish I had my papers properly about me.[27]

Copeland readily agreed to look over pages in proof to check their factual accuracy: Newman would render a service if he could dispel the myth of dishonesty among the Tractarians, an accusation for which Isaac Williams's *Tracts* 'On Reserve in Communicating Religious Knowledge' had been largely to blame. On 10 April Newman's diary reads, 'beginning of my hard work for my Apologia'.[28] The educated world of London knew he was not a liar, but Newman was well aware that the average Evangelical or 'Brummagem', for example, really did imagine he was 'a clever knave'. A 'History of my Opinions' would enable him to defend himself for the first time on such matters as *Tract 90*. The public lectures he had 'all but determined on',[29] and which St John had urged, would be unsuitable for such a personal history. The *Apologia* was to have another crucial dimension; perhaps it was a letter from Acton which first suggested it to Newman. On the same day that he began work in earnest, Acton wrote to say that brilliantly as Newman had defended himself personally, the fact that he had not attempted to defend the integrity of the Catholic clergy had been noted and explained on the ground that a defence of the Catholic Church's love of truth would be very difficult to sustain; in this sense, the controversy had shown the Church up in as bad a light as it had shown Newman in a good light. On 15 April Newman tersely accepted the challenge:

Your letter is a very valuable one to me. I am writing from morning till night, and against time, which is not pleasant—this is the cause that I have not thanked you before, and why I do not write longer now. I get so tired.

As to the points you mention, you may be sure I shall go as far as ever I can[.][30]

We can see the last great chapter of the *Apologia*, 'Position of my Mind since 1845', already, as it were, conceived in this last pregnant sentence, full of significance for the future struggle against Ultramontanism.

Newman had decided to bring out the book in weekly pamphlets, which the publisher wanted to appear as soon as possible while the

---

[27] *LD* xxi. 90–1.   [28] Ibid. 92.   [29] Ibid. 93.   [30] Ibid. 94.

controversy was still news. A complete book would reach fewer people because of its length and because there would be less interest by the time it was published. The first of the pamphlets was published on Thursday 21 April, followed by six more on consecutive Thursdays, and ending with an appendix, which appeared two weeks later. It was an astonishing feat: 'the most arduous work . . . I ever had in my life', and 'one of the most terrible trials that I have had'.[31] As Newman wrote, he consulted not only Copeland (who in turn consulted Keble), but also Frederic Rogers and William Froude about the portrait of Hurrell Froude. He warned Copeland that it was not a history of the Oxford Movement, but 'an egotistical matter from beginning to end', intended 'to prove that I did not act *dishonestly*'. As he wrote the part which dealt with his early life up to 1833, he 'kept bursting into tears', and when he read it out aloud to St John he 'could not get on from beginning to end'. Rogers's response to the first part or pamphlet, which, like the second, dealt with Kingsley (both were eventually consigned to appendices) worried him considerably: he appreciated that people might feel he had already vanquished Kingsley and that he was now displaying 'a savageness which will provoke a reaction'—but he had 'considered all this, before I began'. At any rate, he had completed his polemic against Kingsley. If he had been 'too severe', he was 'in for it'.[32]

Encouraged by Copeland, he also wrote to R. W. Church, with whom he had not been in contact since he said goodbye to him when he left Littlemore in 1846. He explained that he was involved 'in one of the most painful trials in which I have ever been in my life, and I think you can help me'. He had always been aware that one day he might 'be called on to defend my honesty while in the Church of England'. There had been endless attacks, but they had been anonymous, 'or else a sentence or two on some particular point has been the whole'. But he had decided that 'if any one with [a] name made an elaborate charge on me, I was bound to speak'.[33] He knew, of course, that Kingsley was 'a furious foolish fellow—but he has a name'. Kingsley's pamphlet, absurd as it was, needed to be answered for the benefit of the Evangelicals, who had never trusted him, as well as for the Catholics and ordinary people in Birmingham, who knew nothing about his history. He had to 'speak strongly', too, otherwise he would not seem to be 'in earnest'. He was afraid of making mistakes and omissions in matters of fact, but still more of 'making bold generalizations without suspicion that they are not to the letter tenable'.[34] Church, who had seen so much of him from 1840 onwards, could help him by correcting any mistakes in that part of his story, as well as by lending any of Newman's contemporary letters that

---

[31] Ibid. 96–7. [32] Ibid. 97–9. [33] Ibid. 100. [34] Ibid. 100.

he might have. He confessed that he needed Church for 'the dullest part of the whole', where he explained why he had written *Tract 90*. He did not want to argue or defend himself, although he would have to give the general reasons for his conversion; but his real object was to show that he had not been dishonest and to explain 'the stages in my change, and the impediments which kept me from going faster'. The whole account would not be long, but 'parts I write so many times over'. Church promised every assistance he could, but begged Newman not to be in such a hurry as to leave out anything important. Newman replied that he was not attempting to write a history of the Oxford Movement—nor, if he had delayed even a month, could he have written the story at all ('It has been a great misery to me').[35] He told Keble, who also gladly agreed to help in any way he could, that when he saw the part he wanted him to look at (1833 to 1840), he would 'wonder how I ever could get myself to write it'. But for some 'very great stimulus' he never could have written it, and now he only wanted 'to tell the truth, and to leave the matter in God's hands'. He was 'writing from morning to night, hardly having time for my meals'.[36] He realized that friends would be astonished and startled by what they read; he had never written in this kind of autobiographical vein before. He could hardly use his pen for correspondence: 'My fingers have been *walking* nearly 20 miles a day.' It was not that the bulk of what he was writing was so large, 'but I have to write parts over and over again, from the necessity of digesting and compressing'.[37] He appreciated that his account would appear to be unfavourable to Anglicanism; this was not his intention, but it made him feel awkward about asking Anglican friends for their help. His one aim was to state the true facts to clear his own character; he had no desire to attack the Church of England, so long as it continued to uphold orthodox Christianity.

Never before had any book cost him so much as this. Not only had he never been in such 'a stress of brain', but also he had never suffered such 'pain of heart' as well. He had been 'constantly in tears, and constantly crying out with distress': he could never have written what he had 'in cold blood', or if he had delayed.[38] It was strange: not only was he now reunited with old Anglican friends, at least in spirit, but he was once again with them reliving the Oxford Movement. And, in a sense, they were collaborating in writing the first (partial) history of it, both by the letters they lent (which he promised to return: 'I want you to have them,' he assured Church, 'that you may not forget me'),[39] and also by their criticisms.

On 20 May Newman's diary records that he worked on the manu-

---

[35] *LD* xxi. 102.   [36] Ibid. 103.   [37] Ibid. 105.
[38] Ibid. 107.   [39] Ibid. 106.

script 'for 22 hours running'.[40] By now five parts or pamphlets had been published, and the sixth and seventh appeared the two following weeks. Finally, after another fortnight, the eighth appeared on 16 June, an appendix called 'Answer in Detail to Mr. Kingsley's Accusations'. Newman himself had sent off the last proof four days earlier. It had 'involved', he wrote, 'a more imperious call upon my time, and a heavier burden upon my mind, now for from ten to twelve weeks, than it has been my lot to experience from any former engagement of a literary nature'.[41] He had only had a fortnight or three weeks' 'capital' before the first pamphlet was due to be published—'but it soon went—and I was soon compelled to live from hand to mouth'. He had had to work so continuously and so hard that at times he had been afraid he might seriously damage his health. Sometimes he 'had to sweep away what I had written ruthlessly, and saw the day of publication yawning close upon me'; nor was it easy to finish the separate parts, as 'my matter grew under my hands', with the result that 'manuscript and proof got jammed together, as in a stoppage in the streets of London—and the proof almost got ahead of the manuscript, if that can be'.[42] He had written pamphlets in the course of a single day or night during the Oxford Movement, but never before a substantial book 'all at a heat'. It was as though he were 'ploughing in very stiff clay. It was moving on at the rate of a mile an hour, when I had to write and print and correct a hundred miles by the next day's post.' Every week a pamphlet had to be ready for publication—'and Thursday would come round once a week—so I was like a man who had fallen overboard and had to swim to land, and found the distance he had to go greater and greater. At last I am ashore, and have crawled upon the beach, and there I lie . . .'.[43] As he rested at Rednal he could only look back upon the whole exercise as 'an extreme pain' from 'first to last'.[44]

4

The eight parts or pamphlets were published together as a single volume in 1864 under the title *Apologia pro Vita Sua: Being a Reply to a Pamphlet entitled 'What, Then, Does Dr. Newman Mean?'* The second edition, which appeared the following year, was simply entitled *History of My Religious Opinions*; it omitted the first two polemical parts (which were replaced by a brief preface) and shortened and recast the appendix in the form of a series of notes, in which all reference to Kingsley was dropped and

---

[40] Ibid. 111. [41] Ibid. 115. [42] Ibid. 126.
[43] Ibid. 131–2. [44] Ibid. 117.

additional matter was added. In 1873 Newman restored the original title, while retaining as a subtitle, 'Being a History of his Religious Opinions'; in the course of various revisions, the preface was also enlarged with further extracts from the first two pamphlets, and additional notes were added at the end.

In the preface, Newman explains that his one object is to refute Kingsley's charge of untruthfulness ('*How can I tell that I shall not be the dupe of some cunning equivocation?*'), by which Kingsley had attempted 'to cut the ground from under my feet;—to poison by anticipation the public mind against me . . . and to infuse into the imaginations of my readers, suspicion and mistrust of everything that I may say . . . This I call *poisoning the wells*.'[45] But although some 'dirt sticks longer than other dirt . . . no dirt is immortal'.[46] It is not, however, Kingsley's 'articles of impeachment which he has framed from my writings, and which I shall easily crumble into dust, but the bias of the court' which Newman has to overcome. It is not that he doubts the justice of his fellow countrymen, who are his judges and who 'are as generous, as they are hasty'—indeed, 'I had rather be an Englishman . . . than belong to any other race under heaven.' What he has to contend with is 'the state of the atmosphere. . . . the vibration all around, which will echo his bold assertion of my dishonesty; it is that prepossession against me which takes it for granted that, when my reasoning is convincing it is only ingenious, and that when my statements are unanswerable, there is always something put out of sight or hidden in my sleeve'.[47] It is a popular tradition of twenty years, which at last he has to confront openly, that 'I was for years where I had no right to be; that I was "Romanist" in Protestant livery and service; that I was doing the work of a hostile Church in the bosom of the English Establishment, and knew it, or ought to have known it'. The 'knavery of a conspiracy such as this' was felt the more because 'craft and intrigue' were, after all, in the popular mind 'the very instruments to which the Catholic Church has in these last centuries been indebted for her maintenance and extension'. As for the 'reticence, and half-speaking, and apparent indecision' of the Tractarians, this was plainly part of the plot 'to open the gate of that city, of which they were the sworn defenders, to the enemy who lay in ambush outside of it'.[48] How could he 'now . . . be trusted, when long ago I was trusted, and was found wanting?'[49]

The idea that Newman was simply 'a *liar*' not only appealed to popular prejudice, but had the great advantage of being 'a positive idea'. Argument was not enough: the only way of dislodging a false idea was to put a true one in its place.

[45] *Apo.* 6. [46] Ibid. 8. [47] Ibid. 8, 10–11.

[48] Ibid. 403–4. [49] Ibid. 10.

'What does Dr. Newman mean?' . . . He asked what I *mean*; not about my words, not about my arguments, not about my actions, as his ultimate point, but about that living intelligence, by which I write, and argue, and act. He asks about my Mind and its Beliefs and its sentiments; and he shall be answered . . .

He knew what he had to do, though he 'shrank from both the task and the exposure it would entail': he must 'give the true key' to his 'whole life',[50] if he wished 'to be known as a living man, and not as a scarecrow which is dressed up in my clothes'.[51]

It is not at all pleasant for me to be egotistical; nor to be criticized for being so. It is not pleasant to reveal to high and low, young and old, what has gone on within me from my early years. It is not pleasant to be giving to every shallow or flippant disputant the advantage over me of knowing my most private thoughts, I might even say the intercourse between myself and my Maker. But I do not like to be called to my face a liar and a knave . . .[52]

As in his notorious letter to the *Globe*, he felt that unless he 'wrote with the keen feeling which I really had, though it is ordinarily one's duty not to show it, people would not believe me; they would say that my book was written for me, or corrected by revisers, or that I was not in earnest, but exerting myself in an intellectual fence'.[53] The actual polemic against Kingsley recalls the satirical exuberance of the early 1850s. Modern readers, without the Victorian taste for controversy, who are shocked by the superb invective of some of the polemical passages, especially those which Newman eventually omitted, should look at Kingsley's own pamphlet, which contains some splendid sneers ('While he tried to destroy others' reason, he was at least fair enough to destroy his own'), as well as some marvellously outraged indignation—which is often funny in a way Kingsley did not intend (' . . . he will remain upon his trial as long as Englishmen know how to guard the women whom God has committed to their charge . . . I trust there will be always one man left in England to inform them of the fact, for the sake of the ladies of this land').[54] Newman's own polemic revives themes from *Present Position of Catholics*, like the imaginary Russian who reads about the British Constitution without knowing anything of Britain. Startlingly tactile imagery is deployed, too:

He need not commit himself to a definite accusation against me, such as requires definite proof and admits of definite refutation; for he has two strings to his bow;—when he is thrown off his balance on the one leg, he can recover himself by the use of the other. If I demonstrate that I am not a knave, he may exclaim, 'Oh, but you are a fool!' and when I demonstrate that I am not a fool, he may turn round and retort, 'Well, then, you are a knave.'[55]

---

[50] Ibid. 12.   [51] Ibid. 406.   [52] Ibid. 14.
[53] *LD* xxi. 260.   [54] *Apo.* 370, 377.   [55] Ibid. 388.

As Newman counter-attacks, we are vividly reminded of the hapless Achilli; but there is a significant difference, for not only is it 'very difficult to get up resentment towards persons whom one has never seen', but 'I wish to impute nothing worse to Mr. Kingsley than that he has been furiously carried away by his feelings.'[56] Moreover, instead of merely defending the Catholic Church against calumny, Newman has to vindicate the conversion to it of one 'who has given up much that he loved and prized and could have retained, but that he loved honesty better than name, and Truth better than dear friends'.[57] For (as in *Present Position of Catholics*) the object is not simply to disprove slanderous allegations, but to show how ludicrously misplaced they are. Again, as in the earlier satirical writings, the tone ranges freely from the earnestly moving to the scathing, almost ribald. And the variety of style is matched by the rich profusion of metaphor.

I am sitting at home without a thought of Mr. Kingsley; he wantonly breaks in upon me . . . '. . . If you have not broken one commandment, let us see whether we cannot convict you of the breach of another. If you are not a swindler or forger, you are guilty of arson or burglary . . . What does it matter to you who are going off the stage, to receive a slight additional daub upon a character so deeply stained already?'[58]

He was lucky that in Kingsley's scenario 'the scene of my labours was not at Moscow or Damascus'—fortunately, he had only been accused of 'mere quibbling and lying' at Oxford: 'in Spain I should have been an Inquisitor, with my rack in the background; I should have had a concealed dagger in Sicily; at Venice I should have brewed poison; in Turkey I should have been . . . with my bowstring . . .'.[59]

5

The replacement of the first two original polemical pamphlets with a shortened preface means that the *Apologia* is what it says it is, 'a history of his religious opinions'. To call the book an autobiography, even a religious autobiography, could be misleading, as it is hardly more concerned with the author's spiritual life than with his personal life. In this sense it is quite unlike St Augustine's *Confessions*, and much more like *The Force of Truth*, the story of Newman's old mentor Thomas Scott's progress from Unitarianism to Calvinism. For the *Apologia* is an intellectual—or rather, theological—autobiography. It is unique among Newman's published works, not only in its form and content, but

[56] *Apo.* 394.   [57] Ibid. 396.   [58] Ibid. 389.   [59] Ibid. 415.

also in its style and tone. This is not surprising when one considers that far from attempting to persuade by argument, the main autobiographical part of the book convinces by deliberately abandoning all argument in favour of facts, by adopting an almost dry documentation in the place of polemical rhetoric in order to prove the integrity of the author's own life. It is thus a curious anomaly that the very book on which Newman's literary reputation is usually presumed principally to rest, itself so strikingly differs from his other works of controversy, which give him so distinctive a place in the history of English literature. Its power lies indeed in the (almost) disconcertingly calm, limpid tone of the author's conversational, indeed confidential, voice. Eloquence is as rigorously excluded as self-defence: 'I am not setting myself up as a pattern of good sense or of any thing else: I am but giving a history of my opinions, and that, with the view of showing that I have come by them through intelligible processes of thought and honest external means.'[60] Nor is there any overt appeal to the reader's sympathy—'I have no romantic story to tell.'[61]

The story which Newman does tell has already been told in these pages. There remains the final fifth chapter, 'Position of My Mind since 1845', where he reverts to current, pressing, theological preoccupations. Less marked than the transition from controversy to documentary, the change of style is still noticeable as the plain facts of a religious history give way to the subtle arguments of a controversial theologian. There is also a crucial enlargement of perspective as the author looks beyond the general Protestant reader to sceptics and Ultramontane opponents. He had already in the previous chapter hinted at what was to come. Referring to the sermons of St Alfonso Liguori, which Dr Russell had lent him, he boldly declared that he could not 'fully enter' into certain Marian devotional writings—'they are suitable for Italy, but they are not suitable for England.'[62] And then, a little later, talking of his theory of development, he described how he 'came to the conclusion that there was no medium . . . between Atheism and Catholicity', since 'I am a Catholic by virtue of my believing in God; and if I am asked why I believe in a God, I answer that it is because I believe in myself, for I feel it impossible to believe in my own existence . . . without believing also in the existence of Him, who lives as a . . . Being in my conscience.'[63]

Newman begins the fifth chapter with an oblique reference to the rumours of his disillusion with the Catholic Church—'I have been in perfect peace and contentment; I never have had one doubt.' On the other hand, he denies that his conversion brought him a 'firmer faith in the fundamental truths of Revelation'. Nor, again, has he 'given up

---

[60] Ibid. 39.   [61] Ibid. 44.   [62] Ibid. 176–7.   [63] Ibid. 179–80.

thinking on theological subjects'. This chapter, which is perhaps the most brilliantly subtle of all Newman's writings, continues in the same highly antithetical vein. On the one hand, Newman affirms he had no 'trouble about receiving those additional articles, which are not found in the Anglican Creed'. On the other hand, 'I am far of course from denying that every article of the Christian Creed ... is beset with intellectual difficulties', which 'I cannot answer'. But he immediately points out: 'Ten thousand difficulties do not make one doubt ... difficulty and doubt are incommensurate.'[64] Thus, in particular, 'the being of a God is, to my own apprehension, encompassed with most difficulty, and yet borne in upon our minds with most power.'[65] The next paragraph evinces the same pattern of argument, although in a simpler way. Transubstantiation 'is difficult to believe; I did not believe the doctrine till I was a Catholic'. But 'I had no difficulty in believing it, as soon as I believed that the Roman Catholic Church was the oracle of God.' Not that it is not 'difficult, impossible, to imagine'—but 'how is it difficult to believe?'[66]

The argument proceeds in the same general way (by thesis, antithesis, and synthesis), although the question now is not whether it is possible to believe honestly in particular Catholic doctrines, but whether, more fundamentally, the Catholic 'system' as such is dishonest. Newman begins by stating, 'the being of a God ... is as certain to me as the certainty of my own existence.' But the 'world seems simply to give the lie to that great truth, of which my whole being is so full', for when 'I look out of myself into the world of men ... I see a sight which fills me with unspeakable distress'. It is as if 'I looked into a mirror, and did not see my face', when 'I look into this living busy world, and see no reflexion of its Creator'. It is not that he wishes to underrate the usual arguments for God's existence, 'but these do not warm me or enlighten me; they do not take away the winter of my desolation, or make the buds unfold and the leaves grow within me, and my moral being rejoice', as he looks out at a world without God, 'a vision to dizzy and appal'. There is only one resolution of the dilemma which does justice to both truths: '*if* there be a God, *since* there is a God, the human race is implicated in some terrible aboriginal calamity.'[67]

This is the background to the explanation of infallibility which follows and which contains much the same movement of argument. Granted that 'truth is the real object of our reason', then 'right reason' when 'correctly exercised' arrives at religious truth. But unfortunately, 'reason as it acts in fact and concretely in fallen man' has a 'tendency ... towards a simple unbelief', and there is no denying 'the all-corroding,

---

[64] *Apo.* 214.   [65] Ibid. 215.   [66] Ibid.   [67] Ibid. 216–18.

all-dissolving scepticism of the intellect', which has resulted in an 'anarchical condition of things'. Just as 'in the pagan world, when our Lord came, the last traces of the religious knowledge of former times were all but disappearing from those portions of the world in which the intellect had been active and had had a career,' so too, in the modern world, 'What a scene, what a prospect, does the whole of Europe present at this day!' The necessity 'to arrest fierce wilful human nature in its onward course' in order to preserve 'some form of religion for the interests of humanity' led to the establishment of religion at the Reformation in Protestant countries, 'but now the crevices of those establishments are admitting the enemy'; nor can the Bible as 'a book . . . make a stand against the wild living intellect of man'. The conflict between the claims of reason and religion is resolved through 'the Church's infallibility, as a provision, adapted by the mercy of the Creator, to preserve religion in the world, and to restrain that freedom of thought, which of course in itself is one of the greatest of our natural gifts, and to rescue it from its own suicidal excesses'. This 'power . . . is happily adapted to be a working instrument . . . for smiting hard and throwing back the immense energy of the aggressive, capricious, untrustworthy intellect'.[68] There follows a severely uncompromising exposition of the Church's authority 'viewed in its fulness' and 'viewed in the concrete, as clothed and surrounded by the appendages of its high sovereignty . . . a supereminent prodigious power sent upon earth to encounter and master a giant evil'. Although infallibility strictly only belongs to solemn dogmatic definitions, Newman professes to submit not only to the traditions of the Church, but also 'to those other decisions of the Holy See, theological or not . . . which, waiving the question of their infallibility, on the lowest ground come to me with a claim to be accepted and obeyed'. Nor does he feel any 'temptation at all to break in pieces the great legacy of thought' which the Church has inherited from her greatest thinkers.

This unequivocal statement of the 'thesis' provokes the 'antithesis', the obvious objection that 'the restless intellect of our common humanity is utterly weighed down' by such an authority, 'so that, if this is to be the mode of bringing it into order, it is brought into order only to be destroyed'. This leads to the 'synthesis', the claim that in fact the 'energy of the human intellect . . . thrives and is joyous, with a tough elastic strength, under the terrible blows of the divinely-fashioned weapon, and is never so much itself as when it has lately been overthrown'. The resolution of the conflict lies in the remarkable argument that far from being mutually contradictory, authority and

---

[68] Ibid. 218–20.

reason need each other precisely because, paradoxically, each is actually sustained by conflict with the other:

... it is the vast Catholic body itself, and it only, which affords an arena for both combatants in that awful, never-dying duel. It is necessary for the very life of religion ... that the warfare should be incessantly carried on. Every exercise of Infallibility is brought out into act by an intense and varied operation of the Reason, both as its ally and as its opponent, and provokes again, when it has done its work, a re-action of Reason against it; and, as in a civil polity the State exists and endures by means of the rivalry and collision, the encroachments and defeats of its constituent parts, so in like manner Catholic Christendom is no simple exhibition of religious absolutism, but presents a continuous picture of Authority and Private Judgment alternately advancing and retreating as the ebb and flow of the tide;—it is a vast assemblage of human beings with wilful intellects and wild passions, brought together into one by the beauty and the Majesty of a Superhuman Power,—into what may be called a large reformatory or training-school, not as if into a hospital or into a prison, not in order to be sent to bed, not to be buried alive, but (if I may change my metaphor) brought together as if into some moral factory, for the melting, refining, and moulding, by an incessant, noisy process, of the raw material of human nature, so excellent, so dangerous, so capable of divine purposes.[69]

The startling chain of imagery that concludes this richly metaphorical passage hints at a new, divergent movement of argument, and reminds us that Newman has other than Protestant or unbelieving readers also in mind. The infallible authority, he insists with a typically secular metaphor, 'is a supply for a need, and it does not go beyond that need', for its purpose is 'not to enfeeble the freedom or vigour of human thought in religious speculation, but to resist and control its extravagance'. Having begun by freely admitting the wide powers enjoyed by ecclesiastical authority, he now emphasizes both the narrow limits of infallibility in defining as explicit doctrine what is already implicit in revelation, and also its rare occurrence (normally by a 'Pope in Ecumenical Council'). But, more important, he recognizes what '*is* the great trial to the Reason', namely, that the Church claims jurisdiction over a wide area of 'secular matters which bear upon religion'. These disciplinary rather than doctrinal judgements are not, however, infallible—but they do claim obedience (although not faith). Again, 'because there is a gift of infallibility in the Catholic Church', it does not necessarily follow that 'the parties who are in possession of it are in all their proceedings infallible'. Indeed, 'I think history supplies us with instances in the Church, where legitimate power has been harshly used.' The unequivocal assertion of the Church's legitimate authority is thus sharply qualified by these reminders of its limits and limitations. But the

[69] *Apo.* 224–6.

apparent discrepancy is resolved by the consideration that it does not 'follow that the substance of the acts of the ruling power is not right and expedient, because its manner may have been faulty'. In fact, Newman remarks tartly, 'high authorities act by means of instruments', and 'we know how such instruments claim for themselves the name of their principals, who thus get the credit of faults which really are not theirs'.[70]

The pages that follow are probably unrivalled in Newman's works for their sharply antithetical style of argument, brilliantly deployed to hold a carefully poised balance between two diametrically opposed points of view. But the object is not to play a balancing-trick between, for example, Manning and Ward on the one side and Acton and Simpson on the other. Nor is the pattern of thought no more than a rhetorical device designed to reach a compromise between the claims of both parties. For what emerges is that truth is attained not in spite of but through the conflict of opposites, which forces the crucial shift of perspective that allows the dilemma to be seen in a new light and so to be resolved.

Newman begins by reinforcing the case for authority and the need for submission. Even Protestants 'have before now obeyed the royal command to abstain from certain theological questions'. Moreover, despite all abuses, Newman insists that ecclesiastical authority has been 'mainly in the right, and that those whom they were hard upon were mainly in the wrong'. For example, Origen (whose name 'I love') 'was wrong' and 'his opponents were right'. And yet—'who can speak with patience of his enemy and the enemy of St. John Chrysostom, that Theophilus, bishop of Alexandria? who can admire or revere Pope Vigilius?' The contradiction is resolved by a completely fresh perspective, at once enlightening and provocative:

In reading ecclesiastical history, when I was an Anglican, it used to be forcibly brought home to me, how the initial error of what afterwards became heresy was the urging forward some truth against the prohibition of authority at an unseasonable time. There is a time for every thing, and many a man desires a reformation of an abuse, or the fuller development of a doctrine, or the adoption of a particular policy, but forgets to ask himself whether the right time for it is come: and knowing that there is no one who will be doing any thing towards its accomplishment in his own lifetime unless he does it himself, he will not listen to the voice of authority, and he spoils a good work in his own century, in order that another man, as yet unborn, may not have the opportunity of bringing it happily to perfection in the next. He may seem to the world to be nothing else than a bold champion for the truth and a martyr to free opinion, when he is just one of those persons whom the competent authority ought to silence; and, though the case may not fall within that subject-matter in which that authority

[70] Ibid. 226, 229–31.

is infallible, or the formal conditions of the exercise of that gift may be wanting, it is clearly the duty of authority to act vigorously in the case.

This, Newman admits, will arouse criticism, especially 'if the ruling power happens in its proceedings to evince any defect of prudence or consideration'. Mindful, no doubt, of his own difficulties with liberal Catholics who disliked his insistence on obedience, Newman adds that 'all those who take the part of that ruling authority will be considered as time-servers, or indifferent to the cause of uprightness and truth'. But that is not the conclusion of the sentence. The surprise, or rather the sting, lies in the second half, directed not at Acton and Simpson, but at Manning and Ward: 'while, on the other hand, the said authority may be accidentally supported by a violent ultra party, which exalts opinions into dogmas, and has it principally at heart to destroy every school of thought but its own'. The personal allusion, however, is clear enough even without Newman's privately expressed view that 'What I aim at may be real and good, but it may be God's will it should be done a hundred years later'—'discouraging' as it is 'to be out of joint with the time, and to be snubbed and stopped as soon as I begin to act'.[71]

This 'state of things' may well provoke and discourage people of moderate views, as well as 'such as keenly perceive, and are honestly eager to remedy, existing evils'—'evils', Newman comments acidly, 'of which divines in this or that foreign country know nothing at all, and which even at home, where they exist, it is not every one who has the means of estimating'. The bewildering progress in modern knowledge raises the critical question, 'how are the respective claims of revelation and of natural science to be adjusted', particularly out of 'tenderness for those many souls who, in consequence of the confident tone of the schools of secular knowledge, are in danger of being led away into a bottomless liberalism of thought'. This 'deep, plausible scepticism', which is 'the development of human reason, as practically exercised by the natural man', is no longer confined to that theological party Newman had once known at Oxford ('of a dry and repulsive character, not very dangerous in itself, though dangerous as opening the door to evils which it did not itself either anticipate or comprehend'), but is now simply 'the educated lay world'. However, Newman is not intent on attacking the 'Liberal religionists of this day' ('a very mixed body'), or contemporary scientists and scholars, some of whom may be hostile to religion, but many of whom pursue their researches in a completely disinterested spirit and should not be blamed (as if one 'were afraid of truth of any kind') for pursuing 'secular facts, by means of the reason which God has given them, to their logical conclusions'. Rather, he is

[71] *LD* xix. 179–80.

concerned for those educated believers 'who are simply perplexed,—frightened or rendered desperate . . . by the utter confusion into which late discoveries or speculations have thrown their most elementary ideas of religion'. Beneath the warm compassion runs a cold undercurrent of contempt for the heartlessness of obscurantist dogmatism:

Who does not feel for such men? who can have one unkind thought of them? Let them be fierce with you who have no experience of the difficulty with which error is discriminated from truth, and the way of life is found amid the illusions of the world.

'How many a Catholic', exclaims Newman, 'has in his thoughts followed such men, many of them so good, so true, so noble! how often has the wish risen in his heart that some one from among his own people should come forward as the champion of revealed truth against its opponents!' Indeed, he has himself been asked to do so by both Catholics and Protestants. But there is a serious objection: 'at the moment it is so difficult to say precisely what it is that is to be encountered and overthrown . . . hypotheses rise and fall.' It is so 'difficult to anticipate which of them will keep their ground' that 'it has seemed to me to be very undignified for a Catholic to commit himself to the work of chasing what might turn out to be phantoms'. Nor would such an attempt be likely to find favour with the authorities of the Church, whose 'recent acts' (like the Munich Brief) may be interpreted, Newman suggests politely, as 'tying the hands of a controversialist . . . and teaching us that true wisdom, which Moses inculcated on his people, when the Egyptians were pursuing them, "Fear ye not, stand still; the Lord shall fight for you, and ye shall hold your peace." ' The exhortation to patience sounds (especially if we substitute Persian for Egyptian slave-masters) ironically like that very counsel Newman was wont to offer to the victims not of secularism, but of religious authoritarianism. However, the conclusion is innocent enough: 'And so far from finding a difficulty in obeying in this case, I have cause to be thankful and to rejoice to have so clear a direction in a matter of difficulty.'

In reality, Newman argues, there never has in the past been any conflict between religion and science. But immediately he qualifies the point both by admitting that it is too soon to pronounce on the relation between modern science and theology, and by freely conceding the one notorious exception to the rule, the case of Galileo. With this ambivalent allusion, the anti-Ultramontane undercurrent begins to swell to a veritable undertow, stronger than the ostensible drift of the argument against objections to an infallible authority. The proof, Newman continues, that infallibility has not crushed intellectual freedom in the Church is that it is 'individuals, and not the Holy See, that have taken the initiative, and given the lead to the Catholic mind, in theological inquiry'. 'Indeed', he points out with studied irony, 'it is one of the reproaches against the Roman Church, that it has originated nothing, and has only served as a sort of *remora* or break in the development of doctrine. And it is an objection which I really embrace as a truth; for such I conceive to be the main purpose of its extraordinary gift.' The historical examples that follow are unrelentingly negative. The fact is that 'the Church of Rome possessed no great mind in the whole period of persecution'. There was not a single doctor till St Leo, who anyway taught only 'one point of doctrine'. Not even Pope St Gregory has a place in the history of theology. The greatest Western theologian, St Augustine, belonged, like the best early Latin theologians, to the African Church. Western theology, in fact, was formed to a considerable extent by heterodox theologians such as Tertullian and Origen and Eusebius, with the result that actual heretical 'questionings' became 'salutary truths'. Even Ecumenical Councils were guided by the 'individual reason' of a mere presbyter like Malchion, or a young deacon like Athanasius. At Trent, too, particular theologians 'had a critical effect on some of the definitions of dogma'. The real, albeit hidden, conclusion is that history gives little support to the Ultramontane view of Rome as a kind of oracle of truth.

History, too, shows how little authority has interfered with the freedom of theologians. Again, beneath the apparent movement of the argument, there runs a contrary, stronger undercurrent, for what really concerns Newman, of course, is that what was true of the past is no longer true of the present. But he is not only protesting against the present by means of the past; he is also stating with great deliberateness his considered view on the crucial balance to be maintained between theology and the teaching authority of the Church. He begins by referring (provocatively) to that theocratic society so idealized by many of his fellow converts.

There never was a time when the intellect of the educated class was more active, or rather more restless, than in the middle ages. And then again all through Church history from the first, how slow is authority in interfering! Perhaps a local teacher, or a doctor in some local school, hazards a proposition, and a controversy ensues. It smoulders or burns in one place, no one interposing; Rome simply lets it alone. Then it comes before a Bishop; or some priest, or some professor in some other seat of learning takes it up; and then there is a second stage of it. Then it comes before a University, and it may be condemned by the theological faculty. So the controversy proceeds year after year, and Rome is still silent. An appeal perhaps is next made to a seat of authority inferior to Rome; and then at last after a long while it comes before the supreme power. Meanwhile, the question has been ventilated and turned over and over again, and viewed on every side of it, and authority is called upon to pronounce a decision, which has already been arrived at by reason. But even then, perhaps the supreme authority hesitates to do so, and nothing is determined on the point for years; or so generally and vaguely, that the whole controversy has to be gone through again, before it is ultimately determined.

Newman, even at this point, when his own personal interest is almost palpable, refrains from outright criticism of the abuse of authority in the contemporary Church. But the rhetoric of reticence has its own eloquence:

It is manifest how a mode of proceeding, such as this, tends not only to the liberty, but to the courage, of the individual theologian or controversialist. Many a man has ideas, which he hopes are true, and useful for his day, but he is not confident about them, and wishes to have them discussed. He is willing, or rather would be thankful, to give them up, if they can be proved to be erroneous or dangerous, and by means of controversy he achieves his end. He is answered, and he yields; or on the contrary he finds that he is considered safe. He would not dare to do this, if he knew an authority, which was supreme and final, was watching every word he said, and made signs of assent or dissent to each sentence, as he uttered it. Then indeed he would be fighting, as the Persian soldiers, under the lash, and the freedom of his intellect might truly be said to be beaten out of him.

Typically, even now he is ready to undermine his own indignation with the frank qualification that 'when controversies run high' then 'an interposition may . . . advisably take place; and again, questions may be of that urgent nature, that an appeal must, as a matter of duty, be made at once to the highest authority in the Church'. But the insistent emphasis on the universal character of the Church that follows barely conceals an unfavourable allusion to the Italian monopoly of the Holy See.

. . . the multitude of nations which are within the fold of the Church will be found to have acted for its protection, against any narrowness, on the supposition of narrowness, in the various authorities at Rome, with whom lies the practical decision of controverted questions . . . Then, again, such national influences have a providential effect in moderating the bias which the local influences of Italy may exert on the See of St. Peter. It stands to reason that . . . Rome must have in it an element of Italy; and it is no prejudice to the zeal and devotion with which we submit ourselves to the Holy See to admit this plainly . . . Catholicity is not only one of the notes of the Church, but . . . one of its securities.

And the conclusion is daringly ambiguous, if not sarcastic:

. . . I trust that all European races will ever have a place in the Church, and assuredly I think that the loss of the English, not to say the German element, in its composition has been a most serious misfortune. And certainly, if there is one consideration more than another which should make us English grateful to Pius the Ninth, it is that, by giving us a Church of our own, he has prepared the way for our own habits of mind, our own manner of reasoning, our own tastes, and our own virtues, finding a place and thereby a sanctification, in the Catholic Church.[72]

This final chapter was written in response to Acton's complaint that it was not enough for Newman merely to vindicate his own personal integrity. Acton wanted him to defend both the integrity of the Church and also the honesty of the clergy. And so the *Apologia* ends where it began—with Kingsley's impugnment of the truthfulness of Catholic priests. As with his own personal history, Newman refuses to enter into any formal defence, but prefers to give his own 'testimony . . . and there to leave it'. On becoming a Catholic, 'nothing struck' him 'more at once than the English out-spoken manner of the Priests', who seemed to be 'more natural and unaffected than many an Anglican clergyman'. Again, he was impressed by their 'simple faith', the very opposite of any kind of hypocrisy and the most obvious cause of their remarkable 'self-devotion' and 'discipline'. It is true that St Alfonso Liguori permitted equivocation under certain circumstances, but then even English Protestant moralists like Dr Johnson allow that lying may sometimes be permissible, and Catholic moral theology books, which assume that 'there is a way of winning men from greater sins by winking for the time at the less', are misinterpreted because they are 'intended for the Confessor, and Protestants view them as intended for the Preacher'. However, Newman admits disarmingly, 'in this department of morality, much as I admire the high points of the Italian character, I like the English rule of conduct better'.[73] Such frank admissions were calculated as much to allay Protestant fears as to excite Ultramontane antagonism.

But to end on that note might be misleading, for what is so impressive ultimately about this last chapter is its refusal to adopt any one particular point of view to the exclusion of other considerations and factors. The result is not a superficially clever exercise in ambiguity or compromise or evasion, but rather, a complex and subtle exploration of the creative interaction of authority and freedom, of the necessary interdependence of the theologian and the magisterium. It is also a crucial stage in the growth of Newman's theology of the Church, a theology which was to reach its full development during the next decade and which was to be the most important theological achievement of his Catholic period.

Another reason why we should not leave the *Apologia* at this point is

[72] *Apo.* 231–41.   [73] Ibid. 242–4, 248.

simply that this would be to ignore the actual end of the book. The famous dedication, like the other personal allusions, conceals as much as it reveals. But there were certainly readers who would have understood the significance of the meagre roll-call of the six surviving members of the depleted Birmingham Oratory, 'who have been so faithful to me . . . who have carried me through so many trials'. It would have been noted that though the name of St Philip is thrice reiterated in the opening sentence, there is no mention at all of St Philip's other, more prominent English followers who had once been with and under Newman. It would have been appreciated how the name of Ambrose St John, 'whom God gave me, when He took every one else away; who are the link between my old life and my new', is used to 'gather up and bear in memory those familiar and affectionate companions and counsellors, who in Oxford were given to me, one after another, to be my daily solace and relief'— but who are now either dead or more or less estranged. And finally, the tribute to 'those many younger men . . . who have never been disloyal to me by word or deed' would have been a reminder of those converts who had once been disciples and now were critics.[74] As much a fond eulogy of faithful friends present as a poignant elegy for erstwhile friends now deceased or disloyal or separated, these closing lines form a fitting conclusion to the studied ambivalence of this last great chapter of the *Apologia*.

[74] Ibid. 252–3.

15

Return to Oxford?

NEVER had Newman thought that he would 'have to write such a book'. Certainly, he had been ready to 'accept the challenge' if anyone well known had made a 'formal attack' on him, but he had 'never fancied' that he would 'meet with more than that casual pelting, as if from idle boys who shie stones, which had so long been going on'.[1] His 'great reward', he told Keble, had been to 'please readers in both communions'.[2] But he turned down suggestions from Catholic friends that he should take the opportunity to start writing again. In the prevailing climate of Ultramontane opinion, 'One cannot speak ten words without ten objections being made to each.'[3] The Church was faced with a crisis, 'and at such seasons extreme views alone are in favour, and a man who is not extravagant is thought treacherous. I sometimes think of King Lear's daughters—and consider that they after all may be found the truest, who are in speech the most measured.'[4] He was well aware, too, of the hostile gossip at Rome, including not only the rumour of his impending defection from the Church, but also the remarkable report of Mgr. Talbot that he had contributed money to the cause of Garibaldi! He had no intention of becoming involved in further controversy than the *Apologia* itself was likely to arouse. Not everything he had said there was likely to please all his co-religionists. But at least there were no signs of a continuation of the controversy with Kingsley, who was bitterly resentful at Newman's success and wrote angrily to Alexander Macmillan that he had no intention of replying; he had deliberately 'struck as hard' as he could, but he had no intention of putting himself 'a second time, by any fresh act of courtesy, into the power of one who, like a treacherous ape, lifts to you meek and suppliant eyes, till he thinks he has you within his reach, and then springs, gibbering and biting, at your face'.[5]

Meanwhile there was no sign of any slackening in the sales of the *Apologia*, the reviews of which had been almost universally favourable. Newman attributed its success to the circumstances of its publication: 'I fancy I write better when I am led to write by what comes in my way—

---

[1] *LD* xxi. 134.   [2] Ibid. 143.   [3] Ibid. 144.
[4] Ibid. 160.   [5] Ibid. 120 n. 1.

or rather I am sure to make failures if I go out of my work.'[6] The opportunity to write his own history had proved to be far more effective than any argument or controversy could have been. Surprisingly, the most favourable response came from Nonconformist reviewers. But there was no doubt of the overwhelming support of most of the Catholic clergy (including even the redoubtable John Gillow of Ushaw). As for Anglicans, Frederic Rogers remarked on how charitably the Church of England had been treated by Newman. It was indeed a turning-point, and not only in terms of Newman's reputation: the enormous sales of the book meant that he no longer had to worry about money. Only five years before he had lamented, 'I lose by every thing I print—and scrape together the money for the outlay, from a sort of feeling, that at a future day people may treat me better than they do now.'[7]

In July 1864, while Newman was away for a few days in London, the egregious Mgr. Talbot paid a visit to the Birmingham Oratory. He wanted to know if Newman agreed with the 'worldly' gentry who were in favour of Catholics going to Oxford. He also wanted to know what Newman '*did*—did I read?' He was told gravely that Newman had certainly been seen to 'take out books from the library'. Talbot followed up his visit with a pompous invitation to preach next Lent at Rome, which 'I think myself you will derive great benefit from revisiting . . . and again showing yourself to the Ecclesiastical Authorities there, who are anxious to see you'. It was, Newman later noted, 'an insolent letter', with its insinuation that he should 'rub up' his Catholicism.[8] However, it had the merit of drawing from him one of his own most famous letters:

I have received your letter, inviting me to preach next Lent in your Church at Rome, to 'an audience of Protestants more educated than could ever be the case in England.'

However, Birmingham people have souls; and I have neither taste nor talent for the sort of work, which you cut out for me: and I beg to decline your offer[.][9]

At the beginning of August, Newman was offered a five-acre plot of ground in Oxford (the site of the old workhouse and the present Wellington Square), which an elderly Catholic ('the patriarch of the Oxford congregation')[10] had bought in the hope that it could be used for a Catholic college. The possibility of founding an Oratory at Oxford immediately occurred to Newman. He had till Christmas to find the money. The opportunity of acquiring such a piece of land freehold in Oxford was hardly likely to occur again, and if the college idea proved to be impractical there would be no difficulty in reselling it at a profit. Newman immediately began to put out feelers to see if the sum could be

[6] Ibid. 178.   [7] Ibid. xix. 243.   [8] Ibid. xxii. 338.
[9] Ibid. xxi. 165-7.   [10] Ibid. 271.

raised. He had his doubts, though, about the feasibility of a Catholic college, which did not lessen as time went on:

It will cost so much; and, when provided, perhaps will not fill. It will attract attention; and shortcomings, whether on the part of tutors or young men, will be jealously noted. It will be impeded in its free action by a number of petty semi-monastic regulations, and will not be in a condition to compete fairly with the Protestant bodies. It will either be looked down upon, or it will kindle fierce controversy and opposition. It will be regarded with great suspicion by an influential portion of the Catholic body; and will bring odium and disrepute on those who take part in it.[11]

The one difference from Ireland was that in England there were Catholics who had the necessary financial means and the capability of bringing influence to bear on the bishops. Towards the end of the month Bishop Ullathorne called to discuss the plan and also to say that he wanted himself to set up a mission and church in Oxford. On Newman referring to his own hope of founding an Oratory there, the bishop promptly offered him the mission. Newman was taken aback by the suggestion, as he had never envisaged going himself to Oxford—although much later he learned that this was what Ullathorne had understood his intention to be. He noted then, 'I saw at once to my surprise and for the first time that a way was offered to me of going to Oxford, a step which I simply disliked and shrank from, but which I could not, as a matter of conscience, when put before me, peremptorily refuse.'[12] Perhaps the five acres might ultimately accommodate not only a college, but also a church and an Oratory too. Cautious as he was about the college plan, Newman saw the advantage of undertaking the mission for the bishop: it would give the projected Oratory an ostensible justification, apart from the idea of the college (towards which a beginning might be made by taking in student lodgers).

Tempting as the prospect was in some ways, Newman remained highly cautious, not to say sceptical. At his age he felt 'sick of all plans', with 'little energy, and declining strength'. They were 'so few' in the existing community and with 'so many irons in the fire'. How could he 'mix again with Oxford men' and 'throw' himself 'into what might be such painful reawakening animosities'? How could he 'adjust' his 'position with dear Pusey, and others who at present are my wellwishers'? Quite apart from all the work involved, he might get into 'hot water' with Propaganda and be summoned only 'to kick my heels at its door for a whole year'. He ought to have '*a view*' on all the theological controversies of the day—but if he did, he 'might get a rap on the knuckles from Propaganda for divulging' it. Finally, he had had enough

---

[11] *LD* xxi. 298.   [12] Ibid. 206 n. 2.

'disappointment and anxiety' over all his other abortive projects.[13] Still, he could not reject the idea out of hand; as an Oratory they were *'called to education'*.[14] It would, however, be out of the question to raise the money for the whole five-acre plot by advertising a prospective college, because a college could not be advertised without the hierarchy's sanction. Half an acre would be needed by the bishop for the mission, and the Birmingham Oratory could purchase two and a half acres (which could either be used for a college one day, or else for lodgings for Catholic students); the rest of the land would have to be acquired by private subscription as an investment.

Further discussion with Ullathorne in September proved far from encouraging. The bishop made it clear that he would only countenance an Oratory at Oxford for the sake of the mission there. There were, he told Newman, objections to a Catholic college, and even more to opening a lodging-house for Catholic undergraduates. Ullathorne, it transpired, had already received a warning from Propaganda (at Manning's instigation, in fact) against Catholics attending English universities. He reminded Newman (rather unkindly) that Newman himself had once asked for a ban on Catholics going to Oxford and Cambridge, for the sake of the Irish University, adding that such a prohibition would be enacted in the not impossible event of a Catholic university being founded in England. The idea of an Oxford Oratory simply for the sake of a parish of about a hundred Catholics hardly appealed to Newman. The purpose of going to Oxford must be to provide care for Catholic students there. Nor did he relish the bishop's suggestion that there would be the possibility of making converts among undergraduates and of forming an alliance with liberal Nonconformists in the city: 'We should be in the false position of being supported by radical dissenters who were envious of the University, and should be expected by Catholics to earn their applause by kidnapping Undergraduates.'[15] However, he agreed in the end to take on the mission for the sake of a future Oxford Oratory, at the same time undertaking that he would not offer accommodation to Catholic undergraduates. His real reason for thinking of an Oratory at all was the hope of attracting much-needed novices, although there would always be work for an Oratory at Oxford so long as there were Catholic undergraduates still there. He was very diffident about his own return to the Oxford scene; he felt distinctly *passé*.

In October came news of the sudden death of the Catholic benefactor in Oxford. To forestall a bid from St John's College to buy the land, Newman was forced to make an offer, without further delay and without

---

[13] Ibid. 212.   [14] Ibid. 217.   [15] Ibid. 232.

the necessary money in hand. He had till the first of January to pay, with only the private means of the wealthier members of the community to fall back on. Since there was no prospect of a college being built, it was necessary to resell the greater part of the plot as fast as possible. On the other hand, he was more enthusiastic about the prospects of a parish: Oxford was growing as professors increased in number and wealth and as fellows and tutors, who were now allowed to marry, were free to move out of college into houses. He intended to launch an appeal for a church to commemorate the conversions that had resulted from the Oxford Movement. He had no intention of moving permanently to Oxford himself, but he meant to take some part in the parish, and in particular in the pastoral care of Catholic undergraduates. Some controversy might be unavoidable, but he certainly had no thought of any 'mission' to non-Catholic undergraduates. His aim was not at 'immediate conversions but to influence, as far as an old man can, the tone of thought in the place'.[16] The important point, however, was to look after the Catholics who were already at the existing colleges, and who would presumably continue to go there. The bishops might not approve, but they could hardly forbid it, when there was no likelihood of a Catholic university in England and when the idea of a Catholic college at Oxford had been rejected.

Newman was nervous, but also excited at the prospect: the situation at Oxford would be novel to him, but then it was a novel experience for him to find himself engaged for a change on an undertaking that seemed so flourishing and full of promise. It still remained unclear, however, how he could combine a role in Oxford with his position at Birmingham (not that physically there was much problem, as the train journey was only an hour and a half, about the same time that it took to get to the Oratory's country cottage at Rednal). There was no doubt that the *Apologia* had aroused an enormous interest and sympathy, not least at Oxford, which gave him an altogether new position and which it seemed foolish not to take advantage of. He told Pusey that he need not worry— 'I have no hostile feeling towards the Anglican Communion—and nothing but love for Oxford.' The mere foundation of an Oratory there might be all he could manage—'even to see Oxford, would be to me inexpressibly painful, as the coming to life again of men who have been apparently drowned.'[17] Pusey was less sanguine: the return of Newman would mean controversy that could only damage the high-church party. But Newman had now set his heart on the idea of 'a centre and School of Catholicism in the heart of the University', something which would 'last and . . . grow'.[18]

[16] *LD* xxi. 283.   [17] Ibid. 304.   [18] Ibid. 306.

Unfortunately, others had set their heart on the very opposite. In September Manning had written to the Vatican asking for a definite instruction to stop more Catholics going to Oxford and Cambridge, and in October Wiseman was asked by Propaganda to call a special meeting of the bishops to settle the matter. Manning was delighted, and seized the opportunity to warn ominously that the people behind the agitation for Catholics to go to English universities were precisely those who had spoken against or failed to support the Temporal Power and the Munich Brief. He seemed indeed more afraid of their baleful influence than of the dangers of Protestant Oxford. He ended by denouncing Newman's plan for an Oxford Oratory, which he claimed was responsible for the sudden increase of interest in the idea of a Catholic college. In November came a specific order, approved by the Pope, for an extraordinary meeting of the bishops. It was obvious to Newman that 'unless the Catholic gentry make themselves heard at Rome, a small active clique will carry the day.'[19] It was also evident to him what the real objection to Catholics going to Oxford was:

I see clearly that the real root of the difficulty is *myself*. There are those who cannot endure the thought that I should have the *forming* of the young Catholic mind at Oxford. This is the one point of battle.[20]

It explained why Wiseman had been so cold when he had called, at Patterson's request, earlier in the month. Bishop Ullathorne nervously enquired if the appeal for an Oratory church at Oxford contained any reference to the University. Apparently he had forgotten that the only reason Newman had agreed to undertake the mission was for the sake of Catholic undergraduates there. The circular appeal was indeed alarmingly explicit: the projected Oratory was intended expressly to provide pastoral care for Catholics at the University, a work, Newman was careful to emphasize, particularly suitable for the English Oratory. He agreed not to issue the circular till after the bishops' meeting in December.

Meanwhile, in the middle of November, Manning published a pamphlet ostensibly directed against Pusey, who had called the Church of England a 'bulwark against infidelity', but really aimed at Newman, who had called it, in the *Apologia*, 'a serviceable breakwater against doctrinal errors, more fundamental than its own'.[21] Manning also deplored what he saw as the denial of the rational proofs for the existence of God implicit in the idea that the only logical alternative to Catholicism was atheism. Newman noted privately, 'what *I really* say is that the *same bad logic* which leads to the rejection of Catholicism necessarily leads also to the rejection of Theism.'[22] For 'the sort of

[19] Ibid. 309.   [20] Ibid. 319.   [21] *Apo.* 298.   [22] *Phil.N.* ii. 46.

argument by which it is proved that the Catholic Church comes from God, is of the same kind, and of the same force, as that by which it is proved . . . that there is a God at all'.[23] (In fact, of course, he also thought that people were 'logically inconsistent'[24] and 'settle down into something or other . . . short of the two extremes'.[25])

The opposition to his going to Oxford was also, he saw very clearly, closely bound up with that 'same dreadful jealousy of the laity, which has ruined things in Dublin', and which was 'at the root' of the dislike of Catholics going to the universities. It was not so much that certain bishops were afraid that Catholics would lose their faith, but that they were simply terrified of 'the natural influence' an educated laity could exercise—an influence 'which would be their greatest, or (humanly speaking) is rather their only, defence against the world'.[26] Newman's insistence on the rights of the laity rested, in fact, on a deeper insight into human motivation, which he summed up with striking succinctness:

Nothing great or living can be done except when men are self governed and independent: this is quite consistent with a full maintenance of ecclesiastical supremacy. St Francis Xavier wrote to St Ignatius on his knees; but who will say that St Francis was not a real centre of action?[27]

As for himself personally, he had 'been so often balked,—brought into undertakings—then left in the lurch, that I wish, if I can, to guard against any such new mis-hap now'.[28] It was only too likely that the bishops would fail to agree on a definite policy, and then there would be a long delay while reference was made to Rome. In theory, the best solution was to found a Catholic university, and the worst to allow Catholics to go to Protestant colleges. But what was the 'most practicable' solution? To say nothing at all, in fact, would 'commit the Church least'.[29] The most practical and sensible course of action seemed to be to leave things as they were, with the possibility later of reviewing the situation. He began to feel that 'if you wish to succeed, you must show your teeth, that the more in this world you yield, the less you get, and the more you claim, the more you are considered'.[30] As it was, it looked strangely as if Manning and Ward were 'co-operating to fulfil *Pusey*'s wish of keeping me out of Oxford'.[31] It was said they were responsible for the tendentious questionnaire which was sent to convert graduates of the English universities (though, pointedly, not to Newman) shortly before the bishops met. Newman's answer to indignant complaints was that the 'unknown persons who mislead Propaganda, put the screw on the Bishops and would shut up our school

[23] *LD* xx. 495.   [24] Ibid. xix. 286.   [25] Ibid. 296.
[26] Ibid. xxi. 327.   [27] Ibid. 331.   [28] Ibid. 330.
[29] Ibid. 339.   [30] Ibid. 333.   [31] Ibid. 340.

if they could' had to be firmly confronted by the laity: 'Such persons will bully, if they are allowed to do so; but will not show fight, if they are resisted.'[32] He himself had recently heard that Ward had refused to allow any further discussion of the *Apologia* in the *Dublin Review*: if Newman could not be openly attacked, at least he could be ignored. His own view was that Ward's 'intellectual complexion has something morbid about it'. But it was not only Ward: 'The present state of things is very sad—and would make me unhappy, had I not got callous to balks and rebuffs. Things must be worse before they are better . . .'.[33]

At their meeting on 13 December the bishops were unanimously against the idea of a Catholic college and in favour of a warning against the danger of Catholics going to Protestant universities. But with the exception of Wiseman and one other bishop, who insisted on making their views known at Rome, all the bishops were against a formal prohibition. It was clear to Newman that but for Ullathorne (who had sharply opposed the Cardinal) offering him the Oxford mission there would never have been a meeting. The effective result of the meeting was that Rome was now officially involved; Propaganda might have kept silent, but now it would have to reiterate its opposition to 'mixed' education.

About the same time, in the middle of December, Pius IX promulgated the notorious *Syllabus of Errors*. Newman noted with surprise that the condemned propositions were not taken from specific Catholic publications, but were abstract propositions about secular ideas like 'progress' and 'liberalism' (terms which were left undefined). But although there was little in the document that would not have been said by 'high churchmen thirty years ago' or 'Keble now', the fact was that 'the advisers of the Holy Father seem determined to make our position in England as difficult as ever they can', and if 'the matter and form of it are unprecedented, I do not know how we can rejoice in its publication'.[34] In England they were 'certainly under a tyranny'— although it was an English tyranny: 'one or two persons, such as Manning seem to do everything.'[35] The Pope seemed only concerned with what might be true in theory, but apparently was quite unconcerned with what was expedient in practice. Nor was it so much its contents as its '*animus*—that is so alarming'. The only comfort was that 'Every thing is good which brings matters to a crisis.' Sooner or later, as had happened so often in the Church's history, there was bound to be a reaction. 'Will not the next century', Newman wondered wistfully, 'demand Popes who are not Italians?'[36] In the meantime, it was fortunate that 'Dogmatic documents are so burdened with jealous forms

---

[32] Ibid. 343. [33] Ibid. 361. [34] Ibid. 378.
[35] Ibid. 383. [36] Ibid. 386.

and exceptions, that, when zealots would do their worse, they *cannot* commit the Church', for such documents had to respect 'the traditions and doctors of the Church'.[37]

Newman decided to sell the original plot of land he had bought in Oxford, and instead to buy privately a smaller plot opposite Christ Church, which might be used later if the situation changed. As it was, he had been 'left in the lurch' once again, and even if he were permitted to go ahead with building a church he might well, after spending thousands of pounds on it, receive a letter from Propaganda 'to the effect of "Pray, Fr Newman, why are you at Oxford? why are you not at Birmingham?"' He was annoyed that the laity, who 'could do any thing, if they chose', had done so little to bring pressure on the bishops.[38] 'Our only hope', he remarked bleakly, 'is in the laity knowing their own strength and exerting themselves.'[39] There had never been any objection to Catholics going to Cambridge (where subscription to the Thirty-nine Articles was only required before taking a degree and not, as at Oxford, on matriculation), nor had Catholics there become Protestants. Again, there had been apostasies among Catholics at Trinity College, Dublin, but they were still allowed to go there. A proper Catholic university would be the obvious answer, but it was not practical. An absolute prohibition on Catholics attending English universities, without any viable alternative, would effectively bar Catholics from taking their place in public life. It was absurd to pretend that Oxford and Cambridge were more 'dangerous' places than a London office or the army. In spite of a lay petition against any prohibition, early in February came news that Propaganda had ordered the bishops to dissuade Catholics from going to Protestant universities. (The letter to Ullathorne was accompanied by a message from Barnabò that Newman's 'good intentions would have their reward in heaven'—'a cheap consolation' which 'did not tell me how to get back my £8000'.[40]) But at least the abortive petition showed that the laity were capable of acting as a body. Newman also received private confirmation that Manning was behind the ban and that his real object was to prevent Newman from going to Oxford. In spite of Manning's growing influence in Rome, Newman refused to believe the rumour that he would succeed Wiseman, who was now close to death. To a letter of condolence from Ambrose Phillipps de Lisle (as he was now called), he replied, 'it is our duty to submit.' Unlike de Lisle he had felt unable to join the 'Association for the Promotion of the Unity of Christendom', which had been condemned by Rome in the September of the previous year, but he thought its members had 'been treated cruelly'.[41]

[37] *LD* xxi. 436.   [38] Ibid. 384.   [39] Ibid. 398.
[40] Ibid. xxii. 62.   [41] Ibid. xxi. 415.

Newman's attitude to ecumenism was typically mixed—uncompromising but pragmatic, critical but open, hopeful yet realistic. For example, he was very alive to Rome's capacity to make significant concessions 'to regain a *population*'—but could one see, as some enthusiastic Catholic ecumenists seemed to believe, 'the true fire' of Catholicism 'glimmering amid the ashes' of English popular religion?[42] However, although it seemed impossible to pretend that Anglicanism was anything 'else than a tomb of what once was living, the casket of a treasure which has been lost',[43] he could also draw the radical conclusion (of considerable relevance to more general ecumenical endeavour) that 'all other truths and acts of religion are included' in mere repentance and faith in Christ.[44] Unlike some of his narrow-minded co-religionists, he did not think that 'in order to be in invincible ignorance one must be out of sight and hearing of Catholicism', for there were psychological barriers which were 'as real walls of separation as mountains'.[45] While it could not be denied that some of the most Catholic-minded leaders of the Church of England 'cannot speak of Rome or of Catholics without calling names',[46] equally, 'one of the most affecting and discouraging elements in the action of Catholicism just now on English society, is the scorn with which some of us treat proceedings and works among Protestants which it is but Christian charity to ascribe to the influence of divine grace.'[47] The hope for the future lay in the Church of England becoming more 'Catholic' and the Roman Catholic Church more 'Christian'. But if Newman had no doubt that there would sooner or later be a reaction against the bigotry of his own Church, he was less convinced that the Church of England might not become so 'radically liberalized . . . as to become a simple enemy of the Truth'.[48]

2

On 15 February 1865 Wiseman finally died. A week later, on the eve of the funeral, Newman made another entry in his private journal, the first since the lengthy review of his life two years previously. His feelings now were greatly changed.

First, I have got hardened against the opposition made to me, and have not the soreness at my ill treatment on the part of certain influential Catholics which I had then—and this simply from the natural effect of time—just as I do not feel that anxiety which I once had that we have no novices—I don't know that this

[42] Ibid. xx. 70–1.
[43] Ibid. xxi. 249.
[44] Ibid. xx. 172.
[45] Ibid. 268–9.
[46] Ibid. 71.
[47] Ibid. xxi. 228.
[48] Ibid. 299.

recklessness is a better state of mind than that anxiety. Every year I feel less and less anxiety to please Propaganda, from a feeling that they *cannot* understand England. Next, the two chief persons, whom I felt to be unjust to me, are gone— the Cardinal and Faber. Their place has been taken by Manning and Ward; but somehow, from my never having been brought closely into contact with either of them, as with the Cardinal and Faber, I have not that sense of their cruelty which I felt so much as regards the last two mentioned. Thirdly, in the last year a most wonderful deliverance has been wrought in my favour, by the controversy, of which the upshot was my Apologia. It has been marvellously blest, for, while I have regained, or rather gained, the favour of Protestants, I have received the approbation . . . of good part of the English clerical body . . . and I stand with them, as I never did before.

His sharp letters of June 1862 rebutting the rumour that he was leaving the Church had brought him to his 'lowest point, as regards popularity', yet it was 'the turning point', for 'by the very force of my descent, I prepared the way for a rebound'. Now his 'temptation' was to 'value the praise of men too highly, especially of Protestants'. He still felt 'keenly the way in which I am kept doing nothing', but 'I am not so much pained at it—both because, by means of my Apologia, I am (as I feel) *indirectly* doing a work, and because its success has put me in spirits to look out for other means of doing good, whether Propaganda cares about them or no'. It was certainly 'very singular that the same effective opposition to me does go on, thwarting my attempts to *act*'. The failure of the Oxford project meant that he was 'thrown back again on my do-nothing life here'—and yet, 'from habit, from recklessness, and from my late success, my feeling of despondency and irritation seems to have gone'.[49] Indeed, if only he could get out of his mind the notion that there was something he could do but was not doing, 'nothing could be happier, more peaceful, or more to my taste, than the life I lead'. It was a 'constant source of sadness' that he had achieved so little since he became a Catholic, but at least he had always 'tried to act, as *others* told me'. The Oratory in Birmingham, the University in Dublin, the translation of the Bible, the *Rambler* editorship, and finally the Oxford mission were all undertakings committed to him by his superiors; he could not in conscience feel that, in so far as they had failed, it was his fault. If he had not done more, 'it has been because I have not been put to do more, or have been stopped when I attempted more'.[50]

As for Cardinal Wiseman, he had 'done a great work and . . . gone to his reward'. It was a pity that 'his last act' had been 'to extinguish a hope of a great future and an opening for a wide field of religious action'.[51] In a way, it was inconsistent, for although 'he was too busy to be strenuous about any thing', still, he was 'a man of large views, and full of resource

---

[49] *AW* 260–1.   [50] *LD* xxi. 434.   [51] Ibid. 424.

and suggestion—but he lived for the day—and every fresh event seemed to wipe out from his mind those which preceded it'.[52] He had 'always meant kindly, but his impulses, kind as they were, were evanescent, and he was naturally influenced by those who got around him and occupied his ear'.[53] That was where the danger lay—in the 'soft and sly ways on the part of some persons in England'.[54] The Roman authorities themselves would be more careful in future; the significance of the petition would not be lost on them. On this occasion, however, Manning had already persuaded Propaganda, and the bishops had been forced to fall into line. The actual directive to the clergy, which was issued in March, only advised them to dissuade parents from sending their sons to Protestant universities; but although not an absolute order or prohibition, it was enough to prevent the Oratory School, for example, from preparing boys for entry. Newman was drily amused by the contrast between the bishops' indifference to the laity's concern about a university education for their children and their own anxiety about the activities of Catholic Members of Parliament: sarcastically he advised William Monsell, who had introduced a bill to change the offensive oath of allegiance still demanded of Catholics (but without removing the denial of the temporal power of the Papacy over other countries, a point insisted on in the *Syllabus*), to tell Archbishop Cullen not to worry but to 'look on with serene compassion at your untheological gambollings'.[55] While rejecting as absurd a plea that he should personally make a protest to Rome, he was firmly 'indisposed to suppress my own judgment in order to satisfy objectors'[56] in the last part of the *Apologia*, which Dr Russell had suggested he should modify. In particular, he was not prepared 'to withdraw the statement that the Pope in Ecumenical Council is the normal seat of Infallibility or to throw doubt upon my conviction that certain Italian devotions to our Lady are not suitable to England'.[57] To a further plea from Russell to allow wider scope for the Pope's infallibility, he insisted, 'with my best lights, I do not see that the Pope's judgments out of Council are other than extraordinary statements': thus a Council would have 'formally to receive and repeat' the papal definition of the Immaculate Conception, which was certainly 'valid and licit, but extraordinary'.[58]

The only consolation was 'the logic of facts'—for 'Catholics won't stand such standing-still for ever.' Newman remembered how Ulla-thorne had once insisted in a memorable interview that the laity were 'peaceable'—by which, 'I understood him to mean "They are grossly ignorant and unintellectual—and we need not consult or consult for

[52] Ibid. xxiii. 360. [53] Ibid. xxi. 426. [54] Ibid. 436.
[55] Ibid. 442. [56] Ibid. 447–8. [57] Ibid. 400.
[58] Ibid. 470.

them at all." '[59] Not surprisingly, the parents of the older boys at the Oratory School, who had no academic stimulus in the shape of any English university to go on to, wondered if their sons were supposed not 'to have a taste for any thing beyond that for shooting pheasants'.[60] They certainly could not understand, any more than Newman, why Oxford was supposed to be such a specially dangerous place for losing one's faith. The school, in fact, was continuing to improve, but it was far from financially viable, nor was it a help to be in Edgbaston, which was fast becoming a built-up area of Birmingham (when they had first come, it was still separated from the city by fields).

The official news of Manning's succession as Archbishop of Westminster reached London on 8 May. The favoured name sent to Rome by the Westminster Chapter, with the approval of the bishops, had been that of Archbishop Errington, who had unfortunately had a row with the Pope on the occasion of his removal as Wiseman's coadjutor. His candidature was seen as an insult by Pius IX, who decided that the new head of the English Church should be a sound Ultramontane. It was a 'marvellous' rise—'in fourteen years a Protestant Archdeacon is made Catholic Archbishop of Westminster, with the whole body of old Catholics, Bishops and all, under him. At the moment he is very unpopular—but, I suppose, there will be a re-action.' His 'great qualifications' would, Newman observed drily, 'overcome the laity', and moreover, 'he has such powers of persuasion that, if he chooses it, he will be able to bring over the Bishops'.[61] Perhaps Manning would take a more 'moderate line' now that he was 'at the top of the tree, and has to conciliate the little men who are under its branches, while he keeps well with powers at Rome'. It was hard to tell, 'he is so mysterious, that I don't know how one can ever have confidence in him.'[62] In answer to a pressing personal invitation to attend the consecration, Newman replied that he would be happy to do so, provided Manning promised to drop a reported attempt to make him a bishop 'in partibus' (or 'honorary' bishop without a diocese). He suspected that Manning wanted to 'put' him 'in the House of Lords and muzzle' him.[63] Manning agreed; he had already been warned by Ullathorne that such an offer would be open to misinterpretation. Newman himself suspected that it would be very convenient for Manning, as well as creating a good impression, if he put 'all the onus of discovering and providing a substitute' for an Oxford education upon Newman himself—but now he had 'by anticipation thrown cold water upon any overtures that way. It would be a case of hot chestnuts—and chestnuts of his own heating.'[64] When T. W. Allies reproached Newman for 'personal feeling' against the new Archbishop, he replied that he

[59] *LD* xxi. 457.   [60] Ibid. 453.   [61] Ibid. 471.
[62] Ibid. 477.   [63] Cit. in *Ward* ii. 88.   [64] *LD* xxi. 492.

certainly 'could not trust him', by which he meant that he had no 'confidence' in him. It was not that he 'doubted Manning felt kindly to me', but 'I never can trust he has not an arrière pensée, in any profession or offer he makes. It is not *my* feeling alone; I have long defended him: I am one of the last who have given into it . . .'.[65] He told Monsell that if Manning 'really wished to do us a service for our sakes, which (mind, "for our sakes") I doubt,—he would simply speak a good word for our *School*'. Episcopal approval would make all the difference: they had nearly seventy boys and only needed another ten or twenty to make ends meet. But Manning's idea would be to make use of him in 'some great scheme of education perhaps, which I cannot stomach, and in which I must be somewhere, with the alternative, if I don't agree, of being no where any where'. And Newman could not help thinking that 'he is afraid of any influence I might exert on the rising generation of Catholics, and that he would break up or transform our school, if he could'. As for the offer of a bishopric, it would be like 'Saul's armour on David'.[66]

Symbolically, when he went to London for the consecration, he stayed with Frederic Rogers, in whose house he met R. W. Church for the first time since 1846. Rogers was much less sceptical than he had feared, but he suspected that Rogers thought he himself was 'a profoundly sceptical thinker, who, determined on not building on an abyss, have, by mere strength of will, bridged it over, and built upon my bridge—but that my bridge, like Mahomet's coffin, is self suspended, by the action of the will'.[67] Unlike the offer of a bishopric, the gift of a violin from his two old Anglican friends was more than welcome, even if it caused a twinge of conscience.

I only fear that I may give time to it more than I ought to spare. I could find solace in music from week to week's end. It will be curious, if I get a qualm of conscience for indulging in it, and as a set off, write a book. I declare I think it is more likely to do so than anything else—I am so lazy . . . it strikes me that, in penance for the violin, I suddenly may rush into work in a fit of contrition.[68]

But music had more than just a penitential effect on Newman. Returning to Beethoven's quartets, which he had played once with Blanco White, he 'thought them more exquisite than ever—so that I was obliged to lay down the instrument and literally cry out with delight'. He had never possessed such a fine violin, and he concluded,

I really think it will add to my power of working, and the length of my life. I never wrote more than when I played the fiddle. I always sleep better after music. There must be some electric current passing from the strings through the

[65] Ibid. xxi. 483.   [66] Ibid. 499.   [67] Ibid. xxii. 26.
[68] Ibid. xxi. 502.

fingers into the brain and down the spinal marrow. Perhaps thought is music.[69]

He had once wondered whether 'musical sounds and their combinations', although 'momentary', were 'not some momentary opening and closing of the Veil which hangs between the worlds of spirit and sense', and movingly compared them to 'the ten thousand little details and complications of daily life and family history', which had no more record than 'the fall of the leaves in Autumn', but which were perhaps 'some reflexion, as in an earthly mirror, of some greater truths above'.[70]

He found the reunion with his friends 'very pleasant, but very painful too'—'It is so cruel not to have the chance of being able to impart to another one's own convictions.'[71] After the service of consecration he was startled to discover that he was expected to kneel and kiss the new Archbishop's hand, a continental custom which even Wiseman had never introduced and which Newman, in spite of having practised it with Manning before the ceremony, performed with awkward embarrassment.

Another event in May, of a very different kind, was the publication of the first part of *The Dream of Gerontius* in the *Month* (the second part was published in June), which 'on the 17th of January last it came into my head to write . . . I really cannot tell how, and I wrote on till it was finished, on small bits of paper'.[72] The magazine, which had now been taken over by the Jesuits, had received Newman's support from its inception the previous year. He had already contributed two (revised) poems about his sister Mary and had begun a series of pithy sayings of the Fathers, called 'Saints of the Desert' (which came to an end in March 1866 after being good-humouredly parodied in *Punch*). He welcomed it as a step in the right direction towards improving the intellectual level of Catholics. In the modern world nothing was more important than education, and nothing more desirable than a 'first-rate journal' which would deal with secular subjects rather than directly with religion, for 'what is to be aimed at, is to lay a Catholic *foundation* of thought—and *no* foundation is above ground. And next, to lay it with Protestant bricks . . . as St Paul at Athens appealed to the Altar of the Unknown God.' There was another important consideration:

. . . Protestants are accustomed to look upon Catholics, as an un-English body, who take no interest in national questions, nay, are unable to do so, and useless or hostile to the public, and the mere instruments of a foreign power. A magazine then, which, without effort or pretence, in a natural way, took part in all questions of the day, not hiding that it was Catholic to the back bone, but showing a real good-will towards the institutions of the country . . . showing

---

[69] *LD* xxii. 9.   [70] Ibid. xix. 415.   [71] Ibid. xxi. 503.
[72] Ibid. xxii. 72.

that it understood them, and could sympathise in them . . . would create in the public mind a feeling of respect and deference for the opinion of the Catholic body, which at present does not exist.[73]

He did not want a light magazine, nor did he want a theological journal: he wanted a periodical comparable to the *Cornhill* or the *Quarterly* or *Edinburgh Review*, in which, for example, he himself could write something philosophical on faith and reason. He was sorry when he found that the *Month* was to include theology proper, which would only deprive it of influence among Protestants. And he told the editor, Father Henry James Coleridge, the convert son of the Achilli trial judge who had lectured him, that 'theology, even when introduced, should always be *in undress*, and should address itself to common sense, reason . . . not to authority or technical data.'[74]

The fame of *The Dream of Gerontius* derives, of course, from the oratorio which Edward Elgar completed in 1900, while the verses which form the hymn 'Praise to the Holiest in the Height' are familiar to countless people who have never read a word of Newman. The poem itself contains the most accomplished verse Newman ever wrote, apart from 'Lead, Kindly Light'. But it is also important as the reflection of his own far from conventional view of death and the afterlife. There is a hint of the possible alleviation of eternal punishment in the idea that eternity need not involve the consciousness of the duration of endless time, a point that was to be developed soon in the *Grammar of Assent*. The actual notion of disembodied souls in purgatory awaiting the final resurrection is conveyed by a piercingly physical parallel:

> Hast thou not heard of those, who after loss
> Of hand or foot, still cried that they had pains
> In hand or foot, as though they had it still?
> So is it now with thee, who hast not lost
> Thy hand or foot, but all which made up man.[75]

But the pain of purgatory itself is both intensified and justified in terms not of material fire but of God's spiritual love:

> It is the face of the Incarnate God
> Shall smite thee with that keen and subtle pain;
> And yet the memory which it leaves will be
> A sovereign febrifuge to heal the wound;
> And yet withal it will the wound provoke,
> And aggravate and widen it the more.

A doctrine which was popularly conceived of in crudely physical terms is, like the concept of hell in *Callista*, realized by Newman as a supremely

---

[73] Ibid. xxxi. 80*.   [74] Ibid. xxi. 496.   [75] *VV* 350.

spiritual reality:

> The longing for Him, when thou seest Him not;
> The shame of self at thought of seeing Him,—
> Will be the veriest, sharpest purgatory.[76]

And so the angel expresses not so much pity as envy at Gerontius's purgatory, the contradictory nature of which is evoked in a superbly concentrated and poised image—

> O happy, suffering soul! for it is safe,
> Consumed, yet quicken'd, by the glance of God.

And the soul's final prayer is the poignantly paradoxical

> Take me away, and in the lowest deep
> There let me be . . .[77]

3

At the general election in the summer of 1865, both Acton and Sir John Simeon were elected to Parliament for English constituencies. Newman hoped that they might become 'rallying points' for a liberal Catholic movement and help offset Manning's appointment.[78] His own important critique of theological 'Liberalism', which he had added as the first 'note' to the second edition of the *Apologia* (published in May), had recently been sharply attacked by James Fitzjames Stephen (the brother of Leslie Stephen). Newman wondered with a wry amusement 'whether the wounds I have received will do me any good with the people in London who go about saying I am a liberal'.[79]

W. G. Ward, who lived in Simeon's constituency, had openly supported Simeon's blatantly anti-Catholic Conservative opponent on the ground that a Protestant was better than a disloyal Catholic who had failed to support the Pope's claim to temporal power. Ward explained to the *Weekly Register* that there was no doubt that the Pope had spoken infallibly in the recent *Syllabus* which affirmed that Catholics must support the doctrine of the Temporal Power. Newman was strongly tempted to send a disclaimer to the paper. He was anxious that such extremism would have a disastrous effect on potential converts, as well as on converts like Thomas Arnold, who had recently stopped practising as a Catholic because he could no longer believe in the Church's claim to infallibility. But he was also afraid that controversy might harm the Oratory. He had no doubt there would be a reaction

---

[76] *VV* 358–60.   [77] Ibid. 366.   [78] *LD* xxii. 15.   [79] Ibid. 4–5.

against Ultramontane extremism, but a reaction could only grow out of opposition. And there was a danger that Ward's dogmatism would become the received view, which it would be much more difficult to oppose in ten years' time than now. What Newman objected to, he told Pusey, was not so much Ward's theological opinions, as the fact that he wanted to impose them on others. He himself had no desire that the authorities should be intolerant towards Marian devotions, which he personally found 'unnatural and forced'. Unlike the Anglican bishops, who were indulgent to the liberals but persecuted the ritualists, 'the Church of Rome is severe on the freethinkers and indulgent towards devotees'.[80] He accepted Pusey's offer to send him a copy of his reply to Manning's 1864 pamphlet *The Workings of the Holy Spirit in the Church of England, a Letter to the Rev. E. B. Pusey*; it was called *The Church of England a Portion of Christ's One Holy Catholic Church, and a Means of Restoring Visible Unity. An Eirenicon, in a Letter to the Author of 'The Christian Year'.*

Earlier in the summer Newman had proposed a visit to Keble, but it had had to be postponed. Now, on 12 September, he called in at the vicarage at Hursley, near Southampton, on his way to the Isle of Wight. He had asked Keble to ensure that he did not come at the same time as Pusey, as he felt he could not meet them both together after so long a time. The extraordinary encounter drew from Newman one of his most evocative descriptions, dramatic, poignant, and sharply defined in its closely observed details.

Keble was at the door, he did not know me, nor I him. How mysterious that first sight of friends is! for when I came to contemplate him, it was the old face and manner, but the first effect and impression was different. His wife had been taken ill again in the night, and at the first moment he, I *think*, and *certainly* I, wished myself away. Then he said, Have you missed my letters? meaning Pusey is here, and I wrote to stop you coming. He said I must go and prepare Pusey. He did so, and then took me into the room. I went in rapidly, and it is strange how action overcomes pain. Pusey, as being passive, was evidently shrinking back into the corner of the room—as I should have done if he had rushed in upon me. He could not help contemplating the look of me narrowly and long— Ah, I thought, you are thinking how old I am grown and I see myself in you— though you, I do think, are more altered than I am. Indeed, the alteration in him shocked me . . . it pained and grieved me. I should have known him any where—his face is not changed, but it is as if you looked at him through a prodigious magnifier. I recollect him short and small—with a round head— smallish features—flaxen curly hair—huddled up together from his shoulders downward—and walking fast. This was as a young man—but comparing him even when last I saw him, when he was slow in his motions and staid in his figure, still there is a wonderful change. His head and his features are half as large again—his chest is very broad—and he has, I think, a paunch—His voice

---

[80] Ibid. 45.

is the same—with my eyes shut, I should not have been sensible of any lapse of time. As we three sat together at one table, I had as painful thoughts as I ever recollect, though it was a pain, not acute, but heavy. There were three old men, who had worked together vigorously in their prime. This is what they have come to—poor human nature—after 20 years they meet together round a table, but without a common cause, or free outspoken thoughts—but, though kind yet subdued, and antagonistic in their mode of speaking, and all of them with broken prospects. Pusey is full of his book which is all but out—against Manning . . . He is full of polemics and of hope. Keble is as different as possible; he is as delightful as ever—and, it *seemed* to me as if he felt a sympathy and intimacy with me which he did not find with Pusey.[81]

The visit lasted about four hours, and after an early dinner he left at 4 o'clock when the bell rang for evensong.

Just before my time for going, Pusey went to read the Evening Service in Church, and I was left in the open air with Keble by himself . . . We walked a little way, and stood looking in silence at the Church and Churchyard, so beautiful and calm. Then he began to converse with me in more than his old tone of intimacy, as if we had never been parted, and soon I was obliged to go.[82]

Two odd aspects of the meeting struck Newman. The first was that when 'I got to Keble's door, he happened to be at it, but we did not know each other, and I was obliged to show him my card. Is not this strange? it is imagination mastering reason.'[83] The second was that 'we three dined together—tête a tête—a thing we had never (I suppose) done in our lives before.'[84]

At one point the conversation had turned to Gladstone's recent failure to be re-elected as the Member of Parliament for Oxford University. Newman remarked that if he had still been there, he would have had to vote against him because of his withdrawal of support for the establishment of the Church of Ireland. 'On this Keble gave me one of his remarkable looks, so earnest and so sweet, came close to me, and whispered in my ear . . . "And is not that just?" '[85] Keble's sympathy for the real 'Church of the Irish' rather than the Establishment was part of his readiness 'to try to enter into the mind and feelings of others'. It was, Newman wrote to him, 'what I love so much in you . . . but I much desiderate it in this new book of Pusey's'. It was astonishing that Pusey should have called it an '*Eirenicon*'—if he 'is writing to hinder his own people from joining us, well and good, he had a right to write as he has done—but how can he fancy that to exaggerate, instead of smoothing contrarieties, is the way to make us listen to him?' Thus, for example, it was one thing to say that no one is saved without the intercession of the

[81] *LD* xxii. 52.   [82] Ibid. xxiv. 143.   [83] Ibid. xxii. 76.
[84] Ibid. 60.   [85] Ibid. xxiv. 143.

Virgin Mary (meaning simply that she 'is *the* Intercessor', who prays according to the will of her Son and is therefore the 'channel by which that will is carried out'), but quite another to conclude from this that without invocation of Mary no one is saved.[86] One did not have to have a devotion to Mary to be saved, but nevertheless, the Church believed that 'Mary's *intercession* is a necessary part of the economy of redemption, just as Eve co-operated in Adam's fall.'[87] It was, in Newman's view, a 'rhetorical and unfair' book, which, however, it would be difficult to answer 'except at the expense of theories and doctrines, which the Archbishop thinks of vital importance, and which I cannot receive'. Indeed, it would be hard for the Ultramontanes themselves to respond to it, because they 'will not like to say out all they hold, yet cannot disown any part of it, so I don't expect any thing bold and straightforward'.[88] At their Hursley meeting, Pusey had certainly been 'full of plans, full of meetings', but not surprisingly he had been reticent about the contents of his so-called *Eirenicon*, which was calculated to make Catholics 'very angry—and justly angry'.[89] He had quoted indiscriminately and from extreme writers, some of whom Newman had never even heard of. Newman agreed that it was 'a mere doctrinaire view to enter a Church without taking up its practical system', but it was not necessary to accept every detail and emphasis of it 'as represented by its popular catechisms and books of devotion'.[90] Using St Alfonso Liguori's moral theology and spirituality, for example, did not necessarily imply accepting his theory of equivocation and his particular Marian piety.

4

Newman was under pressure from many quarters to speak out against Ward and the *Dublin Review*, which was generally assumed to be the voice of Manning. But he felt that he had already spoken his mind on infallibility in the last chapter of the *Apologia*, which had been approved by his own bishop. He could not help blaming 'intemperate writers' in the *Rambler* and the *Home and Foreign Review* for the intellectual monopoly enjoyed by the *Dublin Review*. 'We have lost our position—we have got our heads under water—we cannot get ourselves into a position in which we might use our arms—and why? because we have been very extravagant, very high and mighty, very dictatorial, very provoking; and now we must patiently suffer the consequences.'[91] Pusey's book,

---

[86] Ibid. xxii. 68.   [87] Ibid. 90.   [88] Ibid. 72.
[89] Ibid. 76.   [90] Ibid. 100.   [91] Ibid. 85.

however, which took for granted a certain kind of extreme devotion-alism and dogmatism, provided an opening, for 'it has struck me it will be the most inoffensive way of alluding to Faber and Ward, if I can write without hurting Pusey'.[92] And so on 28 November Newman went out to the peace and quiet of Rednal to write his *Letter to Pusey*. On 7 December (the day he returned to the Oratory) he 'cut it short' and decided he would only publish half the pamphlet he had originally intended, having found that it would 'not come into the right number of pages'.[93] By the time he had seen it through the press, he was too tired even to think of beginning the projected second part, which was to have dealt specifically with infallibility, and for which some notes had already been jotted down. He expected people to be disappointed, as he had only considered one of the subjects raised by Pusey's *Eirenicon*. Publication was delayed by Christmas, three days before which, Newman fell seriously ill—'For thirty years I have not had so anxious an illness. And the worst is, it came on so suddenly and without notice, that it makes me dread to leave home ever again, lest I should be seized in a railway carriage, or at a friend's house.'[94] He was ill for nearly a month, only recovering in the middle of January, when he also comp-leted the proofs of the *Letter to Pusey*, which was published at the end of the month.

The pamphlet begins with praise of Pusey's desire for unity between the churches, towards which his *Eirenicon* was supposed to contribute. 'Even were you an individual member of that Church, a watchman upon a high tower in a metropolis of religious opinion, we should naturally listen with interest to what you had to report of the state of the sky and the progress of the night, what stars were mounting up or what clouds gathering . . .'.[95] It continues with an eulogy of Pusey's own personal prestige, whose influence is without parallel as the religious leader of so many Anglo-Catholics—'and I cannot pay them', Newman suddenly interjects with a typical twist, 'a greater compliment than to tell them they ought all to be Catholics . . .'. But, far from speaking as an unsympathetic outsider, he knows well 'what an outcast I seemed to myself, when I took down from the shelves of my library the volumes of St. Athanasius or St. Basil . . . and how, on the contrary, when at length I was brought into Catholic communion, I kissed them with delight, with a feeling that in them I had more than all that I had lost . . .'. However, although he is sure that such 'would be the joy of the persons I speak of, if they could wake up one morning, and find themselves rightfully possessed of Catholic traditions and hopes', he is quick to stipulate: 'without violence to their own sense of duty', for 'the claims of conscience are ... paramount'.[96] Again, he knows from bitter experience what hard and unfeeling things Roman Catholics are capable of saying against Anglo-Catholics. On the other hand, he undermines the admission (which he supports with a couple of particularly virulent quotations) by coming to the point at last quietly but devastatingly:

But we at least have not professed to be composing an Irenicon, when we were treating you as foes. There was one of old time who wreathed his sword in myrtle; excuse me—you discharge your olive-branch as if from a catapult.

It was right that difficulties and objections should be honestly stated, but 'I am confident, my very dear friend, that at least you will not be angry with me if I say . . . that there is much, both in the matter and in the manner of your Volume, calculated to wound those who love you well, but love truth more.' The concession that immediately follows characteristically contains its own negation: 'This may be a salutary castigation of us, if any of us have fairly provoked it; but it is not making the best of matters; it is not smoothing the way for an understanding or a compromise.'[97] Again Newman appeals to personal friendship and former ties to urge that Pusey had always been less outspoken against Rome than he himself in the past; but now Pusey, who had recently opposed Newman's return to Oxford on the ground that it would renew controversy, had actually revived one of Newman's strongest statements as an Anglican against the idolatry of Rome. More seriously, Pusey had given the impression that Newman had called the Church of England a 'bulwark' against unbelief. In fact, as he had already pointed out in a letter to the *Weekly Register*, what he had said in the *Apologia* was that the Church of England was 'a serviceable breakwater against errors more fundamental than its own'.

A bulwark is an integral part of the thing it defends; whereas the word 'breakwater' implies such a protection of the Catholic truth, as is, in its nature, accidental and *de facto*,—and again, such a protection as does not utterly exclude error, but detracts from its volume and force. 'Serviceable,' too, implies a something external to the thing served. Again, in saying that the Anglican Church is a defence against 'errors more fundamental than its own,' I imply that it has errors, and those fundamental.[98]

This unaccommodating denial, however, is directed not only at Pusey but also more pointedly at Manning, who had already picked up an earlier, similar reference by Pusey to 'breakwater' in his own pamphlet, where he was 'generally considered' (Newman openly acknowledges)

---

[96] Ibid. 3–4.   [97] Ibid. 6–7.   [98] Ibid. 11.

'to be really glancing at my *Apologia*, and correcting it'.[99] The convincing demonstration of positive ecumenical thinking that follows is as much a rebuke to Pusey as it is to Manning. Pusey had implied that Rome denied that 'the whole Christian faith is contained in Scripture', but Newman boldly maintains that the difference between Anglicans and Catholics 'is merely one of words', depending on what is meant by 'proof': 'We mean that not every article of faith is so contained there, that it may thence be logically proved, *independently* of the teaching and authority of the Tradition; but Anglicans mean that every article of faith is so contained there, that it may thence be proved, *provided* there be added the illustrations and compensations supplied by the Tradition.'[100] If there was only really a verbal disagreement, then genuine agreement could be reached on this particular vexed theological issue.

Pusey's remarks about the duty of converts to accept the religious system of their adopted church provide Newman with his opening, as he proceeds to explain his motive and purpose in writing. On the one hand, he readily accepts that a convert 'comes to Catholicism as to a living system, with a living teaching, and not to a mere collection of decrees and canons', while to embrace only 'the framework, not the body and substance of the Church' would 'not only be unreal, but would be dangerous, too, as arguing a wrong state of mind'. On the other hand, by 'not risking the loss of revealed truth altogether by attempting by a private rule to discriminate every moment its substance from its accidents', the convert 'is gradually so indoctrinated in Catholicism, as at length to have a right to speak as well as to hear'. He becomes aware of 'the fact and the nature of the differences of theologian from theologian, school from school, nation from nation, era from era' and that 'there is much of what may be called fashion in opinions and practices'—and, Newman adds significantly, 'that fashions change'. Not only that, but he even discovers that 'sometimes what is denounced in one place as a great offence, or preached up as a first principle, has in another nation been immemorially regarded in just a contrary sense'. With his tongue somewhat in his cheek, Newman remarks that it may actually be 'disloyal' to the Church authorities not to make known one's views, when they need to know all sides of the question before coming to a decision. Given these differences, he feels 'no delicacy' in stating frankly that 'I prefer English habits of belief and devotion to foreign.' And he adds, 'In following those of my people, I show less singularity, and create less disturbance than if I made a flourish with what is novel and exotic.'

The reference to Faber is made explicit when he takes the opportunity to admit that he may have made a mistake all those years ago over the translations of the lives of the saints:

---

[99] *Diff.* ii. 10.   [100] Ibid. 12.

If at that time I was betrayed into any acts which were of a more extreme character than I should approve now, the responsibility of course is my own; but the impulse came, not from old Catholics or superiors, but from men whom I loved and trusted, who were younger than myself. But to whatever extent I might be carried away, and I cannot recollect any tangible instances, my mind in no long time fell back to what seems to me a safer and more practical course.

Kingsley's outburst had enabled him to make his first veiled allusions in print to the Ultramontane party; Pusey's curious peace-offering now offered him the opportunity not only to speak out much more boldly, but also to dissociate himself at last publicly from Faber and the London Oratory.

Though I am a convert, then, I think I have a right to speak out; and that the more because other converts have spoken for a long time, while I have not spoken . . . in the charges you bring, the only two English writers you quote in evidence, are both of them converts, younger in age than myself. I put aside the Archbishop of course, because of his office.

The smooth dismissal of Manning leads on to an urbane disparagement of Faber, whose popularity is attributed to 'his poetical fancy, his engaging frankness, his playful wit, his affectionateness, his sensitive piety'—rather than to any 'general sympathy with his particular sentiments about the Blessed Virgin'. The depreciation of Ward is hardly less ironic: 'And as to our other friend, do not his energy, acuteness, and theological reading, displayed on the vantage ground of the historic "Dublin Review," fully account for the sensation he has produced, without supposing that any great number of our body go his lengths in their view of the Pope's infallibility?' But the iron fist can be felt through the velvet glove as Newman insists peremptorily on the paramount importance of the Fathers, that common ecumenical authority to which Pusey and all Anglo-Catholics also appealed—but, conversely, to whom Newman owed his own conversion to Rome and from whom he derives the Catholic doctrine of Mary:

I cannot, then, without remonstrance, allow you to . . . assume, as you do, that, because they [Faber and Ward] are thorough-going and relentless in their statements, therefore they are the harbingers of a new age, when to show a deference to Antiquity will be thought little else than a mistake. For myself, hopeless as you consider it, I am not ashamed still to take my stand upon the Fathers, and do not mean to budge. The history of their times is not yet an old almanac to me . . . The Fathers made me a Catholic, and I am not going to kick down the ladder by which I ascended into the Church. It is a ladder quite as serviceable for that purpose now, as it was twenty years ago.[101]

So far as Newman is concerned, the essential Marian doctrines are all to be found in antiquity: devotion to Mary has increased, but there has

[101] Ibid. 18–24.

been no 'growth' in doctrine, for 'it has been in substance one and the same from beginning'.[102]

The sun in the spring-time will have to shine many days before he is able to melt the frost, open the soil, and bring out the leaves; yet he shines out from the first notwithstanding, though he makes his power felt but gradually. It is one and the same sun, though his influence day by day becomes greater; and so in the Catholic Church it is the one Virgin Mother, one and the same from first to last, and Catholics may have ever acknowledged her; and yet, in spite of that acknowledgement, their devotion to her may be scanty in one time and place, and overflowing in another.

Far from Italianate devotions being obligatory for English Catholics, the 'distinction is forcibly brought home to a convert, as a peculiarity of the Catholic religion', that while the 'faith is everywhere one and the same', nevertheless, 'a large liberty is accorded to private judgment and inclination as regards matters of devotion'.[103] And far from devotional practices having any kind of absolute character, Newman emphasizes that in fact they vary a lot from age to age, some declining, others arising.

His exposition of the Catholic teaching about Mary begins with the Fathers' view of her as the 'Second Eve'. This he had already explained in his *Essay on the Development of Christian Doctrine*, from which 'the greater part' of the pamphlet was taken—'I have done little more than throw it into a more popular form.'[104] The most important and original part of the *Letter to Pusey* is, not surprisingly, the last part, where Newman turns to discuss the devotions as opposed to the beliefs of Catholics. He begins by pointing out that ordinary people would find it hard to distinguish logically between the patristic view of Mary held by Pusey and the modern Catholic views he criticizes. Granted that there are real distinctions, still, it is very hard to draw the line exactly—a consideration which stimulates a particularly eloquent passage expressive of one of Newman's deepest insights into the nature of life, and one which tells as much against Pusey as against Faber and Ward.

It is impossible, I say, in a doctrine like this, to draw the line clearly between truth and error, right and wrong. This is ever the case in concrete matters, which have life. Life in this world is motion, and involves a continual process of change. Living things grow into their perfection, into their decline, into their death. No rule of art will suffice to stop the operation of this natural law, whether in the material world or in the human mind. We can indeed encounter disorders, when they occur, by external antagonism and remedies; but we cannot eradicate the process itself, out of which they arise. Life has the same right to decay, as it has to wax strong. This is specially the case with great ideas.

---

[102] *Diff.* ii. 26.   [103] Ibid. 28.   [104] *LD* xxii. 149.

You may stifle them; or you may refuse them elbow-room; or again you may torment them with your continuing meddling; or you may let them have free course and range, and be content, instead of anticipating their excesses, to expose and restrain those excesses after they have occurred. But you have only this alternative; and for myself, I prefer much wherever it is possible, to be first generous and then just; to grant full liberty of thought, and to call it to account when abused.

And Newman concludes specifically: 'If what I have been saying be true of energetic ideas generally, much more is it the case in matters of religion. Religion acts on the affections; who is to hinder these, when once roused, from gathering in their strength and running wild?'[105]

Taking ordinary human love as an analogy, Newman argues that religious devotion which 'is abstractedly extravagant, may in particular persons be becoming and beautiful, and only fall under blame when it is found in others who imitate them. When it is formalized into meditations or exercises, it is as repulsive as love-letters in a police report.'[106] He now proceeds to make a more generalized observation which in itself represents a further stage in his developing theology of the Church—and one which also provides a key to one enigmatic aspect of Catholicism:

. . . the religion of the multitude is ever vulgar and abnormal; it ever will be tinctured with fanaticism and superstition, while men are what they are. A people's religion is ever a corrupt religion, in spite of the provisions of Holy Church . . . You may beat religion out of men, if you will, and then their excesses will take a different direction; but if you make use of religion to improve them, they will make use of religion to corrupt it. And then you will have effected that compromise of which our countrymen report so unfavourably from abroad:—a high grand faith and worship which compels their admiration, and puerile absurdities among the people which excite their contempt.[107]

As he explained once in a letter, 'a popular religion is necessarily deformed by the errors and bad taste of the multitude', for 'the religion of a nation will ever partake of the peculiar faults of the national character': 'The most sublime truths take a vulgar shape and bear a forbidding aspect, when reflected back by the masses of human society—nay, often cannot be made intelligible to them, or at least cannot be made to reach them, till thrown into words or actions which are offensive to educated minds.' Disapprove as the Church may, 'she may find it quite impossible to root out the tares without rooting out the wheat with them.'[108]

Newman's developed ecclesiology includes a theology of the corruption of the Church not simply for apologetic purposes, but because

---

[105] *Diff.* ii. 78–9.   [106] Ibid. 80.   [107] Ibid. 81.   [108] *LD* xx. 470–1.

corruption is seen as inseparable from a living Church—'things that do not admit of abuse have very little life in them.'[109] As he was to explain a few years later, 'since the world is ever corrupt, therefore when it has poured into the Church, it has insulted and blasphemed the religion which it professed, in a special way, in which heathenism cannot insult it. I *grant* that a Protestant world cannot commit that sin which a Catholic world can . . .'. It is when ordinary human weaknesses are 'coupled with that intense absolute faith which Catholics have, and Protestants have not', that one finds 'acts of inconsistency, of superstition, violence etc which are not to be looked for external to the Catholic Church'.[110] It was impossible to think of a time when 'the greatest scandals did not exist in the Church, and act as impediments to the success of its mission', scandals which had been 'the occasion of momentous secessions and schisms'. But in spite of these scandals, 'the Church has ever got on and made way, to the surprise of the world; as an army may fight a series of bloody battles, and lose men, and yet go forward from victory to victory'. The 'seceding bodies', on the other hand, 'have sooner or later come to nought'—'At this very time we are witnessing the beginning of the end of Protestantism, the breaking of that bubble of "Bible-Christianity" which has been its life.' Not only had Jesus Christ predicted scandals, but he had spoken of his Church 'as in its very constitution made up of good and bad'. The corruption of the Church had existed from the time of Judas Iscariot, and was 'bound up with the very idea of Christianity', and was 'almost a dogma'.[111]

As for distortions and exaggerations in Marian devotions, Newman notes that it is those countries that 'have lost their faith in the divinity of Christ, who have given up devotion to His Mother', while 'those on the other hand, who had been foremost in her honour, have retained their orthodoxy'. 'In the Catholic Church', Newman insists, 'Mary has shown herself, not the rival, but the minister of her Son; she has protected Him, as in his infancy, so in the whole history of the Religion.'[112] The corruption of this vitality lies in certain 'extravagances'—from which, Newman dares to say, 'I suppose we owe it to the national good sense, that English Catholics have been protected'. It is these 'curiosities of thought', he remarks severely, 'which are both so attractive to undisciplined imaginations and so dangerous to grovelling hearts'.[113] While it would be 'a simple purism' to 'insist upon minute accuracy of expression in devotional and popular writings'—as though 'we . . . disparage Divine Providence when we say that we are indebted to our parents for our life'—nevertheless, Newman admits that a few of Pusey's quotations from foreign devotional writers 'affected me with

[109] *Diff.* ii. 89.   [110] *LD* xxvii. 139.   [111] Ibid. xx. 465.
[112] *Diff.* ii. 92–3.   [113] Ibid. 99–100.

grief and almost anger'. Still, what appeared like idolatry might be justifiable in certain contexts or senses. Where there have clearly been excesses, but where it is 'not easy to convict them of definite error logically', then it may be hard for authority to take action, as in a court of law 'when the commission of an offence is morally certain, but the government prosecutor cannot find legal evidence sufficient to insure conviction'.[114] However, he insists that Marian 'intercession is one thing, devotion is another'—and they must not be confused (implicitly, either by Pusey or extreme Catholic writers). Otherwise, 'there would be grave reasons for doubting of the salvation of St. Chrysostom or St. Athanasius'; indeed, he wonders 'whether St. Augustine, in all his voluminous writings, invokes her once'. But none of this alters the fact that Mary 'intercedes for those Christians who do not know her'.[115]

The conclusion is typically even-handed. On the one hand, some of Pusey's quotations 'seem to me like a bad dream' and, in the English context at any rate, 'calculated to prejudice inquirers, to frighten the unlearned, to unsettle consciences, to provoke blasphemy, and to work the loss of souls'. On the other hand, Pusey himself is not spared, because paradoxically his own work points in the same direction:

Have you not been teaching us on a very tender point in a very rude way? is it not the effect of what you have said to expose her to scorn and obloquy, who is dearer to us than any other creature? Have you even hinted that our love for her is anything else than an abuse? Have you thrown her one kind word yourself all through your book?[116]

Newman leaves Pusey with an analogy to ponder: 'Supposing an opponent of a doctrine for which you so earnestly contend, the eternity of punishment, instead of meeting you with direct arguments against it, heaped together a number of extravagant descriptions of the place, mode, and circumstances of its infliction', quoting indiscriminately from all manner of disparate Christian writers—'would you think this an equitable determination, or the procedure of a theologian?' He ends with a double-edged ecumenical prayer for the season of Christmas: 'May it quench all jealous, sour, proud, fierce antagonism on our side; and dissipate all captious, carping, fastidious refinements of reasoning on yours!'[117]

5

By the middle of February two thousand copies of *A Letter to Pusey* had been sold. A second edition was then published, with some corrections.

---

[114] Ibid. 106–7.   [115] Ibid. 105.   [116] Ibid. 115–16.   [117] Ibid. 117–18.

The reception among Anglo-Catholics had been very favourable, nor had Pusey been offended. Newman had his own theory as to why Pusey had written as he had:

. . . it is harsh to call any mistakes of his, untruthfulness. I think they arise from the same slovenly habit which some people would recognise in his dress, his beard, etc. He never answers letters, I believe, which do not lie in the line of the direct *work* which he has on hand. And so, in composing a book, he takes uncommon pains about some points . . . but he will combine this with extreme carelessness in respect of other statements.

Linked to the moral implication of this is the criticism that Pusey was too 'academic', out of touch with reality: 'Then, from that radical peculiarity of mind which interferes with his being a Catholic, he goes by books, not by persons.' Added to that was his peculiar position as the leader of a movement within the Church of England, which gave him a unique authority to a number of people and explained his 'habit of carelessness in stating and ruling points': 'He goes into print with the same heedless readiness and decisiveness with which he would say words in conversation.'[118] He had survived so many blows as an Anglican, remaining always optimistic and sanguine, that it was unlikely he would ever lose faith in the Church of England, and if he did, Newman thought, it would more likely end in his death than in his conversion to Rome—'he has lived and thrived upon hope, and for him to lose hope is to lose life.'[119]

The Catholic clergy generally welcomed the pamphlet, including Bishop Brown and the redoubtable Dr Gillow (who had also approved of the *Apologia*). Manning guardedly confined himself to praise of Newman's patristic scholarship and his criticism of Pusey. Ward, typically, wrote much more candidly: 'I need not say how keen a grief it is to me that we are thrown more and more into the position of opponents . . . You will well have known beforehand what parts of your new book I thoroughly like; what parts less thoroughly; and what parts not at all.' In his reply, Newman refused to 'feel our differences to be such a trouble, as you do'. Casually, but pointedly, he wrote:

for such differences always have been, always will be, in the Church, and Christians would have ceased to have spiritual and intellectual life, if such differences did not exist. It is part of their militant state. No human power can hinder it; nor, if it attempted it, could do more than make a solitude and call it peace. And, thus thinking that man cannot hinder it, however much he try, I have no great anxiety or trouble. Man cannot, and God will not. He means such differences to be an exercise of charity. Of course I wish as much as possible to

[118] *LD* xxii. 158.				[119] Ibid. xxvi. 44.

agree with all my friends; but, if, in spite of my utmost efforts, they go beyond me or come short of me, I can't help it, and take it easy.[120]

He had more or less given up the idea of writing a second pamphlet on doctrinal development with particular reference to papal infallibility—'I have ever thought it likely to be true, never thought it certain. I think too, its definition inexpedient and unlikely; but I should have no difficulty in accepting it, were it made.'[121] The problem was that it was one thing to attack devotional extravagances when the doctrine itself was clearly defined, but quite another to criticize exaggerations in the theory of infallibility, especially when there was 'no one received doctrine on the Church', and when the theology in question was 'so highly sanctioned at Rome' and could not be dismissed merely as 'foreign'.[122] Simply to attempt to uphold freedom of opinion on the subject would be 'the most offensive thing of all to some influential people'.[123] It was not people like Ward he feared, but Rome, he told Emily Bowles (the convert sister of Frederick Bowles), who urged him to speak out:

. . . to write theology is like dancing on the tight rope some hundred feet from the ground. It is hard to keep from falling, and the fall is great . . . The questions are so subtle, the distinctions so fine, and critical jealous eyes so many. Such critics would be worth nothing, if they had not the power of writing to Rome, now that communication is made so easy—and you may get into hot water, before you know where you are. The necessity of defending myself at Rome would almost kill me with the fidget.

Apart from the fact that the subject of infallibility was a large and difficult one, he had already aroused enough controversy and wanted 'the waves to subside' first. There was another, more interesting, tactical reason why he had decided not to write the second pamphlet:

. . . I was intending to make a great change. I thought at length my time had come. I had introduced the narrow end of the wedge—and made a split—I feared it would split fiercely and irregularly—and I thought by withdrawing the wedge,—the split might [be] left at present more naturally to increase *itself*. Every thing I see confirms me in my view. I have various letters from all parts of the country approving of what I have already done. . . . The less I do myself, the more others will do . . . Englishmen don't like to be driven.[124]

Manning's response to Pusey's *Eirenicon* had been to issue an uncompromising pastoral letter on 'The Reunion of Christendom', which dismayed enthusiastic ecumenists like Phillipps de Lisle. But Newman's own attitude to the corporate reunion of Canterbury and Rome was sceptical, to say the least. It would be, he told de Lisle,

---

[120] Ibid. xxii. 157. [121] Ibid. [122] *TP* ii. 111–12.
[123] *LD* xxii. 167. [124] Ibid. 215–16.

a miracle,—in the same sense in which it would be miracle for the Thames to change its course . . . Of course in the course of ages such a change of direction might take place without miracle—by the stopping up of a gorge or the alteration of a level. But I should not pray for it; and, if I wished to divert the stream from London, I should cut a canal . . . I should carry the innumerable drops of water my own way by forming a new bed by my own labour . . . Now the Anglican Church . . . is not a collection of individuals—but it is a bed, a river bed, formed in the course of ages, depending on external facts, such as political, civil, and social arrangements. Viewed in its structure it has never been more than partially Catholic. If its ritual has been mainly such, yet its Articles are the historical offspring of Luther and Calvin. And its ecclesiastical organisation has ever been, in its fundamental principle, Erastian. To make that actual, visible, tangible body Catholic, would be simply to make a new creature—it would be to turn a panther into a hind. There are very great similarities between a panther and a hind. Still they are possessed of separate natures, and a change from one to the other would be a destruction and reproduction, not a process. It could be done without a miracle in a succession of ages, but in any assignable period, no.

Years before, he had said that Anglicanism and Catholicism were two different religions proceeding on 'different *ideas*', so that whatever they might appear to have in common, 'yet the way in which those doctrines are held, and the whole internal structure in the two religions is different'.[125] Nor was the continuing spread of Anglo-Catholicism inevitable; rather, it was probable that what was a reaction itself would provoke a reaction, perhaps from the growing Liberal wing. Then, too, of course, there were the Evangelicals to contend with—not to mention 'the Erastian party, which embraces all three, and against which there is no re-action at present, which ever *has* been, which is the *foundation* of Anglicanism'. Of the laity, only 'a fraction' was Anglo-Catholic, 'a great portion evangelical, a greater liberal, and a still greater, alas, without any faith at all'. Finally, the Anglican Church was the national Church of *England*, of which nearly half the population were Dissenters. It was indeed hard to see how the Established Church could 'rise above the level of its source (Henry viii, *I* say)'. But still, that did not mean one would wish 'it destroyed till England got *something better*'.[126]

On Palm Sunday Bishop Ullathorne called at the Oratory. He expressed his approval of the letter of Bishop Clifford of Clifton defending the *Letter to Pusey* against a violent attack in the correspondence columns of the *Tablet*. He was himself about to publish a similar letter. He told Newman that he had refused Manning's request to look over an article by Ward which was severely critical of parts of the *Letter to Pusey* and was intended for publication in the *Dublin Review*. Privately,

[125] *LD* xii. 234.   [126] Ibid. xxii. 170–1.

Newman noted that the object appeared to be to gain Ullathorne's 'sanction, and preoccupy the ground against me'. As for Manning, he was prepared to 'do *any* thing he *can*, *every* thing he *can*, to check us'.[127] There was still the very real danger, from the Archbishop's point of view, that after all Newman might still return to Oxford. Indeed, part of the purpose of Ullathorne's call was again, for the third time, to offer the Oxford mission. The land Newman had bought opposite Christ Church might not be suitable for a permanent parish church, but it might do for an Oratory chapel where Mass could be celebrated through the year and where Oratory services could take place in term-time. Newman was half-inclined to accede to the bishop's request.

On Thursday of Holy Week, Keble died, after hearing that his wife had herself not long to live. Newman's view was that he had 'from a youth a great drawing to Catholicism'[128]—such as Pusey had never had—and he was astonished how close he seemed to the Catholic Church at their last meeting. Keble appeared to accept all Catholic doctrine, except for actual communion with Rome. His wife lingered on till May; 'it struck me', Newman wrote, '(I trust it is a really charitable thought) that she was to be kept awhile to do penance for having kept Keble from being a Catholic.'[129] He was delighted with Fr Coleridge's obituary article in the *Month* which showed that a Catholic periodical 'is able to recognise facts as facts, and is not afraid for the Catholic religion, if moral goodness is to be found in bodies not Catholic'. It took him back to those distant days at Oriel when 'Whately used to spit into the fire, between two friends sitting opposite to him at table. Such is the character of some men's minds. Even if they bring out what is true and good, still they spit; but Keble was like the dew from a fountain, as you say.'[130] He was less happy with Coleridge's criticisms, in another article, of Pusey, and offered some advice on the art of controversial writing. To call names and impute motives was as wrong as 'using poisoned weapons in war'.[131] It was fine to show that 'Pusey's facts are wrong, but don't abuse him. Abuse is as great a mistake in controversy, as panegyric in biography.' It was simply bad tactics, 'as if you were to load your gun carefully, and then deliberately to administer some drops of water at the touch hole'.[132] Abuse, after all, was 'accusation without proof—or condemnation before proof—and such a process of putting the cart before the horse defeats itself'. He was to complain later about an article in the *Month* which called the Anglican sacrament a slice of bread—'if there is one thing more than another likely to shock and alienate those whom we wish to convert, it is to ridicule their objects of worship.' It was

---

[127] Ibid. 190–1.   [128] Ibid. 202.   [129] Ibid. 234.

[130] Ibid. 217–18.   [131] Ibid. 203.   [132] Ibid. 211–12.

illogical, too, because 'They may have a false conscience, but, if they are obeying it, it is laughing at them for being religious.'[133]

On 18 April the Birmingham Oratory decided formally to undertake the Oxford mission, but on certain conditions. They were ready to build on the piece of land opposite Christ Church a church which would one day belong to an Oxford Oratory. Most of the expense would fall on them, but the church could be used for the mission, which would contribute to its upkeep. A missioner (or parish priest) would be provided by the Birmingham Oratory, which would also take responsibility for the pastoral care of Catholic undergraduates. But the bishop would have to ensure that Propaganda recognized the house and church at Oxford as an integral part of the Birmingham Oratory during Newman's lifetime and for three years afterwards; otherwise there would be the risk again of laying out money on a potentially abortive project. The bishop thought there would be no problem about this. Newman was once again explicit to Ullathorne about his motive in agreeing—to further Catholicism at Oxford as far as he could and in whatever way he could. He needed, however, some assurance that the present policy of discouraging rather than forbidding Catholics to go to Oxford would continue; this time, of course, there was no intention of announcing publicly that they were going to Oxford for the sake of Catholic students. Ullathorne replied that the present decisions by the bishops would remain in force unless there was a substantial increase in the numbers, in which case more stringent measures might be taken. Newman half-wished he had never got involved again: the Catholic parishioners in Oxford would be annoyed that they were not to have their own church built for them, while the University would look askance at the ostensible reason for their coming, given how few Catholics were in residence. Personally, he told Pusey, 'it would be as painful a step as I could be called to make. Oxford never can be to me what it was. It and I are severed, it would be like the dead visiting the dead. I should be a stranger in my dearest home.'[134] He felt he could not refuse this third overture from the bishop, but, he told Copeland, 'the notion of getting into hot water, is most distasteful to me, now when I wish to be a little quiet. I cannot be in a happier position than I am.' Even if he could be 'sure of incurring no collisions with persons I love, still the mere publicity is a great trial to me'. 'Oh dear,' he groaned, 'how I dread it—but it seems to be the will of God, and I do not know how to draw back.'[135]

At the beginning of the year Newman had ordered a copy of Sir John Seeley's *Ecce Homo*. Although, he confessed to Rogers, 'I see very few

---

[133] *LD* xxii. 306.   [134] Ibid. 227.   [135] Ibid. 241.

books—indeed I have not time', as well as having 'a great laziness about reading books', he was interested in seeing the new publication which had caused such a sensation by concentrating exclusively on the humanity of Christ—and not out of mere curiosity or sense of disapproval:

We are in a strange time. I have not a shadow of a misgiving that the Catholic Church and its doctrine are directly from God—but then I know well that there is in particular quarters a narrowness which is not of God. And I believe great changes before now have taken place in the direction of the Church's course, and that new aspects of her aboriginal doctrines have suddenly come forth, and all this coincidentally with changes in the world's history, such as are now in progress; so that I never should shut up, when new views are set before me, though I might not take them as a whole.[136]

By April he had begun a review article on *Ecce Homo* for the *Month*, which was completed in May and published in June. He had found difficulty in finishing the book: 'There seemed to me little new in it, but what was questionable, or fanciful. And it seemed to me that the author treated things as discoveries, when they were only new to him.' But he admitted to Rogers that it was 'full of interest as a sign of the times—and as likely to influence the course of thought, as it is now running in the religious world'.[137] He did not feel that he had had time to do justice to it. His general feeling was that 'Catholics are both deeper and shallower than Protestants; but in neither case have they any call for a treatise such as this *Ecce Homo*.' The faith of Catholics, he argued, 'is as indelible as the pigment which colours the skin, even though it is skin-deep'. For although 'individual Catholics may be harassed with doubts, particularly in a day like this', still, 'viewed as a body, Catholics . . . are either too deep or too shallow' to suffer from the kind of difficulties Protestants were liable to experience. Seeley seemed to think that 'the faith of a Catholic is the mere profession of a formula', whereas

what Catholics . . . have ever lived on, is not any number of theological canons or decrees, but . . . the Christ Himself, as He is represented in concrete existence in the Gospels. Theological determinations about our Lord are far more of the nature of landmarks or buoys to guide a discursive mind in its reasonings, than to assist a devotional mind in its worship.

And it is Christ's 'Presence in the sacred Tabernacle, not as a form of words, or as a notion, but as an Object as real as we are real', which is the focus of worship in every Catholic church.[138] The chief fault, he thought, of *Ecce Homo* was its eclecticism: any revelation involves 'almost in its very idea as being something new, a collision with the human intellect,

---

[136] Ibid. 129–30.   [137] Ibid. 231.   [138] *DA* 386–8.

and demands accordingly . . . a sacrifice of private judgment'—'Take Christianity, or leave it . . . do not gamble and patch it' or 'dishonestly pick and choose'.[139]

On 8 June the Birmingham Oratory finally decided to undertake the Oxford mission—even though for Newman himself it would be 'opening wounds which are quite healed'.[140] Towards the end of July, however, he heard from Ullathorne that Propaganda had delayed its reply because it was worried that the foundation of an Oratory at Oxford might attract Catholic students to the University. Meanwhile, with Ambrose St John, he left for a holiday in Switzerland on the advice of his doctor, who had recommended a long vacation in view of his serious illness the preceding winter. From there he wrote to Ullathorne, once more reiterating:

I feel no calling whatever to go to Oxford, except it be in order to take care of Catholic undergraduates or to convert graduates. Such care, such conversion, is at Oxford the chief and most important missionary work. If in future there are no undergraduates to care for, at least there will be graduates to convert.

But he disputed a damagingly imprecise statement by the bishop in his reply to Propaganda, in which he said that he had suppressed Newman's circular in 1864 because it contained a reference to undertaking educational work at Oxford—when in fact it had only referred to pastoral care of Catholic students. He ended by tartly remarking that there was 'only one thing which would be more trying' to him than accepting the mission, and that would be 'to be allowed to build the Church there, and, as soon as that preparatory work was over, to be told from Rome that I had now done my part, and might retire'. Privately, he now believed that Ullathorne only really wanted a

Church built, by my name and influence—and he has no *wish* at all that I should have any thing more whatever to do with Oxford . . . Not that *he himself* . . . would be against my being at all at Oxford, but he thinks I am very unpopular at Rome, and he does not wish to get into the scrape of placing me there; so he apologises to the Cardinal [Barnabò] on the ground that it is very desirable to have a good church there and that I have friends who will build one for me.[141]

He had other things on his mind as he toured the Alps,[142] including the difficulty of getting a decent night's sleep at a Swiss hotel, which he describes with relish in almost gloating detail:

For myself, it arises, I think, from the food. I cannot digest such a nagging meal as a table d'hote dinner is . . . first a small piece of boiled, then a cold lobster salad, then a wing of a pigeon, then some hard beef, then an impossible sweet bread, then some beans, and, to finish, some cruel ice, which simply destroys the

---

[139] *DA* 397–8.   [140] *LD* xxii. 249.   [141] Ibid. 277, 279–80.
[142] See below, Chapter 16.

working power of the stomach—and all these at vast intervals, and then the uncertainty, when it is put before you, whether you should be able to manage the particular dish or not, the suspicion with which you begin to eat and the impossibility of your getting your will to cooperate with your jaws, which is a great secret of food digesting well, the disgust at what you don't like, and the desire to get rid of it off your plate into your stomach as soon as you can, all this, in the event, not only does not answer the purpose of food, but murders sleep, when night comes . . . Then the beds, though new and good, are intolerable to me . . . They make me restless. I wake with a crick in my neck—or a pain in my shoulders—or with my foot bare, from the blanket etc being pulled too much over my shoulders—and above all, they are so wonderfully hot. At this time my mattress lies against my wall, as I take it off my bed, before going to bed—the under mattress being harder. The upper mattress is springy, and I can't lie even—At Champéry I had to lie like a serpent in and out . . . The mattresses are new, filled with hair—there is no fault to be found with them, except that I cannot sleep on them.[143]

On his return to Birmingham in September, Newman found a letter awaiting him from Gerard Manley Hopkins, then an undergraduate at Oxford, saying that he wished to see him with a view to becoming a Catholic. Hopkins described to his friend Robert Bridges how 'genial and almost . . . unserious', as well as highly practical, he found the great man to be. (Another visitor at this time remarked on the ease with which he used ordinary conversational slang.) Hopkins, who had been a disciple of Pusey, was struck by Newman's remarking that far from the learned having no excuse, it was they who were most likely to be in 'invincible ignorance'.[144] A month or so later he returned to the Oratory and was received into the Church by Newman.

Towards the end of September, Ullathorne called and casually mentioned that he had decided not to correct any mistaken impression he might have given at Rome about Newman's original intentions in going to Oxford, as it might suggest that Newman was unduly anxious about going. 'The Bishop [fixed] his eyes steadily upon me and smiling in a gracious way, meaning (as it seemed to me) "So you felt I had kicked your shins in my letter to his Eminence,—well you may have borne it pretty well." ' Newman mused, 'I think Bishops fancy that, as justice does not exist between the Creator and His creatures, between man and the brute creation, so there is none between themselves and their subjects.' It was rather a question of whether 'the aggrieved' accepted their acts 'as an opportunity for gaining merit'.[145]

On the first Sunday of October Newman preached 'The Pope and the

[143] *LD* xxii. 283.
[144] *The Letters of Gerard Manley Hopkins to Robert Bridges*, ed. Claude Colleer Abbot (London, 1935), 5–6.
[145] *LD* xxii. 293.

Revolution' (which he immediately had printed), in deference to the bishop's call for special sermons and prayers for Pius IX as Garibaldi was now threatening the city of Rome itself, all that remained of the Temporal Power. It was a careful blend of loyalty to the person of the Pope with a pointed refusal 'to mix up Christ's Vicar with this or that party of men'; while an acknowledgement that ecclesiastical and temporal power had been effectively joined together in the Middle Ages is offset by the admission that 'there are sincere Catholics so dissatisfied with things as they were in Italy, as they are in Rome, that they are brought to think that no social change can be for the worse.'[146] The conclusion is unambiguous—that though the Temporal Power has long been the guarantee of the Church's independence, it need not be in the future. Nor can Newman resist pointing to the irony that there is more loyalty to the Holy See among the disestablished Catholics of England than those of Italy! He was quite prepared, he said privately, to support the Temporal Power while it lasted, but to make it an article of faith was 'simply unbelieving'; and it was 'most undignified to shriek' as if 'mortal man can do us real harm'—after all, the 'Apostles did not shriek when they were put into prison'.[147] Nor, to do him credit, had the Pope, whose 'spirit is simply that of martyrdom—and is utterly different from that implied in these gratuitous shriekings which surround his throne'. Judging from the shrill reaction to Garibaldi's threat, an actual assault on Rome might turn out to be the best thing that could happen:

> . . . I view with equanimity the prospect of a thorough routing out of things at Rome—not till some great convulsions take place . . . and religion is felt to be in the midst of trials, red-tapism will go out of Rome, and a better spirit come in . . . At present things are in appearance . . . effete . . . We are sinking into a sort of Novatianism, the heresy which the early Popes so strenuously resisted. Instead of aiming at being a world-wide power, we are shrinking into ourselves, narrowing the lines of communion, trembling at freedom of thought, and using the language of disarray and despair at the prospect before us, instead of, with the high spirit of the warrior, going out conquering and to conquer.[148]

As for his friend Bishop Moriarty's horror at the prospect of a secular government at Rome intercepting the Vatican's correspondence, Newman could not help remarking that even that would bring great benefits to the Church, for 'it would cut off a great deal of unprofitable gossip sent to Rome . . . and of crude answers sent back from Rome by men who seem to have authority, but have none—and it would throw power into the hands of the local Bishops every where'.[149] People who were surprised at his attitude to the Temporal Power question, should

---

[146] *OS* 287, 303.   [147] *LD* xxii. 305.   [148] Ibid. 314–15.
[149] Ibid. 317.

remember that the Tractarian movement had begun as a protest against Erastianism.

Newman could hardly have been surprised to hear that his sermon had not gone down very well in certain quarters, especially his unflattering comparison of Italian with English Catholics. He heard that his former companion Robert Coffin, now a Redemptorist, was vocal in his criticism. Coffin, who had advocated Manning's appointment, had acted as a guide to the Roman Cardinal who had visited England in the summer for a first-hand investigation into the Oxford Oratory plan; he had arranged for him to meet W. G. Ward (with whom he stayed for three days), but not Newman. It was, in fact, remarkable that Newman had never been consulted officially about the Oxford question, although all sorts of others had been. He did not attribute Manning's opposition to

any animosity to me—but I think he is of a nature to be determined to *crush* or to *melt* every person who stands in his way. He has views and is determined to carry them out—and I must either go with him or be annihilated. I say this, because he long wished to get me made a Bishop (in partibus)—I believe because he knew it would be (as it were) putting me 'in the House of Lords'. When he found that I should not accept the offer, as feeling it would interfere with my independence, his only remaining policy is to put me out.'[150]

The new Archbishop was very different from his predecessor, who, by contrast, 'was a man of general temper and large mind, and was averse to harsh measures'.[151] But although Manning had 'taken this strong part' against him, he was 'as bland and smooth as ever in word and writing'.[152] Now, surprisingly, it seemed that the Archbishop had lost the battle to prevent him from going to Oxford. On Christmas Day Ullathorne wrote to say that Propaganda had given its permission for the Oxford Oratory, and enclosed a copy of Barnabò's letter. Unfortunately, he deliberately omitted one key sentence. This was the famous 'secret instruction' which actually directed Ullathorne 'blandly and smoothly' ('blande suaviterque') to discourage Newman from any idea of taking up residence himself at Oxford (on the ground that it would encourage Catholics to send their sons to the University).[153]

Blissfully ignorant of this, Newman began the new year with a feeling of excitement at the prospect at last of a 'fruitful and important' work. He confided to St John, 'if I had spirit enough to do the Oxford matter well, we need not care one fig for . . . any thing else—for Oxford would be our theatre and our organ.' The problem was that at his age he felt he had 'spirt rather than spirit—that is, I can make an occasional effort, but not a sustained one'. He had the impression that the bishop 'really'

---

[150] Ibid. 329.   [151] Ibid. 318.   [152] Ibid. 334.   [153] Ibid. 331 n. 2.

was 'hand and glove with us'.[154] But although he did not know about the 'secret instruction', he remained cautious about the real intentions of the Roman authorities, who had only given 'provisional' permission (on the condition particularly that it was understood there was no relaxation of the ban on Catholics entering the University). Ullathorne appeared full of confidence, pointing out it was only because it was part of the Oratorian Rule that Newman needed special leave to work in Oxford without leaving Birmingham that Propaganda had become involved—too involved, as it lay within his own power to recognize the foundation of a new Oratory in his own diocese.

Newman, however, did not underestimate Manning's determined opposition. To the suggestion of Emily Bowles that a personal meeting might help, he replied that merely to 'meet him would but increase alienation. He never came to me except he had a purpose . . . He left off seeing me, when he found I was on my guard.' It was not a personal matter, anyway—'he wishes me no ill, but he is determined to bend or break all opposition. He has an iron will, and resolves to have his own way.' He had offered to make Newman a bishop (without a diocese), because he 'wanted to gain me over'. Newman's refusal to lose his independence meant that 'now, he will break me, if he can'. The one obvious sphere for Newman was Oxford, which 'he is doing all he can to keep me from'.[155] Newman was also well aware of the 'lasting suspicion' that his *Rambler* article had caused at Rome (although he had received an assurance from Wiseman through Manning that the matter had been dropped). But he was not prepared, he told Emily Bowles, to try and defend himself now at Rome. Self-defence was a duty only when one's faith or integrity was impugned:

did I go out and battle commonly, I should lose my time, my peace, my strength, and only show a detestable sensitiveness. I consider that Time is the great remedy and Avenger of all wrongs, as far as this world goes. If only we are patient, God works for us—He works for those who do not work for themselves. Of course an inward brooding over injustices is *not* patience, but a recollecting with a view to the future is prudence.[156]

But this did not stop him from writing flatly to Ullathorne, 'I will say to your Lordship frankly, that I cannot trust the Archbishop.' Ullathorne himself had once warned him to be on his guard. 'It seems to me he never wishes to see a man except for his own ends.' He was also two-faced: for example, he had written to thank Newman for his *Letter to Pusey*, but behind his back he had tried to get Ullathorne to approve Ward's article of censure on it in the *Dublin Review*. He was not impressed by Ullathorne's report of friendly overtures on the part of the Archbishop,

---

[154] *LD* xxiii. 3–4.   [155] Ibid. 9–10.   [156] Ibid. 16.

who was obviously anxious not to let himself appear in a bad light now that his treatment of Newman was becoming public knowledge.

I cannot act towards him as if I trusted him—and I think that, as a matter of prudence, I never shall trust him till he has gone through purgatory . . . Certainly I have no wish to see him now; first because I don't like to be practised on; secondly, because I cannot in conversation use smooth words which conceal, not express thoughts; thirdly because I am not sorry he should know that I am dissatisfied with him. Of course his conduct to me is not special, but such as his conduct is to every one . . .'[57]

Newman began preparing a new circular to solicit donations for the proposed Oratory and church. Architecturally, he favoured the Byzantine style, which would be cheaper than Gothic, which he thought was unsuitable anyway for a small building and would turn what he envisaged as a 'real working Church' into a 'mantel piece ornament'. 'There are pretty gothic Churches in the country so crowded with details, that you cannot kneel without falling down some steps, and cannot rise without knocking your head against an image. Our contracted limits demand simplicity; and gothic, when simple, is bald.'[58] He carefully refrained from all mention of Catholic students attending the University, but he specifically referred to the University itself as an appropriate reason for the erection of an Oratory in Oxford (after all, there had to be some reason for it). He assured Pusey he had no intention of setting out to convert undergraduates—besides, 'it is quite uncertain what influence I *could* exert, and, when I think of myself at Oxford again, I think of those actors and singers, who, having retired from the public scenes, in their old age come back again . . . and make deplorable failures . . . and I anticipate that I may be a nine days wonder and then break down.' At any rate, he expressed the hope that if his 'coming produced any effect . . . it would tell more, or at least not less, against scepticism than against the Anglican Church'.[59] He was already under pressure from friends who were subscribing to the new Oratory church to begin building as soon as possible to forestall any attempt by Manning to get the decision of Propaganda reversed. When it proved impossible to start before the middle of the summer, he obtained the bishop's permission to commence the mission by preaching every Sunday in term at the existing chapel in St Clement's. No doubt, had he carried out his intention, a crisis would soon have arisen through his unwitting transgression of the 'secret instruction'.

On 18 March 1867 a letter arrived from Cardinal Barnabò complaining that Propaganda had received a report that Newman was preparing a number of youths for admission to Oxford (where already

[57] Ibid. 17.   [58] Ibid. 59.   [59] Ibid. 29–30.

several Catholics had lost their faith). A similar letter was sent to Ullathorne warning that the permission for an Oratory did not mean any relaxation of the ban on Catholics going to Oxford, and directing the bishops once again to send their views on the subject to Rome. Newman replied that there were indeed two boys at the school who intended going to Oxford, one of whom had been recommended to him by a Catholic bishop in New Zealand, that he was unaware that the Holy See had spoken officially on the subject, and that he was doing nothing more than was being done at colleges like Oscott and Stonyhurst. He was more than ready to comply with the directives of Propaganda, but 'I will not conceal my surprise . . . that, after my twenty years of most faithful service, your Eminence reposes so little confidence in me in the matter:— but God will see to it.'[160] The report that a number of Catholics had had their faith destroyed at Oxford seemed to be based solely on the fact that one undergraduate had 'ducked a Puseyite' in the fountain at Christ Church's 'Tom Quad', and another had talked indiscreetly on the Temporal Power question at Rome![161]

Manning's closest collaborator, Herbert Vaughan (who was to succeed him at Westminster), reported back to the Archbishop from Rome that Barnabò had made fun of Newman's indignation, which Barnabò took as a compliment to himself, attributing it to Newman's disappointment in not being made a bishop. Vaughan also mentioned that he had reason for suspecting that the Oxford Oratory was only a first step to setting up a Catholic college there, and that it was possible Newman had been deceiving his bishop. He concluded that there was no need to feel any scruple 'at removing him from Oxford even with a pitchfork'.[162] To Ullathorne, Newman observed simply that he could not 'run a race, as he would expect me, of rival exaggerations' with Barnabò—so 'I answered his letter sentence by sentence simply and categorically.'[163] He warned the bishop that donations were being made towards the new Oratory on the assumption that no absolute ban was placed on Catholics going to Oxford, in which event (or if further restrictions were placed on himself personally) he would definitely withdraw from the undertaking. He already realized that boys at the Oratory School who wanted to go to Oxford would have to go elsewhere in future for the special tuition necessary for admission.

It was a measure of Newman's intellectual consistency and integrity that at the very moment he was suffering at the hands of the Roman Curia, he was also insisting to Pusey on the Pope's 'unlimited' and 'despotic' jurisdiction as a 'principle' rather than 'doctrine' of the

[160] *LD* xxiii. 94.   [161] Ibid. 88.   [162] Ibid. 93 n.   [163] Ibid. 104.

Catholic 'system'. Principles could be converted into doctrines by being defined, but since they belong to the '*substance*' of the Church, 'they live as necessities before definition, and are the less likely to be defined, *because* they are so essential to life'. Newman's exposition of the actual role of the papacy evinces the usual careful balance and blend of the practical and theoretical. Thus he modifies his initial statement of the limitless jurisdiction of the Pope by quickly pointing out that it is more an 'abstract power' than a 'practical fact'. It was also true that Councils had been fairly vague on the Pope's actual powers, for not only was the Church traditionally anxious to avoid restricting 'the liberty of thinking and judging more than was absolutely necessary', but it also wanted to encourage 'a more generous faith than was imperative on the conscience'. Again, 'to cut clean between doctrine revealed and doctrine not revealed' was in fact impossible, because the Church 'actually *cannot* do so at any given moment, but is illuminated from time to time as to what was revealed in the beginning on this or that portion of the whole mass of teaching which is now received'. To make such a distinction was impossible without a foreknowledge of the questions in the future which would require dogmatic definitions. More important—and this was a crucial consideration which cut across all attempts to try and 'pin down' the exact doctrines Catholics are required to believe—the Church 'would be misrepresenting the real character of the dispensation' and 'abdicating her function' by transferring the faith of Catholics 'from resting on herself as the organ of revelation . . . simply to a code of certain definite articles or a written creed'.[164] He was emphatic to Pusey that the Catholic position is that 'the object of faith is *not* simply certain articles . . . contained in dumb documents, but the whole word of God, explicit and implicit, as dispensed by His living Church', and that 'it marks a fundamental, elementary difference between the Anglican view and ours.' Moreover, he continued, with typical forthrightness,

there is no use in a Pope at all, except to bind the whole of Christendom into one polity; and . . . to ask us to give up his universal jurisdiction is to invite us to commit suicide . . . An honorary head . . . does not affect the real force, or enter into the essence, of a political body, and is not worth contending about. We do not want a man of straw, but a bond of unity . . . Now the Church is a Church Militant, and, as the commander of an army is despotic, so must the visible head of the Church be . . .[165]

The absolute refusal to acquiesce in Ultramontane exaggerations is matched by a no less scrupulous care to reject any attempt to minimize either the practical or the theoretical reality of the papacy.

---

[164] Ibid. 98–100.   [165] Ibid. 105–7.

On 29 March Newman heard from Ullathorne that there had been a division of opinion at Rome over the original Oxford application and that the permission which had been granted had been vehemently attacked by Talbot, Manning, and others. The bishop had also been told that Vaughan was busy spreading the report that the Oratory School was deliberately preparing boys for Oxford. It was a strange irony that only three days previously Newman had been asked by a Jesuit professor at the Collegio Romano (where he was also under attack) to contribute to a collection of pieces on St Peter to be presented to the Pope—which he did by sending passages from his eulogy of the Petrine office from the beginning of the Dublin *Discourses*—a eulogy he somewhat modified in 1873 when he published the *Idea of a University*. (Later he regretted that 'like a fool' he had offered the piece, which admittedly reflected his own belief in papal infallibility, to a volume which was deliberately intended to be used as part of a campaign to force through a definition of the doctrine.[166]) Ullathorne advised Newman to go to Rome to defend himself. Newman was in no doubt about the gravity of the situation. He thought it quite likely that they would even have to give up the school, as they could always be accused of indirectly helping boys to go to Oxford simply by providing an education for the sons of parents who particularly insisted on their going to the University. It was decided that Ambrose St John should go to Rome: as headmaster of the school, it was appropriate that he should undertake its defence, as well as representing Newman, who was not such a good linguist and who doubted how far his personal presence would have a conciliatory effect. Anyway, Newman was needed in England if a start was to be made on the Oxford mission. He gave St John a memorandum to be presented to Propaganda, which recounted the history of the school and defended it against various attacks, as well as proudly claiming that it had 'led the way in a system of educational improvement on a large scale through the Catholic community'.[167]

Surprisingly, perhaps, Newman pressed Ullathorne to allow a start to be made at Oxford as soon as possible, preferably before the bishops met. This was not from any 'personal feeling or wish to go'—rather, 'it would be a great comfort to back out of the whole, for peace is the greatest of earthly blessings.' But he had 'no thought of any such cowardice', and was 'determined to fight it out'.[168] He was under no illusion, he told Bishop Moriarty, about the nature and strength of the opposition, 'who wish me kept from the place at any price', although 'they give other reasons': 'They are sorry I have had an opportunity of gaining the

---

[166] *LD* xxvi. 356.　　　　[167] Ibid. xxiii. 117.　　　　[168] Ibid. 122.

public ear lately by writing—and, if I had a pulpit in Oxford, it would be a great blow to them.'[169]

In the first week of April, E. R. Martin, the Rome correspondent of the *Weekly Register* (the same who had denounced the *Letter to Pusey* in the *Tablet*), reported that the Pope had decided that Newman should not go to Oxford; such a delicate mission could only be entrusted to a trusted Ultramontane, not to someone who was the author of certain passages in the *Apologia* and the recent sermon on the Temporal Power. This 'inspired' piece, which linked Newman's name more than once with that of Döllinger, was so virulent in its tone that Newman began to wonder, 'what is the worth of my voice at Oxford, if I am under a cloud? Already the Protestant periodicals have said that I am not a sound Catholic. I am told so every day.'[170] He expected his bishop to defend him against the attack, but the immediate effect was Ullathorne's disclosure of the 'secret instruction', which he felt Newman ought to know about now that the whole affair was becoming public knowledge, but which he had withheld previously on the ground that it was intended only for his own ears and concerned an eventuality which was not contemplated.

Newman's misgivings about the provisional nature of the original permission from Propaganda had been overruled by the rest of the community; now, certainly, if it had been up to him he would have retired from the undertaking altogether. Had he known about the 'secret instruction' he would never have agreed to go; it would be 'an invisible fetter, just as I found in Dublin . . . to stop me in my course when I attempt to act freely'. To accept the restriction would also be to give the impression that he was intent on going to Oxford. He realized, he wrote to St John, who was on his way to Rome, that 'all that about the School was a pretence; and now they have thrown off the mask and attack, not the school, but me and my teaching'. His opponents could insist on his writings being examined, which 'would be a process of years and keep me under a cloud, and perhaps I should be dead before I was acquitted'.[171] He was tempted to tell St John to return and to abandon the Oxford plan. He told William Monsell:

You may be sure they are determined to put me down at all hazards—and, if in no other way, by a charge of heresy. No matter if it is untenable; an inquiry may be drawn out for a year or two, when they think the chances are that I shall be too old to undertake any new plan . . . if they put me down, of course they have inclusively put down all who dare to think otherwise than the pharisees of the pharisees.[172]

Certainly it was not for any personal reasons that the opposition was moving against him; it was rather a case of 'If they can manage to silence

[169] Ibid. 125.   [170] Ibid. 128.   [171] Ibid. 129–30.   [172] Ibid. 132.

me, who can make a stand?' But there was a sense of relief, as well as sadness, as he concluded with weary resignation: 'No: it looks as if I never should see Oxford again. I have never wished to see it.'[173]

As he reflected cynically but penetratingly on the psychological peculiarities of Roman officialdom, he saw less and less point in St John's mission:

While I am an unknown and strange person *here*, they fear me—as a vicious animal—they address me blandè suaviterque lest I should kick out, or jump at their throat—but, if *you* went to Rome and people saw what third rate men we are, as being so very obedient, then . . . we should be kicked into space without any delay. I think it salutary to keep up this ignorance of me—for the more they knew of me the more they would look down on me.

Nor did he accept the bishop's view of the 'secret instruction': there was no point in even talking of moving or not moving residence when the whole idea had been that the new Oratory was to be an integral part of the Birmingham Oratory. He remarked sarcastically to St John: 'I doubt not the Bishop has got immense credit at Propaganda for years for his wonderful skill in keeping a wild beast like me in order . . . [with] his blanditiae et suavitates . . . It is something superhuman to have kept me in order for . . . twenty years.'[174]

When, however, Ullathorne came to see him, he assured Newman that he intended 'to have it all out' with Manning. He had already accused the Archbishop of being at the bottom of the whole affair, which he had denied. Newman's response was that he knew that Manning would never show his hand openly; his avowed regret at the article in the *Weekly Register* was no doubt real enough, for it had 'let the cat out of the bag'. Ullathorne allowed that Newman 'generally did get to the bottom of things'. He had written to Barnabò to defend Newman and proposed making public all the transactions that had taken place. He still hoped Newman would accept the Oxford mission, the start of which he had wanted to delay until he had been able to go himself to Rome to get the 'secret instruction' cancelled and what was only a conditional and provisional permission confirmed.[175] It so happened that on the day before Ullathorne's visit, the indefatigable Vaughan had an audience with Pius IX; when, in answer to accusations against Newman, the Pope reminded him that Newman had pledged his loyalty and obedience, Vaughan triumphantly produced his trump-card—the delated *Rambler* article, which Vaughan claimed he had never retracted. As Manning had assured Ullathorne, he had hardly taken part in the proceedings against Newman at Rome; Vaughan was doing all that was necessary. Unfortunately for them, the report in the *Weekly Register* ('the best luck

[173] *LD* xxiii. 133.   [174] Ibid. 135–6.   [175] Ibid. 136–8.

we have had a long time', commented Newman[176]) had given the game away. It had also provoked an important reaction in the form of a lay address, which was signed by every Catholic Member of Parliament, nearly all the Catholic peers, and a large number of prominent laymen. It was published in both the *Tablet* and the *Weekly Register*, and contained the following protest: 'we feel that every blow that touches you inflicts a wound upon the Catholic Church in this country.'[177] It began to look as if the Ultramontane party might have overplayed its hand.

Newman wrote to Ambrose St John that he had been unfair to the bishop, who was 'badgered on all sides'[178]—'He is quite with us, and is quite to be relied on.'[179] It was hard to see what else he could have done in the circumstances. Certainly he was almost their only friend in high places; he was not to be alienated.[180] Newman's first reaction had been to wash his hands immediately of the whole Oxford project. But he felt now he had to wait to see how things developed and not take any precipitate action himself, if only so as not to disappoint well-wishers and those who had subscribed to the new Oratory. It was possible, too, he recognized, to interpret the 'secret instruction' about residence in a less drastic sense than he had done on first reading it. However, the bishops at their forthcoming meeting after Easter would no doubt issue a stronger prohibition against Catholics going to Oxford, which would settle the matter once and for all.

Whatever the outcome, it had been proved that what James Hope-Scott had called his ' "sensitiveness" was not timidity, or particularity, or touchiness, but a true instinct of the state of the ecclesiastical atmosphere'. Hope-Scott had urged him to ignore the opposition, but the inescapable fact was that someone like the odious Martin was 'an index of the state of the weather at Rome, as the insects swarming near the earth is a sign of rain'. Ever since the premature death of his only friend at Rome, Mgr. Palma, Newman had become accustomed to 'neglect and unkind usage': it was his 'cross, and the easiest one I could have—how much easier than illhealth or bereavement, or poverty! I would not change it for any other—and somehow I don't think it will ever leave me.'[181]

Emily Bowles, full of indignation against Manning, wondered why Newman had not accepted the opportunity which Talbot's earlier invitation had offered him to make himself heard at Rome. Newman

---

[176] Ibid. 141.   [177] Ibid. 139 n.   [178] Ibid. 148.   [179] Ibid. 143.

[180] Newman's later, reconsidered (private) judgement was closer to his initial reaction: 'Since this time I have got to understand our Bishop better . . . I quite believe him well disposed to me, but justice, truth, kindness, paternity, generosity would have no chance with him, if Pope or Propaganda spoke otherwise' (*LD* xxiii. 165 n. 2).

[181] Ibid. 150–1.

dismissed the idea that the suggestion had come from the Pope; Talbot had obviously simply mentioned the possibility of Newman giving some sermons—'and the Pope of course said, "A very good thought," as he would have said if Mgr T. had said "I wish to bring your Holiness some English razors." ' As for Barnabò, he had resolved the dilemma of whether Newman should or should not be allowed to go to Oxford by means of a secret clause 'as imbecile as it is crooked and cruel'.[182] Among sophisticated Italian ecclesiastics, 'doubledealing' had become a veritable 'tradition', according to which 'fine craft is the true weapon of Churchmen', so that the Prefect of Propaganda had merely 'been trying his hand on my barbarism'.[183] Still, he might yet be, if not outwitted, at least corrupted by a mere barbarian. Newman suggested wickedly to St John: 'Every man has his price . . . a Cardinal or Monsignor's price is English snuff. I am serious—could you not borrow a quantity . . . and on leaving Cardinal Barnabo, slip the fragrant douceur into his hand as you kiss it.'[184] He heard that Manning was very agitated by the lay address: 'I believe the whole clique feels, that I am becoming a power which will break them—and this must not be.'[185]

Writing to thank John Wallis, the editor of the *Tablet*, for his leading article supporting him against the report in the *Weekly Review*, he again emphasized that he saw nothing personal in the opposition to him; it was more serious than that. 'If . . . they are strong enough to put down me, simply on the ground of my not succumbing to the clique, no one else has a chance of not being put down, and a reign of terror has begun, a reign of denunciation, secret tribunals, and moral assassination.' As for 'the actual attack upon me, I shall outlive it, as I have outlived other attacks—but it is not at all easy to break that formidable conspiracy, which is in action against the theological liberty of Catholics'.[186] Slander, he firmly insisted to a lady who wrote to express her sympathy, was 'the lightest of trials', and when 'compared with ill health, with loss of friends, or with poverty, it weighs as nothing'.[187] But he was determined, he candidly informed Mgr. Patterson, to fight against 'tyranny and terrorism', because he could not 'endure narrowing the terms of Catholicity, as some would narrow them'. His own strongly held maxim was 'In necessariis unitas, in dubiis libertas, in omnibus charitas.'[188] Nor again was there anything personal in Barnabò's treatment of him; he was a Roman bureaucrat, 'to whom routine, and dispatch, are every thing and gentleness, courteousness, frankness, and considerateness are words without meaning'. Nevertheless, 'I shall always give a hearty obedience to Rome, but I never expect in my life time any recognition of it.'[189] What remained 'intolerable' was that 'we

[182] *LD* xxiii. 156–7.   [183] Ibid. 165.   [184] Ibid. 177.   [185] Ibid. 178.
[186] Ibid. 187.   [187] Ibid. 188.   [188] Ibid. 189–90.   [189] Ibid. 191.

should be placed at the mercy of a secret tribunal, which dares to speak in the name of the Pope, and would institute, if it could, a regime of espionage, denunciation and terrorism'.[190]

At the end of April Ignatius Ryder (who would succeed Newman as superior of the Birmingham Oratory) published *Idealism in Theology, a Review of Dr. Ward's Scheme of Dogmatic Authority*. Newman appreciated, he sarcastically told St John, that on his arrival in Rome this 'awful pamphlet' might be 'thrown in your teeth' with its 'great flourish of lies'. It hardly mattered—'we don't want to get any thing—and my monkey is up.' He had already informed Ullathorne that St John, together with Henry Bittleton, who was to join him, were not now going to petition Propaganda for anything, but merely to defend their Superior against slander. Whatever trouble they incurred it was 'worth the suffering, if we effectually oppose them'.[191] He instructed St John to tell Barnabò that his 'precious instruction' had made Newman 'unwittingly collect money on fake pretences'—'Far as it was from the intentions of the Most Eminent Prince, he co-operated in a fraud. Distil this blandè suaviterque into his ears.' He sent Ward a copy of the pamphlet, expressing his agreement with it, but adding that it had been written independently of him; it was, however, he warned, a sign of the impatience among a number of younger Catholics who resented the intolerance and narrowness of the Ultramontane party. He wrote to St John that he had heard Mrs Ward compared to Trollope's Mrs Proudie; also, they were not the only ones to wonder if Ward was quite right in the head. 'Ward says that he loves me so, that he should like to pass an eternity with me, but that whenever he sees Manning he makes him creep . . . yet that Manning has the truth and I have not.' It was odd how Newman could attract such professed adulation, and yet at the same time such downright hostility. Ward's response to the pamphlet was quite mild, but he informed Newman that in spite of his liking for him, they had no option but to regard each other's theological views with 'the greatest aversion', since they belonged to 'different religions'![192] Newman replied sharply that he felt bound once again to protest—'ineffectual' as he knew it would be—against Ward's persistence in exaggerating their theological differences as 'of great moment', when within the whole context of the Church's teaching they were 'unimportant, allowable, inevitable differences (which must ever exist between mind and mind)'. This was an 'utterly uncatholic . . . feeling and sentiment' in which Ward had grown over the years. Now he was falling into 'worse excesses':

Pardon me if I say that you are making a Church within a Church, as the

[190] Ibid. 193.   [191] Ibid. 195.   [192] Ibid. 202.

Novatians of old did within the Catholic pale, and as, outside the Catholic pale, the Evangelicals of the Establishment. As they talk of 'vital religion' and 'vital doctrines,' and will not allow that their brethren 'know the Gospel' or are 'Gospel preachers' unless they profess the small shibboleths of their own sect, so you are doing your best to make a party in the Catholic Church . . . by exalting your opinions into dogmas . . .

I protest then again, not against your tenets, but against what I must call your schismatical spirit.[193]

By now St John had reached Rome. From there Newman's old critic Bishop Brown of Newport wrote to express his sympathy and support, as well as that of Frederick Neve, the convert Rector of the English College. Newman replied that for consolation he had no need to look beyond the founder of the Oratory, St Philip Neri, who had also suffered at the hands of the authorities in Rome. St John was able to confirm what Newman already guessed, that Barnabò was only concerned with implementing the policy against 'mixed' education; the hostility to what Newman stood for theologically came from the English Ultramontanes. Barnabò's chief complaint against Newman was the old grievance of the *Rambler* article, which, through Wiseman's fault, had been left unresolved: Barnabò claimed not to know of Newman's letter to Wiseman offering to explain and vindicate the article's orthodoxy, although in fact Wiseman did pass its contents on to Propaganda, which in turn prepared the list of questions that Wiseman failed to send on to Newman. He also complained that Newman had stood on his rights in the row with the London Oratory, and had been jealous because Manning had been made a bishop. St John's impression was that the English converts in general were regarded as 'a lot of queer quarrelsome Inglesi'.[194] As a consolation, Barnabò suggested that Newman was a saint and that saints must expect to be persecuted. The two Oratorians saw the Pope twice, who warned them that he could not countenance Catholics going to Protestant colleges at Oxford.

The Pope might have a policy against 'mixed' education in general, but Newman saw that what people like Manning really objected to was Catholics mixing with Protestants; that was why a Catholic college at Oxford had also to be made to seem unacceptable to the Pope.

I think a number of people wish Catholics to remain a distant caste among the Protestant gentry—and, if inferiority in mind be the necessary consequence or condition of such isolation, well, never mind, it must be accepted by us. It is not that Oxford will corrupt Catholic youths more than Woolwich or London, but

---

[193] *LD* xxiii. 216–17.   [194] Ibid. 209.

that it will improve their intellectual powers, or create a mutual understanding between them and Protestants.

Manning himself put it like this to Talbot: 'I see much danger of an English Catholicism of which Newman is the highest type. It is the old Anglican, patristic, literary, Oxford tone transplanted into the Church.'[195] Newman had no illusions about trying to put across another point of view at Rome; the Pope had advisers like Talbot round him, who 'would soon wipe out any new impression, even if made'.[196] At home they suffered from having no regular organ for their views. They had to resort to pamphlets like that of Ryder, which Newman admitted was not satisfactory: 'He is ever in deep Devonshire lanes—you never know the lie of the country from him—he never takes his reader up to an eminence, whence he could make a map of it.' But in so far as this was deliberate, it was not necessarily a fault. Newman had 'thought it was good generalship for various reasons directly to attack Ward, not in the first place his opinions—I wanted him to show from Ward's character how untrustworthy he was.'[197] He could not help smiling at the lay address to the Pope, which appeared at the end of May at Manning's instigation:

Here am I called to task for saying something strong in favour of the consensus fidelium in the Rambler, and . . . Laymen are signing a new Profession of faith embodying received dogmas, theological opinions, political maxims, in *one* document, as a standard which we, poor Priests, must follow . . . in holding, else we shall appear less orthodox than our flocks.[198]

He received a pompous letter from Talbot, saying that in spite of his personal affection and love for Newman, he could no longer support him when he 'found there was a dangerous party rising in England, who quoted your name', but had been 'obliged to modify my views, and stand up for Ecclesiastical authority in preference of worshipping great intellectual gifts'.[199] The absurdity of extreme Ultramontanism certainly had its comical side. Thus Ward had announced with what 'extreme surprise' he had discovered the full extent of the infallibility claimed by the Pope—a truth he had professedly not been aware of during his years as a lecturer in theology, although he was 'now imposing it on all under pain of mortal sin'.[200] Newman also heard from Rome that his sermon on the Temporal Power had been denounced, but that no action was to be taken because a favourable report on the orthodoxy of his writings had been received from none other than Archbishop, now Cardinal, Cullen.

---

[195] Ibid. 230. [196] Ibid. 231. [197] Ibid. 227.
[198] Ibid. 239. [199] Ibid. 242 n. 1. [200] Ibid. 247.

6

On 18 June the so-called 'Murphy Riots' broke out in Birmingham. They were named after William Murphy, an Irish apostate from Catholicism, who was the principal of the 'lecturers' sent out by the 'Protestant Electoral Union' to assail Catholics and Anglican ritualists. An obscene attack on the confessional enraged the Catholic Irish community and serious rioting broke out. It was feared that the Oratory would be attacked by a Protestant mob during three days of disturbances, and Newman went down to the police station, where he was shown how quickly the new telegraph system could summon the military if necessary. Unfortunately, the outbreak coincided with a visit from his sister Jemima. However, the visit went off without incident. Jemima came to lunch and afterwards played Beethoven's sonatas on Mrs Wootten's piano, accompanied by her brother on the violin. The one in A minor, wrote Newman, 'had, and has had since, an effect on me I can't describe. Often Beethoven transports me, but I cannot express, or analyze, the strange effect which its first movement had on me. I could hardly go on playing.'[201] How extraordinary, he mused, that 'Mary would now be in her 59th year . . . But she, taken away young, looks always young to us . . . And to think that that picture, vivid as it is to us, is now confined to the imaginations of half a dozen persons, and does not exist out of them . . .'.[202]

On 26 June the Pope suddenly announced that a General Council was to be convened. Newman was delighted at first, if only because 'it is the normal way of doing things'.[203] He had heard that one of the purposes of the Council would be 'to recognise and re-affirm the Immaculate Conception, not as throwing doubt on the previous definition, but as normalizing the ecclesiastical proceeding'. This was plausible and desirable 'as showing that the *normal* mode of deciding a point of faith is a Council, not the Pope speaking ex cathedrâ'. There was also a need to update an obsolete code of canon law. Then, too, there was the possibility of progress towards reunion with the Eastern Orthodox, and perhaps also Anglo-Catholics. But there was another, distinctly ominous prospect—that the Ultramontane party 'would push for the Pope's Infallibility, and be unscrupulous in doing so'. Whether the bishops would really accept this 'as part of the original faith, I cannot divine'. He would be surprised if they did. But the eventuality did not alarm him: whatever happened would be God's will and 'they cannot go beyond the divine will and revealed truth'. On the other hand, he told Pusey, he felt confident that 'if the alternative lay between defining it and the

---

[201] *LD* xxiii. 255.   [202] Ibid. 234.   [203] Ibid. 265.

reconciliation of the Anglican Church', then for reasons of expediency there would be no definition. Even the chance of a large body of Anglo-Catholic clergy going over to Rome on the condition that there was no dogmatic definition would surely make the bishops think twice—not that this would be a very logical or satisfactory way of entering the Church. But, he reminded Pusey, the Church was capable of making very large concessions when circumstances justified it. And he urged:

If you have strong points, let them be put forward—for myself I do not sympathise at all in the policy of suppression. I have no fear that it will harm the cause of what I think truth, that some things, nay strong things can be adduced against it. There are objections, and grave objections, to the simplest truths, and the cause of Truth gains by their being stated clearly and considered carefully.[204]

He knew perfectly well that the reason why Pusey was not a Catholic was because he did not see the necessity of communion with the Pope. And he could sympathize with that, because this was '*not* the consideration which made me a Catholic, but the visible fact that the modern Roman Communion was the heir and the image of the primitive Church'.[205]

Unfortunately, the activities of extremists like Ward were hardly calculated to draw Anglicans to the Church. Apart from anything else, they tended to destroy the 'aboriginal, unanswerable note in favour of Catholicism', its clarity and definiteness of belief. Of course, it was true that there had always been 'furious' debates among theologians ('and it is in this way, out of the collision of flint and steel, that the light of truth has been struck and elicited'); what was extraordinary and new was that controversy should pass from the theological schools (which no longer existed) to periodicals run by self-taught lay theologians 'with an appeal to the private judgment of all readers'. The Jesuits agreed with Ward's theological opinions, but they did not call their opponents heretics. It was almost as bad, Newman lamented with understandable exaggeration, as living at the time of the Arian heresy. Infallibility had never been an important issue for him, but he was prepared to go further than Ryder in allowing that this infallibility extended to dogmatic facts 'because all our faith is in concrete doctrine, not abstract merely'. But, he was careful to add, 'this is only *my* view'.[206]

At the beginning of August he received a letter from Manning expressing a wish to resume friendly relations and to clear up any misunderstandings that might have arisen. Newman knew that the Archbishop could truthfully deny that he had played any direct role in the Oxford affair; others had acted on his behalf. He wrote back that it

---

[204] Ibid. 284. [205] Ibid. 288. [206] Ibid. 274–6.

was a 'duty of friendship' to tell him that it was not his ecclesiastical policy (of which he disapproved) that had caused Newman's change of feeling towards him, but 'a distressing mistrust' (which was 'a general feeling') 'that you are difficult to understand'. There was no point in their meeting, as Manning had suggested: 'It is only as time goes on, that new deeds can reverse the old. There is no short cut to a restoration of confidence, when confidence has been seriously damaged.'[207] Of course, Newman knew that he appeared to put himself 'in the wrong' by refusing to meet him—'but I seriously think it would do more harm than good. I do not trust him, and his new words would be the cause of fresh distrust.'[208] Manning replied that he felt exactly the same about Newman and it was a feeling that others shared, which he could not describe better than by using Newman's own words: 'I have felt you difficult to understand, and that your words have not prepared me for your acts.'[209] Frederick Oakeley (now a priest of the Westminster diocese, having with Newman become a Catholic in October 1845) also received a letter from the Archbishop. Manning gave Oakeley, who had offered himself as an intermediary, his reasons for his lack of confidence in Newman. The latter in turn sent his reply to Oakeley. The chief point at issue was an article in the *Rambler* for 1862 attacking a pamphlet by Manning on the subject of the Temporal Power; Manning claimed that not only was it discourteous, but that somebody closely connected with the *Rambler* had stated that the article had been seen and approved before publication by Newman, a fact which 'became extensively known, and was the first cause of the constant contrast of his name, and mine in private and public'.[210] Newman rejoined that not only did he know nothing of the article, but it was only 'extensively' known to 'the endemic gossip of London, which happily never reaches Birmingham, or is widely effective'.[211] It was significant that Manning should so easily have believed that he was still in 1862 closely involved in a periodical that had been severely censured by the bishops. He had told Oakeley that if Manning really wanted a reconciliation then he should arrange for the 'secret instruction' to be rescinded; Manning, of course, ignored the suggestion, pointing out he had always been opposed to Catholics going to Oxford and that therefore he had never been in favour of the proposed Oratory or of Newman going there. It was something of an achievement, Newman drily noted, to have elicited at least this admission from the careful Archbishop. The upshot of the exchange, Newman felt, was that it had 'increased as well as defined our antagonism', although he was glad he had had the opportunity of speaking his mind.[212]

[207] *LD* xxiii. 290.   [208] Ibid. 296.   [209] Ibid. 305.
[210] Ibid. 306.   [211] Ibid. 322.   [212] Ibid. 330.

The English bishops had told Propaganda in May that they were opposed to a formal prohibition of Catholics going to non-Catholic universities, for the sake of Protestant undergraduates who were converted; they merely wanted a repetition of the instruction to the clergy to dissuade as far as possible parents from sending their sons there. Manning was naturally anxious for something more explicit; and in August Propaganda ordered the hierarchy to issue pastoral letters warning Catholics of the grave moral danger of attending Protestant universities. Bishop Ullathorne had published the correspondence relevant to the proposed Oxford Oratory to vindicate Newman's position; Newman appreciated his goodwill, but he could not help feeling that 'to stand well with people at Rome supersedes in his mind every other wish. So he is a coward.' For a few weeks in June and July Oratorians from Birmingham had looked after the Oxford mission while the priest there was ill. But without Newman (who was also needed in the school) it would be impossible to undertake the mission properly. Newman's health, too, was again giving grounds for anxiety; there were disturbing symptoms suggesting the recurrence of his last serious illness, when he had felt after 'it was passed and over . . . overcome as the drunken man who next morning went to see the leap his horse had taken the night before with him in the dark'.[213]

On 18 August he formally resigned the Oxford mission; he told Ullathorne he was only acting on the resolve which he had formed when he first heard of the 'secret instruction'. The bishop replied that he completely understood his decision and deeply deplored the campaign of vilification against him at Rome; but he had to point out that the conclusion to Newman's letter to Barnabò had not helped those who had tried to defend him. Newman confided to St John that it was quite possible the school would be closed or he would be summoned to Rome—perhaps even the Oratory itself was in danger. No doubt Propaganda had interpreted his protest to Barnabò as a sign that he 'meant to turn Protestant. It is quite certain that, any one, who chooses to tell any lie about me at Rome, will find a willing ear in the highest quarters.' Neve, the Rector of the English College, had just been removed by Manning with Talbot's help, because he was 'a Newmanite'.[214] But it seemed the Ultramontane party was nervous. There was fear of an opposition party emerging, particularly among the French bishops. On 23 August Mgr. Nardi, a high Vatican official, called at the Oratory. Newman wrote an amusing account of his Italian visitor's diplomatic skills:

[213] Ibid. 296.   [214] Ibid. 316.

I was a great man—no denying it—a great writer—good style—good strong logic—my style went very easily into Italian—it was a classical style. Of course I had my enemies—they are in England or Englishmen—but all Catholics, to speak as a whole, were my friends. He did not speak from flattery—no—he always spoke his mind, even to the Pope . . . There were things in what I had written which he did not like . . . about a people's religion being a corrupt religion—But perhaps this vehemence of writing could not be helped. I had very good friends. Fr St John was a good friend of mine, very—and a great gentleman. Cardinal Cullen was a good friend, yes—a very good friend . . . I ought to send persons from time to time to explain things . . . I ought to go to Rome myself. It would rejoice the Holy Father—I ought to be a bishop, archbishop—yes, yes—I ought, I ought—yes, a very good bishop—it *is* your line, it *is*, it *is*—it was no good my saying it was not.

I ought to take the part of the Pope. 'We have *very* few friends' he said—'very few'—he spoke in a very grave earnest mournful tone . . .

What we wanted in England for Catholics was education . . . There was no chance of a Catholic University. He seemed to agree with me that London was as bad as Oxford—worse, he had been in the neighbourhood of (I think) Charing Cross lately in the evening, no priest could walk there—no—he was obliged to call a cab.

. . . He wanted my photograph. I gave him two.

These overtures 'brought out both the extremity to which [the Ultra] party is reduced and their wish, or his wish rather, to get me, very strongly'.[215]

At the beginning of September, however, Newman felt the force of the iron fist inside the Roman velvet glove. He received a letter from Barnabò in reply to one he had sent in connection with St John's mission. With singular ungraciousness, as Ullathorne remarked, the Cardinal Prefect of Propaganda took the opportunity to inform Newman that his school was still on trial and had not yet been approved because of the likelihood of its encouraging boys to go on to Oxford. Obviously, Rome considered it to be a remarkable coincidence that 'on the one hand a new school should have been set up, professedly founded on the type of Protestant public schools, and on the other a desire to send to Oxford springing up in the minds of Catholic parents'.[216] It seemed likely in the end that the school would be closed down, if only to keep Newman out of Catholic education. Not only had the school had a marked effect on Catholic education (which was resented by other schools and viewed with suspicion by Rome, merely because it was innovative), but it had given the Birmingham Oratory an important sphere of influence. There was another threat from a different quarter: not only had the Jesuits started a new school at Beaumont, near Windsor, which, with a better situation and lower fees, was already

---

[215] *LD* xxiii. 318–19.   [216] Ibid. 334.

larger in numbers than the undersubscribed Oratory School, but now they were contemplating a college of higher studies, which would no doubt draw away boys over 17 who had stayed on at the Oratory School. The idea was to combine lay students with Jesuit scholastics studying philosophy and theology. The Jesuit provincial wondered if clerical students might suffer from the secular contact. Newman wondered if parents would want to send their sons 'to a sort of Jesuit noviceship'—or whether the young men themselves would want it. Years before, he had heard of a similar experiment in Italy from the Rector of the College of Propaganda; mischievously he wondered whether certain leading political despoilers of the Papal States had been amongst the pious lay youths praised so enthusiastically by Father Bresciani. To force young men destined for careers in the world to study scholastic textbooks alongside aspiring clerics was manifestly absurd. It was a pity the ecclesiastical authorities behaved like strict, unimaginative parents forbidding an imprudent engagement when 'it may be a greater madness to prohibit it'. It was the old principle he had so often enunciated in Dublin.

It does not do to beat the life out of a youth—the life of aspiration excitement and enthusiasm. Older men live by reason habit and self-control, but the young live by visions. I can fancy cases in which Oxford would be the salvation of a youth; when he would be far more likely to rise up against authority, murmur against his superiors, and (more) to become an unbeliever, if he is kept from Oxford than if he is sent there.[217]

Ullathorne's pastoral against Catholics attending non-Catholic universities was issued in October. The uneasy reluctance of most of the bishops to act on the directive from Rome was reflected in Bishop Brown's less than flattering reference to Manning in a letter to Ullathorne: 'No one can have witnessed the behaviour of our Chief in Rome when he has higher ecclesiastics in the room, without being afraid of intrigues.'[218] Newman himself was disgusted by Manning's most recent attempt through a pastoral letter to impose 'extreme views . . . all with a view of anticipating and practising upon the judgments of the Bishops . . . Of course what the General Council speaks is the word of God—but still we may feel indignant at the intrigue, trickery, and imperiousness which is the human side of its history.'[219] Far warmer in praise of the Archbishop was, ironically, Newman's free-thinking brother Francis, who had shared the platform with Manning at a meeting in Manchester, when he spoke against the drink trade. Delighted to find seemingly some common ground with his brother, he was disappointed by the laconic reply he received: 'As to what you tell

[217] Ibid. 366.   [218] Ibid. 332 n. 1.   [219] Ibid. 367.

me of Archbishop Manning, I have heard that some also of our Irish bishops think that too many drink-shops are licensed. As for me, I do not know whether we have too many or too few.'[220] (Newman's misgivings in fact were at least partly based on his antipathy to the separation of morality from religion, as is clear from his response over a decade later to the proposal that local Catholic clergy should co-operate in the temperance movement, when he complained: 'since 1827, there has been a formidable movement among us towards assigning in the national life political or civil motives for social and personal duties, and thereby withdrawing matters of conduct from the jurisdiction of religion. Men are to be made virtuous . . . on purely secular motives. We are having a wedge thrust into us, which tends to the destruction of religion altogether; and this is our misery that there is no definite point at which we can logically take our stand, and resist encroachment on principle.'[221])

At the end of October Newman recorded in his private journal that, like Job, his complaints were now finally

ended too—I have said to Cardinal Barnabò 'Viderit Deus [God will see to it].' I have lodged my cause with Him—and, while I hope ever by His grace to be obedient, I have now as little desire, as I have hope, to gain the praise of such as him in any thing I shall do henceforth. Faber and others have been too much for me. They have too deeply impressed the minds of authorities at Rome against me, to let the truth about me have fair play while I live; and when one ceases to hope, one ceases to fear. They have done their worst—and, as Almighty God in 1864 cleared up my conduct in the sight of Protestants at the end of twenty years, so as regards my Catholic course, at length, after I am gone hence, Deus viderit! I did not use the words lightly, though they seem to have rested most unfortunately on his mind (C. Barnabò's)—nor do I dream of retracting them.

He allowed that his new calm resignation was not without an element of cynicism—'I fear that in one sense the iron has entered into my soul. I mean that confidence in any superiors whatever never can blossom again within me.' But 'since I do not want to initiate any new plan of any kind', he hoped now 'they would keep their hands off me'. He was ready for his part to 'obey them, as Scribes and Pharisees were to be obeyed, as God's representatives'—although, as he remarked tartly on a later occasion, 'they don't like any appeal which implies there is any power in heaven or earth greater than themselves.' As for the frustrations like that of the Oxford scheme, he could honestly say they had actually increased his own 'inward happiness':

I never was in such simply happy circumstances as now . . . I am my own master—I have my time my own—I am surrounded with comforts and

---

[220] *LD* xxiii. 363.   [221] Ibid. xxviii. 363–4.

conveniences—I am in easy circumstances, I have no cares, I have good health—I have no pain of mind or body. I enjoy life only too well. The weight of years falls on me as snow, gently tho' surely, but I do not feel it yet. I am surrounded with dear friends—my reputation has been cleared by the Apologia.[222]

The year ended with the surprise news that the liberal Bishop Dupanloup of Orleans wished to take Newman as his personal theologian to the Council. 'I cannot sufficiently thank him. His act is one of a noble independent Bishop, who dares do what he thinks right.' With the exception of Bishop Clifford of Clifton, such courage was not to be looked for among the English bishops.

But I can't accept . . . *I am too old for it* . . . I think the Roman diet would most seriously compromise my health . . . Then again there are men, and some of them have been Saints, whose vocation does not lie in such ecclesiastical gatherings. St Gregory Nazianzen, and St Chrysostom, not to say St Basil, are instances . . . I am their disciple. I am too old to learn the ways of other great Saints, as St Athanasius, St Augustine, and St Ambrose, whom I admire, but cannot run with. They are race-horses—I am a broken-kneed poney.[223]

[222] *AW* 262–3; *LD* xxvi. 8. [223] *LD* xxiii. 396.

16

The Justification of Religious Belief

At the beginning of January 1868 Newman published a collected volume of his poetry. *Verses on Various Occasions* was favourably received by both Catholic and Protestant reviewers. The change in public opinion, which had begun with the success of the *Apologia*, made him feel rather nervous, 'as if a nemesis would come, if I am not careful'. As for the hostility of Manning and Propaganda, 'I should be so out of my element if I were without that cold shade on the side of ecclesiastical authority, in which I have dwelt nearly all my life, my eyes would be so dazed, and my limbs so relaxed, were I brought out to bask in the full sun of ecclesiastical favour, that I should not know how to act and should make a fool of myself.' Musing on the remarkable change in the public attitude towards him, Newman wondered what the Providential significance of it might be. Perhaps his writings would now begin to have an influence, or perhaps his name was 'to be turned to account as a sanction and outset by which others, who agree with me in opinion, should write and publish instead of me, and thus begin the transmission of views in religious and intellectual matters congenial with my own, to the generation after me'.[1] Ignatius Ryder, for example, had just brought out a second pamphlet against Ward. It was a subject Newman had himself, of course, intended once to deal with. But it was eminently suitable that the dogmatic monopoly Ward enjoyed in the *Dublin Review* should now be challenged by a member of Newman's Oratory. On the other hand, friends and well-wishers were constantly urging him to write on various subjects. Actually he already knew what his next book was likely to be about: 'The chance is, if I work any thing more, it would be on some metaphysical point, which half the world would not read, and the other half would differ from.'[2]

Back in 1851[3] he had recorded how for twenty years he had 'been working on towards a philosophical polemic, suited to these times'.[4] He continued to do so, in spite of all his other preoccupations and problems.

[1] *AW* 264–5.   [2] *LD* xxiv. 26.

[3] The following account as well as the later discussion of the *Grammar of Assent* are based on part of the introduction to my critical edition of *An Essay in aid of a Grammar of Assent* (Oxford, 1985).

[4] *LD* xiv. 206.

Two years later he seriously thought of writing 'a work embodying all the principles I have implied in my books'.[5] By 1859 this had turned into the more modest plan of 're-issuing' the *Oxford University Sermons* 'with a new Preface, drawing up what I have said in it into propositions with something of system'.[6] At the beginning of 1860 he exchanged letters on the possibility of certainty in religious belief with William Froude, whose wife and children had become Catholics. He told him he had 'long meditated' on the problem and was 'habitually praying to God to direct me whether to take up the line of subjects on which it lies, or to devote my remaining years to some other undertaking'.[7] When Froude urged him to take up the subject, he commented:

It is a cause of great sadness to me, when I look back at my life, to consider how my time has been frittered away, and how much I might have done, had I pursued one subject. Had not each year brought its own duties, I should have turned to the subject . . . long ago—but it is not one to be taken up by halves, and now, how many years have I![8]

He felt at this point '*more* inclined to do *something or other* on the subject, but *less* certain whether or not to re-issue the Sermons': if he 'wrote a new work, it would be on "the popular, practical, and personal evidence of Christianity—" i.e. as contrasted to the scientific, and its object would be to show that a given individual, high or low, has as much right (has as real rational grounds) to be certain, as a learned theologian who knows the scientific evidence'.[9]

During the first half of 1860, as his theological papers show, he wrote more on the problem of certainty, but the attempts came to nothing, as he was simply too 'overworked'.[10] In 1861 he admitted wearily that while for 'years and years, indeed, I have wished to write on Faith and Reason', unfortunately 'the good time for it has never come, and now I am too old; too weary, too weak, and too busy'.[11] Three years later he wondered if he would ever write the book he so much wanted to write: the subject was so complex, and he found difficulty anyway in writing 'without an urgent or compulsive force applied to me'.[12] He continued to draft papers on certainty, but 'each in turn intermitted by the stress of little work or odd jobs'.[13]

The book which he had first begun to write in the *Oxford University Sermons*, and which he had attempted 'more times than I can count', was so hard it was 'like tunnelling through the Alps'. Paradoxically, though, the 'beginning' of his 'success' dated from 1866, 'when in Switzerland'.[14]

At last, when I was up at Glion over the lake of Geneva, it struck me 'You are

---

[5] Ibid. xv. 381.   [6] Ibid. xix. 256.   [7] Ibid. 272.   [8] Ibid. 284.
[9] Ibid. 294.   [10] Ibid. 360.   [11] Ibid. 500.   [12] Ibid. xxi. 245.
[13] Ibid. xxii. 175.   [14] Ibid. xxv. 35.

wrong in beginning with certitude—certitude is only a kind of assent—you should begin with contrasting assent and inference.'[15]

When he went on his Swiss holiday in August 1866, he had taken with him some notes made the previous year for the projected work on certitude. But now at length he found 'the point from which to begin'— even if 'the work was not less like tunnelling than before'.[16] It was not that his 'fundamental ideas' had not been 'ever the same', but 'I could not carry them out'.[17] Now he thought he had discovered 'the clue, the "Open Sesame", of the whole subject'.[18] He must begin with assent, not certitude. A letter written on 12 August from Champéry contains the first unmistakable reference to what was to become the *Grammar of Assent*: 'I have done some certitude—little enough in quantity—but, (unless my whole theory be a maresnest, of which I am not sure) good in quality. I can do it when lying down, or travelling.'[19]

Over the years he had slowly but steadily continued to develop the central insights of the *Oxford University Sermons*, the most 'original' of which he thought was the argument that 'antecedent probability is the great instrument of conviction in religious (nay in all) matters'.[20] It was, he claimed, the way 'you convert factory girls as well as philosophers'.[21] In the *Essay on the Development of Christian Doctrine*, he spoke of a 'collection of weak evidences' which 'makes up a strong evidence', and 'a converging evidence' amounting to 'proof'. He also referred to 'a prudent judgment' which decides when probability is sufficient for conviction.[22] In 1846 he argued that 'the measure of probability necessary for certainty' must vary 'with the individual mind'.[23] But his encounters with theologians at Rome during 1846–7 made him acutely aware of the Church's insistence on 'a rational faith . . . built upon right reason'. And he began to wonder if this might not 'be the result of converging probabilities, and a cumulative proof' from 'cumulating probabilities'.[24] Non-logical truths, he argued, were reached 'not by one direct simple and sufficient proof' through a syllogism, 'but by a complex argument consisting of accumulating and converging probabilities'.[25] The 'proof of Religion', he wrote in 1861, using a striking analogy, 'I liken . . . to the mechanism of some triumph of skill . . . where all display is carefully avoided, and the weight is ingeniously thrown in a variety of directions, upon supports which are distinct from, or independent of each other.'[26] Or, as he explained by another analogy, 'The best illustration . . . is that of a *cable* which is made up of a number of separate threads, each feeble, yet together as sufficient as an iron rod',

[15] *AW* 270.　　　[16] *LD* xxv. 35.　　　[17] Ibid. 29.
[18] Ibid. 199.　　　[19] Ibid. xxii. 274.　　　[20] Ibid. xi. 293.
[21] Ibid. xv. 381.　　　[22] *Dev.* 107, 123, 115, 327.　　　[23] *LD* xi. 289.
[24] Ibid. xv. 457–8.　　　[25] *TP* i. 19.　　　[26] *LD* xix. 460.

the latter of which 'represents mathematical or strict demonstration'.²⁷ Or again, the cumulation of probabilities is like a 'bundle of sticks, each of which . . . you could snap in two, if taken separately from the rest'.²⁸ In the *Apologia*, Newman explained how in his Anglican writings he had 'tried to complete' Keble's version of Bishop Butler's famous dictum that 'probability is the guide of life', with 'its tendency to destroy . . . absolute certainty', by arguing that 'absolute certitude' in religion is 'the result of an *assemblage* of concurring and converging probabilities'.²⁹

The idea of 'cumulating probabilities' leading to 'subjective certainty' had been suggested in a seminal 1848 paper entitled 'On the Certainty of Faith'. This forty-page manuscript contains further thoughts on certainty which Newman proceeded to develop during the next few years. For example, in a sermon of 1849, he wrote:

Conviction is a state of mind, and it is something beyond and distinct from the mere arguments of which it is the result; it does not vary with their strength or their number. Arguments lead to a conclusion, and when the arguments are stronger, the conclusion is clearer; but conviction may be felt as strongly in consequence of a clear conclusion, as of one which is clearer.³⁰

It is not, as he put it in a letter of the same year, 'the mere perception of a conclusion, for then it would vary about with the strength of the premisses'.³¹

By 1853 the term 'assent' had acquired a firm place in Newman's philosophical vocabulary: '*Assent* is the acceptance of a proposition as true.' The crucial distinction between assent and inference is also clearly grasped: 'Assent follows on inference, and that *by an act of the will*.' (He held, needless to say, to the traditional Catholic teaching that 'reason proves that Catholicism *ought to be* believed, and that in that form it comes before *the Will*, which accepts it or rejects it, as moved by grace or not', with the corollary that faith 'is not a conclusion from premises, but the result of an act of the *will*, following upon a *conviction* that to believe is a *duty*'.³²) In contradistinction, certainty is 'an assent of the intellect to an assent', and since 'an assent does not admit of degrees, neither does certainty'. But if 'we cannot be more or less *certain* of a truth', still 'we can be certain of it with more vigour, keenness, and directness', a distinction which seems to anticipate the later contrast between the 'notional' and the 'real'. These fragmentary 1853 drafts also distinguish between reasoning which is involved in 'demonstration' or 'proof', and the reasoning which is associated with faith and which is called 'judgment'. This latter is 'the action of the individual mind' which operates by 'practical expertness' rather than by 'rule'. The possession of this

²⁷ Ibid. xxi. 146. ²⁸ Ibid. xxiv. 146. ²⁹ *Apo.* 30–1.
³⁰ *Mix.* 234. ³¹ *LD* xiii. 267. ³² Ibid. xii. 289, 228.

judgement 'in one subject matter is no guarantee for a person's possessing it in another'. Thus it was Newton's 'judgment' in mathematics that enabled him to ascertain his great discoveries before he could prove them. In religious belief, on the other hand, judgement may be exercised by people of all kinds, although the educated require a 'far greater' power of judgement in proportion to their greater knowledge.[33] In a paper of 1860, Newman insisted that 'faith must rest on reason, nay even in the case of children and of the most ignorant and dull peasant'; but he was no less emphatic that 'the faith and reason, of which I speak, are subjective, private, personal, and unscientific'.[34] Although the famous term 'illative sense' does not occur prior to the *Grammar*, he does use the Greek word *phronesis* (or judgement) in his philosophical notebook (in 1865) for the 'wisdom in determining *when* we ought to be certain', which includes assembling and evaluating the arguments.[35]

The year 1865 saw important developments in the concept of what Newman now called 'certitude'. The parallel with conscience is suggested, 'which judges by a sort of instinct derived from moral practice, and reasons without scientific generalizations'. It is as impossible to live without conscience as it is 'without some exercise of certitude'. But, like breathing, acts of certitude and conscience 'are free and depend upon our will'. Both certitude and conscience may turn out to be false, but there is no 'test' to discriminate. However, the possibility of making a mistake is no excuse for not adhering to certitude and conscience. And Newman emphasizes that acts of certitude 'generally succeed', and that even when they do not they 'are more consistent with our nature and our position in the world than a simple suspense of assent'.[36] Certitude is now clearly defined as 'an assent deliberate, unconditional, and conscious, to a proposition as true'. This does not mean that we cannot 'allow that in the abstract it is possible that we are wrong'. But there can be no 'degrees' of certitude. The key distinction between assent and inference is again implied when Newman writes that certitude, which is 'already a full assent', 'cannot be immediately dependent on the reasons which are its antecedents', unlike 'conclusions', which 'may be strengthened' by further arguments. Additional evidence cannot make one more certain if one is already certain, but equally, a cast-iron proof may not entail assent, since assent is a personal act. Certitude 'is not the passive admission of a conclusion as necessary, but the recognition of it as true'.[37]

The realization in August 1866 that certitude was only a kind of assent and that the crucial distinction was between assent and inference marks

---

[33] *TP* i. 11, 31–2, 20, 22, 24–5, 29.			[34] Ibid. 86, 84.			[35] *Phil. N.* ii. 163.
[36] *TP* i. 121–2.						[37] Ibid. 122–4, 126.

the beginning of nearly four years of laborious work on the *Grammar of Assent*. Newman's gradual but slow progress can be traced from the various drafts that are extant. He continued writing on his return to England, but the following eventful year of 1867 provided little leisure for philosophical thought. What was to become the first part of the *Grammar* did not begin to take final shape till the spring of 1868. Once again, it seems, he decided that he had been premature in dealing with certitude, on which he had already sketched out a chapter, but which was now deferred for treatment in the second part of the book.

2

Newman could not help but be conscious of the increasing secularization of society. Even the disestablishment of the Church of Ireland, which Gladstone was advocating and which would become law in 1869, aroused some unease in him, welcome of course as it was in other obvious ways. The fact was that the world was rapidly changing, and nobody could predict the consequences. True, people had exaggerated the dangers of the first Reform Bill. And now Newman, with typical realism, admitted that he was prepared, however grudgingly, to acquiesce in the necessity even of a secular school system—although he was, 'as a matter of principle, utterly opposed to education without religion', and had 'opposed projects tending that way for the greater part of my life'. Forty years earlier, the passing of the Test and Corporation Acts had marked the end of the theoretical union of Church and State. Compulsory secular education now seemed inevitable. Certainly, it was 'cowardly to abandon a principle which you uphold as good and true, because you have suffered one or two defeats in maintaining it—but surely the time may come, after a long warfare steadily carried out in successive great reverses and uniform disappointments of your hopes, when it is . . . unwise and . . . headstrong to continue the war'. Characteristically, he added that it was all 'very well for the Holy See, which is divinely intended to be the principle of immobility to continue its protests and to spurn the notion of concurrence or compromise; but that as little makes it its duty to forbid local hierarchies, according to their greater insight into local necessities, to act on their discretion, and as little justifies local hierarchies to refuse to political expedience what they cannot in principle originate or approve, what the Holy See cannot sanction, and must ignore . . .'.[38] There were other considerations which would set in a new light the abandonment by the Church of its traditional insistence on

[38] *LD* xxiv. 31–2.

Catholic schools. Separate church schools encouraged anti-Catholic bigotry, as well as being a heavy burden on the parishes, which after all could arrange religious instruction for children on Sundays, as had to be done in parts of Italy. Otherwise, the likelihood was that Catholics would not only have to support their own parochial schools without state aid, but would also have to pay taxes for schools which they could not use. No one was more insistent than Newman on ideals and principles, but no one was more ruthlessly and radically pragmatic in practice.

So far as religious belief was concerned, he was convinced that the serious intellectual threat came from 'hard-headed logicians', particularly 'if they address themselves to the young and mentally unformed'. Conscious of his own work, he wrote to one correspondent: 'An evil time is before us. Principles are being adopted as starting points, which contradict what we know to be axioms. It follows that the only controversy which is likely to do good, is *philosophical*.'[39] But he was confident that, just as in its beginning Christianity had triumphed over the force of persecution, so now it would triumph over the reason of the world (as indeed it had also had to do in the time of St Paul, and not with total success by any means). He was even less worried by scientific objections. Darwinism, for example, was not necessarily atheistic: 'It does not seem to me to follow that creation is denied because the Creator, millions of years ago, gave laws to matter.'[40] He could not see why evolution, any more than human generation, was incompatible with the doctrine of creation. As for Adam being literally created from dust, the Bible also said that all men are created from dust, and seemed to say that the sun goes round a stationary earth. Again, there might well have been a 'pre-adamite man' with reason but without conscience, and therefore without 'a natural knowledge of God, till he had a revelation', since 'all the mental faculties are but latent, till elicited by external means, as invisible ink is brought out by heat.' Christianity was certainly 'on trial', but he knew of no objection such that he 'could not fancy either that a fuller investigation would countermine it, or that the original mine when sprung would end in an abortive explosion'; whatever the 'residium of truth' in the objections, 'the greater part of it will vanish before long like the froth and spray of the breakers on a coast'.[41]

In May Newman sent (somewhat cryptic) congratulations to Gerard Manley Hopkins, who had decided to become a Jesuit:

I think it is the very thing for you. You are quite out, in thinking that when I offered you a 'home' here, I dreamed of your having a vocation for us. This I

---

[39] *LD* xxiv. 74.   [40] Ibid. 77.   [41] Ibid. xxi. 394–6.

clearly saw you had *not*, from the moment you came to us. Don't call 'the Jesuit discipline hard', it will bring you to heaven. The Benedictines would not have suited you.[42]

Hopkins had joined the staff at the Oratory School the preceding September. Thomas Arnold too was no longer on the staff, but for different reasons. He had left after three years in 1865, and was now at Oxford taking private pupils. Newman's delight at his conversion had turned into disappointment:

He is a very good amiable fellow, but weak and henpecked. His wife is a Xantippe. From Australia, before he was received there, she sent me two abusive letters, and vowed he never should be a Catholic. When he was received there, she threw a brick through the Church window. When I gave him a professorship at Dublin, she was still unmittigated—and when he came to Edgbaston, she used to nag, nag, nag him, till he almost lost his senses. She preached against Catholicism to her children, and made them unmanageable. Tho' we gave him a large salary, she took care to make him feel he had nothing, and was out at elbows. He did not take enough to eat and to drink—and got ill . . . He is a non-practising Catholic, if he is any thing . . . I fear he *never* has had *faith*.[43]

On 16 June Newman, accompanied by Ambrose St John, paid a last, nostalgic visit to Littlemore. He had always wanted to 'see it once before I died'. When he saw the monument to his mother, he wept. It was forty years since he had gone to the parish. Some people, not surprisingly, remembered him better than he remembered them. It was gratifying to see the fruits of his own planting all those years ago: the village looked quite '*green*'. It was twenty-two years since he had left: 'It was a most strange vision—I could hardly believe it real. It was the past coming back, as it might in the intermediate state.'[44]

Unhappily, old friends who had died could never be seen again. The death of Edward Badeley was

a heavy, sudden, unexpected blow—I shall not see him now, till I cross the stream which he has crossed. How dense is our ignorance of the future, a darkness which can be felt, and the keenest consequence and token of the Fall. Till we remind ourselves of what we are,—in a state of punishment,—such surprises makes us impatient, and almost angry, alas![45]

He comforted Isy Froude, William Froude's eldest daughter, on the early death of her brother with the consolation that God 'takes away our loved ones as hostages, that we may be compelled, even by our earthly affections, to lift up our hearts to Him'.[46]

[42] Ibid. xxiv. 73. [43] Ibid. 34. [44] Ibid. 89, 94.
[45] Ibid. 56. [46] Ibid. 63.

By the end of July he had completed a draft of what he envisaged as the first of three parts of the projected work. It was on assent: 'As to what I have done, I cannot tell whether it is a Truism, a Paradox, or a Mare'snest.'[47] At last he was occupied on the subject 'I have wished to do all my life'—but 'I have the same fidget about it, as a horseman might feel about a certain five feet stone wall which he passes by means of a gate every day of his life, yet is resolved he must and will some day clear—and at last breaks his neck in attempting.'[48] He told Henry Wilberforce that he knew that 'however honest are my thoughts, and earnest my endeavours to keep rigidly within the lines of Catholic doctrine, every word I publish will be malevolently scrutinized, and every expression which can possibly be perverted sent straight to Rome,—that I shall be fighting *under the lash*, which does not tend to produce vigorous efforts in the battle or to inspire either courage or presence of mind'. Not only did he feel surrounded by 'a host of ill wishers', but the subject was difficult, and he tired easily at his age. Nor was his time all his own: there were barely enough priests to cover the various works of the Oratory, with the result that the 'great *domestic* works, the care of the Library, the Sacristy, the Accounts, necessarily in great measure fall to me, at least at intervals'.[49] He also confided to Wilberforce his astonishment two years before to find himself cut dead in the street in London by William Anderdon, Manning's nephew and now secretary, who had come under Newman's influence at Oxford, and after becoming a Catholic had worked for him in Dublin.

News from Ireland of the oppression of the peasantry by unscrupulous landlords prompted Newman to exclaim, 'I don't think there is such a peasant class in the world.' He had heard from Flanagan, now a parish priest there, that practically everybody practised their faith and there was scarcely a crime committed. 'Whatever bitterness there is in them, we are the cause of it, and whether we ever can undo what we have done, is more than any statesman can say.'[50] Elsewhere in Europe, he was aware, the religious situation was very different. He was quite 'prepared for a break up of religion every where, as far as establishment goes, nay as far as consistent profession, but still, as in France and England, so in Italy there will be a remnant, the purer in that it is smaller'. The kind of 'close despotic system' which resulted from the establishment of Catholicism as the state religion of Italy did 'not suit this age of the world, and, however dreadful sacrilege and blasphemy are, I cannot weep that there is a prospect of its being broken up'. In England, he felt the Methodists were 'more likely to make a stand against infidelity' than any other church—'narrow-minded, self-sufficient, and conceited' as

---

[47] *LD* xxiv. 104.   [48] Ibid. 112.   [49] Ibid. 121.   [50] Ibid. 127.

they were. They at least appeared homogeneous and united, he told Pusey, unlike the poor, divided Church of England. The Catholic Church, he felt, was like Noah's Ark, which 'did not hinder or destroy the flood but rode upon it, preserving the hopes of the human family within its fragile planks'.[51]

Meanwhile, the Ultramontane obsession with defining papal infallibility was upsetting converts and discouraging others from joining the Church. Newman himself held 'the Pope's formal definitions of faith to be infallible', but only as a theological opinion not as a dogma, as a probability not as a certainty. He wrote to congratulate the author of a pamphlet which argued against the doctrine from the circumstances concerning the notorious condemnation of Pope Honorius. He was delighted at any opposition to the extreme party, whose control over the Catholic press was still further consolidated at the end of 1868 when the *Tablet* passed into the control of Herbert Vaughan. He was not, however, convinced by the argument: although the Honorius case was certainly a grave objection, it still on balance seemed to him 'the least of difficulties to maintain that, if we knew *all about* Honorius's case, something would be found to turn up to make it compatible with the doctrine'.[52] Whatever the unique teaching authority of the Pope might or might not be, he had to admit to Pusey that the 'routine at Rome is the routine of 1000 years—nay Rome, except in the case of some great Popes, has never shown any great gift of origination'.

Cardinal Barnabò says that only three countries give him trouble—viz. the Turks much, the English more, and the French most. That is to say, routine won't do in those countries. Under these circumstances it is a great thing for him to have an Archbishop like Manning, who makes every thing easy to him, by doing his best to work by routine and to *make* routine work in England.[53]

Disgust, however, with the methods of Roman bureaucracy was one thing; quite another thing was the sober theological recognition that the papacy's primary role was not to initiate, but to conserve: 'The central authority cannot *profess* to relax.' Moves towards Christian unity, for example, he warned Pusey, should come from the local bishops, with Rome reserving the right of veto—'and, if it is *obliged* to speak, it speaks according to the strictest rule of ecclesiastical principle and tradition'. Unfortunately, whereas it was the duty of the English bishops 'to soften difficulties not to increase them', it could not be denied that Manning had done everything in his power to increase them. Again, while it was true that Rome would never make concessions to individual Anglo-Catholics, still, if there was the chance of the reconciliation of a whole

[51] Ibid. 126–7.   [52] Ibid. 91–2.   [53] Ibid. 137–8.

body of people he had no doubt that the Holy See would be prepared to compromise.[54]

On 14 October Newman received a letter from Ullathorne informing him that the Pope had invited him to attend the forthcoming Council as a theological consultor. It was a special mark of favour, but Newman refused. He was busy with the *Grammar of Assent*, and he wanted time to continue sorting out his letters and papers. His experience in Dublin was a 'warning . . . of what will come of my throwing myself into a work foreign to my talents, and among strange persons'. He had never felt at home with ecclesiastical superiors, 'from my shyness, and a sort of nervous continual recollection that I am bound to obey them, which keeps me from being easy with them, speaking my mind without effort, and lucidly and calmly arguing with them'. Nor had he ever 'succeeded with boards or committees. I always have felt out of place, and my words unreal.' There was also his strong sense that he was '*not* a theologian' in the proper, professional sense. Work on a theological committee required 'a strong memory for theological passages and a quick eye in turning over pages—and I have neither'. He joked to Maria Giberne:

Like St Gregory Nazianzen I like going on my own way, and having my time my own, living without pomp or state, or pressing engagements. Put me into official garb, and I am worth nothing; leave me to myself, and every now and then I shall do something. Dress me up and you will soon have to make my shroud—leave me alone, and I shall live the appointed time.

His conclusion was, 'There are some things I *can* do—others that I *can't*. I should, by accepting this invitation, lose my independence and gain nothing.'[55] He hoped that those bishops who, like himself, were opposed to any definition of papal infallibility would have '*facts* to produce'— 'Definite, tangible evidence of the inexpediency of touching the question is what is wanted.'[56]

Towards the end of November Copeland wrote to say that *Parochial and Plain Sermons*, which he was republishing for Newman, were selling extremely well. On rereading them Newman had been disappointed with a number of sermons he had once thought highly of; he was no longer even sure what their relevance was supposed to be. The fact that the volumes were bought even by Nonconformists did not surprise him: it was possible to have different 'ecclesiastical principles' and yet to share 'ethical and religious sentiments'; indeed, he thought that 'the first step towards unity was a unison of feeling', as a 'necessary foundation, on which higher strata of truth might be deposited at some future day'.[57] The important point was that 'Whatever tends to create a unity of heart between men of different communions, lays the ground for advances

---

[54] *LD* xxiv. 78–9.   [55] Ibid. 162, 200, 212–13.   [56] Ibid. 171.   [57] Ibid. 177.

towards a restoration of that visible unity, the absence of which among Christians is so great a triumph, and so great an advantage to the enemies of the Cross.'[58] But to attempt, for example, to reach agreement on the papacy was like building 'St. Peter's from the cross and ball. We must begin from the bottom—not even only from the foundations of the building, but from the soil in which the foundations must be placed.' It would be something to 'succeed merely in this, to contribute to the creation of a sound material on which the stone work of the edifice of faith is to be placed'.[59] This kind of 'levelling up' was important for another reason: 'If we are to convert souls savingly they must have the due preparation of heart, and if England is to be converted, there must be a great move of the national mind to a better sort of religious sentiment.'[60] The 'first step' in the process, Newman thought, was to 'show that there is a true philosophy of religion', such as he himself was attempting in what was to become the *Grammar of Assent*.[61]

The first six volumes of *Parochial and Plain Sermons* were reprinted from the six volumes of *Parochial Sermons*, and the last two from Newman's (fifth) volume in *Plain Sermons*. It was Perrone, the Roman theologian, who had assured him years ago that there was no need to alter the text, provided his own name was not too closely involved in the republication; Copeland's offer to republish the Anglican sermons afforded the appropriate opportunity for a reprint. Such revisions as there were were corrections rather than changes, but Copeland pointed out in his preface that the reproduction of the original text did not imply that Newman still agreed with all that he had once written. In 1869 Copeland also republished *Sermons Bearing on Subjects of the Day* (with a useful list at the end of the dates of all the sermons).

On the last day of November Newman referred again in his journal to 'the wonderful change that has taken place in men's estimation of me'.[62] There was a widespread consciousness of how unfairly he had been treated in the past. Now not only were his Anglican sermons selling extraordinarily well, but the *Dream of Gerontius* was the subject of a lecture by the Professor of Poetry at Oxford. He realized, however, that if his views on the forthcoming Council were to become public, he would be involved in fresh controversy with fellow Catholics.

3

Meanwhile, he was still occupied with the 'one work of a literary kind I want to do'. But, he told Hope-Scott, it was 'like tunnelling through a

---

[58] Ibid. 22.   [59] Ibid. 391.   [60] Ibid. xxv. 3–4.
[61] Ibid. 250.   [62] *AW* 266.

mountain—I have begun it, and it is almost too much for my strength—
it is half theological, half philosophical . . . Perhaps the tunnell will
break in, when I get fairly into my work.' The only other thing he
wanted to do before he died was to put his letters in order, although
there was 'nothing so sad, so piercing as to look over old letters'. 'I used
to say, I will do it before I am sixty, and then I shall be ready for
whatever God wills—now I say, I will do it before I am seventy.'[63]
Although his unfinished book could be said to be on a 'metaphysical
point', he nevertheless refused an invitation from Richard Holt Hutton
to join the newly formed 'Metaphysical Society' in London. The idea
was to include all shades of opinion from Manning to John Stuart Mill.
Newman replied modestly that he had 'no pretensions to receive such an
honour' as it had been his 'misfortune through life to have dabbled in
many things, and to have mastered nothing'; he had 'lived from hand to
mouth, doing nothing but what' he had been 'forced to do'.[64]

This, however, was not true of his present work, which he had chosen
for himself and about which he felt 'sadly discouraged'.[65] He was afraid
that he was going to have to rewrite all or much of what he had thought
was completed. His usual experience was that he was 'obliged to take
great pains with everything I have written, and I often write chapters
over and over again, besides innumerable corrections and interlinear
additions'. Not being 'a good speaker' he had 'to correct laboriously'
what he 'put on paper'. It was not that he had ever

been in the practice since I was a boy of attempting to write well, or to form an
elegant style. I think I never have written for writing sake; but my one and
single desire and aim has been to do what is so difficult—viz. to express clearly
and exactly my meaning; this has been the motive principle of all my
corrections and re-writings. When I have read over a passage which I
had written a few days before, I have found it so obscure to myself that I have
either put it altogether aside or fiercely corrected it; but I don't get any
better for practice. I am as much obliged to correct and re-write as I was thirty
years ago.

When asked about influences on his prose style, he replied, 'the only
master of style I have ever had (which is strange considering the
differences of the languages) is Cicero', to whom he owed 'a great deal'
and 'as far as I know to no one else'. He added significantly, 'His great
mastery of Latin is shown especially in his clearness.'[66]

The general difficulty of religious belief in a sceptical age was not
helped by Ultramontane extremism, which seemed aimed at 'inculcating as necessary to be believed what is not necessary, circumscribing the

[63] *LD* xxiv. 183–4.   [64] Ibid. 225–6.   [65] Ibid. 242.
[66] Ibid. 241–2.

allowable liberty of the mind, at making certain political views as virtually de fide, at tying down Catholic action to what is obsolete and effete, and thereby at unsettling the faith of Catholic youth and talent, and making a dreadful breach between society and religion'.[67] Newman was sensitive to the difficulties of a younger generation of Catholics, like the grown-up children of converts, who had found themselves in the Church rather than found their way to it. But it is striking that he advised, for example, Sir John Simeon's daughter to try 'a course of Tractarianism', and in particular to read his own Anglican *Parochial and Plain Sermons*.[68] This somewhat unexpected recommendation was followed up by the advice both to meditate on the Gospels and also, in order 'to ascertain the starting points for arriving at religious truth', to 'interrogate' the heart or conscience, or, in other words, to interrogate 'the God who dwells there'. The 'attempt to *see*' religious first principles 'by means of the intellect' rather than the conscience, Newman explained, was parallel to the mistake of 'attempting by the intellect to see the physical facts' which are perceived by the senses, which in turn '*enable* the intellect to act, by giving it something to act upon'.[69] The modern insistence on starting with the intellect in religious inquiry, he claimed, was analogous to the medieval Schoolmen's use of syllogistic reasoning in place of empirical observation in scientific investigation.

Newman's opposition to Ultramontanism did not inhibit him from bluntly warning Pusey: 'As to promising that the Church will never increase its definitions, who can say that to the "Spirit who bloweth where He listeth"?' Pusey seemed (if it was not irreverent to say so) to wish 'to bind over the Holy Ghost to keep the peace'.[70] Certainly there was a peace that was greatly preferable to the agitation of extremists, but there was another sort of 'peace' in the sense of immobility, that had always been thoroughly uncongenial to Newman: thus, only a few days before, he had remarked with exasperation of Allies as an historian: 'he always seems in the same place, prancing like a cavalry soldier's horse, without advancing, in the face of a mob.'[71]

At the beginning of July Newman sent Charles Meynell, who was professor of philosophy at Oscott College, the first proofs of the *Grammar of Assent* for his criticism. The book was 'weighing heavy' on his thoughts, he told Edward Bellasis.[72] His anxiety is reflected in several draft prefaces (which were never used) acknowledging that he had not written in the received tradition of scholastic philosophy. Meynell's criticisms seemed to confirm his forebodings. Despairingly, he wrote: 'I have spent so much time and thought upon it, that it comes upon me as another of those great failures which have befallen me for many years,

---

[67] Ibid. 247–8.   [68] Ibid. 248.   [69] Ibid. 275–6.
[70] Ibid. 267–8.   [71] Ibid. 265.   [72] Ibid. 285.

whenever I have attempted any thing for the Catholic cause.'[73] Time and again, he groaned to Henry Wilberforce, 'plan after plan, has crumbled under my hands and come to nought'. He did not feel threatened by Meynell's objections because they actually told against the book, but because they represented the kind of reaction he was likely to receive from Catholic philosophers of religion.

Our theological philosophers are like the old nurses who wrap the unhappy infant in swaddling bands or boards—put a lot of blankets over him—and shut the windows that not a breath of fresh air may come to his skin—as if he were not healthy enough to bear wind and water in due measures. They move in a groove, and will not tolerate any one who does not move in the same. So it breaks upon me, that I shall be doing more harm than good in publishing. What influence should I have with Protestants and Infidels, if a pack of Catholic critics opened at my book fiercely . . .[74]

In the event, although Newman did make some minor corrections as a result of the comments, his worst fears proved to be unfounded and his scholastic critic turned to other, comparatively trivial points. Still, it was a foretaste of the Catholic reviews to come.

Meanwhile, the prospect of a definition of papal infallibility at the impending Council was increasingly occupying Newman's thoughts. He reminded one anxious, bewildered lady, who had felt drawn to Catholicism, that there had been a gradual development in the Church's understanding of the revelation made known to the Apostles. If the infallibility of the Pope were defined, then there would be reasons for its being done now rather than at another time: 'for instance, in the present state of the world, the Catholic body may require to be like an army in the field, under strict and immediate disipline.' True, he himself could see more reasons against a definition than for one, but if it were passed he would then accept as an article of faith what at the moment he only held as a theological opinion. As always, in spite of all the objections to the Church, he fell back upon the reason for his own conversion, 'because the present Roman Catholic Church is *the only Church* which is like, and it is very like, the primitive Church'—'It is almost like a photograph of the primitive Church; or at least it does not differ from the primitive Church near so much as the photograph of a man of 40 differs from his photograph when 20. *You know that it is the same man.*'[75] As for the scandalous lives of Popes, this did not stop them, any more than Balaam or Caiaphas, from speaking religious truth. 'But to say that history is fatal to Roman Catholicism is the saying of one who should recollect that those who live in glass houses should not throw stones at one which has only glass windows, and those of plate glass.'[76]

[73] *LD* xxiv. 306.   [74] Ibid. 316.   [75] Ibid. 325.   [76] Ibid. 330.

He confided to William Monsell, who inquired on behalf of Bishop Dupanloup, that except for Clifford none of the English bishops could be relied on to oppose a definition, although at least two had misgivings; as for Ullathorne, he had the monk's natural instinct of obedience and, although he had no time for the Ultramontane party, he could not be depended on ('he has no spirit, when it comes to the point'). He was confident that if the doctrine were defined, infallibility would be limited to 'evolving' the deposit of faith. Extreme Ultramontanes like Ward, however, placed no such limitations. A very serious situation could arise, therefore, if the French bishops, for example, concentrated on opposing the personal infallibility of the Pope, holding (in accordance with the usual French theological view) that the infallibility of the Church itself had to be extended beyond the development of revelation to include pronouncements on 'dogmatic facts', such as the condemnation of heretical propositions (which, Newman argued, were in fact 'only doctrine *in concreto*'), thus creating an additional '*province* of infallibility'. If papal infallibility were defined with its application extended in this way, the Pope would be given 'an enormous power', since he would not be '*restrained even by the Depositum*'. This was the great danger.[77]

Not surprisingly, one extreme bred another, on which Newman was no less harsh. The famous French Carmelite preacher Father Hyacinthe Loyson published a violent broadside against Ultramontanism. Sympathetic to some extent as Newman obviously was, he was shocked by Loyson's apparent *naïveté* in sending the letter of protest to an ultra-liberal Protestant newspaper. To Miss Holmes Newman sighed, 'but monks always get into scrapes, when they go out of their convents, because they are not men of the world—don't know what's what— mistake chalk for cheese'. But Loyson (who would eventually found his own church) had been worse than simple-minded—'why should he *prejudge* the Council? What an insult to all the Bishops who compose it! and to appeal from the Church to our Lord in a matter of faith is sheer Protestantism. The Church is the *voice* of our Lord.'[78] Deeply perturbed as he might be by the apparently irresistible advance of Ultramontanism, his faith in the *Church* remained unshakeable, as is shown by his eloquent explanation to Mrs Helbert, his worried Anglican correspondent, of the significance of those words of St Augustine which had had so much to do with his own conversion. But not only is it a striking exposition of the Catholicity of the Church, it also anticipates an important new strand in his ecclesiology which was to become more and more prominent in his reaction to the Vatican Council.

—Securus judicat orbis terrarum—'the Christian commonwealth judges

---

[77] Ibid. 327.   [78] Ibid. 346–7.

without misgiving.' That is the maxim . . . on which all depends. The Christian commonwealth is one organized body—from time to time local disturbances rise in it—branches of it rise up separately from the rest, and claim to be heard in matters of discipline or doctrine—they appeal to the Fathers—so did the Donatists, so did the Arians, the Monophysites, the Protestants, the Anglicans—but the Christian State, Commonwealth, Kingdom judicat securus, has the right, the power, the certitude of deciding the rights and the wrongs of the matter. How do we know that Pius ix is true Pope? Securus judicat orbis terrarum. How shall we know that the coming Council is a true Council—but by the after assent and acceptance of it on the part of that Catholic organization which is lineally descended, as one whole, from the first ages?—How can we interpret the decisions of that Council, how the Pope's decisions in any age, except by the Schola Theologorum, the great Catholic school of divines dispersed all over the earth? This is why I am a Catholic— because our Lord set up the Church—and that one Church has been in the world ever since—because in every age bodies have fallen off from her, and have shown in the event that that falling off was death—that they tended to lose all definite faith, *as* bodies . . . the Arians came to nought, and the Donatists— and the Greeks show no signs of life, but remain shut up as if in the sepulchre of the past—and now the Anglican Church is gradually losing any definite faith . . .[79]

The insistence on the reception by the whole Church of the definitive judgements of Councils and Popes, including in particular their interpretation by the theologians, was to form the keynote of Newman's own theology of infallibility in the months and years ahead.

Still he persisted in his resolute refusal to attend the Council, even after repeated requests from Bishop Brown of Newport that he should go as his theological adviser. Finally, he tartly reminded the bishop that the 'prejudice' at Rome against him, which was a sufficient reason for his not going, was due to 'an English Bishop, just ten years ago, who, without a word to me, (which would have settled every thing,) and in spite of the sacred direction, Matth. xviii, 15, denounced a writing of mine to the Authorities' there.[80] To Manning, who also wrote on the eve of his departure for the Council, assuring him that 'the friendship of so many years, though of late unhappily clouded, is still dear to me', Newman repeated simply: 'I do not know whether I am on my head or my heels, when I have active relations with you. In spite of my friendly feelings, this is the judgment of my intellect.'[81] Manning was engaged in a bitter public controversy with a convert called E. S. Ffoulkes (whom he had just excommunicated), into which Newman's name had been dragged. Newman could not 'help being amused' at the melodramatic way in which Ffoulkes had exaggerated the part played by Manning in the delation of *On Consulting the Faithful in Matters of Doctrine*: 'There are

[79] *LD* xxiv. 354–5.   [80] Ibid. 361.   [81] Ibid. 362–3.

those who have been taking matters with a very high hand and with much of silent intrigue for a considerable time, and such ways of going on bring with them their retribution.' Ffoulkes's behaviour was deplorable, but he was 'the "nemesis" . . . of a policy, which I cannot admire'. Nor did he approve of the new *North British Review* which had just appeared—but that too was 'the retributive consequence of tyranny'. He told T. F. Weatherell, its editor, that while he would not expect a Catholic review 'to be religious, or even to profess Catholicity', this new organ of the liberal Catholics gave the impression of being 'written by liberal Scotchmen, religious in a way, who looked at the Church as a fiction of past times'.[82]

Towards the end of November he put down on paper his considered objections to the threatened definition. It was not necessary—there was no heresy to be resisted. Even early Councils which had been necessary had left much confusion and dissension in the wake of their decisions. A definition would lead not only to enormous controversy, but also 'to an alteration of the *elementary constitution* of the Church', because it would encourage the Pope to act alone without the bishops. Finally, because any definition would be 'a retrospective doctrine', it would bring up a host of difficult questions about past papal teachings. 'If any thing', he concluded bitterly, 'could throw religion into confusion, make sceptics, encourage scoffers, and throw back inquirers, it will be the definition of this doctrine.' Any definition would be 'most unseasonable and unwise'. The Church was not 'protected against inexpedient acts'—even if they had to be respected as providential in the sense that God, who could always 'overrule' them, had not prevented them.[83] He could not believe that Manning, fanatical as he was, was under any illusion: 'He says what he thinks, and knows what he is about. I cannot help thinking he holds that the world is soon coming to an end—and that he is in consequence careless about the souls of future generations which will never be brought into being.' It was possible to imagine somebody 'thinking it a grand termination . . . to destroy every ecclesiastical power but the Pope, and let Protestants shift for themselves'.[84]

On 22 November Newman's diary records, 'went out to Rednal to finish my book'.[85] During the fortnight or so he was there he did not complete the *Grammar*, but the end was now in sight. He thought it would 'disappoint friends and opponents when it appears'; it was not on a controversial subject of the day, but on 'a dry logical subject, or semi-logical'.[86] There had been false reports in the papers about what he was writing, which had been followed by the equally false news that it had been 'suppressed for some reason or other'. Ill-wishers had spread

[82] Ibid. 366–7. [83] Ibid. 377–8. [84] Ibid. 379.

[85] Ibid. 381. [86] Ibid. xxv. 19.

the rumour that he was writing on rationalism. 'A lie', he commented drily, 'is like a shuttlecock, which two battledoors can keep up with great success, if skilfully used, without its falling to the ground.'[87] (He had once before remarked that 'nothing has such vitality as a lie—and I have often been astonished how it is capable of being cut in pieces, like some reptiles, yet without substantial injury to its power of action.'[88])

The book would only be a 'small one', but it had taken him 'an immensity of time'. He always said that writing a book was 'like child birth'. He calculated that he had written and rewritten the *Grammar*, or at least a great part of it, 'over ten or fifteen times', perhaps more than any other of his books.[89] He told Edward Bellasis, to whom he was dedicating it, that it would probably be his last book. He thought it was one of the five 'constructive' works he had written—the others being 'My prophetical office (which has come to pieces)—Essay on Justification—Development of Doctrine—University Lectures'. He felt it was the one which had 'tried' him 'most of all'. Although he had 'now got up to' his 'highest point—I mean, I could not do better did I spend a century on it', he had not yet completed the last chapter, in which he was still 'wedged fast' on the eve of Christmas 1869.[90] Jokingly, he compared his work to the recent inauguration of the Suez Canal—'though I have got so far as to let the water in to the canal, there is an awkward rock in mid channel near the mouth which takes a deal of picking and blasting . . . Thus I can't name a day for the opening.'[91] He was but 'a few yards from the shore', he groaned, varying the metaphor, but 'the waves beat me back'.[92] On 16 January 1870 he announced joyfully, but somewhat prematurely, that he had written the last sentence of the book—the 'blasting' was over, but the 'hard work' of correcting and rewriting remained: the work was 'ended, but not finished'.[93] There were sixty or seventy pages of print still to be completed. He had never before felt so uncertain 'of the practical good and use' of anything he had written. There had been times when he had 'been quite frightened lest the labour of thought might inflict on me some terrible retribution at my age.—It is my last work—I say *work* because "work" implies effort—and there are many things I can do without an effort.'[94] For some years he had not had either of his old ailments, a cold or a cough, and he felt in excellent health; his only fear was paralysis if he took on too much work at his age. On 24 January he sent off the last pages and the dedication to the printers. And on 12 February he really did write the very last sentence. 'For twenty years', he told R. H. Hutton, 'I have begun and left off an inquiry again and again . . . but, though my fundamental ideas were

[87] *LD* xxiv. 370.   [88] Ibid. xxii. 266.   [89] Ibid. xxiv. 389.
[90] Ibid. 390–1, 393.   [91] Ibid. xxv. 4.   [92] Ibid. 8.
[93] Ibid. 9.   [94] Ibid. 11.

ever the same, I could not carry them out.'[95] Now at last, after three years of work, he had. He assured Hutton, who was still searching for a religious faith, that he had 'never had a doubt' about Catholicism; 'it has never occurred to me to have a doubt, I could not, without a cruel effort which would be as painful to me as a sin of impurity . . .'.[96]

On 21 February he wrote to thank his sister Jemima for writing on his birthday: 'Birthdays now are like strokes of a passing bell. I am so wonderfully well, that one fancies it may be the rapids before the fall. This cold weather I have used a severe shower bath with nothing but good effect. I have had no cold—and I sleep like a top.' He reiterated that he was sure people would be disappointed by his new book, which would seem 'dry and humdrum'. Although it touched 'on a number of subjects, on which there has been much written in this day', he had carefully refrained from reading other writers, 'because I wished to bring out my own view, and I was sure that, if once I began to read, I should so get confused in the terms and language of others, so mixed up in their controversies, and carried away with the views which they opened, that my own work would vanish'.[97] There was always the danger, of course, of saying what had already been said or refuted by others. The book had run to a hundred pages more than he intended. The hitch over the last chapter had held up the printing, and publication was delayed till the middle of March. Again he warned that it was definitely his 'last work—I say "work," for though I may fiddle-faddle henceforth, a real piece of labour will be beyond me . . . An old horse, or an old piece of furniture will last a long time, if you take care of it—so will the brain—but if you forget that it is old, it soon reminds you of the fact by ceasing to be.'[98] On 15 March the book finally appeared and, to Newman's surprise, was sold out on the first day. It continued to sell extremely well, and before the year was out two further editions had been published.

4

The Catholic response to the *Grammar* was not very helpful. Predictably, it was criticized in the *Month* and the *Tablet* for its obvious lack of conformity with scholastic philosophy. Newman was not very concerned: it was clear to him that syllogistic reasoning would not solve the problem he had attempted to meet. This was also plain to W. G. Ward, who wrote to congratulate Newman, delighted that at least they could agree on their philosophical approach to Christianity. Unfortunately,

---

[95] Ibid. 29.   [96] Ibid. 32.   [97] Ibid. 35–6.   [98] Ibid. 43.

illness prevented him from reviewing the book; but later he was to write that he thought that Newman's approach was substantially the only answer to the problem of the justification of religious belief. In contrast, Richard Simpson, who did review it, was much less enthusiastic, in particular about Newman's treatment of assent.

The reviews in secular journals were not concerned with the absence of scholastic philosophy, but they noted that the *Grammar* was in the tradition of Butler's *Analogy* and the Oriel 'Noetics' rather than of contemporary thought. Naturally there were reservations expressed about the author's Catholicism, but the general reaction was enthusiastic and favourable. Reviewers as different as J. B. Mozley, R. H. Hutton, and J. A. Froude praised the book's originality and subtlety. Where non-Christian (as opposed to high Anglican) critics joined forces with the Catholic reviewers was in criticizing the failure to provide a theory of truth which would enable true certitudes to be distinguished from false certitudes. Newman was well aware that this was the weak point of the book; but it was not exactly a failure, since he had not even attempted to provide one. What, in fact, had he attempted to do?

The *Grammar* is divided into two parts. The first part deals with the relation of assent to apprehension, and seeks to show that it is legitimate to believe what one cannot wholly understand. The opening chapter (which commences with a somewhat disconcerting lack of any introductory explanation) begins by stating the key distinction between assent, which is unconditional, and inference, which is conditional. Apprehension of the terms of a proposition is necessary for assent, but not for inference. Apprehension is something less than understanding, since it is 'simply an intelligent acceptance of the idea, or of the fact which a proposition enunciates'.[99] 'Notional' propositions, involving 'common nouns . . . standing for what is abstract, general, and non-existing', require notional apprehension; whereas 'real' propositions, 'which are composed of singular nouns, and of which the terms stand for things external to us, unit and individual', require real apprehension. Newman makes the important reservation that a given proposition may have 'a notional sense as used by one man, and a real as used by another'; words which are 'a mere common-place', an 'expression of abstractions' to one person, may bring a 'living image' before the imagination of another person. Real apprehension, then, is 'stronger' in the sense of being 'more vivid and forcible', since 'intellectual ideas cannot compete in effectiveness with the experience of concrete facts'.[100] The corollary is that assent is 'stronger', though equally 'unreserved', when the apprehension is of an 'image' rather than an abstract truth,

---

[99] *GA* 20.   [100] Ibid. 13–14.

and so keener and more energetic.[101] The third chapter develops the crucial distinction: 'according as language expresses things external to us, or our own thoughts, so is apprehension real or notional.'[102]

The terms of a proposition do or do not stand for things. If they do, then they are singular terms, for all things that are, are units. But if they do not stand for things they must stand for notions, and are common terms. Singular nouns come from experience, common from abstraction. The apprehension of the former I call real, and of the latter notional.

Even past experiences of concrete things are susceptible of real apprehension through memory, which 'consists in a present imagination of things that are past', which remain 'things still, as being the reflections of things in a mental mirror'. These impressions of past experiences include mental acts which are also 'things', the images of which may be much more vivid than those of sensible objects. It may not always be easy to differentiate memory from abstraction, but wherever we have 'images of things individual' we have real apprehension. What is true of memory is also true of imaginative creation, for we are able 'to form, out of such passive impressions as experience has . . . left on our minds, new images, which, though mental creations, are in no sense abstractions, and though ideal, are not notional'.[103]

Our experience, then, is of individual things, but our inevitable comparison of them means our 'rising from particulars to generals, that is from images to notions'.[104] We move away from the real apprehension of things in order to achieve breadth of mind and make progress in knowledge—even though real apprehension still 'has the precedence, as being the scope and end and the test of notional'. It is the 'variation of vividness' in the two kinds of apprehension which accounts for apparent degrees in the act of assent, for as 'notions come of abstractions' and 'images come of experiences', 'the more fully the mind is occupied by an experience, the keener will be its assent to it, if it assents, and on the other hand, the duller will be its assent and the less operative, the more it is engaged with an abstraction'.[105] Notional assent can look very like inference, which is normally accompanied by notional apprehension just as assent is normally accompanied by real apprehension; whereas 'when inferences are exercised on things, they tend to be conjectures or presentiments, without logical force; and when assents are exercised on notions, they tend to be mere assertions without any personal hold on them on the part of those who make them.'[106] This is why the clearer the inference, the less forcible the assent tends to be, and the more intense the assent, the less distinct the inference. While in notional assents 'the

---

| [101] Ibid. 18. | [102] Ibid. 20. | [103] Ibid. 22–5. |
| [104] Ibid. 27. | [105] Ibid. 30. | [106] Ibid. 33–4. |

mind contemplates its own creations instead of things', 'in real, it is directed towards things, represented by the impressions which they have left on the imagination'.[107] Of course, imagination may usurp reason and create assent where it is only intended to intensify it, so that 'the distinctness of the images . . . is no warrant for the existence of the objects which those images represent'.[108] Because real, unlike notional, assents are not common but personal and individual, they may be divisive and unreliable, but ultimately they are what give us our intellectual moorings, as well as stimulating us to action through the power of the imagination.

The first part of the *Grammar* concludes, like the second part, with an attempt to apply its conclusions to religious faith. A dogma is defined as a proposition which stands for either a notion and a truth or a thing and a reality: if the former, then the assent one gives will be a notional and theological assent of the intellect; if the latter, then the assent will be a real and religious assent of the imagination. Just as our knowledge of the external world is derived instinctively through and in the sense phenomena we experience, 'so from the perceptive power which identifies the intimations of conscience with the reverberations or echoes . . . of an external admonition, we proceed on to the notion of a Supreme Ruler and Judge, and then again we image Him and His attributes in those recurring intimations, out of which, as mental phenomena, our recognition of His existence was originally gained'. Conscience itself has two aspects—'it is a moral sense, and a sense of duty; a judgment of the reason and a magisterial dictate', it 'has both a critical and judicial office'. It is in the latter aspect of a 'sanction' rather than a 'rule' of right conduct that conscience is primary, for it is as 'a voice, or the echo of a voice, imperative and constraining', that conscience is unique in our experience. Newman admits that recognizing God 'in the dictate of conscience' and 'imaging the thought of Him in the definite impressions which conscience creates' would probably be impossible without some 'extrinsic help'. Our image of God is clarified through revelation and deepened through devotion. It is possible to assent to a personal God either as a theological truth or as a religious reality. But a dogmatic creed, far from being alien to a living, personal faith, is necessary because there is a need for facts to be expressed in language and for the exposition of 'the truths on which the religious imagination has to rest'; likewise, because 'knowledge must ever precede the exercise of the affections', religion cannot do without theology. Thus our apprehension of, and assent to, the Trinity as a complex whole or mystery is notional, because 'though we can image the separate propositions, we cannot

---

[107] *GA* 55.　　　　　[108] Ibid. 58.

altogether'.[109] As for the many dogmatic propositions to which a Catholic is required to give notional assent, his assent is implicitly given when he gives a real assent to the Church.

Before proceeding to the second half of the *Grammar*, it is important to clarify the fundamental distinction between notional and real apprehension and assent. First of all, it is worth noting that it would be wrong to try and erect any division between the terms of the proposition in question and its actual apprehension, for 'we cannot draw the line between the object and the act . . . as is the thing apprehended, so is the apprehension.'[110] What is in question is not the subjective apprehension of the objective proposition, but the sense of the proposition as used by different people or by the same person in two different ways. For Newman there could be no separation of the meaning from the use of a proposition.

On the other hand, Newman has been criticized for making too rigid a distinction of kind between the notional and the real, when in fact there is only a distinction of degree. Thus it has been objected that by saying that sight is the most vivid kind of sense experience, Newman seems to be saying that people who lack visual imagery are incapable of real apprehension and assent. This would appear to imply that one person's visual image of an event he has never seen cannot be more vivid than that of another person who has seen it, when this is manifestly not the case. What must be emphasized is that real apprehension and assent, far from being necessarily tied to the visual sense, are not even bound up with sense experience at all. The confusion seems to arise from Newman's saying that real propositions are 'more vivid and forcible' because 'intellectual ideas cannot compete in effectiveness with the experience of concrete facts'.[111] This, not unnaturally, has misled critics into thinking that real assent is concerned only with concrete propositions, and notional with abstract, whereas it is clear that people can be far more excited by intellectual ideas than by the most physical of experiences. But Newman does not deny this. At the very beginning of the book he points out that 'a mere common-place, a terse expression of abstractions' may be 'the record of experiences, a sovereign dogma, a grand aspiration, inflaming the imagination, piercing the heart'. In other words, it may indeed be the object of a real assent. For in this case the general idea becomes 'a living image'—though there is no mental image of a visual or sensory kind.[112] In fact, Newman states categorically that an apprehension of a definite mental act is an apprehension of a 'thing' (as opposed to 'notion'), conceivably with 'an individuality and completeness which outlives the impressions made by sensible objects'.

---

[109] Ibid. 72–6, 79, 82–3, 88.   [110] Ibid. 31.   [111] Ibid. 14.
[112] Ibid. 13.

Similarly, it is possible out of the 'passive impressions' of experience to form images 'which, though mental creations, are in no sense abstractions, and though ideal, are not notional'.[113] What makes propositions concrete and enables assent to be real is 'experience' and the element of the 'personal'.[114]

If, then, we take something as notional as Newman's beloved 'first principles', which are 'notions, not images, because they express what is abstract, not what is individual and from direct experience', these may elicit a *real* assent 'when we apply our general knowledge to a particular instance of that knowledge', for 'these so-called first principles . . . are really conclusions or abstractions from particular experiences; and an assent to their existence is not an assent to things or their images, but to notions, real assent being confined to the propositions directly embodying these experiences.' Such is the difference between knowing 'the received rules' of a profession and entering into them in practice, between 'intellectually recognizing' a truth and seeing or feeling it, between 'accepting a notion' and 'realizing a fact'. Even so abstract a principle as 'the inviolability of the laws of nature' may become a 'vivid impression', a 'distinct and eloquent' image, to a philosopher of the school of Hume. Assents 'as given to moral objects . . . are perhaps as real as they are powerful', and 'till we have them, in spite of a full apprehension and assent in the field of notions, we have no intellectual moorings . . . These beliefs . . . form the mind out of which they grow.'[115] Indeed, for Newman the most important real assent a person is capable of is to the existence of God—and here there is nothing remotely 'concrete' in the usual sense of the word. For it is conscience which 'provides for the mind a real image of God', an image which is in no way sensory, but which is experienced and vivid.[116] The whole theory of real assent demands that there should be notional concepts so vividly realized as to become facts in the imagination, that is, in Newman's terminology, images.

The second part of the *Grammar* is almost a different book, although of course it depends on the theory of assent developed in the first half. At last Newman turns to his central concern: how is one justified in believing what one cannot prove? He begins by returning to his initial distinction between assent and inference. The problem is whether, given that non-logical reasoning never rises above probability (as opposed to logical certainty), the assent in such cases also varies in degree according to the strength of the probability. In formal logical propositions the unconditional assent merely satisfies logically necessary conclusions. But in practice we find there are 'many truths in concrete matter, which no

---

[113] *GA* 24–5.   [114] Ibid. 36, 42.   [115] Ibid. 45, 48–9, 55–6, 58, 62–3.
[116] Ibid. 251.

one can demonstrate, yet every one unconditionally accepts'.[117] Far from being merely the conclusion without the premises to an inference, assent does not depend upon the inference any more than the strongest inference necessarily elicits assent. In the case of logical truths, assent immediately follows on the demonstration, because 'the correlative of ascertained truth is unreserved assent'[118]—although the assent is still distinct from the inference. A mathematician, for instance, may not assent to the conclusion of his own proof until he has the support of another judgement besides his own. However, just as there are no degrees of truth, so there are no degrees of assent. Suspicion and conjecture, for example, are unconditional assents to the probability of a proposition. A 'half-assent'[119] is not an assent at all, but only an inclination to assent. The argument that assent to non-logical truths must be conditional arises from a confusion between the act of assenting to a conclusion and the relation between the conclusion and its premises, for assent is related to a conclusion as sensation of cold or heat is related to the reading of the thermometer in the room. There are apparent exceptions: assent upon the authority of others is often not a true assent at all; 'a *primâ facie* assent is an assent to an antecedent probability of a fact not to the fact itself'; a 'conditional'[120] assent means an assent only under certain circumstances; a deliberate or slow assent refers to the circumstance of the assenting; an uncertain assent is an assent which may be given up because it is not habitual; a strong assent refers to the emotional concomitants of the assent; a luminous assent is an assent where the arguments in its favour are numerous and strong.

Newman now differentiates 'simple' assent, which is unconscious, from 'complex' or 'reflex' assent, which is conscious and deliberate.[121] It is not investigation as such but inquiry which is incompatible with assent. It is true that an investigation may lead to a loss of assent, but the sense of the possibility of this loss is not the same as doubt—nor does assent imply an intention never to change one's mind, but, instead, the absence of any idea of ever changing. Assent to an assent is 'certitude', the proposition is a 'certainty', and the assenting is 'knowing'.[122] False certitudes are less common than is supposed. Certitude implies the confidence that even if certitude failed the certainty would remain, a requirement which disqualifies many so-called certitudes. There are various emotional signs which indicate a lack of real certitude, whereas a feeling of intellectual security signifies real certitude.

Newman at last arrives at the climax of the *Grammar*, the justification of religious certitude. He begins with the assent of faith, which, while unquestioning, is absolutely firm. Some assents of this kind may be lost

---

[117] Ibid. 106.   [118] Ibid. 112.   [119] Ibid. 116.
[120] Ibid. 120.   [121] Ibid. 124.   [122] Ibid. 128.

in the process of trying to turn them into certitudes. The reflex assent of certitude is always notional because it is an assent to the truth of the simple assent. Just as the freshness and vigour of the original assent may be lost in the gaining of certitude, so too the argumentation prior to certitude may disturb the normal thought processes, encouraging doubt and reducing imaginative realities to notions. Certitude may not always be characterized by calm serenity, because of some unexpected surprise or temptation to doubt. The 'human mind is made for truth',[123] and so certitude includes the idea of indefectibility: the failure of certitude is the exception. But the fact is that there is no test for distinguishing true from false certitudes. Unlike infallibility, certitude is not a gift or a faculty, but a disposition of mind relative to a particular case. Thus one can be certain (but not infallible) about the infallibility of the Church. If certitude is unfounded, then it is the prior reasoning, not the actual assent, that is at fault, since to have refused assent in the face of a conclusion would have been to act against one's nature. The intellect may not be infallible, but it is capable of being certain. For example, one must be entitled to be certain that after all one has made a mistake in being certain about something. False certitudes are faults not because they are certitudes, but because they are false:

The sense of certitude may be called the bell of the intellect; and that it strikes when it should not is a proof that the clock is out of order, no proof that the bell will be untrustworthy and useless, when it comes to us adjusted and regulated . . . conscience too may be said to strike the hours, and will strike them wrongly, unless it be duly regulated for the performance of its proper function.[124]

Not all so-called certitudes, however, are true certitudes, which should only follow after examination and proof, as well as being restricted to certain occasions and subject-matter. Opinion is far more attainable than certitude, but even probability presupposes the certainty of first principles. An acceptance of a religious faith involves different kinds of assents, but a change of religion may merely mean the realization and development of one or more basic and continuing certitudes. It would be quibbling to say that certitude is a conviction of what is true and that a false certitude is not a certitude at all. But it is generally true that indefectibility is a negative test of certitude: to lose one's conviction is to show that one never had certitude, because certitude is impregnable against all shocks.

The discussion now turns to the question of how in fact certitude is normally attained. Newman begins by contrasting informal reasoning with formal inference, of which the most logical form is the syllogism. The perfection of strictly logical reasoning lies in the fact that words

---

[123] *GA* 145.   [124] Ibid. 152.

which denote things and which have innumerable implications are stripped of their concrete meanings precisely in order to be abstract and notional. But the abstract cannot reach the concrete. Logical inference cannot produce proof in concrete matters because its premisses are assumed and ultimately depend upon first principles, wherein lies the real problem of attaining to truth. For logic cannot prove the first principles which it assumes. Abstract arguments reach probability but not certainty in concrete matters, because they do not touch the particular. The language of logic has its obvious advantages in the pursuit of knowledge, but human thought is too personal and complex to 'admit of the trammels of any language'.[125]

We have now reached the heart of the book. It is in fact, Newman argues, the cumulation of probabilities, which cannot be reduced to a syllogism, that leads to certainty in the concrete. Many certitudes depend on informal proofs, whose reasoning is more or less implicit. As we view the objects of sense, so we grasp the proof of a concrete truth as a whole 'by a sort of instinctive perception of the legitimate conclusion in and through the premisses'.[126] Such implicit reasoning is too personal for logic. The rays of truth stream through the medium of our moral as well as our intellectual being. As we gain a perspective of a landscape, so we personally grasp a truth with a 'real ratiocination and present imagination' which reaches beyond the 'methodical process of inference'. Such 'supra-logical judgment' is an 'individual perception' under the influence of 'an intellectual conscientiousness'.[127] In religion, the 'moral state' of the inquirer is also very important. But otherwise, in all subjects 'the principle of concrete reasoning is parallel to the method of proof which is the foundation of modern mathematical science', in which the conclusion 'is foreseen and predicted rather than actually attained; foreseen in the number and direction of accumulated premisses, which all converge to it . . . yet do not touch it logically . . . on account of the nature of its subject-matter, and the delicate and implicit character of at least part of the reasonings on which it depends'.[128] And so the mind in concrete matters progresses from probable antecedents to sufficient proof, and finally to certitude.

'Natural' inference, or the implicit, unconscious, and instinctive movement from antecedent to consequent, proceeds not from propositions to propositions, but from concrete things to concrete things, without conscious recognition of the antecedent or the process of inference. This is in fact our natural way of reasoning, employed both by the peasant and the genius; it is an instinctive perception, although not a natural instinct, which is one and the same in all. It may be damaged by

[125] Ibid. 185.   [126] Ibid. 196.   [127] Ibid. 205–6.   [128] Ibid. 207–8.

learning rules or resorting to artificial aids. Like our taste, our reasoning is spontaneous and unselfconscious. It varies according to the subject-matter and has many different forms. 'Judgment then in all concrete matters is the architectonic faculty; and what may be called the Illative Sense, or right judgment in ratiocination, is one branch of it.'[129]

Newman insists that his purpose is not metaphysical, like that of the idealists who defend the certainty of knowledge against sceptical empiricists, but is 'of a practical character, such as that of Butler in his *Analogy*', namely, to ascertain the nature of inference and assent. Certitude, it has been shown, is 'an active recognition of propositions as true' in response to a proof. And 'the sole and final judgment on the validity of an inference in concrete matter is committed to the personal action of the ratiocinative faculty, the perfection or virtue of which I have called the Illative Sense, a use of the word "sense" parallel to our use of it in "good sense".'[130] We have to accept our nature as it is, for it is 'a fact not admitting of question, all things being of necessity referred to it, not it to other things': 'I cannot think . . . about my being, without starting from the very point which I aim at concluding.'[131] Certainly, 'there is no ultimate test of truth besides the testimony born to truth by the mind itself'.[132] Thought is always thought, but it varies according to the subject-matter, and there is no 'ultimate test of truth and error' apart from the illative sense.[133] The mind outstrips language, contemplating first principles without words or any process of analysis, with the illative sense determining the beginning, the middle, and the end of any investigation.

Like the first part, the second part too ends with an attempt to apply its conclusions specifically to religious faith. Christianity may be 'demonstrably true', but it is not 'true irresistibly', because truth, like light, cannot be seen by the blind. Where assumptions are needed, Newman prefers to 'attempt to prove Christianity in the same informal way in which I can prove for certain that I have been born'.[134] First principles are all-important, and here 'belief in revealed truths depends on belief in natural'.[135] Acceptance of the arguments for Christianity rests on acceptance of certain general religious truths. The Christian revelation is 'the completion and supplement of Natural Religion, and of previous revelations'.[136] Without denying its uniqueness, Newman is categorical not only that Christianity fulfils natural religion, but that it is the continuation of a revelation that goes back to the beginning of time—what he calls elsewhere 'a primeval tradition which is universal' and which must exist 'if there was an Adam, a father of men, in direct

---

[129] *GA* 221.　　[130] Ibid. 222–3.　　[131] Ibid. 224.　　[132] Ibid. 226.
[133] Ibid. 231.　　[134] Ibid. 264.　　[135] Ibid. 266.　　[136] Ibid. 250.

communication with his Creator'.[137] The rest of the chapter is concerned first with Christianity as the fulfilment of Judaism, and then with its extraordinary conversion of the Roman Empire, which he saw as 'the most supernatural event in the history of Christianity' and as 'our main proof of the divinity of the gospel now'.[138] He was only able to give a sketch of it here, although he would have liked to write a treatise on it; it was a subject, he had once said, which had 'long interested' him 'more than any other subject'.[139] The secret of that astonishing victory over paganism, he insists with great eloquence, lay in the idea or image of Christ that created and sustained the faith of the early Christians.

Various objections have been made to different parts of the argument. First, the difference between assenting and inferring has not always been clearly grasped. Newman intends a logical distinction between two different kinds of act and the linguistic forms of propositions expressing them. It is not, for example, the difference between recognizing reasons for assenting and actually assenting. 'Conditional' propositions express conclusions and imply a dependence on other propositions; whereas 'categorical' propositions simply assert without any such implication. A conclusion is as distinct from an assertion 'as a word of command is from a persuasion or recommendation'.[140] Where the conclusion of an argument is crystal clear,

though assent would not in consequence be the same act as inference, yet it would certainly follow immediately upon it. I allow then as much as this, that, when an argument is in itself and by itself conclusive of a truth, it has by a law of our nature the same command over our assent, or rather the truth which it has reached has the same command, as our senses have. Certainly our intellectual nature is under laws, and the correlative of ascertained truth is unreserved assent.[141]

In other words, however inevitably assertion may follow conclusion, there are different kinds of intellectual and verbal acts involved in assent and inference. And this difference is embodied in the difference between unconditional and conditional propositions: 'Inference is always inference; even if demonstrative, it is still conditional; it establishes an incontrovertible conclusion on the condition of incontrovertible premises. To the conclusion thus drawn, assent gives its absolute recognition.'[142] It is, then, quite misleading to see the choice as between conditional inference characterized by reservations on the one hand and confident, undoubting assent on the other. Thus, while it is true that there can be no 'variation of an assent to an inference', there are 'assents to a variation in inferences'. It is, in other words, possible to be 'certain of an uncertainty'.[143] Again, while it is true that 'inference is ordinarily the

---

[137] *LD* xxviii. 257.   [138] Ibid. xxx. 207, 259.   [139] Ibid. xx. 454.
[140] *GA* 9–10.   [141] Ibid. 112.   [142] Ibid. 114.   [143] Ibid. 116.

antecedent of assent', that does not interfere with 'the unconditional character of the assent, viewed in itself'.[144]

Second, the intellectual character of the illative sense has not always been fully appreciated. Defined as 'right judgment in ratiocination',[145] the elements both of evaluating and reasoning need to be emphasized. In 'informal reasoning', a man comes to a conclusion which is supported but not demonstrated by the evidence and for which he is 'responsible to himself'.[146] 'Just as', Newman argues, 'there is no sufficient test of poetical excellence, heroic action, or gentleman-like conduct, other than the particular mental sense, be it genius, taste, sense of propriety, or the moral sense, to which those subject-matters are severally committed,' so 'in no class of concrete reasonings, whether in experimental science, historical research, or theology, is there any ultimate test of truth and error in our inferences besides the trustworthiness of the Illative Sense that gives them its sanction.'[147] The use of the word 'sense', then, is justified by the need to emphasize the 'element of the personal' in the 'living intellect', for our conclusions in informal reasoning are judgements arrived at by 'the action of our own minds, by our own individual perception of the truth in question, under a sense of duty to those conclusions and with an intellectual conscientiousness'.[148]

Third, Newman's theory of probability has been insufficiently understood. It has nothing to do with any kind of mechanical procedure for counting probabilities in some sort of numerical scale, for 'a cumulation of probabilities, over and above their implicit character, will vary both in their number and their separate estimated value, according to the particular intellect which is employed upon it.'[149] And so 'proof' in concrete reasoning will always have an 'element of the personal, because "prudence" is not a constituent part of our nature, but a personal endowment'.[150] Ordinary reasoning is carried out by 'dealing with things directly ... in the concrete, with an intrinsic and personal power, not a conscious adoption of an artificial instrument or expedient'.[151] Newman also makes it quite clear that the cumulative argument from probability will vary in kind and method according to the nature of the subject-matter. Thus, for example, we prove that Great Britain is an island in a very different kind of way from that by which we prove that one day I shall die.

Fourth, and most often voiced ever since the first reviews, is the objection to the claim that certitude is indefectible. Now it is perfectly true that Newman says that certitude 'carries with it an inward assurance ... that it shall never fail'. But this confidence only reflects a general rule to which exceptions are always possible; Newman's

---

[144] *GA* 105. [145] Ibid. 221. [146] Ibid. 228. [147] Ibid. 231.
[148] Ibid. 228, 205–6. [149] Ibid. 190. [150] Ibid. 205. [151] Ibid. 214.

concern, in his own words, is merely 'to show, that, as a general rule, certitude does not fail'. He qualifies this 'inward assurance' by adding: 'Indefectibility almost enters into its very idea, enters into it at least so far as this, that its failure, if of frequent occurrence, would prove that certitude was after all and in fact an impossible act.' Actually, he argues, 'failures of what was taken for certitude are the exception'.[152] However, even though the possibility of error is freely admitted, still, 'if we are never to be certain, after having been once certain wrongly, then we ought never to attempt a proof because we have once made a bad one.' And indeed, error itself presupposes certitude, because if 'I have been mistaken in my certitude, may I not at least be certain that I have been mistaken?'[153] But the fact remains that for Newman false certitudes are conceivable 'in many cases', even as 'false consciences abound'.[154] Nevertheless, he holds to the general principle: 'Premising that all rules are but general, especially those which relate to the mind, I observe that indefectibility may at least serve as a negative test of certitude, or *sine quâ non* condition, so that whoever loses his conviction on a given point is thereby proved not to have been certain of it.'[155] That the rule is only a general one is clear from what he says concerning changes of religious belief: 'I will not urge . . . that certitude is a conviction of what is true, and that these so called certitudes have come to nought, because, their objects being errors, not truths, they really were not certitudes at all.'[156] And even after pointing to cases where ostensible certitude in religion transpires to be something less, Newman does not hesitate to admit: 'All concrete laws are general, and persons, as such, do not fall under laws. Still, I have gone a good way, as I think, to remove the objections to the doctrine of the indefectibility of certitude in matters of religion, though I cannot assign to it an infallible token.'[157] In other words, while the indefectibility of religious certitude is generally sustained, there is no absolute guarantee that it will not fail, for the simple reason that there are no absolute tests of true and false certainty.

In the last analysis, then, the *Grammar* is not a 'metaphysical' work. But that does not mean it is a 'psychological' study. Rather, it is a philosophical analysis of that state of mind which we ordinarily call certitude or certainty and of the cognitive acts associated with it; and, as such, it has come to be recognized as a classic by philosophers of religion. Religious certainty becomes one of many kinds of certainty which are not 'proved' in the formal sense of the word. The justification of religious belief merges into a much more general justification of the validity of ordinary processes of thought leading to conviction. Finally, it must be said that no attempt to summarize the book can do justice to the richness

---

[152] Ibid. 145.   [153] Ibid. 150–1.   [154] Ibid. 153.
[155] Ibid. 167.   [156] Ibid. 165.   [157] Ibid. 166.

of the examples adduced of variegated intellectual activity, which, far from being mere illustrations, to a considerable extent constitute the matter and movement of the argument itself.

After the reviews had appeared, Newman was more confident that while the *Grammar* might be 'full of defects, certainly characterized by incompleteness and crudeness', still it was 'something to have started a problem, and mapped in part a country, if I have done nothing more'.[158] He never had the slightest doubt, whatever his other misgivings, that 'I have done my best—both in the way of argument, and of bringing out my meaning': as to 'objections, I have said the book ought to defend itself and answer all the objections, for I expended myself upon it—if it does not, so much the worse for the book'.[159] He did not, however, expect to know its 'worth' in his own lifetime—'No work on which one has bestowed great pains can meet with an early verdict.'[160] He certainly had no illusions about its scope: it was neither comprehensive nor conclusive. He called it 'an *Essay*, as it really is, because it is an analytical inquiry—a Grammar ought to be synthetical'. To have 'put it in synthetical form' would have required 'a new book'; but 'it is enough for me to have attempted an investigation'—'What is the good of building a house with girders which have not previously been tested?'[161] To one typical scholastic objection from a Jesuit, he responded that it was not 'necessary to be exactissimus in a work which is a conversational essay, not a dialectic treatise. It is like a military reconnaissance, or a party in undress, or a house in committee . . . it is a preliminary opening of the ground.'[162] He was, in fact, very conscious that the book was a 'fat' one and a hundred pages longer than intended—'it would not come to an end.'[163] Indeed, if it had not 'already grown so fat, and I was so desperately tired of the whole subject, I had intended to sum up in a last chapter'.[164] As it is, the book ends without a conclusion, as abruptly as it began without an introduction.

[158] *LD* xxv. 280. [159] Ibid. xxvii. 10. [160] Ibid. 44.
[161] Ibid. xxv. 84. [162] Ibid. 131. [163] Ibid. 39, 48.
[164] Ibid. 83–4.

17
Papal Infallibility

❧

During the last stages of writing the *Grammar* Newman had been distracted by the unfolding drama at Rome. It seemed that the extreme Ultramontane party had found itself to be, if anything, smaller than the liberal party led by Bishop Dupanloup. Most of the bishops were in the middle, and Manning was trying to secure a compromise definition which would at least define the Pope to be infallible in matters of faith. It was less than what he and Ward had hoped for, but it went a good deal further than what Dupanloup was prepared to admit. In view of the Gallican theory that infallibility resided in the Church but extended beyond matters of faith, Newman did not see how the definition could be passed. It was essential to gain time, hopefully to extend the Council for another year. The Ultramontanes were pressing hard for a definition, but Manning seemed to be 'over shooting his mark, and losing influence'. True, he had 'a wonderful gift of ingratiating himself with people', but it was 'a difficult thing to retain that kind of influence'.[1]

Towards the end of January 1870 Newman received a letter from Ullathorne in Rome deploring the Ultramontane lobbying but expressing optimism about the eventual outcome of the Council. In reply, Newman wrote one of his most famous letters, perhaps the most indignant he ever wrote.

Rome ought to be a name to lighten the heart at all times, and a Council's proper office is, when some great heresy or other evil impends, to inspire the faithful with hope and confidence; but now we have the greatest meeting which ever has been, and that at Rome, infusing into us . . . little else than fear and dismay.

When we are all at rest, and have no doubts, and at least practically, not to say doctrinally, hold the Holy Father to be infallible, suddenly there is thunder in the clear sky, and we are told to prepare for something we know not what to try our faith we know not how. No impending danger is to be averted, but a great difficulty is to be created. Is this the proper work for an Ecumenical Council? As to myself personally, please God, I do not expect any trial at all; but I cannot help suffering with the various souls which are suffering, and I look with anxiety at the prospect of having to defend decisions, which may be not difficult to my private judgment, but may be most difficult to maintain logically

[1] *LD* xxv. 15.

in the face of historical facts. What have we done to be treated, as the faithful never were treated before? When has definition of doctrine de fide been a luxury of devotion, and not a stern painful necessity? Why should an aggressive insolent faction be allowed to 'make the heart of the just to mourn, whom the Lord hath not made sorrowful?' Why can't we be let alone, when we have pursued peace, and thought no evil? I assure you, my dear Lord, some of the truest minds are driven one way and another, and do not know where to rest their feet . . .

He went on to complain that the Ultramontane agitation would only help to revive past scandals of the papacy; it would also undermine the efforts of high Anglicans to leaven the Protestant lump. He wondered if he should make his feelings public, but he felt all he could do was to pray that 'so great a calamity' should be averted: 'If it is God's will that the Pope's infallibility should be defined, then it is His blessed Will to throw back "the times and the moments" of that triumph which He has destined for His Kingdom; and I shall feel I have but to bow my head to His adorable, inscrutable Providence.'[2]

However, he had not the slightest hesitation in sharply rejecting a demand from Herbert Vaughan to sign a petition for the definition. 'In the Catholic Church', he remarked tartly, 'I consider *rest* to be the better thing.'[3] He agreed with Ullathorne that the Council would have one very beneficial result: by bringing together bishops from all over the world it would enable them to get to know each other, as well as enable the Roman authorities to become better informed ('and since the Italian apprehension is most imaginative and vivid, this will be a wonderful gain')[4]—all of which would surely have an influence on the election of the next Pope. He told Bishop Moriarty that inopportunists like himself were a 'special band of confessors', who, if they could not prevent, would at least diminish 'the nature and weight of the blow which is intended by those whom you oppose, and also because your resistance must bear fruit afterwards, even though it fails at the moment'. Newman himself would continue to pray that there was no definition, but he would accept it if one was passed. He was well aware that his own *Essay on Development* was being enlisted on the Ultramontane side: 'It has been my fate to have my book attacked by various persons, praised by none—till at last it is used against me.'[5] (It was rather like his complaint some years previously that 'through my life, those persons who have done me harm by their tongues, have been by me myself put into those very positions and situations from which they have been able to use their tongues against me.'[6])

In the middle of March a report of Newman's letter to Ullathorne

[2] *LD* xxv. 18–19.   [3] Ibid. 20.   [4] Ibid. 37.   [5] Ibid. 58.
[6] Ibid. xx. 200.

appeared in the *Standard* newspaper. Newman wrote immediately to the editor to deny that he had referred to the Ultramontane party as an 'aggressive insolent faction', while admitting that he deeply deplored its activities. A week later he wrote again to acknowledge that he had indeed used the words in question, but had missed them when he had first consulted his rough copy. He now discovered that copies of the letter were circulating; sooner or later the whole letter would get into the papers; it would be better if it got in before rather than after any definition; it might do some good now, whereas later it could only cause trouble. Perhaps he ought to publish it himself straightaway: he would certainly get into 'very hot water' if he did, but the water would not get less hot if he delayed.[7] It was not his responsibility that 'one of the most confidential letters' which he had ever written had become public knowledge.[8] Nor was it the fault of the bishop, who was clearly deeply embarrassed. Newman himself had never intended to make any public statement about the Council: he felt it could only do harm and it was not his place to do so. But he was certainly not averse to his views becoming known in this way; he would never have dared write so vehemently for publication. He had unburdened himself to his own bishop, 'with great deliberation in one of the most passionate and confidential letters' that he had ever written.[9] His mistake about the words attributed to him had given him the opportunity to make a public avowal of his sentiments. This dissemination of his letter had enabled him to make just the protest which he wanted to make; there was nothing more he could or ought to do. The agitation was so sudden that all one could do was 'cry out, bawl, make violent gestures, as you would do if you saw a railway engine running over some unhappy workmen on the line'.[10]

In the meantime, his attitude remained that a definition was impossible, but if he were proved wrong he would accept it as God's will. He reminded Döllinger that intrigue was not the sole prerogative of the present Council, but was a feature of Ecumenical Councils and did not affect their authority. At the same time he told Robert Whitty, now a leading Jesuit in Rome, that it was enough for Pius IX to have defined the Immaculate Conception, which had ripened gradually into a dogma: 'We do not move at railroad pace in theological matters, even in the 19th century.' Ultramontanism was a new development; the Church, which 'moves as a whole', as a communion rather than an ideology, had 'no right rudely to wipe out the history of centuries, and to substitute a bran new view of the doctrine imported from Rome and the South'. Bluntly he warned, 'we are not ripe yet for the Pope's Infallibility.' To force a dogma in this surreptitious way on the Church

---

[7] Ibid. xxv. 64.   [8] Ibid. 67.   [9] Ibid. 69.   [10] Ibid. 98.

was 'crooked'. Extensive and lengthy research and theological discussion were essential preliminaries. It looked suspiciously as if 'a grave dogmatic question was being treated merely as a move in ecclesiastical politics'.[11] It was as if 'certain parties wished to steal a march upon Catholics. Nothing is above board—nothing is told to the bishops generally before hand—the gravest innovation possible, (for it is a change in the hitherto recognized basis of the Church,) is to be carried by acclamation.'[12] The prospect of the definition was already proving most awkward for English Catholics, who were facing a resurgence of 'No Popery'. As for the enemies of Catholicism, they were delighted, as it seemed to prove what they had all along maintained.

On 6 April the *Standard* published the copy Newman sent of his letter to Ullathorne. Newman's only regret was that he had not included the 'awful text' from St Matthew's Gospel about causing scandal to the 'little ones' of Christ.[13] Its appearance provoked an indignant outburst from Dalgairns in the French newspaper *Le Monde*, which was reprinted approvingly by the *Tablet*. Newman commented to Bishop Moriarty that ever since his conversion to Catholicism Dalgairns had 'shown an ingrained self conceit and arrogance which I think I never found in such a degree in any one else'.[14] For years they had had virtually no contact, and it was odious for Dalgairns now to write as if they were old friends and as if it was Newman who had broken off relations. Not that this and other attacks could 'plague an old soldier, whose skin has been hardened by 40 years of warfare'.[15] On the other hand, it was gratifying to learn that his letter had delighted the great French liberal Catholic Montalembert just before his death. Newman continued to believe that no definition would be made by the Council, and that if one were passed it would be 'in so mild a form as, practically to mean little or nothing'.[16] But although the Council would be protected by the Holy Spirit from teaching error, it was not divinely prevented from acting inopportunely. Even that eventuality, however, Newman could believe must be in the long run be expedient in God's providence, however inexpedient it might seem at the time. He was well aware that General Councils had 'ever been times of great *trial*', but also that 'the conduct of individuals who composed them was no measure of the authority of their result'.[17] Church history showed that they had 'generally two characteristics—a great deal of violence and intrigue on the part of the actors in them, and a great resistance to their definitions on the part of portions of Christendom'.[18]

On 23 July Newman saw the definition of papal infallibility which

---

[11] *LD* xxv. 93–5.   [12] Ibid. 100.   [13] Ibid. 102.   [14] Ibid. 122.
[15] Ibid. 132.   [16] Ibid. 150.   [17] Ibid. 158.   [18] Ibid. xxvi. 281.

had been passed five days earlier. He was 'pleased at its moderation'; the 'terms used' were 'vague and comprehensive', and he personally had no difficulty in accepting it; the only question was, 'does it come to me with the authority of an Ecumenical Council?' It certainly appeared to do so, but there were factors in favour of suspending judgement on its validity. Opposition to defining the dogma had led to more than eighty bishops leaving the Council before the vote was taken. At least 'moral' unanimity seemed necessary for validity. It all depended on what the dissentient minority (who had not actually voted against the definition) now did: if they 'allege in detail acts of violence and deceit used against the Fathers, if they declare they have been kept in the dark and been practised on, then there will be the gravest reasons for determining that the Definition is not valid'. If, on the other hand, they failed to persist in united opposition as a body, then there could be said to have been moral unanimity and there would be no justification for resisting the definition. Finally, and most important, 'if the definition is eventually received by the whole body of the faithful . . . then too it will claim our assent by the force of the great dictum, "Securus judicat orbis terrarum".' After all, 'the general acceptance, judgment of Christendom' was not only 'the broad principle by which all acts of the rulers of the Church are ratified', but also 'the ultimate guarantee of revealed truth'.[19] The celebrated aphorism which had once rung so insistently in his ears now sounded solemnly again at this great potential crisis of faith in the Church. For some converts it was a point of return to old allegiances; to one such, Newman wrote that twenty-five years of unwavering faith in the Catholic Church led him 'to trust that in me will never be fulfilled the woe pronounced on back-sliders'.[20] He was, however, perceptive enough to foresee that the definition would tend to 'create in educated Catholics a habit of scepticism or secret infidelity as regards all dogmatic truth'.[21]

There were, nevertheless, good reasons for immediately accepting the definition, mild as it was, even if not on the authority of the Council. For centuries the Pope had 'been allowed by God to assert virtually his infallibility',[22] and the doctrine had now been confirmed by the Pope and 500 bishops and should probably be received on their authority alone. Newman tried to find crumbs of comfort for worried correspondents who wrote to him. Perhaps it was '*necessary*, in time to come, for the seat of government to be strengthened'; if 'terrible times' were imminent, an increase in papal authority might be 'absolutely necessary to keep things together'. Perhaps the result of the definition would actually be to '*limit* the Pope's power',[23] because its limit at least was now

[19] Ibid. xxv. 164–5, 172.   [20] Ibid. 161.   [21] Ibid. 166.
[22] Ibid. 168.   [23] Ibid. 170, 204.

defined. Certainly the 'abstract shape and formal definition of things' was very different from their 'practical working'; it was hardly likely, whatever the Ultramontanes might hope, that dogmas would now 'become as plenty as blackberries';[24] but from one practical point of view, the definition would not change things, as the Popes had for at least 300 years been exercising such an authority in practice. The cloud of dust raised by the definition would eventually settle: 'there has seldom been a Council without great confusion after it.' But none of this altered the alarming fact that

> it is a new and most serious precedent in the Church that a dogma . . . should be passed *without definite and urgent cause*. This to my mind is the serious part of the matter. You put an enormous power into the hands of one man, without check, and at the very time, by your act, you declare that he may use it without special occasion.[25]

Personally, Newman accepted the somewhat circular argument that if the Pope himself enforced the definition as a dogma of faith, then 'I should consider that the fact of the Pope being able by his power of jurisdiction practically to enforce his claim of infallibility . . . was a providential intimation that the claim was well founded, and I should receive the dogma as a dogma'. He could not help thinking that 'the self-assertion, the ipse dixit of the Popes for 1800 years' was 'a great and imposing argument for the validity of their claims'.[26] True, it was only for 300 years that the Church had actually 'acted on the doctrine'; but from the very beginning the Pope had 'so intervened and interposed in all parts of Christendom, so authoritatively, so magisterially, that it is very perplexing to suppose he had no divine gift of direction and teaching'.[27] Privately, he confided to Ambrose St John that he would not know what to say to anxious enquirers if the Pope did in fact take advantage of what was 'a precedent and a suggestion to use his power without necessity, when ever he will, when not called on to do so'. He was so concerned, he admitted, at the danger of an attempt to extend the definition, that 'we must hope, for one is obliged to hope it, that the Pope will be driven from Rome, and will not continue the Council, or that there will be another Pope'.[28]

There was renewed speculation in the newspapers that Newman might be on the point of returning to the Church of England. Denials, he now knew, were in vain: however much he publicly denied the rumour, 'it has too tough a vitality to dread any thing I may say of it. It defies me.'[29] To one Anglo-Catholic friend he nevertheless wrote forcibly, 'Be sure there is as much chance of my turning an Anglican again as of my

---

[24] *LD* xxv. 174. [25] Ibid. 175. [26] Ibid. 186.
[27] Ibid. 200. [28] Ibid. 192. [29] Ibid. 225.

being ... the King of Clubs.' He could not help 'smiling' at the 'invitation' to return, 'as I should have laughed if I had been the chicken, to whom the good-wife said "Chick, chick, come and be killed." ' More seriously, he reiterated that he had never had one 'passing doubt' since he became a Catholic that 'the Church in communion with Rome is the successor and representative of the Primitive Church'; and he was just 'as certain that the Anglican Church is *not*', but rather 'a mere collection of men, a mere national body, a human society'. In short, he would 'be the most asinine, as well as the most ungrateful of men, if I left that Gracious Lord who manifests Himself in the Catholic Church, for those wearisome Protestant shadows, out of which of His mercy he has delivered me'.[30] In fact, he was even more sceptical about the Church of England's ecclesial position than he had been in 1845, because then 'I had not that utter distrust of the Anglican Orders which I feel in 1870'.[31] There was no question of denying the corruptions of the Roman Catholic Church, but if there was a 'great deal to deplore in the history of the Popes', there was also 'a bright side as well as a dark', which was at least 'as prominent as the dark'. Whatever one's feelings about the human side of the papacy, it was hard to see how a universal Church could be held together without a head. But 'where you have power, you will have the abuse of power— and the more absolute, the stronger, the more sacred the power, the greater and more certain will be its abuse.'[32]

While the papacy was acquiring new spiritual power, it was in the process of losing another, very different kind of power. On 20 September 1870 Pius IX at last surrendered Rome to the Italian forces. Whatever the merits or demerits of the Pope being a temporal ruler, Newman was

---

[30] Ibid. 195.

[31] Ibid. 160. He could not conceive that they were valid, although he could not be certain that they were not. He only felt sure that they could not be proved to be valid and that they were therefore, at least, doubtful, which meant that in practice they had to be treated as invalid. He also felt strongly that the whole subject was 'dreary'—'for it is dreary surely to have to grope into the minute intricate passages and obscure corners of past occurrences'. Apart from the dubious historical evidence, a long record of poor sacramental practice as well as a lack of regard for Apostolic succession suggested that Anglican orders were not valid in the Catholic sense. The mere fact that they required defending was a prima-facie argument against them. The somewhat unkind analogy that struck Newman was that of 'a boat with water in it', in which there must be 'a leak somewhere', even though there might be dispute about where the leak was and whether there was more than one leak (*LD* xxiv. 116, 239). Finally, because he was unhappy about restricting the definition of a sacrament to the Tridentine categories of matter and form, and because he thought that each sacramental rite should be seen as an indivisible whole (including the Eucharist, as to which he had always held the advanced view that it was impossible to say for certain at what point the sacrifice took place), he no more saw how the rite of ordination could be 'cut up into bits . . . or split into essentials and non-essentials' (*Ess.* ii. 82–3) than the Anglican eucharistic rite, which had been 'mortally wounded by alterations' at the Reformation, 'and can no more have life breathed into it again, than a corpse by galvinism be revivified' (*LD* xxviii. 216).

[32] *LD* xxv. 203–4.

hopeful that 'gradually, not at once, a new system must supersede the old; and one better suitable to modern times'.[33] He was clear that it was 'a great scandal' that 'the Holy Father should be protected against his own people by foreign bayonets'; anything was preferable to that, especially considering that it was his 'proper place' to be persecuted, not to persecute.[34] At least 'open infidelity' was not as bad as 'secret, and the state of Rome was such as to honeycomb the population of Italy with deep unbelief, under the outward profession of Christianity'.[35] Perhaps, too, Providence did not intend the same man to be 'both infallible in spirituals and absolute in temporals', so that one might argue that the 'definition of July involved the dethronement of September'.[36] Perhaps for 'one man to be spiritually infallible and temporally despotic, is too much for human nature—and the Papacy cannot mount to the summit in things ecclesiastical, without a secular downfall'.[37] To a request from the *Tablet* to deny a report in an Anglican paper that a sermon against the Temporal Power had been preached by one of the priests at the Oratory, Newman responded with superb disdain: 'I have been thinking . . . what I can possibly at any time have done, to raise in the breast of the Editor of the Tablet, a gentleman known to me only by his articles, the imagination, that he might venture to put me through an interrogation on a matter connected with the Oratory Church.'[38]

Closer study of the definition showed that the Council had only taught the moderate view of infallibility which Ryder, for example, had maintained against Ward. All Catholic theologians had always held

that what the Pope said ex cathedrâ, was true, *when* the Bishops had received it—what has been passed, is to the effect that what he determines ex cathedrâ is true *independently* of the reception by the Bishops—but nothing has been passed as to *what is meant* by 'ex cathedrâ'—and this falls back to the Bishops and the Church to determine quite as much as before. Really therefore nothing has been passed of consequence.

Again, the degree is linked to 'faith and morals'—whereas what the Ultra party wished to pass was political principles.

There was no doubting the Ultramontane party was deeply disappointed that the definition could not be used, in particular, to enforce rigorously the *Syllabus of Errors*. Newman's feelings about Pius IX himself had changed greatly from those early, enthusiastic days after his conversion: 'The present Pope cannot live long—he has lived too long—but, did he live Methuselah's age, he could not in his acts go beyond the limit which God has assigned to him—nor *has* he, though he wished it.'[39] Typically, Manning's pastoral letter in October gave the exaggerated

[33] *LD* xxv. 213. [34] Ibid. 217. [35] Ibid. 239. [36] Ibid. 245.
[37] Ibid. 297. [38] Ibid. 219. [39] Ibid 224.

impression that the Pope's infallibility was unlimited. Newman's hope was that things had got so bad that they could not get worse, but only better:

We have come to a climax of tyranny. It is not good for a Pope to live 20 years. It is anomaly and bears no good fruit; he becomes a god, has no one to contradict him, does not know facts, and does cruel things without meaning it. For years past my only consolation personally has been in our Lord's Presence in the Tabernacle. I turn from the sternness of external authority to Him who can immeasurably compensate trials which after all are not real . . .[40]

He advised Hyacinth Loyson, now excommunicated and about to leave the Church, to be patient; though 'the turn of things may not take place in our time', still 'there will be surely, sooner or later, an energetic and a stern nemesis of imperious acts, such as now afflict us'.[41] As always, Newman's advice to people was not to despair of the present but to look to the future:

What changes are slowly but surely coming in! a new world is rising out of the old—It may take some generations to get into shape—as in former ages of the Church—but we should find, had we the gift of prophecy, that it was quite as happy a state for her, perhaps a happier than any of those former states which are accounted so happy.[42]

The optimism came not from a facile desire to offer cheap comfort, but from an imagination extraordinarily sensitive to the unexpected ways in which apparently ineluctable situations can take on a wholly new aspect under the pressure of historical changes and events. As usual, too, Newman refused to ignore what was true and acceptable in a development which he deplored for other reasons. Disgust with Ultramontane excesses should not be allowed to obscure the original, valid Ultramontanism of, for example, Montalembert, who had opposed Gallicanism as allowing the state to interfere with the spiritual independence of the Church. The freedom of the local Church from political domination depended on Rome's central authority. And while Newman had 'always inclined to the notion that a General Council was the magisterial exponent of the Creed', unfortunately, it had to be admitted that 'a General Council may be hampered and hindered by the action of infidel Governments upon a weak or time-serving episcopate'. The argument that papal authority required strengthening was not lost on Newman, who was even prepared to admit—now that the definition had not only been passed, but by the end of the year had clearly been accepted by the body of bishops—that

It is . . . better that the individual command of Christ to Peter to teach the

---

[40] Ibid. 231.   [41] Ibid. 235.   [42] Ibid. 257.

nations, and to guard the Christian structure of society, should be committed to his undoubted successor. By this means there will be no more of those misunderstandings out of which Jansenism and Gallicanism have arisen, and which in these latter days have begotten here in England the so-called Branch Theory . . .[43]

Although, however, the wording of the definition was quite unexceptionable and could be welcomed in theory, still that did not alter the fact that 'considered in its effects both upon the Pope's mind and that of his people, and in the power of which it puts him in practical possession, it is nothing else than shooting Niagara'. But then again, perhaps the loss of the Pope's temporal power would 'oblige him to court that Catholic body in its separate nations with a considerateness and kindness, which of late years the Holy see has not shown, and which may effectually prevent a tyrannous use of his spiritual power'.[44] It was not a question of wavering between two positions; it was, rather, that the situation had to be considered from every point of view. It was, he insisted, impossible to foresee the future, which was in God's hands. He was sure that it was divine intervention which had prevented the extreme Ultramontanes, including the Pope, from getting through a much stronger definition. It was a pity that Döllinger and others persisted in exaggerating what actually had been defined, however scandalous the proceedings. But it was not the first scandal at a Council, and good would come out of it. The important thing was to be patient and not to despair: 'Remedies spring up naturally in the Church, as in nature, if we wait for them.' Part of the problem, he pointed out, was that the 'definition was taken out of its order—it would have come to us very differently, if those preliminaries about the Church's power had first been passed, which . . . were intended'. If the Council did reassemble, it would hopefully 'occupy itself in other points' which would 'have the effect of qualifying and guarding the dogma'.[45] If this was not to be, then the Council would be completed and modified by another Council, as had happened before in the history of the Church. Characteristically, Newman turned for guidance to the history of the early Church, where it seemed 'as if the Church moved on to the perfect truth by various successive declarations, alternately in contrary directions, and thus perfecting, completing, supplying each other'. It was not so much that the recent definition needed to be 'undone, as to be completed'. 'Let us be patient,' he concluded, 'let us have faith, and a new Pope, and a re-assembled Council may trim the boat.'[46] In the meantime, deplorable as was the treatment meted out to Döllinger (amongst others), who was being pressed (under pain of excommunica-

---

[43] *LD* xxv. 259.   [44] Ibid. 262.   [45] Ibid. 278.   [46] Ibid. 310.

tion) to accept papal infallibility, Newman could not accept the validity of his arguments against the actual definition. Even if the supporting Scripture texts were not convincing (as Newman thought they were), this did not affect the truth of the actual decisions of a Council, which alone were guaranteed. The concept of infallibility was a negative one: as the teacher of a revelation, the Church had to enjoy divine protection from error in teaching revealed truths, but because she was not 'inspired', she had to use ordinary human means (which might be flawed) to arrive at the truth. Nor was the Pope inspired; but like Balaam who 'wished to curse, but opened his mouth with blessings, so a Pope may all his life be in error, but if he attempts to put it forth, he will be cut off, or be deterred, or find himself saying what he did not mean to say'.[47]

At this juncture, Newman had no idea himself of writing on the subject. In fact, he had no intention of publishing anything more. He was now busy editing and republishing his already published writings, as well as sorting out his letters. He wanted to spend the time left to him 'sweeping up, dusting, putting my house in order'.[48] In the previous year he had republished his *Essays on Miracles*; now he was reprinting the *Arians* (with a new appendix) and a collection of articles, nearly all from the *British Critic*, in two volumes (*Essays Critical and Historical*). He had revised the texts, but without making any changes in the argument; he felt free to omit anything which he now regarded as mere anti-Catholic abuse, as opposed to genuine arguments against the Church which he had no intention of altering, although he added notes criticizing his earlier views. He would have liked to 'mend' the *Arians*, which was his first book, 'the work of a year', and 'inexact in thought and incorrect in language'—but he found that if he tried to 'it would come to pieces' and he would 'have to write it over again'.[49]

2

In February 1871 Newman reached his seventieth birthday: 'By fits and starts I realize it; but usually it seems incredible to me.' It was odd how many of his friends had died around this time of year. 'I wonder', he mused with chilling precision, 'what day I shall die on—One passes year by year over one's death day, as one might pass over one's grave.'[50] The longer one lived, the shorter it seemed to be: 'ten years ago is as yesterday, as the pebbles at the bottom of a river seem close to you, when

[47] Ibid. 299.   [48] Ibid. 277.   [49] Ibid. xxx. 105.
[50] Ibid. xxv. 294.

it is clear.'[51] A couple of years before, he had expressed his sense of God's providence watching over him, when he wrote in his private journal that he could only repeat what he had written in 1820, 'that among the ordinary mass of men, *no one* has sinned so much, *no one* has been so mercifully treated, as I have; no one has such cause for humiliation, such cause for thanksgiving'. When he looked again over his journal entries the next year, he found it 'unpleasant' to do so—they seemed so 'affected, unreal, egotistical, petty, fussy'.[52] There was a sense, however, in which it was hard for him not to write down his thoughts: 'I think best when I write. I cannot in the same way think while I speak.'[53] So literally true was this that, when he had a pen which wrote badly, it even affected his style and thought.

The Ultramontanes had not achieved all that they wanted at the Council. But their victory was fairly complete throughout the Church and the repercussions were various. At home at the Oratory School, for example, the senior boys lost interest in their work for want of the stimulus a university would have provided; of that there was no prospect, ever since Manning had 'turned' Wiseman 'round his finger' and persuaded him that it was inadvisable for the laity to be better educated than their priests. At the end of April Newman sent Emily Bowles a marvellously sarcastic commentary on the state of the Church, concluding, however, with a dramatic prophecy of the Second Vatican Council:

This was one chief reason why it was decided that Catholic youths might not have a career. There are those who wish Catholic women, not nuns, to have no higher pursuit than that of dress, and Catholic youths to be shielded from no sin so carefully as from intellectual curiosity. All this is the consequence of Luther, and the separation off of the Teutonic races—and of the imperiousness of the Latin. But the Latin race will not always have a monopoly of the magisterium of Catholicism. We must be patient in our time; but God will take care of His Church—and, when the hour strikes, the reform will begin—Perhaps it *has* struck, though we can't yet tell.[54]

Meanwhile, Newman had no intention of making any public statement about the recent excommunication of Döllinger, whose ruthless treatment by the authorities he deplored, but whose views on the truth of the doctrine and on the validity of the definition he rejected. There was no doubt, though, that Döllinger had an impressive theological tradition behind him, which was diametrically opposed to the present dominant tendency in the Church. In England, Newman had no such support; the failure of the laity to back up his letter to Ullathorne had convinced him it would do more harm than good to

[51] *LD* xxv. 295.   [52] *AW* 268.   [53] *LD* xxv. 300.   [54] Ibid. 326–7.

speak out any more strongly. But he continued to insist that the Church's early dogmas 'were not struck off all at once but piecemeal— one Council did one thing, another a second—and so the whole dogma was built up'. It was precisely because 'the first portion of it looked extreme' that controversies arose which led to subsequent Councils which '*explained* and *completed* what was first done'.[55] (The Second Vatican Council, nearly a century later, was to do exactly that, by placing the primacy of the Pope within the larger context of the whole body of bishops.) Although the longer he lived, the more clear it seemed to Newman that 'there is but one Church, and that is the Roman communion', this could not blind his eyes to its corruptions and scandals; it was at least a 'great relief' that the immediate responsibility for the recent action against Döllinger lay not with the authorities at Rome, but with the Archbishop of Munich.[56] To an enquirer who wondered whether Newman would join the Roman Catholic Church now if he had stayed in the Church of England, he replied simply that if he had refused 'the grace of conversion' which God had offered him, it would have been withdrawn, and he would no doubt have been 'left, a worthless stump, to cumber the ground and to remain where I was till I died'. Yet again, he reiterated that he had not left the Church of England 'from despair', but for the two concurrent reasons which he had given in the *Apologia*: first, his study of the Fathers had raised the alarming question whether the Anglican Church was not in the equivalent position of the Arian and Monophysite Churches; second, the bishops' opposition to *Tract 90* '*confirmed* the interpretation which I had put upon the Fathers, that they *who loved the Fathers, could have no place in the Church of England*'.[57]

In July he wrote to his sister Jemima about a volume of violin music containing his name and the date 1817, which a friend of the family had just given him, after finding it, to her surprise, in an auction. Years before, as Newman remembered only too well, it had been auctioned among the contents of 17 Southampton Street, when his father had gone bankrupt. It was an embarrassing as well as poignant reminder of the past. He had no intention of saying anything which would reflect on his father, who had urged him to remove all his possessions to Oxford just before the bankruptcy. The 'poor book' was 'like a voice from the grave'. It was well worn and was full of associations. 'What a world of history', he sighed, 'has any single family in it, which perishes like the leaves in Autumn.'[58]

Not only was Newman increasingly concerned with death, but for some time he had been thinking about the afterlife, or, more

---

[55] Ibid. 330.   [56] Ibid. 341.   [57] Ibid. 352–3.   [58] Ibid. 352.

particularly, about the problems raised for religious belief by the doctrine of hell. In the *Grammar of Assent* he suggested that the force of 'eternal' punishment was not self-evident:

Eternity, or endlessness, is in itself mainly a negative idea, though the idea of suffering is positive. Its fearful force, as an element of future punishment, lies in what it excludes; it means never any change of state, no annihilation or restoration; but what, considered positively, it adds to suffering, we do not know. For what we know, the suffering of one moment may in itself have no bearing, or but a partial bearing, on the suffering of the next; and thus, as far as its intensity is concerned, it may vary with every lost soul. This may be so, unless we assume that the suffering is necessarily attended by a consciousness of duration and succession, by a present imagination of its past and its future, by a sustained power of realizing its continuity.[59]

Damnation without pain might be a possibility, or the pain might diminish in time. Newman was keenly aware that the idea of hell was a 'tremendous stumbling-block', hence his anxiety 'to soften the difficulty'. But while it was 'the great crux in the Christian system', still (he had once gone so far as to assert) it was 'the turning point between Christianity and pantheism'.[60] What he had said in the *Grammar* had been said 'with fear and trembling'; in years to come it might be condemned at Rome.[61] Certainly the Catholic doctrine of purgatory, which implied there were 'innumerable degrees of grace and sanctity among the saved',[62] meant that there was a less awful alternative to hell. But he rejected the suggestion that the possibility of salvation might be extended beyond death, if only because this would presumably involve the period of probation being extended for all, including those who had already been saved in this life.

If the traditional Christian doctrine of hell had become an obstacle to modern, thinking people, Roman Catholicism presented its own peculiar problems. On the one hand, Newman explained to R. H. Hutton, its claims were more circumscribed than might be supposed. Thus, a Catholic could no more list the contents of revelation than the details of morality, for

there are many things which we know on the whole, but of which we cannot tell the boundaries. I know what is morally right, yet I cannot draw a sharp line in matters of detail between what is right and what is wrong. And so there may be points in Revelation which do not positively and undeniably command my faith, while yet there are points which certainly do.

The Church was like 'a standing Apostolic committee—to answer questions, which the Apostles are not here to answer, concerning what

---

[59] *GA* 271–2.   [60] *LD* xiii. 319.   [61] Ibid. xxv. 292–3.
[62] Ibid. 362.

they received and preached'. But because 'the Church does not know more than the Apostles knew, there are many questions which the Church cannot answer'.[63] On the other hand, the extreme Ultramontanes were now agitating for an extension of the Church's claims as far as possible in the direction of omniscience. There was still the threat of the Council reassembling and drawing up a definition which would extend the range of the Church's infallibility to questions of politics and science, for example. Newman guessed correctly that, since the definition which had been passed attributed to the Pope the same infallibility which the Church possessed, the Ultramontanes would now turn their attention from the question of papal infallibility to that of the Church, since whatever was defined about the Church would also apply to the Pope. Faced with that dire possibility, Newman speculated hopefully that 'so great a change' might be 'accompanied by the throwing open of St Peter's Chair to all nations', as well as by an enlargement of the college of cardinals and 'many other extensions' which would 'trim St Peter's boat'.[64]

A high Anglican clergyman wrote to Newman to express amazement at the peremptory pressure put on the elderly Döllinger to accept the definition, which had led to his leaving the Church and the beginning of the schismatic 'Old Catholic' movement. He also contrasted the devout German Catholics, who crowded the churches on weekdays as well as Sundays, with half-empty Italian masses, celebrated perfunctorily and attended mostly by women and children. Newman not only agreed, but added a scathing denunciation of the devaluation of faith which Ultramontane attitudes involved:

Every consideration, the fullest time should be given to those who have to make up their minds to hold an article of faith which is new to them. To take up at once such an article may be the act of a vigorous faith; but it may also be the act of a man who will believe anything because he believes nothing, and is ready to profess whatever his ecclesiastical, that is, his political party requires of him. There are too many high ecclesiastics in Italy and England, who think that to believe is as easy as to obey—that is, they talk as if they did not know what an act of faith is. A German who hesitates may have more of the real spirit of faith than an Italian who swallows.[65]

But he continued to think Döllinger '*wrong* in making the worst of the definition instead of making the best'. It was simply playing into the hands of the extremists to exaggerate the terms of the definition, which in fact had been a 'defeat' for the Ultramontanes.[66]

Newman never wavered in his confident prophecy, even certainty, that the Church's present situation, both internally and externally,

---

[63] Ibid. 418.   [64] Ibid. 420.   [65] Ibid. 430.   [66] Ibid. 438.

would sooner or later undergo a radical transformation. Not only would there be a natural reaction against Ultramontanism, but revolutionary changes in the political and social order would necessitate corresponding developments in the Church. In reply to a letter from Matthew Arnold, he agreed with him about the special danger which the modern world presented for the Church of England, in so far as it was essentially anti-democratic in a way that the Roman Catholic Church was not. As an Anglican he had agreed with Hurrell Froude that the Established Church must alter its political position; but both of them had been vehemently opposed to anything in the nature of a rebellion against the state, and had counselled patience on the question of establishment. 'It often happens that those who will not bide their time, fail, not because they are not substantially right, but because they are thus impatient.' Perhaps Lamennais, about whom Froude had been so enthusiastic, would turn out to be 'a true prophet after all'. It was true 'the present Papacy' was hardly likely to adopt 'such a line of action', but it had happened before in the time of Hildebrand (Pope Gregory VII), 'and, though we may have a season of depression, as there was a hideous degradation before Gregory, yet it may be in the counsels of Providence that the Catholic Church may at length come out unexpectedly as a popular power'.[67] As for contemporary political developments, Newman thought a democracy needed, like other political forms, 'a drag or regulator'—for 'when was a demos other than a tyrant?'[68]

This was not the first time Arnold had written to him. A few years earlier he had written to say how much he owed to Newman's 'influence and writings'—'the impression of which is so profound, and so mixed up with all that is most essential in what I do and say'. Considering Arnold's special position as the prophet of culture as a replacement for religion, it was a remarkable testimony. Arnold now reiterated his earlier acknowledgement, explaining that 'nothing can ever do away the effect you have produced upon me, for it consists in a general disposition of mind rather than in a particular set of ideas.'[69] Newman was clearly as gratified by this unexpected bouquet as he was irritated by yet another brickbat from his co-religionist W. G. Ward, who wrote with typical extravagance to Emily Bowles that he had had to 'choose between submitting my intellect to *Fr Newman* on the one hand or to *Pope and Bishops* on the other'. It would have been, he declared, a 'formal mortal sin' to have sided with Newman ('the most attractive person I ever came across'), and he was very grateful for the active part he had been able to play in the 'sacred cause' of preventing him from going to Oxford.[70] The vein of this was reminiscent of the old declarations of Faber and

[67] *LD* xxv. 440, 442.   [68] Ibid. xxxi. 106.   [69] Ibid. xxv. 440–1.
[70] Ibid. 452 n. 1.

Dalgairns. But Newman could not bring himself to be indignant with the eccentric Ward: he was at least 'thoroughly honest and above board—which other persons are not—He says out all he thinks—and in the mildest, most affectionate manner would call me an unmistakeable heretic'. As for his prominent role in the Oxford affair, he had at any rate not been guilty of 'smooth words' and secret intrigue. Newman felt that Ward had 'ever in feeling been kinder to me than I to him'.[71] The hostile gossip (in which he knew, for example, that Ward's wife took part) was certainly painful. But it had taken twenty years for the Protestant legend that he had been a crypto-Papist while in the Church of England to be laid; eventually the Catholic myth that he was a crypto-heretic would suffer a similar fate.

If only he could complete the republication of his books and the sorting out of his letters and papers, he felt he would then 'have no excuse for living'.[72] In the middle of December he finished 'Trials of Theodoret' to add to his life of St John Chrysostom, which he had originally written for the *Rambler* and which he was to republish in the second of three volumes of *Historical Sketches*. He had intended there to be four volumes, but he was at last forced to abandon his original idea of including other biographical sketches of St Ambrose, St Jerome, and (perhaps) St Athanasius to complete the work he had planned back in 1859 on the 'Ancient Saints'. The completed essay on Theodoret reflects the crisis of the time in the form of several critical references to Councils, which, however, culminate in this carefully balanced judgement on the Council of Ephesus: 'As to the dogmatic authority of the doctrine which was defined in the Council, it is not at all affected by the scandals . . . because it is the law of Divine Providence . . . that truth is wrought out by the indirect operation of error and sin, and that the supernatural gifts of the Gospel are held in "earthen vessels", and do not guarantee moral perfection in their possessors.'[73]

As the year drew to a close, Newman lamented that the Pope had remained in Rome after the fall of the city. He was 'in a false position'.[74] Having refused to compromise earlier, he ought to have left rather than expose himself to humiliation. The dignified course would have been to say to the people of Rome, 'I don't want to force myself on you. I am not your tyrant or conqueror, but your Father.'[75] On the other hand, it was most unlikely that any serious threat was posed to the Church by the departure of the Old Catholics, who would never be anything more than a sect—although Döllinger's intention had been to introduce reform inside the Church, not to create a new church. There was one ray of light in the darkness: however bad things might look for the Church, at least

---

[71] Ibid. 445.　　　[72] Ibid. 450.　　　[73] *HS* ii. 213.
[74] *LD* xxv. 455.　　　[75] Ibid. 454.

open irreligion was preferable to the hypocrisy of the nominal religious profession so widespread when the Church was in a position of strength. Anyway, numerical triumphalism as always seemed unrealistic to Newman: was there ever really more than a small faithful remnant in the Church?

3

In February 1872 Newman completed the draft of an essay on 'Causes of the Rise and Successes of Arianism', a heresy which was 'nothing less than one passage in the history of the perpetual conflict, which ever has been waged, and which ever will be waged, between the Church and the secular power'.[76] He had long ago intended to write a kind of introduction to his *Select Treatises of St Athanasius*, and it seemed opportune now that he was preparing a collected volume of *Tracts Theological and Ecclesiastical*, which would include the four Latin dissertations that he had published in Rome in 1847, the English version of which was in his original translation of St Athanasius. In January he had put the final touches to *Discussions and Arguments on Various Subjects*. It consisted of his 1836 *British Magazine* article 'Home Thoughts Abroad' (which he thought an ambiguous and vague title, so he renamed it 'How to Accomplish it'), a couple of the *Tracts, The Tamworth Reading Room, Who's to Blame?*, and his review of Seeley's *Ecce Homo* (entitled 'An Internal Argument for Christianity'). He was rather afraid the volume lacked unity. Early in the year, too, a new edition of *Oxford University Sermons* was published; an additional sermon was added, as well as a new preface (containing a useful summary of the treatment of the relation of faith and reason) and also notes. The next project was to collect together three volumes of *Historical Sketches* (they appeared out of order, beginning with the third in 1872 and ending with the second in 1873), incorporating a number of his Anglican and Catholic writings, including *Lectures on the Turks, Church of the Fathers*, and *Office and Work of Universities* (now entitled 'Rise and Progress of Universities'). The volume of *Tracts Theological and Ecclesiastical* was published two years later in 1874, when Newman was greatly relieved by the reaction of a theologian like Dr Russell to the essay on Arianism, where he had gone further than anywhere else in his application of the principle of doctrinal development.

The problem of university education for Catholics remained a festering sore. In 1868 the bishops had recognized that some provision

[76] *TT* 142.

had to be made, although a Catholic university seemed out of the question. But it was not until the autumn of 1871 that a meeting was held to try and implement ideas put forward by the bishops. Newman declined an invitation to attend. He told J. Spencer Northcote, the President of Oscott, who was a member of the committee set up to explore possibilities, that he despaired of any solution so long as the present policy was in force, which would 'impose restraints . . . destructive of the very life of a University', and which refused to acknowledge that of its nature the 'cultivation of the intellect' involved 'a risk to the faith'.[77] Nor could he now support the idea of a Catholic college at Oxford, which Northcote advocated, for two reasons. First, 'it seems to me that the Anglican Church and the University are almost or quite in a whirlpool of unbelief, even if they be as yet at some distance from the gulf and its abyss.' Second, and more serious,

The two main instruments of infidelity just now are physical science and history; physical science is used against Scripture, and history against dogma; the Vatican Council by its decrees about the inspiration of Scripture and the Infallibility of the Pope has simply thrown down the gauntlet to the science and the historical research of the day.

The problem was that there had been 'no intellectual scrutiny, no controversies as yet over the Vatican definitions, and their sense will have to be wrought out not in friendly controversy, but in a mortal fight at Oxford, in the presence of Catholics and Protestants, between Protestant Professors and Tutors and a Catholic College'. Up until recently, Trent had been the last Council, 'and our theologians during a long 300 years had prepared us for the fight—now we are new born children, the birth of the Vatican Council . . . We do not know what exactly we hold—what we may grant, what we must maintain.'[78] Councils 'generally acted as a lever, displacing and disordering portions of the existing theological system', and were often followed by bitter controversies within the Church.[79] Newman's conclusion was that a Catholic university or college for higher studies was undesirable because 'our present rulers would never give us a real one', while a Catholic college at Oxford 'would be challenging controversy, and committing Catholic theologians most dangerously in the religious difficulties of the day'. In the absence of any satisfactory alternative, he could only say that 'the Bishops ought to have let things alone seven years ago, and that, in our present straits, they will do best to undo their own work, and to let Catholics go to Protestant Colleges . . . and to provide . . . a strong Jesuit mission'.[80] As for the bishops' suggestion of a board of examiners with the power to confer degrees, he repeated what he had said in the

---

[77] *LD* xxvi. 34, 59.   [78] Ibid. 59–60.   [79] Ibid. 76.   [80] Ibid. 61.

Idea of a University, that 'a residence without Examinations comes nearer to the idea of a University Education than examinations without residence'. Examinations by themselves, he insisted, were only likely to 'promote cramming and create prigs'.[81] Perhaps delay was the best policy: 'Great changes are taking place at Rome.' As for Manning, he seemed to think 'only an ignorant laity to be manageable', and that 'the Church in modern England could thrive in mental stagnation'.[82] It would be no problem for so astute an ecclesiastic as the Archbishop to relax the university ban without appearing to abandon the principle of Catholic education. The fact was they were 'driven into a corner', and it was hard to avoid the conclusion that 'mixed education in the higher schools is as much a necessity now in England, as it was in the East in the days of St Basil and St Chrysostom'. Apart from inviting invidious comparisons, the discipline of a Catholic college at Oxford 'would not really counteract the temptations to unbelief and sin'; the only real 'antagonist of the world, the flesh, and the devil is the direct power of religion', which could only come from a strong Catholic spiritual presence. Indeed, a small community like a 'close' Catholic college could be more easily spoilt by one bad member in it and so be more dangerous than an 'open' university.[83]

A speech in February by A. C. Tait, the Archbishop of Canterbury, expressing reservations about the Athanasian creed, aroused great controversy. Newman advised high Anglican defenders of the creed to try and achieve a stronger unity among themselves. This, of course, was difficult without 'belief in an external authority to make men think and act together'. But while unity was 'not indispensible for the destructive party', it was 'a first necessity for the conservative'.[84] His own view was that it was 'only a matter of time, how long the Anglican Church retains any part of the faith—but that is no reason why I should not wish it to keep what it has kept so long, as long as possible—but how will it stand against the new world rising up in the midst of it?' He had to admit that what reconciled him to the definition of papal infallibility was the current crisis of belief which required 'a strong force . . . to bind men together—that they may act together'. He warned a high Anglican correspondent that this was 'not a time for the practical tolerance of a hundred opinions'.[85]

Liberal ideas about the creeds were easily developed into a general relativism about doctrine itself, as Newman was reminded by another letter from Matthew Arnold, which accompanied a copy of Arnold's new selection for elementary schools from the book of Isaiah. Newman's response was to deplore treating the Bible 'as 'literature in the first

---

[81] *LD* xxvi. 26.   [82] Ibid. 65–6.   [83] Ibid. 75–6.
[84] Ibid. 48.   [85] Ibid. 55–6.

place'. It was all very well for a religious person to appreciate the poetry of Scripture and to study its text in a scholarly way. But most children were not naturally 'devout', and important doctrinal parts of the Bible, like the prophecies of Christ in Isaiah, came to them 'in the garb of poetry'. Study of the literal text and its historical and geographical background might supersede or dislodge this kind of religious learning. Similarly, in a Protestant country like England, the 'great dogmatic truths of the gospel are inculcated on them in the medium of the imagination and the affections'.[86] Unlike the Church, the Bible might not be able to teach doctrine ('a book does not speak; it is shut till it is opened'),[87] but it bestowed other advantages from which continental Catholics in particular could benefit. Many years' experience had shown Newman that his early enthusiasm for the simple, objective faith of Catholics was only one side of the picture, and that a Bible religion had its value.

It is the best book of meditations which can be, because it is divine. This is why we see such multitudes in France and Italy giving up religion altogether. They have not impressed upon their hearts the life of our Lord and Saviour as given us in the Evangelists. They believe merely with the intellect, not with the heart. Argument may overset a mere assent of the reason, but not a faith founded in a personal love for the Object of Faith. They quarrel with their priests, and then they give up the Church. We can quarrel with men, we cannot quarrel with a book.[88]

As for the Old Testament, it was a closed book to Catholics, to whom it meant nothing at all.

Towards Döllinger, whose quarrel with the Council had become a quarrel with the Church, Newman was still sympathetic, but critical. Characteristically, he diagnosed Döllinger's crisis as fundamentally a failure of imagination. Döllinger was not 'a philosophical historian', in the sense that 'He does not throw himself into the state of things which he reads about—he does not enter into the position of Honorius, or of the Council 40 years afterwards. He ties you down like Shylock to the letter of the bond, instead of realizing what took place as a scene.' Newman could not understand how Döllinger could accept the Council of Ephesus, for example, which was notorious for intrigue and violence, and not the recent one. Perhaps, he shrewdly guessed, 'by this time the very force of logic, to say nothing of philosophy, has obliged him to give up Councils altogether'. His own depressing conclusion was that if the proceedings of Councils 'are to be the measure of their authority, they are, with few exceptions, a dreary, unlovely phenomenon in the Church'.[89] A few years later he felt even more pessimistic about

---

[86] Ibid. 95. [87] *SN* 53. [88] *LD* xxvi. 87. [89] Ibid. 120.

Councils, but correspondingly much more positive about the papacy: 'The more one examines the Councils, the less satisfactory they are . . . [but] the less satisfactory *they*, the more majestic and trust-winning, and the more imperatively necessary, is the action of the Holy See.'[90] However, the human frailties of even the highest authorities in the Church were no argument against the truth of the Church's doctrines— because the patriarch Joseph 'by a gross deceit, obtained the blessing which was *due* to him', this did not alter the fact that 'it had already been promised to him and was by a divine right his'.[91]

In July Newman paid another visit to Abbotsford. Hope-Scott was in poor health, and it was to be the last meeting between the two men. Among the many changes in the world since Newman's first visit was the rise of tourism. 'There are those excursionists again', he grumbled to St John: 'Cooke's—walking past the windows—You can't conceive the state of this place in this point of view. Yesterday men of that kidney were before the windows at 6 o'clock in the morning—and they go on all day. Some poke their heads into the windows—'[92] There was no sign of Hope-Scott's recovering, and Newman remarked to Henry Wilberforce, who was himself to die next year, a few days before Hope-Scott: 'I sometimes think how dreary it would be for me to be left only with younger men, my contemporaries and old friends being gone.'[93] Before travelling to Scotland Newman had visited London, where he was 'turned out' of St Paul's by a verger. He reported to the recently appointed Dean, his old friend R. W. Church:

I stood just inside the door listening to the chanting of the Psalms, of which I am so fond. First came Verger one, a respectful person, inquiring if I wanted a seat in the choir, half a mile off me. No, I said—I was content where I was. Then came a second, not respectful, with a voice of menace—I still said No. Then came a third, I don't recollect much about him, except that he said he could provide me with a seat. Then came Number 2 again, in a compulsory mood, on which I vanished.

Church, who was annoyed by the unfortunate incident, must have been mortified by Newman's comment: 'I am sure if I was a dissenter . . . nothing would attract me more to the Church of England than to be allowed to stand at the door of a Cathedral—did not St Augustine while yet a Manichee, stand and watch St Ambrose? No verger turned him out.' Knowing vergers as he did from his Anglican days, Newman was only amused. But, he assured the Dean, the newspaper report that he had been turned away because he was shabbily dressed was not true: 'On the contrary it was simply a bran new coat, which I never put on till

---

[90] *LD* xxviii. 172.   [91] Ibid. xxvi. 366, 377.   [92] Ibid. 140.
[93] Ibid. 157.

I went on that visit to you . . . I thought it due to London. Indeed, all my visiting clothes are new, for I do not wear them here . . . *They* (the clothes) . . . wear out a weary time themselves in a dark closet . . .'[94] He apologized to Church for sending him a copy of the *Grammar of Assent*; it seemed like 'talking shop'—something Anglican clergymen who were primarily 'gentlemen' did not do, unlike Catholic priests, who were professional men; he himself had 'a great dislike of this shopping personally', and he remembered how George Richmond, 'when he took my portrait', found 'I was the only person he could not draw out'.[95]

September saw the publication of another of Newman's famous public letters. In a leading article, *The Times* claimed that the Pope had never disowned responsibility for the Massacre of St Bartholomew's Day, and would now be prevented from doing so by the infallibility definition. Newman felt bound to speak out, when nobody in authority was apparently prepared to. He did so, eloquently and unequivocally.

No Pope can make evil good. No Pope has any power over those eternal moral principles which God has imprinted on our hearts and consciences. If any Pope has, with his eyes open, approved of treachery or cruelty, let those defend that Pope, who can . . . Craft and cruelty . . . eventually strike the heads of those who are guilty of them.[96]

Whether Pope Gregory XIII had any share in the massacre was for historians to decide. But even if he were guilty, this would not compromise his infallibility—after all, even Caiaphas had prophesied, and infallibility was not the same as impeccability. Newman also wrote to the *Guardian* sharply denying the allegation of J. M. Capes that he did not really believe in papal infallibility, and citing a number of passages in his writings, beginning with the *Essay on Development*, for more or less explicit avowals of the doctrine.

The dogma itself he continued to explain and interpret to people who wrote to him for advice and information. The only infallibility the Pope possessed was the infallibility of the Church. It was a negative gift; unlike the Apostles, the Popes were not inspired but merely protected from error. Nor did definitions involving infallibility 'come of a positive divine guidance, but of human means, research, consulting theologians'.[97] But he told Bishop Moriarty that he did not see how he could write a pamphlet in defence and elucidation of the doctrine, as he had done in his *Letter to Pusey*. There were many historical objections to papal infallibility which would require careful and lengthy answering. He wished, however, he 'could do something against that dreadful

[94] Ibid. 218, 221.   [95] Ibid. 218–19.   [96] Ibid. 163–4.
[97] Ibid. 171.

growth of Indifferentism among Catholics which will be, and is already, the fruit of the transactions at Rome in 1870'.[98]

Then, too, there was the alarming abandonment and rejection of ordinary Christian beliefs among educated English people: 'Either the end of the world is coming, or a great purifying and perfecting of religious belief and ethics, which it may take centuries to complete. Trial does good, though it involves many cruel defections.'[99] It was amazing to find a newspaper 'calmly meditating what is to be done' when 'Christianity has vanished from the earth'.[100] Newman feared for the next generation: 'I look at our poor boys here with anxiety and compassion, feeling what sophistries and temptations of the intellect and social perplexities may be in store for them in middle life.' There was a real danger that all religion would be eventually excluded from the educational system. Where would the process stop? Once 'the moral and religious instincts of the mind' were given up as 'superstitions', Newman did not see how 'the most logical arguments in behalf of their truth' would restore them. He had 'often thought' that if he had killed several people, he 'might get over the sense that murder, as such, is a sin'. It might well be that 'the idea of a God' would simply disappear.[101] One surprising new development was the growth of 'spiritualism':

That it is the work of bad spirits is very likely—but Satan casts out Satan so far as this, that the phenomena are a great puzzle to men like Professor Huxley . . . One of the more curious and arresting prospects of the coming years is how the materialists will meet the challenge—tho' I suppose Satan will take care that, when it comes to the point, the two parties will not eat each other up.[102]

Once more Newman insisted that the right way to counter unbelief was by putting before people the person of Christ in the Gospels. Philip's remark to Nathaniel 'Come and see' was still as pertinent as ever, but was just what freethinkers wanted to prevent. In ordinary human affairs the personal factor was regarded as indispensable—affidavits were no substitute for real live witnesses, for example. On the other hand, the fact that the Gospels were the basis for a living faith and for union between Christians did not seem to Newman to alter the apparently unbridgeable gap between Catholics and those Protestants who regarded the Catholic Church as 'the work of the evil one'—and, he remarked flatly, 'how is either party to give up their own tenet on the point without losing their Christianity?'[103] It was quite true that 'unreal, and but verbal, differences do exist between religious men—but such are not the differences which exist between Catholics and their opponents'; and 'nothing is more unmeaning, as well as more untrue, than compromises and comprehensions.'[104]

[98] *LD* xxvi. 198.   [99] Ibid. 222.   [100] Ibid. 227.   [101] Ibid. 268.
[102] Ibid. 228.   [103] Ibid. 233.   [104] Ibid. 234.

The republication of the works (in 'groups, as far as possible')[105] in a uniform edition was going ahead. After five years, twenty-three volumes had been completed and there were plans for another eleven. Newman was grateful to Copeland for 'breaking the ice': for himself to have begun republishing his Anglican writings would have been very difficult, as alterations would have alienated public opinion, while leaving the text as it stood would have caused scandal to Catholics. The solution he had adopted of adding critical notes seemed to have worked well, and he had even dedicated a volume of *Historical Sketches*, half of which he had written as an Anglican, to a Catholic bishop without causing comment. As a general principle, he felt it was far better 'to answer, not to suppress, what is erroneous', for truth 'has a power of its own, which makes its way'.[106]

At the end of April 1873 Henry Wilberforce died. He was Newman's 'oldest friend', and at Oriel he had been closer to him than to any other undergraduate. Newman vividly remembered first meeting him in 1826—'What a new world has come in since that! yet it seems all gone and that alone to remain—'[107] At the end of the funeral Mass he was asked to say a few words, which he managed, although he broke down twice. Less than a week later he preached at the requiem Mass for Hope-Scott at the Jesuit church in Farm Street. His panegyric included the characteristic praise that his old friend had not been one of those who are 'practical and sensible in all things save in religion'; instead, he had been 'consistent' in 'instinctively' turning from 'bye-ways and cross-paths' and taking 'a broad, intelligible view' of the issues, evincing the same 'straightforward, clear, good sense which he showed in secular matters' when it came to considering the claims of the Catholic Church.[108] In July Henry Wilberforce's older brother, Bishop Samuel Wilberforce, was killed in a riding accident. 'There is something', Newman mused, 'inexpressibly sad in the picture of a man going out on a beautiful Saturday, with a few friends, in a beautiful country, with every thing calm and joyous and heavenly around him, and suddenly being carried off to the awful darkness of the other world.'[109]

At the beginning of October he preached a prophetic sermon called 'The Infidelity of the Future' at the opening of a new seminary at Olton, near Birmingham. Sombrely, he warned the students 'that the trials which lie before us are such as would appal and make dizzy even such courageous hearts as St Athanasius, St Gregory I, or St Gregory VII. And they would confess that, dark as the prospect of their own day was to them severally, ours has a darkness different in kind from any that has been before it.' Individual unbelievers were no new phenomenon, but

---

[105] Ibid. xxviii. 108.   [106] Ibid. xxvi. 294.   [107] Ibid. 278.
[108] *OS* 276.   [109] *LD* xxvi. 342.

their theories had hitherto not been 'current and popular ideas'. The fact was that 'Christianity has never yet had experience of a world simply irreligious.' The orthodoxy of Protestants could no longer be relied upon, while English Catholics were likely to be seen as 'the enemies' of 'civil liberty' and 'national progress', and to face discrimination, particularly since they were too prominent to be ignored and yet too weak to defend themselves. The best defence of religious belief, he concluded, was 'a clear consistent idea of revealed truth', since consistency 'is a persuasive argument for a system being true'. Certainty and completeness of doctrine were only to be found in the Catholic Church, and there was no missionary like a well-instructed Catholic.[110] An eye-witness account tells us that Newman used neither his manuscript text nor notes, 'but held a small Bible in his hand, where he sought out in a curiously eager fashion the texts which he was about to recite. His voice sounded low and clear, with exquisite modulations, as if he were thinking aloud.'[111]

Also in October the Irish bishops announced various reforms at the Catholic University, including for the first time the appointment of laymen to the episcopal board of management and to a newly established finance committee, something the former Rector had often vainly requested. Perhaps the university in Dublin could become 'a middle station at which clergy and laity can meet, so as to learn to understand and to yield to each other—and from which, as from a common ground, they may act in unison upon an age, which is running headlong into infidelity'. As it was, there seemed to Newman to be 'ecclesiastics all over Europe, whose policy it is to keep the laity at arms-length; and hence the laity have been disgusted and become infidel, and only two parties exist, both ultras in opposite directions'.[112] In England, Manning was going ahead with his plans for a Catholic university college at Kensington, which was to be under close clerical control. In November Newman received an invitation to serve on its senate. The proposal to obtain degrees from London University offered an excuse to decline on the grounds of his lifelong opposition to an institution which was the antithesis, educationally and religiously, of his own idea of a university. It was 'a body', he tartly reminded Manning, 'which has been the beginning, and source, and symbol of all the Liberalism existing in the educated classes for the last forty years'.[113] He was invited to preach at the opening of the college in 1875, but refused on the same grounds.

In April 1874 Newman began a correspondence about Catholicism with his nephew John Rickards Mozley, Jemima's son. The Catholic

---

[110] *CS* 121, 123, 128, 133. [111] *LD* xxvi. 373 n. 1. [112] Ibid. 394.
[113] Ibid. 390.

Church, he maintained, was the 'embodiment' of a revelation which was intended to complete and protect the basic moral and religious truths, which, unlike the 'truths of science', cannot 'take care of themselves', but are 'delicate, subtle, fitful, mysterious, incapable of being grasped, easily put down and trampled underfoot'.[114] He had made the same point years before in a memorable passage in his lecture 'Christianity and Medical Science'[115] (which he had republished the previous year in *The Idea of a University*).

The great argument in favour of the Christian revelation, he told his nephew a year later, was that at least it recognized and confronted, even if it did not explain, the insoluble problem of evil. Christ died to destroy sin; yet strangely it continued to exist, even in the Church. Indeed, the history of the Catholic Church exhibited the most serious scandals; but, he insisted, 'the great question to me is, not what evil is left in the Church, but what good has energized in it and been practically exercised in it, and has left its mark there for all posterity'.[116] There was no doubting that dreadful crimes had been committed in the name of the Church at the time of the Reformation, which had 'frightened the Court of Rome out of its wits'. The conviction that 'the one thing needful was to put it down anyhow' had led to political involvement of an unsavoury kind: 'A large society, such as the Church, is necessarily a political power, and to touch politics is to touch pitch.' Since that time the Church 'has sustained a severe loss, as well as the English and German nationalities themselves, by their elimination from it; not the least of the evil being that in consequence the Latin element, which is in the ascendant, does not, cannot know, how great the loss is'. The general disestablishment of the Church might remedy the evil: 'Influential portions of the Latin races may fall off; and, if Popes are chosen from other nationalities, other ideas will circulate among us and gradually gain influence.' But the fact was that at present the Church was 'encumbered by its connection with moribund nations' such as Italy and Spain.[117] For the first 1,500 years of its existence, Newman claimed, the Church had 'always been in advance of the age'; but just as the Jews had been allowed divorce as a practical necessity 'to avoid worse evils, so it has not always been possible for the Church to do upon the spot that which was abstractedly best'.[118]

His nephew complained that the Roman Catholic Church seemed opposed to all forms of modern progress. Newman's reply was carefully nuanced. While distancing himself from certain contemporary Catholic attitudes, he agreed there was an important element of truth in Mozley's charge, which needed to be highlighted, not denied. It was certainly

[114] Ibid. xxvii. 54–5.   [115] *Idea*, 413.   [116] *LD* xxvii. 261.
[117] Ibid. 264–6.   [118] Ibid. 283.

true that there was indeed an 'ethical' difference between Catholicism and Protestantism—although at the same time 'opposition to physical science or to social and political progress, on the part of Catholics, is only an accidental and clumsy form in which this vital antagonism energizes—a form, to which in its popular dress and shape, my own reason does not respond'. The distinction was, of course, one he had drawn out on previous occasions. Early Christianity had an 'ethical system' which 'is the living principle also of present Catholicism, and not of any form of Protestantism whatever'. Regardless of doctrinal and ecclesiastical divergences, 'still the *ethos* of the Catholic Church is what it was of old time, and whatever and whoever quarrels with Catholicism now, quarrels virtually, and would have quarrelled, if alive, 1800 years ago, with the Christianity of Apostles and Evangelists'. This 'ethical character', whether of modern Catholicism or of primitive Christianity, was characterized by its 'utter variance with the ethical character of human society at large as we find it at all times'. Whether it was the martyrs of the first centuries, or the battle against the Arians in the fourth century, or the reforms of Hildebrand, or the more recent history of the Jesuits, 'I say the Catholic Church is emphatically and singularly, in her relation to human philosophy and statesmanship, as was the Apostolic Church, "the Church militant here on earth".' The 'direct and prime aim' of the Church was the worship of God, whereas 'the sole object . . . of the social and political world everywhere, is to make the most of this life'.[119] Advances in secular progress were not to be despised or rejected, but they were secondary to the spiritual priorities of the Gospel, loyalty to which was more important for the Church than keeping up with the times.

In the middle of August Newman suffered an unpleasant bout of diarrhoea which kept him in bed for a week. He wrote to Ambrose St John, who was away on holiday: 'I have been down in my spirits, which is very unusual with me.'[120] He was more specific in his journal entry: 'I have so depressed a feeling that I have done nothing through my long life—and especially that now I am doing nothing at all.' He knew he was more highly regarded by Anglicans than before, but he felt unappreciated in Catholic intellectual circles, particularly by the Jesuits. He reckoned that they thought he had failed to contribute anything of value to the great religious questions of the day, or rather, that the line he had taken was 'too free and sceptical' and conceded too much. The Jesuits had always given him moral support, but he sensed their attitude towards him had changed since the *Grammar of Assent* and the Vatican Council. So influential and powerful were the Jesuits (too

---

[119] *LD* xxvii. 386–8.   [120] Ibid. 111.

much so for the good of the Church, Newman thought) that dissension from their views implied one was not taking 'the Catholic line'.[121]

Six weeks later he wondered what he had been doing for the last fifteen years, during which time he had only written two full-length books. There were, of course, other writings, and during the last few years he had been busy republishing his works. Still, before 1859 he calculated he had written almost a book a year. One obvious reason he had not written between 1859 and 1864 was, of course, the trouble he had got into over the *Rambler*. Mgr. Talbot had been kind enough to say to Ambrose St John three years after the *Apologia* appeared: 'He had ceased writing, and a good riddance—Why did he ever begin again?' Another reason was that he hardly ever wrote 'without a *call*'. The *Grammar* was practically 'the only exception', but even that he had written out of a sense of 'duty'. Without a definite 'stimulus' he found it very difficult to put pen to paper.[122] What he did not know then was that, as so often before in his life, a new controversy was about to break out, which would force him to produce one of his most important and famous writings.

4

In October 1874 Gladstone published an article which referred, in passing, to the 'effort to Romanise the Church and the people of England'. According to Gladstone, there was no chance of it any longer, now that 'no one can become her convert without renouncing his moral and mental freedom, and placing his civil loyalty and duty at the mercy of another'. Newman welcomed the outburst, which was understandable in view of Manning's provocative Ultramontanism, as it was possible to 'speak against Gladstone, while it would not be decent to speak against Manning'.[123] As before in the controversies with Kingsley and Pusey, there was a chance to strike a blow indirectly against Catholic extremists. And during the next few weeks Newman tried to write something in answer to Gladstone, but without success. Then on 5 November Gladstone published his pamphlet *The Vatican Decrees in their bearing on Civil Allegiance: A Political Expostulation*. Gladstone thought (mistakenly) that the Pope had been behind the Irish bishops' opposition to his Irish University Bill, which had failed to get through Parliament after Irish Members had voted against it. His sense of grievance over this defeat in March 1873, which led to the fall of the government in 1874, had been aggravated a few months afterwards by the resignation of the Marquis of Ripon from the Cabinet, as a prelude

---

[121] *AW* 270.   [122] Ibid. 272–3.   [123] *LD* xxvii. 122–3.

to his becoming a Catholic. Gladstone's pamphlet, then, which was popular in tone and became a best-seller, was no mere academic exercise, and Newman saw immediately that it would have to be answered. Once again he attempted without success to meet the challenge; although this time there was something substantial to answer, Gladstone was too 'rambling and slovenly' to answer 'with any logical exactness'. He felt the same difficulty as with his lectures in Dublin, when he had been addressing people he did not know; not only was he no politician, but he felt he had too 'little knowledge of the world at large, Protestant and Catholic'.[124] He called it 'the toughest job I ever had';[125] unless he was really effective, he would only harm the Catholic cause.

At last on 23 November, after working in vain for five or six hours a day for five or six weeks, he began 'a new arrangement of matter' and started on the first introductory section.[126] He wrote without stopping— 'life seemed to come into me of a sudden.'[127] The subject really demanded a whole book, and a weak pamphlet would only make matters worse. It was the most strenuous work he had undertaken since the *Apologia*, and he wondered if his health would stand up. He had never thought he would ever write against Gladstone, but however provocative the Ultramontanes, there was no excuse for accusing Catholics of being 'moral and mental slaves'—it was 'as unfair and untrue' as it was 'cruel'.[128] The pamphlet was to be in the form of a letter to the leading Catholic layman, the young Duke of Norfolk, who had been at the Oratory School, for 'I cannot write at all, except in the form of a letter, and he who is good enough to let me address him, must also be good enough to let me say, that he was one of those who asked me to write'.[129] He finished on 21 December after a month's continuous writing, and the 'pamphlet', which was actually 150 pages of close print, was published on 14 January 1875, the very day on which Gladstone retired as leader of the Liberal Party. A few days later, St John's translation of Bishop Fessler's *True and False Infallibility* also appeared; Fessler had been Secretary-General at the Council, and his book, which maintained a strictly moderate interpretation of papal infallibility, had received the official approval of Pius IX. It had already dealt 'a blow over the knuckles' to Newman's opponents, both to the 'outspeakers' like Ward (who 'is so above board, and outspoken, that he is quite charming'), and the 'whisperers, from whom especially I have long suffered' and 'whom (as Dickens says) I "object to" '.[130]

Right at the very beginning of *A Letter to the Duke of Norfolk*, Newman emphasizes a point he had already made with some force, before the

---

[124] *LD* xxvii. 156.   [125] Ibid. 158.   [126] Ibid. 159.   [127] Ibid. 194.
[128] Ibid. 170.   [129] Ibid. 171.   [130] Ibid. 183.

definition of papal infallibility, in a letter of March 1870, where he pointed out that however infallible the Pope might turn out to be, his pronouncements would still require interpretation. The same was true of a Council's definitions, which—just as 'lawyers explain acts of Parliament'—had to be explained by theologians. Obvious as the fact might be, the conclusion to be drawn from it had serious consequences for the fantasies of extreme Ultramontanism. 'Hence, I have never been able to see myself that the ultimate decision rests with any but the general Catholic intelligence.' Such a realistic theology of 'reception' was simply a further implication of Newman's cherished maxim, 'Securus judicat orbis terrarum.' (Later, in the *Letter to the Duke of Norfolk*, he was careful to emphasize that he simply meant that the whole Church ratified a definition as 'authentic', not that the 'subsequent reception' actually entered into the 'necessary conditions' of a dogmatic decision.[131]) In the same private letter he also noted that abstract definitions could not 'determine particular fact': the doctrine, for example, that there was no salvation outside the Church did not apply to people in 'invincible ignorance'.[132] For 'it does not follow, because there is no Church but one, which has the Evangelical gifts and privileges to bestow, that therefore no one can be saved without the intervention of that one Church'. And it was 'possible to belong to the soul of the Church without belonging to the body'.[133] Other teachings of the Church admitted of exceptions in practice, like the condemnations in theory of mixed education and usury. In the case of usury, moreover, as in that of the doctrine of absolute predestination, distinctions had been drawn between different connotations of the words in question, which had led to the serious modification, even suspension, of the abstract teaching. Such changes and qualifications in the Church's official teaching 'show what caution is to be observed' in interpreting her pronouncements.[134] But, on the other hand, because general doctrines cannot be divorced from concrete circumstances and contexts, it did not follow that condemnations of 'the very wording' of particular doctrinal deviations in books may not be infallible, since otherwise 'neither Pope nor Council could draw up a dogmatic definition at all, for the right exercise of words is involved in the right exercise of thought'.[135]

He continued to insist after the definition that 'the voice of the Schola Theologorum, of the whole Church diffusive' would 'in time make itself heard', and that 'Catholic instincts and ideas' would eventually 'assimilate and harmonize' it into the wider context of Catholic belief.[136] As time went on, too, theologians would 'settle the force of the wording of the dogma, just as the courts of law solve the meaning and bearing of

---

[131] *Diff.* ii. 372. [132] *LD* xxv. 71. [133] *Diff.* ii. 335.
[134] Ibid. 337. [135] Ibid. 330. [136] *LD* xxv. 284.

Acts of Parliament'.[137] While it was hardly more than common sense that ultimately the only way in which the solemn declarations of Councils and Popes could be authenticated was by the acceptance and recognition by the Church that they were indeed what they purported to be, nevertheless their interpretation involved necessarily the technicalities of theological science: the meaning of dogmatic statements was not self-evident, but they were 'always made with the anticipation and condition of this lawyer-like, or special-pleader-like, action of the intellect upon them'.[138] All human statements required interpretation. In defining doctrines, Popes and Councils enjoyed an 'active infallibility', but more was involved in the infallibility of the Church than that, since a *'passive infallibility'* belonged to the whole Catholic people, who had to determine the force and meaning of these doctrinal definitions, although the chief responsibility for this lay with the theologians, whose discussions and investigations assured a clear distinction between 'theological truth' and 'theological opinion', which was essential for preventing 'dogmatism'. The differences between theologians maintained 'liberty of thought', whilst their consensus on points of dogma was 'the safeguard of the infallible decisions of the Church'.[139] Infallibility (itself a comparatively recent term) resided in its fullness in the whole Church (although this had always been assumed and never formally defined)—*securus judicat orbis terrarum.*

As Newman was quick to point out in *A Letter to the Duke of Norfolk*, it is the difficulty of 'getting people' to 'put off the modes of speech and language which are usual with them, and to enter into scientific distinctions and traditionary rules of interpretation' which is his biggest problem. He is also frank enough about the difficulty of coping with the 'chronic extravagancies' of certain Catholic extremists on the one side, and on the other, the 'vehement rhetoric' of Gladstone, which only exacerbated the intense prejudice against Catholics which already existed. It had, however, to be admitted that the responsibility for alienating 'so religious a mind' lay with Catholics themselves, or rather, with those 'who have stated truths in the most paradoxical form, and stretched principles till they were close upon snapping; and who at length, having done their best to set the house on fire, leave to others the task of putting out the flame'. With quiet irony, he adds: 'The English people are sufficiently sensitive of the claims of the Pope, without having them, as if in defiance, flourished in their faces.' He is certainly not going to deny those 'claims' ('I have never denied them'), but he intends to 'uphold them as heartily as I recognize my duty of loyalty to the constitution, the laws and the government of England'.[140] Nor does

[137] *LD* xxv. 447.   [138] Ibid. xxvi. 35.   [139] Ibid. xxvii. 338.
[140] *Diff.* ii. 176–7.

Catholic loyalty preclude his admitting, 'there has been of late years a fierce and intolerant temper abroad, which scorns and virtually tramples on the little ones of Christ.'[141] He stands by his letter to Ullathorne ('one of the most confidential I ever wrote in my life'), deploring 'the violence and cruelty' of the 'very unworthy means' adopted to push through the definition. But this did not 'necessarily' mean he was opposed to the formal declaration of a doctrine which he already believed to be true—'I do not call it inopportune, for times and seasons are known to God alone, and persecution may be as opportune, though not so pleasant as peace.'[142] The implication is clear enough: while not to be dismissed as an unmitigated disaster, the definition was at best a necessary evil. As usual, there is a studied refusal on Newman's part to simplify conclusions and evaluations, however evident some strands in the complicated tissue of events and issues may appear to be.

In his treatment of the role of theology, Newman repeats and develops the points he had already made in private correspondence. He does not hesitate to say that the 'definite rules' and 'traditional principles of interpretation' needed for interpreting dogmatic statements are 'as cogent and unchangeable' as the definitions themselves.[143] Central to this process, he claims, is the 'principle of minimizing',[144] whereby theologians explain 'in the concrete' a pronouncement of the teaching authority, 'by strict interpretation of its wording, by the illustration of its circumstances, and by the recognition of exceptions, in order to make it as tolerable as possible, and the least of a temptation, to self-willed, independent, or wrongly educated minds'. After all, he insists, the virtue of faith is 'so difficult', and 'so difficult is it to assent inwardly to propositions, verified to us neither by reason nor experience, but depending for their reception on the word of the Church as God's oracle, that she has ever shown the utmost care to contract, as far as possible, the range of truths and the sense of propositions, of which she demands this absolute reception.'[145] This 'legitimate minimizing' takes advantage on the one hand of the 'intensely concrete character of the matters condemned' in 'negative' pronouncements, and on the other hand of the abstract nature of 'affirmative' definitions of doctrine ('excepting such as relate to persons'), which 'admit of exceptions in their actual application'.[146] These principles have to be applied to the definition of papal infallibility, the scope of which is carefully limited to deliberate and actual definitions of faith and morals, which are referable either to revelation or to the moral law, and which are intended to be authoritative teachings, binding on the whole Church as pertaining to salvation. In the event, however, of 'a false interpretation' of the

---

[141] Ibid. 339.　　　　[142] Ibid. 193, 299–300.　　　[143] Ibid. 280.
[144] Ibid. 332.　　　　[145] Ibid. 320–1.　　　　[146] Ibid. 334.

infallibility definition, then 'another Leo will be given us for the occasion'. The reference is to Pope St Leo's Council of Chalcedon, which, 'without of course touching the definition' of the preceding Council of Ephesus, 'trimmed the balance of doctrine by completing it'.[147] The warning is an exact prophecy both of the theology of 'creeping infallibility' that came in the wake of the First Vatican Council, and of the Second Vatican Council, which Pope John XXIII convoked nearly a hundred years later.

As regards the relation between history and theology, Newman is unequivocal in his criticism of Döllinger and his followers. While it 'is a tragical event, both for them and for us, that they have left us' and 'robs us of a great *prestige*', for 'they have left none to take their place', still, 'I think them utterly wrong in what they have done and are doing; and, moreover, I agree as little in their view of history as in their acts.' It is not a matter of questioning the accuracy of their historical knowledge, but 'their use of the facts they report' and 'that special stand-point from which they view the relations existing between the records of History and the communications of Popes and Councils'. Newman sums up the essence of the problem: 'They seem to me to expect from History more than History can furnish.' The opposite was true of the Ultramontanes, who simply found history an embarrassing inconvenience.

As the Church is a sacred and divine creation, so in like manner her history, with its wonderful evolution of events, the throng of great actors who have a part in it, and its multiform literature, stained though its annals are with human sin and error, and recorded on no system, and by uninspired authors, still is a sacred work also; and those who make light of it, or distrust its lessons, incur a grave responsibility.

But he wondered why 'private judgment' should 'be unlawful in interpreting Scripture against the voice of authority, and yet be lawful in the interpretation of history?' The Church certainly made use of history, as she also used Scripture, tradition, and human reason; but her doctrines could not be 'proved' by any of these 'informants', individually or in combination. No Catholic doctrine could be fully proved (or, for that matter, disproved) by historical evidence—'in all cases there is a margin left for the exercise of faith in the word of the Church.' Indeed, anyone 'who believes the dogmas of the Church only because he has reasoned them out of History, is scarcely a Catholic'.[148]

On the actual history of the papacy, Newman certainly does not mince his words: 'Assuredly there are certain acts of Popes in which no one would like to have part.'[149] He has no intention of 'saying that Popes

[147] *Diff.* ii. 307.   [148] Ibid. 309, 311–12.   [149] Ibid. 187.

are never in the wrong, and are never to be resisted'.[150] The Popes' policies towards England, for instance, were not necessarily always the right ones. Worse, the lives of the Renaissance Popes had precipitated 'a moral earthquake', as a result of which half of Europe was lost to the Church.[151] As for present papal attitudes to the modern world, Newman's carefully nuanced judgement mocks both the intransigence of Pio Nono and the inconsistency of a politician like Gladstone. Regret for the past merges with acceptance of the present, while the conclusion characteristically consists of the hope for a reconciliation and integration of both conservative and liberal elements in the political and social order of the future.

The Pope has denounced the sentiment that he ought to come to terms with 'progress, liberalism, and the new civilization'. I have no thought at all of disputing his words. I leave the great problem to the future. God will guide other Popes to act when Pius goes, as He has guided him. No one can dislike the democratic principle more than I do. No one mourns, for instance, more than I, over the state of Oxford, given up, alas! to 'liberalism and progress', to the forfeiture of her great medieval motto, 'Dominus illuminatio mea', and with a consequent call on her to go to Parliament or the Heralds' College for a new one; but what can we do? All I know is, that Toryism, that is, loyalty to persons, 'springs immortal in the human breast'; that religion is a spiritual loyalty; and that Catholicity is the only divine form of religion. And thus, in centuries to come, there may be found out some way of uniting what is free in the new structure of society with what is authoritative in the old, without any base compromise with 'Progress' and 'Liberalism'.

However, it is hardly fitting for 'Englishmen, who within fifty years kept up the Pope's system . . . to throw stones at the Pope for keeping it up still'.[152] On the profound implications for morality and religion of the break-up of the old-established political order in England, Newman is typically realistic:

Though I profess to be an admirer of the principles now superseded in themselves . . . nevertheless I say frankly I do not see how they could possibly be maintained in the ascendant. When the intellect is cultivated, it is as certain that it will develope into a thousand various shapes, as that infinite hues and tints and shades of colour will be reflected from the earth's surface, when the sun-light touches it . . . During the last seventy years, first one class of the community, then another, has awakened up to thought and opinion. Their multiform views on sacred subjects necessarily affected and found expression in the governing order . . . The State ought to have a conscience; but what if it happened to have half-a-dozen, or a score, or a hundred, in religious matters, each different from each?[153]

[150] Ibid. 216.   [151] Ibid. 254.   [152] Ibid. 268–9.   [153] Ibid. 267.

Gladstone's complaints about the reactionary influence of the Pope are unreal because of an inconsistency: the established Anglican system in which he and Newman had grown up 'was called Toryism, and men gloried in the name; now it is called Popery and reviled'. The 'old idea of a Christian Polity', in which 'there was one true religion', was then in force. A younger generation might be 'shocked to witness in the abiding Papal system the words, ways, and works of their grandfathers', but that 'old world' had only comparatively recently departed. The 'plea of conscience' had not then permitted the kind of freedom of speech and thought now taken for granted in England. Whether this was progress or not did not alter the fact that the tradition which had been broken was 'the tradition of fifteen hundred years', which had been inherited and retained at the Reformation. The state certainly then 'had a conscience' and 'Christianity was the law of the land'.[154] In short, the principles on which the Pope still acted were also assumed at that time in England. As usual in his controversial writings, Newman employs analogy to prove inconsistency. Gladstone jibbed at the Pope's claim to 'supreme' authority over Catholics—but the 'Law is *supreme*' in this country, though that does not imply that the 'free-born Englishman' is literally a slave of the law.[155] Again, 'we are all of us in this age under the control of public opinion and the public prints', but this does not mean that we are the 'slaves' of 'journalism'. The Pope's 'sway' extends not to '*every*, but *any*' act of a Catholic, simply in the sense that his 'general utterances may come to have a bearing upon some personal act of ours'.[156] Any human society necessarily curtails individual freedom 'for the sake of a common security', and therefore English Catholics acquiesce in certain infringements on their liberty.[157]

Frankness about the limitations of the Popes does not inhibit Newman from some plain speaking about the anti-papal prejudices of England, where it has for centuries been 'the official rule' to 'ignore the existence of the Pope'. It might have been thought that 'the greatest, the oldest power in Europe', which is also 'the mother of English Christianity', would merit some respect instead of being 'absolutely cut'.[158] As for Gladstone's 'sixpenny tract', 'Surely Nana Sahib will have more justice done to him by the English people, than has been shown to the Father of European civilization.' The real objection, Newman considers, of English Protestants is not to the papacy but to the Church—'they do not believe that Christ set up a visible society, or rather kingdom, for the propagation and maintenance of His religion, for a necessary home and a refuge for His people; but we do.'[159] So, too, for Gladstone, 'It is not the existence of a Pope, but of a Church, which is his aversion.' The

---

[154] *Diff.* ii. 262–4. [155] Ibid. 227–8. [156] Ibid. 232.
[157] Ibid. 270. [158] Ibid. 191–2. [159] Ibid. 207.

development of the papacy has meant a concentration of power in one centre, but the extent of the powers claimed by the Church has not changed ('A triangle is the same in its substance and nature, whichever side is made its base').[160] Far from repudiating the early Church's traditions, as Gladstone claimed, the Church of Rome, unlike the Anglican and Orthodox Churches, retains as one of her Notes or credentials her traditional independence of state control, with the result that she 'is now the one faithful representative, and thereby is heir and successor, of that free-spoken dauntless Church of old', a 'luminous fact which more than any other turned men's minds at Oxford forty years ago to look towards her with reverence, interest, and love'. Invoking the 'deadly antagonism' of the first Tractarians to Erastianism, Newman issues a challenge:

Go through the long annals of Church History, century after century, and say, was there ever a time when her Bishops, and notably the Bishop of Rome, were slow to give their testimony in behalf of the moral and revealed law and to suffer for their obedience to it? ever a time when they forgot that they had a message to deliver to the world,—not the task merely of administering spiritual consolation, or of making the sick-bed easy, or of training up good members of society . . . —but specially and directly, a definite message to high and low, from the world's Maker, whether men would hear or whether they would forbear?[161]

It is impossible, he argues, to separate the question of infallibility from the nature of the Gospel, which 'is no mere philosophy thrown upon the world at large, no mere quality of mind and thought, no mere beautiful and deep sentiment or subjective opinion, but a substantive message from above, guarded and preserved in a visible polity'.[162] And it was because the founder of Christianity 'willed the Gospel to be a revelation acknowledged and authenticated, to be public, fixed, and permanent', that 'He framed a Society of men to be its home, its instrument, and its guarantee', so that the 'rulers of that Association are the legal trustees, so to say, of the sacred truths which He spoke to the Apostles by word of mouth'.[163] The Church's teachers had to be supernaturally protected from error if the revelation was to be safeguarded and handed down intact through the ages by human instruments. Infallibility was therefore in principle involved from the beginning in the very idea of Christianity.

Again, there was no mistaking the New Testament's insistence on obedience to Church authorities—'and it should be Mr Gladstone's business, before telling us that we are slaves, because we obey the Pope, first of all to tear away those texts from the Bible'.[164] Newman sets out

[160] Ibid. 209–10.   [161] Ibid. 197–8.   [162] Ibid. 236.
[163] Ibid. 322.   [164] Ibid. 226.

very clearly the limits of this obedience. Writing before the acute ethical problems raised by advances in medical knowledge, he can say without embarrassment, 'So little does the Pope come into this whole system of moral theology by which (as by our conscience) our lives are regulated, that the weight of his hand upon us, as private men, is absolutely unappreciable.' 'Indeed,' he concludes, with wholly unintended irony, 'if my account . . . be correct, I do not see what he takes away at all from our private consciences.'[165] Since 'the field of morals', he adds, with blissful lack of prescience, 'contains so little that is unknown and unexplored, in contrast with revelation and doctrinal fact', it is not clear 'what positions of moral teaching in the course of 1800 years actually have proceeded from the Pope, or from the Church, or where to look for such'.[166]

At the heart of *A Letter to the Duke of Norfolk* is the celebrated treatment of the sovereignty of conscience. Newman, of course, had often written on conscience as the basis of religious belief. But here he discusses the individual believer's conscience in its relation to legitimate ecclesiastical authority. He first defines conscience as the law of God 'as apprehended in the minds of individual men'—which, 'though it may suffer refraction in passing into the intellectual medium of each . . . is not therefore so affected as to lose its character of being the Divine Law, but still has, as such, the prerogative of commanding obedience'. On this view of conscience it is 'the voice of God', whereas the world regards it as little more than 'a creation of man'. Far from being 'a long-sighted selfishness' or 'a desire to be consistent with oneself', Newman declares in ringing tones that 'Conscience is the aboriginal Vicar of Christ, a prophet in its informations, a monarch in its peremptoriness, a priest in its blessings and anathemas, and, even though the eternal priesthood throughout the Church could cease to be, in it the sacerdotal principle would remain and would have a sway.' In earlier times 'its supremacy was assailed by the arm of physical force', but 'now the intellect is put in operation to sap the foundations of a power which the sword could not destroy'. The threat is grandiloquently conveyed, but for all its fragile vulnerability, conscience has a strange, indestructible life:

All through my day there has been a resolute warfare, I had almost said conspiracy against the rights of conscience, as I have described it. Literature and science have been embodied in great institutions in order to put it down. Noble buildings have been reared as fortresses against that spiritual, invisible influence which is too subtle for science and too profound for literature. Chairs in Universities have been made the seats of an antagonist tradition.

The secularized idea of conscience merely concerns 'the right of

---

[165] *Diff.* ii. 229, 231.   [166] Ibid. 332.

thinking, speaking, writing, and acting' as one sees fit, 'without any thought of God at all'. Paradoxically, it has become 'the very right and freedom of conscience to dispense with conscience'. In effect, conscience 'has been superseded by a counterfeit', namely, 'the right of self-will'.[167] Were the Pope himself to 'speak against Conscience in the true sense of the word, he would commit a suicidal act. He would be cutting the ground from under his feet.' Indeed, continues Newman, 'we shall find that it is by the universal sense of right and wrong, the consciousness of transgression, the pangs of guilt, and the dread of retribution, as first principles deeply lodged in the hearts of men, it is thus and only thus, that he has gained his footing in the world and achieved his success'. It is the 'championship of the Moral Law and of conscience' which is 'his *raison d'être*', and the 'fact of his mission is the answer to the complaints of those who feel the insufficiency of the natural light; and the insufficiency of that light is the justification of his mission'. Once again Newman emphasizes the precarious nature of the moral sense, which 'is at once the highest of all teachers, yet the least luminous; and the Church, the Pope, the Hierarchy are . . . the supply of an urgent demand'. But if revelation is the fulfilment of natural religion, it is in no sense 'independent of it': 'The Pope, who comes of Revelation, has no jurisdiction over Nature.'[168]

Turning to the crucial question of the relation of the individual conscience to authority, Newman begins by laying down that since 'conscience is not a judgment upon any speculative truth, any abstract doctrine, but bears immediately . . . on something to be done or not done', it 'cannot come into direct collision with the Church's or the Pope's infallibility; which is engaged on general propositions, and in the condemnation of particular and given errors'. But because conscience is 'a practical dictate', conflict is possible 'only when the Pope legislates, or gives particular orders, and the like'. However, 'a Pope is not infallible in his laws, nor in his commands, nor in his acts of state, nor in his administration, nor in his public policy.' After all, St Peter was not infallible at Antioch when St Paul disagreed with him, nor was Liberius when he excommunicated Athanasius. However, the 'dictate' of conscience, 'in order to prevail against the voice of the Pope, must follow upon serious thought, prayer, and all available means of arriving at a right judgment on the matter in question'. The onus of proof, then, lies on the individual conscience: 'Unless a man is able to say to himself, as in the Presence of God, that he must not, and dare not, act upon the Papal injunction, he is bound to obey it, and would commit a great sin in disobeying it.'[169] As usual, the bold admission about the fallibility of the

---

[167] Ibid. 247–50. [168] Ibid. 252–4. [169] Ibid. 256–8.

first Pope in no way excludes a rigorous emphasis on loyalty and obedience to a legitimate superior. But on the other hand, to obey a papal order which one seriously thinks is wrong would be a sin—even if one is culpably mistaken (a person may be to blame for having a false conscience, but not for acting in accordance with it). In the last analysis, conscience, however misguided, is supreme; and Newman concludes the discussion calmly, even casually, with the famous declaration:

I add one remark. Certainly, if I am obliged to bring religion into after-dinner toasts, (which indeed does not seem quite the thing) I shall drink—to the Pope, if you please—still, to Conscience first, and to the Pope afterwards.[170]

5

A Letter to the Duke of Norfolk was not Newman's last word on the theology of the Church—there was another extremely important essay to come—but it was his last book and his last sustained work of controversy. Characteristically, it ends with two nicely balanced ripostes. On the one hand, the notorious disagreements among Catholics over their view of the definition cannot be denied, but every 'note of triumph over the differences' only refutes Gladstone's 'reproach that we are captives and slaves of the Pope'. On the other hand, there is only one Pope, and 'I think it a usurpation, too wickedly to be comfortably dwelt upon, when individuals use their own private judgment . . . for the purpose of anathematizing the private judgment of others.'[171] It was to be his last real salvo in print against the Ultramontanes.

As a defence and explanation of infallibility, it was received with general enthusiasm by Catholics. Even Manning had to admit that its substance was basically sound, and he warned Rome that any public censure would have disastrous consequences. As for Ward, who was very upset by Newman's strictures on the Ultramontanes, Newman remarked: 'He had never whispered against me—he has spoken out as a man, and he had a right to do so. But I have a right to speak too, and they who play at bowls must expect rubbers.'[172] In print, however, in the *Dublin Review*, Ward was forced to admit that Newman was right about the limited scope of the definition.

Ward might have been even more upset if he had known that Newman thought that theology was in fact 'the regulating principle of the Church'—just as the law maintained 'the tradition of the British Constitution, in spite of King, Lords, and Commons'. He had not yet said anything quite so bold and daring in print. He was also as clear now

---

[170] *Diff.* ii. 261.   [171] Ibid. 346.   [172] *LD* xxvii. 216.

as he had ever been since first becoming a Catholic that the 'great want' of the Church was the 'theological schools' destroyed by the French Revolution.

This has been the occasion of our late and present internal troubles. Where would Ward have been, if there had been theological Schools in England? Again, the Archbishop is not a theologian, and, what is worse, the Pope is not a theologian, and so theology has gone out of fashion. This is the only reason which made me regret not going to Oxford ... I don't profess to be a theologian, but at all events I should have been able to show a side of the Catholic religion more theological ...

Given his lack of theology, he could not be sure he was 'out of the wood' and would not 'receive some cuff from the political ultra-devotional party'. But he was beginning to feel more and more confident about the reception of the book. He wrote to one well-wisher: 'I felt as if up in a balloon, and till I got down safe, I could not be easy. I might be turned upside down by a chimney pot, left atop a tree, or carried out to sea.'[173] But the only real theological school left in the Church was that of the Jesuits; and, while they had not always agreed with him (particularly over the *Grammar of Assent*), they had always supported him. An approving pastoral letter by Cardinal Cullen seemed to clinch the matter.

A high Anglican correspondent wrote to say that he had heard at a party an Ultramontanist say that he wished the *Letter* could be put on the Index, 'whereupon a strong "Protestant" retorted that "Rome would not dare to offer such an affront to *England*"!' The general public had come to regard Newman 'as an English possession of which they are proud'. The change in the climate of opinion was nothing less than a 'revolution'. Newman replied that there had been general acceptance of the *Letter* in the Church, but that one of the 'disadvantages of a General Council, is that it throws individual units through the Church into confusion and sets them at variance', with the resulting danger of schism and heresy; he was not in the least surprised at the rise of the Old Catholics or the extremism of the Ultramontane party.[174] As for Gladstone's *Vaticanism* (his reply to the responses provoked by his original *Expostulation*), Newman had no intention of trying to answer the burden of the argument, which was directed against Manning rather than himself. To go back into the early history of the Church and to try to prove that the doctrine of papal infallibility had always been held 'would be to enter into the general controversy between Catholics and Protestants, in which each party has its own texts and its own facts, and has had them, and flourished them, for the last 300 years'.[175] It was

[173] Ibid. 212, 215.   [174] Ibid. 240.   [175] Ibid. 243.

simply unrealistic to imagine one could prove the Catholic case from an examination of historical facts. The fact was that the Church

has had to be piloted thro' very difficult straits and shallows with hidden rocks and without buoys and light-houses with next to no human means: and, though her Divine Guide has taken care she should not suffer material damage, and she has escaped in every peril, yet she has not much more than escaped; and it is natural and not very difficult for rival shipbuilders and shipowners to maintain that she had suffered. Three centuries have taught us that a case may be made against us, and tho' we have the right on our side, it is God's will that an opportunity and a call is left for faith.[176]

Charles Kingsley died only a few days after the publication of the *Letter*. Newman was shocked to hear of his early death. He could honestly say he had never felt anger against him. He had, after all, never even seen him. But experience had shown that it was only by speaking out strongly that people would believe him. This was why he had felt that 'it would not do to be tame, and not to show indignation' at Kingsley's charges.[177] He said Mass for his old adversary, who he heard had preached about him in a kindly, if critical, way in Chester Cathedral a few years previously. By his 'passionate attack' on him, Kingsley had inadvertently become one of his 'best friends, whom I always wished to shake hands with when living, and towards whose memory I have much tenderness'.[178]

His own birthday came round again in February; he was now 74. As he thought of all his friends who were dead, he reflected sombrely that just as the 'idea of a judgment is the first principle of religion, as being involved in the sentiment of conscience', so 'as life goes on, it becomes very overpowering'. The 'more one has received, the more one has to answer for. We can but throw ourselves on the mercy of God, of which one's whole life is a long experience.'[179] He told an enquirer that 'The proof which comes home to my own mind that God is good, is His dealings with myself. This proof any man may have—for it is a personal proof. Nothing can get rid of it, and it grows the more it is cultivated.'[180] A visitor to the Oratory described how he was received by Newman—

very kindly, with a sort of grave sweet simplicity which coming from so old a man, has in it something inexpressibly touching . . . He looks very aged, hair more white than silvery, body stooped, a very large and prominent nose and large chin, brow which seems good, though one can't see it for the tangled hair falling over it; an air of melancholy, as of one who has passed through terrible struggles, yet of serenity, as of one who had found peace. Not a priest in his manner—still an Englishman more than a R. Catholic.[181]

---

[176] *LD* xxvii. 248.   [177] Ibid. 219.   [178] Ibid. xxix. 388.
[179] Ibid. xxvii. 227.   [180] Ibid. 232.   [181] Ibid. 238 n. 1.

As he showed his guest, a professor of law from Oxford, round the library, Newman had no suspicion of the cruellest of blows that was about to strike him, suddenly and practically without warning.

18

Oxford and Rome Again

THE success of the *Letter to the Duke of Norfolk* had taken Newman by surprise. He told William Neville that they must now expect some great reverse. He hardly dreamed what form it would take. He had, however, had a premonition three years before: 'so many of us are getting old, that one is tempted to ask "O Lord, how long?" How long are we to enjoy that calm and happy time which Thou hast granted us so long? When is it to be, that that tranquil unity is to be broken up which we have so long enjoyed, and we are to be parted one from another . . .?'[1]

Towards the end of April 1875 Ambrose St John began to show signs of nervous strain. On 28 April he apparently suffered sunstroke from walking in the scorching heat to the opening of the new Passionist chapel in neighbouring Harborne. It soon became clear that he was having a nervous breakdown, and before long he had lost his reason. Violent for a time, he then appeared to be making a recovery, but he died peacefully on the night of 24 May out at the Oratory farm at Ravenhurst, where the school playing-fields were. Newman left a detailed and moving account of his illness and death. He was convinced that St John died from overwork. He was in his sixtieth year and a chronic sufferer from asthma. He was heavily involved in both the church and the school, as well as being the minister (or bursar) at the Oratory. On top of all that, he had undertaken the translation of Fessler's important book on infallibility at Newman's request and had been working up to six hours a day on it. For thirty years he had devoted himself to Newman. At his confirmation at Oscott he had asked Wiseman if he could take a vow of obedience to Newman. The request, of course, was refused, but he had always acted as if he had taken one. His last labour of love had proved to be 'the last load upon the camel's back'.[2]

The legend that 'Newman threw himself on the bed by the corpse and spent the night there'[3] has no foundation, but, as Newman remarked in another context at this time, 'lies have a wonderful vitality, like weeds, and I suppose are self sown, or rather sown, by the evil spirit, and find soil among human hearts for a large growth.'[4] He was referring to

---

[1] *LD* xxvi. 52. [2] Ibid. xxvii. 412. [3] *Ward* i. 22.
[4] *LD* xxvii. 295.

reports about himself—but not, of course, to Wilfrid Ward's story, which had not yet been penned. We know from Neville's eye-witness account that Newman said the customary office for the dead beside the body and then came downstairs and 'wrote telegrams and letters, so calmly'.[5] Neville was amazed at Newman's resilience in the midst of his overpowering grief and shock. Ward, who tended only to see the sensitive or feminine side of Newman's personality, presumably imagined or at least gave credence to a fanciful exaggeration of a normal priestly action, and in doing so typically missed the sheer masculine toughness which sustained Newman even at his darkest hour. 'His loss is the greatest affliction I have had in my life', Newman commented simply.[6] In 1845, when 'I had to stand alone, he came to me as Ruth to Naomi'.[7] It was impossible to imagine those early, difficult days at Oscott and Rome without St John's support. Since then, he had been constantly at hand, ready to undertake any work whenever necessary, not least the headmastership of the school. He and Mrs Wootten had been 'the life and the making' of it, and now Mrs Wootten herself seemed unlikely to live much longer (she died in January 1876). 'How life is being stripped of all that makes it bright!'[8]

2

Early in the new year, 1876, Newman heard from Ambrose Phillipps de Lisle of a scheme, which appeared to have some backing from Manning, for an Anglican 'uniate' church which would allow a married clergy, on the model of the Eastern rite churches in communion with Rome. Newman did not think it very practicable: the difficulties of such a complicated ecclesial arrangement would hardly commend it to the Holy See, unless there was a chance of bringing over a large part of the Church of England. But he could not help but be sympathetic to any 'means of drawing to us so many good people, who are now shivering at our gates'.[9] He had always been distressed at the 'scandal' of married clerical converts being 'cast out as useless into idleness and hopeless obscurity'.[10] The plan, which soon collapsed, involved accepting not only papal infallibility, but also conditional reordination; it appeared unlikely to commend itself to many Anglo-Catholics. Newman's attitude to Anglo-Catholics managed to encompass two very different perspectives. On the one hand, he was uncompromisingly adamant that just as 'the Roman Communion is the only True Church, the Ark of

5 Ibid. 301.   6 Ibid. 313.   7 Ibid. 321.

8 Ibid. 390.   9 Ibid. xxviii. 20.   10 Ibid. 33.

Salvation' and is the only 'religious body . . . in which *is* salvation', so Anglicans no more receive grace from the Church of England, 'which is a human work and a political institution', than 'an infant could receive nourishment from the breast of its dead mother', but rather are saved 'by a superabundant mercy of God which He has not promised and covenanted'.[11] It would be idle to try and find any hint of the later understanding of the Second Vatican Council that other churches are not devoid of ecclesial significance but enjoy some, although imperfect, communion with the Catholic Church. But on the other hand, Newman had none of the harsh intolerance of so many of his co-religionists. He saw 'the wonderful revival of religion in the Established Church' as coming 'from God'. He was even prepared to acknowledge that Anglo-Catholics were providentially 'kept where they are, with no more light than they have, being Anglicans in good faith in order gradually to prepare their hearers and readers in greater numbers than otherwise would be possible for the true and perfect faith', since if they were all 'to become Catholics at once now, the work of conversion would simply come to an end'. Although he had to admit that he thought they lacked 'an intellectual foundation', which, for 'practical purposes', the Evangelicals could be said to have, he had every admiration and sympathy for them, particularly when they were persecuted for ritualism. It reminded him of his own experience in the Church of England. And when extreme Anglo-Catholic clergy were in fact facing imprisonment for their practices, he could only 'heartily wish a good number . . . may get into prison' to show up their 'liberal' opponents as 'flagrant persecutors'. So far as he was concerned, they were on the same side as Roman Catholics 'in this evil day of scepticism and infidelity'.[12] The one compensation indeed for 'the cruel overthrow of faith' was that 'as the setting of the sun brings out the stars, so great principles are found to shine out, which are hailed by men of various religions as their own in common, when infidelity prevails'.[13]

Never had the desire for reunion been stronger between Christians, but 'never were the obstacles greater or stronger which divide them'.[14] Newman could only wonder that the 'science necessary for a theologian and the *responsibility* weighing upon an ecclesiastical ruler' had not inhibited Manning from indulging in the extraordinary 'rhetoric' which he had used concerning the infallibility issue.[15] He comforted de Lisle with his usual point that the study of church history showed how often it happened that 'a thing is in itself good, but the time has not come for it. Heretics and schismatics have sometimes been preachers of a neglected truth, which they were impatient and disobedient in insisting on, in their

---

[11] *LD* xxvi. 364; xxx. 33–4.   [12] Ibid. xxv. 129, 260; xxviii. 167–8; xxx. 120.
[13] Ibid. xxvii. 188.   [14] Ibid. xxvi. 187.   [15] Ibid. xxvii. 383.

day . . . And thus I reconcile myself to many, many things, and put them into God's hands.'[16] To the convert biologist St George Jackson Mivart, who had been attacked by Ward, he remarked sarcastically:

Those who would not allow Galileo to reason 300 years ago, will not allow any one else now. The past is no lesson for them for the present and the future: and their notion of stability in faith is ever to be repeating errors and then repeating retractations of them.[17]

When Mivart defended himself, only to be attacked again by Ward, Newman wrote sympathetically, 'I have suffered from him quite as much as you.' Ward had denounced him before now to Rome, but any attempt to reply was useless, if only because he could always have the last word in the *Dublin Review*. 'Controversy is his meat and drink—and he seems to consider it his mission to pick as many holes in others as he can . . .'[18]

In February his birthday came round again: 'I have now lived three quarters of a century, and I call men and angels to hear my witness that much as I have failed Him, He never has failed me—nor will He ever.'[19] April brought another spring. R. W. Church's daughter Helen had, with her sisters, sent him Lewis Carroll's recently published *The Hunting of the Snark* as a birthday present (they had already given him *Alice in Wonderland*, which he had enjoyed). A passage in it reminded Newman of his 'own thoughts and feelings' as a small boy when 'I lay in my crib in the early spring, with outdoor scents, sounds and sights wakening me up, and especially the cheerful ring of the mower's scythe on the lawn'. He looked forward, he told Helen, to the day 'of which Easter is the promise, when that first spring, may return to us, and a sweetness which cannot die may gladden our garden'.[20] His own love of spring was now mixed with other feelings:

. . . it is too intense in its nature, to be unaccompanied with pain, I may say, great pain . . . now especially as life is waning, and friends dropping away, the extreme beauty of the ever-recurring triumphant spring seems to have something of young mockery in it, till one recollects that that beauty is an image and a promise of something more sweet and more lasting than itself.[21]

Another young lady who met him at this time wrote years later that it was 'impossible to describe his fascination of voice and manner . . . his voice was low and very sweet; it had a wonderful ring of sympathy in it'.[22] Lady Coleridge's mysteriously evocative drawing (which is reproduced as the frontispiece) strikingly conveys the kind of impression his expression and manner made on strangers who met him for the first time. Newman had first sat for Lady Coleridge, who was the sister-in-

[16] Ibid. xxviii. 66.   [17] Ibid. 71–2.   [18] Ibid. 195.   [19] Ibid. 31.
[20] Ibid. 52–3.   [21] Ibid. 55.   [22] Ibid. 32 n. 2.

law of Father Coleridge, in June 1874, and was to sit again for the third
and last time in June 1876.

On 23 July 1876 Newman wrote down instructions for William
Neville in the event of his death. 'I wish, with all my heart,' he began, 'to
be buried in Father Ambrose St John's grave—and I give this as my last,
my imperative will.' For his memorial tablet in the cloister to the church,
he wanted the inscription 'Ex umbris et imaginibus in veritatem'—
provided the idea of passing from shadows to reality did not seem to
smack in any way of scepticism.[23] The next day he wrote down directions
for the disposal of his property, followed by a memorandum on any
future biography, which he thought should be divided into two parts, of
which the first half should be entrusted to an Anglican.

In 1872 he had noted privately, 'I don't wish my life written—
because there is so little to say.' This rather remarkable thought was
followed by the consideration that a biographer would have 'to pad—
and then readers are both disappointed at the meagreness of the
composition, and angry with the padding'. He had already 'virtually'
told the story of his life up to 1845 in the *Apologia*—'and there is little or
nothing to say since'. Preposterous as that might sound, there was a
certain important literal truth in it: 'Little or nothing—for if anything is
attempted other men's toes will be trod upon, and the Life will be
answered and a controversy ensue—or if nothing is said in the Life, *then
again* there is a sure opening for controversy, for a reason must be given
by the writer, *why* there is nothing to say—and this cannot be without
throwing the blame on others, as bringing it about that there is nothing
to say.'[24] Perhaps a volume or two of letters and papers might be brought
out, while it would be easy to fill a volume of mostly theological letters.
He had already begun collecting together letters that related to
controversial matters in his Catholic life, which were definitely not for
publication, but were there ready to be used as a defence against
posthumous attacks. Quite apart from his own case, his decided view
was that biographies were 'generally very dull', and had to be padded
out because most people's lives were not 'worth relating'; the only true
'life' was told in a person's own letters.[25] Two years later, in 1874, he had
left an instruction for Ambrose St John, attached to the autobiographical memoir which he had been sketching out to serve as a model for the
kind of biography he wanted St John to write if necessary. Although he
would have preferred nothing but a collection of letters connected by the
slightest of narratives, he realized that a more extensive biography
might prove unavoidable. The private papers he was leaving behind
would give any future biographer 'elbow-room' to make the necessary

---

[23] *MD* 439.   [24] *LD* xxvi. 200.   [25] Ibid. 375.

assessments. He added a postscript in June 1876 to the effect that St John's sudden death, 'together with a growing interest in my subject',[26] had led him to enlarge the sketch into a fuller memoir, which began with his birth and ended with the Oriel tutorship row.[27] The years 1833 to 1845 were already covered by the *Apologia*.

Now he declared that he did not 'want a panegyric written of me, which would be sickening but a real fair downright account of me'. (He once wrote that he preferred 'something *real*' for the life of a saint as opposed to 'the practice so common of cutting up a Saint into virtues and of distributing him into pigeon holes'.) Again he pointed out that it would be hard to say much about his Catholic life without provoking controversy and scandal; and (in a later note) he insisted that nothing should be published which reflected on others 'unless and until reflections are published in any quarter against me'.[28] He stuck to this view, commenting a few years later, 'no account of my *Catholic* life can ever be given, for it would involve the saying things which would be disadvantageous to the reputation of men who for their writings (and or) their works, are in merited esteem.'[29]

Newman's trials and tribulations never seemed to come singly. In September Edward Caswall suffered a heart attack while visiting Norway. He was the last of the 'three men, two of them strangers to me, who in past years gave themselves up to me generously and unreservedly'; he, Ambrose St John, and Joseph Gordon had been 'the life and centre of the Oratory'.[30] The other loyal friend who had given her life to the Oratory was Mrs Wootten, and she too had died in January. 'I always say "No one has ever had such friends as I have had!" '[31] It was 'the penalty of living, to lose the great props of life'.[32] The pain, however, of losing friends for one to whom friendship meant so much was almost unbearable: 'There is some thing awful in the silent resistless sweep of time—and, as years go on, and friends are taken away, one draws the thought of those who remain about one, as in cold weather one buttons up great coats and capes, for protection.' (He had once used a similar protective image in rebuke to an old Anglican friend who had failed to keep in touch after 1845—'friendships are not put on, put off, put on again, like a glove.')[33] In the midst of his own sorrows he had time for those of others; he wrote to a domestic servant: 'I too know what it is to lose a sister. I lost her 49 years ago, and, though so many years have past, I still feel the pain.'[34]

His private griefs hardly affected his stream of correspondence, which took up so much of his time, as he answered the countless questions posed

[26] *AW* 23–4. [27] Ibid. 29–107. [28] *LD* xxiv. 262; xxviii. 92–3.
[29] Ibid. xxx. 303. [30] Ibid. xxviii. 118. [31] Ibid. 151.
[32] Ibid. xxv. 45. [33] Ibid. xix. 277; xxii. 121. [34] Ibid. xxviii. 159.

to him by correspondents of every and no religion. The same problems recurred and the same easy answers were rejected. Thus we find him again insisting that the fact that 'the Church is in the world, and the world in the Church' meant that it could not be assumed that the medieval world, which was outwardly Christian, was necessarily morally and spiritually better than the modern world: 'Man abused supernatural truths in the medieval time, as well as used them; and now man uses natural truths, as well as abuses them.' Whichever of the two abuses was worse, 'I only say that the one age is not all light, the other all darkness.'[35] To the other, very different, question as to whether England would have made the same technological progress if it was still Catholic, Newman replied that, although the Anglo-Saxon race would have been 'eminently practical' whatever its religion, it was true not only that their practicality 'had something to do with their being Protestants, as indisposing them to listen to the claims whether of Authority or of Dogmatic Faith', but also that 'the Catholic Church having for its province exclusively religion and morals, does in fact so earnestly enforce the claims of the unseen world as to put a wet blanket on the energetic enthusiasm with which men who are not Catholics, that is, who have not vivid faith or definite practical creed, pursue purely secular ends.'[36] Theory, of course, was not quite the same as practice, and one should not be surprised if Catholics seemed 'worse' than Protestants, if only on the principle that 'the corruption of the best is the worst': 'And in our Lord's day, though "salvation was of the Jews," they seem to have been as a people in a worse state than the Samaritans.'[37] Even the invading Goths appeared to have had better morals than the Roman Christians.

There was one happy event during these dark months. On 16 October Thomas Arnold called. He wanted to come back to the Church. Afterwards he wrote to Newman to thank him for his kindness and to tell him that he had heard that he had failed to be elected to the chair of Anglo-Saxon at Oxford because of his return to Catholicism. He was now looking for lodgings near the British Museum, in order to escape from the fury of his wife. She herself wrote a splendidly vituperative letter to Newman:

Sir,

You have now for the second time been the cause of my husband's becoming a member of the Church of Rome and from the bottom of my heart I curse you for it. You know well how very weak and unstable he is, and you also know that he has a wife and eight children. You know well that he did nothing for the Roman Catholic Church in the ten years he belonged to it before, and you know

---

[35] *LD* xxviii. 95–6.   [36] Ibid. 109.   [37] Ibid. 223.

well that he will do nothing for it now, but the temptation of having one of *his father's sons* under your direction was too much for you, and for the second time you counselled him to ignore every social duty and become a pervert. He has brought utter ruin upon us all, but what is that to you?

Newman confided drily to a mutual friend of his and Arnold's that it 'was fitting, by way of bright contrast, that so sweet and amiable a fellow as Arnold should have such a yoke fellow—but, except as an aesthetic contrast, it is marvellous that such a pair should be'.[38] He was 'a very good amiable fellow, but weak and henpecked'—quite unlike his formidable wife, who had thrown a brick through the window of the church when he became a Catholic in Australia, and had proceeded to 'nag, nag, nag him, till he almost lost his senses'.[39]

3

At the end of November 1876 Newman began to edit his 'two volumes on the Via Media'.[40] The second volume was to consist of various tracts and letters, while the first volume was to be his third edition of the *Lectures on the Prophetical Office*. On 26 February 1877 he went out to Rednal to prepare a preface for this first volume. The resulting essay was to be his last great contribution towards a theology of the Church. He had 'long wished' to write an essay 'on the conflicting interests, and therefore difficulties of the Catholic Church, because she is at once, first a devotion, secondly a philosophy, thirdly a polity'. At the moment, as at other times, it was clear that 'the philosophical instinct' had been eclipsed by the other two aspects.[41]

He begins by observing that controversial writings have three main elements, only one of which is strictly logical. Of the other two, one is the use of hypothesis 'as a substitute for direct evidence and hard reasoning'. Hypotheses may be 'altogether legitimate, and often necessary; for representations may be true, which nevertheless are not or cannot be proved; and probabilities, when accumulated, tell'. But still they 'appeal to the imagination more than to the reasoning faculty'. The old *Via Media* was just such a hypothesis—'a possible road, lying between a mountain and a morass, to be driven through formidable obstacles . . . by the boldness and skill of the engineers'. The object was to find 'a broad, intellectual, intelligible theory' to justify the position of the Anglican Church—rather than 'a logical and historical foundation' for such a theory. The appeal was to its 'consistency' and its

[38] Ibid. 157–8.   [39] Ibid. xxiv. 34.   [40] Ibid. xxviii. 141.
[41] Ibid. xxvii. 70.

'reasonableness', to its 'innate persuasiveness'—not to the early Church or the Fathers, for it was clear that the 'theory had never been realized'. But nevertheless, he had hoped that 'the Anglican hypothesis could shoot up and thrive in the gaps between the trees which were the pride of the Eden of primitive truth, neither choking nor choked by their foliage'.[42] The other rhetorical element in controversy is 'the coarse rhetoric of hard names and sweeping implications in advance of proof'. Such rhetoric may be justifiable when 'it stands for a token or symbol of earnestness in an assailant', but on the whole it is more suited to public meetings and courts of law than works of theology. Unfortunately, the lectures in question contained much 'reprehensible polemic', of which Newman was now ashamed.[43] As for the third 'argumentative' element, he had leaned too much on the views of the standard Anglican theologians on the Fathers and Rome, 'systematizing' what they said rather than investigating for himself.[44] Characteristically, he felt embarrassed by his inconsistencies—in insisting on the consistency of the *Via Media*, while denouncing Rome for emphasizing consistency at the expense of truth; in referring to 'Romanists' and 'Romanism', while sensitive to Anglicans being called 'Protestants'; and in indulging in the controversial methods of Exeter Hall Evangelicalism.

Newman now proceeds to explain that his object is to provide an answer to one of the two important and plausible objections to the Roman Catholic Church which he had reproduced from Anglican writers in those lectures forty years ago. In the *Development of Doctrine* he had already dealt with 'the contrast which modern Catholicism is said to present with the religion of the Primitive Church'. Now he proposes to consider 'the difference which at first sight presents itself between its formal teaching and its popular and political manifestations'. It is no mere academic problem for him, as he will be 'explaining, as I have long wished to do, how I myself get over difficulties which I formerly felt'. And far from these difficulties decreasing since his own conversion, 'It is so ordered on high that in our day Holy Church should present just that aspect to my countrymen which is most consonant with their ingrained prejudices against her.'[45]

Newman's simple answer to the problem is that 'such an apparent contrariety between word and deed, the abstract and the concrete, could not but take place', since the Church's 'organization cannot be otherwise than complex, considering the many functions which she has to fulfil'. By way of analogy, he points out how difficult it is for one and the same person to perform different roles in different public and private situations. The Church is the mystical body of Christ, who 'is Prophet,

---

[42] *VM* i., pp. xx–xxv.   [43] Ibid., pp. xxvii–xxviii.   [44] Ibid., pp. xxxii–xxxiii.
[45] Ibid., pp. xxxvi–xxxvii.

Priest and, King; and after His pattern, and in human measure, Holy Church has a triple office too; not the Prophetical alone and in isolation, as [the *Lectures on the Prophetical Office*] virtually teach, but three offices, which are indivisible, though diverse, viz. teaching, rule, and sacred ministry'. It follows that Christianity 'is at once a philosophy, a political power, and a religious rite: as a religion, it is Holy; as a philosophy, it is Apostolic; as a political power, it is imperial, that is, One and Catholic. As a religion, its special centre of action is pastor and flock; as a philosophy, the Schools; as a rule, the Papacy and its Curia.' Although the Church has always exercised the three offices,

they were developed in their full proportions one after another, in a succession of centuries; first, in the primitive time it was recognized as a worship, springing up and spreading in the lower ranks of society ... Then it seized upon the intellectual and cultivated class, and created a theology and schools of learning. Lastly it seated itself, as an ecclesiastical polity, among princes, and chose Rome for its centre.

The three different offices are based on different principles, use different means, and are liable to different corruptions:

Truth is the guiding principle of theology and theological inquiries; devotion and edification, of worship; and of government, expedience. The instrument of theology is reasoning; of worship, our emotional nature; of rule, command and coercion. Further, in man as he is, reasoning tends to rationalism; devotion to superstition and enthusiasm; and power to ambition and tyranny.

The difficulty of combining all three offices is well illustrated by the question, 'What line of conduct, except on the long, the very long run, is at once edifying, expedient, and true?' Certainly, the gift of infallibility protects the Church from error not only directly in teaching but also 'indirectly' in 'worship and political action also'; however, 'nothing but the gift of impeccability granted to her authorities would secure them from all liability to mistake in their conduct, policy, words and decisions.' The problem of exercising these three very different functions 'supplies the staple of those energetic charges and vivid pictures of the inconsistency, double-dealing, and deceit of the Church of Rome.'[46]

Without attempting to deny the corruptions of the Church, Newman is anxious to correct his mistake in the *Prophetical Office* in blaming them on Catholic theology, by pointing out that 'ambition, craft, cruelty, and superstition are not commonly the characteristic of theologians', whereas the alleged corruptions in fact 'bear on their face the marks of having a popular or a political origin', and 'theology, so far from encouraging them, has restrained and corrected such extravagances as

[46] Ibid., pp. xxxviii–xliii.

have been committed, through human infirmity, in the exercise of the regal and sacerdotal powers.' Indeed, he adds almost dramatically, religion is never 'in greater danger than when, in consequence of national or international troubles, the Schools of theology have been broken up and ceased to be'. He then gives the reason for this in some of the most original and penetrating words he ever wrote:

I say, then, Theology is the fundamental and regulating principle of the whole Church system. It is commensurate with Revelation, and Revelation is the initial and essential idea of Christianity. It is the subject-matter, the formal cause, the expression, of the Prophetical Office, and, as being such, has created both the Regal Office and the Sacerdotal. And it has in a certain sense a power of jurisdiction over those offices, as being its own creations, theologians being ever in request and in employment in keeping within bounds both the political and popular elements in the Church's constitution,—elements which are far more congenial than itself to the human mind, are far more liable to excess and corruption . . .[47]

After this remarkable eulogy of theology and theologians, the reader should be prepared for one of Newman's characteristic shifts of perspective—'Yet theology cannot always have its own way; it is too hard, too intellectual, too exact, to be always equitable, or to be always compassionate . . .'. Sometimes even a theologian in his writings has to 'let his devout nature betray itself between the joints of his theological harness'. Popular religion may, for example, reject a more accurate translation of the Bible because to 'the devotional mind what is new and strange is as repulsive, often as dangerous, as falsehood is to the scientific. Novelty is often error to those who are unprepared for it, from the refraction with which it enters into their conceptions.' However wrong the condemnation of Galileo, nevertheless

there was nothing wrong in censuring abrupt, startling, unsettling, unverified disclosures . . . at once uncalled for and inopportune, at a time when the limits of revealed truth had not as yet been ascertained. A man ought to be very sure of what he is saying, before he risks the chance of contradicting the word of God. It was safe, not dishonest, to be slow in accepting what nevertheless turned out to be true. Here is an instance in which the Church obliges Scripture expositors, at a given time or place, to be tender of the popular religious sense.

People's 'imaginations' have to become accustomed to religious changes, whereas 'when science crosses and breaks the received path of Revelation', religious people are criticized if 'they show hesitation to shift at a minute's warning their position, and to accept as truths shadowy views at variance with what they have ever been taught and have held'. The modern idea is that it is 'a great moral virtue to be fearless and thorough in inquiry into facts', whereas the 'pursuit of truth in the subject-matter of religion . . . must always be accompanied by the fear of error'.[48] Elsewhere, Newman says: 'What the genius of the Church cannot bear is, changes in thought being hurried, abrupt, violent—out of tenderness to souls, for unlearned and narrow minded men get unsettled and miserable. The great thing is to move all together and then the change, as geological changes, must be very slow.' In another letter, however, he emphasizes the role of theology in preparing the Church for changes—'it is the arena on which questions of development and change are argued out . . . it prepares the way, accustoming the mind of Catholics to the idea of the change.' Because theology also, he explains in the same letter, 'protects' dogma by 'forming a large body of doctrine which must be got through before an attack can be made on the dogma', without theology 'the dogma of the Church would be the raw flesh without skin—nay or a tree without leaves—for, as devotional feelings clothe the dogma on the one hand, so does the teaching of [theology] on the other'.[49]

The Preface continues with an attack on the dogma of free speech, which may be a virtue or a vice depending on the circumstances. In the contemporary world it may be 'the worst charity, and the most provoking, irritating rule of action, and the most unhappy policy, not to speak out', and 'concealment, accommodation, and evasion is to co-operate with the spirit of error'. But against this is the consideration that truth 'lies in a mean'. Truth certainly 'is the rule of Society'—'but not necessarily the whole truth'. Concealment or evasion is often a duty. It is all very well for certain 'sublime sciences, which work out their problems apart from the crowding and jostling, the elbowing and the toe-treading of actual life, to care for nobody and nothing but themselves, and to preach and practise the cheap virtue of devotion to what they call truth, meaning of course facts'. But actually the plain fact is that ever since 'the Creator clothed Adam, concealment is in some sense the necessity of our fall'. The operation of a 'necessary economy' is evident in the Old Testament, as the fullness of revelation was only gradually disclosed; among the 'accommodations' allowed was Moses's toleration even of divorce, which was contrary to the divine law. The relevance of this apparent digression can now be seen. In an analogous way, Catholics have 'to be forebearing and to be silent in many cases, amid the mistakes, excesses, and superstitions of individuals and of classes of our brethren'. No doubt the 'abstract standard of religion and morals' in Catholic theology is 'higher than that which we witness in her children in particular countries or at particular times; but doubtless also, she, like

---

[48] Ibid., pp. xlviii–l, lii–lvi.   [49] *LD* xxv. 31–2; xxii. 99.

the old prophets before her, from no fault of hers, is not able to enforce it'. Again, 'truth and error in religion may be so intimately connected as not to admit of separation', as in the parable of the wheat and the cockle.[50]

The distinction between theology and popular religion, Newman argues, may be traced to the Gospel itself, and he cites the case of the woman with the haemorrhage who hoped to be cured by touching the cloak of Jesus, who 'passed over the superstitious act' and healed her because of her faith. In fact, he praised her for 'what might, not without reason, be called an idolatrous act'. Actually the Gospels show that the 'idolatry of ignorance' is not regarded on a level with other idolatries (of wealth, for example), which, however, are not normally 'shocking to educated minds'. Jesus constantly insisted on the necessity of faith—'but where does He insist on the danger of superstition?' However, the fact remains that this and other incidents in the Gospels 'form an aspect of Apostolic Christianity very different from that presented' by the epistles of St Paul. 'Need men wait for the Medieval Church in order to make their complaint that the theology of Christianity does not accord with its religious manifestations?' Does 'a poor Neapolitan crone, who chatters to the crucifix' do anything inherently more superstitious than the woman with the haemorrhage? Given 'the ethical intelligence of the world at large', Newman remarks that he would wonder 'whether that nation really had the faith, which is free in all its ranks and classes from all kinds and degrees of what is commonly considered superstition'. There is no reason to be surprised if the Catholic Church, in the face of popular religion, finds it difficult 'to make her Sacerdotal office keep step with her Prophetical'. This applies obviously to the cult of the angels and saints, which, 'though ever to be watched with jealousy by theologians, because of human infirmity and perverseness . . . has a normal place in revealed Religion'. For monotheism implies beings inferior to God but superior to human beings, that are able to bridge 'the vast gulf which separates Him from man'. And so polytheism is only 'a natural sentiment corrupted'. The Church's mission is not 'to oppose herself to impulses' which are 'both natural and legitimate', though previously 'the instruments of sin, but to do her best, by a right use, to moderate and purify them'. The fact that she has not always been successful simply shows that 'there will ever be a marked contrariety between the professions of her theology and the ways and doings of a Catholic country'. Moreover, the Church allows much more freedom in devotion, which is 'of a subjective and personal nature', than in doctrine. This contrast is accentuated if 'ecclesiastical authority takes

---

[50] *VM* i. lvii–lx, lxii, lxiv.

part with popular sentiment against a theological decision'. A very early example would be the occasion at Antioch when St Peter stopped associating with converts from paganism because of pressure from converts from Judaism, a lapse for which he was rebuked by St Paul. However, Paul himself was ready to conform to Jewish customs when necessary, and the principle of 'accommodation'—though it may be misapplied, as perhaps in the case of the Jesuit missionaries' adoption of Chinese customs—has always been practised by Christians since the earliest time.[51]

The theological office of the Church, then, may find itself in opposition to both the so-called political and pastoral offices. But equally, the political office may come into conflict with the other two offices. This office is, in fact, essential if the Church is to preserve her independence and freedom of action—as is illustrated by the Orthodox Church, 'which has lost its political life, while its doctrine, and its ritual and devotional system, have little that can be excepted against'. Like 'a sovereign State', the Church has 'to consolidate her several portions, to enlarge her territory, to keep up and to increase her various populations in this ever-dying, ever-nascent world, in which to be stationary is to lose ground, and to repose is to fail'. So important is this aspect of the Church that a point of theology may at times actually be 'determined on its expediency relatively to the Church's Catholicity', that is, 'by the logic of facts, which at times overrides all positive laws and prerogatives, and reaches in its effective force to the very frontiers of immutable truths'.[52] The interests of the Church may override apparently decisive theological arguments, as when Pope St Stephen decided that heretical baptisms were after all valid (a view later accepted by theologians).

The essay concludes with the reflection that 'whatever is great refuses to be reduced to human rule, and to be made consistent in its many aspects with itself.' There should be no cause for surprise, then, if the Church 'is an instance of the same law, presenting to us an admirable consistency and unity in word and deed, as her general characteristic, but crossed and discredited now and then by apparent anomalies'.[53] That the Church, however, has a diversity of offices no more detracts from her essential oneness than the fact that she includes laity as well as hierarchy in her constitution. Like his idea of the university, Newman's idea of the Church is of a wholeness and unity comprising a variety of elements and parts held together in creative tension, each sustained by mutual dependence rather than threatened by the collision of interaction. The keynote in both cases is equipoise as opposed to encroachment.

[51] Ibid., pp. lxvi–lxxi, lxxiv–lxxvi.   [52] Ibid., pp. lxxx–lxxxi, lxxxvi.
[53] Ibid., p. xciv.

4

In May 1877 Newman was sent one of the three drawings of him made by Lady Coleridge. It was a 'beautiful present'.[54] Back in 1866 he had been asked by a group of Birmingham notables to sit for a public portrait. He hesitated then, because he was 'deeply conscious' that he had 'been of no use whatever to this great Town'; indeed, he had 'almost been a stranger amid its large population'.[55] At the same time, however, he did agree to sit in London for his bust by the sculptor Thomas Woolner. Finally, in 1867 he acceded to the renewed request that he should allow his portrait to be painted by a local artist, W. T. Roden, adding again, however, that he had 'done nothing' for Birmingham—'I have paid my rates as an honest man, but have no claim on the place for any sort of service done for it of any kind.'[56] (His real 'personal reason was that I had no wish at all to be put in a collection together with a set of liberal party men or town celebrities with whom I had nothing in common'.[57]) In fact, the portrait was not painted till several years later. In reply to a solicitous letter from a stranger about the picture, Newman wrote deploring the sacrifice of realism to a theory:

If you saw me and talked with me you never would consider me sad or distressed—though the advance of years and the loss of friends of course have a depressing effect on mind and body. My painter, a man of genius, made, like men of genius, a great mistake. He acted on a theory. He caught at some passage of my Apologia, in which I speak of my sorrow at my loss of my Oxford friends and determined to represent me as mourning for them.

John Hungerford Pollen had already noted how the 'peculiar firmness, occasionally perhaps the sternness' of Newman's mouth had been 'enfeebled' in the portrait.[58] It was an early example of how easily the keen sensitivity was emphasized to the exclusion of the resoluteness and strength which formed that other pronounced side of his character. It was the unusual integration of these two powerful qualities that Lady Coleridge had glimpsed in her attempt to evoke the mystery of his personality.

Newman was well aware how he laid himself open to misunderstanding by the frankness with which he expressed his feelings. In September 1876, for example, he had made a note in his private journal, for the benefit of friends who might be 'perplexed' after his death by the way he had complained to people like Wiseman and Barnabò about the treatment he had received in return for his labours on behalf of the Church. But he had not, he insisted, been expressing 'disappointed

[54] *LD* xxviii. 198. [55] Ibid. xxii. 230. [56] Ibid. xxiii. 379.
[57] Ibid. xxviii. 178. [58] Ibid. xxvii. 199–200.

ambition', but 'a scorn and wonder at the *injustice* shown me, and at the demand of toadyism on my part, if I was to get their favour, and the favour of Rome'. Of course, he

knew perfectly well . . . that such language would look like disappointment at having received no promotion, and moreover was the worst way of getting it. But I had no wish to get it, and it was my very consciousness that I never had had such aspiration, nor felt any such disappointment, and was simply careless whether they thought I had or no, that made me thus speak. And at other times of my life also I have used words which, when I used them, I saw could be used against me, but did not care whether they were so used or not, from a clear conscience that it would be a mistaken use of them, if they were.

Although he had received 'no recognition in high quarters', he had nevertheless been wonderfully rewarded by the appreciation shown by so many for his writings. As he ended the entry, he remarked:

I am dissatisfied with the whole of this book. It is more or less a complaint from one end to the other. But it represents what has been the real state of my mind, and what my Cross has been.

But 'how light a Cross—think what the Crosses of others are! And think of the compensation, compensation in even this world . . . ' After this entry only one further line was written—the delightfully amused exclamation, 'Since writing the above I have been made a Cardinal!'[59] Taken together, these last two entries sum up so much of Newman—not only the sensitivity and self-consciousness on the one hand, and the realism and toughness on the other, but also the ironic humour.

The first volume of the *Via Media* was published in August 1877. Newman had already begun work at the end of June on a new, extensively revised *Essay on the Development of Christian Doctrine*. He was 'half re-writing, or rather whole-rearranging' it.[60] Generally, he was 'full of business, racing with time, not knowing how long' his life would last.[61] Other, younger lives among his friends' families were tragically passing away, like that of the wife of his godson Richard Hurrell Froude, who died in India after childbirth. Newman comforted Mrs William Froude with the piercing consolation:

This I have observed, that such dreadful blows do issue in great blessings, and when we look back upon them years afterwards, we see what mercy there is in them, and learn with all our hearts to kiss the scourge . . . which has made our hearts bleed. This is after the wound is healed, but oh! long it will be in healing.[62]

He preferred cruel to cosy comfort in the face of painfully inexplicable suffering: he once remarked that those whom God 'singularly and

---

[59] *AW* 273–5.   [60] *LD* xxviii. 247.   [61] Ibid. 234.   [62] Ibid. 235–6.

specially loves, He pursued with His blows, sometimes on one and the same wound, till perhaps they are tempted to cry out for mercy'.[63]

At the beginning of November not only was the second volume of the *Via Media* finished, but the new revised edition of the *Essay on Development* was ready for the printer; in the preface to the latter it was explained that 'various important alterations have been made in the arrangement of its separate parts, and some, not indeed in its matter, but in its text'.[64] In fact, although he had 'made no substantial alterations in it', he had 'nearly turned it inside out, as far as arrangement goes'.[65] He considered the rearrangement an 'improvement', although he was aware it might have led to 'serious mistakes in logic, references', and so on. It would be irritating if this was the case, as he did not 'mean to open the book again'.[66] Newman was also busy helping Copeland prepare a volume of selected *Parochial and Plain Sermons.* Any sermons that might jar on Catholic ears were to be excluded, for 'the object of the selection is to cultivate a unity of [ethos] among those who otherwise differ'.[67]

5

On 15 December 1877 Newman received out of the blue an invitation from S. W. Wayte, the President of Trinity College, Oxford, to become the college's first honorary fellow. He replied at once:

No compliment could I feel more intimately, or desire more eagerly at once to seize and appropriate than that which is the subject of your letter just received. Trinity College is ever, and ever has been, in my habitual thoughts. Views of its buildings are at my bed side and bring before me morning and evening my undergraduate days, and those good friends, nearly all now gone, whom I loved so much during them, and my love of whom has since their death ever kept me in affectionate loyalty to the college itself.[68]

However, he asked for time, to consider and consult whether he could appropriately accept the honour, particularly in view of the Catholic position on 'mixed' education. Three days later he wrote to Ullathorne, 'I have just received a very great compliment, perhaps the greatest I ever received.' Trinity, he added, 'has been the one and only seat of my affections at Oxford, and to see once more, before I am taken away, what I never thought I should see again, the place where I began the battle of life . . . is a prospect almost too much for me to bear'.[69] After thinking about it, he could not see any objection to accepting. The

---

[63] *LD* xxviii. xxxi. 53–4*.   [64] *Dev.*, p. viii.   [65] *LD* xxviii. 288–9.
[66] Ibid. 304.   [67] Ibid. 248.   [68] Ibid. 279.
[69] Ibid. 283–4.

bishop agreed, and declared that it would be Newman who would be honouring the college, not the other way round. With obvious delight, Newman wrote to the President to accept: 'It is indeed a most strange good fortune, after a long sixty years and more, to become again a freshman of my first and dear College.'[70]

He had had 'a lifelong affection' for the place, 'greater than for any thing in Oxford'.[71] It was true that he had 'more and more intimately personal Oriel friends'—but 'There was too much painful at Oriel . . . hence I rejoice that it is Trinity, not Oriel, that has reclaimed me.' He could not remember when he had 'been so much pleased'. It was yet another sign of the extraordinary 'change of feeling' about him which had begun with the publication of the *Apologia*.[72] There he had concluded his 'History of my Religious Opinions' by recounting how he had called on Dr Ogle, his old tutor at Trinity, before leaving Oxford:

In him I took leave of my first College, Trinity, which was so dear to me, and which held on its foundation so many who had been kind to me both when I was a boy, and all through my Oxford life. Trinity had never been unkind to me. There used to be much snap-dragon growing on the walls opposite my freshman's rooms there, and I had for years taken it as the emblem of my own perpetual residence even unto death in my University.

The next and last chapter of the book, 'Position of my Mind since 1845', had also ended with a poignant tribute—to his 'dearest brothers' of his new home, the Birmingham Oratory—although it was hardly meant to be a farewell.[73] Among them was Edward Caswall, who died on 2 January 1878. He was buried at Rednal, in the grave next to Ambrose St John: 'So now the three most energetic and influential of the first Fathers of our Oratory lie together; and the three who from the first threw in their lot with me . . .'.[74] It was a curious twist of fate. He had said goodbye, he had thought, over thirty years ago to Trinity, but now he was taking leave of those younger companions, who had taken the place of his old Oxford friends and who should have outlived him. St John's death had been a warning, and now Caswall's death was a melancholy confirmation that the 'first generation' of Oratorians was 'passing away'.[75] How 'strange' it was, he wrote to Henry Wilberforce's widow, that he was

going into the world again, and the Oxford world—and, tho' I suppose it will be only for a day or two now and then, yet it is strangely out of keeping with my morning and evening, with the mementos of the departed in my Mass, with my bed at night which is hung around with dear faces which, as far as this life is

[70] Ibid. 285.   [71] Ibid. 285, 288.   [72] Ibid. 290, 292.
[73] *Apo*. 213, 252.   [74] *LD* xxviii. 300.   [75] Ibid. 298.

concerned, I shall never see again. And this is independent of the trial it will be to go to new Oxford with my associations with the old.

However, there was no question that the honorary fellowship was a great honour, and it was 'wonderful that such a recognition of my past should have happened in my life time'.[76] Perhaps even more wonderful was the fact that he was to end his life in the world as he had begun it, as a member of Trinity. Back in 1859 he had thought he had lost his 'last tie' with Oxford when Manuel Johnson died: he had spent his last night at Oxford in his house, and when he travelled by train between Birmingham and London he had always 'been accustomed to salute the Observatory in my thoughts, as a friend', but Johnson's death meant that even that was 'all over'.[77]

As if the recognition by Trinity was not enough, he now heard that there was talk of Oriel commissioning a portrait of him by the well-known portrait painter W. W. Ouless. He began to think that such honours had 'a grave significancy'—as though they were 'an anointing for the burial'.[78]

At the end of February Newman spent a couple of nights in Oxford. He had been invited by the President of Trinity to pay a formal visit, but he 'wanted to break the ice quietly, which in 32 years had got so solid, that it could not be got through without a great effort'.[79] He had lunch with the fellows at Trinity and dinner with the President. He saw his old tutor Thomas Short, who was now nearly 90, and called on Pusey. He visited Oriel and went to see the new college called after Keble. As a way of expressing his gratitude to Trinity, he had taken the 'bold' step of dedicating the new edition of the *Development of Doctrine* to its President.[80] In the dedication he was careful to dissociate both the Head and the college from any sympathy with the contents of the work, but he noted the coincidence that its initial publication in 1846 had marked his departure from Oxford, while its republication coincided with his return to Oxford.

At the end of March he heard that Pusey was very seriously ill. He wrote an almost impassioned letter to H. P. Liddon, Pusey's disciple and future biographer:

If his state admits of it, I should so very much wish to say to my dearest Pusey, whom I have loved and admired for over fifty years, that the Catholic Roman Church solemnly lays claim to him as her child, and to ask him in God's sight, whether he does not acknowledge her right to do so.

If Pusey did still really believe that the Anglican was part of the Catholic

---

[76] *LD* xxviii. 303–4.   [77] Ibid. xix. 58–9, 62.   [78] Ibid. xxviii. 307.
[79] Ibid. 319–20.   [80] Ibid. 324.

Church, then Newman would 'gain this comfort from it, that he died in simple good faith'. But 'I cannot let him die, if such is God's will, with the grave responsibility lying upon me of such an appeal to him.'[81] Liddon replied that Pusey was better, and had no doubts about his religious position.

Privately, Newman admitted to Anne Mozley, his sisters' sister-in-law, his reservations about Pusey's character. Asked whether he remembered an Easter dinner at the Puseys in 1837, he replied that he well remembered 'bitterly complaining that we had only roast veal without a drop of melted butter or other sauce'. Did this kind of asceticism indicate a lack of ordinary human feeling, he wondered, or perhaps a kind of religious ostentation ('unction')? He also confided to Anne Mozley the rather devastating confidence: 'Another, *real* SERIOUS, secret—the contrast of Pusey and Mrs Pusey, so much in favour of the latter, made Mrs Wootten, in spite of her great attachment to the former, a Catholic.'[82] The unattractive side of Pusey's personality had unfortunately adversely affected his reputation, but there was no doubting his greatness.

Anne Mozley was editing the essays of her brother James Mozley, who had just died, and Newman was helping her with advice and information. He told her he had no objection at all to her republishing her brother's critical review of the *Development of Christian Doctrine*. He had no doubts about his own argument ('my faith in it has been rekindled by my recent perusal of it'), but he would welcome any good criticism of it. It was personalizing issues that he deplored:

I never have minded my friends writing against me—what I have complained of is their imputing motives . . . Pusey pained me, for in print he attributed my conversion to 'oversensitiveness—' . . . I don't think I have myself ever imputed motives—or at least my principle has been not to do so.[83]

This did not mean that all personal considerations were to be excluded in explaining another person's views, but they should only be introduced into the argument when they were clearly relevant. Otherwise it was 'like punching a man in the stomach'.[84] To impute motives was to judge somebody personally, as opposed to their actions or writings.

Newman himself was about to start sorting out Keble's letters to him, which he was to give to Keble College. It was tiring work, during some hot summer days. As usual, he was also burdened down with his own correspondence—'if I had any ideas to communicate, they have oozed out, unobserved, at the end of my fingers.'[85] For years and years he had

[81] Ibid. 337.   [82] Ibid. 352.   [83] Ibid. 379–80.
[84] Ibid. 393.   [85] Ibid. 377.

complained of the sheer physical pain of handwriting; the only consolation was that it had not actually got worse. He could not understand why the quality of his handwriting varied so much—sometimes very shaky and weak, at other times firm and strong, for no apparent reason.

In October he wrote to Pusey to say that he had finally, after some misgivings, decided to include his *Treatises of St Athanasius* in the uniform edition of his works, but with a number of changes which would make it almost a new edition, so that it would not 'interfere' with the original work in the Library of the Fathers. One treatise would be omitted as not directly relevant to Arianism, and also several of his own theological tracts now contained in *Tracts Theological and Ecclesiastical*. At the time of the original edition a literal translation was absolutely necessary to allay suspicions about the intentions of the Tractarians, but now he proposed to bring out the meaning of Athanasius more clearly with a freer translation, which would remain faithful 'to his theological teaching, but not necessarily to his controversial text'. He also extended to Pusey his condolences on the death of his eldest granddaughter, adding, 'I do not exaggerate when I say that I have not even now got over my Sister's death.'[86] He intended the new translation of Athanasius to complete the uniform edition and to be his last published work. The study of St Athanasius had been his first and was now his last 'passion'.[87] His anticipation that the revision would take him a year was to be upset by the most extraordinary of events.

6

Pius IX had died at last in February 1878, and had been succeeded by Leo XIII. Newman thought the letter the new Pope had published outlining the policy of his pontificate 'a most excellent one, and [I] have followed with great love and sympathy every act which the Papers have told us of him since his elevation, I only wish he was 10 years younger—that he is not, is his only fault'.[88] Leo's declared intention was to work for reconciliation between the Church and the modern world (although he was still not prepared to accept the new situation in Italy).

Christmas brought a present from the new Pope—a signed holy picture from his personal breviary. It was sent by one of Newman's penitents, now a governess in Rome. She had received it from an official at the Vatican, who was himself a penitent of Newman's old Oratorian mentor, Father Rossi, and who had arranged for her to meet the Pope at

---

[86] *LD* xxviii. 406.   [87] Ibid. xxvii. 56–7.   [88] Ibid. xxviii. 415.

an audience. The little gift was a harbinger of a much greater honour.

At the end of January 1879 Manning received a letter from the Papal Secretary of State asking him to find out how Newman would react to an invitation to become a Cardinal. Manning promptly sent on the enquiry to Ullathorne, adding that he had already forwarded to the Pope a petition to this effect from the Duke of Norfolk and other Catholic peers. There had been rumours since the beginning of the pontificate that the new Pope intended to confer this highest honour. And at the beginning of December 1878, before Manning's letter reached Rome, the Duke of Norfolk had himself personally submitted the suggestion to the Pope. The Duke's explicit object was to secure Rome's recognition of Newman's loyalty and orthodoxy. Such a vindication was not only personally due to Newman, but was important for removing among non-Catholics the suspicion that his immensely persuasive and popular apologetic writings were not really properly Catholic. It looks in fact as if Leo XIII had already had the idea himself, as Newman was later given to believe. As Nuncio in Brussels he had become familiar with the Oxford Movement, and he had met Dominic Barberi in Belgium in 1845 immediately after Barberi had received Newman into the Church. After being elected Pope, he is supposed to have said that the policy of his pontificate would be revealed by the name of the first Cardinal he created. Several years later he told an English visitor: 'My Cardinal! it was not easy, it was not easy. They said he was too liberal, but I had determined to honour the Church in honouring Newman. I always had a cult for him. I am proud that I was able to honour such a man.'[89]

Ullathorne strongly urged Newman to accept the extraordinary honour. The chief difficulty from Newman's point of view was the fear that he might have to leave the Oratory and go and live in Rome, as was then normal for cardinals who were not diocesan bishops. His formal reply, therefore, to Ullathorne, which Manning was to send to Rome, expressed not only his deep gratitude, but also his plea that he might end his days in the Oratory. It was agreed that Ullathorne's covering letter, which was also intended to be sent to the Secretary of State, would make it clear that Newman was in fact ready to accept the honour, but was reluctant to seem to make his continuing residence in Birmingham a condition. When Manning replied that he was forwarding Newman's letter to Rome, but did not mention the covering letter of explanation, Ullathorne wrote again more explicitly. Meanwhile, Manning sent Newman the English original of the letter he had written to Rome at the request of the Duke of Norfolk and the other peers, saying that he wanted Newman to see this token of his friendship towards him now that

---

[89] Ibid. xxix. 426.

they were both coming to the end of their lives. Newman replied simply that he was ready to accept the honour, provided he could stay at the Oratory. A few days later Manning wrote to tell the Duke of Norfolk that Newman had declined the offer, and that the letter giving his reasons had been sent to Rome. Hearing of a rumour in London that Newman had refused, Ullathorne then took it upon himself to write directly to the Secretary of State to explain Newman's feelings. Manning had sent on Newman's letter, keeping Ullathorne's covering letter, which he took with him to Rome, where he arrived a few days after writing to the Duke of Norfolk. Shortly afterwards *The Times* also reported that Newman had refused the red hat. Newman himself noted privately that it was 'to say the least a great impertinence' for anyone to circulate his own interpretation of a letter intended for the Pope before it even reached him.[90] There was no doubting who the source of the reports was, and Newman wrote to the Duke of Norfolk to protest against the way in which 'some one' (he did not mention Manning's name) had not only read his letter 'but, instead of leaving the *Pope* to interpret it, took upon himself to put an interpretation upon it, and published that interpretation to the world'. 'Would it not look odd,' he commented acidly to John Hungerford Pollen, 'if the Postman here, not only read this my letter before it got to the receiving office, but put his own interpretation on it, and told first his particular friends about it, and then the general public, leaving you to receive it next morning?'[91] To T. W. Allies he wrote, 'I have no hesitation in saying, that, were a Cardinal's Hat offered me, it would be a most piercing trial to have to accept it—perhaps the greatest I have had in my life.'[92] He had a great dread of 'the dignity, publicity, and ceremonial state' which would be involved in 'such a new life'.[93] As for the prospect of having to leave the Oratory and become a distinguished ecclesiastic, it would be as absurd as Caligula's horse being appointed Consul!

Meanwhile, on 21 February *The Times* carried a public announcement of a resolution by the Catholic Union congratulating Newman on the offer of the red hat, but without indicating whether he had accepted or not. The news caused a stream of congratulatory letters. But, Newman told his well-wishers, an offer had neither been formally made nor had it been declined. While Catholic friends urged him to accept the honour, Anglicans like Copeland and Pusey were glad to hear the report that he had declined. But there were special reasons why he felt he had to accept, reasons that outweighed all personal inhibitions.

For 20 or 30 years ignorant or hot-headed Catholics had said almost that I was a heretic . . . I knew and felt that it was a miserable evil that the One True

[90] *LD* xxix. 29.   [91] Ibid. 32.   [92] Ibid. 29.   [93] Ibid. 160.

Apostolic Religion should be so slandered as to cause men to suppose that my portrait of it was not the true—and I knew that many would become Catholics, as they ought to be, if only I was pronounced by Authority to be a *good* Catholic. On the other hand it had long riled me, that Protestants should condescendingly say that I was only half a Catholic, and too good to be what they were at Rome. I therefore felt myself constrained to accept.[94]

A puzzled Duke of Norfolk wrote to Manning in Rome, wondering who had told him that Newman had refused and asking him to make it clear to the Pope that the report was false. The Archbishop acknowledged that he himself had so interpreted Newman's letter to Ullathorne. Once again he claimed that he had acted as a sincere friend of Newman and that once again it had ended in a disastrous misunderstanding. He did not mention Ullathorne's covering letter. However, he undertook to explain the situation to the Pope, who, on hearing of Newman's hesitation, immediately waived the usual requirement to reside in Rome, something which apparently had not been done since the seventeenth century. Newman heard the news on 1 March: 'It puts an end to all those reports that my teaching is not Catholic or my books trustworthy, which has been so great a trial to me so long.' To have refused the honour 'would have created a suspicion that it was true that I was but a half and half Catholic, who dared not commit himself to a close union with the Church of Rome, and who wished to be independent'. It would have upset Catholics and deterred potential converts. It would also have 'disheartened so many zealous well-wishers' anxious that his name 'should be vindicated, and who felt that a refusal would be most ungracious to the Pope . . . and would be shrinking from aiding him in my place when he was pursuing the very line of policy which for so many years I had desiderated at Rome'.[95]

A few days later Newman heard that the rumour persisted in circles close to the Archbishop in London that he was still refusing to accept the red hat. He had already, on Ullathorne's advice, written to Manning in Rome to say that he gratefully accepted the Pope's permission to stay in the Oratory. He now wrote to Manning still more explicitly to say, with reference to the report, that as soon as he was officially informed of the intention to elevate him to the Sacred College of Cardinals, he would immediately send his acceptance to Rome. Manning promptly wrote back to say that he had genuinely misunderstood Newman's original meaning. As for the covering letter of Ullathorne, he had taken that merely to signify that Newman 'might' accept the offer if the condition about his continuing residence in Birmingham were met.[96] Whatever Manning's intentions and motives, the meaning of Ullathorne's letter

---

[94] Ibid.   [95] Ibid. 50.   [96] Ibid. 61.

could not have been clearer—'I am thoroughly confident that nothing stands in the way of his most grateful acceptance except . . . having to leave the Oratory.'[97] Nor is it easy to see how Newman's subsequent letter to Manning, saying he could not be so 'ungracious' as to decline the Pope's honour 'provided' he could remain an Oratorian, could have 'confirmed' Manning's misapprehension, as he now claimed.[98] His later explanation to the Duke of Norfolk, who said that he could not see how Newman's letter could have been read as an unconditional refusal, was that it seemed to him to amount to a refusal because it was unprecedented for Cardinals who were not diocesan bishops not to reside at Rome. The charitable judgement on Manning's misunderstanding must be that he was guilty of a certain wishful thinking.

Well aware that old Anglican friends might be surprised that he should accept such an ecclesiastical position, he wrote to R. W. Church that he had not 'dared' to 'refuse the offer. A good Providence gave me an opportunity of clearing myself of former calumnies in my Apologia—and I dared not refuse it—And now He gave me a means . . . to set myself right as regards other calumnies which were directed against me—how could I neglect so great a loving kindness?' But however out of character such a high dignity might seem, there was a certain mischievous glee in accepting it which was very much in character—'Poor Ward can no longer call me a heretic . . .'. It was indeed the 'end' of 'all those stories which have gone about of my being a half Catholic, a liberal Catholic, under a cloud, not to be trusted'.[99] As for Manning, Newman merely wrote to thank him for conveying his answer to the Pope. To the secretary of the Catholic Union he wrote that he wished 'to give a contradiction to any ideas that may be afloat as to any dissatisfaction on my part with any step taken by Cardinal Manning. He has been kind enough to go out of his way to write to me, and I wish every such report swept away for good and all.'[100] His personal victory over the Ultramontanes would be marked by magnanimity.

The official letter to Newman came from the Secretary of State and was dated 15 March. It was enclosed in a letter from Manning, who expressed his joy at Newman's elevation, but did not mention the embarrassing slip in the Vatican letter which addressed Newman as a priest of the London Oratory! The mistake would be repeated at the public consistory. One can only speculate how Father Faber would have enjoyed this final irony.

Newman was now overwhelmed with letters of congratulation, 'yet letters so joyful and affectionate that I should be as hard as a stone, and as cruel as an hyena, and as ungrateful as a wild cat, if I did not welcome

---

[97] *LD* xxix. 20.   [98] Ibid. 22, 61.   [99] Ibid. 72.   [100] Ibid. 76.

them, but they try me much, and I have my new edition of Athanasius, the last of my revisions on my hands, and I much fear lest, while it adds portentously to my daily labour, it should be itself made by those other calls on me a great failure'.[101] He could not help thinking of all those now dead who would have rejoiced at the extraordinary event. He had always thought that in time he would be vindicated—'But the Pope has superseded Time.'[102]

On 16 April he set off for London en route to Rome. An hour or two before he left, he wrote to William Froude to acknowledge an extremely lengthy letter on religion and certainty, promising that he would try and reply from Rome, but without any guarantee that he would be able to say anything very helpful. For he strongly agreed with Froude that 'men must have chronic familiarity to understand each other, and that truth slowly sinks into the mind, and that therefore paper argument is most disappointing—indeed this is one of the "morals" of my Essay on Assent'.[103]

On arriving in Rome a week or so later he wrote to Birmingham to ask one of the community to check if the words 'cor ad cor loquitur' ('heart speaks to heart') were to be found in the Vulgate version of the Bible or in Thomas à Kempis. He had forgotten that he had already quoted the saying from St Francis de Sales in the *Idea of a University*. It was, of course, to be the motto on his cardinal's coat of arms.

A few days later he began a long reply to Froude. The justification of religious belief had always been the subject closest to his heart, and all the excitement of arriving in Rome and making preparations for the consistory did not prevent him from once again expounding his basic approach to the problem. The arguments were familiar, but he stressed to Froude, who was an engineer and naval architect, that like believers, scientists too are certain of truths which they cannot actually prove. But conversely, he was also prepared to 'say emphatically of theology' what Froude had said of science, that it 'makes progress by being always alive to its own fundamental uncertainties'.[104] It was permissible to argue against any doctrines which had not been defined as part of revelation. Great theologians like St Bernard and St Thomas had once disputed the doctrine of the Immaculate Conception, while Jesuit theologians had refuted St Augustine's teaching on predestination. In the event, news of Froude's death early in May in South Africa stopped the letter from being sent.

On Sunday, 27 April at midday Newman had an audience with the Pope. Leo received him 'most affectionately—keeping my hand in his'. Newman sent an account of the meeting to the community:

---

[101] Ibid. 91.   [102] Ibid. 106.   [103] Ibid.   [104] Ibid. 118.

He asked me various questions—was our house a good one? was our Church? how many were we? of what age? when I said, we had lost some, he put his hand on my head and said 'Don't cry.' He asked 'had we any lay brothers'? 'how then did we do for a cook?' I said we had a widow woman, and the kitchen was cut off from the house. He said 'bene.' Where did I get my theology? at Propaganda? etc etc . . . I certainly did not think his mouth large till he smiled, and then the ends turned up, but not unpleasantly—he has a clear white complexion his eyes somewhat bloodshot—but this might have been the accident of the day. He speaks very slowly and clearly and with an Italian manner.[105]

Newman had had a bad cold and a cough since arriving in Rome, and at the beginning of May he retired to bed. Fortunately he was well enough on the twelfth to receive from the Secretary of State the *biglietto* informing him that at a consistory that morning the Pope had elevated him to the College of Cardinals.

The famous speech he gave in reply was highly characteristic. He begins by referring to the 'many trials' he had suffered, noting pointedly that the Pope's action was designed not only to 'give pleasure to English Catholics', but 'even to Protestant England'. Typically, a vindication of his own liberal Catholicism turns into an uncompromising attack on a very different kind of religious liberalism—that liberalism which he had described in the *Apologia* as 'false liberty of thought, or the exercise of thought upon matters, in which, from the constitution of the human mind, thought cannot be brought to any successful issue, and therefore is out of place', and which include first principles, especially religious ones that cannot be subjected to 'human judgment' because they are 'revealed doctrines which are in their nature beyond and independent of it'.[106] The rhetorical implication now is that the two kinds of liberalism are never to be confused, and that in his unswerving opposition to the latter kind Newman is totally at one with his Church.

In a long course of years I have made many mistakes. I have nothing of that high perfection, which belongs to the writings of Saints, *viz.*, that error cannot be found in them; but what I trust that I may claim all through what I have written, is this,—an honest intention, an absence of private ends, a temper of obedience, a willingness to be corrected, a dread of error, a desire to serve Holy Church, and, through Divine Mercy, a fair measure of success. And I rejoice to say, to one great mischief I have from the first opposed myself. For thirty, forty, fifty years I have resisted to the best of my powers the spirit of liberalism in religion. Never did Holy Church need champions against it more sorely than now, when, alas! it is an error overspreading, as a snare, the whole earth . . .

As the Cardinal-elect warmed to his theme, we hear very distinctly the voice of a younger Newman:

---

[105] *LD* xxix. 121.   [106] *Apo.* 256.

Liberalism in religion is the doctrine that there is no positive truth in religion, but that one creed is as good as another, and this is the teaching which is gaining substance and force daily. It is inconsistent with any recognition of any religion, as *true*. It teaches that all are to be tolerated, for all are matters of opinion. Revealed religion is not a truth, but a sentiment and a taste; not an objective fact, not miraculous; and it is the right of each individual to make it say just what strikes his fancy. Devotion is not necessarily founded on faith. Men may go to Protestant Churches and to Catholic, may get good from both and belong to neither. They may fraternize together in spiritual thoughts and feelings, without having any views at all of doctrine in common, or seeing the need of them.

There is an echo of the early *Tamworth Reading Room* as Newman denounces the rejection of religion as 'the bond of society' and the encroaching secularization whereby 'that goodly framework of society which is the creation of Christianity, is throwing off Christianity'.

Instead of the Church's authority and teaching, they would substitute first of all a universal and a thoroughly secular education, calculated to bring home to every individual that to be orderly, industrious and sober is his personal interest . . . As to Religion, it is a private luxury, which a man may have if he will; but which of course he must pay for, and which he must not obtrude upon others, or indulge in to their annoyance.

But he does not hesitate, in the heart of Catholic Rome, to introduce the important modification, 'that there is much in the liberalistic theory which is good and true; for example, not to say more, the precepts of justice, truthfulness, sobriety, self-command, benevolence, which . . . are among its avowed principles, and the natural laws of society'. The surprise, however, lies in the conclusion: it is precisely because of the positive aspects of liberalism that 'There never was a device of the Enemy, so cleverly framed, and with such promise of success.' But that is not the end of the speech, which closes on the optimistic note that 'Christianity has been too often in what seemed deadly peril, that we should fear for it any new trial now.' It is not its survival which is in doubt, but rather the unexpected manner in which it will win through: 'Commonly the Church has nothing more to do than to go on in her own proper duties, in confidence and peace, to stand still and to see the salvation of God.'[107]

The vicissitudes of the Church were a favourite idea of Newman's: the Church always 'seemed dying', but then 'triumphed, against all human calculation'. It was 'impossible to forecast the future' when there were 'no precedents—and the history of Christianity is a succession of fresh and fresh trials—never the same twice'. There was 'a continuous history

[107] *Campaign* 393–400.

of fearful falls and as strange and successful recoveries'. The sheer variety of the catastrophies, 'each unlike the others', was a 'pledge that the present ordeal, though different from any of the preceding, will be overcome'. It seemed they were now 'entering on quite a new course—for which the civil ignoring of Christianity may be the necessary first step, and we may have centuries of confusion—but the Church has steadily worked her way out of overwhelming misfortunes in time past, and will . . . again'. This strong sense of the Church constantly dying and rising only reflected what was almost an obsession with Newman, that it is 'the rule of God's Providence that we should succeed by failure'.[108]

The day after the *biglietto* speech Newman went to the Vatican to receive the cardinal's biretta from the Pope, and two days later there was the public consistory at which the cardinal's hat was actually presented. In Newman's own later words, the 'wonderful attention' he received from Leo XIII 'astonished all there'.[109] He was now both a fellow of an Oxford college and a Cardinal of the Church of Rome. The two halves of his life had come together in an astonishing way at the very end.

Among the many congratulatory messages was one from Cardinal Manning, writing on behalf of the English bishops. It would have been impossible for Newman not to have enjoyed the irony of being able to express his 'great satisfaction to be told . . . that even when there was not such a bias in my favour, equally as when there was, I have through so many years, and under such varying circumstances, and by such men, been so tenderly and considerately regarded'. There was a 'gratification'—but no doubt a surprise too—in 'learning that my honest pains to please them have not been taken in vain; and I have nothing more to desire'.[110] He could also afford to be conciliatory towards the London Oratory; he was now in a position to visit them, he told the Duke of Norfolk, having 'an opportunity of returning good for evil': 'As soon as I knew I was to be a Cardinal, I felt that my position . . . was quite changed, and that I might put myself in relations to them, from which, while I was a lesser man, I abstained.'[111] He arrived back in Birmingham on 1 July. A large crowd of people met him at the station. In the church of the Oratory he presided at a short service and spoke of the joy of returning home and how the idea of home was at the heart of the community life of the Oratory, which was meant to be a model of family life. The cold he had caught before arriving in Rome had turned to pneumonia the day after the consistory, and he still looked very frail and weak after suffering a relapse on the way back.

[108] *LD* xxviii. 196, 91; xxx. 142.   [109] Ibid. xxix. 160.   [110] Ibid. 137.
[111] Ibid. 142.

7

During the weeks that followed, a number of formal congratulatory addresses were presented to Newman. Perhaps none was so gratifying, though, as the story he heard later in November of

a working man, unknown to the friend who met him as she was coming out of a London church. 'Are you a Catholic? Is this Cardinal Newman's church? Do you know him? Tell him the workmen of England are rejoiced to know that the Pope has done so good a deed as to make him a Cardinal.'

It was, Newman soberly reflected, 'so wonderful a change as to cow one'.[112]

A vivid little incident earlier in the autumn, however, was sharply reminiscent of those early trials of community life after his return from Rome more than thirty years ago as the founder of the English Oratory. He had been asked by Arthur Hutton, a young convert Anglican clergyman, who had joined the Oratory three years previously and was about to be ordained a priest, to write a preface to a book he was publishing against the validity of Anglican Orders. He had agreed to do so, but had insisted on certain changes being made in the text. Hutton wrote in October from his ordination retreat to complain about the sharp way Newman had spoken to him and about his reluctance to make what he regarded as unnecessary and expensive corrections. Clearly, the cardinalate had not changed things very much: Hutton's letter could have been written by one of those first members of the Oratory who had suffered a similar rebuke for similar failings. All that had changed was Newman's own manner, which was now gentler and mellower.

If you knew how, all thro' my life, I have hated what I criticized in those passages . . . as savouring both of unkindness and uppishness, you would not wonder at my earnestness with you about them; and you again, who have upon you that token of a generous and affectionate nature, sensitiveness, should be the last man to say unnecessarily, in the way of scorn or scoffing, what may wound the feelings of men whose sensitiveness, for what you know, is as keen as your own.

He confessed to two other reasons for 'speaking with a peremptoriness beyond my wont, as I hope'. He felt that Hutton had 'habitually a liking to have your own way'.[113] He was also afraid that what Hutton had written about corporate reunion would offend F. G. Lee, an Anglo-Catholic promoter of the cause, who was (unsuccessfully) trying at that very moment to organize an Anglican address of congratulation. It was

---

[112] Ibid. 201.   [113] Ibid. 188.

as well that Newman was accustomed to religious instability, to enthusiasm followed by a reaction. Exactly four years later Hutton abandoned not only the priesthood and Catholicism, but also Christianity, and married a teacher at the Oratory School. He eventually resumed the Anglican Orders he had once vilified. After Newman's death he penned some bitter reminiscences of him. Perhaps Newman would not have been surprised either by this or by the fact that Lee, on the other hand, years later left the Church of England and joined the Roman Catholic Church. Only ten days before he had warned an enquirer against the 'temptation' for some of joining the Catholic Church for the wrong reasons ('merely because they can pray better in it, or have more fervency than in the Anglican Church'), and then falling away because they never in fact 'had faith'.[114]

At the end of November he told T. W. Allies that he did not see how he could act on his suggestion that he should present the Pope with a set of his works. He was uncertain of their importance, for one thing—'a man must be dead, and time elapse, before a satisfactory judgment can be arrived at about him.' There were other difficulties: not only could the Pope not read English, but the books themselves were so very much in the English tradition of Bishop Butler that it was doubtful what value if any they would have on the Continent. Finally, there was his own distinct lack of interest in the books he had published:

I took great pains with what I have published, and am as fierce in my heart now as ever against Liberalism on the one hand and . . . extreme [Ultramontane] views . . . on the other, but it has always been a great pain to me to write (I have been used to call it an intellectual child birth,) and it has left no pleasant memories behind, and (most unnaturally!) I have no love for my intellectual children. I have had no pleasure in composing, and no temptation to read over and dwell upon that I have composed. What I thought good and happy at the time of writing, palls upon me when I read it now.[115]

(Nearly twenty years before, he had commented that he had 'hardly, if ever, written a book without being fixed to it by external circumstances', and 'To write a book for the sake of writing would be to me an impossibility.' The sheer labour of thinking and writing had been a 'great pain, pain reaching to the body as well as the mind'. What had made him write was 'the sight of a truth and the desire to show it to others', and the experience was 'mingled satisfaction and distress of being rid of pain *by* pain', like 'the painful relieving of an irritation' one got from going to the dentist.[116])

On Christmas Day he received a telegram announcing the death of

---

[114] *LD* xxviii. 185.   [115] Ibid. 207.   [116] Ibid. xx. 343, 368, 169.

his sister Jemima at the age of 72. She had been ill for some time, so there was no surprise in the news. He told Anne Mozley,

What I miss and shall miss Jemima in is this—she alone, with me, had a memory of dates—I knew quite well, as anniversaries of all kinds came round, she was recollecting them, as well as I—e.g. my getting into Oriel—now I am the only one in the world who know a hundred things most interesting to me. E.G. yesterday was the anniversary of Mary's death—my mind turned at once to Jemima, but she was away.[117]

Back in 1846 he had complained to Jemima that in his 'great trial' of 1845 she 'only' had had 'the heart, or the want of reverence, to write censoriously to me'. But there had been a reconciliation in 1865, and visits had been exchanged later.[118]

Newman himself was nearly 80, as he was reminded by a letter from Rome describing an audience two members of the community had had with the Pope. Leo sent his love and told the Oratorians that they must look after Newman very carefully. On being reminded of his great age, a look of sadness came over the Pope's face and he was silent, before brightening up and declaring with a smile that they would have to make sure that he lived till he was 90!

Around October Newman had managed to resume work on his new edition of St Athanasius. The notes were too long for the size of the uniform edition volumes, so he was putting them together as an appendix. The interruption caused by the cardinalate had upset his plans and 'spoilt the revision': he had intended to make 'a free translation', but lack of time had meant it was 'neither one thing nor the other'. He was 'ashamed of it' and it was 'very mortifying'.[119] He worked away on it through the autumn, but at the beginning of the new year he felt as despondent as ever: 'Going to Rome broke all the principles, memories, traditions, rules, on which I was working, and my work will be sadly out of keeping with itself.'[120] Apart from the never-ending work of sorting out his letters, he saw it as the last task of his life. He told Pusey that it seemed 'likely to equal' the trouble the *Arians* had given him (which 'tried me more than any book since').[121] The edition finally appeared in February 1881, the last two volumes in the uniform series. He was very disappointed at the result, which he thought was inferior to the original Oxford edition: the only thing he could see in its favour was that it was easier to read the notes as a continuous text rather than 'overgrown' footnotes in small print. But he had found the work of conversion 'more laborious than a translation into a foreign language'.[122] As with most of the other reprints, he would not recover

---

[117] Ibid. xxix. 226. [118] Ibid. xxxi. 9*. [119] Ibid. xxix. 173.
[120] Ibid. 220. [121] Ibid. 297. [122] Ibid. 334–5.

from the sales the full cost of republication. The uniform edition was now complete and contained everything he thought 'worth preserving'. He was not very hopeful about future sales: apart from changes in fashion ('books die yearly as leaves in October'), there was the added difficulty that his writings were ' "occasional" even in their titles. They are the record of accidental controversies, they are full of allusions which in little time it will require a commentary to explain.'[123]

On 8 May 1880 Newman went to London to stay at Norfolk House in St James's Square, where the Duke gave a series of dinners and public receptions. The convert Lord Ripon came to say goodbye on the eve of his departure for India as Viceroy. But it was not only Catholics who came to be presented. Matthew Arnold, for instance, who was invited at Newman's own request, came because he 'wanted to have spoken once in my life to Newman'; he did not kneel, but 'made a deferential bow, and Newman took my hand in both of his and was charming'.[124] Newman also gave addresses to the Brompton Oratory and the Catholic Union, as well as holding a reception for 200 clergy.

This triumphant visit was followed by one to Oxford later in the month. There was a splendid reception at Trinity on his arrival on Saturday, 22 May. On the Sunday he preached in the morning and evening at the new Jesuit Church of St Aloysius. In the afternoon, accompanied by the President and some of the fellows, he went to see his old rooms in college. They were then occupied by the future traveller and writer Douglas Sladen, who later remembered Newman as 'a wan little old man with a shrivelled face and a large nose, and one of the most beautiful expressions which ever appeared on a human being', who talked 'to me for a couple of hours, prostrating me with his exquisite modesty'.[125] Newman wanted to know whether the snapdragon still grew on the wall between Trinity and Balliol and how contemporary undergraduate life compared with that of the beginning of the century.

In November an article on Positivism appeared in the *St. James's Gazette*, which contained a remark to the effect that Newman had done as much for encouraging unbelief as any other contemporary writer, by never attempting to argue against it and by confining his defence of Catholicism to the argument that it was the only alternative to atheism. In December Newman added a note to the *Grammar of Assent*, dismissing the first part of the allegation as a patent absurdity and explaining what he had meant by his somewhat stark assertion in the *Apologia*. It was a question of first principles: it was because 'logic leads to right conclusions when principles are right and to wrong conclusions when

[123] *LD* xxviii. 348; xxx. 328.
[124] *Letters of Matthew Arnold 1848–1888*, ed. G. W. E. Russell (London, 1901), ii. 195–6.
[125] Douglas Sladen, *My Long Life* (London, 1939), 46–7.

the principles started with are wrong' that it was possible for him to say 'that there is no medium logically, between atheism and Catholicity'. The same bad principles, or lack of good ones, he claimed, 'which lead men to reject the Catholic Church, would, if fairly fully carried out, lead them on also to disbelieve in the existence of God'. For belief in God leads to belief in the revelation of God in Christianity, which in turn leads to belief in the Catholic Church as containing this revelation. However, in practice as opposed to theory, it is not simply a question of alternatives, since people are not consistent and not only do not 'follow out their reasonings to their legitimate conclusions', but 'commonly they have bad principles and good, and while the bad keep them from going on to Catholicity, their good keep them from going on to Atheism'.[126]

W. S. Lilly, the convert secretary to the Catholic Union, who had compiled a popular anthology of Newman's writings a few years previously, sent a letter in answer to the paper. But when it became known that the author of the offending piece was James Fitzjames Stephen, he urged Newman to write an article replying to the attack. Newman declined: he preferred to leave this distortion, like others, to time to refute. (As he had calmly remarked of some earlier criticism by Leslie Stephen, 'I shall cheerfully leave it to Time to do for me what Time has so often done in the last 40 or 50 years. Time has been my best friend and champion: and to the future I lovingly commit myself with much resignation to its award.'[127]) Anyway, he had already told his critic years ago that 'It is no good our disputing; it is like a battle between a dog and a fish—we are in different elements.'[128] On the basis of this conversation, James Fitzjames Stephen had claimed that Newman was unable to answer his objections.

In February 1881 Newman reached his eightieth birthday. 'A long life', he remarked to one well-wisher, 'is like a long ladder, which sways and jumps dangerously under the feet of the man who mounts it, the higher he goes . . .'.[129] Towards the end of June he went down to London for another, more private visit and stayed at the Oratory for nearly a fortnight. While he was there he sat for his portrait by Millais, which the painter finished 'in a few short sittings', regarding it as 'the best' he had done.[130] Certainly it was generally judged to be the best portrait of Newman that had been painted.

In the autumn of 1880 serious trouble had broken out in Ireland as a result of the agricultural depression. Eviction of tenants on a far larger scale than before led to widespread lawlessness and violence. Newman wanted the Irish bishops to condemn the murders of landowners that followed, but he had little sympathy for the government, which now

---

[126] *LD* xxix. 317–18.   [127] Ibid. xxviii. 270.   [128] Ibid. xxix. 337.
[129] Ibid. 340.   [130] Ibid. 398.

recognized too late that the unjust land laws should be reformed. England would gain no gratitude for doing now what she ought to have done years ago in justice to Ireland, which would have prevented the present situation from arising. Newman felt strongly that his country-men should recognize Ireland's 'right to be a *nation*', but he was not convinced that the repeal of the union between the two countries would necessarily make things better, if it was true that this would weaken the British Empire and so in turn damage Ireland.[131] Certainly the present misery of the Irish peasantry was the result of English sins in the past and suggested a parallel with France before the French Revolution.

A year later the situation was no less serious. In October 1881 Newman told his nephew John Rickards Mozley that he disagreed with Gladstone's denunciation of the Catholic gentry and middle class for not supporting the new land law—far from being 'cowards' they were 'patriots'. The undeniable fact was that the gross ill-treatment of the Irish over the centuries had 'burned into the national heart a deep hatred of England, and . . . the sentiment of patriotism and the latent sense of historical wrongs will hinder even the more rational, and calm judging, the most friendly to England, from separating themselves from their countrymen'. There was no doubting their friendliness to 'individual Englishmen, of that I have clear experience in my own case'—but he had never come across 'one *Anglo-philist* in the nation'. English rule had consisted in forcing on them English laws like that of 'property, founded on the feudal system, instead of their own communism'. There had also been the 'stupid forcing on their catholicism' by English politicians of 'our godless education'.[132] Like other European nations, Newman had long been convinced that the Irish would gain their freedom 'in some shape'. Why was it that Ireland had not been treated like Scotland?—'The old woman shied her stool at the Parson's head, and forthwith Presbyterianism was established.'[133] Instead, England had spent vast sums of money in the attempt to impose Protestantism on the Irish and persecute Catholicism. Irish Catholics were quite right to regard the money taken from them for the established Church of Ireland as money that rightfully belonged to their own Church, 'which Church was proscribed by English law'.[134] Protestant education in Ireland had also been more than generously supported, while Catholics had had to pay for their own university, which was not even granted the right to confer degrees. There was in fact no mystery about the glaring contrast between England's treatment of Scotland and her treatment of Ireland: it was nothing else but the '*dread* of the *power* of the Catholic Religion'.[135] This explained why there was such

---

[131] *LD* xxix. 313.   [132] Ibid. xxx. 9–10.   [133] Ibid. xxxi. 76.
[134] Ibid. xxx. 12.   [135] Ibid. 18.

opposition to Catholic education: 'England was to be liberalistic, and therefore Ireland must be an exception to the rule.'[136]

A few days before Christmas Gladstone wrote to ask Newman as a Cardinal to bring to the attention of Leo XIII evidence of seditious sermons and statements by Irish priests, remarking bitterly that the Pope would certainly silence these advocates of lawlessness if they spoke out publicly against the definition of papal infallibility. Before replying, Newman asked the President of Maynooth to say whether 'It is a probable opinion and therefore may be acted on by an individual, that the Irish people has never recognized, rather have and continuously . . . protested against and rejected the sovereignty of England, and have seemingly admitted it only when they were too weak to resist; and therefore it is no sin to be what would be commonly called a rebel.'[137] This remarkable letter (the draft of which has survived) Newman begged the President to burn, promising in turn to burn his reply. He refrained from saying anything so radical in his response to the Prime Minister, commenting merely that the Pope did not have the kind of power in practical politics that Gladstone imagined. Even in purely ecclesiastical matters (as opposed to doctrinal teaching), he added, the Pope's authority was much more circumscribed than was commonly supposed—'Its exercise is a matter of great prudence, and depends upon times and circumstances.'[138] As for individual priests, they came under the immediate authority of their bishop, not the Pope.

Less formal correspondence continued as before with old disciples and friends. There was the usual problem of religious faith. He admitted to Emily Bowles, who asked for advice on how to reply to a Catholic friend troubled by religious doubts, that 'were I, deliberately to frequent the society, the parties of clever infidels, I should expect all sorts of imaginations contrary to Revealed Truth, not based on reason, but fascinating or distressing, unsettling visions, to take possession of me'.[139] Imagination, so important for Newman for creating the assent of faith, could also destroy faith by hiding its rational basis. Contemporary unbelief was like an epidemic, 'wonderfully catching' and spreading not 'by the reason, but by the imagination', which 'presents a possible, plausible view of things which haunts and at length overcomes the mind'. He could only 'look with keen compassion on the next generation and with, I may say, awe'.[140] It was not, he insisted, 'reason that is against us, but imagination': the contemporary mind, 'after having, to the utter neglect of the Gospels, lived in science, experiences, on coming back to Scripture, an utter strangeness in what it reads, which seems to it a better argument against Revelation than any formal proof from

[136] Ibid. xxxi. 76.   [137] Ibid. xxx. 32–3.   [138] Ibid. 37.

[139] Ibid. 48.   [140] Ibid. 102.

definite facts or logical statements'.[141] (It was an interesting and unusual argument, on the other hand, for the study of the Classics, particularly Horace, that they had a religious influence on the imagination, inasmuch as 'they bring before us most vividly and piteously, our state by nature, they increase in us a sense of our utter dependence and natural helplessness, they arm us against the fallacious promises of the world, especially at this day, the promises of science and literature to give us light and liberty'.[142]) Argument, then, was of 'little use', while 'personal experience of the power of the Gospel is our great, or our only defence from scepticism'. Even an infallible Church was no 'safeguard' where 'minds are wilful'. The prospect for the younger generation was 'dreadful'. But still, 'error cannot last, and light will come after the darkness.'[143] One very encouraging sign was that unbelief 'cannot believe in itself', in the sense that 'in the majority of unbelievers there is a deep misgiving that they are wrong or probably wrong'. This showed in their 'feverish restlessness' and their obsessive hostility to religion, indicating a deep insecurity. The case of people like J. S. Mill, 'who, as they get older, are seen drifting towards belief', indicated that 'utter unbelief has no root in the human heart' but was 'an unnatural state'.[144] Such thinkers arrogantly ignored religious first principles, but assumed 'first principles of their own, without any compunction'. The result of their dogmatism was that there was 'a general antecedent leaning to the side of unbelief, as the more reasonable and probable'. Ordinary people were influenced by arguments 'derived from sight and reason and experience', but they had 'no love of religion, no aspirations after sanctity, no desire, no hope or fear of a future state—and therefore it is that they do not admit the reasonings on which the great positive Catholic system of philosophy and theology rests'.[145]

Membership of the Sacred College of Cardinals did not inhibit him from giving some down-to-earth advice about diet to Maria Giberne, now a nun in France and into her eightieth year:

If you have not teeth, you *cannot* eat hard substances without danger. Unchewed meat is as dangerous to the stomach as brick and stone, or a bunch of keys. You are not an ostrich. I am *very serious*. As to myself I have for years lived mainly on soup and milk. Any doctor would recommend you such a diet—and peas pudding very well boiled, and eggs in the shape of omelet—but not with the white in lumps.[146]

On a more topical note he told Frederic Rogers, now Lord Blachford, that he felt 'very much tempted' by his 'own fears and feelings' to add his name to the protest made against the proposed Channel tunnel—'But

[141] *LD* xxx. 159–60.   [142] Ibid. xxvi. 389.   [143] Ibid. xxx. 186.
[144] Ibid. xxix. 169.   [145] Ibid. xxviii. 278, 207, 241.   [146] Ibid. xxx. 49.

am held back by my utter ignorance of political and military matters, and that in such an act I run the risk of its being refracted, like a stick in water, by being poked into a medium of which I have no experience and which I do not understand.'[147] The only advantage he could see in the tunnel might be 'the saving travellers from sea sickness and an increase of French visitors', while the possible disadvantage would be 'the utter ruin of the British Power'.[148]

Meanwhile the Oratory itself was flourishing: the days when there were no novices were over; although the old members of the community were 'going off, like the slides in a Magic Lantern', young men were now 'coming forward'.[149] The school had proved to be decisive here: 'of our 12 Fathers *seven* have come to the Oratory *through* the School, having been Masters in it, or boys.'[150] Without it, the situation would have been very different, given the unpromising character of the locality for attracting Oratorian novices.

At the beginning of June 1882 Newman received from Thomas Mozley an inscribed copy of his *Reminiscences chiefly of Oriel College and the Oxford Movement*. This unwelcome present touched a very raw nerve in its references to his father's unhappy career—'so cruel as well as untrue'. Stung to the quick by those of the book's notorious inaccuracies which related to the early family history, he cried out in pain to his brother Francis, 'he is a wild beast who rends one's hand when put up to defend one's face.'[151] He had no intention of protesting publicly, and he hoped Francis would not do so either. What upset his free-thinking brother more, however, was the assertion that their mother had given them a Calvinist upbringing, which Francis regarded as a slur on her good sense! His own rather bitter reminiscences, the *Early History of Cardinal Newman*, were to appear a year after the latter's death.

In August a letter came from the Irish convert writer Aubrey de Vere, who had been appointed by Newman to a chair at the Catholic University, inviting him to visit the Tennysons in Surrey, with whom de Vere was staying. Five years earlier, another mutual friend, Lady Simeon, had tried to arrange a meeting between the two great Victorians. Now, as then, Newman wrote directly to Tennyson saying how pleased he would be to meet him, but excused himself from accepting the invitation on the ground of old age. Tennyson replied that since he was the younger of them he ought to try to come to see Newman himself some day—'for though, I dare say, there are a hundred things on which we might differ, there is no man on this side of the grave, more worthy of honour and affection than yourself'.[152]

The gift of a recently published book, containing extracts from a

[147] Ibid. 73.   [148] Ibid. 74.   [149] Ibid. 94.
[150] Ibid. 54.   [151] Ibid. 99.   [152] Ibid. 121.

religious lady's journal, which recorded conversations with various distinguished figures, including John Stirling, Mill, and Carlyle, caused Newman to refer again to the spiritual dangers of consorting with unbelievers. More interestingly, it prompted him to remark to the donor that he had 'a natural dislike of literary and scientific society *as such*, or what Hurrell Froude . . . used to call "the aristocracy of talent" ', adding that it was not only 'a peculiarity' common to himself and Froude, but also a characteristic they shared with Keble and Pusey 'more than any other quality, and has, as much as anything else united us together'.[153] No doubt this aversion had something to do with his repeated refusal to join the Metaphysical Society. Two years after his first invitation, R. H. Hutton had again pressed him to join in 1871, but again he had politely refused: 'In some things I have a good memory— but for books, for doctrines, for views and arguments, I have none . . . I am not a ready man, and should spoil a good cause. And then, I am so dreadfully shy, that I never show to advantage, and feel it myself acutely all the time.'[154] A few years later he was franker about his real reason for not joining, when he expressed his astonishment to R. W. Church that the Dean of St Paul's was prepared to listen, along with the Archbishop of York, Cardinal Manning, and other churchmen, to a paper by Thomas Huxley in refutation of the Resurrection: 'How can this possibly come under the scope of a Metaphysical Society. I thank my stars that, when asked to accept the honour of belonging to it, I declined.' He wondered mischievously whether Manning's participation was perhaps 'a ruse . . . to bring the Professor into the clutches of the Inquisition'![155]

In October 1882 Newman thought that he had preached his last sermon. He was in good health, but lacked strength: 'I speak with difficulty; I can hardly walk, never without the chance of tripping up; I with great difficulty go up and down stairs—I read with discomfort. I cannot write except very slowly—and I am deaf.' His brain did not work as quickly as before, but 'except in failure of memory, and continual little mistakes in the use of words, and confusion in the use of names, I am not conscious that my mind is weaker than it was'. However, 'like other old men, I am so much the creature of hours, rooms, and of routine generally, that to go from home is almost like tearing off my skin, and I suffer from it afterwards.'[156]

In September Pusey had died, and his disciple H. P. Liddon resigned his Scripture chair in November. There was now a religious vacuum at Oxford which Newman thought the Catholic Church should try and fill. The Jesuits, who were running the mission there, should 'seize an

[153] *LD* xxx. 129.   [154] Ibid. xxv. 303–4.   [155] Ibid. xxviii. 11.
[156] Ibid. xxx. 134, 141.

opportunity which never may come again'. As it was, 'The Liberals are sweeping along in triumph, without any Catholic or religious influence to stem them now that Pusey and Liddon are gone.' Unfortunately, the failure to take any initiative was 'only one out of various manifestations of what may be called Nihilism in the Catholic Body, and in its rulers. They forbid, but they do not direct or create.'[157] The Pope ought to reopen the question of Catholic university education in England by sending an impartial representative to investigate the situation.

November brought news of the death of Edward Hawkins. 'What a wonderful kindness', Newman wrote to his widow, 'it is in you to write to me in your present deep distress; it has touched me deeply.' He had thought of writing himself as soon as he heard, 'but on second thoughts I did not dare'. He had never forgotten the kindness Hawkins had shown him in his early days at Oriel. 'May God be with you, and make up to you by His grace this supreme desolation.'[158]

Among the letters Newman received on his eighty-second birthday in February 1883 was one from Gerard Manley Hopkins, now a Jesuit priest teaching at Stonyhurst College. He wanted to bring out a commentary on the *Grammar of Assent*. But Newman refused to allow him to undertake a work 'at once onerous and unnecessary'. After twelve years the book had been far more successful than he had anticipated: it had gone through five editions and been extensively reviewed and commented on. Obviously, 'those who only read so much of it as they can while cutting open the leaves, will make great mistakes about it . . . but if it is worth anything, it will survive the paper cutters, and if it [be] worthless, a comment, however brilliant, will not do more than gain for it a short galvanic life, which has no charms for me.'[159]

The increasing secularization of English society continued with an attempt by Gladstone's government to introduce an Affirmation Bill, which would have replaced the usual oath invoking the name of God, which was incumbent on Members of Parliament, with a simple affirmation of allegiance. It was specifically designed to allow the atheist Charles Bradlaugh to take his seat. Newman refused to join other church leaders, including Manning, in agitating against the bill. He saw no point in 'protesting against abolishing the Parliamentary recognition of Almighty God', when the God of Christianity had long ceased anyway to be the 'God of Parliament'.[160] There was another reason which is worth noting: 'It never has been my line to take up political or social questions, unless they came close to me as matters of personal duty.' The present bill, 'by being rejected, would bring so little gain to religion, and by being passed would be so little loss, that I do not see reason for taking

---

[157] Ibid. 143.   [158] Ibid. 152–3.   [159] Ibid. 191.   [160] Ibid. 206.

a side'.[161] As he had argued anyway years ago in one of the Discourses in the *Idea of a University*, 'what the political and social world means by the word "God" is too often not the Christian God . . . not a personal God, but an unknown God.' What difference did it make, he concluded with typical pragmatic irony, 'whether Mr Bradlaugh swears by no God with the Government or swears by an Impersonal, or Material, or abstract Ideal Something or other'?[162]

The threat to the survival of religion did not worry Newman unduly. He had always 'anticipated a great battle between good and evil', and both the Bible and history showed that all 'the champions of truth' had to do was to stand firm and trust in God. The Roman Empire had been 'overturned' by a small, insignificant sect.[163] The barbarian Arian invaders from the north, bitterly hostile to the Church, had miraculously become Catholics. Not only had the Church recovered from the Reformation, but 'the outburst of Saints in 1500–1600 after the monstrous corruption' was 'one of the great arguments for Christianity'.[164] It had come through more recent upheavals, like the French Revolution. It would surely survive the new crisis of unbelief. This very 'pestilence', which Newman was well aware 'threatened the next generation', had now actually spread into 'St Philip's household' with the announcement at the end of October by Arthur Hutton that he had lost all belief in the existence of a personal God.[165]

Not all aspects of the contemporary world were bad. Some changes were positively to be welcomed. In February 1884 Newman remarked to his niece Jane Mozley, 'It is one of the best points of this unhappy age, that it has made so many openings for the activity of women.'[166]

Developments, on the other hand, that raised problems for religious belief had to be honestly faced. The most important of these was the controversy over the interpretation of Scripture, which had been occasioned by the publication of *Essays and Reviews* in 1860. As a result, Newman began seriously studying the subject in 1861.[167] Three years earlier, he had written that for Catholics the reconciliation between the Bible and modern scientific discoveries and theories was not a serious difficulty, 'because so little is determined about the inspiration of Scripture, except in matters of faith and morals'.[168] The Galileo affair should also have taught the Church authorities to beware of insisting on traditional ideas which could not be maintained to be part of revelation. But it was foolish, too, to try and answer all the alleged scientific facts which were 'confidently urged against Scripture', only to be 'found by

---

[161] *LD* xxx. 209.   [162] Ibid. 216.   [163] Ibid. 220.
[164] Ibid. 264.   [165] Ibid. 271.   [166] Ibid. 316.
[167] The draft papers have been published in *TP* ii. 1–98.   [168] *LD* xviii. 322.

scientific men not to hold water'; it was better to wait patiently, for 'error will eat up error'.[169]

Certain points seemed clear to Newman as he pondered the subject in the early 1860s. Not only had the Church rarely given an authoritative interpretation of any Biblical passage, but the inspiration of Scripture was not even formally an article of faith. All that the Church had defined was that God is the 'auctor' of the Old and New 'Testamenta', which seemed to mean that he was the 'originator' of the Old and New Covenants rather than literally the 'author' of the Old and New Testaments. The Scripture writers were spoken of as inspired, but not the actual writings themselves, which had to be interpreted in the sense intended by the writer. Newman's confidence that the meaning of the Bible was not a serious problem for Catholics was shaken by the teaching of the Vatican Council which declared that Scripture was inspired and that God was the 'auctor' of the books comprising the Old and New Testaments. He thought that the subject had not been considered fully enough and that 'the whole church platform seems to me likely to be off its ancient moorings. It is like a ship which has swung round or taken up a new position.'[170]

The papers Newman drafted in 1861 and 1863 for a work on Biblical inspiration never came to anything. The ecclesiastical climate of the time was not favourable to any original initiatives. And it was not until January 1883, after a letter of his on inspiration, pre-dating the Vatican Council, had been published in more than one periodical and implicitly criticized for being incompatible with the recent Council's definitions, that he began to work on an article called 'On the Inspiration of Scripture'. He consulted Bishop Clifford, who had recently written an article arguing that the beginning of the Book of Genesis was a religious hymn and was not intended to be a scientific account. Newman was delighted with 'an interpretation which ignores science altogether'.[171] After taking into account the criticisms of Clifford, as well as of Archbishop Errington, he published the article in February 1884 in the *Nineteenth Century*.

Newman makes two principal points. First, he argues that 'there always have been two minds in the process of inspiration, a divine *Auctor*, and a human *Scriptor*.' This allows for the obvious human element, but does not deny God's inspiration. It is more realistic and sophisticated than the prevailing Catholic theory of the time, which introduced a crude dichotomy between the divinely inspired content of the Bible and its merely human expression. Newman's way of avoiding a simplistic fundamentalism is to insist that God did not 'immediately' inspire the

---

[169] Ibid. xxx. 359.   [170] Ibid. xxv. 140.   [171] Ibid. xxx. 176.

Scripture writings themselves but 'the men who wrote them. The books are inspired, because the writers were inspired to write them.'[172] His approach anticipates the modern Catholic view of inspiration which was confirmed by the Second Vatican Council. The second point Newman makes is that the Bible contains 'unauthoritative *obiter dicta*', that is, 'not doctrinal, but mere unimportant statements of fact'[173] mentioned in passing.

Given the dangerous and delicate nature of the subject, it hardly came as a surprise when a severe criticism of the article, by a professor at Maynooth called John Healy, appeared in March. Healy complained that while historical facts in the Bible might not be a matter of faith, they had to be accepted as true because Scripture was inspired. Newman replied to the attack in a 'Postscript', which was published in May. He maintained that the history of revelation showed that 'divine gifts' had 'a particular service and application' and were 'given for precise and definite purposes', so that it was reasonable to suppose that there was also 'a distribution and a limitation in the bestowal' of inspiration.[174] As he had put it in one of the drafts of 1861, St Paul was not more or less inspired in different epistles, but in some he had a 'larger opportunity for exercising his gift'.[175] And so, while 'Scripture is inspired in its length and breadth . . . still we may ask the question, In what respect, and for what purpose?'[176] Again, this perspective anticipates the modern Catholic position, which aims to transcend both the literal and the liberal approaches to the Bible by stressing that the purpose of the Scriptures is to teach the truth of revelation.[177]

8

In March 1884 an old wound was painfully reopened. Newman received a letter from the Duke of Norfolk begging him to accept an impending invitation from the London Oratory to attend the opening of their new church. The Duke, who had been at the Oratory School, was only a small boy at the time of the rift between the two Oratories, but of course he knew all about the row and had now heard from the present superior, Philip Gordon, the brother of Joseph Gordon, that he was afraid Newman would refuse to come. Newman resented what he saw as an attempt to bring pressure on him from the leading Catholic layman in England, who had such close ties with himself personally but who knew

---

[172] *SE* 17–18.
[173] Ibid. 29–30.   [174] Ibid. 43.   [175] *TP* ii. 23.   [176] *SE* 63.
[177] For a full discussion of Newman's views on inspiration, see J. Derek Holmes and Robert Murray, SJ (eds.), *On the Inspiration of Scripture: John Henry Newman* (London, 1967), 3–96.

the Brompton rather than the Birmingham side of the story (since Newman had enjoined silence on his own community). His immediate response was to write a protest to Gordon:

Why could you not have sounded me, before you let the Duke write to me? Why did you so little consult for me as not to hinder his making a request to me, which I am obliged for so many reasons not to entertain? Have I shown anything but kindness to you personally?

On being made a Cardinal he had been 'the first to move' by visiting and then staying at the Brompton Oratory. But he had done this in his position as a Cardinal rather than as founder of the Oratory in England, and in the inscription to the set of his works which he had presented to the Brompton community he had been careful to describe himself simply as a Cardinal. Now he was 'appealed to in the name of St Philip to renew a tie' which had been broken thirty years ago, and 'to take part in an act, which concerns intimately and solely the London Oratory'.[178]

Carefully and tactfully, he pointed out to the Duke of Norfolk that the reason for the Duke's intervening in the first place was precisely because it was already clearly appreciated that he would be most unwilling to accept such an invitation. There were 'many and various reasons' why he felt bound to refuse, but 'I will not say more, lest I should say too much; and, though I should say too little, this is the safer mistake.'[179] It was certainly a 'mistake', inasmuch as the Duke (who simply assumed Newman must be jealous of the London Oratory's success) was left exclaiming to Gordon, 'What can one do with such an extraordinary mind.'[180] The emphasis on the 'mind' was right, however. Whatever his feelings, the refusal was not an emotional reaction, but a deliberate decision based both on the fact that in his view he (and his Oratory) had been seriously wronged and had never received an apology, and on the principle that to forgive is not to condone. His unwillingness to explain his reasons to the Duke was also quite deliberate and founded on the determination not to cast a slur on the reputation of Faber and the community by allowing damaging facts to be disseminated.

The severe refusal to compromise on what appeared a matter of principle was characteristic; but intransigence (if that is what it was) should be clearly distinguished from oversensitivity. Nevertheless, if the refusal was not a display of hurt feeling, it was so far as Newman was concerned a strictly personal matter between himself and the London Oratory, which need cause no public remark at all in view of his age and his repeated insistence over the years on the traditional lack of contact between Italian Oratories. Gordon, who of course knew far more than

---

[178] *LD* xxx. 329–30.   [179] Ibid. 334.   [180] Ibid. 337 n. 1.

the Duke about the past history of relations between the two English Oratories, could only apologize for the Duke's gaffe in blurting out the invitation, which he was well aware should have come first from himself; it was true he had spoken to the Duke, but he had not intended him to contact Newman. As for Newman, he could only bewail his mistake in saying anything at all to the Duke; it would have been far better merely to have made his excuses on the grounds of ill health and old age, but he had felt at the time that it would have been less than frank to have done so.

As regards his own private family life, Newman made no bones about his extreme sensitivity. The so-called 'reminiscences' of Tom Mozley had 'knocked' him 'down', and he had 'not got on' his 'legs again yet'; he took it as 'a penance from above . . . so full of untruths that it is safe from having an answer'. It seemed to have 'set the fashion', as now there was talk in the papers of his unfortunate brother Charles, who had recently died, which reflected on both his surviving brothers.[181] Still, he could hardly expect that 'the purveyors of gossip of the past should refrain from tearing off my morbidly sensitive skin, while they can with public interest'.[182]

More and more he was feeling his age. Although there was nothing wrong with his mental faculties, he was slowed down by increasing feebleness. 'The weakness and stiffness of my fingers react upon my brain', he complained, explaining that he had never been able to think well without a pen in his hand, 'and now that I cannot use it freely, I cannot use my mind'.[183] He found that before he got to the second half of a sentence he had forgotten what he was going to say: 'I have always held that thought was instantaneous—that it takes no time—and now that doctrine is confirmed to me, when I want a subtle shorthand to record what otherwise, like a flash of lightning, goes as rapidly as it comes.'[184] He could no longer keep abreast of correspondence, which was left to 'accumulate unanswered', and 'after any unusual exertion' he was 'often obliged to lie down'.[185] What was especially irritating was that he did not have time to reply to 'those letters which would be really pleasant to me, or excite from their importance a real interest, but the way is blocked up by a set of missives from strangers, of very little importance, but which must be answered'.[186]

He was disappointed by the poor sales of William Palmer's *Notes of a Visit to the Russian Church in the Years 1840, 1841*, which he had published with a preface nearly two years previously in 1882. Palmer, who had become a Catholic in 1855, had died in 1879 after making Newman his literary executor. Included among his papers was the account of the

181 *LD* xxx. 350.   182 Ibid. 356.   183 Ibid. 358.
184 Ibid. 390.   185 Ibid. 385.   186 Ibid. 420.

Russian trip which he had undertaken as a Tractarian and while still a fellow of Magdalen to try and prove that the Church of England was a branch of the Catholic Church by receiving Communion in the Church of Russia. He had taken with him his own paper on the Thirty-nine Articles which was on the lines of Newman's *Tract 90* (the condemnation of which upset Palmer's own conversations with Orthodox ecclesiastics). He failed in his mission, but he had painted a 'vivid' picture of the Russian Orthodox Church, which Newman felt would make readers 'not only know Russia, but feel love, interest, and tenderness towards it and its people'.[187] Palmer also introduced among the Orthodox he met 'the idea and the desirableness of Unity', as well as enlightening them on the Catholic movement in the Church of England.[188] It appeared that the Russians 'had all but given up the idea of unity, or of the Catholicity of the Church', their view being that although there had once been 'One Catholic Church' in the world, it had 'died, and the Russo-Greek Church is all that remains of it'.[189] The trouble with this 'Orthodox Church' was that it had 'no political life, such as an ecclesiastical body ought to have'.[190]

There was an annoying little incident in October, although it had a very satisfactory conclusion. A derogatory passage about Newman was quoted in several newspaper reviews of the recently published autobiography of Lord Malmesbury, who had held high office in several Conservative governments. Malmesbury, who had been an undergraduate at Oriel, recounted how Newman had been tormented by his pupils, and told a humiliating story of Provost Copleston publicly rebuking him for mangling a haunch of venison. Lord Blachford immediately wrote to the *Daily News* denying the credibility of Malmesbury's portrait and suggesting that the peer had confused the formidably determined Newman with another tutor celebrated for his easy-going ways. When Malmesbury failed to retract, Newman himself sent a letter to the paper. Back in 1858 he had regretted having 'so unmercifully snubbed' Malmesbury as an undergraduate, whose support he could otherwise have tried to enlist in his attempt to secure a charter for the Catholic University.[191] Now he wrote:

I am sorry that, at the end of nearly sixty years, he should not let bygones by bygones. I have never said a word against him, and his account of me is as discourteous as it is utterly unfounded. If I was as cowardly as he represents I never ought to have been a college tutor.

The truth is, that when I came into office the discipline was in a very lax state, and I, like a new broom, began sweeping very vigorously, as far as my opportunities went. This aroused the indignation of certain high and mighty

---

[187] Ibid. 68.   [188] Ibid. 6.   [189] Ibid. 109, 112.

[190] Ibid. xxv. 5.   [191] Ibid. xviii. 459.

youths, who, relying on the claims of family and fortune, did their best to oppose me and to spread tales about me. I don't consider that on the whole I got the worst of it in the conflict; and what Lord Malmesbury calls 'helpless resignation' and 'painful tolerance,' I interpret to have been the conduct of a gentleman under great provocation.

As for the story about the venison, Newman 'did not recollect that we had such generous fare, even at the Provost's table'. Malmesbury claimed that he had 'witnessed' Newman 'nearly driven' from the table by Copleston—

What? That I was 'nearly' driven. How could he see me 'nearly driven'? He may take my word for it, I should either have been driven out and out, or not driven at all. So much, however, may be true—not that the statement is a fact, but that it is a mythical representation of what was the fact—viz., that I was not supported in my reforms by the high authorities of the college.[192]

The great controversialist's rapier had flashed again, perhaps for the last time.

Towards the end of October, Newman wrote to congratulate Anne Mozley on her edition of the letters of her brother, James Mozley. Explaining that he had decided long ago that 'if a memoir was to be published of me, a Protestant Editor must take the Protestant part' (the Catholic half could not be 'written for many years'), he wondered if she would be willing to look over the memoir he had written in 1874 for the years up to 1833 and to see how far it needed to be illustrated by other papers and letters (the remaining years up to 1845 were already covered by the *Apologia*).[193] Excited at the prospect of this new, important editorial work, she begged Newman to extend the memoir, which he had originally intended as 'a mere specimen', at least down to 1843.[194] But Newman refused: his purpose in writing it in the first place had been

to protest against such biographies as the present morbid taste of the public requires. If indeed there is more which it is reasonable and open to say, say it— but then it should be short; whereas a memoir commonly is *padded* . . . and that either with irrelevant matter or matter too private. Again, this padding is not only culpable in itself, but, breaks the thread of the narrative and is illogical and distracting, and leading to dipping into the pages instead of reading outright.[195]

Years before he had insisted that 'a man's life lies in his letters', while 'Biographers varnish; they assign motives; they conjecture feelings . . . they palliate or defend.'[196] However, he wanted to give Anne Mozley a completely free hand in writing his Anglican life, which he did not want

[192] *LD* xxx. 422–3.   [193] Ibid. 417–18.   [194] Ibid. xxxi. 14.
[195] Ibid. 20.   [196] Ibid. xx. 443.

even to see, let alone collaborate in, and which was not to be published until after his death. The memoir he had sent her represented his own idea of what such a memoir should be, but she should not feel bound by it. Obviously, he would never have asked her to attempt the work if he had not thought she held similar views to himself on the writing of biography. And so at the end of January 1885 Anne Mozley began work on the book which would be published in two volumes a year after Newman's death as *Letters and Correspondence of John Henry Newman during his Life in the English Church with a brief Autobiography*. Newman's hope was that it would forestall 'the chance of the book making by strangers which pays so well' and which would be 'sure to be full of errors'.[197] Already accounts of his life were beginning to appear, about which he felt 'very sensitive'—'as if my skin was torn off (metaphorically)'.[198]

At the beginning of April he received a letter from the sister of Frank Power, the *Times* correspondent in Khartoum who had been murdered the previous September while trying to obtain relief for the beleaguered garrison of General Gordon. The letter accompanied a copy of the pocket edition of *The Dream of Gerontius*, which had belonged to Gordon and which he had presented to Power. Gordon had made pencil marks in the text. Newman immediately replied by return of post that the 'letter and its contents took away my breath. I was deeply moved to find that a book of mine had been in General Gordon's hands, and that, the description of a soul preparing for death.'[199] What 'struck' him 'so much' about Gordon's use of the poem was that 'he was always on his death bed, fulfilling the common advice that we should ever pass the day, as if it was to be our last'.[200] Newman himself had followed events with anguished concern, remaining glued to the map of the route taken by the abortive relief expedition. So intense was the interest in the fate of Gordon of Khartoum that William Neville transcribed the pencil markings into several copies of the *Dream*, one of which was sent to Dean Church.

Another old friend, John Hungerford Pollen, wrote to say that he had taken the *Grammar of Assent* with him as a companion on his visit to India, where his son was aide-de-camp to Lord Ripon, the Viceroy. The idea, Newman confessed, of 'having recourse' to such a book 'as a refuge from the palm trees and apes' lay outside his 'sympathy': his 'imagination' simply could 'not take it in, except as a pendant to that great [Christ Church] Greek scholar who to relieve himself of the excitement of the [subjunctive] mood, used to take up a volume of the Tracts of the Times'.[201]

May saw the beginning of the last of Newman's controversies, in the

[197] Ibid. xxxi. 81–2. [198] Ibid. 81, 83. [199] Ibid. 51.
[200] Ibid. 67. [201] Ibid. 61.

form of an article in the *Contemporary Review* by A. M. Fairbairn, a
Congregationalist theologian (shortly to become the first Principal of
Mansfield College, Oxford), accusing him of philosophical scepticism in
removing the proofs of religion from the sphere of reason into that of
conscience and imagination. Newman left off sorting out letters for Anne
Mozley and during July and August worked on a reply, which he
completed early in September. As usual, he found composition very
difficult, although harder now because of old age: 'My memory goes
before I have set down what I have in my mind, and I have been fagging
six hours and more every day to find by next morning that it won't do—
and I must do it over again.'[202] The article was published in the October
number of the review under the title 'The Development of Religious
Error' (it was later republished as 'Revelation in its Relation to Faith').

Newman's reply amounted to a denial that he had ever impugned
reason, meaning 'the faculty of Reasoning in a large sense', except to the
extent that it has 'this drawback' that 'it depends for success upon the
assumption of prior acts'. It follows that reason cannot arrive at religious
truth if it starts from 'false premisses', in which case it is not reason which
is to blame, but the first principles which are the assumptions from
which it proceeds. So triumphant has human reason been in extending
the frontiers of knowledge that 'there never was a time since Christianity
was' when the world 'had the opportunity of being a worse enemy to
religion' than 'it is likely to be in the years now opening upon mankind'.
Faced, for example, with the 'greatest of mysteries', the existence of evil,
'relentless "reason", under the assumptions of educated society,' will
end in a denial of theism. 'To the World,' after all, 'its own principles are
infallible, and need no proof.' It is the failure to recognize that it is these
hidden and implicit first principles which govern our reasoning that is
responsible for so much confusion and superfluous controversy.[203]

Fairbairn replied in the December issue of the *Contemporary Review*.
Newman was doubtful whether to continue the controversy: the idea
that he had become a Catholic to escape from scepticism was patently
absurd. But on the other hand he did want to emphasize in print that the
doubts he had voiced in the past about the argument from final causes
(in so far as it rested on an unproved assumption) did not affect either
the argument that the existence of the universe implies a first cause, or
the argument from design in the broader sense of an order in the world.
In the end he decided not to publish his reply, but had it printed
privately, sending a copy to Fairbairn early in March 1886.[204] At his age,
he did not want to seem to be indulging in controversy for its own sake,

[202] *LD* xxxi. 80.   [203] *TP* i. 141–2, 145, 148.

[204] It was included at the end of the original article in *SE* and has been republished in *TP* i.
149–57.

but equally he did not wish Catholics to be scandalized by his failure to refute damaging charges.

At the end of March Newman stayed for a couple of nights with Dean Church in London. Church found little change in the Cardinal apart from the fact that he easily tired now. He was 'cautious and reticent, as he should be. But the old smile and twinkle of the eye, and bright, meaning [irony], are all still there, and all seemed to belong to the old days.'[205] The poet Francis Turner Palgrave, the editor of the well-known anthology *The Golden Treasury*, who visited the Oratory in the following January, noted that his voice had 'much of its old strange sweetness'. Palgrave, who had heard him preach more than forty years before at Littlemore, noticed how 'the look of almost anxious searching had passed into the look of perfect peace. His mind was not only bright as ever, but with the cheerfulness and humour of youth.' He was almost overwhelmed by the 'great and perfect humility' with which Newman thanked him for his 'kindness' in coming to visit him.[206]

Although his fingers were finding it increasingly hard even to form the letters, Newman managed to maintain to some extent his vast correspondence. Familiar subjects still cropped up, sometimes eliciting new and striking responses. The unremitting spread of religious indifference and unbelief led him to hope that

a silent and secret process is going on in the hearts of many, which, though it may not reach its limit and scope in this generation or the next, is a definite work of Divine Providence, in prospect of a state of religion such as the world has never yet seen; issuing, not indeed in a millenium, but in a public opinion strong enough for the vigorous spread and exaltation, and thereby the influence and prosperity of Divine Truth all over the world. The world may not in the Divine Decree last long enough for a work so elaborate and multiform. Or without indulging in such great conceptions, one can fancy such a return to primitive truth to be vouchsafed to particular countries which at present are divided and broken up into a hundred sects and at war with each other.[207]

No doubt the second of these rather cryptic speculations is to be seen as a prophecy of the Second Vatican Council and the movement for Christian unity.

He could still, however, write with all his old uncompromising directness and frankness, as when he told Gerard Manley Hopkins, now teaching classics in Dublin, that he ought to moderate his feelings about Irish nationalism by remembering that 'Irish Patriots hold that they never have yielded themselves to the sway of England and therefore never have been under her laws, and never have been rebels'. His capacity to surprise, not to say shock, was not lost: 'If I were an

[205] *LD* xxxi. 128 n.   [206] Ibid. 184 n. 5.   [207] Ibid. 181.

Irishman, I should be (in heart) a rebel.'[208] His general theological position remained the same—a cautious openness, combined with deference to authority: with regard, for example, to the problem of conflict between Scripture and science, he urged: 'Surely it becomes us to imitate the Church's patience, not rudely to attempt to force the hand of authority, but to *prepare the way* for a final decision *by collecting points* which may or may not be taken up in it.'[209]

From the latter half of 1886 Newman's physical powers began to fail. But his mental faculties remained. During the first half of 1887 he was busy preparing a third edition of his *Select Treatises of St Athanasius*, hoping to try to improve a work of whose 'imperfection' he had 'a deep sense'.[210] In August Ullathorne, who had announced his retirement, came to see him. As 'I was rising to leave', wrote the bishop,

an action of his caused a scene I shall never forget . . . He said in low and humble accents, 'My dear Lord, will you do me a great favour?' 'What is it?' I asked. He glided down on his knees, bent down his venerable head, and said, 'Give me your blessing.' What could I do with him before me in such a posture? I could not refuse without giving him great embarrassment. So I laid my hand on his head and said: 'My dear Lord Cardinal, notwithstanding all laws to the contrary, I pray God to bless you, and that His Holy Spirit may be full in your heart.' As I walked to the door, refusing to put on his biretta as he went with me, he said: 'I have been indoors all my life, whilst you have battled for the Church in the world.' I felt annihilated in his presence: there is a Saint in that man!'[211]

In June 1888 Newman went to London to make his last will, under which William Neville was appointed his literary executor. In July he took his last holiday, a short trip to north Wales. At the end of October he had a fall and received the last sacraments, but quickly recovered. In March 1889 Ullathorne died. The immense flow of letters, spanning almost the entire century, but now increasingly dictated, was at last petering out. But Manning's historic intervention in the settlement of the London dockers' strike in September was acknowledged by a letter of congratulation, albeit in another's hand. And in November Newman himself had an opportunity to intercede in a dispute, admittedly of a somewhat less important and public nature. The work-force at the local Cadbury chocolate works, who were all women, were expected by their Quaker employers to attend daily Bible classes. When the local priest heard about the rule and forbade Catholics to attend, an appeal was made to Newman for a more liberal-minded ruling. Although the snow was thick on the ground, he drove straight to Bournville to see the Cadbury brothers, who were 'charmed by the loving Christian spirit

---

[208] *LD* xxxi. 195.   [209] Ibid. 220.   [210] Ibid. 200.
[211] Cuthbert Butler, *The Life and Times of Bishop Ullathorne 1806–1889* (London, 1926), ii. 283–4.

with which he entered into the question'.[212] As a result, a room was specially set aside for Catholic prayers.

Towards the end of November came news of Lord Blachford's death. No one else, not even Hurrell Froude, had been so intimate a friend as Frederic Rogers, who had been his pupil and then colleague at Oriel. Their friendship had been extremely close until the fateful day when Newman revealed that he might become a Roman Catholic. According to Neville, Newman thought he was the most able and intelligent of all his friends. Less than four years before, he had been consulting him about the possibility of a further reply to Fairbairn.

Newman's own end was now near. On Christmas Day 1889 he celebrated Mass for the last time. But, as he entered his ninetieth year, he had still by no means lost all the use of his mental and physical faculties. At the beginning of July 1890 he managed to make a short speech in reply to an address from the Catholic Truth Society, which was meeting in Birmingham. And towards the end of the month he gave away the prizes at the Oratory School; as usual, he also gave a private interview to those who were leaving. On the afternoon of Saturday, 9 August his niece Grace Langford (the only child of his estranged sister Harriett), whom he had not seen since 1843 (when she was 3 years old), came to see him on a visit to England (from Australia, where she had emigrated with her husband). Hearing she wanted to meet him, he had written her a brief note of welcome a week before. It was his last letter; it ended with the simple final postscript 'I am sometimes engaged with the doctor.'[213] In the early hours of the morning of Sunday, 10 August he was taken ill, and he died of pneumonia on the evening of Monday, 11 August.

He was buried on the nineteenth at Rednal in the grave of Ambrose St John. The pall over the coffin bore his cardinal's motto 'cor ad cor loquitur'. On his memorial-tablet were inscribed the words he had chosen—'Ex umbris et imaginibus in veritatem'. Out of unreality into Reality.

---

[212] *LD* xxxi. 278 n.   [213] Ibid. 299.

AFTERWORD

In the Preface to this biography, first published in 1988, I wrote that 'my reading and re-reading of his writings over the years has only deepened my conviction that John Henry Newman is to be numbered among the Doctors of the Church'. When I wrote those words, I was well aware that the Roman Catholic Church would not declare Newman to be a Doctor of the Church unless he had first been canonized as a saint. My words began to come true when, three years later in 1991, Pope John Paul II declared Newman to be 'Venerable' or a figure to be venerated for the 'heroic virtues' that he displayed in his life. This formal papal recognition followed the completion in 1986 of a thorough study of his life and writings conducted by a historical commission established by the diocese in which he lived and worked following his founding of the Birmingham Oratory. The results of this process were sent to Rome to the Congregation for the Causes of Saints, which subsequently confirmed the conclusion reached by the commission. The Catholic Church canonizes people not for leading exceptionally blameless lives but for leading lives of exceptional moral heroism, even in spite of flaws and weaknesses. The formal recognition by the Pope of Newman as 'Venerable' still required divine confirmation in order for him to reach the next rung, so to speak, in the ladder to sainthood, that of beatification.

Although there had never, not surprisingly, been the kind of popular cult of Newman the theologian and writer that a figure like Mother Teresa inspired with her obvious works of heroic charity, over the years the belief that Newman was a saint had been growing all over the Catholic world. As a result, more and more people were praying for his intercession. And then on 15 August 2001, the feast of the Assumption of the Blessed Virgin Mary, an American magistrate, living in Marshfield near Boston, was inexplicably cured of a severe spinal disorder that had left him bent doubled over. Jack Sullivan claimed it was the result of his seeking in prayer the intercession of Newman, ever since watching a television interview with me a year previously in June 2000. Thereupon the archdiocese of Boston established a tribunal that interviewed witnesses and collected all the evidence available, which was then forwarded to the Congregation for the Causes of Saints in Rome. In April 2008 the Congregation's medical board announced that they could not find any natural explanation for the cure. Exactly a year later the Congregation's theological consultors confirmed that the cure was a miracle, a decision that led to Pope Benedict XVI signing a decree in

July 2009 authorizing Newman's beatification. On 19 September 2010 Pope Benedict XVI beatified Newman while on a state visit to Britain.

In clear anticipation of the beatification, the Congregation for Saints instructed that Newman's remains should be exhumed, to allow for their public veneration in accordance with usual Catholic practice. It was then discovered that Newman had been buried in a wooden coffin that, along with his remains, had entirely decomposed in the damp soil, apart from a brass plate (with his name and date of death), the brass handles with some bits of cloth attached, a brass replica of his cardinal's hat, and a wooden crucifix inlaid in silver. This discovery had no implications for the beatification, only for the projected public veneration. One is tempted to feel that Newman's 'disappearance' from this earth was his final fulfilment of the maxim of St Philip Neri, the founder of the Congregation of the Oratory, which he so cherished: *amare nesciri*, 'to love not to be known'. Indeed, the 20 August 1890 report in *The Birmingham Daily Post* of Newman's funeral and burial ended: 'and then the coffin was covered with mould of a softer texture than the marly [clay and lime] stratum in which the grave is cut. This was done in studious and affectionate fulfilment of a desire of Dr Newman's which some may deem fanciful, but which sprang from his reverence for the letter of the Divine Word; which, as he conceived, enjoins us to facilitate rather than impede the operation of the law "Dust thou art, and unto dust shalt thou return." '

Twelve years later on 15 May 2013 another American, living in Chicago, a lawyer by profession, Melissa Villalobos, who had become interested in Newman after watching the same television programme, and who was bleeding in pregnancy from a partially detached placenta, for which there was no medication or medical treatment but only the possibility of healing after resting in bed for a considerable amount of time, began to bleed even more seriously. She desperately prayed, 'Please Cardinal Newman make the bleeding stop!' Thereupon the bleeding immediately stopped. Following the same kind of investigation that was carried out in the case of Jack Sullivan, Pope Francis decreed Newman's canonization on 13 October 2019.

When it became generally known that Newman had been buried, in accordance with his strict instructions, in the same grave as his faithful friend and collaborator, Father Ambrose St John, there was widespread speculation in the international media that there might have been some kind of homosexual relationship between the two friends. In an age that has almost lost the concept of affectionate friendship untouched by sexual attraction, such speculation was no doubt inevitable. Certainly, the assumption that the desire to be buried in the same grave as someone else may, if not must, indicate some sort of sexual attraction would have greatly astonished previous generations. G. K. Chesterton's devoted secretary, Dorothy Collins, whom he and his wife regarded as a daughter, while thinking it presumptuous to ask to be buried in the same grave as the Chestertons, nevertheless directed that she be cremated and her ashes buried in the same grave. C. S. Lewis and his brother Warnie are buried in the same grave in accordance with both brothers' wishes. For Newman, Ambrose St John, a fellow priest of the Birmingham Oratory, was the equivalent of a brother: for thirty years he had been his most faithful and loyal supporter, from the days of his virtual exile at Littlemore through all his trials and tribulations as a Catholic. The last work that Newman had asked him to undertake was to translate the Austrian theologian Joseph Fessler's important book on infallibility in the wake of the First Vatican Council, a labour of love that Newman felt had proved too much for his already overworked friend. There was nothing more natural – then at least – than that Newman should want humbly to show his gratitude by directing that he, a famous cardinal, should be buried in the same grave as that of a comparatively unknown priest, his faithful friend and collaborator.

There were, however, almost certainly two other reasons why Newman was so insistent on the place of his burial. First, he must have feared that as a cardinal, and therefore 'prince of the Church', his Oratorian community, or for that matter the Church authorities, might wish to erect the kind of tomb that would normally have been erected for a cardinal, almost certainly away from the privacy of the community cemetery in what was then countryside and in a prominent public place in the Oratory church in Edgbaston, Birmingham. And second, by being buried in the same grave as St John, between the graves of Joseph Gordon and Edward Caswall, he would lie among the three men 'who in past years gave themselves up to me generously and unreservedly' and who had been 'the life and centre of the Oratory'. After Caswall died and was buried in a grave next to St John's, Newman had written sadly: 'So now the three most energetic and influential of the first Fathers of the Oratory lie together; and the three who from the first threw in their lot with me'.[1] Nothing was more natural than that he, the founder of the Birmingham Oratory, should wish to lie among them.

The publication in 1957, more than fifty years ago, of Newman's *Autobiographical Writings* made available all the evidence necessary to disprove any notion that Newman was homosexual in his inclinations, a suggestion that was first made by Geoffrey Faber, ironically the great-nephew of Father Faber, in his Freudian psychobiography *Oxford Apostles* (1933), where he claimed that Newman's earlier friendship with Hurrell Froude was at least subconsciously homosexual. There had also long been available the testimony of Newman's *Apologia pro Vita sua*.

In December 1816, following his Evangelical conversion in the preceding summer and autumn, we find Newman, aged fifteen, praying in his

---

[1] *LD* xxviii. 118, 300. See pp. 699, 711.

private journal to be preserved from the temptations that awaited him on his return home from boarding school for the Christmas holidays. The only two temptations he specifically mentions are dances and parties. The implication is clear: there he will meet girls, from whom he is shielded at a boys' boarding school. In a later entry at the end of December, by which time he has returned home, he condemns dances and all parties of this kind, again writing discreetly in Latin, and hopes that his parents will respect his scruples.[2] That he has reached the age of puberty is clear from his references to the sins and temptations of the flesh. Clearly the school holidays presented temptations to an adolescent boy that were not present in a boys' boarding school – provided, of course, the adolescent boy was not homosexually inclined. Had the pious Evangelical Newman been so inclined in the slightest way – and adolescent boys in all-male boarding school environments are often sexually confused – we would have found him praying fervently for the school holidays and the accompanying release from an all-male society.

The adolescent Newman's disinclination to mingle in young female society was not only out of a fear for his chastity, but also because of a 'deep imagination' that had taken 'possession' of him in the autumn of 1816 that 'it would be the will of God' that he 'should lead a single life'. In the *Apologia*, he explained why he felt this call to celibacy:

This anticipation, which has held its ground almost continuously ever since, – with the break of a month now and a month then, up to 1829, and, after that date, without any break at all, – was more or less connected in my mind with the notion, that my calling in life would require such a sacrifice as celibacy involved; as, for instance, missionary work among the heathen, to which I had a great drawing for some years. It also strengthened my feeling of separation from the visible world...[3]

A modern reader should not need to be reminded that in nineteenth-century England homosexuality was illegal and generally considered to be immoral. The only 'sacrifice' that Newman could possibly be referring to was that of marriage. And he readily acknowledges that from time to time he continued to feel the natural attraction to marriage that any heterosexual man would feel.

Twenty-four years before he wrote those words, he completed on 25 March 1840 his extraordinary account of his near-fatal illness in Sicily in 1833. And, almost bitterly, he counted the cost of the sacrifice he had made in voluntarily embracing celibacy:

The thought keeps pressing on me, while I write this, what am I writing it for?...

Whom have I, whom can I have, who would take interest in it?...This is the sort of interest which a wife takes and none but she – it is a woman's interest – and that interest, so be it, shall never be taken in me...I willingly give up the possession of that sympathy, which I feel is not, cannot be, granted to me. Yet, not the less do I feel the need of it.[4]

These words are unmistakeably the words of a man who feels called to a life of celibacy, while still a clergyman in the Church of England and therefore fully free to get married. But they are also the words of a man who feels the deep pain of sacrificing the love of a woman in marriage.

When I wrote this biography, the question of the exhumation of Newman's remains had not yet, of course, arisen. I naturally knew of Geoffrey Faber's speculations, which had had some influence – not surprisingly in a culture where the very concept of friendship as opposed to 'relationship' was dying, and where the close affectionate friendships of an all-male environment, such as Oxford was in the first half of the nineteenth century, were certain to arouse suspicions. I also knew that eyebrows had been raised at the fact that Newman was buried in the same grave as Ambrose St John. But this, I reasoned, clearly proved the very opposite of what was insinuated: after all, Newman would scarcely have left such an instruction had he even dreamed that it could ever be interpreted as having any significance beyond the significance which he attached to it – nor would the Oratory or the Church authorities have ever permitted such a joint burial if they had had the slightest suspicion about what must have seemed to them a totally innocent, not to say praiseworthy gesture. Newman had plenty of critics, not to say enemies, in his time; yet not one of them, not one newspaper, not one casual observer even dreamed of reading a significance into an act of loving friendship, and indeed of humility, such as was left to the twentieth century to read into it.

As I said in my original Preface to the biography, I wanted to allow Newman to speak for himself, and 'to present the evidence fairly and squarely so that readers [might] make up their own minds' about Newman's character and personality.[5] I was not thinking at all, when I wrote that, about the speculation as to his sexuality because I knew it was baseless. But in so far as I had it in mind at all, I thought that I had presented sufficient evidence to refute it. It may be that I was wrong in not dealing specifically with it. If that is the case, then this Afterword, which includes the evidence of the 1816 private journal that is not in the biography, will have served a purpose.

Ian Ker
Burford
January 2009

---

[4] *AW* 137–8. See pp. 196–7.   [5] See pp. vii–viii.

INDEX